CASES AND MATERIALS ON
MODERN ANTITRUST LAW AND ITS ORIGINS
Sixth Edition

■ ■ ■

Thomas D. Morgan

S. Chesterfield Oppenheim Professor Emeritus
of Antitrust and Trade Regulation Law
The George Washington University School of Law

Richard J. Pierce, Jr.

Lyle T. Alverson Professor of Law
The George Washington University School of Law

AMERICAN CASEBOOK SERIES®

American Casebook Series is a trademark registered in the U.S. Patent and Trademark Office.

© 1993 West Publishing Co.
© West, a Thomson business, 2001, 2005
© 2009 Thomson Reuters
© 2014 LEG, Inc. d/b/a West Academic
© 2018 LEG, Inc. d/b/a West Academic
     444 Cedar Street, Suite 700
     St. Paul, MN 55101
     1-877-888-1330

West, West Academic Publishing, and West Academic are trademarks of West Publishing Corporation, used under license.

Printed in the United States of America

ISBN: 978-1-68328-941-8

To Kathryn and Lynda

PREFACE

When my friend and colleague, Tom Morgan, announced his retirement, I was happy for him. He and his lovely wife, Kathryn, are enjoying their new life in Florida. From a selfish perspective, however, I was distressed. I have long taught from his wonderful casebook on antitrust law. I share his strong belief that no student can understand modern antitrust law without understanding the complicated process through which it has evolved. I did not want to switch to a casebook that I considered inferior to Tom's book.

This Sixth Edition of Cases and Materials on Modern Antitrust Law and its Origins is my response to the problem that Tom's retirement presented. I hope that it continues to further the goal of helping law students understand this important body of law.

Antitrust law at its best represents a national commitment to the free market's ability to stimulate economic growth and direct economic activity. The development of antitrust thinking thus provides a unique window on what preceding and current generations have thought constituted market imperfections that require correction. Antitrust law also illustrates the formation, development and rejection of a number of important economic hypotheses. In these pages, you will see the issues debated in the Justices' opinions, tested in the world of experience, and modified or abandoned as better (or simply newer) ideas replace them.

To try to convey the intellectual richness of this field, this book departs from the usual practice of examining discrete lines of antitrust doctrine from the adoption of the Sherman Act in 1890 to the present. Instead, it takes up the material in successive chronological periods during which the courts employed important contrasting approaches to antitrust issues.

In each successive period, the Supreme Court tried to correct the mistakes it had made in prior periods. In half a dozen cases, the Court made the corrections in opinions in which it overruled a precedent and replaced one doctrine with another. In most cases, however, the Court used the process of disingenuous distinction of precedents as a means of replacing one doctrine with an inconsistent doctrine without acknowledging that it was changing the doctrine.

This method of correcting its past errors presents challenges to lower courts, lawyers and the public. It is impossible to understand the meaning of a modern opinion without understanding the many prior opinions in which the Court gradually changed the principles it applied to resolve a class of antitrust disputes.

We begin in the Introduction by looking at the adoption of the Sherman Act in the context of the law that preceded it and the economic theory that supported it.

Chapter I examines the period 1890 to 1914 and introduces the judicial debates over what it was that Congress had wrought. Many of the debates were among Justices who were well-versed in law but had little knowledge of economics. They made many mistakes because they believed that legal analysis alone could make sense of the Sherman Act. The early period ended in 1914 with the passage of the other two major antitrust statutes—the Clayton Act and the Federal Trade Commission Act.

Chapter II, the second 25 years of antitrust law, 1915–1939, illustrates a period in which the Court sought to apply what it called a "rule of reason" to antitrust questions. The cases we consider from the period are good illustrations of the original version of the rule of reason in action and of ideas that continue to influence the law's development. The original version of the rule of reason was so open-ended, however, that it was extremely difficult to apply. Its application to a particular set of facts was difficult to predict. Its application often required seemingly endless trials.

Chapter III, the third period in our antitrust history, ran for about 35 years, beginning with the decision in United States v. Socony-Vacuum in 1940 and ending in the mid-1970s. It was a time of aggressive expansion of antitrust doctrine, much of it born of depression-era economics and premised on the idea that American business had become too powerful and American industries too concentrated.

In many cases, the Court replaced the original version of the rule of reason with a per se prohibition on a practice. This approach was based in part on the Court's well-founded belief that the original version of the rule of reason was too open-ended to be susceptible to efficient application or to deter firms from engaging in anticompetitive practices. However, it was also based in part on the Court's mistaken belief that there are many practices that almost always harm competition and rarely have socially beneficial effects.

Chapter IV examines the present era of antitrust thinking, now over 40 years long. The current period represents an appropriate response to genuine concerns that prior antitrust doctrine had inhibited efficient business practices and penalized legitimate success. It has been characterized by replacement of the per se approach that dominated the third period with a new, more predictable and more tractable version of the rule of reason.

As in all of the prior periods, the doctrines created during the modern period have evoked criticism from many able lawyers and economists. When the tenth edition of this book is published, it almost certainly will describe a fifth period in which the Justices corrected the mistakes they made during what we now call the modern period.

Antitrust is a course about cases; indeed, the study of it tends to be more case-oriented than almost any advanced field except Constitutional Law. These materials make a serious attempt to communicate the full richness of the main cases. The procedural context of each case has been left in the opinions, the facts are fully developed, and the Justices' individual efforts to wrestle with unsettled points are retained. Dissents are given almost as much prominence as majority opinions in an effort to help you see the full clash of ideas. Notes and questions that follow each case draw out its historical context, the ongoing debates within the Court, and conflicting economic visions the Justices' positions may reflect. Longer notes provide descriptions of other important cases and economic principles not developed in the opinions.

Special thanks go to Professors Bill Kovacic, George Priest, Todd Seelman, Roy Simon and others who used or commented on the first five editions of these materials, and to Henry Manne who made law and economics come alive for so many now in law teaching.

RICHARD J. PIERCE, JR.

Washington D.C.
October 2017

SUMMARY OF CONTENTS

TABLE OF CONTENTS

TABLE OF CASES

The principal cases are in bold type.

TABLE OF STATUTES

CASES AND MATERIALS ON

MODERN ANTITRUST LAW AND ITS ORIGINS

Sixth Edition

INTRODUCTION

COMMON LAW ANTECEDENTS
OF THE SHERMAN ACT

■ ■ ■

Americans sometimes talk as though we created all that is good in modern law. One cannot really understand current antitrust law, however, without understanding that the concern about monopolies and restraints of trade did not begin with the Sherman Act. The concern extends at least as far back as early periods of the developing British law of property and commercial transactions.

THE CASE OF MONOPOLIES
King's Bench, 1603
Trin. 44 Eliz., 11 Co. Rep. 84b, 77 Eng.Rep. 1260

Edward Darcy, Esquire, a groom of the Privy Chamber to Queen Elizabeth brought an action on the case against T. Allein, haberdasher, of London, and declared, that Queen Elizabeth, intending that her subjects being able men to exercise husbandry, should apply themselves thereunto, and that they should not employ themselves in making playing cards, which had not been any ancient manual occupation within this realm, and that by making such a multitude of cards, card-playing was become more frequent and especially among servants and apprentices, and poor artificers; and to the end her subjects might apply themselves to more lawful and necessary trades; by her letters patent under the Great Seal of the same date granted to Ralph Bowes, Esq. full power, license and authority * * * to provide and buy in any parts beyond the sea, all such playing cards as he thought good, and to import them into this realm, and to sell and utter them within the same, and [provided] that * * * none other should have the making of playing cards within the realm * * * for twelve years; and by the same letters patent, the Queen charged and commanded, that no person or persons besides the said Ralph Bowes, & c. should bring any cards within the realm during those twelve years; nor should buy, sell, or offer to be sold within the said realm, within the said term, any playing cards, nor should make, or cause to be made any playing cards within the said realm, upon pain of the Queen's highest displeasure, and of such fine and punishment as offenders in the case of voluntary contempt deserve. And afterwards the said Queen, by her letters patent reciting the former grants made to Ralph Bowes, granted the plaintiff, his executors, and administrators, and their deputies, the same privileges, authorities, and other the said premises, for twenty-one years after the end of the former term, rendering to the Queen 100 marks per annum; and further granted to him a seal to mark the cards. [The plaintiff] further declared, that after the end of the said term of twelve years, [he] caused to be made 400 grosses of cards for the necessary uses of the subjects, to be sold within this realm, and had expended in making them 5000 l., and that the defendant knowing of the said grant and prohibition in the plaintiff's letters patent, * * * without the Queen's license, or the plaintiff's, at Westminster caused to be [imported or] made [180] grosses of playing cards, * * * none of which were made within the realm, or imported within the realm by the plaintiff * * * nor marked with his seal, and them had sold and uttered to sundry persons unknown, * * * wherefore the plaintiff could not utter his playing cards, & c. * * * The defendant, except to one half gross pleaded not guilty, and as to that pleaded, that the City of London is an ancient city, and that within the same, from time whereof, & c. there has been a society of Haberdashers, and that within the said city there was a custom [that members of that society were free to sell all manner of merchandise and that he] * * * sold the said half gross of playing cards, being made within the realm & c. as he lawfully might; upon which the plaintiff demurred in law.

* * *

* * * [I]t was * * * resolved by Popham, Chief Justice, [and the whole court] that the said grant to the plaintiff of the sole making of cards within the realm was utterly void, and that for two reasons:—1. That it is a monopoly, and against the common law. 2. That it is against divers Acts of Parliament. Against the common law for four reasons:—1. All trades, as well mechanical as others, which prevent idleness (the bane of the commonwealth) and exercise men and youth in labour, for the maintenance of themselves and their families, and for the increase of their substance, to serve the Queen when occasion shall require, are profitable for the commonwealth, and therefore the grant to the plaintiff to have the sole making of them is against the common law, and the benefit and liberty of the subject * * * .

And a case was adjudged in this Court * * * [2. that a grant of any] monopoly, is not only a damage and prejudice to those who exercise the same trade, but also to all other subjects, for the end of all these monopolies is for the private gain of the patentees; and * * * there are three inseparable incidents to every monopoly against the commonwealth, *sc.* 1. That the price of the same commodity will be raised, for he who has the sole selling of any commodity, may and will make the price as he pleases * * * . * * * The 2d incident to a monopoly is, that after the monopoly [is] granted, the commodity is not so good and merchantable as it was before: for the patentee having the sole trade, regards only his private benefit, and not the common wealth. 3. It tends to the impoverishment of divers artificers and others, who before, by the labour of their hands in their art or trade, had maintained themselves and their families, who now will of necessity be constrained to live in idleness and beggary; * * * . * * * 3. The Queen was deceived in her grant; for the Queen, as by the preamble appears, intended it to be for the weal public, and it will be employed for the private gain of the patentee, and for the prejudice of the weal public; * * * and therefore * * * this grant is void jure regio. 4. This grant is [first impression] for no such was ever seen to pass by letters patent under the great Seal before these days, and therefore it is a dangerous innovation, as well without any precedent, for example, as without authority of law, or reason. * * * And it cannot be intended, that Edward Darcy an Esquire, and a groom of the Queen's Privy Chamber, has any skill in this mechanical trade of making cards; and then it was said, that the patent made to him was void; for to forbid others to make cards who have the art and skill, and to give him the sole making of them who has no skill to make them, will make the patent utterly void. And although * * * it may be said he may appoint deputies who are expert, yet if the grantee is not expert, and the grant is void as to him, he cannot make any deputy to supply his place * * * . And as to what has been said, that playing at cards is a vanity, it is true, if it is abused, but the making of them is neither a vanity nor a pleasure, but labour and pains. * * * [T]he importation of foreign cards was prohibited at the grievous complaint of the poor artificers cardmakers, who were not able to live of their trades, if foreign cards should be imported; as appears by the preamble, by which it appears, that the said Act provides remedy for the maintenance of the said trade of making cards, forasmuch as it maintained divers families by their labour and industry; * * * . And therefore it was resolved, that the Queen could not suppress the making of cards within the realm, no more than the making of dice, bowls, balls, hawks' hoods, bells, lures, dog-couples, and other the like, which are works of labour and art, although they serve for pleasure, recreation, and pastime, and cannot be suppressed but by Parliament, nor a man restrained from exercising any trade, but by Parliament. * * *

* * *

* * * [T]he dispensation or license to have the sole importation and merchandizing of cards (without any limitation or stint) notwithstanding the said Act of [Parliament] is utterly against law * * * . * * * [W]hen the wisdom of the Parliament has made an Act to restrain pro bono publico the importation of many foreign manufactures, to the intent that the subjects of the realm might apply themselves to the making of the said manufactures, & c. and thereby maintain themselves and their families with the labour of their hands; now for a private gain to grant the sole importation of them to one, or divers (without any limitation) notwithstanding the said Act, is a monopoly against the common law, and against the end and scope of the Act itself; for this is not to maintain and increase the labours of the poor card-makers within the realm, at whose

petition the Act was made, but utterly to take away and destroy their trade and labours * * * . And judgment was given and entered * * * .

NOTES AND QUESTIONS

1.   Reports of old British cases tend to be hard to read, but this one is worth the effort. What had happened to upset the plaintiff?

2.   The scope of the Crown's authority to grant monopolies was an important constitutional issue of the day, and what we now read as *The Case of Monopolies* is not an opinion written by the judges. What we have is the report of Edward Coke who, as Queen Elizabeth's Attorney General, had argued in defense of Darcy's grant. Coke's report, purportedly based on talks with the judges, was not published until 1615, over a decade into the reign of James I, and its criticism of the late-Queen's attempt to assert her royal prerogative was controversial even when written.[1]

a.   Why might there have been a battle between the authority of the monarch and that of Parliament in the grant of special privileges? To put the matter in partial context, forty years earlier in 1563, the Statute of Artificers had required workers to serve a seven year apprenticeship before entry into local trades. Then, pursuant to the Poor Relief Act of 1601, local communities had to guarantee a minimum income to the unemployed. Thus, among other things, nobles and other members of Parliament had an interest in not having the monarch throw people out of work to benefit her friends.[2]

b.   Do you suppose that authority to grant monopoly privileges can be translated into political or economic support today? Might the grant of a monopoly cable television or taxicab franchise have significant economic value, for example? Think back to this subject when we ask later to what extent federal antitrust policy should yield to whatever regulatory policies state legislatures might adopt.

c.   In a postscript to this case, Reporter Coke noted with pleasure that "our lord the King that now is * * * has published, that monopolies are things against the laws of this realm; and therefore expressly commands, that no suitor presume to move him to grant any of them." 77 Eng.Rep. at 1266. In 1623, eight years after Coke's report of The Case of Monopolies, the Statute of Monopolies largely abolished royal grants of monopoly and reserved to Parliament the right to make new grants.

---

[1]   A superb discussion of the context of the controversy and the many procedural and other issues before the Court, based in part on Coke's own unpublished notes, can be found in Jacob I. Corré, The Argument, Decision and Reports of Darcy v. Allen, 45 Emory L.J. 1261 (1996).

[2]   For an excellent discussion of this period, see Michael J. Trebilcock, The Common Law of Restraint of Trade: A Legal and Economic Analysis 3–8 (1986); William Letwin, Law and Economic Policy in America: The Evolution of the Sherman Antitrust Act 27–32 (1965); Hans B. Thorelli, The Federal Antitrust Policy: Origination of an American Tradition 20–26 (1955). The battle between the Crown and Parliament had been going on for over two hundred years prior to The Case of Monopolies. Edward III granted John Pecche right to sell sweet wine at retail in London in 1373; by 1376, Parliament had punished Pecche for allegedly extortionate pricing. See Letwin, supra, at 19–22.

3.   Is his effort to defend allowing the monarch to grant monopolies, what did Darcy cite as the public interest justification for his royal grant? Were you convinced by his argument that restricting the output of cards was morally praiseworthy? Were you convinced that, if playing cards was "a vanity," monopolizing production of the cards was a virtue?

4.   Did Darcy go to jail as a result of the court's finding his monopoly invalid? As was true here, the usual common law response to agreements in restraint of trade was simply not to enforce them. We will later see that at least one justification for the Sherman Act likely was an effort to broaden the range of remedies for use against such restraints of trade.

5.   It is always a mistake to think that a court sitting almost 400 years ago was commenting on our present situation. However, the report does outline reasons that the Court believed the public should be concerned about monopolies. What are they? Are the same reasons sound today?

a.   Do monopolists tend to increase the price of goods? Is their ability to raise prices unlimited?

b.   Do monopolists tend to reduce the quality of goods they produce? Is that any more than another way of saying that monopolies tend to raise prices?

c.   Do monopolists tend to reduce production of the goods monopolized? Does that tend to reduce total employment in the industries monopolized? Is that the principal failing?

These questions—and others—will be explored in the following note and throughout the remainder of these materials.

———————

A NOTE ON THE ECONOMICS OF MONOPOLY

One often hears that there is a controversy over whether economic theory is central to antitrust analysis and indeed which of several conflicting economic theories is most sound.[3] It is true that the *implications* of economic analysis for the result in particular cases are often

———————

[3]   The economic analysis of antitrust cases intimidates many students. As supplements for the notes in this book, you may want to consult, e.g., David W. Barnes & Lynn A. Stout, Economic Foundations of Regulation and Antitrust Law (1992); Ernest Gellhorn, William E. Kovacic & Stephen Calkins, Antitrust Law and Economics in a Nutshell (5th Ed. 2004); Keith N. Hylton, Antitrust Law: Economic Theory & Common Law Evolution (2003); John E. Kwoka, Jr. & Lawrence J. White, The Antitrust Revolution: Economics, Competition and Policy (5th Ed. 2008); E. Thomas Sullivan & Jeffrey L. Harrison, Understanding Antitrust and its Economic Implications (5th Ed. 2008). See also, Robert H. Bork, The Antitrust Paradox: A Policy At War With Itself (1978); Richard A. Posner, Antitrust Law (2nd Ed. 2001); Richard A. Posner, The Chicago School of Antitrust Analysis, 127 U. Pennsylvania L. Rev. 925 (1979). A rigorous public-choice analysis of antitrust doctrine is provided in Fred S. McChesney & William F. Shughart, II, The Causes and Consequences of Antitrust (1995). Doubts about the "Chicago School" approach to economics are raised in Robert Pitofsky, ed., How the Chicago School Overshot the Mark: The Effect of Conservative Economic Analysis on U.S. Antitrust (2008); Herbert Hovenkamp, Antitrust Policy After Chicago, 84 Michigan L. Rev. 213 (1985); Symposium, Neo-Chicago Antitrust, 78 Antitrust L. J. 37 (2012).

controversial and it is also true that economists are forever refining their analytic tools.[4] But the basic terms of economic analysis are not in significant dispute, and a lawyer needs to understand the analysis in order to assess what the purpose and effect of a practice might be, whether the practice is likely to be challenged, and if so, how most courts today will react to it.

Throughout this book we will see many different applications of economic theory. This note introduces some basic assumptions underlying economic analysis and applies them to issues of competition and monopoly.

1.   The Principle of Scarcity

When most of us were young, we probably imagined that our lives would involve simultaneously being an astronaut, a professional athlete, a parent, a firefighter, a television personality, and maybe even a lawyer. As we grew up, however, we learned the hard truth that life involves choices. We cannot do as many things as we would like. Similarly, we cannot have as many material goods as we might wish a perfect world would provide.

Economists call this reality the principle of scarcity and it is the central problem with which economics deals. Put simply, economists suggest ways to order human activity so as to give as many people as much of what they would like to have as possible—whether they prefer material goods, career satisfaction, leisure, close friendships, or something else. Sometimes economists express preferences in terms of the money required to buy those items that are for sale, but economic principles are not so limited. Analysis of how people can more fully realize their objectives is much broader than analysis of cash transfers.[5]

2.   People Act So as to Maximize Their Own Self Interest

The pursuit of self interest is both an assertion of fact and a normative principle. The factual assertion says that individuals, left alone, will seek to exchange the skills and money they have for the mix of goods or services they want.[6] The normative principle says that the freedom to do so is

---

[4]   The notes and comments after cases in this book will often "cheat" and ask contemporary economic questions about cases that arose in earlier years because the questions illuminate issues that are important to us today. For more about the evolution of economic understanding, see, e.g., Herbert Hovenkamp, The Antitrust Movement and the Rise of Industrial Organization, 68 Texas L.Rev. 105 (1989); Bruce H. Kobayashi & Timothy J. Muris, Chicago, Post-Chicago and Beyond: Time to Let Go of the 20th Century, 78 Antitrust L.J. 147 (2012).

[5]   Professor Gary Becker received the 1992 Nobel Prize in Economics for his work describing the breadth of the insights of economic analysis. See, e.g., Gary S. Becker, The Economic Approach to Human Behavior (1976). The most extensive application of economics to legal issues, however, remains that found in Richard A. Posner, Economic Analysis of Law (7th Ed. 2007).

[6]   The careful reader will have noted that this analysis assumes that the individuals in our economy all have initial endowments of goods and talents that, if not equal, are at least great enough to be able to engage in the trading of goods and services here supposed. Nothing in this note should be read to minimize the consequences of the fact that that is not true. General issues of wealth redistribution would take us far beyond the subject of this book, but regularly ask yourself whether and how particular rules of antitrust law might increase the wealth of some

fundamental and allows members of a diverse society to experience the lives they prefer for themselves and their loved ones.

Understood as upholding freedom to choose among alternatives, the pursuit of self interest is neither cynical nor materialistic. For generations, parents have nursed their children through illness or taken second and third jobs to put them through school. People volunteer to work in hospitals or the arts because they take satisfaction in knowing that they are helping build a stronger community. Similarly, people buy homes, buy automobiles or indulge hobbies. They work because they receive satisfaction from it, seek to change jobs if they do not, or maximize their pursuit of leisure instead. Each of these activities is consistent with overcoming the problem of scarcity; each is consistent with activity in a free society.

3.   Life Is Lived at the Margin

In thinking about scarcity, a careful reader might say: "But life doesn't present only either-or choices. I can be a parent as well as a lawyer; I can also be an amateur athlete and possibly even a volunteer firefighter." That is exactly right and it illustrates a further point economists make: The choices we make in pursuit of our self interest typically are not profound or dramatic; they consist of doing a little more of this and a little less of that. How much more or less is itself a product of our individual choice; economists describe those choices as being made "at the margin."

To take but one example, when you decided to go to law school, you knew it would cost a lot of money. You would face a tuition expense and you would also forego some of the income you would have received by working full time. To finance your education, you may have decided to spend part of your savings, you may have taken out loans, you may have decided to work part time, or you may have decided to extend the time it would take you to graduate so that you could work and obtain current income. Most likely, however, you did some of each.

Similarly, when someone goes into the restaurant business, he or she will try to predict whether that decision will prove profitable over all. Once in business, however, decisions will tend to be marginal. "If I close on Mondays will I save more in expenses than I lose in income?" "If I add live music on Saturday nights will I attract more customers than the musicians cost me?"

As economists describe such questions, people are asking themselves whether the marginal revenue from doing something will exceed the marginal cost of doing it. Do you recognize that as how you make important decisions? Even if you accept the basic idea, do you always accurately balance marginal cost and marginal benefit? The fact that information is often costly to obtain and that people's preferences can be manipulated by

---

persons or groups at the expense of others. See, e.g., Herbert Hovenkamp, Distributive Justice and the Antitrust Laws, 51 George Washington L. Rev. 1 (1982).

clever marketing has caused some analysts to doubt this fundamental principle of economics.[7] But the importance of economic models does not depend on whether all individuals *actually* make such analyses; it is enough that the model predicts effectively how groups of people in general will behave as legal rules or other incentives are changed, and so far most courts have not given up on the idea of rational producers and consumers.[8]

4.   We Deal with Each Other in Markets

Probably no concept is more central to economic discussions than the concept of transactions occurring in markets. Don't be fooled. The concept is a metaphor.[9] The mental image it creates is of vendors hawking their wares in a public square. The courts in antitrust cases speak of "product markets" and "geographic markets" as if all east coast steel producers, for example, did all of their business on a street corner in Pittsburgh.

The "market" described in economic theory and in antitrust cases, however, has neither a street address, a website, nor a FAX number. What is critical for purposes of economic theory is that sometimes people can realistically deal with one another, and sometimes they cannot. Those that can deal are said to be participating in the market.

What the market metaphor does is allow economists to speak of the enormous number of ways in which free exchanges of goods and services might occur. As we have seen, the freedom to choose among alternatives is necessary to let us express our differences and reduce the problem of scarcity experienced by each of us. You may want my ball point pen more than I want it, and I may want your candy bar more than you do. If we can trade what we have with each other, we will not have added a single physical item to the world but we will each consider ourselves better off.

5.   The Quest for Allocative Efficiency

The problem of scarcity will never be completely overcome. In principle, we would know, however, that we had come as close as possible

---

[7]   One term used to describe the alternative to the rationality assumption is "behavioral economics." See, e.g., Jeffrey L. Harrison, Egoism, Altruism, and Market Illusions: The Limits of Law and Economics, 33 UCLA L. Rev. 1309 (1986); Herbert Hovenkamp, Rationality in Law & Economics, 60 George Washington L. Rev. 293 (1992); Christine Jolls, Cass R. Sunstein & Richard Thaler, A Behavioral Approach to Law and Economics, 50 Stanford L. Rev. 1471 (1998); Russell B. Korobkin & Thomas S. Ulen, Law & Behavioral Science: Removing the Rationality Assumption from Law & Economics, 88 California L. Rev. 1051 (2000); Christopher R. Leslie, Rationality Analysis in Antitrust, 158 U. Pennsylvania L. Rev. 261 (2010); Amanda Reeves & Maurice E. Stucke, Behavioral Antitrust, 86 Indiana L.J. 1527 (2011).

[8]   See, e.g., James C. Cooper & William E. Kovacic, Behavioral Economics and Its Meaning for Antitrust Agency Decision Making, 8 J. Law, Economics & Policy 779 (2012); Daniel A. Crane, Chicago, Post-Chicago, and Neo-Chicago, 76 U. Chicago L. Rev. 1911 (2009); Richard A. Epstein, Behavioral Economics: Human Errors and Market Corrections, 73 U. Chicago L. Rev. 111 (2006).

[9]   Probably the best single account of the rhetoric of economics is Donald N. McCloskey, If You're So Smart: The Narrative of Economic Expertise (1990). The impact of the rhetoric in antitrust is also explored in Michael Boudin, Antitrust Doctrine and the Sway of Metaphor, 75 Georgetown L.J. 395 (1986), and John J. Flynn, Antitrust Policy and the Concept of a Competitive Process, 35 N.Y. Law School L. Rev. 893 (1990).

when there was no combination of production or exchange that could make anyone better off without making someone else worse off.[10] That so-called "optimal" state is the north star of economics—it is too distant ever to reach, but staying oriented toward it keeps us pointed in the right direction.

You will often see that optimal state described as "efficient." "Efficiency" is a term you will see both in the antitrust cases and in analyses of those cases. Be careful! It is a term used in antitrust economics in at least three importantly different ways.

What we have been describing is "allocative efficiency." All goods and services would be appropriately allocated, and preferences for leisure met, because, by definition, no further acts or exchanges could make the situation better. Before describing the two other meanings of "efficiency", however, it may be helpful to understand where competition and monopoly—the primary focus of antitrust law—fit into this analysis.

6.   How Prices Are Set in Competition

Suppose you have decided to become an entrepreneur, say a pencil manufacturer. May you set a price of $10 on each pencil you have to sell? Of course you may; nothing forbids your setting any price you wish on such a product. Your problem is likely to be that you will not sell any pencils; your potential customers will have so many sources of better, cheaper writing instruments that someone who charges $10 will sell few pencils, if any.

The Demand Side of Setting Your Price

At what price will you sell your pencils? That will be determined in largest part by your buyer's alternatives. Will the number of pencils you sell tend to increase or decrease when the price of each pencil goes up? That's easy, isn't it? The number will decrease at each higher price level as some of your customers make decisions at the margin that they would rather switch from pencils to pens and others decide they would rather play golf than write at all.

---

[10]   The technical description of maximum economic "welfare", what we call here "optimal" in terms of "allocative efficiency," turns out to have been a challenging intellectual puzzle. The text uses the test developed by economist Vilfredo Pareto early in the 20th century. However, because relatively few actions in a society make literally *everyone* better off, it can be argued that the Pareto-optimal conditions might be met before all production or transactions that would increase total societal welfare had been made. Professors Nicholas Kaldor and J.R. Hicks, writing in the 1930s, suggested that a transaction moves the economy in the direction of efficiency—even if one person profits at the expense of another as Pareto specified could not happen—if the gain of the person benefitted is sufficient to reimburse the other for the loss, whether or not such reimbursement is required. The point is that such a transaction, by definition, increases total welfare in the society. It is this Kaldor-Hicks version of efficiency that Richard Posner and many other students of law and economics use in their analyses. For the most part, economic analysis of antitrust questions does not turn on which definition of the optimal result is chosen—just as we usually do not care that north on a compass does not point directly at the north star—but keep an eye out for situations in which the distinction may prove important.

Figure 1 is a simple graph showing this relationship. All graphs in this book show quantity increasing along the horizontal axis and price increasing along the vertical. Thus, when the price is high, the quantity demanded is shown as lower than the quantity demanded as the price comes down. P is the price per package of 100 pencils (here called a "unit"); Q is the number of thousand units sold.

Figure 1

Sales of Pencils
(in 1000 units of 100 pencils each).

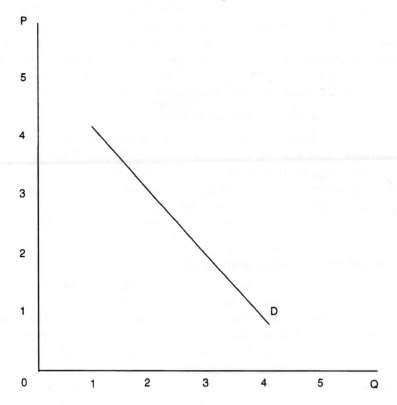

The Supply Side of Price Setting

Assuming that you believe you know something about the demand for pencils, how will you decide how many pencils to manufacture? The short answer, of course, is that you will assess what it would cost you to produce pencils and try to make your venture as profitable as possible.

Is your cost likely to be a constant figure? Of course not. You will have to pay a high initial cost to buy the equipment with which to make pencils, but you will expect a reduction in the cost of making each pencil thereafter. The cost will tend to fall rapidly at first, be basically constant for a time, and then start to increase again as your rate of production pushes your machines, your building, and your workers beyond their most efficient limits.

Table 1 helps us visualize this. It uses Q (quantity) to describe the number of units produced, FC (fixed cost) to describe costs incurred before any goods are produced, and MC (marginal cost) to describe the cost incurred to produce each additional unit the firm produces. TC (total cost) is simply the sum of FC and the total of all MCs, and ATC (average total cost) is TC divided by Q.

Table 1

Q	FC	MC	TC	ATC
1000	$5,000	$2.00	$ 7,000	$7.00
2000	6,000	$1.00	$ 8,000	$4.00
3000		$3.00	$11,000	$3.67
4000		$4.00	$15,000	$3.75
5000		$5.00	$20,000	$4.00
6000		$6.00	$26,000	$4.33

If we put this information on a graph (Figure 2), we will see the same information in another form. Notice that the curves of both ATC and MC are U-shaped.

Which cost, ATC or MC, will be more relevant to your decision whether or not to produce more pencils? If you knew in advance that you could never produce pencils at or above your average total cost, you would not enter the business; by definition, you would be throwing money away. If you were already in business, however, what would be the relevant measure of cost? Do you see that it would be marginal cost? You would continue to produce until the next item you sold cost more to produce than you could charge for it.

Thus, as the price of pencils increases, if all other alternatives available to sellers remain constant, they will produce more pencils. For existing manufacturers, that will be because most are producing under conditions in which their marginal costs are constant or increasing. Their individual supply schedules will be the flat or upward portions of their marginal cost schedules. In addition, firms not now producing pencils will do so if the price increases. The industry supply curve will connect the points of the marginal cost curves at the points where those other firms in the industry would begin production if prices rose.

Figure 2

Costs of Making Pencils
(per 1000 units of 100 pencils each).

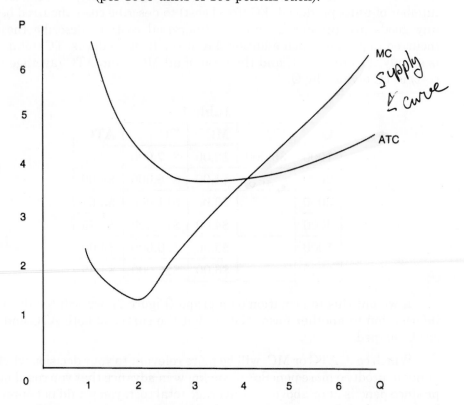

Throughout this discussion of cost, you may have noticed that we have not mentioned "profit." An economist recognizes that you, the business person, must invest both time and capital in the production of pencils. If you weren't making pencils, you could earn a salary doing something else. The money you invested in machinery, if invested in something else, could be earning interest or dividends. You must make what an accountant would call "profits" equal to those alternative sources of return that you have, adjusted for the increased risks of being in business for yourself, or you will leave the pencil industry. Thus, to an economist, such profits are really "costs" and are so treated in this model.

Setting the Price Based on Both Supply and Demand

Now combining both supply and demand schedules into the graph shown as Figure 3, at what price will the pencils be sold? How many units will be sold?

Figure 3

Sales of Pencils
(in 1000 units of 100 pencils each).

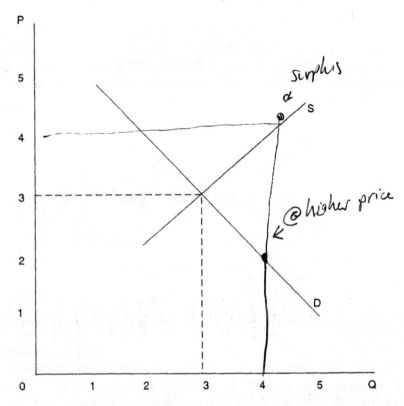

Do you see why, based on the graphs shown, the quantity produced will be 3000 units of pencils and the price set will be $3 per unit?

What would happen if by law the price of pencils were held at $2 per unit? That's right. Customers would perceive a shortage. You can read the result off Figure 3. People would demand 4000 units at that price but producers would supply only 2000 units.

What would happen if one firm set its own price at $4 per unit? Do you see that it would soon be awash in surplus pencils? People would buy their pencils from those who were willing to sell for $3 instead.

We initially passed over it, but Figure 3 shows us something else. Although the market price of pencils is $3 per unit, there are some buyers out there who would have paid $5. In effect, those latter buyers have money in their pockets to spend on something else. That is not a mistake in the graph. The gap between what people actually have to pay for an item and the benefit they receive (as measured by what they would have been willing to pay) is called the "consumer surplus." Its existence is one of the often-unsung virtues of a competitive economy.

7.   The Distortions Imposed by Monopoly

In order to see why sellers would tend to prefer the status of monopolist, we need to think about another concept—the difference between price and "marginal revenue." Taking our data from Figures 1 & 3, we can prepare Table 2 in which TR is the total revenue received for all the items sold and MR is the marginal revenue, i.e., the revenue attributable to the next item sold.

Table 2

Q	P	TR	MR
1000	$5	$5000	$5000
2000	$4	$8000	$3000
3000	$3	$9000	$1000
4000	$2	$8000	−$1000
5000	$1	$5000	−$3000

Do you see what Table 2 is telling us? If a firm can sell 1000 units at $5 or 2000 units at $4, it will make more money selling the 2000 units, but not $4000 more (1000 more units at $4). Instead, it will have to give up some revenue from those people who would have paid $5 to make sales at $4 or less. Indeed, this loss of earlier per unit revenue as the seller tries to increase volume gets so bad that the seller in our example would actually lose *total* revenue selling more items after about 3000 units.

Figure 4 adds marginal revenue to the information shown on Figure 3. It then shows the quantity that will be produced and the selling price under the assumed monopoly conditions.

Figure 4 shows a lot about monopoly. First, because of the divergence between marginal revenue and price, the Supply (S), i.e., Marginal Cost (MC) schedule intersects the Marginal Revenue (MR) schedule at a different point than it intersects the Demand (D) schedule. As a result, what has happened to the price charged by the monopolist? The quantity sold? Do you see that price has gone up and quantity down? Do you now see that *The Case of Monopolies* was right about the effect of monopoly on price? Do you see why?

Figure 4

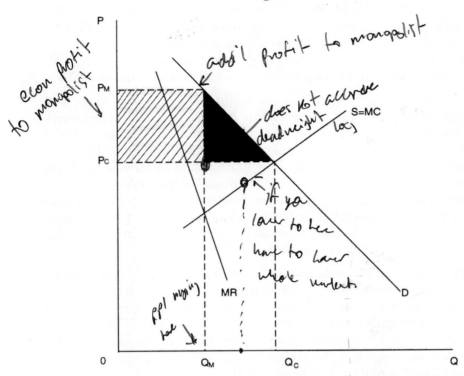

Has some "consumer surplus," indeed "total welfare" disappeared? Look at the darkened triangle at the left of the demand curve and above Pc, the competitive price. Does anyone possess that welfare now that the quantity produced has moved from Qc, the amount produced under competitive conditions, to Qm, the amount produced when the seller has a monopoly? Economists call that area the "welfare loss triangle"; it represents what at minimum they consider to be the social loss from having an industry in the hands of a monopolist.[11]

But it is a mistake to leave the matter there. Do you see what else has happened to the consumer surplus between Figure 3 and Figure 4? Remember that consumer surplus is represented by the area below the

---

[11]   The extent of the welfare loss, indeed the existence and extent of each of the consequences of monopoly, differs from case to case depending on something economists call "elasticity" of demand. If a monopolist knew that raising the price of a product 1% would cause demand for the product to decline 2%, for example, the monopolist would lose money if it raised the price at all. Demand elasticity is calculated by dividing the percentage change in quantity demanded caused by a given percentage gain in price. In our example, dividing a 2% decline in quantity by a 1% price decline would yield an elasticity of 2.0. If raising the price 2% caused demand to decline only 1%, however, the elasticity would be 0.5. We say this latter situation—an elasticity of less than 1.0—represents "inelastic" demand and we would expect to see the seller raise the price to take advantage of the chance to increase its total revenue. Indeed, ceteris paribus, the more inelastic the demand, the greater the benefits to the monopolist of having a monopoly will be. See, e.g., Gregory J. Werden, Demand Elasticities in Antitrust Analysis, 66 Antitrust L. J. 363 (1998).

demand schedule and above the competitive price, P_c. Do you see that in Figure 4 the rectangle bounded by P_c and the higher monopoly price, P_m, has become producer income instead of consumer surplus? Should that offend you? Does it matter whether you believe producers are all rich and consumers poor? Suppose the producer's stock is owned by a miners' pension fund and the product's purchasers are all wealthy consumers?[12]

Furthermore, think of the costs one might incur to be able to act as a monopolist, costs that might be incurred to form a cartel, obtain protective legislation, or seek to drive a competitor from an industry. Suppose that if you had a monopoly, each year you could convert a million dollars of consumer surplus to your own use. How much would you invest in efforts to obtain that monopoly? That's right. It would be profitable for you to invest any amount up to $1 million per year to do so. The concern that resources will be wasted in efforts to seek a monopoly position thus causes some observers to say the costs to society created by monopoly are much larger than the welfare loss triangle.[13]

Further, think of the costs imposed on a firm that would otherwise be a competitor of the monopolist. Imagine the firm driven into bankruptcy or simply engaged in activity different than what its management would choose if the monopolist were not dominating its industry. Think, too, of the concentration of political power that may be associated with substantial economic power. All of these "costs" are cited by some observers as they total up the real costs of monopoly.[14]

8.   The Matter of Productive Efficiency—Economies of Scale and Transaction Costs

We promised to come back to the other meanings of efficiency. For all the reality of the costs of monopoly and all the importance of understanding them, ask yourself how often perfectly competitive markets are a practical possibility. Almost certainly, the times will be rare. Two reasons involve the concepts of economies of scale and transaction costs.

---

[12]   An economic assumption we have not yet discussed is that of the declining marginal utility of goods. For example, you may crave a hot fudge sundae, but after having one sundae, your desire to have a second one will be less. The principle of the *constant* marginal utility of money, however, says that the utility of money does *not* decline. If that is true, the value of a dollar to a homeless person looking for his next meal is no greater than the value of that same dollar to the person who already has a million of them. Before you react with shock that anyone would assert such a thing, remember that money simply represents the capacity to buy what a person would most prefer that he or she does not already have. Rich people want things too, the argument goes, and there is no objective, external standard for saying that the homeless person's preference for a warm bed is more important than the millionaire's preference for a larger suite. Regardless of what you think of the analytic virtue of this argument, watch to see if it indeed underlies what is sometimes called the conflict between "efficiency" and "equity" in antitrust.

[13]   E.g., Richard A. Posner, Antitrust Law: An Economic Perspective 11 (1976).

[14]   E.g., Herbert Hovenkamp, Federal Antitrust Policy: The Law of Competition and its Practice 17–26 (3rd Ed. 2005); Lawrence A. Sullivan & Warren S. Grimes, The Law of Antitrust: An Integrated Handbook 18–19 (2006); Robert Pitofsky, The Political Content of Antitrust, 127 U. Pennsylvania L. Rev. 1051 (1979).

In talking about "allocative efficiency", i.e., getting goods and services to the people who value them most, we have largely ignored "productive efficiency." You could go into law practice by yourself, for example, but most likely you will join or form a partnership. Will you thereby reduce competition in the legal community? Yes, there will be perceptibly fewer competitive entities in the marketplace. Should the law deny two or more persons the right to form a more productive unit? Surely not. In a great many industries—from fast food to steel mills—efficient production of goods and services requires relatively large-scale production units, even if that means a somewhat smaller number of competing firms.

Then, too, your law firm could call "Temps-R-Us" every time you need a secretary or you could send someone down to the coin-operated machine at the public library every time you need copies, but most firms would find that an expensive, awkward way to support their operations. The cost of contracting for services and training new personnel are real costs of doing business that tend to decrease productive efficiency. We now accept as obvious the fact that people form "firms" when it is cheaper for them to do that than it is to incur the "transaction costs" associated with acting atomistically.[15] Each such firm in some small measure reduces the amount of competition in a society, yet few would wish to exchange the often-considerable productive efficiency thus achieved for the often-infinitesimal allocative efficiency thus lost.[16]

9. *Dynamic Efficiency—or—Regulation Can Do More Harm than Good*

But even that is not the end of the story of efficiency. Both allocative and productive efficiency tend to involve "static" determinations, i.e., snapshots of economic activity. When you think about it, however, such an approach is inadequate. Allocative efficiency has to have room for changes in tastes; productive efficiency has to reward innovation. In the real world, change is constant. "Dynamic efficiency" seeks to focus on the conditions in

---

[15] Lest you think this was always obvious, the description of this phenomenon in The Nature of the Firm, 4 Economica (n.s.) 386 (1937), was part of the basis for award of the 1991 Nobel Prize for Economics to Professor Ronald H. Coase.

[16] A related issue of productive efficiency, of particular interest in recent years, goes by the names of "network effects" and "two-sided markets." In a two-sided market, what sellers sell is access to other people. The value of a telephone system, for example, is that people can use it to interconnect with each other; indeed, the more people who are part of the system, the greater its value to them all. A credit card system may be yet another example of a service in which the value of the service to buyers and sellers depends on the number of the other category to whom they get access. Productive efficiency in such a system might cause one firm to get at least a short-term monopoly of service, and because people on each side of the market might have different levels of demand for the services, pricing might depart widely from practices in more traditional markets. See, e.g., David S. Evans, The Antitrust Economics of Multi-Sided Platform Markets, 20 Yale J. on Regulation 325 (2003); Mark A. Lemley & David McGowan, Legal Implications of Network Effects, 86 California L. Rev. 479 (1998); Timothy J. Muris, Payment Card Regulation and the (Mis)application of the Economics of Two-Sided Markets, 2005 Columbia Business L. Rev. 515. We will not develop the implications of such ideas at this point in the course, but watch for two-sided markets as we look at later cases.

which economic life in fact takes place—including the limited information we tend to have and the practical limits on achieving productive and allocative efficiency.[17]

In order to encourage creativity and innovation, for example, patent law creates explicit protection against competition within the scope of a patent for a limited term. Sometimes, patent and antitrust law are said to be in tension, but in reality, it is no more tension than when the law allows a firm to grow in pursuit of productive efficiency. What we will see is repeated efforts by patent holders to extend the limits of the rewards they may get from their patent monopoly. One might also argue that patent law allows more monopoly profit than necessary to encourage the desired level of innovation, but the role of dynamic efficiency in antitrust analysis is not in doubt.[18]

Another insight from examining dynamic efficiency is that people in a constantly changing world behave strategically. Rather than simply asking whether lowering the price $1 would produce more sales today, a producer may ask what the response of its competitors may be to that price reduction and whether offering it would be a money-losing decision. Similarly, a store with no competition in a neighborhood faces some pricing options open to a monopolist. What keeps it from raising its prices may be the fact—even the threat—that if it tries to do so, new firms will enter into competition with it. Thus, analysis of dynamic efficiency might ask whether there are "barriers" to the entry of new competitors, and whether existing firms may have tried to prevent such entry. Such dynamic analysis might even conclude that some aspects of monopoly are self-correcting and that the law itself can create consequences worse than the problems it seeks to solve.[19]

---

[17]   For many years, the idea of "dynamic efficiency" was less central to antitrust analysis than allocative efficiency and productive efficiency. But now that "innovation" is recognized as a key element in economic growth, dynamic efficiency has moved again to prominence. See, e.g., Jonathan Baker, Beyond Schumpeter vs. Arrow: How Antitrust Fosters Innovation, 74 Antitrust L. J. 575 (2007); Richard Gilbert & Steven Sunshine, Incorporating Dynamic Efficiency Concerns in Merger Analysis: The Use of Innovation Markets, 63 Antitrust L. J. 569 (1995); Douglas H. Ginsburg & Joshua D. Wright, Dynamic Analysis and the Limits of Antitrust Institutions, 78 Antitrust L. J. 1 (2012).

[18]   For an overview of issues at the interface between patent and antitrust law, see, e.g., Ward S. Bowman, Patent and Antitrust Law: A Legal and Economic Appraisal (1973); U.S. Department of Justice & Federal Trade Commission, Antitrust Guidelines for the Licensing of Intellectual Property (April 1995); U.S. Department of Justice & Federal Trade Commission, Antitrust Enforcement and Intellectual Property Rights: Promoting Innovation and Competition (April 2007); Federal Trade Commission, The Evolving IP Marketplace: Aligning Patent Notice and Remedies with Competition (March 2011).

[19]   Game theory has become an important tool for the analysis of dynamic efficiency, as well as many other antitrust issues. "Games" are logical analyses of how particular kinds of interactions such as business dealings might proceed. They can provide at least tentative insights about behavior reported in the cases and the likely effects of regulatory changes. For more about game theory, see, e.g., Douglas Baird, Robert H. Gertner & Randal C. Picker, Game Theory and the Law (1994); Ken Binmore, Fun and Games, A Text on Game Theory (2nd Ed. 2003); Eric Rasmusen, Games and Information: An Introduction to Game Theory (3rd Ed. 2003). See also, Willard K. Tom, Application of Game Theory to Antitrust: Game Theory in the Everyday Life of the Antitrust Practitioner, 5 George Mason L. Rev. 457 (1997).

10. The Competence Problem: How Much Can Economic Activity Be Analyzed?

We have seen that allocative efficiency, productive efficiency, and dynamic efficiency are not inevitably at war with each other. Often, all will point toward the same appropriate resolution of antitrust questions. But sometimes they will not, and don't let the single term "efficiency" allow one form of the concept to distract you from also considering the others.

Above all, be modest about what *either* legal or economic analysis can contribute to just resolution of the cases we will consider. Economic activity happens; the number of transactions in any large city runs into the billions each day. Lawyers and judges analyze; we are trained to act as though a great deal turns on detailed understanding of individual events. It is flatly inconceivable that any lawsuit could dissect any significant economic activity sufficiently to determine all of its near and long-term causes or consequences.

The ultimate problem for antitrust law, then, is how to analyze economic information in a way that is sufficiently general to be practical, yet sufficiently accurate to avoid making matters worse instead of better.[20] Economists suggest a useful distinction between types of errors the law can make. Type 1 errors occur when the law convicts the innocent, i.e., prohibits economically productive activity out of an excessive concern to prohibit misconduct. Type 2 errors occur when the law fails to prohibit genuinely harmful conduct. Other writers describe a Type 3 error caused when the complexity of legal rules increases the burden of antitrust compliance and enforcement. As applied to antitrust law, all these types of errors necessarily reduce efficiency to some degree, but Type 2 errors can sometimes be partly corrected by new entry and other market reactions.[21]

As you go through these materials, ask yourself whether a court has adequately considered the issues raised in this note as it applies the antitrust laws to the facts before it. What more would you have wanted to know to be sure you agree with the decision? Have the results reached and the rules adopted made consumers' lives richer or more impoverished?

---

[20]   See, e.g., Daniel A. Crane, Chicago, Post-Chicago, and Neo-Chicago, 76 U. Chicago L. Rev. 1911 (2009); Frank H. Easterbrook, The Limits of Antitrust, 63 Texas L. Rev. 1 (1984); Max Huffman, Marrying Neo-Chicago with Behavioral Antitrust, 78 Antitrust L. J. 105 (2012); Joshua D. Wright, Abandoning Antitrust's Chicago Obsession: The Case for Evidence-Based Antitrust, 78 Antitrust L. J. 241 (2012).

[21]   See, e.g., Alan A. Fisher & Robert H. Lande, Efficiency Considerations in Merger Enforcement, 71 California L. Rev. 1582, 1670–77 (1983); Fred S. McChesney, Talking 'Bout My Antitrust Generation: Competition For and In the Field of Competition Law, 52 Emory L. J. 1401 (2003). For an effort to minimize these errors through application of decision theory, see C. Frederick Beckner III & Steven C. Salop, Decision Theory and Antitrust Rules, 67 Antitrust L. J. 41 (1999).

In the century following The Case of Monopolies, common law courts gained more experience dealing with a wide variety of restraints of trade. Our next case is representative of the way the law developed.

MITCHEL V. REYNOLDS

King's Bench, 1711
1 P. Wms. 181, 24 Eng.Rep. 347

Debt upon a bond. The defendant * * * recited that * * * the defendant had assigned to the plaintiff a lease of a * * * bakehouse in Liquorpond Street, in the parish of St. Andrew's Holborn, for the term of five years [on the condition that] the defendant should not exercise the trade of a baker within that parish during the said term, or, in case he did, should within three days after proof thereof made, pay to the plaintiff the sum of fifty pounds, then the said obligation to be void. * * * [The defendant] pleaded that he was a baker by trade, that he had served an apprenticeship to it, * * * the said bond was void in law, [and therefore] he did trade * * * . Whereupon the plaintiff demurred in law.

* * * Parker, C. J., delivered the resolution of the court.

The general question upon this record is, whether this bond, being made in restraint of trade, be good?

And we are all of opinion, that a special consideration being set forth * * * which shews it was reasonable for the parties to enter into [the arrangement], the same is good * * * ; and that wherever a sufficient consideration appears to make it a proper and an useful contract, and such as cannot be set aside without injury to a fair contractor, it ought to be maintained * * * .

* * *

* * * I come now to make some observations that may be useful in the understanding of [the] cases. And they are—

1st, That to obtain the sole exercise of any known trade throughout England, is a complete monopoly, and against the policy of the law.

2dly, That when restrained to particular places or persons (if lawfully and fairly obtained), the same is not a monopoly.

3dly, That since these restraints may be by custom, and custom must have a good foundation, therefore the thing is not absolutely, and in itself, unlawful.

4thly, That it is lawful upon good consideration, for a man to part with his trade.

* * *

6thly, That where the law allows a restraint of trade, it is not unlawful to enforce it with a penalty.

7thly, That no man can contract not to use his trade at all.

8thly, That a particular restraint is not good without just reason and consideration.

* * *

As to involuntary restraints, the first reason why such of these, as are created by grants and charters from the Crown and by-laws, generally are void, is drawn from the encouragement which the law gives to trade and honest industry, and that they are contrary to the liberty of the subject.

2dly, Another reason is drawn from Magna Charta, which is infringed by these acts of power * * * .

But * * * here no man is abridged of his liberty, or disseised of his freehold; * * * and as to [patents for] new invented arts, no body can be said to have a right to that which was not in being before; and therefore it is but a reasonable reward to ingenuity and uncommon industry.

* * * [T]he true reasons of the distinction upon which the [prohibitions] of voluntary restraints are founded are, 1st, the mischief which may arise from them, 1st, to the party, by the loss of his livelihood, and the subsistence of his family; 2dly, to the public, by depriving it of an useful member.

Another reason is, the great abuses these voluntary restraints are liable to; as for instance, from corporations, who are perpetually laboring for exclusive advantages in trade, and to reduce it into as few hands as possible; as likewise from masters who are apt to give their apprentices much vexation on this account, and to use many indirect practices to procure such bonds from them, lest they should prejudice them in their custom, when they come to set up for themselves.

3dly, Because in a great many instances, they can be of no use to the obligee; which holds in all cases of general restraint throughout England; for what does signify to a tradesman in London, what another does at Newcastle, and surely it would be unreasonable to fix a certain loss on one side, without any benefit to the other. * * *

4thly, The fourth reason is in favor of these contracts, and is, that there may happen instances wherein they may be useful and beneficial, as to prevent a town from being over-stocked with any particular trade; or in case of an old man, who finding himself under such circumstances either of body or mind, as that he is likely to be a loser by continuing his trade, in this case it will be better for him to part with it for a consideration, that by selling his custom, he may procure to himself a livelihood which he might probably have lost, by trading longer.

* * *

The application of this to the case at bar is very plain: here the particular circumstances and consideration are set forth, upon which the court is to judge, whether it be a reasonable and useful contract.

The plaintiff took a baker's house, and the question is, whether he or the defendant shall have the trade in this neighborhood; the concern of the public is equal on both sides.

What makes this the more reasonable is, that the restraint is exactly proportioned to the consideration, viz. the term of five years.

To conclude: In all restraints of trade, where nothing more appears, the law presumes them bad; but if the circumstances are set forth, that presumption is excluded, and the Court is to judge of those circumstances, and determine accordingly; and if upon them it appears to be a just and honest contract, it ought to be maintained.

For these reasons we are of opinion that the plaintiff ought to have judgment.

NOTES AND QUESTIONS

1.   What was the underlying business arrangement here? Were you surprised that the baker might want to sell his business? Is it in the interest of consumers that business people have the ability to do so? Does that ability encourage bakers such as this one to run an efficient and popular business prior to the date of sale?

2.   Were you shocked that the buyer demanded a covenant not to compete from the first baker? If there had been no such covenant, would the buyer have been buying anything of value? Would he likely have paid as much for the bakery premises as he was willing to pay for the premises plus the "good will" of the bakery? Will the price of baked goods rise because the first baker has been paid for such "good will"? Why or why not?

3.   Why is it significant that the geographic scope and temporal duration of this covenant were limited? Does it have to do with the relative lack of ability in early 18th Century England for a person in one trade to go into another one, i.e., if the covenant were unlimited in scope, might the seller have had to leave England or do no work at all?

4.   Does the covenant upheld here create any of the problems discussed in the previous note as being presented by monopoly? After the sale, are there any fewer bakers in town than before the sale? Indeed, if the seller goes into business elsewhere in England, won't the total supply of baked goods in the nation be increased?

5.   Should it be significant that this covenant prevents there being one *more* baker in this town than before, i.e., is this a contractual barrier to the

kind of entry that an economy looks to as protection against the evils of monopoly?

———————

A NOTE ON THE COMMON LAW CONTEXT
FOR THE SHERMAN ACT

Both The Case of Monopolies and Mitchel v. Reynolds were well-known decisions at the time the Sherman Act was adopted and both are still cited today. The common law of restraint of trade consisted of many other cases as well, however, from both England and the United States. Toward the end of the 19th Century, the U.S. cases tended to be the more critical of cartels, mergers and monopoly.

Craft v. McConoughy, 79 Ill. 346 (1875), for example, found that the five grain dealers in a small Illinois town had contracted to operate as separate businesses. However, they agreed that their prices would be identical, and all of their receipts and expenses would be reported to a common manager. Profits were to be divided according to an agreed formula. When one of the parties died and his son sought to receive the father's share under the contract, the court refused to grant him relief. "So long as competition was free," the Illinois Supreme Court said, "the interest of the public was safe. * * * [B]ut the secret combination created a monopoly against which the public interest had no protection. * * * [A] court of equity will not lend its aid in the division of the profits of an illegal transaction between associates." 79 Ill. at 350.

In Richardson v. Buhl, 77 Mich. 632, 43 N.W. 1102 (1889), the Diamond Match Company, a Connecticut corporation, had sought to buy up all companies producing matches in the United States. As it did so, it obtained covenants that the sellers would not produce matches in competition with Diamond for at least 20 years. This lawsuit concerned a loan allegedly made to assist the general manager of a formerly independent match producer to buy stock in the new Diamond organization. Matches are a "necessity", Chief Justice Sherwood wrote for the Michigan Supreme Court, "in every household in the land." "Monopoly in trade or in any line of business in any line of business in this country is odious to our form of government. * * * Its tendency is * * * repugnant to the instincts of a free people * * * and is not allowed to exist under express provision in several of our state constitutions. Indeed, it is doubtful if free government can long exist in a country where such enormous amounts of money are allowed to be accumulated in the vaults of corporations." 43 N.W. at 1110. Because the monopoly to be created was thus against public policy, the court refused to enforce a transaction designed to help a firm become part of it.

In Chicago Gas-Light & Coke Co. v. People's Gas-Light & Coke Co., 121 Ill. 530, 13 N.E. 169 (1887), two firms had been granted corporate charters to sell natural gas in the city of Chicago. The firms entered into an agreement whereby Chicago Gas was to serve the North and South Divisions of the city while People's Gas was to serve the Western Division. Thereafter, Chicago Gas started to lay lines to serve the West and People's Gas sought an injunction. The companies had been granted monopoly territories at the time they were created, the Court found, but those had expired. The new contract "tends to create and perpetuate a monopoly in the furnishing of gas to the city, the Court held, and is, therefore, against public policy" and unenforceable. 121 Ill. at 544, 13 N.E. at 174.

Such cases were not at all unusual in the last half of the 19th century and they were cited in the Sherman Act debates.[22] In short, state common law had taken aim at "combinations" and "monopolies" well before federal law did so. As in the earlier English cases, the most common remedy was the state court's unwillingness to aid or enforce the arrangements.

At about the same time in England, however, the common law placed greater emphasis upon freedom of contract than upon legal protection of freedom of trade. Thus, practices were upheld in England that arguably would not have been upheld in the American states. For example, in Mogul Steamship Co. v. McGregor, Gow & Co., [1892] A.C. 25, [1891–94] All E.R. Rep. 263, owners of ships formed an association that limited the number of ships to be sent to particular ports, how cargoes would be divided among them, and the rates to be charged. A rebate of 5% was given to shippers who shipped only with association members. For a time, association members were alleged to have charged rates that were so low that non-members could not compete without being driven out of business. When the excluded shipowners filed suit, however, the Court of Appeal ruled that because the defendants' motive for acting in concert had been to increase their profits, the agreement was lawful.

The English approach was modified only somewhat in Nordenfelt v. Maxim Nordenfelt Guns & Ammunition Co., [1894] A.C. 535, [1891–94] All E.R. Rep. 1 (H.L.), where the House of Lords upheld a covenant ancillary to the sale of a business whereby the seller agreed not to compete with the buyer anywhere in the world for a period of 25 years. The general rule was said to be that "all interference with liberty of action in trading, and all restraints of trade themselves, if there is nothing more, are contrary to public policy, and therefore void," Lord Macnaghten wrote. However, the restraints could be justified by special circumstances in a particular case. "It is a sufficient justification, and indeed it is the only justification, if the restriction is reasonable—reasonable, that is, in reference to the interests of the parties concerned and reasonable in reference to the interests of the public, so framed and so guarded as to afford adequate protection to the

---

[22]   See, in particular, 21 Cong. Rec. at 2457–60 (1890) (remarks of Senator Sherman).

party in whose favor it is imposed, while at the same time it is in no way injurious to the public." [1894] A.C. at 565.[23]

A NOTE ON THE ADOPTION OF THE SHERMAN ACT

As you struggle with interpretation of the Sherman Act, you like many others may be tempted to try to ascertain the Congressional intent underlying it. No matter how much you research the history of the Act, however, you are unlikely to find convincing answers.[24]

As American industrial development accelerated during the last half of the 19th Century, small firms consolidated into larger and larger enterprises. While probably inevitable, the development was also frightening to many. In the Presidential campaign of 1888, both parties' platforms condemned "trusts" and few in public life had much good to say publicly about the consolidations that had occurred.[25]

Senator John Sherman had been a candidate for the Republican Presidential nomination in 1888. He ultimately lost to Benjamin Harrison, but in attacking the trusts, Sherman had found a popular issue. As Chair of the Senate Finance Committee, he introduced S. 3445 after returning from the 1888 convention. Sherman's bill premised jurisdiction over trusts on the federal taxing power, observing that the trusts were often found in industries protected by tariffs against foreign competition. That basis of jurisdiction, of course, gave Sherman's committee authority to consider the bill.

Ultimately, nothing happened in the last days of the 50th Congress, so a new round of bills was considered beginning in 1889. In addition to

---

[23]   The development of English law in this period is traced in Trebilcock, supra n. 2, at pp. 26 & 38–53; Letwin, supra n. 2, at 44–52.

[24]   The best single source for the primary documents in the legislative history of the Sherman Act is Earl W. Kintner, The Legislative History of the Federal Antitrust Laws and Related Statutes, Vol. 1 (1978). Excellent books describing the history include Hans B. Thorelli, The Federal Antitrust Policy: Origination of an American Tradition 164–232 (1955); William Letwin, Law and Economic Policy in America: The Evolution of the Sherman Antitrust Act 53–99 (1965); Robert H. Bork, The Antitrust Paradox: A Policy At War With Itself 50–71 (1978). Articles addressing the legislative history include Robert H. Bork, Legislative Intent and the Policy of the Sherman Act, 9 J. Law & Economics 7 (1966); Thomas C. Arthur, Farewell to the Sea of Doubt: Jettisoning the Constitutional Sherman Act, 74 California L. Rev. 263 (1986).

[25]   See, e.g., Kintner, supra n. 24, at 9–13; Thorelli, supra n. 24, at 108–163. Americans have long been concerned about monopolies. Massachusetts had a statute and Virginia had a provision in its state constitution prohibiting monopoly. Jefferson favored such a provision in the Federal Constitution and several states were reluctant to ratify the Constitution because it lacked such a provision. Letwin, supra n. 24, at 59–60. Indeed, Jacksonian Democrats had opposed creation of private corporations because they were state-charted for specific purposes and had unlimited life and were thus characterized as "monopolies." Even when there were so many corporations that the term "monopoly" clearly did not apply, many opposed their ability to accumulate wealth. Id. at 65–66. For a thoughtful modern assessment of this period, see Alfred D. Chandler, Jr., Scale and Scope: The Dynamics of Industrial Capitalism 18–36 (1990).

Sherman's own S. 1, there were two other proposals before the Senate and twelve before the House. Sherman got most of the bills considered by his committee.

Sherman's bill, S. 1, had declared two broad categories of "arrangements, contracts, trusts, or combinations" to be illegal. First were those formed to "prevent full and free competition." Second were those which tended to "advance the cost to the consumer." This language is consistent with the contention of Judge Bork and others that the fundamental purpose of the Sherman Act was to enhance the welfare of consumers. Senator Sherman reinforced this interpretation, saying that his bill sought "only to prevent and control combinations made with a view to prevent competition, or for the restraint of trade, or to increase the profits of the producer at the cost of the consumer."[26]

The standard by which courts would judge business arrangements would not be a novel one according to Sherman. His bill adopted the common law of restraint of trade: "It does not announce a new principle of law, but applies old and well recognized principles of the common law to the complicated jurisdiction of our State and Federal Governments."[27] The states had for some time applied their own statutory or common law against certain business combinations. Sherman asserted that because unlawful combinations now extended beyond state lines, "only the General Government can secure relief."[28]

In order to give full effect to any new federal law in this field, Sherman realized that the courts would play a vital role:

> [I]t is difficult to define in legal language the precise line between lawful and unlawful combinations. This must be left for the courts to determine in each particular case. All that we, as lawmakers, can do is to declare general principles, and we can be assured that the courts will apply them as to carry out the meaning of the law * * * . This bill is only an honest effort to declare a rule of action.[29]

Commentators have seized on this language as evincing a broad delegation of authority to the courts to infuse their notions of what is "lawful" or "unlawful" into the federal antitrust law. Others, however, contend that the courts were circumscribed by the goal of consumer welfare, while still others argue that this language merely indicated that

---

[26]   21 Cong. Rec. 2457 (1890). For divergent interpretations of this history, compare Robert H. Bork, The Antitrust Paradox: A Policy at War with Itself (1978), with Robert H. Lande, Wealth Transfers as the Original and Primary Concern of Antitrust: The Efficiency Interpretation Challenged, 34 Hastings L.J. 67 (1982).

[27]   Id. at 2456. At pp. 2457–60, he went on to discuss the state cases included in our earlier note on the common law context of the Sherman Act.

[28]   Id. at 2456.

[29]   Id. at 2460.

the federal courts were bound to decide the "precise line" in the same manner as state courts, which were guided by the common law.[30]

Considering the potential impact of an antitrust law on American business, it is not surprising that Sherman's bill met intense scrutiny. In an early, extended speech in support of the bill, Sherman anticipated the criticism that the bill would interfere with customary and legitimate business practices. He said he was not unmindful of the tremendous economic advances in the American economy that had resulted from aggregations of capital and resources. Corporations "ought to be encouraged and protected as tending to cheapen the cost of production * * * [as] they are the most useful agencies of modern civilization * * * enabl[ing] individuals to unite to undertake great enterprises only attempted in former times by powerful governments." Furthermore, they "tend to cheapen transportation, lessen the cost of production, and bring within the reach of millions comforts and luxuries formerly enjoyed by thousands."[31]

Unfortunately for persons seeking a single motive or rationale behind the Sherman Act, however, the members of the 51st Senate did not unanimously endorse a goal of unfettered competition. Several Senators expressed concern for the small businessman in a market of large corporate entities, however efficient they might be. Others perceived a value in cooperation among those producers who faced sour economic conditions. Senator Platt declared:

> "[T]his bill proceeds upon the false assumption that all competition is beneficent to the country, and that every advance of price is an injury to the country. There never was a greater fallacy in the world. * * * The great corporations of this country * * * are every one of them built upon the graves of weaker competitors that have been forced to their death by remorseless competition."[32]

Platt urged that arrangements among competitors were often necessary to preserve them all from bankruptcy. This concern for firms in "failing" industries was echoed earlier by Senator Stewart:

> If producers did not have the power to make such an agreement [of limiting production] in times like these, when prices are declining * * * if they could not make an agreement to check production and wait for better times to bridge over the trouble, they would be ruined; and this bill would probably, if carried out

---

[30]   See, e.g., Arthur, supra n. 24, and authorities discussed there.

[31]   The full text of this speech, delivered on March 21, 1890, may be found at 21 Cong.Rec. 2456–63 (1890). It is reprinted in Kintner, supra n. 24, at 113–29.

[32]   Id. at 2729.

literally, in times of depression, break up half the manufacturing establishments in the country.[33]

Senator George stated his view of the status of the American economy which any antitrust bill needed to address:

> [T]he present system of production and of exchange is having that tendency which is sure at some not very distant day to crush out all small men, all small capitalists, all small enterprises * * *. We find everywhere over our land the wrecks of small independent enterprises thrown in our pathway * * *. Is production, is trade, to be taken away from the great mass of the people and concentrated in the hands of a few men who * * * have been enabled to aggregate to themselves large, enormous fortunes?[34]

An interesting question surfaced during the debates as to whether an antitrust statute was necessary at all. A few Senators asserted that high protective tariffs lay at the root of the problems facing the American economy. These tariffs sheltered certain industries from foreign competition, the argument ran, and allowed domestic manufacturers to arrange restrictions on production among themselves. Reducing or removing the tariffs would force American producers to compete with lower-priced imports.

Senator George addressed this concern during the first day of debates on Sherman's original bill:

> [Sherman and the Finance Committee] seek to make two inconsistent, even repellant, things coexist and harmonize, to wit: a high protective tariff, which shuts out foreign competition, and the vain prohibition that the protected parties shall not avail themselves of the advantage thus given them. * * * The attempt to do this must fail. * * * By our tariff laws we hold out to the owners of the protected industries the offer of 47 per cent advance in price. We tell them they are entitled to it; that it is right and just. By this bill we say to them, "You must not take the offer."[35]

Others, however, pointed to the absence of a consistent relation between those products which enjoyed tariff protection and those industries which were suspected of combining into trusts. Senator Allison concluded that national legislation was needed to combat "combinations

---

[33]   Id. at 2606.

[34]   Id. at 2598. Robert Bork suggests that Senator George was offering sympathy for such small producers but not offering a standard for construction of the Act different than a preference for competition and a desire to further consumer welfare. See Bork, supra n. 24, at 41.

[35]   Id. at 1768.

and trusts," and that the Congress could not achieve that goal "by merely modifying or changing existing tariff rates."[36]

Other Senators speculated as to the effect of Sherman's bill on cooperative enterprises, such as labor unions and farmers' associations. Senator Teller inquired, "If * * * a class of laborers should combine to raise the price of their labor, and thus have a tendency to increase the price of the product, whether it was in a mill or in a shop or on a farm, would it not fall within the inhibition of this bill * * * ?" Sherman responded that his bill did "not interfere in the slightest degree with voluntary associations made to affect public opinion to advance the interest of a particular trade or occupation."[37] However, not until adoption of the Clayton Act in 1914 did both labor and agricultural associations receive express exemptions from coverage under the antitrust laws.

Sherman's original bill shortly became the recipient of numerous amendments, which, among others, included an amendment giving the state courts concurrent jurisdiction, and an amendment regulating the options and futures markets. Perhaps sensing the unwieldy nature of the bill before it, the Senate referred Sherman's bill to the Judiciary Committee with instructions to return a redrafted version within 20 days. The Committee wasted little time, and after six days it presented to the Senate a substitute version of the Sherman Act in the form that ultimately became law.

The substitute version represented a major revision of Sherman's original proposal. Section 1 generally followed the form of Sherman's bill by prohibiting "every contract, combination in the form of trust or otherwise, or conspiracy, in restraint of trade or commerce." However, Section 2 offered a completely new proscription against the offenses of monopolization, attempted monopolization, and conspiracy to monopolize. Furthermore, the remedial section was expanded to allow private parties injured by reason of a violation of the act to collect treble damages. The substance of all amendments which were offered before referral to the Judiciary Committee was completely missing.

Senate debate on this version was surprisingly limited. Despite the wholesale changes in language, Senator Hoar introduced the debate by stating that he would not explain the whole bill, which was "well understood." Sherman remarked that he would vote for the redrafted bill, even though it was not "precisely what I want."[38]

Even newly created Section 2 merited scant attention from the Senate. Senator Hoar offered a definition of "monopoly" that went unchallenged: "It is the sole engrossing to a man's self by means which prevent other men

---

[36] Id. at 2471.

[37] Id. at 2561–62.

[38] Id. at 3145.

from engaging in fair competition with him." He added that a person who "merely by superior skill and intelligence" accumulated all of the trade in one industry "because nobody could do it as well as he could" would not be considered a monopolist, "but that it involved something like the use of means which made it impossible for other persons to engage in fair competition, like the * * * buying up of all other persons engaged in the same business."[39]

The Senate passed this substitute version of the Sherman Act 52–1, and then sent it to the House for consideration. Representative Bland offered an amendment that would have prohibited all agreements whose purpose was to prevent competition in the sale of commodities transported in interstate commerce, or for preventing competition in the transportation of persons or commodities between states.[40]

The House adopted the bill with Bland's amendment and sent it to the Senate, which referred it to the Judiciary Committee. The committee reported back a version that would have made illegal arrangements entered into for the purpose of preventing competition in transportation, "so that the rates of such transportation may be raised above what is just and reasonable." Following conference committee reports that recommended adoption of the Senate language, the House entered into extended debate over whether the "just and reasonable" clause would permit pooling and thereby decrease competition in the transportation industry and effectively override the anti-pooling clause of the Interstate Commerce Act.[41] The conference committee was unable to find satisfactory compromise language, and in the end both houses agreed to recede from their respective amendments.

In the end the House passed the Sherman Act in the form in which it returned from the Senate Judiciary Committee. It was signed into law by President Harrison on July 2, 1890. Its key provisions were as follows:

THE SHERMAN ACT

"An Act to Protect Trade and Commerce Against Unlawful Restraints and Monopolies"

26 Stat. 209

no examples

SEC. 1. Every contract, combination in the form of trust or otherwise, or conspiracy, in restraint of trade or commerce among the several States, or with foreign nations, is hereby declared to be illegal. Every person who shall make any such contract or engage in any such combination or conspiracy, shall be deemed guilty of a misdemeanor, and, on conviction thereof, shall be punished by fine not exceeding five thousand dollars, or

"Laws of several States"

---

[39]   Id. at 3152.

[40]   Id. at 4099.

[41]   Id. at 5951–61.

by imprisonment not exceeding one year, or by both said punishments, in the discretion of the court.

SEC. 2. Every person who shall monopolize, or attempt to monopolize, or combine or conspire with any other person or persons, to monopolize any part of the trade or commerce among the several States, or with foreign nations, shall be deemed guilty of a misdemeanor, and, on conviction thereof, shall be punished by fine not exceeding five thousand dollars, or by imprisonment not exceeding one year, or by both said punishments, in the discretion of the court.

Conspiracy = 2+

monopoly can be 1 actor

* * *

SEC. 4. The several Circuit Courts of the United States are hereby invested with jurisdiction to prevent and restrain violations of this act * * * . * * * [T]he court may at any time make such temporary restraining order or prohibition as shall be deemed just in the premises.

* * *

SEC. 7. Any person who shall be injured in his business or property by any other person or corporation by reason of anything forbidden or declared to be unlawful by this act, may sue therefor in any Circuit Court of the United States in the district in which the defendant resides or is found, without respect to the amount in controversy, and shall recover threefold the damages by him sustained, and the costs of suit, including a reasonable attorney's fee.

SEC. 8. That the word "person," or "persons," wherever used in this act shall be deemed to include corporations and associations existing under or authorized by the laws of either the United States, the laws of any of the Territories, the laws of any State, or the laws of any foreign country.

Most likely, Congress in 1890 was not unlike Congress today. Members saw several issues as important and in a single vote they hoped to compromise these different concerns and take a symbolic stand for what they hoped their constituents would see as "right" and "just."

As you look at the Sherman Act and the cases arising under it, however, try to sort out which of the following possible goals do or should underlie the analysis in the cases you will be reading:

1. "Allocative efficiency", the allocation of economic goods to the people who value them most, i.e., most of the issues discussed in the earlier economic note.

2. "Productive efficiency", i.e., letting firms achieve the size at which the cost of production is least, even if that means there will be only a relatively few, large firms in some industries.

3.   "Dynamic efficiency", i.e., the desire to protect the competitive process itself and especially to preserve the opportunity for new firms to enter existing markets or create new ones.

4.   The desire to break up large firms so as to advance the interests of small business and prevent the concentration of economic and political power.[42]

ORGANIZING THE CONCEPTS THAT YOU WILL SEE IN ANTITRUST LAW

To help you keep straight which modern cases build on which earlier ones, organize your thinking around the following antitrust concepts that you will find in the remainder of these materials:

Horizontal Arrangements	Vertical Arrangements	Jurisdiction/ Procedural Issues
Price fixing	Resale price maintenance	Interstate commerce
Market division	Territorial allocation	Private litigant standing
Group boycotts	Vertical integration	Antitrust injury
Monopolization	Exclusive dealing	Summary judgment standards
Mergers	Tying	Interplay between antitrust and other federal & state regulatory policies

You may find yourself adding additional concepts to this list as you work through these materials, but most of the cases and economic theories you consider are likely to fit under one or more of these headings.

---

[42]   Further background on the economic and non-economic goals of antitrust may be found in the essays reprinted in E. Thomas Sullivan, ed., The Political Economy of the Sherman Act (1991). See also, e.g., Hans B. Thorelli, The Federal Antitrust Policy: Origination of an American Tradition 108–163 (1954); Robert H. Lande, Proving the Obvious: The Antitrust Laws Were Passed to Protect Consumers (Not Just to Increase Efficiency), 50 Hastings L. J. 959 (1999). For an account of the new federal law through the eyes of a contemporaneous observer, see S.C.T. Dodd, The Present Legal Status of Trusts, 7 Harvard L.Rev. 157 (1893–94).

CHAPTER I

THE FIRST 25 YEARS UNDER THE
SHERMAN ACT: 1890 TO 1914

■ ■ ■

Once the Sherman Act was adopted, the modern era of antitrust law began. It soon became clear, however, that the focus, coverage and even the constitutionality of the Act remained to be determined. Indeed, the following case, the first to reach the Supreme Court, left some concern that the Act had been utterly stillborn.[1]

A. JURISDICTION AND SCOPE OF THE ACT

UNITED STATES V. E.C. KNIGHT COMPANY

Supreme Court of the United States, 1895
156 U.S. 1, 15 S.Ct. 249, 39 L.Ed. 325

[Prior to March, 1892, the American Sugar Refining Co., a New Jersey corporation with its headquarters in New York, had acquired all but five of the sugar refineries in the United States. During March 1892, in separate transactions, American Sugar Refining acquired the four of the "holdouts" that were based in Philadelphia by exchanging shares of its own stock for shares of theirs. Together, the four firms had produced about 33% of the total amount of sugar refined in the United States and had been in active competition with American Sugar Refining. The fifth firm, left unacquired, refined only 2% of U.S. sugar. By the time of this suit, the amount of sugar refined in Philadelphia had increased, the price was below that which had prevailed for some years before the acquisition, and the portion of U.S. sugar not refined by American Sugar Refining had risen to 10%.

counter-intuitive

[The Government's complaint charged a violation of both §§ 1 & 2 of the Sherman Act, sought a declaration that the transactions were illegal and sought an injunction against their consummation. The trial court

---

[1] No antitrust division was created in the Justice Department after passage of the Sherman Act. Instead, enforcement was left to individual U.S. Attorneys. The first such case was filed by John Ruhm in Nashville against the Jellico Mountain Coal and Coke Company, a local cartel that sought to fix the price of Kentucky and Tennessee coal. The permanent injunction sought by the government was granted, 46 Fed. 432 (M.D. Tenn. 1891), and no appeal was taken. The case against the "Sugar Trust" (*E.C. Knight*) was filed near the end of the Harrison administration but taken to the Supreme Court by the administration of Grover Cleveland. See, e.g., William Letwin, Law and Economic Policy in America: The Evolution of the Sherman Act 106–116 (1965); Hans B. Thorelli, The Federal Antitrust Policy: Origination of an American Tradition 371–380 (1954).

dismissed the complaint and the Court of Appeals for the Third Circuit affirmed.]

MR. CHIEF JUSTICE FULLER * * * delivered the opinion of the court.

By the purchase of the stock of the four Philadelphia refineries with shares of its own stock the American Sugar Refining Company acquired nearly complete control of the manufacture of refined sugar within the United States. * * *

* * *

The fundamental question is, whether conceding that the existence of a monopoly in manufacture is established by the evidence, that monopoly can be directly suppressed under the act of Congress in the mode attempted by this bill.

* * * The relief of the citizens of each state from the burden of monopoly and the evils resulting from the restraint of trade among such citizens was left with the states to deal with, and this court has recognized their possession of that power even to the extent of holding that an employment or business carried on by private individuals, when it becomes a matter of such public interest and importance as to create a common charge or burden upon the citizen; in other words, when it becomes a practical monopoly, to which the citizen is compelled to resort and by means of which a tribute can be exacted from the community, is subject to regulation by state legislative power. On the other hand, the power of Congress to regulate commerce among the several states is also exclusive. * * * "Commerce, undoubtedly, is traffic," said Chief Justice Marshall, "but it is something more; it is intercourse. It describes the commercial intercourse between nations and parts of nations in all its branches, and is regulated by prescribing rules for carrying on that intercourse." That which belongs to commerce is within the jurisdiction of the United States, but that which does not belong to commerce is within the jurisdiction of the police power of the state. Gibbons v. Ogden, [22 U.S. (9 Wheat.) 1, 6 L.Ed. 23 (1824)].

The argument is that the power to control the manufacture of refined sugar is a monopoly over a necessary of life, to the enjoyment of which by a large part of the population of the United States interstate commerce is indispensable, and that, therefore, the general government in the exercise of the power to regulate commerce may repress such monopoly directly and set aside the instruments which have created it. But this argument cannot be confined to necessaries of life merely, and must include all articles of general consumption. Doubtless the power to control the manufacture of a given thing involves, in a certain sense, the control of its disposition, but this is a secondary and not the primary sense * * * . Commerce succeeds to manufacture, and is not a part of it. * * *

* * *

* * * Contracts to buy, sell, or exchange goods to be transported among the several States, the transportation and its instrumentalities, and articles bought, sold, or exchanged for the purposes of such transit among the states, or put in the way of transit, may be regulated, but this is because they form part of interstate trade or commerce. The fact that an article is manufactured for export to another state does not of itself make it an article of interstate commerce, and the intent of the manufacturer does not determine the time when the article or product passes from the control of the state and belongs to commerce. * * *

* * *

* * * [A]ll the authorities agree that, in order to vitiate a contract or combination, it is not essential that its result should be a complete monopoly; it is sufficient if it really tends to that end and to deprive the public of the advantages which flow from free competition. Slight reflection will show that if the national power extends to all contracts and combinations in manufacture, agriculture, mining, and other productive industries, whose ultimate result may affect external commerce, comparatively little of business operations and affairs would be left for state control.

It was in the light of well-settled principles that the act of July 2, 1890, was framed. Congress did not attempt thereby to assert the power to deal with monopoly directly as such; * * * or to make criminal the acts of persons in the acquisition and control of property which the states of their residence or creation sanctioned or permitted. * * * It is true that the bill alleged that the products of these refineries were sold and distributed among the several states, and that all the companies were engaged in trade or commerce with the several states and with foreign nations; but this was no more than to say that trade and commerce served manufacture to fulfil its function. Sugar was refined for sale, and sales were probably made at Philadelphia for consumption, and undoubtedly for resale by the first purchasers throughout Pennsylvania and other states, and refined sugar was also forwarded by the companies to other states for sale. Nevertheless it does not follow that an attempt to monopolize, or the actual monopoly of, the manufacture was an attempt, whether executory or consummated, to monopolize commerce, even though, in order to dispose of the product, the instrumentality of commerce was necessarily invoked. * * *

* * *

Decree affirmed.

MR. JUSTICE HARLAN, dissenting.

* * *

* * * If it be true that a combination of corporations or individuals may, so far as the power of Congress is concerned, subject interstate trade, in

any of its stages, to unlawful restraints, the conclusion is inevitable that the constitution has failed to accomplish one primary object of the Union, which was to place commerce among the states under the control of the common government of all the people * * * .

* * *

* * * [I]t will not be doubted that it would be competent for a state, under the power to regulate its domestic commerce and for the purpose of protecting its people against fraud and injustice, to make it a public offence punishable by fine and imprisonment, for individuals or corporations to make contracts, form combinations, or engage in conspiracies, which unduly restrain trade or commerce carried on within its limits, and also to authorize the institution of proceedings for the purpose of annulling contracts of that character, as well as of preventing or restraining such combinations and conspiracies.

But there is a trade among the several states which is distinct from that carried on within the territorial limits of a state. * * * Under the power with which it is invested, Congress may remove unlawful obstructions, of whatever kind, to the free course of trade among the states. In so doing it would not interfere with the "autonomy of the states," because the power thus to protect interstate commerce is expressly given by the people of all the states. * * * Any combination, therefore, that disturbs or unreasonably obstructs freedom in buying and selling articles manufactured to be sold to persons in other states or to be carried to other states—a freedom that cannot exist if the right to buy and sell is fettered by unlawful restraints that crush out competition—affects, not incidentally, but directly, the people of all the states; and the remedy for such an evil is found only in the exercise of powers confided to a government which, this court has said, was the government of all, exercising powers delegated by all, representing all, acting for all.

* * *

We have before us the case of a combination which absolutely controls, or may, at its discretion, control the price of all refined sugar in this country. Suppose another combination, organized for private gain and to control prices, should obtain possession of all the large flour mills in the United States; another, of all the grain elevators; another, of all the oil territory; another, of all the salt-producing regions; another, of all the cotton mills; and another, of all the great establishments for slaughtering animals, and the preparation of meats. What power is competent to protect the people of the United States against such dangers except national power—one that is capable of exerting its sovereign authority throughout every part of the territory and over all the people of the nation?

* * * The common government of all the people is the only one that can adequately deal with a matter which directly and injuriously affects the

entire commerce of the country, which concerns equally all the people of the Union, and which, it must be confessed, cannot be adequately controlled by any one state. Its authority should not be so weakened by construction that it cannot reach and eradicate evils that, beyond all question, tend to defeat an object which that government is entitled, by the constitution, to accomplish. * * *

* * *

For the reasons stated I dissent from the opinion and judgment of the court.

NOTES AND QUESTIONS

1.   There is a tendency today to see old cases discussing the commerce power as too archaic to have modern relevance. In *E.C. Knight*, however, the Court was most of all facing the question of what the new Sherman Act was intended to address.

a.   Remember that Craft v. McConoughy and the other cases cited in the introductory chapter showed that state courts were already dealing with such situations when they involved "necessaries of life." Does Justice Harlan identify any matters that one or more states could *not* have reached without a federal statute?[2]

b.   It is worth remembering that the Court had relatively recently decided several cases upholding state power to regulate all manner of business within their borders. In Munn v. Illinois, 94 U.S. 113, 24 L.Ed. 77 (1877), for example, the Court said "the governments of the States possess all the powers of the Parliament of England, except such as have been delegated to the United States or reserved by the people." The Court there found that a state could regulate any activity "affected with a public interest," i.e., virtually anything.

2.   Is Justice Harlan right that the Court's construction of the Sherman Act, followed logically, would remove all federal power to deal with national manufacturing monopolies? Can this case be limited by saying that all the firms being acquired here had their headquarters in a single state? Indeed, did that fact seem to be central to the decision at all?

3.   Do Chief Justice Fuller and the majority have a positive theory of what activities the Sherman Act *does* prohibit? Notice the majority opinion's concern that all contracts are potentially covered by § 1. Do you share its concern that a narrow construction of the commerce power was necessary to avoid finding that federal power extends to all aspects of commercial law?

4.   While no one considers *E.C. Knight* controlling today, it did not stand alone.

a.   In Hopkins v. United States, 171 U.S. 578, 19 S.Ct. 40, 43 L.Ed. 290 (1898), for example, an association of traders at the Kansas City Live Stock

---

2   See, e.g., Herbert Hovenkamp, Enterprise and American Law, 1836–1937 (1991), at 261–63.

Exchange was held not to be engaged in interstate commerce even though sales on the Kansas City Exchange were simply a part of the process of shipping large numbers of cattle, hogs and sheep from many mid-western states to locations all over the country.

b.   Even a quarter-century later, the Court construed the interstate commerce standard of the Sherman Act narrowly. When a team owner charged professional baseball with monopolizing the "baseball business," Justice Homes wrote for a unanimous court:

> "The business is giving exhibitions of baseball, which are purely state affairs. It is true that, in order to attain for these exhibitions the great popularity that they have achieved, competitions must be arranged between clubs from different cities and States. But the fact that in order to give the exhibitions the Leagues must induce free persons to cross state lines and must arrange and pay for their doing so is not enough to change the character of the business."

Federal Baseball Club of Baltimore v. National League, 259 U.S. 200, 42 S.Ct. 465, 66 L.Ed. 898 (1922).[3]

FOREIGN COMMERCE JURISDICTION:
A CASE OF BANANAS

Remember that the Sherman Act purports to regulate both interstate and *foreign* commerce. The reach of the latter term was tested in American Banana Co. v. United Fruit Co., 213 U.S. 347, 29 S.Ct. 511, 53 L.Ed. 826 (1909).

The events took place in Latin America. The defendant had long achieved a monopoly of the "banana trade" as a result of buying up most of the competition. With the rest of its competitors, it had formed a cartel to sell bananas at what were conceded for purposes of this case to be jointly-set, unreasonably-high prices.

A man named McConnell (whom the plaintiff succeeded) started a banana plantation in what is now Panama. When McConnell began to build a railway to get his products to market, the United Fruit Company demanded that he join the cartel. When he refused, the defendant allegedly conspired with the governments of Panama and Costa Rica to have Costa Rican soldiers come into Panama, physically stop the building of the railroad, and seize the plantation.

The plaintiff argued that these acts by the defendant constituted acts of monopolization in violation of § 2 of the Sherman Act. The Court refused

---

[3]   A half-century later, Flood v. Kuhn, 407 U.S. 258, 92 S.Ct. 2099, 32 L.Ed.2d 728 (1972), again refused to hold professional baseball subject to antitrust scrutiny. This anomaly was partially corrected by the Curt Flood Act of 1998, now codified at 15 U.S.C. § 27a.

to so extend the application of the Act. The events took place outside the United States, the Court observed, and they were not tortious in the country where they occurred. Indeed, they were done in concert with local authorities. The Sherman Act, the Court said, could not render acts illegal that were legal in the nation where they were committed. This time, Justice Harlan concurred in the result.

American Banana was an early case, and later the Court found the constitutional reach of Sherman Act to be more extensive.[4] As you can imagine, however, as United States firms compete in the global economy, the question of how far around the world the United States should seek to apply its antitrust policy remains vitally important.

B. HORIZONTAL COMBINATIONS IN RESTRAINT OF TRADE

UNITED STATES v. TRANS-MISSOURI FREIGHT ASSOCIATION

Supreme Court of the United States, 1897
166 U.S. 290, 17 S.Ct. 540, 41 L.Ed. 1007

[On March 15, 1889, the defendant railroads formed the Trans-Missouri Freight Association and agreed to be governed by its articles of agreement. All competitive traffic between member railroads was to be included if it originated west of a line running from eastern Texas, along the Red River, then north to Kansas City, then along the Missouri River to the eastern boundary of Montana, then north to Canada.

[A committee was created to establish rates and regulations affecting this traffic. Proposed rate reductions had to be filed at least five days before a committee meeting. If unanimously approved, changes could be implemented immediately; otherwise, they were subject to arbitration. Any member railroad could give written notice that, despite disapproval of the rate decrease, it would be implemented ten days later. The Association, in turn, reserved the right to match the decreased rates. In addition, any member railroad could, without notice to anyone, make a rate or rule change necessary to meet the competition of a line that was not a member of the Association. However, if it were later determined that such a rate change had not been made in good faith to meet such competition, the offending railroad would have to pay a fine of up to $100. A railroad could withdraw from the Association by giving thirty days notice to the others.

---

[4]   See, e.g., United States v. Sisal Sales Corp., 274 U.S. 268, 47 S.Ct. 592, 71 L.Ed. 1042 (1927); Continental Ore Co. v. Union Carbide & Carbon Corp., 370 U.S. 690, 82 S.Ct. 1404, 8 L.Ed.2d 777 (1962); Hartford Fire Insurance Co. v. California, 509 U.S. 764, 113 S.Ct. 2891, 125 L.Ed.2d 612 (1993). See also, United States v. Aluminum Co. of America, 148 F.2d 416 (2nd Cir. 1945).

[The Government filed its complaint on January 6, 1892, alleging that the defendants were common carriers who, prior to the agreement, had operated separately and in competition. They were alleged to be operating in interstate commerce and to have as their purpose "unjustly and oppressively" increasing rates. The complaint asked for an injunction against future coordinated ratemaking by Association members.

[The defendants admitted they were common carriers engaged in the interstate transportation of persons and property. However, they alleged that, as such, they were subject to the Interstate Commerce Act of 1887, and thus not subject to the Sherman Act. They further admitted that prior to the organization of the association they furnished separate and competitive lines of transportation and communication and alleged that they still did so. They denied any intent to increase rates unjustly, and denied that the agreement destroyed, prevented or illegally limited or influenced competition. They denied that they charged arbitrary rates, that rates had been increased as a result of their agreement, or that the effect of free competition had been counteracted. They alleged that the proper object of the association had been simply to establish and maintain reasonable rates, rules and regulations on all freight traffic.

[The trial court dismissed the Government's complaint and the Eighth Circuit affirmed. The Government appealed.]

* * *

MR. JUSTICE PECKHAM * * * delivered the opinion of the court.

* * *

* * * [T]here are two important questions which demand our examination. They are, first, whether the * * * trust act applies to and covers common carriers by railroad; and, if so, second, does the agreement set forth in the bill violate any provision of that act?

As to the first question:

The language of the act includes every contract, combination in the form of trust or otherwise, or conspiracy, in restraint of trade or commerce among the several States or with foreign nations. * * * The point urged on the defendants' part is that the statute was not really intended to reach that kind of an agreement relating only to traffic rates entered into by competing common carriers by railroad; that it was intended to reach only those who were engaged in the manufacture or sale of articles of commerce, and who by means of trusts, combinations and conspiracies were engaged in affecting the supply or the price or the place of manufacture of such articles. The terms of the act do not bear out such construction. Railroad companies are instruments of commerce, and their business is commerce itself. An act which prohibits the making of every contract, etc., in restraint of trade or commerce among the several States, would seem to cover by such language a contract between competing railroads * * * .

We have held that the trust act did not apply to a company engaged in one State in the refining of sugar under the circumstances detailed in the case of United States v. E.C. Knight Company because the refining of sugar under those circumstances bore no distinct relation to commerce between the States or with foreign nations. To exclude agreements as to rates by competing railroads for the transportation of articles of commerce between the States would leave little for the act to take effect upon.

* * *

But it is maintained that an agreement like the one in question on the part of the railroad companies is authorized by the Commerce Act, which is a special statute applicable only to railroads, and that a construction of the Trust Act (which is a general act) so as to include within its provisions the case of railroads, carries with it the repeal by implication of so much of the Commerce Act as authorized the agreement. * * * On a line with this reasoning it is said that if Congress had intended to in any manner affect the railroad carrier as governed by the Commerce Act, it would have amended that act directly and in terms, and not have left it as a question of construction to be determined whether so important a change in the commerce statute had been accomplished by the passage of the statute relating to trusts.

The first answer to this argument is that, in our opinion, the Commerce Act does not authorize an agreement of this nature. It may not in terms prohibit, but it is far from conferring either directly or by implication any authority to make it. * * * The general nature of a contract like the one before us is not mentioned in or provided for by the act. The provisions of that act look to the prevention of discrimination, to the furnishing of equal facilities for the interchange of traffic, to the rate of compensation for what is termed the long and the short haul, to the attainment of a continuous passage from the point of shipment to the point of destination, at a known and published schedule, * * * to procuring uniformity of rates charged by each company to its patrons, and to other objects of a similar nature. The act was not directed to the securing of uniformity of rates to be charged by competing companies, nor was there any provision therein as to a maximum or minimum of rates. * * * As the Commerce Act does not authorize this agreement, argument against a repeal by implication, of the provisions of the act which it is alleged grant such authority, becomes ineffective. There is no repeal in the case, and both statutes may stand, as neither is inconsistent with the other.[5]

---

5   [Ed. note] The Court acknowledged that, as discussed in the note on the Sherman Act debates, the House and Senate adopted and then receded from amendments that would have clearly forbidden agreements of this kind. The Court concluded that Congress believed the statute forbade them in its present form.

* * *

It is said that Congress had very different matters in view and very different objects to accomplish in the passage of the [Sherman Act]; that a number of combinations in the form of trusts and conspiracies in restraint of trade were to be found throughout the country, and that it was impossible for the state governments to successfully cope with them because of their commercial character and of their business extension through the different States of the Union. Among these trusts it was said in Congress were the Beef Trust, the Standard Oil Trust, the Steel Trust, the Barbed Fence Wire Trust, the Sugar Trust, the Cordage Trust, the Cotton Seed Oil Trust, the Whiskey Trust and many others, and these trusts it was stated had assumed an importance and had acquired a power which were dangerous to the whole country, and that their existence was directly antagonistic to its peace and prosperity. To combinations and conspiracies of this kind it is contended that the act in question was directed, and not to the combinations of competing railroads to keep up their prices to a reasonable sum for the transportation of persons and property. It is true that many and various trusts were in existence at the time of the passage of the act, and it was probably sought to cover them by the provisions of the act. Many of them had rendered themselves offensive by the manner in which they exercised the great power that combined capital gave them. But a further investigation of "the history of the times" shows also that those trusts were not the only associations controlling a great combination of capital which had caused complaint at the manner in which their business was conducted. There were many and loud complaints from some portions of the public regarding the railroads and the prices they were charging for the service they rendered, and it was alleged that the prices for the transportation of persons and articles of commerce were unduly and improperly enhanced by combinations among the different roads. * * * A reference to this history of the times does not, as we think, furnish us with any strong reason for believing that it was only trusts that were in the minds of the members of Congress, and that railroads and their manner of doing business were wholly excluded therefrom.

* * *

* * * The points of difference between the railroad and other corporations are many and great * * * [but] it must be remembered they have also some points of resemblance. Trading, manufacturing and railroad corporations are all engaged in the transaction of business with regard to articles of trade and commerce, each in its special sphere, either in manufacturing or trading in commodities or in their transportation by rail. A contract among those engaged in the latter business by which the prices for the transportation of commodities traded in or manufactured by the others is greatly enhanced from what it otherwise would be if free competition were the rule, affects and to a certain extent restricts trade

and commerce, and affects the price of the commodity. * * * It is true the results of trusts, or combinations of that nature, may be different in different kinds of corporations, and yet they all have an essential similarity, and have been induced by motives of individual or corporate aggrandizement as against the public interest. In business or trading combinations they may even temporarily, or perhaps permanently, reduce the price of the article traded in or manufactured, by reducing the expense inseparable from the running of many different companies for the same purpose. Trade or commerce under those circumstances may nevertheless be badly and unfortunately restrained by driving out of business the small dealers and worthy men whose lives have been spent therein, and who might be unable to readjust themselves to their altered surroundings. Mere reduction in the price of the commodity dealt in might be dearly paid for by the ruin of such a class, and the absorption of control over one commodity by an all-powerful combination of capital. In any great and extended change in the manner or method of doing business it seems to be an inevitable necessity that distress and, perhaps, ruin shall be its accompaniment in regard to some of those who were engaged in the old methods. A change from stage coaches and canal boats to railroads threw at once a large number of men out of employment; changes from hand labor to that of machinery, and from operating machinery by hand to the application of steam for such purpose, leave behind them for the time a number of men who must seek other avenues of livelihood. These are misfortunes which seem to be the necessary accompaniment of all great industrial changes. It takes time to effect a readjustment of industrial life so that those who are thrown out of their old employment, by reason of such changes as we have spoken of, may find opportunities for labor in other departments than those to which they have been accustomed. It is a misfortune, but yet in such cases it seems to be the inevitable accompaniment of change and improvement.

It is wholly different, however, when such changes are effected by combinations of capital, whose purpose in combining is to control the production or manufacture of any particular article in the market, and by such control dictate the price at which the article shall be sold, the effect being to drive out of business all the small dealers in the commodity and to render the public subject to the decision of the combination as to what price shall be paid for the article. In this light it is not material that the price of an article may be lowered. It is in the power of the combination to raise it, and the result in any event is unfortunate for the country by depriving it of the services of a large number of small but independent dealers who were familiar with the business and who had spent their lives in it, and who supported themselves and their families from the small profits realized therein. Whether they be able to find other avenues to earn their livelihood is not so material, because it is not for the real prosperity of any country that such changes should occur which result in transferring an independent business man, the head of his establishment, small though it might be, into a mere servant or agent of a corporation for selling the commodities which he once manufactured or dealt in, having no voice in shaping the business policy of the company and bound to obey orders issued by others. Nor is it for the substantial interests of the country that any one commodity should be within the sole power and subject to the sole will of one powerful combination of capital. Congress has, so far as its jurisdiction extends, prohibited all contracts or combinations in the form of trusts entered into for the purpose of restraining trade and commerce. The results naturally flowing from a contract or combination in restraint of trade or commerce, when entered into by a manufacturing or trading company such as above stated, while differing somewhat from those which may follow a contract to keep up transportation rates by railroads, are nevertheless of the same nature and kind, and the contracts themselves do not so far differ in their nature that they may not all be treated alike and be condemned in common. * * * We see nothing either in contemporaneous history, in the legal situation at the time of the passage of the statute, in its legislative history, or in any general difference in the nature or kind of these trading or manufacturing companies from railroad companies, which would lead us to the conclusion that it cannot be supposed the legislature in prohibiting the making of contracts in restraint of trade intended to include railroads within the purview of that act.

* * *

Second. The next question to be discussed is as to what is the true construction of the statute, assuming that it applies to common carriers by railroad. * * *

* * *

It is now with much amplification of argument urged that the * * * common law meaning of the term "contract in restraint of trade" includes only such contracts as are in unreasonable restraint of trade, and when that term is used in the Federal statute it is not intended to include all contracts in restraint of trade, but only those which are in unreasonable restraint thereof.

The term is not of such limited signification. Contracts in restraint of trade have been known and spoke of for hundreds of years both in England and in this country, and the term includes all kinds of those contracts which in fact restrain or may restrain trade. Some of such contracts have been held void and unenforceable in the courts by reason of their restraint being unreasonable, while others have been held valid because they were not of that nature. A contract may be in restraint of trade and still be valid at common law. * * * When, therefore, the body of an act pronounces as illegal every contract or combination in restraint of trade or commerce among the several States, etc., the plain and ordinary meaning of such language is not limited to that kind of contract alone which is in unreasonable restraint of trade, but all contracts are included in such language, and no exception or limitation can be added without placing in the act that which has been omitted by Congress.

Proceeding, however, upon the theory that the statute did not mean what its plain language imported, and that it intended in its prohibition to denounce as illegal only those contracts which were in unreasonable restraint of trade, the courts below have made an exhaustive investigation as to the general rules which guide courts in declaring contracts to be void as being in restraint of trade, and therefore against the public policy of the country. In the course of their discussion of that subject they have shown that there has been a gradual though great alteration in the extent of the liberty granted to the vendor of property in agreeing, as part consideration for his sale, not to enter into the same kind of business for a certain time or within a certain territory. So long as the sale was the bona fide consideration for the promise and was not made a mere excuse for an evasion of the rule itself, the later authorities, both in England and in this country, exhibit a strong tendency towards enabling the parties to make such a contract in relation to the sale of property, including an agreement not to enter into the same kind of business, as they may think proper, and this with the view to granting to a vendor the freest opportunity to obtain the largest consideration for the sale of that which is his own. A contract which is the mere accompaniment of the sale of property, and thus entered into for the purpose of enhancing the price at which the vendor sells it, which in effect is collateral to such sale, and where the main purpose of the whole contract is accomplished by such sale, might not be included, within the letter or spirit of the statute in question. But we cannot see how the statute can be limited, as it has been by the courts below, without reading into its text an exception which alters the natural meaning of the language used, and that, too, upon a most material point, and where no sufficient reason is shown for believing that such alteration would make the statute more in accord with the intent of the law-making body that enacted it.

The great stress of the argument for the defendants on this branch of the case has been to show, if possible, some reason in the attendant circumstances, or some fact existing in the nature of railroad property and business upon which to found the claim, that * * * [their agreements were reasonable]. In order to do this, the defendants call attention to many facts which they have already referred to in their argument, upon the point that railroads were not included at all in the statute. They again draw attention to the fact of the peculiar nature of railroad property. When a railroad is once built, it is said, in must be kept in operation; it must transport property, when necessary in order to keep its business, at the smallest price and for the narrowest profit, or even for no profit, provided running expenses can be paid, rather than not to do the work; that railroad property cannot be altered for use for any other purpose, at least without such loss as may fairly be called destructive; that competition while, perhaps, right and proper in other business, simply leads in railroad business to financial ruin and insolvency, and to the operation of the road by receivers in the interest of its creditors instead of in that of its owners and the public * * * .

To the question why competition should necessarily be conducted to such an extent as to result in this relentless and continued war, to eventuate only in the financial ruin of one or all of the companies indulging in it, the answer is made that if competing railroad companies be left subject to the sway of free and unrestricted competition the results above foreshadowed necessarily happen from the nature of the case; that competition being the rule, each company will seek business to the extent of its power, and will underbid its rival in order to get the business, and such underbidding will act and react upon each company until the prices are so reduced as to make it impossible to prosper or live under them; that it is too much to ask of human nature for one company to insist upon charges sufficiently high to afford a reasonable compensation, and while doing so to see its patrons leave for rival roads who are obtaining its business by offering less rates for doing it than can be afforded and a fair profit obtained therefrom. Sooner than experience ruin from mere inaction, efforts will be made in the direction of meeting the underbidding of its rival until both shall end in ruin. The only refuge, it is said, from this wretched end lies in the power of competing roads agreeing among themselves to keep up prices for transportation to such sums as shall be reasonable in themselves so that companies may be allowed to save themselves from themselves, and to agree not to attack each other, but to keep up reasonable and living rates for the services performed. It is said that as railroads have a right to charge reasonable rates it must follow that a contract among themselves to keep up their charges to that extent is valid. Viewed in the light of all these facts it is broadly and confidently asserted that it is impossible to believe that Congress or any other intelligent and honest legislative body could ever have intended to include all contracts or combinations in restraint of trade, and as a consequence thereof to prohibit competing railways from agreeing among themselves to keep up prices for transportation to such a rate as should be fair and reasonable.

* * *

There is another side to this question, however, and it may not be amiss to refer to one or two facts which tend to somewhat modify and alter the light in which the subject should be regarded. If only that kind of contract which is in unreasonable restraint of trade be within the meaning of the statute, and declared therein to be illegal, it is at once apparent that the subject of what is a reasonable rate is attended with great uncertainty. What is a proper standard by which to judge the fact of reasonable rates? Must the rate be so high as to enable the return for the whole business done to amount to a sum sufficient to afford the shareholder a fair and reasonable profit upon his investment? If so, what is a fair and reasonable profit? That depends sometimes upon the risk incurred, and the rate itself differs in different localities: which is the one to which reference is to be made as the standard? Or is the reasonableness of the profit to be limited to a fair return upon the capital that would have been sufficient to build and equip the road, if honestly expended? Or is still another standard to be created, and the reasonableness of the charges tried by the cost of the carriage of the article and a reasonable profit allowed on that? And in such case would contribution to a sinking fund to make repairs upon the roadbed and renewal of cars, etc., be assumed as a proper item? Or is the reasonableness of the charge to be tested by reference to the charges for the transportation of the same kind of property made by other roads similarly situated? If the latter, a combination among such roads as to rates would, of course, furnish no means of answering the question. It is quite apparent, therefore, that it is exceedingly difficult to formulate even the terms of the rule itself which should govern in the matter of determining what would be reasonable rates for transportation. While even after the standard should be determined there is such an infinite variety of facts entering into the question of what is a reasonable rate, no matter what standard is adopted, that any individual shipper would in most cases be apt to abandon the effort to show the unreasonable character of a charge, sooner than hazard the great expense in time and money necessary to prove the fact, and at the same time incur the illwill of the road itself in all his future dealings with it. To say, therefore, that the act excludes agreements which are not in unreasonable restraint of trade, and which tend simply to keep up reasonable rates for transportation, is substantially to leave the question of reasonableness to the companies themselves.

* * *

The general reasons for holding agreements of this nature to be invalid even at common law, on the part of railroad companies are quite strong, if not entirely conclusive.

Considering the public character of such corporations, the privileges and franchises which they have received from the public in order that they might transact business, and bearing in mind how closely and immediately the question of rates for transportation affects the whole public, it may be urged that Congress had in mind all the difficulties which we have before suggested of proving the unreasonableness of the rate, and might, in consideration of all the circumstances, have deliberately decided to prohibit all agreements and combinations in restraint of trade or commerce, regardless of the question whether such agreements were reasonable or the reverse.

* * * Upon the subject now under consideration it is well said by Judge Oliver P. Shiras, United States District Judge, Northern District of Iowa,

in his very able dissenting opinion in this case in the United States Circuit Court of Appeals, as follows:

"As to the majority of the community living along its line, each railway company has a monopoly of the business demanding transportation as one of its elements. By reason of this fact the action of this corporation in establishing the rates to be charged largely influences the net profit coming to the farmer, the manufacturer and the merchant, from the sale of the products of the farm, the workshop and manufactory, and of the merchandise purchased and resold, and also largely influences the price to be paid by every one who consumes any of the property transported over the line of railway. There is no other line of business carried on in our midst which is so intimately connected with the public as that conducted by the railways of the country. * * * It may be entirely true that as we proceed in the development of the policy of public control over railway traffic, methods will be devised and put in operation by legislative enactment whereby railway companies and the public may be protected against the evils arising from unrestricted competition and from rate wars which unsettle the business of the community, but I fail to perceive the force of the argument that because railway companies through their own action cause evils to themselves and the public by sudden changes or reductions in tariff rates they must be permitted to deprive the community of the benefit of competition in securing reasonable rates for the transportation of the products of the country. Competition, free and unrestricted, is the general rule which governs all the ordinary business pursuits and transactions of life. * * * There are benefits and there are evils which result from the operation of the law of free competition between railway companies. The time may come when the companies will be relieved from the operation of this law, but they cannot, by combination and agreements among themselves, bring about this change. * * * "

* * *

* * * It may be that the policy evidenced by the passage of the act itself will, if carried out, result in disaster to the roads and in a failure to secure the advantages sought from such legislation. Whether that will be the result or not we do not know and cannot predict. These considerations are, however, not for us. If the act ought to read as contended for by defendants, Congress is the body to amend it and not this court, by a process of judicial legislation wholly unjustifiable. * * *

The conclusion which we have drawn from the examination above made into the question before us is that the Anti-Trust Act applies to railroads, and that it renders illegal all agreements which are in restraint of trade or commerce as we have above defined that expression, and the question then arises whether the agreement before us is of that nature.

* * * In the view we have taken of the question, the intent alleged by the Government is not necessary to be proved. The question is one of law in regard to the meaning and effect of the agreement itself, namely: Does the agreement restrain trade or commerce in any way so as to be a violation of the act? We have no doubt that it does. * * * [A]lthough the parties have a right to withdraw from the agreement on giving thirty days' notice of a desire so to do, yet while in force and assuming it to be lived up to, there can be no doubt that its direct, immediate and necessary effect is to put a restraint upon trade or commerce as described in the act.

* * *

For the reasons given, the decrees of the United States Circuit Court of Appeals and of the Circuit Court for the District of Kansas must be reversed, and the case remanded to the circuit court for further proceedings in conformity with this opinion.

MR. JUSTICE WHITE, with whom concurred MR. JUSTICE FIELD, MR. JUSTICE GRAY and MR. JUSTICE SHIRAS, dissenting.

* * *

The contract between the railway companies which the court holds to be void because it is found to violate the [Sherman Act] substantially embodies only an agreement between the corporations by which a uniform classification of freight is obtained, by which the secret undercutting of rates is sought to be avoided, and the rates as stated in the published rate sheets, and which, as a general rule, are required by law to be filed with the Interstate Commerce Commission, are secured against arbitrary and sudden charges. * * *

The theory upon which the contract is held to be illegal is that even though it be reasonable, and hence valid, under the general principles of law, it is yet void, because it conflicts with the act of Congress already referred to. * * * But this proposition, I submit, is tantamount to an assertion that the act of Congress is itself unreasonable. * * *

* * *

* * * I think a brief consideration of the history and development of the law on the subject will * * * demonstrate that the words "restraint of trade" embrace only contracts which unreasonably restrain trade, and, therefore, that reasonable contracts, although they, in some measure, "restrain trade," are not within the meaning of the words. * * * The rudiments of the doctrine of contracts in restraint of trade are found in the common law at a very early date. The first case on the subject is * * * known as Dier's Case [1415]. That was an action of damages upon a bond conditioned that the defendant should not practice his trade as a dyer at a particular place

during a limited period, and it was held that the contract was illegal. The principle upon which this case was decided was not described as one forbidding contracts in restraint of trade, but was stated to be one by which contracts restricting the liberty of the subject were forbidden. The doctrine declared in that case was applied in subsequent cases in England prior to the case of Mitchel v. Reynolds, decided in 1711. There the distinction between general restraints and partial restraints was first definitely formulated, and it was held that a contract creating a partial restraint was valid and one creating a general restraint was not. The theory of partial and general restraints established by that case was followed in many decided cases in England, not, however, without the correctness of the difference between the two being in some instances denied and in others questioned, until the matter was set finally at rest by the House of Lords in Nordenfelt v. The Maxim Nordenfelt Guns and Ammunition Co. [1894]. In that case it was held that the distinction between partial and general restraint was an incorrect criterion, but that whether a contract was invalid because in restraint of trade must depend upon whether, on considering all the circumstances, the contract was found to be reasonable or unreasonable. If reasonable, it was not a contract in restraint of trade, and if unreasonable it was.

The decisions of the American courts substantially conform to both the development and ultimate results of the English cases. * * *

* * *

But, admitting arguendo the correctness of the proposition by which it is sought to include every contract, however reasonable, within the inhibition of the law, the statute, considered as a whole, shows, I think, the error of the construction placed upon it. Its title is "An act to protect trade and commerce against unlawful restraints and monopolies." The word "unlawful" clearly distinguishes between contracts in restraint of trade which are lawful and those which are not. In other words, between those which are unreasonably in restraint of trade, and consequently invalid, and those which are reasonable and hence lawful. * * * Whilst it is true that the title of an act cannot be used to destroy the plain import of the language found in its body, yet when a literal interpretation will work out wrong or injury, or where the words of the statute are ambiguous, the title may be resorted to as an instrument of construction. * * *

* * *

* * * The well-settled rule is that where technical words are used in an act, and their meaning has previously been conclusively settled, by long usage and judicial construction, the use of the words without an indication of an intention to give them a new significance is an adoption of the generally accepted meaning affixed to the words at the time the act was passed. Particularly is this rule imperative where the statute in which the

words are used creates a crime, as does the statute under consideration, and gives no specific definition of the crime created. * * *

* * *

The plain intention of the law was to protect the liberty of contract and the freedom of trade. Will this intention not be frustrated by a construction which, if it does not destroy, at least gravely impairs, both the liberty of the individual to contract and the freedom of trade? * * * Secured no longer by the law of reason, all these rights become subject, when questioned, to the mere caprice of judicial authority. * * *

* * *

But conceding for the sake of argument that the words "every contract in restraint of trade," as used in the act of Congress in question, prohibits all such contracts however reasonable they may be, * * * it remains to consider whether the provisions of the act of 1890 were intended to apply to agreements made between carriers for the purpose of classifying the freight to be by them carried, or preventing secret cutting of the published rates * * *. * * * The statute, commonly known as the Interstate Commerce Act, was a special act, and it was intended to regulate interstate commerce transported by railway carriers. All its provisions directly and expressly related to this subject. The act of 1890, on the contract, is a general law, not referring specifically to carriers of interstate commerce. The rule is that a general will not be held to repeal a special statute unless there be a clear implication unavoidably resulting from the general law that it was the intention that the provisions of the general law should cover the subject-matter previously, expressly and specifically provided for by particular legislation. * * *

* * *

* * * That the [ICC] act did not contemplate that the relations of the carrier should be confined to his own line and to business going over such line alone, is conclusively shown by the fact that the [ICC] act specifically provides for joint and continuous lines; in other words, for agreements between several roads to compose a joint line. That these agreements are to arise from contract is also shown by the fact that the law provides for the filing of such contracts with the commission. And it was also contemplated that the agreements should cover joint rates, since it provides for the making of such joint tariffs and for their publication and filing with the commission. * * * That the interstate commerce rates, all of which are controlled by the provisions as to reasonableness, were not intended to fluctuate hourly and daily as competition might ebb and flow, results from the fact that the published rates could not either be increased or reduced, except after a specified time. It follows, then, that agreements as to reasonable rates and against their secret reduction conform exactly to the terms of the act. * * * To illustrate, suppose three joint lines of

railroads between Chicago and New York, each made up of many roads. How could a joint rate be agreed on by the roads composing one of these continuous lines, without an ascertainment of the rate existing on the other continuous line? What contract could be made with safety for transportation over one of the lines without taking into account the rate of all the others? There certainly could be no prevention of unjust discrimination as to the persons and places within a given territory, unless the rates of all competing lines within the territory be considered and the sudden change of the published rates of all such lines be guarded against. * * *

It is, I submit, therefore not to be denied that the agreement between the carriers, the validity of which is here drawn in question, * * * is in accord with the plain text of the Interstate Commerce Act, and is in harmony with the views of the purposes of that law contemporaneously expressed to Congress by the body immediately charged with its administration, and tacitly approved by Congress.

* * *

* * * The answers to the bill of complaint specially denied the allegations as to the improper motives of the parties to the contract, and also expressly averred their lawful and innocent intention. As the case was heard upon bill and answer, improper motives cannot therefore be imputed. Indeed, the opinion of the court sustains this view, since it eliminates all consideration of improper motives and holds that the validity of the contract must depend upon its face, and deduces as a legal conclusion from this premise that the contract is invalid, because even reasonable contracts are embraced within the purview of the act of 1890. To my mind, the judicial declaration that carriers cannot agree among themselves for the purpose of aiding in the enforcement of the provisions of the interstate commerce law, will strike a blow at the beneficial results of that act, and will have a direct tendency to produce the preferences and discriminations which it was one of the main objects of the act to frustrate. The great complexity of the subject, the numerous interests concerned in it, the vast area over which it operates, present difficulties enough without, it seems to me, its being advisable to add to them by holding that a contract which is supported by the text of the law is invalid, because, although it is reasonable and just, it must be considered as in restraint of trade.

* * *

NOTES AND QUESTIONS

1.   Were you convinced by the majority that the failure of Congress to use the term "unreasonable" meant that "every" contract that in any manner restrained trade was rendered illegal? Don't all contracts in some sense restrain trade? For example, if you agree to sell my hardware store 200 cases

of paint, doesn't that eliminate your right to sell the same 200 cases to someone else? Doesn't it limit my practical latitude to buy paint from other suppliers? Clearly, either of us could breach our contract if we were willing to pay damages, but was that not also true of the *Trans-Missouri* agreement?

2.   Unless the Sherman Act literally makes it illegal to enter into *any* contract, the question becomes how to separate lawful contracts from the unlawful.

a.   How did *E.C. Knight* determine which contracts were beyond the reach of the Sherman Act? Remember the majority's concern there that the Act not become a federal commercial law; the Justices were seemingly already concerned about the "all contracts" language. Does limiting what is meant by "interstate commerce" serve as a good way to prevent outlawing all commercial agreements? Is it in fact a very clumsy way to do so?

b.   Do you agree that "restraint of trade" is the statute's key operative phrase as the majority declares? May one simply say that the term means whatever it meant at common law in 1890? Did the majority reject such a possibility? Indeed, did Justice Peckham admit that Mitchel v. Reynolds might be decided the same way under the Sherman Act?

c.   Is Justice White correct that the key test should be the "reasonableness" of the contractual arrangement? Is "reasonable" a self-defining term? Do most people in fact use "reason" to decide whether something is "reasonable"? When you say to someone: "That seems reasonable to me," are you usually making a judgment based more on your judgment and experience than your "reason"?

3.   Were you convinced that the Court should not allow the defendants to show that their agreed-upon rates were reasonable? If there is no clear harm done by an arrangement of this kind, what is the point of condemning it?

a.   Is the point that the benefits of ascertaining reasonableness or the lack of it are less than the costs of doing so? Indeed, would one's judgment of reasonableness one day necessarily be the same the next day when costs of the firms' factors of production might have changed?

b.   At the outset of the opinion, in a portion deleted here, the Court rejected a contention that, because the Association had now been dissolved, the case was moot. Was the Court justified in retaining authority to decide the case? If dissolution were to divest the Court of jurisdiction in such cases, could defendant organizations simply dissolve whenever they were charged with wrongdoing and recreate themselves thereafter?

4.   Was the Court too quick to reject the defendants' view that the Sherman Act was not meant to apply to railroads?

a.   Might railroads have more need than many firms to engage in multi-firm setting of rates and rules? As Justice White observed, many shipments must travel over two or more railroads. Unlike trucks, a train can only go where its tracks go. "Joint rates" for railroads, i.e., rates covering shipments that travel on two or more lines, are essential.

b.   Is there any good way to arrive at joint rates other than by agreement among the affected railroads? Do you agree with Justice Peckham that that problem goes only to the wisdom or "policy" of the Act?[6]

5.   Did Justice Peckham persuade you that Congress intended to prohibit railroad agreements such as this one because of the harm railroads had caused small competitors like stagecoaches and ferry lines?

a.   Does this reference to competitors suggest that protection of small business was a central objective of the Sherman Act? Do you agree that that was historically accurate?

b.   Even if accurate as history, is such a concern misplaced here? Are such small competitors the parties that are harmed by a cartel? If your competitors had such an arrangement, would you complain? Would you seek to join a cartel or remain outside it?

A NOTE ON NATURAL MONOPOLIES

Railroads have long been considered to have "natural monopolies." By definition, a natural monopoly is a market in which firms' marginal cost of production does not increase with an increase in output, at least not over the relevant ranges of production. Thus, there are always further economies of scale—or at least no diseconomies—if such firms increase production. In the case of a railroad, for example, once the track is laid and equipment purchased, it is as cheap or cheaper per ton-mile to carry 100,000 ton-miles as 1,000. A related effect of this phenomenon is that the marginal cost of a firm in an industry with natural monopoly characteristics is consistently below its average cost as shown here:

---

[6]   Gabriel Kolko, Railroads and Regulation: 1877–1916 (1965) provides a good discussion of pooling agreements and similar cartel practices that led to passage of the I.C.C. Act, as well as the perception that the I.C.C. Act changed little about railroad behavior. See also, William Z. Ripley, Railroads: Finance and Organization 575–607 (1923). For evidence that the *Trans-Missouri* decision did not prevent agreements among railroads for very long, see John J. Binder, The Sherman Antitrust Act and Railroad Cartels, 31 J. Law & Economics 443 (1988).

Figure 5

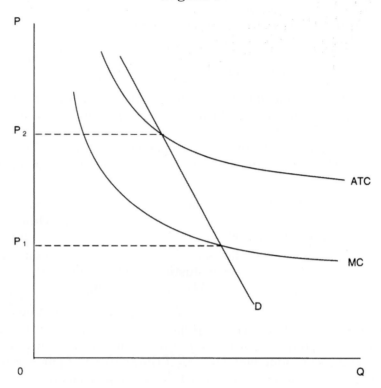

The result is that, if forced to price competitively, a firm in a natural monopoly situation will tend to be willing to sell its goods or services at any price at or above marginal cost rather than lose the business and get no revenue at all. That means that such a firm will consistently be willing to price such goods or services below average total cost. If the firm cannot charge above average total cost for something else, it will ultimately go out of business. Does that give more credence to the "cut-throat competition" argument that the court dismissed here as so much special pleading?[7]

On the other hand, what rates would the I.C.C. and state regulatory agencies have tended to set for the railroads? Are those necessarily the same rates an organization such as the Trans-Missouri Freight Association would be expected to propose?

---

[7] The real problem may have been that *many* industries at this time claimed to have declining marginal costs and to face this problem. Most did not have declining marginal costs, but if the Court had acknowledged the argument here, lower courts would have had to take evidence on the issue again and again. See generally, Herbert Hovenkamp, Enterprise and American Law, 1836–1937 (1991), at 308–22.

A NOTE ON THE *JOINT-TRAFFIC ASSOCIATION* CASE

To say the least, railroads were unhappy with the *Trans-Missouri* decision and in its very next term, the Supreme Court was in effect asked to reconsider it in United States v. Joint-Traffic Association, 171 U.S. 505, 19 S.Ct. 25, 43 L.Ed. 259 (1898).

This time the defendants were the railroads operating *east* of the Mississippi River. The price and rulemaking operations of this association were much like those in *Trans-Missouri*, although here there was also an effort to allocate an "equitable" proportion of the traffic to each participating railroad. Again, Justice Peckham wrote the opinion for a five-member majority.

Counsel had argued that the Court in *Trans-Missouri* could not have meant that "every" contract in restraint of trade was illegal. Otherwise, the Sherman Act would deny the constitutional guarantee of freedom of contract by striking down thousands of contractual relationships long recognized as proper. In response, Justice Peckham implicitly recognized that the Court's prior language had been too sweeping.

> "[W]e might say that the formation of corporations for business or manufacturing purposes has never, to our knowledge, been regarded in the nature of a contract in restraint of trade or commerce. The same may be said of the contract of partnership. It might also be difficult to show that the appointment by two or more producers of the same person to sell their goods on commission was a matter in any degree in restraint of trade.

> "We are not aware that it has ever been claimed that a lease or purchase by a farmer, manufacturer, or merchant of an additional farm, manufactory, or shop, or the withdrawal from business of any farmer, merchant, or manufacturer, restrained commerce or trade, within any legal definition of that term; and the sale of good will of a business with an accompanying agreement not to engage in a similar business was instanced in the Trans-Missouri Case as a contract not within the meaning of the act, and it was said that such a contract was collateral to the main contract or sale, and was entered into for the purpose of enhancing the price at which the vendor sells his business. * * * To suppose, as is assumed by counsel, that the effect of the decision in the Trans-Missouri Case is to render illegal most business contracts or combinations, however indispensable and necessary they may be, because, as they assert, they all restrain trade in some remote and indirect degree, is to make a most violent assumption, and one not called for or justified by the decision mentioned, or any other decision of this court."

Justices Gray, Shiras and White again noted their dissent. Justice McKenna, who had joined the Court to replace former dissenter, Justice Field, did not participate in the decision.

———————

Justice Peckham's new recognition that not "every contract" in restraint of trade is illegal was not entirely original. A few months earlier, a young Court of Appeals judge had said as much in an opinion that offered a different rationale for Sherman Act decisions, a rationale that continues to persuade many analysts today.

UNITED STATES V. ADDYSTON PIPE & STEEL CO.

United States Court of Appeals, Sixth Circuit, 1898
85 Fed. 271

Before HARLAN, CIRCUIT JUSTICE, and TAFT and LURTON, CIRCUIT JUDGES.

[The United States filed suit to enjoin six manufacturers of cast-iron pipe from allocating among themselves the right to serve particular customers. Their arrangements took four forms.

[First, the firms designated "reserved cities" in which one of their number was granted the right to make all pipe sales. Addyston Pipe, for example, was given the right to win bids for pipe needed by the Cincinnati gas and water companies. The other five firms agreed to bid such higher prices as Addyston might request to assure that the process appeared legal and that the contract was awarded to Addyston.

[Second, firms who won bids and received contracts paid part of their income as a "bonus" into a pool to be divided among the others. Third, the firms established specific "bonuses" they would pay into a common fund if they sold outside their own territory. Both plans tended to discourage price cutting to get new business and to discourage members outside a "bonus" area from competing with members within the area.

[Fourth, later in the life of the group, the members bid among themselves for the right to get particular business. Thus, if Addyston promised to pay the most—say, $5 per ton—into the bonus pool for the right to win the contract for water pipe in Louisville, bids of others would be orchestrated as they were for reserved cities.

[The evidence showed that occasionally members of the group set their price so high that a firm from outside the group could underbid their designated winner. Further, when member firms sold in "free" territory, i.e., distant states not subject to the bonus system, they sold for less than they did in "pay" territory even though they faced higher shipping costs on those sales.

[On these stipulated facts, the trial judge dismissed the complaint on the merits.]

TAFT, CIRCUIT JUDGE, after stating the case as above, delivered the opinion of the court.

* * *

Two questions are presented in this case for our decision: First. Was the association of the defendants a contract, combination, or conspiracy in restraint of trade, as the terms are to be understood in the act? Second. Was the trade thus restrained trade between the states?

The contention on behalf of defendants is that the association would have been valid at common law, and that the federal anti-trust law was not intended to reach any agreements that were not void and unenforceable at common law. It might be a sufficient answer to this contention to point to the decision of the Supreme Court of the United States in U.S. v. Trans-Missouri Freight Ass'n, in which it was held that contracts in restraint of interstate transportation were within the statute, whether the restraints would be regarded as reasonable at common law or not. * * * [Moreover,] it is certain that, if the contract of association which bound the defendants was void and unenforceable at the common law because in restraint of trade, it is within the inhibition of the statute if the trade it restrained was interstate. Contracts that were in unreasonable restraint of trade at common law were not unlawful in the sense of being criminal, or giving rise to a civil action for damages in favor of one prejudicially affected thereby, but were simply void, and were not enforced by the courts. The effect of the act of 1890 is to render such contracts unlawful in an affirmative or positive sense, and punishable as a misdemeanor, and to create a right of civil action for damages in favor of those injured thereby, and a civil remedy by injunction in favor of both private persons and the public against the execution of such contracts and the maintenance of such trade restraints.

The argument for defendants is that their contract of association was not, and could not be, a monopoly, because their aggregate tonnage capacity did not exceed 30 per cent of the total tonnage capacity of the country; that the restraints upon the members of the association, if restraints they could be called, did not embrace all the states, and were not unlimited in space; that such partial restraints were justified and upheld at common law if reasonable, and only proportioned to the necessary protection of the parties; that in this case the partial restraints were reasonable, because without them each member would be subjected to ruinous competition by the other, and did not exceed in degree of stringency or scope what was necessary to protect the parties in securing prices for their product that were fair and reasonable to themselves and the public; that competition was not stifled by the association because the prices fixed by it had to be fixed with reference to the very active competition of pipe companies which were not members of the association, and which had more than double the defendants' capacity; that in this way the association only modified and restrained the evils of ruinous competition, while the public had all the benefit from competition which public policy demanded.

From early times it was the policy of Englishmen to encourage trade in England, and to discourage those voluntary restraints which tradesmen were often induced to impose on themselves by contract. Courts recognized this public policy by refusing to enforce stipulations of this character. The objections to such restraints were mainly two. One was that by such contracts a man disabled himself from earning a livelihood with the risk of becoming a public charge, and deprived the community of the benefit of his labor. The other was that such restraints tended to give to the covenantee, the beneficiary of such restraints, a monopoly of the trade, from which he had thus excluded one competitor, and by the same means might exclude others.

* * *

The inhibition against restraints of trade at common law seems at first to have had no exception. * * * After a time it became apparent to the people and the courts that it was in the interest of trade that certain covenants in restraint of trade should be enforced. It was of importance, as an incentive to industry and honest dealing in trade, that, after a man had built up a business with an extensive good will, he should be able to sell his business and good will to the best advantage, and he could not do so unless he could bind himself by an enforceable contract not to engage in the same business in such a way as to prevent injury to that which he was about to sell. It was equally for the good of the public and trade, when partners dissolved, and one took the business, or they divided the business, that each partner might bind himself not to do anything in trade thereafter which would derogate from his grant of the interest conveyed to his former partner. Again, when two men became partners in a business, although their union might reduce competition, this effect was only an incident to the main purpose of a union of their capital, enterprise, and energy to carry on a successful business, and one useful to the community. Restrictions in the articles of partnership upon the business activity of the members, with a view of securing their entire effort in the common enterprise, were, of course, only ancillary to the main end of the union, and were to be encouraged. Again, when one in business sold property with which the buyer might set up a rival business, it was certainly reasonable that the seller should be able to restrain the buyer from doing him an injury which, but for the sale, the buyer would be unable to inflict. This was not reducing competition, but was only securing the seller against an increase of competition of his own creating. * * * Again, it was of importance that business men and professional men should have every motive to employ the ablest assistants, and to instruct them thoroughly; but they would naturally be reluctant to do so unless such assistants were able to bind themselves not to set up a rival business in the vicinity after learning the details and secrets of the business of their employers.

* * *

For the reasons given, then, covenants in partial restraint of trade are generally upheld as valid when they are agreements (1) by the seller of property or business not to compete with the buyer in such a way as to derogate from the value of the property or business sold; (2) by a retiring partner not to compete with the firm; (3) by a partner pending the partnership not to do anything to interfere, by competition or otherwise, with the business of the firm; (4) by the buyer of property not to use the same in competition with the business retained by the seller; and (5) by an assistant, servant, or agent not to compete with his master or employer after the expiration of his time of service. Before such agreements are upheld, however, the court must find that the restraints attempted thereby are reasonably necessary (1, 2, and 3) to the enjoyment by the buyer of the property, good will, or interest in the partnership bought; or (4) to the legitimate ends of the existing partnership; or (5) to the prevention of possible injury to the business of the seller from use by the buyer of the thing sold; or (6) to protection from the danger of loss to the employer's business caused by the unjust use on the part of the employee of the confidential knowledge acquired in such business. * * *

It would be stating it too strongly to say that these five classes of covenants in restraint of trade include all of those upheld as valid at the common law; but it would certainly seem to follow from the tests laid down for determining the validity of such an agreement that no conventional restraint of trade can be enforced unless the covenant embodying it is merely ancillary to the main purpose of a lawful contract, and necessary to protect the covenantee in the enjoyment of the legitimate fruits of the contract, or to protect him from the dangers of an unjust use of those fruits by the other party. * * *

This very statement of the rule implies that the contract must be one in which there is a main purpose, to which the covenant in restraint of trade is merely ancillary. The covenant is inserted only to protect one of the parties from the injury which, in the execution of the contract or enjoyment of its fruits, he may suffer from the unrestrained competition of the other. The main purpose of the contract suggests the measure of protection needed, and furnishes a sufficiently uniform standard by which the validity of such restraints may be judicially determined. In such a case, if the restraint exceeds the necessity presented by the main purpose of the contract, it is void for two reasons: First, because it oppresses the covenantor, without any corresponding benefit to the covenantee; and, second, because it tends to a monopoly. But where the sole object of both parties in making the contract as expressed therein is merely to restrain competition, and enhance or maintain prices, it would seem that there was nothing to justify or excuse the restraint, that it would necessarily have a tendency to monopoly, and therefore would be void. In such a case there is no measure of what is necessary to the protection of either party, except the vague and varying opinion of judges as to how much, on principles of political economy, men ought to be allowed to restrain competition. * * *

* * * It is true that certain rules for determining whether a covenant in restraint of trade ancillary to the main purpose of a contract was reasonably adapted and limited to the necessary protection of a party in the carrying out of such purpose have been somewhat modified by modern authorities. In Mitchel v. Reynolds, the leading early case on the subject, in which the main object of the contract was the sale of a bake house, and there was a covenant to protect the purchaser against competition by the seller in the bakery business, Chief Justice Parker laid down the rule that it must appear before such a covenant could be enforced that the restraint was not general, but particular or partial, as to places or persons, and was upon a good and adequate consideration, so as to make it a proper and useful contract. * * * More recently the limitation that the restraint could not be general or unlimited as to space has been modified in some cases by holding that, if the protection necessary to the covenantee reasonably requires a covenant unrestricted as to space, it will be upheld as valid. * * * But these cases all involved contracts in which the covenant in restraint of trade was ancillary to the main and lawful purpose of the contract, and was necessary to the protection of the covenantee in the carrying out of that main purpose. They do not manifest any general disposition on the part of the courts to be more liberal in supporting contracts having for their sole object the restraint of trade than did the courts of an earlier time. It is true that there are some cases in which the courts, mistaking, as we conceive, the proper limits of the relaxation of the rules for determining the unreasonableness of restraints of trade, have set sail on a sea of doubt, and have assumed the power to say, in respect to contracts which have no other purpose and no other consideration on either side than the mutual restraint of the parties, how much restraint of competition is in the public interest, and how much is not.

The manifest danger in the administration of justice according to so shifting, vague, and indeterminate a standard would seem to be a strong reason against adopting it. * * *

* * *

* * * [W]e can have no doubt that the association of the defendants, however reasonable the prices they fixed, however great the competition they had to encounter, and however great the necessity for curbing themselves by joint agreement from committing financial suicide by ill-advised competition, was void at common law, because in restraint of trade, and tending to a monopoly. But the facts of the case do not require us to go

so far as this, for they show that the attempted justification of this association on the grounds stated is without foundation.

The defendants, being manufacturers and vendors of cast-iron pipe, entered into a combination to raise the prices for pipe for all the states west and south of New York, Pennsylvania, and Virginia, constituting considerably more than three-quarters of the territory of the United States, and significantly called by the associates "pay territory." Their joint annual output was 220,000 tons. The total capacity of all the other cast-iron pipe manufacturers in the pay territory was 170,500 tons. Of this, 45,000 tons was the capacity of mills in Texas, Colorado, and Oregon, so far removed from that part of the pay territory where the demand was considerable that necessary freight rates excluded them from the possibility of competing, and 12,000 tons was the possible annual capacity of a mill at St. Louis, which was practically under the same management as that of one of the defendants' mills. Of the remainder of the mills in pay territory and outside of the combination, one was at Columbus, Ohio, two in northern Ohio, and one in Michigan. Their aggregate possible annual capacity was about one-half the usual annual output of the defendants' mills. They were, it will be observed, at the extreme northern end of the pay territory, while the defendants' mills at Cincinnati, Louisville, Chattanooga, and South Pittsburg, and Anniston, and Bessemer, were grouped much nearer to the center of the pay territory. The freight upon cast-iron pipe amounts to a considerable percentage of the price at which manufacturers can deliver it at any great distance from the place of manufacture. Within the margin of the freight per ton which Eastern manufacturers would have to pay to deliver pipe in pay territory, the defendants, by controlling two-thirds of the output in pay territory, were practically able to fix prices. * * * Much evidence is adduced upon affidavit to prove that defendants had no power arbitrarily to fix prices, and that they were always obliged to meet competition. To the extent that they could not impose prices on the public in excess of the cost price of pipe with freight from the Atlantic seaboard added, this is true; but, within that limit, they could fix prices as they chose. The most cogent evidence that they had this power is the fact, everywhere apparent in the record, that they exercised it. * * * The defendants were, by their combination, therefore able to deprive the public in a large territory of the advantages otherwise accruing to them from the proximity of defendants' pipe factories, and, by keeping prices just low enough to prevent competition by Eastern manufacturers, to compel the public to pay an increase over what the price would have been, if fixed by competition between defendants, nearly equal to the advantage in freight rates enjoyed by defendants over Eastern competitors. * * * Now, the restraint thus imposed on themselves was only partial. It did not cover the United States. There was not a complete monopoly. It was tempered by the fear of competition, and it affected only a part of the price. But this certainly does not take the contract of association out of the annulling effect of the rule against monopolies. In U.S. v. E.C. Knight Co., Chief Justice Fuller, in speaking for the court, said:

> "Again, all the authorities agree that, in order to vitiate a contract or combination, it is not essential that its result should be a complete monopoly. It is sufficient if it really tends to that end, and to deprive the public of the advantages which flow from free competition."

* * *

Another aspect of this contract of association brings it within the term used in the statute, "a conspiracy in restraint of trade." A conspiracy is a combination of two or more persons to accomplish an unlawful end by lawful means or a lawful end by unlawful means. In the answer of the defendants, it is averred that the chief way in which cast-iron pipe is sold is by contracts let after competitive bidding invited by the intending purchaser. It would have much interfered with the smooth working of defendants' association had its existence and purposes become known to the public. A part of the plan was a deliberate attempt to create in the minds of the members of the public inviting bids the belief that competition existed between the defendants. * * * The largest purchasers of pipe are municipal corporations, and they are by law required to solicit bids for the sale of pipe in order that the public may get the benefit of competition. One of the means adopted by the defendants in their plan of combination was this illegal and fraudulent effort to evade such laws, and to deceive intending purchasers. No matter what the excuse for the combination by defendants in restraint of trade, the illegality of the means stamps it as a conspiracy, and so brings it within that term of the federal statute.

The second question is whether the trade restrained by the combination of the defendants was interstate trade. The mills of the defendants were situated, two in Alabama, two in Tennessee, one in Kentucky, and one in Ohio. The invariable custom in sales of pipe required the seller to deliver the pipe at the place where it was to be used by the buyer, and to include in the price the cost of delivery. The contracts, as the answer of the defendants avers, were invariably made after public letting at the home, and in the state, of the buyer. * * * In cases of pipe to be purchased in any state of the 36 in pay territory, except 4, each one of the defendants, by his contract of association, restrained his freedom of trade in respect to making a contract in that state for the sale of pipe to be delivered across state lines. * * * [N]o sale or proposed sale can be suggested within the scope of the contract of association with respect to which that contract did not restrain at least three, often four, more often five, and usually all, of the defendants in the exercise of the freedom, which but for the contract would have been theirs, of selling in one state pipe to be delivered from another state at any price they might see fit to fix. Can there be any doubt that this was a restraint of interstate trade and commerce? * * *

* * *

The learned judge who dismissed the bill at the circuit was of opinion that the contract of association only indirectly affected interstate commerce, and relied chiefly for this conclusion on the decision of the Supreme Court in the case of U.S. v. E.C. Knight Co. * * *

* * *

* * * It seems to us clear that, from the beginning to the end of the [*E.C. Knight*] opinion, the chief justice draws the distinction between a restraint upon the business of manufacturing and a restraint upon the trade or commerce between the states in the articles after manufacture, with the manifest purpose of showing that the regulating power of Congress under the constitution could affect only the latter, while the former was not under federal control, and rested wholly with the states. Among the subjects of commercial regulation by Congress, he expressly mentions "contracts to buy, sell, or exchange goods to be transported among the several states," and leaves it to be plainly inferred that the statute does embrace combinations and conspiracies which have for their object to restrain, and which necessarily operate in restraint of, the freedom of such contracts. * * * It can hardly be that a combination in restraint of what is interstate commerce does not directly affect and burden that commerce. The error into which the circuit court fell, it seems to us, was in not observing the difference between the regulating power of Congress over contracts and negotiations for sales of goods to be delivered across state lines, and that over the merchandise, the subject of such sales and negotiations. The goods are not within the control of Congress until they are in actual transit from state to another. But the negotiations and making of sales which necessarily involve in their execution the delivery of merchandise across state lines are interstate commerce, and so within the regulating power of Congress even before the transit of the goods in performance of the contract has begun.

* * *

Much has been said in argument as to the enlargement of the federal governmental functions in respect of all trade and industry in the states if the view we have expressed of the application of the anti-trust law in this case is to prevail, and as to the interference which is likely to follow with the control which the states have hitherto been understood to have over contracts of the character of that before us. We do not announce any new doctrine in holding either that contracts and negotiations for the sale of merchandise to be delivered across state lines are interstate commerce, or that burdens or restraints upon such commerce Congress may pass appropriate legislation to prevent, and courts of the United States may in proper proceedings enjoin. If this extends federal jurisdiction into fields not before occupied by the general government, it is not because such jurisdiction is not within the limits allowed by the constitution of the United States.

* * *

For the reasons given, the decree * * * dismissing the bill must be reversed, with instructions to enter a decree for the United States perpetually enjoining the defendants from maintaining the combination in cast-iron pipe * * * .

NOTES AND QUESTIONS

1.   This is only a court of appeals decision but it is one of the most important opinions in the development of a rationale for distinguishing among trade restraints. The 41-year-old author of the opinion, of course, went on to develop one of the most impressive resumes of the 20th Century, becoming both President of the United States and, later, Chief Justice.

2.   The opinion takes seriously the relationship between common law ideas of restraint of trade and the scope and meaning of the Sherman Act. Indeed, it sees the latter as in large part creating federal jurisdiction and a federal remedy for the former. What exceptions did Judge Taft believe the common law recognized?

3.   More important, what integrating principle did Judge Taft believe explained the common law exceptions? What makes one purpose "ancillary" to another? Do even most personal dealings have multiple purposes? How does one distinguish after the fact which was the "main" purpose and which the "ancillary" one?

4.   Is Judge Taft doing something other than adopting the distinction between "reasonable" and "unreasonable" restraints of trade that Justice White had advocated? What does Judge Taft say about such a "rule of reason"? Do you agree with him that it amounts to "set[ting] sail on a sea of doubt"?

5.   This is just the first of many cases you will see in which the size of the market and the defendant's place in it are at issue. Always remember that the "market" is a useful metaphor, not an actual place, and that its size is an important conclusion based on facts, not an observed fact itself.

a.   Do you agree with Judge Taft that it should not be relevant here that the defendants sold only 30% of the nation's output of cast-iron pipe? Is that because an agreement should be illegal even if the conspirators are doomed to fail, i.e., if we assume that competition will undercut their agreed-upon price?

b.   Did the Court perhaps simply believe the 30% figure understated the market position of these firms with respect to the customers on whose work they bid?

6. Should it be relevant for antitrust purposes that by rigging the winner of the bid in advance, the defendants had committed a fraud on their customers? Why should that be a matter for federal as opposed to state law?

a. Is the antitrust concern that if prices are higher there inevitably will be less pipe sold? Is it because if prices were lower, water companies would pay less and taxes or water rates would be reduced?

b. Suppose you knew that neither of those consequences was likely. May we say that if a business arrangement simply has no discernable public-serving purpose, there is no social cost to declaring it to be illegal?

7. Do you agree with Judge Taft that we cannot simply assume that market forces will cure any problems created by this arrangement? Why can't we assume that other pipe producers will hear of the high prices being bid in this region and offer to sell pipe in competition with the defendants? Is the high cost of transportation a complete answer? Would such reasoning make every convenience store a monopolist because its customers' alternative would be driving several miles to a discount mall?[8]

8. When the case got to the Supreme Court, the firms argued principally that bidding on a city's business took place in the city itself and thus not in interstate commerce. Justice Peckham rejected that view in an opinion for a unanimous court. 175 U.S. 211, 20 S.Ct. 96, 44 L.Ed. 136 (1899). This was not, he wrote, a case in which only a local operation was involved. Here, the pipe was often to be shipped from the manufacturer's state to the buyer's and thus the conspiracy had a "direct, immediate, and intended relation to and effect upon" the price of pipe generally and upon interstate commerce in pipe. But in deference to *E.C. Knight*, the Court ordered the decree modified so as not to prohibit price fixing and market division by firms within a single state for deliveries within that state, even if some of the other firms with which they were competing for such business were from out-of-state. The Sherman Act was said to reach only the interstate sales.

9. As a final attempt to deflect the charges, the defendants told the Supreme Court that their agreement could not be "restraining trade" because their customers continued to buy their pipe. Do you see the fallacy in this argument? Would you expect a firm ever knowingly to set a price so high that everyone quit buying? Justice Peckham explained, "Total suppression of the trade in the commodity is not necessary in order to render the combination one in restraint of trade. It is the effect of the combination in limiting and restricting the right of each of the members to transact business * * * as well as its effect upon the volume or extent of the dealing in the commodity" that made this conspiracy illegal.

---

[8]   Clearly, not every convenience store is a monopolist, but as you will see later, it may be useful to say that such a store has some "market power" if it can sustain higher than competitive prices over a significant period of time. The "market power" concept will be significant in a number of later cases.

A NOTE ON THE ECONOMICS AND OPERATION OF CARTELS

Addyston Pipe is an illustration of a classic cartel, a group of competitors who conspire to raise prices above those that would prevail in competition. The firms act as one to do together what any one would do if it were a monopolist.

For most Americans, the clearest example of a current cartel is the Organization of Petroleum Exporting Countries (OPEC). Every few months, we read that OPEC ministers have again met to try to raise the price of oil above prevailing prices. In doing so, as one would expect, they have to get their members to cut oil production to an amount that can be sold at the target price.[9]

OPEC provides a convenient example of problems faced by virtually any cartel. The first problem is determining the group's objectives. At any given time, members' needs for cash and expectations about future demand may differ. Further, they may have different cost structures, amounts of excess capacity, and the like. Getting an agreement on a common strategy for a cartel is often almost impossible. When, out of fear of the Sherman Act, such agreements have to be achieved in secret, the cost is greatly increased. Indeed, one reason the railroads were caught in *Trans-Missouri* is that they acted openly, believing they weren't violating the law.

Second, the cartel may not include all of the firms in the market. Prices set by U.S. firms, for example, are not dictated by the OPEC cartel, and producers of pipe not within the *Addyston Pipe* conspiracy sometimes won the bids. The point is that if a cartel raises prices, consumers may often buy from firms outside the cartel instead.

A third and often greater problem does not come from outside the cartel; it is the problem of cheating by parties to the cartel agreement. Think about it. If your cost of production were $5.00 and the cartel price were $7.00, might you be willing to cut your price to $6.75 if you could thereby increase your sales by 20%? Even if *you* would not "cheat", could you say the same for your competitor? Such cheating on a cartel agreement benefits consumers, of course, but successful cartels have to find ways to do business that maximize the chances of fellow cartel members' detecting the cheating.[10]

---

[9]   Suit was brought against OPEC in the United States, but courts held it is immune from suit because it constitutes the acts of sovereign nations. International Ass'n of Machinists v. Organization of Petroleum Exporting Countries, 649 F.2d 1354 (9th Cir.1981). Congress periodically threatens to reverse that result and grant federal courts' jurisdiction over such a case, but such legislation has not been adopted.

[10]   See, e.g., Christopher R. Leslie, Trust, Distrust, and Antitrust, 82 Texas L. Rev. 515 (2004); James M. Griffen & Weiwen Xiong, The Incentive to Cheat: An Empirical Analysis of OPEC, 40 J. Law & Economics 289 (1997). Cf. Ian Ayres, How Cartels Punish: A Structural Theory of Self-Enforcing Collusion, 87 Columbia L. Rev. 295 (1987).

How did the firms in *Addyston Pipe* avoid the problem of cheating? Remember that the pipe was sold through public competitive bids. All cartel members knew what price their competitors were supposed to bid and could verify whether or not they did so.[11] That is probably why, to this day, bid rigging is a popular form of conspiracy and why it is the antitrust violation most likely to be prosecuted as a crime.

Yet a fourth problem may be "assigning" production within the cartel to firms that can produce most efficiently and thus receive maximum benefit from the monopoly price. Do you remember how the firms in *Addyston Pipe* ultimately dealt with this problem? That's right; they had an auction among themselves for the right to get a contract. The effect was that the winner was forced to share some of its monopoly profit with the other members of the cartel.

Keep an eye out for similar problems and methods of overcoming them in later cases involving alleged cartels. In part it may help you decide whether it is plausible to believe cartel behavior is in fact involved.

––––––––––

A NOTE ON SOME EARLY GROUP BOYCOTTS

Trans-Missouri illustrated an alleged conspiracy to fix prices. *Addyston Pipe* added an element of allocating customers to whom individual conspirators would sell. Two other early cases add a third traditional category of "combination or conspiracy"—an agreement among competitors to "boycott" certain other firms.

W.W. Montague & Co. v. Lowry, 193 U.S. 38, 24 S.Ct. 307, 48 L.Ed. 608 (1904), involved an association of California wholesalers and eastern manufacturers of tiles and other fireplace fixtures. The wholesalers agreed not to buy from non-members of the association and the manufacturers agreed not to sell to non-members at less than retail prices. The plaintiff, a wholesale dealer who had not been invited to join the group, complained that it could not get products to sell except from manufacturers in other states whose prices were higher. Justice Peckham, in a relatively brief opinion for a unanimous Court, found the § 1 violation "plain."

In Eastern States Retail Lumber Dealers' Ass'n v. United States, 234 U.S. 600, 34 S.Ct. 951, 58 L.Ed. 1490 (1914), the combination involved retail lumber dealers. Some local wholesale dealers had apparently begun selling directly to building contractors and other volume users whom the retailers saw as their own customers. The members of the defendant association circulated a list of such wholesalers to each other, and although there was no direct proof of the effect of the list, it was understood that

––––––––––

[11]   In the *Trans-Missouri* case as well, rail rates had to be published and the I.C.C. had a staff to enforce those rates.

members would not buy from listed wholesalers. The Justice Department charged a violation of § 1 and the Supreme Court unanimously agreed. Any individual retail dealer could refuse to deal with any wholesaler, Justice Day wrote, but circulation of this list "tended directly to restrain the freedom of commerce" by intimidating the wholesalers from selling at retail.

1.   Do you agree that such "group boycotts" should be illegal? Why? Do they allow the conspirators to limit production in the industry? Do they allow non-competitive price setting?

2.   Do group boycotts impair the ability of non-member firms to enter the market with better service, lower prices, or both? Was that probably what was going on in *Montague*? In *Eastern States*?

3.   Why would the large wholesalers in *Eastern* States have felt intimidated by the small retailers? Weren't the retailers more in need of the wholesalers' good will than the other way around?

We will not stop to consider these issues in detail at this point, but you will see later that group boycott questions recur frequently in the evolution of antitrust doctrine.

LABOR UNIONS AND THE SHERMAN ACT

If every combination in restraint of trade is illegal, and if group boycotts constitute such restraints of trade, it is not much of a step to conclude that labor strikes necessarily violate Sherman Act § 1. Business people who might otherwise have condemned the Sherman Act were more than willing to take that step, and in the early days of the Sherman Act the courts agreed.

In 1894, for example, the year before *E.C. Knight* declared the new statute inadequate to condemn the Sugar Trust, it was more than adequate to support an injunction against the Pullman strike. United States v. Debs, 64 F. 724 (N.D. Ill. 1894), aff'd sub nom. In re Debs, 158 U.S. 564 (1895). See also, e.g., Loewe v. Lawlor, 208 U.S. 274, 28 S.Ct. 301, 52 L.Ed. 488 (1908), and Gompers v. Buck's Stove & Range So., 221 U.S. 418, 31 S.Ct. 492, 55 L.Ed. 797 (1911).

What do you think of this use of antitrust principles? Given its "every * * * combination" construction of the Sherman Act, could the Court have come out any other way? It took a statutory change, adoption of Clayton Act § 6, to moderate the use of Sherman Act § 1 in labor settings. See, e.g.,

Apex Hosiery Co. v. Leader, 310 U.S. 469, 60 S.Ct. 982, 84 L.Ed. 1311 (1940).[12]

C. MONOPOLIZATION AND MERGER

We sometimes hear the *Microsoft* case of the 1990s described as the "antitrust case of the century." Ours is not the first generation to have that hubris. Indeed, citizens thought they saw such a landmark case as the 20th century began.

NORTHERN SECURITIES COMPANY V. UNITED STATES

Supreme Court of the United States, 1904
193 U.S. 197, 24 S.Ct. 436, 48 L.Ed. 679

MR. JUSTICE HARLAN announced the affirmance of the decree of the Circuit Court, and delivered the following opinion:

This suit was brought by the United States against the Northern Securities Company, * * * the Great Northern Railway Company, * * * the Northern Pacific Railway Company, * * * James J. Hill, * * * and * * * J. Pierpont Morgan * * *. * * * By the decree below the United States was given substantially the relief asked by it in the bill.

* * *

The Great Northern Railway Company and the Northern Pacific Railway Company owned, controlled and operated separate lines of railway * * * [from St. Paul, MN to Portland, OR]. The two lines, main and branches, about 9,000 miles in length, were and are parallel and competing lines across the continent through the northern tier of States between the Great Lakes and the Pacific, and the two companies were engaged in active competition for freight and passenger traffic, each road connecting at its respective terminals with lines of railway, or with lake and river steamers, or with seagoing vessels.

* * *

Prior to November 13, 1901, defendant Hill and associate stockholders of the Great Northern Railway Company, and defendant Morgan and

---

[12] William Howard Taft defended use of the Sherman Act against secondary boycotts (but not lawful strikes) in his post-Solicitor General, post-Sixth Circuit, post-Presidential, pre-Chief Justice years as a Yale law professor. See W. H. Taft, The Antitrust Act and the Supreme Court 96–99 (1914). Another discussion of this use of the Sherman Act can be found in Herbert Hovenkamp, Labor Conspiracies in American Law 1880–1930, 66 Texas L. Rev. 919 (1988).

The Clayton Act exception is actually narrower than the language might suggest. Union activity in support of improper concerted employer behavior can still violate the Sherman Act. Compare, e.g., Allen Bradley Co. v. Local Union No. 3, 325 U.S. 797, 65 S.Ct. 1533, 89 L.Ed. 1939 (1945) (efforts to exclude out-of-state contractors from market), with Local Union No. 189 v. Jewel Tea Co., 381 U.S. 676, 85 S.Ct. 1596, 14 L.Ed.2d 640 (1965) (coordination of hours grocery store meat departments would be open). See also, American Steel Erectors v. Local Union No. 7, 536 F.3d 68 (1st Cir. 2008) (effort to deny work to non-union firms).

associate stockholders of the Northern Pacific Railway Company, entered into a combination to form, under the laws of New Jersey, a holding corporation, to be called the Northern Securities Company * * * . * * * [T]he interests of individual stockholders in the property and franchises of the two independent and competing railway companies were to be converted into an interest in the property and franchises of the holding corporation. Thus, * * * "all inducement for competition between the two systems was to be removed, a virtual consolidation effected, and a monopoly of the interstate and foreign commerce formerly carried on by the two systems as independent competitors established."

* * *

The government charges that if the combination was held not to be in violation of the act of Congress, then all efforts of the national government to preserve to the people the benefits of free competition among carriers engaged in interstate commerce will be wholly unavailing, and all transcontinental lines, indeed the entire railway systems of the country, may be absorbed, merged and consolidated, thus placing the public at the absolute mercy of the holding corporation.

* * *

In our judgment, the evidence fully sustains the material allegations of the bill, and shows a violation of the act of Congress. * * *

* * * Necessarily, * * * the constituent companies ceased, under such a combination, to be in active competition for trade and commerce along their respective lines * * * . * * * No scheme or device could more certainly come within the words of the act * * * . This combination is, within the meaning of the act, a "trust;" but if not, it is a combination in restraint of interstate and international commerce; and that is enough to bring it under the condemnation of the act. The mere existence of such a combination, and the power acquired by the holding company as its trustee, constitute a menace to, and a restraint upon, that freedom of commerce which Congress intended to recognize and protect * * * . If such combination be not destroyed, all the advantages that would naturally come to the public under the operation of the general laws of competition, as between the Great Northern and Northern Pacific Railway companies, will be lost, and the entire commerce of the immense territory in the northern part of the United States between the Great Lakes and the Pacific at Puget Sound will be at the mercy of a single holding corporation, organized in a State distant from the people of that territory.

* * *

It is said that whatever may be the power of a State over such subjects Congress cannot forbid single individuals from disposing of their stock in a state corporation, even if such corporation be engaged in interstate and international commerce * * * . It is unnecessary in this case to consider such abstract, general questions. * * *

* * * What the Government particularly complains of—indeed, all that it complains of here—is the existence of a combination among the stockholders of competing railroad companies which in violation of the act of Congress restrains interstate and international commerce through the agency of a common corporate trustee designated to act for both companies in repressing free competition between them. Independently of any question of the mere ownership of stock or of the organization of a state corporation, can it in reason be said that such a combination is not embraced by the very terms of the anti-trust act? * * * If Congress legislates for the protection of the public, may it not proceed on the ground that wrongs when effected by a powerful combination are more dangerous and require more stringent supervision than when they are to be effected by a single person? * * *

* * *

* * * Whether the free operation of the normal laws of competition is a wise and wholesome rule for trade and commerce is an economic question which this court need not consider or determine. * * * Congress has, in effect, recognized the rule of free competition by declaring illegal every combination or conspiracy in restraint of interstate and international commerce. As in the judgment of Congress the public convenience and the general welfare will be best subserved when the natural laws of competition are left undisturbed by those engaged in interstate commerce, and as Congress has embodied that rule in a statute, that must be, for all, the end of the matter * * * .

* * *

The rule of competition, prescribed by Congress, was not at all new in trade and commerce. And we cannot be in any doubt as to the reason that moved Congress to the incorporation of that rule into a statute. * * * [W]hen Congress declared contracts, combinations and conspiracies in restraint of trade or commerce to be illegal, it did nothing more than apply to interstate commerce a rule that had been long applied by the several States when dealing with combinations that were in restraint of their domestic commerce. * * * It may well be assumed that Congress, when enacting that statute, shared the general apprehension that a few powerful corporations or combinations sought to obtain, and, unless restrained, would obtain such absolute control of the entire trade and commerce of the country as would be detrimental to the general welfare.

* * *

Now, the court is asked to adjudge that, if held to embrace the case before us, the Anti-Trust Act is repugnant to the Constitution of the United

States. In this view we are unable to concur. * * * If, as the court has held, Congress can strike down a combination between private persons or private corporations that restrains trade among the States in iron pipe (as in Addyston Pipe & Steel Co. v. United States), or in tiles, grates and mantles (as in Montague & Co. v. Lowry), surely it ought not to be doubted that Congress has power to declare illegal a combination that restrains commerce among the States, and with foreign nations, as carried on over the lines of competing railroad companies exercising public franchises, and engaged in such commerce. * * *

* * *

Many suggestions were made in argument based upon the thought that the anti-trust act would in the end prove to be mischievous in its consequences. Disaster to business and wide-spread financial ruin, it has been intimated, will follow the execution of its provisions. Such predictions were made in all the cases heretofore arising under that act. But they have not been verified. It is the history of monopolies in this country and in England that predictions of ruin are habitually made by them when it is attempted, by legislation, to restrain their operations and to protect the public against their exactions. * * *

But even if the court shared the gloomy forebodings in which the defendants indulge, it could not refuse to respect the action of the legislative branch of the Government if what it has done is within the limits of its constitutional power. * * *

* * *

It is said that this statute contains criminal provisions and must therefore be strictly construed. The rule upon that subject is a very ancient and salutary one. It means only that we must not bring cases within the provisions of such a statute that are not clearly embraced by it, nor by narrow, technical or forced construction of words, exclude cases from it that are obviously within its provisions. What must be sought for always is the intention of the legislature, and the duty of the court is to give effect to that intention as disclosed by the words used.

* * *

The judgment of the court is that the decree below be and hereby is affirmed, with liberty to the Circuit Court to proceed in the execution of its decree as the circumstances may require.

MR. JUSTICE BREWER, concurring.

* * *

* * * [W]hile I was with the majority of the court in the decision in United States v. Trans-Missouri Freight Association, followed by the cases of United States v. Joint Traffic Association, [and] Addyston Pipe & Steel

Company v. United States, * * * I think that in some respects the reasons given for the judgments cannot be sustained. Instead of holding that the Anti-Trust Act included all contracts, reasonable or unreasonable, in restraint of interstate trade, the ruling should have been that the contracts there presented were unreasonable restraints of interstate trade, and as such within the scope of the act. That act, as appears from its title, was leveled at only "unlawful restraints and monopolies." * * *

Further, the general language of the act is also limited by the power which each individual has to manage his own property and determine the place and manner of its investment. Freedom of action in these respects is among the inalienable rights of every citizen. If, applying this thought to the present case, it appeared that Mr. Hill was the owner of a majority of the stock in the Great Northern Railway Company he could not by any act of Congress be deprived of the right of investing his surplus means in the purchase of stock of the Northern Pacific Railway Company, although such purchase might tend to vest in him through that ownership a control over both companies. * * *

But no such investment by a single individual of his means is here presented. There was a combination by several individuals separately owning stock in two competing railroad companies to place the control of both in a single corporation. * * * That combination is as direct a restraint of trade by destroying competition as the appointment of a committee to regulate rates. * * *

* * *

MR. JUSTICE WHITE, with whom concur MR. CHIEF JUSTICE FULLER, MR. JUSTICE PECKHAM, and MR. JUSTICE HOLMES, dissenting.

* * *

The plenary authority of Congress over interstate commerce, its right to regulate it to the fullest extent, to fix the rates to be charged for the movement of interstate commerce, to legislate concerning the ways and vehicles actually engaged in such traffic, and to exert any and every other power over such commerce which flows from the authority conferred by the Constitution, is * * * conceded. But the concessions thus made do not concern the question in this case, which is not the scope of the power of Congress to regulate commerce, but whether the power extends to regulate the ownership of stock in railroads, which is not commerce at all. * * *

* * *

In United States v. E.C. Knight Co., the facts and the relief based on them were thus stated by Mr. Chief Justice Fuller, delivering the opinion of the court:

"By the purchase of the stock of the four Philadelphia refineries, with shares of its own stock, the American Sugar

Refining Company acquired nearly complete control of the manufacture of refined sugar within the United States. * * *

* * *

* * * [P]ointing out that the power of Congress over interstate commerce and the fact that its failure to legislate over subjects requiring uniform legislation expressed the will of Congress that the State should be without power to act on that subject, the court came to consider whether the power of Congress to regulate commerce embraced the authority to regulate and control the ownership of stock in the state sugar refining companies, because the products of such companies when manufactured might become the subject of interstate commerce. Elaborately passing upon that question and reaffirming the definition of Chief Justice Marshall of commerce, in the constitutional sense, it was held that, whilst the power of Congress extended to commerce as thus defined, it did not embrace the ownership of stock in state corporations, because the products of such manufacture might subsequently become the subject of interstate commerce.

The parallel between the two cases is complete. * * *

* * *

MR. JUSTICE HOLMES, with whom concurred the CHIEF JUSTICE, MR. JUSTICE WHITE, and MR. JUSTICE PECKHAM, dissenting.

* * *

Great cases, like hard cases, make bad law. For great cases are called great, not by reason of their real importance in shaping the law of the future, but because of some accident of immediate overwhelming interest which appeals to the feelings and distorts the judgment. * * * What we have to do in this case is to find the meaning of some not very difficult words. * * *

* * *

The statute of which we have to find the meaning is a criminal statute. * * * The words cannot be read one way in a suit which is to end in fine and imprisonment and another way in one which seeks an injunction. * * * [A]ll agree that before a statute is to be taken to punish that which always has been lawful it must express its intent in clear words. So I say we must read the words before us as if the question were whether two small exporting grocers should go to jail.

* * *

This act is construed by the Government to affect the purchasers of shares in two railroad companies because of the effect it may have, or, if you like, is certain to have, upon the competition of these roads. If such a remote result of the exercise of an ordinary incident of property and personal freedom is enough to make that exercise unlawful, there is hardly any transaction concerning commerce between the States that may not be made a crime by the finding of a jury or a court. * * *

* * *

* * * The court below argued as if maintaining competition were the expressed object of the act. The act says nothing about competition. I stick to the exact words used. * * * Contracts in restraint of trade are dealt with and defined by the common law. They are contracts with a stranger to the contractor's business, (although in some cases carrying on a similar one,) which wholly or partially restrict the freedom of the contractor in carrying on that business as otherwise he would. The objection of the common law to them was primarily on the contractor's own account. * * *

Combinations or conspiracies in restraint of trade, on the other hand, were combinations to keep strangers to the agreement out of the business. The objection to them was not an objection to their effect upon the parties making the contract, the members of the combination or firm, but an objection to their intended effect upon strangers to the firm and their supposed consequent effect upon the public at large. In other words, they were regarded as contrary to public policy because they monopolized or attempted to monopolize some portion of the trade or commerce of the realm. * * * All that is added to the first section by § 2 is that like penalties are imposed upon every single person who, without combination, monopolizes or attempts to monopolize commerce among the States; and that the liability is extended to attempting to monopolize any part of such trade or commerce. It is more important as an aid to the construction of § 1 than it is on its own account. It shows that whatever is criminal when done by way of combination is equally criminal if done by a single man. * * *

* * *

If the statute applies to this case it must be because the parties, or some of them, have formed, or because the Northern Securities Company is, a combination in restraint of trade among the States, or, what comes to the same thing in my opinion, because the defendants, or some or one of them, are monopolizing or attempting to monopolize some part of the commerce between the States. But the mere reading of those words shows that they are used in a limited and accurate sense. According to popular speech, every concern monopolizes whatever business it does, and if that business is trade between two States it monopolizes a part of the trade among the States. Of course the statute does not forbid that. * * * A single railroad down a narrow valley or through a mountain gorge monopolizes all the railroad transportation through that valley or gorge. Indeed every railroad monopolizes, in a popular sense, the trade of some area. Yet I suppose no one would say that the statute forbids a combination of men into a corporation to build and run such a railroad between the States.

* * *

There is a natural feeling that somehow or other the statute meant to strike at combinations great enough to cause just anxiety on the part of those who love their country more than money, while it viewed such little ones as I have supposed with just indifference. * * * [I]t has occurred to me that it might be that when a combination reached a certain size it might have attributed to it more of the character of a monopoly merely by virtue of its size than would be attributed to a smaller one. * * * [However, in] the first place size in the case of railroads is an inevitable incident and if it were an objection under the act, the Great Northern and the Northern Pacific already were too great and encountered the law. * * * [E]ven a small railroad will have the same tendency to exclude others from its narrow area that great ones have to exclude others from a greater one, and the statute attacks the small monopolies as well as the great. The very words of the act make such a distinction impossible in this case * * * .

* * *

* * * I am happy to know that only a minority of my brethren adopt an interpretation of the law which in my opinion would make eternal the bellum omnium contra omnes and disintegrate society so far as it could into individual atoms. If that were its intent I should regard calling such a law a regulation of commerce as a mere pretense. It would be an attempt to reconstruct society. I am not concerned with the wisdom of such an attempt, but I believe that Congress was not entrusted by the Constitution with the power to make it and I am deeply persuaded that it has not tried.

NOTES AND QUESTIONS

1. Here is yet another 5–4 decision. Justice Harlan, the dissenter in *E.C. Knight* and author of the plurality opinion here, was part of the majority in *Trans-Missouri*. Justices Brown and Brewer are still aligned with Justice Harlan, although the latter denies the Court a majority position by saying that § 1 only reaches "unreasonable" restraints of trade.

a. Justices Field, Gray and Shiras, all dissenters in *Trans-Missouri*, have now left the Court. President Theodore Roosevelt, a compulsive "trust buster" has replaced two of them with Justices Day and McKenna, both here voting with the plurality.

b. Justice White is still in dissent, and now Justice Peckham, author of most of the Court's earlier opinions, has joined him along with Chief Justice Fuller. They are joined, in turn, by a surprise vote, the third Roosevelt appointee, Justice Oliver Wendell Holmes, who here turns on his benefactor, demonstrating what the President is said later to have called "all the backbone of a banana."[13]

2.   What had happened to cause such an intense reaction from the President and members of the Court?[14]

a.   In part, the reaction arose from concern about a wave of business consolidations in the late-19th and early-20th centuries, triggered in part by the apparent license the Court had given in *E.C. Knight*. Firms such as Standard Oil, United States Steel and American Tobacco—all defendants in later antitrust cases—grew by merger during this period, and it took the result in *Northern Securities* (and a timely stock market crash in 1903) to slow that process.

b.   In part the reaction was to what Holmes suggested was a "great case." The defendants were some of the wealthiest men in America and stories of their business dealings were the stuff of tabloids. It was as though Donald Trump were accused of combining with Bill Gates to monopolize the music industry. To try, as Holmes urged, to decide this as an abstract matter of statutory construction was to ignore reality.

3.   We, however, are less emotionally involved in the facts. How did the Justice Department, and Justice Harlan for the Court majority, characterize what had happened? Do you agree that formerly competing railroads were here made one and that such a merger is automatically a "combination in the form of trust or otherwise * * * in restraint of trade"? Do you agree that *Trans-Missouri* and *Joint-Traffic Association* decided that the Government need not show that all competition had been eliminated, i.e., that all it need show is that the arrangement has a tendency to restrain or limit the benefits of free competition?

4.   Do you agree with Justice White that, this case should be controlled by *E.C. Knight*, i.e., that a merger of two companies is by definition not a transaction in interstate commerce? Is the distinction that the railroads owned by these firms crossed state lines? Are you a potential antitrust offender each time you buy a share of stock in a national company? Would holding that stock purchases are *not* in interstate commerce create a loophole that would render the statute much less effective at controlling monopoly?

5.   Do you agree with Justice Holmes that the Sherman Act should be interpreted as if every case were a criminal case, i.e., narrowly and literally? Might one better realize the purposes of the statute by construing it as a civil

---

[13]   Eleanor M. Fox & Lawrence A. Sullivan, Cases and Materials on Antitrust 69 (1989), citing C.D. Bowen, Yankee From Olympus 370 (1944). We will see later evidence of Justice Holmes' strong views on several antitrust issues. The interesting literature on those views includes Alfred S. Neely, "A Humbug Based on Economic Ignorance and Incompetence": Antitrust in the Eyes of Justice Holmes, 1993 Utah L. Rev. 1; Spencer Weber Waller, The Modern Antitrust Relevance of Oliver Wendell Holmes, 59 Brooklyn L. Rev. 1443 (1994).

[14]   The importance President Roosevelt placed on this prosecution is discussed in Hans B. Thorelli, The Federal Antitrust Policy: Origination of an American Tradition 411–431 (1954).

provision unless the fact that a case is actually brought as a criminal matter requires a narrower construction?[15]

a.   Do you agree with Justice Holmes that because the Sherman Act does not use the word "competition," competition should not be an important concept in interpreting the statute?

b.   Are you persuaded that the only effect of § 1 is to restrict contracts whereby a person limits his or her own freedom of action? Are you persuaded that § 2 only makes it illegal for one person to do what it would be illegal for multiple people to do together?

6.   Should it be relevant here that the Northern Pacific railroad was on the verge of insolvency when this union occurred? What does the Court believe the Northern Pacific management should have done?

a.   Would the northern tier of states have been better served if the Northern Pacific tracks had rusted away and the Great Northern had been a smaller, but still monopoly carrier? Was the inevitable consequence of this decision that another source of keeping the Northern Pacific alive would be found?[16]

b.   The principal other bidder for the Northern Pacific had been E.H. Harriman, owner of the Union Pacific whose line ran from Chicago to Omaha to Salt Lake City and then connected with lines to the west coast. Harriman seems to have wanted to preserve his as the *only* transcontinental railroad. Can one argue that James J. Hill's effort to prevent *that* monopoly by formation of Northern Securities was thus the lesser of two evils? Even if that were true, should it make this combination lawful? Why or why not?

7.   If you decided it was a good idea to permit coordination of activities by these railroads, would you rather have them form joint ventures when they need to work together rather than merge for all purposes into a single firm? In an important sense, Justice Holmes' position won in that most mergers are now evaluated under Clayton Act § 7, adopted a decade later in 1914, rather than under Sherman Act § 1. But proceeding in that way meant that often in history we have given firms more latitude to merge than to coordinate their conduct. That may have tended to push some firms into more permanent arrangements than they or we would otherwise prefer.[17]

---

[15]   Justice Holmes later wrote the opinion for the Court expressly holding that the Sherman Act is not an unconstitutionally vague criminal statute. Nash v. United States, 229 U.S. 373, 33 S.Ct. 780, 57 L.Ed. 1232 (1913). Sixty-five years later, the Court held that there is a higher mens rea requirement when a Sherman Act case is brought as a criminal instead of a civil charge. United States v. United States Gypsum Co., 438 U.S. 422, 98 S.Ct. 2864, 57 L.Ed.2d 854 (1978).

[16]   Ironically, in the Transportation Act of 1920, Congress ordered the ICC to plan the consolidation of U.S. railways into a limited number of "systems." The Great Northern and Northern Pacific were identified as appropriate for consolidation under this plan. D. Philip Locklin, Economics of Transportation 86–89 (1938).

[17]   George Bittlingmayer, Did Antitrust Policy Cause the Great Merger Wave?, 28 J. Law & Economics 77 (1985). But the Sherman Act is still potentially applicable to mergers. E.g., United States v. Reading Co., 253 U.S. 26, 40 S.Ct. 425, 64 L.Ed. 760 (1920); United States v. First Nat'l Bank & Trust Co. of Lexington, 376 U.S. 665, 84 S.Ct. 1033, 12 L.Ed.2d 1 (1964).

STANDARD OIL COMPANY OF NEW JERSEY V. UNITED STATES

Supreme Court of the United States, 1911
221 U.S. 1, 31 S.Ct. 502, 55 L.Ed. 619

MR. CHIEF JUSTICE WHITE delivered the opinion of the court.

The Standard Oil Company of New Jersey and 33 other corporations, John D. Rockefeller, William Rockefeller and five other individual defendants prosecute this appeal to reverse a decree of the court below. Such decree was entered upon a bill filed by the United States under authority of § 4, of the act of July 2, 1890, known as the anti-trust act * * * . * * *

* * * The bill was divided into thirty numbered sections, and sought relief upon the theory that the various defendants were engaged in conspiring "to restrain the trade and commerce in petroleum, commonly called 'crude oil,' in refined oil, and in the other products of petroleum, * * * and to monopolize the said commerce." The conspiracy was alleged to have been formed in or about the year 1870 by three of the individual defendants, viz: John D. Rockefeller, William Rockefeller and Henry M. Flagler. The detailed averments concerning the alleged conspiracy were arranged with reference to three periods, the first from 1870 to 1882, the second from 1882 to 1899, and the third from 1899 to the time of the filing of the bill.

The general charge concerning the period from 1870 to 1882 was * * * that John D. and William Rockefeller and several other named individuals, who, prior to 1870, composed three separate partnerships engaged in the business of refining crude oil and shipping its products in interstate commerce, organized in the year 1870, a corporation known as the Standard Oil Company of Ohio and transferred to that company the business of the said partnerships, the members thereof becoming, in proportion to their prior ownership, stockholders in the corporation. It was averred that the other individual defendants soon afterwards became participants in the illegal combination and either transferred property to the corporation or to individuals to be held for the benefit of all parties in interest in proportion to their respective interests in the combination; that is, in proportion to their stock ownership in the Standard Oil Company of Ohio. By the means thus stated, it was charged that by the year 1872, the combination had acquired substantially all but three or four of the thirty-five or forty oil refineries located in Cleveland, Ohio. By reason of the power thus obtained and in further execution of the intent and purpose to restrain trade and to monopolize the commerce, interstate as well as intrastate, in petroleum and its products, the bill alleged that the combination and its members obtained large preferential rates and rebates in many and devious ways over their competitors from various railroad companies, and that by means of the advantage thus obtained many, if not virtually all, competitors were forced either to become members of the combination or were driven out of business; and thus, it was alleged, during the period in question the following results were brought about:

a.   That the combination, in addition to the refineries in Cleveland which it had acquired as previously stated, and which it had either dismantled to limit production or continued to operate, also from time to time acquired a large number of refineries of crude petroleum, situated in New York, Pennsylvania, Ohio and elsewhere. The properties thus acquired, like those previously obtained, although belonging to and being held for the benefit of the combination, were ostensibly divergently controlled, some of them being put in the name of the Standard Oil Company of Ohio, some in the name of corporations or limited partnerships affiliated therewith, or some being left in the name of the original owners who had become stockholders in the Standard Oil Company of Ohio and thus members of the alleged illegal combination.

b.   That the combination had obtained control of the pipe lines available for transporting oil from the oil fields to the refineries in Cleveland, Pittsburg, Titusville, Philadelphia, New York and New Jersey.

c.   That the combination during the period named had obtained a complete mastery over the oil industry, controlling 90 per cent of the business of producing, shipping, refining and selling petroleum and its products, and thus was able to fix the price of crude and refined petroleum and to restrain and monopolize all interstate commerce in those products.

The averments bearing upon the second period (1882 to 1899) had relation to the claim [that by the terms of a trust agreement] * * * the stock of forty corporations, including the Standard Oil Company of Ohio, * * * was vested in the trustees and their successors, "to be held for all parties in interest jointly." * * *

* * * The agreement provided for the issue of Standard Oil Trust certificates to represent the interest arising under the trust in the properties affected by the trust, which of course in view of the provisions of the agreement and the subject to which it related caused the interest in the certificates to be coincident with and the exact representative of the interest in the combination, that is, in the Standard Oil Company of Ohio. Soon afterwards it was alleged the trustees organized the Standard Oil Company of New Jersey and the Standard Oil Company of New York * * * . The bill alleged that pursuant to said trust agreement the said trustees * * * [acquired many other, smaller companies]. For the stocks and property so acquired the trustees issued trust certificates. * * *

The bill charged that during the second period quo warranto proceedings were commenced against the Standard Oil Company of Ohio, which resulted in the entry by the Supreme Court of Ohio, on March 2, 1892, of a decree adjudging the trust agreement to be void, not only because the Standard Oil Company of Ohio was a party to the same, but also because the agreement in and of itself was in restraint of trade and amounted to the creation of an unlawful monopoly. It was alleged that shortly after this decision, seemingly for the purpose of complying therewith, voluntary proceedings were had apparently to dissolve the trust, but that these proceedings were a subterfuge and a sham because they simply amounted to a transfer of the stock held by the trust in 64 of the companies which it controlled to some of the remaining 20 companies, it having controlled before the decree 84 in all, thereby, while seemingly in part giving up its dominion, yet in reality preserving the same by means of the control of the companies as to which it had retained complete authority. It was charged that especially was this the case, as the stock in the companies selected for transfer was virtually owned by the nine trustees or the members of their immediate families or associates. The bill further alleged that in 1897 the Attorney-General of Ohio instituted contempt proceedings in the quo warranto case based upon the claim that the trust had not been dissolved as required by the decree in that case. * * *

The result of these proceedings, the bill charged, caused a resort to the alleged wrongful acts asserted to have been committed during the third period * * * .

* * *

It was alleged that in or about the month of January, 1899, the individual defendants caused the charter of the Standard Oil Company of New Jersey to be amended; "so that the business and objects of said company were stated as follows, to wit: 'To do all kinds of mining, manufacturing, and trading business; transporting goods and merchandise by land or water in any manner; to buy, sell, lease, and improve land; build houses, structures, vessels, cars, wharves, docks, and piers; to lay and operate pipe lines; to erect lines for conducting electricity; to enter into and carry out contracts of every kind pertaining to its business; to acquire, use, sell, and grant licenses under patent rights; to purchase or otherwise acquire, hold, sell, assign, and transfer shares of capital stock and bonds or other evidences of indebtedness of corporations, and to exercise all the privileges of ownership, including voting upon the stock so held; to carry on its business and have offices and agencies therefor in all parts of the world, and to hold, purchase, mortgage, and convey real estate and personal property outside the State of New Jersey.' "

The capital stock of the company—which since March 19, 1892, had been $10,000,000—was increased to $110,000,000; and the individual defendants, as theretofore, continued to be a majority of the board of directors.

Reiterating in substance the averments that both the Standard Oil Trust from 1882 to 1899 and the Standard Oil Company of New Jersey since 1899 had monopolized and restrained interstate commerce in petroleum and its products, the bill at great length additionally set forth various means by which during the second and third periods, in addition to the effect occasioned by the combination of alleged previously independent concerns, the monopoly and restraint complained of was continued. Without attempting to follow the elaborate averments on these subjects * * * , it suffices to say that such averments may properly be grouped under the following heads: Rebates, preferences and other discriminatory practices in favor of the combination by railroad companies; restraint and monopolization by control of pipe lines, and unfair practices against competing pipe lines; contracts with competitors in restraint of trade; unfair methods of competition, such as local price cutting at the points where necessary to suppress competition; espionage of the business of competitors, the operation of bogus independent companies, and payment of rebates on oil, with the like intent; the division of the United States into districts and the limiting of the operations of the various subsidiary corporations as to such districts so that competition in the sale of petroleum products between such corporations had been entirely eliminated and destroyed; and finally reference was made to what was alleged to be the "enormous and unreasonable profits" earned by the Standard Oil Trust and the Standard Oil Company as a result of the alleged monopoly; which presumably was averred as a means of reflexly inferring the scope and power acquired by the alleged combination.

* * *

[The defendants admitted the acquisitions of property and formation of the trusts and corporations, but denied "all the allegations respecting combinations or conspiracies to restrain or monopolize the oil trade; and particularly that the so-called trust of 1882, or the acquisition of the shares of the defendant companies by the Standard Oil Company of New Jersey in 1899, was a combination of independent or competing concerns or corporations."]

* * *

On June 24, 1907, * * * a special examiner was appointed to take the evidence, and his report was filed March 22, 1909. It was heard * * * before a Circuit Court consisting of four judges.

The court decided in favor of the United States. In the opinion delivered, all the multitude of acts of wrongdoing charged in the bill were put aside, in so far as they were alleged to have been committed prior to the passage of the anti-trust act, "except as evidence of their (the defendants') purpose, of their continuing conduct and of its effect."

By the decree which was entered it was adjudged that the combining of the stocks of various companies in the hands of the Standard Oil Company of New Jersey in 1899 constituted a combination in restraint of trade and also an attempt to monopolize and a monopolization under § 2 of the anti-trust act. * * *

* * *

The Standard Oil Company of New Jersey was enjoined from voting the stocks or exerting any control over [its] * * * thirty-seven subsidiary companies, and the subsidiary companies were enjoined from paying any dividends as to the Standard Oil Company or permitting it to exercise any control over them by virtue of the stock ownership or power acquired by means of the combination. * * * Further, the individual defendants, the Standard Oil Company, and the thirty-seven subsidiary corporations were enjoined from engaging or continuing in interstate commerce in petroleum or its products during the continuance of the illegal combination.

* * *

Both as to the law and as to the facts the opposing contentions pressed in the argument are numerous and in all their aspects are so irreconcilable that it is difficult to reduce them to some fundamental generalization, which by being disposed of would decide them all. For instance, as to the law. While both sides agree that the determination of the controversy rests upon the correct construction and application of the first and second sections of the anti-trust act, yet the views as to the meaning of the act are as wide apart as the poles, since there is no real point of agreement on any view of the act. * * *

So also is it as to the facts. Thus, on the one hand * * * it is insisted that the facts establish that the assailed combination took its birth in a purpose to unlawfully acquire wealth by oppressing the public and destroying the just rights of others, and that its entire career exemplifies an inexorable carrying out of such wrongful intents, since, it is asserted, the pathway of the combination from the beginning to the time of the filing of the bill is marked with constant proofs of wrong inflicted upon the public and is strewn with the wrecks resulting from crushing out, without regard to law, the individual rights of others. Indeed, so conclusive, it is urged, is the proof on these subjects that it is asserted that the existence of the principal corporate defendant—the Standard Oil Company of New Jersey—with the vast accumulation of property which it owns or controls, because of its infinite potency for harm and the dangerous example which its continued existence affords, is an open and enduring menace to all freedom of trade and is a byword and reproach to modern economic methods. On the other hand, in a powerful analysis of the facts, it is insisted that they demonstrate that the origin and development of the vast business which the defendants control was but the result of lawful competitive methods, guided by economic genius of the highest order, sustained by courage, by a keen insight into commercial situations, resulting in the acquisition of great wealth, but at the same time serving to stimulate and increase production, to widely extend the distribution of the products of petroleum at a cost largely below that which would have otherwise prevailed, thus proving to be at one and the same time a benefaction to the general public as well as of enormous advantage to individuals. * * *

Duly appreciating the situation just stated, it is certain that only one point of concord between the parties is discernable, which is, that the controversy in every aspect is controlled by a correct conception of the meaning of the first and second sections of the anti-trust act. * * *

First. The text of the act and its meaning.

* * *

The debates show that doubt as to whether there was a common law of the United States which governed the subject in the absence of legislation was among the influences leading to the passage of the act. They conclusively show, however, that the main cause which led to the legislation was the thought that it was required by the economic condition of the times, that is, the vast accumulation of wealth in the hands of corporations and individuals, the enormous development of corporate organization, the facility for combination which such organizations afforded, the fact that the facility was being used, and that combinations known as trusts were being multiplied, and the widespread impression that their power had been and would be exerted to oppress individuals and injure the public generally. Although debates may not be used as a means for interpreting a statute, that rule in the nature of things is not violated by resorting to debates as a means of ascertaining the environment at the time of the enactment of a particular law, that is, the history of the period when it was adopted.

There can be no doubt that the sole subject with which the first section deals is restraint of trade as therein contemplated, and that the attempt to monopolize and monopolization is the subject with which the second section is concerned. It is certain that those terms, at least in their rudimentary meaning, took their origin in the common law, and were also familiar in the law of this country prior to and at the time of the adoption of the act in question.

* * *

a.   It is certain that at a very remote period the words "contract in restraint of trade" in England came to refer to some voluntary restraint put by contract by an individual on his right to carry on his trade or calling. Originally all such contracts were considered to be illegal, because it was deemed they were injurious to the public as well as to the individuals who made them. In the interest of the freedom of individuals to contract this doctrine was modified so that it was only when a restraint by contract was so general as to be coterminous with the kingdom that it was treated as void. * * *

b.   * * * The frequent granting of monopolies and the struggle which led to a denial of the power to create them, * * * is known to all and need not be reviewed. The evils which led to the public outcry against monopolies and to the final denial of the power to make them may be thus summarily stated: 1. The power which the monopoly gave to the one who enjoyed it to fix the price and thereby injure the public; 2. The power which it engendered of enabling a limitation on production; and, 3. The danger of deterioration in quality of the monopolized article which it was deemed was the inevitable resultant of the monopolistic control over its production and sale. As monopoly as thus conceived embraced only a consequence arising from an exertion of sovereign power, no express restrictions or prohibitions obtained against the creation by an individual of a monopoly as such. But as it was considered, at least so far as the necessaries of life were concerned, that individuals by the abuse of their right to contract might be able to usurp the power arbitrarily to enhance prices, one of the wrongs arising from monopoly, it came to be that laws were passed [prohibiting any] contract or course of dealing of such a character as to give rise to the presumption of an intent to injure others through the means, for instance, of a monopolistic increase of prices. * * *

* * *

And by operation of the mental process which led to considering as a monopoly acts which although they did not constitute a monopoly were thought to produce some of its baneful effects, so also because of the impediment or burden to the due course of trade which they produced, such acts came to be referred to as in restraint of trade. * * * [S]ee especially the opinion of Parker, C.J., in Mitchel v. Reynolds where a classification is made of monopoly which brings it generically within the description of restraint of trade.

Generalizing these considerations, the situation is this: 1. That by the common law monopolies were unlawful because of their restriction upon individual freedom of contract and their injury to the public. 2. That as to necessaries of life the freedom of the individual to deal was restricted where the nature and character of the dealing was such as to engender the presumption of intent to bring about at least one of the injuries which it was deemed would result from monopoly, that is an undue enhancement of price. 3. That to protect the freedom of contract of the individual not only in his own interest, but principally in the interest of the common weal, a contract of an individual by which he put an unreasonable restraint upon himself as to carrying on his trade or business was void. * * *

* * *

In this country also the acts from which it was deemed there resulted a part if not all of the injurious consequences ascribed to monopoly, came to be referred to as a monopoly itself. In other words, here as had been the case in England, practical common sense caused attention to be concentrated not upon the theoretically correct name to be given to the condition or acts which gave rise to a harmful result, but to the result itself and to the remedying of the evils which it produced. * * *

* * *

Let us consider the language of the first and second sections, guided by the principle that where words are employed in a statute which had at the time a well-known meaning at common law or in the law of this country they are presumed to have been used in that sense unless the context compels to the contrary.

As to the first section * * * .

In view of the common law and the law in this country as to restraint of trade, which we have reviewed, and the illuminating effect which that history must have under the rule to which we have referred, we think it results:

a.   That the context manifests that the statute was drawn in the light of the existing practical conception of the law of restraint of trade, because it groups as within that class, not only contracts which were in restraint of trade in the subjective sense, but all contracts or acts which theoretically were attempts to monopolize, yet which in practice had come to be considered as in restraint of trade in a broad sense.

b.   That in view of the many new forms of contracts and combinations which were being evolved from existing economic conditions, it was deemed essential by an all-embracing enumeration to make sure that no form of contract or combination by which an undue restraint of interstate or foreign commerce was brought about could save such restraint from condemnation. * * *

c.   And as the contracts or acts embraced in the provision were not expressly defined, since the enumeration addressed itself simply to classes of acts, those classes being broad enough to embrace every conceivable contract or combination which could be made concerning trade or commerce or the subjects of such commerce, and thus caused any act done by any of the enumerated methods anywhere in the whole field of human activity to be illegal if in restraint of trade, it inevitably follows that the provision necessarily called for the exercise of judgment which required that some standard should be resorted to for the purpose of determining whether the prohibitions contained in the statute had or had not in any given case been violated. Thus not specifying but indubitably contemplating and requiring a standard, it follows that it was intended that the standard of reason which had been applied at the common law and in this country in dealing with subjects of the character embraced by the statute, was intended to be the measure used for the purpose of determining whether in a given case a particular act had or had not brought about the wrong against which the statute provided.

And a consideration of the text of the second section serves to establish that it was intended to supplement the first and to make sure that by no possible guise could the public policy embodied in the first section be frustrated or evaded. * * *

* * *

Undoubtedly, the words "to monopolize" and "monopolize" as used in the section reach every act bringing about the prohibited results. The ambiguity, if any, is involved in determining what is intended by monopolize. But this ambiguity is readily dispelled in the light of the previous history of the law of restraint of trade to which we have referred and the indication which it gives of the practical evolution by which monopoly and the acts which produce the same result as monopoly, that is, an undue restraint of the course of trade, all came to be spoken of as, and to be indeed synonymous with, restraint of trade. * * * And, of course, when the second section is thus harmonized with and made as it was intended to be the complement of the first, it becomes obvious that the criteria to be resorted to in any given case for the purpose of ascertaining whether violations of the section have been committed, is the rule of reason guided by the established law and by the plain duty to enforce the prohibitions of the act and thus the public policy which its restrictions were obviously enacted to subserve. And it is worthy of observation [that the Sherman Act] * * * indicates a consciousness that the freedom to contract, when not unduly or improperly exercised, was the most efficient means for the prevention of monopoly, since the operation of the centrifugal and centripetal forces resulting from the right to freely contract was the means by which monopoly would be inevitably prevented if no extraneous or sovereign power imposed it and no right to make unlawful contracts having a monopolistic tendency were permitted. * * *

* * *

Second. The contentions of the parties as to the meaning of the statute and the decisions of this court relied upon concerning those contentions.

In substance, the propositions urged by the Government are reducible to this: That the language of the statute embraces every contract, combination, etc., in restraint of trade, and hence its text leaves no room for the exercise of judgment, but simply imposes the plain duty of applying its prohibitions to every case within its literal language. The error involved lies in assuming the matter to be decided. * * * [J]udgment must in every case be called into play in order to determine whether a particular act is embraced within the statutory classes, and whether if the act is within such classes its nature or effect causes it to be a restraint of trade within the intendment of the act. To hold to the contrary would require the conclusion either that every contract * * * was within the statute, and thus the statute would be destructive of all right to contract or agree or combine in any respect whatever as to subjects embraced in interstate trade or commerce, or if this conclusion were not reached, then the contention would require it to be held that as the statute * * * excluded resort to the only means by which the acts to which it relates could be ascertained—the light of reason—the enforcement of the statute was impossible because of its uncertainty. * * *

But, it is said, persuasive as these views may be, they may not be here applied, because the previous decisions of this court have given to the statute a meaning which expressly excludes the construction which must result from the reasoning stated. The cases are United States v. [Trans-Missouri] Freight Association, and United States v. Joint Traffic Association. * * * It is undoubted that in the opinion in each case general language was made use of, which, when separated from its context, would justify the conclusion that it was decided that reason could not be resorted to for the purpose of determining whether the acts complained of were within the statute. It is, however, also true that the nature and character of the contract or agreement in each case was fully referred to and suggestions as to their unreasonableness pointed out in order to indicate that they were within the prohibitions of the statute. As the cases cannot by any possible conception be treated as authoritative without the certitude that reason was resorted to for the purpose of deciding them, it follows as a matter of course that it must have been held by the light of reason * * * that the assailed contracts or agreements were within the general enumeration of the statute, and that their operation and effect brought about the restraint of trade which the statute prohibited. * * * This being true, the rulings in the cases relied upon when rightly appreciated were therefore this and nothing more: That as considering the contracts or agreements, their necessary effect and the character of the parties by whom they were made, they were clearly restraints of trade within the purview of the statute, they could not be taken out of that category by indulging in general reasoning as to the expediency or non-expediency of having made the contracts or the wisdom or want of wisdom of the statute which prohibited their being made. * * *

* * *

* * * [I]n order not in the slightest degree to be wanting in frankness, we say that in so far, however, as by separating the general language used in the opinions in the *Freight Association* and *Joint Traffic* cases from the context and the subject and parties with which the cases were concerned, it may be conceived that the language referred to conflicts with the

construction which we give the statute, they are necessarily now limited and qualified. * * *

* * *

Third. The facts and the application of the statute to them.

* * *

* * * [T]he proof, we think, establishes that the result of enlarging the capital stock of the New Jersey company and giving it the vast power to which we have referred produced its normal consequence, that is, it gave to the corporation, despite enormous dividends and despite the dropping out of certain corporations enumerated in the decree of the court below, an enlarged and more perfect sway and control over the trade and commerce in petroleum and its products. * * *

* * * [T]he court below held that the acts and dealings established by the proof operated to destroy the "potentiality of competition" which otherwise would have existed to such an extent as to cause the transfers of stock which were made to the New Jersey corporation and the control which resulted over the many and various subsidiary corporations to be a combination or conspiracy in restraint of trade in violation of the first section of the act, but also to be an attempt to monopolize and a monopolization bringing about a perennial violation of the second section.

We see no cause to doubt the correctness of these conclusions * * * for the following reasons:

a.   Because the unification of power and control over petroleum and its products which was the inevitable result of the combining in the New Jersey corporation by the increase of its stock and the transfer to it of the stocks of so many other corporations, aggregating so vast a capital, gives rise, in and of itself, in the absence of countervailing circumstances, * * * to the prima facie presumption of intent and purpose to maintain the dominancy over the oil industry, not as a result of normal methods of industrial development, but by new means of combination which were resorted to in order that greater power might be added than would otherwise have arisen had normal methods been followed, the whole with the purpose of excluding others from the trade and thus centralizing in the combination a perpetual control of the movements of petroleum and its products in the channels of interstate commerce.

b.   Because the prima facie presumption of intent to restrain trade, to monopolize and to bring about monopolization resulting from the act of expanding the stock of the New Jersey corporation and vesting it with such vast control of the oil industry, is made conclusive by considering, (1), the conduct of the persons or corporations who were mainly instrumental in bringing about the extension of power in the New Jersey corporation before the consummation of that result and prior to the formation of the trust agreements of 1879 and 1882; (2), by considering the proof as to what was done under those agreements and the acts which immediately preceded the vesting of power in the New Jersey corporation as well as by weighing the modes in which the power vested in that corporation has been exerted and the results which have arisen from it.

Recurring to the acts done by the individuals or corporations who were mainly instrumental in bringing about the expansion of the New Jersey corporation during the period prior to the formation of the trust agreements of 1879 and 1882, * * * we think no disinterested mind can survey the period in question without being irresistibly driven to the conclusion that the very genius for commercial development and organization which it would seem was manifested from the beginning soon begot an intent and purpose to exclude others which was frequently manifested by acts and dealings wholly inconsistent with the theory that they were made with the single conception of advancing the development of business power by usual methods, but which on the contrary necessarily involved the intent to drive others from the field and to exclude them from their right to trade and thus accomplish the mastery which was the end in view. And, considering the period from the date of the trust agreements of 1879 and 1882, up to the time of the expansion of the New Jersey corporation, the gradual extension of the power over the commerce in oil which ensued, the decision of the Supreme Court of Ohio, the tardiness or reluctance in conforming to the commands of that decision, the method first adopted and that which finally culminated in the plan of the New Jersey corporation, all additionally serve to make manifest the continued existence of the intent which we have previously indicated and which among other things impelled the expansion of the New Jersey corporation. The exercise of the power which resulted from that organization fortifies the foregoing conclusions, * * * the acquisition here and there which ensued of every efficient means by which competition could have been asserted, the slow but resistless methods which followed by which means of transportation were absorbed and brought under control, the system of marketing which was adopted by which the country was divided into districts and the trade in each district in oil was turned over to a designated corporation within the combination and all others were excluded, all lead the mind up to a conviction of a purpose and intent which we think is so certain as practically to cause the subject not to be within the domain of reasonable contention.

The inference that no attempt to monopolize could have been intended, and that no monopolization resulted from the acts complained of, since it is established that a very small percentage of the crude oil produced was controlled by the combination, is unwarranted. As substantial power over the crude product was the inevitable result of the absolute control which existed over the refined product, the monopolization of the one carried with it the power to control the other, and if the inferences which this situation suggests were developed, which we deem it unnecessary to do, they might well serve to add additional cogency to the presumption of intent to monopolize which we have found arises from the unquestioned proof on other subjects.

* * *

Fourth. The remedy to be administered.

It may be conceded that ordinarily where it was found that acts had been done in violation of the statute, adequate measure of relief would result from restraining the doing of such acts in the future. But in a case like this, where the condition which has been brought about in violation of the statute, in and of itself, is not only a continued attempt to monopolize, but also a monopolization, the duty to enforce the statute requires the application of broader and more controlling remedies. As penalties which are not authorized by law may not be inflicted by judicial authority, it follows that to meet the situation with which we are confronted the application of remedies two-fold in character becomes essential: 1st. To forbid the doing in the future of acts like those which we have found to have been done in the past which would be violative of the statute. 2d. The exertion of such measure of relief as will effectually dissolve the combination found to exist in violation of the statute, and thus neutralize the extension and continually operating force which the possession of the power unlawfully obtained has brought and will continue to bring about.

In applying remedies for this purpose, however, the fact must not be overlooked that injury to the public by the prevention of an undue restraint on, or the monopolization of trade or commerce is the foundation upon which the prohibitions of the statute rest, and moreover that one of the fundamental purposes of the statute is to protect, not to destroy, rights of property.

* * *

The court below * * * commanded the dissolution of the combination, and therefore in effect, directed the transfer by the New Jersey corporation back to the stockholders of the various subsidiary corporations entitled to the same of the stock which had been turned over to the New Jersey company in exchange for its stock. * * *

* * *

* * * We think that in view of the magnitude of the interests involved and their complexity that the delay of thirty days allowed for executing the decree was too short and should be extended so as to embrace a period of at least six months. * * *

* * * The court below to retain jurisdiction to the extent necessary to compel compliance in every respect with its decree.

MR. JUSTICE HARLAN concurring in part, and dissenting in part.

A sense of duty constrains me to express the objections which I have to certain declarations in the opinion just delivered on behalf of the court.

* * *

In my judgment, the decree below should have been affirmed without qualification. * * *

* * * [T]he court by its decision, when interpreted by the language of its opinion, has not only upset the longsettled interpretation of the act, but has usurped the constitutional functions of the legislative branch of the Government. With all due respect for the opinions of others, I feel bound to say that what the court has said may well cause some alarm for the integrity of our institutions. * * *

All who recall the condition of the country in 1890 will remember that there was everywhere, among the people generally, a deep feeling of unrest. The Nation had been rid of human slavery—fortunately, as all now feel— but the conviction was universal that the country was in real danger from another kind of slavery sought to be fastened on the American people, namely, the slavery that would result from aggregations of capital in the hands of a few individuals and corporations controlling, for their own profit and advantage exclusively, the entire business of the country, including the production and sale of the necessaries of life. Such a danger was thought to be then imminent, and all felt that it must be met firmly and by such statutory regulations as would adequately protect the people against oppression and wrong. Congress therefore took up the matter and gave the whole subject the fullest consideration. * * *

* * * [T]o the end that the people, so far as interstate commerce was concerned, might not be dominated by vast combinations and monopolies, having power to advance their own selfish ends, regardless of the general interests and welfare, Congress passed the anti-trust act of 1890 * * * .

* * *

* * * [F]ifteen years ago [in the *Trans-Missouri* case], when the purpose of Congress in passing the Anti-trust Act was fresh in the minds of courts, lawyers, statesmen and the general public, this court expressly declined to indulge in judicial legislation, by inserting in the act the word "unreasonable" or any other word of like import. * * * The public press, magazines and law journals, the debates in Congress, speeches and addresses by public men and jurists, all contain abundant evidence of the general understanding that the meaning, extent and scope of the anti-trust act had been judicially determined by this court, and that the only question remaining open for discussion was the wisdom of the policy declared by the act—a matter that was exclusively within the cognizance of Congress. But at every session of Congress since the decision of 1896, the lawmaking branch of the Government, with full knowledge of that decision, has refused to change the policy it had declared or to so amend the act of 1890 as to except from its operation contracts, combinations and trusts that reasonably restrain interstate commerce.

* * *

The question whether the court should again consider the point decided in the *Trans-Missouri Case*, was disposed of in the most decisive language [in United States v. Joint Traffic Association (1898)] * * * . * * * "As we have twice already deliberately and earnestly considered the same arguments which are now for a third time pressed upon our attention, it could hardly be expected that our opinion should now change from that already expressed."

* * *

* * * The court says that the previous cases, above cited, "cannot by any possible conception be treated as authoritative without the certitude that reason was resorted to for the purpose of deciding them." And its opinion is full of intimations that this court proceeded in those cases, so far as the present question is concerned, without being guided by the "rule of reason," or "the light of reason." * * * [T]his court * * * has now done what it then said it could not constitutionally do. It has, by mere interpretation, modified the act of Congress, and deprived it of practical value as a defensive measure against the evils to be remedied. * * *

* * * When counsel in the present case insisted upon a reversal of the former rulings of this court, and asked such an interpretation of the anti-trust act as would allow reasonable restraints of interstate commerce, this court, in deference to established practice, should, I submit, have said to them: "That question, according to our practice, is not open for further discussion here." * * * Such a course, I am sure, would not have offended the "rule of reason."

But my brethren, in their wisdom, have deemed it best to pursue a different course. They have now said to those who condemn our former decisions and who object to all legislative prohibitions of contracts, combinations and trusts in restraint of interstate commerce, "You may now restrain such commerce, provided you are reasonable about it; only take care that the restraint in not undue." The disposition of the case under consideration, according to the views of the defendants, will, it is claimed, quiet and give rest to "the business of the country." On the contrary, I have a strong conviction that it will throw the business of the country into confusion and invite widely extended and harassing litigation, the injurious effects of which will be felt for many years to come. When Congress prohibited every contract, combination or monopoly, in restraint of commerce, it prescribed a simple, definite rule that all could understand, and which could be easily applied by everyone wishing to obey the law, and not to conduct their business in violation of law. But now, it is to be feared, we are to have, in cases without number, the constantly recurring inquiry—difficult to solve by proof—whether the particular contract, combination, or trust involved in each case is or is not an "unreasonable" or "undue" restraint of trade. * * *

* * *

After many years of public service at the National Capital, and after a somewhat close observation of the conduct of public affairs, I am impelled to say that there is abroad, in our land, a most harmful tendency to bring about the amending of constitutions and legislative enactments by means alone of judicial construction. * * * To overreach the action of Congress merely by judicial construction, that is, by indirection, is a blow at the integrity of our governmental system, and in the end will prove most dangerous to all. * * *

NOTES AND QUESTIONS

1.   After years of 5–4 decisions coming out the other way as to application of the "rule of reason," what has happened?

a.   Who is the lone dissenter from the Court's reasoning? Fifteen years after *Trans-Missouri*, Justice Harlan, age 78, is the only survivor of the majority coalition who is still on the Court, just as now-Chief Justice White is the only remaining former dissenter.

b.   Meanwhile, four new Justices have been appointed in the seven years since *Northern Securities*—Lurton, Lamar, Van Devanter and Hughes. All four plus White, the Justice now elevated to Chief, have been put in their seats by none other than William Howard Taft, the author of *Addyston Pipe*, critic of the reasoning in *Trans-Missouri*, but the President whose Administration did the heavy lifting in the prosecution of Standard Oil.[18]

2.   This case is widely seen as a major turning point in the Court's approach to the Sherman Act, a clear rejection of Peckham's "all contracts" rhetoric.

a.   Does Chief Justice White's analysis ring more true here than it had in his *Trans-Missouri* dissent? Were you persuaded by his historical references and his construction of the Act in light of its common law origins?

b.   Is Chief Justice White here proposing the same test that he had advocated earlier? In the interim, has he apparently seen the need to define more clearly how a rule of reason would be applied?

3.   Were you sympathetic to Justice Harlan's anger at the Court's rejection of its prior cases? Were you any more persuaded than he was by Chief Justice White's effort to distinguish them? Do you agree with Justice Harlan

---

[18]   Does Justice Lurton's name sound familiar. That's right, he was the third member of the Sixth Circuit panel that decided *Addyston Pipe* and was appointed to the Supreme Court by his former colleague.

that the Court may have underestimated the litigation it would be likely to engender by having an imprecise rule? Can you argue that the "all contracts" test was not precise either?

4.   Is this a fair case in which to assess practices under a rule of reason? Put another way, was there anything reasonable about what John D. Rockefeller and Standard Oil had done?

a.   Don't be too quick about your answer. Was Rockefeller a villain ever since his earliest days in Cleveland? Were the "rebates" that he got from the railroad in fact initially pro-competitive, i.e., a way that a poor guy living on the west side of the oil fields could enter the refining business and sell his product in the east?[19]

b.   When did Rockefeller's actions turn anti-social? Was it when he tried to form the Standard Oil Trust? Was there something about that legal device that made the situation worse? Might the trust have simply been an imaginative way to avoid archaic state corporation laws that made it hard for firms to become large enough to produce and distribute products efficiently?

c.   How much discussion did you find in this opinion of Rockefeller's predatory pricing? Was there a lot of evidence that he ran competitors out of business?[20] Would your judgment of Rockefeller be changed if the record showed that most of his competitors were eager to become part of the Standard Oil Company? Would such evidence properly help his case or hurt it?

5.   Was the real evil here Rockefeller's unwillingness to be a "good" monopolist and live off his millions in retirement? Ask yourself that question again after you read the *United States Steel* case in the next chapter.

a.   Do you agree that there is something wrong with hoping to dominate the oil industry, not by "normal methods of industrial development, but by new means of combination"? What are the acceptable "normal methods"?

b.   Is the problem that Rockefeller had a wish to maintain dominance over the oil industry "with the purpose of excluding others from the trade"? Should *wishing* to be a monopolist be illegal? Why is an aggressive spirit something the law should condemn? Put another way, is the Court here condemning acts that hurt the *consumers* of gasoline and oil products? Should the Court be concerned about Rockefeller's business competitors at all? Why or why not?

c.   Was there a time before the turn of the century when the Justice Department should have headed off the development of this "monopoly"? That is, could a suit have successfully challenged any of the mergers that brought

---

[19]   See, e.g., Ron Chernow, Titan: The Life of John D. Rockefeller, Sr. 129–155 (1998); Harold F. Williamson & Arnold R. Daum, The American Petroleum Industry 301–366 (1959); Ralph W. & Muriel E. Hidy, Pioneering in Big Business 13–23 (1954).

[20]   Much of the public perception of this "fact" came from Ida M. Tarbell, The History of the Standard Oil Company (1904). See also, Matthew Josephson, The Robber Barons (1934). For a contrasting view, see Allan Nevins, John D. Rockefeller: The Heroic Age of American Enterprise (1940).

the company to its current size? Was the problem likely that none of the mergers was itself as dramatic as the one in *Northern Securities*?

6.   Was this an appropriate case for the remedy of divestiture? Why was it a more practical remedy here than it might be in many other cases? Many of the 34 firms into which Standard Oil was divided survive and are still household names, e.g., Exxon, Atlantic Richfield, Arco, Chevron, Conoco, Marathon, Mobil and Pennzoil.[21]

ANOTHER LOOK AT MONOPOLIZATION—
THE *AMERICAN TOBACCO* CASE

An authority in 1913 reports that "the decision in the *Standard Oil* case, * * * in wide extended notoriety, was only excelled by that in the *Dred Scott* case * * * . It was the belief of the legal profession and of the general public that it was revolutionary in its character."[22] Less than two weeks later the Supreme Court had an opportunity to take another crack at describing what constituted monopolization in United States v. American Tobacco Co., 221 U.S. 106, 31 S.Ct. 632, 55 L.Ed. 663 (1911). American Tobacco had grown by acquisition of smaller companies to where at one point it sold 86% of all cigarettes produced in the U.S., 26% of all the smoking tobacco, and 51% of all the small cigars.

Chief Justice White explained that *Standard Oil* had held, "not that acts which the statute prohibited could be removed from the control of its prohibitions by a finding that they were reasonable, but * * * that the words 'restraint of trade' should be given a meaning which would not destroy the individual right to contract, and render difficult, if not impossible, any movement of trade in the channels of interstate commerce * * * ."

Thus, the size that American Tobacco had attained was not itself to be condemned, but rather the fact that "the history of the combination is so replete with the doing of acts which it was the obvious purpose of the statute to forbid, so demonstrative of the existence from the beginning of a purpose to acquire dominion and control of the tobacco trade, not by the mere exertion of the ordinary right to contract and to trade, but by methods devised in order to monopolize the trade by driving competitors out of the business, which were ruthlessly carried out upon the assumption that to work upon the fears or play upon the cupidity of competitors would make success possible."

---

[21]   For a discussion of Standard Oil (New Jersey) after the decree, see George S. Gibb & Evelyn H. Knowlton, The Resurgent Years 1911–1927 (1956).

[22]   W.W. Thornton, A Treatise on The Sherman Anti-Trust Act iii (1913).

As evidence of such misconduct, the Court pointed out that the combination (a) began as a way to settle a price war, (b) then fomented its own price wars which drove small producers from the industry, (c) vertically integrated its operations, "serving as perpetual barriers to the entry of others into the tobacco trade," (d) bought up plants of other firms "not for the purpose of utilizing them," but in order to close them, and (e) entered into covenants not to compete with persons who sold their businesses to American Tobacco.

Do the acts identified by the Court convince you that a violation of the Sherman Act should have been found? Does the violation seem to have been based on the "intent" that the acts reveal? Was it based on the fact that American Tobacco actually *did* acquire a large market share?

A WORD ABOUT ATTEMPT TO MONOPOLIZE— THE *SWIFT* CASE

Section 2 of the Sherman Act prohibits an "attempt to monopolize," as well as monopolization itself. The necessity and sufficiency of intent as an element of proof of a Section 2 violation was central to the decision in Swift & Co. v. United States, 196 U.S. 375, 25 S.Ct. 276, 49 L.Ed. 518 (1905). According to the allegations, a cartel in the meat packing industry manipulated cattle prices to the detriment of both farmers and consumers. The defendants were charged with bidding up the price of livestock periodically to induce farmers to ship their animals to market. Then, when the animals arrived, the defendants were said to have agreed together to bid artificially low prices. They also allegedly conspired on prices for cartage of the meat and received favorable shipping rates from the railroads.

The question for the Court was whether the trial court had been correct to enjoin these practices. Justice Holmes, for a unanimous court, said yes. The complaint alleged a scheme so vast, the Court recognized, that precisely pleading all its elements was impossible. Indeed, some of the practices standing alone would not be illegal. Nevertheless, "they are alleged sufficiently as elements of the scheme."

In terms that continue to describe the offense of attempted monopolization, Justice Holmes wrote:

> "The statute gives this proceeding against combinations in restraint of commerce * * * and against attempts to monopolize the same [elements]. Intent is almost essential to such a combination, and is essential to such an attempt. Where acts are not sufficient in themselves to produce a result which the law seeks to prevent—for instance, the monopoly—but require further

acts in addition to the mere forces of nature to bring that result to pass, an intent to bring it to pass is necessary in order to produce a dangerous probability that it will happen. But when that intent and dangerous probability exist, this statute, like many others, and like the common law in some cases, directs itself against that dangerous probability as well as against the completed result."

Do you agree that wanting a monopoly should not be a crime, i.e., that intent to monopolize alone should not violate Section 2? Why or why not? Might intent always be ambiguous? Does a secret desire to dominate an industry lurk in the heart of almost every entrepreneur? If not, should we wish that it did?

In the years since *Swift*, the principal question determining liability has been how "dangerous" the probability must be that the defendants will obtain the monopoly. Watch for that issue as it arises again later in these materials.[23]

THE PROBLEM OF REMEDY—A LOOK AT THE *TERMINAL RAILROAD* DECISION

What to do about an illegal monopoly is often as important as determining whether there has been a violation of § 2. Very often, the defendant firm will have a large market share in an important industry. The productive resources must be preserved even as the "monopoly" itself is rendered harmless. In *Swift*, *Standard Oil* and *American Tobacco*, the remedy chosen was divestiture, i.e., the formation of multiple companies out of the assets of the former firm. That is often relatively easy where the defendant has been composed of several formerly separate firms and has retained multiple production facilities. However, the costs of divestiture may sometimes exceed the benefits.

United States v. Terminal Railroad Association of St. Louis, 224 U.S. 383, 32 S.Ct. 507, 56 L.Ed. 810 (1912), took a different approach. Financier Jay Gould and owners of fourteen of the twenty-four railroads that converged at St. Louis had bought the Union Station, the switching yards on both sides of the Mississippi River, and the only three means of crossing the river. The group then operated all of them as an integrated system for getting rail traffic into and out of St. Louis.

"It cannot be controverted," Justice Lurton wrote for the Court, "that, in ordinary circumstances, a number of independent companies might combine for the purpose of controlling or acquiring terminals for their

---

[23] The continuing viability of *Swift* was reconfirmed in Spectrum Sports, Inc. v. McQuillan, 506 U.S. 447, 113 S.Ct. 884, 122 L.Ed.2d 247 (1993).

common but exclusive use."[24] Anyone not included in the combine could simply create its own facility.

The Court found that geographic conditions at St. Louis, however, made that alternative impractical. The Mississippi River was wide and the hills near its western bank made it preferable that trains cross the river at a single point and have switching operations contained within a common facility. Access to the preferred yard was essential to competitive railroad operations, and because membership in the Terminal Railroad Association was not open to all lines operating in St. Louis, it could not "escape condemnation as a restraint upon commerce." Allegedly discriminatory billing practices tended to confirm the unfairness of the arrangement.

The Government sought divestiture of the defendant into its component parts, but the Court devised an "equally adequate" remedy. The combination would be rendered lawful, the Court said, "if it were what is claimed for it, a proper terminal association acting as the impartial agent of every line which is under compulsion to use its instrumentalities." Thus, non-member railroads had to be given the right to buy an ownership interest, and even those that did not buy an interest had to be given access to the facilities on non-discriminatory terms.

NOTES AND QUESTIONS

1.   *Terminal Railroad* was long cited as creating an "essential facilities" doctrine that would give firms a right of access to property without which they would not be able to compete.[25] Would you favor frequent invocation of such a doctrine as a way to increase competition and benefit consumers? On the other hand, might we say that one aspect of a property right is the freedom not to deal except on terms satisfactory to the owner of the property?

2.   Given the finding of a violation of the Sherman Act, should the defendants be grateful for this relatively non-intrusive way to eliminate their problem? Should shippers be concerned that the cartel controlling St. Louis rail transport has now been judicially enlarged and confirmed?[26]

---

[24]   One might have thought this case would be controlled by *Northern Securities*, i.e., competing firms had all been merged into one that monopolized rail services in and around St. Louis, but the Supreme Court treated that issue as foreclosed by a decision of the Missouri Supreme Court that had held that "the merger of mere railway terminals used to facilitate the public convenience by the transfer of cars from one line of railway to another * * * [did not violate state] statutes forbidding combinations between competing or parallel lines of railroad." 224 U.S. at 402, 32 S.Ct. at 512–13, citing State ex inf. Attorney General v. Terminal Association of St. Louis, 182 Mo. 284, 81 S.W. 395 (1904).

[25]   See, e.g., Associated Press v. United States, 326 U.S. 1, 65 S.Ct. 1416, 89 L.Ed. 2013 (1945) (news gathering organization); Otter Tail Power Co. v. United States, 410 U.S. 366, 93 S.Ct. 1022, 35 L.Ed.2d 359 (1973) (electric power distribution system); Paddock Publications, Inc. v. Chicago Tribune Co., 103 F.3d 42 (7th Cir. 1996) (popular comic strips not essential facilities for newspaper publication). See also Phillip Areeda, Essential Facilities: An Epithet in Need of Limiting Principles, 58 Antitrust L. J. 841 (1990).

[26]   See, e.g., David Reiffen & Andrew N. Kleit, Terminal Railroad Revisited: Foreclosure of an Essential Facility or Simple Horizontal Monopoly, 33 J.Law & Economics 419 (1988).

3. Might a remedy of this kind force the trial court to retain jurisdiction and potentially permanently monitor compliance with this order? Do we really want a Federal District Court to become a mini-I.C.C.?

D. VERTICAL RESTRAINTS OF TRADE— RESALE PRICE MAINTENANCE

DR. MILES MEDICAL COMPANY V. JOHN D. PARK & SONS COMPANY

Supreme Court of the United States, 1911
220 U.S. 373, 31 S.Ct. 376, 55 L.Ed. 502

* * *

The complainant Dr. Miles Medical Company, an Indiana corporation, is engaged in the manufacture and sale of proprietary medicines, prepared by means of secret methods and formulas and identified by distinctive packages, labels and trademarks. It has established an extensive trade throughout the United States and in certain foreign countries. It has been its practice to sell its medicines to jobbers and wholesale druggists who in turn sell to retail druggists for sale to the consumer. In the case of each remedy, it has fixed not only the price of its own sales to jobbers and wholesale dealers, but also the wholesale and retail prices. The bill alleged that most of its sales were made through retail druggists and that the demand for its remedies largely depended upon their good will and commendation, and their ability to realize a fair profit; that certain retail establishments, particularly those known as department stores, had inaugurated a "cut-rate" or "cut-price" system which had caused "much confusion, trouble and damage" to the complainant's business and "injuriously affected the reputation" and "depleted the sales" of its remedies; that this injury resulted "from the fact that the majority of retail druggists as a rule cannot, or believe that they cannot realize sufficient profits" by the sale of the medicines "at the cut-prices announced by the cut-rate and department stores," and therefore are "unwilling to, and do not keep" the medicines "in stock" or "if kept in stock, do not urge or favor sales thereof, but endeavor to foist off some similar remedy or substitute, and from the fact that in the public mind an article advertised or announced at 'cut' or 'reduced' price from the established price suffers loss of reputation and becomes of inferior value and demand."

It was further alleged that for the purpose of protecting "its trade sales and business" and of conserving "its good will and reputation" the complainant had established a method "of governing, regulating and controlling the sale and marketing" of its remedies * * * .

* * *

* * * [W]ritten contracts were required with all retailers of * * * said proprietary remedies, medicines and cures, as follows:

"Retail Agency Contract

"The Dr. Miles Medical Company

"This agreement between The Dr. Miles Medical Company of Elkhart, Indiana, and, [Retailer's Name] * * * hereinafter referred to as retail agent, witnesseth:

"Appointed Agent.

"The said Dr. Miles Medical Company hereby appoints said retail dealer as one of the retail distributing agents of its proprietary medicines and agrees that said retail agent may purchase the proprietary medicines manufactured by said Dr. Miles Medical Company (each retail package of which the said company will cause to be identified by a number) at the following prices, to wit:

"Wholesale Prices.

"Medicines, of which the retail price is $1.00; $8.00 per dozen.

"Medicines, of which the retail price is 50 cents; $4.00 per dozen.

"Medicines, of which the retail price is 25 cents; $2.00 per dozen.

* * *

"Full Price.

"In consideration whereof said retail agent agrees in no case to sell or furnish the said proprietary medicines to any person, firm or corporation whatsoever, at less than the full retail price as printed on the packages, without reduction for quantity; and said retail agent further agrees not to sell the said proprietary medicines at any price to wholesale or retail dealers not accredited agents of the Dr. Miles Medical Company.

"Violation.

"It is further agreed between the parties hereto that the giving of any article of value, or the making of any concession by means of trading stamps, cash register coupons, or otherwise, for the purpose of reducing the price above agreed upon shall be considered a violation of this agreement, and further it is agreed between the parties hereto that the Dr. Miles Medical Company will sustain damage in the sum of twenty-five dollars ($25.00) for each violation of any provision of this agreement, it being otherwise impossible to fix the measure of damage.

"This contract will take effect when a duplicate thereof, duly signed by the Retail Agent, has been received and approved by The Dr. Miles Company, at its office at Elkhart, Indiana."[27]

* * *

As an aid to the maintenance of the prices thus fixed the company devised a system for tracing and identifying, through serial numbers and cards, each wholesale and retail package of its products.

It was alleged that all wholesale and retail druggists, "and all dealers in proprietary medicines," had been given full opportunity, without discrimination, to sign contracts in the form stated, and that such contracts were in force between the complainant "and over four hundred jobbers and wholesalers and twenty-five thousand retail dealers in proprietary medicines in the United States."

The defendant is a Kentucky corporation conducting a wholesale drug business. The bill alleged that the defendant had formerly dealt with the complainant and had full knowledge of all the facts relating to the trade in its medicines; that it had been requested, and refused, to enter into the wholesale contract required by the complainant; that in the city of Cincinnati, Ohio, where the defendant conducted a wholesale drug store, there were a large number of wholesale and retail druggists who had made contracts, of the sort described, with the complainant, and kept its medicines on sale pursuant to the agreed terms and conditions. It was charged that the defendant, "in combination and conspiracy with a number of wholesale and retail dealers in drugs and proprietary medicines, who have not entered into said wholesale and retail contracts" required by the complainant's system and solely for the purpose of selling the remedies to dealers "to be advertised, sold and marketed at cut-rates," and "to thus attract and secure custom and patronage for other merchandise, and not for the purpose of making or receiving a direct money profit" from the sales of the remedies, had unlawfully and fraudulently procured them from the complainant's "wholesale and retail agents" by means "of false and fraudulent representations and statements, and by surreptitious and dishonest methods, and by persuading and inducing, directly and indirectly," a violation of their contracts.

It is further charged that the defendant, having procured the remedies in this manner, had advertised and sold them at less than the jobbing and retail prices established by the complainant; and that for the purpose of concealing the source of supply the identifying serial numbers, which had been stamped upon the labels and cartons, had been obliterated by the

---

[27] [Ed. note] A different but substantially parallel version of this agreement was required of all wholesalers of Dr. Miles' products.

defendant or by those acting in collusion with the defendant, and the labels and cartons had been mutilated thus rendering the list of ailments and directions for use illegible, and that the remedies in this condition were sold both to the wholesale and retail dealers and ultimately to buyers for use at cut rates.

The bill prayed for an injunction restraining the defendant from inducing or attempting to induce any party to any of the said "wholesale or retail agency contracts" to "violate or break the same * * * ." * * *

* * *

The Circuit Court sustained the demurrers and dismissed the bill and its judgment was affirmed by the Circuit Court of Appeals.

MR. JUSTICE HUGHES, after making the above statement, delivered the opinion of the court.

The complainant, a manufacturer of proprietary medicines which are prepared in accordance with secret formulas, presents by its bill a system, carefully devised, by which it seeks to maintain certain prices fixed by it for all the sales of its products both at wholesale and retail. Its purpose is to establish minimum prices at which sales shall be made by its vendees and by all subsequent purchasers who traffic in its remedies. Its plan is thus to govern directly the entire trade in the medicines it manufactures, embracing interstate commerce as well as commerce within the States respectively. * * *

* * * The complainant invokes the established doctrine that an actionable wrong is committed by one who maliciously interferes with a contract between two parties and induces one of them to break that contract to the injury of the other and that, in the absence of an adequate remedy at law, equitable relief will be granted.

The principal question is as to the validity of the restrictive agreements.

* * * The complainant insists that the [wholesale] "consignment contract" contemplates a true consignment for sale for account of the complainant, and that those who make sales under it are the complainant's agents and not its vendees. The court below did not so construe the agreement and considered it an effort "to disguise the wholesale dealers in the mask of agency * * * ."

* * *

The other form of contract, adopted by the complainant, while described as a "retail agency contract," is clearly an agreement looking to sale and not to agency. The so-called "retail agents" are not agents at all, either of the complainant or of its consignees, but are contemplated purchasers who buy to sell again, that is, retail dealers. It is agreed that they may purchase the medicines manufactured by the complainant at stated prices. There follows this stipulation:

> "In consideration whereof said retail agent agrees in no case to sell or furnish the said proprietary medicines to any person, firm or corporation whatsoever, at less than the full retail prices as printed on the packages, without reduction for quantity; and said retail agent further agrees not to sell the said proprietary medicines at any price to wholesale or retail dealers not accredited agents of the Dr. Miles Medical Company." * * *

The bill asserts complainant's "right to maintain and preserve the aforesaid system and method of contracts and sales adopted and established by it." It is, as we have seen, a system of interlocking restrictions by which the complainant seeks to control not merely the prices at which its agents may sell its products, but the prices for all sales by all dealers at wholesale or retail, whether purchasers or subpurchasers, and thus to fix the amount which the consumer shall pay, eliminating all competition. * * *

That these agreements restrain trade is obvious. That, having been made, as the bill alleges, with "most of the jobbers and wholesale druggists and a majority of the retail druggists of the country" and having for their purpose the control of the entire trade, they relate directly to interstate as well as intrastate trade, and operate to restrain trade or commerce among the several states, is also clear.

But it is insisted that the restrictions are not invalid either at common law or under the act of Congress of July 2, 1890, upon the following grounds, which may be taken to embrace the fundamental contentions for the complainant: (1) That the restrictions are valid because they relate to proprietary medicines manufactured under a secret process; and (2) that, apart from this, a manufacturer is entitled to control the prices on all sales of his own products.

First. The first inquiry is whether there is any distinction, with respect to such restrictions as are here presented, between the case of an article manufactured by the owner of a secret process and that of one produced under ordinary conditions. The complainant urges an analogy to rights secured by letters patent. Bement v. National Harrow Company, 186 U.S. 70 [1902]. In the case cited, there were licenses for the manufacture and sale of articles covered by letters patent with stipulations as to the prices at which the licensee should sell. The court said, referring to the act of July 2, 1890: "But that statute clearly does not refer to that kind of restraint of interstate commerce which may arise from reasonable and legal conditions imposed upon the assignee or licensee of a patent by the owner thereof, restricting the terms upon which the article may be used and the price to be demanded therefor. * * * "

But whatever rights the patentee may enjoy are derived from statutory grant under the authority conferred by the Constitution. This grant is based upon public considerations. The purpose of the patent law is to stimulate invention by protecting inventors for a fixed time in the advantages that may be derived from exclusive manufacture, use and sale. * * *

The complainant has no statutory grant. * * * The complainant has not seen fit to make the disclosure required by the statute and thus to secure the privileges it confers. Its case lies outside the policy of the patent law, and the extent of the right which that law secures is not here involved or determined.

* * *

If a manufacturer, in the absence of statutory privilege, has the control over the sales of the manufactured article, for which the complainant here contends, it is not because the process of manufacture is kept secret. In this respect, the maker of so-called proprietary medicines, unpatented, stands on no different footing from that of other manufacturers. The fact that the article is represented to be curative in its properties does not justify a restriction of trade which would be unlawful as to compositions designed for other purposes.

Second. We come, then, to the second question, whether the complainant, irrespective of the secrecy of its process, is entitled to maintain the restrictions by virtue of the fact that they relate to products of its own manufacture.

The basis of the argument appears to be that, as the manufacturer may make and sell, or not, as he chooses, he may affix conditions as to the use of the article or as to the prices at which purchasers may dispose of it. The propriety of the restraint is sought to be derived from the liberty of the producer.

But because a manufacturer is not bound to make or sell, it does not follow that in case of sales actually made he may impose upon purchasers every sort of restriction. Thus a general restraint upon alienation is ordinarily invalid. * * *

Nor can the manufacturer by rule and notice, in the absence of contract or statutory right, even though the restriction be known to purchasers, fix prices for future sales. It has been held by this court that no such privilege exists under the copyright statutes, although the owner of the copyright has the sole right to vend copies of the copyrighted production. Bobbs-Merrill Co. v. Straus, 210 U.S. 339 [1908]. * * * It will hardly be contended, with respect to such a matter, that the manufacturer of an article of commerce, not protected by any statutory grant, is in any better case. * * *

With respect to contracts in restraint of trade * * * the public interest is still the first consideration. To sustain the restraint, it must be found to be reasonable both with respect to the public and to the parties and that it is limited to what is fairly necessary, in the circumstances of the particular case, for the protection of the convenantee. Otherwise restraints of trade are void as against public policy. * * *

* * *

The present case is not analogous to that of a sale of good will, or of an interest in a business, or of the grant of a right to use a process of manufacture. The complainant has not parted with any interest in its business or instrumentalities of production. It has conferred no right by virtue of which purchasers of its products may compete with it. It retains complete control over the business in which it is engaged, manufacturing what it pleases and fixing such prices for its own sales as it may desire. Nor are we dealing with a single transaction, conceivably unrelated to the public interest. The agreements are designed to maintain prices, after the complainant has parted with the title to the articles, and to prevent competition among those who trade in them.

The bill asserts the importance of a standard retail price and alleges generally that confusion and damage have resulted from sales at less than the prices fixed. But the advantage of established retail prices primarily concerns the dealers. The enlarged profits which would result from adherence to the established rates would go to them and not to the complainant. It is through the inability of the favored dealers to realize these profits, on account of the described competition, that the complainant works out its alleged injury. If there be an advantage of a manufacturer in the maintenance of fixed retail prices, the question remains whether it is one which he is entitled to secure by agreements restricting the freedom of trade on the part of dealers who own what they sell. As to this, the complainant can fare no better with its plan of identical contracts than could the dealers themselves if they formed a combination and endeavored to establish the same restrictions, and thus to achieve the same result, by agreement with each other. If the immediate advantage they would thus obtain would not be sufficient to sustain such a direct agreement, the asserted ulterior benefit to the complainant cannot be regarded as sufficient to support its system.

But agreements or combinations between dealers, having for their sole purpose the destruction of competition and the fixing or prices, are injurious to the public interest and void. They are not saved by the advantages which the participants expect to derive from the enhanced price to the consumer.

The complainant's plan falls within the principle which condemns contracts of this class. It, in effect, creates a combination for the prohibited purposes. * * * [W]here commodities have passed into the channels of trade and are owned by dealers, the validity of agreements to prevent competition and to maintain prices is not to be determined by the circumstance whether they were produced by several manufacturers or by one, or whether they were previously owned by one or by many. The complainant having sold its product at prices satisfactory to itself, the public is entitled to whatever advantage may be derived from competition in the subsequent traffic.

* * *

Judgment affirmed.

MR. JUSTICE LURTON took no part in the consideration and decision of this case.

MR. JUSTICE HOLMES, dissenting.

This is a bill to restrain the defendant from inducing, by corruption and fraud, agents of the plaintiff and purchasers from it to break their contracts not to sell its goods below a certain price. There are two contracts concerned. The first is that of the jobber or wholesale agent to whom the plaintiff consigns its goods * * * . That they are agents and not buyers I understand to be conceded, and I do not see how it can be denied. * * *

The second contract is that of the retail agents, so called, being really the first purchasers, fixing the price below which they will not sell to the public. * * * [T]he only question is whether the law forbids a purchaser to contract with his vendor that he will not sell below a certain price. * * * I suppose that in the case of a single object such as a painting or a statue the right of the artist to make such a stipulation hardly would be denied. In other words, I suppose that the reason why the contract is held bad is that it is part of a scheme embracing other similar contracts each of which applies to a number of similar things, with the object of fixing a general market price. This reason seems to me inadequate in the case before the court. In the first place by a slight change in the form of the contract the plaintiff can accomplish the result in a way that would be beyond successful attack. If it should make the retail dealers also agents in law as well as in name and retain the title until the goods left their hands I cannot conceive that even the present enthusiasm for regulating the prices to be charged by other people would deny that the owner was acting within his rights. * * *

* * * I think that, at least, it is safe to say that the most enlightened judicial policy is to let people manage their own business in their own way, unless the ground for interference is very clear. What then is the ground upon which we interfere in the present case? Of course, it is not the interest of the producer. No one, I judge, cares for that. * * * Perhaps it may be assumed to be the interest of the consumers and the public. On that point I confess that I am in a minority as to larger issues than are concerned

here. I think that we greatly exaggerate the value and importance to the public of competition in the production or distribution of an article * * * as fixing a fair price. What really fixes that is the competition of conflicting desires. We, none of us, can have as much as we want of all the things that we want. Therefore, we have to choose. As soon as the price of something that we want goes above the point at which we are willing to give up other things to have that, we cease to buy it and buy something else. Of course, I am speaking of things that we can get along without. There may be necessaries that sooner or later must be dealt with like short rations in a shipwreck, but they are not Dr. Miles's medicines. With regard to things like the latter it seems to me that the point of most profitable returns marks the equilibrium of social desires and determines the fair price in the only sense in which I can find meaning in those words. The Dr. Miles Medical Company knows better than we do what will enable it to do the best business. * * * I cannot believe that in the long run the public will profit by this court permitting knaves to cut reasonable prices for some ulterior purpose of their own and thus to impair, if not to destroy, the production and sale of articles which it is assumed to be desirable that the public should be able to get.

The conduct of the defendant falls within a general prohibition of the law. It is fraudulent and has no merits of its own to recommend it to the favor of the court. * * * The analogy relied upon to establish [the] evil effect [of Dr. Miles' contracts] is that of combinations in restraint of trade. I believe that we have some superstitions on that head, as I have said; but those combinations are entered into with intent to exclude others from a business naturally open to them * * * . I venture to say that there is no likeness between them and this case. * * * I think also that the importance of the question and the popularity of what I deem mistaken notions makes it my duty to express my view in this dissent.

NOTES AND QUESTIONS

1.   Here we have another case alleging a violation of § 1, but as you can see, there is a fundamental difference. Instead of firms at one level of the distribution process forming a cartel, this "restraint" is imposed by a manufacturer on its own dealers. Because different levels of distribution are involved, such a restraint is said to be "vertical." Keep this distinction in mind; it is fundamental to many of the cases that follow.

2.   Does a vertical restraint such as the "resale price maintenance" seen here present the problems of monopoly outlined in the introductory economic note in these materials? Put another way, did Dr. Miles' resale price agreements cause retail sales to be made at higher than competitive prices?

a.   Why does the majority believe that it did? Would resale price maintenance seem to cost a manufacturer sales? Is it really plausible to believe, as the majority suggests, that Dr. Miles was a victim of hundreds of retail dealers who conspired to require it to impose restraints on their independent pricing?

b.   Whom does Justice Holmes believe these restraints were designed to benefit? Indeed, what does Justice Holmes believe will determine the price that Dr. Miles will set for the tonic? Isn't it obviously the price of competing tonics and the next-best alternatives to tonic?

3.   Are there plausible reasons to believe that a manufacturer such as Dr. Miles might itself benefit from setting retail prices?[28]

a.   How about the idea that a high price suggests higher quality? With a patent medicine like Dr. Miles', might one suggest that image is everything? Might a cut-rate price cause people to lose confidence in the curative powers of the elixir?

b.   Would the desire to preserve a wide dealer network be a possible explanation for these arrangements? Might dealers' costs vary so much that it would be necessary to keep the retail price high to avoid someone undercutting a dealer whom the manufacturer wants to have carry the product? Indeed, might Dr. Miles have been concerned that the discount department stores seen here would act as "free riders" on the promotional efforts of smaller firms?[29]

c.   Might Dr. Miles have thought it could buy promotional effort and other dealer services by giving retailers a guaranteed spread between the wholesale and retail prices? To persons concerned about restraints of trade, should it matter whether a manufacturer gives a retailer a discount in exchange for its doing local advertising, a check to pay for the advertising, a protected spread between the wholesale and retail price out of which to pay for the advertising, or whether the manufacturer does the advertising itself?

4.   Are there, however, some negative features of resale price maintenance that neither the majority nor the dissent adequately considered here?

a.   Might retail price maintenance facilitate manufacturer collusion, i.e., collusion between Dr. Miles and its competitors? When one has enforced, published prices, might it be harder for firms to cheat on a cartel agreement?

b.   Should the fact that, under a system of resale price maintenance, many consumers *believe* they pay higher retail prices be sufficient to render the practice illegal?

---

[28]   Lest you think this is some obscure company, not now part of your life, Dr. Franklin Miles later named his company Miles Laboratories; its leading products have included Alka-Seltzer (which originally rose to popularity as a hangover cure), and vitamins such as "One-a-Day" and "Flintstones." Later, it was acquired by the world-wide pharmaceutical firm, Bayer A.G.

[29]   The classic article asserting arguments such as these is Lester G. Telser, Why Should Manufacturers Want Fair Trade?, 3 J. Law & Economics 86 (1960). See also, Herbert Hovenkamp, Federal Antitrust Policy: The Law of Competition and its Practice 450–58 (3rd Ed. 2005); Richard A. Posner, Antitrust Law 171–189 (2nd ed. 2001). For a contrary view, see Robert Pitofsky, In Defense of Discounters: The No-Frills Case for a Per Se Rule Against Vertical Price Fixing, 71 Georgetown L.J. 1487 (1983).

5. Was *Dr. Miles* really a lawyer malpractice case? That is, was the failure to find these were consignment arrangements with the dealers largely the result of bad drafting? What were the drafter's biggest mistakes? What changes in language could have changed this result?

6. How did this case get to Court? Is it at all significant that it was a proceeding for an injunction, i.e., one in which the plaintiff's clean hands might have been at issue? If the court had been *balancing* equities here, do you agree with Justice Holmes that the court should not have rewarded the defendant's inducing breaches of contract?

7. What was the point of Dr. Miles' argument that its processes were secret? As the Court notes and as we will see, patent holders are often held to have rights that ordinary producers do not have. Is there any good reason for not granting Dr. Miles those same rights? Why do you suppose Dr. Miles did not just apply for a patent on this tonic?

8. While resale price maintenance remains a major symbolic issue, do you suppose many manufacturers would now institute such a system if they were free to do so? Given the importance of national advertising and of moving large quantities of products through mass merchandisers, may one assume the practice would have few proponents? On the other hand, if only a few firms would institute it, can one argue that little social harm would be caused by allowing it?

AN IMPORTANT QUALIFICATION OF THE
DR. MILES RULE—THE *COLGATE* CASE

While the *Dr. Miles* prohibition of resale price maintenance long affected the development of antitrust law, just eight years later, the Court noted an important qualification on its potential scope.

In United States v. Colgate & Co., 250 U.S. 300, 39 S.Ct. 465, 63 L.Ed. 992 (1919), the defendant had allegedly circulated lists to its dealers

"showing uniform prices to be charged; urging [dealers] to adhere to such prices and notices, stating that no sales would be made to those who did not; requests, often complied with, for information concerning dealers who had departed from specified prices; investigation and discovery of those not adhering thereto and placing their names upon 'suspended lists'; requests to offending dealers for assurances and promises of future adherence to prices, which were often given; uniform refusals to sell to any who failed to give the same; sales to those who did; similar assurances and promises required of, and given by, other dealers followed by sales to them; unrestricted sales to dealers with established accounts who had observed established prices, etc."

As a result, the Government alleged, retailers charged uniform prices for Colgate products throughout the United States.

Colgate was largely a case of prosecutor malpractice. In an indictment alleging a combination under Sherman Act § 1, the prosecutor had named Colgate as the only defendant. At least as read by the Supreme Court, the indictment alleged no contract between Colgate and its dealers, nor did it identify any conspiracy. *Dr. Miles* had involved "contracts which undertook to prevent dealers from freely exercising the right to sell," a unanimous Supreme Court said. Colgate had only done what any firm may do:

> "In the absence of any purpose to create or maintain a monopoly, the act does not restrict the long recognized right of trader or manufacturer engaged in an entirely private business, freely to exercise his own independent discretion as to parties with whom he will deal; and, of course, he may announce in advance the circumstances under which he will refuse to sell."

This so-called "*Colgate* rule" continued to be extremely important. Watch for it to come up often in the cases that follow, but be careful also to note how frequently the Government, private plaintiffs and the courts tried to avoid and modify its reach.

E. ADOPTION OF THE CLAYTON AND FEDERAL TRADE COMMISSION ACTS

Throughout the early history of the Sherman Act, various people and groups were eager to clarify and strengthen it.[30] The *E.C. Knight* decision, for example, had raised fears that a narrow construction of the interstate commerce requirement might make the law a dead letter and had led to pressure to make clear that a broad reach for the law had been intended.

Theodore Roosevelt, who assumed the Presidency in 1901, was clearly an important figure asserting the importance of antitrust issues. He was not a lawyer, but he understood good political rhetoric and the power of the bully pulpit. Roosevelt asserted that one had to distinguish industrial combinations that were the cause and product of efficiency from those that wrongfully hurt their competitors. As President, in 1903, he created a Bureau of Corporations that published important studies of organizations such as the Standard Oil Company and American Tobacco Co., later of course broken up by suits under Section 2 of the Sherman Act.[31]

---

[30]   The best single set of primary sources about adoption of the Clayton Act is Earl W. Kintner, The Legislative History of the Federal Antitrust Laws and Related Statutes, Vols. 2–4 (1978). The legislative history of the Federal Trade Commission Act is equally well covered in Volume 5 of the same series. For an outstanding history of this period, see Marc Winerman, The Origins of the FTC: Concentration, Cooperation, Control, and Competition, 71 Antitrust L. J. 1 (2003).

[31]   The earliest proposal to expand the functions of the Bureau of Corporations was the Hepburn Bill in 1908. See Thomas K. McCraw, Prophets of Regulation 119 (1984). See also, Gabriel Kolko, The Triumph of Conservatism: A Reinterpretation of American History 1900–1916 57–158

Pressure to amend and strengthen the Sherman Act was then dramatically revived by the 1911 decision in *Standard Oil*. Many feared the "rule of reason" would impair or eliminate antitrust enforcement.[32]

Antitrust policy was a major issue in the 1912 election campaign which pitted Woodrow Wilson against former-President Roosevelt and the incumbent, William Howard Taft. The principal economic adviser to candidate Wilson was the "people's lawyer," Louis Brandeis, formerly general counsel to the United Shoe Machinery Co., a frequent antitrust defendant. The Wilson campaign had been built upon a program called the "New Freedom." It stressed freeing up opportunities for small business and restricting the power and influence of large corporations. Once in office, the Wilson administration put together a package of proposals including one to specifically address certain issues that had arisen under the Sherman Act and one to institutionalize the Bureau of Corporations concept in a Federal Trade Commission.[33]

In January 1914, President Wilson gave a speech to a joint session of Congress that began the serious legislative effort. He made two points:

> "Surely we are sufficiently familiar with the actual processes and methods of monopoly and of the many hurtful restraints of trade to make definition possible * * * . These practices * * * can be explicitly and item by item forbidden by statute in such terms as will practically eliminate uncertainty, the law itself and the penalty being made equally plain.

> "And the business men of the country desire something more than that the menace of legal process in these matters be made

---

(1963); Hans B. Thorelli, The Federal Antitrust Policy: Origination of an American Tradition 411–421 (1954).

[32] This view was reinforced the next year by the decision in Henry v. A.B. Dick Co., 224 U.S. 1, 32 S.Ct. 364, 56 L.Ed. 645 (1912). A.B. Dick, had sold Ms. Christina Skou a mimeograph machine; the defendant, Mr. Henry, had sold her some ink for use in it. On the patented machine, however, A.B. Dick had placed a notice that all stencil paper, ink and other supplies for use in the machine had to be purchased from the machine manufacturer. Thus, A.B. Dick contended, by selling the ink, Henry had been guilty of "contributory infringement" of Dick's patent. In an opinion by Justice Lurton, a five member majority of the Supreme Court agreed. Patent law by definition grants a monopoly, the Court said, so any burden created by this condition is not inconsistent with the command of the antitrust law. Indeed, *Dr. Miles* expressly distinguished patent cases like E. Bement & Sons v. National Harrow Co., in which even control over the resale price of a patented item was upheld. Chief Justice White, for himself and Justices Hughes and Lamar, disagreed. The patent covered the machine, not the ink, they reasoned. Ms. Skou had purchased the mimeograph machine and A.B. Dick had no legitimate reason to affect her subsequent buying decisions. It is fine to protect the inventor's monopoly of the invention, they argued, but this decision gave inventors control over commodities only incidentally related to their invention. It was as though the seller of a coffee pot could require the purchaser to buy a particular brand of coffee.

[33] Brandeis' role in the development of both of these statutes is described in McCraw, supra n. 31, at 81–142. See also, Earl W. Kintner, supra n. 30, vol. 2, at 994–95. As President, William Howard Taft had aggressively enforced the Sherman Act. When Wilson succeeded him as President and proposed new legislation, Taft (by then Kent Professor of Law at Yale) gave a series of lectures summarizing the state of antitrust law at that time and expressing doubts about the need for new legislation. Those lectures are collected as William Howard Taft, The Anti-Trust Act and the Supreme Court (1914).

explicit and intelligible. They desire the advice, the definite guidance and information which can be supplied by an administrative body, an interstate trade commission."[34]

Thus, one legislative proposal was to deal specifically with particular antitrust issues that the courts had not handled adequately to date. The other would create an administrative agency capable of "directing and shaping" remedies "not only in aid of the courts but also by independent suggestion, if necessary."[35] Early legislative leadership was provided by Senator Robert M. LaFollette, with whom Brandeis worked closely. Henry D. Clayton was Chairman of the House Judiciary Committee and it was his bill that was ultimately adopted.[36]

The Clayton Act ultimately contained provisions that have had continuing significance. Section 2 dealt with price discrimination and Section 3 with the problem of *Henry v. A.B. Dick*.[37] Section 6 exempted labor unions from antitrust attack and Section 7 regulated stock acquisition mergers. Sections 4 & 5 expanded the practical availability of private treble damage actions and Section 16 gave a comparable private right to injunctive relief.

The Federal Trade Commission Act, in turn, dealt primarily with creation of the agency. The controlling substantive concept was that of "unfair methods of competition," a term that Congress left for the new agency to define.[38]

CLAYTON ANTITRUST ACT

38 Stat. 730
October 15, 1914

Be it enacted by the Senate and House of Representatives of the United States of America in Congress Assembled, * * *

Sec. 2. That it shall be unlawful for any person engaged in commerce, in the course of such commerce, either directly or indirectly to discriminate in price between different purchasers of commodities, which commodities are sold for use, consumption, or resale within the United States * * * where the effect of such discrimination may be to substantially lessen competition or tend to create a monopoly in any line of commerce: *Provided,*

---

[34]   Address by President Woodrow Wilson, 51 Cong.Rec. 1962–64 (Jan. 20, 1914), reprinted in Kintner, supra n. 30, vol. 5, at 3748.

[35]   Ibid.

[36]   In fact, Congressman Clayton was the sponsor of both the bill to amend the Sherman Act and the one to create the Federal Trade Commission. The latter was assigned to the Commerce Committee, however, instead of to Clayton's Judiciary Committee, so it does not bear his name.

[37]   Discussed supra n. 32.

[38]   "It is impossible to frame definitions which will embrace all unfair practices. There is no limit to human inventiveness in this field. If Congress were to adopt the method of definition, it would undertake an endless task." H.R. Rep. No. 1142, 63d Cong., 2d Sess. 19 (1914), reprinted in Kintner, supra n. 30, at 4694.

That nothing herein contained shall prevent discrimination in price between purchasers of commodities on account of differences in the grade, quality, or quantity of the commodity sold, or that makes only due allowance for differences in the cost of selling or transportation, or discrimination in price in the same or different communities made in good faith to meet competition: *And provided further*, That nothing herein contained shall prevent persons engaged in selling goods, wares, or merchandise in commerce from selecting their own customers in bona fide transactions and not in restraint of trade.

Sec. 3. That it shall be unlawful for any person engaged in commerce, *no price fixing* in the course of such commerce, to lease or make a sale or contract for sale of goods * * * or other commodities, whether patented or unpatented, for use, consumption or resale within the United States * * *, or fix a price charged therefor, or discount from, or rebate upon, such price, on the condition, agreement or understanding that the lessee or purchaser thereof shall not use or deal in the goods * * * or other commodities of a competitor or competitors of the lessor or seller, where the effect of such lease, sale, or contract for sale or such condition, agreement or understanding may be to substantially lessen competition or tend to create a monopoly in any line of commerce.

Sec. 4. That any person who shall be injured in his business or property by reason of anything forbidden in the antitrust laws may sue therefor in [United States District Court] * * * without respect to the amount in controversy, and shall recover threefold the damages by him sustained, and the cost of suit, including a reasonable attorney's fee.

Sec. 5. That a final judgment or decree hereafter rendered in any criminal prosecution or in any suit or proceeding in equity brought by or on behalf of the United States under the antitrust laws to the effect that a defendant has violated said laws shall be prima facie evidence against such defendant in any suit or proceeding brought by any other party against such defendant under said laws as to all matters respecting which said judgment would be an estoppel as between the parties thereto: *Provided*, This section shall not apply to consent judgments or decrees entered before any testimony has been taken. * * *

Sec. 6. That the labor of a human being is not a commodity or article of commerce. Nothing contained in the antitrust laws shall be construed to forbid the existence and operation or labor, agricultural, or horticultural organizations, instituted for the purposes of mutual help, * * * nor shall such organizations or the members thereof be held or construed to be illegal combinations or conspiracies in restraint of trade * * *.

Sec. 7. That no corporation engaged in commerce shall acquire, directly or indirectly, the whole or any part of the stock or other share capital of another corporation engaged also in commerce, where the effect of such acquisition may be to substantially lessen competition between the corporation whose stock is so acquired and the corporation making the acquisition, or to restrain such commerce in any section or community, or tend to create a monopoly of any line of commerce.

* * *

Sec. 16. That any person, firm, corporation, or association shall be entitled to sue for and have injunctive relief, in any court of the United States having jurisdiction over the parties, against threatened loss or damage by a violation of the antitrust laws * * * .

FEDERAL TRADE COMMISSION ACT
38 Stat. 717
September 26, 1914

Sec. 5. Unfair methods of competition in or affecting commerce, and unfair or deceptive acts or practices in or affecting commerce, are hereby declared unlawful.

The Commission is hereby empowered and directed to prevent persons, partnerships, or corporations, except banks, and common carriers subject to the Act to regulate commerce, from using unfair methods of competition in or affecting commerce and unfair or deceptive acts or practices in or affecting commerce.

Whenever the Commission shall have reason to believe that any such person * * * has been or is using any unfair method of competition in commerce, and if it shall appear to the Commission that a proceeding by it in respect thereof would be to the interest of the public, it shall issue and serve upon such person * * * a complaint * * * . * * * If [after hearing] the Commission shall be of the opinion that the method of competition in question is prohibited by this Act, it shall make a report in writing * * * and shall issue * * * an order requiring [the defendant] * * * to cease and desist from using such method of competition. * * *

CHAPTER II

THE RULE OF REASON PERIOD: 1915 TO 1939

■ ■ ■

In Chapter I, we watched the Court and later Congress try to craft a coherent body of doctrine out of the Delphic concepts of the Sherman Act. We also saw the initial creation of categories such as horizontal price fixing (*Trans-Missouri*), market division (*Addyston Pipe*), merger (*Northern Securities*), monopolization (*Standard Oil*), and vertical resale price maintenance (*Dr. Miles*) that still structure antitrust thinking.

The first 25 years after adoption of the Clayton and FTC Acts correspond closely to the period in which the rule of reason, first articulated in *Standard Oil*, provided the dominant model for antitrust analysis. It was a time in which the new laws were not irrelevant, but the Sherman Act was still the primary benchmark for antitrust thinking.

In this Chapter, we examine four groups of cases. The first are two cases that defined the dominant approach to Sherman Act §§ 1 and 2 during this 25 year period. The next case suggests practical issues involving trade associations, but also illustrates the more general problem of dealing with firms whose conduct is interdependent but falls short of the agreement that underlies a classic cartel. The third set of cases raise problems in the interplay of patent and antitrust law, while the final pair tested the boundaries of the rule of reason.

The period from 1915–1939 might also be called the "Brandeis era" of antitrust thinking. Justice Louis Brandeis, President Wilson's principal adviser on antitrust matters, was appointed to the Court by Wilson in 1916 where he served until 1939, writing some of the Court's most important rule of reason opinions. Indeed, in our next case, he defined the nature of rule of reason analysis in a way that affected all the cases that followed and still is influential today.

A. CASES GIVING DEFINITION TO THE RULE OF REASON

BOARD OF TRADE OF CITY OF CHICAGO V. UNITED STATES
Supreme Court of the United States, 1918
246 U.S. 231, 38 S.Ct. 242, 62 L.Ed. 683

MR. JUSTICE BRANDEIS delivered the opinion of the court.

Chicago is the leading grain market in the world. Its Board of Trade is the commercial center through which most of the trading in grains is done. * * * Its 1600 members include brokers, commission merchants, dealers, millers, maltsters, manufacturers of corn products and proprietors of elevators. * * * The standard forms of trading are: (a) Spot sales; that is, sales of grain already in Chicago in railroad cars or elevators for immediate delivery by order on carrier or transfer of warehouse receipt. (b) Future sales; that is, agreements for delivery later in the current or in some future month. (c) Sales "to arrive"; that is, agreements to deliver on arrival grain which is already in transit to Chicago or is to be shipped there within a time specified. On every business day sessions of the Board are held at which all bids and sales are publicly made. Spot sales and future sales are made at the regular sessions of the Board from 9:30 A.M. to 1:15 P.M., except on Saturdays, when the session closes at 12 M. Special sessions, termed the "call," are held immediately after the close of the regular session, at which sales "to arrive" are made. These sessions are not limited as to duration, but last usually about half an hour. At all these sessions transactions are between members only; but they may trade either for themselves or on behalf of others. Members may also trade privately with one another at any place, either during the sessions or after, and they may trade with non-members at any time except on the premises occupied by the Board.

Purchases of grain "to arrive" are made largely from country dealers and farmers throughout the whole territory tributary to Chicago, which includes besides Illinois and Iowa, Indiana, Ohio, Wisconsin, Minnesota, Missouri, Kansas, Nebraska, and even South and North Dakota. The purchases are sometimes the result of bids to individual country dealers made by telegraph or telephone either during the sessions or after; but most purchases are made by the sending out from Chicago by the afternoon mails to hundreds of country dealers offers to buy, at the prices named, any number of carloads, subject to acceptance before 9:30 A.M. on the next business day.

In 1906 the Board adopted what is known as the "call" rule. By it members were prohibited from purchasing or offering to purchase, during the period between the close of the call and the opening of the session on the next business day, any wheat, corn, oats or rye "to arrive" at a price other than the closing bid at the call. The call was over, with rare exceptions, by two o'clock. The change effected was this: Before the adoption of the rule, members fixed their bids throughout the day at such prices as they respectively saw fit; after the adoption of the rule, the bids had to be fixed at the day's closing bid on the call until the opening of the next session.

In 1913 the United States filed * * * this suit against the Board and its executive officers and directors, to enjoin the enforcement of the call rule * * * . The defendants admitted the adoption and enforcement of the call rule, and averred that its purpose was not to prevent competition or to control prices, but to promote the convenience of members by restricting their hours of business and to break up a monopoly in that branch of the grain trade acquired by four or five warehousemen in Chicago. On motion of the Government the allegations concerning the purpose of establishing the regulation were stricken from the record. The case was then heard upon evidence; and a decree was entered which * * * enjoined them from acting upon the same or from adopting or acting upon any similar rule.

* * * The government proved the existence of the rule and described its application and the change in business practice involved. It made no attempt to show that the rule was designed to or that it had the effect of limiting the amount of grain shipped to Chicago; or of retarding or accelerating shipment; or of raising or depressing prices; or of discriminating against any part of the public; or that it resulted in hardship to anyone. The case was rested upon the bald proposition, that a rule or agreement by which men occupying positions of strength in any branch of trade, fixed prices at which they would buy or sell during an important part of the business day, is an illegal restraint of trade under the Anti-Trust Law. But the legality of an agreement or regulation cannot be determined by so simple a test, as whether it restrains competition. Every agreement concerning trade, every regulation of trade, restrains. To bind, to restrain, is of their very essence. The true test of legality is whether the restraint imposed is such as merely regulates and perhaps thereby promotes competition or whether it is such as may suppress or even destroy competition. To determine that question the court must ordinarily consider the facts peculiar to the business to which the restraint is applied; its condition before and after the restraint was imposed; the nature of the restraint and its effect, actual or probable. The history of the restraint, the evil believed to exist, the reason for adopting the particular remedy, the purpose or end sought to be attained, are all relevant facts. This is not because a good intention will save an otherwise objectionable regulation or the reverse; but because knowledge of intent may help the court to interpret facts and to predict consequences. The District Court erred, therefore, in striking from the answer allegations concerning the history and purpose of the call rule and in later excluding evidence on that subject.

But the evidence admitted makes it clear that the rule was a reasonable regulation of business consistent with the provisions of the Anti-Trust Law.

First: The nature of the rule: The restriction was upon the period of price-making. It required members to desist from further price-making after the close of the call until 9:30 A.M. the next business day: but there was no restriction upon the sending out of bids after close of the call. Thus it required members who desired to buy grain "to arrive" to make up their minds before the close of the call how much they were willing to pay during the interval before the next session of the Board. The rule made it to their interest to attend the call; and if they did not fill their wants by purchases there, to make the final bid high enough to enable them to purchase from country dealers.

Second: The scope of the rule: It is restricted in operation to grain "to arrive." It applies only to a small part of the grain shipped from day to day to Chicago, and to an even smaller part of the day's sales: members were left free to purchase grain already in Chicago from anyone at any price throughout the day. It applies only during a small part of the business day; members were left free to purchase during the sessions of the Board grain "to arrive," at any price, from members anywhere and from non-members anywhere except on the premises of the Board. It applied only to grain shipped to Chicago: members were left free to purchase at any price throughout the day from either members or non-members, grain "to arrive" at any other market. Country dealers and farmers had available in practically every part of the territory called tributary to Chicago some other market for grain "to arrive." * * *

Third: The effects of the rule: As it applies to only a small part of the grain shipped to Chicago and to that only during a part of the business day and does not apply at all to grain shipped to other markets, the rule had no appreciable effect on general market prices; nor did it materially affect the total volume of grain coming to Chicago. But within the narrow limits of its operation the rule helped to improve market conditions thus:

(a) It created a public market for grain "to arrive." Before its adoption, bids were made privately. Men had to buy and sell without adequate knowledge of actual market conditions. This was disadvantageous to all concerned, but particularly so to country dealers and farmers.

(b) It brought into the regular market hours of the Board sessions more of the trading in grain "to arrive."

(c) It brought buyers and sellers into more direct relations; because on the call they gathered together for a free and open interchange of bids and offers.

(d) It distributed the business in grain "to arrive" among a far larger number of Chicago receivers and commission merchants than had been the case there before.

(e) It increased the number of country dealers engaging in this branch of the business; supplied them more regularly with bids from Chicago; and also increased the number of bids received by them from competing markets.

(f) It eliminated risks necessarily incident to a private market, and thus enabled country dealers to do business on a smaller margin. In that way the rule made it possible for them to pay more to farmers without raising the price to consumers.

(g) It enabled country dealers to sell some grain to arrive which they would otherwise have been obliged either to ship to Chicago commission merchants or to sell for "future delivery."

(h) It enabled those grain merchants of Chicago who sell to millers and exporters to trade on a smaller margin and, by paying more for grain or selling it for less, to make the Chicago market more attractive for both shippers and buyers of grain.

(i) Incidentally it facilitated trading "to arrive" by enabling those engaged in these transactions to fulfil their contracts by tendering grain arriving at Chicago on any railroad, whereas formerly shipments had to be made over the particular railroad designated by the buyer.

* * * Every Board of Trade and nearly every trade organization imposes some restraint upon the conduct of business by its members. Those relating to the hours in which business may be done are common; and they make a special appeal where, as here, they tend to shorten the working day or, at least, limit the period of most exacting activity. The decree of the District Court is reversed with directions to dismiss the bill.

MR. JUSTICE MCREYNOLDS took no part in the consideration or decision of this case.

NOTES AND QUESTIONS

1. The Court is unanimous here in its application of the rule of reason. Were you persuaded by Justice Brandeis' argument that all contracts restrain trade and that they cannot all be illegal? Do you remember earlier cases in which judges had tried in vain to make that same point?

2. Does it follow that in each case the court should take evidence on "whether the restraint imposed is such as merely regulates and perhaps thereby promotes competition or whether it is such as may suppress or even destroy competition"? Is there any limit to the kind of evidence a court should consider?

a.   Do you agree that "to determine that question the court must ordinarily consider the facts peculiar to the business to which the restraint is applied; its condition before and after the restraint was imposed; the nature of the restraint and its effect, actual or probable"? Should "the history of the restraint, the evil believed to exist, the reason for adopting the particular remedy, [and] the purpose or end sought to be attained, all [be] relevant facts"? How long do you suppose a trial thoroughly investigating all those issues might last?

b.   Procedurally, the key distinction between the "rule of reason" and the "per se" rule is whether evidence seeking to explain a business practice may be introduced. Will the added understanding gained through a full scale inquiry into possible justifications for a restraint always justify the added costs of the inquiry? Might such an inquiry be so diffuse, wide-ranging and unstructured as to yield little definitive information?[1] Does it necessarily follow that the rule of reason should be rejected? Might any other approach be even worse?

3.   Do you believe Justice Brandeis that the "call rule" was not anticompetitive?

a.   Would buyers and sellers normally prohibit themselves from reaching mutually satisfactory prices at which to buy and sell grain? Why or why not?

b.   Were you persuaded by the Court's argument that so little grain was affected by this rule that there was little effect on the market price? Would you be less persuaded if you thought that about 40% of the grain traded in Chicago was sold "to arrive"?[2]

c.   Might we ask in each Section 1 case what prices would have been absent the restraint? Do you suppose economic theory is refined enough to provide an answer to that question even if we wanted to ask it?

4.   Assuming there may be some anticompetitive effects associated with this agreement, were you convinced by the reasons Justice Brandeis gave to justify the call rule?

a.   What about the argument based on the "convenience" of Board of Trade members, i.e., that the rule let them sleep soundly and not worry that someone would outbid them during the night? Should the convenience of some

---

[1]   Later, in National Association of Window Glass Manufacturers v. United States, 263 U.S. 403, 44 S.Ct. 148, 68 L.Ed. 358 (1923), the Court implied that a lengthy factual record might not be necessary. Hand-blown window glass was considered higher quality and sold at a higher price than machine-made glass. Manufacturers of hand-blown glass had reached an agreement with the glassblowers union that not only set wages but also allocated the supply of glassblowers to each company at specific times of the year. This allegedly restricted the supply of hand-blown glass, and if so, could have violated the Sherman Act in spite of Clayton Act § 6. In a unanimous opinion by Justice Holmes, however, the Court dismissed the charge. It noted that hand-blown glass was a dying industry and the agreement made it possible for plants to run at full capacity (and peak efficiency) for limited periods each year instead of at partial capacity for longer periods. That alone was enough to make any collateral effect on supply and price a reasonable restraint of trade.

[2]   See Peter C. Carstensen, The Board of Trade Case and the Rule of Reason, Research in Law & Economics 1, 35 (1992).

sellers be permitted to trump possible benefits to everyone else if the call rule were struck down?

b.   How about the argument based upon improving information in the hands of farmers and country grain dealers? In the absence of the call rule, were rural residents without defenses against unscrupulous Chicago purchasers?

c.   How could this rule increase the number of dealers "engaging in this branch of the business"? Why would this effect be important to someone like Justice Brandeis? Would it be important to farmers?

d.   Do you agree that this rule helped make the Chicago market more competitive? What features of the rule, if any, would contribute to the "break up [of the] monopoly in that branch of the grain trade acquired by four or five warehousemen in Chicago"? Why would this rule make it possible to "trade on a smaller margin" and thus make "the Chicago market more attractive for both shippers and buyers of grain"?

5.   Something not discussed by the Court may have been going on here. This was a period in which commissions on the Board of Trade were fixed by agreement, so Board members had an incentive to want trades to occur there.

a.   Suppose the large traders were making off-market deals in the hours after the market closed that avoided the Board of Trade commission, thus potentially benefitting the farmers and rural dealers but hurting the smaller dealers who dealt primarily on the exchange. Would the call rule inhibit such off-market transactions? If it did, would that affect your judgment about whether the rule should have been sustained by the Court?

b.   Suppose the rule were procompetitive in the sense of increasing open trading, but anticompetitive in the sense of requiring more farmers to deal at fixed commission rates. Could such effects be balanced under a rule of reason? Should we even try to do so?

UNITED STATES V. UNITED STATES STEEL CORPORATION

Supreme Court of the United States, 1920
251 U.S. 417, 40 S.Ct. 293, 64 L.Ed. 343

MR. JUSTICE MCKENNA delivered the opinion of the court.

Suit against the Steel Corporation and certain other companies which it directs and controls by reason of the ownership of their stock * * * .

It is prayed that it and they be dissolved because [they are] engaged in illegal restraint of trade and the exercise of monopoly.

* * *

The Steel Corporation is a holding company only; the other companies are the operating ones, manufacturers in the iron and steel industry, 12 in number. There are, besides, other corporations and individuals * * * that are alleged to be instruments or accomplices in [defendants'] activities * * * extend[ing] from 1901 to 1911, when the bill was filed * * * .

* * *

The case was heard in the District Court by four judges. They agreed that the bill should be dismissed; they disagreed as to the reasons for it. One opinion (written by Judge Buffington and concurred in by Judge McPherson) expressed the view that the Steel Corporation was not formed with the intention or purpose to monopolize or restrain trade * * * . The corporation, in the view of the opinion, was an evolution, a natural consummation of the tendencies of the industry on account of changing conditions, * * * tending to combinations of capital and energies rather than diffusion in independent action. * * * Indeed an important purpose of the organization of the corporation was the building up of the export trade in steel and iron which at that time was sporadic, the mere dumping of the products upon foreign markets.

Not monopoly, therefore, was the purpose of the organization of the corporation, but concentration of efforts with resultant economies and benefits.

The tendency of the industry and the purpose of the corporation in yielding to it were expressed in comprehensive condensation by the word "integration," which signifies continuity in the processes of the industry from ore mines to the finished product.

* * * [W]hile conceding that the Steel Corporation, after its formation in times of financial disturbance, entered into informal agreements or understandings with its competitors to maintain prices, they * * * had ceased to exist, [so] the court was not justified in dissolving the corporation.

The other opinion, by Judge Woolley and concurred in by Judge Hunt, was in some particulars, in antithesis to Judge Buffington's. The view was expressed that neither the Steel Corporation nor the preceding combinations, which were in a sense its antetypes, had the justification of industrial conditions, nor were they * * * compelled to unite in comprehensive enterprise because such had become a condition of success under the new order of things. On the contrary, * * * the organizers of the corporation and the preceding companies had illegal purpose from the very beginning, and the corporation became "a combination of combinations, by which, directly or indirectly, approximately 180 independent concerns were brought under one business control," which, measured by the amount of production, extended to 80% or 90% of the entire output of the country, and that its purpose was * * * to accomplish permanently what those combinations had demonstrated could be accomplished temporarily, and thereby monopolize and restrain trade.[3]

The organizers, however (we are still representing the opinion), underestimated the opposing conditions and at the very beginning the corporation instead of relying upon its own power sought and obtained the assistance and the cooperation of its competitors (the independent companies). In other words * * * the testimony did "not show that the corporation in and of itself ever possessed or exerted sufficient power when acting alone to control prices of the products of the industry." Its power was efficient only when in cooperation with its competitors, and hence it concerted with them in the expedients of pools, associations, trade meetings, and finally in a system of dinners inaugurated in 1907 by the president of the company, E. H. Gary, and called "the Gary Dinners." The dinners were * * * instituted first in "stress of panic," but, their potency being demonstrated, they were afterwards called to control prices "in periods of industrial calm." "They were pools without penalties" and more efficient in stabilizing prices. But it was the further declaration that "when joint action was either refused or withdrawn the corporation's prices were controlled by competition."

The corporation, it was said, did not at any time abuse the power or ascendency it possessed. It resorted to none of the brutalities or tyrannies that the cases illustrate of other combinations. It did not secure freight rebates; it did not increase its profits by reducing the wages of its employees—whatever it did was not at the expense of labor; it did not increase its profits by lowering the quality of its products, nor create an artificial scarcity of them; it did not oppress or coerce its competitors—its competition, though vigorous, was fair; it did not undersell its competitors in some localities by reducing its prices there below those maintained elsewhere, or require its customers to enter into contracts limiting their purchases or restricting them in resale prices; it did not obtain customers by secret rebates or departures from its published prices; there was no evidence that it attempted to crush its competitors or drive them out of the market, nor did it take customers from its competitors by unfair means, and in its competition it seemed to make no difference between large and small competitors. Indeed it is said in many ways and illustrated that

---

[3]   As bearing upon the power obtained and what the corporation did we give other citations from Judge Woolley's opinion as follows:

* * *

    " * * * [L]arge as was the corporation, and substantial as was its proportion of the business of the industry, the corporation was not able in the first ten years of its history to maintain its position in the increase of trade. During that period, its proportion of the domestic business decreased from 50.1 per cent to 40.9 per cent and its increase of business during that period was but 40.6 per cent of its original volume. Its increase of business, measured by percentage, was exceeded by eight of its competitors, whose increase of business, likewise measured by percentage, ranged from 63 to 3779. * * * " [Court's fn. 1] "instead of relying upon its own power to fix and maintain prices, the corporation, at its very beginning sought and obtained the assistance of others." It combined its power with that of its competitors. * * * Its offense, therefore, such as it was, was not different from theirs and was distinguished from theirs "only in the leadership it assumed in promulgating and perfecting the policy." This leadership it gave up, and it had ceased to offend against the law before this suit was brought. It was hence concluded that * * * it "in and of itself is not now and has never been a monopoly or a combination in restraint of trade," and a decree of dissolution should not be entered against it.

* * *

* * * [O]ur consideration should be of not what the corporation had power to do or did, but what it has now power to do and is doing, and what judgment shall be now pronounced—whether its dissolution, as the government prays, or the dismissal of the suit, as the corporation insists.

* * * [I]t is against monopoly that the statute is directed, not against an expectation of it, but against its realization, and it is certain that it was not realized. * * * The power attained was much greater than that possessed by any one competitor—it was not greater than that possessed by all of them. Monopoly, therefore, was not achieved, and competitors had to be persuaded by pools, associations, trade meetings, and through the social form of dinners, all of them, it may be, violations of the law, but transient in their purpose and effect. They were scattered through the years from 1901 (the year of the formation of the Corporation), until 1911, but, after instances of success and failure, were abandoned nine months before this suit was brought. There is no evidence that the abandonment was in prophecy of or dread of suit; and the illegal practices have not been resumed, nor is there any * * * "dangerous probability" of their resumption, the test for which Swift & Co. v. United States is cited. * * *

What, then, can now be urged against the corporation? * * * [I]ts power over prices was not and is not commensurate with its power to produce.

* * *

* * * The company's officers and, as well, its competitors and customers, testified that its competition was genuine, direct and vigorous, and was reflected in prices and production. No practical witness was produced by the Government in opposition. Its contention is based on the size and asserted dominance of the Corporation—alleged power for evil, not the exertion of the power in evil. * * * [I]t is admitted "no competitor came forward and said he had to accept the Steel Corporation's prices." But this absence of complaint counsel urge against the Corporation. Competitors, it is said, followed the Corporation's prices because they made money by the

imitation. Indeed the imitation is urged as an evidence of the Corporation's power. * * *

* * *

* * * The government, therefore, is reduced to the assertion that the size of the corporation, the power it may have, not the exertion of the power, is an abhorrence to the law * * * . "A wrongful purpose," the government adds, is "matter of aggravation." * * * To assent to that, to what extremes should we be led? Competition consists of business activities and ability—they make its life; but there may be fatalities in it. Are the activities to be encouraged when militant, and suppressed or regulated when triumphant because of the dominance attained? * * *

* * *

* * * The corporation is undoubtedly of impressive size and it takes an effort of resolution not to be affected by it or to exaggerate its influence. But we must adhere to the law and the law does not make mere size an offence or the existence of unexerted power an offence. It, we repeat, requires overt acts and trusts to its prohibition of them and its power to repress or punish them. It does not compel competition nor require all that is possible.

Admitting, however, that there is pertinent strength in the propositions of the government, and in connection with them, we recall the * * * *Standard Oil* Case * * * . * * *

Are the case and its precepts applicable here? The Steel Corporation by its formation united under one control competing companies and thus, it is urged, a condition was brought about in violation of the statute, and therefore illegal and became a "continually operating force" with the "possession of power unlawfully obtained."

But there are countervailing considerations. We have seen whatever there was of wrong intent could not be executed, whatever there was of evil effect, was discontinued before this suit was brought; and this, we think, determines the decree. * * *

* * *

The government, however, tentatively presents a proposition which has some tangibility. It submits that certain of the subsidiary companies are so mechanically equipped and so officially directed as to be released and remitted to independent action and individual interests and the competition to which such interests prompt, without any disturbance to business. * * * They are fully integrated, it is said—possess their own supplies, facilities of transportation, and distribution. They are subject only to the Steel Corporation, is in effect the declaration, in nothing but its control of their prices. * * *

* * * The prayer of the government calls for, not only a disruption of present conditions, but the restoration of the conditions of 20 years ago, if not literally, substantially. Is there guidance to this in the *Standard Oil* Case and the *Tobacco* Case? * * *

The Standard Oil Company had its origin in 1882 and through successive forms of combinations and agencies it progressed in illegal power to the day of the decree, even attempting to circumvent by one of its forms the decision of a court against it. And its methods in using its power was of the kind that Judge Woolley described as "brutal," and of which practices, he said, the Steel Corporation was absolutely guiltless. * * * [O]f the [Standard Oil] practices this court said no disinterested mind could doubt that the purpose was "to drive others from the field and to exclude them from their right to trade and thus accomplish the mastery which was the end in view." * * *

* * *

The *Tobacco* Case has the same bad distinctions as the *Standard Oil* Case. The illegality in which it was formed * * * continued, indeed progressed in intensity and defiance to the moment of decree. And it is the intimation of the opinion if not its direct assertion that the formation of the company * * * was preceded by the intimidation of a trade war "inspired by one or more of the minds which brought about and became parties to that combination." In other words the purpose of the combination was signalled to competitors and the choice presented to them was submission or ruin, to become parties to the illegal enterprise or be driven "out of the business." * * * In the *Tobacco* Case, therefore, as in the *Standard Oil* Case, the court had to deal with a persistent and systematic lawbreaker masquerading under legal forms, and which not only had to be stripped of its disguises but arrested in its illegality. A decree of dissolution was the manifest instrumentality and inevitable. We think it would be a work of sheer supererogation to point out that a decree in that case or in the *Standard Oil* Case furnishes no example for a decree in this.

In conclusion we are unable to see that the public interest will be served by yielding to the contention of the government respecting the dissolution of the company or the separation from it of some of its subsidiaries; and we do see in a contrary conclusion a risk of injury to the public interest, including a material disturbance of, and, it may be serious detriment to, the foreign trade. And in submission to the policy of the law and its fortifying prohibitions the public interest is of paramount regard.

We think, therefore, that the decree of the District Court should be affirmed.

MR. JUSTICE MCREYNOLDS and MR. JUSTICE BRANDEIS took no part in the consideration or decision of the case.

MR. JUSTICE DAY dissenting.

This record seems to me to leave no fair room for a doubt that the defendants, the United States Steel Corporation and the several subsidiary corporations which make up that organization, were formed in violation of the Sherman Act. I am unable to accept the conclusion which directs a dismissal of the bill instead of following the well-settled practice, sanctioned by previous decisions of this court, requiring the dissolution of combinations made in direct violation of the law.

* * *

The contention must be rejected that the combination was an inevitable evolution of industrial tendencies compelling union of endeavor. * * *

For many years, as the record discloses, this unlawful organization exerted its power to control and maintain prices by pools, associations, trade meetings, and as the result of discussion and agreements at the so-called "Gary Dinners," where the assembled trade opponents secured cooperation and joint action through the machinery of special committees of competing concerns, and by prudent prevision took into account the possibility of defection, and the means of controlling and perpetuating that industrial harmony which arose from the control and maintenance of prices.

It inevitably follows that the corporation violated the law in its formation and by its immediate practices. * * *

* * *

I agree that the act offers no objection to the mere size of a corporation, nor to the continued exertion of its lawful power, when that size and power have been obtained by lawful means and developed by natural growth, although its resources, capital and strength may give to such corporation a dominating place in the business and industry with which it is concerned. * * * But I understand the reiterated decisions of this court construing the Sherman Act to hold that this power may not legally be derived from conspiracies, combinations, or contracts in restraint of trade. * * * Trans-Missouri Freight Assn. Case; Northern Securities Case; Addyston Pipe Co. v. United States. While it was not the purpose of the act to condemn normal and usual contracts to lawfully expand business and further legitimate trade, it did intend to effectively reach and control all conspiracies and combinations or contracts of whatever form which unduly restrain competition and unduly obstruct the natural course of trade, or which from their nature, or effect, have proved effectual to restrain interstate commerce. Standard Oil Co. v. United States; United States v. American Tobacco Co.

This statute has been in force for nearly 30 years. * * * [T]he nature and character of the relief to be granted against combinations found guilty of violations of it have been the subject of much consideration. Its interpretation has become a part of the law itself, and, if changes are to be made now in its construction or operation, it seems to me that the exertion of such authority rests with Congress and not with the courts.

* * *

It is said that a complete monopolization of the steel business was never attained by the offending combinations. To insist upon such result would be beyond the requirements of the statute and in most cases practicably impossible. As we said in dealing with the Packers' combination in Swift & Co. v. United States: " * * * [When] intent [to monopolize] and the consequent dangerous probability exist, this statute, like many others and like the common law in some cases, directs itself against that dangerous probability as well as against the completed result."

* * * We have here a combination in control of one-half of the steel business of the country. If the plan were followed, as in the *American Tobacco* Case, of remanding the case to the District Court, a decree might be framed restoring competitive conditions as far as practicable. * * * In my judgment the principles there laid down if followed now would make a very material difference in the steel industry. Instead of one dominating corporation, with scattered competitors, there would be competitive conditions throughout the whole trade which would carry into effect the policy of the law.

* * *

MR. JUSTICE PITNEY and MR. JUSTICE CLARKE concur in this dissent.

NOTES AND QUESTIONS

1.   *Standard Oil* had announced the rule of reason but had found the defendant's practices illegal. *Board of Trade* showed a defendant could win a § 1 case under the rule of reason; this case illustrates the same result under § 2. Why do you suppose the government brought this case? What was the situation in the steel industry the Justice Department observed in 1911?[4]

---

[4]   The U.S. Steel combination was the work of J.P. Morgan; that's right, he was one of the defendants in *Northern Securities*. This "super-combination" of almost 200 companies was overwhelmingly large even in a period of rapid consolidation. See, e.g., Hans B. Thorelli, The Federal Antitrust Policy: Origination of an American Tradition 285–308 (1954). Perhaps ironically, however, the decision by President Taft (the author of *Addyston Pipe*) to charge U.S. Steel was not politically popular. It appeared to be an attack on one of the country's most successful industries, and it is sometimes cited as a factor in Woodrow Wilson's defeat of Taft in 1912. See William Kolasky, The Election of 1912: A Pivotal Moment in Antitrust History, 25 Antitrust 82 (Summer 2011).

2. Is this 4–3 decision in fact consistent with *Standard Oil*? What does the majority (Chief Justice White, and Justices Van Devanter, Holmes & McKenna) seem to believe are the elements of the offense of monopolization?

a. What does the majority mean when it says: "The power attained was much greater than that possessed by any one competitor—it was not greater than that possessed by all of them. Monopoly, therefore, was not achieved." Does it mean that, by definition, a firm with less than a 50% market share cannot "monopolize" an industry within the meaning of § 2?

b. What is the significance of the assertion that a corporation's possession of market power is not a measure of whether it monopolizes an industry? Does that mean that proof of "exertion of the power" is essential in any § 2 case? Would that be the functional equivalent of saying that if a cartel fixes a reasonable price, there is no violation of § 1?

c. What would you advise a client would constitute improper "exertion" of size and power? Negotiating a labor agreement paying lower wages than competitors pay? Creating a new, lower-quality line of products? Requiring its dealers to sign resale price maintenance agreements? Each of these is mentioned by the Court in this opinion; do you agree that any of them implicate the concerns underlying § 2?

3. How do the dissenters characterize what happened here? Indeed, does even the majority agree that U.S. Steel probably exploited its market position for high profits as long as it was able, while trying at the same time to slow its loss of market share?

a. Do you agree with the dissenters that one should not have expected competitors to complain about an arrangement which contributed to their wealth as well? Did they likely come to the Gary Dinners solely because the food was good? See William H. Page, The Gary Dinners and the Meaning of Concerted Action, 62 SMU L.Rev. 597 (2009).

b. Do you agree with the dissenters that once a firm has been shown to have grown or maintained its size improperly, the appropriate remedy is dissolution? Otherwise, could a firm such as U.S. Steel be said to "get away with" a violation of the Act?

4. Is the division between majority and dissent primarily about whether dissolution of U.S. Steel would do more harm than good? Do you agree that at least some division of U.S. Steel into smaller entities could have been accomplished with relatively little loss of efficiency? Do you agree that the defendant's market share was now small enough that risking injury to its efficient operation was not justified by whatever symbolic benefits might have been expected?

A NOTE ON *EASTMAN KODAK v. SOUTHERN PHOTO MATERIALS*

Section 2 was not entirely moribund in the 1920s and 30s, in spite of *U.S. Steel*. One case identifying alleged "bad practices" of a market-leading firm was Eastman Kodak Co. v. Southern Photo Materials, 273 U.S. 359, 47 S.Ct. 400, 71 L.Ed. 684 (1927).

The plaintiff was a retail dealer in Atlanta that sold film and other supplies to photographers in several southern states. Kodak had allegedly purchased both competing manufacturers of such supplies and the dealers through which they had distributed their products. Kodak had also allegedly imposed requirements for resale price maintenance on its own dealers and restrictions on handling competing goods.

In 1910, the plaintiff alleged, Kodak tried to buy it out. When the plaintiff refused to sell, Kodak refused to grant it the discount given to other dealers and required it to pay full retail prices for Kodak supplies. No other sources of Kodak products were available, the plaintiff said, and as a result the profits of its business were much lower than they otherwise would have been. The Supreme Court unanimously affirmed a jury verdict for the plaintiff. The issue was one of Kodak's motive, the Court said, and on such a question, the jury's verdict was conclusive.

a.   What do you think of this result? Is it consistent with *U.S. Steel*? Does it make sense to distinguish good economic behavior from bad based on the psychology of the actors?

b.   Can the distinction between "good" firms and "bad" ones be used effectively by lawyers in counseling their clients?

c.   How might a firm fearful of an adverse jury's verdict tend to behave after this case? Are the incentives it would have necessarily desirable for consumers? Might the rule asserted here tend to discourage innovation and vigorous competitive conduct that would increase the firm's sales and lower prices? Might any other social values justify such consequences?

B. THE TRADE ASSOCIATION CASES

The price fixing cases we looked at from the pre-1914 period—*Trans-Missouri* and *Addyston Pipe*—clearly involved attempts to establish specific prices. Often, however, the first step in cases is even characterizing the parties' conduct as price fixing.

The activities of the firms in *Board of Trade* required characterization, as did those of the firms in this section. The cases involve the activities of trade associations. At their best, such associations give small firms the benefits of research, marketing, and the like, that might otherwise come only from consolidation into larger firms. In other situations, however, trade associations might be seen as little more than sophisticated cartels.

AMERICAN COLUMN & LUMBER COMPANY V. UNITED STATES

Supreme Court of the United States, 1921
257 U.S. 377, 42 S.Ct. 114, 66 L.Ed. 284

MR. JUSTICE CLARKE delivered the opinion of the Court.

The unincorporated "American Hardwood Manufacturers' Association" was formed in December, 1918, * * * [and adopted an] "Open Competition Plan" * * * .

Participation in the Plan was optional with the members of the Association, but, at the time this suit was commenced, of its 400 members, 365, operating 465 mills, were members of the Plan. The importance and strength of the Association are shown by the [fact] * * * that while the defendants operated only five per cent of the number of mills engaged in hardwood manufacture in the country, they produced one-third of the total production of the United States. The places of business of the * * * members of the Plan, were located in many states from New York to Texas, but chiefly in the hardwood producing territory of the Southwest. The defendants are the members of the Plan, * * * and F. R. Gadd, its "Manager of Statistics."

The bill alleged, in substance, that the Plan constituted a combination and conspiracy to restrain interstate commerce in hardwood lumber by restricting competition and maintaining and increasing prices * * * .

The answer denied that the Plan had any such purpose and effect as charged, and averred that it promoted competition, especially among its own members.

A temporary injunction, granted by the District Court, restricting the activities of the Plan in specified respects, by consent of the parties was made permanent and a direct appeal brings the case here for review.

The activities which we shall see were comprehended within the "Open Competition Plan," * * * have come to be widely adopted in our country * * * .

There is very little dispute as to the facts. * * *

The record shows that the Plan was evolved by a committee, which, in recommending its adoption, said:

> "The purpose of this plan is to disseminate among members accurate knowledge of production and market conditions so that each member may gauge the market intelligently instead of guessing at it; to make competition open and above board instead

of secret and concealed; to substitute, in estimating market conditions, frank and full statements of our competitors for the frequently misleading and colored statements of the buyer."

* * *

* * * [A] further explanation of the objects and purposes of the Plan was made in an appeal to members to join it, in which it is said:

"The theoretical proposition at the basis of the Open Competition plan is that knowledge regarding prices actually made is all that is necessary to keep prices at reasonably stable and normal levels.

"The Open Competition plan is a central clearing house for information on prices, trade statistics and practices. By keeping all members fully and quickly informed of what the others have done, the work of the plan results in a certain uniformity of trade practice. There is no agreement to follow the practice of others, although members do naturally follow their most intelligent competitors, if they know what these competitors have been actually doing."

* * *

And in another later, and somewhat similar, appeal sent to all the members, this is found:

"Competition, blind, vicious, unreasoning, may stimulate trade to abnormal activity but such condition is no more sound than that medieval spirit some still cling to of taking a club and going out and knocking the other fellow and taking away his bone.

"The keynote to modern business success is mutual confidence and co-operation. Co-operative Competition, not Cut-throat Competition. Co-operation is a matter of business because it pays, because it enables you to get the best price for your product, because you come into closer personal contact with the market.

"Co-operation will only replace undesirable competition as you develop a co-operative spirit. For the first time in the history of the industry, the hardwood manufacturers are organized into one compact, comprehensive body, equipped to serve the whole trade in a thorough and efficient manner. * * * With co-operation of this kind we will very soon have enlisted in our efforts practically every producing interest, and you know what that means."

Thus, the Plan proposed a system of cooperation among the members, consisting of the interchange of reports of sales, prices, production, and practices, and in meetings of the members for discussion, for the avowed purpose of substituting "Co-operative Competition" for "Cut-throat Competition," of keeping "prices at reasonably stable and normal levels," and of improving the "human relations" among the members. But the purpose to agree upon prices or production was always disclaimed.

* * *

[The Plan] required each member to make six reports to the secretary, viz:

1.   A *daily* report of all sales actually made, with the name and address of the purchaser, the kind, grade and quality of lumber sold and all special agreements of every kind, verbal or written with respect thereto. "These reports are to be exact copies of orders taken."

2.   A *daily* shipping report, with exact copies of the invoices, all special agreements as to terms, grade, etc. The classification shall be the same as with sales.

3.   A *monthly* production report, showing the production of the member reporting during the previous month, with the grades and thickness classified as prescribed in the Plan.

4.   A *monthly* stock report by each member, showing the stock on hand on the first day of the month, sold and unsold, green and dry, with the total of each kind, grade and thickness.

5.   Price-lists. Members must file at the beginning of each month price-lists showing prices f.o.b. shipping point, which shall be stated. New prices must be filed with the association as soon as made.

6.   Inspection reports. These reports are to be made to the association by a service of its own, established for the purpose of checking up grades of the various members and the Plan provides for a chief inspector and sufficient assistants to inspect the stocks of all members from time to time.

* * *

All of these reports by members are subject to complete audit by representatives of the association. Any member who fails to report *shall not receive the reports* of the secretary * * * .

Plainly it would be very difficult to devise a more minute disclosure of everything connected with one's business than is here provided for by this Plan and very certainly only the most attractive prospect could induce any man to make it to his rivals and competitors.

But, since such voluminous disclosures to the secretary would be valueless unless communicated to the members in a condensed and interpreted form * * * :

The secretary is required to send to each member:

1.   A *monthly* summary showing the production of each member for the previous month, "subdivided as to grade, kind, thickness," etc.

2.   A *weekly* report, not later than Saturday, of all sales, to and including the preceding Tuesday, giving each sale and the price, and the name of the purchaser.

3.   On Tuesday of each week the secretary must send to each member a report of each shipment by each member, complete up to the evening of the preceding Thursday.

4.   He must send a *monthly* report, showing the individual stock on hand of each member and a summary of all stocks, green and dry, sold and unsold. This report is very aptly referred to by the managing statistician as a monthly inventory of the stock of each member.

5.   Not later than the 10th of each month the secretary shall send a summary of the price-lists furnished by members, showing the prices asked by each, and any changes made therein must be immediately transmitted to all the members.

6.   A market report letter shall be sent to each member of the association (whether participating in the Plan or not) pointing "out changes in conditions both in the producing and consuming sections, giving a comparison of production and sales and in general an analysis of the market conditions."

7.   Meetings shall be held once a month at Cincinnati "or at points to be agreed upon by the members." "It is intended that the regular meetings shall afford opportunity for the discussion of all subjects of interest to the members."

* * *

This extensive interchange of reports, supplemented as it was by monthly meetings at which an opportunity was afforded for discussion "of all subjects of interest to the members," very certainly constituted an organization through which agreements, actual or implied, could readily be arrived at and maintained, if the members desired to make them.

Such, in outline, was the paper plan adopted by the association, but elaborate though it was, in practice three important additions were made to it.

First of all, the Southwestern territory for meeting purposes was divided into four districts, and instead of the monthly meeting provided for in the Plan, "in order that members could more conveniently attend," the record shows that 49 of these meetings were held between January 31, 1919, and February 19, 1920,—approximately one for each week, in some part of the territory.

Second. Before each of these meetings a questionnaire was sent out to the members, and from the replies received, supplementing the other reports, the statistician compiled an estimate of the condition of the market, actual and prospective, which was distributed to the members attending each meeting, and was mailed to those not present. There were eleven questions on this list of which the most important were:

> "(4)   What was your total production of hardwood during the last month? What do you estimate your production will probably be for the next two months?"

> "(10) Do you expect to shut down within the next few months on account of shortage of logs or for any other reason? If so, please state how long you will be idle."

> "(11) What is your view of market conditions for the next few months and what is the general outlook for business? State the reasons for your conclusion."

The Plan on paper provided only for reports of past transactions and much is made of this in the record and in argument—that reporting to one another past transactions cannot fix prices for the future. But each of these three questions plainly invited an estimate and discussion of future market conditions by each member, and a coordination of them by an expert analyst could readily evolve an attractive basis for cooperative, even if unexpressed, "harmony" with respect to future prices.

Third. The Plan provided for a monthly "market report letter" to go to all members of the association. In practice this market report letter was prepared by F.R. Gadd, manager of statistics, but his review of the market and forecast for the future were contained, almost from the beginning, not only in these market letters but also in the weekly sales reports, so that they were sent out to all of the members 19 times between February 1 and December 6, 1919, and they were discussed at all but one or two of the 49 meetings which were held. All the activities of the Plan plainly culminated in the counsels contained in these letters and reports.

* * * It is plain that the only element lacking in this scheme to make it a familiar type of the competition suppressing organization is a definite agreement as to production and prices. But this is supplied: by the disposition of men "to follow their most intelligent competitors," especially when powerful; by the inherent disposition to make all the money possible,

joined with the steady cultivation of the value of "harmony" of action; and by the system of reports, which makes the discovery of price reductions inevitable and immediate. The sanctions of the plan obviously are, financial interest, intimate personal contact, and business honor, all operating under the restraint of exposure of what would be deemed bad faith and of trade punishment by powerful rivals.

* * *

Obviously, the organization of the defendants constitutes a combination and confessedly they are engaged in a large way in the transportation and sale of lumber in interstate commerce so that there remains for decision only the question whether the system of doing business adopted resulted in that direct and undue restraint of interstate commerce which is condemned by [the] anti-trust statute.

* * *

In the first quarter of the year the problem was to maintain the war prices then prevailing rather than to advance them, and although the minutes of the various meetings were kept in barest outline, we find that * * * the members of the Plan began actively to cooperate, through the meetings, to suppress competition by restricting production. * * *

* * *

[In a market letter, Mr. Gadd] quotes from an editorial in the Southern Lumberman, in which, among other things, it is said:

"The danger which we see lurking in the future for the lumber industry is overproduction. When the demand for lumber is keen and the prices are good * * * [t]he desire to cash in while the cashing is good is natural and easy to understand; but every sawmill man who contemplates putting on a night shift should stop long enough to reflect on the past history of the lumber business. * * * Overproduction has always been the curse of the lumber industry in America. It has caused more trouble and hardship than any other one factor. It would be criminal folly, therefore, for the lumber manufacturers to indulge themselves in any such form of commercial suicide." * * *

The managing statistician of the association significantly adds:

"Are we guilty? If so, the warning is timely."

* * *

Much more of like purport appears in the minutes of the meetings throughout the year, but this is sufficient to convincingly show that one of the prime purposes of the meetings, held in every part of the lumber district, and of the various reports, was to induce members to cooperate in

restricting production, thereby keeping the supply low and the prices high
* * * . The cooperation is palpable and avowed, its purpose is clear, and we
shall see that it was completely realized.

Next, the record shows clearly that the members of the combination
were not satisfied to secure, each for himself, the price which might be
obtainable even as the result of cooperative restriction of production, but
that throughout the year they assiduously cultivated, through the letters
of Gadd, speaking for them all, and through the discussions at the
meetings, the general conviction that higher and higher prices were
obtainable and a disposition on the part of all to demand them. * * *

* * *

* * * Men in general are so easily persuaded to do that which will
obviously prove profitable that this reiterated opinion from the analyst of
their association, with all obtainable data before him, that higher prices
were justified and could easily be obtained, must inevitably have resulted,
as it did result, in concert of action in demanding them.

But not only does the record thus show a persistent purpose to
encourage members to unite in pressing for higher and higher prices,
without regard to cost, but there are many admissions by members, not
only that this was the purpose of the Plan, but that it was fully realized.

Within four months of the consolidation, on April 23, 1919, the
Manager of Statistics wrote to members asking each to write him "his
experience with the Plan" and any incidents showing benefits derived from
it.

The replies to this letter are significant confessions. One writes:

> "All those who have access to your reports bring their prices
> to the top."

Another:

> "There seems to be a friendly rivalry among members to see
> who can get the best prices, whereas, under the old plan it was cut
> throat competition."

Another:

> "It has kept us in touch closely with the market and in many
> instances has made us one or more dollars per thousand feet on
> lumber that we have sold and we believe that the plan is going to
> be very successful in carrying out the purposes for which it is
> intended."

* * *

These quotations are sufficient to show beyond discussion that the
purpose of the organization and especially of the frequent meetings was to

bring about a concerted effort to raise prices regardless of cost or merit, and so was unlawful, and that the members were soon entirely satisfied that the Plan was "carrying out the purpose for which it was intended."

As to the price conditions during the year: Without going into detail the record shows that the prices of the grades of hardwood in most general use were increased to an unprecedented extent during the year. Thus, the increases in prices of varieties of oak range from 33.3% to 296% during the year; of gum, 60% to 343%, and of ash, from 55% to 181%. While it is true that 1919 was a year of high and increasing prices generally and that wet weather may have restricted production to some extent, we cannot but agree with the members of the Plan themselves * * * that the united action of this large and influential membership of dealers contributed greatly to this extraordinary price increase.

Such close co-operation, between many persons, firms, and corporations controlling a large volume of interstate commerce, as is provided for in this Plan, is plainly in theory, as it proved to be in fact, inconsistent with that free and unrestricted trade which the statute contemplates shall be maintained; and that the persons conducting the association fully realized this is apparent from their * * * repeated insistence that the Sherman Law "designed to prevent the restraint of trade is itself one of the greatest restrainers of trade, and should be repealed."

To call the activities of the defendants, as they are proved in this record, an "Open Competition Plan" of action is plainly a misleading misnomer.

Genuine competitors do not make daily, weekly and monthly reports of the minutest details of their business to their rivals, as the defendants did; * * * and they do not submit the details of their business to the analysis of an expert, jointly employed, and obtain from him a "harmonized" estimate of the market as it is and as, in his specially and confidentially informed judgment, it promises to be. This is not the conduct of competitors but is * * * clearly that of men united in an agreement, express or implied, to act together and pursue a common purpose under a common guide * * * . To pronounce such abnormal conduct on the part of 365 natural competitors, controlling one-third of the trade of the country in an article of prime necessity, a "new form of competition" and not an old form of combination in restraint of trade, as it so plainly is, would be for this court to confess itself blinded by words and forms to realities which men in general very plainly see and understand and condemn, as an old evil in a new dress and with a new name.

The Plan is, essentially, simply an expansion of the gentlemen's agreement of former days, skillfully devised to evade the law. To call it open competition because the meetings were nominally open to the public, * * * or because no specific agreement to restrict trade or fix prices is proved, cannot conceal the fact that the fundamental purpose of the Plan was to procure "harmonious" individual action among a large number of naturally competing dealers with respect to the volume of production and prices, * * * and to rely for maintenance of concerted action in both respects, not upon fines and forfeitures as in earlier days, but upon what experience has shown to be the more potent and dependable restraints of business honor and social penalties—cautiously reinforced by many and elaborate reports which would promptly expose to his associates any disposition in any member to deviate from the tacit understanding that all were to act together under the subtle direction of a single interpreter of their common purposes * * * .

In the presence of this record it is futile to argue that the purpose of the Plan was simply to furnish those engaged in this industry, with widely scattered units, the equivalent of such information as is contained in the newspaper and government publications with respect to the market for commodities sold on boards of trade or stock exchanges. One distinguishing and sufficient difference is that the published reports go to both seller and buyer, but these reports go to the seller only; and another is that there is no skilled interpreter of the published reports, such as we have in this case, to insistently recommend harmony of action likely to prove profitable in proportion as it is unitedly pursued.

Convinced, as we are, that the purpose and effect of the activities of the Open Competition Plan, here under discussion, were to restrict competition and thereby restrain interstate commerce in the manufacture and sale of hardwood lumber by concerted action in curtailing production and in increasing prices, we agree with the District Court that it constituted a combination and conspiracy in restraint of interstate commerce within the meaning of the Anti-Trust Act of 1890 and the decree of that court must be

Affirmed.

MR. JUSTICE HOLMES, dissenting.

When there are competing sellers of a class of goods, knowledge of the total stock on hand, of the probable total demand, and of the prices paid, of course will tend to equalize the prices asked. But I should have supposed that the Sherman Act did not set itself against knowledge—did not aim at a transitory cheapness unprofitable to the community as a whole because not corresponding to the actual conditions of the country. I should have thought that the ideal of commerce was an intelligent interchange made with full knowledge of the facts as a basis for a forecast of the future on both sides. A combination to get and distribute such knowledge, notwithstanding its tendency to equalize, not necessarily to raise, prices, is very far from a combination in unreasonable restraint of trade. * * * A combination in unreasonable restraint of trade imports an attempt to override normal market conditions. An attempt to conform to them seems to me the most reasonable thing in the world. I see nothing in the conduct of the appellants that binds the members even by merely social sanctions to anything that would not be practiced, if we could imagine it, by an allwise socialistic government acting for the benefit of the community as a whole. * * *

I must add that the decree as it stands seems to me surprising in a country of free speech that affects to regard education and knowledge as desirable. It prohibits the distribution of stock, production, or sales reports, the discussion of prices at association meetings, and the exchange of predictions of high prices. It is true that these acts are the main evidence of the supposed conspiracy, but that to my mind only shows the weakness of the Government's case. I cannot believe that the fact, if it be assumed, that the acts have been done with a sinister purpose, justifies excluding mills in the backwoods from information, in order to enable centralized purchasers to take advantage of their ignorance of the facts.

I agree with the more elaborate discussion of the case by my Brother Brandeis.

MR. JUSTICE BRANDEIS dissenting, with whom MR. JUSTICE MCKENNA concurs.

There are more than 9,000 hardwood lumber mills in that part of the United States which lies east of a line extending from Minnesota to Texas. Three hundred and sixty-five concerns—each separate and independent— are members of an association by means of which they cooperate under the so-called "Open Competition Plan." * * * The question presented for our decision is whether the Open Competition Plan either inherently or as practiced by these concerns violates the Sherman Law. * * *

Restraint of trade may be exerted upon rivals; upon buyers or upon sellers; upon employers or upon employed. Restraint may be exerted through force or fraud or agreement. It may be exerted through moral or through legal obligations; through fear or through hope. It may exist although it is not manifested in any overt act, and even though there is no intent to restrain. Words of advice seemingly innocent and perhaps benevolent, may restrain, when uttered under circumstances that make advice equivalent to command. For the essence of restraint is power; and power may arise merely out of position. Wherever a dominant position has been attained, restraint necessarily arises. And when dominance is attained, or is sought, through combination—however good the motives or the manners of those participating—the Sherman Law is violated; provided, of course, that the restraint be what is called unreasonable.

In the case before us there was clearly no coercion. There is no claim that a monopoly was sought or created. There is no claim that a division of territory was planned or secured. There is no claim that uniform prices were established or desired. There is no claim that by agreement, force, or fraud, any producer, dealer or consumer was to be or has in fact been controlled or coerced. * * * No information gathered under the Plan was kept secret from any producer, any buyer or the public. Ever since its inception in 1917, a copy of every report made and of every market letter published has been filed with the Department of Justice, and with the Federal Trade Commission. The district meetings were open to the public. Dealers and consumers were invited to participate in the discussions and to some extent have done so.

It is claimed that the purpose of the Open Competition Plan was to lessen competition. Competition among members was contemplated and was in vigorous operation. The Sherman Law does not prohibit every lessening of competition; and it certainly does not command that competition shall be pursued blindly, that business rivals shall remain ignorant of trade facts or be denied aid in weighing their significance. * * * The hardwood lumber mills are widely scattered. The principal area of production is the Southern States. But there are mills in Minnesota, New York, New England and the Middle States. Most plants are located near the sources of supply; isolated, remote from the larger cities and from the principal markets. No official, or other public, means have been established for collecting from these mills and from dealers data as to current production, stocks on hand and market prices. Concerning grain, cotton, coal and oil, the government collects and publishes regularly, at frequent intervals, current information on production, consumption and stocks on hand; and boards of trade furnish freely to the public details of current market prices of those commodities, the volume of sales, and even individual sales, as recorded in daily transactions. Persons interested in such commodities are enabled through this information to deal with one another on an equal footing. The absence of such information in the hardwood lumber trade enables dealers in the large centers more readily to secure advantage over the isolated producer. And the large concerns, which are able to establish their own bureaus of statistics, secure an advantage over smaller concerns. Surely it is not against the public interest to distribute knowledge of trade facts, however detailed. * * * Intelligent conduct of business implies not only knowledge of trade facts, but an understanding of them. To this understanding editorial comment and free discussion by those engaged in the business and by others interested are aids. Opinions expressed may be unsound; predictions may be unfounded; but there is nothing in the Sherman Law which should limit freedom of discussion, even among traders.

It is insisted that there was a purpose to curtail production. No evidence of any such purpose was introduced. There was at no time uniformity in the percentage of production to capacity. On the contrary the evidence is uncontradicted that the high prices induced strenuous efforts to increase production. * * * There were, it is true, from time to time, warnings in the "Market Letters" and otherwise, against overproduction— warnings which seem not to have been heeded. But surely Congress did not intend by the Sherman Act to prohibit self-restraint—and it was for self-restraint that the only appeal was made. The purpose of the warnings was to induce mill owners to curb their greed—lest both they and others suffer from the crushing evils of overproduction. Such warning or advice whether given by individuals or the representatives of an association presents no element of illegality.

It is urged that this was a concerted effort to enhance prices. There was at no time uniformity in prices. So far as appears every mill charged for its product as much as it could get. * * * It may be that the distribution of the trade data, the editorial comment and the conferences enabled the producers to obtain, on the average, higher prices than would otherwise have been possible. But there is nothing in the Sherman Law to indicate that Congress intended to condemn cooperative action in the exchange of information, merely because prophecy resulting from comment on the data collected may lead, for a period, to higher marketing prices. * * * [Congress'] purpose, obviously, was not to prevent the making of profits or to counteract the operation of the law of supply and demand. Its purpose was merely to prevent restraint. The illegality of a combination under the Sherman Law lies not in its effect upon the price level, but in the coercion thereby effected. * * *

The co-operation which is incident to this Plan does not suppress competition. On the contrary it tends to promote all in competition which is desirable. By substituting knowledge for ignorance, rumor, guess and suspicion, it tends also to substitute research and reasoning for gambling and piracy, without closing the door to adventure or lessening the value of prophetic wisdom. In making such knowledge available to the smallest concern it creates among producers equality of opportunity. In making it available also to purchasers and the general public, it does all that can actually be done to protect the community from extortion. * * *

The refusal to permit a multitude of small rivals to cooperate, as they have done here, in order to protect themselves and the public from the chaos and havoc wrought in their trade by ignorance, may result in suppressing competition in the hardwood industry. These keen business rivals, who sought through cooperative exchange of trade information to create conditions under which alone rational competition is possible, produce in the aggregate about one-third of the hardwood lumber of the country. This court held in United States v. United States Steel Corporation that it was not unlawful to vest in a single corporation control of 50 per cent of the steel industry of the country * * * . May not these hardwood lumber concerns, frustrated in their efforts to rationalize competition, be led to enter the inviting field of consolidation? And if they do, may not another huge trust with highly centralized control over vast resources, natural, manufacturing and financial, become so powerful as to dominate competitors, wholesalers, retailers, consumers, employees and, in large measure, the community?

NOTES AND QUESTIONS

1.   Trade associations have long been important clients of antitrust counselors. Inevitably, such associations are composed of competitors who come together for reasons of mutual interest. Where did the American Hardwood Association go wrong?

a.   Was it improper for Mr. Gadd to write a newsletter column urging members not to expand their production in response to the increase in post-war prices? Was it the call for a "cooperative spirit" that was illegal? Do you agree with Justice Holmes that making such advocacy illegal would be inconsistent with First Amendment principles?

b.   Was the "smoking gun" here the Association's own claim to have brought increased profits to its members? Should that constitute proof of wrongdoing? Should the accuracy of the claim have to be proved? Did the letters from satisfied members seem to you to be "confessions" of Association misconduct? Was their distribution any more than the "puffing" any group might do in trying to recruit more dues-paying members?

c.   Was intent to restrain trade evidenced by the fact that "the persons conducting the association * * * [repeatedly insisted] that the Sherman Law 'designed to prevent the restraint of trade is itself one of the greatest restrainers of trade and should be repealed' "? Is it normally a crime to express criticism of a federal statute?

2.   What is the economic impact of making more information available to participants in a market? Does information have inherently anticompetitive effects?

a.   What would an economic model assume about what buyers and sellers know? Could one have theoretically "perfect" competition without complete information about the choices the consumer faces? Does it then follow that each increment of accurate information makes the competitive process more nearly perfect?

b.   Was the problem here that the information went to the sellers but not to buyers? Was that in fact true? Did Justice Brandeis satisfy you on this point when he pointed out that meetings were open and both the Justice Department and the Federal Trade Commission were on Mr. Gadd's mailing list?

3.   Was the problem the *kind* of information involved here?

a.   Was all the information equally suspect? Was the monthly report of past production, for example, as consistent with the theory of collusive behavior as the "daily report of all sales actually made"? Why?

b.   Was there something about the information involved here that made it different from the information exchanged about other commodities on the Chicago Board of Trade? Did the Court convince you that it was Mr. Gadd's editorial comments that made the difference?

c.   Would any of the information regularly exchanged here have been a problem in the absence of the district meetings and the questionnaires filled out in advance of each? Can you tell from this opinion whether an exchange of information would be upheld if it were less pervasive than the one involved here? How much less?

4.   Was it relevant here that 365 firms were members of the Plan? That roughly 8000 firms in the industry were *not* members?

a.   How significant should it have been that the members here produced $1/3$ of the nation's hardwood? The Court thought that was a large proportion. Justice Brandeis, however, reminds us that in *U.S. Steel* (decided the preceding year) the Court assumed that a single firm with less than 50% of the market could not exercise monopoly power. Was this diverse an association of firms *more* likely to be able to do so?

b.   Is Justice Brandeis' passion here explained by his long-standing concern to make it possible for small business to survive and prosper? Indeed, is he not right that absent this ability to exchange information, there might be an incentive for firms to consolidate into fewer, larger entities? Should the desire to allow firms to operate efficiently without consolidation affect the Court's reaction to information exchanges such as the one here?

c.   If you had been a member of this Plan, would you have believed it would be possible to cut your output and raise your price with confidence your competitors were doing the same thing? Was there anything about the information Mr. Gadd provided that would tend to increase such confidence? What in particular might do so?

A NOTE ON THE BROADER PROBLEM
OF DEALING WITH OLIGOPOLY

The suspicion that a conspiracy was implicit in *American Column* is part of a broader concern among antitrust enforcers that firms sometimes may be collectively reducing their output and raising their prices even when not formally meeting in ways that would obviously violate the law. Unless we can reach these "implicit" cartels, some believe, the Antitrust Division and FTC will be unable to address an important anticompetitive evil.

Do you agree? Remember the problems even overt conspirators must overcome to have a successful cartel. They must reach agreement on common objectives and methods, and they must have a way to assure that others in the industry are acting in compliance with the plan instead of cheating on the rest of them. Doing all that without directly communicating magnifies those problems, and in an industry with a large number of firms, "implicit" agreement would be almost impossible.

The Berle-Douglas Account of Oligopoly Pricing

"Oligopoly," however, is the term often used to describe an industry with relatively few firms, an industry in which such an implicit agreement might work. In a much later case, Justice Douglas quoted A.A. Berle's description of how large firms engage in a system of what he called "price control":

> " * * * The three or four 'bigs' in any particular line are happy to stay with a good price level for their product. If the price gets too high, some smart vice president in charge of sales may see a chance to take a fat slice of business away from his competitors.

> "But while any one of the two or three bigs knows he can reduce prices and start taking all the business there is, he knows, too, that one or all of his associates will soon drop the price below that. In the ensuing price war, nobody will make money for quite a while.

> "So, an uneasy balance is struck, and everyone's price remains about the same. Shop around for an automobile and you will see how this works. Economists call it 'imperfect competition'—a tacitly accepted price that is not necessarily the price a stiff competitive free market would create. * * * "[5]

Are you convinced by this account? Is it obvious how the firms get the price above a competitive level in the first place? Is it obvious how the "uneasy balance is struck" if no one can communicate directly?

The Cournot Model of How Oligopoly Pricing Might Work

Analysis of oligopoly pricing is not new. Much of it is based on work of Augustin Cournot in the early 19th Century,[6] but it has been further developed over the years by game theorists such as John Nash.[7]

Imagine that you are producing in a two-firm industry. Your competitor has production costs similar to your own. You know the price and output that would maximize your profits, i.e., the production level you

---

[5]   Fn. 8 in Simpson v. Union Oil, 377 U.S. 13, 84 S.Ct. 1051, 12 L.Ed.2d 98 (1964), quoting A.A. Berle, Bigness: Curse or Opportunity? New York Times Magazine, Feb. 18, 1962, pp. 18, 55, 58.

[6]   Augustin Cournot, Studies in the Mathematical Principles of the Theory of Wealth (1838).

[7]   E.g., John F. Nash, Jr., Noncooperative Games, 54 Annals of Mathematics 286 (1951). If the Nash name sounds familiar, he won the Nobel Prize for Economics in 1994, and his life was the subject of the book and later film *A Beautiful Mind* (2001).

would set if you did not have to worry about your competitor selling for less. You produce that output and set that price. What will your competitor do?

Cournot said the competitor would recognize that it too would benefit from the reduced output and higher price. The two of you would not be required to meet together to reach this conclusion; the competitor simply would not rock the boat. That might be particularly true if you and your competitor had factories of finite size that would be costly to expand or some comparable basis for confidence that the other would not suddenly expand output and begin a price war.

The point made by Cournot, and developed by Nash and other game-theorists, is that price and output decisions are rarely wholly unilateral; they are inevitably made in anticipation of decisions that might be made by others. The more firms there are in an industry and the smaller any given firm's share of the output, of course, the harder it will be for any firm to anticipate all the others' moves. Thus, under those conditions, prices will tend to move toward a competitive level. Even then, however, one can imagine market participants evolving strategies to slow price declines, e.g., by promising to meet competitors' lower prices in order to discourage any given competitor from lowering its price.[8]

Professor Turner's Skepticism About Prohibiting Oligopoly Pricing

Even if firms unquestionably consider other firms' possible reactions when they set their prices, however, it does not follow that the antitrust laws can or should prohibit the behavior. There is no multi-firm agreement, for example, so under Sherman Act § 1, it is hard to characterize such conduct as a "contract, combination or conspiracy."

Furthermore, Professor Donald Turner argued in an important article,[9] enforcement agencies and courts have no practical basis for distinguishing "price coordination" behavior of oligopolists from the same firms' "competitive" behavior. Basically, in both cases, the firms would set their prices at what they saw as their profit maximizing point, without consultation with their competitors. Their prices would be "interdependent," i.e., set with regard to what they believed their competitors would do, but as we have seen, *every* firm necessarily so prices.

Even if oligopoly theory explains why prices seem high in some industries, then, Professor Turner argued that there would be no facts to put before a jury that would not be equally consistent with innocent conduct. Furthermore, at the remedy stage of such a case, the court could

---

[8] The literature on oligopoly pricing is too complex to pursue here. Good accounts of it are provided, however, in Herbert Hovenkamp, Federal Antitrust Policy: The Law of Competition and its Practice 159–165 (3rd ed. 2005); Keith N. Hylton, Antitrust Law: Economic Theory & Common Law Evolution 21–22, 76–77, 83–85 (2003).

[9] Donald F. Turner, "The Definition of Agreement Under the Sherman Act: Conscious Parallelism and Refusals to Deal," 75 Harvard L. Rev. 655 (1962).

not come up with a description of how it would want the firms to price. The firms could not be required to ignore the pricing behavior of the others, in short, without making even a competitive price impossible to achieve.

Professor Turner's concern, in short, was consistent with what we earlier called a Type 1 error.[10] Such an error both leads to the unjust conviction of an innocent party and can discourage competitive conduct that is beneficial to the public as a whole. Antitrust law is the wrong weapon, Professor Turner argued, with which to deal with whatever problem oligopoly industries present.

Judge Posner's Efforts to Specify When Antitrust Intervention Might Be Appropriate

As a professor and later as a judge, Richard Posner has taken the problem of identifying and dealing with oligopoly as seriously as any prominent writer in recent years. He argues that it would be better to deal with the oligopoly problem directly, if there is such a problem, rather than indirectly, as you will see we often do by preventing mergers or requiring dissolution of monopoly firms.[11] And, he believes, the courts can properly find an illegal Sherman Act § 1 "conspiracy" even in the absence of a face-to-face agreement.

In order to distinguish "wrongful" from "innocent" oligopoly industries, Judge Posner has suggested a two-step analysis of situations in which one suspects prices are higher than competition would yield. First, one should ask whether conditions in a particular market are even conducive to the kinds of interdependent conduct that might raise prices. If so, one should then ask whether higher than competitive pricing can be observed. Judge Posner cites several conditions favorable to the occurrence of implicit collusion in an industry, but we will combine them here into five.

First is a *concentrated market of sellers and a lack of a fringe market of small firms*. There are no magic numbers to use, but if the largest four firms do not total at least 50% of the market, the need to worry is arguably low. Likewise, four firms with 100% of the market would be likely to find it easier to monitor each other's conduct than would two even larger firms that had to keep track of each other plus the conduct of many smaller competitors.

Second is a *standard product sold primarily on the basis of price*. There is much less to agree upon and more to keep track of when sellers offer different standards of quality, different sales terms, etc. Associated with this is the sellers' operating at the same level of the distribution process

---

[10] Supra, p. 19.

[11] Richard A. Posner, Antitrust Law 51–100 (2nd ed. 2001); Richard A. Posner, Antitrust Law: An Economic Perspective 39–77 (1976). An even earlier version of this work was Richard A. Posner, Oligopoly and the Antitrust Laws: A Suggested Approach, 21 Stanford L. Rev. 1562 (1969).

and with the same degree of vertical integration. Agreement is also easier and thus more likely when all firms have roughly the same costs.[12]

Third are issues going to *the "need" or at least the incentive to collude*. For example, one might be a high ratio of fixed to variable costs such as we saw in the railroad industry with its fear of "destructive competition." Another might be a static or declining demand in which cutting output might seem particularly important to firms' survival.

Fourth is an *inelastic demand at the competitive price*. This factor is true by definition. This condition simply means that at the competitive price, a reduction in output would in fact yield more net revenue.[13]

Fifth is *an industry in which entry takes a long time*. Again, this is true by definition. The point is that entry is rarely impossible but in some industries a higher than competitive price takes longer than usual to self-correct.

An enforcement agency presumably should not waste its time looking for oligopoly pricing in an industry that does *not* have the above characteristics. (Can you think of many that *do* have them?) Even in such an industry, Judge Posner suggests, a court should not sustain a case unless one or more tell-tale signs of implicit collusion are observed. Again, we reduce them to five.

A.   *Fixed relative market shares*. If firms are vigorously competing they will tend to be more successful or less over time. An industry in which that is not observed may be employing some kind of collusion.

B.   *Price discrimination*. This is simply charging higher prices to some customers or in some regions than others. I could not get away with it normally because you would sell at the market price to anyone whom I tried to charge more than that amount. If you and I let each other get away with so charging, then, it may be a sign that we aren't truly competing.

C.   *Exchanges of price information*. We have seen this point before. The point is that while information in general is pro-competitive, under conditions otherwise conducive to collusion, it might be anticompetitive, particularly if it gives industry participants information about price cutting by one firm that the others might want to "punish."

---

[12]   In addition, Judge Posner observes that having products sold by public competitive bidding lends itself especially well to collusion of the sort we saw in *Addyston Pipe*.

[13]   Demand elasticity is calculated by dividing the percentage change in quantity demanded by a given percentage change in price. Thus, for example, if doubling the price of an item from $1 to $2 would cause sales to fall from 150 units to 50, the elasticity would be calculated as 1.5. If doubling the price would lead to a decline from 150 to 100 units, however, the elasticity would be calculated as 0.6. We say the latter situation represents "inelastic" demand and we would expect to see the seller raise the price to take advantage of the chance to increase its total revenue. For more on the calculation of elasticity, see Jeffrey L. Harrison, Thomas D. Morgan & Paul R. Verkuil, Regulation and Deregulation 321–323 (2d Ed. 2004).

D. *Industry-wide resale price maintenance.* Regardless of the justification for resale price maintenance in the case of a single manufacturer, if all of the firms engage in it, it may be a sign of implicit collusion and a way to make cheating harder.

E. *Evidence of new entry and declining market share of leading firms.* Again, this is what one would tend to expect if prices were higher than a competitive level. *U.S. Steel* was a particularly good example; remember the Gary Dinners!

You will see that oligopoly is often seen as a problem in the remainder of these materials. Keep Judge Posner's criteria in mind as the cases come up; they may help you determine whether there is (or is not) something to the plaintiffs' concern.[14]

LIMITING THE REACH OF *AMERICAN COLUMN—* THE *MAPLE FLOORING* CASE

If one can have confidence about anything in antitrust law it is that yesterday's certainties may be tomorrow's fallacies. Only four years later, in Maple Flooring Manufacturers' Assn. v. United States, 268 U.S. 563, 45 S.Ct. 578, 69 L.Ed. 1093 (1925), the Court seemed to do an about face. The defendants included 22 corporations engaged in the business of selling and shipping maple, beech and birch flooring, along with George W. Keehn, this Association's version of Mr. Gadd. In 1922, the defendants produced 70% of the nation's maple, beech and birch flooring.

The Government attacked four activities of the Association:

(1) Computation and distribution to members of the association of the average cost to members of producing all dimensions and grades of flooring, a practice that the Government alleged would tend to lead to price quotations based on those average costs.

(2) Preparation and distribution of a booklet showing freight rates on flooring from Cadillac, Michigan, to between five and six thousand other locations in the United States.

(3) Gathering statistics "giving complete information as to the quantity and kind of flooring sold and prices received by the reporting members, and the amount of stock on hand, which information is summarized by the secretary and transmitted to members without,

---

[14] More insight on these issues is provided in William E. Kovacic, Robert C. Marshall, Leslie M. Marx & Halbert L. White, Plus Factors and Agreement in Antitrust Law, 110 U. Michigan L. Rev. 393 (2011); Gregory J. Werden, Economic Evidence on the Existence of Collusion: Reconciling Antitrust Law with Oligopoly Theory, 71 Antitrust L. J. 719 (2004).

however, revealing the identity of the members in connection with any specific information thus transmitted."

(4) Holding meetings "at which the representatives of members congregate and discuss the industry and exchange views as to its problems."

The Court found that there had been no overt price fixing, although "it was conceded by defendants that the dissemination of information as to cost of the product and as to production and prices would tend to bring about uniformity in prices through the operation of economic law." The Court also found "abundant evidence that * * * the freight rate book served a useful and legitimate purpose in enabling members to quote promptly a delivered price on their product by adding to their mill price a previously calculated freight rate which approximated closely to the actual rate from their own mill towns."

Furthermore, the Court noted, the compiled sales statistics did not report individual sales or the names or purchasers and they were widely reported to the Department of Commerce and to trade journals read by 90 to 95% of Association members' customers. Finally, at Association meetings, the Court said, members discussed "market prices of rough maple flooring", as well as "manufacturing and market conditions," but they did not discuss future pricing.

American Column & Lumber, the Court said, had rested "squarely on the ground that there was a combination on the part of the members to secure concerted action in curtailment of production and increase of price, which actually resulted in a restraint of commerce, producing increase of price." Further, the *Maple Flooring* opinion noted:

> "It is not, we think, open to question that the dissemination of pertinent information concerning any trade or business tends to stabilize that trade or business and to produce uniformity of price and trade practice. * * * But the natural effect of the acquisition of wider and more scientific knowledge of business conditions, on the minds of the individuals engaged in commerce, and its consequent effect in stabilizing production and price, can hardly be deemed a restraint of commerce or if so it cannot, we think, be said to be an unreasonable restraint, or in any respect unlawful."

Finally, the Court noted: "It was not the purpose or the intent of the Sherman Anti-Trust Law to inhibit the intelligent conduct of business operations * * * ." Chief Justice Taft and Justices McReynolds and Sanford dissented, believing the case could not properly be distinguished from the facts and reasoning of *American Column*.

NOTES AND QUESTIONS

1.   Do you agree that *American Column* and *Maple Flooring* can be distinguished? Had the justices simply changed their minds in the four years since the decision in *American Column*? It might seem so looking only at the majority opinion, but in the interim between the decisions, four new members—Butler, Sutherland, Sanford and Stone—had been appointed to the Court by Presidents Harding and Coolidge. Chief Justice Taft, also a Harding appointee, and Justice McReynolds, Wilson's former Attorney General, had gone from the majority in *American Column* to the dissent here, and they picked up Sanford. The previous dissenters, Holmes and Brandeis, now prevailed, bringing along the other three new members. Apparently only Justice Van Devanter thought the results were consistent, voting with the majority each time.

2.   Are the facts of *American Column* and *Maple Flooring* really quite different?

a.   Might you argue that, in *Maple Flooring*, an exchange of information was even *more* likely to reinforce conspiratorial behavior? What was the number of firms to keep track of here, for example, and what was their collective market share?

b.   On the other hand, was the information collected in *Maple Flooring* as detailed as that in *American Column*? Would a firm be able to monitor each of its competitors' adherence to an implicit price and output understanding, for example, if all it had were the firms' average cost of production, and reports of transactions with the names of the parties deleted?

c.   Do you agree it should have been significant in *Maple Flooring* that all information related to past transactions? How about that it was available to both buyers and sellers through trade journals? Why should either of these realities make any difference at all?

3.   Should it be illegal for all the firms in an industry to sell their products with freight charged as if the goods were sent from Cadillac, Michigan? The practice is called "basing point pricing" and the courts have long struggled over whether it should be a matter of concern. See, e.g., Corn Products Refining Co. v. Federal Trade Commission, 324 U.S. 726, 65 S.Ct. 961, 89 L.Ed. 1320 (1945).[15]

4.   Cement Manufacturers' Protective Ass'n v. United States, 268 U.S. 588, 45 S.Ct. 586, 69 L.Ed. 1104 (1925), decided the same day as *Maple Flooring*, involved a group of 19 manufacturers who produced cement along the east coast from New York to Virginia. Cement is a standardized product, about $2/3$ of which typically was sold through retail dealers, the rest directly to contractors. The government showed that association members used a system of "specific job contracts" in their dealings with contractors. The Association

---

[15]   See, e.g., Herbert Hovenkamp, Federal Antitrust Policy: The Law of Competition and its Practice 181–85 (3rd Ed. 2005); David Haddock, Basing-Point Pricing: Competitive v. Collusive Theories, 72 American Economic Rev. 229 (1982).

collected detailed information on orders received by each, allegedly to counteract a practice under which contractors would order their full requirements from each of several dealers, knowing that trade practice allowed them to return whatever they did not use. The Association also complied and distributed a book showing freight rates and monthly information on past production and stock on hand, but without advice or comment. A lawyer was on hand at all meetings "to steer the discussion away from illegal subjects."

The Court reversed an order enjoining these activities. An exchange, even in advance, of specific contract terms is permissible, the Court said, as a defense against multiple orders for the same job. Likewise, the Court upheld the distribution of general statistical information, even assuming it had tended to stabilize prices, because there was no *agreement* to maintain *uniform* prices. Did this case cast *American Column* into even more doubt?

C. THE INTERPLAY BETWEEN PATENTS AND ANTITRUST LAW

Now we turn to two cases involving the special issues surrounding patents and patented products. The rule of reason period was not the first in which such issues were raised; the interplay of patents and the antitrust law had been a problem for the courts since the earliest days of the Sherman Act. However, this was the period in which important principles were established that in many cases are still applicable today.

Briefly, to obtain or defend a patent, an inventor must demonstrate that an invention is a "new and useful process, machine, manufacture, or composition of matter, or any new and useful improvement thereof." 35 U.S.C. § 101. In addition, the invention must be "novel" (§ 102), and "non-obvious" (§ 103). The application also must fully describe the invention (§ 112) so that the public receives the benefit of the insight the patented invention represents.

If the Patent Office agrees that these criteria have been met, a patent will issue giving the inventor the "right to exclude others from making, using, or selling the invention throughout the United States" for a period of twenty years from the date of the original application (§ 154). If someone infringes the patent (§ 271), the inventor may seek an injunction (§ 283), damages (§ 284), or both, plus reasonable attorney fees (§ 285). A patent is presumed valid (§ 282), but the defendant may argue that the patent was not infringed, that it is invalid (i.e., should not have been issued in the first place), or that it should not be enforceable because the inventor has "misused" the patent.

The problem of reconciling patent and antitrust law, of course, arises primarily from the fact that a patent is a legal monopoly. The persistent question is thus where the monopoly rights so granted end and where antitrust principles applicable to everyone else begin. Put another way, once one has conceded that a patent holder is entitled to earn a monopoly profit, the question becomes whether there is any principled reason to limit the ways it seeks to earn it.[16]

UNITED STATES V. GENERAL ELECTRIC COMPANY

Supreme Court of the United States, 1926
272 U.S. 476, 47 S.Ct. 192, 71 L.Ed. 362

MR. CHIEF JUSTICE TAFT delivered the opinion of the Court.

This is a bill in equity brought by the United States * * * to enjoin the General Electric Company [hereafter the Electric Company], [and] the Westinghouse Electric and Manufacturing Company * * * from further violation of the Anti-Trust Act of July 2, 1890. The bill made two charges * * * . * * *

The Government [first] alleged that the system of distribution adopted was merely a device to enable the Electric Company to fix the resale prices of lamps in the hands of purchasers, that the so-called agents were in fact wholesale and retail merchants, and the lamps passed through the ordinary channels of commerce in the ordinary way * * * . The Electric Company answered that its distributors were bona fide agents, that it had the legal right to market its lamps and pass them directly to the consumer by such agents, and at prices and by a system prescribed by it and agreed upon between it and its agents, there being no limitation sought as to resale prices upon those who purchased from such agents.

The second question in the case involves the validity of a license granted March 1, 1912, by the Electric Company to the Westinghouse Company to make, use and sell lamps under the patents owned by the former. It was charged that the license in effect provided that the Westinghouse Company would follow prices and terms of sales from time to time fixed by the Electric Company and observed by it, and that the Westinghouse Company would, with regard to lamps manufactured by it under the license, adopt and maintain the same conditions of sale as observed by the Electric Company in the distribution of lamps manufactured by it.

The District Court upon a full hearing dismissed the bill for want of equity and this is an appeal * * * .

There had been a prior litigation between the United States and the three defendants and 32 other corporations, in which the Government sued to dissolve an illegal combination in restraint of interstate commerce in electric lamps, in violation of the Anti-Trust Act, and to enjoin further

---

[16]   See, e.g., Louis Kaplow, The Patent-Antitrust Intersection: A Reappraisal, 97 Harvard L.Rev. 1815 (1984); Ward S. Bowman, Patent and Antitrust Law: A Legal and Economic Appraisal (1973).

violation. A consent decree was entered in that cause by which the combination was dissolved, the subsidiary corporations surrendered their charters, and their properties were taken over by the General Electric Company. * * * After the decree was entered, a new sales plan, which was the one here complained of, * * * was adopted and has been in operation since 1912.

The government insists that these circumstances tend to support the government's view that the new plan was a mere evasion of the restrictions of the decree and was intended to carry out the same evil result that had been condemned in the prior litigation. * * *

The General Electric Company is the owner of three patents—one of 1912 to Just & Hanaman, the basic patent for the use of tungsten filaments in the manufacture of electric lamps; the Coolidge patent of 1913, covering a process of manufacturing tungsten filaments by which their tensile strength and endurance are greatly increased; and, third, the Langmuir patent of 1916, which is for the use of gas in the bulb by which the intensity of the light is substantially heightened. These three patents cover completely the making of the modern electric lights with the tungsten filaments, and secure to the Electric Company the monopoly of their making, using and vending.

The total business in electric lights for the year 1921 was $68,300,000, and the relative percentages of business done by the companies were, General Electric, 69 per cent; Westinghouse, 16 per cent; other licensees, 8 per cent; and manufacturers not licensed, 7 per cent. The plan of distribution by the Electric Company divides the trade into three classes. The first class is that of sales to large consumers readily reached by the Electric Company, negotiated by its own salaried employees and the deliveries made from its own factories and warehouses. The second class is of sales to large consumers under contracts with the Electric Company, negotiated by agents, the deliveries being made from stock in the custody of the agents; and the third is of the sales to general consumers by agents under similar contracts. The agents under the second class are called B agents, and the agents under the third class are called A agents. * * * [Contracts with B agents provide] that the company is to maintain on consignment in the custody of the agent a stock of lamps, the sizes, types, classes and quantity of which, and the length of time which they are to remain in stock, to be determined by the company. * * * The consigned stock, or any part of it, is to be returned to the company as it may direct. The agent is to keep account books and records giving the complete information as to his dealings for the inspection of the company. All of the lamps in such consigned stock are to be and remain the property of the company until the lamps are sold, and the proceeds of all lamps are to be held in trust for the benefit and for the account of the company until fully accounted for. The B agent is authorized to deal with the lamps on consignment with him in three ways—first to distribute the lamps to the company's A agents as authorized by the company; second, to sell lamps from the stock to any consumer to the extent of his requirements for immediate delivery at prices specified by the company; third, to deliver lamps from the stock to any purchaser under written contract with the company to whom the B agent may be authorized by the company to deliver lamps at the prices and on the terms stated in the contract. The B agent has no authority to dispose of any of the lamps, except as above provided and is not to control or attempt to control prices at which any purchaser shall sell any of such lamps. * * * The agent guarantees the return to the company of all unsold lamps in the custody of the agent within a certain time after the termination of his agency. The agent is to pay over to the company not later than the 15th of each month an amount equal to the total sales value, less the agent's compensation, of all of the company's lamps sold by him * * * . This is to comply with the guaranty of the agent of due and prompt payment for all lamps sold by him from his stock. Third, the agent is to pay to the company the value of all of the company's lamps lost or missing from or damaged in the stock in his custody. There is a basic rate of commission payable to the agent, and there are certain special supplemental and additional compensations for prompt and efficient service. If the agent becomes insolvent, or fails to make reports and remittances, or fails in any of his obligations, the appointment may be terminated; and, when terminated, either at the end of the year or otherwise, the consigned lamps remaining unsold are to be delivered to the manufacturer. It appears in the evidence that since 1915, * * * the company has assumed all risk of fire, flood, obsolescence, and price decline, and carries whatever insurance is carried on the stocks of lamps in the hands of its agents, and pays whatever taxes are assessed. This is relevant as a circumstance to confirm the view that the so-called relation of agent to the company is the real one. There are 400 of the B agents, the large distributors. They recommend to the company efficient and reliable distributors, in the localities with which they are respectively familiar, to act as A agents whom the company appoints. There are 21,000 or more of the A agents. They are usually retail electrical supply dealers in smaller places. The only sales which the A agent is authorized to make are to consumers for immediate delivery and to purchasers under written contract with the manufacturer, just as in the case of the B agents. * * * The question is whether, in view of the arrangements made by the company with those who ordinarily and usually would be merchants buying from the manufacturer and selling to the public, such persons are to be treated as agents or as owners of the lamps consigned to them under such contracts. * * *

We find nothing in the form of the contracts and the practice under them which makes the so-called B and A agents anything more than genuine agents of the company, or the delivery of the stock to each agent anything more than a consignment to the agent for his custody and sale as such. He is not obliged to pay over money for the stock held by him until it is sold. As he guarantees the account when made, he must turn over what should have been paid whether he gets it or not. This term occurs in a frequent form of pure agency known as sale by del credere commission. There is no conflict in the agent's obligation to account for all lamps lost, missing, or damaged in the stock. It is only a reasonable provision to secure his careful handling of the goods entrusted to him. * * * The agent has no power to deal with the lamps in any way inconsistent with the ownership of the lamps retained by the company. When they are delivered by him to the purchasers, the title passes directly from the company to those purchasers. * * * The circumstance that the agents were in their regular business wholesale or retail merchants, and under a prior arrangement had bought the lamps and sold them as their owners, did not prevent a change in their relation to the company. We find no reason in this record to hold that the change in this case was not in good faith and actually maintained.

But it is said that the system of distribution is so complicated and involves such a very large number of agents, distributed throughout the entire country, that the very size and comprehensiveness of the scheme brings it within the Anti-Trust Law. We do not question that in a suit under the Anti-Trust Act the circumstance that the combination effected secures domination of so large a part of the business affected as to control prices is usually most important in proof of a monopoly violating the act. But under the patent law the patentee is given by statute a monopoly of making, using and selling the patented article. The extent of his monopoly in the articles sold and in the territory of the United States where sold is not limited in the grant of his patent, and the comprehensiveness of his control of the business in the sale of the patented article is not necessarily an indication of illegality of his method. * * * The validity of the Electric Company's scheme of distribution of its electric lamps turns, therefore, on the question whether the sales are by the company through its agents to the consumer, or are in fact by the company to the so-called agents at the time of consignment. The distinction in law and fact between an agency and a sale is clear. For the reasons already stated, we find no ground for inference that the contracts made between the company and its agents are, or were intended, to be other than what their language makes them.

The Government relies in its contention for a different conclusion on the case of Dr. Miles Medical Company v. John D. Park & Sons Company. * * *

The plan of distribution of the Miles Medical Company resembled in many details the plan of distribution in the present case, except that the subject-matter there was medicine by a secret formula, and not a patented article. But there were certain vital differences. * * * This Court * * * found in the contracts themselves and their operation plain provision for purchases by the so-called agents which necessarily made the contracts as to an indefinite amount of the consignments to them, contracts of sale rather than of agency. The Court therefore held that the showing made was of an attempt by the Miles Medical Company, through its plan of distribution to hold its purchasers after the purchase at full price to an obligation to maintain prices on a resale by them. This is the whole effect of the *Miles Medical* case. * * *

* * *

We are of opinion, therefore, that there is nothing as a matter of principle or in the authorities which requires us to hold that genuine contracts of agency like those before us, however comprehensive as a mass or whole in their effect, are violations of the Anti-Trust Act. The owner of an article patented or otherwise is not violating the common law or the Anti-Trust Act, by seeking to dispose of his article directly to the consumer and fixing the price by which his agents transfer the title from him directly to such consumer. The first charge in the bill can not be sustained.

Second. Had the Electric Company as the owner of the patents, entirely controlling the manufacture, use and sale of the tungsten incandescent lamps, in its license to the Westinghouse Company, the right to impose the condition that its sales should be at prices fixed by the licensor and subject to change according to its discretion? * * *

The owner of a patent may assign it to another and convey (1) the exclusive right to make, use, and vend the invention throughout the United States; or (2) an undivided part or share of that exclusive right, or (3) the exclusive right under the patent within and through a specific part of the United States. But any assignment or transfer short of one of these is a license giving the licensee no title in the patent and no right to sue at law in his own name for an infringement. * * * It is well settled, as already said, that where a patentee makes the patented article, and sells it, he can exercise no future control over what the purchaser may wish to do with the article after his purchase. * * * But the question is a different one * * * when we consider what a patentee who grants a license to one to make and vend the patented article may do in limiting the licensee in the exercise of the right to sell. The patentee may make and grant a license to another to make and use the patented articles but withhold his right to sell them. The licensee in such a case acquires an interest in the articles made. He owns the material of them and may use them. But if he sells them he infringes the right of the patentee, and may be held for damages and enjoined. If the patentee goes further and licenses the selling of the articles, may he limit the selling by limiting the method of sale and the price? We think he may do so provided the conditions of sale are normally and reasonably adapted to secure pecuniary reward for the patentee's monopoly. One of the valuable elements of the exclusive right of a patentee is to acquire profit by the price at which the article is sold. The higher the price, the greater the profit, unless it is prohibitory. When the patentee licenses another to make and vend and retains the right to continue to make and vend on his own account, the price at which his licensee will sell will necessarily affect the price at which he can sell his own patented goods. It would seem entirely reasonable that he should say to the licensee, "Yes, you may make and sell articles under my patent, but not so as to destroy the profit that I wish to obtain by making them and selling them myself." He does not thereby sell outright to the licensee the articles the latter may make and sell, or vest absolute ownership in them. He restricts the property and interest the licensee has in the goods he makes and proposes to sell.

This question was considered by this Court in the case of Bement v. National Harrow Company, 186 U.S. 70 [1902]. A combination of manufacturers owning a patent to make float spring tool harrows licensed others to make and sell the products under the patent on condition that they would not during the continuance of the license sell the products at a less price or on more favorable terms of payment and delivery to purchasers than were set forth in a schedule made part of the license. That was held to be a valid use of the patent rights of the owners of the patent. * * *

* * *

Nor do we think that [a different result is compelled by] the decisions of this Court holding * * * that a patentee may not attach to the article made by him or with his consent a condition running with the article in the hands of purchasers limiting the price at which one who becomes its owner for full consideration shall part with it. They do not consider or condemn a restriction put by a patentee upon his licensee as to the prices at which the latter shall sell articles which he makes and only can make legally under the license. * * *

For the reasons given, we sustain the validity of the license granted by the Electric Company to the Westinghouse Company. The decree of the District Court dismissing the bill is affirmed.

NOTES AND QUESTIONS

1.   The first issue the Court considers is General Electric's use of agency agreements as a way of keeping control of the distribution of their bulbs. Were you convinced by the Court's distinction of *Dr. Miles*? Had that case really turned only on the fact of a badly-drafted contract?

a.   Of course, almost a quarter-century before this case and almost a decade before *Dr. Miles*, the Court had decided in Bement v. National Harrow Company that a patent holder may set the price at which a patented product may be resold. Was the holding here thus a foregone conclusion?

b.   Should it be relevant that General Electric itself was a corporate entity only formed after a number of smaller firms had lost a price fixing case? If it would have been a crime for multiple manufacturers or dealers in patented products to fix prices horizontally, why shouldn't it be equally improper to merge the manufacturers into one company and impose uniform prices vertically?

c.   This, of course, is what the Government argued, and you see that the Government lost. Indeed, does the Court here even limit its holding to patent cases?

d.   Does the Court's language mean that *Dr. Miles* is an easily-avoided dead letter? Think back to the questions we raised about whether resale price maintenance should be prohibited at all; might quietly burying *Dr. Miles* in this way have been desirable? As you will see later, in fact it was *General Electric*, not *Dr. Miles*, that the Court long sought to avoid.

2.   The other issue in *General Electric* is its licensing of Westinghouse to make bulbs under an arrangement that set the minimum price Westinghouse could charge for the bulbs.

a.   Why would G.E. license its principal competitor to make its product? Is doing so per se suspicious? Suppose General Electric otherwise would have had to construct costly new facilities to meet the demand for its product, for example. Isn't it likely that patent holders will often find that other firms can exploit the patent more efficiently than they themselves can?

b.   Does it follow that a patent holder needs the kind of price protection that General Electric required of Westinghouse here? How else could General Electric have tried to assure that Westinghouse could not undersell it? Might General Electric have made Westinghouse its agent for manufacture and then sold the bulbs as if they were G.E.'s own? Chief Justice Taft says that that clearly would have been legal. Would the public have been better served by requiring General Electric to proceed that way?

c.   But that still doesn't explain why this approach was chosen. It should trouble you. Assume that it costs Westinghouse $1 to make a light bulb and General Electric wants bulbs sold for at least $2.50 each. What mechanism does General Electric already have to make Westinghouse's costs at least that high? That's right, the royalty rate. In this example, if General Electric had set the royalty at $1.50, it would not have had to set the resale price and could have avoided a lawsuit.

d.   Why, then, did it do what it did? We have implied that the patent holder can set any royalty it chooses; in fact, it has to get the licensee to agree. Perhaps Westinghouse knew it would be costly for General Electric to make the bulbs itself and demanded a lower royalty rate so as to give itself a higher profit. Perhaps, instead, General Electric did not know Westinghouse's real cost of manufacture and thus was not confident that setting the royalty rate would fully protect it against being undersold.

e.   But suppose General Electric believed Westinghouse was going to enter light bulb production anyway using methods that would not clearly violate GE patents. Suppose General Electric and Westinghouse would prefer to avoid head-to-head competition. Could the licensing arrangement chosen here be a way to mask a price-fixing agreement that would otherwise clearly violate the law? Could a court ever tell the parties' *real* motivations? Just such concerns lie behind our next case.

STANDARD OIL COMPANY (INDIANA) v. UNITED STATES

Supreme Court of the United States, 1931
283 U.S. 163, 51 S.Ct. 421, 75 L.Ed. 926

MR. JUSTICE BRANDEIS delivered the opinion of the Court.

This suit was brought by the United States * * * to enjoin further violation of § 1 and § 2 of the Sherman Anti-Trust Act. * * * After a hearing, * * * the District Court granted some of the relief asked. The * * * defendants appealed to this Court. * * *

* * * The violation of the Sherman Act now complained of rests substantially on the making and effect of three contracts entered into by the primary defendants. The history of these agreements may be briefly stated. For about half a century before 1910, gasoline had been manufactured from crude oil exclusively by distillation and condensation at atmospheric pressure. When the demand for gasoline grew rapidly with the widespread use of the automobile, methods for increasing the yield of gasoline from the available crude oil were sought. It had long been known that from a given quantity of crude, additional oils of high volatility could be produced by "cracking"; that is, by applying heat and pressure to the residuum after ordinary distillation. But a commercially profitable cracking method and apparatus for manufacturing additional gasoline had not yet been developed. The first such process was perfected by the Indiana Company in 1913; and for more than seven years this was the only one practiced in America. During that period the Indiana Company not only manufactured cracked gasoline on a large scale, but also had licensed fifteen independent concerns to use its process * * * .

Meanwhile, since the phenomenon of cracking was not controlled by any fundamental patent, other concerns had been working independently to develop commercial processes of their own. Most prominent among these were the three other primary defendants * * * . Each of these secured numerous patents covering its particular cracking process. Beginning in 1920, conflict developed among the four companies concerning the validity, scope, and ownership of issued patents. One infringement suit was begun; cross-notices of infringement, antecedent to other suits, were given; and interferences were declared on pending applications in the Patent Office. The primary defendants assert that it was these difficulties which led to their executing the three principal agreements which the United States attacks; and that their sole object was to avoid litigation and losses incident to conflicting patents.

* * * The three agreements differ from one another only slightly in scope and terms. Each primary defendant was released thereby from liability for any past infringement of patents of the others. Each acquired the right to use these patents thereafter in its own process. Each was empowered to extend to independent concerns, licensed under its process, releases from past, and immunity from future claims of infringement of patents controlled by the other primary defendants. And each was to share in some fixed proportion the fees received under these multiple licenses. * * *

First. The defendants contend that the agreements assailed relate solely to the issuance of licenses under their respective patents; that the granting of such licenses * * * is not interstate commerce; and that the Sherman Act is therefore inapplicable. This contention is unsound. Any agreement between competitors may be illegal if part of a larger plan to control interstate markets. * * *

Second. The Government contends that the three agreements constitute a pooling by the primary defendants of the royalties from their several patents; that thereby competition between them in the commercial exercise of their respective rights to issue licenses is eliminated; that this tends to maintain or increase the royalty charged secondary defendants and hence to increase the manufacturing cost of cracked gasoline; that thus the primary defendants exclude from interstate commerce gasoline which would, under lower competitive royalty rates, be produced * * * . There is no provision in any of the agreements which restricts the freedom of the primary defendants individually to issue licenses under their own patents alone or under the patents of all the others; and no contract between any of them, and no license agreement with a secondary defendant executed pursuant thereto, now imposes any restriction upon the quantity of gasoline to be produced, or upon the price, terms, or conditions of sale, or upon the territory in which sales may be made. The only restraint thus charged is that necessarily arising out of the making and effect of the provisions for cross-licensing and for division of royalties.

The Government concedes that it is not illegal for the primary defendants to cross-license each other and the respective licensees; and that adequate consideration can legally be demanded for such grants. But it contends that the insertion of certain additional provisions in these agreements renders them illegal. It urges, first, that the mere inclusion of the provisions for the division of royalties, constitutes an unlawful combination under the Sherman Act because it evidences an intent to obtain a monopoly. This contention is unsound. Such provisions for the division of royalties are not in themselves conclusive evidence of illegality. Where there are legitimately conflicting claims or threatened interferences, a settlement by agreement, rather than litigation, is not precluded by the Act. An interchange of patent rights and a division of royalties according to the value attributed by the parties to their respective patent claims is frequently necessary if technical advancement is not to be blocked by threatened litigation.[17] If the available advantages are open on reasonable terms to all manufacturers desiring to participate, such interchange may promote rather than restrain competition.[18]

Third. The Government next contends that the agreements to maintain royalties violate the Sherman Law because the fees charged are onerous. The argument is that the competitive advantage which the three primary defendants enjoy of manufacturing cracked gasoline free of royalty, while licensees must pay to them a heavy tribute in fees, enables these primary defendants to exclude from interstate commerce cracked gasoline which would, under lower competitive royalty rates, be produced by possible rivals. This argument ignores the privileges incident to ownership of patents. Unless the industry is dominated, or interstate commerce directly restrained, the Sherman Act does not require cross-licensing patentees to license at reasonable rates others engaged in interstate commerce. Compare Bement v. National Harrow Co.; United States v. General Electric Co. The allegation that the royalties charged are onerous is, standing alone, without legal significance; and, as will be shown, neither the alleged domination, nor restraint of commerce has been proved.

Fourth. The main contention of the Government is that even if the exchange of patent rights and division of royalties are not necessarily improper and the royalties are not oppressive, the three contracts are still obnoxious to the Sherman Act because specific clauses enable the primary defendants to maintain existing royalties and thereby to restrain interstate commerce. * * * Licenses granting rights under the patents of both are to be issued at a fixed royalty—approximately that charged by the Indiana Company when its process was alone in the field. * * *

---

[17]   This is often the case where patents covering improvements of a basic process, owned by one manufacturer, are granted to another. A patent may be rendered quite useless, or "blocked," by another unexpired patent which covers a vitally related feature of the manufacturing process. Unless some agreement can be reached, the parties are hampered and exposed to litigation. And, frequently, the cost of litigation to a patentee is greater than the value of a patent for a minor improvement. [Court's fn. 5]

[18]   Such agreements, varying in purpose, scope, and validity, are not uncommon. Conflict of patents in the automobile industry, and the early difficulties encountered with an alleged basic patent, led to an agreement in 1915 by which the members of the National Automobile Chamber of Commerce cross-licensed each other without royalty for the use of all patent improvements. This agreement was renewed as to existing patents in 1925. Interchange of basic aviation patents was made during the world war, at the suggestion of the National Advisory Committee for Aeronautics; and this agreement, providing for fixed royalties, was approved by the Attorney-General. In 1928 the arrangement was modified and renewed. * * * [Court's fn. 6]

The rate of royalties may, of course be a decisive factor in the cost of production. If combining patent owners effectively dominate an industry, the power to fix and maintain royalties is tantamount to the power to fix prices. Where domination exists, a pooling of competing process patents, or an exchange of licenses for the purpose of curtailing the manufacture and supply of an unpatented product, is beyond the privileges conferred by the patents and constitutes a violation of the Sherman Act. * * * But an agreement for cross-licensing and division of royalties violates the Act only when used to effect a monopoly, or to fix prices, or to impose otherwise an unreasonable restraint upon interstate commerce. * * *

Fifth. No monopoly, or restriction of competition, in the business of licensing patented cracking processes resulted from the execution of these agreements. Up to 1920 all cracking plants in the United States were either owned by the Indiana Company alone, or were operated under licenses from it. In 1924 and 1925, after the cross-licensing arrangements were in effect, the four primary defendants owned or licensed, in the aggregate, only 55% of the total cracking capacity, and the remainder was distributed among twenty-one independently owned cracking processes. This development and commercial expansion of competing processes is clear evidence that the contracts did not concentrate in the hands of the four primary defendants the licensing of patented processes for the production of cracked gasoline. Moreover, the record does not show that after the execution of the agreements there was a decrease of competition among them in licensing other refiners to use their respective processes.

No monopoly, or restriction of competition, in the production of either ordinary or cracked gasoline has been proved. The output of cracked gasoline in the years in question was about 26% of the total gasoline production. Ordinary or straight run gasoline is indistinguishable from cracked gasoline and the two are either mixed or sold interchangeably. Under these circumstances the primary defendants could not effectively control the supply or fix the price of cracked gasoline by virtue of their alleged monopoly of the cracking processes, unless they could control, through some means, the remainder of the total gasoline production from all sources. Proof of such control is lacking. * * *

No monopoly, or restriction of competition, in the sale of gasoline has been proved. On the basis of testimony relating to the marketing of both cracked and ordinary gasoline, the master found that the defendants were in active competition among themselves and with other refiners; that both kinds of gasoline were refined and sold in large quantities by other companies; and that the primary defendants and their licensees neither individually nor collectively controlled the market price or supply of any gasoline moving in interstate commerce. There is ample evidence to support these findings.

* * * In the absence of proof that the primary defendants had such control of the entire industry as would make effective the alleged domination of a part, it is difficult to see how they could by agreeing upon royalty rates control either the price or the supply of gasoline, or otherwise restrain competition. By virtue of their patents they had individually the right to determine who should use their respective processes or inventions and what the royalties for such use should be. To warrant an injunction which would invalidate the contracts here in question, and require either new arrangements or settlement of the conflicting claims by litigation, there must be a definite factual showing of illegality. Chicago Board of Trade v. United States.

Sixth. In the District Court, the Government undertook to prove the violation charged by showing that the three agreements challenged were made by the primary defendants in bad faith. * * * The master found, after an elaborate review of the entire art, that the presumption of validity attaching to the patents had not been negatived in any way; that they merited a broad interpretation; that they had been acquired in good faith; and that the scope of the several groups of patents overlapped sufficiently to justify the threats and fear of litigation. The District Court stated that the particular claims should be interpreted narrowly, and that the respective inventions might be practiced without infringement of adversely owned patents. But it confirmed the finding of presumptive validity and did not question the finding of good faith. It held that the patents were adequate consideration for the cross-licensing agreements and that the violation charged could not be predicated on patent invalidity. * * *

* * *

* * * The bill should have been dismissed. * * *

* * *

MR. JUSTICE STONE took no part in the consideration or decision of this case.

NOTES AND QUESTIONS

1.   If you had been representing the Government, how would you have described what was wrong with what these companies had done?

a.   Would you have conceded, as the Government did here, that the firms could cross-license each other to use the patents? Would cross-licensing have had any anticompetitive effects? Would it have made matters any worse if the firms had paid each other royalties when they produced gasoline under such an arrangement?

b.   Would you have allowed the defendants only to license each other? Wouldn't competition normally be increased by sub-licensing even more firms to use the package of rights?

c.   Would you have challenged, as the Government did here, the division of royalties among the firms granting the licenses? Assuming that a royalty could be set by each patent holder for sub-licenses of the patents, would you have thought there was anything to be gained by rewarding the first firm to grant sub-licenses by letting it keep the total amount of the royalties?

d.   Would you have alleged that the royalties charged were "onerous"? Was that argument likely to be a winner given the patent holder's right to earn a monopoly return?

2.   What would the royalties have been here if the firms had not been allowed to do what they did?

a.   Suppose two people have patents that do not conflict and that will produce cracked gasoline equally well. What royalty will each be able to charge? Won't competition tend to drive the royalty down to the marginal cost of allowing use of the patent?

b.   What will that be? Sure, it will be little or nothing. The cost of invention might have been high, but once a discovery is made, the cost of allowing use of it a million times—as opposed to only once—will often be low or non-existent. Never forget that the patent law grants a monopoly over *use* of the patented invention, but it does not guarantee any given level of economic return.

c.   What incentive does that give firms who have competing patents? It certainly gives each an incentive to assert that it has the only valid patent, because then it can get all the royalties. Less good is to assert that the patents are blocking and cross-license each other so that at least neither has to pay royalties to the other. Even better is to do what was done here, i.e., cross-license with the right to sub-license at agreed royalties. That way, competition can indeed be avoided.

d.   Do you suppose it is easy for a judge to tell whether patents are in fact "blocking" without significant investigation and possible litigation? Might firms have an incentive to settle such a case early under the approach taken here? Might they indeed have an incentive to see conflict where none exists? Should the only test to which they are subject be "bad faith"?

3.   Did Justice Brandeis convince you that no one was hurt by this arrangement?

a.   Was the correct test to use whether the defendants had obtained a "monopoly" of cracking? Should the only illegal cartels be those that involve all the firms in an industry?

b.   Should it have been seen as significant that only 55% of the cracking capacity in the country was licensed under these patents, i.e., that 45% used competing, non-infringing processes? Would the significance be affected by whether there were large differences in cost associated with the various methods of cracking?

c.   Should it have been important that only 26% of the country's gasoline was produced by cracking? Do you suppose that that figure was immutable, i.e., unrelated to the cost of cracking and unaffected by the royalty rates charged here?

4.   Justice Brandeis observes that the problem presented in this case is particularly common when there are follow-on or improvement patents. One firm comes up with a better way of exploiting a patented technique but a licensee cannot use it without a license under the original patent as well.

a.   Should patent pooling be permitted in such situations? Might you fear that such pools might cartelize entire industries in which technology is important?

b.   Might that be especially true if the principles of *General Electric* and *Standard Oil (Indiana)* were combined? That is, once one has a patent pool, does *G.E.* allow the sublicensees to specify the prices at which the finished products embodying the patented ideas will be sold? The Court has said "no"; that is the point at which the line must be drawn. United States v. Masonite Corp., 316 U.S. 265, 62 S.Ct. 1070, 86 L.Ed. 1461 (1942); United States v. Line Material Co., 333 U.S. 287, 68 S.Ct. 550, 92 L.Ed. 701 (1948).[19]

A BRIEF NOTE ON THE PATENT-TYING "MISUSE" CASES

Patent "misuse" has long described a way that an inventor may lose his or her patent rights, and cases alleging such misuse have long influenced antitrust doctrine. Indeed, you may remember from an earlier note that the 1912 decision in Henry v. A.B. Dick Co. was one reason for adoption of the Clayton Act. There, the patent holder had tried to make the buyer of a patented mimeograph machine purchase all of her unpatented ink from him. The Court upheld the requirement, but then Section 3 of the Clayton Act effectively reversed that result.

Motion Picture Patents Co. v. Universal Film Mfg. Co., 243 U.S. 502, 37 S.Ct. 416, 61 L.Ed. 871 (1917), confirmed the change in the law. The manufacturer of a film projector containing a patented film feeder required purchasers only to use film in it that was made using a second patent owned by the firm. The Court held that the two patents were unrelated; the effect was the same as requiring use of unpatented "supplies" in a patented product. Justice Clarke, writing for the Court, was adamant: "A restriction which would give to the plaintiff such a potential power for evil

---

[19]   Cf. Ethyl Gasoline Corp. v. United States, 309 U.S. 436, 60 S.Ct. 618, 84 L.Ed. 852 (1940) (generally prohibiting resale price maintenance of patented items); United States v. Singer Manufacturing Co., 374 U.S. 174, 83 S.Ct. 1773, 10 L.Ed.2d 823 (1963) (condemning cross-license arrangement designed to exclude Japanese manufacturers from American market). See also Ward S. Bowman, Patent and Antitrust Law: A Legal and Economic Appraisal 192–197 (1973); George Priest, Cartels and Patent License Agreements, 20 J.Law & Econ. 309 (1977); Steven C. Carlson, Patent Pools and the Antitrust Dilemma, 16 Yale J. on Regulation 359 (1999).

over an industry * * * is plainly void, because wholly without the scope and purpose of our patent laws * * * ."

However, Justices Holmes, McKenna and Van Devanter dissented. The holder of a patent may forbid another to use it, and thus may permit use on any terms. "[I]f the owner prefers to keep the * * * feeder unless you will buy his * * * films," Holmes wrote, "I cannot see, in allowing him to do so, anything more than an ordinary incident of ownership * * * ." Do you agree?

Later, in International Business Machines Corp. v. United States, 298 U.S. 131, 56 S.Ct. 701, 80 L.Ed. 1085 (1936), the manufacturer of a patented tabulating machine tried to require lessees of its tabulating machines to purchase all the cards to be used in the machines from it. The patent holder raised a quality control issue and said that its reputation was based on the machines working well. If people used cards that jammed or led to inaccurate results, it argued, the machine maker would get the blame. A unanimous Court was unimpressed. Others could make the cards to I.B.M. specifications, it reasoned, and I.B.M. could warn users about the dangers of cheap imitations. The Clayton Act was clear and acknowledged no exceptions.

We will not stop here to analyze these cases, but you will want to keep them in mind when we examine tying arrangements in the next chapter.[20]

A NOTE ON THE RELATED ISSUE OF EXCLUSIVE DEALING ARRANGEMENTS

Exclusive dealing is another issue frequently encountered in the context of patent misuse charges. Early in the rule-of-reason period, Standard Fashion Company v. Magrane-Houston Company, 258 U.S. 346, 42 S.Ct. 360, 66 L.Ed. 653 (1922), confirmed that Clayton Act § 3 prohibits many exclusive dealing arrangements.

Standard created and distributed clothing patterns; Magrane sold those patterns at its retail store and agreed not to sell the patterns of any other company. Later, Magrane decided it would rather sell McCall's patterns instead. Standard sued to enjoin such sales, and Magrane's defense was that the contract limiting it to sale of Standard's patterns had been illegal.

Clayton Act § 3 prohibits exclusive dealing contracts whose effects *may* be to substantially limit competition or create a monopoly, the Court said. "But we do not think that the purpose in using the word 'may' was to

---

[20]   The patent law doctrine of patent misuse has itself been amended by the Patent Misuse Reform Act of 1988. See 35 U.S.C. § 271.

prohibit the mere possibility of the consequences described. It was intended to prevent such agreements as would under the circumstances disclosed *probably* lessen competition, or create an *actual* tendency to monopoly." 258 U.S. at 356–57, 42 S.Ct. at 362 (emphasis added).

On the other hand, the Court noted that in an industry with 52,000 retail pattern outlets, Standard and two other firms had used exclusive dealing contracts to control 40% of them. That gave the top firms substantial power to "give fashions their vogue," the Court said, and could facilitate their obtaining an even greater market share in the future. Thus, the Court held, in this case Clayton Act § 3 prohibited Standard's exclusivity requirement.

D. TESTING THE LIMITS OF THE RULE OF REASON

The preceding cases in this chapter have shown us the rule of reason's creation and application in important kinds of settings. Our final two cases remind us that problems of characterizing practices and clarifying issues for antitrust juries were not eliminated by the rule of reason. Indeed, if anything, they were made more perplexing.

UNITED STATES v. TRENTON POTTERIES COMPANY

Supreme Court of the United States, 1927
273 U.S. 392, 47 S.Ct. 377, 71 L.Ed. 700

MR. JUSTICE STONE delivered the opinion of the Court.

Respondents, twenty individuals and twenty-three corporations, were convicted in the district court for southern New York of violating the Sherman Anti-Trust Law. The indictment was in two counts. The first charged a combination to fix and maintain uniform prices for the sale of sanitary pottery, in restraint of interstate commerce; the second, a combination to restrain interstate commerce by limiting sales of pottery to a special group known to respondents as "legitimate jobbers." On appeal, the Court of Appeals for the Second Circuit reversed the judgment of conviction on both counts * * * . This Court granted certiorari.

Respondents, engaged in the manufacture or distribution of 82 per cent. of the vitreous pottery fixtures produced in the United States for use in bathrooms and lavatories, were members of a trade organization known as the Sanitary Potters' Association. Twelve of the corporate respondents had their factories and chief places of business in New Jersey; one was located in California and the others were situated in Illinois, Michigan, West Virginia, Indiana, Ohio and Pennsylvania. * * *

There is no contention here that the verdict was not supported by sufficient evidence * * * .

* * * It is urged that the court below erred in holding in effect that the trial court should have submitted to the jury the question whether the price agreement complained of constituted an unreasonable restraint of trade * * * .

The trial court charged, in submitting the case to the jury that, if it found the agreements or combination complained of, it might return a verdict of guilty without regard to the reasonableness of the prices fixed, or the good intentions of the combining units, whether prices were actually lowered or raised or whether sales were restricted to the special jobbers, since both agreements of themselves were unreasonable restraints. * * * In particular the court refused the request to charge the following:

> "The essence of the law is injury to the public. It is not every restraint of competition and not every restraint of trade that works an injury to the public; it is only an undue and unreasonable restraint of trade that has such an effect and is deemed to be unlawful."

Other requests of similar purport were refused including a quotation from the opinion of this Court in Chicago Board of Trade v. United States.

The court below held specifically that the trial court erred in refusing to charge as requested and held in effect that the charge as given on this branch of the case was erroneous. This determination was based upon the assumption that the charge and refusals could be attributed only to a mistaken view of the trial judge, expressed in denying a motion at the close of the case to quash and dismiss the indictment, that the "rule of reason" announced in Standard Oil Co. v. United States, and in American Tobacco Co. v. United States, which were suits for injunctions, had no application in a criminal prosecution.

This disposition of the matter ignored the fact that the trial judge plainly and variously charged the jury that the combinations alleged in the indictment, if found, were violations of the statute as a matter of law, saying:

> " * * * the law is clear that an agreement on the part of the members of a combination controlling a substantial part of an industry, upon the prices which the members are to charge for their commodity, is in itself an undue and unreasonable restraint of trade and commerce; * * * "

If the charge itself was correctly given and adequately covered the various aspects of the case, the refusal to charge in another correct form or to quote to the jury extracts from opinions of this court was not error, nor should the court below have been concerned with the wrong reasons that may have inspired the charge, if correctly given. The question therefore to be considered here is whether the trial judge correctly withdrew from the jury the consideration of the reasonableness of the particular restraints charged.

That only those restraints upon interstate commerce which are unreasonable are prohibited by the Sherman Law was the rule laid down by the opinions of this court in the *Standard Oil* and *Tobacco* cases. But it does not follow that agreements to fix or maintain prices are reasonable restraints and therefore permitted by the statute, merely because the prices themselves are reasonable. * * * Our view of what is a reasonable restraint of commerce is controlled by the recognized purpose of the Sherman Law itself. Whether this type of restraint is reasonable or not must be judged in part at least in the light of its effect on competition, for, whatever difference of opinion there may be among economists as to the social and economic desirability of an unrestrained competitive system, it cannot be doubted that the Sherman Law and the judicial decisions interpreting it are based upon the assumption that the public interest is best protected from the evils of monopoly and price control by the maintenance of competition. See United States v. Trans-Missouri Freight Association; Standard Oil Co. v. United States; American Column Co. v. United States.

* * * The power to fix prices, whether reasonably exercised or not, involves power to control the market and to fix arbitrary and unreasonable prices. The reasonable price fixed today may through economic and business changes become the unreasonable price of tomorrow. * * * Agreements which create such potential power may well be held to be in themselves unreasonable or unlawful restraints without the necessity of minute inquiry whether a particular price is reasonable or unreasonable as fixed and without placing on the government in enforcing the Sherman Law the burden of ascertaining from day to day whether it has become unreasonable through the mere variation of economic conditions. Moreover, in the absence of express legislation requiring it, we should hesitate to adopt a construction making the difference between legal and illegal conduct in the field of business relations depend upon so uncertain a test as whether prices are reasonable—a determination which can be satisfactorily made only after a complete survey of our economic organization and a choice between rival philosophies. * * *

That such was the view of this court in deciding the *Standard Oil* and *Tobacco* cases, and that such is the effect of its decisions both before and after those cases, does not seem fairly open to question. Beginning with United States v. Trans-Missouri Freight Association [and] United States v. Joint Traffic Association, where agreements for establishing reasonable and uniform freight rates by competing lines of railroad were held unlawful, it has since often been decided and always assumed that uniform price-fixing by those controlling in any substantial manner a trade or business in interstate commerce is prohibited by the Sherman Law, despite the reasonableness of the particular prices agreed upon. * * *

* * *

Respondents rely upon Chicago Board of Trade v. United States, in which an agreement by members of the Chicago Board of Trade controlling prices during certain hours of the day in a special class of grain contracts and affecting only a small proportion of the commerce in question was upheld. * * * That decision, dealing as it did with a regulation of a board of trade, does not sanction a price agreement among competitors in an open market such as is presented here.

The charge of the trial court, viewed as a whole, fairly submitted to the jury the question whether a price-fixing agreement as described in the first count was entered into by the respondents. Whether the prices actually agreed upon were reasonable or unreasonable was immaterial in the circumstances charged in the indictment and necessarily found by the verdict. The requested charge which we have quoted, and others of similar tenor, while true as abstract propositions, were inapplicable to the case in hand and rightly refused.

* * *

It follows that the judgment of the Circuit Court of Appeals must be reversed and the judgment of the District Court reinstated.

MR. JUSTICE VAN DEVANTER, MR. JUSTICE SUTHERLAND and MR. JUSTICE BUTLER dissent.

MR. JUSTICE BRANDEIS took no part in the consideration or decision of this case.

NOTES AND QUESTIONS

1. Why were the defendants not permitted to present their defense? What happened to the rule of reason? Were these accused criminals denied due process of law?

2. At bottom, of course, this case was about a proffered jury instruction, not about the right to present a defense. The defendant wanted to have the judge tell the jury:

> "The essence of the law is injury to the public. It is not every restraint of competition and not every restraint of trade that works an injury to the public; it is only an undue and unreasonable restraint of trade that has such an effect and is deemed to be unlawful."

a. Is that an accurate statement of the law circa 1927? Even if it is true as far as it goes, does it suggest that the jury has more latitude to define what is "unreasonable" than it ever really had?

b.   When Justice White and Justice Brandeis talked about "reason" in earlier cases, did they assume that the jury had the ability to exercise such reason? Did they believe reasonableness was a question for the trier of fact or was it really a matter of law?

3.   Look at what the trial judge *did* tell the jury:

"[It] might return a verdict of guilty without regard to the reasonableness of the prices fixed, or the good intentions of the combining units, [or] whether prices were actually lowered or raised * * * ."

Is there anything to criticize about that statement? Indeed, is it consistent with *Board of Trade*?

4.   *Trenton Potteries* has long been seen as an important case in antitrust history because it seems to many to reject the rule of reason and to be an early assertion of what we will come to call the per se rule. Certainly the Court later so viewed it. Perhaps its most important message, however, is that even in a period (like the present one) when the Court recognizes the reasonableness of certain restraints of trade, there will likely be many restraints that have no redeeming virtues. As to these, a jury perhaps should not be permitted to, in Judge Taft's words, "set sail on a sea of doubt."[21]

THE INTERPLAY BETWEEN ANTITRUST AND DIRECT REGULATION: THE *KEOGH* CASE

As we have noted before, the antitrust laws are only some of many laws regulating business. The Interstate Commerce Act, for example, adopted three years *before* the Sherman Act, required railroads to file rates with the I.C.C., answer any challenge to the rates as unreasonable, and then adhere to the rates until changed.

Keogh v. Chicago & Northwestern Railway Co., 260 U.S. 156, 43 S.Ct. 47, 67 L.Ed. 183 (1922), was a private antitrust action challenging railroad rates established in meetings of the Western Trunk Line Committee. That's right. It was basically the Trans-Missouri Freight Association with a new name.

Keogh manufactured and shipped "excelsior and flax tow." He asked for treble damages—three times the overcharges he alleged he had been forced to pay—because the railroads had established rates collectively instead of individually. In a unanimous opinion written by Justice Brandeis, the Supreme Court denied relief. There was no question the railroads had acted illegally, the Court said, citing *Trans-Missouri* and

---

[21]   For a similar reading of *Trenton Potteries* and its application to current problems, see Thomas G. Krattenmaker, Per Se Violations in Antitrust Law: Confusing Offenses With Defenses, 77 Georgetown L. J. 165 (1988).

Joint Traffic Association, but a private treble damage action was an inappropriate way to challenge the behavior of regulated railroads.

First, once a railroad's rates are approved by the I.C.C., the railroad is legally required to charge them. An award of treble damages would sanction the railroad for obeying that requirement of the law. Second, ratemaking is not a mechanical process; for the court to determine how high the "overcharge" was it would have to know what rates would have been proposed and approved if they had not been set collectively. Because a court could not know that, damage awards would always be arbitrary. Finally, rate regulation is designed to assure that shippers similarly situated pay the same rates. Inconsistent damage awards would undercut that policy of the Interstate Commerce Act.

The case illustrates a problem of accommodating the antitrust laws with often inconsistent federal regulatory policies that continues to the present day.[22] Watch for it throughout this course.

Trenton Potteries represented per se illegality in a rule of reason period, but our next case showed that, even after *Trenton Potteries*, the rule of reason remained alive and well.

APPALACHIAN COALS, INC. v. UNITED STATES

Supreme Court of the United States, 1933
288 U.S. 344, 53 S.Ct. 471, 77 L.Ed. 825

MR. CHIEF JUSTICE HUGHES delivered the opinion of the Court.

This suit was brought to enjoin a combination alleged to be in restraint of interstate commerce in bituminous coal and in attempted monopolization of part of that commerce, in violation of sections 1 and 2 of the Sherman Anti-Trust Act. The District Court * * * made detailed findings of fact and entered [a] final decree granting the injunction. The case comes here on appeal.

Defendants, other than Appalachian Coals, Inc., are 137 producers of bituminous coal in eight districts (called for convenience Appalachian territory) lying in Virginia, West Virginia, Kentucky and Tennessee. * * * In 1929 * * * defendants' production * * * was found to amount to 74.4 per cent [of all the coal produced in the Appalachian region].

The challenged combination lies in the creation by the defendant producers of an exclusive selling agency. This agency is the defendant

---

[22] *Keogh* itself was reaffirmed by the Court in Square D Co. v. Niagara Frontier Tariff Bureau, 476 U.S. 409, 106 S.Ct. 1922, 90 L.Ed.2d 413 (1986). See also, Georgia v. Pennsylvania R.R., 324 U.S. 439, 65 S.Ct. 716, 89 L.Ed. 1051 (1945) (state may sue to enjoin collective ratemaking); and 49 U.S.C. § 10706 (current statutory regulation of collective ratemaking).

Appalachian Coals, Inc., which may be designated as the Company. Defendant producers own all its capital stock, their holdings being in proportion to their production. * * * By uniform contracts, separately made, each defendant producer constitutes the Company an exclusive agent for the sale of all coal * * * which the producer mines in Appalachian territory. The Company agrees to establish standard classifications, to sell all the coal of all its principals at the best prices obtainable and, if all cannot be sold, to apportion orders upon a stated basis. The plan contemplates that prices are to be fixed by the officers of the Company at its central office * * * . The Company is to be paid a commission of ten per cent. of the gross selling prices f.o.b. at the mines, and guarantees accounts. * * * The Company has not yet begun to operate as selling agent * * * .

The Government's contention, which the District Court sustained, is that the plan violates the Sherman Anti-Trust Act—in the view that it eliminates competition among the defendants themselves and also gives the selling agency power substantially to affect and control the price of bituminous coal in many interstate markets. On the latter point the District Court made the general finding that this elimination of competition and concerted action will affect market conditions, and have a tendency to stabilize prices and to raise prices to a higher level than would prevail under conditions of free competition. The court added that the selling agency will not have monopoly control of any market nor the power to fix monopoly prices.

Defendants insist that the primary purpose of the formation of the selling agency was to increase the sale, and thus the production, of Appalachian coal through better methods of distribution, intensive advertising and research, to achieve economies in marketing, and to eliminate abnormal, deceptive and destructive trade practices. They disclaim any intent to restrain or monopolize interstate commerce, and in justification of their design they point to the statement of the District Court that "it is but due to defendants to say that the evidence in the case clearly shows that they have been acting fairly and openly, in an attempt to organize the coal industry and to relieve the deplorable conditions resulting from overexpansion, destructive competition, wasteful trade practices, and the inroads of competing industries." Defendants contend that the evidence establishes that the selling agency will not have the power to dominate or fix the price of coal in any consuming market; that the price of coal will continue to be set in an open competitive market; and that their plan by increasing the sale of bituminous coal from Appalachian territory will promote, rather than restrain, interstate commerce.

First. There is no question as to the test to be applied in determining the legality of the defendants' conduct. The purpose of the Sherman Anti-Trust Act is to prevent undue restraints of interstate commerce, to maintain its appropriate freedom in the public interest, to afford protection from the subversive or coercive influences of monopolistic endeavor. As a charter of freedom, the Act has a generality and adaptability comparable to that found to be desirable in constitutional provisions. It does not go into detailed definitions which might either work injury to legitimate enterprise or through particularization defeat its purposes by providing loopholes for escape. The restrictions the Act imposes are not mechanical or artificial. Its general phrases, interpreted to attain its fundamental objects, set up the essential standard of reasonableness. * * *

In applying this test, a close and objective scrutiny of particular conditions and purposes is necessary in each case. Realities must dominate the judgment. The mere fact that the parties to an agreement eliminate competition between themselves is not enough to condemn it. * * * The familiar illustrations of partnerships, and enterprises fairly integrated in the interest of the promotion of commerce, at once occur. The question of the application of the statute is one of intent and effect, and is not to be determined by arbitrary assumptions. * * *

Second. The findings of the District Court, upon abundant evidence, leave no room for doubt as to the economic condition of the coal industry. That condition, as the District Court states, "for many years has been indeed deplorable." Due largely to the expansion under the stimulus of the Great War, "the bituminous mines of the country have a developed capacity exceeding 700,000,000 tons" to meet a demand "of less than 500,000,000 tons." * * * The actual decrease is partly due to the industrial condition but the relative decrease is progressing, due entirely to other causes. Coal has been losing markets to oil, natural gas and water power and has also been losing ground due to greater efficiency in the use of coal. * * *

This unfavorable condition has been aggravated by particular practices. One of these relates to what is called "distress coal." The greater part of the demand is for particular sizes of coal such as nut and slack, stove coal, egg coal, and lump coal. Any one size cannot be prepared without making several sizes. According to the finding of the court below, one of the chief problems of the industry is thus involved in the practice of producing different sizes of coal even though orders are on hand for only one size, and the necessity of marketing all sizes. Usually there are no storage facilities at the mines and the different sizes produced are placed in cars on the producer's tracks, which may become so congested that either production must be stopped or the cars must be moved regardless of demand. This leads to the practice of shipping unsold coal to billing points or on consignment to the producer or his agent in the consuming territory. If the coal is not sold by the time it reaches its destination, and is not unloaded promptly, it becomes subject to demurrage charges which may exceed the amount obtainable for the coal unless it is sold quickly. The court found that this type of "distress coal" presses on the market at all times, includes all sizes and grades, and the total amount from all causes is of substantial quantity.

"Pyramiding" of coal is another "destructive practice." It occurs when a producer authorizes several persons to sell the same coal, and they may in turn offer it for sale to other dealers. In consequence "the coal competes with itself, thereby resulting in abnormal and destructive competition which depresses the price for all coals in the market." * * *

In addition to these factors, the District Court found that organized buying agencies, and large consumers purchasing substantial tonnages, "constitute unfavorable forces." "The highly organized and concentrated buying power which they control and the great abundance of coal available have contributed to make the market for coal a buyers' market for many years past."

It also appears that the "unprofitable condition" of the industry has existed particularly in the Appalachian territory where there is little local consumption as the region is not industrialized. * * * And in a graphic summary of the economic situation, the court found that "numerous producing companies have gone into bankruptcy or into the hands of receivers, many mines have been shut down, the number of days of operation per week have been greatly curtailed, wages to labor have been substantially lessened, and the States in which coal producing companies are located have found it increasingly difficult to collect taxes."

Third. * * * The serious economic conditions had led to discussions among coal operators and state and national officials, seeking improvement of the industry. Governors of States had held meetings with coal producers. The limits of official authority were apparent. * * * [At a] general meeting in December, 1931, * * * a report which recommended the organization of regional sales agencies, and was supported by the opinion of counsel as to the legality of proposed forms of contract, was approved. Committees to present the plan to producers were constituted for eighteen producing districts including the eight districts in Appalachian territory. Meetings of the representatives of the latter districts resulted in the organization of defendant Appalachian Coals, Inc. It was agreed that a minimum of 70 per cent. and a maximum of 80 per cent. of the commercial tonnage of the territory should be secured before the plan should become effective. Approximately 73 per cent. was obtained. * * * The maximum of 80 per cent. was adopted because a majority of the producers felt that an organization with a greater degree of control might unduly restrict competition in local markets. The minimum of 70 per cent. was fixed because it was agreed that the organization would not be effective without the degree of control. The court below also found that it was the expectation that similar agencies would be organized in other producing districts including those which were competitive with Appalachian coal * * *.

When, in January, 1932, the Department of Justice announced its adverse opinion, the producers outside Appalachian territory decided to hold their plans in abeyance pending the determination of the question by the courts. The District Court found that "the evidence tended to show that other selling agencies with a control of at least 70 per cent. of the production in their respective districts will be organized if the petition in this case is dismissed * * * but the testimony tends to show that there will still be substantial, active competition in the sale of coal in all markets in which Appalachian coal is sold."

* * *

No attempt was made to limit production. The producers decided that it could not legally be limited and, in any event, it could not be limited practically. The finding is that "it was designed that the producer should produce and the selling agent should sell as much coal as possible." The importance of increasing sales is said to lie in the fact that the cost of production is directly related to the actual running time of the mines.

Fourth. Voluminous evidence was received with respect to the effect of defendants' plan upon market prices. As the plan has not gone into operation, there are no actual results upon which to base conclusions. The question is necessarily one of prediction. The court below found that, as between defendants themselves, competition would be eliminated. * * *

The more serious question relates to the effect of the plan upon competition between defendants and other producers. * * * [A]n examination of [the evidence] fails to disclose an adequate basis for the conclusion that the operation of the defendants' plan would produce an injurious effect upon competitive conditions, in view of the vast volume of coal available, the conditions of production, and the network of transportation facilities at immediate command. * * *

* * *

Fifth. We think that the evidence requires the following conclusions:

(1) With respect to defendants' purposes, we find no warrant for determining that they were other than those they declared. Good intentions will not save a plan otherwise objectionable, but knowledge of actual intent is an aid in the interpretation of facts and prediction of consequences. Chicago Board of Trade v. United States. The evidence leaves no doubt of the existence of the evils at which defendants' plan was aimed. * * * The unfortunate state of the industry would not justify any attempt unduly to restrain competition or to monopolize, but the existing situation prompted defendants to make, and the statute did not preclude them from making, an honest effort to remove abuses, to make competition fairer, and thus to promote the essential interests of commerce. The interests of producers and consumers are interlinked. When industry is

grievously hurt, when producing concerns fail, when unemployment mounts and communities dependent upon profitable production are prostrated, the wells of commerce go dry. * * *

(2) The question thus presented chiefly concerns the effect upon prices. * * * [W]e think that the proof clearly shows that, wherever their selling agency operates, it will find itself confronted by effective competition backed by virtually inexhaustible sources of supply, and will also be compelled to cope with the organized buying power of large consumers. The plan cannot be said either to contemplate or to involve the fixing of market prices.

The contention is, and the court below found, that while defendants could not fix market prices, the concerted action would "affect" them, that is, that it would have a tendency to stabilize market prices and to raise them to a higher level than would otherwise obtain. But the facts found do not establish, and the evidence fails to show, that any effect will be produced which in the circumstances of this industry will be detrimental to fair competition. A cooperative enterprise, otherwise free from objection, which carries with it no monopolistic menace, is not to be condemned as an undue restraint merely because it may effect a change in market conditions, where the change would be in mitigation of recognized evils and would not impair, but rather foster, fair competitive opportunities. * * * The intelligent conduct of commerce through the acquisition of full information of all relevant facts may properly be sought by the cooperation of those engaged in trade, although stabilization of trade and more reasonable prices may be the result. Maple Flooring Association v. United States; Cement Manufacturers Association v. United States. Putting an end to injurious practices, and the consequent improvement of the competitive position of a group of producers is not a less worthy aim and may be entirely consonant with the public interest, where the group must still meet effective competition in a fair market and neither seeks nor is able to effect a domination of prices.

Decisions cited in support of a contrary view were addressed to very different circumstances from those presented here. * * * In Addyston Pipe & Steel Company v. United States, the combination was effected by those who were in a position to deprive, and who sought to deprive, the public in a large territory of the advantages of fair competition and was for the actual purpose and had the result of enhancing prices—which in fact had been unreasonably increased. In United States v. Trenton Potteries Company, defendants, who controlled 82 per cent. of the business of manufacturing and distributing vitreous pottery in the United States, had combined to fix prices. It was found that they had the power to do this and had exerted it. * * *

(3) * * * Defendants insist that on the evidence adduced as to their competitive position in the consuming markets, and in the absence of proof of actual operations showing an injurious effect upon competition, either through possession or abuse of power, no valid objection could have been interposed under the Sherman Act if the defendants had eliminated competition between themselves by a complete integration of their mining properties in a single ownership. United States v. United States Steel Corporation. We agree that there is no ground for holding defendants' plan illegal merely because they have not integrated their properties and have chosen to maintain their independent plants, seeking not to limit but rather to facilitate production. We know of no public policy, and none is suggested by the terms of the Sherman Act, that in order to comply with the law those engaged in industry should be driven to unify their properties and businesses in order to correct abuses which may be corrected by less drastic measures. Public policy might indeed be deemed to point in a different direction. * * *

* * * We recognize, however, that the case has been tried in advance of the operation of defendants' plan, and that it has been necessary to test that plan with reference to purposes and anticipated consequences without the advantage of the demonstrations of experience. If in actual operation it should prove to be an undue restraint upon interstate commerce, if it should appear that the plan is used to the impairment of fair competitive opportunities, the decision upon the present record should not preclude the Government from seeking the remedy which would be suited to such a state of facts. * * *

* * *

MR. JUSTICE MCREYNOLDS thinks that the court below reached the proper conclusion and that its decree should be affirmed.

NOTES AND QUESTIONS

1. Was there any basis to deny that 137 companies were engaged in price fixing when they formed Appalachian Coals? Hadn't 137 individual price setters become one?

a. Don't be too quick! Why wasn't Appalachian Coals like a partnership? The Court had been saying for years that formation of partnerships is not a Sherman Act violation.

b. Was Appalachian Coals, Inc., merely another trade association trying to stimulate demand for its members' product? Was the Court's reliance on *Maple Flooring* appropriate and convincing?

2. How varied do you suppose the price of coal was on any given day *before* Appalachian Coals was formed?

a.   Might coal be a fungible product—like corn or wheat—that is sold at a market price not set by any of the 137 producers? If so, wouldn't Appalachian Coals, Inc. be as subject to those market forces as were its individual members?

b.   Does that ignore shipping costs and the consequent advantages firms have selling to customers near to them? Does this case turn on the finding that not much coal was bought for use in Appalachia?

3.   Were you convinced there were special "destructive practices" in the coal market?

a.   What does it mean to say that the market was flooded with "distress coal"? Aren't the falling prices mines faced exactly the signal the market is supposed to give to people who are overproducing? Weren't the falling prices a *good* thing for homeowners who lacked money to heat their homes? Was homeowners' preference for oil and gas heat an "evil" calling out for correction?

b.   Was the real problem a "pyramiding" of coal, i.e., selling it through more than one agent? Can one really attribute the decline in market prices to confusion about how much coal was for sale? Do you suppose market professionals were confused for very long about what was going on?

c.   Then was the fact that some buyers bought large amounts of coal among the "unfavorable forces" affecting this market? Were any individual large buyers likely monopsonists? Could any of them likely have affected the market price of coal?

4.   Did Appalachian Coals have even close to a monopoly of coal in the country? What significance should be given to the fact that its members produced 54–74% of the coal in the Appalachian region and 12% of the coal mined east of the Mississippi?

a.   There were similar sales organizations already formed and only waiting for the go ahead from the Supreme Court to proceed. What effect should a trend toward use of common selling agents have on the Court's view of them? That is, might forming one agency be innocuous but forming eight to sell all the coal in the country create a problem of oligopoly?

b.   May one set aside concerns about formation of this selling agency because there are no limits set on members' production? That is, can one rest easy because if Appalachian Coals, Inc., does not have better storage facilities than its members did, the increasing supply of coal will prevent efforts to increase price?

c.   Is "stabilizing" price a permitted practice even if price fixing is not? Should mere "effect" on price be enough to render an agreement illegal? Was some likely effect on price largely conceded by the Court here? Before you answer too confidently, wait until you read United States v. Socony-Vacuum Oil Co. at the outset of the next chapter.

d.   Indeed, what issue did the Court say could only be determined after the new entity was in operation? Was it whether there would be an effect on price? Look again. It was whether it would create an "undue restraint upon interstate commerce." Do you have any clear idea what the Court meant by that phrase?

5.   Do you agree with Chief Justice Hughes that: "As a charter of freedom, the Act has a generality and adaptability comparable to that found to be desirable in constitutional provisions. It does not go into detailed definitions * * * "? Is the capacity to change as conditions and as economic theories change part of the genius of the Sherman Act? Are you uncomfortable about the content of a criminal statute being that adaptable?[23]

6.   Do you agree that holding this plan illegal might have tended to cause firms to merge as a way of getting the same result without § 1 liability? Does your answer depend on whether Section 7 of the Clayton Act would prohibit such mergers? If they were not clearly prohibited, should we be worried about such combinations?

7.   Should it be relevant that the economic policy of the New Deal was consistent with formation of such joint selling agencies? Should firms acting pursuant to an order of a federal agency have a complete defense to a charge of restraint of trade? How about when they are acting pursuant to the order of a state agency? What relevance should be given to the fact that, as the Court noted, "Governors of States had held meetings with coal producers"?

8.   Agricultural cooperatives perform a function similar to Appalachian Coals and have a specific statutory exemption from the Sherman Act.[24] Is there any policy basis for treating agricultural cooperatives differently from Appalachian Coals, Inc.?

MORE ON PROOF OF AGREEMENT: *SUGAR INSTITUTE* AND *INTERSTATE CIRCUIT*

Earlier in this chapter, we looked at cases from the mid-1920s trying to deal with pricing by firms that was interdependent but not conspiratorial. In the mid-1930s, the Supreme Court decided two other important cases that helped define when firms could be said to have "agreed" on prices in violation of Sherman Act § 1.

In Sugar Institute v. United States, 297 U.S. 553, 56 S.Ct. 629, 80 L.Ed. 859 (1936), the fifteen Institute members refined 70–80% of the sugar used in the United States. Prices had fallen after World War I and

---

[23]   For trenchant criticism of Chief Justice Hughes' approach to Sherman Act construction, see Thomas C. Arthur, Farewell to the Sea of Doubt: Jettisoning the Constitutional Sherman Act, 74 California L. Rev. 263 (1986); Thomas C. Arthur, Workable Antitrust Law: The Statutory Approach to Antitrust, 62 Tulane L. Rev. 1163 (1988). For contrast, see, e.g., Paul H. Brietzke, The Constitutionalization of Antitrust: Jefferson, Madison, Hamilton, and Thomas C. Arthur, 22 Valparaiso U. L. Rev. 275 (1988); Robert Pitofsky, The Political Content of Antitrust, 127 U. Pennsylvania L. Rev. 1051 (1979).

[24]   It is Clayton Act § 6, 15 U.S.C. § 17, the same statutory section that protects labor unions against most antitrust prosecution.

"unethical" refiners had started giving discounts on their announced prices. As a result, the Institute's Code of Ethics forbade members from changing prices until after a "move," i.e. a publicly announced price change. Any seller could announce such a move to take place typically a day later. No consultation occurred before the announcement, but in practice, if other firms did not similarly announce a "move" raising their prices, the first firm would withdraw its own "move" to avoid losing sales. "[T]he endeavor to put a stop to illicit practices must not itself become illicit," the Court said. Companies may announce price changes in advance, but Institute steps to enforce adherence to those prices violated Sherman Act § 1.[25]

In Interstate Circuit v. United States, 306 U.S. 208, 59 S.Ct. 467, 83 L.Ed. 610 (1939), defendants Interstate Circuit and Texas Consolidated ran a total of 130 movie theaters in Texas and New Mexico. Some were "first run" theaters and charged 40 cents or more for a ticket. Some were "subsequent run" theaters that ran films whose initial popularity had waned and thus charged less per ticket. These two firms "dominated" exhibition in the cities in which they operated and together they paid over 74% of the movie license fees in their territories. The two firms were affiliated with each other and with Paramount Pictures, a major movie distributor. In 1934, the common manager of Interstate and Consolidated wrote a letter to each of eight "distributors"—in effect wholesalers of movies—stating that, as a condition of Interstate's and Consolidated's continuing to show their films, a distributor must agree not to make films available to any subsequent run theater that charged less than 25 cents per ticket, or any theater that ran first run films as part of a "double feature." The letters clearly showed each addressee that all of its competitors had received the same letter. The distributors individually agreed to the demand.

The Supreme Court upheld the District Court's conclusion that the contracts between Interstate and each distributor were in restraint of trade, but that was not the interesting part of the case. The Court also found that each of the distributors was guilty of conspiring with each of the others even though they had never communicated with one another; they had only responded to Interstate. Justice Stone wrote:

> "Acceptance by competitors, without previous agreement, of an invitation to participate in a plan, the necessary consequence of which, if carried out, is in restraint of interstate commerce, is sufficient to establish an unlawful conspiracy under the Sherman Act."

---

[25]   On just such a theory, the Justice Department challenged the practice whereby airlines "announce" future price changes by putting them into the industry's computerized reservation systems. United States v. Airline Tariff Publishing Co., 836 F.Supp. 9 (D.D.C.1993). What do you think of the charge?

Does this result surprise you? Do you agree that action undertaken with the knowledge that others will act the same way should constitute an "agreement"? The Court cited *American Column & Lumber Co.* in support of this proposition. Do you agree that *American Column* went that far?

A NOTE ON ECONOMIC THINKING DURING THE DEPRESSION

The Great Depression, which began in about 1929 and lasted at least until World War II, was a time of reexamination of economic assumptions in this country. The virtue of "rugged individualism" and the expectation of inexhaustible wealth generated by big business were both cast into doubt. In addition, to some analysts, the new economic program in the Soviet Union seemed a promising source of alternate approaches.

It is impossible to capture such widely diverse ideas in a page or two, but one cannot properly understand the next thirty years of antitrust law without recognizing the intellectual and policy upheaval the Great Depression caused. Some of the ideas may even sound familiar—albeit often marketed under new labels—today.

Basically, two propositions had to be made to coexist. The first idea was that excessive concentration within industries and excessive concentrations of private wealth lead to an economic system that is sluggish and a political system that serves the rich at the expense of the poor.[26] As President Roosevelt put it in his 1938 Message to Congress, "The liberty of a democracy is not safe if the people tolerate the growth of private power to a point where it becomes stronger than their democratic state itself."

The second was that widely distributed economic and political power is inefficient. It needs to be organized and coordinated by government, with subsidies granted to especially promising or worthy enterprises. Only as businesses and industries are organized and managed democratically, it was argued, can they realize economies of scale but function for the common good.[27]

Thus, government policy proceeded on two fronts. One was action against the "trusts" of the day, whether by filing antitrust actions against large firms like Alcoa (a case we will examine in the next chapter), by creating new federal agencies such as the Federal Power Commission, or

---

[26] Among the important books expressing this theme were Charles A. Beard, The Myth of Rugged American Individualism (1931); Adolf A. Berle, Jr. & Gardiner C. Means, The Modern Corporation and Private Property (1933). The period is described in Ellis W. Hawley, The New Deal and the Problem of Monopoly (1966).

[27] See, e.g., William O. Douglas, Protecting the Investor, 23 The Yale Review 521 (1934).

by creating new government enterprises such as the Tennessee Valley Authority.

The other front was symbolized by the National Industrial Recovery Act, adopted as the centerpiece of his economic program within 100 days after President Roosevelt took office in 1933.

> "The NIRA promised to extract the United States from the continuing depression through cooperative action: promoting cartels to aid industry and promoting unions to aid employees. Within one year, codes of 'fair competition' were passed for four hundred and fifty individual industries, covering twenty-three million workers. By the time the law was declared unconstitutional on 27 May 1935, over five hundred and fifty codes had been passed covering almost the entire private, nonagricultural economy."[28]

The National Recovery Administration saw itself as in the "process of building a new industrial democracy."[29] Codes created an "executive and administrative organization chosen from within the industry itself," which was seen as "one of the ideals which industry itself has sought from the beginning of time." The codes contained provisions prohibiting "the abuses of the past, the chiseling, cut-throat competition, dishonest practices of all sorts"; this was to be industry's "quid pro quo for its efforts in behalf of labor and for its cooperation with the country."[30]

One of the biggest problems the NRA addressed was the creation of industry trade associations that would seek creation of a Code. Such associations that been "hampered in their legitimate aims by the antitrust laws."[31] The point is that this second front of the battle against the depression was inconsistent with most of the pro-competitive philosophy that had undergirded the antitrust laws, both in their early years and under the rule of reason.

It is small wonder, then, that the creators of Appalachian Coals, Inc., saw themselves in the vanguard of a new movement. Keep the same sense in mind as you read *Socony-Vacuum*, *Alcoa*, Parker v. Brown, and other depression-era cases in the next chapter.

---

[28]　Michael M. Weinstein, Recovery and Redistribution Under the NIRA 1 (1980).

[29]　A. Heath Onthank, How Codes are Made, in Clair Wilcox, et al., eds., American's Recovery Program 68 (1934).

[30]　Id. at 72.

[31]　Id. at 73. See also, Bruno Burn, Codes, Cartels, National Planning (1934); George Terborgh, Price Control Devices in NRA Codes (1934).

CHAPTER III

THE PER SE RULE AND FOCUS ON MARKET STRUCTURE: 1940 TO 1974

■ ■ ■

This chapter is longer than the first two combined. The period from 1940 to the early 1970s developed many of the important principles to which the cases in the modern period respond. It was also the period during which many of today's senior practitioners received their antitrust training.

In order to see the doctrinal development somewhat better, this chapter is subdivided into five parts. The first looks at horizontal price fixing, market division and group boycott cases brought under Sherman Act § 1. The second examines alleged monopolization under Sherman Act § 2. The third considers which vertical arrangements, if any, deny other firms business opportunities in violation of Clayton Act § 3, while the fourth examines vertical price fixing and market division alleged to be in violation of Sherman Act § 1. The fifth and final part considers mergers under the standards of Clayton Act § 7.

Within each of these lines of cases, notice that doctrine was rarely static. It evolved as the Court tried to give warning of practices considered illegal, avoid prohibiting practices that might in fact be procompetitive, and make the issues in antitrust cases simple enough that they could be tried before ordinary judges and juries.

Finally, pay close attention to economic assumptions underlying the Court's decisions. The Great Depression lasted over a decade, and it became more and more tempting to believe that such a significant event had exposed something fundamentally wrong in the American economy. In 1932, Adolf Berle and Gardiner Means blamed much of the problem on the control of about one-half the corporate wealth in the United States by the 200 largest non-banking corporations.[1] All of the elements that favored concentration still existed, they reported, and many of their readers were convinced that legal intervention was required.

In 1937, Professor Thurman Arnold blamed the concentration on the then-current approach to antitrust law. He explained:

---

[1]   Adolf A. Berle and Gardiner Means, The Modern Corporation and Private Property 19 (1932). This period is summarized well in Lee Loevinger, Antitrust and the New Economics, 37 Minnesota L.Rev. 505 (1953).

"The actual result of the antitrust laws was to promote the growth of great industrial organizations by deflecting the attack on them into purely moral and ceremonial channels. * * * [T]he courts soon discovered that it was only 'unreasonable' combinations which were bad, just as any court would decide that a big, strong neighbor should not be incarcerated so long as he acted reasonably. * * * [This occurred] not because the courts were composed of wicked and hypocritical people, anxious to evade the law, but because such a process is inevitable when an ideal meets in head-on collision with a practical need. * * * In this way the antitrust laws became the greatest protection to uncontrolled business dictatorships."[2]

In 1938, President Roosevelt appointed Arnold to head the Justice Department's antitrust division. That same year, Congress created a Temporary National Economic Committee whose report later called for restoration of a competitive economy to head off the need for "concentrated government authority which might easily destroy democracy."[3]

That was the context in 1939 when the Supreme Court was joined by a 41-year-old recent chairman of the SEC. He would serve for 36 years and his period of service would closely track and significantly define the third great period of antitrust law. His name was William O. Douglas, and in one of his first important opinions he completely transformed much of the law we have seen to this point.

A. HORIZONTAL COMBINATIONS IN RESTRAINT OF TRADE

1. PRICE FIXING

UNITED STATES v. SOCONY-VACUUM OIL CO.

Supreme Court of the United States, 1940
310 U.S. 150, 60 S.Ct. 811, 84 L.Ed. 1129

MR. JUSTICE DOUGLAS delivered the opinion of the Court.

Respondents were convicted by a jury, under an indictment charging violations of § 1 of the Sherman Anti-Trust Act. The Circuit Court of Appeals reversed and remanded for a new trial. The case is here on * * * certiorari * * * .

---

[2]   Thurman Arnold, The Folklore of Capitalism 212–214 (1937). Arnold's strategy and vigor in this transformative period of antitrust enforcement are described in Spencer Weber Waller, The Antitrust Legacy of Thurman Arnold, 78 St. John's L. Rev. 569 (2004).

[3]   Final Report and Recommendations of the Temporary National Economic Committee, S.Doc. No. 35, 77th Cong., 1st Sess., p. 25 (1941).

I. THE INDICTMENT.

The indictment * * * charges that certain major oil companies,[4] selling gasoline in the Mid-Western area, * * * (1) "combined and conspired together for the purpose of artificially raising and fixing the tank car prices of gasoline" in the "spot markets" in the East Texas and Mid-Continent fields; (2) "have * * * maintained said prices at artificially high and non-competitive levels" * * * ; (3) "have arbitrarily," by reason of the provisions of the prevailing form of jobber contracts which made the price to the jobber dependent on the average spot market price, "exacted large sums of money from thousands of jobbers with whom they have had such contracts in said Mid-Western area"; and (4) "in turn have intentionally raised the general level of retail prices prevailing in said Mid-Western area."

The manner and means of effectuating such conspiracy are alleged in substance as follows: Defendants, from February 1935 to December 1936 "have knowingly and unlawfully engaged and participated in two concerted gasoline buying programs" for the purchase "from independent refiners in spot transactions of large quantities of gasoline in the East Texas and Mid-Continent fields at uniform, high, and at times progressively increased prices." * * *

* * *

The methods of marketing and selling gasoline in the Mid-Western area are set forth in the indictment in some detail. * * * Each defendant major oil company owns, operates or leases retail service stations in this area. It supplies those stations, as well as independent retail stations, with gasoline from its bulk storage plants. All but one sell large quantities of gasoline to jobbers in tank car lots under term contracts. * * * The price to the jobbers under those contracts with defendant companies is made dependent on the spot market price * * * . And the spot market tank car prices of gasoline directly and substantially influence the retail prices in the area. In sum, it is alleged that defendants by raising and fixing the tank car prices of gasoline in these spot markets could and did increase * * * the retail prices of gasoline sold in the Mid-Western area. * * *

* * *

II. BACKGROUND OF THE ALLEGED CONSPIRACY.

* * *

Beginning about 1926 there commenced a period of production of crude oil in such quantities as seriously to affect crude oil and gasoline markets

---

[4]   The major oil companies, in the main, engage in every branch of the business—owning and operating oil wells, pipelines, refineries, bulk storage plants, and service stations. Those engaging in all such branches are major integrated oil companies; those lacking facilities for one or more of those branches are semi-integrated. "Independent refiners" describes companies engaged exclusively in refining. [Court's fn. 4]

throughout the United States. Overproduction was wasteful, reduced the productive capacity of the oil fields and drove the price of oil down to levels below the cost of production from pumping and stripper wells. When the price falls below such cost, those wells must be abandoned. Once abandoned, subsurface changes make it difficult or impossible to bring those wells back into production. Since such wells constitute about 40% of the country's known oil reserves, conservation requires that the price of crude oil be maintained at a level which will permit such wells to be operated. As Oklahoma and Kansas were attempting to remedy the situation through their proration laws, the largest oil field in history was discovered in East Texas. That was in 1930. The supply of oil from this field was so great that at one time crude oil sank to 10 or 15 cents a barrel, and gasoline was sold in the East Texas field for $2\frac{1}{8}$ cents a gallon. Enforcement by Texas of its proration law was extremely difficult. Orders restricting production were violated, the oil unlawfully produced being known as "hot oil" and the gasoline manufactured therefrom, "hot gasoline." Hot oil sold for substantially lower prices than those posted for legal oil. Hot gasoline therefore cost less and at times could be sold for less than it cost to manufacture legal gasoline. The latter, deprived of its normal outlets, had to be sold at distress prices. The condition of many independent refiners using legal crude oil was precarious. In spite of their unprofitable operations they could not afford to shut down, for if they did so they would be apt to lose their oil connections in the field and their regular customers. Having little storage capacity they had to sell their gasoline as fast as they made it. As a result their gasoline became "distress" gasoline—gasoline which the refiner could not store, for which he had no regular sales outlets and which therefore he had to sell for whatever price it would bring. Such sales drove the market down.

In the spring of 1933 conditions were acute. The wholesale market was below the cost of manufacture. As the market became flooded with cheap gasoline, gasoline was dumped at whatever price it would bring. On June 1, 1933, the price of crude oil was 25 cents a barrel; the tank car price of regular gasoline was $2\frac{5}{8}$ cents a gallon. In June 1933 Congress passed the National Industrial Recovery Act. Sec. 9(c) of that Act authorized the President to forbid the interstate and foreign shipment of petroleum and its products produced or withdrawn from storage in violation of state laws. By Executive Order the President on July 11, 1933, forbade such shipments. On August 19, 1933, a code of fair competition for the petroleum industry was approved. The Secretary of the Interior was designated as Administrator of that Code. He established a Petroleum Administrative Board to "advise with and make recommendations" to him. A Planning and Coordination Committee was appointed, of which respondent Charles E. Arnott, a vice-president of Socony-Vacuum, was a member, to aid in the administration of the Code. In addressing that Committee in the fall of 1933 the Administrator said: "Our task is to stabilize the oil industry upon a profitable basis." * * * In April 1934 an amendment to the Code was adopted [which] * * * authorized the Planning and Coordination Committee, with the approval of the President, to make suitable arrangements for the purchase of gasoline from non-integrated or semi-integrated refiners and the resale of the same through orderly channels. Thereafter four buying programs were approved by the Administrator. These permitted the major companies to purchase distress gasoline from the independent refiners. * * *

The flow of hot oil out of East Texas continued. Refiners in the field could procure such oil for 35 cents or less a barrel and manufacture gasoline from it for 2 or 2 1/2 cents a gallon. This competition of the cheap hot gasoline drove the price of legal gasoline down below the cost of production. * * * In October 1934 the Administrator set up a Federal Tender Board and issued an order making it illegal to ship crude oil or gasoline out of East Texas in interstate or foreign commerce unless it were accompanied by a tender issued by that Board certifying that it had been legally produced or manufactured. Prices rose sharply. But the improvement was only temporary as the enforcement of § 9(c) of the Act was enjoined in a number of suits. On January 7, 1935, this Court held § 9(c) to be unconstitutional. Panama Refining Co. v. Ryan, 293 U.S. 388. Following that decision there was a renewed influx of hot gasoline into the Mid-Western area and the tank car market fell.

Meanwhile the retail markets had been swept by a series of price wars. These price wars affected all markets—service station, tank wagon, and tank car. Early in 1934 the Petroleum Administrative Board tried to deal with them—by negotiating agreements between marketing companies and persuading individual companies to raise the price level for a period. On July 9, 1934, that Board asked respondent Arnott, chairman of the Planning and Coordination Committee's Marketing Committee, if he would head up a voluntary, cooperative movement to deal with price wars. * * * On July 20, 1934, the Administrator wrote Arnott, described the disturbance caused by price wars and said:

"Under Article VII, Section 3 of the Code it is the duty of the Planning and Coordination Committee to cooperate with the Administration as a planning and fair practice agency for the industry. I am, therefore, requesting you, as Chairman of the Marketing Committee of the Planning and Coordination Committee, to take action which we deem necessary to restore markets to their normal conditions in areas where wasteful competition has caused them to become depressed. * * * "

After receiving that letter Arnott appointed a General Stabilization Committee * * * . Over fifty state and local committees were set up. * * * The Petroleum Administrative Board worked closely with Arnott and the committees until the end of the Code near the middle of 1935. The effort (first local, then state-wide, and finally regional) was to eliminate price wars by negotiation * * * . * * * It was at [one of those] meetings that the groundwork for the alleged conspiracy was laid.

III. THE ALLEGED CONSPIRACY.

* * *

A. *Formation of the Mid-Continent Buying Program.*

* * * [A] meeting of the General Stabilization Committee was held in Chicago on January 4, 1935, and was attended by all of the individual respondents, by representatives of the corporate respondents, and by others. * * * Views were expressed to the effect that "if we were going to have general stabilization in retail markets, we must have some sort of a firm market in the tank car market." As a result of the discussion Arnott appointed a Tank Car Stabilization Committee to study the situation and make a report, or, to use the language of one of those present, "to consider ways and means of establishing and maintaining an active and strong tank car market on gasoline." Three days after this committee was appointed, this Court decided Panama Refining Co. v. Ryan. * * *

The first meeting of the Tank Car Committee was held February 5, 1935, and the second on February 11, 1935. At these meetings the alleged conspiracy was formed, the substance of which, so far as it pertained to the Mid-Continent phase, was as follows:

It was estimated that there would be between 600 and 700 tank cars of distress gasoline produced in the Mid-Continent oil field every month by about 17 independent refiners. These refiners, not having regular outlets for the gasoline, would be unable to dispose of it except at distress prices. Accordingly, it was proposed and decided that certain major companies (including the corporate respondents) would purchase gasoline from these refiners. The Committee would assemble each month information as to the quantity and location of this distress gasoline. Each of the major companies was to select one (or more) of the independent refiners having distress gasoline as its "dancing partner," and would assume responsibility for purchasing its distress supply. In this manner buying power would be coordinated, purchases would be effectively placed, and the results would be much superior to the previous haphazard purchasing. There were to be no formal contractual commitments to purchase this gasoline, either between the major companies or between the majors and the independents. Rather it was an informal gentlemen's agreement or understanding whereby each undertook to perform his share of the joint undertaking. Purchases were to be made at the "fair going market price."

* * *

B. *The Mid-Continent Buying Program in Operation.*

* * *

The concerted action under this program took the following form:

The Tank Car Stabilization Committee had A.V. Bourque, Secretary of the Western Petroleum Refiners' Association, make a monthly survey, showing the amount of distress gasoline which each independent refiner would have during the month. * * * Each member of the Committee present would indicate how much his company would buy and from whom. * * * Throughout, persuasion was apparently used to the end that all distress gasoline would be taken by the majors and so kept from the tank car markets. As the program progressed, most of the major companies continued to buy from the same "dancing partners" with whom they had started.

One of the tasks of the Mechanical Sub-Committee was to keep itself informed as to the current prices of gasoline and to use its persuasion and influence to see to it that the majors paid a fair going market price and did not "chisel" on the small refiners. It did so. * * *

* * *

The major companies regularly reported to Bourque, the trade association representative of the Mid-Continent independent refiners, the volume of their purchases under the program and the prices paid. * * * [T]hough the arrangement was informal, it was nonetheless effective, as we shall see. * * *

* * *

C. *Formation and Nature of the East Texas Buying Program.*

In the meetings when the Mid-Continent buying program was being formulated it was recognized that it would be necessary or desirable to take the East Texas surplus gasoline off the market so that it would not be a "disturbing influence in the Standard of Indiana territory." * * * With East Texas spot market prices more than $1/8$ cents a gallon below Mid-Continent spot market prices, there might well be a resulting depressing effect on the Mid-Continent spot market prices.

* * *

Every Monday morning the secretary of the East Texas association ascertained from each member the amount of his forthcoming weekly surplus gasoline and the price he wanted. He used the consensus of opinion as the asking price. He would call the major companies; they would call him. He exchanged market information with them. * * * Very few cars were purchased through the Association by others than the major oil companies. * * *

D.   Scope and Purpose of the Alleged Conspiracy.

As a result of these buying programs it was hoped and intended that both the tank car and the retail markets would improve. The conclusion is irresistible that defendants' purpose was not merely to raise the spot market prices but, as the real and ultimate end, to raise the price of gasoline in their sales to jobbers and consumers in the Mid-Western area. * * *

But there was no substantial competent evidence that defendants, as charged in the indictment, induced the independent refiners to curtail their production.

E.   Marketing and Distribution Methods.

* * *

The defendant companies sold about 83% of all gasoline sold in the Mid-Western area during 1935. * * * During the greater part of the indictment period the defendant companies owned and operated many retail service stations through which they sold about 20% of their Mid-Western gasoline in 1935 and about 12% during the first seven months of 1936. Standard Oil Company (Indiana) was known during this period as the price leader or market leader throughout the Mid-Western area. It was customary for retail distributors, whether independent or owned or controlled by major companies, to follow Standard's posted retail prices. Its posted retail price in any given place in the Mid-Western area was determined by computing the Mid-Continent spot market price and adding thereto the tank car freight rate from the Mid-Continent field, taxes and 5 $1/2$ cents. The 5 $1/2$ cents was the equivalent of the customary 2 cents jobber margin and 3 $1/2$ cents service station margin. In this manner the retail price structure throughout the Mid-Western area during the indictment period was based in the main on Mid-Continent spot market quotations, or, as stated by one of the witnesses for the defendants, the spot market was a "peg to hang the price structure on."

* * *

F.   The Spot Market Prices During the Buying Program.

* * *

Major company buying began under the Mid-Continent program on March 7, 1935. * * * The low quotation on third grade gasoline was 3 $1/2$ cents on March 6, 1935. It rose to 4 $3/4$ cents early in June. That advance was evidenced by ten successive steps. * * * By the middle of January the low again had risen, this time to 5 $1/4$ cents. It held substantially at that point until the middle of February 1936. By the end of February it had dropped to 5 cents. * * * [I]t had declined to 4 $1/2$ cents before the middle of September. It stayed there until early October when it rose to 4 $5/8$ cents, continuing at that level until middle November when it rose to 4 $3/4$ cents.

The low remained at substantially that point throughout the balance of 1936.

* * *

During this period there were comparable movements on the Mid-Continent spot market for regular gasoline. * * *

* * *

G.   Jobber and Retail Prices During the Buying Programs.

That the spot market prices controlled prices of gasoline sold by the majors to the jobbers in the Mid-Western area during the indictment period is beyond question. * * * [T]he vast majority of jobbers' supply contracts during that period contained price formulae which were directly dependent on the Mid-Continent spot market prices. Hence, as the latter rose, the prices to the jobbers under those contracts increased.

* * *

Retail prices in the Mid-Western area kept close step with Mid-Continent spot market prices during 1935 and 1936, though there was a short lag between advances in the spot market prices and the consequent rises in retail prices. * * * [T]he contours of the retail prices [also] conformed in general to those of the tank car spot markets. The movements of the two were not just somewhat comparable; they were strikingly similar. Irrespective of whether the tank car spot market prices controlled the retail prices in this area, there was substantial competent evidence that they influenced them—substantially and effectively. * * *

IV.   OTHER CIRCUMSTANCES ALLEGEDLY RELEVANT
TO THE OFFENSE CHARGED IN THE INDICTMENT

* * *

A.   Alleged Knowledge and Acquiescence
of the Federal Government.

* * * [A]dmittedly the authorization under the National Industrial Recovery Act necessary for [antitrust] immunity had not been obtained. [But] respondents' offers of proof were made in order to show the circumstances which, respondents argue, should be taken into consideration in order to judge the purpose, effect and reasonableness of their activities in connection with the buying program.

Arnott testified that on January 8 or 9, 1935, he reported the appointment of the Tank Car Stabilization Committee to officials of the Petroleum Administrative Board who, he said, expressed great interest in it. * * * There was evidence that at least general information concerning the meetings of the Tank Car Stabilization Committee was given a representative of the Board in February 1935. In March 1935 the Code authorities with the approval of the Administrator, asked the major companies to curtail their manufacture of gasoline during that month by 1,400,000 barrels. The purpose was said to be to aid the small refiners by forcing the majors to buy part of their requirements from them. A voluntary curtailment of some 960,000 barrels was made.

On March 12, 1935, Arnott saw the Chairman and at least one other representative of the Board. Among other things the buying programs were discussed. Arnott did not ask for the Board's approval of these programs nor its "blessing." * * * The Chairman of the Board asked Arnott if the programs violated the anti-trust laws. Arnott said he did not believe they did and described what his group was doing. Arnott testified that he felt that the Board thought the program was sound and hoped it would work; and that if he had thought they disapproved, he would have discontinued his activities. There was no evidence that the Board told Arnott to discontinue the program. * * *

* * *

On April 2, 1935, the Administrator wrote Arnott, referred to his letter of July 20, 1934 and stated, inter alia:

> "The matter that at present concerns me is the necessity of complying with the requirements of the basic law. * * * I know you will appreciate that agreements between supplying companies which might be in conflict with the anti-trust laws of the United States require specific approval after due consideration if companies are to receive the protection afforded by Sections 4 and 5 of the National Industrial Recovery Act.

* * *

On April 22, 1935, the Petroleum Administrative Board wrote a letter to Arnott imposing three conditions on general stabilization work: (1) there should be no stabilization meeting without a representative of the Board being present; (2) every element in the industry should be heard from before any decisions were made; (3) no general instructions should be given under the July 20, 1934 letter. A meeting of Arnott's committee and members of the Board was held on May 8, 1935. A representative of the Board testified that they called Arnott "on the carpet to request him to explain" to them "what he had been doing." * * * [Arnott gave the Board only] a general explanation of the buying programs, stating that the majors were continuing informally to buy; that there was no pool; that no one was obliged to make purchases; that they were trying to lift from independent refiners distress gasoline which was burdening the market.

Respondents also offered to prove that on May 14, 1935, the Chairman of the Petroleum Administrative Board asked Arnott to undertake to stabilize the Pennsylvania refinery market in the way that he had stabilized the Mid-Continent refinery market; that in connection with this request the Board evinced support and approval of the Mid-Continent buying program; and that Arnott undertook to do what he could in the matter and called a meeting of the Pennsylvania refiners for May 28, 1935. Apparently the *Schechter* decision[5] terminated that undertaking.

* * *

In sum, respondents by this and similar evidence offered to establish that the Petroleum Administrative Board knew of the buying programs and acquiesced in them. And respondents by those facts * * * undertook to show that their objectives under the buying programs were in line with those of the federal government under the Code * * * .

* * *

V.   APPLICATION OF THE SHERMAN ACT

A.   *Charge to the Jury*

The court charged the jury that it was a violation of the Sherman Act for a group of individuals or corporations to act together to raise the prices to be charged for the commodity which they manufactured where they controlled a substantial part of the interstate trade and commerce in that commodity. The court stated that where the members of a combination had the power to raise prices and acted together for that purpose, the combination was illegal; and that it was immaterial how reasonable or unreasonable those prices were or to what extent they had been affected by the combination. It further charged that if such illegal combination existed, it did not matter that there may also have been other factors which contributed to the raising of the prices. * * * The court then charged that, unless the jury found beyond a reasonable doubt that the price rise and its continuance were "caused" by the combination and not caused by those other factors, verdicts of "not guilty" should be returned. It also charged that there was no evidence of governmental approval which would exempt the buying programs from the prohibitions of the Sherman Act; and that knowledge or acquiescence of officers of the government or the good intentions of the members of the combination would not give immunity from prosecution under that Act.

The Circuit Court of Appeals held this charge to be reversible error, since it was based upon the theory that such a combination was illegal per se. In its view respondents' activities were not unlawful unless they constituted an unreasonable restraint of trade. Hence, since that issue had not been submitted to the jury and since evidence bearing on it had been excluded, that court reversed and remanded for a new trial * * * . * * *

---

5   [Ed. note] The Court was referring here to A.L.A. Schechter Poultry Corp. v. United States, 295 U.S. 495, 55 S.Ct. 837, 79 L.Ed. 1570 (1935), in which the attempt of the National Industrial Recovery Act to give the President authority to approve "codes of fair competition" was declared unconstitutional because it was said improperly to delegate legislative power to the executive branch and to industrial and other private associations.

In United States v. Trenton Potteries Co., this Court sustained a conviction under the Sherman Act where the jury was charged that an agreement on the part of the members of a combination, controlling a substantial part of an industry, upon the prices which the members are to charge for their commodity is in itself an unreasonable restraint of trade without regard to the reasonableness of the prices or the good intentions of the combining units. * * * This Court pointed out that the so-called "rule of reason" announced in Standard Oil Co. v. United States had not affected this view of the illegality of price-fixing agreements. * * *

* * *

But respondents claim that other decisions of this Court afford them adequate defenses to the indictment. Among those on which they place reliance are Appalachian Coals, Inc. v. United States; Chicago Board of Trade v. United States; and the *American Tobacco* and *Standard Oil* cases.

* * *

* * * [W]e are of the opinion that Appalachian Coals, Inc. v. United States, is not in point.

In that case certain producers of bituminous coal created an exclusive selling agency for their coal. * * * The occasion for the formation of the agency was the existence of certain so-called injurious practices and conditions in the industry. * * * The agency was to promote the systematic study of the marketing and distribution of coal, its demand and consumption; to maintain an inspection and an engineering department to demonstrate to customers the advantages of this type of coal and to promote an extensive advertising campaign; to provide a research department to demonstrate proper and efficient methods of burning coal and thus to aid producers in their competition with substitute fuels; * * * and to make the sale of coal more economical. * * * This Court concluded that so far as actual purpose was concerned, the defendant producers were engaged in a "fair and open endeavor to aid the industry in a measurable recovery from its plight." And it observed that the plan did not either contemplate or involve "the fixing of market prices"; that defendants would not be able to fix the price of coal in the consuming markets; that their coal would continue to be subject to "active competition." To the contention that the plan would have a tendency to stabilize market prices and to raise them to a higher level, this Court replied:

> "The fact that the correction of abuses may tend to stabilize a business, or to produce fairer price levels, does not mean that the abuses should go uncorrected or that cooperative endeavor to correct them necessarily constitutes an unreasonable restraint of trade. The intelligent conduct of commerce through the acquisition of full information of all relevant facts may properly be sought by the cooperation of those engaged in trade, although

stabilization of trade and more reasonable prices may be the result."

* * *

Thus in reality the only essential thing in common between the instant case and the *Appalachian Coals* case is the presence in each of so-called demoralizing or injurious practices. The methods of dealing with them were quite divergent. * * * Unlike the plan in the instant case, the plan in the *Appalachian Coals* case was not designed to operate vis-a-vis the general consuming market and to fix the prices on that market. Furthermore, the effect, if any, of that plan on prices was not only wholly incidental but also highly conjectural. For the plan had not then been put into operation. Hence this Court expressly reserved jurisdiction in the District Court to take further proceedings if, inter alia, in "actual operation" the plan proved to be "an undue restraint upon interstate commerce." And as we have seen it would per se constitute such a restraint if price-fixing were involved.

* * *

Nor can respondents find sanction in Chicago Board of Trade v. United States for the buying programs here under attack. * * * [There,] no attempt was made to show that the purpose or effect of the rule was to raise or depress prices. The rule affected only a small proportion of the commerce in question. And among its effects was the creation of a public market for grains under that special contract class, where prices were determined competitively and openly. Since it was not aimed at price manipulation or the control of the market prices and since it had "no appreciable effect on general market prices," the rule survived as a reasonable restraint of trade.

* * *

Thus for over forty years this Court has consistently and without deviation adhered to the principle that price-fixing agreements are unlawful per se under the Sherman Act and that no showing of so-called competitive abuses or evils which those agreements were designed to eliminate or alleviate may be interposed as a defense. * * *

* * *

Respondents seek to distinguish the *Trenton Potteries* case from the instant one. They assert that in that case the parties substituted an agreed-on price for one determined by competition * * * . Respondents contend that in the instant case there was no elimination in the spot tank car market of competition which prevented the prices in that market from being made by the play of competition in sales between independent refiners and their jobber and consumer customers; * * * and that if respondents had tried to do more than free competition from the effect of distress gasoline and to set an arbitrary non-competitive price through their purchases, they would have been without power to do so.

But we do not deem those distinctions material.

In the first place, there was abundant evidence that the combination had the purpose to raise prices. And likewise, there was ample evidence that the buying programs at least contributed to the price rise and the stability of the spot markets, and to increases in the price of gasoline sold in the Mid-Western area during the indictment period. That other factors also may have contributed to that rise and stability of the markets is immaterial. * * * So far as cause and effect are concerned it is sufficient in this type of case if the buying programs of the combination resulted in a price rise and market stability which but for them would not have happened. For this reason the charge to the jury that the buying programs must have "caused" the price rise and its continuance was more favorable to respondents than they could have required. Proof that there was a conspiracy, that its purpose was to raise prices, and that it caused or contributed to a price rise is proof of the actual consummation or execution of a conspiracy under § 1 of the Sherman Act.

Secondly, the fact that sales on the spot markets were still governed by some competition is of no consequence. For it is indisputable that that competition was restricted through the removal by respondents of a part of the supply which but for the buying programs would have been a factor in determining the going prices on those markets. But the vice of the conspiracy was not merely the restriction of supply of gasoline by removal of a surplus. * * * The timing and strategic placement of the buying orders for distress gasoline played an important and significant role. * * * Sellers were assigned to the buyers so that regular outlets for distress gasoline would be available. The whole scheme was carefully planned and executed to the end that distress gasoline would not overhang the markets and depress them at any time. * * * Competition was not eliminated from the markets; but it was clearly curtailed * * * .

The elimination of so-called competitive evils is no legal justification for such buying programs. * * * Ruinous competition, financial disaster, evils of price cutting and the like appear throughout our history as ostensible justifications for price-fixing. If the so-called competitive abuses were to be appraised here, the reasonableness of prices would necessarily become an issue in every price-fixing case. In that event the Sherman Act would soon be emasculated; * * * it would not be the charter of freedom which its framers intended.

The reasonableness of prices has no constancy due to the dynamic quality of business facts underlying price structures. * * * [T]he thrust of the rule * * * reaches more than monopoly power. Any combination which tampers with price structures is engaged in an unlawful activity. Even though the members of the price-fixing group were in no position to control the market, to the extent that they raised, lowered, or stabilized prices they would be directly interfering with the free play of market forces. The Act places all such schemes beyond the pale and protects that vital part of our economy against any degree of interference. * * * [Congress] has no more allowed genuine or fancied competitive abuses as a legal justification for such schemes than it has the good intentions of the members of the combination. * * * There was accordingly no error in the refusal to charge that in order to convict the jury must find that the resultant prices were raised and maintained at "high, arbitrary and noncompetitive levels." The charge in the indictment to that effect was surplusage.

Nor is it important that the prices paid by the combination were not fixed in the sense that they were uniform and inflexible. Price-fixing as used in the *Trenton Potteries* case has no such limited meaning. An agreement to pay or charge rigid, uniform prices would be an illegal agreement under the Sherman Act. But so would agreements to raise or lower prices whatever machinery for price-fixing was used. * * * Hence, prices are fixed within the meaning of the *Trenton Potteries* case if the range within which purchases or sales will be made is agreed upon, if the prices paid or charged are to be at a certain level or on ascending or descending scales, if they are to be uniform, or if by various formulae they are related to the market prices. They are fixed because they are agreed upon. And the fact that, as here, they are fixed at the fair going market price is immaterial. For purchases at or under the market are one species of price-fixing. In this case, the result was to place a floor under the market—a floor which served the function of increasing the stability and firmness of market prices. That was repeatedly characterized in this case as stabilization. But in terms of market operations stabilization is but one form of manipulation. And market manipulation in its various manifestations is implicitly an artificial stimulus applied to (or at times a brake on) market prices, a force which distorts those prices, a factor which prevents the determination of those prices by free competition alone. * * *

* * *

Under the Sherman Act a combination formed for the purpose and with the effect of raising, depressing, fixing, pegging, or stabilizing the price of a commodity in interstate or foreign commerce is illegal per se. Where the machinery for price-fixing is an agreement on the prices to be charged or paid for the commodity in the interstate or foreign channels of trade, the power to fix prices exists if the combination has control of a substantial part of the commerce in that commodity. Where the means for price-fixing are purchases or sales of the commodity in a market operation or, as here, purchases of a part of the supply of the commodity for the purpose of keeping it from having a depressive effect on the markets, such power may be found to exist though the combination does not control a substantial part of the commodity. In such a case that power may be established if as a result of market conditions, the resources available to the combinations, the timing and the strategic placement of orders and the like, effective means are at hand to accomplish the desired objective. But there may be effective influence over the market though the group in question does not control it. Price-fixing agreements may have utility to members of the group though the power possessed or exerted falls far short of domination and control. * * * Proof that a combination was formed for the purpose of fixing prices and that it caused them to be fixed or contributed to that result is proof of the completion of a price-fixing conspiracy under § 1 of the Act.[6] The indictment in this case charged that this combination had that purpose and effect. And there was abundant evidence to support it. * * *

As to knowledge or acquiescence of officers of the Federal Government little need be said. The fact that Congress through utilization of the precise methods here employed could seek to reach the same objectives sought by respondents does not mean that respondents or any other group may do so without specific Congressional authority. * * * Though employees of the

---

[6]   Under this indictment proof that prices in the Mid-Western area were raised as a result of the activities of the combination was essential, since sales of gasoline by respondents at the increased prices in that area were necessary in order to establish jurisdiction in the Western District of Wisconsin. Hence we have necessarily treated the case as one where exertion of the power to fix prices (i.e. the actual fixing of prices) was an ingredient of the offense. But that does not mean that both a purpose and a power to fix prices are necessary for the establishment of a conspiracy under § 1 of the Sherman Act. That would be true if power or ability to commit an offense was necessary in order to convict a person of conspiring to commit it. But it is well established that a person "may be guilty of conspiring, although incapable of committing the objective offense." And it is likewise well settled that conspiracies under the Sherman Act are not dependent on any overt act other than the act of conspiring. It is the "contract, combination * * * or conspiracy in restraint of trade or commerce" which § 1 of the Act strikes down, whether the concerted activity be wholly nascent or abortive on the one hand, or successful on the other. See United States v. Trenton Potteries Co. And the amount of interstate or foreign trade involved is not material since § 1 of the Act brands as illegal the character of the restraint not the amount of commerce affected. In view of these considerations a conspiracy to fix prices violates § 1 of the Act though no overt act is shown, though it is not established that the conspirators had the means available for accomplishment of their objective, and though the conspiracy embraced but a part of the interstate or foreign commerce in the commodity. Whatever may have been the status of price-fixing agreements at common law * * * the Sherman Act has a broader application to them than the common law prohibitions or sanctions. See United States v. Trans-Missouri Freight Assn. Price-fixing agreements may or may not be aimed at complete elimination of price competition. The group making those agreements may or may not have power to control the market. But the fact that the group cannot control the market prices does not necessarily mean that the agreement as to prices has no utility to the members of the combination. The effectiveness of price-fixing agreements is dependent on many factors, such as competitive tactics, position in the industry, the formula underlying price policies. Whatever economic justification particular price-fixing agreements may be thought to have, the law does not permit an inquiry into their reasonableness. They are all banned because of their actual or potential threat to the central nervous system of the economy.

The existence or exertion of power to accomplish the desired objective (United States v. United States Steel Corp.) becomes important only in cases where the offense charged is the actual monopolizing of any part of trade or commerce in violation of § 2 of the Act. An intent and a power to produce the result which the law condemns are then necessary. As stated in Swift & Co. v. United States, " * * * when that intent and the consequent dangerous probability exist, this statute, like many others and like the common law in some cases, directs itself against that dangerous probability as well as against the completed result." But the crime under § 1 is legally distinct from that under § 2 though the two sections overlap in the sense that a monopoly under § 2 is a species of restraint of trade under § 1. Standard Oil Co. v. United States. Only a confusion between the nature of the offenses under those two sections would lead to the conclusion that power to fix prices was necessary for proof of a price-fixing conspiracy under § 1. [Court's fn. 59]

government may have known of those programs and winked at them or tacitly approved them, no immunity would have thereby been obtained. For Congress had specified the precise manner and method of securing immunity. None other would suffice. * * *

* * *

The judgment of the Circuit Court of Appeals is reversed and that of the District Court affirmed. * * *

The CHIEF JUSTICE and MR. JUSTICE MURPHY did not participate in the consideration or decision of this case.

MR. JUSTICE ROBERTS [with whom MR. JUSTICE MCREYNOLDS joins], dissenting.

* * *

The Government relies on United States v. Trenton Potteries Co. That case is clearly not in point. There the conspiracy was to fix the prices of the commodity manufactured and sold by the defendants and to adhere to the prices so fixed. * * * Neither pleading nor proof [here] goes to any such conspiracy.

* * *

I think the defendants were entitled to have the jury charged that, in order to convict them, the jury must find that, although defendants knew the result of their activities would be a rise in the level of prices, nevertheless, if what they agreed to do, and did, had no substantial tendency to restrain competition in interstate commerce in transactions in gasoline the verdict should be not guilty.

* * *

* * * [C]oncerted action to remove a harmful and destructive practice in an industry, even though such removal may have the effect of raising the price level, is not offensive to the Sherman Act if it is not intended and does not operate unreasonably to restrain interstate commerce; and such action has been held not unreasonably to restrain commerce if, as here, it involves no agreement for uniform prices but leaves the defendants free to compete with each other in the matter of price.

No case decided by this court has held a combination illegal solely because its purpose or effect was to raise prices. The criterion of legality has always been the purpose or effect of the combination unduly to restrain commerce.

I think Appalachian Coals, Inc. v. United States a controlling authority sustaining the defendants' contention that the charge foreclosed a defense available to them under the Sherman Act. It is said that their combination had the purpose and effect of putting a floor under the spot market for gasoline. But that was precisely the purpose and effect of the plan in the *Appalachian* case. True, the means adopted to overcome the effect of the dumping of distress products on the market were not the same in the two cases, but means are unimportant provided purpose and effect are lawful.

NOTES AND QUESTIONS

1.   You have read lots of price fixing cases by now—*Trans-Missouri, Addyston Pipe, Board of Trade, American Column & Lumber, General Electric, Standard Oil (Indiana), Trenton Potteries,* and *Appalachian Coals.* If you had been representing these defendants, would you have been surprised by the result the court reached here?[7]

a.   Had the defendants been engaged in price fixing as you have come to understand the term? Had any specific prices been set, either prices at which gasoline would be purchased or prices at which it would be resold? Is Justice Roberts correct that without such specific price setting, the Court's reference to *Trenton Potteries* is inapposite? Did Justice Douglas have any other precedent he could have cited to Justice Roberts on this point?

b.   Was the agreement that the majors would not "chisel" and would pay the independents "fair" prices illegal? Could the majors then have passed on those higher-than-distress prices to consumers? Instead, would the principal cost of dealing "fairly" have been borne by the stockholders of the major oil companies? Would someone like Justice Brandeis have thought that dealing fairly with small firms was bad social policy? Do you think so?

c.   Was there any agreement here that restricted output by either the majors or the independents? Indeed, does the court concede that there was "no substantial competent evidence" of any such restriction? Would such a restriction of output normally have been an essential part of any price fixing scheme? Should finding a lack of any such restriction have been the end of the court's inquiry?[8]

2.   Was "price stabilization" the evil found to be illegal here? Why?

a.   Would consumers prefer substantial swings in the price of gasoline? Think of your own buying habits. Does the pattern of gasoline prices matter to you? Are you usually in a position to buy lots of gas when the price is low and use it later when the price is high?

---

[7]   Justice Douglas was not the only newcomer to the Court between the *Appalachian Coals* decision and this one. Justice Black had been appointed in 1937, Justice Reed in 1938, and Justice Frankfurter in 1939. All joined Justice Douglas in the majority. Justice Stone was in the majority in both cases. Justice McReynolds would have condemned Appalachian Coals, Inc., but voted to uphold the practices here. Justice Roberts believed the defendants in both cases had acted properly.

[8]   Doubts about the lack of output restrictions are expressed in D. Bruce Johnsen, Property Rights to Cartel Rents, 34(1) J.Law & Econ. 177 (1991). Professor Johnsen documents previous state prorationing laws, New Deal "Codes" and the Connolly "Hot Oil" Act and suggests that this buying program can best be explained as an effort to restrict quantities of oil refined while preserving the brand-name leadership of the major companies.

b.   Was the time of storage or degree of price stabilization likely to be significant? Did it prove to be so? Do you suppose the majors' storage capacity was infinite? That it involved little costs to the majors?

c.   On the other hand, if there really was nothing in this program to benefit the major oil companies, why did they devote so much effort to it? Was patriotism the only motive?

3.   What part of the District Judge's instruction did the Court find to be incorrect? Look again at the Court's footnote 59 and the text of the opinion surrounding it. How many different tests for illegality does Justice Douglas articulate?

a.   Suppose Socony-Vacuum had not undertaken this effort with its fellow oil companies. Suppose it had simply bought distress gas from the independents because it thought it was a good investment, i.e., it could buy such gas for a price lower than the cost of refining it. Would that be a practice the antitrust laws should condemn? Would there be any "victim" of such behavior?

b.   Does the result here really constitute a condemnation of the majors' *hope* that this program would help stabilize or even increase prices in the industry? Should bad motives, i.e., wishing for an economic result that the firm is in no position to achieve, make an otherwise innocent act per se illegal? After this case, how should a jury be charged in a case where an intent to affect price is alleged but no actual effect on price has been proved?

4.   Do you think that *Appalachian Coals* dictated a different result here?

a.   What were the factual differences between how these defendants had conducted their stabilization program and the manner in which Appalachian Coals, Inc. had operated? Do you agree with Justice Roberts that those differences were not significant?

b.   Indeed, which program was likely to have had the greater effect on prices paid by consumers? Do you agree with the Court that the form a practice takes should be more relevant than its actual effect on price?

c.   How would *Appalachian Coals* have been decided if this court's test in footnote 59 had been the controlling standard? Was the joint selling agency there created with the "intent or effect of affecting price"? Was it likely created for any other reason?

5.   Should the result here have been affected by the fact that this case involved a criminal indictment, as had *Trenton Potteries*? That is, might one suggest that an agreement on a specific price is required to sustain a criminal conviction, while an injunction could be obtained against any attempt to affect price? Does the Sherman Act or Clayton Act give any support to drawing distinctions depending on the remedy sought? More than thirty years after these cases, the Court added an element of intent when a defendant has been charged with a criminal violation of the Sherman Act. See United States v. United States Gypsum Co., 438 U.S. 422, 98 S.Ct. 2864, 57 L.Ed.2d 854 (1978).

6.   What may make a rule like that in *Socony-Vacuum* attractive to judges?

a.   Do you agree that some practices are so likely to be anticompetitive and so unlikely to be justifiable that courts should not allow defendants to offer a defense? Even if some such cases come to mind, e.g., bid-rigging, was *Socony-Vacuum* such a case?

b.   Are you persuaded by the argument that a per se rule makes antitrust cases shorter and cheaper to try? Can you think of other contexts in which we deny criminal defendants the right to put on a defense because of our concern for judicial economy?

c.   Is it important that a per se rule is relatively certain, i.e., that lawyers can give clear advice and clients need not wonder how a court will react to the economic factors involved. Might one argue that it is patronizing to deny actual defendants the right to explain their conduct because of our desire to simplify the counseling tasks facing lawyers?

d.   Can the same arguments of judicial economy and ease in counseling be made in favor of per se rules of *legality*? Are there any reasons not to identify conduct that will always be held to be lawful?[9]

7.   Was the Court too quick to dismiss the argument that the defendants had been lured into this program by federal officials?

a.   Was there any doubt here that the effort to stabilize, indeed raise, oil prices was New Deal policy? Should the burden have been on the companies to anticipate that large portions of the New Deal program would be held unconstitutional?

b.   Did Socony-Vacuum's Mr. Arnott take matters beyond what the statute authorized? Should he have read the newspapers and realized that the NRA had been held unconstitutional? Should he have been more cautious when the Chairman of the Petroleum Administrative Board spoke well of what he was doing but expressly raised doubts about whether it was consistent with the antitrust laws?

That *Socony-Vacuum* did not eliminate questions about the interplay between regulation and the antitrust laws is revealed clearly in our next case.

PARKER V. BROWN

Supreme Court of the United States, 1943
317 U.S. 341, 63 S.Ct. 307, 87 L.Ed. 315

MR. CHIEF JUSTICE STONE delivered the opinion of the Court.

The questions for our consideration are whether the marketing program adopted for the 1940 raisin crop under the California Agricultural

---

[9]   Judges Richard Posner and Frank Easterbrook have made important efforts to suggest such rules of per se legality. See Richard A. Posner, The Next Step in the Antitrust Treatment of Restricted Distribution: Per Se Legality, 48 U. Chicago L. Rev. 6 (1981); Frank H. Easterbrook, The Limits of Antitrust, 63 Texas L.Rev. 1 (1984).

Prorate Act is rendered invalid (1) by the Sherman Act, or (2) by the Agricultural Marketing Agreement Act of 1937, or (3) by the Commerce Clause of the Constitution.

Appellee, a producer and packer of raisins in California, brought this suit in the district court to enjoin appellants—the State Director of Agriculture, Raisin Proration Zone No. 1, the members of the State Agricultural Prorate Advisory Commission and of the Program Committee for Zone No. 1, and others charged by the statute with the administration of the Prorate Act—from enforcing, as to appellee, a program for marketing the 1940 crop of raisins produced in "Raisin Proration Zone No. 1." After a trial * * *, the [three judge] district court held that the 1940 raisin marketing program was an illegal interference with and undue burden upon interstate commerce and gave judgment for appellee granting the injunction prayed for. The case * * * comes here on appeal.

As appears from the evidence and from the findings of the district court, almost all the raisins consumed in the United States, and nearly one-half of the world crop, are produced in Raisin Proration Zone No. 1. Between 90 and 95 per cent of the raisins grown in California are ultimately shipped in interstate or foreign commerce.

* * *

The California Agricultural Prorate Act authorizes the establishment, through action of state officials, of programs for the marketing of agricultural commodities produced in the state, so as to restrict competition among the growers and maintain prices in the distribution of their commodities to packers. The declared purpose of the Act is to "conserve the agricultural wealth of the State" and to "prevent economic waste in the marketing of agricultural products" of the state. It authorizes the creation of an Agricultural Prorate Advisory Commission of nine members, of which a state official, the Director of Agriculture, is ex-officio a member. * * *

Upon the petition of ten producers for the establishment of a prorate marketing plan for any commodity within a defined production zone, and after a public hearing, and after making prescribed economic findings * * *, the Commission is authorized to grant the petition. The Director, with the approval of the Commission, is then required to select a program committee from among nominees chosen by the qualified producers within the zone, to which he may add not more than two handlers or packers who receive the regulated commodity from producers for marketing.

* * * If the proposed program, as approved by the Commission, is consented to by 65 per cent in number of producers in the zone owning 51 per cent of the acreage devoted to production of the regulated crop, the Director is required to declare the program instituted.

Authority to administer the program, subject to the approval of the Director of Agriculture, is conferred on the program committee. Section 22.5 declares that it shall be a misdemeanor, which is punishable by fine and imprisonment, for any producer to sell or any handler to receive or possess without proper authority any commodity for which a proration program has been instituted. * * *

The seasonal proration marketing program for raisins, with which we are now concerned, became effective on September 7, 1940. This provided that the program committee should classify raisins as "standard," "substandard," and "inferior"; "inferior" raisins are those which are unfit for human consumption, as defined in the Federal Food, Drug and Cosmetic Act. The committee is required to establish receiving stations within the zone to which every producer must deliver all raisins which he desires to market. The raisins are graded at these stations. All inferior raisins are to be placed in the "inferior raisin pool," to be disposed of by the committee "only for assured by-product and other diversion purposes." All substandard raisins, and at least 20 per cent of the total standard and substandard raisins produced, must be placed in a "surplus pool." Raisins in this pool may also be disposed of only for "assured by-product and other diversion purposes," except that under certain circumstances the program committee may transfer standard raisins from the surplus pool to the stabilization pool. Fifty per cent of the crop must be placed in a "stabilization pool."

Under the program the producer is permitted to sell the remaining 30 per cent of his standard raisins, denominated "free tonnage," through ordinary commercial channels, subject to the requirement that he obtain a "secondary certificate" authorizing such marketing * * *. * * * Raisins in the stabilization pool are to be disposed of by the committee "in such manner as to obtain stability in the market and to dispose of such raisins," but no raisins (other than those subject to special lending or pooling arrangements of the Federal Government) can be sold by the committee at less than the prevailing market price for raisins of the same variety and grade on the date of sale. Under the program the committee is to make advances to producers of from $25 to $27.50 a ton, depending upon the variety of raisins, for deliveries into the surplus pool, and from $50 to $55 a ton for deliveries into the stabilization pool. The committee is authorized to pledge the raisins held in those pools in order to secure funds to finance pool operations and make advances to growers.

Appellee's bill of complaint challenges the validity of the proration program as in violation of the Commerce Clause and the Sherman Act; in support of the decree of the district court he also urges that it conflicts with and is superseded by the Federal Agricultural Marketing Agreement Act of 1937. * * *

Appellee's allegations of irreparable injury are * * * that he * * * expected to sell, if the challenged program were not in force, 3,000 tons of the 1940 crop at $60 a ton * * * . * * *

VALIDITY OF THE PRORATE PROGRAM UNDER THE SHERMAN ACT.

* * * We may assume for present purposes that the California prorate program would violate the Sherman Act if it were organized and made effective solely by virtue of a contract, combination or conspiracy of private persons, individual or corporate. We may assume also, without deciding, that Congress could, in the exercise of its commerce power, prohibit a state from maintaining a stabilization program like the present because of its effect on interstate commerce. Occupation of a legislative "field" by Congress in the exercise of a granted power is a familiar example of its constitutional power to suspend state laws.

But it is plain that the prorate program here was never intended to operate by force of individual agreement or combination. It derived its authority and its efficacy from the legislative command of the state and was not intended to operate or become effective without that command. We find nothing in the language of the Sherman Act or in its history which suggests that its purpose was to restrain a state or its officers or agents from activities directed by its legislature. In a dual system of government in which, under the Constitution, the states are sovereign, save only as Congress may constitutionally subtract from their authority, an unexpressed purpose to nullify a state's control over its officers and agents is not lightly to be attributed to Congress.

The Sherman Act makes no mention of the state as such, and gives no hint that it was intended to restrain state action or official action directed by a state. The Act is applicable to "persons" including corporations, and it authorizes suits under it by persons and corporations. A state may maintain a suit for damages under it, but the United States may not, conclusions derived not from the literal meaning of the words "person" and "corporation" but from the purpose, the subject matter, the context and the legislative history of the statute.

There is no suggestion of a purpose to restrain state action in the Act's legislative history. The sponsor of the bill which was ultimately enacted as the Sherman Act declared that it prevented only "business combinations." That its purpose was to suppress combinations to restrain competition and attempts to monopolize by individuals and corporations, abundantly appears from its legislative history.

True, a state does not give immunity to those who violate the Sherman Act by authorizing them to violate it, or by declaring that their action is lawful, and we have no question of the state or its municipality becoming a participant in a private agreement or combination by others for restraint of trade. Here the state command to the Commission and to the program committee of the California Prorate Act is not rendered unlawful by the Sherman Act since, in view of the latter's words and history, it must be taken to be a prohibition of individual and not state action. It is the state which has created the machinery for establishing the prorate program. Although the organization of a prorate zone is proposed by producers, and a prorate program, approved by the Commission, must also be approved by referendum of producers, it is the state, acting through the Commission, which adopts the program and which enforces it with penal sanctions, in the execution of a governmental policy. The prerequisite approval of the program upon referendum by a prescribed number of producers is not the imposition by them of their will upon the minority by force of agreement or combination which the Sherman Act prohibits. The state itself exercises its legislative authority in making the regulation and in prescribing the conditions of its application. The required vote on the referendum is one of these conditions.

The state in adopting and enforcing the prorate program made no contract or agreement and entered into no conspiracy in restraint of trade or to establish monopoly but, as sovereign, imposed the restraint as an act of government which the Sherman Act did not undertake to prohibit.

VALIDITY OF THE PROGRAM UNDER THE AGRICULTURAL MARKETING AGREEMENT ACT.

The Agricultural Marketing Agreement Act of 1937 authorizes the Secretary of Agriculture to issue orders limiting the quantity of specified agricultural products, including fruits, which may be marketed "in the current of * * * or so as directly to burden, obstruct, or affect interstate or foreign commerce." * * *

We may assume that the powers conferred upon the Secretary would extend to the control of surpluses in the raisin industry through a pooling arrangement such as was promulgated under the California Prorate Act in the present case. We may assume also that a stabilization program adopted under the Agricultural Marketing Agreement Act would supersede the state act. But the federal act becomes effective only if a program is ordered by the Secretary. * * * Since the Secretary has not * * * proposed or promulgated any order regulating raisins, it must be taken that he has no reason to believe that issuance of an order will tend to effectuate the policy of the Act.

* * *

It is evident * * * that the Marketing Act contemplates the existence of state programs at least until such time as the Secretary shall establish a federal marketing program, unless the state program in some way conflicts with the policy of the federal act. * * *

* * * The only possibility of conflict would seem to be if a State program were to raise prices beyond the parity price prescribed by the Federal Act, a condition which has not occurred.

That the Secretary has reason to believe that the state act will tend to effectuate the policies of the federal act so as not to require the issuance of an order under the latter is evidenced by the approval given by the Department of Agriculture to the state program by the loan agreement between the state and the Commodity Credit Corporation. * * *

* * *

We have no occasion to decide whether the same conclusion would follow if the state program had not been adopted with the collaboration of officials of the Department of Agriculture * * * .

VALIDITY OF THE PROGRAM UNDER THE COMMERCE CLAUSE.

* * * [S]ince 95 per cent of the crop is marketed in interstate commerce, the program may be taken to have a substantial effect on the commerce * * * .

The question is thus presented whether in the absence of congressional legislation prohibiting or regulating the transactions affected by the state program, the restrictions which it imposes upon the sale within the state of a commodity by its producer to a processor who contemplates doing, and in fact does, work upon the commodity before packing and shipping it in interstate commerce, violate the Commerce Clause.

* * * This Court has repeatedly held that the grant of power to Congress by the Commerce Clause did not wholly withdraw from the states the authority to regulate the commerce with respect to matters of local concern, on which Congress has not spoken. * * * Whether we resort to the mechanical test sometimes applied by this Court in determining when interstate commerce begins with respect to a commodity grown or manufactured within a state and then sold and shipped out of it—or whether we consider only the power of the state in the absence of Congressional action to regulate matters of local concern * * *—we think the present regulation is within state power.

In applying the mechanical test to determine when interstate commerce begins and ends this Court has frequently held that for purposes of local taxation or regulation "manufacture" is not interstate commerce even though the manufacturing process is of slight extent. * * *

All of these cases proceed on the ground that the taxation or regulation involved, however drastically it may affect interstate commerce, is nevertheless not prohibited by the Commerce Clause where the regulation is imposed before any operation of interstate commerce occurs. Applying that test, the regulation here controls the disposition, including the sale and purchase, of raisins before they are processed and packed preparatory to interstate sale and shipment. The regulation is thus applied to transactions wholly intrastate * * * .

* * *

* * * But courts are not confined to so mechanical a test. When Congress has not exerted its power under the Commerce Clause, and state regulation of matters of local concern is so related to interstate commerce that it also operates as a regulation of that commerce, the reconciliation of the power thus granted with that reserved to the state is to be attained by the accommodation of the competing demands of the state and national interests involved.

* * *

Examination of the evidence in this case and of available data of the raisin industry in California, of which we may take judicial notice, leaves no doubt that the evils attending the production and marketing of raisins in that state present a problem local in character and urgently demanding state action for the economic protection of those engaged in one of its important industries. Between 1914 and 1920 there was a spectacular rise in price of all types of California grapes, including raisin grapes. The price of raisins reached its peak, $235 per ton, in 1921, and was followed by large increase in acreage with accompanying reduction in price. The price of raisins in most years since 1922 has ranged from $40 to $60 per ton but acreage continued to increase until 1926 and production reached its peak * * * in 1938. Since 1920 there has been a substantial carry over of 30 to 50% of each year's crop. The result has been that at least since 1934 the industry, with a large increase in acreage and the attendant fall in price, has been unable to market its product and has been compelled to sell at less than parity prices and in some years at prices regarded by students of the industry as less than the cost of production.

The history of the industry, at least since 1929, is a record of a continuous search for expedients which would stabilize the marketing of the raisin crop and maintain a price standard which would bring fair return to the producers. It is significant of the relation of the local interest in maintaining this program to the national interest in interstate commerce, that throughout the period from 1929 until the adoption of the prorate program for the 1940 raisin crop, the national government has contributed to these efforts either by its establishment of marketing programs pursuant to Act of Congress or by aiding programs sponsored by the state. * * *

* * *

This history shows clearly enough that the adoption of legislative measures to prevent the demoralization of the industry by stabilizing the marketing of the raisin crop is a matter of state as well as national concern and, in the absence of inconsistent Congressional action, is a problem whose solution is peculiarly within the province of the state. In the exercise of its power the state has adopted a measure appropriate to the end sought. The program was not aimed at nor did it discriminate against interstate commerce, although it undoubtedly affected the commerce by increasing the interstate price of raisins and curtailing interstate shipments to some undetermined extent. * * *

In comparing the relative weights of the conflicting local and national interests involved, it is significant that Congress, by its agricultural legislation, has recognized the distressed condition of much of the agricultural production of the United States, and has authorized marketing procedures, substantially like the California prorate program, for stabilizing the marketing of agricultural products. * * * All involved attempts in one way or another to prevent over-production of agricultural products and excessive competition in marketing them, with price stabilization as the ultimate objective. Most if not all had a like effect in restricting shipments and raising or maintaining prices of agricultural commodities moving in interstate commerce.

* * *

We conclude that the California prorate program for the 1940 raisin crop is a regulation of state industry of local concern which, in all the circumstances of this case which we have detailed, does not impair national control over the commerce in a manner or to a degree forbidden by the Constitution.

Reversed.

NOTES AND QUESTIONS

1. Are these facts starting to sound familiar to you? Prices rose in an industry during the period of reduced supply during World War I; they stayed high during the 1920s. The prices have now fallen, a result the producers attribute to "overproduction;" thus, the industry seeks to reduce quantities marketed in order to raise the price.

a. Was the special rationale proffered here convincing to you? In what sense was a limit on the number of raisins sold a "conservation" measure? Was there a limit on the number of acres of grapes that could be planted?

b. Did the raisin prorate program bear the signs of a classic cartel? Was there a process for reaching agreement and a way to protect against cheating? Indeed, is obtaining a legally-enforceable regulation from a state or federal agency the ideal way to assure cartel members that their agreement will be implemented?

c. Could this program have been upheld under *Appalachian Coals*? Was this simply a cooperative marketing arrangement? Was it just another scheme to persuade people to eat more raisins?

d.   Absent the state regulation, was this program clearly in violation of the principles of *Socony-Vacuum*? Was there an intent to affect the price of raisins? Was there probably also success in that effort?

2.   Were you persuaded that this regulation should not have been held to violate the commerce clause?

a.   Did this regulation burden any commerce *but* the interstate variety? How large a portion of the California raisin crop was sold outside California? Should it be relevant for Sherman Act purposes whether a state's own citizens bear a significant share of the cost of the regulation, i.e., whether there is a genuine political constituency in a position to see that the regulation had been fairly considered before it was adopted?

b.   Was the Court's real point here that the state had simply followed federal policy? Did the fact that the Secretary of Agriculture had done nothing tend to confirm that conclusion or undercut it? How much success did Mr. Arnott of Socony-Vacuum have relying on ambiguous inaction by federal officials?

3.   On what basis did the Court say that this cartel-like behavior did not violate the Sherman Act?

a.   Was this regulation *imposed* on the raisin industry? Should it have to be? Indeed, does the Court acknowledge that this program—like many regulatory schemes—was sought by the regulated producers?

b.   Is it then convincing to say that the Sherman Act only addresses the behavior of business firms, not states? Could one equally have said that where the firms were the moving parties, a state should not be able to immunize their conspiracy simply by "forcing" firms to participate in it?

4.   Was Parker v. Brown an aberration, a case upholding state implementation of federal policy in a time of economic crisis when the Court had only recently departed from its practice of closely reviewing and often striking down state regulations? See Paul R. Verkuil, State Action, Due Process and Antitrust: Reflections on Parker v. Brown, 75 Columbia L.Rev. 328 (1975).

a.   Authority for so limiting *Parker* seemed to be provided by Schwegmann Brothers v. Calvert Distillers Corp., 341 U.S. 384, 71 S.Ct. 745, 95 L.Ed. 1035 (1951). There, a Louisiana state law required retailers to adhere to the resale prices stipulated by manufacturers. As you remember, resale price maintenance contracts had been held to violate the Sherman Act in *Dr. Miles*. The Miller-Tydings Act, 50 Stat. 693 (1937), however, specially authorized state laws upholding such "Fair Trade" agreements.[10] What Miller-Tydings did not authorize were state laws extending resale price maintenance to firms that refused to sign the contracts. Thus, the state law was held unenforceable to the extent it exceeded the federal authorization. "The fact that a state authorizes

---

[10]   The Miller-Tydings Act, in turn, was repealed by the Consumer Goods Pricing Act of 1975, 89 Stat. 801, so that today there is no federal legislation authorizing resale price maintenance.

* * * price fixing does not * * * give immunity to the scheme, absent approval by Congress."

b.   If Parker v. Brown were indeed thus limited, we would likely no longer even read it. As you will see in the next chapter, however, the extent to which state regulation can authorize acts that would otherwise clearly violate federal law is one of the most litigated areas of antitrust law today.

ANTITRUST IMMUNITY FOR SEEKING REGULATORY CHANGE—THE *NOERR* AND *CALIFORNIA MOTOR TRANSPORT* CASES

As things now stand, the antitrust laws make it costly to engage in collective private conduct tending to reduce industry output or raise price. Get a state to "require" firms to do the same thing, however, and there may be no such liability. As a result, the incentive to seek such regulation is tremendous. Parties injured by that regulation have a corresponding desire to condemn the effort to obtain it as itself an antitrust violation.

In Eastern Railroad Presidents Conference v. Noerr Motor Freight, Inc., 365 U.S. 127, 81 S.Ct. 523, 5 L.Ed.2d 464 (1961), a group of 41 Pennsylvania truckers charged 24 Eastern railroads with conspiracy to restrain trade and monopolize long-distance freight hauling. The railroads had engaged a public relations firm to conduct a publicity campaign designed to foster the adoption of laws against long, heavy trucks, and to increase enforcement of the current laws. The campaign was alleged to be "vicious, corrupt, and fraudulent," using a "third-party technique" in which positions taken were made to appear as spontaneously expressed views of independent persons and civic groups when, in fact, they were prepared by the railroads.

In some instances, the railroads had attempted to influence legislation by means of their publicity campaign. In another case, the railroads had succeeded in "persuading the Governor of Pennsylvania to veto a measure known as the 'Fair Truck Bill,' which would have permitted truckers to carry heavier loads over Pennsylvania roads." The complaint sought treble damages and an injunction against dissemination of any "arguments of the railroads against the truckers or their business."

In an opinion by Justice Black, the Court unanimously asserted that "no violation of the [Sherman] Act can be predicated upon mere attempts to influence the passage or enforcement of laws. * * * [U]nder our form of government the question whether a law of that kind should pass, or if passed be enforced, is the responsibility of the appropriate legislative or executive branch of government * * * ."[11]

---

[11]   365 U.S. at 135–36, 81 S.Ct. at 528–29.

Further, the Court said, "we think it equally clear that the Sherman Act does not prohibit two or more persons from associating together in an attempt to persuade the legislature or the executive to take particular action with respect to a law that would produce a restraint or a monopoly." *Noerr* was not decided on Constitutional grounds but "to hold that the government retains the power to act in this representative capacity and yet hold, at the same time, that the people cannot freely inform the government of their wishes would impute to the Sherman Act a purpose to regulate, not business activity, but political activity, a purpose which would have no basis whatever in the legislative history of that Act."[12]

But the Court added: "There may be situations in which a publicity campaign, ostensibly directed toward influencing governmental action, is a mere sham to cover what is actually nothing more than an attempt to interfere directly with the business relationships of a competitor * * * ."[13] Such a situation *would* justify antitrust liability, but this was not such a case.[14]

The "mere sham" exception was largely undefined until the Court's decision in California Motor Transport v. Trucking Unlimited, 404 U.S. 508, 92 S.Ct. 609, 30 L.Ed.2d 642 (1972). Defendants were national truckers who operated in California. They were sued by truckers who operated *only* in California. Defendants allegedly intervened in administrative proceedings trying to keep plaintiffs from getting new operating rights. If they lost the first time, they would allegedly seek rehearing, appeal, and otherwise make life hard for intrastate truckers.

One might ask why this conduct wasn't clearly protected under the *Noerr-Pennington* doctrine. The Court concluded that there was a difference between aggressive advocacy seeking legislation and unethical conduct in an adjudicative proceeding.

There have long been rules against abuse of civil process and courts have long sanctioned misbehavior before them, Justice Douglas wrote. Any carrier may petition a court or agency, using proper procedures, to defeat a route application. Intent is irrelevant to that right, i.e., the purpose may be to improve one's own wealth or even to create a monopoly, but a combination to harass competitors and deny them "free and unlimited

---

[12]   Id. at 137, 81 S.Ct. at 529.

[13]   Id. at 144, 81 S.Ct. at 533.

[14]   *Noerr* was followed four years later by United Mine Workers v. Pennington, 381 U.S. 657, 85 S.Ct. 1585, 14 L.Ed.2d 626 (1965). The mine workers union and leading coal companies had gotten together (1) to lobby the Secretary of Labor to establish minimum wages for coal miners, and (2) to lobby the TVA not to make spot purchases of coal that weren't subject to Walsh-Healy prevailing wage requirements. The Supreme Court held: "Joint efforts to influence public officials do not violate the antitrust laws even though intended to eliminate competition. Such conduct is not illegal, either standing alone or as part of a broader scheme itself violative of the Sherman Act." You will often see references to the results in these two cases cited as the "*Noerr-Pennington*" doctrine.

access" to agencies and courts can be prohibited consistent with the First Amendment and was here held to be prohibited by the Sherman Act.

Does this distinction make sense to you? Is the distinction real? Aren't general industry policies often tested and evaluated in individually-adjudicated cases?[15]

2. GROUP BOYCOTTS

FASHION ORIGINATORS' GUILD OF AMERICA
v. FEDERAL TRADE COMMISSION

Supreme Court of the United States, 1941
312 U.S. 457, 61 S.Ct. 703, 85 L.Ed. 949

MR. JUSTICE BLACK delivered the opinion of the Court.

The Circuit Court of Appeals * * * affirmed a Federal Trade Commission decree ordering petitioners to cease and desist from certain practices found to have been done in combination and to constitute "unfair methods of competition" tending to monopoly. * * *

Some of the members of the combination design, manufacture, sell and distribute women's garments—chiefly dresses. Others are manufacturers, converters or dyers of textiles from which these garments are made. Fashion Originators' Guild of America (FOGA), an organization controlled by these groups, is the instrument through which petitioners work to accomplish the purposes condemned by the Commission. The garment manufacturers claim to be creators of original and distinctive designs of fashionable clothes for women, and the textile manufacturers claim to be creators of similar original fabric designs. After these designs enter the channels of trade, other manufacturers systematically make and sell copies of them, the copies usually selling at prices lower than the garments copied. Petitioners call this practice of copying unethical and immoral, and give it the name of "style piracy." And although they admit that their "original creations" are neither copyrighted nor patented, and indeed assert that existing legislation affords them no protection against copyists, they nevertheless urge that sale of copied designs constitutes an unfair trade practice and a tortious invasion of their rights. Because of these alleged wrongs, petitioners, while continuing to compete with one another in many respects, combined among themselves to combat and, if possible, destroy all competition from the sale of garments which are copies of their "original creations." They admit that to destroy such competition they have in combination purposely boycotted and declined to sell their products to retailers who follow a policy of selling garments copied by other

---

[15]   You will see in Chapter IV that the Supreme Court has revisited this issue in Professional Real Estate Investors v. Columbia Pictures, 508 U.S. 49, 113 S.Ct. 1920, 123 L.Ed.2d 611 (1993), and held that to constitute a sham, litigation must be "objectively baseless in the sense that no reasonable litigant could realistically expect success on the merits."

manufacturers from designs put out by Guild members. As a result of their efforts, approximately 12,000 retailers throughout the country have signed agreements to "cooperate" with the Guild's boycott program, but more than half of these signed the agreements only because constrained by threats that Guild members would not sell to retailers who failed to yield to their demands—threats that have been carried out by the Guild practice of placing on red cards the names of non-cooperators (to whom no sales are to be made), placing on white cards the names of cooperators (to whom sales are to be made), and then distributing both sets of cards to the manufacturers.

The one hundred and seventy-six manufacturers of women's garments who are members of the Guild occupy a commanding position in their line of business. In 1936, they sold in the United States more than 38% of all women's garments wholesaling at $6.75 and up, and more than 60% of those at $10.75 and above. The power of the combination is great; competition and the demand of the consuming public make it necessary for most retail dealers to stock some of the products of these manufacturers. And the power of the combination is made even greater by reason of the affiliation of some members of the National Federation of Textiles, Inc.— that being an organization composed of about one hundred textile manufacturers, converters, dyers, and printers of silk and rayon used in making women's garments. Those members of the Federation who are affiliated with the Guild have agreed to sell their products only to those garment manufacturers who have in turn agreed to sell only to cooperating retailers.

The Guild maintains a Design Registration Bureau for garments, and the Textile Federation maintains a similar Bureau for textiles. The Guild employs "shoppers" to visit the stores of both cooperating and non-cooperating retailers, "for the purpose of examining their stocks, to determine and report as to whether they contain * * * copies of registered designs * * * ." An elaborate system of trial and appellate tribunals exists, for the determination of whether a given garment is in fact a copy of a Guild member's design. In order to assure the success of its plan of registration and restraint, and to ascertain whether Guild regulations are being violated, the Guild audits its members' books. And if violations of Guild requirements are discovered, as, for example, sales to red-carded retailers, the violators are subject to heavy fines.

In addition to the elements of the agreement set out above, all of which relate more or less closely to competition by so-called style copyists, the Guild has undertaken to do many things apparently independent of and distinct from the fight against copying. Among them are the following: the combination prohibits its members from participating in retail advertising; regulates the discount they may allow; prohibits their selling at retail; cooperates with local guilds in regulating days upon which special sales shall be held; prohibits its members from selling women's garments to persons who conduct businesses in residences, residential quarters, hotels or apartment houses; and denies the benefits of membership to retailers who participate with dress manufacturers in promoting fashion shows unless the merchandise used is actually purchased and delivered.

If the purpose and practice of the combination of garment manufacturers and their affiliates runs counter to the public policy declared in the Sherman and Clayton Acts, the Federal Trade Commission has the power to suppress it as an unfair method of competition. * * * The relevance of [Section 3] of the Clayton Act [making it unlawful to sell goods on the condition that the buyer will not deal in the goods of the seller's competitor] to petitioners' scheme is shown by the fact that the scheme is bottomed upon a system of sale under which (1) textiles shall be sold to garment manufacturers only upon the condition and understanding that the buyers will not use or deal in textiles which are copied from the designs of textile manufacturing Guild members; (2) garment manufacturers shall sell to retailers only upon the condition and understanding that the retailers shall not use or deal in such copied designs. And the Federal Trade Commission concluded in the language of the Clayton Act that these understandings substantially lessened competition and tended to create a monopoly. We hold that the Commission, upon adequate and unchallenged findings, correctly concluded that this practice constituted an unfair method of competition.

Not only does the plan in the respects above discussed thus conflict with the principles of the Clayton Act; the findings of the Commission bring petitioners' combination in its entirety well within the inhibition of the policies declared by the Sherman Act itself. * * * [A]mong the many respects in which the Guild's plan runs contrary to the policy of the Sherman Act are these: it narrows the outlets to which garment and textile manufacturers can sell and the sources from which retailers can buy; subjects all retailers and manufacturers who decline to comply with the Guild's program to an organized boycott; takes away the freedom of action of members by requiring each to reveal to the Guild the intimate details of their individual affairs; and has both as its necessary tendency and as its purpose and effect the direct suppression of competition from the sale of unregistered textiles and copied designs. In addition to all this, the combination is in reality an extra-governmental agency, which prescribes rules for the regulation and restraint of interstate commerce, and provides extra-judicial tribunals for determination and punishment of violations, and thus "trenches upon the power of the national legislature and violates the statute." Addyston Pipe & Steel Co. v. United States.

Nor is it determinative in considering the policy of the Sherman Act that petitioners may not yet have achieved a complete monopoly. For "it is sufficient if it really tends to that end and to deprive the public of the advantages which flow from free competition." United States v. E.C. Knight Co.; Addyston Pipe & Steel Co. v. United States. It was, in fact, one of the hopes of those who sponsored the Federal Trade Commission Act that its effect might be prophylactic and that through it attempts to bring about complete monopolization of an industry might be stopped in their incipiency.

Petitioners, however, argue that the combination cannot be contrary to the policy of the Sherman and Clayton Acts, since the Federal Trade Commission did not find that the combination fixed or regulated prices, parceled out or limited production, or brought about a deterioration in quality. But action falling into these three categories does not exhaust the types of conduct banned by the Sherman and Clayton Acts. And as previously pointed out, it was the object of the Federal Trade Commission Act to reach not merely in their fruition but also in their incipiency combinations which could lead to these and other trade restraints and practices deemed undesirable. In this case, the Commission found that the combination exercised sufficient control and power in the women's garments and textile businesses "to exclude from the industry those manufacturers and distributors who do not conform to the rules and regulations of said respondents, and thus tend to create in themselves a monopoly in the said industries." While a conspiracy to fix prices is illegal, an intent to increase prices is not an ever-present essential of conduct amounting to a violation of the policy of the Sherman and Clayton Acts; a monopoly contrary to their policies can exist even though a combination may temporarily or even permanently reduce the price of the articles manufactured or sold. For as this Court has said, "Trade or commerce under those circumstances may nevertheless be badly and unfortunately restrained by driving out of business the small dealers and worthy men whose lives have been spent therein, and who might be unable to readjust themselves to their altered surroundings. Mere reduction in the price of the commodity dealt in might be dearly paid for by the ruin of such a class, and the absorption of control over one commodity by an all-powerful combination of capital." [United States v. Trans-Missouri Freight Assn.]

But petitioners further argue that their boycott and restraint of interstate trade is not within the ban of the policies of the Sherman and Clayton Acts because "the practices of FOGA were reasonable and necessary to protect the manufacturer, laborer, retailer and consumer against the devastating evils growing from the pirating of original designs and had in fact benefited all four." The Commission declined to hear much of the evidence that petitioners desired to offer on this subject. As we have pointed out, however, the aim of petitioners' combination was the intentional destruction of one type of manufacture and sale which competed with Guild members. The purpose and object of this combination, its potential power, its tendency to monopoly, the coercion it could and did practice upon a rival method of competition, all brought it within the policy of the prohibition declared by the Sherman and Clayton Acts. For this reason, the principles announced in Appalachian Coals, Inc. v. United States * * * have no application here. Under these circumstances it was not error to refuse to hear the evidence offered, for the reasonableness of the methods pursued by the combination to accomplish its unlawful object is no more material than would be the reasonableness of the prices fixed by unlawful combination. Cf. United States v. Trenton Potteries Co.; United States v. Socony-Vacuum Oil Co. Nor can the unlawful combination be justified upon the argument that systematic copying of dress designs is itself tortious, or should now be declared so by us. In the first place, whether or not given conduct is tortious is a question of state law * * * . In the second place, even if copying were an acknowledged tort under the law of every state, that situation would not justify petitioners in combining together to regulate and restrain interstate commerce in violation of federal law. * * * The decision below is accordingly

Affirmed.

NOTES AND QUESTIONS

1. This case is the first we have considered that was brought by the Federal Trade Commission and decided under § 5 of the FTC Act. Does the Court rest its judgment on the Commission's power to define practices to be "unfair methods of competition"? Would the case have come out the same way if it had been filed by the Justice Department?

2. The decision is brief and unanimous. Was the case really that easy? Was it the defendants' motives or the choice of "boycott" behavior that was found to be illegal here?

a. Should it be relevant for antitrust purposes that the defendants sincerely believed that they were defending themselves against the "piracy" of their creative efforts? Should the sole measure of the legitimacy of that claim be the extent of federal copyright or patent protection afforded such designs?

b. Suppose the Guild had induced state legislatures to create a tort remedy for infringement of their designs; would that have rendered the antitrust law powerless to condemn this kind of self-help? See Sears, Roebuck & Co. v. Stiffel Co., 376 U.S. 225, 84 S.Ct. 784, 11 L.Ed.2d 661 (1964) (state design piracy law held preempted by federal patent and antitrust laws).

3. What's wrong with group boycotts? Do they in fact restrain trade in a meaningful way? Did the Court virtually concede that no prices were agreed upon here?

a. What if the Guild had not demanded a boycott of "style pirates" but had put a label saying "Made in the U.S.A. by a member of F.O.G.A." into each of their garments. Could anyone have complained?

b. Suppose instead that Guild members had demanded that retailers sew a "Made in a Low-Wage Country by a Style Pirate" label into goods made by non-Guild members. Assuming the label reported the facts accurately, why wouldn't the Guild action clearly be helpful to consumers in making informed choices?

c. Was the likely effect of the Guild boycott greater than the achievement of a clear differentiation between Guild and non-Guild dresses? Why should we be concerned if the only effect of this boycott were to require that non-Guild dresses be sold in different stores than "original" dresses? Be careful! If that were all that was going on, why would the Guild have gone to the expense of instituting and policing its system?

4. Suppose the Guild were successful here? Would that mean low-priced dresses could not be sold at all? Can you imagine circumstances in which no meaningful number of stores would handle non-Guild products? What would have to be true about the industry before a boycott of the kind instituted here would in fact exclude non-Guild members from all or most outlets?

a. Suppose that only Guild members produced a full line of dresses, for example, and that a retailer could not stock an entire dress department from the odds and ends available from non-members. Would that be a circumstance in which a group boycott by the Guild could have the desired effect? Can you think of any other circumstances in which the Guild boycott would be effective?

b. If the number of such situations is relatively few, why should a group's use of the boycott technique be per se illegal? That is, why shouldn't it be the government's burden to prove in each case that the conditions are such that the boycott could lead to genuine public harm?

c. If no such burden is imposed, might the antitrust laws become a basis for redressing disputes between private firms for which state tort remedies already exist? Might the antitrust laws' holding out treble damages plus attorneys' fees stimulate such filing of antitrust claims? Should the public view that as a matter primarily of interest to overworked federal judges? Are the implications any broader?

5. Look at the last paragraph of the Court's opinion. Does Justice Black convince you that a group boycott case should be treated as per se illegal? How was this attempt to have retailers boycott style pirates the same as price fixing? Did these designers want to protect their high-prices by excluding from the market the low-priced products that the public might prefer to buy?

6. Does this case mean that all concerted self-help is illegal?

a. You may remember from Chapter I that, absent the express exemption in § 6 of the Clayton Act, every strike called by a labor union could violate the Sherman Act. Is that really the kind of conduct the antitrust laws were designed to prohibit?

b. Suppose the National Organization for Women tried to get its members to encourage groups to which they belonged not to hold conventions in states that had not ratified the Equal Rights Amendment? See Missouri v. National Organization for Women, 620 F.2d 1301 (8th Cir.1980) (political protest not reached by the Sherman Act). We will come back to this question again in the next chapter.

A NOTE ON STANDARDS SETTING

The conduct in *Fashion Originators* was relatively easy to characterize as self-serving. Suppose, however, that the Guild had published lists of manufacturers who used flammable fabrics and that retailers had agreed with Guild members not to carry such unsafe apparel. Should an agreement with such a genuine public interest component also be subject to group boycott challenge?

Radiant Burners, Inc. v. Peoples Gas Light & Coke Co., 364 U.S. 656, 81 S.Ct. 365, 5 L.Ed.2d 358 (1961), raised that kind of issue. The American Gas Association is a membership organization composed of natural gas pipeline companies, public utilities that sell natural gas to consumers, and companies that make products that burn the gas. One of the Association's activities was the operation of a testing laboratory that evaluated the safety, utility and durability of gas burners. Products that passed the laboratory's tests received the agency's "seal of approval."

The plaintiff in *Radiant Burners* produced a burner that failed the AGA test. Utility members of AGA would not sell gas for use in an unapproved burner and, not surprisingly, consumers were not interested in buying a burner for which they could not buy gas. When the plaintiff asserted it was the victim of a group boycott, however, the lower courts did not agree. The Seventh Circuit wrote (273 F.2d 196, 200):

> "[T]he Sherman Act protects the individual injured competitor * * * only under circumstances where there is such general injury to the competitive process that the public at large suffers economic harm. * * * [T]he allegations of [the] plaintiff's complaint fail to establish that there has been any appreciable lessening in the sale of conversion gas burners or gas furnaces or that the public has been deprived of a product of overall superiority."

In a per curiam opinion, the Supreme Court reinstated the complaint. A "conspiratorial refusal" to sell gas for burners lacking the AGA seal of approval "falls within one of the classes of restraints" that are per se illegal. Any refusal to deal of this kind has a "monopolistic tendency," the Court asserted, and no safety justification for this refusal to deal could be heard.

Will this decision make you feel better the next time you hear the burner in your gas furnace fire up? Does the decision reflect sound economic theory? Does *Radiant Burners* represent the kind of unreality that makes people wonder aloud about lawyers and judges? There are, of course, still private standards setting agencies. Imagine yourself advising one. What would you suggest your client do to avoid running afoul of *Radiant Burners?*

ANTITRUST AND THE NEWS BUSINESS: THE *ASSOCIATED PRESS* CASE

Only four years after *Fashion Originators*, the Supreme Court heard a particularly celebrated group boycott case, Associated Press v. United States, 326 U.S. 1, 65 S.Ct. 1416, 89 L.Ed. 2013 (1945). The Associated Press was a cooperative of over 1200 newspapers from all around the country. Although the Associated Press had some reporters of its own, most of its stories came from its members. Whenever a reporter wrote a local news story, it would be put on the AP wire and sent to the other member papers. Thus, for example, the Peoria Journal Star or Omaha World Herald could publish stories of interest to Peoria or Omaha readers no matter where the events had occurred.

The AP's By-Laws prohibited AP members from selling news to non-members. In addition, as a practical matter, any AP member could block admission to the cooperative of any newspaper with which the member was in competition. It was this ability to block new members that the Government described as a group boycott. The District Court had granted summary judgment for the Government and enjoined enforcement of the By-Law.

While recognizing the important place of the press in our society, Justice Black, writing for the Court, made clear that the news media had no "peculiar constitutional sanctuary" from the reach of the antitrust laws. Newspaper publishers are in business for profit, and like producers of "food, steel, aluminum, or anything else people need or want", they are required to comply with the Sherman Act.

Even though several newspapers did not *want* to be AP members and even though both the United Press and International News Service provided alternative cooperative sources of news, the Court found that "inability to buy news from the largest news agency, or any one of its multitude of members, can have most serious effects on the publication of competing newspapers, both those presently published and those which, but for these restrictions, might be published in the future." Thus, the By-Law was per se illegal.

In dissent, Justice Roberts and Chief Justice Stone argued that the stories of each reporter are the property of his or her newspaper. The Sherman Act should not be read to require that they be shared with other papers. If two newspapers could agree to exchange stories only with each other, they reasoned, twelve hundred should be able to do so as well.

Further, Justice Murphy pointed out that there was no showing that the Associated Press "monopolizes or dominates the newspaper field." Where that was not true, he argued, to characterize its By-Law as a group boycott and to apply a per se rule to its operations created a weapon in the hands of government that was dangerous to the future of the news media.

NOTES AND QUESTIONS

1.   What do you suppose the problem was that the Associated Press was trying to solve with its By-Law?

a.   Suppose the Chicago Tribune and Chicago Sun-Times could run each other's stories without cost. What would that do to the Tribune's incentive to send a reporter to a story it knew the Sun-Times was covering? And what would the Sun-Times do next time? Soon, both papers would realize the potential for cost savings and neither would be eager to duplicate the other's production of news.

b.   Should an organization's concern about another's getting a "free ride" on its efforts be sufficient to justify a restraint such as that imposed by the Associated Press? Can you argue that such a restraint in fact increases rather than decreases competition? You will see later that restraints designed to deal with this "free rider" problem have been treated more sympathetically in recent antitrust cases.

2.   Should the antitrust law permit a contract between the Chicago Tribune and Chicago Sun-Times whereby they divide possible story sites—e.g., City Hall, the courthouse, etc.—and each supplies the other with stories originating at their assigned locations? What is different between that kind of arrangement and the Associated Press By-Law?

3.   Could NBC require Brian Williams to agree not to moonlight at ABC? The Court expressly noted that such a requirement might be upheld as reasonable. What makes denial of access to a reporter permissible but denial of access to his stories per se unlawful?

4.   Was the remedy here indeed just a modern version of the *Terminal R.R.* decree? Is the Associated Press like the St. Louis rail yard? The latter was found to be physically a natural monopoly, i.e., there was only one way in and out of town. Was there anything analogous about the Associated Press? Indeed, did the rise of the United Press and I.N.S. demonstrate that the newspaper business lacked natural monopoly characteristics?

5.   Is there any underlying economic theory that supports the illegality of group boycotts in a case like this? Did the AP by-law reduce the amount of news collected, for example? Did it raise the price of news? Did it make it harder to enter the industry? Did it tend to reinforce the oligopolistic pricing of newspapers? Did it reinforce local newspaper monopolies?

6.   Do you believe this case would have come out the same way in an industry other than the news media? Do we have special reason not to want monopolies of our sources of news? On the other hand, should the mass communications industry be entitled to more latitude today, if only because of newspapers' financial troubles? Cf. The Newspaper Preservation Act, 15 U.S.C. § 1801 et seq. (1970).

A NOTE ON DUE PROCESS IN EXCLUSION FROM ORGANIZATIONS

Even if a case like *Associated Press* says that organizations may not arbitrarily or for anti-competitive reasons be excluded from essential services, the question arises whether and under what conditions non-arbitrary criteria for exclusion may be employed. That issue was at the heart of Silver v. New York Stock Exchange, 373 U.S. 341, 83 S.Ct. 1246, 10 L.Ed.2d 389 (1963).

Harold Silver had formed companies to trade municipal bonds and over-the-counter securities. The firms were registered broker-dealers but not members of the New York Stock Exchange. In Silver's business, private wire connections to municipal bond departments and securities departments of other organizations were required. Some of the connections were to NYSE member firms. The Stock Exchange's rules required approval for such connections, and Silver received temporary approval in 1958. The next year, however, the Exchange ordered its members to terminate both the private-wire links to Silver and his access to the NYSE stock ticker. No reason was given for the action.

Silver filed suit alleging a group boycott, and the district court granted summary judgment that the collective refusal to grant Silver's private wire connections was a per se violation of § 1. The Supreme Court agreed that this was indeed a group boycott, citing *Fashion Originators*, *Associated Press* and *Radiant Burners*. "[I]mportant business advantages were taken away from petitioners by the group action of the Exchange and its members," the Court said, and this has long been held to be "forbidden."

Indeed, the only real question for the Court was whether the self-regulation of the stock exchange changed its exposure to antitrust liability. The Court said no. In order to claim the protection from antitrust liability afforded by its obligations to comply with regulatory requirements, the Exchange would have had to grant Silver due process before his termination. Because it failed to do that, the termination was per se illegal.

What do you think about this result? Should a lack of due process before essential services are removed constitute a per se antitrust violation? Do private firms normally have to grant due process to persons or firms with whom they deal? Should the court ignore the due process issue and focus only on the substantive reasons for the termination and the possible anticompetitive effects flowing from it?

3. MARKET DIVISION

TIMKEN ROLLER BEARING CO. V. UNITED STATES

Supreme Court of the United States, 1951
341 U.S. 593, 71 S.Ct. 971, 95 L.Ed. 1199

MR. JUSTICE BLACK delivered the opinion of the Court.

The United States brought this civil action to prevent and restrain violations of the Sherman Act by appellant, Timken Roller Bearing Co., an Ohio corporation. The complaint charged that appellant, in violation of §§ 1 and 3 of the Act, combined, conspired and acted with British Timken, Ltd. (British Timken), and Societe Anonyme Francaise Timken (French Timken) to restrain interstate and foreign commerce by eliminating competition in the manufacture and sale of antifriction bearings in the markets of the world. After a trial * * * the District Court made detailed findings of fact which may be summarized as follows:

As early as 1909 appellant and British Timken's predecessor had made comprehensive agreements providing for a territorial division of the world markets for antifriction bearings. These arrangements were somewhat modified and extended in 1920, 1924 and 1925. Again in 1927 the agreements were substantially renewed in connection with a transaction by which appellant and one Dewar, an English businessman, cooperated in purchasing all the stock of British Timken. Later some British Timken stock was sold to the public with the result that appellant now holds about 30% of the outstanding shares while Dewar owns about 24%. In 1928 appellant and Dewar organized French Timken and since that date have together owned all the stock in the French company. Beginning in that year, appellant, British Timken and French Timken have continuously kept operative "business agreements" regulating the manufacture and sale of antifriction bearings by the three companies and providing for the use by the British and French corporations of the trademark "Timken." Under these agreements the contracting parties have (1) allocated trade territories among themselves; (2) fixed prices on products of one sold in the territory of the others; (3) cooperated to protect each other's markets and to eliminate outside competition; and (4) participated in cartels to restrict imports to, and exports from, the United States.

On these findings, the District Court concluded that appellant had violated the Sherman Act as charged, and entered a comprehensive decree designed to bar future violations. The case is before us on appellant's direct appeal * * * .

* * *

Appellant * * * contends that the restraints of trade so clearly revealed by the District Court's findings can be justified as "reasonable," and therefore not in violation of the Sherman Act, because they are "ancillary" to allegedly "legal main transactions," namely, (1) a "joint venture" between appellant and Dewar, and (2) an exercise of appellant's right to license the trademark "Timken."

We cannot accept the "joint venture" contention. That the trade restraints were merely incidental to an otherwise legitimate "joint venture" is, to say the least, doubtful. The District Court found that the dominant purpose of the restrictive agreements into which appellant, British Timken and French Timken entered was to avoid all competition either among themselves or with others. Regardless of this, however, appellant's argument must be rejected. Our prior decisions plainly establish that agreements providing for an aggregation of trade restraints such as those existing in this case are illegal under the Act. United States v. Socony-Vacuum Oil Co.; United States v. American Tobacco Co., 221 U.S. 106 (1911); Associated Press v. United States. See also United States v. Aluminum Co. of America, 148 F.2d 416 (2d Cir.1945). The fact that there is common ownership or control of the contracting corporations does not liberate them from the impact of the antitrust laws. E.g., Kiefer-Stewart Co. v. Seagram & Sons, 340 U.S. 211 (1951). Nor do we find any support in reason or authority for the proposition that agreements between legally separate persons and companies to suppress competition among themselves and others can be justified by labeling the project a "joint venture." Perhaps every agreement and combination to restrain trade could be so labeled.

Nor can the restraints of trade be justified as reasonable steps taken to implement a valid trademark licensing system, even if we assume with appellant that it is the owner of the trademark "Timken" in the trade areas allocated to the British and French corporations. Appellant's premise that the trade restraints are only incidental to the trademark contracts is refuted by the District Court's finding that the "trade mark provisions [in the agreements] were subsidiary and secondary to the central purpose of allocating trade territories." Furthermore, while a trademark merely affords protection to a name, the agreements in the present case went far beyond protection of the name "Timken" and provided for control of the manufacture and sale of antifriction bearings whether carrying the mark or not. A trademark cannot be legally used as a device for Sherman Act violation. Indeed, the Trade Mark Act of 1946 itself penalizes use of a mark "to violate the antitrust laws of the United States."

We also reject the suggestion that the Sherman Act should not be enforced in this case because what appellant has done is reasonable in view of current foreign trade conditions. The argument in this regard seems to be that tariffs, quota restrictions and the like are now such that the export and import of antifriction bearings can no longer be expected as a practical matter; that appellant cannot successfully sell its American-made goods abroad; and that the only way it can profit from business in England, France and other countries is through the ownership of stock in companies organized and manufacturing there. This position ignores the fact that the provisions in the Sherman Act against restraints of foreign trade are based on the assumption, and reflect the policy, that export and import trade in commodities is both possible and desirable. Those provisions of the Act are wholly inconsistent with appellant's argument that American business must be left free to participate in international cartels, that free foreign commerce in goods must be sacrificed in order to foster export of American dollars for investment in foreign factories which sell abroad. Acceptance of appellant's view would make the Sherman Act a dead letter insofar as it prohibits contracts and conspiracies in restraint of foreign trade. If such a drastic change is to be made in the statute, Congress is the one to do it.

* * *

* * * [A] majority of this Court, for reasons set forth in other opinions filed in this case, believe that divestiture should not have been ordered by the District Court. * * * As so modified, the judgment of the District Court is affirmed.

MR. JUSTICE BURTON and MR. JUSTICE CLARK took no part in the consideration or decision of this case.

[The concurring opinion of MR. JUSTICE REED and THE CHIEF JUSTICE is omitted.]

MR. JUSTICE FRANKFURTER, dissenting. * * * Even "cartel" is not a talismanic word, so as to displace the rule of reason by which breaches of the Sherman Law are determined. Nor is "division of territory" so self-operating a category of Sherman Law violations as to dispense with analysis of the practical consequences of what on paper is a geographic division of territory.

* * *

MR. JUSTICE JACKSON, dissenting. * * *

The fundamental issue here concerns a severely technical application to foreign commerce of the concept of conspiracy. It is admitted that if Timken had, within its own corporate organization, set up separate departments to operate plants in France and Great Britain, as well as in the United States, "that would not be a conspiracy. You must have two entities to have a conspiracy." * * * The doctrine now applied to foreign commerce is that foreign subsidiaries organized by an American corporation are "separate persons," and any arrangement between them and the parent corporation to do that which is legal for the parent alone is an unlawful conspiracy. I think that result places too much weight on labels.

* * * Timken did not sit down with competitors and divide an existing market between them. It has at all times, in all places, had powerful rivals. It was not effectively meeting their competition in foreign markets, and so it joined others in creating a British subsidiary to go after business best reachable through such a concern and a French one to exploit French markets. Of course, in doing so, it allotted appropriate territory to each and none was to enter into competition with the other or with the parent. Since many foreign governments prohibit or handicap American corporations from owning plants, entering into contracts, or engaging in business directly, this seems the only practical way of waging competition in those areas.

* * * In a world of tariffs, trade barriers, empire or domestic preferences, and various forms of parochialism from which we are by no means free, I think a rule that it is restraint of trade to enter a foreign market through a separate subsidiary of limited scope is virtually to foreclose foreign commerce of many kinds. It is one thing for competitors or a parent and its subsidiaries to divide the United States domestic market which is an economic and legal unit; it is another for an industry to recognize that foreign markets consist of many legal and economic units and to go after each through separate means. I think this decision will restrain more trade than it will make free.

NOTES AND QUESTIONS

1. This is a short case but one that raises a number of important issues. Notice that the charge here was neither price fixing nor group boycott. It was that the world had been divided into markets within each of which only one of the "conspirators" would sell.

a. Should such a division of markets ordinarily be held to restrain trade? You saw it so held in *Addyston Pipe*. Think of the issue in economic terms. Does market division make it easier for each firm to reduce its output and raise its price? Does it make each a monopolist within its territory?

b. Does the effect of a market division depend in part on how large the territory of each firm is and how easy it is for a buyer to travel from the territory of firm A to purchase in the territory of firm B? Does the effect also depend on how many other competitors there are within each of the assigned territories?

c. Would the economic effect of this market division have been different if Timken had licensed British and French firms unrelated to it to produce and sell roller bearings under the Timken trademark? Would the result have been different under antitrust doctrine?

2.   Should calling the defendants' activities a "joint venture" make a difference? Are joint ventures necessarily simply cartels with a different name?

a.   What features of a joint venture might be significant enough to justify evaluating it under something other than a per se rule of illegality? Suppose several otherwise-competing firms formed a joint venture to do basic research that would be available to all. Might such research be in the public interest? Should it at least be assessed under a rule of reason rather than a per se rule?[16]

b.   Were you persuaded by the argument that this market division was "ancillary" to integration of these firms' legitimate activities? After *Socony-Vacuum*, need a court any longer think about the continuing vitality of *Addyston Pipe*?

3.   Even if a conspiracy of firms not to compete with each other within the United States is properly held to be illegal, did it seem odd to you that a conspiracy to decide who can sell roller bearings in Bangladesh should similarly concern the Justice Department?

a.   You remember, of course, that the extraterritorial reach of the Sherman Act had been questioned as long ago as the 1909 decision in *American Banana*. Was it clear here that patterns of Timken imports to and exports from the United States will in fact change as a result of this decision? Does the character of the firms' ownership suggest to you that little is likely to change?

b.   Given the finding of liability, was there any principled basis for not breaking up the Timken corporate family? Do you agree that the cure would have been worse than the disease?

4.   Was the defendants' argument about the requirements of international trade worth a more considered reply than the Court gave it? To what material issue does it relate most directly?

a.   If you knew that corporations doing business in Poland are required to have 50.1% local ownership, for example, might that explain why an enterprise would organize a separate corporation to operate in that country?

b.   Would that affect your assessment of the Court's suggestion that for Sherman Act purposes an organization that works through subsidiary corporations instead of departments within a single corporation has made a voluntary choice and should be stuck with its logical consequences?

———————

Within about a decade of the decision in *Socony-Vacuum*, then, the Court had clearly established that three kinds of horizontal, multi-firm conduct—price fixing, group boycotts and market division—were illegal per

---

[16]   Congress believed such joint ventures were sufficiently different from cartels that it adopted the National Cooperative Research Act of 1984, 15 U.S.C. §§ 4301–4305. The Act provides that many joint ventures will be evaluated under a rule of reason, and if they register their plans with the government, they will not be subject to treble damage liability even if the activities are later found to have violated the Sherman Act. We come back to this issue in Section E of this chapter.

se under § 1 of the Sherman Act. During the same period of the 1940s and 50s, a number of related developments were occurring as well.

FIXING MAXIMUM PRICES

When a case like *Socony-Vacuum* had posited a rule as broad as the per se rule against price fixing, there was not much room for the law to grow. Indeed, the number of price fixing cases that reached the Supreme Court over the next thirty years was relatively small. One such case, however, suggested just how broad this per se rule really was.

In the same term that it decided *Timken*, the Court also decided Kiefer-Stewart Co. v. Joseph E. Seagram & Sons, 340 U.S. 211, 71 S.Ct. 259, 95 L.Ed. 219 (1951). There, the plaintiff, a wholesale liquor dealer, charged that two liquor distillers, Seagram and Calvert, had conspired to sell their products only to retailers who would agree not to exceed the retail prices at which the distillers wished their products to be sold. This, of course, was price fixing with a twist. Instead of setting minimum prices in order to increase their own or their dealers' profits, they set *maximum* prices allegedly so as to improve their image as firms that did not take advantage of shortages after World War II.[17]

The question was whether fixing maximum prices is as illegal under § 1 as fixing minimum prices would be. The Court said yes. "[S]uch agreements, no less than those to fix minimum prices, cripple the freedom of traders and thereby restrain their ability to sell in accordance with their own judgment." Quoting *Socony-Vacuum*, the Court said: "[A] combination formed for the purpose and with the effect of raising, depressing, fixing, pegging, or stabilizing the price of a commodity in interstate or foreign commerce is per se illegal."

Regulating *maximum* price fixing surely constitutes applying the per se rule with a vengeance. Isn't such a rule obviously foolish? Don't answer too quickly. If maximum price fixing were permitted, could firms simply fix a minimum price and call it a "maximum," i.e., would form control substance? Would the agreement firms reached on maximum prices inevitably affect the level of service the sellers could provide for that price? Are consumers sometimes well served when firms are free to charge higher prices than their competitors and to try to convince customers to patronize them because of their personal service, longer hours, more convenient locations, etc.?

---

[17]   Although the Supreme Court did not acknowledge the defendants' rationale because it was applying a per se rule, the Court of Appeals did discuss it. 182 F.2d 228 (7th Cir.1950).

INTRA-ENTERPRISE CONSPIRACY

May the Government charge the members of an integrated corporate family with a conspiracy in restraint of trade? You saw that in *Timken* the answer was yes. Do you agree that it should be illegal for related corporations to coordinate their activities in the way that a single corporation organized into departments clearly could do?

The first case applying this doctrine of "intra-enterprise conspiracy" was apparently United States v. Yellow Cab Co., 332 U.S. 218, 67 S.Ct. 1560, 91 L.Ed. 2010 (1947). There, a family of cabs had been separately incorporated to reduce their tort exposure and reduce required liability insurance. The District Court had dismissed a complaint accusing the enterprise of "conspiring" to monopolize the Chicago taxicab market, but the Supreme Court reversed. The acquisition of these taxicabs by a single corporate entity was part of the conspiracy, the Court held. "[A]ny affiliation of integration flowing from an illegal conspiracy cannot insulate the conspirators from the sanctions which Congress has imposed."

The same issue was also presented in Kiefer-Stewart Co. v. Joseph E. Seagram & Sons. The two liquor companies that had "conspired" to set the maximum retail prices were both wholly-owned subsidiaries of the same corporation. Thereafter, in the Supreme Court's next term, the Justice Department argued that a corporation could be guilty of an agreement with its own officers and directors.[18]

The "intra-enterprise conspiracy" doctrine of *Yellow Cab*, *Kiefer-Stewart*, and *Timken* was widely criticized by antitrust commentators,[19] but it remained the law for over 35 years.

The critics were finally vindicated, however, in Copperweld Corp. v. Independence Tube Corp., 467 U.S. 752, 104 S.Ct. 2731, 81 L.Ed.2d 628 (1984). Copperweld had acquired a company, Regal Tube, that made steel tubing. David Grohne had been Regal's president when it was a division of Lear Siegler. Grohne left Lear Siegler and tried to start a steel tubing business of his own, Independence Tube Corp., but Copperweld made it known to Grohne's potential customers that it would sue Independence if it made use of Regal's trade secrets. Thus, Independence sued Copperweld, accusing it of a conspiracy with its subsidiary, Regal, to damage Independence's business.

Sherman Act § 1 draws a sharp distinction between unilateral and concerted action, Chief Justice Burger wrote for the Court. "[T]he coordinated activity of a parent and its wholly owned subsidiary must be

---

[18] Lorain Journal Co. v. United States, 342 U.S. 143, 72 S.Ct. 181, 96 L.Ed. 162 (1951). The Supreme Court affirmed the finding of an attempt to monopolize under § 2 and thus was able to avoid the question whether § 1 would support a charge of conspiracy between a corporate defendant and its officers.

[19] E.g., Report of Attorney General's National Committee to Study the Antitrust Laws (1955).

viewed as that of a single enterprise for purposes of § 1 of the Sherman Act. A parent and its wholly owned subsidiary have a complete unity of interests." There is no point in having a legal rule that makes something turn on whether or not the subsidiary is separately incorporated, the Court said; it discourages selecting the most efficient form in which to do business.

The Court made clear, however, that "we do not consider under what circumstances, if any, a parent may be liable for conspiring with an affiliated corporation it does not completely own." Note, however, how narrow the *Copperweld* holding really is. Yellow Cab and Kiefer-Stewart presumably should be retroactively exonerated, but the Timken family of companies would presumably still be liable for their agreement because of the public holdings in British Timken.[20]

CONSCIOUS PARALLELISM

A third important dispute during this period centered around how much direct evidence was required to prove a combination or conspiracy under § 1. Remember that Interstate Circuit, Inc. v. United States, 306 U.S. 208, 59 S.Ct. 467, 83 L.Ed. 610 (1939), taken up near the end of the last chapter, had held it was sufficient to show that the "conspirators" had all received copies of the same letter demanding that each exhibitor act in a given way. The simple fact that each exhibitor knew that the others would be similarly constrained was sufficient to convict the exhibitors of a conspiracy with each other.

Federal Trade Commission v. Cement Institute, 333 U.S. 683, 68 S.Ct. 793, 92 L.Ed. 1010 (1948), upheld a finding of conspiracy based on a system of basing point pricing. Institute members had reached a "mutual understanding" to sell cement on a basis of "delivered prices." Thus, instead of pricing the product at the seller's factory and adding a freight charge, producers added a freight charge based on shipping from one of several hypothetical points. The effect of the system was that no buyer could negotiate a better price from a nearby seller; all purchasers in a given area faced uniform prices from all producers. The Court upheld the Commission's finding that such a system improperly facilitated uniform pricing and a consequent lessening of competition.

United States v. Paramount Pictures, Inc., 334 U.S. 131, 68 S.Ct. 915, 92 L.Ed. 1260 (1948), went even farther. It involved another alleged conspiracy among distributors to set minimum prices at which movies

---

[20] For a review of the background of *Copperweld* and its contemporary significance, see Andrew I. Gavil, *Copperweld* 2000: The Vanishing Gap Between Sections 1 and 2 of the Sherman Act, 68 Antitrust L.J. 87 (2000); Stephen Calkins, *Copperweld* in the Courts: The Road to *Caribe*, 63 Antitrust L.J. 345 (1995).

would be shown. The evidence showed that "substantially uniform maximum prices had been established" by each defendant. Justice Douglas wrote that a conspiracy could be inferred simply from a "pattern" of prices. "It is not necessary to find an express agreement in order to find a conspiracy. It is enough that a concert of action is contemplated and that the defendants conformed to the arrangement."

No one could seriously doubt that proof of an antitrust conspiracy could fall short of the transcript of a conversation among defendants. Whether such a conspiracy could in fact be proved merely by evidence that two firms had acted in the same way, however, was a much harder question. Remember *American Column* and *Maple Flooring*. Most of the time, one would expect well-informed firms to behave in similar ways in most competitive markets. Surely, then, such behavior should not always be evidence of conspiracy.

The Supreme Court explicitly recognized that some limit must be set on permissible inferences. The case, Theatre Enterprises, Inc. v. Paramount Film Distributing Corp., 346 U.S. 537, 74 S.Ct. 257, 98 L.Ed. 273 (1954), again involved the movies. Plaintiff was the owner of a theater in a Baltimore suburb. He approached each of the defendant distributors seeking the right to show first-run movies at his theater. However, no defendant agreed to the request. The fact that each gave "exclusive" licenses to show first-run movies suggested a conspiracy, but the fact that each distributor realized it could make more money giving the right to a theater in a prestigious downtown location instead of a "small shopping center" suggested otherwise. Justice Clark wrote for the Court:

> "The crucial question is whether respondents' conduct toward petitioner stemmed from independent decision or from an agreement, tacit or express. To be sure, business behavior is admissible circumstantial evidence from which the fact finder may infer agreement. *Interstate Circuit, Inc.* But this Court has never held that proof of parallel business behavior conclusively establishes agreement or, phrased differently, that such behavior itself constitutes a Sherman Act offense. * * * '[C]onscious parallelism' has not yet read conspiracy out of the Sherman Act entirely."[21]

4. CASES TESTING THE LIMITS OF THE PER SE RULE

There were important Sherman Act § 1 prosecutions for horizontal price fixing, group boycotts and market division during the 1950s and

---

[21] For a sense of the contemporaneous academic treatment of these issues, see, e.g., James A. Rahl, Conspiracy and the Anti-Trust Laws, 44 Illinois L. Rev. 743 (1950); Donald F. Turner, The Definition of Agreement Under the Sherman Act: Conscious Parallelism and Refusals to Deal, 75 Harvard L. Rev. 655 (1962).

60s,[22] but few of them made new law. Two later cases, however, raised difficult problems of characterization and tested just how far the per se rule could be extended.

UNITED STATES V. CONTAINER CORPORATION OF AMERICA

Supreme Court of the United States, 1969
393 U.S. 333, 89 S.Ct. 510, 21 L.Ed.2d 526

MR. JUSTICE DOUGLAS delivered the opinion of the Court.

This is a civil antitrust action charging a price-fixing agreement in violation of § 1 of the Sherman Act. The District Court dismissed the complaint. The case is here on appeal.

The case as proved is unlike any other price decisions we have rendered. There was here an exchange of price information but no agreement to adhere to a price schedule as in Sugar Institute v. United States or United States v. Socony-Vacuum Oil Co. There was here an exchange of information concerning specific sales to identified customers, not a statistical report on the average cost to all members, without identifying the parties to specific transactions, as in Maple Flooring Mfrs. Assn. v. United States. While there was present here, as in Cement Mfrs. Protective Assn. v. United States, an exchange of prices to specific customers, there was absent the controlling circumstance, viz., that cement manufacturers, * * * exchanged price information as a means of protecting their legal rights from fraudulent inducements to deliver more cement than needed for a specific job.

Here all that was present was a request by each defendant of its competitor for information as to the most recent price charged or quoted, whenever it needed such information and whenever it was not available from another source. Each defendant on receiving that request usually furnished the data with the expectation that it would be furnished reciprocal information when it wanted it. That concerted action is of course sufficient to establish the combination or conspiracy, the initial ingredient of a violation of § 1 of the Sherman Act.

There was of course freedom to withdraw from the agreement. But the fact remains that when a defendant requested and received price information, it was affirming its willingness to furnish such information in return.

There was to be sure an infrequency and irregularity of price exchanges between the defendants; and often the data were available from

---

[22] The most visible was the criminal prosecution for price fixing of high-ranking executives of General Electric Co., Westinghouse, and some of the nation's other largest electrical equipment manufacturers. See, e.g., Charles A. Bane, The Electrical Equipment Conspiracies: The Treble Damage Actions (1973). On more general antitrust enforcement during the period, see Theodore Philip Kovaleff, Business and Government During the Eisenhower Administration (1980).

the records of the defendants or from the customers themselves. Yet the essence of the agreement was to furnish price information whenever requested.

Moreover, although the most recent price charged or quoted was sometimes fragmentary, each defendant had the manuals with which it could compute the price charged by a competitor on a specific order to a specific customer.

Further, the price quoted was the current price which a customer would need to pay in order to obtain products from the defendant furnishing the data.

The defendants account for about 90% of the shipment of corrugated containers from plants in the Southeastern United States. While containers vary as to dimensions, weight, color, and so on, they are substantially identical, no matter who produces them, when made to particular specifications. The prices paid depend on price alternatives. Suppliers when seeking new or additional business or keeping old customers, do not exceed a competitor's price. It is common for purchasers to buy from two or more suppliers concurrently. A defendant supplying a customer with containers would usually quote the same price on additional orders, unless costs had changed. Yet where a competitor was charging a particular price, a defendant would normally quote the same price or even a lower price.

The exchange of price information seemed to have the effect of keeping prices within a fairly narrow ambit. Capacity has exceeded the demand from 1955 to 1963, the period covered by the complaint, and the trend of corrugated container prices has been downward. Yet despite this excess capacity and the downward trend of prices, the industry has expanded in the Southeast from 30 manufacturers with 49 plants to 51 manufacturers with 98 plants. An abundance of raw materials and machinery makes entry into the industry easy with an investment of $50,000 to $75,000.

The result of this reciprocal exchange of prices was to stabilize prices though at a downward level. Knowledge of a competitor's price usually meant matching that price. The continuation of some price competition is not fatal to the Government's case. The limitation or reduction of price competition brings the case within the ban, for as we held in United States v. Socony-Vacuum Oil Co., at n. 59, interference with the setting of price by free market forces is unlawful per se. Price information exchanged in some markets may have no effect on a truly competitive price. But the corrugated container industry is dominated by relatively few sellers. The product is fungible and the competition for sales is price. The demand is inelastic, as buyers place orders only for immediate, short-run needs. The exchange of price data tends toward price uniformity. For a lower price does not mean a larger share of the available business but a sharing of the existing business at a lower return. Stabilizing prices as well as raising them is within the ban of § 1 of the Sherman Act. As we said in United States v. Socony-Vacuum Oil Co., "in terms of market operations stabilization is but one form of manipulation." The inferences are irresistible that the exchange of price information has had an anticompetitive effect in the industry, chilling the vigor of price competition. The agreement in the present case, though somewhat casual, is analogous to those in American Column & Lumber Co. v. United States * * * .23

Price is too critical, too sensitive a control to allow it to be used even in an informal manner to restrain competition.

Reversed.

MR. JUSTICE FORTAS, concurring.

I join in the judgment and opinion of the Court. I do not understand the Court's opinion to hold that the exchange of specific information among sellers as to prices charged to individual customers, pursuant to mutual arrangement, is a per se violation of the Sherman Act.

Absent per se violation, proof is essential that the practice resulted in an unreasonable restraint of trade. There is no single test to determine when the record adequately shows an "unreasonable restraint of trade"; but a practice such as that here involved, which is adopted for the purpose of arriving at a determination of prices to be quoted to individual customers, inevitably suggests the probability that it so materially interfered with the operation of the price mechanism of the marketplace as to bring it within the condemnation of this Court's decisions. Cf. Sugar Institute v. United States; American Column & Lumber Co. v. United States.

Theoretical probability, however, is not enough unless we are to regard mere exchange of current price information as so akin to price-fixing by combination or conspiracy as to deserve the per se classification. I am not prepared to do this, nor is it necessary here. In this case, the probability that the exchange of specific price information led to an unlawful effect upon prices is adequately buttressed by evidence in the record. * * *

* * * [T]he exchange of prices made it possible for individual defendants confidently to name a price equal to that which their competitors were asking. The obvious effect was to "stabilize" prices by joint arrangement—at least to limit any price cuts to the minimum necessary to meet competition. In addition, there was evidence that, in some instances, during periods when various defendants ceased

---

23 The *American Column* case was a sophisticated and well-supervised plan for the exchange of price information between competitors with the idea of keeping prices reasonably stable and of putting an end to cutthroat competition. There were no sanctions except financial interest and business honor. But the purpose of the plan being to increase prices, it was held to fall within the ban of the Sherman Act. * * * [Court's fn. 3]

exchanging prices exceptionally sharp and vigorous price reductions resulted.

* * * That being so, there is no need to consider the possibility of a per se violation.

MR. JUSTICE MARSHALL, with whom MR. JUSTICE HARLAN and MR. JUSTICE STEWART join, dissenting.

I agree with the Court's holding that there existed an agreement among the defendants to exchange price information whenever requested. However, I cannot agree that that agreement should be condemned, either as illegal per se, or as having had the purpose or effect of restricting price competition in the corrugated container industry in the Southeastern United States.

Under the antitrust laws, numerous practices have been held to be illegal per se without regard to their precise purpose or harm. * * * Among these practices are price-fixing, United States v. Socony-Vacuum Oil Co.; division of markets, United States v. Addyston Pipe & Steel Co.; group boycotts, Fashion Originators' Guild v. FTC; and tying arrangements, International Salt Co. v. United States, 332 U.S. 392 (1947). * * * This Court has refused to apply a per se rule to exchanges of price and market information in the past. See American Column & Lumber Co. v. United States; Maple Flooring Mfrs. Assn. v. United States; Cement Mfrs. Protective Assn. v. United States. I believe we should follow the same course in the present case.

Per se rules always contain a degree of arbitrariness. They are justified on the assumption that the gains from imposition of the rule will far outweigh the losses and that significant administrative advantages will result. In other words, the potential competitive harm plus the administrative costs of determining in what particular situations the practice may be harmful must far outweigh the benefits that may result. If the potential benefits in the aggregate are outweighed to this degree, then they are simply not worth identifying in individual cases.

I do not believe that the agreement in the present case is so devoid of potential benefit or so inherently harmful that we are justified in condemning it without proof that it was entered into for the purpose of restraining price competition or that it actually had that effect. * * *

Complete market knowledge is certainly not an evil in perfectly competitive markets. This is not, however, such a market, and there is admittedly some danger that price information will be used for anticompetitive purposes, particularly the maintenance of prices at a high level. If the danger that price information will be so used is particularly high in a given situation, then perhaps exchange of information should be condemned.

I do not think the danger is sufficiently high in the present case. Defendants are only 18 of the 51 producers of corrugated containers in the Southeastern United States. Together, they do make up 90% of the market and the six largest defendants do control 60% of the market. But entry is easy; an investment of $50,000 to $75,000 is ordinarily all that is necessary. In fact, the number of sellers has increased from 30 to the present 51 in the eight-year period covered by the complaint. The size of the market has almost doubled because of increased demand for corrugated containers. Nevertheless, some excess capacity is present. The products produced by defendants are undifferentiated. Industry demand is inelastic, so that price changes will not, up to a certain point, affect the total amount purchased. The only effect of price changes will be to reallocate market shares among sellers.

In a competitive situation, each seller will cut his price in order to increase his share of the market, and prices will ultimately stabilize at a competitive level—i.e., price will equal cost, including a reasonable return on capital. Obviously, it would be to a seller's benefit to avoid such price competition and maintain prices at a higher level, with a corresponding increase in profit. In a market with very few sellers, and detailed knowledge of each other's price, such action is possible. However, I do not think it can be concluded that this particular market is sufficiently oligopolistic, especially in light of the ease of entry, to justify the inference that price information will necessarily be used to stabilize prices. Nor do I think that the danger of such a result is sufficiently high to justify imposing a per se rule without actual proof.

* * *

* * * The District Court specifically found that the corrugated container market was highly competitive and that each defendant engaged in active price competition. The Government would have us ignore this evidence and these findings, and assume that because we are dealing with an industry with overcapacity and yet continued entry, the new entrants must have been attracted by high profits. * * * The Government admits that the price trend was down, but asks the Court to assume that the trend would have been accelerated with less informed, and hence more vigorous, price competition.[24] In the absence of any proof whatsoever, I cannot make such an assumption. It is just as likely that price competition was furthered by the exchange as it is that it was depressed.

* * *

---

[24] There was no effort to demonstrate that the price behavior of those manufacturers who did not exchange price information, if any, varied significantly from the price behavior of those who did. In fact, several of the District Court's findings indicate that when certain defendants stopped exchanging price information, their price behavior remained essentially the same, and, in some cases, prices actually increased. [Dissent fn. 3]

The Government is ultimately forced to fall back on the theoretical argument that prices would have been more unstable and would have fallen faster without price information. As I said earlier, I cannot make this assumption on the basis of the evidence in this record. * * * [H]ere, as in *Maple Flooring*, the Government has not proved that the information was [used to support concerted action]. Rather, the record indicates that, while each defendant occasionally received price information from a competitor, that information was used in the same manner as other reliable market information—i.e., to reach an individual price decision based upon all available information. * * * Accordingly, I would affirm the decision of the court below.

NOTES AND QUESTIONS

1.   Here we find an information exchange scrutinized almost 50 years after *American Column & Lumber Co.* Did the Court employ a per se rule here?

a.   Justice Fortas says not, but if it were that clear, why do you suppose the majority would not say so directly? Further, if no per se rule was intended, what is the point of the Court's reliance on *Socony*'s establishing such a per se standard?

b.   Were you surprised how concerned the Court was here with the structure of the market in a price fixing case? Is such an analysis more consistent with a rule of reason than a per se approach? Is such an analysis necessary simply to characterize the intent and effect of the information exchange?

c.   Could one say that Justice Douglas has created a "qualified per se rule"? Would creating such a middle ground between the per se rule and the rule of reason be desirable? In what kinds of cases would it be useful to use such an approach?

2.   What precise conduct was held to be illegal here?

a.   Was it improper for a firm to ask verification of the price its competitor had charged a customer? Was it improper for the firm being called to answer the question? Was it only improper to call *knowing* one would get an honest answer?

b.   Was the problem that the *effect* was "to stabilize prices though at a downward level"? Does that mean that prices fell more slowly or simply that everyone's prices went down at more nearly the same time?

c.   Was the problem that firms' knowledge of each other's prices tends to "lead toward price uniformity"? Aren't stability and uniformity the effects that *all* accurate information tends to create? Think about the stock market; doesn't the fact that the ticker reports transactions tend to make prices of trades more uniform and stable than they would otherwise be? Didn't *Maple Flooring* lay to rest the fallacy of thinking that accurate information is itself an evil?

3.   Part of the problem in reading this case may be the Court's lack of clarity about what had happened in the District Court. Justice Douglas tells us only that the District Court "dismissed the complaint."

a.   That was literally true, but the action came only after there had been a full bench trial. The Government had alleged a "combination and conspiracy" in "unreasonable" restraint of trade in violation of § 1. The Government contended, however, that it would be sufficient to prove a per se violation if it could show an agreement to exchange the price information with a purpose and effect of either the firms' charging similar prices or minimizing price decreases.

b.   The district judge made extensive findings, 273 F.Supp. 18 (M.D.N.C.1967), and concluded that while the competitors occasionally answered each other's questions about price as the Court here describes, there was no "agreement" to do so. Further, the judge found neither an intent nor effect of affecting the market price for containers within the meaning of *Socony-Vacuum*.

4.   Does the Court here conclude that these factual findings were not supported by the evidence?

a.   The entire Court, including Justice Marshall, agreed that there was in fact an "agreement." Do you agree? If reciprocal obligations of courtesy qualify as an agreement, can a firm ever do anything to negate an inference of conspiracy?

b.   Do you agree with Justice Fortas that there was in fact an effect on price? Does either he or the Court itself justify this conclusion by citations to the evidence or findings below?

c.   Does Justice Douglas do so by showing that there has been excess capacity in the industry but the number of firms and plants has almost doubled? Does this prove there are excess profits being earned? Given that this industry was easy to enter, is there any reason to believe excess profits will be more than a transitory phenomenon?

d.   Indeed, is Justice Marshall right that exchanges of information might actually drive prices down? Suppose your price is $1 and your marginal cost is 90 cents. If a buyer says your competitor will sell the item for 95 cents, will you lower your price if you can't verify the claim? Wouldn't doing so invite your buyer to lie with impunity? Might you lower your price *only* if you know your buyer cannot get away with lying?

5.   As it turned out, there was much more to the litigation in the cardboard box industry. In 1978, indictments were returned charging criminal violations of the Sherman Act. Some defendants pleaded nolo contendere; others were acquitted. Private plaintiffs filed what came to be called the Corrugated Container Antitrust Litigation.[25] The ultimate settlements paid by the companies were in excess of $300 million.

---

[25]   The case generated multiple opinions in the District Court and the Court of Appeals. See, e.g., In re Corrugated Container Antitrust Litigation, 643 F.2d 195 (5th Cir.1981), and 756 F.2d 411 (5th Cir.1985). Some of the history of the criminal and later civil litigation may be found in

UNITED STATES V. TOPCO ASSOCIATES, INC.

Supreme Court of the United States, 1972
405 U.S. 596, 92 S.Ct. 1126, 31 L.Ed.2d 515

MR. JUSTICE MARSHALL delivered the opinion of the Court.

The United States brought this action for injunctive relief against alleged violation by Topco Associates, Inc. (Topco), of § 1 of the Sherman Act. Following a trial on the merits, the United States District Court * * * entered judgment for Topco, and the United States appealed directly to this Court * * *. We * * * now reverse the judgment of the District Court.

I

Topco is a cooperative association of approximately 25 small and medium-sized regional supermarket chains that operate stores in some 33 States. Each of the member chains operates independently; there is no pooling of earnings, profits, capital, management, or advertising resources. No grocery business is conducted under the Topco name. Its basic function is to serve as a purchasing agent for its members.[26] In this capacity, it procures and distributes to the members more than 1,000 different food and related nonfood items, most of which are distributed under brand names owned by Topco. The association does not itself own any manufacturing, processing, or warehousing facilities, and the items that it procures for members are usually shipped directly from the packer or manufacturer to the members. * * *

All of the stock in Topco is owned by the members, with the common stock, the only stock having voting rights, being equally distributed. The board of directors, which controls the operation of the association, is drawn from the members and is normally composed of high-ranking executive officers of member chains. * * *

Topco was founded in the 1940's by a group of small, local grocery chains, independently owned and operated, that desired to cooperate to obtain high quality merchandise under private labels in order to compete more effectively with larger national and regional chains.[27] With a line of

---

Note, Derivative Use Immunity in Civil Antitrust Proceedings: The Controversy in the Corrugated Container Cases, 55 Temple L.Q. 132 (1982). See also the economic data on the industry in Don E. Waldman, The Inefficiencies of "Unsuccessful" Price Fixing Agreements, 33 Antitrust Bull. 67 (1988).

[26] In addition to purchasing various items for its members, Topco performs other related functions: e.g., it insures that there is adequate quality control on the products that it purchases; it assists members in developing specifications on certain types of products (e.g., equipment and supplies); and it also aids the members in purchasing goods through other sources. * * * [Court's fn. 2]

[27] The founding members of Topco were having difficulty competing with larger chains. This difficulty was attributable in some degree to the fact that the larger chains were capable of developing their own private-label programs. Private-label products differ from other brand-name products in that they are sold at a limited number of easily ascertainable stores. A & P, for example, was a pioneer in developing a series of products that were sold under an A & P label and that were only available in A & P stores. It is obvious that by using private-label products, a chain can achieve significant cost economies in purchasing, transportation, warehousing, promotion, and

canned, dairy, and other products, the association began. It added frozen foods in 1950, fresh produce in 1958, * * * . By 1964, Topco's members had combined retail sales of more than $2 billion; by 1967, their sales totaled more than $2.3 billion, a figure exceeded by only three national grocery chains.

Members of the association vary in the degree of market share that they possess in their respective areas. The range is from 1.5% to 16%, with the average being approximately 6%. While it is difficult to compare these figures with the market shares of larger regional and national chains because of the absence in the record of accurate statistics for these chains, there is much evidence in the record that Topco members are frequently in as strong a competitive position in their respective areas as any other chain. The strength of this competitive position is due, in some measure, to the success of Topco-brand products. Although only 10% of the total goods sold by Topco members bear the association's brand names, the profit on these goods is substantial and their very existence has improved the competitive potential of Topco members with respect to other large and powerful chains.

* * *

II

* * *

The United States charged that, beginning at least as early as 1960 and continuing up to the time that the complaint was filed, Topco had combined and conspired with its members to violate § 1 in two respects. First, the Government alleged [a division of markets]. * * *

* * * When applying for membership, a chain must designate the type of license that it desires. Membership must first be approved by the board of directors, and thereafter by an affirmative vote of 75% of the association's members. If, however, the member whose operations are closest to those of the applicant, or any member whose operations are located within 100 miles of the applicant, votes against approval, an affirmative vote of 85% of the members is required for approval. Because, as indicated by the record, members cooperate in accommodating each other's wishes, the procedure for approval provides, in essence, that members have a veto of sorts over actual or potential competition in the territorial areas in which they are concerned.

---

advertising. These economies may afford the chain opportunities for offering private-label products at lower prices than other brand-name products. This, in turn, provides many advantages of which some of the more important are: a store can offer national-brand products at the same price as other stores, while simultaneously offering a desirable, lower priced alternative; or, if the profit margin is sufficiently high on private-brand goods, national-brand products may be sold at reduced price. * * * [Court's fn. 3]

Following approval, each new member signs an agreement with Topco designating the territory in which that member may sell Topco-brand products. No member may sell these products outside the territory in which it is licensed. Most licenses are exclusive, and even those denominated "coextensive" or "non-exclusive" prove to be de facto exclusive. Exclusive territorial areas are often allocated to members who do no actual business in those areas on the theory that they may wish to expand at some indefinite future time and that expansion would likely be in the direction of the allocated territory. When combined with each member's veto power over new members, provisions for exclusivity work effectively to insulate members from competition in Topco-brand goods. Should a member violate its license agreement and sell in areas other than those in which it is licensed, its membership can be terminated * * * . * * *

* * *

From the inception of this lawsuit, Topco accepted as true most of the Government's allegations regarding territorial divisions and restrictions on wholesaling, although it differed greatly with the Government on the conclusions, both factual and legal, to be drawn from these facts.

* * *

* * * Topco essentially maintains that it needs territorial divisions to compete with larger chains; that the association could not exist if the territorial divisions were anything but exclusive; and that by restricting competition in the sale of Topco-brand goods, the association actually increases competition by enabling its members to compete successfully with larger regional and national chains.

The District Court, considering all these things relevant to its decision, agreed with Topco. It recognized that the panoply of restraints that Topco imposed on its members worked to prevent competition in Topco-brand products, but concluded that

> "[w]hatever anti-competitive effect these practices may have on competition in the sale of Topco private label brands is far outweighed by the increased ability of Topco members to compete both with the national chains and other supermarkets operating in their respective territories."

The court held that Topco's practices were procompetitive and, therefore, consistent with the purposes of the antitrust laws. But we conclude that the District Court used an improper analysis in reaching its result.

III

On its face, § 1 of the Sherman Act appears to bar any combination of entrepreneurs so long as it is "in restraint of trade." Theoretically, all manufacturers, distributors, merchants, sellers, and buyers could be considered as potential competitors of each other. Were § 1 to be read in the narrowest possible way, any commercial contract could be deemed to violate it. Chicago Board of Trade v. United States (Brandeis, J.). The history underlying the formulation of the antitrust laws led this Court to conclude, however, that Congress did not intend to prohibit all contracts, nor even all contracts that might in some insignificant degree or attenuated sense restrain trade or competition. In lieu of the narrowest possible reading of § 1, the Court adopted a "rule of reason" analysis for determining whether most business combinations or contracts violate the prohibitions of the Sherman Act. * * *

While the Court has utilized the "rule of reason" in evaluating the legality of most restraints alleged to be violative of the Sherman Act, it has also developed the doctrine that certain business relationships are per se violations of the Act without regard to a consideration of their reasonableness. * * *

It is only after considerable experience with certain business relationships that courts classify them as per se violations of the Sherman Act. One of the classic examples of a per se violation of § 1 is an agreement between competitors at the same level of the market structure to allocate territories in order to minimize competition. Such concerted action is usually termed a "horizontal" restraint, in contradistinction to combinations of persons at different levels of the market structure, e.g., manufacturers and distributors, which are termed "vertical" restraints. This Court has reiterated time and time again that "[h]orizontal territorial limitations * * * are naked restraints of trade with no purpose except stifling of competition." White Motor Co. v. United States, 372 U.S. 253 (1963). Such limitations are per se violations of the Sherman Act.

We think that it is clear that the restraint in this case is a horizontal one, and, therefore, a per se violation of § 1. The District Court failed to make any determination as to whether there were per se horizontal territorial restraints in this case and simply applied a rule of reason in reaching its conclusions that the restraints were not illegal. In so doing, the District Court erred.

United States v. Sealy, Inc., [388 U.S. 350 (1967)], is, in fact, on all fours with this case. Sealy licensed manufacturers of mattresses and bedding to make and sell products using the Sealy trademark. Like Topco, Sealy was a corporation owned almost entirely by its licensees, who elected the Board of Directors and controlled the business. Just as in this case, Sealy agreed with the licensees not to license other manufacturers or sellers to sell Sealy brand products in a designated territory in exchange for the promise of the licensee who sold in that territory not to expand its sales beyond the area demarcated by Sealy. The Court held that this was a horizontal territorial restraint, which was per se violative of the Sherman Act.[28]

Whether or not we would decide this case the same way under the rule of reason used by the District Court is irrelevant to the issue before us. The fact is that courts are of limited utility in examining difficult economic problems.[29] Our inability to weigh, in any meaningful sense, destruction of one sector of the economy against promotion of competition in another sector is one important reason we have formulated per se rules.

In applying these rigid rules, the Court has consistently rejected the notion that naked restraints of trade are to be tolerated because they are well intended or because they are allegedly developed to increase competition.

Antitrust laws in general, and the Sherman Act in particular, are the Magna Carta of free enterprise. They are as important to the preservation of economic freedom and our free-enterprise system as the Bill of Rights is to the protection of our fundamental personal freedoms. And the freedom guaranteed each and every business, no matter how small, is the freedom to compete—to assert with vigor, imagination, devotion, and ingenuity whatever economic muscle it can muster. Implicit in such freedom is the notion that it cannot be foreclosed with respect to one sector of the economy because certain private citizens or groups believe that such foreclosure might promote greater competition in a more important sector of the economy. Cf. United States v. Philadelphia National Bank, 374 U.S. 321 (1963).

* * * [T]he Sherman Act gives to each Topco member and to each prospective member the right to ascertain for itself whether or not competition with other supermarket chains is more desirable than competition in the sale of Topco-brand products. Without territorial restrictions, Topco members may indeed "[cut] each other's throats." But, we have never found this possibility sufficient to warrant condoning horizontal restraints of trade.

* * *

* * * If a decision is to be made to sacrifice competition in one portion of the economy for greater competition in another portion, this too is a decision that must be made by Congress and not by private forces or by the

---

[28] It is true that in *Sealy* the Court dealt with price fixing as well as territorial restrictions. To the extent that *Sealy* casts doubt on whether horizontal territorial limitations, unaccompanied by price fixing, are per se violations of the Sherman Act, we remove that doubt today. [Court's fn. 9]

[29] There has been much recent commentary on the wisdom of per se rules. Without the per se rules, businessmen would be left with little to aid them in predicting in any particular case what courts will find to be legal and illegal under the Sherman Act. Should Congress ultimately determine that predictability is unimportant in this area of the law, it can, of course, make per se rules inapplicable in some or all cases, and leave courts free to ramble through the wilds of economic theory in order to maintain a flexible approach. [Court's fn. 10]

courts. Private forces are too keenly aware of their own interests in making such decisions and courts are ill-equipped and ill-situated for such decisionmaking. To analyze, interpret, and evaluate the myriad of competing interests and the endless data that would surely be brought to bear on such decisions, and to make the delicate judgment on the relative values to society of competitive areas of the economy, the judgment of the elected representatives of the people is required.

* * *

We reverse the judgment of the District Court and remand the case for entry of an appropriate decree.

MR. JUSTICE POWELL and MR. JUSTICE REHNQUIST took no part in the consideration or decision of this case.

MR. JUSTICE BLACKMUN, concurring in the result.

The conclusion the Court reaches has its anomalous aspects, for surely as the District Court's findings make clear, today's decision in the Government's favor will tend to stultify Topco members' competition with the great and larger chains. The bigs, therefore, should find it easier to get bigger and, as a consequence, reality seems at odds with the public interest. The per se rule, however, now appears to be so firmly established by the Court that, at this late date, I could not oppose it. Relief, if any is to be forthcoming, apparently must be by way of legislation.

MR. CHIEF JUSTICE BURGER, dissenting.

This case does not involve restraints on interbrand competition or an allocation of markets by an association with monopoly or near-monopoly control of the sources of supply of one or more varieties of staple goods. Rather, we have here an agreement among several small grocery chains to join in a cooperative endeavor which, in my view, has an unquestionably lawful principal purpose; in pursuit of that purpose they have mutually agreed to certain minimal ancillary restraints that are fully reasonable in view of the principal purpose and that have never before today been held by this Court to be per se violations of the Sherman Act.

In joining in this cooperative endeavor, these small chains did not agree to the restraints here at issue in order to make it possible for them to exploit an already established line of products through noncompetitive pricing. There was no such thing as a Topco line of products until this cooperative was formed. * * * The goal sought was the enhancement of the individual members' abilities to compete, albeit to a modest degree, with the large national chains which had been successfully marketing private-label lines for several years. The sole reason for a cooperative endeavor was to make economically feasible such things as quality control, large quantity purchases at bulk prices, the development of attractively printed labels, and the ability to offer a number of different lines of trademarked products.

All these things, of course, are feasible for the large national chains operating individually, but they are beyond the reach of the small operators proceeding alone.

After a careful review of the economic considerations bearing upon this case, the District Court determined that "the relief which the government here seeks would not increase competition in Topco private label brands"; on the contrary, such relief "would substantially diminish competition in the supermarket field." This Court has not today determined, on the basis of an examination of the underlying economic realities, that the District Court's conclusions are incorrect. Rather, the majority holds that the District Court * * * should not have sought to determine whether Topco's practices did in fact restrain trade or commerce within the meaning of § 1 of the Sherman Act; it should have found no more than that those practices involve a "horizontal division of markets" and are, by that very fact, per se violations of the Act.

I do not believe that our prior decisions justify the result reached by the majority. Nor do I believe that * * * the judicial convenience and ready predictability that are made possible by per se rules * * * justify their promulgation without careful prior consideration of the relevant economic realities in the light of the basic policy and goals of the Sherman Act.

* * *

II

* * *

* * * [T]he Court does not tell us what "pernicious effect on competition" the practices here outlawed are perceived to have; nor does it attempt to show that those practices "lack * * * any redeeming virtue." Rather, it emphasizes only the importance of predictability, asserting that "courts are of limited utility in examining difficult economic problems" and have not yet been left free by Congress to "ramble through the wilds of economic theory in order to maintain a flexible approach."

With all respect, I believe that there are two basic fallacies in the Court's approach here. First, while I would not characterize our role under the Sherman Act as one of "rambl[ing] through the wilds," it is indeed one that requires our "examin[ation of] difficult economic problems." We can undoubtedly ease our task, but we should not abdicate that role by formulation of per se rules with no justification other than the enhancement of predictability and the reduction of judicial investigation. Second, from the general proposition that per se rules play a necessary role in antitrust law, it does not follow that the particular per se rule promulgated today is an appropriate one. * * * More specifically, it is far from clear to me why such a rule should cover those division-of-market agreements that involve no price fixing and which are concerned only with trademarked products that are not in a monopoly or near-monopoly position with respect to competing brands. The instant case presents such an agreement; I would not decide it upon the basis of a per se rule.[30]

NOTES AND QUESTIONS

1.   How would you describe Topco? Have we run into any organization like Topco before?

a.   How about Appalachian Coals, Inc.? Did Topco, like Appalachian Coals, perform several functions for its members other than the stabilization of price? Indeed, did Topco's functions include any actions that would allow Topco members to raise their prices?

b.   Was Topco like the Associated Press? Did it perform key central functions that its members needed to survive? Was Topco nearly the dominant force in the industry that the AP had been? On the other hand, was it an organization that would have been as hard for independents to replicate as the Court suggested the AP would have been?

c.   Was Topco like Timken Roller Bearing? Could both have been called joint ventures? Could the term "joint venture" be applied to so many kinds of business arrangements that one necessarily must go beyond that label in analyzing antitrust cases?

2.   The Court was clearly correct that Topco was most like the defendant in United States v. Sealy, Inc., 388 U.S. 350, 87 S.Ct. 1847, 18 L.Ed.2d 1238 (1967). Sealy was a membership organization of 30 mattress producers from around the United States who produced trademarked items, the best known of which was the Sealy "Posturepedic" mattress. Sealy products were advertised nationally but produced locally by member dealers who collectively set retail prices of their Sealy products and allocated exclusive territories to new members.

Justice Fortas, writing for a six member majority, characterized the *Sealy* arrangements as horizontal rather than vertical and thus as per se illegal under *Socony-Vacuum* and *Timken*. The question left open in *Sealy* was whether such an organization would violate the Sherman Act if the element of collective price fixing were not present. *Topco* answers that market division alone is enough.

3.   Conceding that the Court had precedent for its decision, are you disturbed that Topco's activities were held to be illegal? Do you believe consumers were better or worse off as a result of the services it performed for small grocery chains? Was competition in the grocery business increased or decreased?

---

[30]   The national chains market their own private-label products, and these products are available nowhere else than in the stores of those chains. The stores of any one chain, of course, do not engage in price competition with each other with respect to their chain's private-label brands, and no serious suggestion could be made that the Sherman Act requires otherwise. I fail to see any difference whatsoever in the economic effect of the Topco arrangement for the marketing of Topco-brand products and the methods used by the national chains in marketing their private-label brands. * * * [Dissent fn. 11]

a.   Where did Topco go wrong? Was Topco's problem simply that the per se rule was inexorable in its effect, that is, if a practice could be characterized as price fixing, market division, or group boycott, the practice was doomed no matter how procompetitive it might in fact have been?

b.   As you will see in each of the lines of cases in this chapter, by at least the late 1960s or early 70s, the Court had reached a point where the rigid application of the per se rule led to results that even proponents of vigorous antitrust enforcement found hard to defend. When we get to the material on current antitrust cases, you will want to ask whether *Topco* is still good law.

B. MONOPOLIZATION

So far, this chapter has considered the almost 35 years of developments involving multi-firm horizontal arrangements analyzed under § 1 of the Sherman Act. In this section, we turn to the parallel developments arising under Sherman Act § 2. Here as well, you will see that the cases begin with a de facto per se approach, a sharp departure from *Standard Oil* and *U.S. Steel*. You will want to ask yourself here as well whether a so-called "structural" approach to understanding market competitiveness survives analysis and stands the test of time.

UNITED STATES V. ALUMINUM COMPANY OF AMERICA
United States Court of Appeals, Second Circuit, 1945
148 F.2d 416

Before L. HAND, SWAN, and AUGUSTUS N. HAND, CIRCUIT JUDGES.

L. HAND, CIRCUIT JUDGE:

This appeal comes to us by virtue of a certificate of the Supreme Court * * * . The action [asked] * * * the district court to adjudge that the defendant, Aluminum Company of America was monopolizing interstate and foreign commerce, particularly in the manufacture and sale of "virgin" aluminum ingot, and that it be dissolved * * * . The action came to trial on June 1, 1938, and proceeded without much interruption until August 14, 1940 * * * . [It took until July 1942 for the trial judge to issue a final judgment; he dismissed the complaint.] * * * On June 12, 1944, the Supreme Court, declaring that a quorum of six justices qualified to hear the case was wanting, referred the appeal to this court * * * . * * *

I.   "ALCOA'S" MONOPOLY OF "VIRGIN" INGOT

"Alcoa" is a corporation, organized under the laws of Pennsylvania on September 18, 1888 * * * . It has always been engaged in the production and sale of "ingot" aluminum, and since 1895 also in the fabrication of the metal into many finished and semi-finished articles. It has proliferated into a great number of subsidiaries, created at various times between the years 1900 and 1929, as the business expanded. Aluminum is a chemical element; it is never found in a free state, being always in chemical combination with oxygen. One form of this combination is known as alumina; and for practical purposes the most available material from which alumina can be extracted is an ore, called, "bauxite." Aluminum was isolated as a metal more than a century ago, but not until about 1886 did it become commercially practicable to eliminate the oxygen, so that it could be exploited industrially. One, Hall, discovered a process by which this could be done in that year, and got a patent on April 2, 1889, which he assigned to "Alcoa," which thus secured a legal monopoly of the manufacture of the pure aluminum until on April 2, 1906, when this patent expired. Meanwhile Bradley had invented a process by which the smelting could be carried on without the use of external heat, as had theretofore been thought necessary; and for this improvement he too got a patent on February 2, 1892. Bradley's improvement resulted in great economy in manufacture, so that, although after April 2, 1906, anyone could manufacture aluminum by the Hall process, for practical purposes no one could compete with Bradley or with his licensees until February 2, 1909, when Bradley's patent also expired. On October 31, 1903, "Alcoa" and the assignee of the Bradley patent entered into a contract by which "Alcoa" was granted an exclusive license under that patent * * * . Thus until February 2, 1909, "Alcoa" had either a monopoly of the manufacture of "virgin" aluminum ingot, or the monopoly of a process which eliminated all competition.

The extraction of aluminum from alumina requires a very large amount of electrical energy, which is ordinarily, though not always, most cheaply obtained from water power. Beginning at least as early as 1895, "Alcoa" secured such power from several companies by contracts, containing in at least three instances, covenants binding the power companies not to sell or let power to anyone else for the manufacture of aluminum. "Alcoa"—either itself or by a subsidiary—also entered into four successive "cartels" with foreign manufacturers of aluminum by which, in exchange for certain limitations upon its import into foreign countries, it secured covenants from the foreign producers, either not to import into the United States at all, or to do so under restrictions, which in some cases involved the fixing of prices. These "cartels" and restrictive covenants and certain other practices were the subject of a suit filed by the United States against "Alcoa" on May 16, 1912, in which a decree was entered by consent on June 7, 1912, declaring several of these covenants unlawful and enjoining their performance * * * . * * *

None of the foregoing facts are in dispute, and the most important question in the case is whether the monopoly in "Alcoa's" production of "virgin" ingot, secured by the two patents until 1909, and in part perpetuated between 1909 and 1912 by the unlawful practices, * * * continued for the ensuing twenty-eight years; and whether, if it did, it was unlawful under § 2 of the Sherman Act. It is undisputed that throughout this period "Alcoa" continued to be the single producer of "virgin" ingot in the United States; and the plaintiff argues that this without more was enough to make it an unlawful monopoly. It also takes an alternative position: that in any event during this period "Alcoa" consistently pursued unlawful exclusionary practices, which made its dominant position certainly unlawful, even though it would not have been, had it been retained only by "natural growth." * * * "Alcoa's" position is that the fact *Sherman Act* that it alone continued to make "virgin" ingot in the country did not, and does not, give it a monopoly of the market; that it was always subject to the competition of imported "virgin" ingot, and of what is called "secondary" ingot; and that even if it had not been its monopoly would not have been retained by unlawful means, but would have been the result of a growth which the Act does not forbid, even when it results in a monopoly. * * *

* * * In the year 1912 * * * [Alcoa's output] represented nearly ninety-one per cent of the total amount of "virgin" ingot available for sale in this country. This percentage varied year by year up to and including 1938: in 1913 it was about seventy-two per cent; in 1921 about sixty-eight per cent; in 1922 about seventy-two; with these exceptions it was always over eighty per cent of the total and for the last five years 1934–1938 inclusive it averaged over ninety per cent. The effect of such a proportion of the production upon the market we reserve for the time being, for it will be necessary first to consider the nature and uses of "secondary" ingot, the name by which the industry knows ingot made from aluminum scrap. * * * It is true that some of the witnesses * * * testified that at each remelting aluminum takes up some new oxygen which progressively deteriorates its quality for those uses in which purity is important; but other witnesses thought that it had become commercially feasible to remove this impurity, and the judge made no finding on the subject. Since the plaintiff has the burden of proof, we shall assume that there is no such deterioration. Nevertheless, there is an appreciable "sales resistance" * * * [to even the purest kinds of secondary aluminum], and for some uses (airplanes and cables among them), fabricators absolutely insist upon "virgin": just why is not altogether clear. * * * The judge found that the return of fabricated products to the market as "secondary" varied from five to twenty-five years, depending upon the article; but he did not, and no doubt could not, find how many times the cycle could be repeated before the metal was finally used up.

There are various ways of computing "Alcoa's" control of the aluminum market—as distinct from its production—depending upon what one regards as competing in that market. The judge figured its share—during the years 1929–1938, inclusive—as only about thirty-three percent; to do so he included "secondary," and excluded that part of "Alcoa's" own production which it fabricated and did not therefore sell as ingot. If, on the other hand, "Alcoa's" total production, fabricated and sold, be included, and balanced against the sum of imported "virgin" and "secondary," its share of the market was in the neighborhood of sixty-four per cent for that period.

The percentage we have already mentioned—over ninety—results only if we both include all "Alcoa's" production and exclude "secondary." That percentage is enough to constitute a monopoly; it is doubtful whether sixty or sixty-four percent would be enough; and certainly thirty-three per cent is not. Hence it is necessary to settle what we shall treat as competing in the ingot market. That part of its production which "Alcoa" itself fabricates, does not of course ever reach the market as ingot; and we recognize that it is only when a restriction of production either inevitably affects prices, or is intended to do so, that it violates § 1 of the Act. However, even though we were to assume that a monopoly is unlawful under § 2 only in case it controls prices, the ingot fabricated by "Alcoa," necessarily had a direct effect upon the ingot market. All ingot—with trifling exceptions—is used to fabricate intermediate, or end, products; and therefore all intermediate, or end, products which "Alcoa" fabricates and sells, pro tanto reduce the demand for ingot itself. The situation is the same, though reversed, as in Standard Oil Co. [N.J.] v. United States, where the court answered the defendants' argument that they had no control over the crude oil by saying that "as substantial power over the crude product was the inevitable result of the absolute control which existed over the refined product, the monopolization of the one carried with it the power to control the other." We cannot therefore agree that the computation of the percentage of "Alcoa's" control over the ingot market should not include the whole of its ingot production.

As to "secondary," as we have said, for certain purposes the industry will not accept it at all; but for those for which it will, the difference in price is ordinarily not very great; the judge found that it was between one and two cents a pound, hardly enough margin on which to base a monopoly. Indeed, there are times when all differential disappears, and "secondary" will actually sell at a higher price: i.e. when there is a supply available which contains just the alloy that a fabricator needs for the article which he proposes to make. Taking the industry as a whole, we can say nothing more definite than that, although "secondary" does not compete at all in some uses, (whether because of "sales resistance" only, or because of actual metallurgical inferiority), for most purposes it competes upon a substantial equality with "virgin." On these facts the judge found that "every pound of secondary or scrap aluminum which is sold in commerce displaces a pound of virgin aluminum which otherwise would, or might have been, sold." We agree * * * . (This is indeed the same argument which we used a moment ago to include in the supply that part of "virgin" with "Alcoa" fabricates; it is not apparent to us why the judge did not think it applicable to that item as well.) At any given moment therefore "secondary" competes with "virgin" in the ingot market; further, it can, and probably does, set a limit or "ceiling" beyond which the price of "virgin" cannot go, for the cost of its production will in the end depend only upon the expense of scavenging and reconditioning. It might seem for this reason that in estimating "Alcoa's" control over the ingot market, we ought to include the supply of "secondary," as the judge did. Indeed, it may be thought a paradox to say that anyone has the monopoly of a market in which at all times he must meet a competition that limits his price. We shall show that it is not.

In the case of a monopoly of any commodity which does not disappear in use and which can be salvaged, the supply seeking sale at any moment will be made up of two components: (1) the part which the putative monopolist can immediately produce and sell; and (2) the part which has been, or can be, reclaimed out of what he has produced and sold in the past. By hypothesis he presently controls the first of these components; the second he has controlled in the past, although he no longer does. During the period when he did control the second, if he was aware of his interest, he was guided, not alone by its effect at that time upon the market, but by his knowledge that some part of it was likely to be reclaimed and seek the future market. That consideration will to some extent always affect his production until he decides to abandon the business, or for some other reason ceases to be concerned with the future market. Thus, in the case at bar "Alcoa" always knew that the future supply of ingot would be made up in part of what it produced at the time, and, if it was as far-sighted as it proclaims itself, that consideration must have had its share in determining how much to produce. How accurately it could forecast the effect of present production upon the future market is another matter. Experience, no doubt, would help; but it makes no difference that it had to guess; it is enough that it had an inducement to make the best guess it could, and that it would regulate that part of the future supply, so far as it should turn out to have guessed right. The competition of "secondary" must therefore be disregarded, as soon as we consider the position of "Alcoa" over a period of years; it was as much within "Alcoa's" control as was the production of the "virgin" from which it had been derived. This can be well illustrated by the case of a lawful monopoly: e.g. a patent or a copyright. The monopolist cannot prevent those to whom he sells from reselling at whatever prices they please. United States v. General Electric Co. Nor can he prevent their reconditioning articles worn by use, unless they in fact make a new article. At any moment his control over the market will therefore be limited by that part of what he has formerly sold, which the price he now charges may bring upon the market, as second hand or reclaimed articles. Yet no one would think of saying that for this reason the patent or the copyright did not confer a monopoly. Again, consider the situation of the owner of the only supply of some raw material like iron ore. Scrap iron is a constant factor in the iron market; it is scavenged, remelted into pig, and sold in competition with newly smelted pig; an owner of the sole supply of ore must always face that competition and it will serve to put a "ceiling" upon his price, so far as there is enough of it. Nevertheless, no one would say that, even during the period while the pig which he has sold in the past can so return to the market, he does not have a natural monopoly. Finally, if

"Alcoa" is right, precisely the same reasoning ought to lead us to include that part of clippings and trimmings which a fabricator himself saves and remelts—"process scrap"—for that too pro tanto reduces the market for "virgin." * * *

We conclude therefore that "Alcoa's" control over the ingot market must be reckoned at over ninety per cent; that being the proportion which its production bears to imported "virgin" ingot. If the fraction which it did not supply were the produce of domestic manufacture there could be no doubt that this percentage gave it a monopoly—lawful or unlawful, as the case might be. The producer of so large a proportion of the supply has complete control within certain limits. It is true that, if by raising the price he reduces the amount which can be marketed—as always, or almost always, happens—he may invite the expansion of the small producers who will try to fill the place left open; nevertheless, not only is there an inevitable lag in this, but the large producer is in a strong position to check such competition; and, indeed, if he has retained his old plant and personnel, he can inevitably do so. There are indeed limits to his power; substitutes are available for almost all commodities, and to raise the price enough is to evoke them. Moreover, it is difficult and expensive to keep idle any part of a plant or of personnel; and any drastic contraction of the market will offer increasing temptation to the small producers to expand. But these limitations also exist when a single producer occupies the whole market: even then, his hold will depend upon his moderation in exerting his immediate power.

The case at bar is however different, because, for aught that appears, there may well have been a practically unlimited supply of imports as the price of ingot rose. * * * It is entirely consistent with the evidence that it was the threat of greater foreign imports which kept "Alcoa's" prices where they were, and prevented it from exploiting its advantage as sole domestic producer; indeed it is hard to resist the conclusion that potential imports did put a "ceiling" upon those prices. Nevertheless, within the limits afforded by the tariff and the cost of transportation, "Alcoa" was free to raise its prices as it chose, since it was free from domestic competition, save as it drew other metals into the market as substitutes. Was this a monopoly within the meaning of § 2? The judge found that, over the whole half century of its existence, "Alcoa's" profits upon capital invested, after payment of income taxes, had been only about ten per cent * * * . A profit of ten per cent in such an industry, dependent, in part at any rate, upon continued tariff protection, and subject to the vicissitudes of new demands, to the obsolescence of plant and process—which can never be accurately gauged in advance—to the chance that substitutes may at any moment be discovered which will reduce the demand, and to the other hazards which attend all industry: a profit of ten per cent, so conditioned, could hardly be considered extortionate.

There are, however, two answers to any such excuse; and the first is that the profit on ingot was not necessarily the same as the profit of the business as a whole, and that we have no means of allocating its proper share to ingot. * * * But the whole issue is irrelevant anyway, for it is no excuse for "monopolizing" a market that the monopoly has not been used to extract from the consumer more than a "fair" profit. The Act has wider purposes. Indeed, even though we disregarded all but economic considerations, it would by no means follow that such concentration of producing power is to be desired, when it has not been used extortionately. Many people believe that possession of unchallenged economic power deadens initiative, discourages thrift and depresses energy; that immunity from competition is a narcotic, and rivalry is a stimulant, to industrial progress; that the spur of constant stress is necessary to counteract an inevitable disposition to let well enough alone. Such people believe that competitors, versed in the craft as no consumer can be, will be quick to detect opportunities for saving and new shifts in production, and be eager to profit by them. In any event the mere fact that a producer, having command of the domestic market, has not been able to make more than a "fair" profit, is no evidence that a "fair" profit could not have been made at lower prices. True, it might have been thought adequate to condemn only those monopolies which could not show that they had exercised the highest possible ingenuity, had adopted every possible economy, had anticipated every conceivable improvement, stimulated every possible demand. No doubt, that would be one way of dealing with the matter, although it would imply constant scrutiny and constant supervision, such as courts are unable to provide. Be that as it may, that was not the way that Congress chose; it did not condone "good trusts" and condemn "bad" ones; it forbade all. Moreover, in so doing it was not necessarily actuated by economic motives alone. It is possible, because of its indirect social or moral effect, to prefer a system of small producers, each dependent for his success upon his own skill and character, to one in which the great mass of those engaged must accept the direction of a few. These considerations, which we have suggested only as possible purposes of the Act, we think the decisions prove to have been in fact its purposes.

It is settled, at least as to § 1, that there are some contracts restricting competition which are unlawful, no matter how beneficent they may be; no industrial exigency will justify them; they are absolutely forbidden. Chief Justice Taft said as much of contracts dividing a territory among producers, in the often quoted passage of his opinion in the Circuit Court of Appeals in United States v. Addyston Pipe and Steel Co. The Supreme Court unconditionally condemned all contracts fixing prices in United States v. Trenton Potteries Company; and whatever doubts may have arisen as to that decision from Appalachian Coals Inc. v. United States, they were laid by United States v. Socony-Vacuum Co. It will now scarcely be denied that the same notion originally extended to all contracts—

"reasonable," or "unreasonable"—which restrict competition. United States v. Trans-Missouri Freight Association; United States v. Joint Traffic Association. The decisions in Standard Oil Co. v. United States, and American Tobacco Company v. United States, certainly did change this, and since then it has been accepted law that not all contracts which in fact put an end to existing competition are unlawful. Starting, however, with the authoritative premise that all contracts fixing prices are unconditionally prohibited, the only possible difference between them and a monopoly is that while a monopoly necessarily involves an equal, or even greater, power to fix prices, its mere existence might be thought not to constitute an exercise of that power. That distinction is nevertheless purely formal; it would be valid only so long as the monopoly remained wholly inert; it would disappear as soon as the monopoly began to operate; for, when it did—that is, as soon as it began to sell at all—it must sell at some price and the only price at which it could sell is a price which it itself fixed. Thereafter the power and its exercise must needs coalesce. Indeed it would be absurd to condemn such contracts unconditionally, and not to extend the condemnation to monopolies; for the contracts are only steps toward that entire control which monopoly confers: they are really partial monopolies.

* * *

We have been speaking only of the economic reasons which forbid monopoly; but, as we have already implied, there are others, based upon the belief that great industrial consolidations are inherently undesirable, regardless of their economic results. In the debates in Congress Senator Sherman himself in the passage quoted in the margin showed that among the purposes of Congress in 1890 was a desire to put an end to great aggregations of capital because of the helplessness of the individual before them.[31] Another aspect of the same notion may be found in the language of Mr. Justice Peckham in United States v. Trans-Missouri Freight Association. * * * [I]t has been constantly assumed that one of [the Antitrust laws'] purposes was to perpetuate and preserve, for its own sake and in spite of possible cost, an organization of industry in small units which can effectively compete with each other. We hold that "Alcoa's" monopoly of ingot was of the kind covered by § 2.

---

[31] "If the concerted powers of this combination are intrusted to a single man, it is a kingly prerogative, inconsistent with our form of government, and should be subject to the strong resistance of the State and national authorities * * *." 21 Cong. Record 2457.

"The popular mind is agitated with problems that may disturb social order, and among them all none is more threatening than the inequality of condition, of wealth, and opportunity that has grown within a single generation out of the concentration of capital into vast combinations to control production and trade and to break down competition. These combinations already defy or control powerful transportation corporations and reach State authorities. They reach out their Briarean arms to every part of our country. They are imported from abroad. Congress alone can deal with them, and if we are unwilling or unable there will soon be a trust for every production and a master to fix the price for every necessity of life. * * * " 21 Cong. Record 2460. See also 21 Cong. Record 2598. [Court's fn. 1]

It does not follow because "Alcoa" had such a monopoly, that it "monopolized" the ingot market: it may not have achieved monopoly; monopoly may have been thrust upon it. If it had been a combination of existing smelters which united the whole industry and controlled the production of all aluminum ingot, it would certainly have "monopolized" the market. In several decisions the Supreme Court has decreed the dissolution of such combinations, although they had engaged in no unlawful trade practices. * * * We may start therefore with the premise that to have combined ninety per cent of the producers of ingot would have been to "monopolize" the ingot market; and, so far as concerns the public interest, it can make no difference whether an existing competition is put an end to, or whether prospective competition is prevented. * * * Nevertheless, it is unquestionably true that from the very outset the courts have at least kept in reserve the possibility that the origin of a monopoly may be critical in determining its legality * * * . This notion has usually been expressed by saying that size does not determine guilt; that there must be some "exclusion" of competitors; that the growth must be something else than "natural" or "normal"; that there must be a "wrongful intent," or some other specific intent; or that some "unduly" coercive means must be used. * * * What engendered these compunctions is reasonably plain; persons may unwittingly find themselves in possession of a monopoly, automatically so to say: that is, without having intended either to put an end to existing competition, or to prevent competition from arising when none had existed; they may become monopolists by force of accident. Since the Act makes "monopolizing" a crime, as well as a civil wrong, it would be not only unfair, but presumably contrary to the intent of Congress, to include such instances. A market may, for example, be so limited that it is impossible to produce at all and meet the cost of production except by a plant large enough to supply the whole demand. Or there may be changes in taste or in cost which drive out all but one purveyor. A single producer may be the survivor out of a group of active competitors, merely by virtue of his superior skill, foresight and industry. In such cases a strong argument can be made that, although the result may expose the public to the evils of monopoly, the Act does not mean to condemn the resultant of those very forces which it is its prime object to foster * * * . The successful competitor, having been urged to compete, must not be turned upon when he wins. The most extreme expression of this view is in United States v. United States Steel Corporation * * * . * * * But, whatever authority it [has] was modified by the gloss of Cardozo, J. in Swift & Company v. United States, 286 U.S. 106 [1932], when he said: "Mere size * * * is not an offense against the Sherman Act unless magnified to the point at which it amounts to a monopoly * * * but size carries with it an opportunity for abuse that is not to be ignored when the opportunity is proved to have been utilized in the past."[32] "Alcoa's" size was "magnified" to make it a "monopoly"; indeed, it has never been anything else; and its size, not only offered it an "opportunity for abuse," but it "utilized" its size for "abuse," as can easily be shown.

It would completely misconstrue "Alcoa's" position in 1940 to hold that it was the passive beneficiary of a monopoly, following upon an involuntary elimination of competitors by automatically operative economic forces. Already in 1909, when its last lawful monopoly ended, it sought to strengthen its position by unlawful practices, and these concededly continued until 1912. In that year it had two plants in New York, at which it produced less than 42 million pounds of ingot; in 1934 it had five plants (the original two, enlarged; one in Tennessee; one in North Carolina; one in Washington), and its production had risen to about 327 million pounds, an increase of almost eightfold. Meanwhile not a pound of ingot had been produced by anyone else in the United States. This increase and this continued and undisturbed control did not fall undesigned into "Alcoa's" lap; obviously it could not have done so. It could only have resulted, as it did result, from a persistent determination to maintain the control, with which it found itself vested in 1912. There were at least one or two abortive attempts to enter the industry, but "Alcoa" effectively anticipated and forestalled all competition, and succeeded in holding the field alone. True, it stimulated demand and opened new uses for the metal, but not without making sure that it could supply what it had evoked. There is no dispute as to this; "Alcoa" avows it as evidence of the skill, energy and initiative with which it has always conducted its business; as a reason why, having won its way by fair means, it should be commended, and not dismembered. We need charge it with no moral derelictions after 1912; we may assume that all it claims for itself is true. The only question is whether it falls within the exception established in favor of those who do not seek, but cannot avoid, the control of a market. It seems to us that that question scarcely survives its statement. It was not inevitable that it should always anticipate increases in the demand for ingot and be prepared to supply them. Nothing compelled it to keep doubling and redoubling its capacity before others entered the field. It insists that it never excluded competitors; but we can think of no more effective exclusion that progressively to embrace each new opportunity as it opened, and to face every newcomer with new capacity already geared into a great organization, having the advantage of experience, trade connections and the elite of personnel. Only in case we interpret "exclusion" as limited to maneuvers not honestly industrial, but actuated solely by a desire to prevent competition, can such a course, indefatigably pursued, be deemed not "exclusionary." So to limit

---

[32] [Ed. note] The quoted language comes from an opinion considering whether to modify a consent decree that prohibited the defendant's selling groceries at retail. The Court found that while much had changed about the grocery business since the decree was entered, there was still sufficient risk that a firm the size of Swift could "lay a handicap on rivals overweighted at the start" that the agreed-upon injunction should not be set aside.

it would in our judgment emasculate the Act; would permit just such consolidations as it was designed to prevent.

"Alcoa" answers that it positively assisted competitors, instead of discouraging them. That may be true as to fabricators of ingot; but what of that? They were its market for ingot, and it is charged only with a monopoly of ingot. We can find no instance of its helping prospective ingot manufacturers. * * *

We disregard any question of "intent." Relatively early in the history of the Act—1905—Holmes, J. in Swift & Company v. United States, explained this aspect of the Act in a passage often quoted. Although the primary evil was monopoly, the Act also covered preliminary steps, which, if continued, would lead to it. These may do no harm of themselves; but, if they are initial moves in a plan or scheme which, carried out, will result in monopoly, they are dangerous and the law will nip them in the bud. For this reason conduct falling short of monopoly, is not illegal unless it is part of a plan to monopolize, or to gain such other control of a market as is equally forbidden. To make it so, the plaintiff must prove what in the criminal law is known as a "specific intent"; an intent which goes beyond the mere intent to do the act. By far the greatest part of the fabulous record piled up in the case at bar, was concerned with proving such an intent. The plaintiff was seeking to show that many transactions, neutral on their face, were not in fact necessary to the development of "Alcoa's" business, and had no motive except to exclude others and perpetuate its hold upon the ingot market. * * * The plaintiff has so satisfied us, and the issue of intent ceases to have any importance; no intent is relevant except that which is relevant to any liability, criminal or civil: i.e. an intent to bring about the forbidden act. Note 59 of United States v. Socony-Vacuum Oil Co., on which "Alcoa" appears so much to rely, is in no sense to the contrary. Douglas, J. was answering the defendants' argument that, assuming that a combination had attempted to fix prices, it had never had the power to do so, for there was too much competing oil. His answer was that the plan was unlawful, even if the parties did not have the power to fix prices, provided that they intended to do so; and it was to drive home this that he contrasted the case then before the court with monopoly, where power was a necessary element. In so doing he said: "An intent and a power * * * are then necessary," which he at once followed by quoting the passage we have just mentioned from Swift & Co. v. United States. In order to fall within § 2, the monopolist must have both the power to monopolize, and the intent to monopolize. To read the passage as demanding any "specific," intent, makes nonsense of it, for no monopolist monopolizes unconscious of what he is doing. So here, "Alcoa" meant to keep, and did keep, that complete and exclusive hold upon the ingot market with which it started. That was to "monopolize" that market, however innocently it otherwise proceeded. So far as the judgment held that it was not within § 2, it must be reversed.

* * *

IV. THE REMEDIES

Nearly five years have passed since the evidence was closed; during that time the aluminum industry, like most other industries, has been revolutionized by the nation's efforts in a great crisis. That alone would make it impossible to dispose of the action upon the basis of the record as we have it; and so both sides agree * * * . The plaintiff wishes us to enter a judgment that "Alcoa" shall be dissolved, and that we shall direct it presently to submit a plan, whose execution, however, is to be deferred until after the war. * * * On the other hand, "Alcoa" argues that, when we look at the changes that have taken place—particularly the enormous capacity of plaintiff's aluminum plants—it appears that, even though we should conclude that it had "monopolized" the ingot industry up to 1941, the plaintiff now has in its hands the means to prevent any possible "monopolization" of the industry after the war * * * .

* * * We may, and we do, accept the figures of aluminum production in the report of the so-called "Truman Committee" as of March, 1944, which showed that the annual production of "Alcoa's" plants was about 828 million pounds; that the production of plants owned by the plaintiff which it had leased to "Alcoa," was about 1293 million pounds; and that the production of the Reynolds and Olin plants was together, 202 million pounds: a total of about 2300 million pounds. * * *

* * * [I]t is impossible to say what will be "Alcoa's" position in the industry after the war. * * * No one can now forecast in the remotest way what will be the form of the industry after the plaintiff has disposed of [government owned] plants * * * . It may be able to transfer all of them to persons who can effectively compete with "Alcoa"; it may be able to transfer some; conceivably, it may be unable to dispose of any. The measure of its success will be at least one condition upon the propriety of dissolution * * * . * * * Dissolution is not a penalty but a remedy; if the industry will not need it for its protection, it will be a disservice to break up an aggregation which has for so long demonstrated its efficiency. The need for such a remedy will be for the district court in the first instance, and there is a peculiar propriety in our saying nothing to control its decision, because the appeal from any judgment which it may enter, will perhaps be justiciable only by the Supreme Court, if there are then six justices qualified to sit.

But there is another, and even more persuasive, reason why we should not now adjudge a dissolution of any kind. The Surplus Property Act of 1944 provides [that government aluminum plants be disposed of in a manner that favors small business. The court may thus not have to impose a remedy at all]. * * * Therefore we shall merely reverse the judgment, so far as it held that "Alcoa" was not "monopolizing" the ingot market, and remand the case to the district court.

NOTES AND QUESTIONS

1.   This is the only case in which Learned Hand sat as a Justice of the U.S. Supreme Court. Technically, he didn't do so even here, of course, but the case was referred to the Second Circuit when the Supreme Court could not muster a quorum. The authoritative force of the views expressed by Judge Hand was expressly affirmed by the Supreme Court in the *American Tobacco* case, infra.

a.   What is the basis for the Court's decision? Was this a bad practices case like *Standard Oil*? How had Alcoa come to dominate the aluminum industry before the consent decree in 1912? Do you think a case should be decided based on the effects of restrictive contracts the company had terminated over a quarter-century before?

b.   Were there bad effects flowing from Alcoa's market position? That is, were there identifiable competitors who were excluded from the market as a result of Alcoa's practices? Was there a showing that Alcoa had reduced the output of aluminum and raised its price? Indeed, was it found guilty in part of keeping prices so reasonable that no one else had an incentive to enter the market?

2.   Then where did Alcoa go wrong? What transformed it from one of the country's great industrial success stories to a candidate for condemnation and divestiture?

a.   Are you convinced a firm should be criticized for being other than a passive beneficiary of its large market share? Is it wrong for a firm to expand its production eight-fold over 25 years? Is it Alcoa's fault that no one else entered the market because every time demand for aluminum increased, Alcoa expanded to meet it?

b.   Is there force to the idea that "exclusion" of competitors is not limited to methods "not honestly industrial"? Can you "think of no more effective exclusion than progressively to embrace each new opportunity as it opened"?

c.   Consider the competitive picture that faces American firms in world markets. Do we really want American managers *not* to seek to embrace growth opportunities? Suppose you were an Alcoa employee; what kind of job security would you have if Alcoa managers were as passive as Judge Hand seems to imply they should have been?

3.   Then what antitrust policies did the court believe it was furthering with this decision?

a.   Do you agree that it was Congress that had expressed a preference for "a system of small producers, each dependent for his success upon his own skill and character, to one in which the great mass of those engaged must accept the direction of a few"? Was that more accurately the view of some Supreme Court justices in some earlier opinions?

b.   Is monopolization a status offense or a prohibition of certain conduct? Do you agree that Congress meant to condemn "good trusts" as well as bad ones? Apart from the *U.S. Steel* precedent, would you agree with the Court that the task of discerning which trusts are "good" and "bad" is so daunting that the Court here wisely eschews it as a test?

c.   Do you agree that Congress feared that monopolists would get fat and quit innovating? Would a monopolist inevitably have that incentive, at least if it wanted to keep its monopoly? Was Alcoa an illustration of a firm that had gone soft? Indeed, did its conduct cast doubt on this behavioral assumption?

d.   Is the Court implicitly holding that § 2 of the Sherman Act gives courts a license to change the "structure" of American industry? Will restructuring industry along the lines Judge Hand asserts Congress intended help lower prices, create opportunities for new entrepreneurs, and perhaps decrease the need for more direct economic regulation? This view that the structure of an industry determines the competitive performance of that industry was held by many economists and lawyers during this period; watch for it underlying the Court's approach when we get to mergers as well.[33]

4.   Does the Court hold that every firm with a large market share is a monopolist?

a.   Can you think of very many firms that have had monopoly "thrust upon" them? How many firms "unwittingly" get a large market share? Is the number so small that the reference to the possibility only reinforces the sweep of the rule Judge Hand articulates here?

b.   What should be the relevance of intent in monopoly cases? Should it be sufficient to show that Alcoa acted with an intent to make it unattractive for new firms to decide to enter the market?

c.   Can one argue that Alcoa had competitors here even though its market share was very high? Can one say that its competitors were the firms not yet making aluminum, or the foreign firms not yet shipping to the United States, but capable of doing so if Alcoa raised prices above a competitive level? Don't dismiss the idea out of hand; you will see that this concept of "potential competition" plays a large role in the merger cases we will examine later.

5.   To this point, we have assumed that Alcoa had a large market share. As you will come to see, however, measurement of market share is one of the most important issues in both monopolization and merger cases.

a.   Remember that the "market" is a metaphor, not a street corner. We traditionally use two dimensions to define a market whose share is being measured. We speak of both a product market and a geographic market, and we then measure the defendant's share of "X product in Y area."

---

[33]   See, e.g., Joe S. Bain, Barriers to New Competition: Their Character and Consequences in Manufacturing Industries (1956); Carl Kaysen and Donald F. Turner, Antitrust Policy: An Economic and Legal Analysis (1959); F.M. Scherer, Industrial Market Structure and Economic Performance (1970). For contrasting views, see Harold Demsetz, The Market Concentration Doctrine: An Examination of Evidence and a Discussion of Policy (1973).

b.   The geographic market here was agreed to be the United States. The contested issue was what made up the product market. What questions should one ask in defining what is within and outside an economic "market"?

6.   How did Judge Hand reach his conclusion that Alcoa had 90% of the market for aluminum ingot in the United States?

a.   Remember the four possibilities the court identified as making up the market: (a) domestic virgin aluminum ingot made by Alcoa, (b) products fabricated from U.S. virgin aluminum by Alcoa, (c) secondary aluminum, most of which we would today call "recycled", and (d) virgin aluminum produced abroad and sold in this country.

b.   How does one calculate Alcoa's market share at 90%? Here's a hint. Of all the aluminum sold in the United States, category (a) represented 18%, (b) was 46%, (c) was 26%, and (d) was 10%. Judge Hand effectively used the formula a + b + c divided by a + b + c + d. When you work the numbers out, you get 90/100 or 90%.

c.   How had the District Judge taken the same underlying facts and concluded that Alcoa had only 33% of the market? Try treating Alcoa as producing only category a and divide that amount, 18%, by 54%, the sum of categories a + c + d.

d.   What assumptions, in turn, would lead to the 64% market share that Judge Hand rejects and concludes might be too small to constitute monopolization? How about crediting Alcoa with both categories a + b (64%) and then dividing by the sum of all four other categories?

7.   You can clearly see from the numbers here that "market share" is a conclusion based on facts, not a fact itself. Is there a principled way to determine the right market share conclusion to have reached in this case?

a.   Can we conclude that the District Court was incorrect in concluding the market share was 33%? Remember, it ignored all virgin aluminum sold by Alcoa as fabricated products (e.g., pots and pans) rather than as ingots. Did that make sense? Could it have done that if Alcoa had not been vertically integrated, i.e., if the fabricators had been firms other than Alcoa?

b.   Does that mean that Judge Hand was correct? Remember that he treated Alcoa as producing all secondary aluminum anew each year.

c.   Is it really relevant that Alcoa had once sold the aluminum in its virgin state? Can the original producer of a durable product factor the possibility of reuse into production calculations? Think of the law school casebook market. Do you suppose activity of the courts is the only reason there are so many new editions?

d.   Assuming that for a significant number of purposes, secondary aluminum is in fact an acceptable—if not perfect—substitute for the virgin product, is it not clear that Alcoa had to compete against both secondary and foreign aluminum, neither of which it currently controlled, and thus that the 64% market share was correct?

8.   Ironically, this case was filed in 1937 and tried for over two years. It took two more years for the trial court opinion, and another three for this opinion. Why wasn't breaking up Alcoa inevitable here?

a.   Do you suppose that this classic remedy for monopoly can cost jobs as well as market share? Indeed, if productive facilities have been consolidated, might there be few productive assets to spin off to the new firms? Would it ever be worth killing off a large, productive firm to vindicate what Judge Hand saw as the underlying Sherman Act policy in favor of small firms?

b.   Was the remedy phase probably easier in *Standard Oil*? How had that firm been formed and how had it grown? Keep in mind throughout both the monopoly and the merger cases that the issue on the merits is only part of the problem; devising a practical remedy is the real art.

c.   In fact, the facts in *Alcoa* were overtaken by events. The remedy phase in the case took another five years. As Judge Hand suggests, during World War II, the government had built its own aluminum plants and after the War it sold them to both Reynolds and Kaiser Aluminum which increased their productive capacity accordingly. By 1950, Alcoa had less than a 50% market share and no divestiture was ordered. Thus, after 13 years, the lawyers got paid and we have this opinion, but perhaps fortunately for everyone, there was no divestiture.

THE INTERNATIONAL SIDE OF THE *ALCOA* CASE

Alcoa is best remembered for what Judge Hand said about the reach of Sherman Act § 2, but it is also significant for what it said about the impact of U.S. antitrust law on the conduct of foreign cartels.

Alcoa had organized a Canadian company called "Limited" to hold its properties outside the United States. Limited, in turn, had an ownership interest in the "Alliance," a Swiss corporation whose other owners were companies based in France, Germany, Switzerland and Great Britain. An agreement in 1936 established production quotas for each owner in the Alliance; exceeding that quota required the firm to pay royalties to the Alliance to be divided according to the owners' shares.

Judge Hand found that the agreement would have been illegal if it had been reached in this country. Citing *American Banana*, however, he said that the fact that a foreign conspiracy has incidental effects in the United States is not itself enough to create Sherman Act jurisdiction. On the other hand, he said, where as here there is *both* an intent to affect and an actual effect on the quantity of aluminum shipped into the United States to compete with Alcoa's U.S. production, a Sherman Act violation can indeed be found.

A NOTE ON *ALCOA*'S ALLEGED PRICE SQUEEZE

Another issue in *Alcoa* was the government's charge that Alcoa had used a "price squeeze" to try to run Alcoa's "sheet rolling" competitors out of business. Judge Hand described the government's case and the court's analysis of it.

> "The plaintiff's theory is that Alcoa consistently sold ingot at so high a price that the sheet rollers, who were forced to buy from it, could not pay the expenses of rolling the sheet and make a living profit out of the price at which Alcoa itself sold sheet. * * *

> " * * * For all the five gauges of coiled sheet for eight years, 1925–1932, the average profit open to competing rollers was .84 cents a pound, as against 4.7 cents for the five succeeding years, 1933–1937. * * * Moreover, in 31 instances out of 112 there was no spread at all; that is, the cost of ingot plus the cost of rolling was greater than the price at which Alcoa was selling sheet. Obviously, there was in the eight years little or no inducement to continue in the sheet business * * * .

> " * * * That it was unlawful to set the price of sheet so low and hold the price of ingot so high, seems to us unquestionable, provided, as we have held, that on this record the price of ingot must be regarded as higher than a fair price. True, this was only a consequence of Alcoa's control over the price of ingot, and perhaps it ought not to be considered as a separate wrong; moreover, we do not use it as part of the reasoning by which we conclude that the monopoly was unlawful. But it was at least an unlawful exercise of Alcoa's power after it had been put on notice by the sheet rollers' complaints; and this is true, even though we assent to the judge's finding that it was not part of an attempt to monopolize the sheet market. We hold that at least in 1932 it had become a wrong."

Do you agree that such an alleged price squeeze should be improper? Is the impropriety that Alcoa charged too much for the aluminum ingot? How would you determine the price Alcoa could properly charge? Should Alcoa instead have been required to charge consumers more for its own aluminum sheet so as to give its competitors more profit?[34]

---

[34]   The best discussion of the possibility that a price squeeze can raise an antitrust issue is by then-Judge Breyer in Town of Concord v. Boston Edison Co., 915 F.2d 17 (1st Cir. 1990). As you will see in the next chapter, the Supreme Court has now gently rejected Judge Hand's analysis in Pacific Bell Tel. Co. v. Linkline Communications, 555 U.S. 438, 127 S.Ct. 1109, 172 L.Ed.2d 836 (2009), at fn. 3.

THE SUPREME COURT "AFFIRMS" JUDGE HAND—
THE *AMERICAN TOBACCO* CASE

Because the Second Circuit had only heard *Alcoa* when the Supreme Court could not assemble a quorum, the decision we have read was never directly affirmed. However, the Court loudly affirmed Judge Hand's reasoning the following year in American Tobacco Co. v. United States, 328 U.S. 781, 66 S.Ct. 1125, 90 L.Ed. 1575 (1946).

R.J. Reynolds, Liggett & Myers, and American Tobacco were the "Big Three" U.S. cigarette makers. From 1931 to 1939, their combined market shares totaled from 68% to 91% and was usually more than 75%.

The 1930s were the heart of the Great Depression, and some smaller companies that had made their reputation selling cigarettes for 10 cents per pack started making inroads into sales of the Big Three. Indeed, sales of the cheaper brands rose dramatically from .28% in 1931 to 22.78% in 1932. At that point, the Big Three cut their wholesale prices by 20% until their retail prices stabilized at 3 cents per pack more than the 10 cent brands. The smaller firms were not run out of business by this action but their sales fell back to 6.43% of the market.

The Supreme Court said the issue before it was "whether actual exclusion of competitors is necessary to the crime of monopolization * * * under § 2 of the Sherman Act." It found that no actual exclusion was required.[35] Indeed, the structure of the industry was more important than the defendant's acts. Citing *Northern Securities*, the Court said that "the material consideration in determining whether a monopoly exists is not that prices are raised and that competition actually is excluded but that power exists to raise prices or to exclude competition when it is desired to do so."

Thereafter, the Court noted the *ALCOA* case and said, "We find the following statements from the opinion of the court in that case to be especially appropriate here and we welcome this opportunity to endorse them:

* * *

" * * * We may start therefore with the premise that to have combined ninety per cent of the producers of ingot would have been to 'monopolize' the ingot market; and, so far as concerns the public interest, it can make no difference whether an existing

---

[35]   On the question of proof of agreement, the Court was receptive to arguments about conscious parallelism, saying: "No formal agreement is necessary to constitute an unlawful conspiracy. * * * The essential combination or conspiracy in violation of the Sherman Act may be found in a course of dealing or other circumstances as well as in an exchange of words. Where the circumstances are such as to warrant a jury in finding that the conspirators had a unity of purpose or a common design and understanding, or a meeting of minds in an unlawful arrangement, the conclusion that a conspiracy is established is justified."

competition is put an end to, or whether prospective competition is prevented. * * *

"[Alcoa] insists that it never excluded competitors; but we can think of no more effective exclusion than progressively to embrace each new opportunity as it opened, and to face every newcomer with new capacity already geared into a great organization, having the advantage of experience, trade connections and the elite of personnel. Only in case we interpret 'exclusion' as limited to maneuvers not honestly industrial, but actuated solely by a desire to prevent competition, can such a course, indefatigably pursued, be deemed not 'exclusionary.' So to limit it would in our judgment emasculate the Act; would permit just such consolidations as it was designed to prevent.

"In order to fall within § 2, the monopolist must have both the power to monopolize, and the intent to monopolize. To read the passage as demanding any 'specific' intent, makes nonsense of it, for no monopolist monopolizes unconscious of what he is doing."

Judge Hand, in short, really did wind up writing a Supreme Court opinion.

THE SUPREME COURT REFINES ITS TEST FOR MONOPOLIZATION—A LOOK AT *UNITED STATES v. GRIFFITH*

In the development of Supreme Court precedent under § 2 after *Alcoa* and *American Tobacco*, United States v. Griffith, 334 U.S. 100, 68 S.Ct. 941, 92 L.Ed. 1236 (1948), stands out as important in defining the evolving rule.

The case involved defendants who operated movie theaters in 85 small midwestern towns. In 53 of the towns, they owned all the theaters; in the other 32, they had competitors. The defendants had a practice of booking films into their entire circuit of theaters and often demanded exclusive rights to be the first to show new films. The district court found that competitors had difficulty getting rights to desirable films, but the defendants had not tried to put those competitors out of business. Building upon *American Tobacco*, Justice Douglas wrote for the Court:

"Anyone who owns and operates the single theater in a town, or who acquires the exclusive right to exhibit a film, has a monopoly in the popular sense. But he usually does not violate § 2 of the Sherman Act unless he has acquired or maintained his strategic position, or sought to expand his monopoly, or expanded it by means of those restraints of trade which are cognizable under

§ 1. For those things which are condemned by § 2 are in large measure merely the end products of conduct which violates § 1. Standard Oil Co. of New Jersey v. United States. But that is not always true. * * * Section 2 is not restricted to conspiracies or combinations to monopolize * * *. [M]onopoly power, whether lawfully or unlawfully acquired, may itself constitute an evil and stand condemned under § 2 even though it remains unexercised. For § 2 is aimed, inter alia, at the acquisition or retention of effective market control. See United States v. Aluminum Co. of America. * * * Hence the existence of power 'to exclude competition when it is desired to do so' is itself a violation of § 2, provided it is coupled with the purpose or intent to exercise that power. * * * The anti-trust laws are as much violated by the prevention of competition as by its destruction. It follows a fortiori that the use of monopoly power, however lawfully acquired, to foreclose competition, to gain a competitive advantage, or to destroy a competitor, is unlawful."

Booking films for the whole circuit meant that the defendants were using their market power in towns where they had a monopoly to lock up films for other towns in which they otherwise would have had to compete for the rights, the Court concluded. Even acknowledging that no competitors had gone out of business as a result, "it cannot be doubted" that there had been some adverse effect on those other firms and thus that there had been a violation of Sherman Act § 2.

Our next major § 2 case involved a firm that was the acknowledged industry leader in the manufacture of shoemaking machines. We read the District Court opinion by Charles Wyzanski, a prominent judge and the first to use an "economics clerk," Professor Carl Kaysen, to help him understand the evidence and the industry. In a brief per curiam order, the Supreme Court in effect adopted the following opinion as its own.

UNITED STATES V. UNITED SHOE MACHINERY CORP.

United States District Court, D. Mass. 1953
110 F.Supp. 295

WYZANSKI, DISTRICT JUDGE.

* * *

There are 18 major processes for the manufacturing of shoes by machine. Some machine types are used only in one process, but others are used in several * * *. The approximately 1460 shoe manufacturers themselves are highly competitive in many respects, including their choice of processes and other technological aspects of production. Their total demand for machine services * * * constitutes an identifiable market which is a "part of the trade or commerce among the several States."

United, the largest source of supply, is a corporation lineally descended from a combination of constituent companies, adjudged lawful by the Supreme Court of the United States in 1918. * * *

Supplying different aspects of that market are at least 10 other American manufacturers and some foreign manufacturers, whose products are admitted to the United States free of tariff duty. Almost all the operations performed in the 18 processes can be carried out without the use of any of United's machines, and (at least in foreign areas, where patents are no obstacle,) a complete shoe factory can be efficiently organized without a United machine.

Nonetheless, United at the present time is supplying over 75%, and probably 85%, of the current demand in the American shoe machinery market, as heretofore defined. This is somewhat less than the share it was supplying in 1915. In the meantime, one important competitor, Compo Shoe Machinery Corporation, became the American innovator of the cement process of manufacture. In that sub-market Compo roughly equals United.

Machine types in all processes vary greatly in character. The more complex ones are the important revenue producers in the industry. They must be designed with great engineering skill, require large investments of time and money, and demand a knowledge of the art of shoemaking. Otherwise they cannot meet extraordinary elements of variability resulting from the variety of manufacturing processes and sub-processes, the preliminary preparatory stages of manufacture, the lasts, the sizes, the leather, and other aspects of the shoemaking business.

Once designed, a shoe machine can be copied, as German competitors have shown. But the copying is not easy, and an American machine manufacturer unfamiliar with the art of shoemaking would not ordinarily enter the field even if United gave him technical assistance, at least, unless he were assured that he would be encouraged to continue making similar machines for a long time.

United is the only machinery enterprise that produces a long line of machine types, and covers every major process. * * * United's heavy research expenditures, over $3 million annually, have been pro-rated roughly according to those fields where maximum revenue has been or could be attained, and, except in the cement process, often in inverse proportion to actual competition. Through its own research, United has developed inventions many of which are now patented. Roughly 95% of its 3915 patents are attributable to the ideas of its own employees.

Although at the turn of the century, United's patents covered the fundamentals of shoe machinery manufacture, those fundamental patents have expired. Current patents cover for the most part only minor developments, so that it is possible to "invent around" them, to use the words of United's chief competitor. However, the aggregation of patents does to some extent block potential competition. It furnishes a trading advantage. It leads inventors to offer their ideas to United, on the general principle that new complicated machines embody numerous patents. And it serves as a hedge or insurance for United against unforeseen competitive developments.

In the last decade and a half, United has not acquired significant patents, inventions, machines, or businesses from any outside source, and has rejected many offers made to it. Before then, while it acquired no going businesses, in a period of two decades it spent roughly $3,500,000 to purchase inventions and machines. Most of these were from moribund companies * * * .

In supplying its complicated machines to shoe manufacturers, United, like its more important American competitors, has followed the practice of never selling, but only leasing. Leasing has been traditional in the shoe machinery field since the Civil War. So far as this record indicates, there is virtually no expressed dissatisfaction from consumers respecting that system; and Compo, United's principal competitor, endorses and uses it. Under the system, entry into shoe manufacture has been easy. The rates charged for all customers have been uniform. The machines supplied have performed excellently. United has, without separate charge, promptly and efficiently supplied repair service and many kinds of other service useful to shoe manufacturers. * * * The cost to the average shoe manufacturer of its machines and services supplied to him has been less than 2% of the wholesale price of his shoes.

However, United's leases, in the context of the present shoe machinery market, have created barriers to the entry by competitors into the shoe machinery field.

First, the complex of obligations and rights accruing under United's leasing system in operation deter a shoe manufacturer from disposing of a United machine and acquiring a competitor's machine. He is deterred more than if he owned that same United machine, or if he held it on a short lease carrying simple rental provisions and a reasonable charge for cancelation before the end of the term. The lessee is now held closely to United by the combined effect of the 10 year term, the requirement that if he has work available he must use the machine to full capacity, and by the return charge which can in practice * * * be reduced to insignificance if he keeps this and other United machines to the end of the periods for which he leased them.

Second, when a lessee desires to replace a United machine, United gives him more favorable terms if the replacement is by another United machine than if it is by a competitive machine.

Third, United's practice of offering to repair, without separate charges, its leased machines, has had the effect that there are no independent service organizations to repair complicated machines. In turn, this has had the effect that the manufacturer of a complicated machine must either offer repair service with his machine, or must face the obstacle of marketing his machine to customers who know that repair service will be difficult to provide.

Through its success with its principal and more complicated machines, United has been able to market more successfully its other machines, whether offered only for sale, or on optional sale or lease terms. * * * Having business relations with, and a host of contacts with, shoe factories, United seems to many of them the most efficient, normal, and above all, convenient supplier. Finally, United has promoted the sale of these simple machine types by the sort of price discrimination between machine types, about to be stated.

Although maintaining the same nominal terms for each customer, United has followed, as between machine types, a discriminatory pricing policy. * * * United's own internal documents reveal that these sharp and relatively durable differentials are traceable, at least in large part, to United's policy of fixing a higher rate of return where competition is of minor significance, and a lower rate of return where competition is of major significance. * * *

On the foregoing facts, the issue of law is whether defendant in its shoe machinery business has violated that provision of § 2 of the Sherman Act addressed to "Every person who shall monopolize, or attempt to monopolize * * * any part of the trade or commerce among the several States."

The historic development of that statutory section can be speedily recapitulated.

When they proposed the legislation, Senators Hoar and Edmunds thought it did little more than bring national authority to bear upon restraints of trade known to the common law, and it could not apply to one "who merely by superior skill and intelligence * * * got the whole business because nobody could do it as well." They did not discuss the intermediate case where the causes of an enterprise's success were neither common law restraints of trade, nor the skill with which the business was conducted, but rather some practice which without being predatory, abusive, or coercive was in economic effect exclusionary.

Early Supreme Court decisions went in different directions, until Mr. Justice White announced "the 'rule of reason'" * * *. His opinions encouraged the view that there was no monopolization unless defendant had resorted to predatory practices. And this was unquestionably the view to which Mr. Justice McKenna led the Court in United States v. United Shoe Machinery Company of N.J. [1918] and United States v. United

States Steel Corp. [1920]. But a reversal of trend was effectuated through the landmark opinion of Judge Learned Hand in United States v. Aluminum Co. of America.

In *Aluminum* Judge Hand, perhaps because he was cabined by the findings of the District Court, did not rest his judgment on the corporation's coercive or immoral practices. Instead, adopting an economic approach, he defined the appropriate market, found that Alcoa supplied 90% of it, determined that this control constituted a monopoly, and ruled that since Alcoa established this monopoly by its voluntary actions, such as building new plants, though, it was assumed, not by moral derelictions, it had "monopolized" in violation of § 2. Judge Hand reserved the issue as to whether an enterprise could be said to "monopolize" if its control was purely the result of technological, production, distribution, or like objective factors, not dictated by the enterprise, but thrust upon it by the economic character of the industry; and he also reserved the question as to control achieved solely "by virtue of * * * superior skill, foresight and industry." At the same time, he emphasized that an enterprise had "monopolized" if, regardless of its intent, it had achieved a monopoly by maneuvers which, though "honestly industrial," were not economically inevitable, but were rather the result of the firm's free choice of business policies.

* * *

Both the technique and the language of Judge Hand were expressly approved in American Tobacco Co. v. United States. Comparable principles were applied in United States v. Griffith.

* * *

* * * [I]n these recent authorities there are discernible at least three different, but cognate, approaches.

The approach which has the least sweeping implications really antedates the decision in Aluminum. But it deserves restatement. An enterprise has monopolized in violation of § 2 of the Sherman Act if it has acquired or maintained a power to exclude others as a result of using an unreasonable "restraint of trade" in violation of § 1 of the Sherman Act. United States v. Griffith.

A more inclusive approach was adopted by Mr. Justice Douglas in United States v. Griffith. He stated that to prove a violation of § 2 it was not always necessary to show a violation of § 1. And he concluded that an enterprise has monopolized in violation of § 2 if it (a) has the power to exclude competition, and (b) has exercised it, or has the purpose to exercise it. The least that this conclusion means is that it is a violation of § 2 for one having effective control of the market to use, or plan to use, any exclusionary practice, even though it is not a technical restraint of trade. But the conclusion may go further.

Indeed the way in which Mr. Justice Douglas used the terms "monopoly power" and "effective market control", and cited Aluminum suggests that he endorses a third and broader approach, which originated with Judge Hand. It will be recalled that Judge Hand said that one who has acquired an overwhelming share of the market "monopolizes" whenever he does business, apparently even if there is no showing that his business involves any exclusionary practice. * * *

In the case at bar, the Government contends that the evidence satisfies each of the three approaches to § 2 of the Sherman Act, so that it does not matter which one is taken.

If the matter were res integra, this Court would adopt the first approach, and, as a preliminary step to ruling upon § 2, would hold that it is a restraint of trade under § 1 for a company having an overwhelming share of the market, to distribute its more important products only by leases which have provisions that go beyond assuring prompt, periodic payments of rentals, which are not terminable cheaply, which involve discrimination against competition, and which combine in one contract the right to use the product and to have it serviced. But this inferior court feels precluded from so deciding because of the overhanging shadows of * * * [the] cases involving this company's predecessor and itself. * * *

This Court finds it unnecessary to choose between the second and third approaches. For, taken as a whole, the evidence satisfies the tests laid down in both *Griffith* and *Aluminum*. The facts show that (1) defendant has, and exercises, such overwhelming strength in the shoe machinery market that it controls that market, (2) this strength excludes some potential, and limits some actual, competition, and (3) this strength is not attributable solely to defendant's ability, economies of scale, research, natural advantages, and adaptation to inevitable economic laws.

In estimating defendant's strength, this Court gives some weight to the 75 plus percentage of the shoe machinery market which United serves.[36] But the Court considers other factors as well. In the relatively static shoe machinery market where there are no sudden changes in the style of machines or in the volume of demand, United has a network of long-term, complicated leases with over 90% of the shoe factories. These leases

---

[36] * * * This Court does not consider whether this high percentage, by itself, would warrant (but not compel) an inference that United has such overwhelming strength that it could exclude competition. Nor does this Court consider whether, drawing upon United States v. Griffith and United States v. Aluminum Co. of America, a bold, original court, mindful of what legal history teaches about the usual, if not invariable, relationship between overwhelming percentage of the market and control of the market, and desirous of enabling trial judges to escape the morass of economic data in which they are now plunged, might, on the basis of considerations of experience and judicial convenience, announce that an enterprise having an overwhelming percentage of the market was presumed to have monopoly power, * * * and that defendant, to escape liability, must bear the burden of proving that its share of the market was attributable to its ability, natural advantage, legal license, or, perhaps, to others' lack of interest in entering the market. [Court's fn. 1]

assure closer and more frequent contacts between United and its customers than would exist if United were a seller and its customers were buyers. * * * Moreover, United offers a long line of machine types, while no competitor offers more than a short line. Since in some parts of its line United faces no important competition, United has the power to discriminate, by wide differentials and over long periods of time, in the rate of return it procures from different machine types. Furthermore, being by far the largest company in the field, with by far the largest resources in dollars, in patents, in facilities, and in knowledge, United has a marked capacity to attract offers of inventions, inventors' services, and shoe machinery businesses. And, finally, there is no substantial substitute competition from a vigorous secondhand market in shoe machinery.

To combat United's market control, a competitor must be prepared with knowledge of shoemaking, engineering skill, capacity to invent around patents, and financial resources sufficient to bear the expense of long developmental and experimental processes. The competitor must be prepared for consumers' resistance found on their long-term, satisfactory relations with United, and on the cost to them of surrendering United's leases. Also, the competitor must be prepared to give, or point to the source of, repair and other services, and to the source of supplies of machine parts, expendable parts, and the like. Indeed, perhaps a competitor who aims at any large scale success must also be prepared to lease his machines. The considerations would all affect potential competition, and have not been without their effect on actual competition.

Not only does the evidence show United has control of the market, but also the evidence does not show that the control is due entirely to excusable causes. The three principal sources of United's power have been the original constitution of the company, the superiority of United's products and services, and the leasing system. The first two of these are plainly beyond reproach. * * *

* * *

In one sense, the leasing system [and related activities] * * * were natural and normal, for they were, in Judge Hand's words, "honestly industrial." They are the sort of activities which would be engaged in by other honorable firms. And, to a large extent, the leasing practices conform to long-standing traditions in the shoe machinery business. Yet, they are not practices which can be properly described as the inevitable consequences of ability, natural forces, or law. * * * They are contracts, arrangements, and policies which, instead of encouraging competition based on pure merit, further the dominance of a particular firm. * * *

It is only fair to add that * * * United's power does not rest on predatory practices. * * * The violation with which United is now charged depends not on moral considerations, but on solely economic considerations. * * * That those policies are not immoral is irrelevant.

* * *

* * * Concentrations of power, no matter how beneficently they appear to have acted, nor what advantages they seem to possess, are inherently dangerous. * * * Dispersal of private economic power is thus one of the ways to preserve the system of private enterprise. Moreover, well as a monopoly may have behaved in the moral sense, its economic performance is inevitably suspect. The very absence of strong competitors implies that there cannot be an objective measuring rod of the monopolist's excellence, and the test of its performance must, therefore, be largely theoretical. * * * Industrial advance may indeed be in inverse proportion to economic power; for creativity in business as in other areas, is best nourished by multiple centers of activity, each following its unique pattern and developing its own esprit de corps to respond to the challenge of competition. * * *

* * *

The Government's proposal that the Court dissolve United into three separate manufacturing companies is unrealistic. United conducts all machine manufacture at one plant in Beverly, with one set of jigs and tools, one foundry, one laboratory for machinery problems, one managerial staff, and one labor force. It takes no Solomon to see that this organism cannot be cut into three equal and viable parts.

* * *

The Court agrees that it would be undesirable, at least until milder remedies have been tried, to direct United to abolish leasing forthwith. * * * First, if a ban were immediately applied, a substantial number of shoe factories would probably to put out of business, for they have not the assets, nor the capacity to borrow, requisite to purchase machines, even on conditional sales agreements. Second, if this Court forbade United to lease machines, it could not apply a similar ban to its competitors. This would constitute for United a major not a minor competitive handicap * * * . * * *

Although leasing should not now be abolished by judicial decree, the Court agrees with the Government that the leases should be purged of their restrictive features. In the decree filed herewith, the term of the lease is shortened, the full capacity clause is eliminated, the discriminatory commutative charges are removed, and United is required to segregate its charges for machines from its charges for repair service. * * *

The decree does not prohibit United from rendering service, because, in the Court's view, the rendition of service, if separately charged for, has no exclusionary effects. Moreover, the rendition of service by United will keep its research and manufacturing divisions abreast of technological problems in the shoe manufacturing industry; and this will be an economic advantage of the type fostered by the Sherman Act.

Nor does the decree attempt to deal with that feature of United's pricing policy which discriminates between machine types. To try to extirpate such discrimination would require either an order directing a uniform rate of markup, or an order subjecting each price term and each price change to judicial supervision. Neither course would be sound. * * * [W]hile price discrimination has been an evidence of United's monopoly power, a buttress to it, and a cause of its perpetuation, its eradication cannot be accomplished without turning United into a public utility, and the Court into a public utility commission, or requiring United to observe a general injunction of non-discrimination between different products—an injunction which would be contrary to sound theory, which would require the use of practices not followed in any business known to the Court, and which could not be enforced.

The Court also agrees with the Government that if United chooses to continue to lease any machine type, it must offer that type of machine also for sale. * * * Insofar as United's machines are sold rather than leased, they will ultimately, in many cases, reach a second-hand market. From that market, United will face a type of substitute competition which will gradually weaken the prohibited market power which it now exercises. * * *

Furthermore, the creation of a sales market together with the purging of the restrictive features of the leases will, in combination, gradually diminish the magnetic hold now exercised by what United properly describes as the partnership features of the leasing system. As United's relationships with its customers grow feebler, competitors will have an enhanced opportunity to market their wares.

* * *

The Government goes one step further and asks the Court to require defendant to makes its sales terms more attractive to customers than any lease terms it offers. * * * [But] if this Court were to direct United to make its sales terms more favorable than lease terms, and to keep that discrimination effective every time that new terms were set, every time that new machine types were introduced, and every time that money rates changed in the financial world, this Court would be creating administrative problems which would require its continuous judicial supervision. To avoid the difficulties just stated, it seems to the Court sufficient to direct defendant, if it offers any machine type for lease, to set such terms for leasing that machine as do not make it substantially more advantageous for a shoe factory to lease rather than to buy a machine. Admittedly, there is in this direction some flexibility. But defendant is forewarned by the decree itself that if it abuses this flexibility, the Court after the entry of this decree may modify it. * * *

* * *

Jurisdiction of this cause is retained for the purpose of enabling either of the parties to apply to this Court at any time for such further orders and directions as may be appropriate for the correction, construction, or carrying out of this Decree, and to set aside the Decree and take further proceedings if future developments justify that course in the appropriate enforcement of the Anti-Trust Act.

NOTES AND QUESTIONS

1.   What was it that United Shoe Machinery had allegedly done wrong here? Was its undoing the fact that it produced a product measurably better than the products of its nearest competitors?

a.   How had United initially achieved its market share? It, like many other firms, achieved early growth by means of patents. After those patents expire, should we say the name recognition and market position those firms enjoy is somehow illegitimate?

b.   Might patent owners be more likely to moderate their short-run royalty demands if they can capture the reputation advantage that goes with treating customers well? Is that something the antitrust law should discourage?

c.   Could a shoe manufacturer make shoes without using United machines at all? Indeed, did you notice that foreign shoe manufacturing machines could be imported free of duty? Do you doubt that United's success was the result of having the best machines?

2.   Why did United do business as it did? Are the reasons at all suspicious?

a.   Why from United's point of view was it important to lease the machines rather than sell them? Think back to the problem Alcoa had with secondary aluminum. Is leasing the way to avoid competing with oneself? Notice that the Court says creation of a second-hand market is an important reason for the decree's compelling a sales option.[37]

b.   Why did United's customers prefer leasing instead of buying the machines? Does leasing the shoe machines make it easier or harder for a shoemaker to enter the industry? Should we as purchasers of shoes like the fact that the system helped produce a shoe making industry of almost 1500 manufacturers?

---

[37]   On whether leasing should be seen as a problem with which antitrust authorities should be concerned, compare John Shepard Wiley, Jr., The Leasing Monopolist, 37 U.C.L.A. L. Rev. 693 (1990), with Michael Waldman, Eliminating the Market for Secondhand Goods: An Alternative Explanation for Leasing, 40 J. Law & Econ. 61 (1997).

c.   Why did United require lessees to produce all of their shoes on the United machines they had rented? Given the fact that the shoemaker paid United on the basis of shoes produced on the machines, was it only fair that the lessee not use someone else's machines while United's sat idle?

d.   Is it accurate to use the term "price discrimination" to describe the practice of charging more to use machines unique to United than to use machines for which there is competition? Might the "unique" machines be inherently more valuable precisely because of their uniqueness? Note whether the term "price discrimination" is used the same way in Utah Pie and other cases, infra, brought under the Robinson-Patman Act.

e.   Should we be troubled that at the end of the 10-year lease term, United gave customers very favorable terms to renew? Why is that different than saying that United offered fair, reasonable prices for its products? Is that conduct we ordinarily want to discourage?

3.   Might one argue that United Shoe Machinery sounds like the ideal corporate citizen? What was even arguably wrong with its business practices?

a.   Do you agree that the 10-year lease term discouraged lessees from converting their operations to another's machines? Why would having capital tied up in purchased machines less tend to do so? Does your answer depend on whether United would permit subleases of its machines?

b.   Were you convinced that United's providing free repair service both discouraged independent repair firms from growing up and required new entrants to offer similar service? Who would be the real beneficiaries of a requirement that United bill for repairs?

4.   Judge Wyzanski was a friend and admirer of Judge Hand, and the approach they both used became known as the "structural" approach to monopoly, as opposed to a "conduct" approach. What did the Court here find were tests for § 2 illegality? Are the three tests clearly different? Do you agree that the cases cited support the tests the Court discerns in them?

a.   Do you agree that Judge Hand would have found United's conduct illegal here? Are United's huge market share, relations with 90% of shoe manufacturers, and efforts to keep its customers loyal the sorts of things that § 2 was designed to prohibit?

b.   Was this a market in which judicial relief was necessary? Were there genuine barriers to entry if new firms found a better way to make shoes? Remember that Compo had entered the market by coming up with a process for gluing shoe pieces.

c.   Do we want big firms to be wimps who do not seek to make a product so good that everyone will voluntarily choose to deal with them? Should we care that the United States went from 1500 shoe manufacturing firms before this decision to almost none today?

5.   In the remedy phase of the opinion, you can see that Judge Wyzanski was concerned about arbitrarily breaking the firm up into three small

companies because of the way its production facilities, etc., were organized. Thus, the decree eliminated use of the allegedly-restrictive agreements in the name of promoting competition.

  a. As noted earlier, the Supreme Court affirmed this decree per curiam. United Shoe Machinery Corp. v. United States, 347 U.S. 521, 74 S.Ct. 699, 98 L.Ed. 910 (1954).

  b. Thereafter, seeing that its days of market dominance were numbered, the company tried to diversify. It made over fifty acquisitions, most of them in haste, and the overwhelming majority were big money losers. The firm also tried to create new products, among them a baseball stitching machine that none of the baseball manufacturers could be persuaded to buy. Thus, the once prosperous company started to incur debt to stay alive.[38]

  c. Fifteen years later, the Government noted that United's market share had fallen, but only from 62% to 48%. It sought again to break up the firm. Judge Wyzanski refused to do so, but the Supreme Court reversed, United States v. United Shoe Machinery, 391 U.S. 244, 88 S.Ct. 1496, 20 L.Ed.2d 562 (1968).

  d. Thus, Judge Wyzanski ordered United to divest itself of sufficient assets that it would have less than 33% of the market. Forced to sell some of its most profitable products, the decree marked the beginning of the end for the company. Emhart Corp. acquired it in a hostile takeover in 1976, but that buyer could not turn its fortunes around either.[39]

  e. Ultimately, the price of U.S. shoe machinery went up, foreign firms entered the market with computerized equipment, and most production of both shoe machinery and shoes has now gone abroad. American leadership in the industry has effectively been snuffed out. Even if you believe there are firms against which § 2 should be used, is the decline of United Shoe Machinery a victory for sound antitrust policy, or an embarrassing set back?[40]

MARKET DEFINITION REVISITED— THE CELLOPHANE FALLACY

  Market definition was not a major issue in United Shoe Machinery, but it was the central issue two years later in United States v. E.I. du Pont de Nemours & Co., 351 U.S. 377, 76 S.Ct. 994, 100 L.Ed. 1264 (1956).

---

  [38] See Peter Vanderwicken, USM's Hard Life as an Ex-Monopoly, Fortune, October 1972, at 124.

  [39] See, e.g., It's Tough Up There, Forbes, July 13, 1987, at p. 160. (Report on America's 100 largest companies in 1917, only 22 of which remained in the top 100 seventy years later.)

  [40] The case in analyzed in John Shepard Wiley, Jr., Eric Rasmusen & J. Mark Ramseyer, The Leasing Monopolist, 37 U.C.L.A. L. Rev. 693 (1990). The lack of success with divestiture remedies in general is chronicled in William E. Kovacic, Failed Expectations: The Troubled Past and Uncertain Future of the Sherman Act as a Tool for Deconcentration, 74 Iowa L. Rev. 1105 (1989).

E. I. du Pont produced almost 75% of the cellophane sold in the United States, and cellophane constituted less than 20% of all "flexible packaging material" sales. The District Court found the latter was the relevant market and that competition from paper, wax paper, glassine, aluminum foil, and other plastic film denied du Pont the power to raise the price of cellophane without a significant diversion of sales to other packaging products.

The Supreme Court affirmed. The first issue in market definition, the Court said, is whether products are physical substitutes for one another. Each producer of a soft drink is a monopolist of its own product, for example, but that does not put each in violation of § 2 because, at the margin, consumers can and will substitute one soft drink for another. Likewise, some flexible packaging materials are better for some uses than others, but there remains room for choice among materials based on their relative prices. The Court said:

> "[W]here there are market alternatives that buyers may readily use for their purposes, illegal monopoly does not exist merely because the product said to be monopolized differs from others. If it were not so, only physically identical products would be a part of the market. * * * What is called for is an appraisal of the "cross-elasticity" of demand in the trade."

> * * *

> "An element for consideration as to cross-elasticity of demand between products is the responsiveness of the sales of one product to price changes of the other. If a slight decrease in the price of cellophane causes a considerable number of customers of other flexible wrappings to switch to cellophane, it would be an indication that a high cross-elasticity of demand exists between them; that the products compete in the same market. The court below held that the "great sensitivity of customers in the flexible packaging markets to price or quality changes" prevented du Pont from possessing monopoly control over price. The record sustains these findings."[41]

Chief Justice Warren, along with Justices Black and Douglas, strenuously dissented. Lots of things could be used for wrapping, they conceded, but business people bought cellophane even though its cost was from twice to seven times that of the other materials. "That they did so," the dissent argued, "is testimony to cellophane's distinctiveness." The dissenters believed that du Pont treated cellophane as a unique product without significant competition.

---

[41]   351 U.S. at 400, 76 S.Ct. at 1007–10.

* * * "A monopolist seeking to maximize profits cannot raise prices arbitrarily. Higher prices of course mean smaller sales, but they also mean higher per-unit profit. Lower prices will increase sales but reduce per-unit profit. Within these limits a monopolist has a considerable degree of latitude in determining which course to pursue in attempting to maximize profits. * * * It is this latitude with respect to price, this broad power of choice, that the antitrust laws forbid. * * * The findings of fact cited by the majority * * * merely demonstrate that, during the period covered by the complaint, du Pont was a "good monopolist," i.e., that it did not engage in predatory practices and that it chose to maximize profits by lowering price and expanding sales. Proof of enlightened exercise of monopoly power certainly does not refute the existence of that power."[42]

History has not been kind to the majority opinion in *du Pont*.[43] Can you see the ambiguous nature of evidence allegedly showing cross-elasticity of demand? A monopolist, like any other producer, faces a downward sloping demand curve. The monopolist makes every effort to charge at the point where it believes any higher price would cause enough people to turn to an alternative product that its net revenue would fall. Thus, if the monopolist has priced its product correctly, one would expect to see consumers turn to substitutes if relative prices change.

The point is not that the majority's cross-elasticity test is wrong as a matter of theory. It is that we will observe substitution of one product for another under conditions of monopoly as well as under competitive conditions. It is hard to know from substitution alone that products are sensibly grouped in the same market.

Put another way, the "cellophane fallacy" arises when one looks at the effect of a change in a product's actual price instead of a change from what the product's price would be in a competitive market. The problem in avoiding that fallacy, of course, is that proof becomes a battle of economic experts trying to determine the price in a competitive market and what the sales of other firms might be in response to such a price.

---

[42] 351 U.S. at 422–23, 76 S.Ct. at 1021.

[43] See, e.g., Herbert Hovenkamp, Federal Antitrust Policy: The Law of Competition and its Practice § 3.4 (4th Ed. 2011). Contemporaneous criticisms of the Court's analysis may be found in Donald F. Turner, Antitrust Policy and the Cellophane Case, 70 Harvard L.Rev. 281 308–313 (1956); George W. Stocking & Willard F. Mueller, The Cellophane Case and the New Competition, 45 Amer.Econ. Rev. 29 (1955).

TAILORING A MARKET DEFINITION—THE *GRINNELL* CASE

Might one argue that *du Pont* was not exclusively a market definition case, but in part a partial retreat from the extension of monopolization doctrine in *Alcoa, American Tobacco,* and *United Shoe Machinery*? Would such caution about the direction the Court was going have been desirable?[44]

Whatever your answer to those questions, a decade later the Court tailored the market to the defendant's own product in United States v. Grinnell Corp., 384 U.S. 563, 86 S.Ct. 1698, 16 L.Ed.2d 778 (1966).

The case involved a charge of monopolization brought against a national firm that provided property protection service from central locations within a city. The company placed sensors on the client's property and a signal went to the company headquarters if there was a fire, suspicious glass breakage, or the like. Its special selling point was that use of this service would get the insured better rates from some insurance companies. The government proposed to define the product market monopolized as "central station protection service" that was "accredited" by insurance companies.

The defendants sought to define the market to include a number of other kinds of protective services, e.g., guards stationed on the property, guard dogs, and (in the case of fire protection) even sprinkler systems. They also sought to have their share of the geographic market determined in terms of particular cities in which they competed with local firms that lacked the defendants' national scope. The Government, however, asked for a national geographic market and said that each of the proposed product alternatives was either less desirable, more costly, or both.

Judge Charles Wyzanski, again the trial judge, sided with the Government. The Supreme Court, per Justice Douglas, agreed. The relevant product market, the Court ruled, was thus the service as to which the defendant by definition provided 87% of the national market.

Justices Fortas, Harlan and Stewart dissented. In their view, the court had ignored the fact that the kinds of services consumers purchased were very responsive to changes in their relative prices. Justice Fortas concluded, "the relevant geographical and product markets have not been defined on the basis of the economic facts of the industry concerned. They have been tailored precisely to fit defendants' business."

---

[44] Although it does not explicitly urge such caution, the Report of the Attorney General's National Committee to Study the Antitrust Laws (1955) is certainly in that spirit. It was published after the District Court opinion in *du Pont* and before the Supreme Court opinion. The Commission included economists of diverse views such as Walter Adams, Alfred Kahn and George Stigler, and lawyers such as Milton Handler, Earl Kintner, Victor Kramer, Louis Schwartz, and John Paul Stevens. A co-chair of the Committee had been one of the first to call for its creation. See S. Chesterfield Oppenheim, Federal Antitrust Legislation: Guideposts to a Revised National Antitrust Policy, 50 Michigan L.Rev. 1139 (1952).

But in an almost throw-away fashion, the Court restated the test for monopolization in a manner arguably less expansive than some of the Court's prior expressions:

> "The offense of monopoly under § 2 of the Sherman Act has two elements: (1) the possession of monopoly power in the relevant market and (2) the willful acquisition or maintenance of that power as distinguished from growth or development as a consequence of a superior product, business acumen, or historic accident."

Given the market definition it had approved, the Court found the offense of monopolization was a foregone conclusion. But the *Grinnell* test for monopolization has survived. Watch for it in a number of cases even today.

UNILATERAL REFUSAL TO DEAL AS A SECTION 2 OFFENSE— THE *LORAIN JOURNAL* AND *OTTER TAIL* CASES

You remember from *Fashion Originators'* and *Associated Press* that when two or more firms agree not to deal with another, their "group boycott" is likely to violate Sherman Act § 1. *Colgate*, however, made clear that a single firm's refusal to deal is not a § 1 violation. The question then became under what conditions a unilateral refusal to deal might violate Sherman Act § 2.

In Lorain Journal Co. v. United States, 342 U.S. 143, 72 S.Ct. 181, 96 L.Ed. 162 (1951), the publisher of the only newspaper in Lorain, Ohio, had tried but failed to get a license to operate a radio station. When a new radio station was licensed in a nearby town, the publisher was afraid of losing his virtual monopoly as an advertising outlet for local merchants. The newspaper adopted a policy that it would not print advertising from any firm that had advertised or was believed to be about to advertise on the radio station.

In the Court's view, the case was easy. The lower court had found an explicit attempt to destroy the radio competitor. The local dissemination of news and advertising was held to be part of interstate commerce, citing *Associated Press*. Loss of the radio station's advertising base "was a major threat to its existence." Although the radio station had not gone out of business and "the injunction may save it," proof of both intent to monopolize and a dangerous probability that the monopoly would be achieved was sufficient to establish an attempt to monopolize under § 2.[45]

---

[45] More recent analysis suggests the Court's analysis may have been seriously flawed. See John E. Lopatka & Andrew N. Kleit, The Mystery of *Lorain Journal* and the Quest for Foreclosure in Antitrust, 73 Texas L.Rev. 1255 (1995).

Likewise, in Otter Tail Power Co. v. United States, 410 U.S. 366, 93 S.Ct. 1022, 35 L.Ed.2d 359 (1973), the defendant was a large private power company that wanted to sell retail power as well as wholesale it to others. When its local retail power franchises expired, Otter Tail refused either to sell wholesale power, or transmit power bought from others, to municipalities who might want to replace it as the local utility. If the Federal Power Commission or local customers sought injunctions to require Otter Tail to deal with them, Otter Tail allegedly dragged out the litigation so that the municipalities could not issue bonds with which to build the competing systems.

Citing *Griffith* and *Lorain Journal*, the Court said that a firm's use of "strategic dominance" to foreclose potential entrants into an industry constitutes an "attempt to monopolize" in violation of Sherman Act § 2. Its regulation by the Federal Power Commission did not change that result. The Federal Power Act was designed to preserve competition to the maximum extent consistent with the public interest, the Court said, and the Federal Power Commission's power to order interconnections was not enough to "immunize Otter Tail from antitrust regulation."

ATTEMPTED EXCLUSION BY A PATENT HOLDER— THE *WALKER PROCESS* CASE

As we have seen several times before, patent and antitrust law rub against each other at several sensitive points. A patent grants a legal monopoly that, standing alone, ordinarily should not violate Sherman Act § 2. Walker Process Equipment, Inc. v. Food Machinery & Chemical Corp., 382 U.S. 172, 86 S.Ct. 347, 15 L.Ed.2d 247 (1965), however, involved an issued patent allegedly procured by fraud.

Walker alleged that Food Machinery had fraudulently concealed from the Patent Office that its invention had been in public use for more than a year prior to its patent application. If that were true, the patent should not have been issued. Food Machinery's later efforts to enforce its patent then allegedly deprived Walker of business for which it demanded relief under Sherman Act § 2.

Food Machinery conceded for purposes of the litigation that if Walker had been sued for infringing the patent, it could have cited the alleged fraud as a defense. Only the United States may affirmatively sue to invalidate a patent, however, and Food Machinery argued that permitting Walker to maintain an affirmative claim for treble damages should likewise be barred.

A unanimous Supreme Court disagreed. Even a successful antitrust claim would not render the patent invalid, the Court said, so Food

Machinery's technical defense was beside the point. Citing Mercoid Corp. v. Mid-Continent Investment Co., 320 U.S. 661, 64 S.Ct. 268, 88 L.Ed. 376 (1944), the Court said that an injured party may affirmatively sue to enjoin the misuse of patent rights. This was, in turn, simply a claim for treble damages against one who had allegedly attempted to monopolize a market by dishonestly claiming to have a legal monopoly.

A defendant's "honest mistake" or "technical fraud" would not be enough to justify treble damages, the Court said. Indeed, the plaintiff will have to show that the patent had "exclusionary power," i.e., that there was no non-infringing way to be able to compete with the defendant effectively. The Court further refused to reach the question whether the defendant's alleged misconduct should be said to be per se illegal. However, even as it stood, the plaintiff's claim was sufficient to state a cause of action and be the basis for offers of proof.

Remember that one important feature of *American Tobacco* had been the argument that the "big 3" had cut their prices below cost in order to regain market share they had lost. Although the term "predatory pricing" was not used by the Court, and the case expressly held that § 2 does not require proof that firms were actually driven out of business, allegations of predatory behavior have been an important element in several § 2 cases.

Our next case arose 11 years after *du Pont* and 21 after *American Tobacco*. In addition to § 2 of the Sherman Act, it introduces us to § 2 of the Clayton Act, usually called the Robinson-Patman Act. As you will see, that Act prohibits price discrimination with respect to the sale of goods of like kind and quality. Read the case both for what it tells you about "primary-line injury" under the Robinson-Patman Act and what it says about predatory behavior generally. Ask yourself as well whether the Court extends the logic of its prior cases to and even beyond the breaking point.

UTAH PIE CO. v. CONTINENTAL BAKING CO.

Supreme Court of the United States, 1967
386 U.S. 685, 87 S.Ct. 1326, 18 L.Ed.2d 406

MR. JUSTICE WHITE delivered the opinion of the Court.

This suit for treble damages and injunction under §§ 4 and 16 of the Clayton Act, was brought by petitioner, Utah Pie Company, against respondents, Continental Baking Company, Carnation Company and Pet Milk Company. The complaint charged a conspiracy under §§ 1 and 2 of the Sherman Act, and violations by each respondent of § 2(a) of the Clayton

Act, as amended by the Robinson-Patman Act.[46] The jury found for respondents on the conspiracy charge and for petitioner on the price discrimination charge. Judgment was entered for petitioner for damages and attorneys' fees and respondents appealed on several grounds. The Court of Appeals reversed, addressing itself to the single issue of whether the evidence against each of the respondents was sufficient to support a finding of probable injury to competition within the meaning of § 2(a) and holding that it was not. * * * We reverse.

The product involved is frozen dessert pies—apple, cherry, boysenberry, peach, pumpkin, and mince. The period covered by the suit comprised the years 1958, 1959, and 1960 and the first eight months of 1961. Petitioner is a Utah corporation which for 30 years has been baking pies in its plant in Salt Lake City and selling them in Utah and surrounding States. It entered the frozen pie business in late 1957. It was immediately successful with its new line and built a new plant in Salt Lake City in 1958. The frozen pie market was a rapidly expanding one: 57,060 dozen frozen pies were sold in the Salt Lake City market in 1958, 111,729 dozen in 1959, 184,569 dozen in 1960, and 266,908 dozen in 1961. Utah Pie's share of this market in those years was 66.5%, 34.3%, 45.5%, and 45.3% respectively, its sales volume steadily increasing over the four years. Its financial position also improved. Petitioner is not, however, a large company. At the time of the trial, petitioner operated with only 18 employees, nine of whom were members of the Rigby family, which controlled the business. * * *

Each of the respondents is a large company and each of them is a major factor in the frozen pie market in one or more regions of the country. Each entered the Salt Lake City frozen pie market before petitioner began freezing dessert pies. None of them had a plant in Utah. * * * The Salt Lake City market was supplied by respondents chiefly from their California operations. They sold primarily on a delivered price basis.

* * *

The major competitive weapon in the Utah market was price. The location of petitioner's plant gave it natural advantages in the Salt Lake City marketing area and it entered the market at a price below the then going prices for respondents' comparable pies. For most of the period involved here its prices were the lowest in the Salt Lake City market. It was, however, challenged by each of the respondents at one time or another

---

[46]   The portion of § 2(a) relevant to the issue before the Court provides:

    "That it shall be unlawful for any person engaged in commerce, in the course of such commerce, either directly or indirectly, to discriminate in price between different purchasers of commodities of like grade and quality, where either or any of the purchases involved in such discrimination are in commerce * * * where the effect of such discrimination may be substantially to lessen competition or tend to create a monopoly in any line of commerce, or to injure, destroy, or prevent competition with any person who either grants or knowingly receives the benefit of such discrimination, or with customers of either of them * * * ." [Court's fn. 2]

and for varying periods. There was ample evidence to show that each of the respondents contributed to what proved to be a deteriorating price structure over the period covered by this suit, and each of the respondents in the course of the ongoing price competition sold frozen pies in the Salt Lake market at prices lower than it sold pies of like grade and quality in other markets considerably closer to its plants. Utah Pie, which entered the market at a price of $4.15 per dozen at the beginning of the relevant period, was selling "Utah" and "Frost 'N' Flame" pies for $2.75 per dozen when the instant suit was filed some 44 months later. Pet, which was offering pies at $4.92 per dozen in February 1958, was offering "Pet-Ritz" and "Bel-air" pies at $3.56 and $3.46 per dozen respectively in March and April 1961. * * * The price range experienced by Continental during the period covered by this suit ran from a 1958 high of over $5 per dozen to a 1961 low of $2.85 per dozen.[47]

I

We deal first with petitioner's case against the Pet Milk Company. Pet entered the frozen pie business in 1955 * * * and undertook a large advertising campaign to market its "Pet-Ritz" brand of frozen pies. Pet's initial emphasis was on quality, but in the face of competition from regional and local companies and in an expanding market where price proved to be a crucial factor, Pet was forced to take steps to reduce the price of its pies to the ultimate consumer. These developments had consequences in the

---

[47]   The Salt Lake City sales volumes and market shares of the parties to this suit as well as of other sellers during the period at issue were as follows:

1958

Company	Volume (in doz.)	Percent of Market
Carnation	5,863	10.3
Continental	754	1.3
Utah Pie	37,969.5	66.5
Pet	9,336.5	16.4
Others	3,137	5.5
Total	57,060	100.0

1961

Company	Volume (in doz.)	Percent of Market
Carnation	20,067	8.8
Continental	18,799.5	8.3
Utah Pie	102,690	45.3
Pet	66,786	29.4
Others	18,565.5	8.2
Total	226,908	100.0

[Court's fn. 7]

Salt Lake City market which are the substance of petitioner's case against Pet.

First, Pet successfully concluded an arrangement with Safeway, which is one of the three largest customers for frozen pies in the Salt Lake market, whereby it would sell frozen pies to Safeway under the latter's own "Bel-air" label at a price significantly lower than it was selling its comparable "Pet-Ritz" brand in the same Salt Lake market and elsewhere. The initial price on "Bel-air" pies was slightly lower than Utah's price for its "Utah" brand of pies at the time, and near the end of the period the "Bel-air" price was comparable to the "Utah" price but higher than Utah's "Frost 'N' Flame" brand. Pet's Safeway business amounted to 22.8%, 12.3%, and 6.3% of the entire Salt Lake City market for the years 1959, 1960, and 1961, respectively, and to 64%, 44%, and 22% of Pet's own Salt Lake City sales for those same years.

Second, it introduced a 20-ounce economy pie under the "Swiss Miss" label and began selling the new pie in the Salt Lake market in August 1960 at prices ranging from $3.25 to $3.30 for the remainder of the period. This pie was at times sold at a lower price in the Salt Lake City market than it was sold in other markets.

Third, Pet became more competitive with respect to the prices for its "Pet-Ritz" proprietary label. * * * According to the Court of Appeals, in seven of the 44 months Pet's prices in Salt Lake were lower than prices charged in the California markets. This was true although selling in Salt Lake involved a 30- to 35-cent freight cost.

The Court of Appeals first concluded that Pet's price differential on sales to Safeway must be put aside in considering injury to competition because * * * Utah would not in any event have been able to enjoy the Safeway custom. Second, it concluded that the remaining discriminations on "Pet-Ritz" and "Swiss Miss" pies were an insufficient predicate on which the jury could have found a reasonably possible injury either to Utah Pie as a competitive force or to competition generally.

We disagree with the Court of Appeals * * * .

* * *

With respect to whether Utah would have enjoyed Safeway's business absent the Pet contract with Safeway, it seems clear that whatever the fact is in this regard, it is not determinative of the impact of that contract on competitors other than Utah and on competition generally. There were other companies seeking the Safeway business, including Continental and Carnation, whose pies may have been excluded from the Safeway shelves by what the jury could have found to be discriminatory sales to Safeway. * * *

Third, the Court of Appeals almost entirely ignored other evidence which provides material support for the jury's conclusion that Pet's behavior satisfied the statutory test regarding competitive injury. This evidence bore on the issue of Pet's predatory intent to injure Utah Pie.[48] As an initial matter, the jury could have concluded that Pet's discriminatory pricing was aimed at Utah Pie; Pet's own management, as early as 1959, identified Utah Pie as an "unfavorable factor," one which "[dug] holes in our operation" and posed a constant "check" on Pet's performance in the Salt Lake City market. Moreover, Pet candidly admitted that during the period when it was establishing its relationship with Safeway, it sent into Utah Pie's plant an industrial spy to seek information that would be of use to Pet in convincing Safeway that Utah Pie was not worthy of its custom. Pet denied that it ever in fact used what it had learned against Utah Pie in competing for Safeway's business. * * * But even giving Pet's view of the incident a measure of weight does not mean the jury was foreclosed from considering the predatory intent underlying Pet's mode of competition. Finally, Pet does not deny that the evidence showed it suffered substantial losses on its frozen pie sales during the greater part of the time involved in this suit, and there was evidence from which the jury could have concluded that the losses Pet sustained in Salt Lake City were greater than those incurred elsewhere. It would not have been an irrational step if the jury concluded that there was a relationship between price and the losses.

It seems clear to us that the jury heard adequate evidence from which it could have concluded that Pet had engaged in predatory tactics in waging competitive warfare in the Salt Lake City market. Coupled with the incidence of price discrimination attributable to Pet, the evidence as a whole established, rather than negated, the reasonable possibility that Pet's behavior produced a lessening of competition proscribed by the Act.

II

Petitioner's case against Continental is not complicated. Continental was a substantial factor in the market in 1957. But its sales of frozen 22-ounce dessert pies, sold under the "Morton" brand, amounted to only 1.3% of the market in 1958, 2.9% in 1959, and 1.8% in 1960. Its problems were

---

[48]   The dangers of predatory price discrimination were recognized in Moore v. Mead's Fine Bread Co., 348 U.S. 115 [1954], where such pricing was held violative of § 2(a). Subsequently, the Court noted that "the decisions of the federal courts in primary-line-competition cases * * * consistently emphasize the unreasonably low prices and the predatory intent of the defendants." F.T.C. v. Anheuser-Busch, Inc., 363 U.S. 536, 548 [1960]. * * *

Chief Justice Hughes noted in a related antitrust context that "knowledge of actual intent is an aid in the interpretation of facts and prediction of consequences." Appalachian Coals, Inc. v. United States, and we do not think it unreasonable for courts to follow that lead. Although the evidence in this regard against Pet seems obvious, a jury would be free to ascertain a seller's intent from surrounding economic circumstances, which would include persistent unprofitable sales below cost and drastic price cuts themselves discriminatory. See Rowe, Price Discrimination Under the Robinson-Patman Act 141–150 (1962), commenting on the Court's statement in F.T.C. v. Anheuser-Busch, Inc., supra, that "a price reduction below cost tends to establish [predatory] intent." * * * [Court's fn. 12]

primarily that of cost and in turn that of price, the controlling factor in the market. In late 1960 it worked out a co-packing arrangement in California by which fruit would be processed directly from the trees into the finished pie without large intermediate packing, storing, and shipping expenses. Having improved its position, it attempted to increase its share of the Salt Lake City market by utilizing a local broker and offering short-term price concessions in varying amounts. Its efforts for seven months were not spectacularly successful. Then * * * [e]ffective for the last two weeks of June [1961] it offered its 22-ounce frozen apple pies in the Utah area at $2.85 per dozen. It was then selling the same pies at substantially higher prices in other markets. The Salt Lake City price was less than its direct cost plus an allocation for overhead. Utah's going price at the time for its 24-ounce "Frost 'N' Flame" apple pie sold to Associated Grocers was $3.10 per dozen, and for its "Utah" brand $3.40 per dozen. At its new prices, Continental sold pies to American Grocers in Pocatello, Idaho, and to American Food Stores in Ogden, Utah. Safeway, one of the major buyers in Salt Lake City, also purchased 6,250 dozen, its requirements for about five weeks. Another purchaser ordered 1,000 dozen. Utah's response was immediate. It reduced its price on all of its apple pies to $2.75 per dozen. Continental refused Safeway's request to match Utah's price, but renewed its offer at the same prices effective July 31 for another two-week period. Utah filed suit on September 8, 1961. Continental's total sales of frozen pies increased from 3,350 dozen in 1960 to 18,800 dozen in 1961. Its market share increased from 1.8% in 1960 to 8.3% in 1961. The Court of Appeals concluded that Continental's conduct had had only minimal effect, that it had not injured or weakened Utah Pie as a competitor, that it had not substantially lessened competition and that there was no reasonable possibility that it would do so in the future.

We again differ with the Court of Appeals. Its opinion that Utah was not damaged as a competitive force apparently rested on the fact that Utah's sales volume continued to climb in 1961 and on the court's own factual conclusion that Utah was not deprived of any pie business which it otherwise might have had. But this retrospective assessment fails to note that Continental's discriminatory below-cost price caused Utah Pie to reduce its price to $2.75. The jury was entitled to consider the potential impact of Continental's price reduction absent any responsive price cut by Utah Pie. Price was a major factor in the Salt Lake City market. Safeway, which had been buying Utah brand pies, immediately reacted and purchased a five-week supply of frozen pies from Continental, thereby temporarily foreclosing the proprietary brands of Utah and other firms from the Salt Lake City Safeway market. The jury could rationally have concluded that had Utah not lowered its price, Continental, which repeated its offer once, would have continued it, that Safeway would have continued to buy from Continental and that other buyers, large as well as small, would have followed suit. It could also have reasonably concluded that a competitor who is forced to reduce his price to a new all-time low in a market of declining prices will in time feel the financial pinch and will be a less effective competitive force.

Even if the impact on Utah Pie as a competitor was negligible, there remain the consequences to others in the market who had to compete not only with Continental's 22-ounce pie at $2.85 but with Utah's even lower price of $2.75 per dozen for both its proprietary and controlled labels. Petitioner and respondents were not the only sellers in the Salt Lake City market, although they did account for 91.8% of the sales in 1961. The evidence was that there were nine other sellers in 1960 who sold 23,473 dozen pies, 12.7% of the total market. In 1961 there were eight other sellers who sold less than the year before—18,565 dozen or 8.2% of the total— although the total market had expanded from 184,569 dozen to 226,908 dozen. We think there was sufficient evidence from which the jury could find a violation of § 2(a) by Continental.

III

* * * Carnation also quickly found the market extremely sensitive to price. Carnation decided, however, not to enter an economy product in the market, and during the period covered by this suit it offered only its quality "Simple Simon" brand. Its primary method of meeting competition in its markets was to offer a variety of discounts and other reductions, and the technique was not unsuccessful. * * * 1960 was a turnaround year for Carnation in the Salt Lake City market; it more than doubled its volume of sales over the preceding year and thereby gained 12.1% of the market. And while the price structure in the market deteriorated rapidly in 1961 Carnation's position remained important.

We need not dwell long upon the case against Carnation * * * . * * * Carnation's banner year, 1960, in the end involved eight months during which the prices in Salt Lake City were lower than prices charged in other markets. The trend continued during the eight months in 1961 that preceded the filing of the complaint in this case. In each of those months the Salt Lake City prices charged by Carnation were well below prices charged in other markets * * * . * * * We cannot say that the evidence precluded the jury from finding it reasonably possible that Carnation's conduct would injure competition.

IV

Section 2(a) does not forbid price competition which will probably injure or lessen competition by eliminating competitors, discouraging entry into the market or enhancing the market shares of the dominant sellers. But Congress has established some ground rules for the game. Sellers may not sell like goods to different purchasers at different prices if the result may be to injure competition in either the sellers' or the buyers' market unless such discriminations are justified as permitted by the Act. * * * [W]e disagree with [the Court of Appeals'] apparent view that there is no reasonably possible injury to competition as long as the volume of sales in a particular market is expanding and at least some of the competitors in the market continue to operate at a profit. * * * In this case there was some evidence of predatory intent with respect to each of these respondents.[49] There was also other evidence upon which the jury could rationally find the requisite injury to competition. The frozen pie market in Salt Lake City was highly competitive. At times Utah Pie was a leader in moving the general level of prices down, and at other times each of the respondents also bore responsibility for the downward pressure on the price structure. We believe that the Act reaches price discrimination that erodes competition as much as it does price discrimination that is intended to have immediate destructive impact. In this case, the evidence shows a drastically declining price structure which the jury could rationally attribute to continued or sporadic price discrimination. * * * The statutory test is one that necessarily looks forward on the basis of proven conduct in the past. Proper application of that standard here requires reversal of the judgment of the Court of Appeals.

* * *

It is so ordered.

THE CHIEF JUSTICE took no part in the decision of this case.

MR. JUSTICE STEWART, with whom MR. JUSTICE HARLAN joins, dissenting.

* * *

There is only one issue in this case in its present posture: * * * [D]id the respondents' actions have the anticompetitive effect required by the statute as an element of a cause of action?

The Court's own description of the Salt Lake City frozen pie market from 1958 through 1961, shows that the answer to that question must be no. In 1958 Utah Pie had a quasi-monopolistic 66.5% of the market. In 1961—after the alleged predations of the respondents—Utah Pie still had a commanding 45.3%, Pet had 29.4%, and the remainder of the market was divided almost equally between Continental, Carnation, and other, small local bakers. Unless we disregard the lessons so laboriously learned in scores of Sherman and Clayton Act cases, the 1961 situation has to be considered more competitive than that of 1958. Thus, if we assume that the

---

[49] It might be argued that the respondents' conduct displayed only fierce competitive instincts. Actual intent to injure another competitor does not, however, fall into that category, and neither, when viewed in the context of the Robinson-Patman Act, do persistent sales below cost and radical price cuts themselves discriminatory. Nor does the fact that a local competitor has a major share of the market make him fair game for discriminatory price cutting free of Robinson-Patman Act proscriptions. * * * [Court's fn. 14]

price discrimination proven against the respondents had any effect on competition, that effect must have been beneficent.

* * * [T]he Court has fallen into the error of reading the Robinson-Patman Act as protecting competitors, instead of competition * * * .

I cannot hold that Utah Pie's monopolistic position was protected by the federal antitrust laws from effective price competition, and I therefore respectfully dissent.

NOTES AND QUESTIONS

1.   *Utah Pie* was brought under both the Sherman Act and the Robinson-Patman Act. There are real parallels between the court's analysis of injury to competition and the analysis of predatory pricing under Sherman Act § 2.

a.   Notice that the Robinson-Patman Act prohibits price discrimination with respect to the sale of goods of like kind and quality. What constituted the price discrimination here? Were you surprised to learn that manufacturers sold frozen pies for more in cities like Denver and San Francisco than in Utah?

b.   Would you have been surprised to learn that a company did *not* sell its product with an eye to competitive conditions in local markets? Do you see why "price discrimination" is so hard for firms to avoid, and why under the Robinson-Patman Act the "injury to competition" issue thus looms so large?[50]

2.   Were you shocked here by the conduct of the national pie companies? Should we, in general, conclude that competition is "injured" when a firm enters a new market offering lower prices?

a.   Isn't such new entry the essence of competition? If Utah Pie, dominant firm in the market, had tried to sabotage the new entrants by denying them access to stores, for example, might it have found itself answering a § 2 monopolization charge?

b.   Why should the Robinson-Patman Act give Utah Pie a club with which to do essentially the same thing? Of all the facts that might have significance in your assessment of the propriety of what the national firms did here, would the fact that they sold pies for more in San Francisco than in Salt Lake City rank high on your list? Why is that even relevant, much less critical to the question of liability?

c.   Were consumers better off before or after the entry of the national firms? Can one persuasively argue that a vigorous four-firm market was created where there probably had been super-competitive pricing before? What is the Court's answer to that argument? Are you convinced?

---

[50]   We consider a different aspect of the Robinson-Patman Act—secondary-line injury—in more detail, and look at the Act's defenses of cost justification and meeting competition, in part D.4. of this chapter, infra.

3.   The Court suggests that the national firms were using predatory pricing to enter the Salt Lake City market. On what facts did it rely to draw that conclusion?

a.   Was that conclusion demonstrated by the fact that forcing Utah Pie to make an "all time low" offer made it feel a "financial pinch"?

b.   Was the national firms' "predatory intent" evidenced by memos such as Pet's which called Utah Pie an "unfavorable factor" in the Salt Lake City market that cut into Pet's sales growth?

c.   Should we want firms to act in ways that do not offend their competition? Isn't it the essence of competition to make oneself seen by one's rivals as an "unfavorable factor" in the rivals' wish to have an easy life?[51]

The problem of how to distinguish predatory pricing from tough but fair competition has frustrated the courts for many years, as discussed in our next note.

A NOTE ON IDENTIFYING PREDATORY PRICING

The term "predatory pricing" has a sinister ring to it. It must mean something other than setting prices at levels which attract sales and please customers, lest we discourage firms from doing exactly what a competitive market seeks to have them do.

Typically, predatory pricing is said to involve a firm's charging a very low price for a product or service with the aim of forcing someone else out of business. The "predator" is thought to calculate that it can survive losses longer than the victim. After the competitor goes out of business, the theory goes, the predator will charge more than a competitive price to recoup its losses.

John McGee gets credit for observing in his article, "Predatory Price Cutting: The Standard Oil (N.J.) Case", 1 J.Law & Econ. 137 (1958), that this widely-held view of common business practice is highly implausible. What might you say on both a theoretical and practical level is wrong with it? Think about it. It is very costly to get a monopoly that way, and once a firm has it, the threat of new entry will keep the firm from exploiting its advantage for very long.

The opponent one wants to drive out will keep fighting unless it has other uses for its fixed investment. It may be a long war unless the "predator" can survive longer and the victim knows it. Further, the assets

---

[51]   *Utah Pie* ranks high on many critics' lists of counterproductive antitrust decisions. See, e.g., Ward S. Bowman, Restraint of Trade by the Supreme Court: The Utah Pie Case, 77 Yale L.J. 70 (1968). See also, Kenneth G. Elzinga & Thomas F. Hogarty, *Utah Pie* and the Consequences of Robinson-Patman, 21(2) J.Law & Econ. 427 (1978) (reporting that Utah Pie Co. went out of business in 1972, due largely to declining product quality and disputes among the children of the founders).

of the firm driven out don't disappear. That firm, or some other firm, will be on the edge of the market waiting for the predator to increase price so much that it can re-enter the market. Probably the best the predator can do is intimidate the opponent into selling out cheap.

To avoid punishing firms that are simply more efficient than the competition, the price must also be "below cost," i.e., below the cost of the firm charging it and thus irrational except as predation. Philip Areeda and Donald Turner—then both Harvard law professors—posed a test for predatory pricing that is central to analysis of this issue today. The essence of the theory is that if it is rational and profitable for a firm to price in a given way, it should be legal to do so. One cannot infer improper intent from conduct that is equally consistent with a pure heart.

In their article, "Predatory Pricing and Related Practices Under Section 2 of the Sherman Act", 88 Harvard L.Rev. 697 (1975), Areeda and Turner said that no pricing should be deemed predatory if it is above the short run marginal cost of the firm using it. Because real marginal costs are very hard to calculate and probably exist largely in theory, they looked to what they called "reasonably anticipated average variable costs."[52]

Are Areeda & Turner right that firms would find it sensible to price at any level above such long run variable costs? In general, yes. A firm incurs fixed costs thinking it can price to recover them later, but once spent, they are sunk. The firm can get wealthier (or reduce its losses) every time it sells a unit for more than the variable costs of producing it, regardless of its average cost per unit.

The firm will not *enter* the business unless it believes it can cover all its fixed and variable costs. Once in, it will sell for the highest price it can, but it will find it rational to price anywhere above marginal/variable cost that will allow it to sell its product, even if that price is below its average cost.

Should the Areeda-Turner test be dispositive of the determination of when pricing is predatory? The Eleventh Circuit perhaps best summarized the academic and judicial reception of the test when it said: "The Areeda-Turner test is like the Venus de Milo; it is much admired and often discussed, but rarely embraced."[53]

For one thing, calculation of costs is notoriously uncertain; allocation between products in a multi-product line and between long-run and short-

---

[52] To understand the distinction, remember that in our introductory chapter we imagined that the firm produced 100 pencils in each batch. Technically, marginal cost is the difference between the cost of numbers 97 and 98. Average variable cost is the total cost of all 100 units, divided by 100. The latter is obviously easier to determine and examine.

[53] McGahee v. Northern Propane Gas Co., 858 F.2d 1487, 1495 (11th Cir.1988). For approving judicial comments on (but not adoption of) the test, see, e.g., William Inglis & Sons Baking Co. v. ITT Continental Baking Co., Inc., 668 F.2d 1014 (9th Cir.1981); Barry Wright Corp. v. ITT Grinnell Corp., 724 F.2d 227 (1st Cir.1983).

run costs can be equally so. Then, too, a firm with excess capacity necessarily tends to have low marginal costs, but the construction of such capacity might itself be considered a predatory act.[54] The issue of what should constitute predatory pricing—indeed, predatory behavior more generally—continues and we will see it again in the next chapter.

A NOTE ON THE IDEA OF SHARED MONOPOLY

Although *American Tobacco* was a relatively early case in the modern elaboration of § 2, the effort to use circumstantial evidence to prove coordinated activity continued. One major effort along these lines was the effort by the Federal Trade Commission to find a conspiratorial explanation for the increase in gasoline prices during the 1970s. Although several years and millions of dollars were invested in the case, little plausible evidence of actionable conduct could be found.

A second effort was the F.T.C. investigation and prosecution of the big-4 cereal companies, begun in 1972. The respondents were the Kellogg Company, producer of such cereal favorites as "Special K", "Rice Krispies" and "Froot Loops"; General Mills, Inc., producer of "Cheerios" and "Lucky Charms"; General Foods Corporation which sells "Grape Nuts" and "Sugar Crisp", among others, under the "Post" brand; and the Quaker Oats Company, producer of "Quaker Oats" and "Cap'n Crunch."[55]

While the Commission sometimes asserted an actual "conspiracy" theory, its principal reliance was on what came to be called "shared monopoly." The theory is summarized succinctly in the Commission's complaint:

> "5. * * * In 1940, respondents' sales accounted for approximately 68 percent of the RTE [ready-to-eat] cereal market; in 1950, for 84 percent, and in 1970, for 90 percent. In 1969 respondents controlled the following approximate shares of the RTE cereal market: Kellogg, 45 percent; General Mills, 21

---

[54] For a sense of the debate about these issues, see, e.g., F. M. Scherer, Predatory Pricing and the Sherman Act: A Comment, 89 Harvard L.Rev. 869 (1976); Oliver Williamson, Predatory Pricing: A Strategic & Welfare Analysis, 87 Yale L.J. 284 (1977); William J. Baumol, Quasi-Permanence of Price Reductions: A Policy for Prevention of Predatory Pricing, 89 Yale L.J. 1 (1979); Paul Joskow & Alvin Klevorick, A Framework for Analyzing Predatory Pricing Policy, 89 Yale L.J. 213 (1979); John S. McGee, Predatory Pricing Revisited, 23(2) J.Law & Econ. 289 (1980); Joseph F. Brodley & George A. Hay, Predatory Pricing: Competing Economic Theories and the Evolution of Legal Standards, 66 Cornell L.Rev. 738 (1981); Frank H. Easterbrook, Predatory Strategies and Counterstrategies, 48 U.Chicago L.Rev. 263 (1981); Richard O. Zerbe, Jr. & Donald S. Cooper, An Empirical and Theoretical Comparison of Alternative Predation Rules, 61 Texas L.Rev. 655 (1982).

[55] The history of the proceeding is set forth well in the opinion dismissing the matter with prejudice. In re Kellogg Company, 99 F.T.C. 8 (1982). Nabisco, Inc., and the Ralston-Purina Company were not made respondents but they were said to have "contributed by acquiescence" to the noncompetitive structure of the industry.

percent; General Foods, 16 percent; and Quaker, 9 percent. In 1969 Nabisco and Ralston each had an approximate share of four percent of the RTE cereal market.

"6. For at least the past 30 years * * * respondents * * * have engaged in acts or have practiced forbearance with respect to the acts of other respondents, the effect of which has been to maintain a highly concentrated, noncompetitive market structure in the production and sale of RTE cereal."[56]

In addition to acquisition of smaller firms, the acts of which respondents were accused fell into three types. First was "brand proliferation, product differentiation, and trademark promotion." In short, the cereal companies came out with new brands of cereal and emphasized "trivial variations such as color and shape" in their advertising, especially to children. Second were other unfair methods of competition such as implying that a person would be a better athlete if he or she ate "Wheaties," or suggesting that consumption of particular cereals would be helpful in losing weight. Third was Kellogg's alleged control of shelf space, i.e., its assisting grocers to decide where particular cereals should be placed on the grocers' shelves. The effect of these practices—engaged in separately but in a way that everyone within the industry or outside could observe—was said to be to create "artificially high prices," substitute product "imitation" for "innovation," and block "significant entry" into the RTE cereal industry for over 30 years.

You are familiar with the industry; indeed, you probably watch the advertising and consume the products. What do you think of these charges?

1. Should copying a competitor's successful cereal innovation be seen as an act of conspiracy? Would exaggerated advertising claims be expected from firms in a "shared monopoly"? Should heavy advertising be seen as a sign of vigorous competition rather than as an effort to discourage new entry?

2. If the Commission were to have found a violation of § 5 of the FTC Act here, what remedy could have corrected the practices? For example, would consumers be better off if the Commission had ordered the "big 4" producers broken up into 10 or 15 firms, each perhaps with the trademark of a flagship cereal, e.g., "Wheaties, Inc.," "Sugar Smacks Co.," etc.? Such a remedy was initially sought, but ultimately abandoned when, early in the Reagan Administration, the FTC dismissed its complaint with prejudice, 99 F.T.C. 8 (1982).

---

[56] 99 F.T.C. at 11.

C. VERTICAL ARRANGEMENTS PERCEIVED AS EXCLUSIONARY—TYING AND EXCLUSIVE DEALING

So far in Chapter III, we have considered price fixing, group boycotts and market division in violation of Sherman Act § 1, and monopolization, attempts to monopolize and conspiracies to monopolize in violation of Sherman Act § 2. We have raised doubts about the characterization of what was going on in some of the cases, but it was relatively clear in most cases how at least the moving party believed the alleged practices might reduce output and raise the prices paid by consumers.

Now we turn to "vertical" arrangements. They involve transactions between firms that are *not* competitors, but rather are at different levels of the distribution process. As a result, the theoretical impact on competition is less direct. Think back to *Dr. Miles*. There, the Court concluded there was an impact on competition largely because it believed that resale price maintenance was the product of a conspiracy of retail dealers rather than representing a policy that served the interest of Dr. Miles itself.

In this part of the Chapter, we look at two specific kinds of vertical agreements—tying arrangements and exclusive dealing contracts. Often, the courts have believed that these agreements have an exclusionary effect that helps firms to obtain monopoly power or keep it. As you read these cases, ask yourself whether the agreements are indeed anticompetitive. Might they be largely neutral, or even procompetitive in their effect? And, given the diverse possible explanations for many tying arrangements, ask yourself whether it is appropriate to make tying illegal per se.

As we have mentioned, parallel to the evolution of the antitrust laws, there had been a line of cases on patent misuse. Beginning with Leeds & Catlin v. Victor Talking Machine (1909) (records had to be bought from holder of patent on phonograph) and Henry v. A.B. Dick (1912) (ink required to be bought from holder of patent on mimeograph), the cases included Motion Picture Patents Co. v. Universal Film Manufacturing Co. (1917) (licensee of film projector had to buy film from patent holder) and I.B.M. v. United States (1936) (cards for use in patented tabulating machine must be bought from patent holder).

Henry v. A.B. Dick is often credited with adoption of a new provision of the antitrust laws. Clayton Act § 3 prohibits leasing or selling

> "goods * * * or other commodities, whether patented or unpatented * * * on the condition, agreement or understanding that the lessee or purchaser thereof shall not use or deal in the goods * * * or other commodities of a competitor or competitors of the lessor or seller, where the effect * * * may be to substantially lessen competition or tend to create a monopoly."

While many of the cases in this section rely on § 1 of the Sherman Act as well, Clayton Act § 3 is a key provision in tying cases. Watch for it and pay attention to how it is construed.

INTERNATIONAL SALT CO. V. UNITED STATES
Supreme Court of the United States, 1947
332 U.S. 392, 68 S.Ct. 12, 92 L.Ed. 20

MR. JUSTICE JACKSON delivered the opinion of the Court.

The Government brought this civil action to enjoin the International Salt Company * * * from carrying out provisions of the leases of its patented machines to the effect that lessees would use therein only International's salt products. The restriction is alleged to violate § 1 of the Sherman Act, and § 3 of the Clayton Act. Upon appellant's answer and admissions of fact, the Government moved for summary judgment * * *. Judgment was granted and appeal was taken directly to this Court.

It was established * * * that the International Salt Company is engaged in interstate commerce in salt, of which it is the country's largest producer for industrial uses. It also owns patents on two machines for utilization of salt products. One, the "Lixator," dissolves rock salt into a brine used in various industrial processes. The other, the "Saltomat," injects salt, in tablet form, into canned products during the canning process. The principal distribution of each of these machines is under leases which, among other things, require the lessees to purchase from appellant all unpatented salt and salt tablets consumed in the leased machines.

Appellant had outstanding 790 leases of an equal number of "Lixators," all of which leases were on appellant's standard form containing the tying clause and other standard provisions * * *. It also had in effect 73 leases of 96 "Saltomats," all containing the restrictive clause. In 1944, appellant sold approximately 119,000 tons of salt, for about $500,000, for use in these machines.

The appellant's patents confer a limited monopoly of the invention they reward. From them appellant derives a right to restrain others from making, vending or using the patented machines. But the patents confer no right to restrain use of, or trade in, unpatented salt. By contracting to close this market for salt against competition, International has engaged in a restraint of trade for which its patents afford no immunity from the antitrust laws.

Appellant contends, however, that summary judgment was unauthorized because it precluded trial of alleged issues of fact as to whether the restraint was unreasonable within the Sherman Act or substantially lessened competition or tended to create a monopoly in salt within the Clayton Act. We think the admitted facts left no genuine issue.

Not only is price-fixing unreasonable, per se, United States v. Socony-Vacuum Oil Co.; United States v. Trenton Potteries Co., but also it is unreasonable, per se, to foreclose competitors from any substantial market. Fashion Originators' Guild v. Federal Trade Commission. The volume of business affected by these contracts cannot be said to be insignificant or insubstantial and the tendency of the arrangement to accomplishment of monopoly seems obvious. Under the law, agreements are forbidden which "tend to create a monopoly," and it is immaterial that the tendency is a creeping one rather than one that proceeds at full gallop; nor does the law await arrival at the goal before condemning the direction of the movement.

Appellant contends, however, that the "Lixator" contracts are saved from unreasonableness and from the tendency to monopoly because they provided that if any competitor offered salt of equal grade at a lower price, the lessee should be free to buy in the open market, unless appellant would furnish the salt at an equal price; and the "Saltomat" agreements provided that the lessee was entitled to the benefit of any general price reduction in lessor's salt tablets. The "Lixator" provision does, of course, afford a measure of protection to the lessee, but it does not avoid the stifling effect of the agreement on competition. The appellant had at all times a priority on the business at equal prices. A competitor would have to undercut appellant's price to have any hope of capturing the market, while appellant could hold that market by merely meeting competition. We do not think this concession relieves the contract of being a restraint of trade, albeit a less harsh one than would result in the absence of such a provision. The "Saltomat" provision obviously has no effect of legal significance since it gives the lessee nothing more than a right to buy appellant's salt tablets at appellant's going price. All purchases must in any event be of appellant's product.

Appellant also urges that since under the leases it remained under an obligation to repair and maintain the machines, it was reasonable to confine their use to its own salt because its high quality assured satisfactory functioning and low maintenance cost. The appellant's rock salt is alleged to have an average sodium chloride content of 98.2%. Rock salt of other producers, it is said, "does not run consistent in sodium chloride content and in many instances runs as low as 95% of sodium chloride." This greater percentage of insoluble impurities allegedly disturbs the functioning of the "Lixator" machine. A somewhat similar claim is pleaded as to the "Saltomat."

Of course, a lessor may impose on a lessee reasonable restrictions designed in good faith to minimize maintenance burdens and to assure satisfactory operation. We may assume, as matter of argument, that if the "Lixator" functions best on rock salt of average sodium chloride content of 98.2%, the lessee might be required to use only salt meeting such a specification of quality. But it is not pleaded, nor is it argued, that the machine is allergic to salt of equal quality produced by anyone except International. If others cannot produce salt equal to reasonable specifications for machine use, it is one thing; but it is admitted that, at times, at least, competitors do offer such a product. They are, however, shut out of the market by a provision that limits it, not in terms of quality, but in terms of a particular vendor. Rules for use of leased machinery must not be disguised restraints of free competition, though they may set reasonable standards which all suppliers must meet. Cf. International Business Machines Corp. v. United States.

* * *

Judgment affirmed.

[The dissent of JUSTICE FRANKFURTER, joined by JUSTICES REED and BURTON, objecting to the breadth of the injunction entered by the District Court, is omitted.]

NOTES AND QUESTIONS

1. What was the statutory basis for the charge against International Salt?

a. Look at Sherman Act § 1. Does a tying clause have inherently anticompetitive effects and no procompetitive ones?

b. Look at Clayton Act § 3. Was there proof here of a tendency to create a monopoly? If so, a monopoly of what product? Salt?

c. Did the government prove a "substantial lessening of competition"? How was "substantial" defined for this purpose?

2. Were you at all persuaded by the company's arguments that its requirements were narrowly tailored to deal with its reasonable concerns?

a. Is it enough to say that International Salt could sue a user who caused corrosion of a leased machine by using a poor grade of salt? Should it always be illegal for a company to try to *prevent* a problem rather than be required to sue for damages later?

b. Was the Court too quick to dismiss the defense that customers were free to buy other salt if it was cheaper? Do you suppose the customers found this rule oppressive? What purpose is served by giving other salt companies—not parties to the transaction—a basis to object to the arrangement?

3. Does the Court hold that every contract for a package of two or more goods is illegal?

a. Does the Court find that International Salt had unusual market power that allowed it to impose burdens on its customers? Should such a showing be required as part of a finding of liability?

b. May one simply assume that a patent holder has market power because of its legally-granted monopoly? Are you convinced that that is always true? Might even patented products face competition from patented or unpatented products or processes? Remember why firms may have formed the patent pool in *Standard Oil (Indiana)*.

4. Is it even true here that International Salt's competitors would inevitably be denied the market represented by its customers?

a. Suppose International's production facilities were busy; its cost of producing salt tablets was $1.25 per 100 and a competitor's cost was only $1.00. What would you do if you ran International Salt?

b. Lest you think the point is unrealistic, think of I.B.M. and its earlier requirement that customers buy its tabulating cards. Do you suppose that I.B.M. *made* those cards? In short, don't make the mistake of assuming that the firm that makes the tying product is in fact more than a high volume shopper for the product that is tied; its reason for using a tying contract must typically be explained some other way.

c. Should the courts thus *assume* there is no adverse impact on competing salt producers? Should the lack of effect be an available affirmative defense for the maker of the tying product, in this case the machine?

5. What was really going on here? Why was International Salt so insistent on this way of doing business?

a. Might a tying arrangement such as this one be a way to monitor the amount of machine use and thus a way to be able to estimate depreciation of the machines? Should achieving such an objective subject a manufacturer to treble damages?

b. Might the arrangement have helped International Salt charge more to firms that used the machines extensively than to those that did not? Should such "discrimination" among users be illegal? Does this explanation make sense where, as here, the buyer could buy the same grade salt from anyone who sold it cheaper, i.e., where apparently no "excess" profit was being earned on the salt?[57]

WHY MIGHT A FIRM WANT TO ENGAGE IN TYING?

Will a tying arrangement help a firm increase its profits? Why else might the firm find it attractive to package its product in a way that a court would call a tying arrangement?[58]

---

[57] This apparent anomaly is explored in John L. Peterman, The International Salt Case, 22(2) J.Law & Econ. 351 (1979).

[58] Possible reasons have been developed by several authors and in a variety of ways. See, e.g., Robert H. Bork, The Antitrust Paradox: A Policy At War With Itself 372–381 (1978); Meyer L. Burstein, A Theory of Full-Line Forcing, 55 Northwestern U.L.Rev. 62 (1960); Ward S. Bowman, Jr., Tying Arrangements and the Leverage Problem, 67 Yale L.J. 19 (1957). But see, e.g., Lawrence A. Sullivan, Antitrust 445–454 (1977); Louis Kaplow, Extension of Monopoly Power Through

1.   First, if International Salt were the only manufacturer of machines for use in the canning industry, would it also want to obtain a monopoly on the sale of all the nation's salt? Sure. Salt is sold to many more and many different people than use its salt machines. Thus, if a seller of a tying product could "extend" its monopoly of that product to obtain a monopoly of something completely different, it would greatly increase its profits by doing so.

Ask yourself, however, how often that explains the tying you observe in the litigated cases. There is no way that International Salt, for example, could have obtained a monopoly of the sale of all the nation's salt by requiring use of its salt tablets in the Saltomat. The market for the tied product—salt—was far too large for that to be a possibility.

2.   Well, would a manufacturer with a monopoly of one product want to obtain a monopoly of a second product used *only* with the first. Would International Salt, for example, make more money if it could also require buyers of its machines to buy a concrete base that would make the machine operate more quietly?

Do you see why it could not? The value of International Salt's machine is going to be based on how much the machine saves users over adding salt some other way. All the value added by the machine can be recovered by International Salt whether it sells the base of the machine itself or lets others do so. Suppose, for example, the machine that costs $500 to make can be sold for $1000 if it has a base. Suppose the base costs an additional $100 to make and that other firms would compete to sell it for that amount. International Salt could charge $900 for the machine and allow the base to be sold competitively for $100, or it might sell the package for $1000. Either way, International Salt would get the $400 in monopoly profit. If you see package selling in such a case, the reason for it is not necessarily sinister.[59]

3.   Would a manufacturer with a monopoly of one product increase its profits by requiring that purchasers also buy a product used in variable quantities, here the salt tablets used by canners of different quantities of foods? Sure, that would give the manufacturer an ability to charge more to larger users of the machine than to lesser users. It is often the most likely explanation of a tying arrangement.

Should such a use of tying upset us? If the practice is labeled "price discrimination" it sometimes triggers a visceral negative reaction, but if

---

Leverage, 85 Columbia L.Rev. 515 (1985); Donald F. Turner, The Validity of Tying Arrangements Under the Antitrust Laws, 72 Harvard L.Rev. 50 (1958).

[59]   There might be a "sinister" reason to tie purchase of the base to purchase of the machine under some circumstances. Suppose the price of the machine were regulated so that the seller could not realize the full $400 profit in our example. Then, the seller might want also to sell an unregulated item like the base to realize the extra profit. Lest this seem far-fetched, when gasoline was subject to price control in the 1970s, it was not unusual for dealers to try to require gasoline customers to buy something else as well—say, a $10 rabbit's foot—as a condition of being able to buy the gasoline at all.

the manufacturer had leased the machine for a price based on a metering of its usage, we would likely not have thought a thing about it.[60] We would not have imagined that use of a meter illegally allowed the manufacturer to reduce output and raise prices. Then why don't all manufacturers use a mechanical meter? The answer varies, but sometimes it is simply thought to be easier to disable such a meter than to avoid using the "tied" item.

4.   Might it even be possible that the "quality control" argument, rejected in *International Salt*, was better than the Court acknowledged? Would it really be just as easy to specify standards for salt tablets used in the machine as to sell the tablets directly? How could the manufacturer prove that the lessee or purchaser had not used salt of the required quality? Who would have the best access to the evidence? Would it be costly—both in money and goodwill—for the manufacturer to conduct unannounced inspections of the user's facility to verify the quality of salt being used?

If we are right that often—indeed, possibly most often—when a firm sells a package of products or services it does not reduce output or increase the prices paid by consumers, what does that suggest about the wisdom of making tying illegal per se?

STANDARD OIL COMPANY OF CALIFORNIA V. UNITED STATES

Supreme Court of the United States, 1949
337 U.S. 293, 69 S.Ct. 1051, 93 L.Ed. 1371

MR. JUSTICE FRANKFURTER delivered the opinion of the Court.

This is an appeal to review a decree enjoining the Standard Oil Company of California and its wholly-owned subsidiary, Standard Stations, Inc., from enforcing or entering into exclusive supply contracts with any independent dealer in petroleum products and automobile accessories. The use of such contracts was successfully assailed by the United States as violative of § 1 of the Sherman Act and § 3 of the Clayton Act.

The Standard Oil Company of California, a Delaware corporation, owns petroleum-producing resources and refining plants in California and sells petroleum products in what has been termed in these proceedings the "Western area"—Arizona, California, Idaho, Nevada, Oregon, Utah and Washington. It sells through its own service stations, to the operators of independent service stations, and to industrial users. It is the largest seller of gasoline in the area. In 1946 its combined sales amounted to 23% of the

---

[60]   Indeed, there is a significant theoretical argument in *favor* of this kind of price discrimination. If we assume that the firm engaged in tying has significant market power over the tying product and that it must sell to all users at the same price, it will have an incentive to set the price higher than some users who value it less would be willing to pay. Allowing the firm to charge different prices to different customers will mean that the firm will cut output less or not at all, thus giving more users the benefit of its product at prices they find acceptable.

total taxable gallonage sold there in that year: sales by company-owned service stations constituted 6.8% of the total, sales under exclusive dealing contracts with independent service stations, 6.7% of the total; the remainder were sales to industrial users. Retail service-station sales by Standard's six leading competitors absorbed 42.5% of the total taxable gallonage; the remaining retail sales were divided between more than seventy small companies. It is undisputed that Standard's major competitors employ similar exclusive dealing arrangements. In 1948 only 1.6% of retail outlets were what is known as "split-pump" stations, that is, sold the gasoline of more than one supplier.

Exclusive supply contracts with Standard had been entered into, as of March 12, 1947, by the operators of 5,937 independent stations, or 16% of the retail gasoline outlets in the Western area, which purchased from Standard in 1947, $57,646,233 worth of gasoline and $8,200,089.21 worth of other products. Some outlets are covered by more than one contract so that in all about 8,000 exclusive supply contracts are here in issue. These are of several types, but a feature common to each is the dealer's undertaking to purchase from Standard all his requirements of one or more products. * * * Of the written agreements, 2,712 were for varying specified terms; the rest were effective from year to year * * * . * * *

Between 1936 and 1946 Standard's sales of gasoline through independent dealers remained at a practically constant proportion of the area's total sales * * * . * * *

Since § 3 of the Clayton Act was directed to prohibiting specific practices even though not covered by the broad terms of the Sherman Act, it is appropriate to consider first whether the enjoined contracts fall within the prohibition of the narrower Act. The relevant provisions of § 3 are:

> "It shall be unlawful for any person engaged in commerce, in the course of such commerce, to lease or make a sale or contract for sale of goods, wares, merchandise, machinery, supplies, or other commodities, whether patented or unpatented, for use, consumption, or resale within the United States * * * on the condition, agreement, or understanding that the lessee or purchaser thereof shall not use or deal in the goods * * * of a competitor or competitors of the * * * seller, where the effect of such lease, sale, or contract for sale or such condition, agreement, or understanding may be to substantially lessen competition or tend to create a monopoly in any line of commerce."

Obviously the contracts here at issue would be proscribed if § 3 stopped short of the qualifying clause beginning, "where the effect * * * ." [But] * * * it is by no means obvious, in view of Standard's minority share of the "line of commerce" involved, of the fact that that share has not recently increased, and of the claims of these contracts to economic utility, that the effect of the contracts may be to lessen competition or tend to create a monopoly. * * *

The District Court held that the requirement of showing an actual or potential lessening of competition or a tendency to establish monopoly was adequately met by proof that the contracts covered "a substantial number of outlets and a substantial amount of products, whether considered comparatively or not." Given such quantitative substantiality, the substantial lessening of competition—so the court reasoned—is an automatic result, for the very existence of such contracts denies dealers opportunity to deal in the products of competing suppliers and excludes suppliers from access to the outlets controlled by those dealers. Having adopted this standard of proof, the court excluded as immaterial testimony bearing on "the economic merits or demerits of the present system as contrasted with a system which prevailed prior to its establishment and which would prevail if the court declared the present arrangement [invalid]." The court likewise deemed it unnecessary to make findings, on the basis of evidence that was admitted, whether the number of Standard's competitors had increased or decreased since the inauguration of the requirements-contract system, whether the number of their dealers had increased or decreased, and as to other matters which would have shed light on the comparative status of Standard and its competitors before and after the adoption of that system. * * *

The issue before us, therefore, is whether the requirement of showing that the effect of the agreements "may be to substantially lessen competition" may be met simply by proof that a substantial portion of commerce is affected or whether it must also be demonstrated that competitive activity has actually diminished or probably will diminish.[61]

Since the Clayton Act became effective, this Court has passed on the applicability of § 3 in eight cases, in five of which it upheld determinations that the challenged agreement was violative of that Section. Three of these—United Shoe Machinery Corp. v. United States, 258 U.S. 451 [1922]; International Business Machines Corp. v. United States; International Salt Co. v. United States—involved contracts tying to the use of a patented article all purchases of an unpatented product used in connection with the patented article. The other two cases—Standard Fashion Co. v. Magrane-Houston Co., 258 U.S. 346 [1922]; Fashion Originators' Guild v. Federal

---

[61]   It is clear, of course, that the "line of commerce" affected need not be nationwide, at least where the purchasers cannot, as a practical matter, turn to suppliers outside their own area. Although the effect on competition will be quantitatively the same if a given volume of the industry's business is assumed to be covered, whether or not the affected sources of supply are those of the industry as a whole or only those of a particular region, a purely quantitative measure of this effect is inadequate because the narrower the area of competition, the greater the comparative effect on the area's competitors. Since it is the preservation of competition which is at stake, the significant proportion of coverage is that within the area of effective competition. * * * [Court's fn. 5]

Trade Comm'n—involved requirements contracts not unlike those here in issue.

The *Standard Fashion* case, the first of the five holding that the Act had been violated, settled one question of interpretation of § 3. The Court said:

> "Section 3 condemns sales or agreements where the effect of such sale or contract of sale 'may' be to substantially lessen competition or tend to create monopoly. * * * But we do not think that the purpose in using the word 'may' was to prohibit the mere possibility of the consequences described. It was intended to prevent such agreements as would under the circumstances disclosed probably lessen competition, or create an actual tendency to monopoly."

The Court went on to add that the fact that the Section "was not intended to reach every remote lessening of competition is shown in the requirement that such lessening must be substantial," but because it deemed the finding of two lower courts that the contracts in question did substantially lessen competition and tend to create monopoly amply supported by evidence that the defendant controlled two-fifths of the nation's pattern agencies, it did not pause to indicate where the line between a "remote" and a "substantial" lessening should be drawn.

All but one of the later cases also regarded domination of the market as sufficient in itself to support the inference that competition had been or probably would be lessened. * * * It is thus apparent that none of these cases controls the disposition of the present appeal, for Standard's share of the retail market for gasoline, even including sales through company-owned stations, is hardly large enough to conclude as a matter of law that it occupies a dominant position, nor did the trial court so find. The cases do indicate, however, that some sort of showing as to the actual or probable economic consequences of the agreements, if only the inferences to be drawn from the fact of dominant power, is important, and to that extent they tend to support appellant's position.

* * *

But then came International Salt Co. v. United States. That decision, at least as to contracts tying the sale of a nonpatented to a patented product, rejected the necessity of demonstrating economic consequences once it has been established that "the volume of business affected" is not "insignificant or insubstantial" and that the effect of the contracts is to "foreclose competitors from [a] substantial market." * * * It was established * * * that defendant was the country's largest producer of salt for industrial purposes, that it owned patents on the leased machines, that about 900 leases were outstanding, and that in 1944 defendant sold about $500,000 worth of salt for use in these machines. It was not established that equivalent machines were unobtainable, it was not indicated what proportion of the business of supplying such machines was controlled by defendant, and it was deemed irrelevant that there was no evidence as to the actual effect of the tying clauses upon competition. It is clear, therefore, that unless a distinction is to be drawn for purposes of the applicability of § 3 between requirements contracts and contracts tying the sale of a nonpatented to a patented product, the showing that Standard's requirements contracts affected a gross business of $58,000,000 comprising 6.7% of the total in the area goes far toward supporting the inference that competition has been or probably will be substantially lessened.

In favor of confining the standard laid down by the *International Salt* case to tying agreements, important economic differences may be noted. Tying agreements serve hardly any purpose beyond the suppression of competition. The justification most often advanced in their defense—the protection of the good will of the manufacturer of the tying device—fails in the usual situation because specification of the type and quality of the product to be used in connection with the tying device is protection enough. If the manufacturer's brand of the tied product is in fact superior to that of competitors, the buyer will presumably choose it anyway. The only situation, indeed, in which the protection of good will may necessitate the use of tying clauses is where specifications for a substitute would be so detailed that they could not practically be supplied. In the usual case only the prospect of reducing competition would persuade a seller to adopt such a contract and only his control of the supply of the tying device, whether conferred by patent monopoly or otherwise obtained, could induce a buyer to enter one. The existence of market control of the tying device, therefore, affords a strong foundation for the presumption that it has been or probably will be used to limit competition in the tied product also.

Requirements contracts, on the other hand, may well be of economic advantage to buyers as well as to sellers, and thus indirectly of advantage to the consuming public. In the case of the buyer, they may assure supply, afford protection against rises in price, enable long-term planning on the basis of known costs, and obviate the expense and risk of storage in the quantity necessary for a commodity having a fluctuating demand. From the seller's point of view, requirements contracts may make possible the substantial reduction of selling expenses, give protection against price fluctuations, and—of particular advantage to a newcomer to the field to whom it is important to know what capital expenditures are justified—offer the possibility of a predictable market. They may be useful, moreover, to a seller trying to establish a foothold against the counterattacks of entrenched competitors. Since these advantages of requirements contracts may often be sufficient to account for their use, the coverage by such contracts of a substantial amount of business affords a weaker basis for the inference that competition may be lessened than would similar coverage by tying clauses, especially where use of the latter is combined with market control of the tying device. A patent, moreover, although in fact there may be many competing substitutes for the patented article, is at least prima facie evidence of such control. And so we could not dispose of this case merely by citing International Salt Co. v. United States.

Thus, even though the qualifying clause of § 3 is appended without distinction of terms equally to the prohibition of tying clauses and of requirements contracts, pertinent considerations support, certainly as a matter of economic reasoning, varying standards as to each for the proof necessary to fulfill the conditions of that clause. If this distinction were accepted, various tests of the economic usefulness or restrictive effect of requirements contracts would become relevant. Among them would be evidence that competition has flourished despite use of the contracts, and under this test much of the evidence tendered by appellant in this case would be important. Likewise bearing on whether or not the contracts were being used to suppress competition, would be the conformity of the length of their term to the reasonable requirements of the field of commerce in which they were used. Still another test would be the status of the defendant as a struggling newcomer or an established competitor. Perhaps most important, however, would be the defendant's degree of market control, for the greater the dominance of his position, the stronger the inference that an important factor in attaining and maintaining that position has been the use of requirements contracts to stifle competition rather than to serve legitimate economic needs.

Yet serious difficulties would attend the attempt to apply these tests. We may assume, as did the court below, that no improvement of Standard's competitive position has coincided with the period during which the requirements-contract system of distribution has been in effect. We may assume further that the duration of the contracts is not excessive and that Standard does not by itself dominate the market. But Standard was a major competitor when the present system was adopted, and it is possible that its position would have deteriorated but for the adoption of that system. When it is remembered that all the other major suppliers have also been using requirements contracts, and when it is noted that the relative share of the business which fell to each has remained about the same during the period of their use, it would not be farfetched to infer that their effect has been to enable the established suppliers individually to maintain their own standing and at the same time collectively, even though not collusively, to prevent a late arrival from wresting away more than an insignificant portion of the market. If, indeed, this were a result of the system, it would seem unimportant that a short-run by-product of stability may have been greater efficiency and lower costs, for it is the theory of the antitrust laws that the long-run advantage of the community depends upon the removal of restraints upon competition. See Fashion Originators' Guild v. Federal Trade Comm'n; United States v. Aluminum Co. of America.

Moreover, to demand that bare inference be supported by evidence as to what would have happened but for the adoption of the practice that was in fact adopted or to require firm prediction of an increase of competition as a probable result of ordering the abandonment of the practice, would be a standard of proof, if not virtually impossible to meet, at least most ill-suited for ascertainment by courts. Before the system of requirements contracts was instituted, Standard sold gasoline through independent service-station operators as its agents, and it might revert to this system if the judgment below were sustained. Or it might, as opportunity presented itself, add service stations now operated independently to the number managed by its subsidiary, Standard Stations, Inc. From the point of view of maintaining or extending competitive advantage, either of these alternatives would be just as effective as the use of requirements contracts, although of course insofar as they resulted in a tendency to monopoly they might encounter the anti-monopoly provisions of the Sherman Act. See United States v. Aluminum Co. of America. As appellant points out, dealers might order petroleum products in quantities sufficient to meet their estimated needs for the period during which requirements contracts are now effective, and even that would foreclose competition to some degree. So long as these diverse ways of restricting competition remain open, therefore, there can be no conclusive proof that the use of requirements contracts has actually reduced competition below the level which it would otherwise have reached or maintained.

We are dealing here with a particular form of agreement specified by § 3 and not with different arrangements, by way of integration or otherwise, that may tend to lessen competition. To interpret that section as requiring proof that competition has actually diminished would make its very explicitness a means of conferring immunity upon the practices which it singles out. Congress * * * has not left at large for determination in each case the ultimate demands of the "public interest," as the English lawmakers * * * have recently chosen to do.[62] Though it may be that such an alternative to the present system as buying out independent dealers and making them dependent employees of Standard Stations, Inc., would be a greater detriment to the public interest than perpetuation of the system, this is an issue, like the choice between greater efficiency and freer competition, that has not been submitted to our decision. We are faced, not with a broadly phrased expression of general policy, but merely a broadly

---

[62] The Monopolies and Restrictive Practices (Inquiry and Control) Act, 1948, adopted July 30, 1948, provides, as one mode of procedure, for reference of restrictive trade practices by the Board of Trade to a permanent Commission for investigation in order to determine "whether any such things as are specified in the reference * * * operate or may be expected to operate against the public interest." The Act does not define what is meant by "the public interest," although in § 14 it sets up broad criteria to be taken into account. It is noteworthy, however, that, having established so broad a basis for investigation, the Act entrusts the task to an expert body without provision for judicial review. This approach was repeatedly contrasted in debate with that of the United States. * * * [Court's fn. 14]

phrased qualification of an otherwise narrowly directed statutory provision.

* * * If in fact it is economically desirable for service stations to confine themselves to the sale of the petroleum products of a single supplier, they will continue to do so though not bound by contract, and if in fact it is important to retail dealers to assure the supply of their requirements by obtaining the commitment of a single supplier to fulfill them, competition for their patronage should enable them to insist upon such an arrangement without binding them to refrain from looking elsewhere.

We conclude, therefore, that the qualifying clause of § 3 is satisfied by proof that competition has been foreclosed in a substantial share of the line of commerce affected. It cannot be gainsaid that observance by a dealer of his requirements contract with Standard does effectively foreclose whatever opportunity there might be for competing suppliers to attract his patronage, and it is clear that the affected proportion of retail sales of petroleum products is substantial. In view of the widespread adoption of such contracts by Standard's competitors and the availability of alternative ways of obtaining an assured market, evidence that competitive activity has not actually declined is inconclusive. Standard's use of the contracts creates just such a potential clog on competition as it was the purpose of § 3 to remove wherever, were it to become actual, it would impede a substantial amount of competitive activity.

Since the decree below is sustained by our interpretation of § 3 of the Clayton Act, we need not go on to consider whether it might also be sustained by § 1 of the Sherman Act. * * *

The judgment below is affirmed.

MR. JUSTICE DOUGLAS.

The economic theories which the Court has read into the Anti-Trust Laws have favored rather than discouraged monopoly. * * * Cartels have increased their hold on the nation. The trusts wax strong. There is less and less place for the independent.

The full force of the Anti-Trust Laws has not been felt on our economy. It has been deflected. Niggardly interpretations have robbed those laws of much of their efficacy. * * *

* * *

The increased concentration of industrial power in the hands of a few has changed habits of thought. A new age has been introduced. It is more and more an age of "monopoly competition." Monopoly competition is a regime of friendly alliances, of quick and easy accommodation of prices even without the benefit of trade associations, of what Brandeis said was euphemistically called "cooperation." While this is not true in all fields, it has become alarmingly apparent in many.

The lessons Brandeis taught on the curse of bigness have largely been forgotten in high places. Size is allowed to become a menace to existing and putative competitors. Price control is allowed to escape the influences of the competitive market and to gravitate into the hands of the few. But beyond all that there is the effect on the community when independents are swallowed up by the trusts and entrepreneurs become employees of absentee owners. Then there is a serious loss in citizenship. Local leadership is diluted. He who was a leader in the village becomes dependent on outsiders for his action and policy. Clerks responsible to a superior in a distant place take the place of resident proprietors beholden to no one. These are the prices which the nation pays for the almost ceaseless growth in bigness on the part of industry.

These problems may not appear on the surface to have relationship to the case before us. But they go to the very heart of the problem.

It is common knowledge that a host of filling stations in the country are locally owned and operated. Others are owned and operated by the big oil companies. * * *

* * * The method of doing business under requirements contracts at least keeps the independents alive. They survive as small business units. The situation is not ideal from either their point of view or that of the nation. But the alternative which the Court offers is far worse from the point of view of both.

The elimination of these requirements contracts sets the stage for Standard and the other oil companies to build service-station empires of their own. * * *

* * *

Today there is vigorous competition between the oil companies for the market. That competition has left some room for the survival of the independents. But when this inducement for their survival is taken away, we can expect that the oil companies will move in to supplant them with their own stations. There will still be competition between the oil companies. But there will be a tragic loss to the nation. The small, independent business man will be supplanted by clerks. * * *

That is the likely result of today's decision. The requirements contract which is displaced is relatively innocuous as compared with the virulent growth of monopoly power which the Court encourages. The Court does not act unwittingly. It consciously pushes the oil industry in that direction. The Court approves what the Anti-Trust Laws were designed to prevent. It helps remake America in the image of the cartels.

MR. JUSTICE JACKSON, with whom THE CHIEF JUSTICE and MR. JUSTICE BURTON join, dissenting.

* * *

* * * It is indispensable to the Government's case to establish that either the actual or the probable effect of the accused arrangement is to substantially lessen competition or tend to create a monopoly.

* * *

I regard it as unfortunate that the Clayton Act submits such economic issues to judicial determination. It not only leaves the law vague as a warning or guide, and determined only after the event, but the judicial process is not well adapted to exploration of such industry-wide, and even nation-wide, questions.

But if they must decide, the only possible way for the courts to arrive at a fair determination is to hear all relevant evidence from both parties and weigh not only its inherent probabilities of verity but also compare the experience, disinterestedness and credibility of opposing witnesses. This is a tedious process and not too enlightening, but without it a judicial decree is but a guess in the dark. That is all we have here and I do not think it is an adequate basis on which to upset long-standing and widely practiced business arrangements.

I should therefore vacate this decree and direct the court below to complete the case by hearing and weighing the Government's evidence and that of defendant as to the effects of this device.

However, if the Court refuses to do that, I cannot agree that the requirements contract is per se an illegal one under the antitrust law, and that is the substance of what the Court seems to hold. I am not convinced that the requirements contract as here used is a device for suppressing competition instead of a device for waging competition. * * * Many contracts have the effect of taking a purchaser out of the market for goods he already has bought or contracted to take. But the retailer in this industry is only a conduit from the oil fields to the driver's tank, a means by which the oil companies compete to get the business of the ultimate consumer * * *. It means to me, if I must decide without evidence, that these contracts are an almost necessary means to maintain this all-important competition for consumer business, in which it is admitted competition is keen. The retail stations, whether independent or company-owned, are the instrumentalities through which competition for this ultimate market is waged.

* * *

If the courts are to apply the lash of the antitrust laws to the backs of businessmen to make them compete, we cannot in fairness also apply the lash whenever they hit upon a successful method of competing. * * * I would reverse.

NOTES AND QUESTIONS

1.   The government thought it was sure to win this case because of the decision in *International Salt*. What were the points of analogy between the cases? Do you agree that the Court adequately distinguished the methods of dealing?

a.   Do you agree that tying clauses serve almost no purpose other than suppression of competition? Does that mean that no one would ever voluntarily buy two items as a package? Then how does one have to define a tying clause to conclude it is usually anti-competitive?

b.   Do you agree that exclusive dealing contracts require a different legal test than the one applied to tying arrangements? Does the Clayton Act apply different statutory language to the two phenomena?

c.   Does calling Standard's arrangements "requirements contracts" make them sound too innocent? Should the fact that they help both buyer and seller plan production be enough to overcome the risk that they will exclude independent suppliers from some portion of the market for some period?

d.   Is that the wrong question? Are you convinced that, even if some independent suppliers have fewer outlets for their products, it will allow firms like Standard to reduce industry output and raise prices?

e.   Is the real difference between *International Salt* and this case that Standard Oil of California had less market power than International Salt? Is it more likely the opposite was true? Should the fact that International Salt had a patent, while Standard did not, overcome all other indicia of market power?

2.   How would you determine whether the effect on competition of an exclusive dealing arrangement will be "substantial"? What test did the Court use in *International Salt*? Did it use the same test here?

In Tampa Electric Co. v. Nashville Coal Co., 365 U.S. 320, 81 S.Ct. 623, 5 L.Ed.2d 580 (1961), the Court confirmed that in exclusive dealing cases it is market share, not absolute sales, that determines the "substantial[ity]" of effect on competition. The parties had entered into a 20 year requirements contract for supply of what was estimated to be 2,250,000 tons of coal each year to meet the needs of a large electric generating facility. The minimum price was to be $6.40 per ton, and the total value of sales over the 20 years was estimated at $128 million. Apparently the price of coal rose. The seller wanted out of the contract and asserted that it was an impermissible exclusive dealing arrangement in violation of Clayton § 3.

The Supreme Court rejected that conclusion. The fact that $128 million was a big number was not controlling. Nor was the fact that this contract would be for about ¹/₂ of all the coal consumed in Florida each year; most other consumers used oil or natural gas. The firms foreclosed by this contract from sales to Tampa Electric, the court observed, produced and sold most of their coal up and down the east coast. This 2.25 million tons was less than 1% of the total output of the firms that might have sold to Tampa Electric. Such a proportion is not "significant", the Court said, so Nashville Coal was forced to honor its agreement. Would the justices who decided *Standard Oil* have agreed?

3.   What was Standard trying to achieve with this exclusive arrangement?

a.   Are you surprised that a company that allows its name to be placed on the sign out in front of a service station would want to be sure products it can be proud of are sold there? Does such a wish seem unreasonable?

b.   When you yourself buy gasoline, would you feel more secure, or less, knowing that a manufacturer cannot dictate whose products the local dealer will sell? Might the consumer protection side of the Federal Trade Commission be concerned about this result even if the competition bureau initially likes it?

c.   Is it an answer to both points to say that Standard may set quality standards and is only prohibited from requiring that the products be bought from it?

4.   On what basis did the Court find illegality here?

a.   Should it be enough to say that Standard, even if not dominant, was a major firm whose position might have eroded if it had not had these clauses? Is it fair to say that competition was "lessened" because it was not improved?

b.   Is it important that several companies had exclusive dealing clauses, although they were not adopted collusively? Was it reasonable for the Court to fear that the *industry-wide* effect may have been to discourage new entry? Remember that this case was decided only three years after *American Tobacco* and may reflect its great worry about consciously parallel behavior.

c.   Does Justice Frankfurter beg the question to say that one can never know what would have happened without these clauses, so proof of actual effects should not be required? Will the "may lessen competition" language of § 3 *always* be satisfied if one finds that argument persuasive?

5.   Justice Jackson was no amateur in antitrust. In the late 1930's, he had been in charge of the Antitrust Division. What was his concern about the Court's approach?

a.   Do you agree with him that intuition suggests that exclusive dealing is an efficient way to do business? Do you agree that methods of dealing should not be illegal just because they are successful?

b.   Is Justice Jackson correct that the Court's approach takes away all of the factual issues and ignores whether clauses may actually help consumers who ultimately buy the products? Indeed, doesn't the statute seem to require proof of the *actual* effects of requirements?

6.   Cases like this one are often brought by or on behalf of people who want to be gasoline retailers. Should consumers care whether a given arrangement yields more or fewer retail oil dealers? Beyond a certain point does it matter how many there are? If a given consumer may readily choose

from among ten or more gasoline companies, will doubling the number of choices always be preferable?

7.   Justice Douglas is beside himself in his memorandum opinion. What has him so upset?

a.   You have seen a lot of antitrust cases by now. Is Justice Douglas right that there has been a "sell out" to monopoly? Do you agree with him—and with Justice Brandeis and Judge Hand—that a world of small firms is inevitably more in the public interest than a world that has fewer, larger firms?

b.   Do you agree that exclusive dealing contracts were all that was maintaining small gasoline retailers' independence and preventing oil companies' vertical integration? This was before the 1950 amendments to § 7 that we will discuss later; Justice Douglas was right that the oil companies could have bought the assets of the retailers with virtual antitrust impunity.

8.   Where does the truth lie? What did the government seem to think would happen when these contracts were held to be illegal? Why do you suppose that, in spite of this case, there are few "split pump" stations selling two or three brands of gas at each outlet?

9.   Are exclusive dealing arrangements in fact exclusionary? If you were an independent refiner, what could you do? Could you sell to independent retailers, or even wholesale your surplus gas to one of the majors?[63]

THE SINGLE PRODUCT PROBLEM:
A LOOK AT *TIMES-PICAYUNE*

When you buy a car, are you troubled that it comes with tires already on it? Is selling a car complete with tires a tying arrangement? Don't answer too quickly. If you wanted higher performance tires than the manufacturer supplied as original equipment, you might want to argue that you should have a legal right to get a discount off the price of the car so as to purchase the tires you prefer. Might tire makers claim a similar right to compel automakers not to make you buy a car with tires supplied?

Automakers, of course, would answer that they have a right to define the product they are selling. Lots of products are composed of several elements, for example, a box of assorted candy. The task of defining when one is looking at a single product and when something is a "tied" package, then, is a recurring problem in antitrust law.

A leading case on the issue was Times-Picayune Publishing Co. v. United States, 345 U.S. 594, 73 S.Ct. 872, 97 L.Ed. 1277 (1953). New Orleans had three daily newspapers. The Times-Picayune was published in the morning; the Item and the States were evening papers. The Times-

---

[63]   See, e.g., Howard P. Marvel, Exclusive Dealing, 25 J. Law & Economics 1 (1982).

Picayune Publishing Co. also published the States. The Item would sell advertising space to anyone. To put an ad in the morning Times-Picayune, however, the publisher made the advertiser also buy space in the evening States. The Justice Department asserted that this requirement violated Sherman Act § 1 in that the Times-Picayune "monopoly" of the morning newspaper market was being used to compel merchants to buy evening ads they did not want. Further, it alleged, the requirement would make it harder for the evening Item to sell ads to advertisers who did not have the money to buy advertising in both evening papers. The District Court agreed and enjoined the Times-Picayune's practice.

Justice Clark, writing for a five-member majority, reasserted the ban on tying, saying:

> "Tying arrangements, we may readily agree, flout the Sherman Act's policy that competition rule the marts of trade. * * * By conditioning his sale of one commodity on the purchase of another, a seller coerces the abdication of buyers' independent judgment as to the 'tied' product's merits and insulates it from the competitive stresses of the open market. * * * Conversely, the effect on competing sellers attempting to rival the 'tied' product is drastic: to the extent the enforcer of the tying arrangement enjoys market control, other existing or potential sellers are foreclosed from offering up their goods to a free competitive judgment; they are effectively excluded from the marketplace."

The majority, however, found no tying in the case. It concluded that newspaper advertising was fungible; an ad in the morning paper was not something different than an ad in the evening paper.

> " * * * [T]hat readers consciously distinguished between these two publications does not necessarily imply that advertisers bought separate and distinct products when insertions were placed in the Times-Picayune and the States. So to conclude here would involve speculation that advertisers bought space motivated by considerations other than customer coverage; that their media selections, in effect, rested on generic qualities differentiating morning from evening readers in New Orleans. Although advertising space in the Times-Picayune, as the sole morning daily, was doubtless essential to blanket coverage of the local newspaper readership, nothing in the record suggests that advertisers viewed the city's newspaper readers, morning or evening, as other than fungible customer potential. We must assume, therefore, that the readership 'bought' by advertisers in the Times-Picayune was the selfsame 'product' sold by the States and, for that matter, the Item.

> " * * * The common core of the adjudicated unlawful tying arrangements is the forced purchase of a second distinct

commodity with the desired purchase of a dominant 'tying' product, resulting in economic harm to competition in the 'tied' market. Here, however, two newspapers under single ownership at the same place, time, and terms sell indistinguishable products to advertisers; no dominant "tying" product exists (in fact, since space in neither the Times-Picayune nor the States can be bought alone, one may be viewed as 'tying' as the other); no leverage in one market excludes sellers in the second, because for present purposes the products are identical and the market the same. In short, neither the rationale nor the doctrines evolved by the 'tying' cases can dispose of the Publishing Company's arrangements challenged here.[64]

1. Do you agree with the Court? If you had a monopoly of morning advertising space, could you make greater profits by requiring purchase of one evening ad for each one in the morning? Under what conditions might you be able to do so?

2. United States v. Jerrold Electronics Corp., 187 F.Supp. 545 (E.D.Pa.1960), affirmed per curiam, 365 U.S. 567 (1961), raised closely-related issues a few years later. Jerrold sold "master antenna" systems that received over-the-air television signals, boosted them, and transmitted them to subscribers in fringe reception areas. Jerrold concededly had excellent "head end" equipment for receiving and boosting the signals; its equipment for connecting its antenna to subscriber homes was less technologically advanced. Nevertheless, it insisted on installing the entire system because it said subscribers would blame Jerrold if they were unhappy with the service. The District Court held, and the Supreme Court affirmed, that when the industry was in its infancy, it had been reasonable for Jerrold to insist on installing the entire system, but now that there were several suppliers of quality equipment, to insist on sale of the entire system was a violation of Sherman Act § 1. Are you convinced? Was this a wise, practical result, or an intrusion into an industry whose operation a court was probably ill-equipped to improve?

A NOTE ON SINGLE-PRODUCT PROBLEMS IN FRANCHISING

Yet another single-product issue is frequently presented in franchise agreements. Suppose the owner of a franchised store that sells ice cream does not want to buy its ice cream from the firm that granted the franchise. Should it be heard to say the requirement that it do so is an unlawful tying

---

[64] You may also see *Times-Picayune* cited for the proposition that in a tying case brought under Clayton Act § 3 the plaintiff must show *either* that defendant has market power in sales of the tying product *or* that the tying requirement creates a substantial effect on competition, while in a Sherman Act § 1 case *both* must be shown. Although the distinction was once black-letter law, it was rejected in Northern Pacific Railway Co. v. United States, infra.

arrangement? If so, what is the tying product and what has been tied? Two leading cases on the subject in the 1960s approached the problem in contrasting ways.

Susser v. Carvel Corporation, 332 F.2d 505 (2d Cir.1964), involved a franchise selling soft ice cream from a distinctively shaped building. Franchisees were required to buy the ice cream mix from Carvel, as well as specially shaped ice cream cones and spoons. Paper products, machinery and equipment could be bought on the open market as long as they met Carvel specifications. A divided panel of the Second Circuit *upheld* this method of dealing. Judge Lumbard, in dissent, argued that a trademark could be a tying product; thus, requiring purchase of any items as a condition of using the franchise trademark should be per se illegal. Judge Friendly, for the majority, answered that the items Carvel required to be purchased were a single product with the trademark. Uniformity and quality of the ice cream were what the franchise was all about. Further, there was no showing that the trademark had market power anything like the patent in *International Salt*, because Carvel had only a 1% share of the market.

Siegel v. Chicken Delight, Inc., 448 F.2d 43 (9th Cir.1971), on the other hand, involved requirements that franchisees buy their cooking equipment, dry-mix coating for the chicken, and special packaging from the franchisor. The Chicken Delight trademark has market power, the Court held. The franchisor could properly have imposed this requirement when it was just starting, but by the time of this case, the mark was unique and profitable, albeit not "dominant" in the industry. Turning to the single product issue, the Court reasoned that a Chicken Delight franchise does not exist to distribute the franchisor's chicken in the way a Carvel franchise might be said to distribute the franchisor's special ice cream. Chicken Delight retailers sell chicken locally in a uniform, high quality way. That's all. The franchisor is entitled to set performance standards, but may not require its franchisees to buy their supplies from it.

Given these cases, what may a company such as McDonald's require its franchisees to acquire from it? May it require them to lease their building from McDonald's, for example. In Principe v. McDonald's Corp., 631 F.2d 303 (4th Cir.1980), the court said it could:

"* * * Franchising has come a long way since the decision in *Chicken Delight*.

"Without disagreeing with the result in *Chicken Delight*, we conclude that the court's emphasis in that case upon the trademark as the essence of a franchise is too restrictive. Far from merely licensing franchisees to sell products under its trade name, a modern franchisor such as McDonald's offers its franchisees a complete method of doing business. It takes people from all walks of life, sends them to its management school, and teaches them a variety of skills ranging from hamburger grilling to financial planning. It installs them in stores whose market has been researched and whose location has been selected by experts to maximize sales potential. It inspects every facet of every store several times a year and consults with each franchisee about his operations's strengths and weaknesses. Its regime pervades all facets of the business, from the design of the menu board to the amount of catsup on the hamburgers, nothing is left to chance. This pervasive franchisor supervision and control benefits the franchisee in turn. His business is identified with a network of stores whose very uniformity and predictability attracts customers. In short, the modern franchisee pays not only for the right to use a trademark but for the right to become a part of a system whose business methods virtually guarantee his success. It is often unrealistic to view a franchise agreement as little more than a trademark license.

"Given the realities of modern franchising, we think the proper inquiry is not whether the allegedly tied products are associated in the public mind with the franchisor's trademark, but whether they are integral components of the business method being franchised. Where the challenged aggregation is an essential ingredient of the franchised system's formula for success, there is but a single product and no tie in exists as a matter of law."

The Court went on to conclude that the distinctive shape of a McDonald's building was associated with the trademark and the expert selection of locations for the restaurants was part of the formula for success. Thus, McDonald's could require the franchisee to enter into the lease.

Are you convinced by the Court's analysis? On the other hand, even if one were to disagree and say that the standard McDonald's building is not obviously central to the franchise, was there any "victim" in *Principe*? Was McDonald's "overreaching" its franchisees? If so, why do you suppose the plaintiff wanted yet another McDonald's outlet? Did the McDonald's requirement cause harm to consumers? To anyone else?

Our next case presents a virtually unique fact situation, but we read it because the case has had a powerful impact on the development of tying doctrine and on the per se rule generally.

NORTHERN PACIFIC RAILWAY CO. V. UNITED STATES

Supreme Court of the United States, 1958
356 U.S. 1, 78 S.Ct. 514, 2 L.Ed.2d 545

MR. JUSTICE BLACK delivered the opinion of the Court.

In 1864 and 1870 Congress granted the predecessor of the Northern Pacific Railway Company approximately forty million acres of land in several Northwestern States and Territories to facilitate its construction of a railroad line from Lake Superior to Puget Sound. In general terms, this grant consisted of every alternate section of land in a belt 20 miles wide on each side of the track through States and 40 miles wide through Territories. The granted lands were of various kinds; some contained great stands of timber, some iron ore or other valuable mineral deposits, some oil or natural gas, while still other sections were useful for agriculture, grazing or industrial purposes. By 1949 the Railroad had sold about 37,000,000 acres of its holdings, but had reserved mineral rights in 6,500,000 of those acres. Most of the unsold land was leased for one purpose or another. In a large number of its sales contracts and most of its lease agreements the Railroad had inserted "preferential routing" clauses which compelled the grantee or lessee to ship over its lines all commodities produced or manufactured on the land, provided that its rates (and in some instances its service) were equal to those of competing carriers. Since many of the goods produced on the lands subject to these "preferential routing" provisions are shipped from one State to another the actual and potential amount of interstate commerce affected is substantial. Alternative means of transportation exist for a large portion of these shipments including the facilities of two other major railroad systems.

In 1949 the Government filed suit under § 4 of the Sherman Act seeking a declaration that the defendant's "preferential routing" agreements were unlawful as unreasonable restraints of trade under § 1 of that Act. After various pretrial proceedings the Government moved for summary judgment * * *. The district judge * * * granted the Government's motion * * *. * * * The defendant took a direct appeal to this Court * * *.

The Sherman Act was designed to be a comprehensive charter of economic liberty aimed at preserving free and unfettered competition as the rule of trade. It rests on the premise that the unrestrained interaction of competitive forces will yield the best allocation of our economic resources, the lowest prices, the highest quality and the greatest material progress, while at the same time providing an environment conducive to the preservation of our democratic political and social institutions. But even were that premise open to question, the policy unequivocally laid down by the Act is competition. And to this end it prohibits "Every contract, combination * * * or conspiracy, in restraint of trade or commerce among the several States." Although this prohibition is literally all-encompassing, the courts have construed it as precluding only those contracts or combinations which "unreasonably" restrain competition. Standard Oil Co. of New Jersey v. United States; Chicago Board of Trade v. United States.

However, there are certain agreements or practices which because of their pernicious effect on competition and lack of any redeeming virtue are conclusively presumed to be unreasonable and therefore illegal without elaborate inquiry as to the precise harm they have caused or the business excuse for their use. This principle of per se unreasonableness not only makes the type of restraints which are proscribed by the Sherman Act more certain to the benefit of everyone concerned, but it also avoids the necessity for an incredibly complicated and prolonged economic investigation into the entire history of the industry involved, as well as related industries, in an effort to determine at large whether a particular restraint has been unreasonable—an inquiry so often wholly fruitless when undertaken. Among the practices which the courts have heretofore deemed to be unlawful in and of themselves are price fixing, United States v. Socony-Vacuum Oil Co.; division of markets, United States v. Addyston Pipe & Steel Co.; group boycotts, Fashion Originators' Guild v. Federal Trade Comm'n; and tying arrangements, International Salt Co. v. United States.

For our purposes a tying arrangement may be defined as an agreement by a party to sell one product but only on the condition that the buyer also purchases a different (or tied) product, or at least agrees that he will not purchase that product from any other supplier. Where such conditions are successfully exacted competition on the merits with respect to the tied product is inevitably curbed. Indeed "tying agreements serve hardly any purpose beyond the suppression of competition." Standard Oil Co. of California v. United States. They deny competitors free access to the market for the tied product, not because the party imposing the tying requirements has a better product or a lower price but because of his power or leverage in another market. At the same time buyers are forced to forego their free choice between competing products. * * * They are unreasonable in and of themselves whenever a party has sufficient economic power with respect to the tying product to appreciably restrain free competition in the market for the tied product and a "not insubstantial" amount of interstate commerce is affected. International Salt Co. v. United States. Of course where the seller has no control or dominance over the tying product so that it does not represent an effectual weapon to pressure buyers into taking the tied item any restraint of trade attributable to such tying arrangements would obviously be insignificant at most. As a simple example, if one of a dozen food stores in a community were to refuse to sell flour unless the buyer also took sugar it would hardly tend to restrain competition in sugar if its competitors were ready and able to sell flour by itself.

In this case we believe the district judge was clearly correct in entering summary judgment declaring the defendant's "preferential routing" clauses unlawful restraints of trade. We wholly agree that the undisputed facts established beyond any genuine question that the defendant possessed substantial economic power by virtue of its extensive landholdings which it used as leverage to induce large numbers of purchasers and lessees to give it preference, to the exclusion of its competitors, in carrying goods or produce from the land transferred to them. * * *

As pointed out before, the defendant was initially granted large acreages by Congress in the several Northwestern States through which its lines now run. This land was strategically located in checkerboard fashion amid private holdings and within economic distance of transportation facilities. Not only the testimony of various witnesses but common sense makes it evident that this particular land was often prized by those who purchased or leased it and was frequently essential to their business activities. In disposing of its holdings the defendant entered into contracts of sale or lease covering at least several million acres of land which included "preferential routing" clauses. The very existence of this host of tying arrangements is itself compelling evidence of the defendant's great power, at least where, as here, no other explanation has been offered for the existence of these restraints. The "preferential routing" clauses conferred no benefit on the purchasers or lessees. While they got the land they wanted by yielding their freedom to deal with competing carriers, the defendant makes no claim that it came any cheaper than if the restrictive clauses had been omitted. In fact any such price reduction in return for rail shipments would have quite plainly constituted an unlawful rebate to the shipper. So far as the Railroad was concerned its purpose obviously was to fence out competitors, to stifle competition. While this may have been exceedingly beneficial to its business, it is the very type of thing the Sherman Act condemns. * * *

In our view International Salt Co. v. United States, which has been unqualifiedly approved by subsequent decisions, is ample authority for affirming the judgment below. * * *

The defendant attempts to evade the force of *International Salt* on the ground that the tying product there was patented while here it is not. But we do not believe this distinction has, or should have, any significance. In arriving at its decision in *International Salt* the Court placed no reliance on the fact that a patent was involved nor did it give the slightest intimation that the outcome would have been any different if that had not been the case. If anything, the Court held the challenged tying arrangements unlawful despite the fact that the tying item was patented, not because of it. * * * Nor have subsequent cases confined the rule of per se unreasonableness laid down in *International Salt* to situations involving patents.

* * *

While there is some language in the *Times-Picayune* opinion which speaks of "monopoly power" or "dominance" over the tying product as a necessary precondition for application of the rule of per se unreasonableness to tying arrangements, we do not construe this general language as requiring anything more than sufficient economic power to impose an appreciable restraint on free competition in the tied product (assuming all the time, of course, that a "not insubstantial" amount of interstate commerce is affected). To give it any other construction would be wholly out of accord with the opinion's cogent analysis of the nature and baneful effects of tying arrangements and their incompatibility with the policies underlying the Sherman Act. * * *

The defendant contends that its "preferential routing" clauses are subject to so many exceptions and have been administered so leniently that they do not significantly restrain competition. It points out that these clauses permit the vendee or lessee to ship by competing carrier if its rates are lower (or in some instances if its service is better) than the defendant's. Of course if these restrictive provisions are merely harmless sieves with no tendency to restrain competition, as the defendant's argument seems to imply, it is hard to understand why it has expended so much effort in obtaining them in vast numbers and upholding their validity, or how they are of any benefit to anyone, even the defendant. * * * In *International Salt* the defendants similarly argued that their tying arrangements were inoffensive restraints because they allowed lessees to buy salt from other suppliers when they offered a lower price than International. The Court's answer there is equally apt here.

> "[This exception] does, of course, afford a measure of protection to the lessee, but it does not avoid the stifling effect of the agreement on competition. The appellant had at all times a priority on the business at equal prices. A competitor would have to undercut appellant's price to have any hope of capturing the market, while appellant could hold that market by merely meeting competition. We do not think this concession relieves the contract of being a restraint of trade, albeit a less harsh one than would result in the absence of such a provision."

All of this is only aggravated, of course, here in the regulated transportation industry where there is frequently no real rate competition at all and such effective competition as actually thrives takes other forms.

Affirmed.

MR. JUSTICE CLARK took no part in the consideration or decision of this case.

MR. JUSTICE HARLAN, whom MR. JUSTICE FRANKFURTER and MR. JUSTICE WHITTAKER join, dissenting.

* * * In my view, * * * this case should be remanded to the District Court for a trial on the issue whether appellants' landholdings gave them that amount of control over the relevant market for land necessary under this Court's past decisions to make the challenged tying clauses violative per se of the Sherman Act. Further, in light of the Court's disposition of the case and the nature of the findings made below, I think that the Court's discussion of International Salt Co. v. United States is apt to produce confusion as to what proof is necessary to show per se illegality of tying clauses in future Sherman Act cases.

Because the Government necessarily based its complaint on § 1 of the Sherman Act rather than on § 3 of the Clayton Act,[65] it was required to show that the challenged tying clauses constituted unreasonable restraints of trade. As a result, these tying clauses raise legal issues different from those presented by the legislatively defined tying clauses invalidated under the more pointed prohibitions of the Clayton Act. * * *

My primary difficulty with the Court's affirmance of the judgment below is that the District Court made no finding that the appellants had a "dominant position" or, as this Court now puts it, "sufficient economic power," in the relevant land market. Such a finding would indicate that those requiring land of the character owned by the appellants would be driven to them for it, thereby putting appellants in a position to foreclose competing carriers, through the medium of tying clauses, from shipping the produce from the lands sold or leased. The District Court seems to have conceived that no more need be shown on this score than that the appellants owned the particular tracts of land sold or leased subject to a tying clause. * * *

* * *

* * * The District Court should have taken evidence of the relative strength of appellants' landholdings vis-a-vis that of others in the appropriate market for land of the types now or formerly possessed by appellants, of the "uniqueness" of appellants' landholdings in terms of quality or use to which they may have been put, and of the extent to which the location of the lands on or near the Northern Pacific's railroad line, or any other circumstances, put the appellants in a strategic position as against other sellers and lessors of land. * * *

* * * I do not deny that there may be instances where economic coercion by a vendor may be inferred, without any direct showing of market dominance, from the mere existence of the tying arrangements themselves, as where the vendee is apt to suffer economic detriment from the tying

---

[65]   The tying arrangements proscribed by § 3 of the Clayton Act relate only to "goods, wares, merchandise, machinery, supplies or other commodities * * * ." [Dissent fn. 1]

clause because precluded from purchasing a tied product at better terms or of a better quality elsewhere. But the tying clauses here are not cast in such absolute terms. The record indicates that a large majority of appellants' lands were close to the Northern Pacific lines and thus vendees or lessees of these lands might be expected to utilize Northern Pacific as a matter of course. * * * [M]ore is needed than the tying clauses themselves to warrant the inference that acceptance of the tying clauses resulted from coercion exercised by appellants through their position in the land market.

* * *

NOTES AND QUESTIONS

1.   Here we are eleven years after *International Salt* and five after *Times-Picayune*. We have another Sherman § 1 case. The facts are unique but the discussion of the tying rule is still cited as authoritative today.

a.   Does the Court adhere to the rule of *Times-Picayune* that in Clayton § 3 cases one needs *either* power over the tying product or substantial effects in the market for the tied product, but in Sherman § 1 cases like this, one needs both?

b.   Do you agree that the distinction is well ignored? Does it follow that effects should be presumed, i.e., that the defendant should be denied the opportunity to show that there were few real effects flowing from its clauses?

2.   Why in the Court's view are tying arrangements per se illegal?

a.   Is it always true that tying clauses have a negative effect on competition but no positive effects? Is that analysis authoritative because Justice Frankfurter relied on it in *Standard Stations*? Does that mean it is true?

b.   Suppose the railroad had structured these agreements as requirements contracts? That is, suppose the railroad had agreed to carry all the lessees' goods at its published rates or to meet any other carrier's lower price, and the lessees had agreed to use no other carrier. Do you think that exclusive dealing contracts are inherently different from tying agreements?

3.   Exactly when does the per se rule against tying apply?

a.   The key test here seems to be: "They are [illegal] whenever a party has sufficient economic power with respect to the tying product to appreciably restrain free competition in the market for the tied product and a 'not insubstantial' amount of interstate commerce is affected." Are all the terms of that rule self-defining?

b.   What is the basis for the Court's saying that if the tying product is readily available elsewhere, power in the tying product may not be present? Remember its example of one seller of flour requiring buyers to take sugar too, but flour being available from other sellers without sugar.

c.   How did that analysis apply here? Did the Northern Pacific really have a monopoly of Western land? Were you convinced by the Court's assertion that the landholdings were large, strategically located, and that the contracts involved a large number of buyers and lessees? Suppose the seller of flour in the Court's example has large attractive stores; should that detract from the fact that there are many other sellers who do not also require a purchase of sugar?

4.   Were these agreements exclusionary? Whom did they exclude and from what market? Did the exclusion, if any, allow the Northern Pacific to reduce its quality of service or raise its price?

a.   Does the fact that people signed these clauses prove that the railroad had market power? Do you agree that shippers would not otherwise agree to these terms? Given the fact (1) that in a rate regulated industry such as railroading there would be little rate competition, (2) that the Northern Pacific was likely the closest railroad, and (3) that there was an "equal or better" escape clause in the agreements, do you believe lessees and purchasers considered themselves oppressed?

b.   But what about the argument that something must have been going on here or the Northern Pacific would not have fought for the right to enforce these clauses? One article suggests the clause allowed Northern Pacific to monitor which of its competitors were offering to carry goods for less than their published rates. See F. Jay Cummings & Wayne E. Ruhter, The *Northern Pacific* Case, 22 J.Law & Econ. 329 (1979).

c.   Thus the competitors of Northern Pacific were apparently the ones who were upset, not because they were "excluded" but because illegal attempts to provide service for less than published rates would be discovered. Should that interest merit government intervention in the form of finding these clauses per se rule illegal?

5.   Notice who the dissenters are here. Do they surprise you?

a.   Justice Frankfurter, author of *Standard Oil (Calif.)*, member of the majority in *Times-Picayune* and dissenting only as to remedy in *International Salt*, here believes the Court has extended the concept of tying too far. Has the law changed or has Justice Frankfurter?

b.   Note also that this dissent is written by Justice Harlan, recently appointed to the Court to replace Justice Jackson. You will see that throughout his service on the Court from 1955–72, Justice Harlan stood against most of the directions the Court was then taking in antitrust cases.

UNITED STATES V. LOEW'S, INC.

Supreme Court of the United States, 1962
371 U.S. 38, 83 S.Ct. 97, 9 L.Ed.2d 11

MR. JUSTICE GOLDBERG delivered the opinion of the Court.

These consolidated appeals present as a key question the validity under § 1 of the Sherman Act of block booking of copyrighted feature motion pictures for television exhibition. We hold that the tying agreements here are illegal and in violation of the Act.

The United States brought separate civil antitrust actions in the Southern District of New York in 1957 against six major distributors of pre-1948 copyrighted motion picture feature films for television exhibition * * *. The complaints asserted that the defendants had, in selling to television stations, conditioned the license or sale of one or more feature films upon the acceptance by the station of a package or block containing one or more unwanted or inferior films. No combination or conspiracy among the distributors was alleged; nor was any monopolization or attempt to monopolize under § 2 of the Sherman Act averred. The sole claim of illegality rested on the manner in which each defendant had marketed its product. * * *

After a lengthy consolidated trial, the district judge * * * found that the actions of the defendants constituted violations of § 1 of the Sherman Act. * * *

* * *

* * * [D]efendant Loew's, Incorporated, had in two negotiations that resulted in licensing agreements declined to furnish stations KWTV of Oklahoma City and WBRE of Wilkes-Barre with individual film prices and had refused their requests for permission to select among the films in the groups. Loew's exacted from KWTV a contract for the entire Loew's library of 723 films, involving payments of $314,725.20. The WBRE agreement was for a block of 100 films, payments to total $15,000.

* * *

Associated Artists Productions, Inc., negotiated four contracts that were found to be block booked. Station WTOP was to pay $118,800 for the license of 99 pictures, which were divided into three groups of 33 films, based on differences in quality. To get "Treasure of the Sierra Madre," "Casablanca," "Johnny Belinda," "Sergeant York," and "The Man Who Came to Dinner," among others, WTOP also had to take such films as "Nancy Drew Troubleshooter," "Tugboat Annie Sails Again," "Kid Nightingale," "Gorilla Man," and "Tear Gas Squad." A similar contract for 100 pictures, involving a license fee of $140,000, was entered into by WMAR of Baltimore. * * *

Defendant National Telefilm Associates was found to have entered into five block booked contracts. Station WMAR wanted only 10 Selznick films, but was told that it could not have them unless it also bought 24 inferior films from the "TNT" package and 12 unwanted "Fabulous 40's." It bought all of these, for a total of $62,240. * * *

* * *

The court entered separate final judgments against the defendants, wherein each was enjoined from

> "(A) Conditioning or tying, or attempting to condition or tie, the purchase or license of the right to exhibit any feature film over any television station upon the purchase or license of any other film * * * ."

* * *

I

This case raises the recurring question of whether specific tying arrangements violate § 1 of the Sherman Act. This Court has recognized that "[tying] agreements serve hardly any purpose beyond the suppression of competition," Standard Oil Co. of California v. United States. They are an object of antitrust concern for two reasons—they may force buyers into giving up the purchase of substitutes for the tied product, see Times-Picayune Pub. Co. v. United States, and they may destroy the free access of competing suppliers of the tied product to the consuming market, see International Salt Co. v. United States. A tie-in contract may have one or both of these undesirable effects when the seller, by virtue of his position in the market for the tying product, has economic leverage sufficient to induce his customers to take the tied product along with the tying item. The standard of illegality is that the seller must have "sufficient economic power with respect to the tying product to appreciably restrain free competition in the market for the tied product * * * ." Northern Pacific R. Co. v. United States. Market dominance— some power to control price and to exclude competition—is by no means the only test of whether the seller has the requisite economic power. Even absent a showing of market dominance, the crucial economic power may be inferred from the tying product's desirability to consumers or from uniqueness in its attributes.[66]

The requisite economic power is presumed when the tying product is patented or copyrighted, International Salt Co. v. United States; United States v. Paramount Pictures, Inc., 334 U.S. 131 [1948]. This principle grew out of a long line of patent cases which had eventuated in the doctrine that a patentee who utilized tying arrangements would be denied all relief against infringements of his patent. These cases reflect a hostility to use of the statutorily granted patent monopoly to extend the patentee's economic

---

[66] Since the requisite economic power may be found on the basis of either uniqueness or consumer appeal, and since market dominance in the present context does not necessitate a demonstration of market power in the sense of § 2 of the Sherman Act, it should seldom be necessary in a tie-in sale case to embark upon a full-scale factual inquiry into the scope of the relevant market for the tying product and into the corollary problem of the seller's percentage share in that market. This is even more obviously true when the tying product is patented or copyrighted, in which case, as appears in greater detail below, sufficiency of economic power is presumed. Appellants' reliance on United States v. E.I. du Pont de Nemours & Co. is therefore misplaced. [Court's fn. 4]

control to unpatented products. The patentee is protected as to his invention, but may not use his patent rights to exact tribute for other articles.

Since one of the objectives of the patent laws is to reward uniqueness, the principle of these cases was carried over into antitrust law on the theory that the existence of a valid patent on the tying product, without more, establishes a distinctiveness sufficient to conclude that any tying arrangement involving the patented product would have anticompetitive consequences. In United States v. Paramount Pictures, Inc., the principle of the patent cases was applied to copyrighted feature films which had been block booked into movie theaters. The Court reasoned that

> "The copyright law, like the patent statutes, makes reward to the owner a secondary consideration. * * * It is said that reward to the author or artist serves to induce release to the public of the products of his creative genius. But the reward does not serve its public purpose if it is not related to the quality of the copyright. Where a high quality film greatly desired is licensed only if an inferior one is taken, the latter borrows quality from the former and strengthens its monopoly by drawing on the other. The practice tends to equalize rather than differentiate the reward for the individual copyrights. Even where all the films included in the package are of equal quality, the requirement that all be taken if one is desired increases the market for some. Each stands not on its own footing but in whole or in part on the appeal which another film may have. As the District Court said, the result is to add to the monopoly of the copyright in violation of the principle of the patent cases involving tying clauses."

* * *

Appellants cannot escape the applicability of *Paramount Pictures*. A copyrighted feature film does not lose its legal or economic uniqueness because it is shown on a television rather than a movie screen.

The district judge found that each copyrighted film block booked by appellants for television use "was in itself a unique product"; that feature films "varied in theme, in artistic performance, in stars, in audience appeal, etc.," and were not fungible; and that since each defendant by reason of its copyright had a "monopolistic" position as to each tying product, "sufficient economic power" to impose an appreciable restraint on free competition in the tied product was present, as demanded by the *Northern Pacific* decision.[67] We agree. These findings of the district judge, supported by the

---

[67]   To use the trial court's apt example, forcing a television station which wants "Gone With The Wind" to take "Getting Gertie's Garter" as well is taking undue advantage of the fact that to television as well as motion picture viewers there is but one "Gone With The Wind." [Court's fn. 6]

record, confirm the presumption of uniqueness resulting from the existence of the copyright itself.

Moreover, there can be no question in this case of the adverse effects on free competition resulting from appellants' illegal block booking contracts. Television stations forced by appellants to take unwanted films were denied access to films marketed by other distributors who, in turn, were foreclosed from selling to the stations. Nor can there be any question as to the substantiality of the commerce involved. The 25 contracts found to have been illegally block booked involved payments to appellants ranging from $60,800 in the case of Screen Gems to over $2,500,000 in the case of Associated Artists. A substantial portion of the licensing fees represented the cost of the inferior films which the stations were required to accept. These anticompetitive consequences are an apt illustration of the reasons underlying our recognition that the mere presence of competing substitutes for the tying product, here taking the form of other programming material as well as other feature films, is insufficient to destroy the legal, and indeed the economic, distinctiveness of the copyrighted product. * * *

It is therefore clear that the tying arrangements here both by their "inherent nature" and by their "effect" injuriously restrained trade. Accommodation between the statutorily dispensed monopoly in the combination of contents in the patented or copyrighted product and the statutory principles of free competition demands that extension of the patent or copyright monopoly by the use of tying agreements be strictly confined. There may be rare circumstances in which the doctrine we have enunciated under § 1 of the Sherman Act prohibiting tying arrangements involving patented or copyrighted tying products is inapplicable. However, we find it difficult to conceive of such a case, and the present case is clearly not one.

* * *

The judgments are vacated and the causes are remanded to the District Court for further proceedings in conformity with this opinion.

[The dissenting opinion of MR. JUSTICE HARLAN, with whom MR. JUSTICE STEWART joined, which went only to the question of modifying the decree, is omitted.]

NOTES AND QUESTIONS

1. Who was hurt by the contracts at issue in this case?

a. Was it the television stations? Do you agree with the Court that they were forced to pay for films they did not want? Might they have found the price of the package attractive enough that they would pay the full price for the films they *did* want?

b.   Were other distributors of motion pictures hurt? Do you agree with the court that they would tend to be excluded from the television market because stations all had film libraries full of the trash they had been compelled to buy under this plan? Did the fact that the station had bought "Tear Gas Squad" as part of a package, for example, mean that it was compelled to show it? Might it not also buy the other distributors' films if it could get better ratings by showing them?

2.   Why would a film distributor want to sell its films this way?

a.   If everyone wanted "Casablanca" and would pay a high price for it, why would a film studio be able to make more money by requiring the purchaser to buy "Tugboat Annie" as well? Would the incremental amount it could get by adding the latter film to the package ever exceed its incremental value to the purchaser?

b.   Suppose that not every purchaser valued the films equally? That is, suppose that while "Casablanca" would only draw a so-so audience for one station, "Gorilla Man" would attract large ratings. For other stations, however, the relative values would be reversed. What, then, would block booking accomplish?

3.   Consider the following example showing films with their possible values in selected cities:

	New York	Atlanta	Burbank
Gone with the Wind	$ 400	$1000	$ 300
Bedtime for Bonzo	$ 200	$ 100	$1000
Manhattan	$1000	$ 500	$ 300

a.   If you were to price each film individually, what price would you set for each? If you set the price of each at $1000, you would sell one copy of each and receive a total of $3000. Would that be the maximum return you could realize from the films?

b.   Suppose you were willing to lower the price sufficiently to sell two copies of each film. That would require a price of $400 for Gone with the Wind, $200 for Bedtime for Bonzo, and $500 for Manhattan. Even selling two copies of each film at those prices would bring in only $2200 total, so you would not be better off.

c.   Now try selling three copies of each picture. Do you see that the "market" price for each will be the lowest price any of the cities would be willing to pay. Thus, you would get $300 each for Gone with the Wind and Manhattan, but only $100 each for Bonzo. The total would come to only $2100.

d.   But what could you get for the three films if you sold them as a package? Do you see that each city would be willing to pay $1600 for the package of three films. The total you would receive would thus be $4800. Don't be shocked. While the figures are arbitrary, the point is sound. When people value parts of a package differently, they will tend to be willing to pay a higher package price than the sum of the competitive prices of the pieces of the package individually.[68]

e.   Would such a pricing program raise any of the concerns that the prohibition of tying is designed to prevent? Would it tend to exclude anyone from the market? Would it reduce competition or tend to create a monopoly? If the answer to these questions is yes, must Life Savers stop selling packages containing five flavors of candy? Must record companies stop selling albums that contain more than one song?

A NOTE ON THE ISSUE OF END PRODUCT ROYALTIES

Should a patent holder be permitted to base its royalty for use of a patent on a percentage of the sale price of the whole product in which the patented invention is used?

In Zenith Radio Corp. v. Hazeltine Research, Inc., 395 U.S. 100, 89 S.Ct. 1562, 23 L.Ed.2d 129 (1969), the holder of about 500 patents set as its royalty charge a percentage of the price of the licensees' radio and television sets. That was to be the royalty whether the manufacturer's sets contained many patented parts, a few, or none at all. The Supreme Court struck down the practice, holding that it was the same as charging royalties on unpatented items. It was analytically the same as International Salt's requiring the purchase of unpatented salt tablets. Thus, the Court reasoned, the practice should be examined to see if licensees had been coerced into buying what they did not want. If so, it would constitute "patent misuse" and an injunction against it would be upheld.

Do you agree? Why might a patent holder establish such a royalty arrangement? Would such a basis for charging royalties reduce concern about a licensee's cheating better than a charge based on items actually used would? Even the same model of the same set might have slightly different parts based on somewhat different patents. Might a system of end product royalties allow looking at sales data but not opening the backs of sets or arguing about what patented processes have been used?

Would charging royalties on this basis contribute to the optimal use of the patented items? Notice that from the perspective of the licensee, end product royalties eliminate the patent royalty as a marginal cost of a component and thus tend not to discourage a patent's use. When the royalty is the same no matter how often the invention is used, a

---

[68]   In fact, many of the packages apparently did not contain any popular movies at all; they were strictly suitable for showing to insomniacs. The difficulty of setting prices on the individual movies was thus actually even greater than we have hypothesized. See Roy W. Kenney & Benjamin Klein, The Economics of Block Booking, 26 J.Law & Econ. 497 (1983).

manufacturer will use it as often as it saves money or increases quality to do so. That would seem to be the optimal or efficient level of use.

If end-product royalties are good for both licensor and licensee, then, why should the Court ever consider them to be patent misuse? The reason is not clear. The Court had seemed to uphold such royalties in Automatic Radio Manufacturing Co. v. Hazeltine Research, Inc., 339 U.S. 827, 70 S.Ct. 894, 94 L.Ed. 1312 (1950), a case in which *all* the radios had some patented devices, albeit not the same number. In the *Zenith* case, the problem for the Court seemed to be the extension of the principle to products that might use no patented devices at all. Can you see any principles of either patent law or antitrust law that would be violated by such a scheme? See, e.g., William Baxter, Legal Restrictions on Exploitation of the Patent Monopoly: An Economic Analysis, 76 Yale L.J. 267 (1966).

Finally, in the years covered by this chapter, our next case came to be seen as the high (or low) point in the development of the law of tying.

FORTNER ENTERPRISES, INC. V. UNITED STATES STEEL CORP.

Supreme Court of the United States, 1969
394 U.S. 495, 89 S.Ct. 1252, 22 L.Ed.2d 495

MR. JUSTICE BLACK delivered the opinion of the Court.

This case raises a variety of questions concerning the proper standards to be applied by a United States district court in passing on a motion for summary judgment in a civil antitrust action. Petitioner, Fortner Enterprises, Inc., filed this suit seeking treble damages and an injunction against alleged violations of §§ 1 and 2 of the Sherman Act. The complaint charged that respondents, United States Steel Corp. and its wholly-owned subsidiary, the United States Steel Homes Credit Corp., had engaged in a contract, combination, and conspiracy to restrain trade and to monopolize trade in the sale of prefabricated houses. It alleged that there was a continuing agreement between respondents "to force corporations and individuals, including the plaintiff, as a condition to availing themselves of the services of United States Steel Homes Credit Corporation, to purchase at artificially high prices only United States Steel Homes * * * ." Specifically, petitioner claimed that in order to obtain loans totaling over $2,000,000 from the Credit Corp. for the purchase and development of certain land in the Louisville, Kentucky, area, it had been required to agree, as a condition of the loans, to erect a prefabricated house manufactured by U.S. Steel on each of the lots purchased with the loan proceeds. Petitioner claimed that the prefabricated materials were then supplied by U.S. Steel at unreasonably high prices and proved to be defective and unusable, thus requiring the expenditure of additional sums and delaying the completion date for the development. Petitioner sought treble damages for the profits thus lost, along with a decree enjoining respondents from enforcing the requirement of the loan agreement that petitioner use only houses manufactured by U.S. Steel.

After pretrial proceedings * * * the District Court entered summary judgment for respondents * * * . * * * [T]he District Judge held that petitioner had failed to establish the prerequisites of illegality under our tying cases, namely sufficient market power over the tying product and foreclosure of a substantial volume of commerce in the tied product. The Court of Appeals affirmed * * * . Since we find no basis for sustaining this summary judgment, we reverse and order that the case proceed to trial.

We agree with the District Court that the conduct challenged here primarily involves a tying arrangement of the traditional kind. The Credit Corp. sold its credit only on the condition that petitioner purchase a certain number of prefabricated houses from the Homes Division of U.S. Steel. Our cases have made clear that, at least when certain prerequisites are met, arrangements of this kind are illegal in and of themselves, and no specific showing of unreasonable competitive effect is required. The discussion in Northern Pacific R. Co. v. United States is dispositive of this question:

* * *

> "[Tying agreements] deny competitors free access to the market for the tied product, not because the party imposing the tying requirements has a better product or a lower price but because of his power or leverage in another market. At the same time buyers are forced to forego their free choice between competing products. * * * They are unreasonable in and of themselves whenever a party has sufficient economic power with respect to the tying product to appreciably restrain free competition in the market for the tied product and a 'not insubstantial' amount of interstate commerce is affected. International Salt Co. v. United States."

Despite its recognition of this strict standard, the District Court held that petitioner had not even made out a case for the jury. The court held that respondents did not have "sufficient economic power" over credit, the tying product here, because although the Credit Corp.'s terms evidently made the loans uniquely attractive to petitioner, petitioner had not proved that the Credit Corp. enjoyed the same unique attractiveness or economic control with respect to buyers generally. The court also held that the amount of interstate commerce affected was "insubstantial" because only a very small percentage of the land available for development in the area was foreclosed to competing sellers of prefabricated houses by the contract with petitioner. We think it plain that the District Court misunderstood the two controlling standards and misconceived the extent of its authority to evaluate the evidence in ruling on this motion for summary judgment.

A preliminary error that should not pass unnoticed is the District Court's assumption that the two prerequisites mentioned in *Northern Pacific* are standards that petitioner must meet in order to prevail on the merits. On the contrary, these standards are necessary only to bring into play the doctrine of per se illegality. Where the standards were found satisfied in *Northern Pacific*, and in International Salt Co. v. United States, this Court approved summary judgment against the defendants but by no means implied that inability to satisfy these standards would be fatal to a plaintiff's case. A plaintiff can still prevail on the merits whenever he can prove, on the basis of a more thorough examination of the purposes and effects of the practices involved, that the general standards of the Sherman Act have been violated. Accordingly, even if we could agree with the District Court that the *Northern Pacific* standards were not satisfied here, the summary judgment against petitioner still could not be entered without further examination of petitioner's general allegations that respondents conspired together for the purpose of restraining competition and acquiring a monopoly in the market for prefabricated houses. And such an examination could rarely justify summary judgment with respect to a claim of this kind, for as we said in Poller v. Columbia Broadcasting, 368 U.S. 464, 473 (1962):

> "We believe that summary procedures should be used sparingly in complex antitrust litigation where motive and intent play leading roles, the proof is largely in the hands of the alleged conspirators, and hostile witnesses thicken the plot. It is only when the witnesses are present and subject to cross-examination that their credibility and the weight to be given their testimony can be appraised. Trial by affidavit is no substitute for trial by jury which so long has been the hallmark of 'even handed justice.' "

We need not consider, however, whether petitioner is entitled to a trial on this more general theory, for it is clear that petitioner raised questions of fact which, if proved at trial, would bring this tying arrangement within the scope of the per se doctrine. The requirement that a "not insubstantial" amount of commerce be involved makes no reference to the scope of any particular market or to the share of that market foreclosed by the tie * * * . An analysis of market shares might become relevant if it were alleged that an apparently small dollar-volume of business actually represented a substantial part of the sales for which competitors were bidding. But normally the controlling consideration is simply whether a total amount of business, substantial enough in terms of dollar-volume so as not to be merely de minimis, is foreclosed to competitors by the tie * * *. *International Salt.*[69]

The complaint and affidavits filed here leave no room for doubt that the volume of commerce allegedly foreclosed was substantial. It may be true, as respondents claim, that petitioner's annual purchases of houses from U.S. Steel under the tying arrangement never exceeded $190,000, while more than $500,000 in annual sales was involved in the tying arrangement held illegal in *International Salt*, but we cannot agree with respondents that a sum of almost $200,000 is paltry or "insubstantial." In any event, a narrow focus on the volume of commerce foreclosed by the particular contract or contracts in suit would not be appropriate in this context. As the special provision awarding treble damages to successful plaintiffs illustrates, Congress has encouraged private antitrust litigation not merely to compensate those who have been directly injured but also to vindicate the important public interest in free competition. For purposes of determining whether the amount of commerce foreclosed is too insubstantial to warrant prohibition of the practice, therefore, the relevant figure is the total volume of sales tied by the sales policy under challenge, not the portion of this total accounted for by the particular plaintiff who brings suit. * * * In the present case, the annual sales allegedly foreclosed by respondents' tying arrangements throughout the country totaled almost $4,000,000 in 1960, more than $2,800,000 in 1961, and almost $2,300,000 in 1962. These amounts could scarcely be regarded as insubstantial.

The standard of "sufficient economic power" does not, as the District Court held, require that the defendant have a monopoly or even a dominant position throughout the market for the tying product. Our tie-in cases have made unmistakably clear that the economic power over the tying product can be sufficient even though the power falls far short of dominance and even though the power exists only with respect to some of the buyers in the market. See, e.g., *International Salt*; *Northern Pacific*; United States v. Loew's Inc. As we said in the *Loew's* case, "Even absent a showing of market dominance, the crucial economic power may be inferred from the tying product's desirability to consumers or from uniqueness in its attributes."

These decisions rejecting the need for proof of truly dominant power over the tying product have all been based on a recognition that because tying arrangements generally serve no legitimate business purpose that cannot be achieved in some less restrictive way, the presence of any appreciable restraint on competition provides a sufficient reason for invalidating the tie. Such appreciable restraint results whenever the seller can exert some power over some of the buyers in the market, even if his power is not complete over them and over all other buyers in the market.

---

[69]   [Ed. note] Remember that only 8 years earlier, in Tampa Electric Co. v. Nashville Coal Co., the Court had reiterated that in exclusive dealing cases "substantiality" was to be measured as a percentage of the market.

In fact, complete dominance throughout the market, the concept that the District Court apparently had in mind, would never exist even under a pure monopoly. Market power is usually stated to be the ability of a single seller to raise price and restrict output, for reduced output is the almost inevitable result of higher prices. Even a complete monopolist can seldom raise his price without losing some sales; many buyers will cease to buy the product, or buy less, as the price rises. * * * Accordingly, the proper focus of concern is whether the seller has the power to raise prices, or impose other burdensome terms such as a tie-in, with respect to any appreciable number of buyers within the market.

The affidavits put forward by petitioner clearly entitle it to its day in court under this standard. A construction company president stated that competitors of U.S. Steel sold prefabricated houses and built conventional homes for at least $400 less than U.S. Steel's price for comparable models. Since in a freely competitive situation buyers would not accept a tying arrangement obligating them to buy a tied product at a price higher than the going market rate, this substantial price differential with respect to the tied product (prefabricated houses) in itself may suggest that respondents had some special economic power in the credit market. In addition, petitioner's president, A. B. Fortner, stated that he accepted the tying condition on respondents' loan solely because the offer to provide 100% financing, lending an amount equal to the full purchase price of the land to be acquired, was unusually and uniquely advantageous to him. He found that no such financing was available to his corporation on any such cheap terms from any other source during the 1959–1962 period. His views on this were supported by the president of a finance company in the Louisville area * * * .

We do not mean to accept petitioner's apparent argument that market power can be inferred simply because the kind of financing terms offered by a lending company are "unique and unusual." We do mean, however, that uniquely and unusually advantageous terms can reflect a creditor's unique economic advantages over his competitors.[70] Since summary judgment in antitrust cases is disfavored, the claims of uniqueness in this case should be read in the light most favorable to petitioner. They could well mean that U.S. Steel's subsidiary Credit Corp. had a unique economic ability to provide 100% financing at cheap rates. The affidavits show that for a three-to-four-year period no other financial institution in the Louisville area was willing to match the special credit terms and rates of interest available from U.S. Steel. Since the possibility of a decline in

---

[70] Uniqueness confers economic power only when other competitors are in some way prevented from offering the distinctive product themselves. Such barriers may be legal, as in the case of patented and copyrighted products, e.g., *International Salt, Loew's*; or physical, as when the product is land, e.g., *Northern Pacific*. It is true that the barriers may also be economic, as when competitors are simply unable to produce the distinctive product profitably, but the uniqueness test in such situations is somewhat confusing since the real source of economic power is not the product itself but rather the seller's cost advantage in producing it. [Court's fn. 2]

property values, along with the difficulty of recovering full market value in a foreclosure sale, makes it desirable for a creditor to obtain collateral greater in value than the loan it secures, the unwillingness of competing financial institutions in the area to offer 100% financing probably reflects their feeling that they could not profitably lend money on the risks involved. U.S. Steel's subsidiary Credit Corp., on the other hand, may well have had a substantial competitive advantage in providing this type of financing because of economies resulting from the nationwide character of its operations. In addition, potential competitors such as banks and savings and loan associations may have been prohibited from offering 100% financing by state or federal law. Under these circumstances the pleadings and affidavits sufficiently disclose the possibility of market power over borrowers in the credit market to entitle petitioner to go to trial on this issue.

It may also be, of course, that these allegations will not be sustained when the case goes to trial. * * * But on the record before us it would be impossible to reach such conclusions as a matter of law, and it is not our function to speculate as to the ultimate findings of fact. * * *

* * *

* * * [Respondents' argue] that this opinion will somehow prevent those who manufacture goods from ever selling them on credit. But our holding in this case will have no such effect. There is, at the outset of every tie-in case * * * the problem of determining whether two separate products are in fact involved. In the usual sale on credit the seller, a single individual or corporation, simply makes an agreement determining when and how much he will be paid for his product. In such a sale the credit may constitute such an inseparable part of the purchase price for the item that the entire transaction could be considered to involve only a single product. * * * Sales such as that are a far cry from the arrangement involved here, where the credit is provided by one corporation on condition that a product be purchased from a separate corporation, and where the borrower contracts to obtain a large sum of money over and above that needed to pay the seller for the physical products purchased. Whatever the standards for determining exactly when a transaction involves only a "single product," we cannot see how an arrangement such as that present in this case could ever be said to involve only a single product.

* * * Although advantageous credit terms may be viewed as a form of price competition in the tied product, so is the offer of any other tying product on advantageous terms. In both instances, the seller can achieve his alleged purpose, without extending his economic power, by simply reducing the price of the tied product itself.

* * *

In addition, barriers to entry in the market for the tied product are raised since, in order to sell to certain buyers, a new company not only must be able to manufacture the tied product but also must have sufficient financial strength to offer credit comparable to that provided by larger competitors under tying arrangements. If the larger companies have achieved economies of scale in their credit operations, they can of course exploit these economies legitimately by lowering their credit charges to consumers who purchase credit only, but economies in financing should not, any more than economies in other lines of business, be used to exert economic power over other products that the company produces no more efficiently than its competitors.

For all these reasons we can find no basis for treating credit differently in principle from other goods and services. Although money is a fungible commodity—like wheat or, for that matter, unfinished steel—credit markets, like other markets, are often imperfect, and it is easy to see how a big company with vast sums of money in its treasury could wield very substantial power in a credit market. Where this is true, tie-ins involving credit can cause all the evils that the antitrust laws have always been intended to prevent, crippling other companies that are equally, if not more, efficient in producing their own products. Therefore, the same inquiries must be made as to economic power over the tying product and substantial effect in the tied market, but where these factors are present no special treatment can be justified solely because credit, rather than some other product, is the source of the tying leverage used to restrain competition.

The judgment of the Court of Appeals is reversed, and the case is remanded with directions to let this suit proceed to trial.

MR. JUSTICE WHITE, with whom MR. JUSTICE HARLAN joins, dissenting.

* * *

* * * Proscription of the sale of goods on easy credit terms as an illegal tie without proof of market power in credit not only departs from established doctrine but also in my view should not be outlawed as per se illegal under the Sherman Act. Provision of favorable credit terms may be nothing more or less than vigorous competition in the tied product, on a basis very nearly approaching the price competition which it has always been the policy of the Sherman Act to encourage. Moreover, it is far from clear that, absent power in the credit market, credit financing of purchases should be regarded as a tie of two distinct products any more than a commodity should be viewed as tied to its own price. Since provision of credit by sellers may facilitate competition, since it may provide essential risk or working capital to entrepreneurs or businessmen, and since the logic of the majority's opinion does away in practice with the requirement of showing market power in the tying product while retaining that requirement in form, the majority's per se rule is inappropriate. I dissent.

* * *

There is general agreement in the cases and among commentators that the fundamental restraint against which the tying proscription is meant to guard is the use of power over one product to attain power over another, or otherwise to distort freedom of trade and competition in the second product. This distortion injures the buyers of the second product, who because of their preference for the seller's brand of the first are artificially forced to make a less than optimal choice in the second. And even if the customer is indifferent among brands of the second product and therefore loses nothing by agreeing to use the seller's brand of the second in order to get his brand of the first, such tying agreements may work significant restraints on competition in the tied product. The tying seller may be working toward a monopoly position in the tied product[71] and, even if he is not, the practice of tying forecloses other sellers of the tied product and makes it more difficult for new firms to enter that market. They must be prepared not only to match existing sellers of the tied product in price and quality, but to offset the attraction of the tying product itself. Even if this is possible through simultaneous entry into production of the tying product, entry into both markets is significantly more expensive than simple entry into the tied market, and shifting buying habits in the tied product is considerably more cumbersome and less responsive to variations in competitive offers. In addition to these anticompetitive effects in the tied product, tying arrangements may be used to evade price control in the tying product through clandestine transfer of the profit to the tied product; they may be used as a counting device to effect price discrimination; and they may be used to force a full line of products on the customer so as to extract more easily from him a monopoly return on one unique product in the line.[72]

---

[71] If the monopolist uses his monopoly profits in the first market to underwrite sales below market price in the second, his monopoly business becomes less profitable. There remains an incentive to do so nonetheless when he thinks he can obtain a monopoly in the tied product as well, permitting him later to raise prices without fear of entry to recoup the monopoly profit he has forgone. But just as the firm whose deep pocket stems from monopoly profits in the tying product may make this takeover, so may anyone else with a deep pocket, from whatever source. [White fn. 4]

[72] Tie-ins may also at times be beneficial to the economy. Apart from the justifications discussed in the text are the following. They may facilitate new entry into fields where established sellers have wedded their customers to them by ties of habit and custom. They may permit clandestine price cutting in products which otherwise would have no price competition at all because of fear of retaliation from the few other producers dealing in the market. They may protect the reputation of the tying product if failure to use the tied product in conjunction with it may cause it to misfunction. And, if the tied and tying products are functionally related, they may reduce costs through economies of joint production and distribution. These benefits which may flow from tie-ins, though perhaps in some cases a potential basis for an affirmative defense, were not sufficient to avoid the imposition of a per se proscription, once market power has been demonstrated. But in determining whether even the market-power requirement should be eliminated, as the logic of the majority opinion would do, extending the per se rule to absolute

All of these distortions depend upon the existence of some market power in the tying product quite apart from any relationship which it might bear to the tied product. In this case, what proof of any market power in the tying product has been alleged? Only that the tying product—money—was not available elsewhere on equally good terms, and perhaps not at all. Let us consider these possibilities in turn.

First, if enough money to proceed was available elsewhere and U.S. Steel was simply offering credit at a lower price, in terms of risk of loss, repayment terms, and interest rate, surely this does not establish that U.S. Steel had market power by any measure in the money market. There was nothing unique about U.S. Steel's money except its low cost to petitioner. A low price on a product is ordinarily no reflection of market power. It proves neither the existence of such power nor its absence, although absence of power may be the more reasonable inference. One who has such power benefits from it precisely because it allows him to raise prices, not lower them, and ordinarily he does so.

A low price in the tying product—money, the most fungible item of trade since it is by definition an economic counter—is especially poor proof of market power when untied credit is available elsewhere. In that case, the low price of credit is functionally equivalent to a reduction in the price of the houses sold. * * * By cutting the price of his houses, a competitor of U.S. Steel can compete with U.S. Steel houses on equal terms since U.S. Steel's money is no more desirable to the purchaser than money from another source except in point of price. The same money which U.S. Steel is willing to risk or forgo by providing better credit terms it could sacrifice by cutting the price of houses. There is no good reason why U.S. Steel should always be required to make the price cut in one form rather than another, which its purchaser prefers.

* * *

* * * Buyers are not burdened. They may buy both tied and tying products elsewhere on normal terms. Nor are the seller's competitors restrained. The economic advantage of the tie-in to buyers can be matched by other sellers of the tied product by offering lower prices on that product. Promotional tie-ins effected by underpricing the tying product do not themselves prove there is any market power to exercise in that product market, unless the economic resources to withstand lower profit margins and the willingness to compete in this manner are themselves suspect. If they are, however, they should as surely taint and muffle hard price competition in the tied market itself, a result which, short of a § 2 violation, it would be difficult to reach under the Sherman Act.

* * *

---

dimensions, the fact that tie-ins are not entirely unmitigated evils should be borne in mind. [White fn. 9]

MR. JUSTICE FORTAS, with whom MR. JUSTICE STEWART joins, dissenting.

* * *

* * * This is a sale of a single product with the incidental provision of financing. It is not a sale of one product on condition that the buyer will not deal with competitors for another product or will buy the other product exclusively from the seller.

* * *

* * * Almost all modern selling involves providing some ancillary services in connection with making the sale—delivery, installation, supplying fixtures, servicing, training of the customer's personnel in use of the material sold, furnishing display material and sales aids, extension of credit. * * * It is possible that in some situations, such arrangements could be used to restrain competition or might have that effect, but to condemn them out-of-hand under the "tying" rubric, is, I suggest, to use the antitrust laws themselves as an instrument in restraint of competition.

* * *

NOTES AND QUESTIONS

1.   What is the substantive test for tying after this case? Is tying clearly per se illegal if the *Northern Pacific* criteria are met?

a.   What is the standard of "market power" used here? Do you agree that market power was demonstrated by the fact that U.S. Steel was able to get an "appreciable number of buyers within the market" to accept its "burdensome" terms?

b.   How should one measure substantiality of effect on the tied product? Do you agree that an impact on $200,000 worth of purchases is "not insubstantial"? Should share of the market affected be the test of substantiality only in exclusive dealing cases?

2.   Whom does the Court believe get hurt by tying arrangements such as this one?

a.   Are the primary victims the sellers of traditional housing components who cannot afford to provide their own financing for sales? Indeed, would the need to provide such financing constitute a barrier to entering the housing industry?

b.   Are banks and other financial institutions among the victims? Do you agree with the Court that regulatory restrictions on their lending put them at a competitive disadvantage compared to a company like U.S. Steel?

c.   Do you see Mr. Fortner as a victim of U.S. Steel's requirements? Did U.S. Steel put a gun to his head? Indeed, might Mr. Fortner have been pleased to get 100% financing for a house that he could sell at a profit? Then, what is it that should entitle Mr. Fortner to sue U.S. Steel for treble damages plus attorneys' fees?

3.   Are there costs associated with extending the per se rule against tying to an arrangement such as this one?

a.   Were the dissenters right that this decision puts all credit sales at risk? How about all sales under which the seller agrees to deliver the goods to the buyer's home or business?

b.   If U.S. Steel would be willing to sell these houses *without* financing them, would that eliminate the tying issue? If so, why did it not do so? Should the law tend to force firms not to provide collateral services, discounts, and the like?

4.   The Court suggests that there are also instances of tying that are not per se illegal, but tested under the rule of reason.

a.   On the one hand, should *all* tying cases be tested under the rule of reason? Are the motivations for and consequences of package selling sufficiently varied that per se treatment threatens to condemn far too many desirable packages?

b.   On the other hand, what should the Court examine in a rule of reason tying case? What could be the possible anticompetitive effects of trade terms imposed by a firm that lacks the degree of market power required for application of the per se rule?

A NOTE ON SOME PROCEDURAL ISSUES SUGGESTED BY *FORTNER*

Fortner clearly extended tying principles to or beyond the breaking point. The substantive result may have been at least partly dictated by its procedural context and the Court's concern about procedural issues at this time in the development of antitrust doctrine.

Look at the Court's reference to Poller v. Columbia Broadcasting System, 368 U.S. 464, 82 S.Ct. 486, 7 L.Ed.2d 458 (1962), establishing the standard for a grant of summary judgment in an antitrust case. Under the *Poller* standard, it was hard to imagine the Supreme Court *ever* sustaining a grant of summary judgment, and until more recently[73] it rarely did.

However, not everyone agrees that antitrust cases are less appropriate than ordinary cases for granting summary judgment. Indeed, because the cost of litigating them is so high, might one argue that summary remedies should be used whenever possible? Can you think of the political realities of trying to make such a change in approach? Might increased willingness

---

[73]   E.g., Matsushita Electric Industrial Co. v. Zenith Radio Corp., 475 U.S. 574, 106 S.Ct. 1348, 89 L.Ed.2d 538 (1986), that you will read in the next chapter.

to use such remedies tend to decrease the settlement value of plaintiffs' cases? Where would you expect plaintiffs' antitrust lawyers to turn for relief?

Now suppose a firm that had agreed to a tying arrangement changed its mind. Should it be able to seek an injunction against enforcement of the contract, damages, or both? Should it instead be barred by the doctrine of in pari delicto, i.e., "equal fault", because it had accepted the benefit of the contract terms?

In Perma Life Mufflers v. International Parts Corp., 392 U.S. 134, 88 S.Ct. 1981, 20 L.Ed.2d 982 (1968), the Court found no such bar. The private suit serves an important public purpose, the Court held. Benefits the plaintiff gained from the contract could be set off against any damages claimed, but if the signer of an illegal contract were barred from filing suit, the public would be ill-served. Do you agree? Might a better result be to let either party avoid the illegal contract but neither sue for an antitrust violation?

The debate over the value to the public of private treble damage actions is a continuing one. The private action is seen by many as a supplement to often-lax enforcement by public agencies. Others, however, see it largely as a device by which unsuccessful firms harass the more successful, deter efficient conduct, and potentially have the defendants pay all the legal bills.[74] Watch as the debate over these issues recurs throughout these materials.

A POSTSCRIPT ON *FORTNER*

On remand, a jury—and later a judge in a bench trial—had both rendered judgment for Fortner, and the Court of Appeals affirmed. When the case again came to the Supreme Court, however, the Court unanimously reversed both lower courts. Justice Stevens, one of four new justices then on the Court, wrote:

> "[Previous tying cases] focus attention on the question whether the seller has the power within the market for the tying product to raise prices or require purchasers to accept burdensome terms that could not be exacted in a completely competitive market. * * *

---

[74] The scholarly debate is suggested by, e.g., William Breit & Kenneth Elzinga, Private Antitrust Enforcement: The New Learning, 28 J.Law & Econ. 405 (1985); Frank H. Easterbrook, Detrebling Antitrust Damages, 28 J.Law & Econ. 445 (1985); and Robert H. Lande, Are Antitrust "Treble" Damages Really Single Damages?, 54 Ohio St.L.J. 115 (1993).

"Without any such advantage differentiating his product from that of his competitors, the seller's product does not have the kind of uniqueness considered relevant in prior tying-clause cases. * * *

"Quite clearly, if the evidence merely shows that credit terms are unique because the seller is willing to accept a lesser profit— or to incur greater risks—than its competitors, that kind of uniqueness will not give rise to any inference of economic power in the credit market. * * *

"The unusual credit bargain offered to Fortner proves nothing more than a willingness to provide cheap financing in order to sell expensive houses. * * * "

United States Steel Corp. v. Fortner Enterprises, Inc., 429 U.S. 610, 621–23, 97 S.Ct. 861, 868–69, 51 L.Ed.2d 80 (1977).

Are you confused? Had the new justices simply helped change the Court's collective mind? Was *Fortner II* part of the "new wave" of antitrust thinking that we will see later? Or did the result just reflect the Court's longstanding willingness to decide on a full record, questions that it had been unwilling to decide on summary judgment?

D. DEALING WITH DEALERS

In the first three topics examined in this chapter, we have seen a per se rule asserted and developed over a period of 25 to 35 years. Our next series of cases largely assumed that price fixing, group boycotts and market division agreements among competitors were per se illegal. The question presented in these later cases was how those principles applied to dealings among firms who are *not* competitors, i.e., to the manner in which firms deal with entities that distribute their products.

There are at least four different kinds of such cases. The first case we read raises a group boycott issue analogous to what we saw in *Fashion Originators'*. Next we look at resale price maintenance, i.e., the vertical price fixing that we encountered in *Dr. Miles*, *Colgate*, and *General Electric*. The third group of cases deal with "market division", i.e., with firms' creation of exclusive territories for their dealers. Finally, we look briefly at some functionally-related, but doctrinally-different, price discrimination issues that arise under the Robinson-Patman Act.

1. GROUP BOYCOTTS OF PARTICULAR DEALERS

Prominent among antitrust cases since the late 1950s have been those involving firms engaged in discount selling. Particularly important have been private actions brought by dealers terminated ("boycotted") for engaging in or assisting such conduct.

KLOR'S, INC. V. BROADWAY-HALE STORES

Supreme Court of the United States, 1959
359 U.S. 207, 79 S.Ct. 705, 3 L.Ed.2d 741

MR. JUSTICE BLACK delivered the opinion of the Court.

Klor's, Inc., operates a retail store on Mission Street, San Francisco, California; Broadway-Hale Stores, Inc., a chain of department stores, operates one of its stores next door. The two stores compete in the sale of radios, television sets, refrigerators and other household appliances. Claiming that Broadway-Hale and 10 national manufacturers and their distributors have conspired to restrain and monopolize commerce in violation of §§ 1 and 2 of the Sherman Act, Klor's brought this action for treble damages and injunction * * * . In support of its claim Klor's made the following allegations: George Klor started an appliance store some years before 1952 and has operated it ever since either individually or as Klor's, Inc. Klor's is as well equipped as Broadway-Hale to handle all brands of appliances. Nevertheless, manufacturers and distributors of such well-known brands as General Electric, RCA, Admiral, Zenith, Emerson and others have conspired among themselves and with Broadway-Hale either not to sell to Klor's or to sell to it only at discriminatory prices and highly unfavorable terms. Broadway-Hale has used its "monopolistic" buying power to bring about this situation. The business of manufacturing, distributing and selling household appliances is in interstate commerce. The concerted refusal to deal with Klor's has seriously handicapped its ability to compete and has already caused it a great loss of profits, goodwill, reputation and prestige.

The defendants did not dispute these allegations, but sought summary judgment and dismissal of the complaint for failure to state a cause of action. They submitted unchallenged affidavits which showed that there were hundreds of other household appliance retailers, some within a few blocks of Klor's who sold many competing brands of appliances, including those the defendants refused to sell to Klor's. * * * [T]he District Court concluded that the controversy was a "purely private quarrel" between Klor's and Broadway-Hale, which did not amount to a "public wrong proscribed by the [Sherman] Act." On this ground the complaint was dismissed and summary judgment was entered for the defendants. The Court of Appeals for the Ninth Circuit affirmed the summary judgment. * * * The holding, if correct, means that unless the opportunities for customers to buy in a competitive market are reduced, a group of powerful businessmen may act in concert to deprive a single merchant, like Klor, of the goods he needs to compete effectively. * * *

We think Klor's allegations clearly show one type of trade restraint and public harm the Sherman Act forbids, and that defendants' affidavits provide no defense to the charges. * * * In the landmark case of Standard Oil Co. v. United States, this Court read § 1 to prohibit those classes of contracts or acts which the common law had deemed to be undue restraints of trade and those which new times and economic conditions would make unreasonable. The Court construed § 2 as making "the prohibitions of the act all the more complete and perfect by embracing all attempts to reach the end prohibited by the first section * * * ." The effect of both sections, the Court said, was to adopt the common-law proscription of all "contracts or acts which it was considered had a monopolistic tendency * * * " and which interfered with the "natural flow" of an appreciable amount of interstate commerce. The Court recognized that there were some agreements whose validity depended on the surrounding circumstances. It emphasized, however, that there were classes of restraints which from their "nature or character" were unduly restrictive, and hence forbidden by both the common law and the statute. As to these classes of restraints, the Court noted, Congress had determined its own criteria of public harm and it was not for the courts to decide whether in an individual case injury had actually occurred.

Group boycotts, or concerted refusals by traders to deal with other traders, have long been held to be in the forbidden category. They have not been saved by allegations that they were reasonable in the specific circumstances, nor by a failure to show that they "fixed or regulated prices, parcelled out or limited production, or brought about a deterioration in quality." Fashion Originators' Guild v. Federal Trade Comm'n. Cf. United States v. Trenton Potteries Co. Even when they operated to lower prices or temporarily to stimulate competition they were banned. For, as this Court said in Kiefer-Stewart Co. v. Joseph E. Seagram & Sons, "such agreements * * * cripple the freedom of traders and thereby restrain their ability to sell in accordance with their own judgment."

Plainly the allegations of this complaint disclose such a boycott. This is not a case of a single trader refusing to deal with another, nor even of a manufacturer and a dealer agreeing to an exclusive distributorship. Alleged in this complaint is a wide combination consisting of manufacturers, distributors and a retailer. This combination takes from Klor's its freedom to buy appliances in an open competitive market and drives it out of business as a dealer in the defendants' products. It deprives the manufacturers and distributors of their freedom to sell to Klor's at the same prices and conditions made available to Broadway-Hale, and in some instances forbids them from selling to it on any terms whatsoever. It interferes with the natural flow of interstate commerce. It clearly has, by its "nature" and "character," a "monopolistic tendency." As such it is not to be tolerated merely because the victim is just one merchant whose business is so small that his destruction makes little difference to the economy. Monopoly can as surely thrive by the elimination of such small businessmen, one at a time, as it can by driving them out in large groups. In recognition of this fact the Sherman Act has consistently been read to forbid all contracts and combinations "which 'tend to create a monopoly,' " whether "the tendency is a creeping one" or "one that proceeds at full gallop." International Salt Co. v. United States.

The judgment of the Court of Appeals is reversed and the cause is remanded to the District Court for trial.

MR. JUSTICE HARLAN, believing that the allegations of the complaint are sufficient to entitle the petitioner to go to trial, and that the matters set forth in respondents' affidavits are not necessarily sufficient to constitute a defense irrespective of what the petitioner may be able to prove at the trial, concurs in the result.

NOTES AND QUESTIONS

1.   What was going on in the appliance business on Mission Street in San Francisco?

a.   What kind of store was George Klor running? Do you suppose he had a fancy showroom? Do you suppose he had lots of floor samples and explained the features of the appliances he sold? Do you suppose he had lower prices than stores like Broadway-Hale's?

b.   Did the Court dismiss too quickly Broadway-Hale's defense that this was a "purely private quarrel" between stores that did not create a "public harm"? Is there a good argument that not every unfair business practice should constitute a federal antitrust violation? If there is no discernable public harm, would any judicial error necessarily be a Type 1 error?[75]

c.   On the other hand, are most antitrust cases at some level "purely private" disputes? Did San Francisco consumers likely have fewer appliances and higher prices as a result of what Broadway-Hale had done? If this case had come out the other way, could discount retailers like K-Mart and Wal-Mart have gotten started nearly as easily?

2.   Who were Broadway-Hale's co-conspirators alleged to be in this case?

a.   Were the appliance manufacturers co-conspirators of Broadway-Hale or were they also victims of its market power? Should that matter for purposes of construing the § 1 requirement of a "contract, combination or conspiracy"?

b.   Do you suppose that manufacturers were indifferent to the rise of discount merchandising? Would they be likely to have welcomed it or feared it? Quite apart from the fact that Broadway-Hale was bigger than Klor's, might the fact that it performed more customer service have made its good will important to the manufacturers? Indeed, would it be fair to call Klor's a "free rider" if it encouraged customers, in effect, to "look next door, but shop at Klor's"?

c.   Is this case like any other § 2 case that we have seen? Is it like *Standard Oil* in which contract provisions allegedly denied new refiners and

---

[75]   Professor Keith Hylton calls the fact of private injury but lack of public harm "the Klor's paradox." He discusses reasons antitrust law should and should not intervene in such cases in Keith N. Hylton, Antitrust Law: Economic Theory and Common Law Evolution 174–77 (2003).

new drillers the ability to get access to railroads and pipelines? If so, does it matter whether Broadway-Hale had co-conspirators or did not?

3.   On the other hand, should group boycotts such as this be per se illegal? Should the real issues in these cases be whether the objectives of the group action are reasonable and whether their means are no more anticompetitive than necessary? Broadway-Hale might still be found guilty, of course, but the process of getting to that result might reduce the risk of Type 1 error.

2.   RESALE PRICE MAINTENANCE

Discount selling has been a reality in many industries since at least the 1950s, and the firm in our next case tried to address the *Klor's* kind of issue by agreement rather than boycott.

UNITED STATES V. PARKE, DAVIS & CO.

Supreme Court of the United States, 1960
362 U.S. 29, 80 S.Ct. 503, 4 L.Ed.2d 505

MR. JUSTICE BRENNAN delivered the opinion of the Court.

The Government sought an injunction * * * against the appellee, Parke, Davis & Company, on a complaint alleging that Parke Davis conspired and combined, in violation of §§ 1 and 3 of the [Sherman] Act, with retail and wholesale druggists in Washington, D.C., and Richmond, Virginia, to maintain the wholesale and retail prices of Parke Davis pharmaceutical products. After the Government completed the presentation of its evidence at the trial, * * * the District Court * * * dismissed the complaint * * * on the ground that upon the facts and the law the Government had not shown a right to relief. * * *

Parke Davis makes some 600 pharmaceutical products which it markets nationally through drug wholesalers and drug retailers. The retailers buy these products from the drug wholesalers or make large quantity purchases directly from Parke Davis. Sometime before 1956 Parke Davis announced a resale price maintenance policy in its wholesalers' and retailers' catalogues. The wholesalers' catalogue contained a Net Price Selling Schedule listing suggested minimum resale prices on Parke Davis products sold by wholesalers to retailers. The catalogue stated that it was Parke Davis' continuing policy to deal only with drug wholesalers who observed that schedule and who sold only to drug retailers authorized by law to fill prescriptions. Parke Davis, when selling directly to retailers, quoted the same prices listed in the wholesalers' Net Price Selling Schedule but granted retailers discounts for volume purchases. Wholesalers were not authorized to grant similar discounts. The retailers' catalogue contained a schedule of minimum retail prices applicable in States with Fair Trade Laws[76] and stated that this schedule was suggested for use also in States not having such laws. These suggested minimum retail prices usually provided a 50% markup over cost on Parke Davis products purchased by retailers from wholesalers but, because of the volume discount, often in excess of 100% markup over cost on products purchased in large quantities directly from Parke Davis.

There are some 260 drugstores in Washington, D.C., and some 100 in Richmond, Virginia. Many of the stores are units of Peoples Drug Stores, a large retail drug chain. There are five drug wholesalers handling Parke Davis products in the locality who do business with the drug retailers. The wholesalers observed the resale prices suggested by Parke Davis. However, during the spring and early summer of 1956 drug retailers in the two cities advertised and sold several Parke Davis vitamin products at prices substantially below the suggested minimum retail prices; in some instances the prices apparently reflected the volume discounts on direct purchases from Parke Davis since the products were sold below the prices listed in the wholesalers' Net Price Selling Schedule. The Baltimore office manager of Parke Davis in charge of the sales district which included the two cities sought advice from his head office on how to handle this situation. The Parke Davis attorney advised that the company could legally "enforce an adopted policy arrived at unilaterally" to sell only to customers who observed the suggested minimum resale prices. He further advised that this meant that "we can lawfully say 'we will sell you only so long as you observe such minimum retail prices' but cannot say 'we will sell you only if you agree to observe such minimum retail prices,' since except as permitted by Fair Trade legislations [sic] agreements as to resale price maintenance are invalid." Thereafter in July the branch manager put into effect a program for promoting observance of the suggested minimum retail prices by the retailers involved. The program contemplated the participation of the five drug wholesalers. In order to insure that retailers who did not comply would be cut off from sources of supply, representatives of Parke Davis visited the wholesalers and told them, in effect, that not only would Parke Davis refuse to sell to wholesalers who did not adhere to the policy announced in its catalogue, but also that it would refuse to sell to wholesalers who sold Parke Davis products to retailers who did not observe the suggested minimum retail prices. Each wholesaler was

---

76 [Ed. note] Fair Trade Laws were state statutes that allowed the manufacturer of a trademarked item to contract with retail dealers to establish the item's resale price. Originally passed during the depression to protect small retailers against "loss-leader" sales of popular products by larger stores, Fair Trade was specifically acknowledged as an exception to the Sherman Act by the Miller-Tydings Amendment to § 1, 50 Stat. 693 (1937). Soon, all but three states had Fair Trade legislation, and after the Supreme Court decision in Schwegmann Bros. v. Calvert Distillers Corp., Congress passed the McGuire Act, 66 Stat. 632 (1952), to extend the Sherman Act exception even to state legislation that imposed resale price maintenance on non-signers. However, methods of mass retailing have changed and so has Congressional support for Fair Trade. Both exemptions were repealed by the Consumer Goods Pricing Act, 89 Stat. 801 (1975); there are no state Fair Trade Laws today.

interviewed individually but each was informed that his competitors were also being apprised of this. The wholesalers without exception indicated a willingness to go along.

Representatives called contemporaneously upon the retailers involved, individually, and told each that if he did not observe the suggested minimum retail prices, Parke Davis would refuse to deal with him, and that furthermore he would be unable to purchase any Parke Davis products from the wholesalers. Each of the retailers was also told that his competitors were being similarly informed.

Several retailers refused to give any assurances of compliance and continued after these July interviews to advertise and sell Parke Davis products at prices below the suggested minimum retail prices. Their names were furnished by Parke Davis to the wholesalers. Thereafter Parke Davis refused to fill direct orders from such retailers and the wholesalers likewise refused to fill their orders. This ban was not limited to the Parke Davis products being sold below the suggested minimum prices but included all the company's products, even those necessary to fill prescriptions.

The president of Dart Drug Company, one of the retailers cut off, protested to the assistant branch manager of Parke Davis that Parke Davis was discriminating against him because a drugstore across the street, one of the Peoples Drug chain, had a sign in its window advertising Parke Davis products at cut prices. The retailer was told that if this were so the branch manager "would see Peoples and try to get them in line." The branch manager testified at the trial that thereafter he talked to a vice-president of Peoples and that the following occurred:

> "Q. Well, now, you told Mr. Downey [the vice president of Peoples] at this meeting, did you not, Mr. Powers, [the assistant branch manager of Parke Davis] that you noticed that Peoples were cutting prices?
>
> "A. Yes.
>
> "Q. And you told him, did you not, that it had been the Parke, Davis policy for many years to do business only with individuals that maintained the scheduled prices?
>
> "A. I told Mr. Downey that we had a policy in our catalog, and that anyone that did not go along with our policy, we were not interested in doing business with them.
>
> * * *
>
> "Q. * * * Now, Mr. Downey told you on the occasion of this visit, did he not, that Peoples would stop cutting prices and would abide by the Parke-Davis policy, is that right?
>
> "A. That is correct.

* * *

"Q. When you went to call on Mr. Downey, you solicited his support of Parke, Davis policies, is not that right?

"A. That is right.

"Q. And he said, I will abide by your policy?

"A. That is right."

The District Court found, apparently on the basis of this testimony, that "The Peoples' representative stated that Peoples would stop cutting prices on Parke, Davis' products and Parke, Davis continued to sell to Peoples."

But five retailers continued selling Parke Davis products at less than the suggested minimum prices from stocks on hand. Within a few weeks Parke Davis modified its program. Its officials believed that the selling at discount prices would be deterred, and the effects minimized of any isolated instances of discount selling which might continue, if all advertising of such prices were discontinued. In August the Parke Davis representatives again called on the retailers individually. When interviewed, the president of Dart Drug Company indicated that he might be willing to stop advertising, although continuing to sell at discount prices, if shipments to him were resumed. Each of the other retailers was then told individually by Parke Davis representatives that Dart was ready to discontinue advertising. Each thereupon said that if Dart stopped advertising he would also. On August 28 Parke Davis reported this reaction to Dart. Thereafter all of the retailers discontinued advertising of Parke Davis vitamins at less than suggested minimum retail prices and Parke Davis and the wholesalers resumed sales of Parke Davis products to them. However, the suspension of advertising lasted only a month. One of the retailers again started newspaper advertising in September and, despite efforts of Parke Davis to prevent it, the others quickly followed suit. Parke Davis then stopped trying to promote the retailers' adherence to its suggested resale prices, and neither it nor the wholesalers have since declined further dealings with them. A reason for this was that the Department of Justice, on complaint of Dart Drug Company, had begun an investigation of possible violation of the antitrust laws.

The District Court held that the Government's proofs did not establish a violation of the Sherman Act because "the actions of [Parke Davis] were properly unilateral and sanctioned by law under the doctrine laid down in the case of United States v. Colgate & Co."

* * *

The Government concedes for the purposes of this case that under the *Colgate* doctrine a manufacturer, having announced a price maintenance policy, may bring about adherence to it by refusing to deal with customers who do not observe that policy. The Government contends, however, that subsequent decisions of this Court compel the holding that what Parke Davis did here by entwining the wholesalers and retailers in a program to promote general compliance with its price maintenance policy went beyond mere customer selection and created combinations or conspiracies to enforce resale price maintenance in violation of §§ 1 and 3 of the Sherman Act.

The history of the *Colgate* doctrine is best understood by reference to a case which preceded the *Colgate* decision, Dr. Miles Medical Co. v. Park & Sons Co. Dr. Miles entered into written contracts with its customers obligating them to sell its medicine at prices fixed by it. The Court held that the contracts were void because they violated both the common law and the Sherman Act. The *Colgate* decision distinguished *Dr. Miles* on the ground that the *Colgate* indictment did not charge that company with selling its products to dealers *under agreements* which obligated the latter not to resell except at prices fixed by the seller. The *Colgate* decision created some confusion and doubt as to the continuing vitality of the principles announced in *Dr. Miles*.

The Court went on to explain [in United States v. Schrader's Son, Inc., 252 U.S. 85 (1920), however], that the statement from *Colgate* quoted earlier in this opinion meant no more than that a manufacturer is not guilty of a combination or conspiracy if he merely "indicates his wishes concerning prices and declines further dealings with all who fail to observe them * * * "; however there is unlawful combination where a manufacturer "enters into agreements—whether express or implied from a course of dealing or other circumstances—with all customers * * * which undertake to bind them to observe fixed resale prices."

* * *

* * * The Sherman Act forbids combinations of traders to suppress competition. True, there results the same economic effect as is accomplished by a prohibited combination to suppress price competition if each customer, although induced to do so solely by a manufacturer's announced policy, independently decides to observe specified resale prices. So long as *Colgate* is not overruled, this result is tolerated but only when it is the consequence of a mere refusal to sell in the exercise of the manufacturer's right "freely to exercise his own independent discretion as to parties with whom he will deal." When the manufacturer's actions, as here, go beyond mere announcement of this policy and the simple refusal to deal, and he employs other means which effect adherence to his resale prices, this countervailing consideration is not present and therefore he has put together a combination in violation of the Sherman Act. Thus, whether an unlawful combination or conspiracy is proved is to be judged by what the parties actually did rather than by the words they used. * * *

The program upon which Parke Davis embarked to promote general compliance with its suggested resale prices plainly exceeded the limitations of the *Colgate* doctrine * * * . Parke Davis did not content itself with announcing its policy regarding retail prices and following this with a simple refusal to have business relations with any retailers who disregarded that policy. Instead Parke Davis used the refusal to deal with the wholesalers in order to elicit their willingness to deny Parke Davis products to retailers and thereby help gain the retailers' adherence to its suggested minimum retail prices. The retailers who disregarded the price policy were promptly cut off when Parke Davis supplied the wholesalers with their names. The large retailer who said he would "abide" by the price policy, the multi-unit Peoples Drug chain, was not cut off. In thus involving the wholesalers to stop the flow of Parke Davis products to the retailers, thereby inducing retailers' adherence to its suggested retail prices, Parke Davis created a combination with the retailers and the wholesalers to maintain retail prices and violated the Sherman Act. Although Parke Davis' originally announced wholesalers' policy would not under *Colgate* have violated the Sherman Act if its action thereunder was the simple refusal without more to deal with wholesalers who did not observe the wholesalers' Net Price Selling Schedule, that entire policy was tainted with the "vice of * * * illegality," when Parke Davis used it as the vehicle to gain the wholesalers' participation in the program to effectuate the retailers' adherence to the suggested retail prices.

Moreover, Parke Davis also exceeded the "limited dispensation which [*Colgate*] confers" in another way, which demonstrates how far Parke Davis went beyond the limits of the *Colgate* doctrine. With regard to the retailers' suspension of advertising, Parke Davis did not rest with the simple announcement to the trade of its policy in that regard followed by a refusal to sell to the retailers who would not observe it. First it discussed the subject with Dart Drug. When Dart indicated willingness to go along the other retailers were approached and Dart's apparent willingness to cooperate was used as the lever to gain their acquiescence in the program. Having secured those acquiescences Parke Davis returned to Dart Drug with the report of that accomplishment. Not until all this was done was the advertising suspended and sales to all the retailers resumed. In this manner Parke Davis sought assurances of compliance and got them, as well as the compliance itself. It was only by actively bringing about substantial unanimity among the competitors that Parke Davis was able to gain adherence to its policy. It must be admitted that a seller's announcement that he will not deal with customers who do not observe his policy may tend to engender confidence in each customer that if he complies his competitors will also. But if a manufacturer is unwilling to rely on individual self-interest to bring about general voluntary acquiescence which has the collateral effect of eliminating price competition, and takes affirmative action to achieve uniform adherence by inducing each customer to adhere to avoid such price competition, the customers' acquiescence is not then a matter of individual free choice prompted alone by the desirability of the product. The product then comes packaged in a competition-free wrapping—a valuable feature in itself—by virtue of concerted action induced by the manufacturer. The manufacturer is thus the organizer of a price-maintenance combination or conspiracy in violation of the Sherman Act. * * *

* * *

The judgment is reversed and the case remanded to the District Court with directions to enter an appropriate judgment enjoining Parke Davis from further violations of the Sherman Act unless the company * * * refutes the Government's right to injunctive relief established by the present record.

MR. JUSTICE STEWART, concurring.

I concur in the judgment. The Court's opinion amply demonstrates that the present record shows an illegal combination to maintain retail prices. I therefore find no occasion to question, even by innuendo, the continuing validity of the *Colgate* decision * * * .

MR. JUSTICE HARLAN, whom MR. JUSTICE FRANKFURTER and MR. JUSTICE WHITTAKER join, dissenting.

The Court's opinion reaches much further than at once may meet the eye, and justifies fuller discussion than otherwise might appear warranted. Scrutiny of the opinion will reveal that the Court has done no less than send to its demise the *Colgate* doctrine which has been a basic part of antitrust law concepts since it was first announced in 1919 * * * .

* * *

* * * [Here, the District Court] determined with respect to each of the four facets of the alleged conspiracy that "there was no coercion" and that "Parke, Davis did not combine, conspire or enter into an agreement, understanding or concert of action" with the wholesalers, retailers, or anyone else. I cannot detect in the record any indication that the District Court in making these findings applied anything other than the standard which has always been understood to govern prosecutions based on §§ 1 and 3 of the Sherman Act.

* * *

* * * I think that what the Court has really done here is to throw the *Colgate* doctrine into discard.

To be sure, the Government has explicitly stated that it does not ask us to overrule *Colgate*, and the Court professes not to do so. But contrary to the long understanding of bench and bar, the Court treats *Colgate* as turning not on the absence of the concerted action explicitly required by

§§ 1 and 3 of the Sherman Act, but upon the Court's notion of "countervailing" social policies. I can regard the Court's profession as no more than a bow to the fact that *Colgate*, decided more than 40 years ago, has become part of the economic regime of the country upon which the commercial community and the lawyers who advise it have justifiably relied.

If the principle for which *Colgate* stands is to be reversed, it is, as the Government's position plainly indicates, something that should be left to the Congress. It is surely the emptiest of formalisms to profess respect for *Colgate* and eviscerate it in application.

I would affirm.

NOTES AND QUESTIONS

1. This was the case that, at least for a while, made the *Colgate* rule largely an historical artifact.

a. How did Parke Davis organize its distribution system in the Washington/Richmond area and how did it communicate the prices it wanted its distributors to charge?

b. Where did its system break down? Is it almost inevitable that a large organization will first hear about discount pricing through complaints from other dealers?

c. Was the legal advice given the manager sent to deal with this situation sound under then-current law? Was it practical to say Parke Davis would sell to dealers "so long as" they adhered to the net price selling schedule but not to say it will sell "only if" a firm agreed to adhere to the selling schedule?

2. If you had been Parke Davis, how would you have defended what your firm did?

a. Could you have argued that there is no way in real life to act pursuant to *Colgate* other than by talking to people and making one's position clear? Is the Court here inevitably overruling *Colgate* at least as applied to large companies?

b. Was it clear that Parke Davis was doing something *it* wanted to do, not just enforcing a cartel among its dealers? Why would Parke Davis have wanted to prevent discount selling of its products? Wouldn't Parke Davis prosper as the volume of sales went up?

3. Notice that in all of this, the focus is on the method by which Parke Davis acted rather than on whether the scheme restrained trade or had any social value. What is the argument that protecting its non-discounting dealers had few if any negative effects on consumers?

a. Can one argue that the market for vitamins and other over-the-counter drug store items is competitive? If someone cannot get Parke Davis' items inexpensively, can't she get another brand? Isn't Parke Davis' pricing freedom limited by its competitors' prices? Remember, of course, that Justice Holmes made all these points in vain in *Dr. Miles*.

b.   Might one answer that advertising differentiates consumer products so much that Parke Davis products are unique and the market offers little constraint on price?

c.   Suppose you knew that the Parke Davis plan would help keep small pharmacies in business and slow the growth of giant chains. Would that make the market more competitive or less? Would it further or impair other social values?

d.   Should the result in this case be different if Parke Davis had "consigned" its products to the pharmacies, a practice the Court had seemed to approve in *General Electric*? You may want to wait to answer until you have read our next case.

SIMPSON V. UNION OIL CO. OF CALIFORNIA

Supreme Court of the United States, 1964
377 U.S. 13, 84 S.Ct. 1051, 12 L.Ed.2d 98

MR. JUSTICE DOUGLAS delivered the opinion of the Court.

This is a suit for damages under § 4 of the Clayton Act for violation of §§ 1 and 2 of the Sherman Act. The complaint grows out of a so-called retail dealer "consignment" agreement which, it is alleged, Union Oil requires lessees of its retail outlets to sign, of which Simpson was one. The "consignment" agreement is for one year and thereafter until canceled, is terminable by either party at the end of any year and, by its terms, ceases upon any termination of the lease. The lease is also for one year; and it is alleged that it is used to police the retail prices charged by the consignees, renewals not being made if the conditions prescribed by the company are not met. The company, pursuant to the "consignment" agreement, set the prices at which the retailer sells the gasoline. While "title" to the consigned gasoline "shall remain in Consignor until sold by Consignee," and while the company pays all property taxes on all gasoline in possession of Simpson, he must carry personal liability and property damage insurance by reason of the "consigned" gasoline and is responsible for all losses of the "consigned" gasoline in his possession, save for specified acts of God. Simpson is compensated by a minimum commission and pays all the costs of operation in the familiar manner.

The retail price fixed by the company for the gasoline during the period in question was 29.9 cents per gallon; and Simpson, despite the company's demand that he adhere to the authorized price, sold it at 27.9 cents, allegedly to meet a competitive price. Solely because Simpson sold gasoline below the fixed price, Union Oil refused to renew the lease; termination of the "consignment" agreement ensued; and this suit was filed. The terms of the lease and "consignment" agreement are not in dispute nor the method of their application in this case. The interstate character of Union Oil's business is conceded, as is the extensive use by it of the lease-consignment agreement in eight western States.

* * * The District Court, concluding that "all the factual disputes" had been eliminated from the case, entertained * * * motions [for summary judgment]. The District Court granted the company's motion and denied Simpson's, holding as to the latter that he had not established a violation of the Sherman Act and, even assuming such a violation, that he had not suffered any actionable damage. The Court of Appeals affirmed. * * * The case is here on a writ of certiorari.

We disagree * * * that there is no actionable wrong or damage if a Sherman Act violation is assumed. If the "consignment" agreement achieves resale price maintenance in violation of the Sherman Act, it and the lease are being used to injure interstate commerce by depriving independent dealers of the exercise of free judgment whether to become consignees at all, or remain consignees, and, in any event, to sell at competitive prices. The fact that a retailer can refuse to deal does not give the supplier immunity if the arrangement is one of those schemes condemned by the antitrust laws.

There is actionable wrong whenever the restraint of trade or monopolistic practice has an impact on the market; and it matters not that the complainant may be only one merchant. See Klor's v. Broadway-Hale Stores. * * *

The fact that, on failure to renew a lease, another dealer takes Simpson's place and renders the same service to the public is no * * * answer here * * *. For Congress, not the oil distributor, is the arbiter of the public interest; and Congress has closely patrolled price fixing whether effected through resale price maintenance agreements or otherwise. The exclusive requirements contracts struck down in Standard Oil Co. [Calif.] v. United States, were not saved because dealers need not have agreed to them, but could have gone elsewhere. If that were a defense, a supplier could regiment thousands of otherwise competitive dealers in resale price maintenance programs merely by fear of nonrenewal of short-term leases.

We made clear in United States v. Parke, Davis & Co. that a supplier may not use coercion on its retail outlets to achieve resale price maintenance. We reiterate that view, adding that it matters not what the coercive device is. * * * Here we have * * * an agreement; it is used coercively, and, it promises to be equally if not more effective in maintaining gasoline prices than were the Parke, Davis techniques in fixing monopoly prices on drugs.

Consignments perform an important function in trade and commerce, and their integrity has been recognized by many courts, including this one.

Yet consignments, though useful in allocating risks between the parties and determining their rights inter se, do not necessarily control the rights of others, whether they be creditors or sovereigns. * * *

One who sends a rug or a painting or other work of art to a merchant or a gallery for sale at a minimum price can, of course, hold the consignee to the bargain. A retail merchant may, indeed, have inventory on consignment, the terms of which bind the parties inter se. Yet the consignor does not always prevail over creditors in case of bankruptcy, where a recording statute or a "traders act" or a "sign statute" is in effect. The interests of the Government also frequently override agreements that private parties make. Here we have an antitrust policy expressed in Acts of Congress. Accordingly, a consignment, no matter how lawful it might be as a matter of private contract law, must give way before the federal antitrust policy. * * *

We are enlightened on present-day marketing methods by recent congressional investigations. In the automobile field the price is "the manufacturer's suggested retail price," not a price coercively exacted; nor do automobiles go on consignment; they are sold. Resale price maintenance of gasoline through the "consignment" device is increasing. * * * The theory and practice of gasoline price fixing in vogue under the "consignment" agreement has been well exposed by Congress. A Union Oil official in recent testimony before a House Committee on Small Business explained the price mechanism:

> "Mr. ROOSEVELT. Who sets the price in your consignment station, dealer consignment station?
>
> "Mr. RATH. We do.
>
> "Mr. ROOSEVELT. You do?
>
> "Mr. RATH. Yes. We do it on this basis: You see, he is paid a commission to sell these products for us. Now, we go out into the market area and find out what the competitive major price is, what that level is, and we set our house-brand price at that."

Dealers, like Simpson, are independent businessmen; and they have all or most of the indicia of entrepreneurs, except for price fixing. The risk of loss of the gasoline is on them, apart from acts of God. Their return is affected by the rise and fall in the market price, their commissions declining as retail prices drop. Practically the only power they have to be wholly independent businessmen, whose service depends on their own initiative and enterprise, is taken from them by the proviso that they must sell their gasoline at prices fixed by Union Oil. By reason of the lease and "consignment" agreement dealers are coercively laced into an arrangement under which their supplier is able to impose noncompetitive prices on thousands of persons whose prices otherwise might be competitive. The evil of this resale price maintenance program, like that of the requirements contracts held illegal by Standard Oil Co. [Calif.] v. United States, is its inexorable potentiality for and even certainty in destroying competition in retail sales of gasoline by these nominal "consignees" who are in reality small struggling competitors seeking retail gas customers.

As we have said, an owner of an article may send it to a dealer who may in turn undertake to sell it only at a price determined by the owner. There is nothing illegal about that arrangement. When, however, a "consignment" device is used to cover a vast gasoline distribution system, fixing prices through many retail outlets, the antitrust laws prevent calling the "consignment" an agency, for then the end result of United States v. Socony-Vacuum Oil Co. would be avoided merely by clever manipulation of words, not by differences in substance. The present, coercive "consignment" device, if successful against challenge under the antitrust laws, furnishes a wooden formula for administering prices on a vast scale.

Reliance is placed on United States v. General Electric Co., where a consignment arrangement was utilized to market patented articles. Union Oil correctly argues that the consignment in that case somewhat parallels the one in the instant case. The Court in the *General Electric* case did not restrict its ruling to patented articles; it, indeed, said that the use of the consignment device was available to the owners of articles "patented or otherwise." But whatever may be said of the *General Electric* case on its special facts, involving patents, it is not apposite to the special facts here.

The Court in that case particularly relied on the fact that patent rights have long included licenses "to make, use and vend" the patented article "for any royalty or upon any condition the performance of which is reasonably within the reward which the patentee by the grant of the patent is entitled to secure." * * *

* * * Long prior to the *General Electric* case, price fixing in the marketing of patented articles had been condoned (Bement v. National Harrow Co.), provided it did not extend to sales by purchasers of the patented articles.

The patent laws which give a 17-year monopoly on "making, using, or selling the invention" are in pari materia with the antitrust laws and modify them pro tanto. That was the ratio decidendi of the *General Electric* case. We decline the invitation to extend it.

* * *

Hence on the issue of resale price maintenance under the Sherman Act there is nothing left to try, for there was an agreement for resale price maintenance, coercively employed.

The case must be remanded for a hearing on all the other issues in the case, including * * * the damages, if any, suffered. * * * We reserve the question whether, when all the facts are known, there may be any equities that would warrant only prospective application in damage suits of the rule governing price fixing by the "consignment" device which we announce today.

MR. JUSTICE HARLAN took no part in the disposition of this case.

MR. JUSTICE STEWART, dissenting.

* * *

* * * I * * * agree with the Court that the judgment of the Court of Appeals should be set aside and the case remanded to the District Court for a trial on the merits. But I think that upon remand there should be a full trial of all the issues in this litigation, because I completely disagree with the Court that whenever a bona fide consignor, employing numerous agents, sets the price at which his property is to be sold, "the antitrust laws prevent calling the 'consignment' an agency," and transform the consignment into a sale. In the present posture of this case, such a determination, overruling as it does a doctrine which has stood unquestioned for almost 40 years, is unwarranted, unnecessary and premature.

In United States v. General Electric, this Court held that a bona fide consignment agreement of this kind does not violate the Sherman Act. The Court today concedes that "the consignment in that case somewhat parallels the one in the instant case." The fact of the matter is, so far as the record now before us discloses, the two agreements are virtually indistinguishable. Instead of expressly overruling *General Electric*, however, the Court seeks to distinguish that case upon the specious ground that its underpinnings rest on patent law.

It is, of course, true that what was sold in *General Electric* was not gasoline, but lamp bulbs which had been manufactured under a patent. But until today no one has ever considered this fact relevant to the holding in that case that bona fide consignment agreements do not violate the antitrust laws "however comprehensive as a mass or whole in their effect * * * ." In addition to the unambiguous statement in Chief Justice Taft's opinion for a unanimous Court that "[the] owner of an article, patented or otherwise, is not violating the common law, or the Anti-Trust law, by seeking to dispose of his article directly to the consumer and fixing the price by which his agents transfer the title from him directly to such consumer," the Court, throughout that portion of its opinion dealing with the validity of General Electric's consignment agreements, gave no intimation whatsoever that its conclusion would have differed in any respect if the consigned article had been unpatented. * * *

* * *

* * * It is not by virtue of a patent monopoly that a bona fide consignor may control the price at which his consignee sells; his control over price flows from the simple fact that the owner of goods, so long as he remains the owner, has the unquestioned right to determine the price at which he will sell them.

It is clear, therefore, that the Court today overrules *General Electric*. It does so, even though the validity of that decision was not challenged in the briefs or in oral argument in this case. * * * We cannot be blind to the fact that commercial arrangements throughout our economy are shaped in reliance upon this Court's decisions elaborating the reach of the antitrust laws. Everyone knows that consignment selling is a widely used method of distribution all over the country. By our decision today outlawing consignment selling if it includes a price limitation, we inject severe uncertainty into commercial relationships established in reliance upon a decision of this Court explicitly validating this method of distribution. We create, as well, the distinct possibility that an untold number of sellers of goods will be subjected to liability in treble damage suits because they thought they could rely on the validity of this Court's decisions.

* * *

After a trial on the merits it may be determined that the scheme here involved, although on its face a bona fide lease-and-consignment agreement, was in actual operation and effect a system of resale price maintenance. Or the District Court after a trial might find that despite the formal provisions of the lease-and-consignment agreement, there actually existed here some coercive arrangement otherwise violative of the antitrust laws. In either event, the question of the petitioner's damages would then become an issue to be determined. Only if all these issues, and perhaps others, were resolved in favor of the respondent, would there be presented the question of the continuing validity of the *General Electric* doctrine. Consequently, re-examination of that case should certainly await another day.

I would vacate the judgment of the Court of Appeals and remand this case to the District Court for a plenary trial of all the issues.

Memorandum of MR. JUSTICE BRENNAN and MR. JUSTICE GOLDBERG. * * * We * * * agree with MR. JUSTICE STEWART and would vacate the judgment of the Court of Appeals and remand this case to the District Court for a plenary trial of all the issues.

NOTES AND QUESTIONS

1. When all is said and done here, what does the court say is wrong with the consignment system, at least in this industry?

a. Does it seem odd to have the retail dealers portrayed as victims? Was there evidence large numbers of them were complaining about being coerced into having their profit margins protected by Union Oil?

b.   Do you agree that, regardless of the formal structure of the arrangements, the purpose and effect of this method of dealing was to transform the independent decisions of retailers into the single decision of the oil company?

2.   Are there particular reasons we should worry about resale price maintenance in an industry like this one?

a.   Do you agree with Justice Douglas that the system facilitates oligopoly pricing? Instead of gas prices being set by thousands of dealers independently, does this plan mean they will be set by a relatively few companies?

b.   Was Justice Douglas' position here predictable after the position he took on exclusive dealing contracts in *Standard Stations*? Was that also a case about keeping dealers independent?

c.   Is there any kind of consignment that Justice Douglas and the Court would uphold? Do you agree that consignments of paintings or rugs present no similar restraint of trade? Is that because they tend not to facilitate oligopoly pricing? Is there any other reason?

3.   Does Justice Douglas deal fairly with the *General Electric* precedent?

a.   Did the Court that decided *General Electric* mean to limit it to patent cases? Was the rationale used there really based on the special rights of patent holders, in spite of the fact that the Court said its rule was broader? Is Justice Douglas simply adopting the conservative approach of limiting *General Electric* to its holding instead of its reasoning and dicta?

b.   Is Justice Stewart right that the Court here effectively overrules *General Electric*? Should such a result have unfairly surprised well-advised firms? Would you have been surprised to see this case come out the other way?

4.   Are the dissenting justices right that the reality of a particular consignment arrangement is a factual issue that should not be decided on summary judgment? If *Klor's* and *Fortner* were cases that could not be decided on summary judgment, why was there a basis for doing so here?

3.   TERRITORIAL ALLOCATION

About the time it seemed that the per se rule had no exceptions, no less a personage than Justice Douglas showed us the risk of jumping to conclusions.

WHITE MOTOR CO. v. UNITED STATES

Supreme Court of the United States, 1963
372 U.S. 253, 83 S.Ct. 696, 9 L.Ed.2d 738

MR. JUSTICE DOUGLAS delivered the opinion of the Court.

This is a civil suit under the antitrust laws that was decided below on a motion for summary judgment. * * *

* * *

Appellant manufactures trucks and sells them (and parts) to distributors, to dealers, and to various large users. Both the distributors and dealers sell trucks (and parts) to users. Moreover, some distributors resell trucks (and parts) to dealers, selected with appellant's consent. All of the dealers sell trucks (and parts) only to users. The principal practices charged as violations of §§ 1 and 3 of the Sherman Act concern limitations or restrictions on the territories within which distributors or dealers may sell and limitations or restrictions on the persons or classes of persons to whom they may sell. Typical of the territorial clause is the following:

"Distributor is hereby granted the exclusive right, except as hereinafter provided, to sell during the life of this agreement, in the territory described below, White and Autocar trucks purchased from Company hereunder.

"STATE OF CALIFORNIA: Territory to consist of all of Sonoma County, south of a line starting at the western boundary, or Pacific Coast, passing through the City of Bodega, and extending due east to the east boundary line of Sonoma County, with the exception of the sale of fire truck chassis to the State of California and all political subdivisions thereof.

"Distributor agrees to develop the aforementioned territory to the satisfaction of Company, and not to sell any trucks purchased hereunder except in accordance with this agreement, and not to sell such trucks except to individuals, firms, or corporations having a place of business and/or purchasing headquarters in said territory."

Typical of the *customer clause* is the following:

"Distributor further agrees not to sell nor to authorize his dealers to sell such trucks to any Federal or State government or any department or political subdivision thereof, unless the right to do so is specifically granted by Company in writing."

These provisions, applicable to distributors and dealers alike, are claimed by appellee to be per se violations of the Sherman Act. The District Court adopted that view and granted summary judgment accordingly. We noted probable jurisdiction.

Appellant, in arguing for a trial of the case on the merits, made the following representations to the District Court: the territorial clauses are necessary in order for appellant to compete with those who make other competitory [sic] kinds of trucks; appellant could theoretically have its own retail outlets throughout the country and sell to users directly; that method, however, is not feasible as it entails a costly and extensive sales organization; the only feasible method is the distributor or dealer system;

for that system to be effective against the existing competition of the larger companies, a distributor or dealer must make vigorous and intensive efforts in a restricted territory, and if he is to be held responsible for energetic performance, it is fair, reasonable, and necessary that appellant protect him against invasions of his territory by other distributors or dealers of appellant; that appellant in order to obtain maximum sales in a given area must insist that its distributors and dealers concentrate on trying to take sales away from other competing truck manufacturers rather than from each other. * * *

As to the customer clauses, appellant represented to the District Court that one of their purposes was to assure appellant "that 'national accounts,' 'fleet accounts' and Federal and State governments and departments and political subdivisions thereof, which are classes of customers with respect to which the defendant is in especially severe competition with the manufacturers of other makes of trucks and which are likely to have a continuing volume of orders to place, shall not be deprived of their appropriate discounts on their purchases of repair parts and accessories from any distributor or dealer, with the result of becoming discontented with The White Motor Company and the treatment they receive with reference to the prices of repair parts and accessories for White trucks."

* * *

In this Court appellant defends the customer clauses on the ground that "the only sure way to make certain that something really important is done right, is to do it for oneself. The size of the orders, the technicalities of bidding and delivery, and other factors all play a part in this decision."

* * *

Where the sale of an unpatented product is tied to a patented article, that is a per se violation since it is a bald effort to enlarge the monopoly of the patent beyond its terms. International Salt Co. v. United States. If competitors agree to divide markets, they run afoul of the antitrust laws. Timken Roller Bearing Co. v. United States. * * *

* * *

We are asked to extend the holding in Timken Roller Bearing Co. v. United States (which banned *horizontal* arrangements among competitors to divide territory), to a *vertical* arrangement by one manufacturer restricting the territory of his distributors or dealers. We intimate no view one way or the other on the legality of such an arrangement, for we believe that the applicable rule of law should be designed after a trial.

This is the first case involving a territorial restriction in a *vertical* arrangement; and we know too little of the actual impact of both that restriction and the one respecting customers to reach a conclusion on the bare bones of the documentary evidence before us.

Standard Oil Co. v. United States read into the Sherman Act the "rule of reason." That "rule of reason" normally requires an ascertainment of the facts peculiar to the particular business. * * *

* * *

Horizontal territorial limitations, like "[g]roup boycotts, or concerted refusals by traders to deal with other traders" (Klor's v. Broadway-Hale Stores), are naked restraints of trade with no purpose except stifling of competition. A vertical territorial limitation may or may not have that purpose or effect. We do not know enough of the economic and business stuff out of which these arrangements emerge to be certain. They may be too dangerous to sanction or they may be allowable protections against aggressive competitors or the only practicable means a small company has for breaking into or staying in business and within the "rule of reason." We need to know more than we do about the actual impact of these arrangements on competition to decide whether they have such a "pernicious effect on competition and lack * * * any redeeming virtue" (Northern Pac. R. Co. v. United States) and therefore should be classified as per se violations of the Sherman Act.

There is an analogy from the merger field that leads us to conclude that a trial should be had. A merger that would otherwise offend the antitrust laws because of a substantial lessening of competition has been given immunity where the acquired company was a failing one. See International Shoe Co. v. Federal Trade Commission, 280 U.S. 291 [1930]. But in such a case, as in cases involving the question whether a particular merger will tend "substantially to lessen competition," a trial rather than the use of the summary judgment is normally necessary.

We conclude that the summary judgment * * * was improperly employed in this suit. [W]e do not intimate any view on the merits. We only hold that the legality of the territorial and customer limitations should be determined only after a trial.

Reversed.

MR. JUSTICE WHITE took no part in the consideration or decision of this case.

MR. JUSTICE BRENNAN, concurring.

While I join the opinion of the Court, the novelty of the antitrust questions prompts me to add a few words. I fully agree that it would be premature to declare either the territorial or the customer restrictions illegal per se * * * . But it seems to me that distinct problems are raised by the two types of restrictions and that the District Court will wish to have this distinction in mind at the trial.

I

I discuss first the territorial limitations. The insulation of a dealer or distributor through territorial restraints against sales by neighboring dealers who would otherwise be his competitors involves a form of restraint upon alienation, which is therefore historically and inherently suspect under the antitrust laws. See Dr. Miles Medical Co. v. John D. Park & Sons Co. That proposition does not, however, tell us that every form of such restraint is utterly without justification and is therefore to be deemed unlawful per se. * * * To gauge the appropriateness of a per se test for the forms of restraint involved in this case, * * * we must determine whether experience warrants, at this stage, a conclusion that inquiry into effect upon competition and economic justification would be similarly irrelevant. With respect to the territorial limitations of the type at bar, I agree that the courts have as yet been shown no sufficient experience to warrant such a conclusion.

The Government urges, and the District Court found, that these restrictions so closely resemble two traditionally outlawed forms of restraint—horizontal market division and resale price maintenance—that they ought to be governed by the same absolute legal test. Both analogies are surely instructive, * * * but both are, at the same time, misleading. It seems to me that consideration of the similarities has thus far obscured consideration of the equally important differences, which serve in my view to distinguish the practice here from others as to which we have held a per se test clearly appropriate.

* * * If it were clear that the territorial restrictions involved in this case had been induced solely or even primarily by appellant's dealers and distributors, it would make no difference to their legality that the restrictions were formally imposed by the manufacturer rather than through inter-dealer agreement. But for aught that the present record discloses, an equally plausible inference is that the territorial restraints were imposed upon unwilling distributors by the manufacturer to serve exclusively his own interests. * * * In any event, * * * [t]he crucial question whether, despite the differences in form, these restraints serve the same pernicious purpose and have the same inhibitory effects upon competition as horizontal divisions of markets, is one which cannot be answered without a trial.

The analogy to resale price maintenance agreements is also appealing, but is no less deceptive. Resale price maintenance is not only designed to, but almost invariably does in fact, reduce price competition not only *among* sellers of the affected product, but quite as much *between* that product and competing brands. See United States v. Parke, Davis & Co. While territorial restrictions may indirectly have a similar effect upon *intra*-brand competition, the effect upon *inter*-brand competition is not necessarily the same as that of resale price maintenance.

Indeed, the principal justification which the appellant offers for the use of these limitations is that they foster a vigorous inter-brand competition which might otherwise be absent. Thus, in order to determine the lawfulness of this form of restraint, it becomes necessary to assess the merit of this and other extenuations offered by the appellant. Surely it would be significant to the disposition of this case if, as appellant claims, some such arrangement were a prerequisite for effective competition on the part of independent manufacturers of trucks. * * *

There are other situations, not presented directly by this case, in which the possibility of justification cautions against a too hasty conclusion that territorial limitations are invariably unlawful. Arguments have been suggested against that conclusion, for example, in the case of a manufacturer starting out in business or marketing a new and risky product; the suggestion is that such a manufacturer may find it essential, simply in order to acquire and retain outlets, to guarantee his distributors some degree of territorial insulation as well as exclusive franchises. It has also been suggested that it may reasonably appear necessary for a manufacturer to subdivide his sales territory in order to ensure that his product will be adequately advertised, promoted, and serviced. It is, I think, the inappropriateness or irrelevance of such justifications as these to the practices traditionally condemned under the per se test that principally distinguishes the territorial restraints involved in the present case from horizontal market divisions and resale price maintenance.

* * *

Another pertinent inquiry would explore the availability of less restrictive alternatives. In the present case, for example, as the Government suggests, it may appear at the trial that whatever legitimate business needs White advances for territorial limitations could be adequately served, with less damage to competition, through other devices—for example, an exclusive franchise, an assignment of areas of primary responsibility to each distributor, or a revision of the levels of profit pass-over so as to minimize the deterrence to cross-selling by neighboring dealers where competition is feasible. * * *

II

I turn next to the customer restrictions. These present a problem quite distinct from that of the territorial limitations. The customer restraints would seem inherently the more dangerous of the two, for they serve to suppress all competition between manufacturer and distributors for the custom of the most desirable accounts. At the same time they seem to lack any of the countervailing tendencies to foster competition between brands which may accompany the territorial limitations. * * *

The crucial question to me is whether, in any meaningful sense, the distributors could, but for the restrictions, compete with the manufacturer for the reserved outlets. If they could, but are prevented from doing so only by the restrictions, then in the absence of some justification neither presented nor suggested by this record, their invalidity would seem to be apparent. * * *

* * *

* * * On trial, as I see it, the Government will necessarily prevail unless the proof warrants a finding that, even in the absence of the restrictions, the economics of the trade are such that the distributors cannot compete for the reserved accounts.

MR. JUSTICE CLARK, with whom THE CHIEF JUSTICE and MR. JUSTICE BLACK join, dissenting.

* * * I believe that [the] "bare bones" [of this case] really lay bare one of the most brazen violations of the Sherman Act that I have experienced in a quarter of a century.

* * *

The situation in which White Motor finds itself may be summed up in its own words, i.e., that its contracts are "the only feasible way for [it] to compete effectively with its bigger and more powerful competitors * * * ." In this justification it attempts but to make a virtue of business necessity, which has long been rejected as a defense in such cases. See Dr. Miles Medical Co. v. John D. Park & Sons Co.; Fashion Originators' Guild v. Federal Trade Comm'n; and Northern Pac. R. Co. v. United States. * * * These grounds for its action may be good for White Motor but they are disastrous for free competitive enterprise and, if permitted, will destroy the effectiveness of the Sherman Act. For under these contracts a person wishing to buy a White truck must deal with only one seller who by virtue of his agreements with dealer competitors has the sole power as to the public to set prices, determine terms and even to refuse to sell to a particular customer. * * * [The customer] might buy another brand of truck, it is true, but the existence of interbrand competition has never been a justification for an explicit agreement to eliminate competition. Likewise each White Motor dealer is * * * confined to his own economic island.

I have diligently searched appellant's offer of proof but fail to find any allegation by it that raises an issue of fact. All of its statements are economic arguments or business necessities none of which have any bearing on the legal issue. * * * I return to the conclusion, as did Mr. Justice Lurton [in *Dr. Miles*], that "If these contracts leave any room at any point of the line for the usual play of competition between the dealers * * * it is not discoverable."

This Court, it is true, has never held whether there is a difference between market divisions voluntarily undertaken by a manufacturer such as White Motor and those of dealers in a commodity, agreed upon by themselves, such as were condemned in Timken Roller Bearing Co. v. United States. White does not contend that its distribution system has any less tendency to restrain competition among its distributors and dealers than a horizontal agreement among such distributors and dealers themselves. It seems to place some halo around its agreements because they are vertical. But the intended and actual effect is the same as, if not even more destructive than, a price-fixing agreement or any of its per se counterparts. This is true because price-fixing agreements, being more easily breached, must be continually policed by those forming the combination, while contracts for a division of territory, being easily detected, are practically self-enforcing. * * *

* * *

The Court says that perhaps the reasonableness or the effect of such arrangements might be subject to inquiry. But the rule of reason is inapplicable to agreements made solely for the purpose of eliminating competition. United States v. Socony-Vacuum Oil Co. * * * To admit, as does the petitioner, that competition is eliminated under its contracts is, under our cases, to admit a violation of the Sherman Act. No justification, no matter how beneficial, can save it from that interdiction.

* * *

Today the Court does a futile act in remanding this case for trial. In my view appellant cannot plead nor prove an issue upon which a successful defense of its contracts can be predicated. * * * Certainly the decision has no precedential value in substantive antitrust law.

NOTES AND QUESTIONS

1.   This was a 5–3 decision. If Justice Douglas had voted the other way, the Court would have split 4–4 and the District Court's finding of per se illegality would have been affirmed. Were you surprised to see the author of *Socony-Vacuum* writing this opinion? Had Justice Douglas by this time become the modern Brandeis, the defender of small firms in a world he saw as dominated by big business?

a.   Why weren't the government and the dissenters obviously right here? If resale price maintenance is per se illegal by analogy to a cartel among the dealers, why aren't territorial and customer allocations similarly illegal?

b.   Do you agree with Justice Brennan that the effects of price and territorial clauses are likely to be different? That is, might resale price maintenance often facilitate oligopoly pricing while territorial and customer allocations instead tend to increase inter-brand competition?

c.   Should it matter what kind of territorial and customer allocations are involved in a case? Here, for example, dealers were limited to selling to customers who had a business location within their territories; customers could not drive to another territory to shop. Does Justice Brennan help you think of territorial arrangements that would be less restrictive but would help retain the possible pro-competitive interbrand effects the Court mentions?

d. Do you agree that dealers are likely to initiate resale price maintenance while manufacturers are likely to prefer the clauses at issue here? Would White's dealers likely have "required" White to retain the right to serve large customers, for example? Should who initiates such a program make any difference to the decision under § 1?

2. Does this decision cast doubt on per se rules generally? Has the Court let the genie out of the bottle?

a. Once one concedes that White's market share and financial health are relevant in assessing territorial allocation clauses, is there any reason not to make them relevant in other cases? Can a practice ever be per se illegal if the actors, not just the act, must be evaluated as part of the decision?

b. Once one concedes that possible effects on interbrand competition are relevant, can any firm's action be evaluated apart from a full inquiry into the functioning of its market? If such an inquiry is required, is any meaning left to the term "per se illegal"?

3. Is *White Motor* really just another summary judgment case? Has the Court become so cautious about deciding matters without a full trial that this opinion may appear to suggest issues are open that prior law would suggest are not? Might the Court thereby be doing a disservice to the development of the law and to litigants in this and future cases? Might the Court be suggesting instead that even it now recognizes that its per se approach to cases too often had ignored important economic realities?

A NOTE ON *GENERAL MOTORS*

United States v. General Motors Corp., 384 U.S. 127, 86 S.Ct. 1321, 16 L.Ed.2d 415 (1966), decided three years after *White Motors* and two years after *Simpson*, was another colorful case in this series. It combined territorial allocation with the phenomenon of discount selling.

Several G.M. dealers were found to be cooperating with "discount houses" and "referral services." Those were organizations that would sell cars very cheap, having bought them almost at the wholesale price from the cooperating dealers. Buyers were encouraged to take advantage of the showrooms of authorized G.M. dealers to decide what features they wanted, and the regular dealers were often called upon to do the preconditioning and warranty work. As you might imagine, the discounters tended to buy from dealers distant from where they sold, i.e., the wholesaling G.M. dealers tried to get benefits for themselves by imposing burdens on G.M. dealers elsewhere.

The G.M. dealers' association went to company management to complain. General Motors sent out its regional manager who threatened to knock the offending wholesaling dealers' "teeth down their throat." G.M. also invoked the "location clause" in its dealer contracts and reasoned that selling to discounters was in effect opening a showroom at an unauthorized location.

Justice Fortas, writing for the Court, said the case was easy; it was *Klor's* and *Parke-Davis* all over again. The dealers had worked together and with General Motors to cut off the discounters' supply of inventory and thus inhibit entry. Because one of the prime purposes of the practices was to keep prices up, the agreement was per se illegal under *Socony-Vacuum*.

NOTES AND QUESTIONS

1. Do you agree with that analysis? Were G.M.'s location clauses themselves per se illegal? Was it only their use in this case that was improper? Should even their use here have been upheld? Might General Motors have a legitimate interest in preventing acts by which some G.M. dealers try to "free ride" on work they imposed on others?

2. Is it self-evident that the Court should review manufacturer/dealer disputes under the antitrust laws at all? If the manufacturer could sell the item through employees who clearly could be fired for violating company policy, isn't it artificial to say that the company may not terminate a dealer? Contract issues may be presented, of course, but those would be matters of state law.

3. Do cases like *General Motors* present a federal question? Does the alleged conduct affect interstate commerce? How? Because the terminated dealer will be replaced by another, is there even any loss of competition? How did that argument fare in *Klor's* and *Simpson*? Is the real concern that genuine intimidation could never be stopped if dealer terminations were not subject to review?

AND THEN THERE WAS *SCHWINN*

Just a year after *General Motors*, and four years after *White Motors*, the Court hopelessly confused the developing law of vertical restraints by its decision in United States v. Arnold, Schwinn & Co., 388 U.S. 365, 87 S.Ct. 1856, 18 L.Ed.2d 1249 (1967).

Schwinn was a family-owned business that had once been America's largest seller of bicycles.[77] Since after World War II, it had sold bicycles in three ways. First, it sold them to traditional wholesalers and retailers who in turn sold them to the public. Second, it sold them under consignment or

---

[77] In 1951, Schwinn had 22.5% of the U.S. market. By 1961, however, makers of cheaper bicycles had replaced Schwinn as market leaders; Schwinn's market share had fallen to 12.8%.

agency agreements with distributors. Third, it used the "Schwinn Plan" under which customers placed orders through retail dealers to whom the bicycles were shipped by Schwinn for delivery to the identified purchasers. The government did not appeal the District Court's findings that Schwinn did not set the prices at which any of the sales must be made, but the Court accepted that Schwinn did require that its wholesalers and retailers distribute only through "franchised retailers" and not through discount houses or other unfranchised dealers.

Schwinn, in turn, did not appeal from the District Court order invalidating its territorial restrictions as to sales in the first category, i.e., bicycles sold to wholesalers and retailers for later sale to the public. The questions before the Court, therefore, were (1) whether that District Court prohibition should be extended to consignment and Schwinn-Plan sales, and (2) whether agreements by franchised wholesalers and retailers not to sell to unfranchised dealers should themselves be enjoined.

Justice Fortas, writing for the Court, found no prior precedents controlling. Schwinn had been a market leader, not a "failing company" like the defendant in *White Motor*. Thus, Schwinn's method of distribution was not clearly reasonable. However, this was also not a program like the ones in *Klor's* and *General Motors* that had been imposed on manufacturers by retailers.

Turning to the merits, the Court concluded that territorial restraints imposed on wholesalers and retailers who had purchased Schwinn bicycles would constitute "restraints on alienation" like the ones condemned in *Dr. Miles*. On the other hand, the Court said, franchising is an important way for small enterprises to flourish and territorial limitations are often useful in franchising. Thus, unlike the result in *Simpson* where price fixing had been involved, the rule of reason should be used to determine the lawfulness of Schwinn's consignment and Schwinn Plan sales. In this case, the Court found, the District Court had correctly determined that in the case of a relatively small manufacturer whose restrictions went no farther than competitive pressure required, the territorial limitations were reasonable.

Justices Stewart and Harlan's dissent agreed with the Court that the consignment and Schwinn Plan sales were reasonable. They argued, however, that there was no principled basis for failing to apply the same rule to bicycles sold directly to wholesalers and retailers. In failing to apply the same analysis apply to all methods of distribution, the Court had unnecessarily resurrected a distinction that was better left buried.[78]

---

[78] In case you're wondering, there were only two changes of membership on the Court between this case and *White Motor*. Justice Fortas had replaced Justice Goldberg and Justice Marshall had replaced Justice Clark. Neither change seems to explain the result.

NOTES AND QUESTIONS

1.   Why would Schwinn establish the marketing program that it did? Do you believe its method of distribution enhanced consumer choice among bicycles, or diminished it? Who, if anyone, would have considered themselves "victims" of Schwinn's program?

2.   Are the dissenters correct that there is no basis for distinguishing cases where Schwinn parted with title from those where it did not?

a.   Is there any economic significance to the distinction? Are Justices Stewart & Harlan correct that its consequences can be avoided by drafting, i.e., that the distinction is entirely a matter of form, not substance?

b.   Should the Court have considered itself bound by the law's historic concern about restraints on alienation? Might one argue that the doctrine of ancillary restraints, ignored by the Court majority, should have overcome that concern in this case?

c.   If Schwinn had appealed the District Court's holding with respect to the goods that were sold, might the Supreme Court majority have reacted more sympathetically to the positions of Justices Stewart & Harlan?

3.   Was the Court's endorsement of the Schwinn Plan a major victory for manufacturers? Would use of consignment sales be practical for most firms? Might the plan be particularly costly for small firms? Remember that under the plan, the manufacturer winds up being required to finance dealers; it cannot make them pay before the sale to the ultimate consumer.

Our next case involves a "manufacturer" that has simultaneously allocated territories and imposed a system of *maximum* resale price maintenance. As you read the case, ask yourself whether the issues of price and location are as different as the Court has wanted to consider them. Also ask yourself whether here, again, the Court has taken the per se rule too far.

ALBRECHT V. HERALD CO.

Supreme Court of the United States, 1968
390 U.S. 145, 88 S.Ct. 869, 19 L.Ed.2d 998

MR. JUSTICE WHITE delivered the opinion of the Court.

A jury returned a verdict for respondent in petitioner's suit for treble damages for violation of § 1 of the Sherman Act. * * * [T]he Court of Appeals * * * affirmed. * * *

We take the facts from those stated by the Court of Appeals. Respondent publishes the Globe-Democrat, a morning newspaper distributed in the St. Louis metropolitan area by independent carriers who buy papers at wholesale and sell them at retail. There are 172 home delivery routes. Respondent advertises a suggested retail price in its newspaper. Carriers have exclusive territories which are subject to termination if prices exceed the suggested maximum. Petitioner, who had Route 99, adhered to the advertised price for some time but in 1961 raised the price to customers.[79] After more than once objecting to this practice, respondent wrote petitioner on May 20, 1964, that because he was overcharging and because respondent had reserved the right to compete should that happen, subscribers on Route 99 were being informed by letter that respondent would itself deliver the paper to those who wanted it at the lower price. In addition to sending these letters to petitioner's customers, respondent hired Milne Circulation Sales, Inc., which solicited readers for newspapers, to engage in telephone and house-to-house solicitation of all residents on Route 99. As a result, about 300 of petitioner's 1,200 customers switched to direct delivery by respondent. Meanwhile, respondent continued to sell papers to petitioner but warned him that should he continue to overcharge, respondent would not have to do business with him. Since respondent did not itself want to engage in home delivery, it advertised a new route of 314 customers as available without cost. Another carrier, George Kroner, took over the route knowing that respondent would not tolerate overcharging and understanding that he might have to return the route if petitioner discontinued his pricing practice. On July 27 respondent told petitioner that it was not interested in being in the carrier business and that petitioner could have his customers back as long as he charged the suggested price. Petitioner brought this lawsuit on August 12. In response, petitioner's appointment as a carrier was terminated and petitioner was given 60 days to arrange the sale of his route to a satisfactory replacement. Petitioner sold his route for $12,000, $1,000 more than he had paid for it but less than he could have gotten had he been able to turn over 1,200 customers instead of 900.

Petitioner's complaint charged a combination or conspiracy in restraint of trade under § 1 of the Sherman Act. At the close of the evidence the complaint was amended to charge only a combination between respondent and "plaintiff's customers and/or Milne Circulation Sales, Inc. and/or George Kroner." The case went to the jury on this theory, the jury found for respondent, and judgment in its favor was entered on the verdict. The court denied petitioner's motion for judgment notwithstanding the verdict, which asserted that under United States v. Parke, Davis & Co., and like cases, the undisputed facts showed as a matter of law a combination to fix resale prices of newspapers which was per se illegal under the Sherman Act. The Court of Appeals affirmed. * * * The previous decisions of this Court were deemed inapposite to a situation in which a seller establishes maximum prices to be charged by a retailer enjoying an exclusive territory and in which the seller, who would be entitled to refuse

---

[79]   The record indicates that petitioner raised his price by 10 cents a month. [Court's fn. 2]

to deal, simply engages in competition with the offending retailer. We disagree with the Court of Appeals and reverse its judgment.

On the undisputed facts recited by the Court of Appeals respondent's conduct cannot be deemed wholly unilateral and beyond the reach of § 1 of the Sherman Act. That section covers combinations in addition to contracts and conspiracies, express or implied. The Court made this quite clear in United States v. Parke, Davis & Co., where it held that an illegal combination to fix prices results if a seller suggests resale prices and secures compliance by means in addition to the "mere announcement of his policy and the simple refusal to deal." * * *

If a combination arose when Parke, Davis threatened its wholesalers with termination unless they put pressure on their retail customers, then there can be no doubt that a combination arose between respondent, Milne, and Kroner to force petitioner to conform to the advertised retail price. * * * It was through the efforts of Milne, as well as because of respondent's letter to petitioner's customers, that about 300 customers were obtained for Kroner. Milne's purpose was undoubtedly to earn its fee, but it was aware that the aim of the solicitation campaign was to force petitioner to lower his price. Kroner * * * undertook to deliver papers at the suggested price and materially aided in the accomplishment of respondent's plan. Given the uncontradicted facts recited by the Court of Appeals, there was a combination within the meaning of § 1 between respondent, Milne, and Kroner, and the Court of Appeals erred in holding to the contrary.[80]

The Court of Appeals also held there was no restraint of trade, despite the long-accepted rule in § 1 cases that resale price fixing is a per se violation of the law whether done by agreement or combination. United States v. Trenton Potteries Co.; United States v. Socony-Vacuum Oil Co.; Kiefer-Stewart Co. v. Seagram & Sons.

In *Kiefer-Stewart*, liquor distributors combined to set maximum resale prices. The Court of Appeals held the combination legal under the Sherman Act because in its view setting maximum prices " * * * constituted no restraint on trade and no interference with plaintiff's right to engage in all the competition it desired." This Court rejected that view and reversed the Court of Appeals, holding that agreements to fix maximum prices "no less than those to fix minimum prices, cripple the freedom of traders and

---

[80] * * * Under *Parke, Davis* petitioner could have claimed a combination between respondent and himself, at least as of the day he unwillingly complied with respondent's advertised price. Likewise, he might successfully have claimed that respondent had combined with other carriers because the firmly enforced price policy applied to all carriers, most of whom acquiesced in it. See United States v. Arnold, Schwinn & Co. These additional claims, however, appear to have been abandoned by petitioner when he amended his complaint in the trial court. Petitioner's amended complaint did allege a combination between respondent and petitioner's customers. Because of our disposition of this case it is unnecessary to pass on this claim. It was not, however, a frivolous contention. [Court's fn. 6]

thereby restrain their ability to sell in accordance with their own judgment."[81]

We think *Kiefer-Stewart* was correctly decided and we adhere to it. Maximum and minimum price fixing may have different consequences in many situations. But schemes to fix maximum prices, by substituting the perhaps erroneous judgment of a seller for the forces of the competitive market, may severely intrude upon the ability of buyers to compete and survive in that market. Competition, even in a single product, is not cast in a single mold. Maximum prices may be fixed too low for the dealer to furnish services essential to the value which goods have for the consumer or to furnish services and conveniences which consumers desire and for which they are willing to pay. Maximum price fixing may channel distribution through a few large or specifically advantaged dealers who otherwise would be subject to significant nonprice competition. Moreover, if the actual price charged under a maximum price scheme is nearly always the fixed maximum price, which is increasingly likely as the maximum price approaches the actual cost of the dealer, the scheme tends to acquire all the attributes of an arrangement fixing minimum prices. It is our view, therefore, that the combination formed by the respondent in this case to force petitioner to maintain a specified price for the resale of the newspapers which he had purchased from respondent constituted, without more, an illegal restraint of trade under § 1 of the Sherman Act.

We also reject the suggestion of the Court of Appeals that *Kiefer-Stewart* is inapposite and that maximum price fixing is permissible in this case. The Court of Appeals reasoned that since respondent granted exclusive territories, a price ceiling was necessary to protect the public from price gouging by dealers who had monopoly power in their own territories. But neither the existence of exclusive territories nor the economic power they might place in the hands of the dealers was at issue before the jury. Likewise, the evidence taken was not directed to the question of whether exclusive territories had been granted or imposed as the result of an illegal combination in violation of the antitrust laws. Certainly on the record before us the Court of Appeals was not entitled to assume, as its reasoning necessarily did, that the exclusive rights granted by respondent were valid under § 1 of the Sherman Act, either alone or in conjunction with a price-fixing scheme. See United States v. Arnold, Schwinn & Co. The assertion that illegal price fixing is justified because it blunts the pernicious consequences of another distribution practice is

---

[81]   Our Brother Harlan appears to read *Kiefer-Stewart* as prohibiting only combinations of suppliers to squeeze retailers from the top. Under this view, scarcely derivable from the opinion in that case, signed contracts between a single supplier and his many dealers to fix maximum resale prices would not violate the Sherman Act. With all deference, we reject this view, which seems to stem from the notion that there can be no agreement violative of § 1 unless that agreement accrues to the benefit of both parties, as determined in accordance with some a priori economic model. Cf. Comment, The Per Se Illegality of Price-Fixing—Sans Power, Purpose, or Effect, 19 U. Chicago L. Rev. 837 (1952). [Court's fn. 8]

unpersuasive. If, as the Court of Appeals said, the economic impact of territorial exclusivity was such that the public could be protected only by otherwise illegal price fixing itself injurious to the public, the entire scheme must fall under § 1 of the Sherman Act.

In sum, the evidence cited by the Court of Appeals makes it clear that a combination in restraint of trade existed. Accordingly, it was error to affirm the judgment of the District Court which denied petitioner's motion for judgment notwithstanding the verdict. The judgment of the Court of Appeals is reversed and the case is remanded to that court for further proceedings consistent with this opinion.

MR. JUSTICE DOUGLAS, concurring.

While I join the opinion of the Court, there is a word I would add. This is a "rule of reason" case stemming from Standard Oil Co. v. United States. Whether an exclusive territorial franchise in a vertical arrangement is per se unreasonable under the antitrust laws is a much mooted question. A fixing of prices for resale is conspicuously unreasonable, because of the great leverage that price has over the market. The Court quite properly refuses to say whether in the newspaper distribution business an exclusive territorial franchise is illegal.

The traditional distributing agency is the neighborhood newspaper boy. Whether he would have the time, acumen, experience, or financial resources to wage competitive warfare without the protection of a territorial franchise is at least doubtful. Here, however, we have a distribution system which has the characteristics of a large retail enterprise. Petitioner's business requires practically full time. He purchased his route for $11,000, receiving a list of subscribers, a used truck, and a newspaper-tying machine. At the time his dispute with respondent arose, there were 1,200 subscribers on the route, and that route covered "the whole northeast section" of a "big city." Deliveries had to be made by motor vehicle and although they were usually completed by 6 o'clock in the morning, the rest of the workday was spent in billing, receiving phone calls, arranging for new service, or in placing "stop" or "start" orders on existing service. Petitioner at times hired a staff to tie and to wrap newspapers.

Under our decisions the legality of exclusive territorial franchises in the newspaper distribution business would have to be tried as a factual issue; and that was not done here.

The case is therefore close to White Motor Co. v. United States, where before ruling on the legality of a territorial restriction in a vertical arrangement, we remanded for findings on "the actual impact of these arrangements on competition."

MR. JUSTICE HARLAN, dissenting.

* * *

I

The practice of setting genuine price "ceilings," that is maximum prices, differs from the practice of fixing minimum prices, and no accumulation of pronouncements from the opinions of this Court can render the two economically equivalent.

* * *

Resale price maintenance, a practice not involved here, lessens horizontal intrabrand competition. The effects, higher prices, less efficient use of resources, and an easier life for the resellers, are the same whether the price maintenance policy takes the form of a horizontal conspiracy among resellers or of vertical dictation by a manufacturer plus reseller acquiescence. This means two things. First, it is frequently possible to infer a combination of resellers behind what is presented to the world as a vertical and unilateral price policy, because it is the resellers and not the manufacturer who reap the direct benefits of the policy. Second, price floors are properly considered per se restraints, in the sense that once a combination to create them has been demonstrated, no proffered justification is an acceptable defense. Following the rule of reason, combinations to fix price floors are invariably unreasonable: to the extent that they achieve their objective, they act to the direct detriment of the public interest as viewed in the Sherman Act. * * *

Vertically imposed price ceilings are, as a matter of economic fact that this Court's words cannot change, an altogether different matter. Other things being equal, a manufacturer would like to restrict those distributing his product to the lowest feasible profit margin, for in this way he achieves the lowest overall price to the public and the largest volume. When a manufacturer dictates a minimum resale price he is responding to the interest of his customers, who may treat his product better if they have a secure high margin of profits. When the same manufacturer dictates a price ceiling, however, he is acting directly in his own interest, and there is no room for the inference that he is merely a mechanism for accomplishing anticompetitive purposes of his customers.

* * *

* * * The per se treatment of price maintenance is justified because analysis alone, without the burden of a trial in each individual case, demonstrates that price floors are invariably harmful on balance. Price ceilings are a different matter: they do not lessen horizontal competition; they drive prices toward the level that would be set by intense competition, and they cannot go below this level unless the manufacturer who dictates them and the customer who accepts them have both miscalculated. Since price ceilings reflect the manufacturer's view that there is insufficient competition to drive prices down to a competitive level, they have the arguable justification that they prevent retailers or wholesalers from reaping monopoly or supercompetitive profits.

* * * Both practices share the negative attribute that they restrict individual discretion in the pricing area, but only the former imposes upon the public the much more significant evil of lessened competition, and, as just seen, the latter has an important arguable justification that the former does not possess. * * *82

II

The Court's discovery in this case of (a) a combination and (b) a restraint that is per se unreasonable is beset with pitfalls. The Court relies directly on combinations with Milne and Kroner, two third parties who were simply hired and paid to do telephoning and distributing jobs that respondent could as effectively have done itself. Neither had any special interest in respondent's objective of setting a price ceiling. If the critical question is whether a company pays one of its own employees to perform a routine task, or hires an outsider to do the same thing, the requirement of a "combination" in restraint of trade has lost all significant meaning. * * *

* * *

This does not mean, however, that no combination or conspiracy could ever be inferred in such an ostensibly unilateral situation. It would often be proper to infer, in situations in which a manufacturer dictates a minimum price to a retailer, that the manufacturer is the mechanism for enforcing a very real combinatorial restraint among retailers who should be competing horizontally.83 * * *84

---

82 The same points may be made from the perspective of the retailers or wholesalers subject to the price dictation. When the issue is minimum resale prices, those sellers who are more efficient and ambitious are likely to object to price restrictions, while the lazier and less efficient sellers will welcome their protection. When the issue is price ceilings, the matter is different. Assuming the ceilings are high enough to permit a return that will enable the seller to stay in business, a seller will object to price ceilings only because they deny him the supercompetitive return that the imperfections of competition would otherwise permit. [Dissent fn. 4]

83 See Turner, The Definition of Agreement Under the Sherman Act: Conscious Parallelism and Refusals to Deal, 75 Harvard L. Rev. 655. Professor Turner (as he then was) suggested the overruling of United States v. Colgate & Co., arguing, inter alia, that *Colgate* behavior by a manufacturer tends to produce tacit or implied minimum price agreements among otherwise competitive retailers. He suggested that "it should be perfectly clear to any manufacturer that a policy of refusing to deal with *price cutters* is no more nor less than an invitation [to retailers] to agree [with each other as well as with the manufacturer] on * * * a minimum price * * *." (Emphasis added.) [Dissent fn. 5]

84 I thought at the time *Parke, Davis* was decided (see my dissenting opinion in that case) and continue to believe, that the result reached could not be supported on the majority's reasoning. I am frank to say, however, that I now consider that the *Parke, Davis* result can be supported on Professor Turner's rationale. See Turner, supra, [dissent] n. 5. Further reflection on the matter also leads me to say that my statement in dissent to the effect that *Parke, Davis* had overruled the *Colgate* case was overdrawn, and further that I am not yet prepared to say that Professor Turner's rationale necessarily carries the total discard of *Colgate*. [Dissent fn. 7]

* * * [T]he manufacturer who purports to act unilaterally in dictating a maximum price really is acting unilaterally. No one is economically interested in the price squeeze but himself. Had the Court been in the habit of analyzing the economics on which the inference of a combination may be based, it would have seen that even if combinations to fix maximum prices are as illegal as combinations to fix minimum prices the circumstances under which a combination to fix maximum prices may be inferred are different from those which imply a combination to keep prices up.

* * *

Kiefer-Stewart's treatment of the combination requirement is instructive. Any manufacturer is at perfect liberty to set the prices at which he will sell to retailers, and in that way maximize his profits while lessening theirs. Competition, that is the threat that the purchasing seller will simply turn to another manufacturer, prevents the manufacturer from raising his prices beyond a certain point. It is per se unlawful, however, for two manufacturers to combine to raise their prices together, rendering each of them secure because the retailer or wholesaler has nowhere else to turn. From the manufacturer's viewpoint, putting a ceiling on the resale price may be simply an alternative means to the end of maximizing his own profits by lessening distribution costs: instead of squeezing the reseller from the bottom he squeezes from the top. The holding of *Kiefer-Stewart* was that the squeeze from the top, like the squeeze from the bottom, was lawful unless by a combination of persons between whom competition would otherwise have limited the power to squeeze from either direction. No combination of the kind required in *Kiefer-Stewart* exists here, and the Court has found no sensible substitute theory of combination.

The Court's second difficulty in this case is to state why imposition of price ceilings is a per se unlawful restraint. * * *

The Court has not been persuasive. The question in this case is not whether dictation of maximum prices is *ever* illegal, but whether it is *always* illegal. Petitioner is seeking, and now receives, a judgment notwithstanding the verdict of a jury that he had failed to show that the practice was unreasonable in this case. The best the Court can do is to list certain unfortunate consequences that maximum price dictation might have in other cases but was not shown to have here. * * *

* * *

It may well be that the mechanics of newspaper distribution are such that a city quite naturally divides itself into one or more relatively exclusive territories (sometimes called "paper routes"), giving each distributor a large degree of monopoly power. * * *

There is no question that the ideal situation, from the point of view of both the publisher and the public, is to have a very large number of distributors intensely vying with each other in both price and service. This situation, however, may be one that it is impossible to achieve in some, perhaps in all, cities. * * *

Confronted by this situation, the publisher, who is competing with other publishers in, among other things, price and service to the public, will seek to provide efficient distribution service at the lowest possible price. These objectives would be realized by intense competition without the publisher's interference, but in the absence of such competition the publisher must take steps of his own.

The present respondent took two steps. First, it insisted on the right to approve each distributor. * * * Second, it set a maximum home delivery price and enforced it; the price could not be below the level that perfect competition would dictate without driving the distributors out of business and defeating the publisher's whole objective. Hence the price set cannot be supposed to have been unreasonable. Respondent had no need to go to the extreme of cutting off distributors preferring to do a high-profit, low-volume business, and did not do so. It simply advertised the maximum home delivery price and created competition with any distributor not observing it. Today's decision leaves respondent with no alternative but to use its own trucks.

* * * I would affirm the judgment below.

MR. JUSTICE STEWART, with whom MR. JUSTICE HARLAN joins, dissenting. * * *

The case was litigated throughout by both parties upon the premise that the respondent's granting of an exclusive territory to each distributor was a perfectly permissible practice. Upon that premise the judgment of the Court of Appeals was obviously correct. For the respondent's conduct here was in furtherance of, not contrary to, the purposes of the antitrust laws. * * * The cases cited by the petitioner, such as Kiefer-Stewart Co. v. Seagram & Sons and United States v. Parke, Davis & Co., did not involve monopoly products distributed through exclusive territories and are thus totally inapplicable here. The thrust of those decisions is that the reseller should be free to make his own independent pricing determination. But that cannot be a proper objective where the reseller is a monopolist. * * *

But, says the Court, the original grant of an exclusive territory to the petitioner may have itself violated the antitrust laws. * * * I fail to understand how the illegality of the petitioner's exclusive territory could conceivably help his case. * * * If it was illegal in the first place for the petitioner to enjoy a *conditional* monopoly, I am at a loss to understand how the respondent can be liable to the petitioner for not permitting him a *complete* monopoly.

The Court in this case does more, I think, than simply depart from the rule of reason. The Court today stands the Sherman Act on its head.

NOTES AND QUESTIONS

1.   This case merges the issues of territorial allocation and maximum resale prices.

a.   Why did the newspaper feel the need to keep prices low? Are all of a newspaper's profits derived from sales revenue? Might some of its most important revenue come from advertisers who pay based on circulation figures?

b.   How could the newspaper's action fixing maximum prices *not* be in the public interest? Isn't reducing prices and increasing output what the antitrust laws are about?

c.   Were you convinced by the argument that today's price ceiling may become tomorrow's price floor? If identifying that phenomenon were the worst problem the courts faced, would you be worried?

d.   How about the argument that every dealer faces different costs and customer demands for different levels of service? Do you agree that when a producer mandates a resale price, it unduly constrains the range of services that competition would provide?

2.   What was the relation between territorial allocation and maximum resale prices?

a.   Was the carrier's ability to raise prices a result of its having no competition within its territory? Is there any way the newspaper could, by altering the size of territories or in some other manner deny the carrier's ability to act as a monopolist?

b.   Is the newspaper business one in which interbrand competition is relatively unimportant? Do you suppose St. Louis readers would really consider the Chicago Tribune a close substitute? Should that affect our evaluation of the use of exclusive territories in this industry?

c.   Can one argue that the licensing of a second distributor for a territory should always be per se *legal*? A state breach of contract claim might be presented, but isn't it clear that authorizing a second carrier always *increases* competition, not decreases it?

3.   Were you surprised by the result here, given the procedural posture of the case?

a.   Do you agree with Justice Douglas that this was just another rule of reason case like *White Motor* in which the District Court had not developed a sufficient factual record?

b.   What *had* happened in the District Court? Hadn't the plaintiff tried his case to a jury and lost? Was Albrecht arguing that the jury had been improperly instructed? Would you have thought liability here was so clear that the Supreme Court should order entry of judgment for Albrecht notwithstanding the jury's verdict?

4. PRICE DISCRIMINATION

THE ROBINSON-PATMAN ACT

An important limitation in marketing—and frequent trap for the unwary—is presented by § 2 of the Clayton Act, as amended in 1936 by the Robinson-Patman Act. This is the same statute we saw in *Utah Pie* but here we consider its more common application.

The key language is that of § 2(a):

"It shall be unlawful for any person engaged in commerce, in the course of such commerce, either directly or indirectly, to discriminate in price between different purchasers of commodities of like grade and quality, where either or any of the purchases involved in such discrimination are in commerce, where such commodities are sold for use, consumption, or resale within the United States * * * , and where the effect of such discrimination may be substantially to lessen competition or tend to create a monopoly in any line of commerce, or to injure, destroy, or prevent competition with any person who either grants or knowingly receives the benefit of such discrimination, or with customers of either of them: *Provided*, That nothing herein contained shall prevent differentials which make only due allowance for differences in the cost of manufacture, sale, or delivery resulting from the differing methods or quantities in which such commodities are to such purchasers sold or delivered: *Provided, however,* That the Federal Trade Commission may * * * fix and establish quantity limits * * * as to particular commodities or classes of commodities, where it finds that available purchasers in greater quantities are so few as to render differentials on account thereof unjustly discriminatory or promotive of monopoly in any line of commerce * * *: *And provided further,* That nothing herein contained shall prevent price changes from time to time where in response to changing conditions affecting the market for or the marketability of the goods concerned, such as but not limited to actual or imminent deterioration of perishable goods, obsolescence of seasonal goods, distress sales under court process, or sales in good faith in discontinuance of business in the goods concerned."

Section 2(b) continues:

"Upon proof being made * * * that there has been discrimination in price * * * , the burden of rebutting the prima-facie case thus made by showing justification shall be upon the person charged with a violation of this section, and unless justification shall be affirmatively shown, the Commission is authorized to issue an order terminating the discrimination: Provided, however, That nothing herein contained shall prevent a seller rebutting the prima-facie case thus made by showing that his lower price * * * was made in good faith to meet an equally low price of a competitor * * * "

Section 2(c) makes it unlawful for

"any person engaged in commerce, in the course of such commerce, to pay or grant, or to receive or accept, anything of value as a commission, brokerage, or other compensation, or any allowance or discount in lieu thereof, except for services rendered in connection with the sale or purchase of goods * * * [by] the other party to the transaction * * * .

Section 2(d) forbids

"any person engaged in commerce to pay * * * anything of value to or for the benefit of a customer * * * as compensation or in consideration for any services or facilities furnished by or through such customer in connection with the * * * sale * * * of any product or commodities * * * [of] such person, unless such payment or consideration is available on proportionately equal terms to all other customers competing in the distribution of such commodity or commodities."

Section 2(e) prohibits any person's discriminating

"in favor of one purchaser against another purchaser or purchasers of a commodity bought for resale * * * [by] furnishing * * * any services or facilities connected with the processing, handling, sale, or offering for sale of such commodity * * * on terms not accorded to all purchasers on proportionately equal terms."

Finally, Section 2(f) forbids knowingly receiving a discrimination prohibited by the preceding sections.

THE LEGISLATIVE HISTORY OF THE ROBINSON-PATMAN ACT

The Robinson-Patman Act, another piece of Depression-era legislation, was first introduced in the House of Representatives by Congressman Wright Patman, a Texas Democrat, as an amendment to § 2 of the Clayton Act.[85] Its purpose was to prohibit "unfair price discriminations" against the

---

[85]   The Robinson-Patman Act was originally two bills, one in the Senate, called the Robinson Bill, and one in the House of Representatives, called the Patman Bill. When these two bills were introduced they were identical but through amendments in each chamber of Congress the bills were altered. The two bills were then combined into one, the Robinson-Patman Act, by the Conference Committee. That bill was then passed by both Houses.

small independent store owner.[86] Congressman Patman believed the Clayton Act as it stood, was a "feeble gesture against price discrimination * * * because it permits quantity discounts without suggesting any measure or standard to limit their abuse."[87] Many chain stores and mail order houses were receiving discounts because of the large quantity that they were purchasing. There were several ways that the manufacturer could give the discount. One way was for the manufacturer to pay an excessively high commission to a broker that was associated with the purchaser. Another common method was for the manufacturer to pay the chain store to advertise its product.

Either way, the chain store's net price was lower than that charged the independent store which did not get the commission or allowance.[88]

Congressman Patman believed that if the current trend continued, independent merchants would be forced out of business. He explained that in the grocery industry "only 18 percent of the cash business of the food and grocery business was done by the independent stores * * * ."[89] The reason is that the chain store can "put the same goods on their shelves as the independent across the street puts on his shelves at 20 percent less."[90] Although the lower prices might seem beneficial now, in the long run, this practice would allegedly force all independent grocers out of business.

If the independent merchant was forced out of business this would be bad for the economy because "[w]hen you take money from the local community you dry up the reservoir of credit for that community, and the benefit that you get out of the corporate chains are destroyed many times in different ways. * * * It is [the] drying up [of] the reservoir of credit in the local communities throughout this country * * * [that] has caused a big part of this depression from which we have been suffering."[91]

Congressman Patman perceived other long term disadvantages to the chain stores. He believed that "we would have a monopoly and along with that monopoly would come higher prices and oppression * * * of both producers and consumers or Government ownership."[92] Although Congressman Patman's example was about grocers, he was fearful that all industries would end up being controlled by monopolies.

---

[86] 4 Earl W. Kintner, The Legislative History of the Federal Antitrust Laws and Related Statutes 3085 (1980).

[87] Id. at 2927–28.

[88] See, e.g., Federal Trade Commission, Chain Stores: Final Report on the Chain-Store Investigation (1935). The background is also summarized in A.B.A. Section of Antitrust Law, The Robinson-Patman Act: Policy and Law, vol. I. (1980).

[89] Id. at 2930.

[90] Id.

[91] Id. at 2934.

[92] Id. at 2931.

Equal Prices for All

The Robinson-Patman Act was designed to "enable the retailer, when he purchases a certain quantity, to be able to get that merchandise at the same price and on the same terms as his competitor."[93] To accomplish this principle, the Robinson-Patman Act made it unlawful to discriminate in price between different purchasers of commodities of like grade and quality. The word "quantity" was purposely left out of this clause because the Act was expressly designed not to recognize quantity discounts unrelated to cost differences.

The Act further qualified the prohibition by saying a price discrimination was only illegal if "the effect of such discrimination may be substantially to lessen competition or tend to create a monopoly in any line of commerce, or to injure, destroy, or prevent competition with any person who either grants or knowingly receives the benefit of such discrimination." "[U]nder the then prevailing doctrines of constitutional law, a federal statute regulating pricing conduct which did not injuriously affect the interstate economy appeared vulnerable" and might be declared unconstitutional.[94] The other problem was that "a bill banning discrimination, without more, might not reach predatory pricing tactics by sellers who, in order to destroy their competitors, slashed prices across the board in one area without differentiating among competing buyers."[95]

Brokerage Fees, Commissions, and Advertising

Sections 2(c), 2(d), and 2(e) were written into the Robinson-Patman Act to prohibit many of the common business practices of the 1930's— excessive commissions and brokerage fees, contracting for a purchasing party, and advertising allowances, that would give a buyer a net discount in the actual price he would pay for his goods.

Senator M.M. Logan, a Democrat from Kentucky, explained: "One large chain received last year $6,000,000 or $8,000,000, in brokerage fees" and this will give the chain a competitive advantage over the independent store owner.[96] Another "buyer is forcing * * * the payment of $12,000 a month under the cloak of advertising. * * * [There are] hundreds of such instances developed by the FTC in its investigation and also by the House Committee."[97]

Buyer's Liability

To help ensure compliance with the Robinson-Patman Act by buyers, buyers are also held liable if they knowingly "induce or receive a discrimination in price." "[T]he provision establishing legal liability for

---

[93]   Id. at 2932.

[94]   Frederick M. Rowe, Price Discrimination Under the Robinson-Patman Act 121 (1962).

[95]   Id.

[96]   Kintner, supra, at 3071.

[97]   Id.

buyers came only as a belated floor amendment in the final phases of the Senate debate."[98] The purpose was to afford "a valuable support to the manufacturer in his efforts to abide by the intent and purpose of the bill. It makes it easier for him to resist the demand for sacrificial price cuts coming from mass-buyer customers, since it enables him to charge them with knowledge of the illegality of the discount, and equal liability for it."[99] Not only were the Congressmen fearful that the manufacturers would offer discounts to attract large volume customers, they feared that large volume customers would demand a discount in price for their business.

Exceptions to Price Discrimination

Cost Allowance

The allowance to reflect cost differences is part of the Robinson-Patman Act that was taken from Section 2 of the original Clayton Act. Although the Robinson-Patman Act was designed to protect the small businessman from the chain store, there was a limit to that protection. Congress was not willing to protect the small businessman at the expense of efficiency unless the more efficient firm or firms could create a monopoly or oligopoly. The Federal Trade Commission was empowered to restrict the reductions in prices due to cost differentials if the differential is "unjustly discriminatory or promotive of monopoly in any line of commerce."

One Congressional concern was that most freight was transported on railroads. One company might be able to purchase enough freight to use a hundred cars while the small retailer might be able to purchase only one carload. There thus was a concern that "a big buyer would get a reduced rate of freight, and they could put their goods on their shelves at much less cost than * * * the independent."[100] The cost differential clauses were a "compromise instrument ensuring the protection of small merchants while preserving the consumer's stake in the fruits of economical mass distribution."[101]

Change in Market Conditions

The Robinson-Patman Act also provides that a seller may change the price at which the goods are sold if the market conditions change. Examples include the actual or imminent deterioration of perishable goods, obsolescence of seasonal goods, distress sales under court order, or sales in discontinuance of business in the goods concerned.[102]

This part of the Act was added as an amendment because of concerns that a seller could violate the Robinson-Patman Act if he acted in an economically efficient manner. Senator Lewis B. Schellenbach, a Democrat

---

[98]   Rowe, supra, at 423.

[99]   Kintner, supra, at 3375.

[100] Kintner, supra, at 3025.

[101] Rowe, supra, at 268.

[102] Robinson Patman Act § 2(a).

from Washington, was specifically concerned about the owner of a produce store who "goes along until 4 o'clock in the afternoon * * * [and] has sold to his customers at a certain price. He realizes that he has to dispose of all his perishables that afternoon, so he reduces his price; and it is feared that that will be forbidden by the bill. * * * [Senator Schellenbach was concerned that] there will be an interpretation by those who administer [the Robinson-Patman Act], and possibly a judicial interpretation" that would make this practice illegal.[103]

Meeting Competition

The Robinson-Patman Act also allows a manufacturer or retailer to give a customer a reduced price if it is to meet the price of a competitor. This idea was originally in Section 2 of the Clayton Act. "Congressional debates disclose a recurrent belief that this 'meeting competition' provision was a truism which neither added to nor subtracted from the law."[104]

Choosing Customers

The Robinson-Patman Act allows retailers and manufacturers to choose their own customers. This clause was in Section 2 of the original Clayton Act and was carried over to the Robinson-Patman Act because Congress wanted to protect merchants against "customers who are troublesome in their methods or insecure in their credit." However, once a customer has been accepted this clause does not permit the "absolute refusal to sell to particular customers where the facts are such as to show that it is done for the purpose of injuring or destroying them."[105]

Criminal Sanctions

The criminal sanctions in the Robinson-Patman Act were originally a competing bill introduced in the Senate by Senators Borah and Van Nuys. "Section 3 [of the Robinson-Patman Act] was the product of a legislative compromise which, rather than choosing between the civil liabilities of the Patman Bill and the criminal bans proposed by Senators Borah and Van Nuys, avoided the problem by merging and enacting both."[106]

Cooperatives

Section 4 of the Robinson-Patman Act legalized cooperatives and allowed the cooperatives to return to its members the savings that result from the operation of the cooperation. A cooperative is formed when a group of independent merchants "get together and will have one jobber * * * [with] sufficient funds to purchase their goods at quantity prices and

---

[103] Kintner, supra, at 3098. This view was consistent with the views of Congressman Clarence E. Hancock who said, "[w]e all know that the heavy overcoat * * * which I buy in November is worth more and costs more than the same overcoat bought * * * in February." Id.

[104] Rowe, supra, at 209.

[105] Kintner, supra, at 3373.

[106] Rowe, supra, at 453.

warehouse them or form a separate corporation and buy stock in it."[107] This section is designed to assure the independent broker "any real economies and savings to which those mass operations entitle them and which they often do not receive."[108]

A NOTE ON SOME IMPORTANT ROBINSON-PATMAN ACT CASES

Some law schools devote a separate course to the Robinson-Patman Act. Its technical complexity certainly justifies such treatment, but rather than open up that range of issues, we will satisfy ourselves with a brief treatment of a few cases answering some of the major questions arising under the Act.

Federal Trade Commission v. Anheuser-Busch, Inc., 363 U.S. 536, 80 S.Ct. 1267, 4 L.Ed.2d 1385 (1960), resolved perhaps the most basic question of all under the Robinson-Patman Act. To prove "price discrimination" one need only show "a price difference."

Federal Trade Commission v. Morton Salt Co., 334 U.S. 37, 68 S.Ct. 822, 92 L.Ed. 1196 (1948), illustrated the idea of "secondary line" injury. We saw the issue of primary line injury in *Utah Pie*, where the price differences were allegedly used to injure a seller's own competitors. What Morton Salt had done was give better prices to merchants who bought a lot of salt than it gave to those who bought less. The adverse effect was said to be on competition among those Morton Salt customers, i.e., small grocers were less able to compete effectively with larger grocery chains, and the Court found that "Congress was especially concerned with protecting small businesses which were unable to buy in quantities * * * ."[109]

The meaning of the "like grade and quality" language in § 2(a) was examined in Federal Trade Commission v. Borden Co., 383 U.S. 637, 86 S.Ct. 1092, 16 L.Ed.2d 153 (1966). Borden produced evaporated milk and sold it under its own name. At the same time, it put exactly the same milk in cans that bore the private labels of its purchasers. It sold its own Borden brand milk to retailers for more than it sold the private label brands, a distinction justified by the greater preference shoppers showed for the "real" product. The Supreme Court upheld a Federal Trade Commission

---

[107] Kintner, supra, at 2934.

[108] Id. at 3376. We will see reference to Section 4 in Northwest Wholesale Stationers, Inc. v. Pacific Stationery & Printing Co., 472 U.S. 284 (1985), in Chapter IV, infra.

[109] For a discussion of who can be a proper plaintiff in a case of this kind today, and what that plaintiff must prove, see Andrew I. Gavil, Secondary Line Price Discrimination and the Fate of Morton Salt: To Save It, Let It Go, 48 Emory L.J. 1057 (1999). Cf. Volvo Trucks North America v. Reeder-Simco GMC, 546 U.S. 164, 126 S.Ct. 860, 163 L.Ed.2d 663 (2006) (for price differences to have a prohibited "effect on competition" they must be between dealers that compete to resell to the same retail customers).

ruling that chemically identical milk was of "like kind and quality" even if customers did not treat it as such. Do you agree? Justices Stewart and Harlan dissented, saying that the issue of economic significance is "likeness" as discerned by consumers.

Section 2(b) of the Act creates a defense that permits a seller "in good faith to meet the equally low price of a competitor." Notice that the statute permits "meet[ing]", not "beating" the price.[110]

Finally, the propriety of promotional allowances was examined in Federal Trade Commission v. Fred Meyer, Inc., 390 U.S. 341, 88 S.Ct. 904, 19 L.Ed.2d 1222 (1968). The defendant operated a chain of supermarkets that made 25% of the food sales in Portland, Oregon. It came up with a plan for the use of coupon books, each page of which could be turned in for a discount on a product sold in the store. To help with the cost of these discounts, firms that produced the canned goods or other items so promoted were required to pay $350 per item. Some also gave Meyer a discount on the wholesale price of advertised items. The Supreme Court upheld a Commission finding that the program violated §§ 2(a), 2(d) and 2(f) of the Act. It violated § 2(d) because the food producers did not offer to pay a similar $350 to every grocer with whom they dealt. The discounts on the price at which promoted goods were sold to Fred Meyer violated § 2(a), and the § 2(f) violation was based on Meyer's soliciting these allowances and discounts.

Do you agree with this result? Were consumers hurt by this program? Did the Robinson-Patman Act here seem to punish a grocer's imagination and success?[111]

SHOULD WE BE UPSET ABOUT PRICE DISCRIMINATION?

One rarely hears a kind word about price discrimination. Yet the reasons one should be upset about it are not always obvious.

---

[110] Think back to United States v. Container Corp. in which sellers called each other to verify the prices buyers said they had been quoted by the others. Do you see why they called? The *Container* opinion suggested the firms should have just offered their best prices, not simply met the competition. But to have done so might have violated § 2(a) unless the firms always offered an equally low price to all their customers, in which case they would not have needed the § 2(b) "meeting competition" defense. In short, the firms in *Container* argued that they were forced to violate either the Sherman Act or the Robinson-Patman Act if they were to deal at all. Later cases have eased that burden somewhat. See, e.g., United States v. United States Gypsum Co., 438 U.S. 422, 98 S.Ct. 2864, 57 L.Ed.2d 854 (1978) (seller not criminally liable for verifying price unless had intent to fix prices); Great Atlantic & Pacific Tea Co. v. Federal Trade Commission, 440 U.S. 69, 99 S.Ct. 925, 59 L.Ed.2d 153 (1979) (seller acts in "good faith" even when it does not completely verify the alleged competitor's price; buyer may be liable under § 2(f) for lying about another's lower price).

[111] See generally, Kenneth W. Dam, The Economics and Law of Price Discrimination: Herein of Three Regulatory Schemes, 31 U. Chicago L. Rev. 1 (1963).

Most often, one hears the same argument that was made in the Robinson-Patman Act debates, i.e., that price discrimination is unfair to small firms. The effect alleged is that price discrimination makes it hard for small firms to survive in a world in which their large competitors are treated better than they are.[112] One can understand why those *firms* would be upset, but why should consumers generally care? From the earliest days of antitrust litigation, it has been asserted that it is important to preserve small firms in the economy, but whether we want to preserve *all* of them instead of having lower prices charged by big firms is less clear.

More fundamentally, the problem with price discrimination is what it suggests about the market power of the firm engaging in it. That is, in a competitive market, a firm could not get away with charging customers different prices. The competitive price is also the producers' marginal cost in perfect competition, so a producer would only charge someone less than the competitive price if it were indeed cost justified to do so.

If Morton Salt charged you the competitive price of $1 per box for salt but tried to charge me $1.25, I would buy salt from someone else. Indeed, perhaps you would resell your $1 salt to me for $1.20. If Morton Salt can get away with charging me $1.25, it is arguably a sign that that firm has significant market power. The Robinson-Patman Act can be said to get at that power indirectly by making the price discrimination itself illegal.

Ask yourself, however, whether that would be the appropriate response even if Morton Salt had a monopoly. Price discrimination may actually make the situation better for consumers. Remember that in the introductory economic note in these materials we concluded that a monopolist ordinarily will reduce output because it has to give up some sales it could have made at high prices in order to sell everything at a lower, uniform price. Price discrimination allows the firm to minimize what it has to give up by selling greater quantities. It thus may tend to keep its production more nearly at the competitive level. That is not as desirable as having a competitive market, of course, but if one cannot get at a monopoly under Sherman Act § 2, trying to get at it by prohibiting price discrimination may be counterproductive.

Furthermore, it seems likely that courts will make some serious Type 1 errors if they always condemn charging different customers different prices. The effort to overcome barriers to market entry that we saw in *Utah Pie* is certainly one example of such pro-consumer conduct. So are lower prices for movie matinees and "buy-two, get one free" discounts to loyal customers. Indeed, while the Robinson-Patman Act is unlikely to be

---

[112] Wal-Mart is perhaps the quintessential example of a power buyer, and its alleged impact on retailing generally makes this an especially timely question. See, e.g., Symposium, Buyer Power and Antitrust, 72 Antitrust L.J. 505–744 (2005).

repealed anytime soon, it is not unfair to describe it as, in large part, an "anti-competition" and "anti-consumer" antitrust law.[113]

E. MERGERS

Now we come to the final series of cases in this chapter. These cases involve mergers. They not only tended to be litigated later chronologically than many of the other cases in the chapter, but they also integrate the analysis of vertical and horizontal arrangements and present some of the most interesting dialogue within the Court about questions of economic analysis.

Consolidations of large companies, of course, have been a subject of antitrust interest since the prosecution in *E.C. Knight* in the 1890s. Consolidations are traditionally classified as "horizontal," i.e., involving competitors at the same level of the manufacturing and distribution process; "vertical," involving firms at different levels of the process; or "conglomerate," involving unrelated firms who were neither competitors nor buyer/suppliers.

Since at least *Northern Securities* in 1904, it has been clear that some consolidations could be challenged under the Sherman Act. However, *U.S. Steel* and *Standard Oil* seemed to say that even large consolidations of actual competitors, if not accompanied by bad practices of the new firm, might not violate the Sherman Act. Thus, § 7 of the Clayton Act, adopted in 1914, sought to make more certain the ability to challenge such consolidations before they were a fait accompli. The language of § 7, however, originally prohibited only the form of consolidation with which Congress in 1914 was most familiar—acquiring the stock of a competing company.

AN INTRODUCTORY NOTE ON *COLUMBIA STEEL*

United States v. Columbia Steel Co., 334 U.S. 495, 68 S.Ct. 1107, 92 L.Ed. 1533 (1948), tested whether the statutory language should be read also to prohibit functionally similar but formally different kinds of consolidations.

U.S. Steel was the largest rolled steel producer in the country. Columbia Steel, its wholly owned subsidiary, was the largest rolled steel

---

[113] For a contemporary essay on continuing issues under the Robinson-Patman Act, see Herbert Hovenkamp, The Robinson-Patman Act and Competition: Unfinished Business, 68 Antitrust L.J. 125 (2000). See also, William J. Baumol & Daniel G. Swanson, The New Economy and Ubiquitous *Competitive* Price Discrimination: Identifying Defensible Criteria of Market Power, 70 Antitrust L.J. 661 (2003); James C. Cooper, Luke Froeb, Daniel P. O'Brien, & Steven Tschantz, Does Price Discrimination Intensify Competition? Implications for Antitrust, 72 Antitrust L.J. 327 (2005).

producer in the Western United States. Columbia Steel was also the sales agent for some eastern fabricators who wanted to sell steel products in the west.

Columbia and U.S. Steel had contracted to buy the assets of Consolidated Steel, the largest independent fabricator of steel products in the western region. At the end of World War II, U.S. Steel had bought a large government plant in California that it had operated during the war, so it needed outlets for lots of western rolled steel. U.S. Steel produced 50% of all west coast steel, but citing *Alcoa*, the Justice Department had decided its size alone did not make it a monopoly.

Before the war, Consolidated had wanted to let U.S. Steel buy it, and buying the rolled steel plant meant U.S. Steel was now interested. With respect to fabricated steel, the firms ranked numbers 1 & 2 in the 11 western state market. U.S. Steel produced 13% while Consolidated produced 10.6%.

The sale was opposed by the Government for two reasons: (a) U.S. Steel would be able to fabricate more of its own steel and thus not need to use other fabricators, and (b) competition for those fabricated products in which U.S. Steel and Consolidated competed would be eliminated.

The Supreme Court, in an opinion by Justice Reed, saw this transaction as simply allowing a steel producer to find a way to fabricate products in a new territory. "Vertical integration, as such without more," the Court held, "cannot be held violative of the Sherman Act." What might have been thought to be an important issue of Clayton Act coverage was disposed of in a footnote saying that because this was an asset acquisition rather than a stock purchase, the Clayton Act did not apply.[114]

Critics of the decision argued that if Clayton § 7 could not reach further expansion of U.S. Steel, its "loopholes" needed to be closed. Thus, just two years later in 1950, Congress adopted the Celler-Kefauver amendments to § 7. Our next case was the first that reached the Supreme Court under the amended § 7.

BROWN SHOE CO., INC. V. UNITED STATES

Supreme Court of the United States, 1962
370 U.S. 294, 82 S.Ct. 1502, 8 L.Ed.2d 510

MR. CHIEF JUSTICE WARREN delivered the opinion of the Court.

I

This suit was initiated in November 1955 when the Government filed a civil action * * * alleging that a contemplated merger between the G. R. Kinney Company, Inc. (Kinney), and the Brown Shoe Company, Inc.

---

[114] Chief Justice Vinson and Justices Frankfurter, Burton and Jackson joined Justice Reed's majority opinion. Justices Douglas, Black, Rutledge and Murphy dissented.

(Brown), * * * would violate § 7 of the Clayton Act. * * * The complaint sought injunctive relief * * * to restrain consummation of the merger.

* * *

In the District Court, the Government contended that the effect of the merger of Brown—the third largest seller of shoes by dollar volume in the United States, a leading manufacturer of men's, women's, and children's shoes, and a retailer with over 1,230 owned, operated or controlled retail outlets[115]—and Kinney—the eighth largest company, by dollar volume, among those primarily engaged in selling shoes, itself a large manufacturer of shoes, and a retailer with over 350 retail outlets—"may be substantially to lessen competition or to tend to create a monopoly" by eliminating actual or potential competition in the production of shoes for the national wholesale shoe market and in the sale of shoes at retail in the Nation, by foreclosing competition from "a market represented by Kinney's retail outlets whose annual sales exceed $42,000,000," and by enhancing Brown's competitive advantage over other producers, distributors and sellers of shoes. The Government argued that the "line of commerce" affected by this merger is "footwear," or alternatively, that the "line[s]" are "men's," "women's," and "children's" shoes, separately considered, and that the "section of the country," within which the anticompetitive effect of the merger is to be judged, is the Nation as a whole, or alternatively, each separate city or city and its immediate surrounding area in which the parties sell shoes at retail.

In the District Court, Brown contended that the merger would be shown not to endanger competition if the "line[s] of commerce" and the "section[s] of the country" were properly determined. Brown urged that not only were the age and sex of the intended customers to be considered in determining the relevant line of commerce, but that differences in grade of material, quality of workmanship, price, and customer use of shoes resulted in establishing different lines of commerce. While agreeing with the Government that, with regard to manufacturing, the relevant geographic market for assessing the effect of the merger upon competition is the country as a whole, Brown contended that with regard to retailing, the market must vary with economic reality from the central business district of a large city to a "standard metropolitan area" for a smaller community. Brown further contended that, both at the manufacturing level and at the retail level, the shoe industry enjoyed healthy competition and that the vigor of this competition would not, in any event, be diminished by

---

[115] Of these over 1,230 outlets under Brown's control at the time of the filing of the complaint, Brown owned and operated over 470, while over 570 were independently owned stores operating under the Brown "Franchise Program" and over 190 were independently owned outlets operating under the "Wohl Plan." A store operating under the Franchise Program agrees not to carry competing lines of shoes of other manufacturers in return for certain aid from Brown; a store under the Wohl Plan similarly agrees to concentrate its purchases on lines which Brown sells through Wohl in return for credit and merchandising aid. In addition, Brown shoes were sold through numerous retailers operating entirely independently of Brown. [Court's fn. 1]

the proposed merger because Kinney manufactured less than 0.5% and retailed less than 2% of the Nation's shoes.

The District Court rejected the broadest contentions of both parties. The District Court found that "there is one group of classifications which is understood and recognized by the entire industry and the public—the classification into 'men's,' 'women's' and 'children's' shoes separately and independently." On the other hand, "[to] classify shoes as a whole could be unfair and unjust; to classify them further would be impractical, unwarranted and unrealistic."

Realizing that "the areas of effective competition for retailing purposes cannot be fixed with mathematical precision," the District Court found that "when determined by economic reality, for retailing, a 'section of the country' is a city of 10,000 or more population and its immediate and contiguous surrounding area, regardless of name designation, and in which a Kinney store and a Brown (operated, franchise, or plan) store are located."

The District Court rejected the Government's contention that the combining of the manufacturing facilities of Brown and Kinney would substantially lessen competition in the production of men's, women's, or children's shoes for the national wholesale market. However, the District Court did find that the likely foreclosure of other manufacturers from the market represented by Kinney's retail outlets may substantially lessen competition in the manufacturers' distribution of "men's," "women's," and "children's" shoes, considered separately, throughout the Nation. The District Court also found that the merger may substantially lessen competition in retailing alone in "men's," "women's," and "children's" shoes, considered separately, in every city of 10,000 or more population and its immediate surrounding area in which both a Kinney and a Brown store are located.

* * *

The Industry

The District Court found that although domestic shoe production was scattered among a large number of manufacturers, a small number of large companies occupied a commanding position. Thus, while the 24 largest manufacturers produced about 35% of the Nation's shoes, the top 4— International, Endicott-Johnson, Brown (including Kinney) and General Shoe—alone produced approximately 23% of the Nation's shoes or 65% of the production of the top 24.

In 1955, domestic production of nonrubber shoes was 509.2 million pairs, of which about 103.6 million pairs were men's shoes, about 271 million pairs were women's shoes, and about 134.6 million pairs were children's shoes. The District Court found that men's, women's, and children's shoes are normally produced in separate factories.

The public buys these shoes through about 70,000 retail outlets, only 22,000 of which, however, derive 50% or more of their gross receipts from the sale of shoes and are classified as "shoe stores" by the Census Bureau. These 22,000 shoe stores were found generally to sell (1) men's shoes only, (2) women's shoes only, (3) women's and children's shoes, or (4) men's, women's, and children's shoes.

The District Court found a "definite trend" among shoe manufacturers to acquire retail outlets. For example, International Shoe Company had no retail outlets in 1945, but by 1956 had acquired 130; General Shoe Company had only 80 retail outlets in 1945 but had 526 by 1956; Shoe Corporation of America, in the same period, increased its retail holdings from 301 to 842; Melville Shoe Company from 536 to 947; and Endicott-Johnson from 488 to 540. Brown, itself, with no retail outlets of its own prior to 1951, had acquired 845 such outlets by 1956. Moreover, between 1950 and 1956 nine independent shoe store chains, operating 1,114 retail shoe stores, were found to have become subsidiaries of these large firms and to have ceased their independent operations.

And once the manufacturers acquired retail outlets, the District Court found there was a "definite trend" for the parent-manufacturers to supply an ever increasing percentage of the retail outlets' needs, thereby foreclosing other manufacturers from effectively competing for the retail accounts. Manufacturer-dominated stores were found to be "drying up" the available outlets for independent producers.

Another "definite trend" found to exist in the shoe industry was a decrease in the number of plants manufacturing shoes. And there appears to have been a concomitant decrease in the number of firms manufacturing shoes. In 1947, there were 1,077 independent manufacturers of shoes, but by 1954 their number had decreased about 10% to 970.

Brown Shoe

Brown Shoe was found not only to have been a participant, but also a moving factor, in these industry trends. Although Brown had experimented several times with operating its own retail outlets, by 1945 it had disposed of them all. However, in 1951, Brown again began to seek retail outlets by acquiring the Nation's largest operator of leased shoe departments, Wohl Shoe Company (Wohl), which operated 250 shoe departments in department stores throughout the United States. Between 1952 and 1955 Brown made a number of smaller acquisitions * * * . * * *

The acquisition of these corporations was found to lead to increased sales by Brown to the acquired companies. * * *

During the same period of time, Brown also acquired the stock or assets of seven companies engaged solely in shoe manufacturing. As a result, in 1955, Brown was the fourth largest shoe manufacturer in the country, producing about 25.6 million pairs of shoes or about 4% of the Nation's total footwear production.

Kinney

Kinney is principally engaged in operating the largest family-style shoe store chain in the United States. At the time of trial, Kinney was found to be operating over 400 such stores in more than 270 cities. These stores were found to make about 1.2% of all national retail shoe sales by dollar volume. * * *

In addition to this extensive retail activity, Kinney owned and operated four plants which manufactured men's, women's, and children's shoes and whose combined output was 0.5% of the national shoe production in 1955, making Kinney the twelfth largest shoe manufacturer in the United States.

Kinney stores were found to obtain about 20% of their shoes from Kinney's own manufacturing plants. At the time of the merger, Kinney bought no shoes from Brown; however, in line with Brown's conceded reasons for acquiring Kinney, Brown had, by 1957, become the largest outside supplier of Kinney's shoes, supplying 7.9% of all Kinney's needs.

It is in this setting that the merger was considered and held to violate § 7 of the Clayton Act. * * *

* * *

III

Legislative History

This case is one of the first to come before us in which the Government's complaint is based upon allegations that the appellant has violated § 7 of the Clayton Act, as that section was amended in 1950. The amendments adopted in 1950 culminated extensive efforts over a number of years, on the parts of both the Federal Trade Commission and some members of Congress, to secure revision of a section of the antitrust laws considered by many observers to be ineffective in its then existing form. * * *

As enacted in 1914, § 7 of the original Clayton Act prohibited the acquisition by one corporation of the stock of another corporation when such acquisition would result in a substantial lessening of competition between the acquiring and the acquired companies, or tend to create a monopoly in any line of commerce. The Act did not, by its explicit terms, or as construed by this Court, bar the acquisition by one corporation of the assets of another. Nor did it appear to preclude the acquisition of stock in any corporation other than a direct competitor. * * *

* * * Although the bill that was eventually to become amended § 7 was confined to embracing within the Act's terms the acquisition of assets as

well as stock, in the course of the hearings conducted in both the Eightieth and Eighty-first Congresses, a more far-reaching examination of the purposes and provisions of § 7 was undertaken. * * *

The dominant theme pervading congressional consideration of the 1950 amendments was a fear of what was considered to be a rising tide of economic concentration in the American economy. Apprehension in this regard was bolstered by the publication in 1948 of the Federal Trade Commission's study on corporate mergers. Statistics from this and other current studies were cited as evidence of the danger to the American economy in unchecked corporate expansions through mergers. Other considerations cited in support of the bill were the desirability of retaining "local control" over industry and the protection of small businesses. Throughout the recorded discussion may be found examples of Congress' fear not only of accelerated concentration of economic power on economic grounds, but also of the threat to other values a trend toward concentration was thought to pose.

What were some of the factors, relevant to a judgment as to the validity of a given merger, specifically discussed by Congress in redrafting § 7?

First, there is no doubt that Congress did wish to "plug the loophole" and to include within the coverage of the Act the acquisition of assets no less than the acquisition of stock.

Second, by the deletion of the "acquiring-acquired" language in the original text, it hoped to make plain that § 7 applied not only to mergers between actual competitors, but also to vertical and conglomerate mergers whose effect may tend to lessen competition in any line of commerce in any section of the country.

Third, it is apparent that a keystone in the erection of a barrier to what Congress saw was the rising tide of economic concentration, was its provision of authority for arresting mergers at a time when the trend to a lessening of competition in a line of commerce was still in its incipiency. Congress saw the process of concentration in American business as a dynamic force; it sought to assure the Federal Trade Commission and the courts the power to brake this force at its outset and before it gathered momentum.

Fourth, and closely related to the third, Congress rejected, as inappropriate to the problem it sought to remedy, the application to § 7 cases of the standards for judging the legality of business combinations adopted by the courts in dealing with cases arising under the Sherman Act, and which may have been applied to some early cases arising under original § 7.

Fifth, at the same time that it sought to create an effective tool for preventing all mergers having demonstrable anticompetitive effects, Congress recognized the stimulation to competition that might flow from particular mergers. When concern as to the Act's breadth was expressed, supporters of the amendments indicated that it would not impede, for example, a merger between two small companies to enable the combination to compete more effectively with larger corporations dominating the relevant market, nor a merger between a corporation which is financially healthy and a failing one which no longer can be a vital competitive factor in the market. The deletion of the word "community" in the original Act's description of the relevant geographic market is another illustration of Congress' desire to indicate that its concern was with the adverse effects of a given merger on competition only in an economically significant "section" of the country. Taken as a whole, the legislative history illuminates congressional concern with the protection of competition, not competitors, and its desire to restrain mergers only to the extent that such combinations may tend to lessen competition.

Sixth, Congress neither adopted nor rejected specifically any particular tests for measuring the relevant markets, either as defined in terms of product or in terms of geographic locus of competition, within which the anti-competitive effects of a merger were to be judged. Nor did it adopt a definition of the word "substantially," whether in quantitative terms of sales or assets or market shares or in designated qualitative terms, by which a merger's effects on competition were to be measured.

Seventh, while providing no definite quantitative or qualitative tests by which enforcement agencies could gauge the effects of a given merger to determine whether it may "substantially" lessen competition or tend toward monopoly, Congress indicated plainly that a merger had to be functionally viewed, in the context of its particular industry. That is, whether the consolidation was to take place in an industry that was fragmented rather than concentrated, that had seen a recent trend toward domination by a few leaders or had remained fairly consistent in its distribution of market shares among the participating companies, that had experienced easy access to markets by suppliers and easy access to suppliers by buyers or had witnessed foreclosure of business, that had witnessed the ready entry of new competition or the erection of barriers to prospective entrants, all were aspects, varying in importance with the merger under consideration, which would properly be taken into account.

Eighth, Congress used the words "*may* be substantially to lessen competition" (emphasis supplied), to indicate that its concern was with probabilities, not certainties. Statutes existed for dealing with clear-cut menaces to competition; no statute was sought for dealing with ephemeral possibilities. Mergers with a probable anticompetitive effect were to be proscribed by this Act.

It is against this background that we return to the case before us.

IV

The Vertical Aspects of the Merger

Economic arrangements between companies standing in a supplier-customer relationship are characterized as "vertical." The primary vice of a vertical merger or other arrangement tying a customer to a supplier is that, by foreclosing the competitors of either party from a segment of the market otherwise open to them, the arrangement may act as a "clog on competition," Standard Oil Co. of California v. United States, which "[deprives] * * * rivals of a fair opportunity to compete."[116] Every extended vertical arrangement by its very nature, for at least a time, denies to competitors of the supplier the opportunity to compete for part or all of the trade of the customer-party to the vertical arrangement. However, the Clayton Act does not render unlawful all such vertical arrangements, but * * * as we have previously noted,

> "[d]etermination of the relevant market is a necessary predicate to a finding of a violation of the Clayton Act because the threatened monopoly must be one which will substantially lessen competition 'within the area of effective competition.' Substantiality can be determined only in terms of the market affected."[117]

The "area of effective competition" must be determined by reference to a product market (the "line of commerce") and a geographic market (the "section of the country").

The Product Market

The outer boundaries of a product market are determined by the reasonable interchangeability of use or the cross-elasticity of demand between the product itself and substitutes for it.[118] However, within this broad market, well-defined submarkets may exist which, in themselves, constitute product markets for antitrust purposes. The boundaries of such a submarket may be determined by examining such practical indicia as industry or public recognition of the submarket as a separate economic entity, the product's peculiar characteristics and uses, unique production facilities, distinct customers, distinct prices, sensitivity to price changes,

---

[116] In addition, a vertical merger may disrupt and injure competition when those independent customers of the supplier who are in competition with the merging customer, are forced either to stop handling the supplier's lines, thereby jeopardizing the goodwill they have developed, or to retain the supplier's lines, thereby forcing them into competition with their own supplier. [Court's fn. 40]

[117] United States v. E.I. du Pont de Nemours & Co., 353 U.S. 586 [1957]. [Court's fn. 41]

[118] The cross-elasticity of production facilities may also be an important factor in defining a product market within which a vertical merger is to be viewed. However, the District Court made but limited findings concerning the feasibility of interchanging equipment in the manufacture of nonrubber footwear. At the same time, the record supports the court's conclusion that individual plants generally produced shoes in only one of the product lines the court found relevant. [Court's fn. 42]

and specialized vendors. Because § 7 of the Clayton Act prohibits any merger which may substantially lessen competition "in any line of commerce" (emphasis supplied), it is necessary to examine the effects of a merger in each such economically significant submarket to determine if there is a reasonable probability that the merger will substantially lessen competition. If such a probability is found to exist, the merger is proscribed.

Applying these considerations to the present case, we conclude that the record supports the District Court's finding that the relevant lines of commerce are men's, women's, and children's shoes. These product lines are recognized by the public; each line is manufactured in separate plants; each has characteristics peculiar to itself rendering it generally noncompetitive with the others; and each is, of course, directed toward a distinct class of customers.

Appellant, however, contends that the District Court's definitions fail to recognize sufficiently "price/quality" and "age/sex" distinctions in shoes. Brown argues that the predominantly medium-priced shoes which it manufactures occupy a product market different from the predominantly low-priced shoes which Kinney sells. But agreement with that argument would be equivalent to holding that medium-priced shoes do not compete with low-priced shoes. We think the District Court properly found the facts to be otherwise. It would be unrealistic to accept Brown's contention that, for example, men's shoes selling below $8.99 are in a different product market from those selling above $9.00. ← This is stupid.

This is not to say, however, that "price/quality" differences, where they exist, are unimportant in analyzing a merger; they may be of importance in determining the likely effect of a merger. But the boundaries of the relevant market must be drawn with sufficient breadth to include the competing products of each of the merging companies and to recognize competition where, in fact, competition exists. * * *

* * *

The Geographic Market

We agree with the parties and the District Court that insofar as the vertical aspect of this merger is concerned, the relevant geographic market is the entire Nation. * * *

The Probable Effect of the Merger

* * *

Since the diminution of the vigor of competition which may stem from a vertical arrangement results primarily from a foreclosure of a share of the market otherwise open to competitors, an important consideration in determining whether the effect of a vertical arrangement "may be substantially to lessen competition, or to tend to create a monopoly" is the size of the share of the market foreclosed. However, this factor will seldom be determinative. If the share of the market foreclosed is so large that it approaches monopoly proportions, the Clayton Act will, of course, have been violated; but the arrangement will also have run afoul of the Sherman Act. And the legislative history of § 7 indicates clearly that the tests for measuring the legality of any particular economic arrangement under the Clayton Act are to be less stringent than those used in applying the Sherman Act. On the other hand, foreclosure of a de minimis share of the market will not tend "substantially to lessen competition."

Between these extremes, in cases such as the one before us, in which the foreclosure is neither of monopoly nor de minimis proportions, the percentage of the market foreclosed by the vertical arrangement cannot itself be decisive. In such cases, it becomes necessary to undertake an examination of various economic and historical factors in order to determine whether the arrangement under review is of the type Congress sought to proscribe.

A most important such factor to examine is the very nature and purpose of the arrangement. Congress not only indicated that "the tests of illegality [under § 7] are intended to be similar to those which the courts have applied in interpreting the same language as used in other sections of the Clayton Act," but also chose for § 7 language virtually identical to that of § 3 of the Clayton Act, which had been interpreted by this Court to require an examination of the interdependence of the market share foreclosed by, and the economic purpose of, the vertical arrangement. Thus, for example, if a particular vertical arrangement, considered under § 3, appears to be a limited term exclusive-dealing contract, the market foreclosure must generally be significantly greater than if the arrangement is a tying contract before the arrangement will be held to have violated the Act. Compare Tampa Electric Co. v. Nashville Coal Co., and Standard Oil Co. of California v. United States, with International Salt Co. v. United States. * * *

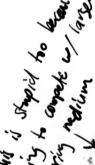

The importance which Congress attached to economic purpose is further demonstrated by the Senate and House Reports on H.R. 2734, which evince an intention to preserve the "failing company" doctrine * * * . Similarly, Congress foresaw that the merger of two large companies or a large and a small company might violate the Clayton Act while the merger of two small companies might not, although the share of the market foreclosed be identical, if the purpose of the small companies is to enable them in combination to compete with larger corporations dominating the market.

The present merger involved neither small companies nor failing companies. In 1955, the date of this merger, Brown was the fourth largest manufacturer in the shoe industry with sales of approximately 25 million pairs of shoes and assets of over $72,000,000 while Kinney had sales of about 8 million pairs of shoes and assets of about $18,000,000. Not only was Brown one of the leading manufacturers of men's, women's, and children's shoes, but Kinney, with over 350 retail outlets, owned and operated the largest independent chain of family shoe stores in the Nation. Thus, in this industry, no merger between a manufacturer and an independent retailer could involve a larger potential market foreclosure. Moreover, it is apparent both from past behavior of Brown and from the testimony of Brown's President, that Brown would use its ownership of Kinney to force Brown shoes into Kinney stores. Thus, in operation this vertical arrangement would be quite analogous to one involving a tying clause.

* * *

The existence of a trend toward vertical integration, which the District Court found, is well substantiated by the record. Moreover, the court found a tendency of the acquiring manufacturers to become increasingly important sources of supply for their acquired outlets. The necessary corollary of these trends is the foreclosure of independent manufacturers from markets otherwise open to them. And because these trends are not the product of accident but are rather the result of deliberate policies of Brown and other leading shoe manufacturers, account must be taken of these facts in order to predict the probable future consequences of this merger. * * *

Brown argues, however, that the shoe industry is at present composed of a large number of manufacturers and retailers, and that the industry is dynamically competitive. But remaining vigor cannot immunize a merger if the trend in that industry is toward oligopoly. * * *

Moreover, as we have remarked above, not only must we consider the probable effects of the merger upon the economics of the particular markets affected but also we must consider its probable effects upon the economic way of life sought to be preserved by Congress. Congress was desirous of preventing the formation of further oligopolies with their attendant adverse effects upon local control of industry and upon small business. Where an industry was composed of numerous independent units, Congress appeared anxious to preserve this structure. * * *

The District Court's findings * * * convince us that the shoe industry is being subjected to just such a cumulative series of vertical mergers which, if left unchecked, will be likely "substantially to lessen competition."

We reach this conclusion because the trend toward vertical integration in the shoe industry, when combined with Brown's avowed policy of forcing its own shoes upon its retail subsidiaries, may foreclose competition from a substantial share of the markets for men's, women's, and children's shoes, without producing any countervailing competitive, economic, or social advantages.

V

The Horizontal Aspects of the Merger

An economic arrangement between companies performing similar functions in the production or sale of comparable goods or services is characterized as "horizontal." The effect on competition of such an arrangement depends, of course, upon its character and scope. Thus, its validity in the face of the antitrust laws will depend upon such factors as: the relative size and number of the parties to the arrangement; whether it allocates shares of the market among the parties; whether it fixes prices at which the parties will sell their product; or whether it absorbs or insulates competitors. * * *

The Product Market

* * *

In Part IV of this opinion we hold that the District Court correctly defined men's, women's, and children's shoes as the relevant lines of commerce in which to analyze the vertical aspects of the merger. For the reasons there stated we also hold that the same lines of commerce are appropriate for considering the horizontal aspects of the merger.

The Geographic Market

The criteria to be used in determining the appropriate geographic market are essentially similar to those used to determine the relevant product market. * * * Moreover, just as a product submarket may have § 7 significance as the proper "line of commerce," so may a geographic submarket be considered the appropriate "section of the country." * * * Congress prescribed a pragmatic, factual approach to the definition of the relevant market and not a formal, legalistic one. The geographic market selected must, therefore, both "correspond to the commercial realities" of the industry and be economically significant. Thus, although the geographic market in some instances may encompass the entire Nation, under other circumstances it may be as small as a single metropolitan area.[119] * * *

The parties do not dispute the findings of the District Court that the Nation as a whole is the relevant geographic market for measuring the anticompetitive effects of the merger viewed vertically or of the horizontal merger of Brown's and Kinney's manufacturing facilities. As to the retail level, however, they disagree.

---

[119] To illustrate: If two retailers, one operating primarily in the eastern half of the Nation, and the other operating largely in the West, competed in but two mid-Western cities, the fact that the latter outlets represented but a small share of each company's business would not immunize the merger in those markets in which competition might be adversely affected. On the other hand, that fact would, of course, be properly considered in determining the equitable relief to be decreed. [Court's fn. 65]

The District Court found that the effects of this aspect of the merger must be analyzed in every city with a population exceeding 10,000 and its immediate contiguous surrounding territory in which both Brown and Kinney sold shoes at retail through stores they either owned or controlled. By this definition of the geographic market, less than one-half of all the cities in which either Brown or Kinney sold shoes through such outlets are represented. The appellant recognizes that if the District Court's characterization of the relevant market is proper, the number of markets in which both Brown and Kinney have outlets is sufficiently numerous so that the validity of the entire merger is properly judged by testing its effects in those markets. However, [Appellant] * * * claims that such areas should, in some cases, be defined so as to include only the central business districts of large cities, and in others, so as to encompass the "standard metropolitan areas" within which smaller communities are found. It argues that any test failing to distinguish between these competitive situations is improper.

We believe, however, that the record fully supports the District Court's findings that shoe stores in the outskirts of cities compete effectively with stores in central downtown areas, and that while there is undoubtedly some commercial intercourse between smaller communities within a single "standard metropolitan area," the most intense and important competition in retail sales will be confined to stores within the particular communities in such an area and their immediate environs.

We therefore agree that the District Court properly defined the relevant geographic markets in which to analyze this merger as those cities with a population exceeding 10,000 and their environs in which both Brown and Kinney retailed shoes through their own outlets. Such markets are large enough to include the downtown shops and suburban shopping centers in areas contiguous to the city, which are the important competitive factors, and yet are small enough to exclude stores beyond the immediate environs of the city, which are of little competitive significance.

* * *

The Probable Effect of the Merger

* * *

* * * An analysis of undisputed statistics of sales of shoes in the cities in which both Brown and Kinney sell shoes at retail, separated into the appropriate lines of commerce, provides a persuasive factual foundation upon which the required prognosis of the merger's effects may be built. * * * They show, for example, that during 1955 in 32 separate cities, ranging in size and location from Topeka, Kansas, to Batavia, New York, and Hobbs, New Mexico, the combined share of Brown and Kinney sales of women's shoes (by unit volume) exceeded 20%. In 31 cities—some the same as those used in measuring the effect of the merger in the women's line—the combined share of children's shoes sales exceeded 20%; in 6 cities their

share exceeded 40%. In Dodge City, Kansas, their combined share of the market for women's shoes was over 57%; their share of the children's shoe market in that city was 49%. In the 7 cities in which Brown's and Kinney's combined shares of the market for women's shoes were greatest (ranging from 33% to 57%) each of the parties alone, prior to the merger, had captured substantial portions of those markets (ranging from 13% to 34%); the merger intensified this existing concentration. In 118 separate cities the combined shares of the market of Brown and Kinney in the sale of one of the relevant lines of commerce exceeded 5%. In 47 cities, their share exceeded 5% in all three lines.

The market share which companies may control by merging is one of the most important factors to be considered when determining the probable effects of the combination on effective competition in the relevant market. In an industry as fragmented as shoe retailing, the control of substantial shares of the trade in a city may have important effects on competition. If a merger achieving 5% control were now approved, we might be required to approve future merger efforts by Brown's competitors seeking similar market shares. The oligopoly Congress sought to avoid would then be furthered and it would be difficult to dissolve the combinations previously approved. Furthermore, in this fragmented industry, even if the combination controls but a small share of a particular market, the fact that this share is held by a large national chain can adversely affect competition. Testimony in the record from numerous independent retailers, based on their actual experience in the market, demonstrates that a strong, national chain of stores can insulate selected outlets from the vagaries of competition in particular locations and that the large chains can set and alter styles in footwear to an extent that renders the independents unable to maintain competitive inventories. A third significant aspect of this merger is that it creates a large national chain which is integrated with a manufacturing operation. The retail outlets of integrated companies, by eliminating wholesalers and by increasing the volume of purchases from the manufacturing division of the enterprise, can market their own brands at prices below those of competing independent retailers. Of course, some of the results of large integrated or chain operations are beneficial to consumers. Their expansion is not rendered unlawful by the mere fact that small independent stores may be adversely affected. It is competition, not competitors, which the Act protects. But we cannot fail to recognize Congress' desire to promote competition through the protection of viable, small, locally owned businesses. Congress appreciated that occasional higher costs and prices might result from the maintenance of fragmented industries and markets. It resolved these competing considerations in favor of decentralization. We must give effect to that decision.

Other factors to be considered in evaluating the probable effects of a merger in the relevant market lend additional support to the District

Court's conclusion that this merger may substantially lessen competition. One such factor is the history of tendency toward concentration in the industry.[120] As we have previously pointed out, the shoe industry has, in recent years, been a prime example of such a trend. * * * By the merger in this case, the largest single group of retail stores still independent of one of the large manufacturers was absorbed into an already substantial aggregation of more or less controlled retail outlets. As a result of this merger, Brown moved into second place nationally in terms of retail stores directly owned. Including the stores on its franchise plan, the merger placed under Brown's control almost 1,600 shoe outlets, or about 7.2% of the Nation's retail "shoe stores" as defined by the Census Bureau, and 2.3% of the Nation's total retail shoe outlets. We cannot avoid the mandate of Congress that tendencies toward concentration in industry are to be curbed in their incipiency, particularly when those tendencies are being accelerated through giant steps striding across a hundred cities at a time. In the light of the trends in this industry we agree with the Government and the court below that this is an appropriate place at which to call a halt.

At the same time appellant has presented no mitigating factors, such as the business failure or the inadequate resources of one of the parties that may have prevented it from maintaining its competitive position, nor a demonstrated need for combination to enable small companies to enter into a more meaningful competition with those dominating the relevant markets. On the basis of the record before us, we believe the Government sustained its burden of proof. We hold that the District Court was correct in concluding that this merger may tend to lessen competition substantially in the retail sale of men's, women's, and children's shoes in the overwhelming majority of those cities and their environs in which both Brown and Kinney sell through owned or controlled outlets.

The judgment is affirmed.

MR. JUSTICE FRANKFURTER took no part in the decision of this case [and] MR. JUSTICE WHITE took no part in the consideration or decision of this case.

MR. JUSTICE HARLAN, * * * concurring in part.

* * * I concur in the judgment of the Court but do not join its opinion, which I consider to go far beyond what is necessary to decide the case.

* * *

---

[120] A company's history of expansion through mergers presents a different economic picture than a history of expansion through unilateral growth. Internal expansion is more likely to be the result of increased demand for the company's products and is more likely to provide increased investment in plants, more jobs and greater output. Conversely, expansion through merger is more likely to reduce available consumer choice while providing no increase in industry capacity, jobs or output. It was for these reasons, among others, Congress expressed its disapproval of successive acquisitions. Section 7 was enacted to prevent even small mergers that added to concentration in an industry. [Court's fn. 72]

The dispositive considerations are, I think, found in the "vertical" effects of the merger, that is, the effects reasonably to be foreseen from combining Brown's manufacturing facilities with Kinney's retail outlets. In my opinion the District Court's conclusions as to such effects are supported by the record, and suffice to condemn the merger under § 7, without regard to what might be deemed to be the "horizontal" effects of the transaction.

* * *

Prior to 1955 Kinney had bought none of its outside-source shoes from Brown, and its records for 1955 reveal that the year's purchases were made from a diverse number of independent shoe manufacturers. * * * Consequently, it appears that Kinney was a substantial purchaser of the shoes produced by many small independent shoe manufacturers throughout the country. In fact, the record affirmatively shows that at least five of Kinney's suppliers, three of which are located in the State of New York, one in Pennsylvania, and one in New Hampshire, each relied upon Kinney to purchase more than 40% of its total production in 1955.

* * *

The vertical affiliation between this shoe manufacturer and a primarily retail organization is surely not, as the dissenters thought the contractual tie in *Standard Stations* to be, "a device for waging competition" rather than "a device for suppressing competition." Since Brown is able by reason of this merger to turn an independent purchaser into a captive market for its shoes it inevitably diminishes the available market for which shoe manufacturers compete. If Brown shoes replace those which had been previously produced by others, the displaced manufacturers have no choice but to enter some other market or go out of business. * * *

Not only may this merger, judged from a vertical standpoint, affect manufacturers who compete with Brown; it may also adversely affect competition on the retailing level. With a large manufacturer such as Brown behind it, the Kinney chain would have a great competitive advantage over the retail stores with which it vies for consumer patronage. As a manufacturer-owned outlet, the Kinney store would doubtless be able to sell its shoes at a lower profit margin and outlast an independent competitor. The merger would also effectively prevent the retail competitor from dealing in Brown shoes, since these might be offered at lower prices in Kinney stores than elsewhere.

* * * When, as here, the foreclosure of what may be considered a small percentage of retailers' purchases may be caused by the combination * * * and when the volume of * * * purchases from independent manufacturers in various parts of the country is large enough to render it probable that these suppliers, if displaced, will have to fall by the wayside, it cannot, in

my opinion, be said that the effect on the shoe industry is "remote" or "insubstantial."

* * *

Accordingly, * * * I join the judgment of affirmance.[121]

NOTES AND QUESTIONS

1.   This is an important case for the law of both horizontal and vertical mergers. What do we know about Brown and Kinney? What did they make and how much did they sell?

a.   Would you have called shoe manufacturing a concentrated industry? What do we know about the number of firms and the market shares of even the largest firms? As you will later see, by almost any standard, shoe manufacturing was one of the *least* concentrated industries in the country.

b.   What do we already know about the recent history of this industry? Think back to the *United Shoe Machinery* case. Was it almost inevitable that this cottage industry would tend to consolidate to some extent? Might the *United Shoe Machinery* decree itself have contributed to that development?

2.   How did the District Court and later this court define markets here?

a.   Were you convinced that the three product markets defined by the Court were accurately drawn? Did the Court justify them in terms of cross-elasticity of demand as it had said was appropriate in the cellophane case (*E.I. duPont*)?

b.   What is the concept of a "submarket"?[122] How does determination of submarkets differ from determination of markets, if at all? Why did Brown want a market definition that took account of price and quality differences within the categories of men's, women's and children's shoes? Should those have been seen to be appropriate submarkets?

c.   Are you convinced that each city with over 10,000 people should be considered a separate geographic market for shoes? Are shoes so inexpensive that people will not travel to a nearby town to shop for a lower price?

d.   Were you persuaded that because Brown and Kinney made 57% of the women's shoe sales in Dodge City, Kansas, their merger could be blocked for that reason alone? What statutory language gives such far reaching effect to such local consequences?

3.   What did the Court have to say about Congress' intent in adopting the antimerger law in general and the 1950 amendments in particular?

---

[121] [Ed. note] The concurring opinion of Mr. Justice Clark, making many of the same points as Justice Harlan, is omitted.

[122] For a later reflection on the concept, see Jonathan B. Baker, Stepping Out in an Old *Brown Shoe*: In Qualified Praise of Submarkets, 68 Antitrust L.J. 203 (2000).

a.   Did the Court suggest that if this merger had been permitted to go through, Brown/Kinney would have monopolized the shoe industry? What then is the standard to be applied to mergers under § 7?

b.   Is Justice Harlan right that § 7 says that mergers must be struck down unless their effect on other firms is "remote" or "insubstantial"?

c.   Whom does Chief Justice Warren say the antitrust laws in general, and § 7 in particular, were designed to benefit? Might the Congressional debates in the late 1940s have reflected the then-recent concerns about concentration that we saw in *Alcoa* and *American Tobacco*? Does Chief Justice Warren ever reconcile the purpose of protecting "competition, not competitors" with the objective of preserving small business?

4.   What sorts of "mitigating factors" does the Court say might be relevant in a merger case?

a.   Should small firms be permitted to merge to reach a size at which they can compete more efficiently? How did the argument about a need to so compete later work in *Topco*?

b.   Should mergers be less stringently reviewed than joint ventures formed to undertake specific projects? Should we encourage absolute combinations, i.e., mergers, rather than more limited combinations? Keep this question in mind when we look at United States v. Penn-Olin Chemical Co., infra.

5.   If firms want to grow or expand, how else does the Court believe they might do so? Do you agree that internal expansion generally serves the public better than growth by acquisition? Why? Might such expansion create problems of its own for the small businesses the court says Congress wanted to protect, i.e., at whose expense will growth by internal expansion occur?

6.   This case also raises problems with the vertical aspects of this merger. Why might someone believe that competition would be reduced if a shoe manufacturer acquired a shoe retailer?

a.   Is the perceived problem the one the Court associated with tying clauses, i.e., exclusion of independent firms from certain market opportunities? Is the argument any better here than it was in the tying cases?

b.   Is there reason to believe that a manufacturer will make its own retailer carry poorer quality, higher priced shoes than the retailer would carry if it were independent? If that does happen, who will bear the consequences of the action? Will shoppers simply turn to other stores to meet their needs?

c.   If the manufacturer "overcharges" its retailer for shoes, can the retailer pass the higher price on to consumers? If the price Brown charges the retail outlets is low, as Justice Harlan posits it might be, will they underprice the other stores? Look at it this way: Will the retailer's price be determined more by the price its books show it paid its parent for shoes or by the price at which its competitors sell comparable shoes?

d.   Should we be concerned that if Brown buys Kinney, some former Kinney suppliers will lose an important customer? Who will sell to the stores to which Brown sold its shoes before it acquired Kinney?[123]

7.   If the Brown-Kinney merger makes the firms more efficient, might consumers receive some of the benefits of that efficiency in the form of lower prices? Should that be irrelevant? Does even Chief Justice Warren acknowledge that "the legislative history illuminates Congressional concern with the protection of competition, not competitors"?

A NOTE ON VERTICAL INTEGRATION— THE *DU PONT-GM* CASE

The issues of vertical integration raised by *Brown Shoe* were raised earlier in United States v. E.I. du Pont de Nemours, 353 U.S. 586, 77 S.Ct. 872, 1 L.Ed.2d 1057 (1957). Some 40 years before, in 1917, du Pont had purchased 23% of the stock of General Motors. Because the purchase had occurred well before 1950, it was challenged as a violation of pre-1950 Clayton Act § 7.

The question before the Court was whether competition in the market for automotive finishes and fabrics was substantially limited by this acquisition. The Court said that it was. The automobile industry is large and GM is a large part of that industry, the Court reasoned, so the effects were by definition "substantial." Du Pont supplied 2/3 of GM's finishes and 1/2 of its fabrics and there was evidence suggesting that one reason for du Pont's purchases of GM stock was to get on the Board and get access to this business. In an opinion by Justice Brennan, the Court held that although price and quality were not irrelevant to GM, du Pont's success in selling to GM could be assumed to have been the result of stock holdings and not simply "competitive merit."

Is the majority's analysis persuasive to you? If you were du Pont, would you want General Motors to buy fabrics from you that you could sell for *more* money to other buyers? Would you want to sell your fabrics to General Motors if it could get the same quality from others for a *lower* cost? Are you surprised that in dissent, Justices Burton and Frankfurter could show that du Pont's sales were to meet specific needs and varied among GM divisions and products? Further, total sales of du Pont paint to

---

[123]   Four years after this case, Brown was again before the Supreme Court. This time, the Federal Trade Commission had objected to the "Brown Franchise Stores' Program" under which independent retailers entered into exclusive dealing arrangements with Brown. Did that program present the same problems raised by the proposed Brown-Kinney merger? Given the result here, it was probably inevitable that the Court would uphold the FTC finding that the program was an "unfair method of competition." See Federal Trade Commission v. Brown Shoe Co., 384 U.S. 316, 86 S.Ct. 1501, 16 L.Ed.2d 587 (1966).

everyone was only 10% of total sales of paint nationally; thus, there was lots of room left for other sellers.

So who could get hurt by the du Pont-GM merger? Perhaps the most likely victims may have been the GM shareholders who did not sell their shares to du Pont. Du Pont *did* have a conflict of interest. If it raised the price of paint charged to GM by $1, it made $1 on paint but lost only 23 cents of profit as a GM shareholder. Thus, there was a fiduciary duty issue of fair dealing presented, but not a problem of harm to purchasers of cars or other sellers of finishes and fabrics.[124]

There was, of course, a statute of limitations problem also raised by these facts that the Court largely passed over. If this so-called "backward sweep doctrine" were actively used today to reach all mergers over the past 40 years, it would eliminate the need for much of § 2. It might be tempting to invoke it today with respect to airline mergers in the 1980s, for example. The "doctrine," which seems to give little or no security to a merged enterprise, has not been repudiated by the Supreme Court but it is not often invoked.

A NOTE ON THE FAILING COMPANY DOCTRINE

The Court in *Brown Shoe* suggests that a merger might be evaluated differently if the acquiring firm were taking over a firm that was about to go out of business. This is the "failing company defense." After all, the argument goes, when a firm fails it necessarily ceases being a competitive force. Thus, its acquisition cannot make matters worse.

Other "public interest" reasons also argue for recognizing such a defense. Perhaps the acquirer can revitalize the company and make its resources productive again. After all, no one likes to see a firm fail and its employees and stockholders get hurt.

However, the question arises whether it is true that there is no less competition when the defense is successfully used? Imagine a firm with 50% of the market and 5 others with 10% each. Assume one of the 10% firms is failing. Should the 50% firm be able to buy it?

Perhaps the most prominent "failing company" case is Citizen Publishing Co. v. United States, 394 U.S. 131, 89 S.Ct. 927, 22 L.Ed.2d 148 (1969), where publishers of two newspapers tried to establish a "joint operating agreement" to prevent one of them from failing. In an opinion by

---

[124] For an unsympathetic treatment of the Court's decision, see Jesse W. Markham, The du Pont-General Motors Decision, 43 Virginia L. Rev. 881 (1957). Analogous issues of vertical integration were raised by Ford Motor Co. v. United States, 405 U.S. 562, 92 S.Ct. 1142, 31 L.Ed.2d 492 (1972). The case involved Ford's attempt to buy Autolite, a producer of spark plugs, allegedly to be able to sell more replacement parts to purchasers of its cars. See generally, Keith N. Hylton, Antitrust Law: Economic Theory & Common Law Evolution 335–44 (2003).

Justice Douglas, the Court affirmed a finding that the agreement would violate § 7, and established a high standard for showing that the proposed acquisition was the failing firm's "last straw."

> "The failing company doctrine plainly cannot be applied in a merger or in any other case unless it is established that the company that acquires the failing company or brings it under dominion is the only available purchaser. For if another person or group could be interested, a unit in the competitive system would be preserved and not lost to monopoly power.

> " * * * The prospects of reorganization of the Citizen in 1940 would have had to be dim or nonexistent to make the failing company doctrine applicable to this case."

Do you agree with the Court's standard? Can one argue that if we simply let the firm fail, its assets and customers will not go to the dominant firm but be distributed throughout the industry? Thus, might there be more concentration in the industry if we recognize the defense than if we do not permit it at all?[125]

THE MOVE TO PRESUMED ILLEGALITY—
THE *PHILADELPHIA BANK* CASE

The proposed merger between Philadelphia National Bank and Girard Trust Corn Exchange Bank was significant on at least two levels. First, it was a merger of the 2nd and 3rd largest of the 42 commercial banks in Philadelphia to form the largest such bank. But second, it was part of the Comptroller of the Currency's effort to create banks large enough to compete with New York banks in making loans to large corporate customers.

The merger was subject to the Comptroller's approval after consultation with the Federal Reserve Board, the Federal Deposit Insurance Corporation and the Justice Department. Each of the other agencies raised doubts about the merger, but the Comptroller declared: "As to effect upon competition, * * * there will remain an adequate number of alternative sources of banking service in Philadelphia, and in view of the beneficial effects of this consolidation upon international and national competition it was concluded that the over-all effect upon competition would not be unfavorable."

---

[125] This point is made in Richard A. Posner & Frank H. Easterbrook, Antitrust: Cases, Economic Notes and Other Materials 471–72 (2d ed. 1981). It was also explicated in Thomas Campbell, The Efficiency of the Failing Company Defense, 63 Texas L.Rev. 251 (1984). A contrary analysis is developed in Fred S. McChesney, Defending the Failing-Firm Defense, 65 Nebraska L.Rev. 1 (1985).

The Justice Department charged that the merger would violate both Sherman Act § 1 and Clayton Act § 7. The District Court denied a motion to enjoin the merger, but the Supreme Court reversed, *United States v. Philadelphia National Bank*, 374 U.S. 321, 83 S.Ct. 1715, 10 L.Ed.2d 915 (1963), finding that the merger violated § 7.

The first issue the Court faced was jurisdictional. The Court explained: "By its terms, the present § 7 reaches acquisitions of corporate stock or share capital by any corporation engaged in commerce, but it reaches acquisitions of corporate assets only by corporations 'subject to the jurisdiction of the Federal Trade Commission.' The FTC, under § 5 of the Federal Trade Commission Act, has no jurisdiction over banks." But that was not a problem, the Court said. *Brown Shoe* held that Congress meant to close loopholes and the FTC jurisdiction requirement could simply be read out of the statute.

The next issue was market definition. Defining the product market was relatively easy; it was "commercial banking," a category that described a "congeries of services," most important of which were "the creation of additional money and credit, the management of the checking account system, and the furnishing of short-term business loans."

The geographic market was harder. The Justice Department said it was Philadelphia and its three contiguous counties; the Comptroller saw it as national and international in scope. The Court answered: "In banking, as in most service industries, convenience of location is essential to effective competition. Individuals and corporations typically confer the bulk of their patronage on banks in their local community; they find it impractical to conduct their banking business at a distance. The factor of inconvenience localizes banking competition as effectively as high transportation costs in other industries." Further, the statute refers to "*any* section of the country," so if the Justice Department can identify one area where problems will arise, that is enough.

Having focused attention on the local market for commercial banking, the Court said that "the resulting bank would be the largest in the four-county area, with (approximately) 36% of the area banks' total assets, 36% of deposits, and 34% of net loans. It and the second largest (First Pennsylvania Bank and Trust Company, now the largest) would have between them 59% of the total assets, 58% of deposits, and 58% of the net loans, while after the merger the four largest banks in the area would have 78% of total assets, 77% of deposits, and 78% of net loans."

But the Court also saw that whether the merger would "substantially lessen competition" requires "not merely an appraisal of the immediate impact of the merger upon competition, but a prediction of its impact upon competitive conditions in the future. * * * Such a prediction is sound only if it is based upon a firm understanding of the structure of the relevant market; yet the relevant economic data are both complex and elusive." To give business people a basis for planning, the Court said, "we must be alert to the danger of subverting congressional intent by permitting a too-broad economic investigation" and should "simplify the test of illegality."

The Court called for use of what was known as a structural analysis that looked to the market share the merged firms were likely to have and presumed illegality if the share was above a prescribed level.[126] It noted that the PNB-Girard merger would mean "a single bank's controlling at least 30% of the commercial banking business in the four-county Philadelphia metropolitan area. Without attempting to specify the smallest market share which would still be considered to threaten undue concentration, we are clear that 30% presents that threat. Further, whereas presently the two largest banks in the area (First Pennsylvania and PNB) control between them approximately 44% of the area's commercial banking business, the two largest after the merger (PNB-Girard and First Pennsylvania) will control 59%. Plainly, we think, this increase of more than 33% in concentration must be regarded as significant."

The burden of justifying the merger thus shifted to the defendants, and in this case, as in most later cases during the period, they were unable to sustain it. In particular, the Court rejected any idea that the benefits flowing from a merger may be weighed against the harms. "A value choice of such magnitude is beyond the ordinary limits of judicial competence, and in any event has been made for us already, by Congress when it enacted the amended § 7. Congress determined to preserve our traditionally competitive economy. It therefore proscribed anti-competitive mergers, the benign and the malignant alike, fully aware, we must assume, that some price might have to be paid."[127]

a.   Do you agree with this approach to mergers? Does it come close to being a per se rule, at least if the merged firms will have greater than a 30% market share in some definable market? Would even Judge Hand have drawn the line for illegality at that level?

b.   Is the view that "competition is likely to be greatest when there are many sellers, none of which has any significant market share" largely a restatement of worries about oligopoly? Does it ignore the other factors that Judge Posner suggested were relevant to identification of industries where oligopoly pricing could occur?

c.   Is it realistic in this industry to say, relying on *Brown Shoe*, that banks should grow by internal expansion if at all? Can one sensibly make

---

[126] The Court cited Carl Kaysen and Donald Turner, Antitrust Policy (1959) and George Stigler, Mergers and Preventive Antitrust Policy, 104 U. Pennsylvania L. Rev. 176, 182 (1955), as saying that its test was "fully consonant with economic theory."

[127] You may remember that the Court later relied upon this language in *Topco* to reject the defendants' claim that their territorial restrictions were needed to build a network strong enough to take on the national grocery chains.

that argument with respect to an industry in which federal deposit insurance will bear the loss if smaller banks are driven out of business?

d.   Would this case have been decided differently under § 1 of the Sherman Act? We don't know for sure, although Justice Goldberg believed it might have been decided the same way. The next year the Court seemed to prove him right. In United States v. First National Bank & Trust Co. of Lexington, 376 U.S. 665, 84 S.Ct. 1033, 12 L.Ed.2d 1 (1964), the Court enjoined a bank merger applying *only* § 1.

TWO SMALL BUT VIGOROUS COMPETITORS:
A NOTE ON *VON'S GROCERY*

Three years after *Philadelphia Bank*, the Supreme Court stopped a merger of even smaller firms in United States v. Von's Grocery Co., 384 U.S. 270, 86 S.Ct. 1478, 16 L.Ed.2d 555 (1966).

Von's was the third largest grocery chain in the Los Angeles area and Shopping Bag Food Stores ranked sixth. Together, however, they sold only 7.5% of the groceries in Los Angeles and their respective operations were centered in different parts of the city. Justice Black, writing for the six-member majority, noted that both chains had roughly doubled in size in the preceding decade, a time when the number of single-owner groceries in Los Angeles had declined by about 30%. Acquisitions and mergers of groceries were proceeding so rapidly in the Los Angeles market, the Court held, that the government could enjoin this merger of small but successful chains. "Where concentration is gaining momentum in a market," the Court wrote, "we must be alert to carry out Congress' intent to protect competition against ever-increasing concentration through mergers."[128]

Justices Stewart and Harlan were aghast at the majority's approach. The majority was making "no effort to appraise the competitive effects of this acquisition in terms of the contemporary economy of the retail food industry," they said. The majority had resorted instead to "a simple exercise in sums." The Court was undertaking no less an effort than "to roll back the supermarket revolution." The Court's opinion was no more than

---

[128]   This is now the third case we have seen in which "ever-increasing concentration" seemed to haunt the Court. In addition to the Celler-Kefauver Act debates themselves, the concern had been enhanced by books such as Joe S. Bain, Barriers to New Competition (1956), and Carl Kaysen & Donald F. Turner, Antitrust Policy: An Economic and Legal Analysis (1959). See also, Derek C. Bok, Section 7 of the Clayton Act and the Merging of Law and Economics, 74 Harvard L.Rev. 226, 308–339 (1960). The concern about concentration was later reiterated in the White House Task Force Report on Antitrust Policy (1969). The Task Force, chaired by Dean Phil C. Neal of the University of Chicago, included Professors William Baxter, Robert Bork, William K. Jones, Paul MacAvoy and James Rahl. By the mid-1970s, however, evidence about the effects of concentration was decidedly more mixed. See, e.g., Harvey J. Goldschmid, H. Michael Mann & J. Fred Weston, Industrial Concentration: The New Learning (1974).

"a requiem for the so-called 'Mom and Pop' grocery stores * * * that are now economically and technologically obsolete in many parts of the country."

With which opinion do you agree? Was the Court engaged in a hopeless effort to stem the tide of progress? Was it instead carrying out the purpose that Congress had created the Celler-Kefauver Act to accomplish?[129]

———————

Our next case considers one of the forms of multi-firm conduct to which we alluded earlier. It involves a joint venture, a combination short of merger. The case also introduces us to the concept of "potential competition," an idea important to merger analysis in this period.

UNITED STATES V. PENN-OLIN CHEMICAL CO.

Supreme Court of the United States, 1964
378 U.S. 158, 84 S.Ct. 1710, 12 L.Ed.2d 775

MR. JUSTICE CLARK delivered the opinion of the Court.

Pennsalt Chemicals Corporation and Olin Mathieson Chemical Corporation jointly formed Penn-Olin Chemical Company to produce and sell sodium chlorate in the southeastern United States. The Government seeks to dissolve this joint venture as violative of both § 7 of the Clayton Act and § 1 of the Sherman Act. This direct appeal * * * raises two questions. First, whether § 7 of the Clayton Act is applicable where two corporations form a third to engage in a new enterprise; and, second, if this question is answered in the affirmative, whether there is a violation of § 1 or § 7 under the facts of this case. The trial court found that the joint venture, on this record, violated neither of these sections and found it unnecessary to reach the first question. * * * We have concluded that a joint venture as organized here would be subject to the regulation of § 7 of the Clayton Act and, reaching the merits, we hold that while on the present record there is no violation of § 1 of the Sherman Act, the District Court erred in dismissing the complaint as to § 7 of the Clayton Act. Accordingly, the judgment is vacated and remanded for further consideration.

1. LINE OF COMMERCE, RELEVANT MARKET, ETC.

At the outset it is well to note that some of the troublesome questions ordinarily found in antitrust cases have been eliminated by the parties. First, the line of commerce is a chemical known as sodium chlorate. * * * All sodium chlorate of like purity is usable interchangeably and is used primarily in the pulp and paper industry to bleach the pulp, making for a brighter and higher quality paper. * * * The chemical is also employed in the production of herbicides, agricultural chemicals and in certain

———————

[129] To get a later report on the fortunes of Von's, Shopping Bag and the rest of the Los Angeles grocery industry, see Kathleen E. McDermott, Whatever Happened to * * * Von's?, 7 Antitrust 46 (Summer 1993).

derivatives, such as ammonium perchlorate. Next, the relevant market is not disputed. It is the southeastern part of the United States. Nor is the fact that Olin has never engaged in the commercial production of sodium chlorate contested. It has purchased and does purchase amounts of the chemical for internal consumption and has acted as sales agent for Pennsalt in the southeastern territory * * * . Olin also owns a patented process for bleaching pulp with chlorine dioxide. This process requires sodium chlorate and has been widely used by paper manufacturers under royalty-free licenses.

* * *

2.   THE COMPANIES INVOLVED.

Pennsalt is engaged solely in the production and sale of chemicals and chemical products throughout the United States. Its assets are around a hundred million dollars and its sales are about the same amount. Its sodium chlorate production is located at Portland, Oregon, with a capacity of some 15,000 tons as of 1959. It occupied 57.8% of the market west of the Rocky Mountains. It has marketed sodium chlorate in the southeastern United States to some extent since 1957. Its shipments into that territory in 1960 were 4,186 tons of which Olin sold 3,202 tons on its sales agency contract.

Olin is a large diversified corporation, the result of a merger of Olin Industries, Inc., and Mathieson Chemical Corporation in 1954. One of its seven divisions operates plants in 15 States and produces a wide range of chemicals and chemical products accounting for about 30% of Olin's revenues. Olin's sales in 1960 grossed some $690,000,000 and its total assets were $860,000,000.

Penn-Olin was organized in 1960 as a joint venture of Olin and Pennsalt. Each owns 50% of its stock and the officers and directors are divided equally between the parents. Its plant at Calvert City, Kentucky, was built by equal contribution of the two parents * * * . It has a capacity to produce 26,500 tons of sodium chlorate annually. Pennsalt operates the plant and Olin handles the sales. Penn-Olin deals in no other chemicals.

3.   BACKGROUND AND STATISTICS OF THE INDUSTRY.

Prior to 1961 the sodium chlorate industry in the United States was made up of three producing companies. The largest producer, Hooker Chemical Corporation, * * * now has two plants, one in the relevant marketing area at Columbus, Mississippi, which originally had a capacity of 16,000 tons * * * . * * * Hooker has assets of almost $200,000,000. American Potash & Chemical Corporation * * * also has two plants, one located at * * * Aberdeen, Mississippi * * * . Its assets are almost $100,000,000. The trial court found that these two corporations "had a virtual monopoly" in the relevant southeast market, holding over 90% of the market.

A third company in the industry was Pennsalt * * * . It entered seriously into the relevant marketing area through a sales arrangement with Olin * * * which was aimed at testing the availability of the southeastern market. Olin as an exclusive seller was to undertake the sale of 2,000 tons of sodium chlorate per year to pulp and paper mills in the southeast * * * . In 1960, 4,186 tons of sodium chlorate were marketed in the relevant market with the aid of this agreement. This accounted for 8.9% of the sales in that market.

During the previous decade no new firms had entered the sodium chlorate industry, and little effort had been made by existing companies to expand their facilities prior to 1957. In 1953 Olin had made available to Pennsalt its Mathieson patented process for bleaching pulp with chlorine dioxide and the latter had installed it 100% in all of the western paper mills. This process uses sodium chlorate. At about the same time the process was likewise made available, royalty free, to the entire pulp and paper industry. By 1960 most of the chlorine dioxide generated by paper manufacturers was being produced under the Olin controlled process. This created an expanding demand for sodium chlorate and by 1960 the heaviest concentration of purchasers was located in the relevant southeastern territory. By 1957 Hooker began increasing the capacity of its Columbus plant and by 1960 it had been almost doubled. American Potash sensed the need of a plant in Mississippi to compete with Hooker and began its Aberdeen plant in 1957. It was completed to a 15,000-ton capacity in 1959, and this capacity was expanded 50% by 1961.

The sales arrangement between Pennsalt and Olin, previously mentioned, was superseded by the joint venture agreement on February 11, 1960, and the Penn-Olin plant operations at Calvert City, Kentucky, began in 1961. In the same year Pittsburgh Plate Glass Company announced that it would build a plant at Lake Charles, Louisiana, with a capacity of 15,000 tons. Pittsburgh Plate Glass had operated a sodium chlorate plant in Canada.

As a result of these expansions and new entries into the southeastern market, the projected production of sodium chlorate there more than doubled. By 1962 Hooker had 32,000 tons; American Potash, 22,500 tons; Penn-Olin, 26,500 tons; and Pittsburgh Glass, 15,000 tons—a total of 96,000 tons as contrasted to 41,150 in 1959. Penn-Olin's share of the expanded relevant market was about 27.6%. * * *

4.   THE SETTING FROM WHICH THE JOINT VENTURE EMERGED.

As early as 1951 Pennsalt had considered building a plant at Calvert City and starting in 1955 it initiated several cost and market studies for a sodium chlorate plant in the southeast. Three different proposals from within its own organization were rejected prior to 1957, apparently because the rate of return was so unattractive that "the expense of refining these figures further would be unwarranted." When Hooker announced in

December 1956 that it was going to increase the capacity of its Columbus plant, the interest of Pennsalt management was reactivated. It appointed a "task force" to evaluate the company's future in the eastern market; it retained management consultants to study that market and its chief engineer prepared cost estimates. However, in December 1957 the management decided that the estimated rate of return was unattractive and considered it "unlikely" that Pennsalt would go it alone. It was suggested that Olin would be a "logical partner" in a joint venture and might in the interim be interested in distributing in the East 2,000 tons of the Portland sodium chlorate production. The sales agreement with Olin, heretofore mentioned, was eventually made. In the final draft the parties agreed that "neither * * * should move in the chlorate or perchlorate field without keeping the other party informed * * * " and that one would "bring to the attention of the other any unusual aspects of this business which might make it desirable to proceed further with production plans." Pennsalt claims that it finally decided, prior to this agreement, that it should not build a plant itself and that this decision was never reconsidered or changed. But the District Court found to the contrary.

During this same period * * * Olin began investigating the possibility of entering the sodium chlorate industry. It had never produced sodium chlorate commercially, although its predecessor had done so years before. However, the electrolytic process used in making sodium chlorate is intimately related to other operations of Olin and required the same general knowledge. Olin also possessed extensive experience in the technical aspects of bleaching pulp and paper and was intimate with the pulp and paper mills of the southeast. In April 1958 Olin's chemical division wrote and circulated to the management a "Whither Report" which stated in part:

> "We have an unparalleled opportunity to move sodium chlorate into the paper industry as the result of our work on the installation of chlorine dioxide generators. We have a captive consumption for sodium chlorate."

And Olin's engineering supervisor concluded that entry into sodium chlorate production was "an attractive venture" since it "represents a logical expansion of the product line of the Industrial Chemicals Division * * * " with respect to "one of the major markets, pulp and paper bleaching, [with which] we have a favorable marketing position, particularly in the southeast."

The staff, however, did not agree with the engineering supervisor or the "Whither Report" and concluded "that they didn't feel that this particular project showed any merit worthy of serious consideration by the corporation at that time." They were dubious of the cost estimates and felt the need to temper their scientists' enthusiasm for new products with the uncertainties of plant construction and operation. But, as the trial court found, the testimony indicated that Olin's decision to enter the joint venture was made without determining that Olin could not or would not be an independent competitor. That question, the president of Penn-Olin testified, "never reached the point of final decision."

This led the District Court to find that "[t]he possibility of individual entry into the southeastern market had not been completely rejected by either Pennsalt or Olin before they decided upon the joint venture."

5.   SECTION 7 OF THE CLAYTON ACT APPLIES TO "JOINT VENTURES."

Appellees argue that § 7 applies only where the acquired company is "engaged" in commerce and that it would not apply to a newly formed corporation, such as Penn-Olin. The test, they say, is whether the enterprise to be acquired is engaged in commerce—not whether a corporation formed as the instrumentality for the acquisition is itself engaged in commerce at the moment of its formation. We believe that this logic fails in the light of the wording of the section and its legislative background. The test of the section is the effect of the acquisition. Certainly the formation of a joint venture and purchase by the organizers of its stock would substantially lessen competition—indeed foreclose it—as between them * * * . This would be true whether they were in actual or potential competition with each other and even though the new corporation was formed to create a wholly new enterprise. Realistically, the parents would not compete with their progeny. Moreover, in this case the progeny was organized to further the business of its parents, * * * and the fact that it was organized specifically to engage in commerce should bring it within the coverage of § 7. In addition, long prior to trial Penn-Olin was actually engaged in commerce. To hold that it was not "would be illogical and disrespectful of the plain congressional purpose in amending § 7 * * * [for] it would create a large loophole in a statute designed to close a loophole." United States v. Philadelphia National Bank. * * *

6.   THE APPLICATION OF THE MERGER DOCTRINE.

This is the first case reaching this Court * * * that directly involves the validity under § 7 of the joint participation of two corporations in the creation of a third as a new domestic producing organization. We are, therefore, plowing new ground. It is true, however, that some aspects of the problem might be found in United States v. Terminal R. Assn., and Associated Press v. United States, where joint ventures with great market power were subjected to control, even prior to the amendment to § 7.

* * *

The joint venture, like the "merger" and the "conglomeration," often creates anticompetitive dangers. * * * Inevitably, the operations of the joint venture will be frozen to those lines of commerce which will not bring it into competition with the parents, and the latter, by the same token will be foreclosed from the joint venture's market.

This is not to say that the joint venture is controlled by the same criteria as the merger or conglomeration. The merger eliminates one of the participating corporations from the market while a joint venture creates a new competitive force therein. The rule of United States v. El Paso Natural Gas Co., 376 U.S. 651 (1964), where a corporation sought to protect its market by acquiring a potential competitor, would, of course, apply to a joint venture where the same intent was present in the organization of the new corporation.

* * *

7.   THE CRITERIA GOVERNING § 7 CASES.

We apply the light of these considerations in the merger cases to the problem confronting us here. The District Court found that "Pennsalt and Olin each possessed the resources and general capability needed to build its own plant in the southeast and to compete with Hooker and [American Potash] in that market. Each could have done so if it had wished." In addition, the District Court found that, contrary to the position of the management of Olin and Pennsalt, "the forecasts of each company indicated that a plant could be operated with profit."

The District Court held, however, that these considerations had no controlling significance, except "as a factor in determining whether as a matter of probability *both* companies would have entered the market as individual competitors if Penn-Olin had not been formed. Only in this event would potential competition between the two companies have been foreclosed by the joint venture." In this regard the court found it "impossible to conclude that as a matter of reasonable probability *both* Pennsalt and Olin would have built plants in the southeast if Penn-Olin had not been created." The court made no decision concerning the probability that one would have built "while the other continued to ponder." It found that this "hypothesized situation affords no basis for concluding that Penn-Olin had the effect of substantially lessening competition." That would depend, the court said, "upon the competitive impact which Penn-Olin will have as against that which might have resulted if Pennsalt or Olin had been an individual market entrant." The court found that this impact could not be determined from the record in this case. "Solely as a matter of theory," it said, " * * * no reason exists to suppose that Penn-Olin will be a less effective competitor than Pennsalt or Olin would have been. The contrary conclusion is the more reasonable."

We believe that the court erred in this regard. Certainly the sole test would not be the probability that *both* companies would have entered the market. Nor would the consideration be limited to the probability that one entered alone. There still remained for consideration the fact that Penn-

Olin eliminated the potential competition of the corporation that might have remained at the edge of the market, continually threatening to enter. Just as a merger eliminates actual competition, this joint venture may well foreclose any prospect of competition between Olin and Pennsalt in the relevant sodium chlorate market. The difference, of course, is that the merger's foreclosure is present while the joint venture's is prospective. Nevertheless, "[p]otential competition * * * as a substitute for * * * [actual competition] may restrain producers from overcharging those to whom they sell or underpaying those from whom they buy * * * . Potential competition, insofar as the threat survives [as it would have here in the absence of Penn-Olin], may compensate in part for the imperfection characteristic of actual competition in the great majority of competitive markets." Wilcox, Competition and Monopoly in American Industry, TNEC Monograph No. 21 (1940) 7–8. Potential competition cannot be put to a subjective test. It is not "susceptible of a ready and precise answer." As we found in United States v. El Paso Natural Gas Co., the "effect on competition * * * is determined by the nature or extent of that market and by the nearness of the absorbed company to it, that company's eagerness to enter that market, its resourcefulness, and so on." The position of a company "as a competitive factor * * * was not disproved by the fact that it had never sold * * * there. * * * [I]t is irrelevant in a market * * * where incremental needs are booming." The existence of an aggressive, well equipped and well financed corporation engaged in the same or related lines of commerce waiting anxiously to enter an oligopolistic market would be a substantial incentive to competition which cannot be underestimated. Witness the expansion undertaken by Hooker and American Potash as soon as they heard of the interest of Olin Mathieson and of Pennsalt in southeast territory. This same situation might well have come about had either Olin or Pennsalt entered the relevant market alone and the other remained aloof watching developments.

8.   THE PROBLEM OF PROOF.

Here the evidence shows beyond question that the industry was rapidly expanding; the relevant southeast market was requiring about one-half of the national production of sodium chlorate; few corporations had the inclination, resources and know-how to enter this market; both parent corporations of Penn-Olin had great resources; each had long been identified with the industry, one owning valuable patent rights while the other had engaged in sodium chlorate production for years; each had other chemicals, the production of which required the use of sodium chlorate; right up to the creation of Penn-Olin, each had evidenced a long-sustained and strong interest in entering the relevant market area; each enjoyed good reputation and business connections with the major consumers of sodium chlorate in the relevant market, i.e., the pulp and paper mills; and, finally, each had the know-how and the capacity to enter that market and could have done so individually at a reasonable profit. * * * Unless we are going to require subjective evidence, this array of probability certainly reaches the prima facie stage. As we have indicated, to require more would be to read the statutory requirement of reasonable probability into a requirement of certainty. This we will not do.

However, despite these strong circumstances, we are not disposed to disturb the court's finding that there was not a reasonable probability that both Pennsalt and Olin would have built a plant in the relevant market area. But we have concluded that a finding should have been made as to the reasonable probability that either one of the corporations would have entered the market by building a plant, while the other would have remained a significant potential competitor. * * * Since the trial court might have been concerned over whether there was evidence on this point, we reiterate that it is impossible to demonstrate the precise competitive effects of the elimination of either Pennsalt or Olin as a potential competitor. * * * There being no proof of specific intent to use Penn-Olin as a vehicle to eliminate competition, nor evidence of collateral restrictive agreements between the joint venturers, we put those situations to one side. * * *

The judgment is therefore vacated and the case is remanded for further proceedings in conformity with this opinion.

MR. JUSTICE WHITE dissents.

MR. JUSTICE DOUGLAS, with whom MR. JUSTICE BLACK agrees, dissenting.

Agreements among competitors to divide markets are per se violations of the Sherman Act. The most detailed, grandiose scheme of that kind is disclosed in Addyston Pipe & Steel Co. v. United States, where industrialists, acting like commissars in modern communist countries, determined what tonnage should be produced by each company and what territory was "free" and what was "bonus." The Court said: "Total suppression of the trade in the commodity is not necessary in order to render the combination one in restraint of trade. It is the effect of the combination in limiting and restricting the right of each of the members to transact business in the ordinary way, as well as its effect upon the volume or extent of the dealing in the commodity, that is regarded."

* * *

In the late 1950's the only producers of sodium chlorate in the United States were Pennsalt, one of the appellees in this case, Hooker Chemical Corporation, and American Potash and Chemical Corporation. No new firms had entered the industry for a decade. Prices seemed to be stable and little effort had been made to expand existing uses or to develop new ones. But during the 1950's the sodium chlorate market began to grow * * * .

Pennsalt, whose only sodium chlorate plant was at Portland, Oregon, became interested in establishing a plant in the rapidly growing southeast sodium chlorate market. * * *

In the early 1950's Olin too was investigating the possibilities of entering the southeast industry. * * *

During the years when Pennsalt and Olin were considering independent entry into the southeast market, they were also discussing joint entry. * * * [An] agreement entered into in February 1958 provided that neither of the two companies would "move in the chlorate or perchlorate field without keeping the other party informed." And each by the agreement bound itself "to bring to the attention of the other any unusual aspects of this business which might make it desirable to proceed further with production plans." * * *

So what we have in substance is two major companies who on the eve of competitive projects in the southeastern market join forces. In principle the case is no different from one where Pennsalt and Olin decide to divide the southeastern market as was done in *Addyston Pipe* * * * . Through the "joint venture" they do indeed divide it fifty-fifty. That division through the device of the "joint venture" is as plain and precise as though made in more formal agreements. As we saw in the *Timken* case, "agreements between legally separate persons and companies to suppress competition among themselves and others" cannot be justified "by labeling the project a 'joint venture.'" And we added, "Perhaps every agreement and combination to restrain trade could be so labeled." What may not be done by two companies who decide to divide a market surely cannot be done by the convenient creation of a legal umbrella—whether joint venture or common ownership and control—under which they achieve the same objective by moving in unison.

An actual division of the market through the device of "joint venture" has, I think, the effect "substantially to lessen competition" within the meaning of § 7 of the Clayton Act. * * *

We do not, of course, know for certain what would have happened if the "joint venture" had not materialized. But we do know that § 7 deals only with probabilities, not certainties. We know that the interest of each company in the project was lively, that one if not both of them would probably have entered that market, and that even if only one had entered at the beginning the presence of the other on the periphery would in all likelihood have been a potent competitive factor. Cf. United States v. El Paso Natural Gas Co. We also know that as between Pennsalt and Olin the "joint venture" foreclosed all future competition by dividing the market fifty-fifty. That could not have been done consistently with our decisions had the "joint venture" been created after Pennsalt and Olin had entered the market or after either had done so. To allow the joint venture to obtain antitrust immunity because it was launched at the very threshold of the entry of two potential competitors into a territory is to let § 7 be avoided by sophisticated devices.

* * *

MR. JUSTICE HARLAN, dissenting.

I can see no purpose to be served by this remand except to give the Government an opportunity to retrieve an antitrust case which it has lost, and properly so. Believing that this Court should not lend itself to such a course, I would affirm the judgment of the District Court.

NOTES AND QUESTIONS

1. What is this case doing in the merger section of this chapter? Was there in fact any merger here? Hadn't these firms in fact *increased* competition among sodium chlorate producers in the southeast?

a. How do Justices Black and Douglas characterize what was going on here? Are they clearly wrong? The Court indirectly answers them by citing *Terminal R.R.* and *Associated Press.* Do those cases provide an answer? Under what statutory provisions were those cases decided?

b. Were you disturbed that Pennsalt and Olin had a marketing agreement which required each to tell the other if it planned to build a plant itself? Does that tend to reinforce the dissenters' suspicions about what was up?

2. In assessing the venture under § 7, the Supreme Court applies the doctrine of potential competition.

a. Were you able to tell from the case the rationale underlying that doctrine? Is the idea that certain firms are "on the edge" of the market requiring the actual competitors to offer their best prices and service consistent with what you know about the role of new entry in economic theory?

b. Do you agree that the potential competition doctrine should have been applied to these facts? What were the firms' histories of interest in expansion into the Southeast and what had each thought about with respect to building facilities there?

c. If each had entered the market, they would have been actual competitors and their merger clearly would have raised § 7 issues. Is it inevitable that using a joint venture as a means of entering the market would raise similar questions?

d. What test does the Court formulate to determine whether this joint venture was a net plus for competition or a net loss? Are you confident that any court can determine from objective data whether one of these firms would have entered and the other would have remained on the fringe as a potential competitor?

3. Should joint ventures be encouraged as a way for American business to respond flexibly to situations without completely merging the parent

institutions? Should we draw any distinction between research joint ventures and production joint ventures?

a. Might one argue that research joint ventures should be encouraged because research is extremely risky and firms may wind up with nothing to show for their efforts?

b. On the other hand, might such joint ventures have an incentive to invent away from areas in which the participating firms are strong, i.e., to avoid invention that will compete with currently successful items? If the joint venture includes most of the industry's competitors, might it freeze technology instead of stimulate competition?

c. If the research is done in cooperation with foreign firms, might exchanges of data give away secrets important for future advances by other U.S. firms? Might there be particular concern about this problem where the basic information was developed under defense contracts?

d. In 1984, Congress passed the National Cooperative Research Act, 15 U.S.C. §§ 4301–05. It says that R & D joint ventures will be evaluated under a rule of reason, and if the joint ventures are registered in advance, any antitrust violation found will be subject to single, not treble, damages.[130]

4. May similar arguments be made in favor of production joint ventures?

a. Indeed, are boundaries between research and production always clear? Does one often (a) do research on production methods and (b) get research information as production proceeds?

b. It is certainly argued that there are significant risks in production as one builds plants to compete in a world economy for a world market. Do you believe that, in the name of helping U.S. firms compete effectively in world markets, Congress should give production joint ventures similar antitrust protection? It did so in 1993 by the National Cooperative Production Amendments to the National Cooperative Research Act.

5. On remand in *Penn-Olin*, the District Court held that the Government had the burden of proving that one or both of the firms would have entered the market other than through the joint venture. It found that the burden had not been met, and so upheld the joint venture. United States v. Penn-Olin Chemical Co., 246 F.Supp. 917 (D.Del.1965). The result was affirmed by an equally divided Supreme Court, Justice Marshall not

---

[130] A comparative look at the treatment of joint ventures is provided in Sara G. Zwart, Innovate, Integrate, and Cooperate: Antitrust Changes and Challenges in the United States and the European Economic Community, 1989 Utah L.Rev. 63 (1989). See also, Re Agreement Between Bayer AG and Gist-Brocades NV, 1 Common Market L.Rep. D98 (1976) (agreement whereby firms agreed to "specialize" their research into penicillin products found to violate EEC Article 85(1), the counterpart to Sherman Act § 1, but exemption granted under Article 85(3) "to promote technical or economic progress"); Re Agreement Between Volkswagenwerk AG and Maschinenfabrik Augsburg-Nurnberg (MAN), 1 Com.Mkt. L.Rep. 621 (1984) (joint research agreement between truck manufacturers found to violate Article 85(1) but Article 85(3) exemption granted for 15 years).

participating. 389 U.S. 308 (1967). There was thus no opinion and we do not know how individual justices voted.

COMPETITION FOR THE MARKET—THE *EL PASO GAS* CASE

Both the Court's opinion, and the dissent of Justices Douglas and Black, made a point of citing United States v. El Paso Natural Gas Co., 376 U.S. 651, 84 S.Ct. 1044, 12 L.Ed.2d 12 (1964), decided earlier in the Court's same term.

El Paso Gas was the only out-of-state seller of natural gas in California. It bought gas in Texas, collected it in New Mexico, and sold large quantities of it to Southern California Edison, a public utility. Pacific Northwest was a relatively new gas company. Its lines ran from New Mexico to Oregon, and it also bought gas from Canada. Its major potential California customer was Pacific Gas & Electric, a utility serving Northern California. However, earlier, Pacific Northwest had engaged in head-to-head bidding with El Paso and forced El Paso to offer a lower price than it had planned in order to get a contract to serve part of Southern California.

El Paso proposed to merge with Pacific Northwest, alleging the merger simply to be a market extension, i.e., a merger of firms operating in different parts of the region. In an opinion by Justice Douglas, the Supreme Court upheld a challenge to the merger under § 7. The Court reasoned that El Paso had to keep in mind the potential entry of Pacific Northwest into the Southern California market whenever it made its bids to extend service to new service areas. Thus, Pacific Northwest was a "potential competitor."

Even if individual contracts are exclusive and run for a long term, as is usually true with service contracts for utilities, in an expanding marketplace, there is always room for competition to get new business as it becomes available. That was clearly true in California in the 1960s. Thus, the proposed merger was found to "substantially limit competition" within the meaning of § 7 of the Clayton Act. The merger would eliminate a firm that was *potentially* able to win contracts. And, even if Pacific Northwest never actually bid again, it would *presently* give El Paso Gas an incentive to service its present and new customers well.

Can you see why Justice Douglas was so upset that the Court seemed to downplay this case in *Penn-Olin*? Do you agree with him that, if the Court was willing to find Pacific Northwest a potential competitor of El Paso Gas, it should also have found that Olin and Pennsalt were potential competitors?

SECTION 7 AND CONGLOMERATE MERGERS:
CONTINENTAL CAN AND *ROME CABLE*

The year 1964 was a big one for merger cases and for development of the idea of potential competition. Two particularly interesting cases involved mergers that appeared to be neither horizontal nor vertical. They seemed to be combinations of firms in different industries that were diversifying their product lines and thus hedging their exposure to risk.

The growth of conglomerate organizations, however, was the subject of significant political concern.[131] The fear was that large aggregations of wealth could exercise disproportionate political influence in the society. Whether existing antitrust laws were up to the task of interdicting such developments was thus a major question.

In United States v. Continental Can Co., 378 U.S. 441, 84 S.Ct. 1738, 12 L.Ed.2d 953 (1964), Continental, which produced 33% of the nation's metal containers (2d largest in the industry), sought to buy Hazel-Atlas, a firm that produced 9.6% of the country's glass jars (3d in its industry). Continental argued that metal cans and glass jars are used for different products and thus that there could be no substantial lessening of competition within any line of commerce.

The Government argued, however, that the potential for packaging tastes to change was significant. Indeed the District Court expressly found that

> "There was substantial and vigorous inter-industry competition between these three industries and between various of the products which they manufactured. Metal can, glass container and plastic container manufacturers were each seeking to enlarge their sales to the thousands of packers of hundreds of varieties of food, chemical, toiletry and industrial products, ranging from ripe olives to fruit juices to tuna fish to smoked tongue; from maple syrup to pet food to coffee; from embalming fluid to floor wax to nail polish to aspirin to veterinary supplies, to take examples at random.

> "Each industry and each of the manufacturers within it was seeking to improve their products so that they would appeal to new customers or hold old ones." 217 F.Supp. at 780–81.

The District Court held, however, that except for the market for beer containers, the Government had made insufficient showing of cross-elasticity of demand to meet the market definition requirements laid down

---

[131] A good example of the concern is provided by Mark J. Green, et al., The Closed Enterprise System: Ralph Nader's Study Group Report on Antitrust Enforcement (1972). A more scholarly treatment of the issues is provided in Harlan M. Blake, Conglomerate Mergers and the Antitrust Laws, 73 Columbia L.Rev. 555 (1973); Donald F. Turner, Conglomerate Mergers and Section 7 of the Clayton Act, 78 Harvard L.Rev. 1313 (1965).

in the cellophane case. The Supreme Court disagreed in an opinion by Justice White.

"Though the 'outer boundaries of a product market are determined by the reasonable interchangeability of use or the cross-elasticity of demand between the product itself and substitutes for it,' there may be 'within this broad market, well-defined submarkets * * * which, in themselves, constitute product markets for antitrust purposes.' Brown Shoe Co. v. United States. * * *

* * *

"Baby food was at one time packed entirely in metal cans. Hazel-Atlas played a significant role in inducing the shift to glass as the dominant container by designing 'what has become the typical baby food jar.' * * *

"In the soft drink business, a field which has been, and is, predominantly glass territory, the court recognized that the metal can industry had 'after considerable initial difficulty * * * developed a can strong enough to resist the pressures generated by carbonated beverages' and 'made strenuous efforts to promote the use of metal cans for carbonated beverages as against glass bottles.' Continental has been a major factor in this rivalry. * * * "

Thus, the Court held, the relevant product market was "the combined glass and metal container industries and all end uses for which they compete." It expressly refused to include plastic, paper, foil and other packaging products within the relevant market. They might be trying equally hard to compete with glass and metal containers and might be within a relevant market in some other case, but "metal-glass" was a sufficiently "well-defined submarket" that the other products could be ignored. With the market so defined, the firms' combined percentage share "approaches that held presumptively bad in United States v. Philadelphia National Bank * * * ."

Justices Harlan and Stewart dissented. Not only had the Court gerrymandered the market definition in their view, but *Philadelphia Bank* could not properly be applied to "shares" of such a market. Do you agree? Is the implication of the Court's analysis in this case that a single firm's having 100% of the can market would have no different competitive effects than its having 50% of the can market and 50% of the glass market?

Some of the Court's concern seemed to turn on the effects of this merger on the incentives of the combined firm to innovate in the uses of both cans and glass for packaging new or different products. Was such a concern well founded? Put yourself in the position of the President of the new "Continental/Hazel-Atlas." Do you now feel free to close the research and development department? Will you be indifferent to changing packaging trends or willing to let Owens-Corning develop the new uses of glass that may render your can assets less valuable? In short, when you are a minority player in *both* industries, can you afford *not* to keep innovating? The Court believes that you will see that in the short run you are simply converting glass sales to cans or vice versa; if you let that control your thinking, however, will you be a success in *any* phase of packaging?

The Court faced similar problems of finding boundaries for the market in United States v. Aluminum Company of America, 377 U.S. 271, 84 S.Ct. 1283, 12 L.Ed.2d 314 (1964). That was a civil action to enjoin Alcoa's purchase of the stock and assets of Rome Cable, a producer of copper electrical cable. As you might imagine, Alcoa produced aluminum cable. Both products were used by electrical utilities for power transmission, but aluminum had cost advantages for overhead lines while copper had much greater consumer acceptance for other uses. Under these circumstances, the Court found that aluminum wire should be seen as its own market or submarket and thus a "line of commerce" within the meaning of § 7.

Such a finding might have seemed to be in Alcoa's interest; certainly Continental would have liked it. It would seem to imply that the merger was a "product extension" for both firms, one that could not reduce competition or tend to create a monopoly. However, the Court was not deterred. Justice Douglas wrote that Rome Cable also sold aluminum conductor, 1.3% to be exact. Adding even this small amount to Alcoa's 38.6% of the market violated § 7. Justices Stewart and Harlan again dissented, this time joined by Justice Goldberg. With whom do you agree?

These were important cases extending the reach of § 7. The rhetoric was familiar but the results were not inevitable. The Government had actually been more conservative in its own theory of how much § 7 ought to prohibit. In *Continental*, the Government argued only that a merger was illegal whenever there is: (a) a substantial degree of competition between two industries, (b) a high degree of concentration in either or both of the competing industries, and (c) a dominant position of each of the merging companies in its respective industry.

Would such a view have been easier to justify under the Court's decisions to date? Is it more consistent with § 7 than the approach taken by the Court? Does the theory help explain why the Government brought our next case?

FEDERAL TRADE COMMISSION V. PROCTER & GAMBLE CO.

Supreme Court of the United States, 1967
386 U.S. 568, 87 S.Ct. 1224, 18 L.Ed.2d 303

MR. JUSTICE DOUGLAS delivered the opinion of the Court.

This is a proceeding initiated by the Federal Trade Commission charging that respondent, Procter & Gamble Co., had acquired the assets of Clorox Chemical Co. in violation of § 7 of the Clayton Act. The charge was that Procter's acquisition of Clorox might substantially lessen competition or tend to create a monopoly in the production and sale of household liquid bleaches.

Following evidentiary hearings, the hearing examiner rendered his decision in which he concluded that the acquisition was unlawful and ordered divestiture. * * * The Commission affirmed the examiner * * *. The Court of Appeals for the Sixth Circuit reversed and directed that the Commission's complaint be dismissed. We find that the Commission's findings were amply supported by the evidence, and that the Court of Appeals erred.

* * * The facts are not disputed * * *.

At the time of the merger, in 1957, Clorox was the leading manufacturer in the heavily concentrated household liquid bleach industry. It is agreed that household liquid bleach is the relevant line of commerce. * * * It is a distinctive product with no close substitutes. Liquid bleach is a low-price, high-turnover consumer product sold mainly through grocery stores and supermarkets. The relevant geographical market is the Nation and a series of regional markets. Because of high shipping costs and low sales price, it is not feasible to ship the product more than 300 miles from its point of manufacture. Most manufacturers are limited to competition within a single region since they have but one plant. Clorox is the only firm selling nationally; it has 13 plants distributed throughout the Nation. Purex, Clorox's closest competitor in size, does not distribute its bleach in the northeast or mid-Atlantic States; in 1957, Purex's bleach was available in less than 50% of the national market.

At the time of the acquisition, Clorox was the leading manufacturer of household liquid bleach, with 48.8% of the national sales—annual sales of slightly less than $40,000,000. Its market share had been steadily increasing for the five years prior to the merger. Its nearest rival was Purex, which manufactures a number of products other than household liquid bleaches, including abrasive cleaners, toilet soap, and detergents. Purex accounted for 15.7% of the household liquid bleach market. The industry is highly concentrated; in 1957, Clorox and Purex accounted for almost 65% of the Nation's household liquid bleach sales, and, together with four other firms, for almost 80%. The remaining 20% was divided among over 200 small producers. Clorox had total assets of $12,000,000; only eight producers had assets in excess of $1,000,000 and very few had assets of more than $75,000.

* * *

Since all liquid bleach is chemically identical, advertising and sales promotion are vital. In 1957 Clorox spent almost $3,700,000 on advertising, imprinting the value of its bleach in the mind of the consumer. In addition, it spent $1,700,000 for other promotional activities. The Commission found that these heavy expenditures went far to explain why Clorox maintained so high a market share despite the fact that its brand, though chemically indistinguishable from rival brands, retailed for a price equal to or, in many instances, higher than its competitors.

Procter is a large, diversified manufacturer of low-price, high-turnover household products sold through grocery, drug, and department stores. Prior to its acquisition of Clorox, it did not produce household liquid bleach. Its 1957 sales were in excess of $1,100,000,000 from which it realized profits of more than $67,000,000; its assets were over $500,000,000. Procter has been marked by rapid growth and diversification. It has successfully developed and introduced a number of new products. Its primary activity is in the general area of soaps, detergents, and cleansers * * * .[132] Procter was the dominant factor in this area. It accounted for 54.4% of all packaged detergent sales. The industry is heavily concentrated—Procter and its nearest competitors, Colgate-Palmolive and Lever Brothers, account for 80% of the market.

In the marketing of soaps, detergents, and cleansers, as in the marketing of household liquid bleach, advertising and sales promotion are vital. In 1957, Procter was the Nation's largest advertiser, spending more than $80,000,000 on advertising and an additional $47,000,000 on sales promotion. Due to its tremendous volume, Procter receives substantial discounts from the media. As a multiproduct producer Procter enjoys substantial advantages in advertising and sales promotion. Thus, it can and does feature several products in its promotions, reducing the printing, mailing, and other costs for each product. It also purchases network programs on behalf of several products, enabling it to give each product network exposure at a fraction of the cost per product that a firm with only one product to advertise would incur.

Prior to the acquisition, Procter was in the course of diversifying into product lines related to its basic detergent-soap-cleanser business. Liquid bleach was a distinct possibility since packaged detergents—Procter's primary product line—and liquid bleach are used complementarily in washing clothes and fabrics, and in general household cleaning. * * *

The decision to acquire Clorox was the result of a study conducted by Procter's promotion department designed to determine the advisability of entering the liquid bleach industry. The initial report noted the ascendancy of liquid bleach in the large and expanding household bleach market, and recommended that Procter purchase Clorox rather than enter independently. Since a large investment would be needed to obtain a

---

[132] [Ed. note] Procter & Gamble was reported to be the industry leader in detergent (Tide), deodorant (Secret), coffee (Folgers), cleanser (Comet), antacid (Pepto-Bismol), toilet paper (Charmin), cough syrup (NyQuil), dishwasher soap (Cascade), peanut butter (Jif), shortening (Crisco), and fabric softener (Downy). Brian Dumaine, P & G Rewrites the Marketing Rules, Fortune, Nov. 6, 1989, p. 34.

satisfactory market share, acquisition of the industry's leading firm was attractive. * * * The initial report predicted that Procter's "sales, distribution and manufacturing setup" could increase Clorox's share of the markets in areas where it was low. The final report confirmed the conclusions of the initial report and emphasized that Procter could make more effective use of Clorox's advertising budget and that the merger would facilitate advertising economies. A few months later, Procter acquired the assets of Clorox * * * in exchange for Procter stock.

The Commission found that the * * * substitution of Procter with its huge assets and advertising advantages for the already dominant Clorox would dissuade new entrants and discourage active competition from the firms already in the industry due to fear of retaliation by Procter. The Commission thought it relevant that retailers might be induced to give Clorox preferred shelf space since it would be manufactured by Procter, which also produced a number of other products marketed by the retailers. There was also the danger that Procter might underprice Clorox in order to drive out competition, and subsidize the underpricing with revenue from other products. * * * Further, the merger would seriously diminish potential competition by eliminating Procter as a potential entrant into the industry. Prior to the merger, the Commission found, Procter was the most likely prospective entrant, and absent the merger would have remained on the periphery, restraining Clorox from exercising its market power. If Procter had actually entered, Clorox's dominant position would have been eroded and the concentration of the industry reduced. * * *

The Court of Appeals said that the Commission's finding of illegality had been based on "treacherous conjecture," mere possibility and suspicion. It dismissed the fact that Clorox controlled almost 50% of the industry, that two firms controlled 65%, and that six firms controlled 80% with the observation that "[t]he fact that in addition to the six * * * producers sharing eighty per cent of the market, there were two hundred smaller producers * * * would not seem to indicate anything unhealthy about the market conditions." It dismissed the finding that Procter, with its huge resources and prowess, would have more leverage than Clorox with the statement that it was Clorox which had the "knowhow" in the industry, and that Clorox's finances were adequate for its purposes. As for the possibility that Procter would use its tremendous advertising budget and volume discounts to push Clorox, the court found "it difficult to base a finding of illegality on discounts in advertising." It rejected the Commission's finding that the merger eliminated the potential competition of Procter because "[t]here was no reasonable probability that Procter would have entered the household liquid bleach market but for the merger." * * *

The Court of Appeals also heavily relied on post-acquisition "evidence * * * to the effect that the other producers subsequent to the merger were selling more bleach for more money than ever before" and that "[t]here [had] been no significant change in Clorox's market share in the four years subsequent to the merger", and concluded that "[t]his evidence certainly does not prove anti-competitive effects of the merger." The Court of Appeals, in our view, misapprehended the standards for its review and the standards applicable in a § 7 proceeding.

Section 7 of the Clayton Act was intended to arrest the anticompetitive effects of market power in their incipiency. The core question is whether a merger may substantially lessen competition, and necessarily requires a prediction of the merger's impact on competition, present and future. See Brown Shoe Co. v. United States; United States v. Philadelphia National Bank. The section can deal only with probabilities, not with certainties. United States v. Penn-Olin Chemical Co. And there is certainly no requirement that the anticompetitive power manifest itself in anticompetitive action before § 7 can be called into play. If the enforcement of § 7 turned on the existence of actual anticompetitive practices, the congressional policy of thwarting such practices in their incipiency would be frustrated.

All mergers are within the reach of § 7, and all must be tested by the same standard, whether they are classified as horizontal, vertical, conglomerate or other. As noted by the Commission, this merger is neither horizontal, vertical, nor conglomerate. * * * [T]he Commission aptly called this acquisition a "product-extension merger":

> "By this acquisition * * * Procter has not diversified its interests in the sense of expanding into a substantially different, unfamiliar market or industry. Rather, it has entered a market which adjoins, as it were, those markets in which it is already established, and which is virtually indistinguishable from them insofar as the problems and techniques of marketing the product to the ultimate consumer are concerned. * * * "

The anticompetitive effects with which this product-extension merger is fraught can easily be seen: (1) the substitution of the powerful acquiring firm for the smaller, but already dominant, firm may substantially reduce the competitive structure of the industry by raising entry barriers and by dissuading the smaller firms from aggressively competing; (2) the acquisition eliminates the potential competition of the acquiring firm.

The liquid bleach industry was already oligopolistic before the acquisition, and price competition was certainly not as vigorous as it would have been if the industry were competitive. Clorox enjoyed a dominant position nationally, and its position approached monopoly proportions in certain areas. The existence of some 200 fringe firms certainly does not belie that fact. Nor does the fact, relied upon by the court below, that, after the merger, producers other than Clorox "were selling more bleach for more money than ever before." In the same period, Clorox increased its share from 48.8% to 52%. The interjection of Procter into the market considerably changed the situation. There is every reason to assume that the smaller firms would become more cautious in competing due to their fear of retaliation by Procter. It is probable that Procter would become the price leader and that oligopoly would become more rigid.

The acquisition may also have the tendency of raising the barriers to new entry. The major competitive weapon in the successful marketing of bleach is advertising. Clorox was limited in this area by its relatively small budget and its inability to obtain substantial discounts. By contrast, Procter's budget was much larger; and, although it would not devote its entire budget to advertising Clorox, it could divert a large portion to meet the short-term threat of a new entrant. Procter would be able to use its volume discounts to advantage in advertising Clorox. Thus, a new entrant would be much more reluctant to face the giant Procter than it would have been to face the smaller Clorox.[133]

Possible economies cannot be used as a defense to illegality. Congress was aware that some mergers which lessen competition may also result in economies but it struck the balance in favor of protecting competition. See Brown Shoe Co. v. United States.

The Commission also found that the acquisition of Clorox by Procter eliminated Procter as a potential competitor. The Court of Appeals declared that this finding was not supported by evidence because there was no evidence that Procter's management had ever intended to enter the industry independently and that Procter had never attempted to enter. The evidence, however, clearly shows that Procter was the most likely entrant. * * * No manufacturer had a patent on the product or its manufacture, necessary information relating to manufacturing methods and processes was readily available, there was no shortage of raw material, and the machinery and equipment required for a plant of efficient capacity were available at reasonable cost. Procter's management was experienced in producing and marketing goods similar to liquid bleach. Procter had considered the possibility of independently entering but decided against it because the acquisition of Clorox would enable Procter to capture a more commanding share of the market.

---

[133] The barriers to entry have been raised both for entry by new firms and for entry into new geographical markets by established firms. The latter aspect is demonstrated by Purex's lesson in Erie, Pennsylvania. In October 1957, Purex selected Erie, Pennsylvania—where it had not sold previously—as an area in which to test the salability, under competitive conditions, of a new bleach. The leading brands in Erie were Clorox, with 52%, and the "101" brand * * * with 29% of the market. Purex launched an advertising and promotional campaign to obtain a broad distribution in a short time, and in five months captured 33% of the Erie market. Clorox's share dropped to 35% and 101's to 17%. Clorox responded by offering its bleach at reduced prices, and then added an offer of a $1-value ironing board cover for 50 cents with each purchase of Clorox at the reduced price. It also increased its advertising with television spots. The result was to restore Clorox's lost market share and, indeed, to increase it slightly. Purex's share fell to 7%. * * * [Court's fn. 3]

It is clear that the existence of Procter at the edge of the industry exerted considerable influence on the market. First, the market behavior of the liquid bleach industry was influenced by each firm's predictions of the market behavior of its competitors, actual and potential. Second, the barriers to entry by a firm of Procter's size and with its advantages were not significant. There is no indication that the barriers were so high that the price Procter would have to charge would be above the price that would maximize the profits of the existing firms. Third, the number of potential entrants was not so large that the elimination of one would be insignificant. Few firms would have the temerity to challenge a firm as solidly entrenched as Clorox. Fourth, Procter was found by the Commission to be the most likely entrant. These findings of the Commission were amply supported by the evidence.

The judgment of the Court of Appeals is reversed and remanded with instructions to affirm and enforce the Commission's order.

* * *

MR. JUSTICE STEWART and MR. JUSTICE FORTAS took no part in the consideration or decision of this case.

MR. JUSTICE HARLAN, concurring.

I agree that the Commission's order should be sustained, but * * * [it] is regrettable to see this Court as it enters this comparatively new field of economic adjudication starting off with what has almost become a kind of res ipsa loquitur approach to antitrust cases.

* * *

I

The Court's opinion rests on three separate findings of anticompetitive effect. The Court first declares that the market here was "oligopolistic" and that interjection of Procter would make the oligopoly "more rigid" because "[t]here is every reason to assume that the smaller firms would become more cautious in competing due to their fear of retaliation by Procter." * * *

But assumption is no substitute for reasonable probability as a measure of illegality under § 7, and Congress has not mandated the Commission or the courts "to campaign against 'super-concentration' in the absence of any evidence of harm to competition." Moreover, even if an effect of this kind were reasonably predictable, the Court does not explain why the effect on competition should be expected to be the substantial one that § 7 demands. * * *

The Court next stresses the increase in barriers to new entry into the liquid bleach field caused primarily, it is thought, by the substitution of the larger advertising capabilities of Procter for those of Clorox. Economic theory would certainly indicate that a heightening of such barriers has taken place. But the Court does not explain why it considers this change to have significance under § 7, nor does it indicate when or how entry barriers affect competition in a relevant market. * * *[134]

Finally, the Court places much emphasis on the loss to the market of the most likely potential entrant, Procter. * * * Certainly the exclusion of what would promise to be an important independent competitor from the market may be sufficient, in itself, to support a finding of illegality under § 7, United States v. El Paso Natural Gas Co., when the market has few competitors. The Commission, however, expressly refused to find a reasonable probability that Procter would have entered this market on its own, and the Sixth Circuit was in emphatic agreement. The Court certainly cannot mean to set its judgment on the facts against the concurrent findings below, and thus it seems clear to me that no consequence can be attached to the possibility of loss of Procter as an actual competitor. Cf. United States v. Penn-Olin Chemical Co.

* * *

II

* * *

At the outset, it seems to me that there is a serious question whether the state of our economic knowledge is sufficiently advanced to enable a sure-footed administrative or judicial determination to be made a priori of substantial anticompetitive effect in mergers of this kind. It is clear enough that Congress desired that conglomerate and product-extension mergers be brought under § 7 scrutiny, but well versed economists have argued that such scrutiny can never lead to a valid finding of illegality. * * *

Lending strength to this position is the fact that such mergers do provide significant economic benefits which argue against excessive controls being imposed on them. The ability to merge brings large firms into the market for capital assets and encourages economic development by holding out the incentive of easy and profitable liquidation to others. Here, for example, the owners of Clorox who had built the business, were able to liquefy their capital on profitable terms without dismantling the enterprise they had created. Also merger allows an active management to move rapidly into new markets bringing with its intervention competitive stimulation and innovation. It permits a large corporation to protect its shareholders from business fluctuation through diversification, and may

---

[134] The need for analysis is even clearer in light of the fact that entry into the market by producers of nonadvertised, locally distributed bleaches was found to be easy. There were no technological barriers to entry, and the capital requirements for entry, with the exception of advertising costs, were small. The Court must at least explain why the threat of such entry and the presence of small competitors in existing regional markets cannot be considered the predominant, and unaffected, form of competition. * * * [Concur fn. 3]

facilitate the introduction of capital resources, allowing significant economies of scale, into a stagnating market.

At the other end of the spectrum, it has been argued that the entry of a large conglomerate enterprise may have a destructive effect on competition in any market. * * * [C]ongressional concern in enacting § 7 extended not only to anticompetitive behavior in particular markets, but also to the possible economic dominance of large companies which had grown through merger. * * *

III

* * *

In its initial decision, the Commission remanded the proceeding to the Examiner for the express purpose of taking additional evidence on the post-merger situation in the liquid bleach industry. * * * The Commission's subsequent opinion, handed down by an almost entirely changed Commission, held post-merger evidence generally irrelevant * * * . Market structure changes, rather than evidence of market behavior, were held to be the key to a § 7 analysis.

* * *

If § 7 is to serve the purposes Congress intended for it, we must, I think, stand with the Commission on this issue. Only by focusing on market structure can we begin to formulate standards which will allow the responsible agencies to give proper consideration to such mergers and allow businessmen to plan their actions with a fair degree of certainty. * * *

Deciding that § 7 inquiry in conglomerate or product-extension merger cases should be directed toward reasonably probable changes in market structure does not, however, determine how that inquiry should be narrowed and focused. The Commission and the Court isolate two separate structural elements, the degree of concentration in the existing market and the "condition of entry." The interplay of these two factors is said to determine the existence and extent of market power, since the "condition of entry" determines the limits potential competition places on the existing market. It must be noted, however, that economic theory teaches that potential competition will have no effect on the market behavior of existing firms unless present market power is sufficient to drive the market price to the point where entry would become a real possibility. So long as existing competition is sufficient to keep the market price below that point, potential competition is of marginal significance as a market regulator. Thus in a conglomerate or product-extension case, where the effects on market structure which are easiest to discover are generally effects on the "condition of entry," an understanding of the workings of the premerger market cannot be ignored, and, indeed, is critical to a determination whether the visible effects on "condition of entry" have any competitive significance.

The Commission pinned its analysis of the premerger market exclusively on its concentration, the large market share enjoyed by the leading firms. In so doing the Commission was following the path taken by this Court in judging more conventional merger cases, e.g., United States v. Philadelphia National Bank * * * . The Court bases its agreement with the Commission * * * on Clorox's alleged domination of the market. But domination is an elusive term, for dominance in terms of percentage of sales is not the equivalent of dominance in terms of control over price or other aspects of market behavior. Just as the total number of sellers in the market is not determinative of its operation, the percentage of sales made by any group of sellers is similarly not conclusive. The determinative issue is, instead, how the sellers interact and establish the pattern of market behavior. The significance of concentration analysis is that it allows measurement of one easily determined variable to serve as an opening key to the pattern of market behavior.

I think that the Commission, on *this* record, was entitled to regard the market as "oligopolistic" and that it could properly ignore the impact of the smaller firms. * * * [However, in] adjudicating § 7 questions in a conglomerate or product-extension merger context where the pattern of behavior in the existing market is apt to be crucial, I would * * * allow the introduction by a defendant of evidence designed to show that the actual operation of the market did not accord with oligopoly theory, or whatever other theory the Commission desires to apply. * * *

* * * But to challenge effectively the presumption which the Commission is entitled to draw from general economic theory, a defendant must present, in my opinion, not only contradictory facts but a more cogent explanation of the pattern of market behavior.

If the proof as a whole establishes that pricing power may be exercised by a firm or firms in the market—that prices may be raised in the long run over competitive prices—then the Commission may legitimately focus on the role of potential competition and the "condition of entry." In so doing, however, a new difficulty is encountered. The threat of potential competition merely affects the range over which price power extends. Potential competition does not compel more vigorous striving in the market, nor advance any other social goal which Congress might be said to have favored in passing § 7. Thus it may legitimately be questioned whether even a substantial increase in entry barriers creates a substantial lessening of competition or tendency to monopoly as required by § 7.

* * *

* * * [H]owever, the problem of efficiencies * * * must still be faced. The Court attempts to brush the question aside by asserting that Congress preferred competition to economies, but neglects to determine whether certain economies are inherent in the idea of competition. If it is conceded,

as it must be, that Congress had reasons for favoring competition, then more efficient operation must have been among them. It is of course true that a firm's ability to achieve economies enhances its competitive position, but adverse effects on competitors must be distinguished from adverse effects on competition. Brown Shoe Co. v. United States. Economies achieved by one firm may stimulate matching innovation by others, the very essence of competition. They always allow the total output to be delivered to the consumer with an expenditure of fewer resources. Thus when the case against a conglomerate or product-extension merger rests on a market-structure demonstration that the likelihood of anticompetitive consequences has been substantially increased, the responsible agency should then move on to examine and weigh possible efficiencies arising from the merger in order to determine whether, on balance, competition has been substantially lessened. * * *

* * *

IV

The Commission's decision did, I think, conform to this analysis. * * *

* * *

Procter was indisputably many times the size of any firm in the liquid bleach industry and had great financial resources. * * * The expenditure on advertising which would have to be undertaken by a potential entrant in order to capture an acceptable market would vary with the tenacity of response to be expected from existing competitors. The greater the expenditure required, the higher the price to be commanded would have to be before entry would be undertaken. In this regard the substitution of Procter for Clorox was a substantial change.

Procter's strong position in other product markets is equally relevant to the probability of change in the "condition of entry." * * * If Procter were hard pressed along all fronts of its operation, competitors could safely assume that increased pressure in the liquid bleach industry would not provoke a strong response, simply because financial resources could not be diverted to that purpose. Procter, however, was conducting highly profitable operations in other markets and had demonstrated its ability to bring large resources to bear in intensive competitive campaigns by its successful introduction of Comet cleanser and various toothpastes on a nationwide scale. * * *

* * *

The Commission's analysis of the economies involved in this case is critical and I regret that the Court refrains from commenting upon it. The Commission—in my opinion quite correctly—seemed to accept the idea that economies could be used to defend a merger, noting that "[a] merger that results in increased efficiency of production, distribution or marketing may, in certain cases, increase the vigor of competition in the relevant market." But advertising economies were placed in a different classification since they were said "only to increase the barriers to new entry" and to be "offensive to at least the spirit, if not the letter, of the antitrust laws." Advertising was thought to benefit only the seller by entrenching his market position, and to be of no use to the consumer.

I think the Commission's view overstated and over-simplified. Proper advertising serves a legitimate and important purpose in the market by educating the consumer as to available alternatives. This process contributes to consumer demand being developed to the point at which economies of scale can be realized in production. The advertiser's brand name may also be an assurance of quality, and the value of this benefit is demonstrated by the general willingness of consumers to pay a premium for the advertised brands. Undeniably advertising may sometimes be used to create irrational brand preferences and mislead consumers as to the actual differences between products, but it is very difficult to discover at what point advertising ceases to be an aspect of healthy competition. It is not the Commission's function to decide which lawful elements of the "product" offered the consumer should be considered useful and which should be considered the symptoms of industrial "sickness." * * *

I do not think, however, that on the record presented Procter has shown any true efficiencies in advertising. Procter has merely shown that it is able to command equivalent resources at a lower dollar cost than other bleach producers. * * * Economies employed in defense of a merger must be shown in what economists label "real" terms, that is in terms of resources applied to the accomplishment of the objective. For this reason, the Commission, I think, was justified in discounting Procter's efficiency defense.

NOTES AND QUESTIONS

1.   If it were true that Procter & Gamble and Clorox neither competed with each other nor sold to each other before the merger, how could competition be reduced by their merging? On the other hand, was this result inevitable after *El Paso Gas*, *Penn-Olin* and *Continental Can*?

a.   Were you persuaded that if Procter owned Clorox, no one else would enter the bleach industry, thus creating an entry barrier by the fact of their merged existence? Is that because Procter was in a related industry?

b.   Would you say the same thing if Apple acquired Clorox, i.e., a pure "conglomerate" merger? Wouldn't all the same "dominant firm" arguments apply? What does the concept of "dominance" add, if anything, to a careful analysis of these issues?

2.   Were you persuaded that Procter & Gamble was indeed a *potential* bleach producer here?

a. Should the FTC's and the Court of Appeals' finding that Procter & Gamble had no actual intention of entering de novo have been the end of the matter? Should "potential competition" be judged from the perspective of the firm on the fringe or the firms already in the market?

b. Were you persuaded by Justice Harlan's analysis of when potential competition is important? Is he right that if existing firms do not have enough market power to raise prices to a level at which potential de novo entrants would find the market worth entering, there is no good reason to find potential competition important in that market?

c. Given the fact that this product is easy to make and that neither Procter nor anyone else seemed to want to enter the market de novo, was there likely any monopoly profit being earned here? Even if there were none, should that be dispositive of the case?

d. Does the majority seem to ignore the potential of small regional firms to discipline this market by threat of entry? Is that possibility consistent with what the Court tells us about how bleach is produced and sold? Is it consistent with Purex's experience in Erie, PA?

e. Why would it be cheaper for Procter to enter an industry by buying the leading firm than by starting a new one? If you were Clorox, would you sell your company for less that it would cost Procter to enter another way? Don't answer too quickly. Might you worry about the losses you would suffer if you had to slug it out with Procter? Might you assess the cost of Procter's next best alternative, e.g., buying Purex, and consider that amount to be the limit you could get for your own company?[135]

f. Is society better off if a firm like Procter actually enters de novo and fights from zero for market share? Who would likely lose if such an approach were compelled? Is a world in which merger is not an available means of entry really the worst of all worlds for the small firms in an industry?

3. Should the experience and economies of scale in advertising possessed by Procter be held against it?

a. Would Procter & Gamble's ability to help Clorox buy chemicals and bottles at quantity discounts "substantially lessen competition or tend to create a monopoly"?

b. Do you share Justice Harlan's view that the fact that Procter & Gamble can buy additional advertising at lower cost does not mean that it is a more efficient advertiser? Justice Harlan's analytic point is very important; the price one pays for something may or may not be equal to the resources used to produce it. But how can "social resources" typically be calculated except by reference to their prices?

---

[135] Blocked in its effort to merge with Procter & Gamble, Clorox later tried developing a combination detergent with bleach (Clorox Super Detergent). The venture was a failure and resulted in a $125 million writeoff in 1989. In addition, Clorox tried to diversify itself by acquiring food businesses such as the maker of Hidden Valley Ranch salad dressing. See Thom Calandra, In the Hot Seat, Forbes, Oct. 12, 1992, p. 126.

A NOTE ON EFFICIENCIES AS AN ANTITRUST DEFENSE

Suppose a merger makes an industry more concentrated; suppose it would even make it possible for the industry to decrease output and raise prices. Should the fact that the merger makes the new combination significantly more efficient have any effect on how we view its social impact?

Professor Oliver Williamson brought the importance of efficiencies back to public attention in his article Efficiencies as an Antitrust Defense: The Welfare Tradeoffs, 58 American Economic Review 18 (1968). The Williamson model is quite simple.[136] Even if a merger reduces marginal cost, price might go up because the firm sets its price where the marginal revenue curve intersects the marginal cost curve rather than where the demand curve intersects the marginal cost curve.

$MR =$ rev. from lunit

$MC =$ cost from 1. unit

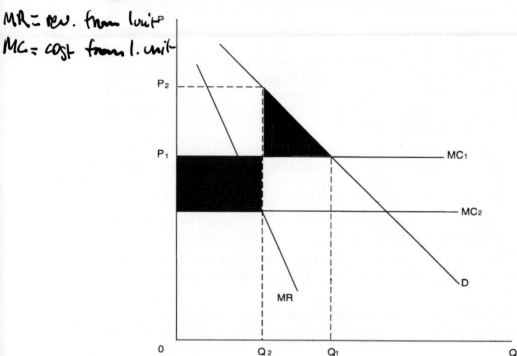

Williamson, however, urges us to focus on the the social *loss* from monopoly pricing. An efficiency-enhancing merger may yield a large *saving* in social resources. Thus, there is reason to take efficiencies seriously if we want to avoid having merger policy do more harm than good. Unfortunately the efficiency and pricing effects of a merger are not usually predictable

---

[136] It was Figure 4 in the Introduction to these materials.

with precision at the time of the merger, so we can only make a rough approximation of the tradeoffs.

THE HIGH POINT OF POTENTIAL COMPETITION:
THE *FALSTAFF BREWING* CASE

Probably the best summary of this line of merger cases was provided in United States v. Falstaff Brewing Corp., 410 U.S. 526, 93 S.Ct. 1096, 35 L.Ed.2d 475 (1973). It was a case of beer. The top 8 brewers in New England sold over 80% of the beer there, and the top 4 sold over 60%. Of the ten largest brewers in the country, only two did not sell in New England. Falstaff was one of them; it now sought to acquire Narragansett, New England's largest brewer.

The District Judge found that Falstaff's management was firmly committed not to enter de novo. Thus, he held that the merger did not lessen competition. The Supreme Court, however, reversed. Justice White wrote for the majority:

> "The District Court erred as a matter of law. The error lay in the assumption that because Falstaff, as a matter of fact, would never have entered the market de novo, it could in no sense be considered a potential competitor. More specifically, the District Court failed to give separate consideration to whether Falstaff was a potential competitor in the sense that it was so positioned on the edge of the market that it exerted beneficial influence on competitive conditions in that market.

> "A similar error was committed by the Court of Appeals in FTC v. Procter & Gamble Co. * * * .

> "The specific question with respect to this phase of the case is not what Falstaff's internal company decisions were but whether, given its financial capabilities and conditions in the New England market, it would be reasonable to consider it a potential entrant into that market. * * * [I]f it would appear to rational beer merchants in New England that Falstaff might well build a new brewery to supply the northeastern market then its entry by merger becomes suspect under § 7. * * * "

The concurring opinion of Justice Douglas was among his last and it was certainly among his most personal.

> " * * * The antitrust laws look with suspicion on the acquisition of local business units by out-of-state companies. For then local employment is apt to suffer, local payrolls are likely to drop off, and responsible entrepreneurs in counties and States are replaced by clerks.

"A case in point is Goldendale in my State of Washington. It was a thriving community—an ideal place to raise a family—until the company that owned the sawmill was bought by an out-of-state giant. In a year or so, auditors in faraway New York City, who never knew the glories of Goldendale, decided to close the local mill and truck all the logs to Yakima. Goldendale became greatly crippled. It is Exhibit A to the Brandeis concern, which became part of the Clayton Act concern, with the effects that the impact of monopoly often has on a community, as contrasted with the beneficent effect of competition.

"A nation of clerks is anathema to the American antitrust dream. So is the spawning of federal regulatory agencies to police the mounting economic power. For the path of those who want the concentration of power to develop unhindered leads predictably to socialism that is antagonistic to our system."

But the clearest analysis of the point to which the Court had come was provided by Justice Marshall, concurring in the result.

"Since 1950, we have repeatedly applied § 7 to cases where the merging firms competed in the same line of commerce, and we have been willing to define the line of commerce liberally so as to reach anticompetitive practices in their "incipiency." But in keeping with the spirit of the Celler-Kefauver Amendment, we have also applied § 7 to cases where the acquiring firm is outside the market in which the acquired firm competes. These cases fall into three broad categories which, while frequently overlapping, can be dealt with separately for analytical purposes.

"1. The Dominant Entrant.—In some situations, a firm outside the market may have overpowering resources which, if brought to bear within the market, could ultimately have a substantial anticompetitive effect. If such a firm were to acquire a company within the relevant market, it might drive other marginal companies out of business, thus creating an oligopoly, or it might raise entry barriers to such an extent that potential new entrants would be discouraged from entering the market. Cf. Ford Motor Co. v. United States, 405 U.S. 562 (1972); FTC v. Procter & Gamble Co. Such a danger is especially intense when the market is already highly concentrated or entry barriers are already unusually high before the dominant firm enters the market.

"2. The Perceived Potential Entrant.—Even if the entry of a firm does not upset the competitive balance within the market, it may be that the removal of the firm from the fringe of the market has a present anticompetitive effect. In a concentrated oligopolistic market, the presence of a large potential competitor on the edge of the market, apparently ready to enter if entry barriers are lowered, may deter anticompetitive conduct within the market. * * * From the perspective of the firms already in the market, the possibility of entry by such a lingering firm may be an important consideration in their pricing and marketing decisions. When the lingering firm enters the market by acquisition, the competitive influence exerted by the firm is lost with no offsetting gain through an increase in the number of companies seeking a share of the relevant market. The result is a net decrease in competitive pressure.[137]

"3. The Actual Potential Entrant.—Since the effect of a perceived potential entrant depends upon the perception of those already in the market, it may in some cases be difficult to prove. Moreover, in a market which is already competitive, the existence of a perceived potential entrant will have no present effect at all.[138] The entry by acquisition of such a firm may nonetheless have an anticompetitive effect by eliminating an actual potential competitor. When a firm enters the market by acquiring a strong company within the market, it merely assumes the position of that company without necessarily increasing competitive pressures. Had such a firm not entered by acquisition, it might at some point have entered de novo. An entry de novo would increase competitive pressures within the market, and an entry by acquisition eliminates the possibility that such an increase will take place in the future. Thus, even if a firm at the fringe of the market exerts no present procompetitive effect, its entry by acquisition may end for all time the promise of more effective competition at some future date."

Justice Marshall proposed remanding the case to the District Court with instructions to use only "objective" evidence of whether Falstaff was an actual potential entrant. "[C]orporations are, after all, profit-making institutions," he observed, "and, absent special circumstances, they can be expected to follow courses of action most likely to maximize profits."

---

[137] Thus, whereas the practical difference between entry by acquisition and entry de novo may be marginal in the case of a dominant entrant, it is crucial in the case of a perceived potential entrant. If the perceived potential entrant enters de novo, its deterrent effect on anticompetitive practices remains and the total number of firms competing for market shares increases. But when such a firm enters by acquisition, it merely steps into the shoes of the acquired firm. The result is no net increase in the actual competition for market shares and the removal of a threat exerting procompetitive influence from outside the market. [Marshall fn. 14]

[138] Still, even if the market is presently competitive, it is possible that it might grow less competitive in the future. For example, a market might be so concentrated that even though it is presently competitive, there is a serious risk that parallel pricing policies might emerge sometime in the near future. In such a situation, an effective competitor lingering on the fringe of the market—what might be called a potential perceived potential entrant—could exert a deterrent force when anticompetitive conduct is about to emerge. As its very name suggests, however, such a firm would be still a further step removed from the exertion of actual, present competitive influence, and the problems of proof are compounded accordingly—particularly in light of the showing of reasonable probability required under § 7. [Marshall fn. 15]

Justice Rehnquist (who had replaced Justice Harlan on the Court) and Justice Stewart joined in dissent. They agreed with Justice Marshall's analysis but argued that, "In the field of economic forecasting in general, and in the area of potential competition in particular, * * * the distinction between 'objective' and 'subjective' evidence is largely illusory."

NOTES AND QUESTIONS

1.   The opinions in this case suggest the multiple strands of doctrine and theory underlying merger law by the early 1970s. Is the distinction between an actual and a perceived potential entrant a useful one?

2.   What evidence should be considered in deciding whether a firm was a potential entrant?

a.   What will you expect to hear from the firms into whose industry a competitor has entered? Are they likely to tell you honestly about their *prior* expectations?

b.   Can one reliably determine intent to enter a market by facts showing it would have been potentially profitable to do so? If the industry is pricing competitively, is Justice Marshall right that one may conclude that a firm outside the industry will not enter?

3.   Are many of these questions simply beyond the competence of courts to answer?

a.   Would you rather have courts make Type 1 errors (convicting too many innocent firms) or Type 2 errors (freeing too many guilty ones)? May the costs of getting right answers exceed the value in helping the courts make better decisions? In short, might we wisely take the risk of making some wrong decisions in exchange for getting quicker, more definitive answers?

b.   If so, are you convinced that the Court had defined the right questions to ask? As a partial answer to that question, in 1968, the Justice Department began issuing "Merger Guidelines."[139] The current version of those Guidelines will be examined in the next chapter.

---

[139] The Assistant Attorney General (Antitrust) at the time the first Merger Guidelines were issued was a highly-respected Harvard antitrust professor, Donald Turner, whom you may remember from the Areeda-Turner test for identifying predatory pricing.

CHAPTER IV

THE MODERN DEVELOPMENT OF ANTITRUST LAW: SINCE 1975

■ ■ ■

By the early 1970s, changes in the nation's approach to antitrust law were probably inevitable. Per se rules were ill-suited to carry the entire load of antitrust analysis for a complex economy. Further, rules that may have seemed to make sense in the context in which they were created often did not lend themselves to logical extension.

Articulate critics such as Robert Bork, Harold Demsetz and Richard Posner, raised questions about the intellectual basis for much antitrust doctrine.[1] Cases such as *Container, Topco, Utah Pie, Fortner,* and *Schwinn* were seen as embarrassments even by many of those who defended expanded antitrust enforcement. The real question became how to approach antitrust issues in a manner consistent with both traditional concerns *and* sound economic analysis.[2]

Early in the 1970s, four new justices took seats on the Supreme Court. Justice Blackmun replaced Justice Fortas in 1970. Justice Rehnquist replaced Justice Harlan in 1972, and Justice Powell replaced Justice Black the same year. Finally, the Douglas era came to an end in 1975 when he was succeeded by Justice Stevens to complete the Court's transformation. In a real sense, however, much of the intellectual leadership in the current period has come from judges of the Courts of Appeals—names like Bork and Posner, Easterbrook and Ginsburg—each the author of influential opinions.

---

[1]   Two of the leading books from the period were Robert H. Bork, The Antitrust Paradox (1978), and Richard A. Posner, Antitrust Law: An Economic Perspective (1976). One of the most important attacks on the concern about industry concentration was Harold Demsetz, The Market Concentration Doctrine: An Examination of Evidence and a Discussion of Policy (1973). See also, Dominick T. Armentano, Antitrust and Monopoly: Anatomy of a Policy Failure (1982); Richard A. Posner, The Chicago School of Antitrust Analysis, 127 U. Pennsylvania L. Rev. 925 (1979); The Goals of Antitrust: A Dialogue on Policy, 65 Columbia L. Rev. 363 (1965) (consisting of Robert H. Bork & Ward S. Bowman, Jr., The Crisis in Antitrust; Harlan M. Blake & William K. Jones, In Defense of Antitrust; Robert H. Bork, Contrasts in Antitrust Theory I; and Ward S. Bowman, Contrasts in Antitrust Theory II). A longer look back at this transition is William H. Page, Legal Realism and the Shaping of Modern Antitrust, 44 Emory L.J. 1 (1995).

[2]   This is not to imply that the task has been without controversy. Compare, e.g., Frank H. Easterbrook, Workable Antitrust Policy, 84 Michigan L.Rev. 1696 (1986), with Herbert Hovenkamp, Antitrust Policy After Chicago, 84 Michigan L.Rev. 213 (1985), and Eleanor Fox, The Politics of Law and Economics in Judicial Decision Making: Antitrust as a Window, 61 N.Y.U. L.Rev. 554 (1986).

We begin this chapter with three cases from the mid-1970s that marked a break from the cases we examined in Chapter III. One was a price fixing case that extended antitrust principles, this time to professional groups that had thought themselves largely exempt. One involved vertical allocation of dealer territories and revisited *White Motor* and *Schwinn*. The third took on antitrust jurisdiction and placed a significant limit on private antitrust actions. All three cases, then, presaged the developments that have remade antitrust law over the last thirty years.

A. THE TRANSITION CASES

GOLDFARB V. VIRGINIA STATE BAR
Supreme Court of the United States, 1975
421 U.S. 773, 95 S.Ct. 2004, 44 L.Ed.2d 572

MR. CHIEF JUSTICE BURGER delivered the opinion of the Court.

We granted certiorari to decide whether a minimum-fee schedule for lawyers published by the Fairfax County Bar Association and enforced by the Virginia State Bar violates § 1 of the Sherman Act. The Court of Appeals held that, although the fee schedule and enforcement mechanism substantially restrained competition among lawyers, publication of the schedule by the County Bar was outside the scope of the Act because the practice of law is not "trade or commerce," and enforcement of the schedule by the State Bar was exempt from the Sherman Act as state action as defined in Parker v. Brown.

I

In 1971 petitioners, husband and wife, contracted to buy a home in Fairfax County, Va. The financing agency required them to secure title insurance; this required a title examination, and only a member of the Virginia State Bar could legally perform that service. Petitioners therefore contacted a lawyer who quoted them the precise fee suggested in a minimum-fee schedule published by respondent Fairfax County Bar Association; the lawyer told them that it was his policy to keep his charges in line with the minimum-fee schedule which provided for a fee of 1% of the value of the property involved. Petitioners then tried to find a lawyer who would examine the title for less than the fee fixed by the schedule. They sent letters to 36 other Fairfax County lawyers requesting their fees. Nineteen replied, and none indicated that he would charge less than the rate fixed by the schedule; several stated that they knew of no attorney who would do so.

The fee schedule the lawyers referred to is a list of recommended minimum prices for common legal services. Respondent Fairfax County Bar Association published the fee schedule although, as a purely voluntary association of attorneys, the County Bar has no formal power to enforce it. Enforcement has been provided by respondent Virginia State Bar which is the administrative agency through which the Virginia Supreme Court regulates the practice of law in that State; membership in the State Bar is required in order to practice in Virginia. Although the State Bar has never taken formal disciplinary action to compel adherence to any fee schedule, it has published reports condoning fee schedules, and has issued two ethical opinions indicating that fee schedules cannot be ignored. The most recent opinion states that "evidence that an attorney habitually charges less than the suggested minimum fee schedule adopted by his local bar Association, raises a presumption that such lawyer is guilty of misconduct * * * ."

Because petitioners could not find a lawyer willing to charge a fee lower than the schedule dictated, they had their title examined by the lawyer they had first contacted. They then brought this class action against the State Bar and the County Bar alleging that the operation of the minimum-fee schedule, as applied to fees for legal services relating to residential real estate transactions, constitutes price fixing in violation of § 1 of the Sherman Act. Petitioners sought both injunctive relief and damages.

After a trial solely on the issue of liability the District Court held that the minimum-fee schedule violated the Sherman Act. The court viewed the fee-schedule system as a significant reason for petitioners' failure to obtain legal services for less than the minimum fee, and it rejected the County Bar's contention that as a "learned profession" the practice of law is exempt from the Sherman Act.

* * *

II

Our inquiry can be divided into four steps: did respondents engage in price fixing? If so, are their activities in interstate commerce or do they affect interstate commerce? If so, are the activities exempt from the Sherman Act because they involve a "learned profession?" If not, are the activities "state action" within the meaning of Parker v. Brown and therefore exempt from the Sherman Act?

A

The County Bar argues that because the fee schedule is merely advisory, the schedule and its enforcement mechanism do not constitute price fixing. Its purpose, the argument continues, is only to provide legitimate information to aid member lawyers in complying with Virginia professional regulations. Moreover, the County Bar contends that in practice the schedule has not had the effect of producing fixed fees. The facts found by the trier belie these contentions, and nothing in the record suggests these findings lack support.

A purely advisory fee schedule issued to provide guidelines, or an exchange of price information without a showing of an actual restraint on trade, would present us with a different question, e.g., American Column Co. v. United States. The record here, however, reveals a situation quite different from what would occur under a purely advisory fee schedule. Here a fixed, rigid price floor arose from respondents' activities: every lawyer who responded to petitioners' inquiries adhered to the fee schedule, and no lawyer asked for additional information in order to set an individualized fee. The price information disseminated did not concern past standards, but rather minimum fees to be charged in future transactions, and those minimum rates were increased over time. The fee schedule was enforced through the prospect of professional discipline from the State Bar, and the desire of attorneys to comply with announced professional norms, see generally *American Column*, the motivation to conform was reinforced by the assurance that other lawyers would not compete by underbidding. This is not merely a case of an agreement that may be inferred from an exchange of price information, United States v. Container Corp., for here a naked agreement was clearly shown, and the effect on prices is plain.

Moreover, in terms of restraining competition and harming consumers like petitioners the price-fixing activities found here are unusually damaging. A title examination is indispensable in the process of financing a real estate purchase, and since only an attorney licensed to practice in Virginia may legally examine a title, consumers could not turn to alternative sources for the necessary service. All attorneys, of course, were practicing under the constraint of the fee schedule. The County Bar makes much of the fact that it is a voluntary organization; however, the ethical opinions issued by the State Bar provide that any lawyer, whether or not a member of his county bar association, may be disciplined for "*habitually* [charging] less than the suggested minimum fee schedule adopted by his local bar Association. . . ." These factors coalesced to create a pricing system that consumers could not realistically escape. On this record respondents' activities constitute a classic illustration of price fixing.

B

The County Bar argues, as the Court of Appeals held, that any effect on interstate commerce caused by the fee schedule's restraint on legal services was incidental and remote. In its view the legal services, which are performed wholly intrastate, are essentially local in nature and therefore a restraint with respect to them can never substantially affect interstate commerce. Further, the County Bar maintains, there was no showing here that the fee schedule and its enforcement mechanism increased fees, and that even if they did there was no showing that such an increase deterred any prospective homeowner from buying in Fairfax County.

These arguments misconceive the nature of the transactions at issue and the place legal services play in those transactions. As the District Court found, "a significant portion of funds furnished for the purchasing of homes in Fairfax County comes from without the State of Virginia," and "significant amounts of loans on Fairfax County real estate are guaranteed by the United States Veterans Administration and Department of Housing and Urban Development, both headquartered in the District of Columbia." Thus in this class action the transactions which create the need for the particular legal services in question frequently are interstate transactions. The necessary connection between the interstate transactions and the restraint of trade provided by the minimum-fee schedule is present because, in a practical sense, title examinations are necessary in real estate transactions to assure a lien on a valid title of the borrower. In financing realty purchases lenders require, "as a condition of making the loan, that the title to the property involved be examined. . . ." Thus a title examination is an integral part of an interstate transaction * * *.

Given the substantial volume of commerce involved, and the inseparability of this particular legal service from the interstate aspects of real estate transactions, we conclude that interstate commerce has been sufficiently affected.

The fact that there was no showing that home buyers were discouraged by the challenged activities does not mean that interstate commerce was not affected. Otherwise, the magnitude of the effect would control, and our cases have shown that, once an effect is shown, no specific magnitude need be proved. Nor was it necessary for petitioners to prove that the fee schedule raised fees. * * * See *Socony-Vacuum.*

Where, as a matter of law or practical necessity, legal services are an integral part of an interstate transaction, a restraint on those services may substantially affect commerce for Sherman Act purposes. * * *

C

The County Bar argues that Congress never intended to include the learned professions within the terms "trade or commerce" in § 1 of the Sherman Act, and therefore the sale of professional services is exempt from the Act. No explicit exemption or legislative history is provided to support this contention; rather, the existence of state regulation seems to be its primary basis. Also, the County Bar maintains that competition is inconsistent with the practice of a profession because enhancing profit is not the goal of professional activities; the goal is to provide services necessary to the community. That, indeed, is the classic basis traditionally advanced to distinguish professions from trades, businesses, and other occupations, but it loses some of its force when used to support the fee control activities involved here.

In arguing that learned professions are not "trade or commerce" the County Bar seeks a total exclusion from antitrust regulation. Whether state regulation is active or dormant, real or theoretical, lawyers would be able to adopt anticompetitive practices with impunity. We cannot find support for the proposition that Congress intended any such sweeping exclusion. The nature of an occupation, standing alone, does not provide sanctuary from the Sherman Act, nor is the public-service aspect of professional practice controlling in determining whether § 1 includes professions. Congress intended to strike as broadly as it could in § 1 of the Sherman Act, and to read into it so wide an exemption as that urged on us would be at odds with that purpose.

The language of § 1 of the Sherman Act, of course, contains no exception. And our cases have repeatedly established that there is a heavy presumption against implicit exemptions, United States v. Philadelphia National Bank (1963). Indeed, our cases have specifically included the sale of services within § 1. Whatever else it may be, the examination of a land title is a service; the exchange of such a service for money is "commerce" in the most common usage of that word. It is no disparagement of the practice of law as a profession to acknowledge that it has this business aspect.[3]

D

In Parker v. Brown, the Court held that an anticompetitive marketing program which "derived its authority and its efficacy from the legislative command of the state" was not a violation of the Sherman Act because the Act was intended to regulate private practices and not to prohibit a State from imposing a restraint as an act of government. Respondent State Bar and respondent County Bar both seek to avail themselves of this so-called state-action exemption.

Through its legislature Virginia has authorized its highest court to regulate the practice of law. That court has adopted ethical codes which deal in part with fees, and far from exercising state power to authorize binding price fixing, explicitly directed lawyers not "to be controlled" by fee schedules. The State Bar, a state agency by law, argues that in issuing fee schedule reports and ethical opinions dealing with fee schedules it was merely implementing the fee provisions of the ethical codes. The County

---

[3]   The fact that a restraint operates upon a profession as distinguished from a business is, of course, relevant in determining whether that particular restraint violates the Sherman Act. It would be unrealistic to view the practice of professions as interchangeable with other business activities, and automatically to apply to the professions antitrust concepts which originated in other areas. The public service aspect, and other features of the professions, may require that a particular practice, which could properly be viewed as a violation of the Sherman Act in another context, be treated differently. We intimate no view on any other situation than the one with which we are confronted today. [Court's fn. 17]

Bar, although it is a voluntary association and not a state agency, claims that the ethical codes and the activities of the State Bar "prompted" it to issue fee schedules and thus its actions, too, are state action for Sherman Act purposes.

The threshold inquiry in determining if an anticompetitive activity is state action of the type the Sherman Act was not meant to proscribe is whether the activity is required by the State acting as sovereign. * * * Respondents have pointed to no Virginia statute requiring their activities; state law simply does not refer to fees, leaving regulation of the profession to the Virginia Supreme Court; although the Supreme Court's ethical codes mention advisory fee schedules they do not direct either respondent to supply them, or require the type of price floor which arose from respondents' activities. Although the State Bar apparently has been granted the power to issue ethical opinions, there is no indication in this record that the Virginia Supreme Court approves the opinions. Respondents' arguments, at most, constitute the contention that their activities complemented the objective of the ethical codes. In our view that is not state action for Sherman Act purposes. It is not enough that, as the County Bar puts it, anticompetitive conduct is "prompted" by state action; rather, anticompetitive activities must be compelled by direction of the State acting as a sovereign.

* * *

III

We recognize that the States have a compelling interest in the practice of professions within their boundaries, and that as part of their power to protect the public health, safety, and other valid interests they have broad power to establish standards for licensing practitioners and regulating the practice of professions. We also recognize that in some instances the State may decide that "forms of competition usual in the business world may be demoralizing to the ethical standards of a profession." United States v. Oregon State Medical Society, 343 U.S. 326, 336, 72 S.Ct. 690, 96 L. Ed. 978 (1952). The interest of the States in regulating lawyers is especially great since lawyers are essential to the primary governmental function of administering justice, and have historically been "officers of the courts." In holding that certain anticompetitive conduct by lawyers is within the reach of the Sherman Act we intend no diminution of the authority of the State to regulate its professions.

The judgment of the Court of Appeals is reversed and the case is remanded to that court with orders to remand to the District Court for further proceedings consistent with this opinion.

MR. JUSTICE POWELL took no part in the consideration or decision of this case.

NOTES AND QUESTIONS

1.   It is tempting to view the modern period as nothing but a retreat from the cases in the previous chapter, but *Goldfarb* shows that is an oversimplification. In the four ways illustrated by this short case, the current period incorporates and even extends prior law. The first issue raised is as to the continued vitality of the per se rule against price fixing and what kind of agreement is required to prove prohibited conduct.

a.   Do you agree that this kind of fee schedule should have been held to be per se illegal under *Socony-Vacuum*? Is there any doubt that it was intended to affect the fees lawyers charged? Was there any doubt that it had at least some of its intended effect?

b.   Should the "voluntary" character of the fee schedule have saved it from illegality? Could more formal enforcement of the schedule have made it any more universally followed than it apparently was here? Are you convinced that what the Court calls a "purely voluntary" fee schedule should present a different question and perhaps produce a different result?

2.   What is the Court's answer to the defense that legal services are not rendered in interstate commerce? Do you agree that the Virginia closing by a Virginia lawyer of the sale of a Virginia house by a Virginia seller to a Virginia buyer should be seen as an interstate transaction?

a.   The preceding year, the Court had decided Gulf Oil Corp. v. Copp Paving Co., 419 U.S. 186, 95 S.Ct. 392, 42 L.Ed.2d 378 (1974), in which a firm had sold "asphaltic concrete" within a single state for use on interstate highways. The Court held that the interstate commerce requirement of the Robinson-Patman Act had *not* been met. The Robinson-Patman Act "extends only to persons and activities that are themselves 'in commerce'," the Court said. Can you see a textual or principled basis for a distinction between the Clayton and Sherman Acts on the interstate commerce issue?

b.   Are the Clayton and Robinson-Patman Acts identical for this purpose? In United States v. American Bldg. Maintenance Industries, 422 U.S. 271, 95 S.Ct. 2150, 45 L.Ed.2d 177 (1975), the Court suggested more transactions might be in commerce under the Clayton Act. Janitorial firms cleaning buildings within a single state were not in commerce just because they cleaned the offices of companies with interstate activities, the Court held, but their purchase of cleaning supplies from other states might establish the jurisdictional link.

c.   Given these precedents, was *Goldfarb* a shock? The Court later applied *Goldfarb* principles to condemn fixed real estate commission rates in McLain v. Real Estate Board of New Orleans, Inc., 444 U.S. 232, 100 S.Ct. 502, 62 L.Ed.2d 441 (1980).

3.   Should it have made a difference that this case involved a "learned profession" like the practice of law?

a.   Before this case, lawyers thought their conduct was basically exempt from antitrust challenge. What was the perceived statutory basis for that alleged exemption?

b.   Do you agree with Chief Justice Burger that it does not disparage lawyers to point out that many of their services are part of the stream of trade and commerce? When lawyers set minimum fees does their work lose the public service character that has made lawyers special?

c.   In his later years, Chief Justice Burger was a critic of lawyer advertising, but one can argue that he set the stage for it with his remarks in this opinion. What does he say here about a "professionalism" defense to challenged conduct? What does it mean to say in the Court's fn. 17 that the fact a profession is involved is "relevant"? Relevant to what?

d.   Watch for the impact the Court's conclusion on the "learned profession" issue has made on antitrust enforcement in the current period. Notice how many cases involve physicians, engineers, dentists and others who also might have thought their "professional ethics" were beyond antitrust scrutiny.

4.   Do you believe that Parker v. Brown should have protected the state bar against liability in this case? In what sense, if any, did the extent of state regulation fall short of what is required for *Parker* protection?

a.   *Parker* later was held to bar antitrust liability for an absolute prohibition of lawyer advertising that was directly imposed by state supreme court rule. Bates v. State Bar of Arizona, 433 U.S. 350, 97 S.Ct. 2691, 53 L.Ed.2d 810 (1977).[4]

b.   *Parker* was also held to bar an antitrust claim against state bar examiners who worked under state supreme court supervision. Hoover v. Ronwin, 466 U.S. 558, 104 S.Ct. 1989, 80 L.Ed.2d 590 (1984).

c.   *Goldfarb* was one of the first major cases to test the reach of *Parker* in the over three decades since *Parker* was decided. Later in this chapter, we will see that considerable *Parker* litigation followed and that *Goldfarb* grants somewhat less *Parker* protection than later cases have recognized.

———————

No single moment immediately alters an approach to antitrust or any other field, but like *Standard Oil* in 1911 and *Socony-Vacuum* in 1940, our next case is usually seen as marking the clearest beginning of the fourth and current chapter in antitrust analysis. This time, it fell to Justice Powell to write the Court's opinion.

———————————————

[4]   If you have taken legal ethics, you will probably remember that, although there was no antitrust liability, *Bates* held the advertising prohibition was an unconstitutional restriction of commercial speech.

CONTINENTAL T.V., INC. V. GTE SYLVANIA INC.

Supreme Court of the United States, 1977
433 U.S. 36, 97 S.Ct. 2549, 53 L.Ed.2d 568

MR. JUSTICE POWELL delivered the opinion of the Court.

Franchise agreements between manufacturers and retailers frequently include provisions barring the retailers from selling franchised products from locations other than those specified in the agreements. This case presents important questions concerning the appropriate antitrust analysis of these restrictions under § 1 of the Sherman Act, and the Court's decision in United States v. Arnold, Schwinn & Co.

I

Respondent GTE Sylvania Inc. (Sylvania) manufactures and sells television sets through its Home Entertainment Products Division. Prior to 1962, like most other television manufacturers, Sylvania sold its televisions to independent or company-owned distributors who in turn resold to a large and diverse group of retailers. Prompted by a decline in its market share to a relatively insignificant 1% to 2% of national television sales, Sylvania conducted an intensive reassessment of its marketing strategy, and in 1962 adopted the franchise plan challenged here. Sylvania phased out its wholesale distributors and began to sell its televisions directly to a smaller and more select group of franchised retailers. An acknowledged purpose of the change was to decrease the number of competing Sylvania retailers in the hope of attracting the more aggressive and competent retailers thought necessary to the improvement of the company's market position.[5] To this end, Sylvania limited the number of franchises granted for any given area and required each franchisee to sell his Sylvania products only from the location or locations at which he was franchised.[6] A franchise did not constitute an exclusive territory, and Sylvania retained sole discretion to increase the number of retailers in an area in light of the success or failure of existing retailers in developing their market. The revised marketing strategy appears to have been successful during the period at issue here, for by 1965 Sylvania's share of national television sales had increased to approximately 5%, and the company ranked as the Nation's eighth largest manufacturer of color television sets.

This suit is the result of the rupture of a franchiser-franchisee relationship that had previously prospered under the revised Sylvania plan. Dissatisfied with its sales in the city of San Francisco,[7] Sylvania

---

[5] The number of retailers selling Sylvania products declined significantly as a result of the change, but in 1965 there were at least two franchised Sylvania retailers in each metropolitan center of more than 100,000 population. [Court's fn. 2]

[6] Sylvania imposed no restrictions on the right of the franchisee to sell the products of competing manufacturers. [Court's fn. 3]

[7] Sylvania's market share in San Francisco was approximately 2.5%—half its national and northern California average. [Court's fn. 4]

decided in the spring of 1965 to franchise Young Brothers, an established San Francisco retailer of televisions, as an additional San Francisco retailer. The proposed location of the new franchise was approximately a mile from a retail outlet operated by petitioner Continental T.V., Inc. (Continental), one of the most successful Sylvania franchisees. Continental protested that the location of the new franchise violated Sylvania's marketing policy, but Sylvania persisted in its plans. Continental then canceled a large Sylvania order and placed a large order with Phillips, one of Sylvania's competitors.

During this same period, Continental expressed a desire to open a store in Sacramento, Cal., a desire Sylvania attributed at least in part to Continental's displeasure over the Young Brothers decision. Sylvania believed that the Sacramento market was adequately served by the existing Sylvania retailers and denied the request.[8] In the face of this denial, Continental advised Sylvania in early September 1965, that it was in the process of moving Sylvania merchandise from its San Jose, Cal., warehouse to a new retail location that it had leased in Sacramento. Two weeks later, allegedly for unrelated reasons, Sylvania's credit department reduced Continental's credit line from $300,000 to $50,000. In response to the reduction in credit and the generally deteriorating relations with Sylvania, Continental withheld all payments owed to John P. Maguire & Co., Inc. (Maguire), the finance company that handled the credit arrangements between Sylvania and its retailers. Shortly thereafter, Sylvania terminated Continental's franchises, and Maguire filed this diversity action in the United States District Court for the Northern District of California seeking recovery of money owed and of secured merchandise held by Continental.

The antitrust issues before us originated in cross-claims brought by Continental against Sylvania and Maguire. Most important for our purposes was the claim that Sylvania had violated § 1 of the Sherman Act by entering into and enforcing franchise agreements that prohibited the sale of Sylvania products other than from specified locations. At the close of evidence in the jury trial of Continental's claims, Sylvania requested the District Court to instruct the jury that its location restriction was illegal only if it unreasonably restrained or suppressed competition. Relying on this Court's decision in United States v. Arnold, Schwinn & Co., the District Court rejected the proffered instruction in favor of the following one:

> "Therefore, if you find by a preponderance of the evidence that Sylvania entered into a contract, combination or conspiracy with one or more of its dealers pursuant to which Sylvania exercised dominion or control over the products sold to the dealer, after having parted with title and risk to the products, you must

---

8   Sylvania had achieved exceptional results in Sacramento, where its market share exceeded 15% in 1965. [Court's fn. 6]

find any effort thereafter to restrict outlets or store locations from which its dealers resold the merchandise which they had purchased from Sylvania to be a violation of Section 1 of the Sherman Act, regardless of the reasonableness of the location restrictions."

In answers to special interrogatories, the jury found that Sylvania had engaged "in a contract, combination or conspiracy in restraint of trade in violation of the antitrust laws with respect to location restrictions alone," and assessed Continental's damages at $591,505, which was trebled * * * to produce an award of $1,774,515.

On appeal, the Court of Appeals for the Ninth Circuit, sitting en banc, reversed by a divided vote. * * * [It] concluded that *Schwinn* was distinguishable on several grounds. Contrasting the nature of the restrictions, their competitive impact, and the market shares of the franchisers in the two cases, the court concluded that Sylvania's location restriction had less potential for competitive harm than the restrictions invalidated in *Schwinn* and thus should be judged under the "rule of reason" rather than the per se rule stated in *Schwinn*. * * *

We granted Continental's petition for certiorari * * * .

II

A

We turn first to Continental's contention that Sylvania's restriction on retail locations is a per se violation of § 1 of the Sherman Act as interpreted in *Schwinn*. The restrictions at issue in *Schwinn* were part of a three-tier distribution system comprising, in addition to * * * [Schwinn], 22 intermediate distributors and a network of franchised retailers. * * *

* * *

* * * [In *Schwinn*] the Court proceeded to articulate the following "bright line" per se rule of illegality for vertical restrictions: "Under the Sherman Act, it is unreasonable without more for a manufacturer to seek to restrict and confine areas or persons with whom an article may be traded after the manufacturer has parted with dominion over it." But the Court expressly stated that the rule of reason governs when "the manufacturer retains title, dominion, and risk with respect to the product and the position and function of the dealer in question are, in fact, indistinguishable from those of an agent or salesman of the manufacturer."

Application of these principles to the facts of *Schwinn* produced sharply contrasting results depending upon the role played by the distributor in the distribution system. With respect to that portion of Schwinn's sales for which the distributors acted as ordinary wholesalers, buying and reselling Schwinn bicycles, the Court held that the territorial and customer restrictions challenged by the Government were per se illegal. * * * Applying the rule of reason to the restrictions that were not imposed in conjunction with the sale of bicycles, the Court had little difficulty finding them all reasonable in light of the competitive situation in "the product market as a whole."

B

In the present case, it is undisputed that title to the television sets passed from Sylvania to Continental. Thus, the *Schwinn* per se rule applies unless Sylvania's restriction on locations falls outside *Schwinn*'s prohibition against a manufacturer's attempting to restrict a "retailer's freedom as to where and to whom it will resell the products." As the Court of Appeals conceded, the language of *Schwinn* is clearly broad enough to apply to the present case. Unlike the Court of Appeals, however, we are unable to find a principled basis for distinguishing *Schwinn* from the case now before us.

* * * In intent and competitive impact, the retail-customer restriction in *Schwinn* is indistinguishable from the location restriction in the present case. In both cases the restrictions limited the freedom of the retailer to dispose of the purchased products as he desired. The fact that one restriction was addressed to territory and the other to customers is irrelevant to functional antitrust analysis and, indeed, to the language and broad thrust of the opinion in *Schwinn*.[9] * * *

III

* * * Although *Schwinn* is supported by the principle of stare decisis, we are convinced that the need for clarification of the law in this area justifies reconsideration. *Schwinn* itself was an abrupt and largely unexplained departure from White Motor Co. v. United States, where only four years earlier the Court had refused to endorse a per se rule for vertical restrictions. Since its announcement, *Schwinn* has been the subject of continuing controversy and confusion, both in the scholarly journals and in the federal courts. The great weight of scholarly opinion has been critical of the decision,[10] and a number of the federal courts confronted with

---

[9] The distinctions drawn by the Court of Appeals and endorsed in Mr. Justice White's separate opinion have no basis in *Schwinn*. The intrabrand competitive impact of the restrictions at issue in *Schwinn* ranged from complete elimination to mere reduction; yet, the Court did not even hint at any distinction on this ground. Similarly, there is no suggestion that the per se rule was applied because of Schwinn's prominent position in its industry. That position was the same whether the bicycles were sold or consigned * * *. * * * [Court's fn. 12]

[10] A former Assistant Attorney General in charge of the Antitrust Division has described *Schwinn* as "an exercise in barren formalism" that is "artificial and unresponsive to the competitive needs of the real world." Baker, Vertical Restraints in Times of Change: From White to Schwinn to Where?, 44 Antitrust L.J. 537 (1975). See, e.g., Handler, The Twentieth Annual Antitrust Review—1967, 53 Virginia L.Rev. 1667 (1967); McLaren, Territorial and Customer Restrictions, Consignments, Suggested Retail Prices and Refusals to Deal, 37 Antitrust L.J. 137 (1968); Pollock, Alternative Distribution Methods After Schwinn, 63 Northwestern U.L.Rev. 595 (1968); Posner, Antitrust Policy and the Supreme Court: An Analysis of the Restricted

analogous vertical restrictions have sought to limit its reach. In our view, the experience of the past 10 years should be brought to bear on this subject of considerable commercial importance.

* * * Per se rules of illegality are appropriate only when they relate to conduct that is manifestly anticompetitive. As the Court explained in Northern Pac. R. Co. v. United States, "there are certain agreements or practices which because of their pernicious effect on competition and lack of any redeeming virtue are conclusively presumed to be unreasonable and therefore illegal without elaborate inquiry as to the precise harm they have caused or the business excuse for their use."[11]

In essence, the issue before us is whether *Schwinn's* per se rule can be justified under the demanding standards of *Northern Pac. R. Co.* The Court's refusal to endorse a per se rule in *White Motor Co.* was based on its uncertainty as to whether vertical restrictions satisfied those standards. * * *

* * *

The market impact of vertical restrictions[12] is complex because of their potential for a simultaneous reduction of intrabrand competition and

---

Distribution, Horizontal Merger and Potential Competition Decisions, 75 Columbia L.Rev. 282 (1975) * * * . But see Louis, Vertical Distributional Restraints Under *Schwinn* and *Sylvania*: An Argument for the Continuing Use of a Partial Per Se Approach, 75 Michigan L. Rev. 275 (1976); Zimmerman, Distribution Restrictions After *Sealy* and *Schwinn*, 12 Antitrust Bull. 1181 (1967). For a more inclusive list of articles and comments, see 537 F.2d, at 988 n. 13. [Court's fn. 13]

[11]   Per se rules thus require the Court to make broad generalizations about the social utility of particular commercial practices. The probability that anticompetitive consequences will result from a practice and the severity of those consequences must be balanced against its procompetitive consequences. Cases that do not fit the generalization may arise, but a per se rule reflects the judgment that such cases are not sufficiently common or important to justify the time and expense necessary to identify them. Once established, per se rules tend to provide guidance to the business community and to minimize the burdens on litigants and the judicial system of the more complex rule-of-reason trials, but those advantages are not sufficient in themselves to justify the creation of per se rules. If it were otherwise, all of antitrust law would be reduced to per se rules, thus introducing an unintended and undesirable rigidity in the law. [Court's fn. 16]

[12]   As in *Schwinn*, we are concerned here only with nonprice vertical restrictions. The per se illegality of price restrictions has been established firmly for many years and involves significantly different questions of analysis and policy. As Mr. Justice White notes, some commentators have argued that the manufacturer's motivation for imposing vertical price restrictions may be the same as for nonprice restrictions. There are, however, significant differences that could easily justify different treatment. In his concurring opinion in White Motor Co. v. United States, Mr. Justice Brennan noted that, unlike nonprice restrictions, "[r]esale price maintenance is not only designed to, but almost invariably does in fact, reduce price competition not only among sellers of the affected product, but quite as much between that product and competing brands." Professor Posner also recognized that "industrywide resale price maintenance might facilitate cartelizing." [S]ee R. Posner, Antitrust: Cases, Economic Notes and Other Materials 134 (1974); E. Gellhorn, Antitrust Law and Economics 252 (1976). Furthermore, Congress recently has expressed its approval of a per se analysis of vertical price restrictions by repealing those provisions of the Miller-Tydings and McGuire Acts allowing fair trade pricing at the option of the individual States. Consumer Goods Pricing Act of 1975. No similar expression of congressional intent exists for nonprice restrictions. [Court's fn. 18]

stimulation of interbrand competition.[13] Significantly, the Court in *Schwinn* did not distinguish among the challenged restrictions on the basis of their individual potential for intrabrand harm or interbrand benefit. * * * The pivotal factor was the passage of title: All restrictions were held to be per se illegal where title had passed, and all were evaluated and sustained under the rule of reason where it had not. * * *

* * *[14]

Vertical restrictions reduce intrabrand competition by limiting the number of sellers of a particular product competing for the business of a given group of buyers. * * * Although intrabrand competition may be reduced, the ability of retailers to exploit the resulting market may be limited both by the ability of consumers to travel to other franchised locations and, perhaps more importantly, to purchase the competing products of other manufacturers. None of these key variables, however, is affected by the form of the transaction by which a manufacturer conveys his products to the retailers.

Vertical restrictions promote interbrand competition by allowing the manufacturer to achieve certain efficiencies in the distribution of his products. These "redeeming virtues" are implicit in every decision sustaining vertical restrictions under the rule of reason. Economists have identified a number of ways in which manufacturers can use such restrictions to compete more effectively against other manufacturers. For example, new manufacturers and manufacturers entering new markets can use the restrictions in order to induce competent and aggressive retailers to make the kind of investment of capital and labor that is often required in the distribution of products unknown to the consumer. Established manufacturers can use them to induce retailers to engage in promotional activities or to provide service and repair facilities necessary

---

[13]   Interbrand competition is the competition among the manufacturers of the same generic product—television sets in this case—and is the primary concern of antitrust law. The extreme example of a deficiency of interbrand competition is monopoly, where there is only one manufacturer. In contrast, intrabrand competition is the competition between the distributors—wholesale or retail—of the product of a particular manufacturer.

The degree of intrabrand competition is wholly independent of the level of interbrand competition confronting the manufacturer. Thus, there may be fierce intrabrand competition among the distributors of a product produced by a monopolist and no intrabrand competition among the distributors of a product produced by a firm in a highly competitive industry. But when interbrand competition exists, as it does among television manufacturers, it provides a significant check on the exploitation of intrabrand market power because of the ability of consumers to substitute a different brand of the same product. [Court's fn. 19]

[14]   The Court also stated that to impose vertical restrictions in sale transactions would "violate the ancient rule against restraints on alienation." This isolated reference has provoked sharp criticism from virtually all of the commentators on the decision, most of whom have regarded the Court's apparent reliance on the "ancient rule" as both a misreading of legal history and a perversion of antitrust analysis. We quite agree with Mr. Justice Stewart's dissenting comment in *Schwinn* that "the state of the common law 400 or even 100 years ago is irrelevant to the issue before us: the effect of the antitrust laws upon vertical distributional restraints in the American economy today." * * * [Court's fn. 21]

to the efficient marketing of their products. Service and repair are vital for many products, such as automobiles and major household appliances. The availability and quality of such services affect a manufacturer's goodwill and the competitiveness of his product. Because of market imperfections such as the so-called "free rider" effect, these services might not be provided by retailers in a purely competitive situation, despite the fact that each retailer's benefit would be greater if all provided the services than if none did.

Economists also have argued that manufacturers have an economic interest in maintaining as much intrabrand competition as is consistent with the efficient distribution of their products. Bork, The Rule of Reason and the Per Se Concept: Price Fixing and Market Division [II], 75 Yale L. J. 373, 403 (1966).[15] Although the view that the manufacturer's interest necessarily corresponds with that of the public is not universally shared, even the leading critic of vertical restrictions concedes that *Schwinn*'s distinction between sale and nonsale transactions is essentially unrelated to any relevant economic impact. Comanor, Vertical Territorial and Customer Restrictions: White Motor and Its Aftermath, 81 Harv. L. Rev. 1419, 1422 (1968).[16] Indeed, to the extent that the form of the transaction is related to interbrand benefits, the Court's distinction is inconsistent with its articulated concern for the ability of smaller firms to compete effectively with larger ones. Capital requirements and administrative expenses may prevent smaller firms from using the exception for nonsale transactions.[17]

We conclude that the distinction drawn in *Schwinn* between sale and nonsale transactions is not sufficient to justify the application of a per se rule in one situation and a rule of reason in the other. The question remains whether the per se rule stated in *Schwinn* should be expanded to include nonsale transactions or abandoned in favor of a return to the rule of reason. We have found no persuasive support for expanding the per se rule. As noted above, the *Schwinn* Court recognized the undesirability of

---

[15] "Generally a manufacturer would prefer the lowest retail price possible, once its price to dealers has been set, because a lower retail price means increased sales and higher manufacturer revenues." Note, 88 Harvard L.Rev. 636, 641 (1975). In this context, a manufacturer is likely to view the difference between the price at which it sells to its retailers and their price to the consumer as its "cost of distribution," which it would prefer to minimize. Posner, supra, n. 13. [Court's fn. 24]

[16] Professor Comanor argues that the promotional activities encouraged by vertical restrictions result in product differentiation and, therefore, a decrease in interbrand competition. This argument is flawed by its necessary assumption that a large part of the promotional efforts resulting from vertical restrictions will not convey socially desirable information about product availability, price, quality, and services. Nor is it clear that a per se rule would result in anything more than a shift to less efficient methods of obtaining the same promotional effects. [Court's fn. 25]

[17] We also note that per se rules in this area may work to the ultimate detriment of the small businessmen who operate as franchisees. To the extent that a per se rule prevents a firm from using the franchise system to achieve efficiencies that it perceives as important to its successful operation, the rule creates an incentive for vertical integration into the distribution system, thereby eliminating to that extent the role of independent businessmen. [Court's fn. 26]

"prohibit[ing] all vertical restrictions of territory and all franchising * * * ." And even Continental does not urge us to hold that all such restrictions are per se illegal.

We revert to the standard articulated in *Northern Pac. R. Co.*, and reiterated in *White Motor*, for determining whether vertical restrictions must be "conclusively presumed to be unreasonable and therefore illegal without elaborate inquiry as to the precise harm they have caused or the business excuse for their use." Such restrictions, in varying forms, are widely used in our free market economy. As indicated above, there is substantial scholarly and judicial authority supporting their economic utility. There is relatively little authority to the contrary.[18] Certainly, there has been no showing in this case, either generally or with respect to Sylvania's agreements, that vertical restrictions have or are likely to have a "pernicious effect on competition" or that they "lack * * * any redeeming virtue."[19] Accordingly, we conclude that the per se rule stated in Schwinn must be overruled. In so holding we do not foreclose the possibility that particular applications of vertical restrictions might justify per se prohibition under *Northern Pac. R. Co.* But we do make clear that departure from the rule-of-reason standard must be based upon demonstrable economic effect rather than—as in *Schwinn*—upon formalistic line drawing.

In sum, we conclude that the appropriate decision is to return to the rule of reason that governed vertical restrictions prior to *Schwinn*. When anticompetitive effects are shown to result from particular vertical restrictions they can be adequately policed under the rule of reason, the standard traditionally applied for the majority of anticompetitive practices challenged under § 1 of the Act. Accordingly, the decision of the Court of Appeals is

Affirmed.

MR. JUSTICE REHNQUIST took no part in the consideration or decision of this case.

---

[18] There may be occasional problems in differentiating vertical restrictions from horizontal restrictions originating in agreements among the retailers. There is no doubt that restrictions in the latter category would be illegal per se, see, e.g., United States v. General Motors Corp.; United States v. Topco Associates, Inc., but we do not regard the problems of proof as sufficiently great to justify a per se rule. [Courts fn. 28]

[19] The location restriction used by Sylvania was neither the least nor the most restrictive provision that it could have used. But we agree with the implicit judgment in *Schwinn* that a per se rule based on the nature of the restriction is, in general, undesirable. Although distinctions can be drawn among the frequently used restrictions, we are inclined to view them as differences of degree and form. We are unable to perceive significant social gain from channeling transactions into one form or another. Finally, we agree with the Court in *Schwinn* that the advantages of vertical restrictions should not be limited to the categories of new entrants and failing firms. Sylvania was faltering, if not failing, and we think it would be unduly artificial to deny it the use of valuable competitive tools. [Court's fn. 29]

MR. JUSTICE WHITE, concurring in the judgment.

Although I agree with the majority that the location clause at issue in this case is not a per se violation of the Sherman Act and should be judged under the rule of reason, I cannot agree that this result requires the overruling of United States v. Arnold, Schwinn & Co. In my view this case is distinguishable from *Schwinn* because there is less potential for restraint of intrabrand competition and more potential for stimulating interbrand competition. As to intrabrand competition, Sylvania, unlike Schwinn, did not restrict the customers to whom or the territories where its purchasers could sell. As to interbrand competition, Sylvania, unlike Schwinn, had an insignificant market share at the time it adopted its challenged distribution practice and enjoyed no consumer preference that would allow its retailers to charge a premium over other brands. In two short paragraphs, the majority disposes of the view, adopted after careful analysis by the Ninth Circuit en banc below, that these differences provide a "principled basis for distinguishing *Schwinn*" * * * [and] that the per se rule established in that case does not apply to location clauses such as Sylvania's. To reach out to overrule one of this Court's recent interpretations of the Sherman Act, after such a cursory examination of the necessity for doing so, is surely an affront to the principle that considerations of stare decisis are to be given particularly strong weight in the area of statutory construction.

* * *

I have, moreover, substantial misgivings about the approach the majority takes to overruling *Schwinn*. The reason for the distinction in *Schwinn* between sale and nonsale transactions was not, as the majority would have it, "the Court's effort to accommodate the perceived intrabrand harm and interbrand benefit of vertical restrictions;" the reason was rather, as Judge Browning argued in dissent below, the notion in many of our cases involving vertical restraints that independent businessmen should have the freedom to dispose of the goods they own as they see fit. * * *

* * *

After summarily rejecting this concern * * * for "the autonomy of independent businessmen," the majority not surprisingly finds "no justification" for Schwinn's distinction between sale and nonsale transactions because the distinction is "essentially unrelated to any relevant economic impact." But while according some weight to the businessman's interest in controlling the terms on which he trades in his own goods may be anathema to those who view the Sherman Act as directed solely to economic efficiency, this principle is without question more deeply embedded in our cases than the notions of "free rider" effects and distributional efficiencies borrowed by the majority from the "new economics of vertical relationships." Perhaps the Court is right in partially abandoning this principle and in judging the instant nonprice vertical restraints solely by their "relevant economic impact"; but the precedents which reflect this principle should not be so lightly rejected by the Court. * * *

I have a further reservation about the majority's reliance on "relevant economic impact" as the test for retaining per se rules regarding vertical restraints. It is common ground among the leading advocates of a purely economic approach to the question of distribution restraints that the economic arguments in favor of allowing vertical nonprice restraints generally apply to vertical price restraints as well. Although the majority asserts that "the per se illegality of price restrictions * * * involves significantly different questions of analysis and policy," I suspect this purported distinction may be as difficult to justify as that of *Schwinn* under the terms of the majority's analysis. Thus Professor Posner, in an article cited five times by the majority, concludes: "I believe that the law should treat price and nonprice restrictions the same and that it should make no distinction between the imposition of restrictions in a sale contract and their imposition in an agency contract." Posner, [Court's fn. 13]. Indeed, the Court has already recognized that resale price maintenance may increase output by inducing "demand creating activity" by dealers (such as additional retail outlets, advertising and promotion, and product servicing) that outweighs the additional sales that would result from lower prices brought about by dealer price competition. Albrecht v. Herald Co. These same output-enhancing possibilities of nonprice vertical restraints are relied upon by the majority as evidence of their social utility and economic soundness, and as a justification for judging them under the rule of reason. The effect, if not the intention, of the Court's opinion is necessarily to call into question the firmly established per se rule against price restraints.

* * * In order to decide this case, the Court need only hold that a location clause imposed by a manufacturer with negligible economic power in the product market has a competitive impact sufficiently less restrictive than the *Schwinn* restraints to justify a rule-of-reason standard, even if the same weight is given here as in *Schwinn* to dealer autonomy. I therefore concur in the judgment.

MR. JUSTICE BRENNAN, with whom MR. JUSTICE MARSHALL joins, dissenting.

I would not overrule the per se rule stated in United States v. Arnold, Schwinn & Co. and would therefore reverse the decision of the Court of Appeals for the Ninth Circuit.

NOTES AND QUESTIONS

1.   Did Justice Powell's majority opinion convince you? It may have been inevitable that such a key antitrust decision would be written by someone who was relatively new to the Court and typically identified as a "moderate," not identified with any political or economic ideology.

a.   Do you agree that *Schwinn*'s per se rule was properly transformed here into a rule of reason? Is it obvious that "the market impact of vertical restrictions is complex," i.e., more complex than horizontal restrictions? Do you agree that one should not condemn such restrictions unless one knows the effect on both *inter*-brand and *intra*-brand competition?

b.   Did you agree with the Ninth Circuit that *Schwinn* could be distinguished? Did Justice White's opinion convince you that it could be? Should we limit the exception to *Schwinn* to cases in which the firm both has a "precarious" position in the market and the practice is needed to expand its market share?

c.   Are financial strength and market share too ephemeral to use as bases for decision? Would it affect your judgment about this plan to know that three years after this decision, Sylvania was sold by GTE to North American Philips Corp., its former competitor, a company with $2 billion in annual sales of consumer electronics products?

2.   Do you agree that reducing intrabrand competition may have "redeeming virtues"?

a.   Should efficiencies in product distribution be significant enough virtues to overcome a loss in retail competition?

b.   Do you agree that a manufacturer's problem of controlling "free riders" should require permitting this limitation?

c.   Were you convinced that Sylvania's warranty obligations should be a significant justification for organizing its distribution network as it had?

3.   Was it self-evident from the Court's opinion that it was making a sharp turn in antitrust analysis? Did Justice White recognize it when he expressed apprehension about a "purely economic approach" to antitrust questions?

a.   If we go as far as the Court does, is Justice White correct that there is no basis for not striking down the per se rule against resale price maintenance as well? Are you convinced that resale price maintenance can facilitate price fixing cartels while allocation of territories cannot?

b.   What is the effect of this case on earlier cases? For example, how about *General Motors* (1966)? *Topco*, decided only 5 years before in 1972? Are you satisfied that those cases simply involved *horizontal* market division and thus are not affected by this decision?

Earlier the same year it decided *GTE Sylvania*, the Court handed down a less-celebrated decision, but one that may have had even more practical impact on the development of modern antitrust practice.

BRUNSWICK CORP. V. PUEBLO BOWL-O-MAT, INC.

Supreme Court of the United States, 1977
429 U.S. 477, 97 S.Ct. 690, 50 L.Ed.2d 701

MR. JUSTICE MARSHALL delivered the opinion of the Court.

This case raises important questions concerning the interrelationship of the antimerger and private damages action provisions of the Clayton Antitrust Act.

I

Petitioner is one of the two largest manufacturers of bowling equipment in the United States. Respondents are three of the 10 bowling centers owned by Treadway Companies, Inc. Since 1965, petitioner has acquired and operated a large number of bowling centers, including six in the markets in which respondents operate. Respondents instituted this action contending that these acquisitions violated various provisions of the antitrust laws.

In the late 1950's, the bowling industry expanded rapidly, and petitioner's sales of lanes, automatic pinsetters, and ancillary equipment rose accordingly. Since this equipment requires a major capital expenditure—$12,600 for each lane and pinsetter * * *—most of petitioner's sales were for secured credit.

In the early 1960's, the bowling industry went into a sharp decline. Petitioner's sales quickly dropped to preboom levels. Moreover, petitioner experienced great difficulty in collecting money owed it; by the end of 1964 over $100,000,000, or more than 25%, of petitioner's accounts were more than 90 days delinquent. Repossessions rose dramatically, but attempts to sell or lease the repossessed equipment met with only limited success. Because petitioner had borrowed close to $250,000,000 to finance its credit sales, it was, as the Court of Appeals concluded, "in serious financial difficulty."

To meet this difficulty, petitioner began acquiring and operating defaulting bowling centers when their equipment could not be resold and a positive cash flow could be expected from operating the centers. During the seven years preceding the trial in this case, petitioner acquired 222 centers, 54 of which it either disposed of or closed. These acquisitions made petitioner by far the largest operator of bowling centers, with over five times as many centers as its next largest competitor. Petitioner's net worth in 1965 was more than eight times greater, and its gross revenue more than seven times greater, than the total for the 11 next largest bowling chains.

Nevertheless, petitioner controlled only 2% of the bowling centers in the United States.

At issue here are acquisitions by petitioner in the three markets in which respondents are located: Pueblo, Colo., Poughkeepsie, N.Y., and Paramus, N.J. In 1965, petitioner acquired one defaulting center in Pueblo, one in Poughkeepsie, and two in the Paramus area. In 1969, petitioner acquired a third defaulting center in the Paramus market, and in 1970 * * * a fourth. * * * [Four of these] centers were operational at the time of trial.

Respondents initiated this action in June 1966, alleging, inter alia, that these acquisitions might substantially lessen competition or tend to create a monopoly in violation of § 7 of the Clayton Act. Respondents sought damages, pursuant to § 4 of the Act, for three times "the reasonably expectable profits to be made [by respondents] from the operation of their bowling centers." Respondents also sought a divestiture order, an injunction against future acquisitions, and such "other further and different relief" as might be appropriate under § 16 of the Act.

* * * To establish a § 7 violation, respondents sought to prove that because of its size, petitioner had the capacity to lessen competition in the markets it had entered by driving smaller competitors out of business. To establish damages, respondents attempted to show that had petitioner allowed the defaulting centers to close, respondents' profits would have increased. At respondents' request, the jury was instructed in accord with respondents' theory as to the nature of the violation and the basis for damages. The jury returned a verdict in favor of respondents in the amount of $2,358,030, which represented the minimum estimate by respondents of the additional income they would have realized had the acquired centers been closed. As required by law, the District Court trebled the damages. It also awarded respondents costs and attorneys' fees totaling $446,977.32, and, sitting as a court of equity, it ordered petitioner to divest itself of the centers involved here. Petitioner appealed.

The Court of Appeals, while endorsing the legal theories upon which respondents' claim was based, reversed the judgment and remanded the case for further proceedings. * * * Both sides petitioned this Court for writs of certiorari. * * *

II

The issue for decision is a narrow one. Petitioner does not presently contest the Court of Appeals' conclusion that a properly instructed jury could have found the acquisitions unlawful. Nor does petitioner challenge the Court of Appeals' determination that the evidence would support a finding that had petitioner not acquired these centers, they would have gone out of business and respondents' income would have increased. Petitioner questions only whether antitrust damages are available where the sole injury alleged is that competitors were continued in business, thereby denying respondents an anticipated increase in market shares.[20]

To answer that question it is necessary to examine the antimerger and treble-damages provisions of the Clayton Act. Section 7 * * * is, as we have observed many times, a prophylactic measure, intended "primarily to arrest apprehended consequences of intercorporate relationships before those relationships could work their evil * * * ." United States v. E.I. du Pont; Brown Shoe Co. v. United States; United States v. Philadelphia Nat. Bank.

Section 4, in contrast, is in essence a remedial provision. It provides treble damages to "[a]ny person who shall be injured in his business or property by reason of anything forbidden in the antitrust laws * * * ." Of course, treble damages also play an important role in penalizing wrongdoers and deterring wrongdoing, as we also have frequently observed. It nevertheless is true that the treble-damages provision, which makes awards available only to injured parties, and measures the awards by a multiple of the injury actually proved, is designed primarily as a remedy.

Intermeshing a statutory prohibition against acts that have a potential to cause certain harms with a damages action intended to remedy those harms is not without difficulty. Plainly, to recover damages respondents must prove more than that petitioner violated § 7, since such proof establishes only that injury may result. Respondents contend that the only additional element they need demonstrate is that they are in a worse position than they would have been had petitioner not committed those acts. The Court of Appeals agreed * * * . Because this holding divorces antitrust recovery from the purposes of the antitrust laws without a clear statutory command to do so, we cannot agree with it.

Every merger of two existing entities into one, whether lawful or unlawful, has the potential for producing economic readjustments that adversely affect some persons. But Congress has not condemned mergers on that account; it has condemned them only when they may produce anticompetitive effects. Yet under the Court of Appeals' holding, once a merger is found to violate § 7, all dislocations caused by the merger are actionable, regardless of whether those dislocations have anything to do with the reason the merger was condemned. This holding would make § 4 recovery entirely fortuitous, and would authorize damages for losses which are of no concern to the antitrust laws.

Both of these consequences are well illustrated by the facts of this case. If the acquisitions here were unlawful, it is because they brought a "deep pocket" parent into a market of "pygmies." Yet respondents' injury—the

---

[20]   * * * In light of our holding, we have no occasion to consider the applicability of the failing-company defense to the conglomerate-like acquisitions involved here. [Court's fn. 9]

loss of income that would have accrued had the acquired centers gone bankrupt—bears no relationship to the size of either the acquiring company or its competitors. Respondents would have suffered the identical "loss"—but no compensable injury—had the acquired centers instead obtained refinancing or been purchased by "shallow pocket" parents, as the Court of Appeals itself acknowledged. Thus, respondents' injury was not of "the type that the statute was intended to forestall."

But the antitrust laws are not merely indifferent to the injury claimed here. At base, respondents complain that by acquiring the failing centers petitioner preserved competition, thereby depriving respondents of the benefits of increased concentration. The damages respondents obtained are designed to provide them with the profits they would have realized had competition been reduced. The antitrust laws, however, were enacted for "the protection of *competition*, not *competitors*," Brown Shoe Co. v. United States. It is inimical to the purposes of these laws to award damages for the type of injury claimed here.

Of course, Congress is free, if it desires, to mandate damages awards for all dislocations caused by unlawful mergers despite the peculiar consequences of so doing. But because of these consequences, "we should insist upon a clear expression of a congressional purpose," Hawaii v. Standard Oil Co., [405 U.S. 251 (1972)], before attributing such an intent to Congress. We can find no such expression in either the language or the legislative history of § 4. To the contrary, it is far from clear that the loss of windfall profits that would have accrued had the acquired centers failed even constitutes "injury" within the meaning of § 4. And it is quite clear that if respondents were injured, it was not "by reason of anything forbidden in the antitrust laws": while respondents' loss occurred "by reason of" the unlawful acquisitions, it did not occur "by reason of" that which made the acquisitions unlawful.

We therefore hold that for plaintiffs to recover treble damages on account of § 7 violations, they must prove more than injury causally linked to an illegal presence in the market. Plaintiffs must prove *antitrust* injury, which is to say injury of the type the antitrust laws were intended to prevent and that flows from that which makes defendants' acts unlawful. The injury should reflect the anticompetitive effect either of the violation or of anticompetitive acts made possible by the violation. It should, in short, be "the type of loss that the claimed violations * * * would be likely to cause."[21]

---

[21]   This does not necessarily mean, as the Court of Appeals feared, that § 4 plaintiffs must prove an actual lessening of competition in order to recover. The short-term effect of certain anticompetitive behavior—predatory below-cost pricing, for example—may be to stimulate price competition. But competitors may be able to prove antitrust injury before they actually are driven from the market and competition is thereby lessened. Of course, the case for relief will be strongest where competition has been diminished. [Court's fn. 14]

III

We come, then, to the question of appropriate disposition of this case. At the very least, petitioner is entitled to a new trial * * * because the District Court's instruction as to the basis for damages was inconsistent with our holding as outlined above. Our review of the record, however, persuades us that a new trial on the [respondents'] damages claim is unwarranted. * * * [T]heir entire proof of damages was based on their claim to profits that would have been earned had the acquired centers closed. Since respondents did not prove any cognizable damages and have not offered any justification for allowing respondents, after two trials and over 10 years of litigation, yet a third opportunity to do so, it follows that petitioner is entitled * * * to judgment on the damages claim notwithstanding the verdict.

* * *

The judgment of the Court of Appeals is vacated, and the case is remanded for further proceedings consistent with this opinion.

NOTES AND QUESTIONS

1.   What was the alleged *substantive* antitrust violation in this case? Was it clear that this acquisition of assets by Brunswick could properly be found by a jury to violate § 7?

a.   Would *Proctor & Gamble* have been authority for finding a violation here? Was Brunswick a similarly "dominant" firm?

b.   Would the "failing company" doctrine, on the other hand, have been a basis on which to defend this acquisition?

c.   When the Court says that any actual harm for which plaintiffs might seek recovery would reflect losses that we *want* more efficient firms to inflict on others, has it simply decided that there was no antitrust violation?

2.   The Court assumes for sake of argument that this acquisition would have been found illegal if the government had brought the case. Thus, the only issue was whether *these competitors* could be the ones to challenge it.

a.   If this merger had been required to be approved by an administrative agency, would Pueblo Bowl-O-Mat have had standing to seek judicial review of a decision upholding the acquisition? What is the standard for determining standing to review administrative decisions?

b.   Was the Court saying here that the Constitution would not permit this action, i.e., that there was no "case or controversy" between Brunswick and Pueblo Bowl-O-Mat?

c.   Then why does Pueblo not have standing to file this action under the Clayton Act? Should the nature of the alleged injury be a substantive defense rather than a jurisdictional standard?

d.   Would *any* private person or firm have a basis for filing a private antitrust action here, i.e., is it only these competitors who are barred?

e.   What should the Court say about private plaintiff standing in cases in which *no* single firm will suffer injury; instead, the injury will be to the public or to the process of competition?

THE PLACE OF PRIVATE LITIGATION
IN ANTITRUST ENFORCEMENT

It is easy to see *Brunswick* as a quirky, minor part of antitrust doctrine. But the reason we read *Brunswick* as a key transitional case is that jurisdictional and procedural issues in the current period have been at least as important as the changes in the substantive law.[22] A study by Professors Salop and White helps clarify the role of private cases by the 1970s.[23]

Antitrust Cases by Decade

	Government	Private
1941–50	437	826
1951–60	514	2208
1961–70	621	3034
1971–80	768	13715

Brunswick certainly did not bring an end to private suits, but it arguably helped reduce their number. The Salop and White study, for example, showed that 1611 private actions had been filed in 1977, the year *Brunswick* was decided, but by 1984, the number had steadily fallen to 1100. A 2012 study shows that by 1990, the number of private cases had gone down to just over 400 annually, and they fluctuated between 400 & 800 during the 1990s. On the other hand, private cases rose steadily to 1300 in 2008 but fell sharply back to about 400 by 2010.[24]

As you read the materials in this chapter, notice how many of them decided questions of jurisdiction and procedure that affected the incentives

----

[22]   Developments since *Brunswick* are discussed in Jonathan M. Jacobson & Tracy Greer, Twenty-One Years of Antitrust Injury: Down the Alley With Brunswick v. Pueblo Bowl-O-Mat, 66 Antitrust L. J. 273 (1998). See also, Roger D. Blair & Jeffrey L. Harrison, Rethinking Antitrust Injury, 42 Vanderbilt L. Rev. 1539 (1989); Ronald W. Davis, Standing on Shaky Ground: The Strangely Elusive Doctrine of Antitrust Injury, 70 Antitrust L.J. 697 (2003).

[23]   Steven C. Salop & Lawrence J. White, Economic Analysis of Private Antitrust Litigation, 74 Georgetown L.J. 1001, 1002 (1986). An earlier study revealing similar insights was Richard A. Posner, A Statistical Study of Antitrust Enforcement, 13 J.Law & Econ. 365 (1970).

[24]   William Kolasky, Antitrust Litigation: What's Changed in Twenty-Five Years?, 27 Antitrust 9 (Fall 2012).

of private litigants to file antitrust cases. Does the public benefit from private suits that allege public harm when they are brought by plaintiffs like Pueblo Bowl-O-Mat who have knowledge of what has happened and a financial incentive to pursue the case vigorously? Is there a corresponding risk that the threat of such cases will deter pro-competitive actions by more efficient firms?[25]

At about the same it was deciding *Brunswick*, the Court was making other, similarly-important changes in the law applicable to private actions.

THE PROBLEM OF "PASSING-ON"

An important line of cases raising issues related to standing was initiated some years earlier by Hanover Shoe v. United Shoe Machinery Corp., 392 U.S. 481, 88 S.Ct. 2224, 20 L.Ed.2d 1231 (1968). *Hanover Shoe* was a private action brought in the wake of the government's § 2 case against a defendant we have seen before. United Shoe Machinery Co. asserted that even if Hanover had been overcharged for machines because United leased but did not sell them, Hanover would have passed the increased cost on to the purchasers of its shoes. Thus, at the very least, Hanover should not be permitted to treat any of the overcharges as damages.

The Court rejected that defense. Even if Hanover had tried to pass the overcharges on, the Court reasoned, the higher prices would have cost it sales and it would have suffered damage. Even if all shoe manufacturers had been overcharged—so that Hanover would not have been worse off than its competitors—there would be no way to know how much had been passed on by each of them. Only if the first purchaser from the defendant had resold the goods under a "cost-plus" contract so that all increased costs were necessarily passed-on would a passing-on defense be available.

Illinois Brick Co. v. Illinois, 431 U.S. 720, 97 S.Ct. 2061, 52 L.Ed.2d 707 (1977), decided the same year as *Brunswick*, raised the next logical question. The state of Illinois, suing on its own behalf and that of some of its citizens, asserted that the defendant had overcharged building contractors for brick used in building projects within the state. The state

---

[25] See, e.g., Donald I. Baker, Revisiting History—What Have We Learned About Private Antitrust Enforcement That We Would Recommend to Others?, 16 Loyola Consumer L. Rev. 379 (2004); Daniel A. Crane, Optimizing Private Antitrust Enforcement, 63 Vanderbilt L. Rev. 675 (2010); Edward A. Snyder & Thomas E. Kauper, Misuse of the Antitrust Laws: The Competitor Plaintiff, 90 Michigan L.Rev. 477 (1991); D. Daniel Sokol, The Strategic Use of Public and Private Litigation in Antitrust as Business Strategy, 85 S. California L. Rev. 689 (2012). But see, Robert H. Lande, Are Antitrust "Treble" Damages Really Single Damages?, 54 Ohio St.L.J. 115 (1993).

sued, in short, as an indirect purchaser—someone whose costs had been raised because the contractor from whom it had bought could be presumed to have passed-on the overcharge.

The Court held that the same logic that said Hanover *could* sue said that Illinois could *not*. If everyone at every level of the distribution process could sue, there would be no end to litigation and a great risk of inconsistent recoveries. The first purchaser not only *may* sue, the Court said, but it is the *only* one who may. Not surprisingly perhaps, indirect purchasers believed that this result gave standing only to companies whose long-term relationships with potential defendants and lack of any real injury might often give them little incentive to sue.

Finally, Kansas v. UtiliCorp United, Inc., 497 U.S. 199, 110 S.Ct. 2807, 111 L.Ed.2d 169 (1990), closed the logical loop. It was a treble-damage action brought against a natural gas pipeline by both a natural gas utility (the first purchaser) and states acting parens patriae on behalf of consumers (subsequent purchasers) from the utility. The question posed was whether a sale to a public utility is the kind of "cost-plus" contract that *Hanover Shoe* had said could justify use of the passing-on defense. The Court held it is *not*. We speak loosely of public utilities being able to pass-on costs to their consumers, the Court said, but in fact they must apply for rate increases and many factors affect whether they get them. Whether or not the public utility has any *incentive* to file suit, *only* it may do so.

As a practical matter, these cases eliminated many suits by consumers, including those filed as class actions.[26] There have been federal legislative attempts to reverse *Illinois Brick*, but to date, those efforts have been unsuccessful.

In California v. ARC America Corp., 490 U.S. 93, 109 S.Ct. 1661, 104 L.Ed.2d 86 (1989), however, the Court considered whether *states* could grant standing to indirect purchasers under their own state antitrust laws. The Court held that they *could*. Definitional problems abound, but by some measures, over half the states have adopted statutes allowing indirect purchasers to sue under state law. Further, federal law does not prevent division of a settlement among both direct and indirect purchasers where both federal and state claims are settled for a single amount.[27] And because

---

[26]   See, e.g., William H. Page, The Limits of State Indirect Purchaser Suits: Class Certification in the Shadow of *Illinois Brick*, 67 Antitrust L.J. 1 (1999). The use of class actions to aggregate private antitrust claims was also complicated by the requirement of Eisen v. Carlisle & Jacquelin, 417 U.S. 156, 94 S.Ct. 2140, 40 L.Ed.2d 732 (1974), that the named plaintiff bear the large cost of notice along with other costs. See, e.g., Kenneth Dam, Class Actions: Efficiency, Compensation, Deterrence and Conflict of Interest, 4 J. Legal Studies 47 (1975); Benjamin DuVal, The Class Action as an Antitrust Enforcement Device: The Chicago Experience, 1976 A.B.F. Research J. 1021.

[27]   See, e.g., ABA Section of Antitrust Law, Indirect Purchaser Litigation Handbook (2007); Ralph Folsom, Indirect Purchasers: State Antitrust Remedies and Roadblocks, 50 Antitrust Bulletin 181 (2005).

the Class Action Fairness Act removes many state law class actions to federal court, federal judges can find themselves being asked to try indirect purchaser cases in spite of *Illinois Brick*.

A NOTE ON SOME OTHER STANDING ISSUES

The "passing-on" cases were only a part of the litigation over the right to bring private actions that took place in the 1970s and early 80s.

Hawaii v. Standard Oil Co. of California, 405 U.S. 251, 92 S.Ct. 885, 31 L.Ed.2d 184 (1972), cited in *Brunswick*, was an action brought by a state (1) to recover damages for injury to the state's economy and (2) parens patriae to recover losses suffered by the state's citizens. The Supreme Court rejected both claims. First, the state was a "person" within the meaning of Clayton Act § 4, but damage to the state's economy was not damage to its "business or property." The parens patriae action was similarly rejected; the state's citizens could themselves sue, the Court said, but allowing the state to sue on their behalf would run the risk of duplicative recovery. It took later legislation adding §§ 4C—4G of the Clayton Act to reverse this result and allow state attorneys general to file such actions on behalf of their citizens.

Reiter v. Sonotone Corp., 442 U.S. 330, 99 S.Ct. 2326, 60 L.Ed.2d 931 (1979), examined whether a consumer who bought a hearing aid could collect damages for injury to her "business or property." Only companies should be able to sue, the defendant argued; if Congress had wanted consumers to be able to sue, it would have used words such as "pecuniary" injury in the statute. The Supreme Court disagreed. Consumers may not have a "business" injury, the Court reasoned, but they certainly have an injury to their "property."[28] Further, denial of the parens patriae remedy in Hawaii v. Standard Oil was based on a concern about duplicative recovery; the Court had assumed there that suits by individual or classes of consumers would be possible.

Blue Shield of Virginia v. McCready, 457 U.S. 465, 102 S.Ct. 2540, 73 L.Ed.2d 149 (1982), was a suit by a insured who had been denied reimbursement for psychotherapy services rendered by a psychologist. She argued that the insurance company's denial of coverage was part of a conspiracy by psychiatrists to injury their competitors. The Court held the patient had standing. There was no risk of duplicative recoveries, Justice Brennan reasoned, and a patient's injury was not so remote from the harm

---

[28] Earlier, Pfizer v. Government of India, 434 U.S. 308, 98 S.Ct. 584, 54 L.Ed.2d 563 (1978), had tested whether *foreign governments* were "persons" under Clayton Act § 4 and thus had standing to sue for damages caused by the defendants' fixing the prices of antibiotics. The Court held that they were; neither the fact they were governments nor the fact they were foreign undercut that conclusion.

to the real targets of the anticompetitive conduct as to deny patients the right to sue.

The Court seemed to take back some of *McCready's* liberality, however, in Associated General Contractors of California, Inc. v. California State Council of Carpenters, 459 U.S. 519, 103 S.Ct. 897, 74 L.Ed.2d 723 (1983). There, the plaintiff unions alleged a conspiracy to boycott union subcontractors. That, in turn, allegedly reduced employment of union members represented by the plaintiff and reduced pension contributions to the union. Such an injury, the Court asserted, was too remote to give the union standing. The question of who "is a proper party to bring a private antitrust action" is not the same as a constitutional standing requirement, the Court said. It requires assessment of three factors.

> First is the causal connection between the defendant's act and the plaintiff's harm; that was clear here.

> Second is the relation between the plaintiff's injury and the type of conduct the antitrust laws were intended to prohibit. Here, the union was neither a consumer or competitor of the defendants, and in many ways, its interests would often be *served* by having employers act together in labor relations.

> Finally, there is the issue of duplicative recovery. That was a real threat here. Unionized subcontractors might be proper plaintiffs in the case, Justice Stevens reasoned, but the unions could not appoint themselves private attorneys general to redress the wrongs as well.

Do these cases seem consistent? Are there common threads running through them? Are there good reasons to limit private actions that are brought to redress alleged wrongs against which government agencies could have proceeded but decided not to oppose?[29]

———————

Now that we have seen some of the important cases that marked the transition to the current period of antitrust law, we look at more recent cases. These cases can be understood in terms of the same broad

———————————————————

[29]   See, e.g., Joseph P. Bauer, The Stealth Assault on Antitrust Enforcement: Raising the Barriers for Antitrust Injury and Standing, 62 U. Pittsburgh L. Rev. 437 (2001); Robert H. Lande & Joshua P. Davis, Benefits From Private Antitrust Enforcement: An Analysis of Forty Cases, 42 U. San Francisco L. Rev. 879 (2008).

Meanwhile, European enforcement authorities are looking more favorably on private actions. On June 11, 2013, the European Commission published a Proposal for a Directive of the European Parliament and of the Council on certain rules governing actions for damages under national law for infringements of the competition law provisions of the Member States and of the European Union. See, http://eur-lex.europa.eu/LexUriServ/LexUriServ.do?uri=COM:2013:0404:FIN:EN: PDF.

substantive categories that we had examined in Chapter III, but in this chapter we organize them slightly differently.

Our first cases examine both the horizontal and vertical issues of price fixing, market division and group boycott as the Court has looked for a consistent way to approach the extraordinary number of ways such issues can arise. The second group of cases looks at the problem of exclusionary conduct as it arises under the headings of monopolization and tying. We follow with the current approach to mergers in which enforcement agencies file relatively few challenges but negotiate conditions to be imposed upon many more proposed deals. Finally, we look at the interplay between antitrust and other regulation, both in domestic jurisdictions and increasingly in the international arena.

B. THE EMERGENCE OF THE RULE OF REASON IN SECTION 1 CASES

In 1977, *GTE Sylvania* moderated the per se rule in cases of vertical market division. Two years earlier in *Goldfarb*, the Court had shown no such moderation. The recurring question after 1977, then, was what other kinds of cases would merit rule of reason treatment and how a rule of reason analysis should proceed. Justice Stevens, himself a former antitrust practitioner, addressed these questions in the Court's next term.

1. HORIZONTAL PRICE FIXING

NATIONAL SOCIETY OF PROFESSIONAL ENGINEERS V. UNITED STATES

Supreme Court of the United States, 1978
435 U.S. 679, 98 S.Ct. 1355, 55 L.Ed.2d 637

MR. JUSTICE STEVENS delivered the opinion of the Court.

This is a civil antitrust case brought by the United States to nullify an association's canon of ethics prohibiting competitive bidding by its members. The question is whether the canon may be justified under the Sherman Act, because it was adopted by members of a learned profession for the purpose of minimizing the risk that competition would produce inferior engineering work endangering the public safety. The District Court rejected this justification without making any findings on the likelihood that competition would produce the dire consequences foreseen by the association. The Court of Appeals affirmed. * * * Because we are satisfied that the asserted defense rests on a fundamental misunderstanding of the Rule of Reason frequently applied in antitrust litigation, we affirm.

I

Engineering is an important and learned profession. * * * Engineering fees, amounting to well over $2 billion each year, constitute about 5% of total construction costs. In any given facility, approximately 50% to 80% of the cost of construction is the direct result of work performed by an engineer concerning the systems and equipment to be incorporated in the structure.

* * *

* * * This case does not * * * involve any claim that the National Society has tried to fix specific fees, or even a specific method of calculating fees. It involves a charge that the members of the Society have unlawfully agreed to refuse to negotiate or even to discuss the question of fees until after a prospective client has selected the engineer for a particular project. Evidence of this agreement is found in § 11(c) of the Society's Code of Ethics * * * .

The District Court found that the Society's Board of Ethical Review has uniformly interpreted the "ethical rules against competitive bidding for engineering services as prohibiting the submission of any form of price information to a prospective customer which would enable that customer to make a price comparison on engineering services." If the client requires that such information be provided, then § 11(c) imposes an obligation upon the engineering firm to withdraw from consideration for that job. The Society's Code of Ethics thus "prohibits engineers from both soliciting and submitting such price information," and seeks to preserve the profession's "traditional" method of selecting professional engineers. Under the traditional method, the client initially selects an engineer on the basis of background and reputation, not price.[30]

* * * The complaint prayed for an injunction terminating the unlawful agreement.

In its answer the Society admitted the essential facts alleged by the Government * * * [but] averred that the standard set out in the Code of Ethics was reasonable because competition among professional engineers was contrary to the public interest. It was averred that it would be cheaper and easier for an engineer "to design and specify inefficient and unnecessarily expensive structures and methods of construction." Accordingly, competitive pressure to offer engineering services at the lowest possible price would adversely affect the quality of engineering. Moreover, the practice of awarding engineering contracts to the lowest bidder, regardless of quality, would be dangerous to the public health,

---

[30] Having been selected, the engineer may then, in accordance with the Society's canons of ethics, negotiate a satisfactory fee arrangement with the client. If the negotiations are unsuccessful, then the client may withdraw his selection and approach a new engineer. [Court's fn. 6]

safety, and welfare. For these reasons, the Society claimed that its Code of Ethics was not an "unreasonable restraint of interstate trade or commerce."

* * *

II

In Goldfarb v. Virginia State Bar, the Court held that a bar association's rule prescribing minimum fees for legal services violated § 1 of the Sherman Act. In that opinion the Court noted that certain practices by members of a learned profession might survive scrutiny under the Rule of Reason even though they would be viewed as a violation of the Sherman Act in another context. The Court said [in footnote 17]:

> "The fact that a restraint operates upon a profession as distinguished from a business is, of course, relevant in determining whether that particular restraint violates the Sherman Act. It would be unrealistic to view the practice of professions as interchangeable with other business activities, and automatically to apply to the professions antitrust concepts which originated in other areas. The public service aspect, and other features of the professions may require that a particular practice, which could properly be viewed as a violation of the Sherman Act in another context, be treated differently. * * * "

Relying heavily on this footnote, and on some of the major cases applying a Rule of Reason—principally Mitchel v. Reynolds, Standard Oil Co. v. United States, Chicago Board of Trade v. United States, and Continental T.V., Inc. v. GTE Sylvania Inc.—petitioner argues that its attempt to preserve the profession's traditional method of setting fees for engineering services is a reasonable method of forestalling the public harm which might be produced by unrestrained competitive bidding. To evaluate this argument it is necessary to identify the contours of the Rule of Reason and to discuss its application to the kind of justification asserted by petitioner.

A.   THE RULE OF REASON.

* * *

Congress * * * did not intend the text of the Sherman Act to delineate the full meaning of the statute or its application in concrete situations. The legislative history makes it perfectly clear that it expected the courts to give shape to the statute's broad mandate by drawing on common-law tradition. The Rule of Reason, with its origins in common-law precedents long antedating the Sherman Act, has served that purpose. It has been used to give the Act both flexibility and definition, and its central principle of antitrust analysis has remained constant. Contrary to its name, the Rule does not open the field of antitrust inquiry to any argument in favor of a challenged restraint that may fall within the realm of reason. Instead, it focuses directly on the challenged restraint's impact on competitive conditions.

* * *

The Rule of Reason suggested by Mitchel v. Reynolds has been regarded as a standard for testing the enforceability of covenants in restraint of trade which are ancillary to a legitimate transaction, such as an employment contract or the sale of a going business. Judge (later Mr. Chief Justice) Taft so interpreted the Rule in his classic rejection of the argument that competitors may lawfully agree to sell their goods at the same price as long as the agreed-upon price is reasonable. United States v. Addyston Pipe & Steel Co. That case, and subsequent decisions by this Court, unequivocally foreclose an interpretation of the Rule as permitting an inquiry into the reasonableness of the prices set by private agreement.

The early cases also foreclose the argument that because of the special characteristics of a particular industry, monopolistic arrangements will better promote trade and commerce than competition. United States v. Trans-Missouri Freight Assn. That kind of argument is properly addressed to Congress and may justify an exemption from the statute for specific industries, but it is not permitted by the Rule of Reason. * * *

The test prescribed in *Standard Oil* is whether the challenged contracts or acts "were unreasonably restrictive of competitive conditions." Unreasonableness under that test could be based either (1) on the nature or character of the contracts, or (2) on surrounding circumstances giving rise to the inference or presumption that they were intended to restrain trade and enhance prices. Under either branch of the test, the inquiry is confined to a consideration of impact on competitive conditions.

In this respect the Rule of Reason has remained faithful to its origins. From Mr. Justice Brandeis' opinion for the Court in *Chicago Board of Trade* to the Court's opinion written by Mr. Justice Powell in *Continental T.V., Inc.*, the Court has adhered to the position that the inquiry mandated by the Rule of Reason is whether the challenged agreement is one that promotes competition or one that suppresses competition. * * *

There are, thus, two complementary categories of antitrust analysis. In the first category are agreements whose nature and necessary effect are so plainly anticompetitive that no elaborate study of the industry is needed to establish their illegality—they are "illegal per se." In the second category are agreements whose competitive effect can only be evaluated by analyzing the facts peculiar to the business, the history of the restraint, and the reasons why it was imposed. In either event, the purpose of the analysis is to form a judgment about the competitive significance of the restraint; it is not to decide whether a policy favoring competition is in the public interest, or in the interest of the members of an industry. Subject to exceptions defined by statute, that policy decision has been made by the Congress.

B. THE BAN ON COMPETITIVE BIDDING.

* * * In this case we are presented with an agreement among competitors to refuse to discuss prices with potential customers until after negotiations have resulted in the initial selection of an engineer. While this is not price fixing as such, no elaborate industry analysis is required to demonstrate the anticompetitive character of such an agreement. It operates as an absolute ban on competitive bidding, applying with equal force to both complicated and simple projects and to both inexperienced and sophisticated customers. As the District Court found, the ban "impedes the ordinary give and take of the market place," and substantially deprives the customer of "the ability to utilize and compare prices in selecting engineering services." On its face, this agreement restrains trade within the meaning of § 1 of the Sherman Act.

The Society's affirmative defense confirms rather than refutes the anticompetitive purpose and effect of its agreement. The Society argues that the restraint is justified because bidding on engineering services is inherently imprecise, would lead to deceptively low bids, and would thereby tempt individual engineers to do inferior work with consequent risk to public safety and health.[31] The logic of this argument rests on the assumption that the agreement will tend to maintain the price level; if it had no such effect, it would not serve its intended purpose. The Society nonetheless invokes the Rule of Reason, arguing that its restraint on price competition ultimately inures to the public benefit by preventing the production of inferior work and by insuring ethical behavior. * * * [T]his Court has never accepted such an argument.

* * *

The Sherman Act does not require competitive bidding; it prohibits unreasonable restraints on competition. Petitioner's ban on competitive

---

[31] The Society also points out that competition, in the form of bargaining between the engineer and customer, is allowed under its canon of ethics once an engineer has been initially selected. See [Court's] n. 6, supra. It then contends that its prohibition of competitive bidding regulates only the timing of competition, thus making this case analogous to *Chicago Board of Trade*, where the Court upheld an exchange rule which forbade exchange members from making purchases after the close of the day's session at any price other than the closing bid price. * * * We find this reliance on *Chicago Board of Trade* misplaced for two reasons. First, petitioner's claim mistakenly treats negotiation between a single seller and a single buyer as the equivalent of competition between two or more potential sellers. Second, even if we were to accept the Society's equation of bargaining with price competition, our concern with *Chicago Board of Trade* is in its formulation of the proper test to be used in judging the legality of an agreement; that formulation unquestionably stresses impact on competition. Whatever one's view of the application of the Rule of Reason in that case, the Court considered the exchange's regulation of price information as having a positive effect on competition. The District Court's findings preclude a similar conclusion concerning the effect of the Society's "regulation." [Court's fn. 19]

bidding prevents all customers from making price comparisons in the initial selection of an engineer, and imposes the Society's views of the costs and benefits of competition on the entire marketplace. It is this restraint that must be justified under the Rule of Reason, and petitioner's attempt to do so on the basis of the potential threat that competition poses to the public safety and the ethics of its profession is nothing less than a frontal assault on the basic policy of the Sherman Act.

The Sherman Act reflects a legislative judgment that ultimately competition will produce not only lower prices, but also better goods and services. * * * The assumption that competition is the best method of allocating resources in a free market recognizes that all elements of a bargain—quality, service, safety, and durability—and not just the immediate cost, are favorably affected by the free opportunity to select among alternative offers. Even assuming occasional exceptions to the presumed consequences of competition, the statutory policy precludes inquiry into the question whether competition is good or bad.

* * * In our complex economy the number of items that may cause serious harm is almost endless—automobiles, drugs, foods, aircraft components, heavy equipment, and countless others, cause serious harm to individuals or to the public at large if defectively made. The judiciary cannot indirectly protect the public against this harm by conferring monopoly privileges on the manufacturers.

* * *

In sum, the Rule of Reason does not support a defense based on the assumption that competition itself is unreasonable. Such a view of the Rule would create the "sea of doubt" on which Judge Taft refused to embark in *Addyston*, and which this Court has firmly avoided ever since.

III

* * * The judgment of the Court of Appeals is affirmed.

MR. JUSTICE BRENNAN took no part in the consideration or decision of this case.

MR. JUSTICE BLACKMUN, with whom MR. JUSTICE REHNQUIST joins, concurring in part and concurring in the judgment.

I join Parts I and III of the Court's opinion and concur in the judgment. I do not join Part II because I would not, at least for the moment, reach as far as the Court appears to me to do in intimating that any ethical rule with an overall anticompetitive effect promulgated by a professional society is forbidden under the Sherman Act. In my view, the decision in Goldfarb v. Virginia State Bar properly left to the Court some flexibility in considering how to apply traditional Sherman Act concepts to professions long consigned to self-regulation. Certainly, this case does not require us to decide whether the "Rule of Reason" as applied to the professions ever could take account of benefits other than increased competition. For even accepting petitioner's assertion that product quality is one such benefit, and that maintenance of the quality of engineering services requires that an engineer not bid before he has made full acquaintance with the scope of a client's desired project, petitioner Society's rule is still grossly overbroad. As petitioner concedes, § 11(c) forbids any simultaneous consultation between a client and several engineers, even where the client provides complete information to each about the scope and nature of the desired project before requesting price information. * * * Though § 11(c) does not fix prices directly, and though the customer retains the option of rejecting a particular engineer's offer and beginning negotiations all over again with another engineer, the forced process of sequential search inevitably increases the cost of gathering price information, and hence will dampen price competition, without any calibrated role to play in preventing uninformed bids. * * *

My skepticism about going further in this case by shaping the Rule of Reason to such a narrow last as does the majority, arises from the fact that there may be ethical rules which have a more than de minimis anticompetitive effect and yet are important in a profession's proper ordering. A medical association's prescription of standards of minimum competence for licensing or certification may lessen the number of entrants. A bar association's regulation of the permissible forms of price advertising for nonroutine legal services or limitation of in-person solicitation may also have the effect of reducing price competition. In acknowledging that "professional services may differ significantly from other business services" and that the "nature of the competition in such services may vary," but then holding that ethical norms can pass muster under the Rule of Reason only if they promote competition, I am not at all certain that the Court leaves enough elbow room for realistic application of the Sherman Act to professional services.

MR. CHIEF JUSTICE BURGER, concurring in part and dissenting in part.

I concur in the Court's judgment to the extent it sustains the finding of a violation of the Sherman Act but dissent from that portion of the judgment prohibiting petitioner from stating in its published standards of ethics the view that competitive bidding is unethical. The First Amendment guarantees the right to express such a position and that right cannot be impaired under the cloak of remedial judicial action.

NOTES AND QUESTIONS

1.   After *Goldfarb*, did the professional engineers reasonably have hope that their standard would survive antitrust challenge? What did fn. 17 mean in *Goldfarb* if not that rules of professional ethics would be judged by standards other than solely their effect on competition?

a.   Did the engineers' rule protect a public interest that the purchaser of their service might not take seriously enough? Is a public agency that builds a bridge indifferent to whether it will collapse? Might the officials who select the engineer have to answer to the voters about cost immediately but calculate that they likely will be out of office by the time defects in the bridge design become apparent?

b.   On the other hand, did the engineers' rule really promote the selection of a competent engineer? What do you suppose would go into an engineer's proposal if the engineer could not mention price? Is selecting an engineer on the basis of pictures of previous projects any more in the public interest than choosing on the basis of the protect's proposed cost?

2.   The Court's discussion of the relation between the per se rule and the rule of reason is important here.

a.   Do you suppose it will always be clear which agreements are so plainly anticompetitive that "no elaborate study" is needed to establish illegality?

b.   Is the only alternative to "no elaborate study" a full-scale rule of reason analysis of the type seen in *Chicago Board of Trade*? The Court is obviously feeling its way here, but you should sense even at this point that the Court will have to make the distinction less sharp.

3.   Having drawn the distinction, was this case decided under the per se rule or the rule of reason? Does the Court say?

a.   Did the Court conclude that the engineers had fixed prices? Is the Court saying that when anyone restricts price competition in any way, it is the same as price fixing and thus per se illegal? Do you agree with Justices Blackmun and Rehnquist that it should have been the fact that the rule increased a buyer's search costs that made the rule illegal?

b.   Does the Court implicitly say that, even if the engineers' rule were evaluated under a rule of reason, the engineers offered no legally cognizable defense for the rule and thus that the full meaning of *Goldfarb*'s footnote 17 need not be decided?

c.   When the competitive effects of most ethical rules are evaluated in the context of an industry and the reasons for the practice, is it likely to be easy to tell whether the rules promote competition? Are they often likely to do so, as opposed to promoting some other values?

4.   What were Justices Blackmun and Rehnquist's concerns about the Court's approach?

a.   Do you agree that professions often need rules to order their conduct that could be seen as restrictions on competition, e.g., educational standards, pro bono obligations, etc.?

b.   Should the rule of reason permit looking at non-economic effects, e.g., public safety or preservation of collegiality, of a given rule? Do you agree with the Court's apparent view that those effects should play no role in antitrust analysis?

c. Would it violate the Sherman Act for a group of stores to agree to close at the same hour each day? Does that sound like *Board of Trade*? Would it reduce the "output" of those merchants in a way that affected their prices? Is a "conspiracy" to reduce sellers' costs per se illegal? See, e.g., Barnett Pontiac-Datsun, Inc. v. FTC, 955 F.2d 457 (6th Cir.), cert. denied 506 U.S. 973 (1992), upholding a finding that such an agreement violates § 5 of the FTC Act.

d. Should a professional association be permitted to adopt an ethical rule forbidding doctors to advertise? Might that tend to raise the cost of medical care? Might it increase patients' costs of finding a doctor and make comparison shopping more difficult? See American Medical Association v. Federal Trade Commission, 638 F.2d 443 (2d Cir.1980), affirmed by equally divided court 455 U.S. 676 (1982), that struck down such restrictions. But see California Dental Ass'n v. Federal Trade Commission, 526 U.S. 756, 119 S.Ct. 1604, 143 L.Ed.2d 935 (1999), revisiting the advertising question later in this chapter.

5. Does Chief Justice Burger convince you that professions have a First Amendment right to articulate their standards? Is there a First Amendment right to engage in a conspiracy? Does his point in any event remind us that inferring conspiracy from otherwise public speech at least tends to threaten important First Amendment values?

Professional Engineers had acknowledged the existence of a rule of reason but not much turned on that acknowledgment. Our next case made clear, however, that the rule of reason could be applied to uphold even some horizontal price fixing agreements that almost certainly would have been held to be per se illegal just a few years earlier.

BROADCAST MUSIC, INC. V. COLUMBIA BROADCASTING SYSTEM, INC.

Supreme Court of the United States, 1979
441 U.S. 1, 99 S.Ct. 1551, 60 L.Ed.2d 1

MR. JUSTICE WHITE delivered the opinion of the Court.

This case involves an action under the antitrust and copyright laws brought by respondent Columbia Broadcasting System, Inc. (CBS), against petitioners, American Society of Composers, Authors and Publishers (ASCAP) and Broadcast Music, Inc. (BMI), and their members and affiliates. The basic question presented is whether the issuance by ASCAP and BMI to CBS of blanket licenses to copyrighted musical compositions at fees negotiated by them is price fixing per se unlawful under the antitrust laws.

I

CBS operates one of three national commercial television networks, supplying programs to approximately 200 affiliated stations and telecasting approximately 7,500 network programs per year. Many, but not all, of these programs make use of copyrighted music recorded on the soundtrack. CBS also owns television and radio stations in various cities. It is "the giant of the world in the use of music rights," the "No. 1 outlet in the history of entertainment."

Since 1897, the copyright laws have vested in the owner of a copyrighted musical composition the exclusive right to perform the work publicly for profit, but the legal right is not self-enforcing. In 1914, Victor Herbert and a handful of other composers organized ASCAP because those who performed copyrighted music for profit were so numerous and widespread, and most performances so fleeting, that as a practical matter it was impossible for the many individual copyright owners to negotiate with and license the users and to detect unauthorized uses. "ASCAP was organized as a 'clearing-house' for copyright owners and users to solve these problems" associated with the licensing of music. As ASCAP operates today, its 22,000 members grant it nonexclusive rights to license nondramatic performances of their works, and ASCAP issues licenses and distributes royalties to copyright owners in accordance with a schedule reflecting the nature and amount of the use of their music and other factors.

BMI, a nonprofit corporation owned by members of the broadcasting industry, was organized in 1939, is affiliated with or represents some 10,000 publishing companies and 20,000 authors and composers, and operates in much the same manner as ASCAP. Almost every domestic copyrighted composition is in the repertory either of ASCAP, with a total of three million compositions, or of BMI, with one million.

Both organizations operate primarily through blanket licenses, which give the licensees the right to perform any and all of the compositions owned by the members or affiliates as often as the licensees desire for a stated term. Fees for blanket licenses are ordinarily a percentage of total revenues or a flat dollar amount, and do not directly depend on the amount or type of music used. Radio and television broadcasters are the largest users of music, and almost all of them hold blanket licenses from both ASCAP and BMI. Until this litigation, CBS held blanket licenses from both organizations for its television network on a continuous basis since the late 1940's and had never attempted to secure any other form of license from either ASCAP or any of its members.

* * * CBS argued that ASCAP and BMI are unlawful monopolies and that the blanket license is illegal price fixing, an unlawful tying arrangement, a concerted refusal to deal, and a misuse of copyrights. * * *

After an 8-week trial, limited to the issue of liability, the court dismissed the complaint, rejecting again the claim that the blanket license was price fixing and a per se violation of § 1 of the Sherman Act, and holding that since direct negotiation with individual copyright owners is available and feasible there is no undue restraint of trade, illegal tying, misuse of copyrights, or monopolization.

Though agreeing with the District Court's factfinding and not disturbing its legal conclusions on the other antitrust theories of liability, the Court of Appeals held that the blanket license issued to television networks was a form of price fixing illegal per se under the Sherman Act. This conclusion, without more, settled the issue of liability under the Sherman Act, established copyright misuse, and required reversal of the District Court's judgment * * * .

ASCAP and BMI petitioned for certiorari, presenting the questions of the applicability of the per se rule and of whether this constitutes misuse of copyrights. * * * We granted certiorari * * * . Because we disagree with the Court of Appeals' conclusions with respect to the per se illegality of the blanket license, we reverse its judgment and remand the cause for further appropriate proceedings.

II

In construing and applying the Sherman Act's ban against contracts, conspiracies, and combinations in restraint of trade, the Court has held that certain agreements or practices are so "plainly anticompetitive," National Society of Professional Engineers v. United States; Continental T.V., Inc. v. GTE Sylvania Inc., and so often "lack * * * any redeeming virtue," Northern Pac. R. Co. v. United States, that they are conclusively presumed illegal without further examination under the rule of reason generally applied in Sherman Act cases. This per se rule is a valid and useful tool of antitrust policy and enforcement. And agreements among competitors to fix prices on their individual goods or services are among those concerted activities that the Court has held to be within the per se category. But easy labels do not always supply ready answers.

A

To the Court of Appeals and CBS, the blanket license involves "price fixing" in the literal sense: the composers and publishing houses have joined together into an organization that sets its price for the blanket license it sells.[32] But this is not a question simply of determining whether

---

[32] CBS also complains that it pays a flat fee regardless of the amount of use it makes of ASCAP compositions and even though many of its programs contain little or no music. We are unable to see how that alone could make out an antitrust violation or misuse of copyrights: "Sound business judgment could indicate that such payment represents the most convenient method of fixing the business value of the privileges granted by the licensing agreement. * * * Petitioner cannot complain because it must pay royalties whether it uses Hazeltine patents or not. What it acquired by the agreement into which it entered was the privilege to use any or all of the patents

two or more potential competitors have literally "fixed" a "price." As generally used in the antitrust field, "price fixing" is a short-hand way of describing certain categories of business behavior to which the per se rule has been held applicable. The Court of Appeals' literal approach does not alone establish that this particular practice is one of those types or that it is "plainly anticompetitive" and very likely without "redeeming virtue." Literalness is overly simplistic and often overbroad. When two partners set the price of their goods or services they are literally "price fixing," but they are not per se in violation of the Sherman Act. See United States v. Addyston Pipe & Steel Co. Thus, it is necessary to characterize the challenged conduct as falling within or without that category of behavior to which we apply the label "per se price fixing." That will often, but not always, be a simple matter.

Consequently, as we recognized in United States v. Topco Associates, Inc., "[i]t is only after considerable experience with certain business relationships that courts classify them as per se violations * * * ." See White Motor Co. v. United States. We have never examined a practice like this one before; indeed, the Court of Appeals recognized that "[i]n dealing with performing rights in the music industry we confront conditions both in copyright law and in antitrust law which are sui generis." And though there has been rather intensive antitrust scrutiny of ASCAP and its blanket licenses, that experience hardly counsels that we should outlaw the blanket license as a per se restraint of trade.

B

* * *

The Department of Justice first investigated allegations of anticompetitive conduct by ASCAP over 50 years ago. A criminal complaint was filed in 1934, but the Government was granted a midtrial continuance and never returned to the courtroom. In separate complaints in 1941, the United States charged that the blanket license, which was then the only license offered by ASCAP and BMI, was an illegal restraint of trade and that arbitrary prices were being charged as the result of an illegal copyright pool. * * * The case was settled by a consent decree that imposed tight restrictions on ASCAP's operations. * * * [T]he 1941 decree was reopened and extensively amended in 1950.

Under the amended decree, which still substantially controls the activities of ASCAP, members may grant ASCAP only nonexclusive rights to license their works for public performance. Members, therefore, retain the rights individually to license public performances, along with the rights to license the use of their compositions for other purposes. * * * ASCAP

---

and developments as it desired to use them." Automatic Radio Mfg. Co. v. Hazeltine Research, Inc., 339 U.S. 827, 834 (1950). See also Zenith Radio Corp. v. Hazeltine Research, Inc., 395 U.S. 100 (1969). [Court's fn. 13]

may not insist on the blanket license, and the fee for the per-program license, which is to be based on the revenues for the program on which ASCAP music is played, must offer the applicant a genuine economic choice between the per-program license and the more common blanket license. If ASCAP and a putative licensee are unable to agree on a fee within 60 days, the applicant may apply to the District Court for a determination of a reasonable fee, with ASCAP having the burden of proving reasonableness.

* * * [T]he District Court found, and in this respect the Court of Appeals agreed, that there are no practical impediments preventing direct dealing by the television networks if they so desire. Historically, they have not done so. Since 1946, CBS and other television networks have taken blanket licenses from ASCAP and BMI. * * *

Of course, a consent judgment, even one entered at the behest of the Antitrust Division, does not immunize the defendant from liability for actions, including those contemplated by the decree, that violate the rights of nonparties. * * * But it cannot be ignored that the Federal Executive and Judiciary have carefully scrutinized ASCAP and the challenged conduct, have imposed restrictions on various of ASCAP's practices, and * * * stand ready to provide further consideration, supervision, and perhaps invalidation of asserted anticompetitive practices. In these circumstances, we have a unique indicator that the challenged practice may have redeeming competitive virtues and that the search for those values is not almost sure to be in vain. Thus, although CBS is not bound by the Antitrust Division's actions, the decree is a fact of economic and legal life in this industry, and the Court of Appeals should not have ignored it completely in analyzing the practice. * * *

* * *

Finally, we note that Congress itself, in the new Copyright Act, has chosen to employ the blanket license and similar practices. * * * Though these provisions are not directly controlling, they do reflect an opinion that the blanket license, and ASCAP, are economically beneficial in at least some circumstances.

* * *

III

Of course, we are no more bound than is CBS by the views of the Department of Justice, the results in the prior lower court cases, or the opinions of various experts about the merits of the blanket license. But while we must independently examine this practice, all those factors should caution us against too easily finding blanket licensing subject to per se invalidation.

A

As a preliminary matter, we are mindful that the Court of Appeals' holding would appear to be quite difficult to contain. If, as the court held, there is a per se antitrust violation whenever ASCAP issues a blanket license to a television network for a single fee, why would it not also be automatically illegal for ASCAP to negotiate and issue blanket licenses to individual radio or television stations or to other users who perform copyrighted music for profit? * * *

Although the Court of Appeals apparently thought the blanket license could be saved in some or even many applications, it seems to us that the per se rule does not accommodate itself to such flexibility and that the observations of the Court of Appeals with respect to remedy tend to impeach the per se basis for the holding of liability.

CBS would prefer that ASCAP be authorized, indeed directed, to make all its compositions available at standard per-use rates within negotiated categories of use. * * * Thus, we are called upon to determine that blanket licensing is unlawful across the board. We are quite sure, however, that the per se rule does not require any such holding.

B

In the first place, the line of commerce allegedly being restrained, the performing rights to copyrighted music, exists at all only because of the copyright laws. Those who would use copyrighted music in public performances must secure consent from the copyright owner or be liable at least for the statutory damages for each infringement and, if the conduct is willful and for the purpose of financial gain, to criminal penalties. Furthermore, nothing in the Copyright Act of 1976 indicates in the slightest that Congress intended to weaken the rights of copyright owners to control the public performance of musical compositions. Quite the contrary is true. Although the copyright laws confer no rights on copyright owners to fix prices among themselves or otherwise to violate the antitrust laws, we would not expect that any market arrangements reasonably necessary to effectuate the rights that are granted would be deemed a per se violation of the Sherman Act. Otherwise, the commerce anticipated by the Copyright Act and protected against restraint by the Sherman Act would not exist at all or would exist only as a pale reminder of what Congress envisioned.

C

More generally, in characterizing this conduct under the per se rule,[33] our inquiry must focus on whether the effect and, here because it tends to

---

[33] The scrutiny occasionally required must not merely subsume the burdensome analysis required under the rule of reason, see National Society of Professional Engineers v. United States,

show effect, the purpose of the practice are to threaten the proper operation of our predominantly free-market economy—that is, whether the practice facially appears to be one that would always or almost always tend to restrict competition and decrease output, and in what portion of the market, or instead one designed to "increase economic efficiency and render markets more, rather than less, competitive." See Continental T.V., Inc. v. GTE Sylvania, Inc.

The blanket license, as we see it, is not a "naked restrain[t] of trade with no purpose except stifling of competition," White Motor Co. v. United States, but rather accompanies the integration of sales, monitoring, and enforcement against unauthorized copyright use. As we have already indicated, ASCAP and the blanket license developed together out of the practical situation in the marketplace: thousands of users, thousands of copyright owners, and millions of compositions. Most users want unplanned, rapid, and indemnified access to any and all of the repertory of compositions, and the owners want a reliable method of collecting for the use of their copyrights. Individual sales transactions in this industry are quite expensive, as would be individual monitoring and enforcement, especially in light of the resources of single composers. Indeed, as both the Court of Appeals and CBS recognize, the costs are prohibitive for licenses with individual radio stations, nightclubs, and restaurants, and it was in that milieu that the blanket license arose.

A middleman with a blanket license was an obvious necessity if the thousands of individual negotiations, a virtual impossibility, were to be avoided. Also, individual fees for the use of individual compositions would presuppose an intricate schedule of fees and uses, as well as a difficult and expensive reporting problem for the user and policing task for the copyright owner. Historically, the market for public-performance rights organized itself largely around the single-fee blanket license, which gave unlimited access to the repertory and reliable protection against infringement. When ASCAP's major and user-created competitor, BMI, came on the scene, it also turned to the blanket license.

With the advent of radio and television networks, market conditions changed, and the necessity for and advantages of a blanket license for those users may be far less obvious than is the case when the potential users are individual television or radio stations, or the thousands of other individuals and organizations performing copyrighted compositions in public. But even for television network licenses, ASCAP reduces costs absolutely by creating a blanket license that is sold only a few, instead of thousands, of times, and that obviates the need for closely monitoring the networks to see that they do not use more than they pay for. ASCAP also provides the necessary resources for blanket sales and enforcement, resources unavailable to the

---

or else we should apply the rule of reason from the start. That is why the per se rule is not employed until after considerable experience with the type of challenged restraint. [Court's fn. 33]

vast majority of composers and publishing houses. Moreover, a bulk license of some type is a necessary consequence of the integration necessary to achieve these efficiencies, and a necessary consequence of an aggregate license is that its price must be established.

D

This substantial lowering of costs, which is of course potentially beneficial to both sellers and buyers, differentiates the blanket license from individual use licenses. The blanket license is composed of the individual compositions plus the aggregating service. Here, the whole is truly greater than the sum of its parts; it is, to some extent, a different product. The blanket license has certain unique characteristics: It allows the licensee immediate use of covered compositions, without the delay of prior individual negotiations,[34] and great flexibility in the choice of musical material. Many consumers clearly prefer the characteristics and cost advantages of this marketable package, and even small performing-rights societies that have occasionally arisen to compete with ASCAP and BMI have offered blanket licenses. Thus, to the extent the blanket license is a different product, ASCAP is not really a joint sales agency offering the individual goods of many sellers, but is a separate seller offering its blanket license, of which the individual compositions are raw material.[35] ASCAP, in short, made a market in which individual composers are inherently unable to compete fully effectively.[36]

E

Finally, we have some doubt—enough to counsel against application of the per se rule—about the extent to which this practice threatens the "central nervous system of the economy," United States v. Socony-Vacuum Oil Co., that is, competitive pricing as the free market's means of allocating resources. Not all arrangements among actual or potential competitors that have an impact on price are per se violations of the Sherman Act or

---

[34] See Timberg, The Antitrust Aspects of Merchandising Modern Music: The ASCAP Consent Judgment of 1950, 19 Law & Contemp. Prob. 294, 297 (1954) ("The disk-jockey's itchy fingers and the bandleader's restive baton, it is said, cannot wait for contracts to be drawn with ASCAP's individual publisher members, much less for the formal acquiescence of a characteristically unavailable composer or author"). Significantly, ASCAP deals only with nondramatic performance rights. Because of their nature, dramatic rights, such as for musicals, can be negotiated individually and well in advance of the time of performance. The same is true of various other rights, such as sheet music, recording, and synchronization, which are licensed on an individual basis. [Court's fn. 37]

[35] Moreover, because of the nature of the product—a composition can be simultaneously "consumed" by many users—composers have numerous markets and numerous incentives to produce, so the blanket license is unlikely to cause decreased output, one of the normal undesirable effects of a cartel. And since popular songs get an increased share of ASCAP's revenue distributions, composers compete even within the blanket license in terms of productivity and consumer satisfaction. [Court's fn. 40]

[36] Cf. United States v. Socony-Vacuum Oil Co. (distinguishing Chicago Bd. of Trade v. United States on the ground that among the effects of the challenged rule there "was the creation of a public market") * * * . [Court's fn. 41]

even unreasonable restraints. Mergers among competitors eliminate competition, including price competition, but they are not per se illegal, and many of them withstand attack under any existing antitrust standard. Joint ventures and other cooperative arrangements are also not usually unlawful, at least not as price-fixing schemes, where the agreement on price is necessary to market the product at all.

Here, the blanket-license fee is not set by competition among individual copyright owners, and it is a fee for the use of any of the compositions covered by the license. But the blanket license cannot be wholly equated with a simple horizontal arrangement among competitors. ASCAP does set the price for its blanket license, but that license is quite different from anything any individual owner could issue. The individual composers and authors have neither agreed not to sell individually in any other market nor use the blanket license to mask price fixing in such other markets. Moreover, the substantial restraints placed on ASCAP and its members by the consent decree must not be ignored. The District Court found that there was no legal, practical, or conspiratorial impediment to CBS's obtaining individual licenses; CBS, in short, had a real choice.

With this background in mind, which plainly enough indicates that over the years, and in the face of available alternatives, the blanket license has provided an acceptable mechanism for at least a large part of the market for the performing rights to copyrighted musical compositions, we cannot agree that it should automatically be declared illegal in all of its many manifestations. Rather, when attacked, it should be subjected to a more discriminating examination under the rule of reason. It may not ultimately survive that attack, but that is not the issue before us today.

* * *

The judgment of the Court of Appeals is reversed, and the cases are remanded to that court for further proceedings consistent with this opinion.

MR. JUSTICE STEVENS, dissenting.

The Court holds that ASCAP's blanket license is not a species of price fixing categorically forbidden by the Sherman Act. I agree with that holding. The Court remands the cases to the Court of Appeals, leaving open the question whether the blanket license as employed by ASCAP and BMI is unlawful under a rule-of-reason inquiry. I think that question is properly before us now and should be answered affirmatively.

* * *

II

Under our prior cases, there would be no question about the illegality of the blanket-only licensing policy if ASCAP and BMI were the exclusive sources of all licenses. A copyright, like a patent, is a statutory grant of monopoly privileges. The rules which prohibit a patentee from enlarging his statutory monopoly by conditioning a license on the purchase of unpatented goods, or by refusing to grant a license under one patent unless the licensee also takes a license under another, are equally applicable to copyrights.[37]

It is clear, however, that the mere fact that the holder of several patents has granted a single package license covering them all does not establish any illegality. This point was settled by Automatic Radio Mfg. Co. v. Hazeltine Research, Inc., 339 U.S. 827 [1950], and reconfirmed in Zenith Radio Corp. v. Hazeltine Research, Inc., 395 U.S. 100 [1969]. * * * But both of those cases identify an important limitation on this rule. In the former, the Court was careful to point out that the record did not present the question whether the package license would have been unlawful if Hazeltine had refused to license on any other basis. And in the latter case, the Court held that the package license was illegal because of such a refusal.

Since ASCAP offers only blanket licenses, its licensing practices fall on the illegal side of the line drawn by the two *Hazeltine* cases. But there is a significant distinction: unlike *Hazeltine*, ASCAP does not have exclusive control of the copyrights in its portfolio, and it is perfectly possible—at least as a legal matter—for a user of music to negotiate directly with composers and publishers for whatever rights he may desire. * * * ASCAP is therefore quite correct in its insistence that its blanket license cannot be categorically condemned on the authority of the blockbooking and package-licensing cases. While these cases are instructive, they do not directly answer the question whether the ASCAP practice is unlawful.

* * * [I]t is well settled that a sales practice that is permissible for a small vendor, at least when no coercion is present, may be unreasonable when employed by a company that dominates the market. We therefore must consider what the record tells us about the competitive character of this market.

III

The market for music at issue here is wholly dominated by ASCAP-issued blanket licenses. Virtually every domestic copyrighted composition is in the repertoire of either ASCAP or BMI. And again, virtually without exception, the only means that has been used to secure authority to perform such compositions is the blanket license.

The blanket all-or-nothing license is patently discriminatory. The user purchases full access to ASCAP's entire repertoire, even though his needs could be satisfied by a far more limited selection. The price he pays for this

---

[37] Indeed, the leading cases condemning the practice of "blockbooking" involved copyrighted motion pictures, rather than patents. See United States v. Paramount Pictures, 334 U.S. 131 [1948]; United States v. Loew's Inc. [Dissent fn. 12]

access is unrelated either to the quantity or the quality of the music he actually uses, or, indeed, to what he would probably use in a competitive system. Rather, in this unique all-or-nothing system, the price is based on a percentage of the user's advertising revenues, a measure that reflects the customer's ability to pay but is totally unrelated to factors—such as the cost, quality, or quantity of the product—that normally affect price in a competitive market. The ASCAP system requires users to buy more music than they want at a price which, while not beyond their ability to pay and perhaps not even beyond what is "reasonable" for the access they are getting, may well be far higher than what they would choose to spend for music in a competitive system. It is a classic example of economic discrimination.

The record plainly establishes that there is no price competition between separate musical compositions. Under a blanket license, it is no more expensive for a network to play the most popular current hit in prime time than it is to use an unknown composition as background music in a soap opera. Because the cost to the user is unaffected by the amount used on any program or on all programs, the user has no incentive to economize by, for example, substituting what would otherwise be less expensive songs for established favorites or by reducing the quantity of music used on a program. * * * Perhaps the prospect is in any event unlikely, but the blanket license does not present a new songwriter with any opportunity to try to break into the market by offering his product for sale at an unusually low price. The absence of that opportunity, however unlikely it may be, is characteristic of a cartelized rather than a competitive market.

The current state of the market cannot be explained on the ground that it could not operate competitively, or that issuance of more limited— and thus less restrictive—licenses by ASCAP is not feasible. The District Court's findings disclose no reason why music-performing rights could not be negotiated on a per-composition or per-use basis, either with the composer or publisher directly or with an agent such as ASCAP. In fact, ASCAP now compensates composers and publishers on precisely those bases. If distributions of royalties can be calculated on a per-use and per-composition basis, it is difficult to see why royalties could not also be collected in the same way. Moreover, the record also shows that where ASCAP's blanket-license scheme does not govern, competitive markets do. A competitive market for "synch" rights exists, and after the use of blanket licenses in the motion picture industry was discontinued, such a market promptly developed in that industry. In sum, the record demonstrates that the market at issue here is one that could be highly competitive, but is not competitive at all.

IV

* * *

The fact that CBS has substantial market power does not deprive it of the right to complain when trade is restrained. Large buyers, as well as small, are protected by the antitrust laws. Indeed, even if the victim of a conspiracy is himself a wrongdoer, he has not forfeited the protection of the law. Moreover, a conclusion that excessive competition would cause one side of the market more harm than good may justify a legislative exemption from the antitrust laws, but does not constitute a defense to a violation of the Sherman Act. * * *

* * *

* * * Even without judicial intervention, the ASCAP monopoly might eventually be broken by CBS, if the benefits of doing so outweigh the significant costs and risks involved in commencing direct dealing.[38] But that hardly means that the blanket-licensing policy at issue here is lawful. An arrangement that produces marketwide price discrimination and significant barriers to entry unreasonably restrains trade even if the discrimination and the barriers have only a limited life expectancy. History suggests, however, that these restraints have an enduring character.

* * * ASCAP itself argues that its blanket license constitutes a product that is significantly different from the sum of its component parts. I agree with that premise, but I conclude that the aggregate is a monopolistic restraint of trade proscribed by the Sherman Act.

NOTES AND QUESTIONS

1.   In what sense do these blanket licenses constitute price fixing? Have composers and publishers set a uniform price where otherwise there would be price competition?

---

[38]   The risks involved in such a venture appear to be substantial. One significant risk, which may be traced directly to ASCAP and its members, relates to music "in the can"—music which has been performed on shows and movies already in the network's inventory, but for which the network must still secure performing rights. The networks accumulate substantial inventories of shows "in the can." And, as the Government has pointed out as amicus curiae: "If they [the networks and television stations] were to discontinue the blanket license, they then would be required to obtain performance rights for these already-produced shows. This attempt would create an opportunity for the copyright owners, as a condition of granting performing rights, to attempt to obtain the entire value of the shows 'in the can.' It would produce, in other words, a case of bilateral monopoly. Because pricing is indeterminate in a bilateral monopoly, television networks would not terminate their blanket licenses until they had concluded an agreement with every owner of copyrighted music 'in the can' to allow future performance for an identified price; the networks then would determine whether that price was sufficiently low that termination of the blanket license would be profitable. But the prospect of such negotiations offers the copyrights owners an ability to misuse their rights in a way that ensures the continuation of blanket licensing despite a change in market conditions that may make other forms of licensing preferable." This analysis is in no sense inconsistent with the findings of the District Court. * * * [Dissent fn. 31]

a.   Assuming per use royalties could have been charged, how high would they likely have been? How much would a radio station pay for one play of a typical song? Are stations short of songs to play if a particular composer or artist wants too much money? While some hit songs might be exceptions, what is the typical marginal value to a station of a typical single song?

b.   Look at the issue through the eyes of the composer and artist. What is their marginal cost of one more play of a record? Isn't it little or nothing? The "cost" to them was in writing and recording the music. How low a price could most people be persuaded to accept for a product the marginal cost of which is zero?

2.   Should the theoretical ability to negotiate with copyright holders individually prevail over the practical limits on such negotiation?

a.   Why would BMI and ASCAP choose to base royalties on station revenues rather than the cost of the music or its specific commercial value?

b.   Why did licensees go along with this system? Do the Court's arguments for the efficiency of the system also show that individual licensing of music was not really the viable option the Court finds that it was? Were you convinced by Justice Stevens' description of the risks to someone bold enough to challenge the system?

3.   How else might copyright royalties be collected? For example, might a certain amount be added to the price stations pay for records that would give the stations a right to play them on the air? Do stations in fact pay for records? Indeed, might record companies have reason to pay the stations to play their records if doing so were not considered to be unethical "payola"?

4.   The court cites desirable features of this plan. What were they?

a.   Do you agree that the arrangement created a new product—the joint license? Why was that different from ASCAP and BMI's being sellers of a package of individual licenses?

b.   Did the arrangement create a market in artists' and composers' rights by reducing the cost of dealing and making it possible for royalties to be charged and collected?

5.   Could the efficiencies created by this system have been sufficient to justify upholding it even if the system allowed ASCAP and BMI to establish a monopoly price for the rights? Look at the graph below.

This graph assumes that the cost of dealing before the joint license was very high, i.e., it was MC_1. Pricing, however, was competitive, i.e., output (Q_1) was set at a level where MC_1 intersects the demand curve (D). There were no monopoly profits and no welfare loss triangle,[39] but the price (P_1) was high. Then, after the joint license was created, the graph assumes the cost of dealing fell to MC_2. The graph also tells us that the pricing was then *not* competitive,

---

[39]   If these concepts still sound foreign to you, look again at the introductory note on economics beginning at page 5 of these materials.

i.e., output (Q_2) was set where marginal cost (MC_2) equals marginal revenue (MR). There are assumed to be both large monopoly profits and a large welfare loss triangle (shown as shaded).

    a.   But are consumers better off? How does P_1 on the graph compare to P_2? Notice that even though the package license is here presumed to have created "monopoly" conditions, on the assumptions reflected in this graph, the reduction in the cost of dealing has made consumers substantially better off. If these assumptions are correct, should the antitrust laws make the package license illegal?

Figure 7

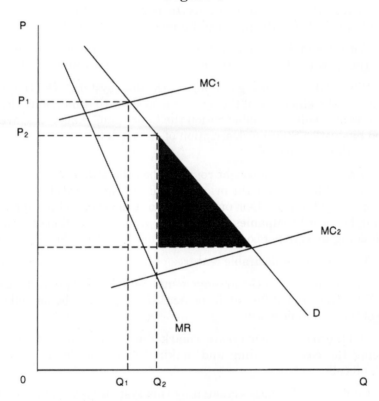

    b.   Might such a system tend to increase output of songs (by increasing the returns to the artists)? Might it also increase the number of plays of each song by lowering the marginal cost of each? Should we take such effects into account in evaluating the rule?

    c.   On the other hand, suppose package licensing reduced somewhat the number of radio stations because the cost of operating a station was increased by the plan. Do we have any measure with which to compare the social loss from one effect against the social gain from another?[40]

---

[40]   See generally, Stanley M. Besen, Sheila N. Kirby & Steven C. Salop, An Economic Analysis of Copyright Collectives, 78 Virginia L.Rev. 383 (1992).

6.   Is there another justification for the decision? Would it have been possible to frame a remedy if the court had found the plan illegal? What could the Court have ordered? Should the question of remedy ever affect the substantive result?[41]

7.   Suppose there were only one multi-artist licensing organization and that it decided to exclude certain new artists from its package license. Would that present an antitrust problem? Would it be a § 1 issue? How about § 2? Could ASCAP be held to be an "essential facility"?

DID *BMI v. CBS* ABOLISH THE PER SE RULE?: THE COURT SAYS "NOT SO FAST"

If lawyers thought that BMI v. CBS had abolished the per se rule, they were corrected the very next year in Catalano v. Target Sales, 446 U.S. 643, 100 S.Ct. 1925, 64 L.Ed.2d 580 (1980). *Catalano* was a private suit brought by beer retailers against a group of their wholesalers who had agreed to eliminate their prior practice of extending retailers trade credit without interest for up to the 30 days permitted by state law.

The wholesalers admitted the agreement but argued that they still competed vigorously on price. Indeed, by eliminating competition on other items, they argued they made price an even more important determinant of sales. Further, they said that the need to grant credit made it harder for new firms to enter wholesaling. Thus the agreement, far from reducing competition, could be said to make the market more competitive.

The district court held that the complaint did not state a case for per se liability, and the 9th Circuit agreed, one judge dissenting. In a unanimous *per curiam* decision, the Supreme Court said the case was obviously an agreement not to grant a discount equal to the value of the money for the 30 days. That was the functional equivalent of price fixing and the Court said that a "horizontal agreement to fix prices is * * * unlawful per se."

Do you see differences between *BMI* and *Catalano*? What are they? Are they sufficient to justify the Court's slamming the door on a rule of reason analysis as firmly as it did?

Two years later, in Arizona v. Maricopa County Medical Society, 457 U.S. 332, 102 S.Ct. 2466, 73 L.Ed.2d 48 (1982), the Court again imposed a

---

[41]   Under the Government's 1950 consent decree with ASCAP, if the parties cannot agree on the amount of a blanket royalty, a court may be asked to do so. Such a process, discussing ASCAP's market power in negotiating royalty rates, is illustrated by American Society of Composers, Authors & Publishers v. Showtime/The Movie Channel, 912 F.2d 563 (2d Cir.1990). See also, United States v. American Society of Composers, Authors & Publishers, 782 F.Supp. 778 (S.D.N.Y.1991), affirmed 956 F.2d 21 (2d Cir.), cert.denied 504 U.S. 914 (1992) (orders ASCAP to make available a per-program license).

per se rule. Doctors in Phoenix had created the Maricopa Foundation for Medical Care in an effort to preserve fee-for-service medicine in the face of competitive gains made by Health Maintenance Organizations (HMOs). The doctors agreed to accept fees for medical procedures based on a schedule that insurers had pre-approved as reasonable. The effect was to allow patients to buy fee-for-service insurance that would be competitive with the cost and service of HMOs.

The doctors said they were limiting fees, not raising them, and that the plan produced a more competitive medical marketplace. By a 4–3 vote, however, the Supreme Court held that "We have not wavered in our enforcement of the per se rule against price fixing." Justice Stevens wrote for the Court that, just as *Goldfarb* said lawyers could not use a minimum fee schedule, doctors could not set maximum fees. The idea that, in context, the plan increased competition and patient choice was deemed irrelevant. "The anticompetitive potential inherent in all price-fixing agreements justifies their facial invalidation even if procompetitive justifications are offered for some."

Justice Powell found the Court's attempt to distinguish *BMI* "unconvincing." Both that case and this "involved competitors and resulted in cooperative pricing. Each arrangement also was prompted by the need for better service to the consumers. And each arrangement apparently makes possible a new product by reaping otherwise unattainable efficiencies." With which of the opinions do you agree?

––––––––––

When is the rule of reason to govern and when the per se rule? Need the choice always be that stark? See if you think our next case better clarifies the rules of the game.

NATIONAL COLLEGIATE ATHLETIC ASSOCIATION V. BOARD OF REGENTS OF THE UNIVERSITY OF OKLAHOMA

Supreme Court of the United States, 1984
468 U.S. 85, 104 S.Ct. 2948, 82 L.Ed.2d 70

JUSTICE STEVENS delivered the opinion of the Court.

The University of Oklahoma and the University of Georgia contend that the National Collegiate Athletic Association has unreasonably restrained trade in the televising of college football games. After an extended trial, the District Court found that the NCAA had violated § 1 of the Sherman Act and granted injunctive relief. The Court of Appeals agreed * * * . We granted certiorari and now affirm.

I

THE NCAA

Since its inception in 1905, the NCAA has played an important role in the regulation of amateur collegiate sports. It has adopted and promulgated playing rules, standards of amateurism, standards for academic eligibility, regulations concerning recruitment of athletes, and rules governing the size of athletic squads and coaching staffs. * * * With the exception of football, the NCAA has not undertaken any regulation of the televising of athletic events.

The NCAA has approximately 850 voting members. The regular members are classified into separate divisions to reflect differences in size and scope of their athletic programs. Division I includes 276 colleges with major athletic programs; in this group only 187 play intercollegiate football. Divisions II and III include approximately 500 colleges with less extensive athletic programs. * * *

Some years ago, five major conferences together with major football-playing independent institutions organized the College Football Association (CFA). The original purpose of the CFA was to promote the interests of major football-playing schools within the NCAA structure. The Universities of Oklahoma and Georgia, respondents in this Court, are members of the CFA.

HISTORY OF THE NCAA TELEVISION PLAN

In 1938, the University of Pennsylvania televised one of its home games. From 1940 through the 1950 season all of Pennsylvania's home games were televised. That was the beginning of the relationship between television and college football.

On January 11, 1951, a three-person "Television Committee," appointed during the preceding year, delivered a report to the NCAA's annual convention in Dallas. Based on preliminary surveys, the committee had concluded that "television does have an adverse effect on college football attendance and unless brought under some control threatens to seriously harm the nation's overall athletic and physical system." The report emphasized that "the television problem is truly a national one and requires collective action by the colleges." * * *

* * *

From 1952 through 1977 the NCAA television committee * * * [had entered into 1-or 2-year contracts with a single television network to broadcast college football games. In 1977, the NCAA] entered into its first 4-year contract granting exclusive rights to the American Broadcasting Co. (ABC) for the 1978–1981 seasons. ABC had held the exclusive rights to network telecasts of NCAA football games since 1965.

THE CURRENT PLAN

The plan adopted in 1981 for the 1982–1985 seasons is at issue in this case. This plan, like each of its predecessors, recites that it is intended to reduce, insofar as possible, the adverse effects of live television upon football game attendance. * * * The plan [this time also] recites that the television committee has awarded rights to negotiate and contract for the telecasting of college football games of members of the NCAA to two "carrying networks." * * *

In separate agreements with each of the carrying networks, ABC and the Columbia Broadcasting System (CBS), the NCAA granted each the right to telecast the 14 live "exposures" described in the plan, in accordance with the "ground rules" set forth therein. Each of the networks agreed to pay a specified "minimum aggregate compensation to the participating NCAA member institutions" during the 4-year period in an amount that totaled $131,750,000. In essence the agreement authorized each network to negotiate directly with member schools for the right to televise their games. * * * Except for differences in payment between national and regional telecasts, and with respect to Division II and Division III games, the amount that any team receives does not change with the size of the viewing audience, the number of markets in which the game is telecast, or the particular characteristic of the game or the participating teams. Instead, the "ground rules" provide that the carrying networks make alternate selections of those games they wish to televise, and thereby obtain the exclusive right to submit a bid at an essentially fixed price to the institutions involved.

The plan also contains "appearance requirements" and "appearance limitations" which pertain to each of the 2-year periods that the plan is in effect. The basic requirement imposed on each of the two networks is that it must schedule appearances for at least 82 different member institutions during each 2-year period. Under the appearance limitations no member institution is eligible to appear on television more than a total of six times and more than four times nationally, with the appearances to be divided equally between the two carrying networks. The number of exposures specified in the contracts also sets an absolute maximum on the number of games that can be broadcast.

* * * No member is permitted to make any sale of television rights except in accordance with the basic plan.

BACKGROUND OF THIS CONTROVERSY

Beginning in 1979 CFA members began to advocate that colleges with major football programs should have a greater voice in the formulation of football television policy than they had in the NCAA. CFA therefore investigated the possibility of negotiating a television agreement of its own, developed an independent plan, and obtained a contract offer from the

National Broadcasting Co. (NBC). This contract, which it signed in August 1981, would have allowed a more liberal number of appearances for each institution, and would have increased the overall revenues realized by CFA members.

In response the NCAA publicly announced that it would take disciplinary action against any CFA member that complied with the CFA-NBC contract. The NCAA made it clear that sanctions would not be limited to the football programs of CFA members, but would apply to other sports as well. * * * [M]ost CFA members were unwilling to commit themselves to the new contractual arrangement with NBC in the face of the threatened sanctions and therefore the agreement was never consummated.

DECISION OF THE DISTRICT COURT

After a full trial, the District Court held that the controls exercised by the NCAA over the televising of college football games violated the Sherman Act. The District Court defined the relevant market as "live college football television" because it found that alternative programming has a significantly different and lesser audience appeal. The District Court then concluded that the NCAA controls over college football are those of a "classic cartel" with an

> "almost absolute control over the supply of college football which is made available to the networks, to television advertisers, and ultimately to the viewing public. Like all other cartels, NCAA members have sought and achieved a price for their product which is, in most instances, artificially high. The NCAA cartel imposes production limits on its members, and maintains mechanisms for punishing cartel members who seek to stray from these production quotas. The cartel has established a uniform price for the products of each of the member producers, with no regard for the differing quality of these products or the consumer demand for these various products."

The District Court found that competition in the relevant market had been restrained in three ways: (1) NCAA fixed the price for particular telecasts; (2) its exclusive network contracts were tantamount to a group boycott of all other potential broadcasters and its threat of sanctions against its own members constituted a threatened boycott of potential competitors; and (3) its plan placed an artificial limit on the production of televised college football.

In the District Court the NCAA offered two principal justifications for its television policies: that they protected the gate attendance of its members and that they tended to preserve a competitive balance among the football programs of the various schools. The District Court rejected the first justification because the evidence did not support the claim that college football television adversely affected gate attendance. With respect to the "competitive balance" argument, the District Court found that the evidence failed to show that the NCAA regulations on matters such as recruitment and the standards for preserving amateurism were not sufficient to maintain an appropriate balance.

DECISION OF THE COURT OF APPEALS

The Court of Appeals held that the NCAA television plan constituted illegal per se price fixing.[42] It rejected each of the three arguments advanced by NCAA to establish the procompetitive character of its plan.[43] * * *

* * *

II

There can be no doubt that the challenged practices of the NCAA constitute a "restraint of trade" in the sense that they limit members' freedom to negotiate and enter into their own television contracts. In that sense, however, every contract is a restraint of trade, and as we have repeatedly recognized, the Sherman Act was intended to prohibit only unreasonable restraints of trade.

It is also undeniable that these practices share characteristics of restraints we have previously held unreasonable. The NCAA is an association of schools which compete against each other to attract television revenues, not to mention fans and athletes. * * * By participating in an association which prevents member institutions from competing against each other on the basis of price or kind of television rights that can be offered to broadcasters, the NCAA member institutions have created a horizontal restraint—an agreement among competitors on the way in which they will compete with one another. A restraint of this type has often been held to be unreasonable as a matter of law. * * * By restraining the quantity of television rights available for sale, the challenged practices create a limitation on output; our cases have held that such limitations are unreasonable restraints of trade. Moreover, the District Court found that the minimum aggregate price in fact operates to preclude any price negotiation between broadcasters and institutions, thereby constituting horizontal price fixing, perhaps the paradigm of an unreasonable restraint of trade.

---

[42] The Court of Appeals rejected the District Court's boycott holding, since all broadcasters were free to negotiate for a contract as carrying networks and the threat of sanctions against members for violating NCAA rules could not be considered a boycott if the rules were otherwise valid. [Court's fn. 13]

[43] In the Court of Appeals as well as the District Court, petitioner argued that respondents had suffered no injury of the type the antitrust laws were designed to prevent, relying on Brunswick Corp. v. Pueblo Bowl-O-Mat, Inc. Both courts rejected its position. Petitioner does not seek review on that question in this Court. [Court's fn. 14]

Horizontal price fixing and output limitation are ordinarily condemned as a matter of law under an "illegal per se" approach because the probability that these practices are anticompetitive is so high; a per se rule is applied when "the practice facially appears to be one that would always or almost always tend to restrict competition and decrease output." Broadcast Music, Inc. v. Columbia Broadcasting System, Inc. In such circumstances a restraint is presumed unreasonable without inquiry into the particular market context in which it is found. Nevertheless, we have decided that it would be inappropriate to apply a per se rule to this case. This decision is not based on a lack of judicial experience with this type of arrangement, on the fact that the NCAA is organized as a nonprofit entity, or on our respect for the NCAA's historic role in the preservation and encouragement of intercollegiate amateur athletics. Rather, what is critical is that this case involves an industry in which horizontal restraints on competition are essential if the product is to be available at all.

* * * What the NCAA and its member institutions market in this case is competition itself—contests between competing institutions. Of course, this would be completely ineffective if there were no rules on which the competitors agreed to create and define the competition to be marketed. A myriad of rules affecting such matters as the size of the field, the number of players on a team, and the extent to which physical violence is to be encouraged or proscribed, all must be agreed upon, and all restrain the manner in which institutions compete. Moreover, the NCAA seeks to market a particular brand of football—college football. The identification of this "product" with an academic tradition differentiates college football from and makes it more popular than professional sports to which it might otherwise be comparable, such as, for example, minor league baseball. In order to preserve the character and quality of the "product," athletes must not be paid, must be required to attend class, and the like. And the integrity of the "product" cannot be preserved except by mutual agreement; if an institution adopted such restrictions unilaterally, its effectiveness as a competitor on the playing field might soon be destroyed. Thus, the NCAA plays a vital role in enabling college football to preserve its character, and as a result enables a product to be marketed which might otherwise be unavailable. In performing this role, its actions widen consumer choice—not only the choices available to sports fans but also those available to athletes—and hence can be viewed as procompetitive.

Broadcast Music squarely holds that a joint selling arrangement may be so efficient that it will increase sellers' aggregate output and thus be procompetitive. Similarly, as we indicated in Continental T.V., Inc. v. GTE Sylvania Inc., a restraint in a limited aspect of a market may actually enhance marketwide competition. Respondents concede that the great majority of the NCAA's regulations enhance competition among member institutions. Thus, despite the fact that this case involves restraints on the ability of member institutions to compete in terms of price and output, a fair evaluation of their competitive character requires consideration of the NCAA's justifications for the restraints.

Our analysis of this case under the Rule of Reason, of course, does not change the ultimate focus of our inquiry. Both per se rules and the Rule of Reason are employed "to form a judgment about the competitive significance of the restraint." National Society of Professional Engineers v. United States. * * *

Per se rules are invoked when surrounding circumstances make the likelihood of anticompetitive conduct so great as to render unjustified further examination of the challenged conduct. But whether the ultimate finding is the product of a presumption or actual market analysis, the essential inquiry remains the same—whether or not the challenged restraint enhances competition.[44] Under the Sherman Act the criterion to be used in judging the validity of a restraint on trade is its impact on competition.

III

Because it restrains price and output, the NCAA's television plan has a significant potential for anticompetitive effects. The findings of the District Court indicate that this potential has been realized. The District Court found that if member institutions were free to sell television rights, many more games would be shown on television, and that the NCAA's output restriction has the effect of raising the price the networks pay for television rights. Moreover, the court found that by fixing a price for television rights to all games, the NCAA creates a price structure that is unresponsive to viewer demand and unrelated to the prices that would prevail in a competitive market.[45] And, of course, since as a practical matter all member institutions need NCAA approval, members have no real choice but to adhere to the NCAA's television controls.

---

[44] Indeed, there is often no bright line separating per se from Rule of Reason analysis. Per se rules may require considerable inquiry into market conditions before the evidence justifies a presumption of anticompetitive conduct. For example, while the Court has spoken of a "per se" rule against tying arrangements, it has also recognized that tying may have procompetitive justifications that make it inappropriate to condemn without considerable market analysis. See Jefferson Parish Hospital Dist. No. 2 v. Hyde, 466 U.S. [2 (1984)]. [Court's fn. 26]

[45] * * * "In a competitive market, each college fielding a football team would be free to sell the right to televise its games for whatever price it could get. The prices would vary for the games, with games between prominent schools drawing a larger price than games between less prominent schools. Games between the more prominent schools would draw a larger audience than other games. Advertisers would pay higher rates for commercial time because of the larger audience. The telecaster would then be willing to pay larger rights fees due to the increased prices paid by the advertisers. Thus, the price which the telecaster would pay for a particular game would be dependent on the expected size of the viewing audience. Clearly, the NCAA controls grossly distort the prices actually paid for an individual game from that to be expected in a free market." [Court's fn. 30]

The anticompetitive consequences of this arrangement are apparent. Individual competitors lose their freedom to compete. Price is higher and output lower than they would otherwise be, and both are unresponsive to consumer preference.[46] * * * Restrictions on price and output are the paradigmatic examples of restraints of trade that the Sherman Act was intended to prohibit. At the same time, the television plan eliminates competitors from the market, since only those broadcasters able to bid on television rights covering the entire NCAA can compete. Thus, as the District Court found, many telecasts that would occur in a competitive market are foreclosed by the NCAA's plan.

Petitioner argues, however, that its television plan can have no significant anticompetitive effect since the record indicates that it has no market power—no ability to alter the interaction of supply and demand in the market. We must reject this argument for two reasons, one legal, one factual.

As a matter of law, the absence of proof of market power does not justify a naked restriction on price or output. To the contrary, when there is an agreement not to compete in terms of price or output, "no elaborate industry analysis is required to demonstrate the anticompetitive character of such an agreement." *Professional Engineers*.[47] * * * This naked restraint on price and output requires some competitive justification even in the absence of a detailed market analysis.

---

[46] "In this case the rule is violated by a price restraint that tends to provide the same economic rewards to all practitioners regardless of their skill, their experience, their training, or their willingness to employ innovative and difficult procedures." Arizona v. Maricopa County Medical Society, 457 U.S. [332 (1982)]. The District Court provided a vivid example of this system in practice:

"A clear example of the failure of the rights fees paid to respond to market forces occurred in the fall of 1981. On one weekend of that year, Oklahoma was scheduled to play a football game with the University of Southern California. Both Oklahoma and USC have long had outstanding football programs, and indeed, both teams were ranked among the top five teams in the country by the wire service polls. ABC chose to televise the game along with several others on a regional basis. A game between two schools which are not well-known for their football programs, Citadel and Appalachian State, was carried on four of ABC's local affiliated stations. The USC-Oklahoma contest was carried on over 200 stations. Yet, incredibly, all four of these teams received exactly the same amount of money for the right to televise their games." [Court's fn. 33]

[47] "The fact that a practice is not categorically unlawful in all or most of its manifestations certainly does not mean that it is universally lawful. For example, joint buying or selling arrangements are not unlawful per se, but a court would not hesitate in enjoining a domestic selling arrangement by which, say, Ford and General Motors distributed their automobiles nationally through a single selling agent. Even without a trial, the judge will know that these two large firms are major factors in the automobile market, that such joint selling would eliminate important price competition between them, that they are quite substantial enough to distribute their products independently, and that one can hardly imagine a pro-competitive justification actually probable in fact or strong enough in principle to make this particular joint selling arrangement 'reasonable' under Sherman Act § 1. The essential point is that the rule of reason can sometimes be applied in the twinkling of an eye." P. Areeda, The "Rule of Reason" in Antitrust Analysis: General Issues 37–38 (Federal Judicial Center, June 1981). [Court's fn. 39]

As a factual matter, it is evident that petitioner does possess market power. The District Court employed the correct test for determining whether college football broadcasts constitute a separate market—whether there are other products that are reasonably substitutable for televised NCAA football games. Petitioner's argument that it cannot obtain supracompetitive prices from broadcasters since advertisers, and hence broadcasters, can switch from college football to other types of programming simply ignores the findings of the District Court. It found that intercollegiate football telecasts generate an audience uniquely attractive to advertisers and that competitors are unable to offer programming that can attract a similar audience. These findings amply support its conclusion that the NCAA possesses market power. Indeed, the District Court's subsidiary finding that advertisers will pay a premium price per viewer to reach audiences watching college football because of their demographic characteristics is vivid evidence of the uniqueness of this product. Moreover, the District Court's market analysis is firmly supported by our decision in International Boxing Club of New York, Inc. v. United States, 358 U.S. 242 (1959), that championship boxing events are uniquely attractive to fans and hence constitute a market separate from that for nonchampionship events. Thus, respondents have demonstrated that there is a separate market for telecasts of college football which "rest[s] on generic qualities differentiating" viewers. It inexorably follows that if college football broadcasts be defined as a separate market—and we are convinced they are—then the NCAA's complete control over those broadcasts provides a solid basis for the District Court's conclusion that the NCAA possesses market power with respect to those broadcasts. * * *

Thus, the NCAA television plan on its face constitutes a restraint upon the operation of a free market, and the findings of the District Court establish that it has operated to raise prices and reduce output. Under the Rule of Reason, these hallmarks of anticompetitive behavior place upon petitioner a heavy burden of establishing an affirmative defense which competitively justifies this apparent deviation from the operations of a free market. * * *

IV

Relying on *Broadcast Music*, petitioner argues that its television plan constitutes a cooperative "joint venture" which assists in the marketing of broadcast rights and hence is procompetitive. While joint ventures have no immunity from the antitrust laws, as *Broadcast Music* indicates, a joint selling arrangement may "mak[e] possible a new product by reaping otherwise unattainable efficiencies." * * * The NCAA does not, however, act as a selling agent for any school or for any conference of schools. The selection of individual games, and the negotiation of particular agreements, is a matter left to the networks and the individual schools. Thus, the effect of the network plan is not to eliminate individual sales of broadcasts, since these still occur, albeit subject to fixed prices and output limitations. Unlike *Broadcast Music*'s blanket license covering broadcast rights to a large number of individual compositions, here the same rights are still sold on an individual basis, only in a non-competitive market.

The District Court did not find that the NCAA's television plan produced any procompetitive efficiencies which enhanced the competitiveness of college football television rights; to the contrary it concluded that NCAA football could be marketed just as effectively without the television plan. * * * The NCAA's efficiency justification is not supported by the record.

Neither is the NCAA's television plan necessary to enable the NCAA to penetrate the market through an attractive package sale. Since broadcasting rights to college football constitute a unique product for which there is no ready substitute, there is no need for collective action in order to enable the product to compete against its nonexistent competitors. * * *

V

Throughout the history of its regulation of intercollegiate football telecasts, the NCAA has indicated its concern with protecting live attendance. This concern, it should be noted, is not with protecting live attendance at games which are shown on television; that type of interest is not at issue in this case. Rather, the concern is that fan interest in a televised game may adversely affect ticket sales for games that will not appear on television.

Although the NORC studies in the 1950's provided some support for the thesis that live attendance would suffer if unlimited television were permitted, the District Court found that there was no evidence to support that theory in today's market. * * * Under the current plan, games are shown on television during all hours that college football games are played. The plan simply does not protect live attendance by ensuring that games will not be shown on television at the same time as live events.

There is, however, a more fundamental reason for rejecting this defense. The NCAA's argument that its television plan is necessary to protect live attendance is not based on a desire to maintain the integrity of college football as a distinct and attractive product, but rather on a fear that the product will not prove sufficiently attractive to draw live attendance when faced with competition from televised games. At bottom the NCAA's position is that ticket sales for most college games are unable to compete in a free market. The television plan protects ticket sales by limiting output—just as any monopolist increases revenues by reducing output. By seeking to insulate live ticket sales from the full spectrum of competition because of its assumption that the product itself is insufficiently attractive to consumers, petitioner forwards a justification that is inconsistent with the basic policy of the Sherman Act. "[T]he Rule of Reason does not support a defense based on the assumption that competition itself is unreasonable." *Professional Engineers.*

VI

Petitioner argues that the interest in maintaining a competitive balance among amateur athletic teams is legitimate and important and that it justifies the regulations challenged in this case. We agree with the first part of the argument but not the second.

Our decision not to apply a per se rule to this case rests in large part on our recognition that a certain degree of cooperation is necessary if the type of competition that petitioner and its member institutions seek to market is to be preserved. It is reasonable to assume that most of the regulatory controls of the NCAA are justifiable means of fostering competition among amateur athletic teams and therefore procompetitive because they enhance public interest in intercollegiate athletics. The specific restraints on football telecasts that are challenged in this case do not, however, fit into the same mold as do rules defining the conditions of the contest, the eligibility of participants, or the manner in which members of a joint enterprise shall share the responsibilities and the benefits of the total venture.

The NCAA does not claim that its television plan has equalized or is intended to equalize competition within any one league.[48] The plan is nationwide in scope and there is no single league or tournament in which all college football teams compete. There is no evidence of any intent to equalize the strength of teams in Division I–A with those in Division II or Division III, and not even a colorable basis for giving colleges that have no football program at all a voice in the management of the revenues generated by the football programs at other schools. The interest in maintaining a competitive balance that is asserted by the NCAA as a justification for regulating all television of intercollegiate football is not related to any neutral standard or to any readily identifiable group of competitors.

The television plan is not even arguably tailored to serve such an interest. It does not regulate the amount of money that any college may spend on its football program, nor the way in which the colleges may use the revenue that are generated by their football programs, whether derived from the sale of television rights, the sale of tickets, or the sale of

---

[48]   It seems unlikely, for example, that there would have been a greater disparity between the football prowess of Ohio State University and that of Northwestern University in recent years without the NCAA's television plan. The District Court found that in fact the NCAA has been strikingly unsuccessful if it has indeed attempted to prevent the emergence of a "power elite" in intercollegiate football. Moreover, the District Court's finding that there would be more local and regional telecasts without the NCAA controls means that Northwestern could well have generated more television income in a free market than was obtained under the NCAA regime. [Court's fn. 62]

concessions or program advertising. The plan simply imposes a restriction on one source of revenue that is more important to some colleges than to others. There is no evidence that this restriction produces any greater measure of equality throughout the NCAA than would a restriction on alumni donations, tuition rates, or any other revenue-producing activity. * * * No other NCAA sport employs a similar plan, and in particular the court found that in the most closely analogous sport, college basketball, competitive balance has been maintained without resort to a restrictive television plan.

Perhaps the most important reason for rejecting the argument that the interest in competitive balance is served by the television plan is the District Court's unambiguous and well-supported finding that many more games would be televised in a free market than under the NCAA plan. The hypothesis that legitimates the maintenance of competitive balance as a procompetitive justification under the Rule of Reason is that equal competition will maximize consumer demand for the product. The finding that consumption will materially increase if the controls are removed is a compelling demonstration that they do not in fact serve any such legitimate purpose.

VII

The NCAA plays a critical role in the maintenance of a revered tradition of amateurism in college sports. There can be no question but that it needs ample latitude to play that role, or that the preservation of the student-athlete in higher education adds richness and diversity to intercollegiate athletics and is entirely consistent with the goals of the Sherman Act. * * * Today we hold only that the record supports the District Court's conclusion that by curtailing output and blunting the ability of member institutions to respond to consumer preference, the NCAA has restricted rather than enhanced the place of intercollegiate athletics in the Nation's life. Accordingly, the judgment of the Court of Appeals is

Affirmed.

JUSTICE WHITE, with whom JUSTICE REHNQUIST joins, dissenting.

* * * Although some of the NCAA's activities, viewed in isolation, bear a resemblance to those undertaken by professional sports leagues and associations, the Court errs in treating intercollegiate athletics under the NCAA's control as a purely commercial venture in which colleges and universities participate solely, or even primarily, in the pursuit of profits. Accordingly, I dissent.

I

* * *

In pursuit of its fundamental goal and others related to it, the NCAA imposes numerous controls on intercollegiate athletic competition among its members * * * . Thus, the NCAA has promulgated and enforced rules limiting both the compensation of student-athletes, and the number of coaches a school may hire for its football and basketball programs; it also has prohibited athletes who formerly have been compensated for playing from participating in intercollegiate competition, restricted the number of athletic scholarships its members may award, and established minimum academic standards for recipients of those scholarships; and it has pervasively regulated the recruitment process, student eligibility, practice schedules, squad size, the number of games played, and many other aspects of intercollegiate athletics. One clear effect of most, if not all, of these regulations is to prevent institutions with competitively and economically successful programs from taking advantage of their success by expanding their programs, improving the quality of the product they offer, and increasing their sports revenues. Yet each of these regulations represents a desirable and legitimate attempt "to keep university athletics from becoming professionalized to the extent that profit making objectives would overshadow educational objectives." Significantly, neither the Court of Appeals nor this Court questions the validity of these regulations under the Rule of Reason.

Notwithstanding the contrary conclusion of the District Court, and the majority, I do not believe that the restraint under consideration in this case—the NCAA's television plan—differs fundamentally for antitrust purposes from the other seemingly anticompetitive aspects of the organization's broader program of self-regulation. * * *

* * *

II

* * *

First, it is not clear to me that the District Court employed the proper measure of output. * * * To the extent that output is measured solely in terms of the number of televised games, I need not deny that it is reduced by the NCAA's television plan. But this measure of output is not the proper one. The District Court found that eliminating the plan would reduce the number of games on network television and increase the number of games shown locally and regionally. It made no finding concerning the effect of the plan on total viewership, which is the more appropriate measure of output or, at least, of the claimed anticompetitive effects of the NCAA plan. This is the NCAA's position, and it seems likely to me that the television plan, by increasing network coverage at the expense of local broadcasts, actually expands the total television audience for NCAA football. The NCAA would surely be an irrational "profit maximizer" if this were not the case. * * *

Second, and even more important, I am unconvinced that respondents have proved that any reduction in the number of televised college football games brought about by the NCAA's television plan has resulted in an anticompetitive increase in the price of television rights. * * * Reductions in output by monopolists in most product markets enable producers to exact a higher price for *the same product*. By restricting the number of games that can be televised, however, the NCAA creates *a new product*—exclusive television rights—that are more valuable to networks than the products that its individual members could market independently.

The television plan makes a certain number of games available for purchase by television networks and limits the incidence of head-to-head competition between football telecasts for the available viewers. Because competition is limited, the purchasing network can count on a larger share of the audience, which translates into a greater advertising revenues and, accordingly, into larger payments per game to the televised teams. There is thus a relationship between the size of the rights payments and the value of the product being purchased by the networks; a network purchasing a series of games under the plan is willing to pay more than would one purchasing the same games in the absence of the plan since the plan enables the network to deliver a larger share of the available audience to advertisers and thus to increase its own revenues. In short, by focusing only on the price paid by the networks for television rights rather than on the nature and quality of the product delivered by the NCAA and its member institutions, the District Court, and this Court as well, may well have deemed anticompetitive a rise in price that more properly should be attributed to an increase in output, measured in terms of viewership.

* * *

IV

Finally, I return to the point with which I began—the essentially noneconomic nature of the NCAA's program of self-regulation. * * *

* * * The Court of Appeals, like the District Court, flatly refused to consider what it termed "noneconomic" justifications advanced by the NCAA in support of the television plan. It was of the view that our decision in National Society of Professional Engineers v. United States precludes reliance on noneconomic factors in assessing the reasonableness of the television plan. This view was mistaken, and I note that the Court does not in so many words repeat this error.

Professional Engineers did make clear that antitrust analysis usually turns on "competitive conditions" and "economic conceptions." Ordinarily, "the inquiry mandated by the Rule of Reason is whether the challenged agreement is one that promotes competition or one that suppresses competition." * * * Broadly read, these statements suggest that noneconomic values like the promotion of amateurism and fundamental educational objectives could not save the television plan from condemnation under the Sherman Act. But these statements were made in response to "public interest" justifications proffered in defense of a ban on competitive bidding imposed by practitioners engaged in standard, profit-motivated commercial activities. The primarily non-economic values pursued by educational institutions differ fundamentally from the "overriding commercial purpose of [the] day-to-day activities" of engineers, lawyers, doctors, and businessmen, and neither *Professional Engineers* nor any other decision of this Court suggests that associations of nonprofit educational institutions must defend their self-regulatory restraints solely in terms of their competitive impact, without regard for the legitimate noneconomic values they promote.

When these values are factored into the balance, the NCAA's television plan seems eminently reasonable. Most fundamentally, the plan fosters the goal of amateurism by spreading revenues among various schools and reducing the financial incentives toward professionalism. * * * The collateral consequences of the spreading of regional and national appearances among a number of schools are many: the television plan, like the ban on compensating student-athletes, may well encourage students to choose their schools, at least in part, on the basis of educational quality by reducing the perceived economic element of the choice * * * . These important contributions, I believe, are sufficient to offset any minimal anticompetitive effects of the television plan.

For all of these reasons, I would reverse the judgment of the Court of Appeals. * * *

NOTES AND QUESTIONS

1.   This was the first Supreme Court case in the modern period that explicitly applied a rule of reason analysis, yet found the practice violated § 1.

a.   Why was a rule of reason analysis required? What kinds of things did the NCAA do without which there almost certainly would have been no college football at all? Cf. Baum Research & Development Co. v. Hillerich & Bradsby Co., 31 F.Supp.2d 1016 (E.D.Mich.1998), upholding an NCAA rule permitting aluminum baseball bats; Gunter Harz Sports, Inc. v. U.S. Tennis Association, Inc., 665 F.2d 222 (8th Cir.1981), upholding an association standard defining the characteristics of a tennis racket.

b.   Did the Court believe a full rule of reason analysis was appropriate? What did it mean to convey when it quoted Professor Areeda in its footnote 39 as saying that "the rule of reason can sometimes be applied in the twinkling of an eye"? This reference has come to be the basis for a "quick look" rule of reason analysis of what courts consider relatively clear cases.

c.   In what sense were the NCAA rules anticompetitive? Can one argue that the rules limiting television appearances of Notre Dame, for example, made possible the survival of football at other schools? Why shouldn't a rule that increases the number of firms in the marketplace receive applause instead of criticism?

d.   How was the public hurt by the NCAA television contract? Was it clear that the agreement reduced the number of college football games on television and raised the prices paid for the right to present them? Do you agree with Justice White that the higher package price may have been a function of a larger and more targeted viewing audience for the package?

2.   What arguments did the NCAA present in defense of its plan? What kinds of arguments would you have made?

a.   Would it have been enough, for example, to say that the contract made more money for NCAA member schools? That it distributed revenues more broadly?

b.   Was the argument that the plan was needed to protect gate receipts one that was dead on arrival? Even though that was in fact the original basis of the plan, isn't it clear that firms may not conspire to prevent competition with their own services?

c.   How about the argument by analogy to *Broadcast Music*? Do you think that a single agent might have been needed to coordinate rights to the great number of possible games? Does the fact that in *Broadcast Music* the artists were free to license their own records end that argument?

3.   Was the argument for competitive balance a better one?

a.   Do you believe people will continue to watch games in which the winner is foreordained because certain teams have gotten richer and thus better? Will that in fact be a problem? Did people watch less golf when Tiger Woods was winning tournaments than when relative unknowns are contending for the lead?

b.   Were the Court's comments about the state of competitive balance in college football convincing? Is Justice Stevens right that the real question is whether the NCAA rules serve to equalize teams in particular conferences? Was it convincing to note that the television plan does not apply to any other sport and that basketball, for example, manages to stay competitively balanced without it?

c.   Was it convincing to note that the NCAA does not regulate what member schools do with other money they have or can raise from other sources such as tuition or donations? Would more comprehensive regulation have made the legality of the television plan a closer antitrust question? Would Justice Stevens likely have considered it an even more obvious violation?

4.   Was the Court too quick to reject the idea that the NCAA has little market power?

a.   Take a look at your television listings. College football competes on Saturday afternoons with auto racing, golf, the end of the professional baseball season, and ubiquitous poker tournaments, not to mention old movies, the Home Shopping Network and MTV. In that kind of competitive environment, what makes college football unique?

b.   How do advertisers decide what they will pay to put their message on a program? Do you suppose advertising managers for beer companies pay based on romantic images of their own college days? Is it more likely that the NCAA can charge no more than the advertisers will pay per head for the demographics of the audience that decide to watch the games? If so, how can the NCAA have market power?

5.   Should the Court have recognized an argument that the NCAA television contract dealt with what economists call "the tragedy of the commons"?

a.   The principle is that when everyone can exploit property held in common, it will be overused, as when owners of a common pool of oil each pump it out quickly so as to get as much as possible for themselves, or when competing fishing fleets together catch more fish than is sustainable environmentally.

b.   Might one argue that we should not want schools to sell all the college football games they can, as fast as they can? Should the law permit allocating rights to television exposure so that the NCAA can reduce the likelihood of overwhelming the public with college football and thus keep the asset popular longer?

6.   Should non-economic values have been relevant here? Does *Professional Engineers* properly make them irrelevant in rule of reason cases?

a.   The NCAA has a rule that schools may not pay their players more than room, board, tuition, and laundry money. A sought after player alleges this is anti-competitive. Is it? See McCormack v. NCAA, 845 F.2d 1338 (5th Cir.1988) (upholding the rule as reasonable to enhance public acceptance of the special "college football" product); Agnew v. NCAA, 683 F.3d 328 (7th Cir.2012) (rejecting objection to caps on scholarships each school may award).

b.   The NCAA has a rule that a player loses eligibility when he or she retains an agent to negotiate with professional teams. Is that rule anticompetitive? Does it reinforce relevant non-economic values? See Banks v. National Collegiate Athletic Ass'n, 977 F.2d 1081 (7th Cir.1992), cert. denied 508 U.S. 908 (1993) (dismissing a challenge to the prohibition).[49]

---

[49]   See, e.g., Gary R. Roberts, The NCAA, Antitrust and Consumer Welfare, 70 Tulane L.Rev. 2631 (1996); Richard E. McKenzie & E. Thomas Sullivan, Does the NCAA Exploit College Athletes? An Economics and Legal Reinterpretation, 22 Antitrust Bulletin 373 (1987). The issues are helpfully generalized as part of the broader problem of dealing with monopsony, i.e., monopoly

c.   The NCAA has promulgated a rule limiting the annual compensation of entry-level assistant coaches to $16,000. Can this rule survive a Sherman Act challenge? See Law v. National Collegiate Athletic Ass'n, 134 F.3d 1010 (10th Cir.), cert. denied 525 U.S. 822 (1998) (rejecting defenses of need to reduce athletic program deficits and preserve competitive equality).

d.   The NCAA has a rule that teams may participate in no more than two so-called "exempt tournaments" every four years. Sports promoters challenged the rules as reducing the number of marquee teams available for such tournaments? What result would you expect? See Worldwide Basketball & Sports Tours, Inc. v. NCAA, 388 F.3d 955 (6th Cir. 2004) (reversing injunction issued after "quick look;" full rule of reason analysis would be required to find the rule illegal).

A NOTE ON AGREEMENT IN THE AWARD
OF NEED-BLIND SCHOLARSHIPS

The *Professional Engineers* rejection of "public interest" factors to justify restraints on competition met the *NCAA* dissenters' view that higher education might be "noneconomic" in United States v. Brown University, 805 F.Supp. 288 (E.D.Pa.1992). M.I.T. and other "elite" colleges had formed an organization called the "Ivy Overlap Group." The Group met each year to establish the methodology by which to measure a student's need for financial aid. Issues considered included the influence on need of the fact that a family had more than one child in school, what to assume about a divorced parent's ability and obligation to provide support, and how much of a family's or student's own assets should be assumed to be available to meet educational expenses. Each school made its own calculation of each admitted student's need. For students admitted to more than one school in the group, the lists were compared and if the figures diverged, an agreed-upon need was determined and the schools agreed not to offer the student more aid than necessary to meet that need.

All schools other than M.I.T. consented to a judgment ordering them to discontinue the practice. M.I.T. argued, however, that what the schools had done was not improper and should not be illegal. Universities are not in "trade or commerce," it argued, and the program made it possible both to allocate scholarship funds more effectively and to permit more needy students to attend college. Competition was not reduced; students simply had to choose which Ivy League school to attend based on something other than price.

---

buyers of goods and services, in Roger D. Blair & Jeffrey L. Harrison, Antitrust Policy and Monopsony, 76 Cornell L.Rev. 297 (1991).

Judge Bechtle rejected M.I.T.'s contentions. The "trade or commerce" issue was clearly settled in *Goldfarb*, he reasoned. The "public service aspect" of an institution does not mean that it is beyond the reach of the antitrust laws. However, Judge Bechtle argued, *Goldfarb* also teaches that "non-business" defendants should not be subjected to "rigid, inflexible rules." Thus, the practices of the Ivy Overlap Group were to be evaluated under a rule of reason rather than a per se rule. In applying the rule of reason, the Court said, *Professional Engineers* teaches that the only inquiry may be whether the restraint "is one that promotes competition." More general arguments about the public-serving character of a practice were not to be considered. M.I.T.'s defense "that competition for students would lead to the erosion of need-blind admissions and need-based aid, 'confirms, rather than refutes the anticompetitive purpose and effect of its agreement.'" 805 F.Supp. at 304, citing *Professional Engineers*.

What do you think of Judge Bechtle's analysis? Under the cases, could he have come out any other way? The Court of Appeals thought the result by no means inevitable and reversed the District Court. United States v. Brown University, 5 F.3d 658 (3d Cir.1993). Judge Bechtle had merely taken a "quick look" approach to applying the rule of reason, the Court decided. He should have recognized that the defendants had not-for-profit status and thus were not motivated by commercial considerations. He should also have given more weight to the schools' argument that the agreement promoted socio-economic diversity among students and improved "consumer choice" for students who could not have gone to an Ivy League school without a scholarship.

The case never reached the Supreme Court, because in December 1993, the government reached a settlement with M.I.T. approving most of the challenged conduct, indeed requiring the participating schools to offer need-blind admissions. Do you think the settlement represented a wise exercise of prosecutorial discretion? Was it instead a major retreat from the teaching of *Professional Engineers* and *NCAA*?

Since 1994, the substance of the settlement has been acknowledged in a special exception to Sherman Act § 1 for the "award of need-based educational aid." The exception was renewed by Pub.L. 110–327, 122 Stat. 3566 (2008), but unless extended again, it expires in 2015.

THE SINGLE ENTITY ISSUE IN PROFESSIONAL SPORTS

Sports leagues have often argued that the league and all its teams make up a single entity and thus fall under the rule of Copperweld Corp. v. Independence Tube Corp., 467 U.S. 752, 104 S.Ct. 2731, 81 L.Ed.2d 628 (1984) (units of a single corporate organization cannot be guilty of conspiracy with other elements of the organization). While not always successful in the sports context, the argument has been better received than one might have expected.

In Chicago Professional Sports Limited Partnership v. National Basketball Association, 95 F.3d 593 (7th Cir. 1996), for example, the National Basketball Association had adopted a rule that no "Superstation", i.e., a local broadcast station carried around the country on cable systems, may carry more than 20 NBA games per season. Chicago's WGN is such a station and wanted to broadcast the Michael Jordan-led Chicago Bulls nationwide. Should the NBA rule fare better than the NCAA television plan? The Seventh Circuit, per Judge Easterbrook, said the argument that the NBA, like a company such as McDonalds, is a single enterprise that issues franchises instead of being an entity formed by otherwise independent teams was plausible enough that the claims required a full rule of reason analysis.

In Fraser v. Major League Soccer, 284 F.3d 47 (1st Cir. 2002), players challenged a plan under which they were all hired by the central league and assigned to the teams that made it up. Here, too, the court rejected the League's plea for automatic application of *Copperweld*, but it also rejected the players' characterization of the League as obviously a device to eliminate competition for players. At worst, Chief Judge Boudin wrote, the teams were joint venturers whose effort to consolidate some functions could be procompetitive and thus deserved rule of reason analysis.

The joint venture analysis became particularly important after the decision in Texaco, Inc. v. Dagher, 547 U.S. 1, 126 S.Ct. 1276, 164 L.Ed.2d 1 (2006), a non-sports case. Texaco and Shell are long-time competitors in the sale of gasoline. They formed a joint venture called Equilon as part of an FTC consent decree. Equilon refined crude oil in the western United States and sold gasoline at a single price to retail stations under the Texaco and Shell brands. Texaco and Shell then split the profits earned.

Dagher represented a class of station owners who said that it was per se illegal for Texaco and Shell to use a joint venture to avoid price competition in sales of their brands to retail stations. The Ninth Circuit used an ancillary restraints analysis and held that sale of refined gasoline at a common price were not ancillary to Equilon's refining activity.

The Supreme Court disagreed. Once they had created Equilon, Justice Thomas wrote for a unanimous Court, Texaco and Shell were no longer competitors; they were simply investors in Equilon, one of whose core activities was gasoline marketing. "[P]ricing decisions of a legitimate joint venture," the Court said, "do not fall within the narrow category or activity that is per se unlawful under § 1 of the Sherman Act."

Dagher set the stage for American Needle, Inc. v. National Football League, 560 U.S. 183, 130 S.Ct. 2201, 176 L.Ed.2d 947 (2010). *American*

Needle was a company that for 20 years had been one of several firms licensed by the NFL to make hats and other clothing bearing the logos of fans' favorite teams. But in 2000, the NFL made producers bid for the right to an exclusive contract to make such apparel. Reebok won the contract and American Needle sued, claiming that the 32 teams who make up the NFL were violating Sherman Act § 1 by collectively denying it licenses to use their trademarked logos.

The District Court and Seventh Circuit found that teams in the NFL have so "integrated their operations" that they should be deemed a single firm, not an association of competitors. The 32 football teams have value only because they compete in the NFL, the courts said. Thus, while in principle each team could license its own logo, nothing prevents them from acting collectively through the NFL to do so.

The Supreme Court, per Justice Stevens, unanimously reversed. "We have long held that concerted action under § 1 does not turn simply on whether the parties involved are legally distinct entities," the Court said. "[W]e have eschewed such formalistic distinctions in favor of a functional consideration of how the parties involved in the alleged anticompetitive conduct actually operate," citing cases such as *Topco*, *NCAA*, and *Goldfarb*. The key question, the Court said, is whether the alleged action "joins together separate decisionmakers" who are separate economic actors pursuing separate economic interests, such that the agreement deprives the marketplace of independent centers of decisionmaking with a diversity of entrepreneurial interests, citing both Fraser v. Major League Soccer and Rothery v. Atlas Van Lines.

NFL teams compete not only on the field, the Court wrote, but also "to attract fans, for gate receipts and for contracts with managerial and playing personnel." They "do not possess either the unitary decisionmaking quality or the single aggregation of economic power characteristic of independent action," and the financial performance of each team, while related to that of the others, does not necessarily rise and fall with that of the others. Team competition includes efforts to increase the value of their intellectual property. "To a firm making hats, the Saints and the Colts are two potentially competing suppliers of valuable trademarks." When teams license their intellectual property, they are acting as separate economic actors pursuing separate economic interests, and each team therefore is a potential independent cente[r] of decisionmaking. When the NFL licenses all teams' logos to only one manufacturer, it deprives the market of actual or potential competition and thus can violate § 1. Although NFL teams do have a common interest in promoting the NFL brand, "they are still separate, profit-maximizing entities, and their interests in licensing team trademarks are not necessarily aligned."

Do you agree with this analysis? Could the same be said for all professional sports leagues? Might enterprises like Major League Soccer and World Team Tennis, for example, that are still struggling to build fan interest be seen functionally as single entities whose teams do not have the independent status of those in the NFL or perhaps the National Basketball Association?[50]

THE LABOR EXEMPTION IN PROFESSIONAL SPORTS

One way that professional sports leagues achieve common ends that would otherwise raise antitrust issues is by taking advantage of Clayton Act § 6's principle that "The labor of a human being is not a commodity or article of commerce." Originally adopted to stop employers' use of the antitrust laws to enjoin unions and break strikes by low-paid laborers, the principle has been extended to permit agreements with often well-paid professional athletes that would otherwise raise antitrust issues. Cases from professional football have been most prominent.

Brown v. Pro Football, Inc., 518 U.S. 231, 116 S.Ct. 2116, 135 L.Ed.2d 521 (1996), involved National Football League teams who each created a "developmental squad" of players that had not made the active roster but continued to practice and might be called up if they were needed later in the season. The NFL Players' Association argued that such players should be free to negotiate salary and other contract terms with the teams, but team owners said each player should be paid $1000 per week. When negotiations over the issue reached an impasse, the owners collectively imposed the $1000 weekly salary. A group of individual players alleged this was a violation of Sherman Act § 1, but the Supreme Court rejected their claim. The Court concluded that where an issue could be the subject of collective bargaining, the "non-statutory" labor exemption prevented the imposition of liability. Any other result, the Court said, would let lawsuits interfere with the bargaining process. Justice Stevens dissented, arguing basically that a principle adopted to protect workers was being used here to protect management.

Clarett v. National Football League, 369 F.3d 124 (2d Cir. 2004), cert. denied 125 S.Ct. 1728 (2005), applied the *Brown* principle. Maurice Clarett had just completed his sophomore year in college when he applied to enter the NFL draft. A District Court held that the NFL rule prohibiting a team's signing a player who was less than three years out of high school violated Sherman Act § 1. The Second Circuit reversed, relying on the non-statutory labor exemption. Eligibility rules do not actually appear in the NFL's

---

[50]   See, e.g., Benjamin Klein, Single Entity Analysis of Joint Ventures After *American Needle*: An Economic Perspective, 78 Antitrust L.J. 669 (2013).

collective bargaining agreement, the court conceded, but they are part of the NFL by-laws referenced in that agreement. Relying on *Brown*, the Court held that union representatives, not federal judges, should determine who should be eligible to play professional football.

Do you agree with the results in these cases?[51] Are they too deferential to large, arguably-monopoly enterprises and unions, the impacts of whose decisions are felt nationwide?

2.   GROUP BOYCOTTS BY COMPETITORS

We have now seen cases from the first seven years after *GTE Sylvania*. We have seen the courts look more to the rule of reason, although noting that some cases are worth only a "quick look." At about this point in the story, related issues arose. Cases came up involving Section 1 challenges to what we have called "group boycotts." We now turn to those cases.

NORTHWEST WHOLESALE STATIONERS, INC. v. PACIFIC STATIONERY & PRINTING CO.

Supreme Court of the United States, 1985
472 U.S. 284, 105 S.Ct. 2613, 86 L.Ed.2d 202

JUSTICE BRENNAN delivered the opinion of the Court.

This case requires that we decide whether a per se violation of § 1 of the Sherman Act occurs when a cooperative buying agency comprising various retailers expels a member without providing any procedural means for challenging the expulsion. The case also raises broader questions as to when per se antitrust analysis is appropriately applied to joint activity that is susceptible of being characterized as a concerted refusal to deal.

I

* * * Petitioner Northwest Wholesale Stationers is a purchasing cooperative made up of approximately 100 office supply retailers in the Pacific Northwest States. The cooperative acts as the primary wholesaler for the retailers. Retailers that are not members of the cooperative can purchase wholesale supplies from Northwest at the same price as members. At the end of each year, however, Northwest distributes its profits to members in the form of a percentage rebate on purchases. Members therefore effectively purchase supplies at a price significantly lower than do nonmembers.[52] Northwest also provides certain warehousing

---

[51]   See generally, Thomas A. Piraino, Jr., A Proposal for the Antitrust Regulation of Professional Sports, 79 Boston U. L. Rev. 889 (1999); Gary R. Roberts, The Evolving Confusion of Professional Sports Antitrust, The Rule of Reason, and the Doctrine of Ancillary Restraints, 61 S. California L. Rev. 943 (1988); Stephen F. Ross, Monopoly Sports Leagues, 73 Minnesota L. Rev. 643 (1989).

[52]   Although this patronage rebate policy is a form of price discrimination, § 4 of the Robinson-Patman Act specifically sanctions such activity by cooperatives. * * * A relevant state-law provision provides analogous protection. [Court's fn. 2]

facilities. The cooperative arrangement thus permits the participating retailers to achieve economies of scale in purchasing and warehousing that would otherwise be unavailable to them. In fiscal 1978 Northwest had $5.8 million in sales.

Respondent Pacific Stationery & Printing Co. sells office supplies at both the retail and wholesale levels. Its total sales in fiscal 1978 were approximately $7.6 million; the record does not indicate what percentage of revenue is attributable to retail and what percentage is attributable to wholesale. Pacific became a member of Northwest in 1958. In 1974 Northwest amended its bylaws to prohibit members from engaging in both retail and wholesale operations. A grandfather clause preserved Pacific's membership rights. In 1977 ownership of a controlling share of the stock of Pacific changed hands, and the new owners did not officially bring this change to the attention of the directors of Northwest. This failure to notify apparently violated another of Northwest's bylaws.

In 1978 the membership of Northwest voted to expel Pacific. * * * No explanation for the expulsion was advanced at the time, and Pacific was given neither notice, a hearing, nor any other opportunity to challenge the decision. Pacific argues that the expulsion resulted from Pacific's decision to maintain a wholesale operation. Northwest contends that the expulsion resulted from Pacific's failure to notify the cooperative members of the change in stock ownership. * * * It is undisputed that Pacific received approximately $10,000 in rebates from Northwest in 1978, Pacific's last year of membership. Beyond a possible inference of loss from this fact, however, the record is devoid of allegations indicating the nature and extent of competitive injury the expulsion caused Pacific to suffer.

Pacific brought suit in 1980 * * * . The gravamen of the action was that Northwest's expulsion of Pacific from the cooperative without procedural protections was a group boycott that limited Pacific's ability to compete and should be considered per se violative of § 1. On cross-motions for summary judgment the District Court * * * held instead that rule-of-reason analysis should govern the case. Finding no anticompetitive effect on the basis of the record as presented, the court granted summary judgment for Northwest.

The Court of Appeals for the Ninth Circuit reversed, holding "that the uncontroverted facts of this case support a finding of per se liability." The court reasoned that the cooperative's expulsion of Pacific was an anticompetitive concerted refusal to deal with Pacific on equal footing, which would be a per se violation of § 1 in the absence of any specific legislative mandate for self-regulation sanctioning the expulsion. The court noted that § 4 of the Robinson-Patman Act specifically approves the price discrimination occasioned by such expulsion and concluded that § 4 therefore provided a mandate for self-regulation. Such a legislative mandate, according to the court, would ordinarily result in evaluation of the challenged practice under the rule of reason. But, drawing on Silver v. New York Stock Exchange, 373 U.S. 341 (1963), the court decided that rule-of-reason analysis was appropriate only on the condition that the cooperative had provided procedural safeguards sufficient to prevent arbitrary expulsion and to furnish a basis for judicial review. Because Northwest had not provided any procedural safeguards, the court held that the expulsion of Pacific was not shielded by Robinson-Patman immunity and therefore constituted a per se group boycott in violation of § 1 of the Sherman Act.

We granted certiorari to examine this * * * area of antitrust law that has not been free of confusion. We reverse.

II

The decision of the cooperative members to expel Pacific was certainly a restraint of trade in the sense that every commercial agreement restrains trade. Chicago Board of Trade v. United States. Whether this action violates § 1 of the Sherman Act depends on whether it is adjudged an unreasonable restraint. Rule-of-reason analysis guides the inquiry, unless the challenged action falls into the category of "agreements or practices which because of their pernicious effect on competition and lack of any redeeming virtue are conclusively presumed to be unreasonable and therefore illegal without elaborate inquiry as to the precise harm they have caused or the business excuse for their use." Northern Pacific R. Co. v. United States. * * *

This Court has long held that certain concerted refusals to deal or group boycotts are so likely to restrict competition without any offsetting efficiency gains that they should be condemned as per se violations of § 1 of the Sherman Act. The question presented in this case is whether Northwest's decision to expel Pacific should fall within this category of activity that is conclusively presumed to be anticompetitive. * * *

A

* * *

The Court in *Silver* framed the issue [before it] as follows:

"[W]hether the New York Stock Exchange is to be held liable to a nonmember broker-dealer under the antitrust laws or regarded as impliedly immune therefrom when, pursuant to rules the Exchange has adopted under the Securities Exchange Act of 1934, it orders a number of its members to remove private direct telephone wire connections previously in operation between their offices and those of the nonmember, without giving the nonmember notice, assigning him any reason for the action, or affording him an opportunity to be heard."

Because the New York Stock Exchange occupied such a dominant position in the securities trading markets that the boycott would devastate the nonmember, the Court concluded that the refusal to deal with the nonmember would amount to a per se violation of § 1 unless the Securities Exchange Act provided an immunity. The question for the Court thus was whether effectuation of the policies of the Securities Exchange Act required partial repeal of the Sherman Act insofar as it proscribed this aspect of exchange self-regulation.

Finding exchange self-regulation—including the power to expel members and limit dealings with nonmembers—to be an essential policy of the Securities Exchange Act, the Court held that the Sherman Act should be construed as having been partially repealed to permit the type of exchange activity at issue. But the interpretive maxim disfavoring repeals by implication led the Court to narrow permissible self-policing to situations in which adequate procedural safeguards had been provided. * * * Thus it was the specific need to accommodate the important national policy of promoting effective exchange self-regulation, tempered by the principle that the Sherman Act should be narrowed only to the extent necessary to effectuate that policy, that dictated the result in *Silver*.

Section 4 of the Robinson-Patman Act is not comparable to the self-policing provisions of the Securities Exchange Act. That section is no more than a narrow immunity from the price discrimination prohibitions of the Robinson-Patman Act itself. * * *

* * * If the challenged concerted activity of Northwest's members would amount to a per se violation of § 1 of the Sherman Act, no amount of procedural protection would save it. If the challenged action would not amount to a violation of § 1, no lack of procedural protections would convert it into a per se violation because the antitrust laws do not themselves impose on joint ventures a requirement of process.

B

This case therefore turns not on the lack of procedural protections but on whether the decision to expel Pacific is properly viewed as a group boycott or concerted refusal to deal mandating per se invalidation. "Group boycotts" are often listed among the classes of economic activity that merit per se invalidation under § 1. Exactly what types of activity fall within the forbidden category is, however, far from certain. * * *

Cases to which this Court has applied the per se approach have generally involved joint efforts by a firm or firms to disadvantage competitors by "either directly denying or persuading or coercing suppliers or customers to deny relationships the competitors need in the competitive struggle." In these cases, the boycott often cut off access to a supply, facility, or market necessary to enable the boycotted firm to compete, and frequently the boycotting firms possessed a dominant position in the relevant market. In addition, the practices were generally not justified by plausible arguments that they were intended to enhance overall efficiency and make markets more competitive. Under such circumstances the likelihood of anticompetitive effects is clear and the possibility of countervailing procompetitive effects is remote.

Although a concerted refusal to deal need not necessarily possess all of these traits to merit per se treatment, not every cooperative activity involving a restraint or exclusion will share with the per se forbidden boycotts the likelihood of predominantly anticompetitive consequences. For example, we recognized last Term in National Collegiate Athletic Assn. v. Board of Regents of University of Oklahoma that per se treatment of the NCAA's restrictions on the marketing of televised college football was inappropriate—despite the obvious restraint on output—because the "case involves an industry in which horizontal restraints on competition are essential if the product is to be available at all."

Wholesale purchasing cooperatives such as Northwest are not a form of concerted activity characteristically likely to result in predominantly anticompetitive effects. Rather, such cooperative arrangements would seem to be "designed to increase economic efficiency and render markets more, rather than less, competitive." Broadcast Music, Inc. v. Columbia Broadcasting System, Inc. The arrangement permits the participating retailers to achieve economies of scale in both the purchase and warehousing of wholesale supplies, and also ensures ready access to a stock of goods that might otherwise be unavailable on short notice. * * *

Pacific, of course, does not object to the existence of the cooperative arrangement, but rather raises an antitrust challenge to Northwest's decision to bar Pacific from continued membership.[53] It is therefore the action of expulsion that must be evaluated to determine whether per se treatment is appropriate. The act of expulsion from a wholesale cooperative does not necessarily imply anticompetitive animus and thereby raise a probability of anticompetitive effect. Wholesale purchasing cooperatives must establish and enforce reasonable rules in order to function effectively. Disclosure rules, such as the one on which Northwest relies, may well provide the cooperative with a needed means for monitoring the creditworthiness of its members. Nor would the expulsion characteristically be likely to result in predominantly anticompetitive effects, at least in the type of situation this case presents. Unless the cooperative possesses market power or exclusive access to an element essential to effective competition, the conclusion that expulsion is virtually

---

[53] Because Pacific has not been wholly excluded from access to Northwest's wholesale operations, * * * [t]o be precise, Northwest's activity is a concerted refusal to deal with Pacific on substantially equal terms. Such activity might justify per se invalidation if it placed a competing firm at a severe competitive disadvantage. See generally Brodley, Joint Ventures and Antitrust Policy, 95 Harvard L.Rev. 1521, 1532 (1982) * * * . [Court's fn. 6]

always likely to have an anticompetitive effect is not warranted. Absent such a showing with respect to a cooperative buying arrangement, courts should apply a rule-of-reason analysis. At no time has Pacific made a threshold showing that these structural characteristics are present in this case.

* * * A plaintiff seeking application of the per se rule must present a threshold case that the challenged activity falls into a category likely to have predominantly anticompetitive effects. The mere allegation of a concerted refusal to deal does not suffice because not all concerted refusals to deal are predominantly anticompetitive. When the plaintiff challenges expulsion from a joint buying cooperative, some showing must be made that the cooperative possesses market power or unique access to a business element necessary for effective competition. Focusing on the argument that the lack of procedural safeguards required per se liability, Pacific did not allege any such facts. Because the Court of Appeals applied an erroneous per se analysis in this case, the court never evaluated the District Court's rule-of-reason analysis rejecting Pacific's claim. A remand is therefore appropriate for the limited purpose of permitting appellate review of that determination.

III

"The per se rule is a valid and useful tool of antitrust policy and enforcement." Broadcast Music, Inc. v. Columbia Broadcasting System, Inc. It does not denigrate the per se approach to suggest care in application. In this case, the Court of Appeals failed to exercise the requisite care and applied per se analysis inappropriately. The judgment of the Court of Appeals is therefore reversed, and the case is remanded for further proceedings consistent with this opinion.

JUSTICE MARSHALL and JUSTICE POWELL took no part in the decision of this case.

NOTES AND QUESTIONS

1. What made this case appropriate for rule of reason analysis? Is the rule Justice Brennan offers—something is per se illegal when "the likelihood of anticompetitive effects is clear and the possibility of countervailing procompetitive effects is remote"—useful for antitrust cases in general?

2. Do you agree—at least on the record we have in this case—that this boycott did not seem to fit Justice Brennan's three more specific tests for per se treatment?

a. Was it clear that this cooperative arrangement was not an essential facility? At what point does a facility go from being essential to merely advantageous? See, e.g., Full Draw Productions v. Easton Sports, Inc., 182 F.3d 745 (10th Cir. 1999) (archery firms' participation in different trade show with intent to destroy plaintiff's show stated claim of group boycott); Rossi v.

Standard Roofing, Inc., 156 F.3d 452 (3d Cir. 1998) (competitors' conspiracy to limit low-price plaintiff's access to supplies made per se analysis of boycott appropriate).

b.   Do you agree that Pacific's competitors lacked market power? Does the fact that each was small inevitably mean that, when joined in this cooperative, they lacked power? Cf. Toys "R" Us, Inc. v. Federal Trade Commission, 221 F.3d 928 (7th Cir. 2000) (large purchaser alleged to have coordinated conspiracy of toy manufacturers not to sell to warehouse clubs).

c.   Was there a plausible pro-competitive justification for the termination of Pacific? Were you persuaded that there was a need to verify creditworthiness or other business justification for the requirement of a notice of change of ownership?

3.   Was the Court right not to make the case turn on process issues? Would a requirement of due process add significantly to the costs of association operation? Might litigation over adequacy of the hearing replace the merits of the termination as the subject of antitrust litigation?

A NOTE ON THE CONCEPT OF MARKET POWER

A term implicit in many of the earlier cases and explicit in many later ones is "market power." It will be of great importance in monopolization and merger cases, and in cases involving tying and exclusive dealing. What is clear in *N.W. Wholesale Stationers* and other cases is that it can be relevant in Sherman Act § 1 cases involving alleged horizontal restraints as well.

For such an important concept, the lack of a simple and agreed definition may seem troubling. Professors Areeda and Turner defined market power as the "ability to raise price without a total loss of sales,"[54] but when you think about it, that simply describes the very common circumstance in which a firm faces a somewhat downward sloping demand curve. Surely it should not be significant for antitrust purposes that a convenience store can get away with charging more for late-night snack items than local grocery stores regularly charge.

Professors Landes and Posner added more nuance when they defined market power as "the ability of a firm (or a group of firms acting jointly) to raise price above the competitive level without losing so many sales so rapidly that the price increase is unprofitable and must be rescinded."[55]

---

[54]   2 Philip Areeda & Donald Turner, Antitrust Law 322 (1978).

[55]   William M. Landes & Richard A. Posner, Market Power in Antitrust Cases, 94 Harvard L.Rev. 937 (1981). The article is the subject of Landes and Posner on Market Power: Four Responses (by Richard Schmalensee, Louis Kaplow, Timothy J. Brennan, and Janusz Ordover, Alan Sykes and Robert Willig), 95 Harvard L.Rev. 1787 (1982).

Their definition acknowledges that lots of firms have this power, at least for some period of time, but once again, the definition encompasses more firms than we would normally want to treat as antitrust miscreants.

The point of both definitions, however, is that "market power" can be something well short of "monopoly power." Monopolists have, by definition, a high degree of market power, but acts of firms with less than a monopoly of a market may be seen as at least capable of competitive harm.[56]

Watch for the concept of market power—or references to its absence—in the cases that follow in this chapter;[57] see if you can tell when it is a useful analytic concept and when it is largely a rhetorical device to justify a given result.

Much of the important work of interpreting and applying prevailing antitrust doctrine, of course, is the work of the lower courts. We next look at such a case. At the same time, we get both a sense of how antitrust might have been influenced if the vote on Judge Bork's nomination to the Supreme Court had come out the other way, and an insight into how Justice Ginsburg looked at such issues when she was on the Court of Appeals.

ROTHERY STORAGE & VAN CO. V. ATLAS VAN LINES, INC.

United States Court of Appeals, District of Columbia Circuit, 1986
792 F.2d 210

Before WALD, GINSBURG and BORK, CIRCUIT JUDGES.

BORK, CIRCUIT JUDGE:

Appellants, plaintiffs below, seek review of the district court's decision dismissing their antitrust action against Atlas Van Lines, Inc. ("Atlas"). Appellants are five present and three former agents of Atlas. For convenience, we will frequently refer to them by the name * * * ("Rothery"). Rothery claims that Atlas and several of the carrier agents affiliated with Atlas adopted a policy constituting a "group boycott" in violation of section 1 of the Sherman Act. * * * The trial court granted Atlas' motion for summary judgment on several alternative grounds. Because we find that

---

[56] See generally, Mark R. Patterson, The Market Power Requirement in Antitrust Rule of Reason Cases: A Rhetorical History, 37 San Diego L.Rev. 1 (2000); George A. Hay, Market Power in Antitrust, 60 Antitrust L.J. 807 (1992); Thomas G. Krattenmaker, Robert H. Lande & Steven C. Salop, Monopoly Power and Market Power in Antitrust Law, 76 Georgetown L.J. 241 (1987).

[57] Important cases to watch for include Aspen Skiing Co. v. Aspen Highlands Skiing Corp., 472 U.S. 585, 105 S.Ct. 2847, 86 L.Ed.2d 467 (1985) (monopolization); Jefferson Parish Hospital Dist. No. 2 v. Hyde, 466 U.S. 2, 104 S.Ct. 1551, 80 L.Ed.2d 2 (1984), and Eastman Kodak Company v. Image Technical Services, Inc., 504 U.S. 451, 112 S.Ct. 2072, 119 L.Ed.2d 265 (1992) (tying). The concept is also central to the Merger Guidelines issued by the Justice Department and the Federal Trade Commission and found in Part D of this chapter.

Atlas' policy is designed to make the van line more efficient rather than to decrease the output of its services and raise rates, we affirm.

I

Atlas operates as a nationwide common carrier of used household goods under authority granted by the Interstate Commerce Commission. * * * Like most national moving companies, Atlas exercises its interstate authority by employing independent moving companies throughout the country as its agents. These companies execute a standard agency contract with Atlas, agreeing to adhere, when making shipments on Atlas' authority, to such things as standard operating procedures, maintenance and painting specifications, and uniform rates. Typically, such an agreement will contain a provision barring an agent affiliated with a particular van line from dealing with any other line. The agency agreement is supplemented by Atlas' bylaws, rules, and regulations governing the agent's interstate operations.

Some of these independent moving companies, the "non-carrier agents," have no interstate authority of their own and can move goods interstate only on Atlas' authority. Until recently, other companies, the "carrier agents," possessed their own interstate authority and could move goods to the extent of that independent authority as principals for their own accounts. Both types of agent may engage in intrastate carriage without Atlas' permission or governance. A carrier agent, however, could act in interstate commerce both as an agent of the van line it serves and as a competitor of that van line. The carrier agents could, and some did, use Atlas equipment, training, and the like for interstate carriage under their own authorities and pay Atlas nothing.

A van line and its agents constitute an enterprise on a scale not easily obtainable by a single carrier. Atlas, which is the sixth largest van line in the nation, provides a network of 490 agents capable of carrying household goods between any two points in the nation. Atlas coordinates and supports the agents' operations. The use of agents spares a van line the necessity of obtaining enormous amounts of capital to perform the same services and, quite possibly, avoids diseconomies of scale, i.e., the inefficiencies of a single management large and complex enough to perform all the functions that are now divided between the van line and its agents. The agents find customers and do the packing, loading, hauling, and storage. Atlas sets the rates, dispatches shipments, chooses routes, arranges backhauls so the agent's truck need not return empty, arranges services at the origin and destination of shipments, collects all revenues and pays the agents, establishes uniform rules for the appearance and quality of equipment, trains salespeople and drivers, purchases and finances equipment for use by the agents, and maintains insurance on all shipments made under Atlas' authority. In addition, Atlas conducts national advertising and promotional forums. With the assistance of agents, it handles customer claims. In short, Atlas, and its agents make up an enterprise or firm integrated by contracts, one which is indistinguishable in economic analysis from a complex partnership.

* * *

The deregulation of the moving industry, beginning in 1979, produced changes that had a profound impact on the relationship between van lines and their agents. Prior to the regulatory changes, independent moving companies had little ability to obtain their own interstate transportation authority. * * * In 1981, * * * the ICC repealed its requirement that carrier agents charge the same rate for agency shipments and shipments carried on their own accounts. Thus, agents could obtain interstate authority and could cut prices to attract business for their own accounts that otherwise might have constituted agency shipments for the van line's account.

This increased potential for the diversion of interstate business to its carrier agents posed two potential problems for Atlas. Each of these problems is a version of what has been called the "free ride." A free ride occurs when one party to an arrangement reaps benefits for which another party pays, though that transfer of wealth is not part of the agreement between them. The free ride can become a serious problem for a partnership or joint venture because the party that provides capital and services without receiving compensation has a strong incentive to provide less, thus rendering the common enterprise less effective. The first problem occurs because, by statute, a van line incurs strict liability for acts of its agents exercising "actual or apparent authority." Thus, an increase of shipments made on the agents' independent authority, but using Atlas' equipment, uniforms, and services would create the risk of increased liability for Atlas although Atlas received no revenue from those shipments. Second, because carrier agents could utilize Atlas services and equipment on non-Atlas interstate shipments, the possible increase of such shipments meant that Atlas might make large outlays for which it received no return. We return to the free-ride problem in Part IV of this opinion.

To meet these problems, Atlas could have amended its pooling agreement to redefine the terms on which it allowed its carrier agents to compete with the principal company. Had Atlas chosen this course and obtained ICC approval of its amended pooling agreement, the new agreement would have enjoyed antitrust immunity * * *. Instead, on February 11, 1982, Atlas announced that it would exercise its statutory right to cancel its pooling agreement and would terminate the agency contract of any affiliated company that persisted in handling interstate carriage on its own account as well as for Atlas. Under the new policy, any carrier agent already affiliated with Atlas could continue to exercise independent interstate authority only by transferring its independent interstate authority to a separate corporation with a new name. These new entities could not use the facilities or services of Atlas or any of its affiliates.

II

Because Atlas and its affiliates refuse to deal with any carrier agent that does not comply, several Atlas carrier agents, appellants here, charged that Atlas' new policy constitutes a "group boycott." They filed this action, and after the completion of discovery on the issue of liability, both sides filed cross motions for summary judgment.

The district court granted summary judgment to Atlas * * * .

* * *

* * * [W]e uphold the trial judge's conclusion that Atlas' new policy does not offend the antitrust laws. The challenged restraint is ancillary to the economic integration of Atlas and its agents so that the rule of per se illegality does not apply. Neither are the other tests of the rule of reason offended since Atlas' market share is far too small for the restraint to threaten competition or to have been intended to do so. * * *

III

* * *

B

Since the restraint on competition within the Atlas system involves an agreement not to deal with those who do not comply with Atlas' policy, and so may be characterized as a boycott, or a concerted refusal to deal, Rothery contends that Supreme Court decisions require a holding of per se illegality. It cannot be denied that the Court has often enunciated that broad proposition. * * *

Despite the seeming inflexibility of the rule as enunciated by the Court, it has always been clear that boycotts are not, and cannot ever be, per se illegal. To apply so rigid and simplistic an approach would be to destroy many common and entirely beneficial business arrangements. As one commentator put it, "[a]ll agreements to deal on specified terms mean refusal to deal on other terms," and the literal application of per se illegality to any situation involving a concerted refusal to deal would mean in practical effect "that every restraint is illegal." See Rahl, Per Se Rules and Boycotts Under the Sherman Act: Some Reflections and the Klor's Case, 45 Virginia L. Rev. 1165, 1172 (1959). For that reason, "any comprehensible per se rule for [group] boycotts * * * is out of the question."[58]

---

[58] The truth of this may be easily demonstrated. When a law firm refuses to hire an applicant there is a concerted refusal to deal since the lawyers in the firm are separate legal entities and capable of practicing law independently. It is also a boycott if the Ivy League refuses to admit a new college to membership or the American League refuses to admit a baseball team. It is no less

The Supreme Court has now made explicit what had always been understood. In Northwest Wholesale Stationers, Inc. v. Pacific Stationery & Printing Co., the plaintiff, a stationer, challenged as per se illegal its expulsion from a wholesale purchasing cooperative for violating the group's bylaws. The Court said that "not all concerted refusals to deal should be accorded per se treatment." * * *

IV

Appellants contend, however, that Atlas' restraints include horizontal price maintenance since the agents must ship on rates established by Atlas. We take this to be a claim that the horizontal elimination of competition within the system is illegal per se or, failing that, is nevertheless unlawful under a rule-of-reason analysis.

Before turning to the case law, we analyze the economic nature and effects of the system Atlas has created. It will be seen to be a system of a very familiar type, one commonly used in many fields of commercial endeavor.

Atlas has required that any moving company doing business as its agent must not conduct independent interstate carrier operations. Thus, a carrier agent, in order to continue as an Atlas agent, must either abandon its independent interstate authority and operate only under Atlas' authority or create a new corporation (a "carrier affiliate") to conduct interstate carriage separate from its operation as an Atlas agent. Atlas' agents may deal only with Atlas or other Atlas agents.

The result of this is an interstate system for the carriage of household goods in which legally separate companies integrate their activities by contract. In this way the participants achieve many of the same benefits or efficiencies that would be available if they were integrated through ownership by Atlas. * * * [T]he system is a contract integration, one identical, in economic terms, to a partnership formed by agreement. Analysis might begin and end with the observation that Atlas and its agents command between 5.1 and 6% of the relevant market, which is the interstate carriage of used household goods.[59] It is impossible to believe

---

a boycott if any of these groups refuses to deal because the applicant's grades are too low, or its football program has standards unacceptable to the Ivy League, or the would-be baseball franchise is currently a slow-pitch softball team in an industrial league. A ruling that concerted refusals to deal are per se illegal would mean that Atlas not only must retain carrier agents that compete with it but must admit as an agent any trucker who applied regardless of the need for an additional agent, the trucker's financial condition, its safety record, or its ability to serve customers. That is what a per se rule means: No group may impose a standard of any kind as a condition of dealing. That nonsensical requirement would destroy all of the groups concerned or force them into one ownership in order to claim the immunity of the *Copperweld* rule. [Court's fn. 1]

[59]   The interstate household goods industry consists of 1100 to 1300 interstate carriers, of which the 15 largest constitute 70% of the market. These carriers employ roughly 8,000 agents. Based on data compiled for 1981, Atlas was the sixth largest interstate carrier, with a 5.86% market share. The market share tapered gradually, from the largest firm's 13.3% share to Atlas' position, after which shares dropped precipitously to 3.19% and 1.99% for the seventh and eighth

that an agreement to eliminate competition within a group of that size can produce any of the evils of monopoly. A monopolist (or those acting together to achieve monopoly results) enhances its revenues by raising the market price. It can do that only if its share of the market is so large that by reducing its output of goods or services the amount offered by the industry is substantially reduced so that the price is bid up. If a group of Atlas' size reduced its output of services, there would be no effect upon market price because firms making up the other 94% of the market would simply take over the abandoned business. The only effect would be a loss of revenues to Atlas. Indeed, so impotent to raise prices is a firm with a market share of 5 or 6% that any attempt by it to engage in a monopolistic restriction of output would be little short of suicidal.

* * *

We might well rest, therefore, upon the absence of market power as demonstrated both by Atlas' 6% national market share and by the structure of the market. If it is clear that Atlas and its agents by eliminating competition among themselves are not attempting to restrict industry output, then their agreement must be designed to make the conduct of their business more effective. No third possibility suggests itself. But we need not rely entirely upon that inference because the record made in the district court demonstrates that the challenged agreement enhances the efficiency of the van line. The chief efficiency, as already noted, is the elimination of the problem of the free ride.

A carrier agent can attract customers because of Atlas' "national image" and can use Atlas' equipment and order forms when undertaking carriage for its own account. The carrier agents "benefit from use of the services of moving and storage firms affiliated with Atlas, for origin or destination work at remote locations, when operating independently of Atlas." * * * To the degree that a carrier agent uses Atlas' reputation, equipment, facilities, and services in conducting business for its own profit, the agent enjoys a free ride at Atlas' expense. The problem is that the van line's incentive to spend for reputation, equipment, facilities, and services declines as it receives less of the benefit from them. That produces a deterioration of the system's efficiency because the things consumers desire are not provided in the amounts they are willing to pay for. In the extreme case, the system as a whole could collapse.

* * *

* * * Rothery suggests free riding does not occur, and that the district court erred in concluding that it did. That argument, however, cannot withstand scrutiny, for Rothery has conceded that the carrier agents

---

largest firms. Thus, the market cannot be said to be heavily concentrated and Atlas is by no means a dominant force in the market. [Court's fn. 3]

associated with Atlas do derive significant benefits from Atlas in dealing with customers for their own profit. We find the district court's conclusion that free riding existed to be amply supported and by no means clearly erroneous.

A few examples will suffice. Plaintiff-appellants conceded below that the carrier agents "benefited" from their association with Atlas' "national image." We cannot rationally infer that this consumer identification advantage did not benefit the carrier agents in operating on their own accounts while using Atlas equipment and personnel trained by Atlas. Rothery also allowed that, while the carrier agents bore the bulk of costs associated with their operations, Atlas did make "some small contributions" to the group advertising programs and "some contributions" to the painting of trucks on which the Atlas logo appeared.

Rothery also credited Atlas with providing a dispatching service, a clearinghouse service for the settlement of accounts among its affiliates, assistance in settling claims among affiliates, certain written forms, sales meetings to provide exposure to national customers, driver and employee training programs, and the screening of the quality and reliability of affiliated firms that provided origin and destination services for the carrier agents.

* * *

If the carrier agents could persist in competing with Atlas while deriving the advantages of their Atlas affiliation, Atlas might well have found it desirable, or even essential, to decrease or abandon many such services. See Continental T.V., Inc. v. GTE Sylvania Inc. ("Because of market imperfections such as the so-called 'free rider' effect, [certain] services might not be provided * * * in a purely competitive situation * * * "). Of that tendency there can be no doubt. When a person or business providing goods or services begins to receive declining revenues, then, other things being equal, that person or firm will provide fewer goods or services. As marginal revenue drops, so does output. Thus, when Atlas' centralized services, equipment, and national image amount to a subsidy of competing carrier agents, this cuts down the marginal revenue derived from the provision of such things so that less will be offered than the market would reward.

On the other side, the firm receiving a subsidized good or service will take more of it. As cost declines, then, other things being equal, demand increases. Carrier agents, that is, will increase the use of Atlas' services, etc., on interstate carriage for their own accounts, over-consuming that which they can obtain at less than its true cost. In this way, free riding distorts the economic signals within the system so that the van line loses effectiveness in serving consumers. The restraint at issue in this case, therefore, is a classic attempt to counter the perceived menace that free riding poses. By compelling carrier agents to transfer their interstate authority to a separate entity, Atlas can continue providing services at optimal levels, confident that it will be paid for those services.

The Atlas agreements thus produce none of the evils of monopoly but enhance consumer welfare by creating efficiency. There seems no reason in the rationale of the Sherman Act, or in any comprehensible policy, to invalidate such agreements. Nevertheless, at one, intermediate, point in the history of antitrust, Supreme Court decisions seemed to require just that result. It seems clear, however, that the law has returned to the original understanding so that the agreements before us are plainly lawful. * * *

* * *

V

* * *

If *Topco* and *Sealy*, rather than *Addyston Pipe & Steel*, state the law of horizontal restraints, the restraints imposed by Atlas would appear to be a per se violation of the Sherman Act. An examination of more recent Supreme Court decisions, however, demonstrates that, to the extent that *Topco* and *Sealy* stand for the proposition that all horizontal restraints are illegal per se, they must be regarded as effectively overruled.

* * *

BMI, *NCAA*, and *Pacific Stationery* dictate the result in this case. All horizontal restraints are alike in that they eliminate some degree of rivalry between persons or firms who are actual or potential competitors. This similarity means that the rules applicable to all horizontal restraints should be the same. At one time, as we have seen, the Supreme Court stated in *Topco* and *Sealy* that the rule for all horizontal restraints was one of per se illegality. The difficulty was that such a rule could not be enforced consistently because it would have meant the outlawing of very normal agreements (such as that of law partners not to practice law outside the firm) that obviously contributed to economic efficiency. The alternative formulation was that of Judge Taft in *Addyston Pipe & Steel*: a naked horizontal restraint, one that does not accompany a contract integration, can have no purpose other than restricting output and raising prices, and so is illegal per se; an ancillary horizontal restraint, one that is part of an integration of the economic activities of the parties and appears capable of enhancing the group's efficiency, is to be judged according to its purpose and effect. In *BMI*, *NCAA*, and *Pacific Stationery*, the Supreme Court returned the law to the formulation of *Addyston Pipe & Steel* and thus effectively overruled *Topco* and *Sealy* as to the per se illegality of all horizontal restraints.

The application of these principles to Atlas' restraints is obvious because * * * these restraints are ancillary to the contract integration of joint venture that constitutes the Atlas van line. The restraints preserve the efficiencies of the nationwide van line by eliminating the problem of the free ride. There is, on the other hand, no possibility that the restraints can suppress market competition and so decrease output. * * * If Atlas should reduce its output, it would merely shrink in size without having any impact upon market price. Under the rule of *Addyston Pipe & Steel*, *BMI*, *NCAA*, and *Pacific Stationery*, therefore, it follows that the Atlas agreements do not violate section 1 of the Sherman Act.

A joint venture made more efficient by ancillary restraints, is a fusion of the productive capacities of the members of the venture. That, in economic terms, is the same thing as a corporate merger. * * * If Atlas bought the stock of all its carrier agents, the merger would not even be challenged under the Department of Justice Merger Guidelines because of inferences drawn from Atlas' market share and the structure of the market. We can think of no good reason not to apply the same inferences to Atlas' ancillary restraints.

The judgment of the district court is affirmed.

WALD, CIRCUIT JUDGE, concurring:

I concur in the result and in much of the reasoning of the panel's opinion. I write separately, however, to point out several concerns that I have about the panel's analysis once it establishes that no per se violation existed and the restraint should be looked at under the rule of reason. I believe that the District Court correctly undertook, in the traditional way, to "carefully balance" the "anticompetitive evils of the challenged practice * * * against its procompetitive virtues." * * *

The panel concludes that no balancing was required here since a defendant lacking significant market power cannot act anticompetitively by reducing output and increasing prices. If, as the panel assumes, the only legitimate purpose of the antitrust laws is this concern with the potential for decrease in output and rise in prices, reliance on market power alone might be appropriate. But, I do not believe that the debate over the purposes of antitrust laws has been settled yet. Until the Supreme Court provides more definitive instruction in this regard, I think it premature to construct an antitrust test that ignores all other potential concerns of the antitrust laws except for restriction of output and price raising.

* * *

* * * I think it more prudent to proceed with a pragmatic, albeit nonarithmetic and even untidy rule of reason analysis, than to adopt a market power test as the exclusive filtering-out device for all potential violators who do not command a significant market share. Under any

analysis, market power is an important consideration; I am not yet willing to say it is the only one.

NOTES AND QUESTIONS

1.   Does Judge Bork deny that one could characterize this as a group boycott? May every refusal to deal involving more than one firm be so characterized? Do you agree with Judge Bork that such an approach to group conduct is incoherent, i.e., that every decision by a partnership not to hire could be characterized as a boycott?

2.   Was Atlas' action here suspect under the standards used in *Northwest Wholesale Stationers*?

a.   Was membership in the Atlas organization necessary to allow Rothery to operate, for example?

b.   Were the agents in the Atlas organization dominant in the marketplace? Were they mostly small firms themselves? Was Atlas' mere 6% market share conclusive on the question of market power?

3.   Were you convinced by Judge Bork that disciplining firms such as Rothery was important to Atlas' efficient operation?

a.   Why are free riders such a problem for national organizations with local agents? Do the agents have an incentive to "shirk" on their responsibilities to the parent firm?

b.   Are you convinced that even if this case had come out differently, Atlas could not have protected itself? Might it have charged the agents for training and other services to discourage overconsumption of them, for example?

4.   Were Atlas' rules best understood as ancillary restraints designed to make possible the integration of economic activity?

a.   Do you agree that *Topco* has effectively been overruled and that *Addyston Pipe* now is the law? Keep that question in mind when you read Palmer v. BRG, infra.

b.   Was Atlas a joint venture that probably should have been analyzed under § 7, not § 1? Would calling Atlas a joint venture in fact advance the analysis at all?

5.   What troubled Judge Wald about Judge Bork's opinion? Did it trouble you?

a.   Was "efficiency" the standard used in Mitchel v. Reynolds? Was Atlas *required* to use these restrictive clauses to get truckers to go into the moving business?

b.   Once one goes beyond "furthering competition" as a justification for an ancillary restraint is he or she into Judge Taft's "sea of doubt"? Can almost any case have an "efficiency" spin placed on the facts? Indeed, can one presuppose that Atlas would not have undertaken the action if it would not have achieved *some* kind of efficiency?

6.   Notice that Atlas could have sought ICC approval for its method of dealing with its agents. Such approval would have given it an express exemption from antitrust liability. Would the ICC have been a preferable forum for evaluating the Atlas program than this Court was? Is it important instead for firms to have access to the kind of "self-help" remedy that Atlas here employed?

A NOTE ON BOYCOTTS AND STANDARDS SETTING

Many boycott cases involve alleged noncompliance with professional or industry standards. A question implicit in those cases is how the standards came to be as they are. A note in the last chapter discussed *Radiant Burners* (1961). There, a cause of action was found stated against an organization that had found the plaintiff's new gas appliance was too dangerous to be marketed. The case illustrated the inherent tension between an antitrust concern about rules that arbitrarily exclude new firms from a market and the work of private groups genuinely trying to assure that potentially dangerous appliances do not leak or explode.

Three years after *Northwest Wholesale Stationers*, the Court revisited such issues in Allied Tube & Conduit Corp. v. Indian Head, Inc., 486 U.S. 492, 108 S.Ct. 1931, 100 L.Ed.2d 497 (1988). The parties were all members of the National Fire Protection Association (NFPA), an organization that establishes electrical code requirements for adoption (usually by cities) in building codes. The plaintiffs made polyvinyl chloride (PVC) pipe while the defendants made the steel conduit that has long been used to carry electric wires throughout a building.

The plaintiffs came to the NFPA annual meeting with a proposal to add PVC pipe to the approved building code's list of types of conduit that could carry electric wire safely. The defendants had anticipated the proposal, however, and had signed up a large number of new NFPA members to bring to the meeting. The proposed change was considered in plenary session and was voted down. As a result, plaintiffs alleged, their potential customers were unable to use PVC products in buildings built under the NFPA-approved code.

The District Court ruled that the defendants' actions were consistent with the *Noerr-Pennington* doctrine because the NFPA's code was effective only when adopted by a city, county or other governmental entity. But the Court of Appeals held that *Noerr-Pennington* did not apply and the Supreme Court agreed. A "quasi-legislative" body like the NFPA is not the same as a state legislature or city council, the Court held. Legislative action may be sought even if it would clearly be anticompetitive, but this self-protective action could only be justified if it did not otherwise violate the antitrust laws. Interference with the process of establishing impartial safety standards, the Court held, constituted a violation of Sherman Act § 1.[60]

Justices White and O'Connor dissented, expressing concern that private standards setting—in their view an important phenomenon—was likely to become so risky that groups would avoid engaging in it.

Do you share the dissenters' concern?[61] How serious is the public harm likely to be that standards setting organizations might cause? Might failing to insulate them from liability result in fewer standards that protect the public from harm? In order to give standards setting organizations more protection against antitrust liability for their work, Congress adopted the Standards Development Organization Advancement Act, P.L. 108–237, 118 Stat. 661, 15 U.S.C. § 4301–4304 (2004). Its primary effect is to cap liability at actual, not treble, damages for standards found to be exclusionary.[62]

BOYCOTTS AS A FORM OF PROTEST

Since at least the Boston Tea Party, Americans have used boycotts as a form of protest against public or private conduct. If more than one person at a time fails to patronize a business, is the action automatically a "group boycott" that is actionable under § 1?

The Eighth Circuit said "no" in State of Missouri v. National Organization for Women, 620 F.2d 1301 (8th Cir.), cert. denied, 449 U.S. 842 (1980). There, a state had challenged as a conspiracy in restraint of trade, an effort by N.O.W. to get national organizations not to hold their conventions in states that had not ratified the Equal Rights Amendment.

---

[60]   See also, American Society of Mechanical Engineers, Inc. v. Hydrolevel Corporation, 456 U.S. 556, 102 S.Ct. 1935, 72 L.Ed.2d 330 (1982) (trade association liable on apparent authority theory for unauthorized opinion issued by one of its committees that plaintiff's device was unsafe). But see, Schachar v. American Academy of Ophthalmology, Inc., 870 F.2d 397 (7th Cir.1989) (characterizing a treatment as "experimental" is not a boycott because the label does not forbid a doctor to use the technique).

[61]   Challenges to industry standards continue, but most of the time, courts have declined to look behind such standards. See, e.g., Brookins v. International Motor Contest Association, 219 F.3d 849 (8th Cir. 2000) (upholding engine standard for auto racing); Super Sulky, Inc. v. U.S. Trotting Ass'n, 174 F.3d 733 (6th Cir. 1999) (upholding the definition of a racing sulky); DM Research, Inc. v. College of American Pathologists, 170 F.3d 53 (1st Cir. 1999) (upholding standard for reagent grade water to be used in clinical laboratories); Jessup v. American Kennel Club, 61 F.Supp.2d 5 (S.D.N.Y. 1999), aff'd 210 F.3d 111 (2nd Cir. 2000) (upholding official definition of the characteristics of a Labrador Retriever). But see, Coalition for ICANN Transparency v. Verisign, 611 F.3d 495 (9th Cir. 2010) (challenge to standards for issuing domain names).

[62]   Another standards setting issue, this time involving the incorporation of patented processes or products into a standard, is discussed later in this chapter.

The Eighth Circuit held that such a boycott was not the kind the Sherman Act sought to prohibit.

A year later, the First Circuit reached the same result when longshoremen refused to unload ships trading with the Soviet Union in order to protest that country's invasion of Afghanistan. Allied International, Inc. v. International Longshoremen's Association, 640 F.2d 1368 (1st Cir.1981), cert. denied 458 U.S. 1120 (1982).

The Supreme Court seemed to agree when it decided NAACP v. Claiborne Hardware Co., 458 U.S. 886, 102 S.Ct. 3409, 73 L.Ed.2d 1215 (1982). Not technically an antitrust case, the action sought damages against the NAACP for a boycott by African-Americans that the NAACP had encouraged against local white merchants. The NAACP was seeking to compel government and business leaders to comply with demands for equality and racial justice. The Supreme Court held the boycott was constitutionally protected. It "was not motivated by any desire to lessen competition or to reap economic benefits but by the aim of vindicating rights of equality and freedom * * * and the boycotters were consumers who did not stand to profit financially from a lessening of competition in the boycotted market."

But in Federal Trade Commission v. Indiana Federation of Dentists, 476 U.S. 447, 106 S.Ct. 2009, 90 L.Ed.2d 445 (1986), the Court drew a line. Some dental insurance companies required dentists to submit patient x-rays along with insurance claims so that the insurers could verify the need for the services provided. The Indiana Dental Association saw the requirement as a threat to dentists' professional independence but it ultimately signed an agreement with the FTC not to resist insurer demands. At that point, about 100 dentists in three cities formed the Indiana Federation of Dentists as a "union,"[63] one of whose "work rules" was that the members would not submit the x-rays. The FTC found the dentists' action was a conspiracy in violation of FTC Act § 5 and the Supreme Court unanimously agreed.

The Court has been slow to find professional rules per se illegal, Justice White wrote, so it would examine these using a rule of reason. But "application of the rule of reason to these facts is not a matter of any great difficulty." The no-x-ray policy was not price fixing, but it interfered with the range of services the market would otherwise offer, made it more expensive for insurers to evaluate dental diagnoses, and had no procompetitive justification. Finally, the Court cited *Professional Engineers* to say the assertion that the dentists' efforts promoted good patient care was "nothing less than a frontal assault on the basic policy of the Sherman Act."

---

[63] The effort to bring this case under the labor exemption was a non-starter, and the dentists made no pretense of being a labor union by the time the case reached the Supreme Court.

So the Court had several approaches it could take when it considered Federal Trade Commission v. Superior Court Trial Lawyers Association, 493 U.S. 411, 110 S.Ct. 768, 107 L.Ed.2d 851 (1990). A group of lawyers who regularly represented indigent defendants in D.C. Superior Court were tired of doing so for the rates established under the Criminal Justice Act of 1964. Those rates were capped at $30 per hour for court time and $20 per hour out of court. The lawyers took their complaints to the DC Bar and to local government officials.

Everyone was sympathetic, but no money was forthcoming. The mayor told them that to muster political support they would have to do something dramatic. Thus, they decided to "strike." They agreed not to come to court to receive assignments in new cases and they issued press releases about what they were doing any why. Very soon, the courts were awash in more cases than the regular D.C. public defenders could handle. Within two weeks, the D.C. City Council had raised the appointed lawyers' pay to $35 per hour and everyone seemed happy.

But members of the FTC saw these events as a classic group boycott. An Administrative Law Judge found the facts to be as alleged, but urged dismissing the complaint on the ground that the efforts had achieved a political solution to a political problem. The Commission disagreed, and issued a cease and desist order.

The Court of Appeals for the D.C. Circuit, in an opinion by Judge Douglas Ginsburg, himself a former head of the Antitrust Division, saw the tension between illegal conspiracy and protected protest activity. Citing United States v. O'Brien, 391 U.S. 367, 88 S.Ct. 1673, 20 L.Ed.3d 672 (1968), a case in which the Supreme Court had found burning a draft card to be a form of speech, the court said the test should be whether the appointed lawyers had market power. If they did *not*, we could say their success had been achieved politically and legally. If they *did* have market power, then the cause of their success would be ambiguous but the Commission's order could be sustained.

The FTC, however, was not content with that. It wanted a per se rule applied to the trial lawyers' conduct, and in an opinion by Justice Stevens, the Supreme Court agreed with the FTC.

First, the fact that Eastern Railroad Presidents Conference v. Noerr Motor Freight permits groups of competitors to seek legislative action did not control this situation. The Court said *Noerr* was a case in which the restraint of trade was the *result* of public action, not the motivation for the action as here. Further, the Court relied on one of the bases for its holding in *Allied Tube & Conduit* that otherwise:

> "Horizontal conspiracies or boycotts designed to exact higher prices or other economic advantages from the government would be immunized on the ground that they are genuinely intended to

influence the government to agree to the conspirators' terms. Firms could claim immunity for boycotts or horizontal output restrictions on the ground that they are intended to dramatize the plight of their industry and spur legislative action."

Claiborne Hardware, in turn, was distinguished as a case in which the boycotters were seeking equal opportunity for all citizens, not primarily benefits for themselves. And applying anything other than a per se rule to these facts, the Court said, would put per se rules too much at risk. Justice Stevens chose an interesting analogy:

> "The per se rules in antitrust law serve purposes analogous to per se restrictions upon, for example, stunt flying in congested areas or speeding. * * * Perhaps most violations of such rules actually cause no harm. No doubt many experienced drivers and pilots can operate much more safely, even at prohibited speeds, than the average citizen.

> "If the especially skilled drivers and pilots were to paint messages on their cars, or attach streamers to their planes, their conduct would have an expressive component. High speeds and unusual maneuvers would help to draw attention to their messages. Yet the laws may nonetheless be enforced against these skilled persons without proof that their conduct was actually harmful or dangerous.

> "In part, the justification for these per se rules is rooted in administrative convenience. They are also supported, however, by the observation that every speeder and every stunt pilot poses some threat to the community. An unpredictable event may overwhelm the skills of the best driver or pilot, even if the proposed course of action was entirely prudent when initiated. A bad driver going slowly may be more dangerous than a good driver going quickly, but a good driver who obeys the law is safer still.

> "So it is with boycotts and price fixing. Every such horizontal arrangement among competitors poses some threat to the free market. A small participant in the market is, obviously, less likely to cause persistent damage than a large participant. Other participants in the market may act quickly and effectively to take the small participant's place. For reasons including market inertia and information failures, however, a small conspirator may be able to impede competition over some period of time. Given an appropriate set of circumstances and some luck, the period can be long enough to inflict real injury upon particular consumers or competitors."

Justices Brennan and Marshall were not impressed with the Court's reasoning. Freedom of speech and protest are based in the Constitution, they said; the right to engage in stunt flying is not. Administrative convenience is not a principled basis for limiting the right to protest and seek political action.

Justice Blackmun also dissented, saying that because D.C. trial judges had inherent power to enlist any D.C. lawyer in the defense of criminal cases, the Superior Court Trial Lawyers could not have sufficient market power to raise an antitrust problem.

NOTES AND QUESTIONS

1.   Which opinion in Superior Court Trial Lawyers makes the most sense to you? Is the majority correct that it is easy to distinguish boycotts that are in the public interest from those that serve only private interests? Are Justices Brennan & Marshall right that making boycotts per se illegal could chill important dissent?

2.   It is important to know, as *Allied Tube* noted, that over 20% of the nation's Gross Domestic Product is spent by agencies of government. Does this mean that boycotts designed to influence government purchasing decisions should be a particularly important target of antitrust enforcement? Should the First Amendment override any such approach?

3.   Where does the law relating to group boycotts stand after this decision? Can we be as sure as we thought we could after *Northwest Wholesale Stationers* that the rule of reason always governs group boycott cases? Were Judge Ginsburg and Justice Blackmun wrong to believe that a boycott by firms without market power should not be held to be per se illegal?

JOINT VENTURES IN NETWORK INDUSTRIES
AS ESSENTIAL FACILITIES

We have seen joint ventures before. The *Penn-Olin* case in 1964, for example, told us that formation of such ventures would be judged by Clayton Act § 7 standards rather than simply ruled per se illegal under Sherman Act § 1. The question we now ask is when or whether a non-member of a joint venture must be permitted access to it, either as a member or as a full participant in its services. Several precedents may come to mind.

In 1911, for example, several railroads formed the Terminal Railroad Association that controlled the switching facilities in St. Louis. The Supreme Court said the joint venture had become a monopolist in violation of Sherman Act § 2, called the joint venture an essential facility, and ordered that all other railroads have access to its services.

More commonly, a group boycott analysis has been employed. In 1945, the Court ruled that the Associated Press—a newspaper joint venture—

could not exclude competing newspapers from membership, while in 1972, similar membership rules of Topco, a joint venture of grocery chains, were declared per se illegal. By 1985, of course, the conduct of Northwest Wholesale Stationers, another buying cooperative, was required to be analyzed under the rule of reason, an approach reinforced in *Rothery*.

When, if ever, should joint ventures be required to admit competitors to membership or otherwise cooperate with them? That question is particularly important in what are sometimes called "two-sided markets," i.e., where companies and products bring producers and consumers together. Think of a joint venture composed of dating services, for example, whose only product is facilitating members' interacting with each other and in which the perceived quality of service provided increases sharply as the number of market participants increases.

This kind of issue arose in United States v. Visa U.S.A., Inc., 344 F.3d 229 (2d Cir. 2003), cert.denied 125 S.Ct. 45 (2004). The Visa cards that most of us carry are actually issued by over 14,000 local banks and financial institutions. Visa, U.S.A., is a joint venture that acts as an intermediary between the banks and the merchants who accept the cards. The more Visa cards that are issued, the more merchants will take them, and the more we all will use them. One of Visa's internal rules is that no one may issue both Visa cards and cards of a competitor other than MasterCard.[64] The primary victims of this rule were American Express and Discover cards, which few banks would issue lest they lose access to Visa and MasterCard.

The court was clear that, because no price fixing or market division was involved, the rule of reason should be the standard for deciding the case. Determining the effect on competition, the court said, first required definition of the market; the court selected "general purpose cards." Other payment media, e.g., cash, checks and merchant-specific cards, were simply no competitive threat to those cards. Measured by dollar volume, Visa had 47% of the card transactions and MasterCard had 26%, for a total of 73%. American Express was used in 20% of transactions, while Discover Card was used in 6%.

Effectively blocking American Express and Discover from banks who might issue their cards, the court said, denied consumers the innovation that competition brings. Justifications offered by the defendants—network cohesion and elimination of free-riding—were held to be inadequate.

Do you agree? Might the characteristics of the credit card industry mean that we would all be better off if the country had only a single type

---

[64]   An earlier decision, Worthen Bank & Trust Co. v. National BankAmericard Inc., 485 F.2d 119 (8th Cir. 1973), cert.denied 415 U.S. 918 (1974), had required Visa to let banks issue the MasterCard as well.

of card?[65] Since this decision, have you seen an explosion in use of American Express and Discover cards?

Should small airlines be able to compel a joint venture of major airlines to give them access to a computerized reservation system? See Alaska Airlines, et al. v. United Airlines and American Airlines, 948 F.2d 536 (9th Cir. 1991), cert.denied 503 U.S. 977 (1992) (denying access). In 2003, the Justice Department concluded that Orbitz, a reservation system established as a joint venture of major airlines, did not have significant anticompetitive effects because the airlines could also sell through Expedia, Travelocity, and their own websites.[66]

3. HORIZONTAL MARKET DIVISION

In the third period, horizontal market division had been just as per se illegal as horizontal price fixing. By now, of course, the rule of reason had become recognized in horizontal price fixing and group boycott cases, and in that light, our next two cases considered the appropriate approach to cases of horizontal market division. The first opinion, issued the same year as *Northwest Wholesale Stationers*, was written by the Court of Appeals judge who, as a lawyer/professor just the year before, had asked the Supreme Court to apply a rule of reason in *NCAA*.

POLK BROS., INC. v. FOREST CITY ENTERPRISES, INC.

United States Court of Appeals, Seventh Circuit, 1985
776 F.2d 185

Before CUMMINGS, CHIEF JUDGE, EASTERBROOK, CIRCUIT JUDGE, and GRANT, SENIOR DISTRICT JUDGE.

EASTERBROOK, CIRCUIT JUDGE.

In 1972 Polk Bros., which owned some land in Burbank, Illinois, discussed with Forest City Enterprises the possibility of building a store large enough for both firms. Polk sells appliances and home furnishings; Forest City sells building materials, lumber, tools and related products. Both have substantial chains of stores. They reached an agreement. Polk

---

[65]　See, e.g., David S. Evans & Richard Schmalensee, Economic Aspects of Payment Card Systems and Antitrust Policy Toward Joint Ventures, 63 Antitrust L.J. 861 (1995); Dennis W. Carlton & Alan S. Frankel, The Antitrust Economics of Credit Card Networks, 63 Antitrust L.J. 643 (1995); Timothy J. Muris, Payment Card Regulation and the (Mis)application of the Economics of Two-Sided Markets, 2005 Columbia Bus.L.Rev. 515 (2005). Visa and MasterCard had prevailed in earlier private litigation that saw the issues differently. See SCFC ILC, Inc. v. Visa USA, Inc., 36 F.3d 958 (10th Cir. 1994), cert. denied 515 U.S. 1152 (1995); Donald I. Baker, Compulsory Access to Network Joint Ventures Under the Sherman Act: Rules or Roulette?, 1993 Utah L.Rev. 999.

[66]　For more discussion of such issues, see Gregory J. Werden, Antitrust Analysis of Joint Ventures: An Overview, 66 Antitrust L.J. 701 (1998); Michael S. McFalls, The Role and Assessment of Classical Market Power in Joint Venture Analysis, 66 Antitrust L.J. 651 (1998); Howard H. Chang, David S. Evans & Richard Schmalensee, Some Economic Principles for Guiding Antitrust Policy Towards Joint Ventures, 1998 Columbia Bus. L.Rev. 223.

built a single building on a large parcel of land. The building is partitioned internally; Polk and Forest City have separate entrances; Polk's store contains 64,000 square feet, Forest City's 68,000 square feet. One parking lot serves both businesses. Forest City became Polk's lessee in 1973. The stores opened in 1975. In 1978 Forest City exercised its option to buy, and Polk took back a mortgage * * * .

The attraction of the arrangement was the complementary nature of the firms' products. The two stores together could offer a full line of goods for furnishing and maintaining a home. Both Polk and Forest City were concerned, however, that competition might replace cooperation. They negotiated a covenant restricting the products each could sell. Forest City promised not to sell "major appliances and furniture," although it reserved the right to sell "built-in appliances in connection with Kitchen-Build-In business." Polk Bros. promised not to "stock or sell Toro materials, lumber and related products, tools, paints and sundries, hardware, garden supplies, automobile supplies or plumbing supplies." The parties agreed on a long list of things that both could sell, including "Gas & Electric Heaters[,] Built-In-Ranges[,] . . . Snow Blowers[,] Lawn Mowers[,] . . . [and] Hardware/Garden Mdse". When Forest City became an owner in 1978 the parties agreed that the restrictions in the lease would become covenants running with the land for 50 years.

Forest City's management changed in 1982. The new managers were concerned about declining profits from its three stores near Chicago. Two stores sold some major appliances; the one at Burbank did not. Forest City found it uneconomical to advertise the large appliances when one of the three outlets could not sell them. Forest City asked to be relieved of its covenant at Burbank. Polk said no. In January 1983 Forest City informed Polk that it considered the covenant invalid; Polk responded with a suit in state court seeking an injunction. Forest City removed the action to the district court * * * .

While the case was pending, Forest City started selling appliances. Polk sought emergency relief * * * . * * * The district court, however, denied Polk's request * * * .

* * *

I

The district court held the covenant invalid under § 3(1)(c) of the antitrust law of Illinois, which declares unlawful contracts "allocating or dividing customers, territories, supplies, sales or markets, functional or geographical, for any commodity." That state's antitrust law, however, refers courts to federal antitrust law as a guide to questions of interpretation. In order to find out what Illinois law forbids, we inquire what federal antitrust law forbids.

Like federal law, Illinois law recognizes a difference between contracts unlawful per se and those that must be assessed under a Rule of Reason. Although federal law treats almost all contracts allocating products and markets as unlawful per se, the per se rule is designed for "naked" restraints rather than agreements that facilitate productive activity. Any firm involves cooperation among people who could otherwise be competitors. Polk Bros. and Forest City each comprise many stores. The managers of each store could set prices independently, competing against each other, but antitrust law does not require this. See *Copperweld.*

Cooperation is the basis of productivity. It is necessary for people to cooperate in some respects before they may compete in others, and cooperation facilitates efficient production. Joint ventures, mergers, systems of distribution—all these and more require extensive cooperation, and all are assessed under a Rule of Reason that focuses on market power and the ability of the cooperators to raise price by restricting output. The war of all against all is not a good model for any economy. Antitrust law is designed to ensure an appropriate blend of cooperation and competition, not to require all economic actors to compete full tilt at every moment. When cooperation contributes to productivity through integration of efforts, the Rule of Reason is the norm. National Collegiate Athletic Association v. Board of Regents of University of Oklahoma.

A court must distinguish between "naked" restraints, those in which the restriction on competition is unaccompanied by new production or products, and "ancillary" restraints, those that are part of a larger endeavor whose success they promote. If two people meet one day and decide not to compete, the restraint is "naked"; it does nothing but suppress competition. If A hires B as a salesman and passes customer lists to B, then B's reciprocal covenant not compete with A is "ancillary." At the time A and B strike their bargain, the enterprise (viewed as a whole) expands output and competition by putting B to work. The covenant not to compete means that A may trust B with broader responsibilities, the better to compete against third parties. Covenants of this type are evaluated under the Rule of Reason as ancillary restraints, and unless they bring a large market share under a single firm's control they are lawful. See United States v. Addyston Pipe & Steel Co.

The evaluation of ancillary restraints under the Rule of Reason does not imply that ancillary agreements are not real horizontal restraints. They are. A covenant not to compete following employment does not operate any differently from a horizontal market division among competitors—not at the time the covenant has its bite, anyway. The difference comes at the time people enter beneficial arrangements. A legal rule that enforces covenants not to complete, even after an employee has launched his own firm, makes it easier for people to cooperate productively in the first place. Knowing that he is not cutting his own throat by doing so, the employer will train the employee, giving him skills, knowledge, and trade secrets that make the firm more productive. Once that employment ends, there is nothing left but restraint—but the aftermath is the wrong focus.

A court must ask whether an agreement promoted enterprise and productivity at the time it was adopted. If it arguably did, then the court must apply the Rule of Reason to make a more discriminating assessment. "It is sometimes difficult to distinguish robust competition from conduct with long-run anti-competitive effects" (*Copperweld*) and so a court must be very sure that a category of acts is anti-competitive before condemning that category per se. See Broadcast Music, Inc. v. Columbia Broadcasting System, Inc. and *NCAA*, both of which assess under the Rule of Reason horizontal agreements that also involve cooperation among rivals that might produce larger output and more desirable products. Both *BMI* and *NCAA* emphasize that condemnation per se is an unusual step, one that depends on confidence that a whole category of restraints is so likely to be anticompetitive that there is no point in searching for a potentially beneficial instance. See also, e.g., Continental T.V., Inc. v. GTE Sylvania Inc.

A restraint is ancillary when it may contribute to the success of a cooperative venture that promises greater productivity and output. See *Addyston*; *BMI*; and *NCAA*; see also Robert H. Bork, The Antitrust Paradox, 26–30 (1978). If the restraint, viewed at the time it was adopted, may promote the success of this more extensive cooperation, then the court must scrutinize things carefully under the Rule of Reason. Only when a quick look reveals that "the practice facially appears to be one that would always or almost always tend to restrict competition and decrease output" (*BMI*), should a court cut off further inquiry. Polk Bros. and Forest City were deciding in 1972–73 whether to embark on a new venture—the building of a joint facility—that would expand output. The endeavor not only would increase the retail selling capacity in Burbank but also would provide a convenience to consumers. Polk Bros. does about 80% of its business in large appliances. If it could bring to the same location building supplies and the other items in which Forest City specializes, shopping would be more convenient for consumers. As the district court put it, the parties "hoped to attract more customers because of the proximity of two stores, selling different but complementary items for the home."

This was productive cooperation. The covenant allocating items between the retailers played an important role in inducing the two retailers to cooperate. The district court found that Polk "would not have entered into this arrangement, however, unless it had received assurances that [Forest City] would not compete with it in the sale of products that are the 'foundation of [Polk's] business'. . . . The agreement not to compete was an integral part of the lease and land sale."

It is easy to see why. Polk spent substantial sums in advertising to attract customers to its stores, where it displayed and demonstrated the appliances. It might be tempting for another retailer to take a free ride on these efforts. Once Polk had persuaded a customer to purchase a color TV, its next door neighbor might try to lure the customer away by quoting a lower price. It could afford to do this if, for example, it simply kept the TV sets in boxes and let Polk bear the costs of sales personnel and demonstrations. Polk would not continue doing the work while its neighbor took the sales. It would do less demonstrating and promotion, to the detriment of consumers who valued the information. The Supreme Court has recognized that the control of free riding is a legitimate objective of a system of distribution. See *Continental T.V.*

The district court nonetheless concluded that the covenant is not ancillary because it was an essential part of the arrangement. It reasoned: "The agreement not to compete was an integral part of the lease and land sale. This was not a sale with an ancillary agreement designed to protect an original owner's established business interests. The lease and land sale would not have been made by Polk Bros. absent an agreement not to compete. . . . Because the covenant not to compete was not merely ancillary to a sale of land or business, it constitutes a horizontal restraint of trade and a per se violation of the Illinois Antitrust Act . . . " There are two possible interpretations of this reasoning. One is that this covenant is not ancillary because it is so important. The other is that the agreement is not ancillary when it is part of the establishment of a new business, as opposed to the sale of an existing business. Neither is correct.

The reason for distinguishing between "ancillary" and "naked" restraints to determine whether the agreement is part of a cooperative venture with prospects for increasing output. If it is, it should not be condemned per se. Only by exalting Webster's Third over the function of antitrust law could a court determine that a restraint is not "ancillary" because it was so important to the productive undertaking. The suggestion that the ancillary restraints doctrine does not apply to new ventures also slights the functions of the rule. The partners of a newly-formed law firm agree on fees and allocate subjects of specialty and clients among them; this "price fixing" and "market division" do not become unlawful just because the firm is new. The benefits of cooperation may be greatest when launching a new venture.

Polk Bros. and Forest City were cooperating to produce, not to curtail output; the cooperation increased the amount of retail space available and was at least potentially beneficial to consumers; the restrictive covenant made the cooperation possible. The Rule of Reason therefore applies. Discriminating analysis is necessary.

The first step in any Rule of Reason case is an assessment of market power. Unless the firms have the power to raise price by curtailing output, their agreement is unlikely to harm consumers, and it makes sense to understand their cooperation as benign or beneficial. Forest City has not argued that the arrangement in question here affects a substantial portion of any market. It governs two stores on a single site. The stores are surrounded by a vast parking lot; the site apparently attracts customers with cars, the very customers who have many other options within a reasonable distance. There was a full trial, and Forest City did not offer evidence from which the court could find market power. It does not suggest that we affirm the judgment on Rule of Reason grounds. Forest City has litigated the antitrust issue as one in which it prevails under the per se rule or not at all. "Not at all" it must be.

* * *

[Part II of the court's opinion, dealing with the clean hands doctrine, is omitted.]

REVERSED.

NOTES AND QUESTIONS

1.   Forest City said this was a classic market division. How was it saying the market had been divided?

a.   Wasn't Polk Bros.' agreement not to carry Toro products clearly an contract to eliminate competition in a popular line of consumer goods? If the two stores had made the same agreement with respect to locations in the same part of the city, but not the same shopping center, would the result have been different?

b.   Why should the fact that a single center is involved render the agreement "ancillary"? Was it because the court found that neither firm would have built this shopping center except for the agreement, i.e., that the agreement contributed to a net increase in the number of stores? Does this case thus have some parallels with *Penn-Olin*?

c.   Were you confident either in *Penn-Olin* or here that a district judge could discern what the firms would have done but for this agreement?

2.   Were you surprised to see the court say: "The war of all against all is not a good model for any economy. Antitrust law is designed to ensure an appropriate blend of cooperation and competition * * * "?

a.   Is the court here largely saying what Judge Taft in *Addyston Pipe* and Justice Brandeis in *Board of Trade* had pointed out, namely that "all contracts in restraint of trade" cannot mean "all contracts"? Is it saying more?

b.   Do you agree that "A court must ask whether an agreement promoted enterprise and productivity at the time it was adopted"? Is only some "promotion" enough? Should a cost-benefit calculation be required with respect to each restraint?

3.   How does Judge Easterbrook say one is to determine whether or not a per se rule applies? Do you agree that it can be done with a "quick look" at whether the "practice facially appears to be one that would always or almost always tend to restrict competition and decrease output"?

4.   What is the court saying here about the relationship between ancillary restraints and market power? Is it that an agreement that reduces total output can never be "ancillary" to an otherwise lawful course of dealing? Should that be the rule?

If you are having trouble making all these cases seem consistent, you are not alone. In our next case, decided the same year as *Superior Court Trial Lawyers*, a unanimous Supreme Court seemed oblivious to the confusion it had created.

JAY PALMER V. BRG OF GEORGIA, INC.

Supreme Court of the United States, 1990
498 U.S. 46, 111 S.Ct. 401, 112 L.Ed.2d 349

PER CURIAM.

In preparation for the 1985 Georgia Bar Examination, petitioners contracted to take a bar review course offered by respondent BRG of Georgia, Inc. (BRG). In this litigation they contend that the price of BRG's course was enhanced by reason of an unlawful agreement between BRG and respondent Harcourt Brace Jovanovich Legal and Professional Publications (HBJ), the Nation's largest provider of bar review materials and lecture services. The central issue is whether the 1980 agreement between respondents violated § 1 of the Sherman Act.

HBJ began offering a Georgia bar review course on a limited basis in 1976, and was in direct, and often intense, competition with BRG during the period from 1977–1979. BRG and HBJ were the two main providers of bar review courses in Georgia during this time period. In early 1980, they entered into an agreement that gave BRG an exclusive license to market HBJ's material in Georgia and to use its trade name "Bar/Bri." The parties agreed that HBJ would not compete with BRG in Georgia and that BRG would not compete with HBJ outside of Georgia.[67] Under the agreement,

----

[67]   The 1980 agreement contained two provisions, one called a "Covenant Not to Compete" and the other called "Other Ventures." The former required HBJ not to "directly or indirectly own, manage, operate, join, invest, control, or participate in or be connected as an officer, employee, partner, director, independent contractor or otherwise with any business which is operating or participating in the preparation of candidates for the Georgia State Bar Examination." The latter required BRG not to compete against HBJ in states in which HBJ currently operated outside the state of Georgia. [Court's fn. 2]

HBJ received $100 per student enrolled by BRG and 40% of all revenues over $350. Immediately after the 1980 agreement, the price of BRG's course was increased from $150 to over $400.

On petitioners' motion for partial summary judgment * * * the District Court held that the agreement was lawful. The United States Court of Appeals for the Eleventh Circuit, with one judge dissenting, agreed with the District Court that per se unlawful horizontal price fixing required an explicit agreement on prices to be charged or that one party have the right to be consulted about the other's prices. The Court of Appeals also agreed with the District Court that to prove a per se violation under a geographic market allocation theory, petitioners had to show that respondents had subdivided some relevant market in which they had previously competed. * * *

In United States v. Socony-Vacuum Oil Co., we held that an agreement among competitors to engage in a program of buying surplus gasoline on the spot market in order to prevent prices from falling sharply was unlawful, even though there was no direct agreement on the actual prices to be maintained. We explained that "under the Sherman Act a combination formed for the purpose and with the effect of raising, depressing, fixing, pegging, or stabilizing the price of a commodity in interstate or foreign commerce is illegal per se." See also Catalano, Inc. v. Target Sales, Inc.; National Society of Professional Engineers v. United States.

The revenue-sharing formula in the 1980 agreement between BRG and HBJ, coupled with the price increase that took place immediately after the parties agreed to cease competing with each other in 1980, indicates that this agreement was "formed for the purpose and with the effect of raising" the price of the bar review course. It was, therefore, plainly incorrect for the District Court to enter summary judgment in respondents' favor. Moreover, it is equally clear that the District Court and the Court of Appeals erred when they assumed that an allocation of markets or submarkets by competitors is not unlawful unless the market in which the two previously competed is divided between them.

In United States v. Topco Associates, Inc., we held that agreements between competitors to allocate territories to minimize competition are illegal:

> "* * * This Court has reiterated time and time again that '[h]orizontal territorial limitations * * * are naked restraints of trade with no purpose except stifling of competition.' Such limitations are per se violations of the Sherman Act."

The defendants in *Topco* had never competed in the same market, but had simply agreed to allocate markets. Here, HBJ and BRG had previously competed in the Georgia market; under their allocation agreement, BRG received that market, while HBJ received the remainder of the United States. Each agreed not to compete in the other's territories. Such agreements are anticompetitive regardless of whether the parties split a market within which both do business or whether they merely reserve one market for one and another for the other. Thus, the 1980 agreement between HBJ and BRG was unlawful on its face.

The petition for writ of certiorari is granted, the judgment of the Court of Appeals is reversed, and the case is remanded for further proceedings consistent with this opinion.

JUSTICE MARSHALL, dissenting:

Although I agree that the limited information before us appears to indicate that the Court of Appeals erred in its decision below, I continue to believe that summary dispositions deprive litigants of a fair opportunity to be heard on the merits and significantly increase the risk of an erroneous decision. I therefore dissent from the Court's decision today to reverse summarily the judgment below.

NOTES AND QUESTIONS

1.   How often have you seen a case the Supreme Court thought was so clear that it did not even have to hear oral argument? This did seem to be a particularly blatant division of markets with respect to a product in which most law students have an interest.

2.   What is the impact of this case on use of the rule of reason in market division cases? Does it cast doubt on *Polk Bros.* and say that all horizontal market division remains per se illegal?

3.   Suppose that instead of dividing the market along state lines, the firms had agreed not to compete in certain fields. Suppose, for example, BRG had agreed to serve the bar review market and not compete with HBJ in preparation materials for the CPA exam. Would that also have been a per se illegal market division?

4.   What does *Palmer* tell us about the viability of some cases that might have seemed irrelevant in the current climate of antitrust thinking? Were you surprised to see *Socony-Vacuum* cited for some of its most sweeping rhetoric? Were you shocked to see *Topco* cited as a centerpiece of the Court's opinion? Had Judge Bork in *Rothery* preached *Topco's* funeral before the body was really dead?

5.   What might *Palmer* foreshadow for a case in which a patent holder pays the producer of a generic drug not to challenge the patent and not to sell the generic? We will look closely at that case later in this chapter. It is Federal Trade Commission v. Actavis, Inc., ___ U.S. ___, 133 S.Ct. 2223, 186 L.Ed.2d 343 (2013).

4. DEALING WITH DEALERS

Contemporaneously with wrestling with the new law of horizontal restraints, the Supreme Court considered price fixing, market division and group boycotts in vertical relationships. The issues were as old as *Dr. Miles* and *Colgate*. They appeared again in *General Electric, Klors, Parke Davis, Simpson, White Motor, Schwinn,* and *Albrecht*. Then, *GTE Sylvania* began the current period by applying the rule of reason to a Sherman Act § 1 complaint involving how a manufacturer organized dealers' territories.

These next cases join the debate over Section § 1 analysis in 1984, the same year the Court decided *NCAA*. As you read the cases, ask yourself whether all vertical practices would best be analyzed under a rule of reason rather than a per se rule of illegality. Indeed, does the Court seem to treat some vertical arrangements as almost per se legal? Should it do so?

These next decisions also have been among the most frustrating to antitrust lawyers who represent private plaintiffs. Can you see why? Pay particular attention to what the cases tell us about proof of agreement and summary judgment standards. Are you troubled or pleased to see additional barriers raised to successful prosecution of private causes of action?

MONSANTO CO. v. SPRAY-RITE SERVICE CORP.

Supreme Court of the United States, 1984
465 U.S. 752, 104 S.Ct. 1464, 79 L.Ed.2d 775

JUSTICE POWELL delivered the opinion of the Court.

This case presents a question as to the standard of proof required to find a vertical price-fixing conspiracy in violation of § 1 of the Sherman Act.

I

Petitioner Monsanto Co. manufactures chemical products, including agricultural herbicides. By the late 1960's, the time at issue in this case, its sales accounted for approximately 15% of the corn herbicide market and 3% of the soybean herbicide market. In the corn herbicide market, the market leader commanded a 70% share. In the soybean herbicide market, two other competitors each had between 30% and 40% of the market. Respondent Spray-Rite Service Corp. was engaged in the wholesale distribution of agricultural chemicals from 1955 to 1972. Spray-Rite was essentially a family business, whose owner and president, Donald Yapp, was also its sole salaried salesman. Spray-Rite was a discount operation, buying in large quantities and selling at a low margin.

Spray-Rite was an authorized distributor of Monsanto herbicides from 1957 to 1968. In October 1967, Monsanto announced that it would appoint distributors for 1-year terms, and that it would renew distributorships according to several new criteria. Among the criteria were: (i) whether the distributor's primary activity was soliciting sales to retail dealers; (ii) whether the distributor employed trained salesmen capable of educating its customers on the technical aspects of Monsanto's herbicides; and (iii) whether the distributor could be expected "to exploit fully" the market in its geographical area of primary responsibility. Shortly thereafter, Monsanto also introduced a number of incentive programs, such as making cash payments to distributors that sent salesmen to training classes, and providing free deliveries of products to customers within a distributor's area of primary responsibility.[68]

In October 1968, Monsanto declined to renew Spray-Rite's distributorship. At that time, Spray-Rite was the 10th largest out of approximately 100 distributors of Monsanto's primary corn herbicide. Ninety percent of Spray-Rite's sales volume was devoted to herbicide sales, and 16% of its sales were of Monsanto products. * * *

Spray-Rite brought this action under § 1 of the Sherman Act. It alleged that Monsanto and some of its distributors conspired to fix the resale prices of Monsanto herbicides. Its complaint further alleged that Monsanto terminated Spray-Rite's distributorship, adopted compensation programs and shipping policies, and encouraged distributors to boycott Spray-Rite in furtherance of this conspiracy. * * *

The case was tried to a jury. The District Court instructed the jury that Monsanto's conduct was per se unlawful if it was in furtherance of a conspiracy to fix prices. In answers to special interrogatories, the jury found that (i) the termination of Spray-Rite was pursuant to a conspiracy between Monsanto and one or more of its distributors to set resale prices * * * . The jury awarded $3.5 million in damages, which was trebled to $10.5 million. * * *

The Court of Appeals for the Seventh Circuit affirmed. * * * The court stated that "proof of termination following competitor complaints is sufficient to support an inference of concerted action." * * *

* * * We reject the statement by the Court of Appeals * * * of the standard of proof required to submit a case to the jury in distributor-termination litigation, but affirm the judgment under the standard we announce today.

II

This Court has drawn two important distinctions that are at the center of this and any other distributor-termination case. First, there is the basic distinction between concerted and independent action—a distinction not

---

[68] These areas of primary responsibility were not exclusive territorial restrictions. Approximately 10 to 20 distributors were assigned to each area, and distributors were permitted to sell outside their assigned area. [Court's fn. 1]

always clearly drawn by parties and courts. * * * Under *Colgate*, the manufacturer can announce its resale prices in advance and refuse to deal with those who fail to comply. And a distributor is free to acquiesce in the manufacturer's demand in order to avoid termination.

The second important distinction in distributor-termination cases is that between concerted action to set prices and concerted action on nonprice restrictions. The former have been per se illegal since the early years of national antitrust enforcement. See Dr. Miles Medical Co. v. John D. Park & Sons Co. The latter are judged under the rule of reason, which requires a weighing of the relevant circumstances of a case to decide whether a restrictive practice constitutes an unreasonable restraint on competition. See Continental T.V., Inc. v. GTE Sylvania Inc.[69]

While these distinctions in theory are reasonably clear, often they are difficult to apply in practice. In *Sylvania* we emphasized that the legality of arguably anticompetitive conduct should be judged primarily by its "market impact." But the economic effect of all of the conduct described above—unilateral and concerted vertical price setting, agreements on price and nonprice restrictions—is in many, but not all, cases similar or identical. And judged from a distance, the conduct of the parties in the various situations can be indistinguishable. For example, the fact that a manufacturer and its distributors are in constant communication about prices and marketing strategy does not alone show that the distributors are not making independent pricing decisions. A manufacturer and its distributors have legitimate reasons to exchange information about the prices and the reception of their products in the market. Moreover, it is precisely in cases in which the manufacturer attempts to further a particular marketing strategy by means of agreements on often costly nonprice restrictions that it will have the most interest in the distributors' resale prices. The manufacturer often will want to ensure that its distributors earn sufficient profit to pay for programs such as hiring and training additional salesmen or demonstrating the technical features of the product, and will want to see that "free-riders" do not interfere. See *Sylvania*. Thus, the manufacturer's strongly felt concern about resale

---

[69] The Solicitor General (by brief only) and several other amici suggest that we take this opportunity to reconsider whether "contract[s], combination[s] * * * or conspirac[ies]" to fix resale prices should always be unlawful. They argue that the economic effect of resale price maintenance is little different from agreements on nonprice restrictions. They say that the economic objections to resale price maintenance that we discussed in *Sylvania*—such as that it facilitates horizontal cartels—can be met easily in the context of rule-of-reason analysis.

Certainly in this case we have no occasion to consider the merits of this argument. This case was tried on per se instructions to the jury. Neither party argued in the District Court that the rule of reason should apply to a vertical price-fixing conspiracy, nor raised the point on appeal. In fact, neither party before this Court presses the argument advanced by amici. We therefore decline to reach the question, and we decide the case in the context in which it was decided below and argued here. [Court's fn. 7]

prices does not necessarily mean that it has done more than the *Colgate* doctrine allows.

Nevertheless, it is of considerable importance that independent action by the manufacturer, and concerted action on nonprice restrictions, be distinguished from price-fixing agreements, since under present law the latter are subject to per se treatment and treble damages. On a claim of concerted price fixing, the antitrust plaintiff must present evidence sufficient to carry its burden of proving that there was such an agreement. If an inference of such an agreement may be drawn from highly ambiguous evidence, there is a considerable danger that the doctrines enunciated in *Sylvania* and *Colgate* will be seriously eroded.

The flaw in the evidentiary standard adopted by the Court of Appeals in this case is that it disregards this danger. Permitting an agreement to be inferred merely from the existence of complaints, or even from the fact that termination came about "in response to" complaints, could deter or penalize perfectly legitimate conduct. As Monsanto points out, complaints about price cutters "are natural—and from the manufacturer's perspective, unavoidable—reactions by distributors to the activities of their rivals." * * * Moreover, distributors are an important source of information for manufacturers. In order to assure an efficient distribution system, manufacturers and distributors constantly must coordinate their activities to assure that their product will reach the consumer persuasively and efficiently. To bar a manufacturer from acting solely because the information upon which it acts originated as a price complaint would create an irrational dislocation in the market. * * *

Thus, something more than evidence of complaints is needed. There must be evidence that tends to exclude the possibility that the manufacturer and nonterminated distributors were acting independently. As Judge Aldisert has written, the antitrust plaintiff should present direct or circumstantial evidence that reasonably tends to prove that the manufacturer and others "had a conscious commitment to a common scheme designed to achieve an unlawful objective." Edward J. Sweeney & Sons [Inc. v. Texaco, Inc., 637 F.2d 105 (3d Cir.1980), cert.denied, 451 U.S. 911 (1981)].[70]

III

A

Applying this standard to the facts of this case, we believe there was sufficient evidence for the jury reasonably to have concluded that Monsanto and some of its distributors were parties to an "agreement" or "conspiracy"

---

[70] The concept of "a meeting of the minds" or "a common scheme" in a distributor-termination case includes more than a showing that the distributor conformed to the suggested price. It means as well that evidence must be presented both that the distributor communicated its acquiescence or agreement, and that this was sought by the manufacturer. [Court's fn. 9]

to maintain resale prices and terminate price cutters. In fact there was substantial direct evidence of agreements to maintain prices. There was testimony from a Monsanto district manager, for example, that Monsanto on at least two occasions in early 1969, about five months after Spray-Rite was terminated, approached price-cutting distributors and advised that if they did not maintain the suggested resale price, they would not receive adequate supplies of Monsanto's new corn herbicide. When one of the distributors did not assent, this information was referred to the Monsanto regional office, and it complained to the distributor's parent company. There was evidence that the parent instructed its subsidiary to comply, and the distributor informed Monsanto that it would charge the suggested price. Evidence of this kind plainly is relevant and persuasive as to a meeting of minds.[71]

An arguably more ambiguous example is a newsletter from one of the distributors to his dealer-customers. The newsletter is dated October 1, 1968, just four weeks before Spray-Rite was terminated. It was written after a meeting between the author and several Monsanto officials, and discusses Monsanto's efforts to "ge[t] the 'market place in order.'" The newsletter reviews some of Monsanto's incentive and shipping policies, and then states that in addition "every effort will be made to maintain a minimum market price level." * * *

B

If, as the courts below reasonably could have found, there was evidence of an agreement with one or more distributors to maintain prices, the remaining question is whether the termination of Spray-Rite was part of or pursuant to that agreement. It would be reasonable to find that it was, since it is necessary for competing distributors contemplating compliance with suggested prices to know that those who do not comply will be terminated. Moreover, there is some circumstantial evidence of such a link. Following the termination, there was a meeting between Spray-Rite's president and a Monsanto official. There was testimony that the first thing the official mentioned was the many complaints Monsanto had received about Spray-Rite's prices. In addition, there was reliable testimony that Monsanto never discussed with Spray-Rite prior to the termination the distributorship criteria that were the alleged basis for the action. By contrast, a former Monsanto salesman for Spray-Rite's area testified that Monsanto representatives on several occasions in 1965–1966 approached Spray-Rite, informed the distributor of complaints from other distributors—including one major and influential one—and requested that

---

[71] In addition, there was circumstantial evidence that Monsanto sought agreement from the distributor to conform to the resale price. The threat to cut off the distributor's supply came during Monsanto's "shipping season" when herbicide was in short supply. The jury could have concluded that Monsanto sought this agreement at a time when it was able to use supply as a lever to force compliance. [Court's fn. 10]

prices be maintained. Later that same year, Spray-Rite's president testified, Monsanto officials made explicit threats to terminate Spray-Rite unless it raised its prices.

IV

We conclude that the Court of Appeals applied an incorrect standard to the evidence in this case. The correct standard is that there must be evidence that tends to exclude the possibility of independent action by the manufacturer and distributor. That is, there must be direct or circumstantial evidence that reasonably tends to prove that the manufacturer and others had a conscious commitment to a common scheme designed to achieve an unlawful objective. Under this standard, the evidence in this case created a jury issue as to whether Spray-Rite was terminated pursuant to a price-fixing conspiracy between Monsanto and its distributors. The judgment of the court below is affirmed.

JUSTICE WHITE took no part in the consideration or decision of this case.

JUSTICE BRENNAN, concurring.

As the Court notes, the Solicitor General has filed a brief in this Court for the United States as amicus curiae urging us to overrule the Court's decision in Dr. Miles Medical Co. v. John D. Park & Sons Co. That decision has stood for 73 years, and Congress has certainly been aware of its existence throughout that time. Yet Congress has never enacted legislation to overrule the interpretation of the Sherman Act adopted in that case. Under these circumstances, I see no reason for us to depart from our long-standing interpretation of the Act. Because the Court adheres to that rule and, in my view, properly applies *Dr. Miles* to this case, I join the opinion and judgment of the Court.

NOTES AND QUESTIONS

1.   What kind of distribution program had Monsanto adopted? Notice that although this case was decided seven years after *GTE Sylvania*, the *events* took place in 1968, nine years *before* that decision. Indeed, Monsanto's plan was implemented one year after *Schwinn*. Do you believe its program was legal as tested by *Schwinn* standards?

a.   What kind of market share did Monsanto have, and what competitors did it face when it began the course of action that got it in trouble? Would anyone seriously argue that it had market power in the sale of herbicides?

b.   Do we have evidence whether Monsanto's plan worked as a marketing matter? What was that evidence?

2.   The Court sees this case as pulling together the *Dr. Miles/Colgate/Parke Davis* line of cases and merging it with the *White/Schwinn/Sylvania* line. What does it see are the key distinctions?

a.   Does the court adequately explain not overruling *Dr. Miles*? Is the line between price and non-price restrictions one that you can defend?

b.   Do you agree that this case was not a good one in which to consider overruling *Dr. Miles*? Will its authority ever get less "longstanding" and, until the Court acts, will any case ever be tried assuming that *Dr. Miles* is not good law?

c.   Were you convinced by Justice Powell's analysis of the interplay between price and non-price restraints? Is he correct that most manufacturers who want dealer help giving service to customers are likely to encounter discounters who will try to lure away the customers others have developed?

3.   Why would Monsanto, with a small market share, cut off one of its largest volume distributors? Was it acting foolishly, such that a loss of profits would provide all the punishment needed to get it to change its ways? Could the public be injured by its action; indeed, might its termination of Spray-Rite make consumers better off?

THE PROBLEM OF PROOF OF AGREEMENT

Issues of coordinated pricing in the absence of overt agreement— issues raised in *American Column, Interstate Circuit, Theatre Enterprises, Container*, and now *Monsanto*—simply will not go away. The issues are far from limited to cases of vertical agreement, of course, but because *Monsanto* addresses the problem so explicitly, we revisit the issues here.

What test did the Court approve for cases that allege an actual conspiracy? What does it mean to "exclude the possibility that the [defendants] were acting independently"? What was the evidence in *Monsanto* that was cited to support the jury's finding of a price fixing conspiracy?

a.   Do you agree that a conspiracy was demonstrated by the fact that *after* Spray-Rite was terminated, Monsanto told other firms to keep their prices up?

b.   Was a conspiracy involving Monsanto proved by the action of a *distributor* who sent a newsletter to its retail customers saying it was sure Monsanto would try to "maintain a minimum price level"?

c.   Could a defendant *ever* get summary judgment if *these* facts support a finding of actual conspiracy? On the other hand, do you think there will often be *no* evidence that tends to exclude the *possibility* of independent action by the manufacturer and distributor?

The shorthand rule in the lower courts has become that the plaintiff must identify "plus factors," i.e., facts in addition to the fact of parallel activity, that tend to prove an agreement.

E.I. du Pont de Nemours & Co. v. Federal Trade Commission, 729 F.2d 128 (2d Cir. 1984), for example, asked whether the Federal Trade Commission could find that the adoption of a business practice by all the firms in an industry was an unfair method of competition under § 5 of the FTC Act. The lead-based anti-knock gasoline industry was down to four firms. Demand was declining because of environmental restrictions, but it was inelastic because, until cars requiring "Ethyl" were taken out of service, drivers had to continue to buy gasoline containing the anti-knock compound. The Commission found that the firms in the industry only sold based on "delivered prices," i.e., the producers absorbed the shipping cost rather than charging for the product plus shipping. Thus, everyone could know exactly what price had to be charged to meet competition; no factor for differences in shipping costs need be calculated.

Further, all the sellers used "most favored nations" clauses, which assured buyers that if the firms granted a discount to one customer, all customers would receive it. Finally, all sellers agreed by contracts with their purchasers to give 30 days advance notice of price changes, a practice that allowed each of them to determine whether competitors were matching the changes or whether the changes should be withdrawn. The Commission concluded that all three practices facilitated oligopoly pricing, but the Court of Appeals found no basis to say the practices had been reached by agreement. While § 5 gives the FTC a right to find more things "unfair" than the Sherman Act condemns, the Court said, without more than the fact of common practices, there was insufficient evidence to sustain a finding that the practices had violated the law.[72]

In re Coordinated Pretrial Proceedings (Petroleum Products Antitrust Litigation), 906 F.2d 432 (9th Cir.1990), cert.denied 500 U.S. 959 (1991), on the other hand, involved actions filed by the Attorneys General of several western states alleging that oil companies coordinated temporary discounts from published tankwagon prices. Three kinds of evidence were cited for the alleged coordination. First was what was described as a "sawtooth" pattern that could be seen on graphs of the prices, i.e., there were sharp decreases in price followed by sharp increases back to about where the prices had begun. This "interdependent" pricing might be observed wholly without coordination where discounts or increases could be quickly changed, the court said, and thus—standing alone—it did not prove a violation of § 1. However, the court also observed that the companies had issued press releases announcing their price changes, allegedly in the hope that the other companies would go along. In addition, there was some evidence that competitors contacted each other directly— even after *Container*—to verify the discounts being granted. As in earlier

---

[72] The case is discussed in George A. Hay, Facilitating Practices: The Ethyl Case (1984), in John E. Kwoka & Lawrence J. White, eds., The Antitrust Revolution: Economics, Competition and Policy (3d Ed. 1999), p. 182.

cases of this type, the defendants asserted that they ultimately made individual decisions in light of publicly available information. The court, however, found sufficient basis to infer coordinated behavior that summary judgment for the defendants was reversed.[73]

United States v. Airline Tariff Publishing Co., 1993–1 CCH Trade Cases ¶ 70,191 (D.D.C.1993), charged the airline industry with indirect coordination of pricing in that all airlines sell tickets to persons who deal through computers. The computer networks, in turn, contain the fare information for all the airlines, including details such as how many seats on each flight are available at discount fares, and starting and ending dates for new or promotional fares. The Justice Department alleged that access to this much detail establishes the conditions necessary for coordinated pricing, particularly in an industry as concentrated as the airline industry has become. Two of the eight defendants agreed to a consent decree forbidding prior announcement of the beginning or end of fare discount programs.[74]

However, other cases have been less prone to see "plus" factors sufficient to find a violation of § 1. In re Baby Food Antitrust Litigation, 166 F.3d 112 (3d Cir. 1999), found the evidence of conspiracy insufficient. It showed an essentially four-firm industry in which one firm, Gerber, made 70% of all sales. Companies tried to distinguish themselves by price, and salespeople of each company reported to management what customers said their competitors planned to do. The result was a series of parallel price changes and, the plaintiffs alleged, a "truce" leading to price increases. Obtaining market information about competitor plans is not conspiratorial, the court reasoned, and any firm with an industry leader like Gerber is likely to follow its leadership. See also, Market Force Inc. v. Wauwatosa Realty Co., 906 F.2d 1167 (7th Cir.1990) (no conspiracy shown where buyers' brokers were paid a referral fee instead of the commission paid to sellers' brokers); Williamson Oil Co. v. Philip Morris USA, 346 F.3d 1287 (11th Cir. 2003) (price cut matched by competitors, followed by industry-wide price increases, not enough to prove conspiracy).

---

[73]   This was particularly significant in light of the Supreme Court's decision in Matsushita Electric Industrial Co. v. Zenith Radio Corp., 475 U.S. 574, 106 S.Ct. 1348, 89 L.Ed.2d 538 (1986), that you will read in Part C of this Chapter. See also, e.g., Isaksen v. Vermont Castings, Inc., 825 F.2d 1158 (7th Cir.1987), cert.denied 486 U.S. 1005 (1988) (court, per Judge Posner, concludes that a showing of actual manufacturer efforts to get dealers to adhere to minimum prices, plus a showing of actual dealer compliance, is sufficient to demonstrate an "agreement" in violation of Sherman Act § 1); Big Apple BMW v. BMW of North America, 974 F.2d 1358 (3d Cir.1992), cert.denied 507 U.S. 912 (1993) (sufficient factual issue to avoid summary judgment on whether dealers conspired with manufacturer to obtain termination of another dealer).

[74]   Cf. Jeffrey L. Kessler & Ronald C. Wheeler, How to Price Without Being a "Price Signaler", 7 Antitrust 26 (Summer 1993); William B. Slowey, Benchmarking: Boon or Buzz Word?, 7 Antitrust 30 (Summer 1993). The private action making the same allegations was settled. But airline passengers received no cash; they got only discount certificates for future flights. In re Domestic Air Transportation Antitrust Litigation, 148 F.R.D. 297 (N.D.Ga.1993).

THE CONTINUING DEBATE ABOUT THE ECONOMICS
OF VERTICAL RESTRAINTS

The almost 75 years between *Dr. Miles* and *Monsanto* had not resolved the controversy over the public interest impact of vertical restraints. You may remember, for example, that the Court in *Dr. Miles* thought resale price maintenance represented a conspiracy of small retailers to protect themselves from competition with larger, more efficient firms.

That view was challenged over 30 years ago on the ground that manufacturers may selfishly want to impose vertical restraints as a way to compensate or reward retailers for providing point of sale services to consumers.[75] The correlative point, that such rewards could stimulate interbrand competition and thus benefit consumers, was then central to the Court's decision in *GTE Sylvania*.

The issues assumed particular importance, in part because a concession that the Court had been wrong all along in its condemnation of vertical restraints might be seen as a victory of economic analysis over legal precedent and properly put other antitrust doctrine at risk. Thus, the debate has continued.

In principle, large firms could employ a sales force to market their goods; that would involve contracts, but we would call them employment contracts. The decision to contract with retail firms represents a manufacturer's decision aimed at lowering the costs inherent in distribution.[76] The terms of the contracts will seek to minimize transaction costs; manufacturers will have no incentive to use terms that take advantage of consumers because that would only make their products less attractive.[77]

The traditional view was that resale price maintenance and territorial allocation worked because they gave a reward to retail dealers which made them willing to offer special service to the consumer. So described, however, the story was incomplete. Dealers who had their price or territory protected did not thereafter provide the required service out of gratitude;

---

[75]   See, e.g., Lester G. Telser, Why Should Manufacturers Want Fair Trade?, 3 J. Law & Econ. 86 (1960). Apparently, however, the basic point had been made within five years of *Dr. Miles*. See F.W. Taussig, Price Maintenance, 6 Am.Econ.Rev. 170 (Supp. 1916).

[76]   E.g., Alan J. Meese, Intrabrand Restraints and the Theory of the Firm, 83 N. Carolina L. Rev. 5 (2004); Douglas H. Ginsburg, Vertical Restraints: De Facto Legality Under the Rule of Reason, 60 Antitrust L. J. 67 (1991); Richard A. Posner, The Next Step in the Antitrust Treatment of Restricted Distribution: Per Se Legality, 48 U. Chicago L. Rev. 6 (1981).

[77]   See, e.g., Oliver E. Williamson, Assessing Vertical Market Restrictions: Antitrust Ramifications of the Transaction Cost Approach, 127 U. Pennsylvania L. Rev. 953 (1979). But see Jean Wegman Burns, Vertical Restraints, Efficiency, and the Real World, 62 Fordham L. Rev. 597 (1993).

their incentive was to let others provide the service and reap the benefits of the others' efforts. The real problem for manufacturers was thus protection of conforming dealers against such "free riders."[78]

As a result, for many, the important judicial issue was not whether the manufacturer imposed restraints or whether a dealer was a "discounter;" it was whether the courts would let manufacturers terminate dealers who did not conform to the agreements that gave them the right to distribute the manufacturer's product in the first place. Under this analysis, Monsanto should have had every right to terminate Spray-Rite because it met none of the important criteria for being a dealer that Monsanto had established.

Not everyone, however, agreed. Economist William S. Comanor, for example, argued that the above analysis loses sight of the fact that the manufacturer will aim most of its efforts at the "marginal" customers, the last ones it can pick up before the cost of reaching them exceeds the revenue they provide the firm. Those are the customers, the argument goes, who need the point-of-sale service. In reality, however, a large part of the world consists of "inframarginal" customers, those who want the product badly, get no benefit from extra service and who would prefer to get the product at the lowest price possible.[79]

Furthermore, others argue, in many markets competing manufacturers sell their products through common retailers. Think of a supermarket, for example, where you see the goods of many manufacturers side by side. Where is the point-of-sale service in such stores, critics ask. All exclusive territories or resale price maintenance is likely to do in such stores is *minimize* interbrand competition as retailers tend to bring the prices of lower-priced items up to those whose price is protected.[80]

Thus, the argument would go, let Spray-Rite sell to inframarginal customers at any prices it wishes. Let Monsanto look for other retailers

---

[78] See, e.g., Andy C. M. Chen & Keith N. Hylton, Procompetitive Theories of Vertical Control, 50 Hastings L.J. 573 (1999); Mark A. Glick & Duncan J. Cameron, When Do Proprietary Aftermarkets Benefit Consumers?, 67 Antitrust L.J. 357 (1999); Benjamin Klein & Kevin M. Murphy, Vertical Restraints as Contract Enforcement Mechanisms, 31 J. Law & Economics 265 (1988).

[79] The principal article is William S. Comanor, Vertical Price Fixing, Vertical Market Restrictions, and the New Antitrust Policy, 98 Harvard L.Rev. 983 (1985). But see Don Boudreaux & Robert B. Ekelund, Jr., Inframarginal Consumers and the Per Se Legality of Vertical Restraints, 17 Hofstra L.Rev. 137 (1988).

[80] See, e.g., Warren S. Grimes, Brand Marketing, Intrabrand Competition, and the Multibrand Retailer: The Antitrust Law of Vertical Restraints, 64 Antitrust L.J. 83 (1995); Barbara Ann White, Black and White Thinking in the Gray Areas of Antitrust: The Dismantling of Vertical Restraints Regulation, 60 George Washington L.Rev. 1 (1991) (citing economic studies); Lawrence A. Sullivan, Section 2 of the Sherman Act and Vertical Strategies by Dominant Firms, 21 Southwestern U. L.Rev. 1227 (1992). The history of the wide swings in public and scholarly analysis of vertical restraints is chronicled in Warren S. Grimes, The Seven Myths of Vertical Price Fixing: The Politics and Economics of a Century-Long Debate, 21 Southwestern U. L.Rev. 1285 (1992).

who will provide the information about application and other service to customers willing to pay extra for it. Or, if it is worried about customers who will shop at the high priced store but buy from Spray-Rite, let Monsanto provide subsidies to retailers who provide services. Then, pass the cost along to everyone, including Spray-Rite, in the wholesale price of the herbicides.

Do any of these arguments persuade you? All of them? See whether the Court adequately deals with them in our next case.

BUSINESS ELECTRONICS CORP. v. SHARP ELECTRONICS CORP.

Supreme Court of the United States, 1988
485 U.S. 717, 108 S.Ct. 1515, 99 L.Ed.2d 808

JUSTICE SCALIA delivered the opinion of the Court.

Petitioner Business Electronics Corporation seeks review of a decision of the United States Court of Appeals for the Fifth Circuit holding that a vertical restraint is per se illegal under § 1 of the Sherman Act only if there is an express or implied agreement to set resale prices at some level. We granted certiorari to resolve a conflict in the Courts of Appeals regarding the proper dividing line between the rule that vertical price restraints are illegal per se and the rule that vertical nonprice restraints are to be judged under the rule of reason.

I

In 1968, petitioner became the exclusive retailer in the Houston, Texas, area of electronic calculators manufactured by respondent Sharp Electronics Corporation. In 1972, respondent appointed Gilbert Hartwell as a second retailer in the Houston area. During the relevant period, electronic calculators were primarily sold to business customers for prices up to $1,000. While much of the evidence in this case was conflicting—in particular, concerning whether petitioner was "free riding" on Hartwell's provision of presale educational and promotional services by providing inadequate services itself—a few facts are undisputed. Respondent published a list of suggested minimum retail prices, but its written dealership agreements with petitioner and Hartwell did not obligate either to observe them, or to charge any other specific price. Petitioner's retail prices were often below respondent's suggested retail prices and generally below Hartwell's retail prices, even though Hartwell too sometimes priced below respondent's suggested retail prices. Hartwell complained to respondent on a number of occasions about petitioner's prices. In June 1973, Hartwell gave respondent the ultimatum that Hartwell would terminate his dealership unless respondent ended its relationship with petitioner within 30 days. Respondent terminated petitioner's dealership in July 1973.

Petitioner brought suit in the United States District Court for the Southern District of Texas, alleging that respondent and Hartwell had conspired to terminate petitioner and that such conspiracy was illegal per se under § 1 of the Sherman Act. The case was tried to a jury. The District Court submitted a liability interrogatory to the jury that asked whether "there was an agreement or understanding between Sharp Electronics Corporation and Hartwell to terminate Business Electronics as a Sharp dealer because of Business Electronics' price cutting." The District Court instructed the jury at length about this question:

> "The Sherman Act is violated when a seller enters into an agreement or understanding with one of its dealers to terminate another dealer because of the other dealer's price cutting. Plaintiff contends that Sharp terminated Business Electronics in furtherance of Hartwell's desire to eliminate Business Electronics as a price-cutting rival.

> * * *

> "If a dealer demands that a manufacturer terminate a price cutting dealer, and the manufacturer agrees to do so, the agreement is illegal if the manufacturer's purpose is to eliminate the price cutting."

The jury * * * awarded $600,000 in damages. The District Court * * * entered judgment for petitioner for treble damages plus attorney's fees.

The Fifth Circuit reversed, holding that the jury * * * instructions were erroneous, and remanded for a new trial. It held that, to render illegal per se a vertical agreement between a manufacturer and a dealer to terminate a second dealer, the first dealer "must expressly or impliedly agree to set its prices at some level, though not a specific one. The distributor cannot retain complete freedom to set whatever price it chooses."

II

A

* * * Ordinarily, whether particular concerted action violates § 1 of the Sherman Act is determined through case-by-case application of the so-called rule of reason—that is, "the factfinder weighs all of the circumstances of a case in deciding whether a restrictive practice should be prohibited as imposing an unreasonable restraint on competition." Continental T. V., Inc. v. GTE Sylvania Inc. * * * We have said that per se rules are appropriate only for "conduct that is manifestly anticompetitive," that is, conduct " 'that would always or almost always tend to restrict competition and decrease output,' " Northwest Wholesale Stationers, Inc. v. Pacific Stationery & Printing Co., quoting Broadcast Music, Inc. v. Columbia Broadcasting System, Inc.

Although vertical agreements on resale prices have been illegal per se since Dr. Miles Medical Co. v. John D. Park & Sons Co., we have recognized that the scope of per se illegality should be narrow in the context of vertical restraints. In Continental T. V., Inc. v. GTE Sylvania Inc., we refused to extend per se illegality to vertical nonprice restraints, specifically to a manufacturer's termination of one dealer pursuant to an exclusive territory agreement with another. We noted that especially in the vertical restraint context "departure from the rule-of-reason standard must be based on demonstrable economic effect rather than * * * upon formalistic line drawing." We concluded that vertical nonprice restraints had not been shown to have such a " 'pernicious effect on competition' " and to be so " 'lac[king] [in] * * * redeeming value' " as to justify per se illegality. Rather, we found, they had real potential to stimulate interbrand competition, "the primary concern of antitrust law." * * *

Moreover, we observed that a rule of per se illegality for vertical nonprice restraints was not needed or effective to protect *intra* brand competition. First, so long as interbrand competition existed, that would provide a "significant check" on any attempt to exploit intrabrand market power. In fact, in order to meet that interbrand competition, a manufacturer's dominant incentive is to lower resale prices. Second, the per se illegality of vertical restraints would create a perverse incentive for manufacturers to integrate vertically into distribution, an outcome hardly conducive to fostering the creation and maintenance of small businesses.

Finally, our opinion in *GTE Sylvania* noted a significant distinction between vertical nonprice and vertical price restraints. That is, there was support for the proposition that vertical price restraints reduce *inter* brand price competition because they " 'facilitate cartelizing.' " The authorities cited by the Court suggested how vertical price agreements might assist horizontal price fixing at the manufacturer level (by reducing the manufacturer's incentive to cheat on a cartel, since its retailers could not pass on lower prices to consumers) or might be used to organize cartels at the retailer level. Similar support for the cartel-facilitating effect of vertical nonprice restraints was and remains lacking.

We have been solicitous to assure that the market-freeing effect of our decision in *GTE Sylvania* is not frustrated by related legal rules. In Monsanto Co. v. Spray-Rite Service Corp., which addressed the evidentiary showing necessary to establish vertical concerted action, we expressed concern that "if an inference of such an agreement may be drawn from highly ambiguous evidence, there is considerable danger that the doctrine enunciated in *Sylvania* * * * will be seriously eroded." We eschewed adoption of an evidentiary standard that "could deter or penalize perfectly legitimate conduct" or "would create an irrational dislocation in the market" by preventing legitimate communication between a manufacturer and its distributors.

Our approach to the question presented in the present case is guided by the premises of *GTE Sylvania* and *Monsanto*: that there is a presumption in favor of a rule-of-reason standard; that departure from that standard must be justified by demonstrable economic effect, such as the facilitation of cartelizing, rather than formalistic distinctions; that interbrand competition is the primary concern of the antitrust laws; and that rules in this area should be formulated with a view towards protecting the doctrine of *GTE Sylvania*. These premises lead us to conclude that the line drawn by the Fifth Circuit is the most appropriate one.

There has been no showing here that an agreement between a manufacturer and a dealer to terminate a "price cutter," without a further agreement on the price or price levels to be charged by the remaining dealer, almost always tends to restrict competition and reduce output. Any assistance to cartelizing that such an agreement might provide cannot be distinguished from the sort of minimal assistance that might be provided by vertical nonprice agreements like the exclusive territory agreement in *GTE Sylvania*, and is insufficient to justify a per se rule. Cartels are neither easy to form nor easy to maintain. Uncertainty over the terms of the cartel, particularly the prices to be charged in the future, obstructs both formation and adherence by making cheating easier. Without an agreement with the remaining dealer on price, the manufacturer both retains its incentive to cheat on any manufacturer-level cartel (since lower prices can still be passed on to consumers) and cannot as easily be used to organize and hold together a retailer-level cartel.[81]

The District Court's rule on the scope of per se illegality for vertical restraints would threaten to dismantle the doctrine of *GTE Sylvania*. Any agreement between a manufacturer and a dealer to terminate another dealer who happens to have charged lower prices can be alleged to have been directed against the terminated dealer's "price cutting." In the vast majority of cases, it will be extremely difficult for the manufacturer to convince a jury that its motivation was to ensure adequate services, since price cutting and some measure of service cutting usually go hand in hand. Accordingly, a manufacturer that agrees to give one dealer an exclusive territory and terminates another dealer pursuant to that agreement, or even a manufacturer that agrees with one dealer to terminate another for failure to provide contractually obligated services, exposes itself to the highly plausible claim that its real motivation was to terminate a price cutter. Moreover, even vertical restraints that do not result in dealer

---

[81] The dissent's principal fear appears to be not cartelization at either level, but Hartwell's assertion of dominant retail power. This fear does not possibly justify adopting a rule of per se illegality. Retail market power is rare, because of the usual presence of interbrand competition and other dealers, and it should therefore not be assumed but rather must be proved. Cf. Baxter, The Viability of Vertical Restraints Doctrine, 75 California L.Rev. 933 (1987). Of course this case was not prosecuted on the theory, and therefore the jury was not asked to find, that Hartwell possessed such market power. [Court's fn. 2]

termination, such as the initial granting of an exclusive territory or the requirement that certain services be provided, can be attacked as designed to allow existing dealers to charge higher prices. Manufacturers would be likely to forgo legitimate and competitively useful conduct rather than risk treble damages and perhaps even criminal penalties.

* * *

* * * [T]he dissent's reasoning hinges upon its perception that the agreement between Sharp and Hartwell was a "naked" restraint—that is, it was not "ancillary" to any other agreement between Sharp and Hartwell. But that is not true, unless one assumes, contrary to *GTE Sylvania* and *Monsanto*, and contrary to our earlier discussion, that it is not a quite plausible purpose of the restriction to enable Hartwell to provide better services under the sales franchise agreement. From its faulty conclusion that what we have before us is a "naked" restraint, the dissent proceeds, by reasoning we do not entirely follow, to the further conclusion that it is therefore a horizontal rather than a vertical restraint. * * *

Finally, we do not agree with petitioner's contention that an agreement on the remaining dealer's price or price levels will so often follow from terminating another dealer "because of [its] price cutting" that prophylaxis against resale price maintenance warrants the District Court's per se rule. Petitioner has provided no support for the proposition that vertical price agreements generally underlie agreements to terminate a price cutter. That proposition is simply incompatible with the conclusion of *GTE Sylvania* and *Monsanto* that manufacturers are often motivated by a legitimate desire to have dealers provide services, combined with the reality that price cutting is frequently made possible by "free riding" on the services provided by other dealers. The District Court's per se rule would therefore discourage conduct recognized by *GTE Sylvania* and *Monsanto* as beneficial to consumers.

B

In resting our decision upon the foregoing economic analysis, we do not ignore common-law precedent concerning what constituted "restraint of trade" at the time the Sherman Act was adopted. But neither do we give that pre-1890 precedent the dispositive effect some would. The term "restraint of trade" in the statute, like the term at common law, refers not to a particular list of agreements, but to a particular economic consequence, which may be produced by quite different sorts of agreements in varying times and circumstances. The changing content of the term "restraint of trade" was well recognized at the time the Sherman Act was enacted.

The Sherman Act adopted the term "restraint of trade" along with its dynamic potential. It invokes the common law itself, and not merely the static content that the common law had assigned to the term in 1890. If it were otherwise, not only would the line of per se illegality have to be drawn today precisely where it was in 1890, but also case-by-case evaluation of legality * * * would have to be governed by 19th-century notions of reasonableness. * * *

* * *

Petitioner's principal contention has been that the District Court's rule on per se illegality is compelled not by the old common law, but by our more recent Sherman Act precedents. First, petitioner contends that since certain horizontal agreements have been held to constitute price fixing (and thus to be per se illegal) though they did not set prices or price levels, see, e.g., Catalano, Inc. v. Target Sales, Inc., it is improper to require that a vertical agreement set prices or price levels before it can suffer the same fate. This notion of equivalence between the scope of horizontal per se illegality and that of vertical per se illegality was explicitly rejected in *GTE Sylvania* * * * .

Second, petitioner contends that per se illegality here follows from our two cases holding per se illegal a group boycott of a dealer because of its price cutting. See United States v. General Motors Corp.; Klor's, Inc. v. Broadway-Hale Stores, Inc. This second contention is merely a restatement of the first, since both cases involved horizontal combinations—*General Motors* at the dealer level, and *Klor's* at the manufacturer and wholesaler levels. Accord, *GTE Sylvania.*

Third, petitioner contends, relying on Albrecht v. Herald Co., and United States v. Parke, Davis & Co., that our vertical price-fixing cases have already rejected the proposition that per se illegality requires setting a price or a price level. We disagree. In *Albrecht*, the maker of the product formed a combination to force a retailer to charge the maker's advertised retail price. * * * It is plain that the combination involved both an explicit agreement on resale price and an agreement to force another to adhere to the specified price. In *Parke, Davis*, a manufacturer combined first with wholesalers and then with retailers in order to gain the "retailers' adherence to its suggested minimum retail prices." * * * This holding also does not support a rule that an agreement on price or price level is not required for a vertical restraint to be per se illegal—first, because the agreement not to advertise prices was part and parcel of the combination that contained the price agreement, and second because the agreement among retailers that the manufacturer organized was a *horizontal* conspiracy among competitors.

In sum, economic analysis supports the view, and no precedent opposes it, that a vertical restraint is not illegal per se unless it includes some agreement on price or price levels. Accordingly, the judgment of the Fifth Circuit is

Affirmed.

JUSTICE KENNEDY took no part in the consideration or decision of this case.

JUSTICE STEVENS, with whom JUSTICE WHITE joins, dissenting.

In its opinion the majority assumes, without analysis, that the question presented by this case concerns the legality of a "vertical nonprice restraint." As I shall demonstrate, the restraint that results when one or more dealers threatens to boycott a manufacturer unless it terminates its relationship with a price-cutting retailer is more properly viewed as a "horizontal restraint." Moreover, an agreement to terminate a dealer because of its price cutting is most certainly not a "nonprice restraint." The distinction between "vertical nonprice restraints" and "vertical price restraints," on which the majority focuses its attention, is therefore quite irrelevant to the outcome of this case. Of much greater importance is the distinction between "naked restraints" and "ancillary restraints" that has been a part of our law since the landmark opinion written by Judge (later Chief Justice) Taft in United States v. Addyston Pipe & Steel Co.

I

* * *

Judge Taft's rejection of an argument that a price-fixing agreement could be defended as reasonable was based on a detailed examination of common-law precedents. * * * The difference between ancillary covenants that may be justified as reasonable and those that are "void" because there is "nothing to justify or excuse the restraint," was described in the opinion's seminal discussion:

> "[T]he contract must be one in which there is a main purpose, to which the covenant in restraint of trade is merely ancillary. The covenant is inserted only to protect one of the parties from the injury which, in the execution of the contract or enjoyment of its fruits, he may suffer from the unrestrained competition of the other. The main purpose of the contract suggests the measure of protection needed, and furnishes a sufficiently uniform standard by which the validity of such restraints may be judicially determined. In such a case, if the restraint exceeds the necessity presented by the main purpose of the contract, it is void for two reasons: First, because it oppresses the covenantor, without any corresponding benefit to the covenantee; and, second, because it tends to a monopoly. * * * "

Although Judge Taft was writing as a Circuit Judge, his opinion is universally accepted as authoritative. We affirmed his decision without dissent, we have repeatedly cited it with approval, and it is praised by a respected scholar as "one of the greatest, if not the greatest, antitrust opinions in the history of the law." R. Bork, The Antitrust Paradox 26

(1978). In accordance with the teaching in that opinion, it is therefore appropriate to look more closely at the character of the restraint of trade found by the jury in this case.

II

It may be helpful to begin by explaining why the agreement in this case does not fit into certain categories of agreement that are frequently found in antitrust litigation. First, * * * [t]he term "vertical nonprice restraint," as used in Continental T.V., Inc. v. GTE Sylvania Inc., and similar cases, refers to a contractual term that a dealer must accept in order to qualify for a franchise. Typically, the dealer must agree to meet certain standards in its advertising, promotion, product display, and provision of repair and maintenance services in order to protect the goodwill of the manufacturer's product. * * * Restrictions of that kind, which are a part of, or ancillary to, the basic franchise agreement, are perfectly lawful unless the "rule of reason" is violated. Although vertical nonprice restraints may have some adverse effect on competition, as long as they serve the main purpose of a procompetitive distribution agreement, the ancillary restraints may be defended under the rule of reason. And, of course, a dealer who violates such a restraint may properly be terminated by the manufacturer.

In this case, it does not appear that respondent imposed any vertical nonprice restraints upon either petitioner or Hartwell. Specifically, respondent did not enter into any "exclusive" agreement, as did the defendant in *Sylvania*. * * * The case is one in which one of two competing dealers entered into an agreement with the manufacturer to terminate a particular competitor without making any promise to provide better or more efficient services and without receiving any guarantee of exclusivity in the future. * * *

Second, this case does not involve a typical vertical price restraint. * * * For purposes of analysis, we should assume that no * * * [agreement on a specific price] existed and that respondent was perfectly willing to allow its dealers to set prices at levels that would maximize their profits. * * *

Third, this is not a case in which the manufacturer acted independently. Indeed, given the jury's verdict, it is not even a case in which the termination can be explained as having been based on the violation of any distribution policy adopted by respondent. * * * The termination was plainly the product of coercion by the stronger of two dealers rather than an attempt to maintain an orderly and efficient system of distribution.

In sum, this case does not involve the reasonableness of any vertical restraint imposed on one or more dealers by a manufacturer in its basic franchise agreement. What the jury found was a simple and naked

" 'agreement between Sharp and Hartwell to terminate Business Electronics because of Business Electronics' price cutting.' "

III

Because naked agreements to restrain the trade of third parties are seldom identified with such stark clarity as in this case, there appears to be no exact precedent that determines the outcome here. There are, however, perfectly clear rules that would be decisive if the facts were changed only slightly.

Thus, on the one hand, if it were clear that respondent had acted independently and decided to terminate petitioner because respondent, for reasons of its own, objected to petitioner's pricing policies, the termination would be lawful. See United States v. Parke, Davis & Co. On the other hand, it is equally clear that if respondent had been represented by three dealers in the Houston market instead of only two, and if two of them had threatened to terminate their dealerships "unless respondent ended its relationship with petitioner within 30 days," an agreement to comply with the ultimatum would be an obvious violation of the Sherman Act. See, e.g., United States v. General Motors Corp.; Klor's, Inc. v. Broadway-Hale Stores, Inc. The question then is whether the two-party agreement involved in this case is more like an illegal three-party agreement or a legal independent decision. For me, the answer is plain.

* * *

* * * [I]f instead of speculating about irrelevant vertical nonprice restraints, we focus on the precise character of the agreement before us, we can readily identify its anticompetitive nature. Before the agreement was made, there was price competition in the Houston retail market for respondent's products. The stronger of the two competitors was unhappy about that competition; it wanted to have the power to set the price level in the market and therefore it "complained to respondent on a number of occasions about petitioner's prices." * * * Although respondent has not granted Hartwell an exclusive dealership * * * its agreement has protected Hartwell from price competition. Indeed, given the jury's finding and the evidence in the record, that is the *sole function* of the agreement found by the jury in this case. It therefore fits squarely within the category of "naked restraints of trade with no purpose except stifling of competition." White Motor Co. v. United States.

* * *

IV

What is most troubling about the majority's opinion is its failure to attach any weight to the value of intrabrand competition. In Continental T. V., Inc. v. GTE Sylvania Inc., we correctly held that a demonstrable benefit to interbrand competition will outweigh the harm to intrabrand competition that is caused by the imposition of vertical nonprice restrictions on dealers. But we also expressly reaffirmed earlier cases in which the illegal conspiracy affected only intrabrand competition. Not a word in the *Sylvania* opinion implied that the elimination of intrabrand competition could be justified as reasonable without any evidence of a purpose to improve interbrand competition.

* * *

Neither the Court of Appeals nor the majority questions the accuracy of the jury's resolution of the factual issues in this case. Nevertheless, the rule the majority fashions today is based largely on its concern that in other cases juries will be unable to tell the difference between truthful and pretextual defenses. * * * Both in its disposition of this case and in its attempt to justify a new approach to agreements to eliminate price competition, the majority exhibits little confidence in the judicial process as a means of ascertaining the truth.

* * *

Although in this case the jury found a naked agreement to terminate a dealer because of its price cutting, the majority boldly characterizes the same agreement as "this nonprice vertical restriction." That characterization is surely an oxymoron when applied to the agreement the jury actually found. * * *

* * *

* * * [T]he "quite plausible purpose" the majority hypothesizes as salvation for the otherwise anticompetitive elimination of price competition—"to enable Hartwell to provide better services under the sales franchise agreement"—is simply not the type of concern we sought to protect in Continental T.V., Inc. v. GTE Sylvania Inc. I have emphasized in this dissent the difference between restrictions imposed in pursuit of a manufacturer's structuring of its product distribution, and those imposed at the behest of retailers who care less about the general efficiency of a product's promotion than their own profit margins. *Sylvania* stressed the importance of the former, not the latter * * * . Thus, while Hartwell may indeed be able to provide better services under the sales franchise agreement with petitioner out of the way, one would not have thought, until today, that the mere possibility of such a result—at the expense of the elimination of price competition and absent the salutary overlay of a manufacturer's distribution decision with the entire product line in mind—would be sufficient to legitimate an otherwise purely anticompetitive restraint. In fact, given the majority's total reliance on "economic analysis," it is hard to understand why, if such a purpose were sufficient to avoid the application of a per se rule in this context, the same purpose should not also be sufficient to trump the per se rule in all other price-fixing cases that arguably permit cartel members to "provide better services."

If, however, we continue to accept the premise that competition in the relevant market is worthy of legal protection—that we should not rely on competitive pressures exerted by sellers in other areas and purveyors of similar but not identical products—and if we are faithful to the competitive philosophy that has animated our antitrust jurisprudence since Judge Taft's opinion in *Addyston Pipe*, we can agree that the elimination of price competition will produce wider gross profit margins for retailers, but we may not assume that the retailer's self interest will result in a better marketplace for consumers. * * *

* * *

I respectfully dissent.

NOTES AND QUESTIONS

1.   Justice Scalia begins his development of post-*Monsanto* analysis of vertical restraints with a discussion of when the rule of reason should be used.

a.   Do you agree that the Court has always indulged a presumption in favor of the rule of reason? Is that true in the case of resale price maintenance? Do you agree that only non-price restraints were present here?

b.   Do you agree that there is no reason to believe that terminating a price cutter, without any further agreement, tends to restrict competition and reduce output? Might one termination "send a message" to other firms?

c.   If the Court had not done what it did here, could any manufacturer give exclusive territories and change distributors without being subject to a price-cutter defense? Is the Court right that reduced service and price cutting are often likely to go together?

2.   Notice that Justice Scalia got five other votes, but Justices Stevens and White, who used to be considered the antitrust experts on the Court, both dissented. On what basis?

a.   Are they right that when a manufacturer terminates a dealer on complaint of other dealers, one has a horizontal and not a vertical restraint? Do *Parke Davis*, *Klors* and *General Motors* leave room for doubt about that point?

b.   Did Sharp convince a jury there was no collusion here? If not, should the Court reverse the jury's finding of fact?

c.   Are the dissenters right that the majority gave no weight to the value of intrabrand competition? How much value should it have been assigned? How would one estimate the effects on such competition?

3.   Both sides want to claim the legacy of *Addyston Pipe*. Who has better claim to it? Do you think Sharp was employing a naked restraint here, or was

its action ancillary to a lawful business arrangement? If *Colgate* still is to have any life, must manufacturers have at least the latitude to decide whom to use as a distributor?[82]

4.   What does it take to win a dealer termination case after *Sharp*?[83] Will the plaintiff have to prove a specific price at which the manufacturer and dealer agreed prices would be set? What does the Court mean when it says an agreement as to "price levels" will suffice?

5.   *Monsanto* and *Sharp* are two of the cases that significantly impacted the work of plaintiffs' antitrust lawyers. Dealer terminations had been relatively easy cases to at least get to a jury based on *Dr. Miles* and *General Motors*. However, even an intense effort by antitrust plaintiffs' lawyers has failed to get Congress to overrule *Monsanto* and *Sharp* legislatively.

VERTICAL GROUP BOYCOTTS—*NYNEX v. DISCON*

Remember *Klor's*? That was the 1960 case of the small retailer who successfully charged its suppliers with conspiracy when they accepted a larger retailer's ultimatum not to ship to the plaintiff. One might have thought *Business Electronics* had already shown that the law on that issue had moderated, but the Supreme Court returned to the question in NYNEX Corp. v. Discon, Inc., 525 U.S. 128, 119 S.Ct. 493, 142 L.Ed.2d 510 (1998).

When competition was introduced into the long-distance telephone business, some local companies had to remove their old call switching equipment and install new. Discon had done removal work for New York Telephone, a subsidiary of NYNEX, but it lost that business when NYNEX switched its business to one its own subsidiaries. In Discon's view, the switch would increase the cost of the removal service, thus benefitting NYNEX and fraudulently passing the burden of the higher cost to telephone users.

The Second Circuit said that while business decisions to switch suppliers were ordinarily upheld as pro-competitive, the theory of this complaint was that there was no such positive rationale. The *Klor's* per se rule is still good law, the court reasoned, where the purchasing decision "has no purpose except stifling competition." 93 F.3d at 1061–62. But the court did invite the defendant to show a pro-competitive rationale as a way of avoiding the per se rule.

---

[82]   See, e.g., Brian R. Henry & Eugene F. Zelek, Jr., Establishing and Maintaining an Effective Minimum Resale Price Policy: A *Colgate* How-To, 17 Antitrust 8 (Summer 2003). Compare Robert Pitofsky, In Defense of Discounters: The No-Frills Case for a Per Se Rule Against Vertical Price Fixing, 71 Georgetown L. Rev. 487 (1983).

[83]   See, e.g., Michael L. Denger, Resale Pricing Issues in Distribution and Franchisor Operations, 60 Antitrust L.J. 419 (1991); Joe Sims & Phillip A. Proger, Litigation Issues in Dealer Termination Pricing Cases, 60 Antitrust L.J. 465 (1991).

A unanimous Supreme Court reversed. The Court acknowledged that *Fashion Originators* and *Klor's* had both applied a per se rule to group boycotts. *Business Electronics*, however, had understood *Klor's* to apply only where there had been a horizontal agreement as well, i.e., there an "agreement" among appliance manufacturers to go along with Broadway-Hale's demand. Quoting *Business Electronics*, the Court said that a vertical restraint "is not illegal per se unless it includes some agreement on price or price levels."

Thus, the Court held, "no boycott-related per se rule applies and * * * the plaintiff here must allege and prove harm, not just to a single competitor, but to the competitive process, i.e., to competition itself." Alleging regulatory fraud was not enough to show injury to competition. Otherwise, any improper purpose such as "nepotism or personal pique" could give rise to a treble-damage antitrust action. Even the threat of such a case could "discourage firms from changing suppliers," a result harmful "to the heart of the competitive process that the antitrust laws seek to encourage." Is all now becoming clear to you?

BREAKING DOWN THE RULE AGAINST RESALE PRICE MAINTENANCE: MAXIMUM RESALE PRICE FIXING

The illegality of fixing *maximum* resale prices was first cast into doubt by Atlantic Richfield Co. v. USA Petroleum, 495 U.S. 328, 110 S.Ct. 1884, 109 L.Ed.2d 333 (1990), the same year the Court decided the group boycott case involving the Superior Court Trial Lawyers. USA Petroleum was a customer of ARCO that sold its gas at "discount" prices; that was USA Petroleum's market persona. ARCO devised a marketing plan with its own stations and its independent ARCO dealers under which they decided to match the prices of such discount dealers. That is, ARCO imposed a cap on ARCO dealers' prices. It worked, and their market share increased as a result.

The prices were not below cost, but USA Petroleum said that the effect of the ARCO plan was to reduce its [USA's] profit margin and damage its ability to remain in the market. It alleged that its demise would reduce competition and thus restrain trade. The District Court threw the case out for lack of antitrust injury. The Ninth Circuit reversed, saying that even non-predatory pricing could create antitrust injury if it caused injury in fact to a competitor. The Supreme Court reversed the Court of Appeals and adopted the "lack of antitrust injury" analysis.

The Court distinguished Albrecht v. Herald Co., saying that *Albrecht* was worried about the effect of maximum prices on customers and dealers, not on other newspapers. Here, the Court stressed the plaintiff's status as competitor, not customer. Further, the Court said, if one considers maximum prices really to be minimums, then USA would be the *beneficiary* of the violation and could have suffered no antitrust injury, citing *Matsushita*. Further, the Court held, price cutting above a predatory level simply constitutes tough competition. Some acts have procompetitive and anticompetitive elements intermixed. The plaintiff may sue only if it is injured by the anti-competitive aspects.

Finally, the Court firmly rejected the plaintiff's argument that actions based on per se violations should not require a showing of antitrust injury. "The per se rule is a presumption of unreasonableness based on 'business certainty and litigation efficiency,' " the Court said. Some per se violations may have procompetitive effects; thus, "insofar as the per se rule permits the prohibition of efficient practices in the name of simplicity, the need for the antitrust injury requirement is underscored."

Justices Stevens and White argued in vain that there was something suspicious about this plan. The Court had put great weight on the vertical character of this agreement, but it might equally have represented a horizontal agreement of ARCO dealers. A plan is no less horizontal, they said, because it is enforced by a party upstream in the production process. The plaintiff claimed injury in fact, they said, and the Court's decision would, at minimum, reduce the deterrent to antitrust violations that the threat of private actions implies.

As events turned out, *ARCO* was simply a transition to State Oil Company v. Khan, 522 U.S. 3, 118 S.Ct. 275, 139 L.Ed.2d 199 (1997), which began: "We conclude that *Albrecht* should be overruled." Khan's arrangement with his lessor/supplier, State Oil, was that he could buy gas for 3.25 cents less than State Oil's suggested retail price. He could sell the gas to customers for any price, but if he earned more than 3.25 cents per gallon, the excess belonged to State Oil. Needless to say, there was no incentive to exceed the suggested retail price and the Court agreed that for all practical purposes this was vertical maximum price fixing.

The Court noted that *GTE Sylvania* and the cases following it had implicitly cast doubt on *Albrecht*, and in *ARCO* the Court had acknowledged in *ARCO* that maximum price fixing could have pro-competitive effects. In any event, anti-competitive effects were sufficiently unlikely as to cast doubt on subjecting it to a per se rule. Indeed, the Court noted, in the years since *Albrecht* was decided in 1968, no enforcement agency had ever brought a challenge to maximum resale price maintenance.

Purported maximum prices, the Court acknowledged, could be used to disguise arrangements to fix minimum prices, but if that arose in a future case, the Court said application of a rule of reason would be sufficient to recognize and punish it. Stare decisis is not an inexorable command, the

Court concluded, and bad rules must give way to "changed circumstances and the lessons of accumulated experience."

Does anything about this decision surprise you? It was unanimous. Even Justice Stevens seemed to realize that some battles are not worth fighting. Now that we know that maximum resale price maintenance is to be analyzed under a rule of reason, what should go into that analysis? Should all maximum resale price maintenance regimes require full-scale rule of reason analysis? Should some simply be subject to a "quick look" before declaring them to be legal or illegal?[84]

But both *ARCO* and *Khan* were simply prologue to our next case, which instantly became seen as one of the most important—and beloved or hated—cases in antitrust history.

LEEGIN CREATIVE LEATHER PRODUCTS, INC. v. PSKS, INC.

Supreme Court of the United States, 2007
551 U.S. 877, 127 S.Ct. 2705, 168 L.Ed.2d 623

JUSTICE KENNEDY delivered the opinion of the Court.

In Dr. Miles Medical Co. v. John D. Park & Sons Co. (1911), the Court established the rule that it is *per se* illegal under § 1 of the Sherman Act, for a manufacturer to agree with its distributor to set the minimum price the distributor can charge for the manufacturer's goods. The question presented by the instant case is whether the Court should overrule the *per se* rule and allow resale price maintenance agreements to be judged by the rule of reason, the usual standard applied to determine if there is a violation of § 1. The Court has abandoned the rule of *per se* illegality for other vertical restraints a manufacturer imposes on its distributors. Respected economic analysts, furthermore, conclude that vertical price restraints can have procompetitive effects. We now hold that *Dr. Miles* should be overruled and that vertical price restraints are to be judged by the rule of reason.

I

Petitioner, Leegin Creative Leather Products, Inc. (Leegin), designs, manufactures, and distributes leather goods and accessories. In 1991, Leegin began to sell belts under the brand name "Brighton." The Brighton brand has now expanded into a variety of women's fashion accessories. It is sold across the United States in over 5,000 retail establishments, for the

---

[84]   See, e.g., Roger D. Blair & John E. Lopatka, The Albrecht Rule After Khan: Death Becomes Her, 74 Notre Dame L.Rev. 123 (1998); Warren S. Grimes, Making Sense of State Oil v. Khan: Vertical Maximum Price Fixing Under a Rule of Reason, 66 Antitrust L.J. 567 (1998).

most part independent, small boutiques and specialty stores. Leegin's president, Jerry Kohl, also has an interest in about 70 stores that sell Brighton products. Leegin asserts that, at least for its products, small retailers treat customers better, provide customers more services, and make their shopping experience more satisfactory than do larger, often impersonal retailers. Kohl explained: "[W]e want the consumers to get a different experience than they get in Sam's Club or in Wal-Mart. And you can't get that kind of experience or support or customer service from a store like Wal-Mart."

Respondent, PSKS, Inc. (PSKS), operates Kay's Kloset, a women's apparel store in Lewisville, Texas. Kay's Kloset buys from about 75 different manufacturers and at one time sold the Brighton brand. It first started purchasing Brighton goods from Leegin in 1995. Once it began selling the brand, the store promoted Brighton. For example, it ran Brighton advertisements and had Brighton days in the store. Kay's Kloset became the destination retailer in the area to buy Brighton products. Brighton was the store's most important brand and once accounted for 40 to 50 percent of its profits.

In 1997, Leegin instituted the "Brighton Retail Pricing and Promotion Policy." Following the policy, Leegin refused to sell to retailers that discounted Brighton goods below suggested prices. The policy contained an exception for products not selling well that the retailer did not plan on reordering. * * * Leegin adopted the policy to give its retailers sufficient margins to provide customers the service central to its distribution strategy. It also expressed concern that discounting harmed Brighton's brand image and reputation.

* * *

In December 2002, Leegin discovered Kay's Kloset had been marking down Brighton's entire line by 20 percent. Kay's Kloset contended it placed Brighton products on sale to compete with nearby retailers who also were undercutting Leegin's suggested prices. Leegin, nonetheless, requested that Kay's Kloset cease discounting. Its request refused, Leegin stopped selling to the store. The loss of the Brighton brand had a considerable negative impact on the store's revenue from sales.

PSKS sued Leegin in the United States District Court for the Eastern District of Texas. It alleged, among other claims, that Leegin had violated the antitrust laws by "enter[ing] into agreements with retailers to charge only those prices fixed by Leegin." Leegin planned to introduce expert testimony describing the procompetitive effects of its pricing policy. The District Court excluded the testimony, relying on the *per se* rule established by *Dr. Miles.* * * * Leegin responded that it had established a unilateral pricing policy lawful under § 1, which applies only to concerted action. See United States v. Colgate & Co. (1919). The jury agreed with PSKS and awarded it $1.2 million. * * * [T]he District Court trebled the damages and * * * entered judgment against Leegin in the amount of $3,975,000.80.

The Court of Appeals for the Fifth Circuit affirmed. On appeal Leegin did not dispute that it had entered into vertical price-fixing agreements with its retailers. Rather, it contended that the rule of reason should have applied to those agreements. The Court of Appeals rejected this argument. It was correct to explain that it remained bound by *Dr. Miles* "[b]ecause [the Supreme] Court has consistently applied the *per se* rule to [vertical minimum price-fixing] agreements." * * * We granted certiorari to determine whether vertical minimum resale price maintenance agreements should continue to be treated as *per se* unlawful.

II

* * *

The rule of reason is the accepted standard for testing whether a practice restrains trade in violation of § 1. "Under this rule, the factfinder weighs all of the circumstances of a case in deciding whether a restrictive practice should be prohibited as imposing an unreasonable restraint on competition." Continental T. V., Inc. v. GTE Sylvania Inc. Appropriate factors to take into account include "specific information about the relevant business" and "the restraint's history, nature, and effect." Whether the businesses involved have market power is a further, significant consideration. See, *e.g.,* Copperweld Corp. v. Independence Tube Corp. * * * . In its design and function the rule distinguishes between restraints with anticompetitive effect that are harmful to the consumer and restraints stimulating competition that are in the consumer's best interest.

The rule of reason does not govern all restraints. Some types "are deemed unlawful *per se.*" The *per se* rule, treating categories of restraints as necessarily illegal, eliminates the need to study the reasonableness of an individual restraint in light of the real market forces at work, Business Electronics Corp. v. Sharp Electronics Corp.; and, it must be acknowledged, the *per se* rule can give clear guidance for certain conduct. Restraints that are *per se* unlawful include horizontal agreements among competitors to fix prices, or to divide markets, see Palmer v. BRG of Ga., Inc. *(per curiam).*

Resort to *per se* rules is confined to restraints, like those mentioned, "that would always or almost always tend to restrict competition and decrease output. To justify a *per se* prohibition a restraint must have "manifestly anticompetitive" effects, and "lack . . . any redeeming virtue," Northwest Wholesale Stationers, Inc. v. Pacific Stationery & Printing Co.

* * *

III

* * *

The reasoning of the Court's more recent jurisprudence has rejected the rationales on which *Dr. Miles* was based. By relying on the common-law rule against restraints on alienation, the Court justified its decision based on "formalistic" legal doctrine rather than "demonstrable economic effect." * * * Yet the Sherman Act's use of "restraint of trade" "invokes the common law itself, * * * not merely the static content that the common law had assigned to the term in 1890." *Business Electronics.* * * * We reaffirm that "the state of the common law 400 or even 100 years ago is irrelevant to the issue before us: the effect of the antitrust laws upon vertical distributional restraints in the American economy today." *GTE Sylvania.*

Dr. Miles, furthermore, treated vertical agreements a manufacturer makes with its distributors as analogous to a horizontal combination among competing distributors. In later cases, however, the Court rejected the approach of reliance on rules governing horizontal restraints when defining rules applicable to vertical ones. See, *e.g., Business Electronics* * * * . Our recent cases formulate antitrust principles in accordance with the appreciated differences in economic effect between vertical and horizontal agreements, differences the *Dr. Miles* Court failed to consider.

The reasons upon which *Dr. Miles* relied do not justify a *per se* rule. As a consequence, it is necessary to examine, in the first instance, the economic effects of vertical agreements to fix minimum resale prices, and to determine whether the *per se* rule is nonetheless appropriate.

A

Though each side of the debate can find sources to support its position, it suffices to say here that economics literature is replete with procompetitive justifications for a manufacturer's use of resale price maintenance. ABA Section of Antitrust Law, Antitrust Law and Economics of Product Distribution 76 (2006) ("[T]he bulk of the economic literature on [resale price maintenance] suggests that [it] is more likely to be used to enhance efficiency than for anticompetitive purposes"); see also H. Hovenkamp, The Antitrust Enterprise: Principle and Execution 184–191 (2005); R. Bork, The Antitrust Paradox 288–291 (1978). * * *

The few recent studies documenting the competitive effects of resale price maintenance also cast doubt on the conclusion that the practice meets the criteria for a *per se* rule. See T. Overstreet, Resale Price Maintenance: Economic Theories and Empirical Evidence 170 (1983) (noting that "[e]fficient uses of [resale price maintenance] are evidently not unusual or rare"); see also Ippolito, Resale Price Maintenance: Empirical Evidence From Litigation, 34 J. Law & Econ. 263, 292–293 (1991). * * *

The justifications for vertical price restraints are similar to those for other vertical restraints. Minimum resale price maintenance can stimulate interbrand competition—the competition among manufacturers selling different brands of the same type of product—by reducing intrabrand competition—the competition among retailers selling the same brand. The promotion of interbrand competition is important because "the primary purpose of the antitrust laws is to protect [this type of] competition." A single manufacturer's use of vertical price restraints tends to eliminate intrabrand price competition; this in turn encourages retailers to invest in tangible or intangible services or promotional efforts that aid the manufacturer's position as against rival manufacturers. Resale price maintenance also has the potential to give consumers more options so that they can choose among low-price, low-service brands; high-price, high-service brands; and brands that fall in between.

Absent vertical price restraints, the retail services that enhance interbrand competition might be underprovided. This is because discounting retailers can free ride on retailers who furnish services and then capture some of the increased demand those services generate. Consumers might learn, for example, about the benefits of a manufacturer's product from a retailer that invests in fine showrooms, offers product demonstrations, or hires and trains knowledgeable employees. Or consumers might decide to buy the product because they see it in a retail establishment that has a reputation for selling high-quality merchandise. If the consumer can then buy the product from a retailer that discounts because it has not spent capital providing services or developing a quality reputation, the high-service retailer will lose sales to the discounter, forcing it to cut back its services to a level lower than consumers would otherwise prefer. Minimum resale price maintenance alleviates the problem because it prevents the discounter from undercutting the service provider. With price competition decreased, the manufacturer's retailers compete among themselves over services.

Resale price maintenance, in addition, can increase interbrand competition by facilitating market entry for new firms and brands. * * * New products and new brands are essential to a dynamic economy, and if markets can be penetrated by using resale price maintenance there is a procompetitive effect.

Resale price maintenance can also increase interbrand competition by encouraging retailer services that would not be provided even absent free riding. It may be difficult and inefficient for a manufacturer to make and enforce a contract with a retailer specifying the different services the retailer must perform. Offering the retailer a guaranteed margin and threatening termination if it does not live up to expectations may be the most efficient way to expand the manufacturer's market share by inducing the retailer's performance and allowing it to use its own initiative and experience in providing valuable services. * * *

B

While vertical agreements setting minimum resale prices can have procompetitive justifications, they may have anticompetitive effects in other cases; and unlawful price fixing, designed solely to obtain monopoly profits, is an ever present temptation. Resale price maintenance may, for example, facilitate a manufacturer cartel. An unlawful cartel will seek to discover if some manufacturers are undercutting the cartel's fixed prices. Resale price maintenance could assist the cartel in identifying price-cutting manufacturers who benefit from the lower prices they offer. Resale price maintenance, furthermore, could discourage a manufacturer from cutting prices to retailers with the concomitant benefit of cheaper prices to consumers.

Vertical price restraints also "might be used to organize cartels at the retailer level." A group of retailers might collude to fix prices to consumers and then compel a manufacturer to aid the unlawful arrangement with resale price maintenance. In that instance the manufacturer does not establish the practice to stimulate services or to promote its brand but to give inefficient retailers higher profits. Retailers with better distribution systems and lower cost structures would be prevented from charging lower prices by the agreement. * * *

A horizontal cartel among competing manufacturers or competing retailers that decreases output or reduces competition in order to increase price is, and ought to be, *per se* unlawful. To the extent a vertical agreement setting minimum resale prices is entered upon to facilitate either type of cartel, it, too, would need to be held unlawful under the rule of reason. This type of agreement may also be useful evidence for a plaintiff attempting to prove the existence of a horizontal cartel.

Resale price maintenance, furthermore, can be abused by a powerful manufacturer or retailer. A dominant retailer, for example, might request resale price maintenance to forestall innovation in distribution that decreases costs. A manufacturer might consider it has little choice but to accommodate the retailer's demands for vertical price restraints if the manufacturer believes it needs access to the retailer's distribution network. A manufacturer with market power, by comparison, might use resale price maintenance to give retailers an incentive not to sell the products of smaller rivals or new entrants. As should be evident, the potential anticompetitive consequences of vertical price restraints must not be ignored or underestimated.

C

Notwithstanding the risks of unlawful conduct, it cannot be stated with any degree of confidence that resale price maintenance "always or almost always tend[s] to restrict competition and decrease output." Vertical agreements establishing minimum resale prices can have either procompetitive or anticompetitive effects, depending upon the circumstances in which they are formed. And although the empirical evidence on the topic is limited, it does not suggest efficient uses of the agreements are infrequent or hypothetical. As the rule would proscribe a significant amount of procompetitive conduct, these agreements appear ill suited for *per se* condemnation.

Respondent contends, nonetheless, that vertical price restraints should be *per se* unlawful because of the administrative convenience of *per se* rules. That argument suggests *per se* illegality is the rule rather than the exception. This misinterprets our antitrust law. *Per se* rules may decrease administrative costs, but that is only part of the equation. Those rules can be counterproductive. They can increase the total cost of the antitrust system by prohibiting procompetitive conduct the antitrust laws should encourage. They also may increase litigation costs by promoting frivolous suits against legitimate practices. The Court has thus explained that administrative "advantages are not sufficient in themselves to justify the creation of *per se* rules," and has relegated their use to restraints that are "manifestly anticompetitive." Were the Court now to conclude that vertical price restraints should be *per se* illegal based on administrative costs, we would undermine, if not overrule, the traditional "demanding standards" for adopting *per se* rules. Any possible reduction in administrative costs cannot alone justify the *Dr. Miles* rule.

Respondent also argues the *per se* rule is justified because a vertical price restraint can lead to higher prices for the manufacturer's goods. * * * Respondent is mistaken in relying on pricing effects absent a further showing of anticompetitive conduct. For, as has been indicated already, the antitrust laws are designed primarily to protect interbrand competition, from which lower prices can later result. The Court, moreover, has evaluated other vertical restraints under the rule of reason even though prices can be increased in the course of promoting procompetitive effects. See, *e.g., Business Electronics.* And resale price maintenance may reduce prices if manufacturers have resorted to costlier alternatives of controlling resale prices that are not *per se* unlawful.

Respondent's argument, furthermore, overlooks that, in general, the interests of manufacturers and consumers are aligned with respect to retailer profit margins. The difference between the price a manufacturer charges retailers and the price retailers charge consumers represents part of the manufacturer's cost of distribution, which, like any other cost, the manufacturer usually desires to minimize. A manufacturer has no incentive to overcompensate retailers with unjustified margins. The retailers, not the manufacturer, gain from higher retail prices. The manufacturer often loses; interbrand competition reduces its competitiveness and market share because consumers will "substitute a different brand of the same product." *GTE Sylvania.* As a general matter, therefore, a single manufacturer will desire to set minimum resale prices only if the "increase in demand resulting from enhanced service . . . will more than offset a negative impact on demand of a higher retail price."

The implications of respondent's position are far reaching. Many decisions a manufacturer makes and carries out through concerted action can lead to higher prices. A manufacturer might, for example, contract with different suppliers to obtain better inputs that improve product quality. Or it might hire an advertising agency to promote awareness of its goods. Yet no one would think these actions violate the Sherman Act because they lead to higher prices. The antitrust laws do not require manufacturers to produce generic goods that consumers do not know about or want. The manufacturer strives to improve its product quality or to promote its brand because it believes this conduct will lead to increased demand despite higher prices. The same can hold true for resale price maintenance.

Resale price maintenance, it is true, does have economic dangers. If the rule of reason were to apply to vertical price restraints, courts would have to be diligent in eliminating their anticompetitive uses from the market. This is a realistic objective, and certain factors are relevant to the inquiry. For example, the number of manufacturers that make use of the practice in a given industry can provide important instruction. When only a few manufacturers lacking market power adopt the practice, there is little likelihood it is facilitating a manufacturer cartel, for a cartel then can be undercut by rival manufacturers. Likewise, a retailer cartel is unlikely when only a single manufacturer in a competitive market uses resale price maintenance. Interbrand competition would divert consumers to lower priced substitutes and eliminate any gains to retailers from their price-fixing agreement over a single brand. Resale price maintenance should be subject to more careful scrutiny, by contrast, if many competing manufacturers adopt the practice.

The source of the restraint may also be an important consideration. If there is evidence retailers were the impetus for a vertical price restraint, there is a greater likelihood that the restraint facilitates a retailer cartel or supports a dominant, inefficient retailer. If, by contrast, a manufacturer adopted the policy independent of retailer pressure, the restraint is less likely to promote anticompetitive conduct. A manufacturer also has an incentive to protest inefficient retailer-induced price restraints because they can harm its competitive position.

As a final matter, that a dominant manufacturer or retailer can abuse resale price maintenance for anticompetitive purposes may not be a serious concern unless the relevant entity has market power. If a retailer lacks market power, manufacturers likely can sell their goods through rival retailers. And if a manufacturer lacks market power, there is less likelihood it can use the practice to keep competitors away from distribution outlets.

The rule of reason is designed and used to eliminate anticompetitive transactions from the market. This standard principle applies to vertical price restraints. A party alleging injury from a vertical agreement setting minimum resale prices will have, as a general matter, the information and resources available to show the existence of the agreement and its scope of operation. As courts gain experience considering the effects of these restraints by applying the rule of reason over the course of decisions, they can establish the litigation structure to ensure the rule operates to eliminate anticompetitive restraints from the market and to provide more guidance to businesses. Courts can, for example, devise rules over time for offering proof, or even presumptions where justified, to make the rule of reason a fair and efficient way to prohibit anticompetitive restraints and to promote procompetitive ones.

For all of the foregoing reasons, we think that were the Court considering the issue as an original matter, the rule of reason, not a *per se* rule of unlawfulness, would be the appropriate standard to judge vertical price restraints.

IV

We do not write on a clean slate, for the decision in *Dr. Miles* is almost a century old. So there is an argument for its retention on the basis of *stare decisis* alone. Even if *Dr. Miles* established an erroneous rule, "*[s]tare decisis* reflects a policy judgment that in most matters it is more important that the applicable rule of law be settled than that it be settled right." *Khan*. And concerns about maintaining settled law are strong when the question is one of statutory interpretation.

Stare decisis is not as significant in this case, however, because the issue before us is the scope of the Sherman Act. From the beginning the Court has treated the Sherman Act as a common-law statute. *Professional Engineers*. Just as the common law adapts to modern understanding and greater experience, so too does the Sherman Act's prohibition on "restraint[s] of trade" evolve to meet the dynamics of present economic conditions. The case-by-case adjudication contemplated by the rule of reason has implemented this common-law approach. Likewise, the boundaries of the doctrine of *per se* illegality should not be immovable. For "[i]t would make no sense to create out of the single term 'restraint of trade' a chronologically schizoid statute, in which a 'rule of reason' evolves with new circumstance and new wisdom, but a line of *per se* illegality remains forever fixed where it was." *Business Electronics.*

A

Stare decisis, we conclude, does not compel our continued adherence to the *per se* rule against vertical price restraints. As discussed earlier, respected authorities in the economics literature suggest the *per se* rule is inappropriate, and there is now widespread agreement that resale price maintenance can have procompetitive effects. It is also significant that both the Department of Justice and the Federal Trade Commission—the antitrust enforcement agencies with the ability to assess the long-term impacts of resale price maintenance—have recommended that this Court replace the *per se* rule with the traditional rule of reason. In the antitrust context the fact that a decision has been "called into serious question" justifies our reevaluation of it.

Other considerations reinforce the conclusion that *Dr. Miles* should be overturned. Of most relevance, "we have overruled our precedents when subsequent cases have undermined their doctrinal underpinnings." The Court's treatment of vertical restraints has progressed away from *Dr. Miles'* strict approach. We have distanced ourselves from the opinion's rationales. This is unsurprising, for the case was decided not long after enactment of the Sherman Act when the Court had little experience with antitrust analysis. Only eight years after *Dr. Miles,* moreover, the Court reined in the decision by holding that a manufacturer can announce suggested resale prices and refuse to deal with distributors who do not follow them. *Colgate.*

In more recent cases the Court, following a common-law approach, has continued to temper, limit, or overrule once strict prohibitions on vertical restraints. * * * While the Court in a footnote in *GTE Sylvania* suggested that differences between vertical price and nonprice restraints could support different legal treatment, the central part of the opinion relied on authorities and arguments that find unequal treatment "difficult to justify."

Continuing in this direction, in two cases in the 1980's the Court defined legal rules to limit the reach of *Dr. Miles* and to accommodate the doctrines enunciated in *GTE Sylvania* and *Colgate.* See *Business Electronics; Monsanto.* In *Monsanto,* the Court required that antitrust plaintiffs alleging a § 1 price-fixing conspiracy must present evidence tending to exclude the possibility a manufacturer and its distributors acted in an independent manner. * * * In *Business Electronics* the Court further narrowed the scope of *Dr. Miles.* It held that the *per se* rule applied only to specific agreements over price levels and not to an agreement between a manufacturer and a distributor to terminate a price-cutting distributor.

Most recently, in 1997, after examining the issue of vertical maximum price-fixing agreements in light of commentary and real experience, the Court overruled a 29-year-old precedent treating those agreements as *per se* illegal. *Khan* (overruling Albrecht v. Herald Co. (1968)). It held instead that they should be evaluated under the traditional rule of reason. Our continued limiting of the reach of the decision in *Dr. Miles* and our recent treatment of other vertical restraints justify the conclusion that *Dr. Miles* should not be retained.

The *Dr. Miles* rule is also inconsistent with a principled framework, for it makes little economic sense when analyzed with our other cases on vertical restraints. If we were to decide the procompetitive effects of resale price maintenance were insufficient to overrule *Dr. Miles,* then cases such as *Colgate* and *GTE Sylvania* themselves would be called into question. * * *

The manufacturer has a number of legitimate options to achieve benefits similar to those provided by vertical price restraints. A manufacturer can exercise its *Colgate* right to refuse to deal with retailers that do not follow its suggested prices. The economic effects of unilateral and concerted price setting are in general the same. See, *e.g., Monsanto.* The problem for the manufacturer is that a jury might conclude its unilateral policy was really a vertical agreement, subjecting it to treble damages and potential criminal liability. Even with the stringent standards in *Monsanto* and *Business Electronics,* this danger can lead, and has led, rational manufacturers to take wasteful measures. A manufacturer might refuse to discuss its pricing policy with its distributors except through counsel knowledgeable of the subtle intricacies of the law. Or it might terminate longstanding distributors for minor violations without seeking an explanation. The increased costs these burdensome measures generate flow to consumers in the form of higher prices.

Furthermore, depending on the type of product it sells, a manufacturer might be able to achieve the procompetitive benefits of resale price maintenance by integrating downstream and selling its products directly to consumers. *Dr. Miles* tilts the relative costs of vertical integration and vertical agreement by making the former more attractive based on the *per se* rule, not on real market conditions. See *Business Electronics.* * * * And integration, unlike vertical price restraints, eliminates all intrabrand competition.

* * *

In sum, it is a flawed antitrust doctrine that serves the interests of lawyers—by creating legal distinctions that operate as traps for the unwary—more than the interests of consumers—by requiring manufacturers to choose second-best options to achieve sound business objectives.

B

Respondent's arguments for reaffirming *Dr. Miles* on the basis of *stare decisis* do not require a different result. Respondent looks to congressional action concerning vertical price restraints. In 1937, Congress passed the Miller-Tydings Fair Trade Act which made vertical price restraints legal if authorized by a fair trade law enacted by a State. Fifteen years later, Congress expanded the exemption to permit vertical price-setting agreements between a manufacturer and a distributor to be enforced against other distributors not involved in the agreement. McGuire Act. In 1975, however, Congress repealed both Acts. That the *Dr. Miles* rule applied to vertical price restraints in 1975, according to respondent, shows Congress ratified the rule.

This is not so. The text of the Consumer Goods Pricing Act did not codify the rule of *per se* illegality for vertical price restraints. It rescinded statutory provisions that made them *per se* legal. * * * Congress could have set the *Dr. Miles* rule in stone, but it chose a more flexible option. We respect its decision by analyzing vertical price restraints, like all restraints, in conformance with traditional § 1 principles, including the principle that our antitrust doctrines "evolv[e] with new circumstances and new wisdom." *Business Electronics*.

* * *

It is also of note that during this time "when the legal environment in the [United States] was most favorable for [resale price maintenance], no more than a tiny fraction of manufacturers ever employed [resale price maintenance] contracts." * * * To the extent consumers demand cheap goods, judging vertical price restraints under the rule of reason will not prevent the market from providing them. * * *

For these reasons the Court's decision in Dr. Miles Medical Co. v. John D. Park & Sons Co. (1911) is now overruled. Vertical price restraints are to be judged according to the rule of reason.

* * *

The judgment of the Court of Appeals is reversed, and the case is remanded for proceedings consistent with this opinion.

It is so ordered.

JUSTICE BREYER, with whom JUSTICE STEVENS, JUSTICE SOUTER, and JUSTICE GINSBURG join, dissenting.

* * * This Court has consistently read *Dr. Miles* as establishing a bright-line rule that agreements fixing minimum resale prices are *per se* illegal. That *per se* rule is one upon which the legal profession, business, and the public have relied for close to a century. Today the Court holds that courts must determine the lawfulness of minimum resale price

maintenance by applying, not a bright-line *per se* rule, but a circumstance-specific "rule of reason." And in doing so it overturns *Dr. Miles.*

The Court justifies its departure from ordinary considerations of *stare decisis* by pointing to a set of arguments well known in the antitrust literature for close to half a century. Congress has repeatedly found in these arguments insufficient grounds for overturning the *per se* rule. And, in my view, they do not warrant the Court's now overturning so well-established a legal precedent.

I

* * *

The case before us asks which kind of approach the courts should follow where minimum resale price maintenance is at issue. Should they apply a *per se* rule (or a variation) that would make minimum resale price maintenance always (or *almost* always) unlawful? Should they apply a "rule of reason"? Were the Court writing on a blank slate, I would find these questions difficult. But, of course, the Court is not writing on a blank slate, and that fact makes a considerable legal difference.

To best explain why the question would be difficult were we deciding it afresh, I briefly summarize several classical arguments for and against the use of a *per se* rule. The arguments focus on three sets of considerations, those involving: (1) potential anticompetitive effects, (2) potential benefits, and (3) administration. The difficulty arises out of the fact that the different sets of considerations point in different directions.

On the one hand, agreements setting minimum resale prices may have serious anticompetitive consequences. *In respect to dealers:* Resale price maintenance agreements, rather like horizontal price agreements, can diminish or eliminate price competition among dealers of a single brand or (if practiced generally by manufacturers) among multibrand dealers. In doing so, they can prevent dealers from offering customers the lower prices that many customers prefer; they can prevent dealers from responding to changes in demand, say falling demand, by cutting prices; they can encourage dealers to substitute service, for price, competition, thereby threatening wastefully to attract too many resources into that portion of the industry; they can inhibit expansion by more efficient dealers whose lower prices might otherwise attract more customers, stifling the development of new, more efficient modes of retailing; and so forth.

In respect to producers: Resale price maintenance agreements can help to reinforce the competition-inhibiting behavior of firms in concentrated industries. In such industries firms may tacitly collude, *i.e.,* observe each other's pricing behavior, each understanding that price cutting by one firm is likely to trigger price competition by all. Where that is so, resale price maintenance can make it easier for each producer to identify (by observing retail markets) when a competitor has begun to cut prices. And a producer who cuts wholesale prices *without* lowering the minimum resale price will stand to gain little, if anything, in increased profits, because the dealer will be unable to stimulate increased consumer demand by passing along the producer's price cut to consumers. In either case, resale price maintenance agreements will tend to prevent price competition from "breaking out"; and they will thereby tend to stabilize producer prices.

Those who express concern about the potential anticompetitive effects find empirical support in the behavior of prices before, and then after, Congress in 1975 repealed the Miller-Tydings Fair Trade Act and the McGuire Act. Those Acts had permitted (but not required) individual States to enact "fair trade" laws authorizing minimum resale price maintenance. At the time of repeal minimum resale price maintenance was lawful in 36 States; it was unlawful in 14 States. Comparing prices in the former States with prices in the latter States, the Department of Justice argued that minimum resale price maintenance had raised prices by 19% to 27%.

After repeal, minimum resale price maintenance agreements were unlawful *per se* in every State. The Federal Trade Commission (FTC) staff, after studying numerous price surveys, wrote that collectively the surveys "indicate[d] that [resale price maintenance] in most cases increased the prices of products sold with [resale price maintenance]." Most economists today agree that, in the words of a prominent antitrust treatise, "resale price maintenance tends to produce higher consumer prices than would otherwise be the case." 8 Areeda & Hovenkamp ¶ 1604b, at 40.

On the other hand, those favoring resale price maintenance have long argued that resale price maintenance agreements can provide important consumer benefits. The majority lists two: First, such agreements can facilitate new entry. For example, a newly entering producer wishing to build a product name might be able to convince dealers to help it do so—if, but only if, the producer can assure those dealers that they will later recoup their investment. Without resale price maintenance, late-entering dealers might take advantage of the earlier investment and, through price competition, drive prices down to the point where the early dealers cannot recover what they spent. By assuring the initial dealers that such later price competition will not occur, resale price maintenance can encourage them to carry the new product, thereby helping the new producer succeed. The result might be increased competition at the producer level, *i.e.*, greater *inter*-brand competition, that brings with it net consumer benefits.

Second, without resale price maintenance a producer might find its efforts to sell a product undermined by what resale price maintenance advocates call "free riding." Suppose a producer concludes that it can succeed only if dealers provide certain services, say, product demonstrations, high quality shops, advertising that creates a certain product image, and so forth. Without resale price maintenance, some dealers might take a "free ride" on the investment that others make in providing those services. Such a dealer would save money by not paying for those services and could consequently cut its own price and increase its own sales. Under these circumstances, dealers might prove unwilling to invest in the provision of necessary services.

Moreover, where a producer and not a group of dealers seeks a resale price maintenance agreement, there is a special reason to believe some such benefits exist. That is because, other things being equal, producers should want to encourage price competition among their dealers. By doing so they will often increase profits by selling more of their product. And that is so, even if the producer possesses sufficient market power to earn a super-normal profit. That is to say, other things being equal, the producer will benefit by charging his dealers a competitive (or even a higher-than-competitive) wholesale price while encouraging price competition among them. Hence, if the producer is the moving force, the producer must have some special reason for wanting resale price maintenance; and in the absence of, say, concentrated producer markets (where that special reason might consist of a desire to stabilize wholesale prices), that special reason may well reflect the special circumstances just described: new entry, "free riding," or variations on those themes.

The upshot is, as many economists suggest, sometimes resale price maintenance can prove harmful; sometimes it can bring benefits. But before concluding that courts should consequently apply a rule of reason, I would ask such questions as, how often are harms or benefits likely to occur? How easy is it to separate the beneficial sheep from the antitrust goats?

Economic discussion, such as the studies the Court relies upon, can *help* provide answers to these questions, and in doing so, economics can, and should, inform antitrust law. But antitrust law cannot, and should not, precisely replicate economists' (sometimes conflicting) views. That is because law, unlike economics, is an administrative system the effects of which depend upon the content of rules and precedents only as they are applied by judges and juries in courts and by lawyers advising their clients. And that fact means that courts will often bring their own administrative judgment to bear, sometimes applying rules of *per se* unlawfulness to business practices even when those practices sometimes produce benefits.

I have already described studies and analyses that suggest (though they cannot prove) that resale price maintenance can cause harms with some regularity—and certainly when dealers are the driving force. But what about benefits? How often, for example, will the benefits to which the Court points occur in practice? I can find no economic consensus on this point. There is a consensus in the literature that "free riding" takes place. But "free riding" often takes place in the economy without any legal effort to stop it. Many visitors to California take free rides on the Pacific Coast Highway. We all benefit freely from ideas, such as that of creating the first supermarket. Dealers often take a "free ride" on investments that others have made in building a product's name and reputation. The question is how often the "free riding" problem is serious enough significantly to deter dealer investment.

* * *

All this is to say that the ultimate question is not whether, but *how much,* "free riding" of this sort takes place. And, after reading the briefs, I must answer that question with an uncertain "sometimes."

How easily can courts identify instances in which the benefits are likely to outweigh potential harms? My own answer is, *not very easily.* For one thing, it is often difficult to identify *who*—producer or dealer—is the moving force behind any given resale price maintenance agreement. * * *

I recognize that scholars have sought to develop check lists and sets of questions that will help courts separate instances where anticompetitive harms are more likely from instances where only benefits are likely to be found. But applying these criteria in court is often easier said than done. * * * One cannot fairly expect judges and juries in such cases to apply complex economic criteria without making a considerable number of mistakes, which themselves may impose serious costs.

Are there special advantages to a bright-line rule? Without such a rule, it is often unfair, and consequently impractical, for enforcement officials to bring criminal proceedings. And since enforcement resources are limited, that loss may tempt some producers or dealers to enter into agreements that are, on balance, anticompetitive.

Given the uncertainties that surround key items in the overall balance sheet, particularly in respect to the "administrative" questions, I can concede to the majority that the problem is difficult. And, if forced to decide now, at most I might agree that the *per se* rule should be slightly modified to allow an exception for the more easily identifiable and temporary condition of "new entry." But I am not now forced to decide this question. The question before us is not what should be the rule, starting from scratch. We here must decide whether to change a clear and simple price-related antitrust rule that the courts have applied for nearly a century.

II ← good for case law

We write, not on a blank slate, but on a slate that begins with *Dr. Miles* and goes on to list a century's worth of similar cases, massive amounts of advice that lawyers have provided their clients, and untold numbers of business decisions those clients have taken in reliance upon that advice.

* * * Those who wish this Court to change so well-established a legal precedent bear a heavy burden of proof. I am not aware of any case in which this Court has overturned so well-established a statutory precedent. Regardless, I do not see how the Court can claim that ordinary criteria for over-ruling an earlier case have been met.

A

I can find no change in circumstances in the past several decades that helps the majority's position. In fact, there has been one important change that argues strongly to the contrary. In 1975, Congress repealed the McGuire and Miller-Tydings Acts. And it thereby consciously *extended Dr. Miles' per se* rule. Indeed, at that time the Department of Justice and the FTC, then urging application of the *per se* rule, discussed virtually every argument presented now to this Court as well as others not here presented. And they explained to Congress why Congress should reject them. Congress fully understood, and consequently intended, that the result of its repeal of McGuire and Miller-Tydings would be to make minimum resale price maintenance *per se* unlawful. * * *

Congress did not prohibit this Court from reconsidering the *per se* rule. But enacting major legislation premised upon the existence of that rule constitutes important public reliance upon that rule. And doing so aware of the relevant arguments constitutes even stronger reliance upon the Court's keeping the rule, at least in the absence of some significant change in respect to those arguments.

* * *

[Reported economic studies,] at most may offer some mild support for the majority's position. But they cannot constitute a major change in circumstances.

* * *

No one claims that the American economy has changed in ways that might support the majority. Concentration in retailing has increased. * * * That change, other things being equal, may enable (and motivate) more retailers, accounting for a greater percentage of total retail sales volume, to seek resale price maintenance, thereby making it more difficult for price-cutting competitors (perhaps internet retailers) to obtain market share.

* * *

In sum, there is no relevant change. And without some such change, there is no ground for abandoning a well-established antitrust rule.

B

* * *

* * * Implementation of the *per se* rule, even with the complications attendant the exception allowed for in United States v. Colgate & Co. (1919), has proved practical over the course of the last century, particularly when compared with the many complexities of litigating a case under the "rule of reason" regime. No one has shown how moving from the *Dr. Miles* regime to "rule of reason" analysis would make the legal regime governing minimum resale price maintenance more "administrable," particularly since *Colgate* would remain good law with respect to *unreasonable* price maintenance.

* * *

* * * [W]hole sectors of the economy have come to rely upon the *per se* rule. A factory outlet store tells us that the rule "form[s] an essential part of the regulatory background against which [that firm] and many other discount retailers have financed, structured, and operated their businesses." The Consumer Federation of America tells us that large low-price retailers would not exist without *Dr. Miles*; minimum resale price maintenance, "by stabilizing price levels and preventing low-price competition, erects a potentially insurmountable barrier to entry for such low-price innovators." * * * New distributors, including internet distributors, have similarly invested time, money, and labor in an effort to bring yet lower cost goods to Americans.

This Court's overruling of the *per se* rule jeopardizes this reliance, and more. What about malls built on the assumption that a discount distributor will remain an anchor tenant? What about home buyers who have taken a home's distance from such a mall into account? What about Americans, producers, distributors, and consumers, who have understandably assumed, at least for the last 30 years, that price competition is a legally guaranteed way of life? The majority denies none of this. It simply says that these "reliance interests . . . , like the reliance interests in *Khan,* cannot justify an inefficient rule."

The Court minimizes the importance of this reliance, adding that it "is also of note" that at the time resale price maintenance contracts were lawful " 'no more than a tiny fraction of manufacturers ever employed' " the practice. By "tiny" the Court means manufacturers that accounted for up to " 'ten percent of consumer goods purchases' " annually. That figure in today's economy equals just over $300 billion. Putting the Court's estimate together with the Justice Department's early 1970's study translates a legal regime that permits all resale price maintenance into retail bills that are higher by an average of roughly $750 to $1000 annually for an American family of four. Just how much higher retail bills will be after the

Court's decision today, of course, depends upon what is now unknown, namely how courts will decide future cases under a "rule of reason." But these figures indicate that the amounts involved are important to American families and cannot be dismissed as "tiny."

* * * [T]he fact that a rule of law has become "embedded" in our "national culture" argues strongly against overruling. The *per se* rule forbidding minimum resale price maintenance agreements has long been "embedded" in the law of antitrust. It involves price, the economy's " 'central nervous system.' " It reflects a basic antitrust assumption (that consumers often prefer lower prices to more service). It embodies a basic antitrust objective (providing consumers with a free choice about such matters). And it creates an easily administered and enforceable bright line, "Do not agree about price," that businesses as well as lawyers have long understood.

* * *

The Court suggests that it is following "the common-law tradition." But the common law would not have permitted overruling *Dr. Miles* in these circumstances. Common-law courts rarely overruled well-established earlier rules outright. Rather, they would over time issue decisions that gradually eroded the scope and effect of the rule in question, which might eventually lead the courts to put the rule to rest. One can argue that modifying the *per se* rule to make an exception, say, for new entry, could prove consistent with this approach. To swallow up a century-old precedent, potentially affecting many billions of dollars of sales, is not. * * *

* * *

The only safe predictions to make about today's decision are that it will likely raise the price of goods at retail and that it will create considerable legal turbulence as lower courts seek to develop workable principles. I do not believe that the majority has shown new or changed conditions sufficient to warrant overruling a decision of such long standing. All ordinary *stare decisis* considerations indicate the contrary. For these reasons, with respect, I dissent.

NOTES AND QUESTIONS

1.   Were you surprised at how close and intense the division among the justices was in this case? Would you have thought the Court would have taken the case if the justices voting to grant certiorari had not thought they had the votes to overrule *Dr. Miles*?[85]

---

[85]   On remand, the District Court again dismissed the complaint, 2009 WL 938561, and again the Fifth Circuit affirmed, 615 F.3d 412 (5th Cir. 2010), finding that the plaintiff had failed to prove the plausible relevant market required to prove a case under the rule of reason. The Supreme Court denied certiorari, 562 U.S. 1217, 131 S.Ct. 1476, 179 L.Ed.2d 301 (2011). But a consumer

2.   Is it significant that no member of the Court suggested that resale price maintenance is per se legal? Is Justice Breyer right that it will be harder to come up with standards for applying a rule of reason in resale price maintenance cases than in territorial allocation cases?

3.   After *Leegin*, may a court or agency presume that resale price maintenance is anti-competitive because it raises prices to consumers and thus immediately require the defendant to prove its practices were justified? This approach was urged on the FTC by a group of 27 states in response to a post-*Leegin* petition by Nine West Group, Inc., for relief from an earlier consent order precluding its use of resale price maintenance. The FTC said that *Leegin* does not support such a presumption of illegality.[86] Do you agree?

4.   Then, what factors might lead a court to conclude that any given resale price maintenance arrangement is in fact anticompetitive?

a.   Proof of actual dealer or manufacturer collusion on price? If one can show horizontal collusion as to price, is there a need for a special rule about resale price maintenance?

b.   Substantial seller market power? How much market power would be enough to let a court presume a violation? How might a seller with market power use resale price maintenance to injure consumers? Would you be concerned, for example, if the seller used resale price maintenance to persuade resellers not to carry products sold by the seller's competitors?

c.   A market with only a few resellers? How few resellers would it take to make collusion and coordination possible, even though presumably not proven in a given case?

5.   What pro-competitive or efficiency-based justifications did Leegin offer for its practices? Were you convinced there was no other way it could have gotten dealers to provide services or preserve the image of its products, for example? Should a company have to pick the least restrictive way to achieve a desired result?

6.   What weight should stare decisis concerns be given in a case like *Leegin*? If such concerns were dispositive, would there ever be a time when the prior precedent would be less long-standing?

7.   And what weight should the states give to *Leegin*? While many states purport to give federal precedent significant weight, for some states, resale price maintenance has become the place to depart from that principle and retain the *Dr. Miles* prohibition.[87]

---

action brought under Kansas law continues, O'Brien v. Leegin Creative Leather Products, 277 P.3d 1062 (Kan. 2012).

[86]   May 6, 2008 Order Granting in Part Petition to Reopen and Modify Order Issued April 11, 2000, In the Matter of Nine West Group, Inc., Fed Trade Comm'n Docket No. C–3937, p. 13.

[87]   For useful tables outlining the state approaches, see Michael A. Lindsay, Resale Price Maintenance and the World After *Leegin*, 22 Antitrust 32 (Fall 2007). See also, Alan M. Barr, Antitrust Federalism in Action—State Challenges to Vertical Price Fixing in the Post-*Leegin* World (Dec. 2009); Michael A. Lindsay, An Update on State RPM Laws Since *Leegin* (Dec. 2010).

a.   In O'Brien v. Leegin Creative Leather Products, Inc., 294 Kan. 318, 277 P.3d 1062 (2012), for example, the Kansas Supreme Court expressly declared that in reading its state law it was not bound by the U.S. Supreme Court's reading of the Sherman Act.

b.   On the other hand, in a blow to the New York Attorney General, at least so far, New York courts have rejected the claim that a statute that makes resale price maintenance contracts unenforceable thereby renders them unlawful or invalidates practices that are consistent with *Colgate*. People v. Tempur-Pedic International, Inc., 944 N.Y.S.2d 518 (Sup.Ct. App.Div. 2012).[88]

8.   The European Union continues to treat resale price maintenance as a "hard core" restraint, not eligible for a block exemption under Article 101. Should the EU now reconsider that position? Should the US and the EU be concerned when their antitrust standards diverge on a recurring question such as this one?

RESALE PRICE MAINTENANCE COORDINATING A CARTEL: THE *APPLE* CASE

Apple is one of the world's great brands, but it came out the loser in United States v. Apple, 2013 WL 3454986 (S.D.N.Y. 2013). As reported by the District Court, when it introduced the iPad, Apple wanted to make an iBookstore available to challenge Amazon, which at that time sold e-books for its own Kindle reader.

Amazon acquired e-books from the major publishers at wholesale prices but then set its own retail price. Amazon chose to sell new-release and best-seller e-books for $9.99, even when that barely covered its costs. The publishers, in turn, feared the $9.99 e-book price would undercut their ability to sell hardcover books often priced at $30 or more.

Enter Apple. The court found that the publishers had been talking to each other about how to raise the price of e-books. Apple proposed an "agency model" under which publishers would set their own e-book retail prices and Apple would charge a fee for distribution on iBooks. Apple then also required the publishers to give it as good a price as every other distributor,[89] thus tending to cause the publishers to force all their distributors—including Amazon—to price using the agency model.

---

[88]   Articles arguing that *Colgate* no longer has force include Mark D. Bauer, Whither *Dr. Miles?*, 20 Loyola Consumer L. Rev. 1, 6–7 (2007); Warren S. Grimes, The Path Forward After *Leegin*: Seeking Consensus Reform of the Antitrust Law of Vertical Restraints, 75 Antitrust L.J. 467, 487–91 (2008). For more on the impact of the *Leegin* case, see Thomas C. Arthur, The Core of Antitrust and the Slow Death of Dr. Miles, 62 SMU L. Rev. 437 (2009); Marina Lao, Resale Price Maintenance: The Internet Phenomenon and Free Rider Issues, 55 Antitrust Bulletin 473 (2010).

[89]   This kind of requirement is known as a Most Favored Nation (MFN) provision, named after a common approach to international trade agreements. Such provisions are controversial today, because while they can reduce bargaining costs and lead to lower prices over time, they can

What this did for the publishers, the court found, was provide a way for them all to move retail sale of e-books—including by Amazon—to a higher price point than Amazon's $9.99 had permitted. In an embarrassing interview, Steve Jobs seemed to admit what was going on and to take pride in it.

Apple said its role in any price increase had been passive; prices had been set by the publishers. But the court found from "compelling direct and circumstantial evidence" that Apple had "participated in and facilitated a horizontal price-fixing conspiracy" of the publishers and that its conduct was *per se* illegal.

The case should be a reminder that the fact that resale price maintenance is subject to the rule of reason does not make it per se illegal. When multiple retailers agree to a form of sale designed to achieve a common goal of higher prices, their conduct can be seen as cartel behavior that *Leegin* does not condone.

BELL ATLANTIC v. TWOMBLY: A NEW PLEADING STANDARD

At an important point in the doctrinal development, Bell Atlantic Corp. v. Twombly, 550 U.S. 544, 127 S.Ct. 1955, 167 L.Ed.2d 929 (2007), raised the standard for proof of agreement issue to new prominence.

Class action plaintiffs alleged that the divestiture of AT&T in 1984 created Verizon, Quest and other "Baby Bell" companies. Each Baby Bell received territories in which to provide local telephone service. Twelve years later, the Telecommunications Act of 1996 gave Baby Bells the right to enter each other's territory to deliver competitive service, but apparently none of them took advantage of that new right. The plaintiff class alleged that the defendants' uniform failure to take advantage of "attractive business opportunities" could best be explained as a conspiracy.

The District Court decided the case on a Rule 12(b)(6) motion to dismiss, i.e., a motion decided prior to discovery based solely on the content of the complaint. The District Court said that "allegations of parallel business conduct, taken alone, do not state a claim under § 1; plaintiffs must allege additional facts that 'ten[d] to exclude independent self-interested conduct as an explanation for defendants' parallel behavior.'" The court found that "the behavior of each ILEC in resisting the incursion of CLECs is fully explained by the ILEC's own interests in defending its

---

also be a way to facilitate collusion among industry participants. See, e.g., Jonathan Baker & Judith A. Chevalier, The Competitive Consequences of Most-Favored-Nation Provisions, 27 Antitrust 20 (Summer 2013); Steven C. Salop & Fiona Scott Morton, Developing an Administrable MFN Enforcement Polity, 27 Antitrust 15 (Summer 2013); W. Stephen Smith, When Most-Favored is Disfavored: A Counselor's Guide to MFNs, 27 Antitrust 10 (Summer 2013) (citing courts who have used the use of MFNs as a "plus factor" indicating collusion).

individual territory," and because the complaint did "not alleg[e] facts . . . suggesting that refraining from competing in other territories as CLECs was contrary to [the ILECs'] apparent economic interests, * * * [it did] not rais[e] an inference that [the ILECs'] actions were the result of a conspiracy."

The 2nd Circuit reversed, saying that a complaint need only give notice of the claim, not specific allegations of plus factors. But in an opinion by Justice Souter, the Supreme Court sided with the District Court, saying:

"[W]e hold that stating such a claim requires a complaint with enough factual matter (taken as true) to suggest that an agreement was made. Asking for plausible grounds to infer an agreement does not impose a probability requirement at the pleading stage; it simply calls for enough fact to raise a reasonable expectation that discovery will reveal evidence of illegal agreement.[90] And, of course, a well-pleaded complaint may proceed even if it strikes a savvy judge that actual proof of those facts is improbable, and "that a recovery is very remote and unlikely." * * * It makes sense to say, therefore, that an allegation of parallel conduct and a bare assertion of conspiracy will not suffice. Without more, parallel conduct does not suggest conspiracy, and a conclusory allegation of agreement at some unidentified point does not supply facts adequate to show illegality. Hence, when allegations of parallel conduct are set out in order to make a § 1 claim, they must be placed in a context that raises a suggestion of a preceding agreement, not merely parallel conduct that could just as well be independent action."

The Court went on, saying:

"[T]he complaint is replete with indications that any CLEC faced nearly insurmountable barriers to profitability owing to the ILECs' flagrant resistance to the network sharing requirements of the 1996 Act. * * * The upshot is that Congress may have expected some ILECs to become CLECs in the legacy territories of other ILECs, but the disappointment does not make conspiracy plausible. We agree with the District Court's assessment that antitrust conspiracy was not suggested by the facts adduced under either theory of the complaint, which thus fails to state a valid § 1 claim."[91]

---

[90] Commentators have offered several examples of parallel conduct allegations that would state a § 1 claim under this standard. * * * The parties in this case agree that "complex and historically unprecedented changes in pricing structure made at the very same time by multiple competitors, and made for no other discernible reason" would support a plausible inference of conspiracy. [Court's fn. 4]

[91] In reaching this conclusion, we do not apply any "heightened" pleading standard, nor do we seek to broaden the scope of Federal Rule of Civil Procedure 9 * * *. Here, our concern is not

Justices Stevens and Ginsburg dissented. They denied that the plaintiffs had alleged no specific instances of conspiracy, and noted: "Many years ago a truly great economist perceptively observed that '[p]eople of the same trade seldom meet together, even for merriment and diversion, but the conversation ends in a conspiracy against the public, or in some contrivance to raise prices.' A. Smith, An Inquiry Into the Nature and Causes of the Wealth of Nations * * * ." They believed discovery should go forward to let plaintiffs see if they could find enough hard evidence to survive a later motion for summary judgment.[92]

LIFE IN THE AFTERMATH OF *TWOMBLY*

Twombly was quickly seen as a potential game changer.[93] How much can a private plaintiff typically know about the details of a cartel's activities before engaging in discovery? Typically, a cartel operates in secret.

Defendants tended to be pleased by the new development. Prevailing on a motion to dismiss rather than waiting for a motion for summary judgment can save millions in defense costs and avoid the need to settle instead of fight.

Critics saw such incentives as making it harder to proceed against cartels and thus making it more likely that firms would take the risks necessary to create them. They sought better ways to allege facts sufficient to infer conspiracy from information observable without discovery.

One such approach is behavioral screening. The idea is to watch for observable behavior that one would not see in the absence of conspiracy. A study in New York, for example, saw that the price of concrete in New York City was 70% higher than in other large cities. Higher New York prices were predictable; 70% higher were highly improbable. In another case,

---

that the allegations in the complaint were insufficiently "particular[ized]"; rather, the complaint warranted dismissal because it failed *in toto* to render plaintiffs' entitlement to relief plausible. [Court's fn. 14]

[92] *Twombly* appears to have had the broad implications that its majority discounted but its dissenters feared. Just two years later, in Ashcroft v. Iqbal, 556 U.S. 662, 129 S.Ct. 1937, 173 L.Ed.2d 868 (2009), a case involving civil liberties rather than antitrust, the Court reaffirmed a distinction drawn in *Twombly* between the factual allegations in a complaint and "conclusions of law" into which the Court put statements about conspiracy. Westlaw notes that *Twombly* and *Iqbal* have been cited several thousand times, in a wide variety of subject matter fields, and only a small minority of the cases seem to limit their application. See, e.g., Gregory G. Wrobel, Michael J. Waters & Joshua Dunn, Judicial Application of Twombly/Iqbal Plausibility Standard in Antitrust Cases, 28 Antitrust 8 (Fall 2011).

[93] See, e.g., Arthur R. Miller, From Conley to Twombly to Iqbal: A Double Play on the Federal Rules of Civil Procedure, 60 Duke L.J. 1 (2010); Randall C. Picker, Twombly, Leegin and the Reshaping of Antitrust, 2007 Sup. Ct. Rev. 161 (2007); Douglas G. Smith, The Twombly Revolution?, 36 Pepperdine L.Rev. 1063 (2009).

seven companies submitted identical bids for a piece of work, a situation unlikely the result of chance.

Inferences can even be drawn from price variance over time; a showing that one area had stable prices while there was greater fluctuation in other areas suggested that the stable prices were the result of an agreement. And stable market shares among a group of providers may imply that their competition has been less intense than one should expect.[94]

Professor Kovacic and three economists suggest looking for clusters of factors—what they call "super plus factors"—from which one can reasonably infer explicit collusion. Some of the factors may seem surprising. Frequent advance announcements of small price increases, for example, are said to represent an industry practice designed to soften customer resistance to higher prices.[95] Parallel decisions to reduce output even as profits are high may also suggest collusion, as may parallel changes in internal rewards made to sales forces, e.g., rewarding higher price instead of sales volumes.

Judge Posner found circumstantial evidence before the court sufficient under *Twombly* in In re Text Messaging Antitrust Litigation, 630 F.3d 622, 628 (7th Cir. 2010):

> "Of note is the allegation in the complaint that the defendants belonged to a trade association and exchanged price information directly at association meetings. This allegation identifies a practice, not illegal in itself, that facilitates price fixing that would be difficult for the authorities to detect. The complaint further alleges that the defendants, along with two other large sellers of text messaging services, constituted and met with each other in an elite leadership council within the association and the leadership council's stated mission was to urge its members to substitute co-opetition for competition.
>
> "The complaint also alleges that in the face of steeply falling costs, the defendants increased their prices. This is anomalous behavior because falling costs increase a seller's profit margin at the existing price, motivating him, in the absence of agreement, to reduce his price slightly in order to take business from his competitors, and certainly not to increase his price. And there is

---

[94] These illustrations come from Rosa Abrantes-Metz & Patrick Bajari, Screens for Conspiracies and their Multiple Applications, 24 Antitrust 66 (Fall 2009). The original idea underlying screening is sometimes traced to Frank Benford, The Law of Anomalous Numbers, 78 Proceedings of the American Philosophy Society 551 (1938). See also, e.g., Joseph E. Harrington, Jr., Behavioral Screening and the Detection of Cartels, in Claus-Dieter Ehlermann & Isabella Atanasiu, eds, European Competition Law Annual 2006 (2007); William H. Page, A Neo-Chicago Approach to Concerted Action, 78 Antitrust L.J. 173 (2012).

[95] See generally, William E. Kovacic, Robert C. Marshall, Leslie M. Marx & Halbert L. White, Plus Factors and Agreement in Antitrust Law, 110 U. Michigan L. Rev. 393 (2011); Robert C. Marshall & Leslie M. Marx, The Economics of Collusion—Cartels and Bidding Rings (2012).

more: there is an allegation that all at once the defendants changed their pricing structures, which were heterogeneous and complex, to a uniform pricing structure, and then simultaneously jacked up their prices by a third. The change in the industry's pricing structure was so rapid, the complaint suggests, that it could not have been accomplished without agreement on the details of the new structure, the timing of its adoption, and the specific uniform price increase that would ensue on its adoption.

"A footnote in *Twombly* had described the type of evidence that enables parallel conduct to be interpreted as collusive: * * * 'The parties in this case agree that "complex and historically unprecedented changes in pricing structure made at the very same time by multiple competitors, and made for no other discernible reason" would support a plausible inference of conspiracy.' That is the kind of 'parallel plus' behavior alleged in this case."

Do you agree that, even after *Twombly*, it remains possible to allege proof of agreement?

CARTEL PROSECUTIONS AND THE PROMISE OF AMNESTY

But no matter how good economic inferences may be, there is nothing like an abject confession as a basis for proving conspiracy. And public prosecution of cartels engaged in naked pricing fixing remains vigorous. Both domestic and international defendants have been hunted down and subjected to surprise raids on corporate facilities. Fines totaling billions of dollars have been collected in the United States and Europe,[96] and guilty executives can expect to serve jail time.

Perhaps the single most effective tool for discovering and terminating cartels has been the Department of Justice's amnesty or leniency program, and its sister program in Europe.[97] The premise of amnesty is simple: Assuming it ceases its own role as soon as responsible officers of the company discover the criminal activity, the first cartel member to report the others will get leniency, or even complete amnesty; the rest of the members will be hunted down and prosecuted.

---

[96] On appropriate fines and other sentences, see, e.g., John M. Connor & Robert H. Lande, The Size of Cartel Overcharges: Implications for U.S. and E.U. Fining Policies, 51 Antitrust Bull. 983 (2006); John M. Connor & Robert H. Lande, Cartel Overcharges and Optimal Cartel Fines, 3 Issues in Competition Law & Policy 2203 (2008).

[97] See U.S. Department of Justice, Frequently Asked Questions Regarding the Antitrust Division's Leniency Program and Model Leniency Letters (Nov. 19, 2008). Proposed revisions to the European policy are at http://ec.europa.eu/comm/competition/cartels/legislation/settlements.html.

That puts an obvious premium on early reporting;[98] in some cases, the first in the door beats the second by only a matter of hours. The Antitrust Division might give a "marker" to a lawyer who turns up evidence that his client is involved in cartel activity so that the lawyer may complete his or her own investigation and turn over additional evidence. Even if the Division has already begun its own investigation, if a cartel member is first in the door, it will qualify for leniency if it terminates its role in the cartel, provides important additional evidence, and makes restitution to injured parties. A corresponding part of the amnesty policy protects individuals who approach the Division on their own behalf, so long as they were not leaders of the conspiracy.

5. PULLING THE SECTION 1 CASES TOGETHER

CAN THE "MODERN" CASES BE RECONCILED?: SOME EFFORTS TO DO SO

By at least the mid-1980s, it was clear that something important was afoot in the development of antitrust principles. While the per se rule continued to be discussed in the cases, its invocation was far from automatic. Yet the problem of efficient resolution of cases remained. The prospect that every antitrust matter would become a full-blown analysis of all the workings of the industry involved had to worry anyone interested in the ability of lawyers to counsel clients, as well as in the prompt resolution of disputes.

An important effort to explain the rules of the new era in antitrust analysis came from the Federal Trade Commission in Massachusetts Board of Registration in Optometry, 110 FTC 549 (1988). Former antitrust professor Terry Calvani wrote for the Commission:

> "Several points flow from the Court's pronouncements. First, the Court expressly states that there is often no bright line that separates per se from rule of reason analysis, thus destroying the neat taxonomy that characterized many an antitrust course outline. Second, the * * * essential inquiry under both is the same, i.e., 'whether or not the challenged restraint enhances competition.' * * *

> "A structure for evaluating horizontal restraints emerges * * * .

> "The structure is readily described as a series of questions to be answered in turn. First, we ask whether the restraint is 'inherently suspect'. In other words, is the practice the kind that

---

[98] See, e.g., Christopher R. Leslie, Trust, Distrust and Antitrust, 82 Texas L. Rev. 515 (2004); Christopher R. Leslie, Antitrust Amnesty, Game Theory, and Cartel Stability, 31 J. Corporation L. 453 (2006).

appears likely, absent an efficiency justification, to 'restrict competition and decrease output? For example, horizontal price-fixing and market division are inherently suspect because they are likely to raise price by reducing output.

"If the restraint is not inherently suspect, then the traditional rule of reason, with attendant issues of market definition and power, must be employed. But if it is inherently suspect, we must pose a second question: Is there a plausible efficiency justification for the practice. That is, does the practice seem capable of creating or enhancing competition (e.g., by reducing the costs of producing or marketing the product, creating a new product, or improving the operation of the market)? Such an efficiency defense is plausible if it cannot be rejected without extensive factual inquiry. If it is not plausible, then the restraint can be quickly condemned.

But if the efficiency justification is plausible, further inquiry—a third inquiry—is needed to determine whether the justification is really valid. If it is, it must be assessed under the full balancing test of the rule of reason. But if the justification is, on examination, not valid, then the practice is unreasonable and unlawful under the rule of reason without further inquiry * * * ."[99]

* * *

Earlier, Professor (now Judge) Frank Easterbrook had used the Texas Law Review as a forum for proposing an approach to cases that would preserve both the virtue of simplicity and the sophistication of modern economic analysis.

"Part of the difficulty in antitrust," Easterbrook wrote, "comes from ambiguity in what we mean by competition. * * * [C]ompetition cannot be defined as the state of maximum rivalry, for that is a formula for disintegration. Today's cooperation creates both today's benefits and tomorrow's competition. * * * The antitrust laws do not supply the time horizon for analysis, and there is no 'right' answer."[100]

Rather than "balancing" things like inter- and intra-brand competition that are not really commensurable, Easterbrook argued, the courts should apply presumptions or "filters" that would quickly screen out cases in which the risk of harm to consumers was small.

First, he suggested, the plaintiff should have to "provide a logical demonstration" that the defendant(s) had market power. Without it, he argued, they could not succeed in their alleged

---

[99] For a reaffirmation of this approach, see Timothy J. Muris, The Federal Trade Commission and the Rule of Reason: In Defense of *Massachusetts Board*, 66 Antitrust L.J. 773 (1998).

[100] Frank H. Easterbrook, The Limits of Antitrust, 63 Texas L.Rev. 1, 13 (1984).

anticompetitive efforts and there was no reason for the law to step in.[101]

Second, the plaintiff should have to "show that the defendant has an incentive to behave in an anticompetitive way and that antitrust sanctions are necessary to correct the defendant's incentives." This, he posited, would eliminate cases alleging conduct that would be unprofitable to the alleged offender, including many vertical arrangements and many predatory pricing cases.[102]

Third, if the case survives the first two filters, the Court should determine whether firms in the industry use different methods of production and distribution; if so, competition between those methods should protect consumers.

Fourth, the Court should look to see if there is evidence output actually was reduced by the challenged practice. And finally, Easterbrook suggested looking at the identity of the plaintiff, positing that if "a business rival brings suit, it is often safe to infer that the arrangement is beneficial to consumers."[103]

What do you think of these analyses? Are they both true to the cases?[104] Which rings more true as a matter of economic theory? Which seems to offer the more workable way to think through fact situations and present matters to judges and juries?[105]

In our next case, the Supreme Court tried to give an authoritative roadmap for the new analysis. In principle, it should render the above analyses moot. However, see if it in fact helps lawyers know any better what to tell a client about how its case will be decided.

---

[101] Id. at 17, 19–23. Professor Easterbrook did not propose requiring defining the relevant market in every case, a task he described as a "fool's errand." He suggested instead that in many cases, e.g., *Topco*, *Fortner*, and *GTE Sylvania*, it was obvious that the defendants lacked market power by any measure.

[102] Id. at 18, 23–29. Further, Professor Easterbrook argued, the Court should determine whether the restraint is "naked", i.e., not part of an integration of productive facilities, but he declined to identify this issue as a "filter." Id. at 18.

[103] Id. at 18, 29–39. See also, Richard S. Markovits, The Limits to Simplifying Antitrust: A Reply to Professor Easterbrook, 63 Texas L.Rev. 41 (1984).

[104] See also, Thomas A. Piriano, Jr., Reconciling the Per Se and Rule of Reason Approaches to Antitrust Analysis, 64 S.California L.Rev. 685 (1991) (proposing a "continuum-based" approach "classifying conduct according to its likely competitive purpose and effect").

[105] For criticism of current developments from someone who believes the Court has taken antitrust law in the wrong direction, see Lawrence A. Sullivan, The Viability of Current Law on Horizontal Restraints, 75 California L.Rev. 835 (1987), and compare, Thomas E. Kauper, Comment: The Sullivan Approach to Horizontal Restraints, 75 California L.Rev. 893 (1987). See also, ABA Antitrust Section, Monograph No. 23, The Rule of Reason (1999); Michael A. Carrier, The Real Rule of Reason: Bridging the Disconnect, 1999 B.Y.U. L.Rev. 1265 (1999).

CALIFORNIA DENTAL ASSOCIATION V. FEDERAL TRADE COMMISSION

Supreme Court of the United States, 1999
526 U.S. 756, 119 S.Ct. 1604, 143 L.Ed.2d 935

JUSTICE SOUTER delivered the opinion of the Court.

There are two issues in this case: whether the jurisdiction of the Federal Trade Commission extends to the California Dental Association (CDA), a nonprofit professional association, and whether a "quick look" sufficed to justify finding that certain advertising restrictions adopted by the CDA violated the antitrust laws. * * *

I

The CDA is a voluntary nonprofit association of local dental societies to which some 19,000 dentists belong, including about three-quarters of those practicing in the State. The CDA * * * lobbies and litigates in its members' interests, and conducts marketing and public relations campaigns for their benefit.

The dentists who belong to the CDA through these associations agree to abide by a Code of Ethics (Code) including the following § 10:

> "Although any dentist may advertise, no dentist shall advertise or solicit patients in any form of communication in a manner that is false or misleading in any material respect. In order to properly serve the public, dentists should represent themselves in a manner that contributes to the esteem of the public. Dentists should not misrepresent their training and competence in any way that would be false or misleading in any material respect."

* * *

Responsibility for enforcing the Code rests in the first instance with the local dental societies, to which applicants for CDA membership must submit copies of their own advertisements and those of their employers or referral services to assure compliance with the Code. The local societies also actively seek information about potential Code violations by applicants or CDA members. Applicants who refuse to withdraw or revise objectionable advertisements may be denied membership; and members who, after a hearing, remain similarly recalcitrant are subject to censure, suspension, or expulsion from the CDA.

The Commission brought a complaint against the CDA, alleging that it applied its guidelines so as to restrict truthful, nondeceptive advertising, and so violated § 5 of the FTC Act. * * * An Administrative Law Judge (ALJ) * * * found that, although there had been no proof that the CDA exerted market power, no such proof was required to establish an antitrust violation * * * since the CDA had unreasonably prevented members and potential members from using truthful, nondeceptive advertising, all to the detriment of both dentists and consumers of dental services. He accordingly found a violation of § 5 of the FTC Act.

The Commission adopted the factual findings of the ALJ except for his conclusion that the CDA lacked market power, with which the Commission disagreed. The Commission treated the CDA's restrictions on discount advertising as illegal per se. In the alternative, the Commission held the price advertising (as well as the nonprice) restrictions to be violations of the Sherman and FTC Acts under an abbreviated rule-of-reason analysis. * * *

The Court of Appeals for the Ninth Circuit affirmed, sustaining the Commission's assertion of jurisdiction over the CDA and its ultimate conclusion on the merits. The court thought it error for the Commission to have applied per se analysis to the price advertising restrictions, finding analysis under the rule of reason required for all the restrictions. But the Court of Appeals went on to explain that the Commission had properly "applied an abbreviated, or 'quick look,' rule of reason analysis designed for restraints that are not per se unlawful but are sufficiently anticompetitive on their face that they do not require a full-blown rule of reason inquiry." See National Collegiate Athletic Assn. v. Board of Regents of Univ. of Okla.

The Court of Appeals thought truncated rule-of-reason analysis to be in order for several reasons. As for the restrictions on discount advertising, they "amounted in practice to a fairly 'naked' restraint on price competition itself." The CDA's procompetitive justification, that the restrictions encouraged disclosure and prevented false and misleading advertising, carried little weight because "it is simply infeasible to disclose all of the information that is required," and "the record provides no evidence that the rule has in fact led to increased disclosure and transparency of dental pricing," As to non-price advertising restrictions, the court said that

> "these restrictions are in effect a form of output limitation, as they restrict the supply of information about individual dentists' services. . . . The restrictions may also affect output more directly, as quality and comfort advertising may induce some customers to obtain nonemergency care when they might not otherwise do so. . . . Under these circumstances, we think that the restriction is a sufficiently naked restraint on output to justify quick look analysis."

The Court of Appeals went on to hold that the Commission's findings with respect to the CDA's agreement and intent to restrain trade, as well as on the effect of the restrictions and the existence of market power, were all supported by substantial evidence. In dissent, Judge Real * * * argued full-bore rule-of-reason analysis was called for, since the disclosure requirements were not naked restraints and neither fixed prices nor banned nondeceptive advertising.

We granted certiorari to resolve conflicts among the Circuits on the * * * occasions for abbreviated rule-of-reason analysis. We now vacate the judgment of the Court of Appeals and remand.

II

The FTC Act gives the Commission authority over "persons, partnerships, or corporations," and defines "corporation" to include "any company . . . or association * * * which is organized to carry on business for its own profit or that of its members." Although the Circuits have not agreed on the precise extent of this definition, the Commission has long held that some circumstances give it jurisdiction over an entity that seeks no profit for itself. * * *

* * * The FTC Act is at pains to include not only an entity "organized to carry on business for its own profit," but also one that carries on business for the profit "of its members." * * *

* * * [P]roximate relation to lucre must appear; the FTC Act does not cover all membership organizations of profit-making corporations without more, and an organization devoted solely to professional education may lie outside the FTC Act's jurisdictional reach, even though the quality of professional services ultimately affects the profits of those who deliver them. There is no line drawing exercise in this case, however, where the CDA's contributions to the profits of its individual members are proximate and apparent. Through for-profit subsidiaries, the CDA provides advantageous insurance and preferential financing arrangements for its members, and it engages in lobbying, litigation, marketing, and public relations for the benefit of its members' interests. This congeries of activities confers far more than de minimis or merely presumed economic benefits on CDA members; the economic benefits conferred upon the CDA's profit-seeking professionals plainly fall within the object of enhancing its members' "profit,"[106] which the FTC Act makes the jurisdictional touchstone. * * *

* * *

III

* * * Because we decide that the Court of Appeals erred when it held as a matter of law that quick-look analysis was appropriate (with the

---

[106] * * * [W]e do not, and indeed, on the facts here, could not, decide today whether the Commission has jurisdiction over nonprofit organizations that do not confer profit on for-profit members but do, for example, show annual income surpluses, engage in significant commerce, or compete in relevant markets with for-profit players. We therefore do not foreclose the possibility that various paradigms of profit might fall within the ambit of the FTC Act. Nor do we decide whether a purpose of contributing to profit only in a presumed sense, as by enhancing professional educational efforts, would implicate the Commission's jurisdiction. [Court's fn. 6]

consequence that the Commission's abbreviated analysis and conclusion were sustainable), we do not reach the question of the substantiality of the evidence supporting the Commission's conclusion.

In National Collegiate Athletic Assn. v. Board of Regents of Univ. of Okla., we held that a "naked restraint on price and output requires some competitive justification even in the absence of a detailed market analysis." Elsewhere, we held that no elaborate industry analysis is required to demonstrate the anticompetitive character of "horizontal agreements" among competitors to refuse to discuss prices, National Soc. of Professional Engineers v. United States * * * . In each of these cases, which have formed the basis for what has come to be called abbreviated or "quick-look" analysis under the rule of reason, an observer with even a rudimentary understanding of economics could conclude that the arrangements in question would have an anticompetitive effect on customers and markets. * * *

The case before us, however, fails to present a situation in which the likelihood of anticompetitive effects is comparably obvious. * * * [I]t seems to us that the CDA's advertising restrictions might plausibly be thought to have a net procompetitive effect, or possibly no effect at all on competition. The restrictions on both discount and nondiscount advertising are, at least on their face, designed to avoid false or deceptive advertising in a market characterized by striking disparities between the information available to the professional and the patient. In a market for professional services, in which advertising is relatively rare and the comparability of service packages not easily established, the difficulty for customers or potential competitors to get and verify information about the price and availability of services magnifies the dangers to competition associated with misleading advertising. What is more, the quality of professional services tends to resist either calibration or monitoring by individual patients or clients, partly because of the specialized knowledge required to evaluate the services, and partly because of the difficulty in determining whether, and the degree to which, an outcome is attributable to the quality of services (like a poor job of tooth-filling) or to something else (like a very tough walnut). * * * The existence of such significant challenges to informed decisionmaking by the customer for professional services immediately suggests that advertising restrictions arguably protecting patients from misleading or irrelevant advertising call for more than cursory treatment as obviously comparable to classic horizontal agreements to limit output or price competition.

The explanation proffered by the Court of Appeals for the likely anticompetitive effect of the CDA's restrictions on discount advertising began with the unexceptionable statements that "price advertising is fundamental to price competition," and that "restrictions on the ability to advertise prices normally make it more difficult for consumers to find a lower price and for dentists to compete on the basis of price" (citing Bates v. State Bar of Ariz.). * * *

But these observations brush over the professional context and describe no anticompetitive effects. * * * Put another way, the CDA's rule appears to reflect the prediction that any costs to competition associated with the elimination of across-the-board advertising will be outweighed by gains to consumer information (and hence competition) created by discount advertising that is exact, accurate, and more easily verifiable (at least by regulators). As a matter of economics this view may or may not be correct, but it is not implausible, and neither a court nor the Commission may initially dismiss it as presumptively wrong.[107]

* * *

The point is not that the CDA's restrictions necessarily have the procompetitive effect claimed by the CDA; it is possible that banning quality claims might have no effect at all on competitiveness if, for example, many dentists made very much the same sort of claims. And it is also of course possible that the restrictions might in the final analysis be anticompetitive. The point, rather, is that the plausibility of competing claims about the effects of the professional advertising restrictions rules out the indulgently abbreviated review to which the Commission's order was treated. The obvious anticompetitive effect that triggers abbreviated analysis has not been shown.

In light of our focus on the adequacy of the Court of Appeals's analysis, Justice Breyer's thorough-going, de novo antitrust analysis contains much to impress on its own merits but little to demonstrate the sufficiency of the Court of Appeals's review. * * * Had the Court of Appeals engaged in a painstaking discussion in a league with Justice Breyer's (compare his 14 pages with the Ninth Circuit's 8), and had it confronted the comparability of these restrictions to bars on clearly verifiable advertising, its reasoning might have sufficed to justify its conclusion. Certainly Justice Breyer's treatment of the antitrust issues here is no "quick look." Lingering is more like it, and indeed Justice Breyer, not surprisingly, stops short of endorsing the Court of Appeals's discussion as adequate to the task at hand.

Saying here that the Court of Appeals's conclusion at least required a more extended examination of the possible factual underpinnings than it received is not, of course, necessarily to call for the fullest market analysis. Although we have said that a challenge to a "naked restraint on price and output" need not be supported by "a detailed market analysis" in order to

---

[107] * * * [B]efore a theoretical claim of anticompetitive effects can justify shifting to a defendant the burden to show empirical evidence of pro-competitive effects, as quick-look analysis in effect requires, there must be some indication that the court making the decision has properly identified the theoretical basis for the anticompetitive effects and considered whether the effects actually are anticompetitive. Where, as here, the circumstances of the restriction are somewhat complex, assumption alone will not do. [Court's fn. 12]

"require some competitive justification," it does not follow that every case attacking a less obviously anticompetitive restraint (like this one) is a candidate for plenary market examination. The truth is that our categories of analysis of anticompetitive effect are less fixed than terms like "per se," "quick look," and "rule of reason" tend to make them appear. We have recognized, for example, that "there is often no bright line separating per se from Rule of Reason analysis," since "considerable inquiry into market conditions" may be required before the application of any so-called "per se" condemnation is justified. "Whether the ultimate finding is the product of a presumption or actual market analysis, the essential inquiry remains the same—whether or not the challenged restraint enhances competition." Indeed, the scholar who enriched antitrust law with the metaphor of "the twinkling of an eye" for the most condensed rule-of-reason analysis himself cautioned against the risk of misleading even in speaking of a 'spectrum' of adequate reasonableness analysis for passing upon antitrust claims: "There is always something of a sliding scale in appraising reasonableness, but the sliding scale formula deceptively suggests greater precision than we can hope for. . . . Nevertheless, the quality of proof required should vary with the circumstances." P. Areeda, Antitrust Law ¶ 1507 (1986). At the same time, Professor Areeda also emphasized the necessity, particularly great in the quasi-common law realm of antitrust, that courts explain the logic of their conclusions. * * * As the circumstances here demonstrate, there is generally no categorical line to be drawn between restraints that give rise to an intuitively obvious inference of anticompetitive effect and those that call for more detailed treatment. What is required, rather, is an enquiry meet for the case, looking to the circumstances, details, and logic of a restraint. The object is to see whether the experience of the market has been so clear, or necessarily will be, that a confident conclusion about the principal tendency of a restriction will follow from a quick (or at least quicker) look, in place of a more sedulous one. And of course what we see may vary over time, if rule-of-reason analyses in case after case reach identical conclusions. For now, at least, a less quick look was required for the initial assessment of the tendency of these professional advertising restrictions. Because the Court of Appeals did not scrutinize the assumption of relative anticompetitive tendencies, we vacate the judgment and remand the case for a fuller consideration of the issue.

It is so ordered.

JUSTICE BREYER, with whom JUSTICE STEVENS, JUSTICE KENNEDY, and JUSTICE GINSBURG join, concurring in part and dissenting in part.

I agree with the Court that the Federal Trade Commission has jurisdiction over petitioner, and I join Parts I and II of its opinion. I also agree that in a "rule of reason" antitrust case "the quality of proof required should vary with the circumstances," that "what is required . . . is an enquiry meet for the case," and that the object is a "confident conclusion about the principal tendency of a restriction." But I do not agree that the Court has properly applied those unobjectionable principles here. In my view, a traditional application of the rule of reason to the facts as found by the Commission requires affirming the Commission—just as the Court of Appeals did below.

I

The Commission's conclusion is lawful if its "factual findings," insofar as they are supported by "substantial evidence," "make out a violation of Sherman Act § 1." To determine whether that is so, I would not simply ask whether the restraints at issue are anticompetitive overall. Rather, like the Court of Appeals (and the Commission), I would break that question down into four classical, subsidiary antitrust questions: (1) What is the specific restraint at issue? (2) What are its likely anticompetitive effects? (3) Are there offsetting procompetitive justifications? (4) Do the parties have sufficient market power to make a difference?

A

The most important question is the first: What are the specific restraints at issue? Those restraints do not include merely the agreement to which the California Dental Association's * * * ethical rule literally refers, namely, a promise to refrain from advertising that is " 'false or misleading in any material respect.' " Instead, the Commission found a set of restraints arising out of the way the Dental Association implemented this innocent-sounding ethical rule in practice, through advisory opinions, guidelines, enforcement policies, and review of membership applications. As implemented, the ethical rule reached beyond its nominal target, to prevent truthful and nondeceptive advertising. In particular, the Commission determined that the rule, in practice:

> (1) "precluded advertising that characterized a dentist's fees as being low, reasonable, or affordable," (2) "precluded advertising . . . of across the board discounts," and (3) "prohibited all quality claims."

Whether the Dental Association's basic rule as implemented actually restrained the truthful and nondeceptive advertising of low prices, across-the-board discounts, and quality service are questions of fact. The Administrative Law Judge (ALJ) and the Commission may have found those questions difficult ones. But both the ALJ and the Commission ultimately found against the Dental Association in respect to these facts. And the question for us—whether those agency findings are supported by substantial evidence—is not difficult.

The Court of Appeals referred explicitly to some of the evidence that it found adequate to support the Commission's conclusions. It pointed out, for example, that the Dental Association's "advisory opinions and guidelines indicate that ... descriptions of prices as 'reasonable' or 'low' do not comply" with the Association's rule; that in "numerous cases" the Association "advised members of objections to special offers, senior citizen discounts, and new patient discounts, apparently without regard to their truth"; and that one advisory opinion "expressly states that claims as to the quality of services are inherently likely to be false or misleading," all "without any particular consideration of whether" such statements were "true or false."

The Commission itself had before it far more evidence. It referred to instances in which the Association, without regard for the truthfulness of the statements at issue, recommended denial of membership to dentists wishing to advertise, for example, "reasonable fees quoted in advance," "major savings," or "making teeth cleaning ... inexpensive." * * *

I need not review the evidence further, for this Court has said that "substantial evidence" is a matter for the courts of appeals, and that it "will intervene only in what ought to be the rare instance when the standard appears to have been misapprehended or grossly misapplied." I have said enough to make clear that this is not a case warranting our intervention. Consequently, we must decide only the basic legal question whether the three restraints described above unreasonably restrict competition.

B

Do each of the three restrictions mentioned have "the potential for genuine adverse effects on competition"? I should have thought that the anticompetitive tendencies of the three restrictions were obvious. An agreement not to advertise that a fee is reasonable, that service is inexpensive, or that a customer will receive a discount makes it more difficult for a dentist to inform customers that he charges a lower price. If the customer does not know about a lower price, he will find it more difficult to buy lower price service. That fact, in turn, makes it less likely that a dentist will obtain more customers by offering lower prices. And that likelihood means that dentists will prove less likely to offer lower prices. But why should I have to spell out the obvious? To restrain truthful advertising about lower prices is likely to restrict competition in respect to price—"the central nervous system of the economy." United States v. Socony-Vacuum Oil Co. The Commission thought this fact sufficient to hold (in the alternative) that the price advertising restrictions were unlawful per se. For present purposes, I need not decide whether the Commission was right in applying a per se rule. I need only assume a rule of reason applies, and note the serious anticompetitive tendencies of the price advertising restraints.

The restrictions on the advertising of service quality also have serious anticompetitive tendencies. This is not a case of "mere puffing," as the FTC recognized. The days of my youth, when the billboards near Emeryville,

California, home of AAA baseball's Oakland Oaks, displayed the name of "Painless" Parker, Dentist, are long gone—along with the Oakland Oaks. But some parents may still want to know that a particular dentist makes a point of "gentle care." Others may want to know about 1-year dental work guarantees. To restrict that kind of service quality advertisement is to restrict competition over the quality of service itself, for, unless consumers know, they may not purchase, and dentists may not compete to supply that which will make little difference to the demand for their services. That, at any rate, is the theory of the Sherman Act. And it is rather late in the day for anyone to deny the significant anticompetitive tendencies of an agreement that restricts competition in any legitimate respect, let alone one that inhibits customers from learning about the quality of a dentist's service.

* * *

C

We must also ask whether, despite their anticompetitive tendencies, these restrictions might be justified by other procompetitive tendencies or redeeming virtues. This is a closer question—at least in theory. * * * The Association, the argument goes, had to prevent dentists from engaging in the kind of truthful, nondeceptive advertising that it banned in order effectively to stop dentists from making unverifiable claims about price or service quality, which claims would mislead the consumer.

The problem with this or any similar argument is an empirical one. Notwithstanding its theoretical plausibility, the record does not bear out such a claim. The * * * Court of Appeals wrote, in respect to the price restrictions, that "the record provides no evidence that the rule has in fact led to increased disclosure and transparency of dental pricing." With respect to quality advertising, the Commission stressed that the Association "offered no convincing argument, let alone evidence, that consumers of dental services have been, or are likely to be, harmed by the broad categories of advertising it restricts." * * *

* * *

In the usual Sherman Act § 1 case, the defendant bears the burden of establishing a procompetitive justification. And the Court of Appeals was correct when it concluded that no such justification had been established here.

D

I shall assume that the Commission must prove one additional circumstance, namely, that the Association's restraints would likely have made a real difference in the marketplace. The Commission, disagreeing with the ALJ on this single point, found that the Association did possess enough market power to make a difference. In at least one region of

California, the mid-Peninsula, its members accounted for more than 90% of the marketplace; on average they accounted for 75%. In addition, entry by new dentists into the market place is fairly difficult. Dental education is expensive (leaving graduates of dental school with $50,000–$100,000 of debt), as is opening a new dentistry office (which costs $75,000–$100,000). And Dental Association members believe membership in the Association is important, valuable, and recognized as such by the public.

These facts, in the Court of Appeals' view, were sufficient to show "enough market power to harm competition through [the Association's] standard setting in the area of advertising." And that conclusion is correct. Restrictions on advertising price discounts in Palo Alto may make a difference because potential patients may not respond readily to discount advertising by the handful (10%) of dentists who are not members of the Association. And that fact, in turn, means that the remaining 90% will prove less likely to engage in price competition. Facts such as these have previously led this Court to find market power—unless the defendant has overcome the showing with strong contrary evidence. I can find no reason for departing from that precedent here.

II

* * *

I would note that the form of analysis I have followed is not rigid; it admits of some variation according to the circumstances. The important point, however, is that its allocation of the burdens of persuasion reflects a gradual evolution within the courts over a period of many years. That evolution represents an effort carefully to blend the procompetitive objectives of the law of antitrust with administrative necessity. It represents a considerable advance, both from the days when the Commission had to present and/or refute every possible fact and theory, and from antitrust theories so abbreviated as to prevent proper analysis. The former prevented cases from ever reaching a conclusion, and the latter called forth the criticism that the "Government always wins." I hope that this case does not represent an abandonment of that basic, and important, form of analysis.

For these reasons, I respectfully dissent from Part III of the Court's opinion.

NOTES AND QUESTIONS

1.   Has the Court now clarified the analysis to be applied in Sherman Act cases? Has it made the analysis less comprehensible than ever?

a.   Where did the Federal Trade Commission go wrong? Was its mistake in thinking that any restraints of trade are per se illegal anymore? Was its mistake in thinking the category of per se violations is significantly broader than naked price fixing?

b.   Where did the Court of Appeals go wrong? Was its mistake in thinking that a "quick look" at the defendants' conduct was sufficient? Does the Supreme Court back away from the quick look approach in principle? How is one to know how much of a look will be required?[108]

2.   When this case came back to the Court of Appeals, it concluded—using what it called a "more-extensive" rule of reason analysis—that the FTC's condemnation of the advertising restrictions was not supported by substantial evidence. California Dental Association v. Federal Trade Commission, 224 F.3d 942 (9th Cir. 2000).

a.   The Court of Appeals found little empirical evidence in the Commission's record that showed an overtly anticompetitive intent or effect of the restrictions. Would you be surprised to see that in a record based on what the Commission thought was a per se offense?

b.   The Court of Appeals directed the Commission to dismiss its case against the CDA. Do you think such an order was warranted? The Court was disturbed that complaint counsel for the Commission had not introduced all the evidence in the agency's possession at the original hearing and thus would be getting a "second bite at the apple" if the case were remanded.

c.   Is the effect of the Court of Appeals order that, whatever the Supreme Court may have thought it was requiring, plaintiffs' counsel will hereafter have to try every case as if it will be reviewed under a full rule of reason analysis, lest they guess wrong about what a reviewing court will say was required? Do you think the Supreme Court majority anticipated such a result?

3.   Might this case have turned on some members of the Court's underlying objection to advertising by professionals?

a.   Is the Court saying that, because consumer confusion about dental pricing might reduce demand, providing less consumer information would increase demand and therefore output?

b.   It may be that the Court was suspicious of professional advertising generally. The Court split almost the same way in holding that the constitutional commercial speech doctrine did not prevent regulation of lawyers' advertising for clients shortly after a plane crash or similar disaster. See The Florida Bar v. Went For It, Inc., 515 U.S. 618, 115 S.Ct. 2371, 132 L.Ed.2d 541 (1995).

---

[108]   There has been no shortage of academics willing to suggest answers to this question. See, e.g., Thomas C. Arthur, A Workable Rule of Reason: A Less Ambitious Role for the Federal Courts, 68 Antitrust L.J. 337 (2000); Willard K. Tom & Chul Pak, Toward a Flexible Rule of Reason, 68 Antitrust L.J. 391 (2000); Stephen Calkins, California Dental Association: Not a Quick Look But Not the Full Monty, 67 Antitrust L.J. 495 (2000). Cf. C. Frederick Beckner III & Steven C. Salop, Decision Theory and Antitrust Rules, 67 Antitrust L.J. 41 (1999) (exploring efforts to limit Type 1, Type 2 and Type 3 errors in antitrust cases).

THE ANTITRUST GUIDELINES FOR COLLABORATIONS AMONG COMPETITORS

If there is a bottom-line message from the cases in this part of the chapter, it is that not all competitor collaborations are anticompetitive. One must carefully distinguish among competitor agreements to determine which represent traditional cartels and which are harmless or even in the public interest.

In an effort to help draw such distinctions and sort through the rules now governing horizontal arrangements after *California Dental*, the Justice Department and Federal Trade Commission jointly issued Antitrust Guidelines for Collaborations Among Competitors (April 2000), one of several such Guidelines described in this chapter. None of the Guidelines purports to change the law or regulate private suits, but each of them helps practitioners predict enforcement policy and can help students organize concepts and understand the cases they have studied.[109]

Under § 1.1 of the Guidelines, "competitors" include both the actual and potential variety, and a "competitor collaboration" is joint economic activity by competitors that falls short of being a merger.[110]

Agreements that remain per se illegal include those to "fix prices or output, rig bids, or share or divide markets." Guidelines § 1.2.

Agreements analyzed under the rule of reason include those "reasonably related to, and reasonably necessary to achieve procompetitive benefits from, an efficiency-enhancing integration of economic activity." In a rule of reason analysis:

> "The Agencies' analysis * * * ask[s] about the business purpose of the agreement and examine[s] whether the agreement, if already in operation, has caused anticompetitive harm. In some cases, the nature of the agreement and the absence of market power together may demonstrate the absence of anticompetitive harm. In such cases, the Agencies do not challenge the agreement. Alternatively, where the likelihood of anticompetitive harm is evident from the nature of the agreement, or anticompetitive harm has resulted from an agreement already in operation, then, absent overriding benefits that could offset the anticompetitive harm, the Agencies challenge such agreements without a detailed market analysis.

---

[109] The complete text of this and other Guidelines can be found on the agency websites—www.justice.gov/ and www.ftc.gov/.

[110] If a competitor collaboration extends over 10 years, the arrangement may be challenged as a merger under Clayton Act § 7. [Guidelines § 1.3].

"If the initial examination of the nature of the agreement indicates possible competitive concerns, but the agreement is not one that would be challenged without a detailed market analysis, the Agencies analyze the agreement in greater depth. The Agencies typically define relevant markets and calculate market shares and concentration as an initial step in assessing whether the agreement may create or increase market power or facilitate its exercise. The Agencies examine the extent to which the participants and the collaboration have the ability and incentive to compete independently. The Agencies also evaluate other market circumstances, e.g. entry, that may foster or prevent anticompetitive harms.

"If the examination of these factors indicates no potential for anticompetitive harm, the Agencies end the investigation without considering procompetitive benefits. If investigation indicates anticompetitive harm, the Agencies examine whether the relevant agreement is reasonably necessary to achieve procompetitive benefits that likely would offset anticompetitive harms."

The Guidelines appreciate that multi-firm activity can have significant procompetitive benefits that lower prices, increase quality, speed invention or justify investments that will increase production. "The Agencies assess the competitive effects of a relevant agreement as of the time of possible harm to competition, whether at formation of the collaboration or at a later time, as appropriate." However, the Agencies will be "sensitive to the reasonable expectations" of collaborators who have made significant sunk cost investments before an agreement becomes anticompetitive. [Guidelines § 2.4].

Effects of a collaboration will be assessed in all relevant product and geographic markets. Where technology agreements are involved, markets will be identified under the standards set out in the Antitrust Guidelines for the Licensing of Intellectual Property (1995). [Guidelines § 3.32]. Ease of entry into the industry in which the collaboration takes place will also be relevant to its evaluation. [Guidelines § 3.35].

The Guidelines close with "safety zones" designed to encourage cooperative ventures:

1.   Except for agreements that are per se illegal or that present other "extraordinary circumstances," the Agencies "do not challenge" a collaboration "when the market shares of the collaboration and its participants collectively account for no more than twenty percent of each relevant market in which competition may be affected." [Guidelines § 4.2].

2.   Again with the above exceptions, the Agencies do not challenge collaborations in an "innovation market where three or more independently controlled research efforts in addition to those of the

collaboration possess the required specialized assets * * * and the incentive to engage in R & D that is a close substitute for the R & D activity of the collaboration." [Guidelines § 4.3].

Will you find it useful to have the reassurance of such Guidelines? Have the agencies retained sufficient discretion to make it unsafe to rely heavily on their guidance? Should the Guidelines be persuasive to a judge who is considering a suit filed by a state attorney general or by a customer or competitor, even if they are not binding on the court in such a case?[111]

THE FTC AND JUDICIAL RESPONSE—
THE THREE TENORS CASE

The Federal Trade Commission's answer to what *California Dental* required in the conduct of litigation was the so-called "Three Tenors" case, 2003 WL 21770765 (FTC 2003), aff'd Polygram Holding, Inc. v. Federal Trade Commission, 416 F.3d 29 (D.C. Cir. 2005). The defendants were distributors of albums of two well-known "Three Tenors" concerts given by Jose Carreras, Placido Domingo and Luciano Pavarotti. The two defendants held joint rights to the tenors' third concert, but found it would contain much of the same music as was in the first two. Afraid the third album would not sell well, they agreed not to advertise or discount either of the first two albums for a six week period after release of the third album.

In an opinion by FTC Chairman Tim Muris, the Commission said that after *California Dental* a plaintiff must make an initial showing that "the conduct at issue is inherently suspect owing to its likely tendency to suppress competition." If it does so, the defendant can avoid losing only by "advancing a legitimate justification for those practices." It must offer both a "legally cognizable" and "facially plausible" case that the practices have no adverse consequences for consumers in the relevant market. At that point, the burden shifts back to the plaintiff to offer proof to counter the defendant's position, whereupon the defense has a chance to respond in kind.

The Court of Appeals read the FTC's approach as basically the one described by the Commission in *Massachusetts Board of Optometry,* supra. "[C]onduct 'inherently suspect' as a restraint of competition—that is, conduct that 'appears likely, absent an efficiency justification, to restrict competition and decrease output'—is to be presumed unreasonable," the court said. "Only if the competitive harm wrought by the restraint is not

---

[111] Cf. Augusta News Co. v. Hudson News Co., 269 F.3d 41 (1st Cir. 2001) (not improper for two local newspapers to set up a new joint regional service; *Guidelines* not cited).

The European Union has published its own "Guidelines on the applicability of Article 101 of the Treaty on the Functioning of the European Union to horizontal cooperation agreements" (Jan. 14, 2011).

readily apparent from the nature of the restraint itself, or the charged party offers a plausible competitive justification for the restraint, must the Commission, under this approach, engage in a more searching analysis of the market circumstances surrounding the restraint." It was reasonable, the court found, for the Commission to conclude that an agreement not to advertise or discount, even for a limited period, was "inherently suspect." The defendants' attempt to justify the agreement was not convincing. "[I]f the only way a new product can profitably be introduced is to restrain the legitimate competition of older products," the court said, "then one must seriously wonder whether consumers are genuinely benefitted by the new product."

Do you agree that the new procedure accurately captures the letter and spirit of *California Dental*? Other courts have affirmed application of the "inherently suspect" test, first to doctors who collectively negotiated rates with health insurers, North Texas Specialty Physicians v. FTC, 528 F.3d 346 (5th Cir. 2008) (describing the process as "quick look" analysis), and a multiple listing service website that limited information provided about "nontraditional" real estate services, Realcomp II, Ltd. v. FTC, 635 F.3d 815 (6th Cir. 2011).[112]

APPLICATION OF ANTITRUST PRINCIPLES TO THE AFFORDABLE CARE ACT

Dental advertising as in *California Dental* is a relatively trivial issue in the application of Sherman Act § 1 to health care. More significant questions have arisen with respect to issues such as multi-hospital purchase of high-technology equipment, hospital agreements to divide provision of specialized surgery and other services, joint purchasing arrangements among hospitals, clinics or both, multi-physician networks that coordinate services vertically, horizontally or both, and provider groups that coordinate dealings with third-party payers.[113] We have already discussed a number of the important cases that have addressed health care over the last 30 years, and we have seen doctors incur antitrust liability at least as often as other professionals.[114]

---

[112] See, e.g., Geoffrey D. Oliver, Of Tenors, Real Estate Brokers and Golf Clubs: A Quick Look at Truncated Rule of Reason Analysis, 24 Antitrust 40 (Spring 2010); David L. Meyer, The FTC's New "Rule of Reason": Realcomp and the Expanding Scope of "Inherently Suspect" Analysis, 24 Antitrust 47 (Spring 2010).

[113] Issues relating to hospital mergers are discussed later in this chapter.

[114] E.g., Arizona v. Maricopa County Medical Society, 457 U.S. 332, 102 S.Ct. 2466, 73 L.Ed.2d 48 (1982) (doctors agreement with insurers about reimbursement schedule held per se illegal); Group Life & Health Insurance Co. v. Royal Drug Co., 440 U.S. 205, 99 S.Ct. 1067, 59 L.Ed.2d 261 (1979) (Blue Shield contracts with pharmacies about payment rates held not to be the "business of insurance"); Union Labor Life Insurance Co. v. Pireno, 458 U.S. 119, 102 S.Ct. 3002, 73 L.Ed.2d 647 (1982) (insurer's use of chiropractic association to review chiropractor charges likewise not the

Important issues in the health care industry were addressed by the Department of Justice and the Federal Trade Commission in their Statements of Antitrust Enforcement Policy in Health Care (August 1996). Briefly, the agencies stressed the importance of preserving competition in the provision of health care but acknowledged that many beneficial practices necessarily involve coordination among health care providers. As in the Guidelines cited earlier, the Health Care Statements defined what they call "antitrust safety zones," i.e., practices unlikely to raise concerns because of low market share or obvious efficiencies. Even practices outside the safety zones are subject to a rule of reason that involves defining the relevant market, evaluating competitive effects of the practice, estimating procompetitive efficiencies, and considering the impact of any collateral agreements.

Later, after two years of hearings, in July 2004 the agencies issued a new report, "Improving Health Care: A Dose of Competition," that was broader and more comprehensive than the 1996 Statements. It acknowledged the place of multiple regulatory and subsidy programs in the health care marketplace, but called in forceful tones for competition as one of the key ways to drive improvements in an industry whose economic impact seems destined only to grow.[115]

It was in that context that the Patient Protection and Affordable Care Act, Pub. L. No. 111–48, 124 Stat. 119, often called "Obamacare," was adopted in 2010. Among its efforts to reduce health expenditures, the Act encourages health care providers to form accountable care organizations (ACOs) to provide coordinated care to groups of Medicare recipients under a "Shared Savings Program." If an ACO can serve its patient group for less than Medicare has been paying on a fee-for-service basis, providers are to share in those savings. Critics fear, however, that if an ACO can raise its rates above a competitive level, it will profit even more and reap its profits from patients well beyond those it serves under Medicare.

In October 2011, coinciding with issuance of a final rule by the Centers for Medicare and Medicaid Services under Sec. 3022 of the Affordable Care Act, the Department of Justice and Federal Trade Commission issued a "Statement of Antitrust Enforcement Policy Regarding [ACOs] * * * ."[116] The Statement announces that rule of reason analysis will be applied to

---

business of insurance); Federal Trade Commission v. Indiana Federation of Dentists, 476 U.S. 447, 106 S.Ct. 2009, 90 L.Ed.2d 445 (1986) (dentists refuse to submit x-rays to insurance companies).

[115] Both the Statements and the new report may be found on the agency websites— www.usdoj.gov and www.ftc.gov. The issues are also discussed in an excellent Symposium: Issues in the Evolution of Health Care Antitrust, 71 Antitrust L. J. 853–1032 (2004).

[116] 76 Fed. Reg. 67,026 (Oct. 28, 2011). The Statement applies only to "collaborations among otherwise independent providers and provider groups." Fully integrated entities will be analyzed under the DOJ/FTC Horizontal Merger Guidelines, discussed in Part D of this Chapter.

ACOs and creates a "safety zone" within which ACOs will be deemed to be "highly unlikely to raise significant competitive concerns."

To be within the safety zone as to a given service, market shares of individual members of an ACO must total less than 30% of the market for that service.[117] ACOs that fall outside the safety zone are not unlawful, but members must be careful not to share competitively sensitive information, encourage private payers to select certain providers, tie sales of some services to others, contract on an exclusive basis with other providers, or deny benefits to non-Medicare patients that it grants under the shared savings program.

In short, the Department of Justice and Federal Trade Commission are not standing in the way of forming Accountable Care Organizations, but lawyers advising those organizations will have to make their clients aware that exposure to significant liability could accompany the operation of such entities.

In 2013, the Supreme Court examined a practice that was controversial for many years and that brings together several issues we have seen before—the interplay of intellectual property and antitrust, the desire to reduce the cost of antitrust litigation, and the effort to minimize both Type 1 and Type 2 errors. The Court's decision provides a fitting end to our look at the current state of the law under Sherman Act § 1.

FEDERAL TRADE COMMISSION V. ACTAVIS, INC.

Supreme Court of the United States, 2013
___ U.S. ___, 133 S.Ct. 2223, 186 L.Ed. 2d 343

JUSTICE BREYER delivered the opinion of the Court.

Company A sues Company B for patent infringement. The two companies settle under terms that require (1) Company B, the claimed infringer, not to produce the patented product until the patent's term expires, and (2) Company A, the patentee, to pay B many millions of dollars. Because the settlement requires the patentee to pay the alleged infringer, rather than the other way around, this kind of settlement agreement is often called a "reverse payment" settlement agreement. And the basic question here is whether such an agreement can sometimes unreasonably diminish competition in violation of the antitrust laws. Cf. Palmer v. BRG of Ga., Inc. (invalidating agreement not to compete).

---

[117] Real life, of course, is more complicated. The Statement goes into detail about how market shares are to be calculated, differences between exclusive and non-exclusive ACOs, different standards for "dominant" providers who had over 50% of the market before joining the ACO, and different standards for ACOs in rural areas.

In this case, the Eleventh Circuit dismissed a Federal Trade Commission (FTC) complaint claiming that a particular reverse payment settlement agreement violated the antitrust laws. In doing so, the Circuit stated that a reverse payment settlement agreement generally is "immune from antitrust attack so long as its anticompetitive effects fall within the scope of the exclusionary potential of the patent." And since the alleged infringer's promise not to enter the patentee's market expired before the patent's term ended, the Circuit found the agreement legal and dismissed the FTC complaint. In our view, however, reverse payment settlements such as the agreement alleged in the complaint before us can sometimes violate the antitrust laws. We consequently hold that the Eleventh Circuit should have allowed the FTC's lawsuit to proceed.

I

A

Apparently most if not all reverse payment settlement agreements arise in the context of pharmaceutical drug regulation, and specifically in the context of suits brought under statutory provisions allowing a generic drug manufacturer (seeking speedy marketing approval) to challenge the validity of a patent owned by an already-approved brand-name drug owner. We consequently describe four key features of the relevant drug-regulatory framework established by the Drug Price Competition and Patent Term Restoration Act of 1984 * * * commonly known as the Hatch-Waxman Act.

First, a drug manufacturer, wishing to market a new prescription drug, must submit a New Drug Application to the federal Food and Drug Administration (FDA) and undergo a long, comprehensive, and costly testing process, after which, if successful, the manufacturer will receive marketing approval from the FDA. * * *

Second, once the FDA has approved a brand-name drug for marketing, a manufacturer of a generic drug can obtain similar marketing approval through use of abbreviated procedures. The Hatch-Waxman Act permits a generic manufacturer to file an Abbreviated New Drug Application specifying that the generic has the "same active ingredients as," and is "biologically equivalent" to, the already-approved brand-name drug. In this way the generic manufacturer can obtain approval while avoiding the "costly and time-consuming studies" needed to obtain approval "for a pioneer drug." The Hatch-Waxman process, by allowing the generic to piggy-back on the pioneer's approval efforts, "speed[s] the introduction of low-cost generic drugs to market," thereby furthering drug competition.

Third, the Hatch-Waxman Act sets forth special procedures for identifying, and resolving, related patent disputes. It requires the pioneer brand-name manufacturer to list in its New Drug Application the "number and the expiration date" of any relevant patent. And it requires the generic manufacturer in its Abbreviated New Drug Application to "assure the FDA" that the generic "will not infringe" the brand-name's patents.

The generic can provide this assurance in one of several ways. It can certify that the brand-name manufacturer has not listed any relevant patents. It can certify that any relevant patents have expired. It can request approval to market beginning when any still-in-force patents expire. Or, it can certify that any listed, relevant patent "is invalid or will not be infringed by the manufacture, use, or sale" of the drug described in the Abbreviated New Drug Application. Taking this last-mentioned route (called the "paragraph IV" route), automatically counts as patent infringement, and often "means provoking litigation." If the brand-name patentee brings an infringement suit within 45 days, the FDA then must withhold approving the generic, usually for a 30-month period, while the parties litigate patent validity (or infringement) in court. If the courts decide the matter within that period, the FDA follows that determination; if they do not, the FDA may go forward and give approval to market the generic product.

Fourth, Hatch-Waxman provides a special incentive for a generic to be the first to file an Abbreviated New Drug Application taking the paragraph IV route. That applicant will enjoy a period of 180 days of exclusivity (from the first commercial marketing of its drug). During that period of exclusivity no other generic can compete with the brand-name drug. If the first-to-file generic manufacturer can overcome any patent obstacle and bring the generic to market, this 180-day period of exclusivity can prove valuable, possibly "worth several hundred million dollars." Hemphill, Paying for Delay: Pharmaceutical Patent Settlement as a Regulatory Design Problem, 81 N.Y.U. L.Rev. 1553, 1579 (2006). Indeed, the Generic Pharmaceutical Association said in 2006 that the " 'vast majority of potential profits for a generic drug manufacturer materialize during the 180-day exclusivity period.' " The 180-day exclusivity period, however, can belong only to the first generic to file. Should that first-to-file generic forfeit the exclusivity right in one of the ways specified by statute, no other generic can obtain it.

B

1

In 1999, Solvay Pharmaceuticals, a respondent here, filed a New Drug Application for a brand-name drug called AndroGel. The FDA approved the application in 2000. In 2003, Solvay obtained a relevant patent and disclosed that fact to the FDA, as Hatch-Waxman requires.

Later the same year another respondent, Actavis, Inc. * * * filed an Abbreviated New Drug Application for a generic drug modeled after AndroGel. Subsequently, Paddock Laboratories, also a respondent, separately filed an Abbreviated New Drug Application for its own generic product. Both Actavis and Paddock certified under paragraph IV that Solvay's listed patent was invalid and their drugs did not infringe it. A fourth manufacturer, Par Pharmaceutical, likewise a respondent, did not file an application of its own but joined forces with Paddock, agreeing to share the patent litigation costs in return for a share of profits if Paddock obtained approval for its generic drug.

Solvay initiated paragraph IV patent litigation against Actavis and Paddock. Thirty months later the FDA approved Actavis' first-to-file generic product, but, in 2006, the patent-litigation parties all settled. Under the terms of the settlement Actavis agreed that it would not bring its generic to market until August 31, 2015, 65 months before Solvay's patent expired (unless someone else marketed a generic sooner). Actavis also agreed to promote AndroGel to urologists. The other generic manufacturers made roughly similar promises. And Solvay agreed to pay millions of dollars to each generic—$12 million in total to Paddock; $60 million in total to Par; and an estimated $19–$30 million annually, for nine years, to Actavis. The companies described these payments as compensation for other services the generics promised to perform, but the FTC contends the other services had little value. According to the FTC the true point of the payments was to compensate the generics for agreeing not to compete against AndroGel until 2015.

2

On January 29, 2009, the FTC filed this lawsuit against all the settling parties, namely, Solvay, Actavis, Paddock, and Par. The FTC's complaint * * * alleged that respondents violated § 5 of the Federal Trade Commission Act, by unlawfully agreeing "to share in Solvay's monopoly profits, abandon their patent challenges, and refrain from launching their low-cost generic products to compete with AndroGel for nine years." The District Court held that these allegations did not set forth an antitrust law violation. It accordingly dismissed the FTC's complaint. * * *

The Court of Appeals for the Eleventh Circuit affirmed the District Court. It wrote that "absent sham litigation or fraud in obtaining the patent, a reverse payment settlement is immune from antitrust attack so long as its anticompetitive effects fall within the scope of the exclusionary potential of the patent." The court recognized that "antitrust laws typically prohibit agreements where one company pays a potential competitor not to enter the market." * * * But, the court found that "reverse payment settlements of patent litigation presen[t] atypical cases because one of the parties owns a patent." Patent holders have a "lawful right to exclude others from the market;" thus a patent "conveys the right to cripple competition." The court recognized that, if the parties to this sort of case do not settle, a court might declare the patent invalid. But, in light of the public policy favoring settlement of disputes (among other considerations) it held that the courts could not require the parties to continue to litigate in order to avoid antitrust liability.

The FTC sought certiorari. Because different courts have reached different conclusions about the application of the antitrust laws to Hatch-Waxman-related patent settlements, we granted the FTC's petition. * * *

II

A

Solvay's patent, if valid and infringed, might have permitted it to charge drug prices sufficient to recoup the reverse settlement payments it agreed to make to its potential generic competitors. And we are willing to take this fact as evidence that the agreement's "anticompetitive effects fall within the scope of the exclusionary potential of the patent." But we do not agree that that fact, or characterization, can immunize the agreement from antitrust attack.

For one thing, to refer, as the Circuit referred, simply to what the holder of a valid patent could do does not by itself answer the antitrust question. The patent here may or may not be valid, and may or may not be infringed. "[A] *valid* patent excludes all except its owner from the use of the protected process or product," United States v. Line Material Co., 333 U.S. 287, 308, 68 S.Ct. 550, 92 L.Ed. 701 (1948) (emphasis added). And that exclusion may permit the patent owner to charge a higher-than-competitive price for the patented product. But an invalidated patent carries with it no such right. And even a valid patent confers no right to exclude products or processes that do not actually infringe. The paragraph IV litigation in this case put the patent's validity at issue, as well as its actual preclusive scope. The parties' settlement ended that litigation. The FTC alleges that in substance, the plaintiff agreed to pay the defendants many millions of dollars to stay out of its market, even though the defendants did not have any claim that the plaintiff was liable to them for damages. That form of settlement is unusual. And, for reasons discussed in Part II–B, infra, there is reason for concern that settlements taking this form tend to have significant adverse effects on competition.

Given these factors, it would be incongruous to determine antitrust legality by measuring the settlement's anticompetitive effects solely against patent law policy, rather than by measuring them against procompetitive antitrust policies as well. And indeed, contrary to the Circuit's view that the only pertinent question is whether "the settlement agreement . . . fall[s] within" the legitimate "scope" of the patent's "exclusionary potential," this Court has indicated that patent and antitrust policies are both relevant in determining the "scope of the patent monopoly"—and consequently antitrust law immunity—that is conferred by a patent.

Thus, the Court in *Line Material* explained that "the improper use of [a patent] monopoly," is "invalid" under the antitrust laws and resolved the antitrust question in that case by seeking an accommodation "between the lawful restraint on trade of the patent monopoly and the illegal restraint prohibited broadly by the Sherman Act." To strike that balance, the Court asked questions such as whether "the patent statute specifically gives a right" to restrain competition in the manner challenged; and whether "competition is impeded to a greater degree" by the restraint at issue than other restraints previously approved as reasonable. * * * In short, rather than measure the length or amount of a restriction solely against the length of the patent's term or its earning potential, as the Court of Appeals apparently did here, this Court answered the antitrust question by considering traditional antitrust factors such as likely anticompetitive effects, redeeming virtues, market power, and potentially offsetting legal considerations present in the circumstances, such as here those related to patents. * * * Whether a particular restraint lies "beyond the limits of the patent monopoly" is a conclusion that flows from that analysis and not, as the Chief Justice suggests, its starting point.

For another thing, this Court's precedents make clear that patent-related settlement agreements can sometimes violate the antitrust laws. In United States v. Singer Mfg. Co., 374 U.S. 174, 83 S.Ct. 1773, 10 L.Ed.2d 823 (1963), for example, two sewing machine companies possessed competing patent claims; a third company sought a patent under circumstances where doing so might lead to the disclosure of information that would invalidate the other two firms' patents. All three firms settled their patent-related disagreements while assigning the broadest claims to the firm best able to enforce the patent against yet other potential competitors. The Court did not examine whether, on the assumption that all three patents were valid, patent law would have allowed the patents' holders to do the same. Rather, emphasizing that the Sherman Act "imposes strict limitations on the concerted activities in which patent owners may lawfully engage," it held that the agreements, although settling patent disputes, violated the antitrust laws. And that, in important part, was because "the public interest in granting patent monopolies" exists only to the extent that "the public is given a novel and useful invention" in "consideration for its grant." * * *

Similarly, both within the settlement context and without, the Court has struck down overly restrictive patent licensing agreements—irrespective of whether those agreements produced supra-patent-permitted revenues. We concede that in United States v. General Elec. Co., the Court permitted a single patentee to grant to a single licensee a license containing a minimum resale price requirement. But in *Line Material*, the Court held that the antitrust laws forbid a group of patentees, each owning one or more patents, to cross-license each other, and, in doing so, to insist that each licensee maintain retail prices set collectively by the patent holders. * * *

Finally in *Standard Oil Co. (Indiana)*, the Court upheld cross-licensing agreements among patentees that settled actual and impending patent litigation, which agreements set royalty rates to be charged third parties for a license to practice all the patents at issue (and which divided resulting revenues). But, in doing so, Justice Brandeis, writing for the Court, warned that such an arrangement would have violated the Sherman Act had the patent holders thereby "dominate[d]" the industry and "curtail[ed] the manufacture and supply of an unpatented product." These cases do not simply ask whether a hypothetically valid patent's holder would be able to charge, e.g., the high prices that the challenged patent-related term allowed. Rather, they seek to accommodate patent and antitrust policies, finding challenged terms and conditions unlawful unless patent law policy offsets the antitrust law policy strongly favoring competition.

Thus, contrary to the dissent's suggestion, there is nothing novel about our approach. What does appear novel are the dissent's suggestions that a patent holder may simply "pa[y] a competitor to respect its patent" and quit its patent invalidity or noninfringement claim without any antitrust scrutiny whatever, and that "such settlements . . . are a well-known feature of intellectual property litigation." * * *

Finally, the Hatch-Waxman Act itself does not embody a statutory policy that supports the Eleventh Circuit's view. Rather, the general procompetitive thrust of the statute, its specific provisions facilitating challenges to a patent's validity, and its later-added provisions requiring parties to a patent dispute triggered by a paragraph IV filing to report settlement terms to the FTC and the Antitrust Division of the Department of Justice, all suggest the contrary. * * *

B

The Eleventh Circuit's conclusion finds some degree of support in a general legal policy favoring the settlement of disputes. The Circuit's related underlying practical concern consists of its fear that antitrust scrutiny of a reverse payment agreement would require the parties to litigate the validity of the patent in order to demonstrate what would have happened to competition in the absence of the settlement. Any such litigation will prove time consuming, complex, and expensive. The antitrust game, the Circuit may believe, would not be worth that litigation candle.

We recognize the value of settlements and the patent litigation problem. But we nonetheless conclude that this patent-related factor should not determine the result here. Rather, five sets of considerations lead us to conclude that the FTC should have been given the opportunity to prove its antitrust claim.

First, the specific restraint at issue has the "potential for genuine adverse effects on competition." The payment in effect amounts to a purchase by the patentee of the exclusive right to sell its product, a right it already claims but would lose if the patent litigation were to continue and the patent were held invalid or not infringed by the generic product. Suppose, for example, that the exclusive right to sell produces $50 million in supracompetitive profits per year for the patentee. And suppose further that the patent has 10 more years to run. Continued litigation, if it results in patent invalidation or a finding of noninfringement, could cost the patentee $500 million in lost revenues, a sum that then would flow in large part to consumers in the form of lower prices.

We concede that settlement on terms permitting the patent challenger to enter the market before the patent expires would also bring about competition, again to the consumer's benefit. But settlement on the terms said by the FTC to be at issue here—payment in return for staying out of the market—simply keeps prices at patentee-set levels, potentially producing the full patent-related $500 million monopoly return while dividing that return between the challenged patentee and the patent challenger. The patentee and the challenger gain; the consumer loses. * * *

But, one might ask, as a practical matter would the parties be able to enter into such an anticompetitive agreement? Would not a high reverse payment signal to other potential challengers that the patentee lacks confidence in its patent, thereby provoking additional challenges, perhaps too many for the patentee to "buy off?" Two special features of Hatch-Waxman mean that the answer to this question is "not necessarily so." First, under Hatch-Waxman only the first challenger gains the special advantage of 180 days of an exclusive right to sell a generic version of the brand-name product. And as noted, that right has proved valuable—indeed, it can be worth several hundred million dollars. Subsequent challengers cannot secure that exclusivity period, and thus stand to win significantly less than the first if they bring a successful paragraph IV challenge. * * * The potential reward available to a subsequent challenger being significantly less, the patentee's payment to the initial challenger (in return for not pressing the patent challenge) will not necessarily provoke subsequent challenges. Second, a generic that files a paragraph IV after learning that the first filer has settled will (if sued by the brand-name) have to wait out a stay period of (roughly) 30 months before the FDA may approve its application, just as the first filer did. These features together mean that a reverse payment settlement with the first filer (or, as in this case, all of the initial filers) "removes from consideration the most motivated challenger, and the one closest to introducing competition." * * *

Second, these anticompetitive consequences will at least sometimes prove unjustified. California Dental Assn. v. FTC (Breyer, J., concurring in part and dissenting in part). As the FTC admits, offsetting or redeeming virtues are sometimes present. The reverse payment, for example, may amount to no more than a rough approximation of the litigation expenses saved through the settlement. * * * Where a reverse payment reflects traditional settlement considerations, such as avoided litigation costs or fair value for services, there is not the same concern that a patentee is using its monopoly profits to avoid the risk of patent invalidation or a finding of noninfringement. * * * But that possibility does not justify dismissing the FTC's complaint. An antitrust defendant may show in the antitrust proceeding that legitimate justifications are present, thereby explaining the presence of the challenged term and showing the lawfulness of that term under the rule of reason.

Third, where a reverse payment threatens to work unjustified anticompetitive harm, the patentee likely possesses the power to bring that harm about in practice. At least, the "size of the payment from a branded drug manufacturer to a prospective generic is itself a strong indicator of power"—namely, the power to charge prices higher than the competitive level. An important patent itself helps to assure such power. Neither is a firm without that power likely to pay "large sums" to induce "others to stay out of its market." In any event, the Commission has referred to studies showing that reverse payment agreements are associated with the presence of higher-than-competitive profits—a strong indication of market power.

Fourth, an antitrust action is likely to prove more feasible administratively than the Eleventh Circuit believed. * * * That is because it is normally not necessary to litigate patent validity to answer the antitrust question (unless, perhaps, to determine whether the patent litigation is a sham). An unexplained large reverse payment itself would normally suggest that the patentee has serious doubts about the patent's survival. And that fact, in turn, suggests that the payment's objective is to maintain supracompetitive prices to be shared among the patentee and the challenger rather than face what might have been a competitive market— the very anticompetitive consequence that underlies the claim of antitrust unlawfulness. The owner of a particularly valuable patent might contend, of course, that even a small risk of invalidity justifies a large payment. But, be that as it may, the payment (if otherwise unexplained) likely seeks to prevent the risk of competition. And, as we have said, that consequence constitutes the relevant anticompetitive harm. In a word, the size of the unexplained reverse payment can provide a workable surrogate for a patent's weakness, all without forcing a court to conduct a detailed exploration of the validity of the patent itself.

Fifth, the fact that a large, unjustified reverse payment risks antitrust liability does not prevent litigating parties from settling their lawsuit. They may, as in other industries, settle in other ways, for example, by allowing the generic manufacturer to enter the patentee's market prior to the patent's expiration, without the patentee paying the challenger to stay out prior to that point. Although the parties may have reasons to prefer settlements that include reverse payments, the relevant antitrust question is: What are those reasons? If the basic reason is a desire to maintain and to share patent-generated monopoly profits, then, in the absence of some other justification, the antitrust laws are likely to forbid the arrangement.

* * *

III

The FTC urges us to hold that reverse payment settlement agreements are presumptively unlawful and that courts reviewing such agreements should proceed via a "quick look" approach, rather than applying a "rule of reason." See *California Dental* ("Quick-look analysis in effect" shifts to "a defendant the burden to show empirical evidence of procompetitive effects"). We decline to do so. In *California Dental*, we held (unanimously) that abandonment of the "rule of reason" in favor of presumptive rules (or a "quick-look" approach) is appropriate only where "an observer with even a rudimentary understanding of economics could conclude that the arrangements in question would have an anticompetitive effect on customers and markets." We do not believe that reverse payment settlements, in the context we here discuss, meet this criterion.

That is because the likelihood of a reverse payment bringing about anticompetitive effects depends upon its size, its scale in relation to the payor's anticipated future litigation costs, its independence from other services for which it might represent payment, and the lack of any other convincing justification. The existence and degree of any anticompetitive consequence may also vary as among industries. These complexities lead us to conclude that the FTC must prove its case as in other rule-of-reason cases.

To say this is not to require the courts to insist, contrary to what we have said, that the Commission need litigate the patent's validity, empirically demonstrate the virtues or vices of the patent system, present every possible supporting fact or refute every possible pro-defense theory. * * *

As in other areas of law, trial courts can structure antitrust litigation so as to avoid, on the one hand, the use of antitrust theories too abbreviated to permit proper analysis, and, on the other, consideration of every possible fact or theory irrespective of the minimal light it may shed on the basic question—that of the presence of significant unjustified anticompetitive consequences. We therefore leave to the lower courts the structuring of the present rule-of-reason antitrust litigation. We reverse the judgment of the Eleventh Circuit. And we remand the case for further proceedings consistent with this opinion.

JUSTICE ALITO took no part in the consideration or decision of this case.

CHIEF JUSTICE ROBERTS, with whom JUSTICE SCALIA and JUSTICE THOMAS join, dissenting.

Solvay Pharmaceuticals holds a patent. It sued two generic drug manufacturers that it alleged were infringing that patent. Those companies counterclaimed, contending the patent was invalid and that, in any event, their products did not infringe. The parties litigated for three years before settling on these terms: Solvay agreed to pay the generics millions of dollars and to allow them into the market five years before the patent was set to expire; in exchange, the generics agreed to provide certain services (help with marketing and manufacturing) and to honor Solvay's patent. The Federal Trade Commission alleges that such a settlement violates the antitrust laws. The question is how to assess that claim.

A patent carves out an exception to the applicability of antitrust laws. The correct approach should therefore be to ask whether the settlement gives Solvay monopoly power beyond what the patent already gave it. The Court, however, departs from this approach, and would instead use antitrust law's amorphous rule of reason to inquire into the anticompetitive effects of such settlements. This novel approach is without support in any statute, and will discourage the settlement of patent litigation. I respectfully dissent.

I

The point of antitrust law is to encourage competitive markets to promote consumer welfare. The point of patent law is to grant limited monopolies as a way of encouraging innovation. Thus, a patent grants "the right to exclude others from profiting by the patented invention." * * * In doing so it provides an exception to antitrust law, and the scope of the patent—i.e., the rights conferred by the patent-forms the zone within which the patent holder may operate without facing antitrust liability.

This should go without saying, in part because we've said it so many times. * * * [A]lthough it is per se unlawful to fix prices under antitrust law, we have long recognized that a patent holder is entitled to license a competitor to sell its product on the condition that the competitor charge a certain, fixed price. See, e.g., General Elec. Co.

We have never held that it violates antitrust law for a competitor to refrain from challenging a patent. And by extension, we have long recognized that the settlement of patent litigation does not by itself violate the antitrust laws. Standard Oil Co. (Indiana) v. United States. Like most litigation, patent litigation is settled all the time, and such settlements—which can include agreements that clearly violate antitrust law, such as licenses that fix prices, or agreements among competitors to divide territory—do not ordinarily subject the litigants to antitrust liability.

The key, of course, is that the patent holder—when doing anything, including settling—must act within the scope of the patent. If its actions go beyond the monopoly powers conferred by the patent, we have held that such actions are subject to antitrust scrutiny. If its actions are within the scope of the patent, they are not subject to antitrust scrutiny, with two exceptions concededly not applicable here: (1) when the parties settle sham litigation, cf. Professional Real Estate Investors, Inc. v. Columbia Pictures Industries, Inc., 508 U.S. 49, 113 S.Ct. 1920, 123 L.Ed.2d 611 (1993); and (2) when the litigation involves a patent obtained through fraud on the Patent and Trademark Office. *Walker Process Equipment.*

Thus, under our precedent, this is a fairly straight-forward case. Solvay paid a competitor to respect its patent—conduct which did not exceed the scope of its patent. * * * As in any settlement, Solvay gave its competitors something of value (money) and, in exchange, its competitors gave it something of value (dropping their legal claims). In doing so, they put an end to litigation that had been dragging on for three years. Ordinarily, we would think this a good thing.

II

Today, however, the Court announces a new rule. * * * According to the majority, if a patent holder settles litigation by paying an alleged infringer a "large and unjustified" payment, in exchange for having the alleged infringer honor the patent, a court should employ the antitrust rule of reason to determine whether the settlement violates antitrust law.

The Court's justifications for this holding are unpersuasive. First, the majority explains that "the patent here may or may not be valid, and may or may not be infringed." Because there is "uncertainty" about whether the patent is actually valid, the Court says that any questions regarding the legality of the settlement should be "measur[ed]" by "procompetitive antitrust policies," rather than "patent law policy." This simply states the conclusion. * * * The problem, as the Court correctly recognizes, is that we're not quite certain if the patent is actually valid, or if the competitor is infringing it. But that is always the case, and is plainly a question of patent law.

* * *

The majority is * * * right to suggest that * * * "precedents make clear that patent-related settlement agreements can sometimes violate the antitrust laws." The key word is sometimes. And those some times are spelled out in our precedents. * * * When the holder steps outside the scope of the patent, he can no longer use the patent as his defense. The majority points to no case where a patent settlement was subject to antitrust scrutiny merely because the validity of the patent was uncertain. Not one. It is remarkable, and surely worth something, that in the 123 years since the Sherman Act was passed, we have never let antitrust law cross that Rubicon.

Next, the majority points to the "general procompetitive thrust" of the Hatch-Waxman Act * * * . The Hatch-Waxman Act surely seeks to encourage competition in the drug market. And, like every law, it accomplishes its ends through specific provisions. * * * But it should by now be trite—and unnecessary—to say that "no legislation pursues its purposes at all costs" and that "it frustrates rather than effectuates legislative intent simplistically to assume that whatever furthers the statute's primary objective must be the law. It is especially disturbing here, where the Court discerns from specific provisions a very broad policy—a "general procompetitive thrust," in its words—and uses that policy to unsettle the established relationship between patent and antitrust law. Indeed, for whatever it may be worth, Congress has repeatedly declined to enact legislation addressing the issue the Court takes on today.

* * *

The majority suggests that "[a]pparently most if not all reverse payment settlement agreements arise in the context of pharmaceutical drug regulation." This claim is not supported empirically by anything the majority cites, and seems unlikely. * * * Whatever one might call them, such settlements—paying an alleged infringer to drop its invalidity claim— are a well-known feature of intellectual property litigation, and reflect an intuitive way to settle such disputes. To the extent there are not scores and scores of these settlements to point to, this is because such settlements— outside the context of Hatch-Waxman—are private agreements that for obvious reasons are generally not appealed, nor publicly available.

* * *

In sum, none of the Court's reasons supports its conclusion that a patent holder, when settling a claim that its patent is invalid, is not immunized by the fact that it is acting within the scope of its patent. And I fear the Court's attempt to limit its holding to the context of patent settlements under Hatch-Waxman will not long hold.

III

The majority's rule will discourage settlement of patent litigation. Simply put, there would be no incentive to settle if, immediately after settling, the parties would have to litigate the same issue—the question of patent validity—as part of a defense against an antitrust suit. In that suit, the alleged infringer would be in the especially awkward position of being for the patent after being against it.

This is unfortunate because patent litigation is particularly complex, and particularly costly. * * * One study found that the cost of litigation in this specific context—a generic challenging a brand name pharmaceutical patent—was about $10 million per suit.

* * *

The majority seems to think that even if the patent is valid, a patent holder violates the antitrust laws merely because the settlement took away some chance that his patent would be declared invalid by a court. This is flawed for several reasons.

First, a patent is either valid or invalid. The parties of course don't know the answer with certainty at the outset of litigation; hence the litigation. But the same is true of any hard legal question that is yet to be adjudicated. Just because people don't know the answer doesn't mean there is no answer until a court declares one. Yet the majority would impose antitrust liability based on the parties' subjective uncertainty about that legal conclusion.

The Court does so on the assumption that offering a "large" sum is reliable evidence that the patent holder has serious doubts about the patent. Not true. A patent holder may be 95% sure about the validity of its patent, but particularly risk averse or litigation averse, and willing to pay a good deal of money to rid itself of the 5% chance of a finding of invalidity. What is actually motivating a patent holder is apparently a question district courts will have to resolve on a case-by-case basis. The task of trying to discern whether a patent holder is motivated by uncertainty about its patent, or other legitimate factors like risk aversion, will be made all the more difficult by the fact that much of the evidence about the party's motivation may be embedded in legal advice from its attorney, which would presumably be shielded from discovery.

Second, the majority's position leads to absurd results. Let's say in 2005, a patent holder sues a competitor for infringement and faces a counterclaim that its patent is invalid. The patent holder determines that the risk of losing on the question of validity is low, but after a year of litigating, grows increasingly risk averse, tired of litigation, and concerned about the company's image, so it pays the competitor a "large" payment, in exchange for having the competitor honor its patent. Then let's say in 2006, a different competitor, inspired by the first competitor's success, sues the patent holder and seeks a similar payment. The patent holder, recognizing that this dynamic is unsustainable, litigates this suit to conclusion, all the way to the Supreme Court, which unanimously decides the patent was valid. According to the majority, the first settlement would violate the antitrust laws even though the patent was ultimately declared valid, because that first settlement took away some chance that the patent would be invalidated in the first go around. Under this approach, a patent holder may be found liable under antitrust law for doing what its perfectly valid patent allowed it to do in the first place; its sin was to settle, rather than prove the correctness of its position by litigating until the bitter end.

Third, this logic—that taking away any chance that a patent will be invalidated is itself an antitrust problem—cannot possibly be limited to reverse-payment agreements, or those that are "large." The Government's brief acknowledges as much, suggesting that if antitrust scrutiny is invited for such cash payments, it may also be required for "other consideration" and "alternative arrangements." * * *

Thus, although the question posed by this case is fundamentally a question of patent law—i.e., whether Solvay's patent was valid and therefore permitted Solvay to pay competitors to honor the scope of its patent—the majority declares that such questions should henceforth be scrutinized by antitrust law's unruly rule of reason. Good luck to the district courts that must, when faced with a patent settlement, weigh the "likely anticompetitive effects, redeeming virtues, market power, and potentially offsetting legal considerations present in the circumstances." * * *

IV

* * *

The majority * * * points out that the first challenger gets a 180-day exclusive period to market a generic version of the brand name drug, and that subsequent challengers cannot secure that exclusivity period—meaning when the patent holder buys off the first challenger, it has bought off its most motivated competitor. There are two problems with this argument. First, according to the Food and Drug Administration, all manufacturers who file on the first day are considered "first applicants" who share the exclusivity period. Thus, if ten generics file an application to market a generic drug on the first day, all will be considered "first applicants." This is not an unusual occurrence. * * *

Second, and more fundamentally, the 180 days of exclusivity simply provides more incentive for generic challenges. Even if a subsequent generic would not be entitled to this additional incentive, it will have as much or nearly as much incentive to challenge the patent as a potential challenger would in any other context outside of Hatch-Waxman, where there is no 180-day exclusivity period. And a patent holder who gives away notably large sums of money because it is, as the majority surmises, concerned about the strength of its patent, would be putting blood in water where sharks are always near.

* * *

The irony of all this is that the majority's decision may very well discourage generics from challenging pharmaceutical patents in the first place. Patent litigation is costly, time consuming, and uncertain. See * * * [a 2010 study showing that generics prevailed in 82 cases and lost in 89 cases]. Generics "enter this risky terrain only after careful analysis of the potential gains if they prevail and the potential exposure if they lose." Taking the prospect of settlements off the table—or limiting settlements to an earlier entry date for the generic, which may still be many years in the future—puts a damper on the generic's expected value going into litigation, and decreases its incentive to sue in the first place. The majority assures us, with no support, that everything will be okay because the parties can settle by simply negotiating an earlier entry date for the generic drug manufacturer, rather than settling with money. But it's a matter of common sense, confirmed by experience, that parties are more likely to settle when they have a broader set of valuable things to trade.

V

The majority today departs from the settled approach separating patent and antitrust law, weakens the protections afforded to innovators by patents, frustrates the public policy in favor of settling, and likely undermines the very policy it seeks to promote by forcing generics who step into the litigation ring to do so without the prospect of cash settlements. I would keep things as they were and not subject basic questions of patent law to an unbounded inquiry under antitrust law, with its treble damages and famously burdensome discovery. I respectfully dissent.

NOTES AND QUESTIONS

1.   The majority and dissent stress their differences, but how much of their disagreement is really substantive? Does the majority doubt that some reverse-payment settlements represent a legitimate way to limit uncertainty and litigation cost? Do the dissenters doubt that the failure to test the validity of patents will wind up transferring some consumer surplus to producers?

2.   Does it seem that the difference in this case turn largely on the justices' relative faith that litigation about the legitimacy of the settlements can be accurate and efficient?

a.   Chief Justice Roberts' dissent, for example, describes the average $10 million cost of an antitrust case and remarks about such cases' "famously burdensome discovery." Do you agree that the benefit associated with antitrust cases cannot justify the cost?

b.   The Court, per Justice Breyer, on the other hand, suggests that a good trial judge can narrow the issues and manage discovery to keep the issues within bounds, even without applying a "quick look" test that would immediately require the defendants to justify the settlement. Do you agree that judicial management of antitrust cases, like that described earlier in cases like *Polygram*, for example, can make cases like these ones in which "the antitrust game * * * [is] worth th[e] litigation candle"?

3.   What issues does the Court suggest the trial judge should examine?

a.   What makes a reverse payment excessively "large"? Will the FTC be required to show any more than that the payment exceeds the likely cost of litigation plus the value of any services to be provided by the generic challenger? Do you suppose that either of those calculations will be non-controversial?

b.   Should the FTC have to show that the patent gives the patent holder market power in a relevant market? We speak loosely about monopoly returns from a patent, but in some markets, there can be non-infringing products competing for market share with a patented product. In such markets, presumably consumer welfare losses from settlement with a generic challenger would be small. Should the FTC be required to negate that possibility as part of its prima facie case?

c.   What does the Court leave open for the defendant to assert in response to the plaintiff's case? May the patent holder try to prove that its patent was indeed valid and infringed? If such a defense is available, is there any basis for the Court's assertion that the antitrust litigation can avoid becoming a complex inquiry into the patent's validity?[118]

d.   Was the Court persuasive in arguing that the size of the reverse payment can itself be a surrogate for its anticompetitive character? The Court says that "the payment (if otherwise unexplained) likely seeks to prevent the risk of competition. And, as we have said, that consequence constitutes the relevant anticompetitive harm."[119] Did the dissent persuade you that, far from making litigation simple, the complexity will simply shift to the defendant's explanation for its payment?

4.   Is the dissent correct that the result in this case likely will lead to fewer generic challenges to existing patents? If a reduced likelihood of a reverse payment makes that true, how would that make consumers worse off? Is the answer that the risk of challenge may be a form of potential competition that tends to cause patent holders to anticipatorily lower prices in an effort to make challenges less profitable?

5.   Should the rule in *Actavis* be limited to reverse-payment settlements? Is the Court's analysis relevant to patent settlements more generally, as the dissent suggests? If holders of allegedly mutually-infringing patents form a patent pool to market their inventions together, for example, should that pooling arrangement be subject to challenge? Is Justice Brandeis, the author of *Standard Oil (Indiana)*, likely turning over in his grave?

6.   Will *Actavis* be limited to cases brought by public agencies? Can you identify any private plaintiffs who would be likely to have both the required

---

[118] A related question may arise as to the court to which a district court decision in one of these cases must be appealed. If patent validity is the central issue in a case, appellate jurisdiction is normally in the Court of Appeals for the Federal Circuit rather than the Court of Appeals for the Circuit in which the district court sits.

[119] See, e.g., Aaron Edlin, Scott Hemphill, Herbert Hovenkamp & Carl Shapiro, Activating Actavis, 28 Antitrust 16 (Fall 2013) (provides an appendix measuring the impact of reverse-payment settlements on competition).

standing and the economic incentive to challenge reverse payment settlements?[120]

C. THE CONTINUING CONCERN ABOUT EXCLUSIONARY CONDUCT

1. MONOPOLIZATION

We have already seen a number of important Sherman Act § 2 cases. There were John D. Rockefeller's alleged foreclosure of the "potentiality of competition" in *Standard Oil* (1911) and Elbert Gary's dinners in *U.S. Steel* (1920). Judge Hand in *ALCOA* (1945) left little freedom of action for firms with dominant market shares, and *Utah Pie* (1967) upheld a questionable jury finding of predatory pricing. Shortly after *Utah Pie*, two other Sherman § 2 prosecutions dominated public concern about issues of monopoly.

The first case, filed by the Justice Department in 1969, charged IBM with monopolization of the market for general-purpose computers. Competitors had complained—mostly unsuccessfully as things turned out[121]—about IBM's alleged dominance of the industry, its allegedly false announcements of new equipment, and its failure to make information available to smaller firms so they could more readily manufacturer IBM-compatible equipment. The Government's case consumed six years of discovery, 700 trial days, 17,000 exhibits, and tens of millions of dollars. It became what some writers called "the Antitrust Division's Vietnam."[122] Thirteen years later, in 1982, the Reagan Administration moved to dismiss the case, having concluded that it was "without merit."[123]

The second case, filed in 1974, sought to break up the American Telephone & Telegraph Company.[124] It was more successful. Since the early part of the century, AT&T had been the nation's only telephone company, and it did not welcome new entry into the field. When a start-up called Microwave Communications, Inc. (MCI) proposed to offer private-line service between Chicago and St. Louis, for example, AT&T resisted

---

[120] See, e.g., In re Nexium (Esomeprazole) Antitrust Litigation, 2013 WL 4832176 (D. Mass. 2013).

[121] See, e.g., Telex Corp. v. IBM, 510 F.2d 894 (10th Cir. 1975); California Computer Products v. IBM, 613 F.2d 727 (9th Cir. 1979).

[122] The massive efforts on the case and the excesses of the Government's claims are described in John E. Lopatka, United States v. IBM: A Monument to Arrogance, 68 Antitrust L.J. 145 (2000).

[123] The trial judge, David Edelstein, delayed approving the dismissal, but he was ultimately directed to do so by the Second Circuit. In re IBM Corp., 687 F.2d 591 (2d Cir. 1982).

[124] The District Court's opinion approving and modifying the proposed settlement is reported at 552 F.Supp. 131 (D.D.C.1982), affirmed 460 U.S. 1001 (1983). An important earlier decision holding that the antitrust charges were not within the exclusive jurisdiction of the Federal Communications Commission is reported at 461 F.Supp. 1314 (D.D.C.1978), and the denial of the defendants' motion to dismiss at the close of the government's case may be found at 524 F.Supp. 1336 (D.D.C.1981).

vigorously.[125] Later, AT&T sought to offer sharply lower prices on services that competed with those of new entrants and continued to resist F.C.C. efforts to permit competition.[126] The Justice Department asserted that AT&T's conduct violated Sherman Act § 2.

The same year as the *IBM* dismissal, this time in the midst of trial, the parties reached a settlement that District Judge Harold Greene approved with modifications.[127] Most significantly, AT&T was divested of its local telephone system subsidiaries and new "Baby Bells" were created. Each Baby Bell, in turn, owned local telephone companies, most of which were subject to state public utility regulation. Meanwhile, other companies were free to make equipment that worked over telephone lines—designer phones, computer modems, FAX machines. Likewise, new firms entered the market to provide long distance telephone service, most prominently, MCI and Sprint.[128]

a. The Big Three Supreme Court Monopolization Cases in the Modern Period

Neither of the two cases just discussed reached the Supreme Court on the merits.[129] The first two Sherman § 2 cases in this chapter laid the groundwork for current Supreme Court ideas about the limits of proper conduct by firms with a large market share.

ASPEN SKIING CO. V. ASPEN HIGHLANDS SKIING CORP.

Supreme Court of the United States, 1985
472 U.S. 585, 105 S.Ct. 2847, 86 L.Ed.2d 467

JUSTICE STEVENS delivered the opinion of the Court.

In a private treble-damages action, the jury found that petitioner Aspen Skiing Company (Ski Co.) had monopolized the market for downhill skiing services in Aspen, Colorado. The question presented is whether that finding is erroneous as a matter of law because it rests on an assumption that a firm with monopoly power has a duty to cooperate with its smaller

---

[125] In re Applications of Microwave Communications, Inc., 18 F.C.C.2d 953 (1969).

[126] See, e.g., Specialized Common Carrier Services, 44 F.C.C.2d 467 (1973), aff'd sub nom. Washington Utilities & Transportation Commission v. F.C.C., 513 F.2d 1142 (9th Cir.1975).

[127] The District Court's opinion approving and modifying the proposed settlement is reported at 552 F.Supp. 131 (D.D.C.1982). An important earlier decision holding that the antitrust charges were not within the exclusive jurisdiction of the Federal Communications Commission is reported at 461 F.Supp. 1314 (D.D.C.1978), and the denial of the defendants' motion to dismiss at the close of the government's case may be found at 524 F.Supp. 1336 (D.D.C.1981).

[128] Scholarly assessments of the impact of the AT&T decree tend to be far from complimentary. See, e.g., Paul W. MacAvoy & Kenneth Robinson, Losing by Judicial Policymaking: The First Year of the AT&T Divestiture, 2 Yale J. on Reg. 225 (1985). The story of the case is described well in Steve Coll, The Deal of the Century: The Breakup of AT&T (1986).

[129] The Supreme Court did review and approve per curiam the entry of the consent decree. Maryland v. United States, 460 U.S. 1001, 103 S.Ct. 1240, 75 L.Ed.2d 472 (1983).

rivals in a marketing arrangement in order to avoid violating § 2 of the Sherman Act.

I

Aspen is a destination ski resort with a reputation for "super powder," "a wide range of runs," and an "active night life," including "some of the best restaurants in North America." Between 1945 and 1960, private investors independently developed three major facilities for downhill skiing: Aspen Mountain (Ajax),[130] Aspen Highlands (Highlands),[131] and Buttermilk.[132] A fourth mountain, Snowmass,[133] opened in 1967.

The development of any major additional facilities is hindered by practical considerations and regulatory obstacles. The identification of appropriate topographical conditions for a new site and substantial financing are both essential. Most of the terrain in the vicinity of Aspen that is suitable for downhill skiing cannot be used for that purpose without the approval of the United States Forest Service. That approval is contingent, in part, on environmental concerns. Moreover, the county government must also approve the project, and in recent years it has followed a policy of limiting growth.

Between 1958 and 1964, three independent companies operated Ajax, Highlands, and Buttermilk. In the early years, each company offered its own day or half-day tickets for use of its mountain. In 1962, however, the three competitors also introduced an interchangeable ticket.[134] The 6-day,

---

[130] Ski Co. developed Ajax in 1946. The runs are quite steep and primarily designed for expert or advanced intermediate skiers. The base area of Ajax is located within the village of Aspen. [Court's fn. 2]

[131] In 1957, the United States Forest Service suggested that Ajax "was getting crowded, and * * * that a ski area ought to be started at Highlands." Whipple V.N. Jones, who owned an Aspen lodge at the time, discussed the project with Ski Co. officials, but they expressed little interest, telling him that they had "plenty of problems at Aspen now, and we don't think we want to expand skiing in Aspen." Jones went ahead with the project on his own, and laid out a well-balanced set of ski runs: 25% beginner, 50% intermediate, 25% advanced. The base area of Highlands Mountain is located 1 ½ miles from the village of Aspen. Respondent Aspen Highlands Skiing Corporation provides the downhill skiing services at Highlands Mountain. Throughout this opinion we refer to both the respondent and its mountain as Highlands. [Court's fn. 3]

[132] In 1958, Friedl Pfeiffer and Arthur Pfister began developing the ranches they owned at the base of Buttermilk Mountain into a third ski area. Pfeiffer, a former Olympian, was the director of the ski school for Ski Co., and the runs he laid out were primarily for beginners and intermediate skiers. More advanced runs have since been developed. The base area of Buttermilk is located approximately 2 ¼ miles from the village of Aspen. [Court's fn. 4]

[133] In the early 1960's William Janss, a former ski racer, and his associates had acquired three ranches in the Snowmass Valley, and had secured Forest Service permits for a ski area. The developer sold the company holding the permits to Ski Co. to allow it to develop a downhill skiing facility for the project, leaving him to develop the land at the base of the site. A fairly balanced mountain was developed with a mixture of beginner, intermediate, and advanced runs. The base area of Snowmass is eight miles from the village of Aspen. [Court's fn. 5]

[134] Friedl Pfeiffer, one of the developers of Buttermilk, initiated the idea of an all-Aspen ticket at a luncheon with the owner of Highlands and the President of Ski Co. Pfeiffer, a native of Austria, informed his competitors that " '[i]n St. Anton, we have a mountain that has three different lift companies—lifts owned by three different lift companies. * * * We sell a ticket that is

all-Aspen ticket provided convenience to the vast majority of skiers who visited the resort for weekly periods, but preferred to remain flexible about what mountain they might ski each day during the visit. It also emphasized the unusual variety in ski mountains available in Aspen.

As initially designed, the all-Aspen ticket program consisted of booklets containing six coupons, each redeemable for a daily lift ticket at Ajax, Highlands, or Buttermilk. The price of the booklet was often discounted from the price of six daily tickets, but all six coupons had to be used within a limited period of time—seven days, for example. The revenues from the sale of the 3-area coupon books were distributed in accordance with the number of coupons collected at each mountain.

In 1964, Buttermilk was purchased by Ski Co., but the interchangeable ticket program continued. In most seasons after it acquired Buttermilk, Ski Co. offered 2-area, 6- or 7-day tickets featuring Ajax and Buttermilk in competition with the 3-area, 6-coupon booklet. Although it sold briskly, the all-Aspen ticket did not sell as well as Ski Co.'s multiarea ticket until Ski Co. opened Snowmass in 1967. Thereafter, the all-Aspen coupon booklet began to outsell Ski Co.'s ticket featuring only its mountains.

In the 1971–1972 season, the coupon booklets were discontinued and an "around the neck" all-Aspen ticket was developed. This refinement on the interchangeable ticket was advantageous to the skier, who no longer found it necessary to visit the ticket window every morning before gaining access to the slopes. Lift operators at Highlands monitored usage of the ticket in the 1971–1972 season by recording the ticket numbers of persons going onto the slopes of that mountain. Highlands officials periodically met with Ski Co. officials to review the figures recorded at Highlands, and to distribute revenues based on that count.

* * *

In the next four seasons, Ski Co. and Highlands used * * * surveys to allocate the revenues from the 4-area, 6-day ticket. Highlands' share of the revenues from the ticket was 17.5% in 1973–1974, 18.5% in 1974–1975, 16.8% in 1975–1976, and 13.2% in 1976–1977. During these four seasons, Ski Co. did not offer its own 3-area, multiday ticket in competition with the all-Aspen ticket. By 1977, multiarea tickets accounted for nearly 35% of the total market. Holders of multiarea passes also accounted for additional daily ticket sales to persons skiing with them.

* * * Nevertheless, for the 1977–1978 season, Ski Co. offered to continue the all-Aspen ticket only if Highlands would accept a 13.2% fixed share of the ticket's revenues.

---

interchangeable.' It was good on any of those lifts; and he said, 'I think we should do the same thing here.' " [Court's fn. 7]

Although that had been Highlands' share of the ticket revenues in 1976–1977, Highlands contended that that season was an inaccurate measure of its market performance since it had been marked by unfavorable weather and an unusually low number of visiting skiers. Moreover, Highlands wanted to continue to divide revenues on the basis of actual usage, as that method of distribution allowed it to compete for the daily loyalties of the skiers who had purchased the tickets. Fearing that the alternative might be no interchangeable ticket at all, and hoping to persuade Ski Co. to reinstate the usage division of revenues, Highlands eventually accepted a fixed percentage of 15% for the 1977–1978 season. * * *

* * *

In March 1978, the Ski Co. management recommended to the board of directors that the 4-area ticket be discontinued for the 1978–1979 season. The board decided to offer Highlands a 4-area ticket provided that Highlands would agree to receive a 12.5% fixed percentage of the revenue— considerably below Highlands' historical average based on usage. Later in the 1978–1979 season, a member of Ski Co.'s board of directors candidly informed a Highlands' official that he had advocated making Highlands "an offer that [it] could not accept."

Finding the proposal unacceptable, Highlands suggested a distribution of the revenues based on usage to be monitored by coupons, electronic counting, or random sample surveys. If Ski Co. was concerned about who was to conduct the survey, Highlands proposed to hire disinterested ticket counters at its own expense—"somebody like Price Waterhouse"—to count or survey usage of the 4-area ticket at Highlands. Ski Co. refused to consider any counterproposals, and Highlands finally rejected the offer of the fixed percentage.

As far as Ski Co. was concerned, the all-Aspen ticket was dead. In its place Ski Co. offered the 3-area, 6-day ticket featuring only its mountains. In an effort to promote this ticket, Ski Co. embarked on a national advertising campaign that strongly implied to people who were unfamiliar with Aspen that Ajax, Buttermilk, and Snowmass were the only ski mountains in the area. For example, Ski Co. had a sign changed in the Aspen Airways waiting room at Stapleton Airport in Denver. The old sign had a picture of the four mountains in Aspen touting "Four Big Mountains" whereas the new sign retained the picture but referred only to three.[135]

Ski Co. took additional actions that made it extremely difficult for Highlands to market its own multiarea package to replace the joint

---

[135] Ski Co. circulated another advertisement to national magazines labeled "Aspen, More Mountains, More Fun." The advertisement depicted the four mountains of Aspen, but labeled only Ajax, Buttermilk, and Snowmass. Buttermilk's label is erroneously placed directly over Highlands Mountain. [Court's fn. 12]

offering. Ski Co. discontinued the 3-day, 3-area pass for the 1978–1979 season,[136] and also refused to sell Highlands any lift tickets, either at the tour operator's discount or at retail.[137] Highlands finally developed an alternative product, the "Adventure Pack," which consisted of a 3-day pass at Highlands and three vouchers, each equal to the price of a daily lift ticket at a Ski Co. mountain. The vouchers were guaranteed by funds on deposit in an Aspen bank, and were redeemed by Aspen merchants at full value. Ski Co., however, refused to accept them.

Later, Highlands redesigned the Adventure Pack to contain American Express Traveler's Checks or money orders instead of vouchers. Ski Co. eventually accepted these negotiable instruments in exchange for daily lift tickets.[138] Despite some strengths of the product, the Adventure Pack met considerable resistance from tour operators and consumers who had grown accustomed to the convenience and flexibility provided by the all-Aspen ticket.

Without a convenient all-Aspen ticket, Highlands basically "becomes a day ski area in a destination resort." Highlands' share of the market for downhill skiing services in Aspen declined steadily after the 4-area ticket based on usage was abolished in 1977: from 20.5% in 1976–1977, to 15.7% in 1977–1978, to 13.1% in 1978–1979, to 12.5% in 1979–1980, to 11% in 1980–1981. Highlands' revenues from associated skiing services like the ski school, ski rentals, amateur racing events, and restaurant facilities declined sharply as well.[139]

---

[136] Highlands' owner explained that there was a key difference between the 3-day, 3-area ticket and the 6-day, 3-area ticket: "with the three day ticket, a person could ski on the * * * Aspen Skiing Corporation mountains for three days and then there would be three days in which he could ski on our mountain; but with the six-day ticket, we are absolutely locked out of those people." As a result of "tremendous consumer demand" for a 3-day ticket, Ski Co. reinstated it late in the 1978–1979 season, but without publicity or a discount off the daily rate. [Court's fn. 13]

[137] In the 1977–1978 negotiations, Ski Co. previously had refused to consider the sale of any tickets to Highlands noting that it was "obviously not interested in helping sell" a package competitive with the 3-area ticket. Later, in the 1978–1979 negotiations, Ski Co.'s vice president of finance told a Highlands official that "[w]e will not have anything to do with a four-area ticket sponsored by the Aspen Highlands Skiing Corporation." When the Highlands official inquired why Ski Co. was taking this position considering that Highlands was willing to pay full retail value for the daily lift tickets, the Ski Co. official answered tersely: "we will not support our competition." [Court's fn. 14]

[138] Of course, there was nothing to identify Highlands as the source of these instruments, unless someone saw the skier "taking it out of an Adventure Pack envelope." For the 1981–1982 season, Ski Co. set its single ticket price at $22 and discounted the 3-area, 6-day ticket to $114. According to Highlands, this price structure made the Adventure Pack unprofitable. [Court's fn. 15]

[139] Highlands' ski school had an outstanding reputation, and its share of the ski school market had always outperformed Highlands' share of the downhill skiing market. Even some Ski Co. officials had sent their children to ski school at Highlands. After the elimination of the 4-area ticket, however, families or groups purchasing 3-area tickets were reluctant to enroll a beginner among them in the Highlands ski school when the more experienced skiers would have to leave to ski at Ajax, Buttermilk, or Snowmass. [Court's fn. 17]

II

In 1979, Highlands filed a complaint in the United States District Court for the District of Colorado naming Ski Co. as a defendant. Among various claims, the complaint alleged that Ski Co. had monopolized the market for downhill skiing services at Aspen in violation of § 2 of the Sherman Act, and prayed for treble damages. The case was tried to a jury which rendered a verdict finding Ski Co. guilty of the § 2 violation and calculating Highlands' actual damages at $2.5 million.

In her instructions to the jury, the District Judge explained that the offense of monopolization under § 2 of the Sherman Act has two elements: (1) the possession of monopoly power in a relevant market, and (2) the willful acquisition, maintenance, or use of that power by anticompetitive or exclusionary means or for anticompetitive or exclusionary purposes. Although the first element was vigorously disputed at the trial and in the Court of Appeals, in this Court Ski Co. does not challenge the jury's special verdict finding that it possessed monopoly power.[140] Nor does Ski Co. criticize the trial court's instructions to the jury concerning the second element of the § 2 offense.

On this element, the jury was instructed that it had to consider whether "Aspen Skiing Corporation willfully acquired, maintained, or used that power by anti-competitive or exclusionary means or for anti-competitive or exclusionary purposes." The instructions elaborated:

> "In considering whether the means or purposes were anti-competitive or exclusionary, you must draw a distinction here between practices which tend to exclude or restrict competition on the one hand and the success of a business which reflects only a superior product, a well-run business, or luck, on the other. The line between legitimately gained monopoly, its proper use and maintenance, and improper conduct has been described in various ways. It has been said that obtaining or maintaining monopoly power cannot represent monopolization if the power was gained and maintained by conduct that was honestly industrial. Or it is said that monopoly power which is thrust upon a firm due to its superior business ability and efficiency does not constitute monopolization.

> "For example, a firm that has lawfully acquired a monopoly position is not barred from taking advantage of scale economies by constructing a large and efficient factory. These benefits are a consequence of size and not an exercise of monopoly power. Nor is

---

[140]   The jury found that the relevant product market was "[d]ownhill skiing at destination ski resorts," that the "Aspen area" was a relevant geographic submarket, and that during the years 1977–1981, Ski Co. possessed monopoly power, defined as the power to control prices in the relevant market or to exclude competitors. [Court's fn. 20]

a corporation which possesses monopoly power under a duty to cooperate with its business rivals. Also a company which possesses monopoly power and which refuses to enter into a joint operating agreement with a competitor or otherwise refuses to deal with a competitor in some manner does not violate Section 2 if valid business reasons exist for that refusal.

"In other words, if there were legitimate business reasons for the refusal, then the defendant, even if he is found to possess monopoly power in a relevant market, has not violated the law. We are concerned with conduct which unnecessarily excludes or handicaps competitors. This is conduct which does not benefit consumers by making a better product or service available—or in other ways—and instead has the effect of impairing competition.

"To sum up, you must determine whether Aspen Skiing Corporation gained, maintained, or used monopoly power in a relevant market by arrangements and policies which rather than being a consequence of a superior product, superior business sense, or historic element, were designed primarily to further any domination of the relevant market or sub-market."

The jury answered a specific interrogatory finding the second element of the offense as defined in these instructions.

Ski Co. filed a motion for judgment notwithstanding the verdict, contending that the evidence was insufficient to support a § 2 violation as a matter of law. * * *[141] The District Court denied Ski Co.'s motion and entered a judgment awarding Highlands treble damages of $7,500,000, costs and attorney's fees.

The Court of Appeals affirmed in all respects. * * * First, relying on United States v. Terminal Railroad Assn. of St. Louis, the Court of Appeals held that the multiday, multiarea ticket could be characterized as an "essential facility" that Ski Co. had a duty to market jointly with Highlands. Second, it held that there was sufficient evidence to support a finding that Ski Co.'s intent in refusing to market the 4-area ticket, "considered together with its other conduct," was to create or maintain a monopoly.

---

[141] Counsel also appears to have argued that Ski Co. was under a legal obligation to refuse to participate in any joint marketing arrangement with Highlands:

"Aspen Skiing Corporation is required to compete. It is required to make independent decisions. It is required to price its own product. It is required to make its own determination of the ticket that it chooses to offer and the tickets that it chooses not to offer."

In this Court, Ski Co. does not question the validity of the joint marketing arrangement under § 1 of the Sherman Act. Thus, we have no occasion to consider the circumstances that might permit such combinations in the skiing industry. See generally National Collegiate Athletic Assn. v. Board of Regents of Univ. of Okla.; Broadcast Music, Inc. v. Columbia Broadcasting System, Inc.; Continental T.V., Inc. v. GTE Sylvania, Inc. [Court's fn. 22]

* * *

III

In this Court, Ski Co. contends that even a firm with monopoly power has no duty to engage in joint marketing with a competitor, that a violation of § 2 cannot be established without evidence of substantial exclusionary conduct, and that none of its activities can be characterized as exclusionary. It also contends that the Court of Appeals incorrectly relied on the "essential facilities" doctrine and that an "anticompetitive intent" does not transform nonexclusionary conduct into monopolization. In response, Highlands submits that, given the evidence in the record, it is not necessary to rely on the "essential facilities" doctrine in order to affirm the judgment.

* * * Ski Co. * * * is surely correct in submitting that even a firm with monopoly power has no general duty to engage in a joint marketing program with a competitor. Ski Co. is quite wrong, however, in suggesting that the judgment in this case rests on any such proposition of law. For the trial court unambiguously instructed the jury that a firm possessing monopoly power has no duty to cooperate with its business rivals.

The absence of an unqualified duty to cooperate does not mean that every time a firm declines to participate in a particular cooperative venture, that decision may not have evidentiary significance, or that it may not give rise to liability in certain circumstances. The absence of a duty to transact business with another firm is, in some respects, merely the counterpart of the independent businessman's cherished right to select his customers and his associates. The high value that we have placed on the right to refuse to deal with other firms does not mean that the right is unqualified.

In Lorain Journal Co. v. United States, 342 U.S. 143 (1951), we squarely held that this right was not unqualified. Between 1933 and 1948 the publisher of the Lorain Journal, a newspaper, was the only local business disseminating news and advertising in that Ohio town. In 1948, a small radio station was established in a nearby community. In an effort to destroy its small competitor, and thereby regain its "pre-1948 substantial monopoly over the mass dissemination of all news and advertising," the Journal refused to sell advertising to persons that patronized the radio station.

* * * The Court approved the entry of an injunction ordering the Journal to print the advertisements of the customers of its small competitor.

In *Lorain Journal*, the violation of § 2 was an "attempt to monopolize," rather than monopolization, but the question of intent is relevant to both offenses. In the former case it is necessary to prove a "specific intent" to accomplish the forbidden objective—as Judge Hand explained, "an intent which goes beyond the mere intent to do the act." United States v. Aluminum Co. of America. In the latter case evidence of intent is merely relevant to the question whether the challenged conduct is fairly characterized as "exclusionary" or "anticompetitive"—to use the words in the trial court's instructions—or "predatory," to use a word that scholars seem to favor. Whichever label is used, there is agreement on the proposition that "no monopolist monopolizes unconscious of what he is doing." As Judge Bork stated more recently: "Improper exclusion (exclusion not the result of superior efficiency) is always deliberately intended."[142]

The qualification on the right of a monopolist to deal with whom he pleases is not so narrow that it encompasses no more than the circumstances of *Lorain Journal*. In the actual case that we must decide, the monopolist did not merely reject a novel offer to participate in a cooperative venture that had been proposed by a competitor. Rather, the monopolist elected to make an important change in a pattern of distribution that had originated in a competitive market and had persisted for several years. The all-Aspen, 6-day ticket with revenues allocated on the basis of usage was first developed when three independent companies operated three different ski mountains in the Aspen area. It continued to provide a desirable option for skiers when the market was enlarged to include four mountains, and when the character of the market was changed by Ski Co.'s acquisition of monopoly power. Moreover, since the record discloses that interchangeable tickets are used in other multimountain areas which apparently are competitive, it seems appropriate to infer that such tickets satisfy consumer demand in free competitive markets.

Ski Co.'s decision to terminate the all-Aspen ticket was thus a decision by a monopolist to make an important change in the character of the market.[143] Such a decision is not necessarily anticompetitive, and Ski Co. contends that neither its decision, nor the conduct in which it engaged to implement that decision, can fairly be characterized as exclusionary in this case. It recognizes, however, that as the case is presented to us, we must interpret the entire record in the light most favorable to Highlands and give to it the benefit of all inferences which the evidence fairly supports, even though contrary inferences might reasonably be drawn.

---

[142] R. Bork, The Antitrust Paradox 160 (1978) (hereinafter Bork). [Court's fn. 29]

[143] "In any business, patterns of distribution develop over time; these may reasonably be thought to be more efficient than alternative patterns of distribution that do not develop. The patterns that do develop and persist we may call the optimal patterns. By disturbing optimal distribution patterns one rival can impose costs upon another, that is, force the other to accept higher costs." Bork 156. In § 1 cases where this Court has applied the per se approach to invalidity to concerted refusals to deal, "the boycott often cut off access to a supply, facility or market necessary to enable the boycotted firm to compete, * * * and frequently the boycotting firms possessed a dominant position in the relevant market." Northwest Wholesale Stationers, Inc. v. Pacific Stationery & Printing Co. [Court's fn. 31]

* * * Since the jury was unambiguously instructed that Ski Co.'s refusal to deal with Highlands "does not violate Section 2 if valid business reasons exist for that refusal," we must assume that the jury concluded that there were no valid business reasons for the refusal. The question then is whether that conclusion finds support in the record.

IV

The question whether Ski Co.'s conduct may properly be characterized as exclusionary cannot be answered by simply considering its effect on Highlands. In addition, it is relevant to consider its impact on consumers and whether it has impaired competition in an unnecessarily restrictive way. If a firm has been "attempting to exclude rivals on some basis other than efficiency," it is fair to characterize its behavior as predatory. It is, accordingly, appropriate to examine the effect of the challenged pattern of conduct on consumers, on Ski Co.'s smaller rival, and on Ski Co. itself.

SUPERIOR QUALITY OF THE ALL-ASPEN TICKET

The average Aspen visitor "is a well-educated, relatively affluent, experienced skier who has skied a number of times in the past * * * ." Over 80% of the skiers visiting the resort each year have been there before—40% of these repeat visitors have skied Aspen at least five times. Over the years, they developed a strong demand for the 6-day, all-Aspen ticket in its various refinements. Most experienced skiers quite logically prefer to purchase their tickets at once for the whole period that they will spend at the resort; they can then spend more time on the slopes and enjoying apres-ski amenities and less time standing in ticket lines. The 4-area attribute of the ticket allowed the skier to purchase his 6-day ticket in advance while reserving the right to decide in his own time and for his own reasons which mountain he would ski on each day. It provided convenience and flexibility, and expanded the vistas and the number of challenging runs available to him during the week's vacation.

While the 3-area, 6-day ticket offered by Ski Co. possessed some of these attributes, the evidence supports a conclusion that consumers were adversely affected by the elimination of the 4-area ticket. In the first place, the actual record of competition between a 3-area ticket and the all-Aspen ticket in the years after 1967 indicated that skiers demonstrably preferred four mountains to three. Highlands' expert marketing witness testified that many of the skiers who come to Aspen want to ski the four mountains, and the abolition of the 4-area pass made it more difficult to satisfy that ambition. A consumer survey undertaken in the 1979–1980 season indicated that 53.7% of the respondents wanted to ski Highlands, but would not; 39.9% said that they would not be skiing at the mountain of their choice because their ticket would not permit it.

* * *

HIGHLANDS' ABILITY TO COMPETE

The adverse impact of Ski Co.'s pattern of conduct on Highlands is not disputed in this Court. Expert testimony described the extent of its pecuniary injury. * * * The size of the damages award also confirms the substantial character of the effect of Ski Co.'s conduct upon Highlands.[144]

SKI CO.'S BUSINESS JUSTIFICATION

Perhaps most significant, however, is the evidence relating to Ski Co. itself, for Ski Co. did not persuade the jury that its conduct was justified by any normal business purpose. Ski Co. was apparently willing to forgo daily ticket sales both to skiers who sought to exchange the coupons contained in Highlands' Adventure Pack, and to those who would have purchased Ski Co. daily lift tickets from Highlands if Highlands had been permitted to purchase them in bulk. The jury may well have concluded that Ski Co. elected to forgo these short-run benefits because it was more interested in reducing competition in the Aspen market over the long run by harming its smaller competitor.

That conclusion is strongly supported by Ski Co.'s failure to offer any efficiency justification whatever for its pattern of conduct. * * *

* * *

Although Ski Co.'s pattern of conduct may not have been as " 'bold, relentless, and predatory' " as the publisher's actions in *Lorain Journal*, the record in this case comfortably supports an inference that the monopolist made a deliberate effort to discourage its customers from doing business with its smaller rival. The sale of its 3-area, 6-day ticket, particularly when it was discounted below the daily ticket price, deterred the ticket holders from skiing at Highlands. The refusal to accept the Adventure Pack coupons in exchange for daily tickets was apparently motivated entirely by a decision to avoid providing any benefit to Highlands even though accepting the coupons would have entailed no cost to Ski Co. itself, would have provided it with immediate benefits, and would have satisfied its potential customers. Thus the evidence supports an inference that Ski Co. was not motivated by efficiency concerns and that it was willing to sacrifice short-run benefits and consumer goodwill in exchange for a perceived long-run impact on its smaller rival.

Because we are satisfied that the evidence in the record,[145] construed most favorably in support of Highlands' position, is adequate to support the

---

[144] In considering the competitive effect of Ski Co.'s refusal to deal or cooperate with Highlands, it is not irrelevant to note that similar conduct carried out by the concerted action of three independent rivals with a similar share of the market would constitute a per se violation of § 1 of the Sherman Act. See Northwest Wholesale Stationers, Inc. v. Pacific Stationery & Printing Co. [Court's fn. 38]

[145] * * * [W]e find it unnecessary to consider the possible relevance of the "essential facilities" doctrine, or the somewhat hypothetical question whether nonexclusionary conduct could ever

verdict under the instructions given by the trial court, the judgment of the Court of Appeals is

Affirmed.

JUSTICE WHITE took no part in the decision of this case.

NOTES AND QUESTIONS

1.   What were Aspen Highlands' complaints? What did it say Aspen Skiing had done illegally?

a.   Did it argue, for example, that Aspen Skiing had tricked it into joining in a four mountain ticket and breached a contract to continue the arrangement?

b.   Did it argue that, because a four mountain ticket was possible, Aspen Skiing had a legal obligation to enter into such an arrangement? If there had been no such ticket before this case, could Aspen Highlands have argued that one must be created?

c.   Was the Court of Appeals correct that the all-Aspen ticket had become an essential facility like the one in *Terminal Railroad*? What makes something "essential"? When should a large firm be permitted unilaterally to refuse to deal? If I want to use your secret process to cut my production costs in half and you fail to tell me the secret, should you be liable to me for three times what I would have saved?[146]

d.   Was Highlands' argument none of the above positions and yet all of them? Was the contention that Aspen Skiing had made it difficult for skiers to deal with Aspen Highlands by making it more expensive for them to do so?

2.   Were you persuaded by Aspen Skiing's argument that it had no right—much less duty—to cooperate with its competitor? Was it frivolous to argue that the antitrust laws forbade such cooperation? Notice that the factual events described in this case occurred in the late 1970s, *before* the Court had handed down BMI v. CBS. They occurred when the per se rule was the dominant approach to § 1 cases.

3.   This case was tried on a § 2 monopolization theory. What is it that the District Court said, and the Supreme Court affirmed, a plaintiff must show to prove a § 2 violation?

---

constitute an abuse of monopoly power if motivated by an anticompetitive purpose. If, as we have assumed, no monopolist monopolizes unconscious of what he is doing, that case is unlikely to arise. [Court's fn. 44]

[146] See, e.g., Philip Areeda, Essential Facilities: An Epithet in Need of Limiting Principles, 58 Antitrust L. J. 841 (1989); Abbott B. Lipsky, Jr. & J. Gregory Sidak, Essential Facilities, 51 Stanford L. Rev. 1187 (1999); Robert Pitofsky, Donna Patterson & Jonathan Hooks, The Essential Facilities Doctrine Under U.S. Antitrust Law, 70 Antitrust L. J. 443 (2002); Glen O. Robinson, On Refusing to Deal with Rivals, 87 Cornell L. Rev. 1177 (2002). See also, MCI Communications Corp. v. AT&T, 708 F.2d 1081 (7th Cir. 1983) (defining when doctrine applies under U.S. law); Commercial Solvents, Case 6/73, [1974] ECR 6211 (applying doctrine under European Community law).

a. Is there anything new in saying that the defendant must have willfully acquired, maintained, or used monopoly power by anticompetitive or exclusionary means or for such purposes? Do you agree that is what happened here?

b. Did Aspen Skiing engage in practices that should be distinguished from success based on luck, a superior product, or a well-run business?

c. What "legitimate business reasons" would have justified Aspen Skiing's failing to cooperate with Aspen Highlands? Should it have been enough to prove that the new system would make it easier for Aspen Skiing to know how many people would be skiing on its mountains on any given day and thus would let it more nearly get the maximum return from its facilities?

d. Could Aspen Skiing have been found guilty of an attempt to monopolize here? What standard would have been applied to reach such a conclusion?

4. How does the Supreme Court analyze and resolve this case?

a. How was the market defined? Did Aspen Skiing have a monopoly of "downhill skiing at destination ski resorts" in the United States? Is this another case in which, once a narrow submarket was defined, the case was virtually decided?

b. Conceding that the all-Aspen ticket had provided a "desirable option for skiers" that satisfies "consumer demand in free competitive markets," where does that leave a successful firm that wants to change its manner of doing business? Should Aspen Skiing have been prohibited from acting to "change the character" of the market?

c. Was the Court correct to ask whether Aspen Skiing's conduct diminished advantages to consumers? This was a private action brought by Highlands. Was Highlands in part acting as a private attorney general here?

d. If a firm has been "attempting to exclude rivals on some basis other than efficiency," is it fair to say as the Court does that the behavior is "predatory"?

5. Suppose Ski Co. could have shown that after its change in policy the number of skiers in Aspen went up, i.e., there was no reduction in output of "downhill skiing." Should that be relevant to the Court's decision?

a. If the skiing market is truly national or international and the trick is to get people to come to Aspen in the first place, is there a different business and legal issue presented than if the only question is what they will do once they get to Aspen?

b. Is part of the problem in these cases that litigation tends to pose an injured competitor against a successful firm? Has the Court here mistaken a business tort for an issue that should raise antitrust concerns?

6. Is this case really saying that big firms must tread lightly, i.e., not do things that would be fine for smaller firms to do?

a.   Is the rule here that if a big firm's rivals get hurt, the burden will be on the big firm to justify what it did? Might such an approach be traced back to the *Grinnell* case?

b.   Is there a danger that such a test will force big firms to do what U.S. Steel did? Will it force them to make avoiding injury to competitors more important than providing benefits to consumers?[147]

c.   Such an approach would move American law more in the direction of Article 102 of the European Union that prohibits "abuse of a dominant position." Abuse is defined in Article 102 to include "imposing unfair selling prices or trading conditions." E.g., Hoffman-LaRoche v. Commission, CCH Common Market Rep. ¶ 8527 (1979) (large vitamin producer requires reciprocal buying); Michelin v. Commission, CCH Common Market Rep. ¶ 14,031 (1983) (tire manufacturer requires dealers to meet high sales quotas).

7.   Can this case be explained by its procedural posture? This case, like *Utah Pie*, came to the Court after a trial and jury verdict for the plaintiff. Must we be careful to suspend our own judgment of the business realities as the Court struggles with whether, under any proper view of the law, a jury could have found Ski Co. liable?

8.   Was the real problem in this case created at the time Aspen Skiing purchased Buttermilk, i.e., when the valley went from three competitors to two? Would a § 7 case have been successful at that time based on the facts as you see them here? Are monopolization cases an awkward way to correct the failure to deal with mergers at the time they happen? On the other hand, would it be inappropriate to prevent all mergers that *might* present problems later?

Although having just decided one Sherman Act § 2 case, *Aspen Skiing*, the Supreme Court took on another the very next year. Since the days of *Utah Pie*—and long before in *Standard Oil*—predatory pricing had been seen as one of the key indicia of exclusionary conduct. Thus, the message of the next case was a welcome surprise to many but a source of concern to others.

MATSUSHITA ELECTRIC INDUSTRIAL CO. V. ZENITH RADIO CORP.

Supreme Court of the United States, 1986
475 U.S. 574, 106 S.Ct. 1348, 89 L.Ed.2d 538

JUSTICE POWELL delivered the opinion of the Court.

This case requires that we again consider the standard district courts must apply when deciding whether to grant summary judgment in an antitrust conspiracy case.

---

[147] See, e.g., John E. Lopatka & William H. Page, Monopolization, Innovation and Consumer Welfare, 69 George Washington L. Rev. 367 (2001).

I

* * *

* * * Since we review only the standard applied by the Court of Appeals in deciding this case, and not the weight assigned to particular pieces of evidence, we find it unnecessary to state the facts in great detail. What follows is a summary of this case's long history.

A

Petitioners, defendants below, are 21 corporations that manufacture or sell "consumer electronic products" (CEPs)—for the most part, television sets. Petitioners include both Japanese manufacturers of CEPs and American firms, controlled by Japanese parents, that sell the Japanese-manufactured products. Respondents, plaintiffs below, are Zenith Radio Corporation (Zenith) and National Union Electric Corporation (NUE). Zenith is an American firm that manufactures and sells television sets. NUE is the corporate successor to Emerson Radio Company, an American firm that manufactured and sold television sets until 1970, when it withdrew from the market after sustaining substantial losses. Zenith and NUE began this lawsuit in 1974, claiming that petitioners had illegally conspired to drive American firms from the American CEP market. According to respondents, the gist of this conspiracy was a " 'scheme to raise, fix and maintain artificially *high* prices for television receivers sold by [petitioners] in Japan and, at the same time, to fix and maintain *low* prices for television receivers exported to and sold in the United States.' " These "low prices" were allegedly at levels that produced substantial losses for petitioners. The conspiracy allegedly began as early as 1953, and according to respondents was in full operation by sometime in the late 1960's. Respondents claimed that various portions of this scheme violated §§ 1 and 2 of the Sherman Act, § 2(a) of the Robinson-Patman Act, § 73 of the Wilson Tariff Act, and the Antidumping Act of 1916.

After several years of detailed discovery, petitioners filed motions for summary judgment on all claims against them. The District Court directed the parties to file, with preclusive effect, "Final Pretrial Statements" listing all the documentary evidence that would be offered if the case proceeded to trial. * * * In three detailed opinions, the District Court found the bulk of the evidence on which Zenith and NUE relied inadmissible.

* * * In an opinion spanning 217 pages, the court found that the admissible evidence did not raise a genuine issue of material fact as to the existence of the alleged conspiracy. At bottom, the court found, respondents' claims rested on the inferences that could be drawn from petitioners' parallel conduct in the Japanese and American markets, and from the effects of that conduct on petitioners' American competitors. After reviewing the evidence both by category and in toto, the court found that any inference of conspiracy was unreasonable, because (i) some portions of the evidence suggested that petitioners conspired in ways that did not injure respondents, and (ii) the evidence that bore directly on the alleged price-cutting conspiracy did not rebut the more plausible inference that petitioners were cutting prices to compete in the American market and not to monopolize it. * * *

B

The Court of Appeals for the Third Circuit reversed. The court began by examining the District Court's evidentiary rulings, and determined that much of the evidence excluded by the District Court was in fact admissible. These evidentiary rulings are not before us.

On the merits, and based on the newly enlarged record, the court found that the District Court's summary judgment decision was improper. The court acknowledged that "there are legal limitations upon the inferences which may be drawn from circumstantial evidence," but it found that "the legal problem * * * is different" when "there is direct evidence of concert of action." Here, the court concluded, "there is both direct evidence of certain kinds of concert of action and circumstantial evidence having some tendency to suggest that other kinds of concert of action may have occurred." Thus, the court reasoned, cases concerning the limitations on inferring conspiracy from ambiguous evidence were not dispositive. Turning to the evidence, the court determined that a factfinder reasonably could draw the following conclusions:

> 1.   The Japanese market for CEPs was characterized by oligopolistic behavior, with a small number of producers meeting regularly and exchanging information on price and other matters. This created the opportunity for a stable combination to raise both prices and profits in Japan. American firms could not attack such a combination because the Japanese Government imposed significant barriers to entry.

> 2.   Petitioners had relatively higher fixed costs than their American counterparts, and therefore needed to operate at something approaching full capacity in order to make a profit.

> 3.   Petitioners' plant capacity exceeded the needs of the Japanese market.

> 4.   By formal agreements arranged in cooperation with Japan's Ministry of International Trade and Industry (MITI), petitioners fixed minimum prices for CEPs exported to the American market. The parties refer to these prices as the "check prices," and to the agreements that require them as the "check price agreements."

5.   Petitioners agreed to distribute their products in the United States according to a "five company rule": each Japanese producer was permitted to sell only to five American distributors.

6.   Petitioners undercut their own check prices by a variety of rebate schemes. Petitioners sought to conceal these rebate schemes both from the United States Customs Service and from MITI, the former to avoid various customs regulations as well as action under the antidumping laws, and the latter to cover up petitioners' violations of the check-price agreements.

Based on inferences from the foregoing conclusions, the Court of Appeals concluded that a reasonable factfinder could find a conspiracy to depress prices in the American market in order to drive out American competitors, which conspiracy was funded by excess profits obtained in the Japanese market. The court apparently did not consider whether it was as plausible to conclude that petitioners' price-cutting behavior was independent and not conspiratorial.

The court found it unnecessary to address petitioners' claim that they could not be held liable under the antitrust laws for conduct that was compelled by a foreign sovereign. * * * The court concluded that this case did not present any issue of sovereign compulsion, because the check-price agreements were being used as "evidence of a low export price conspiracy" and not as an independent basis for finding antitrust liability. The court also believed it was unclear that the check prices in fact were mandated by the Japanese Government, notwithstanding a statement to that effect by MITI itself.

We granted certiorari to determine (i) whether the Court of Appeals applied the proper standards in evaluating the District Court's decision to grant petitioners' motion for summary judgment, and (ii) whether petitioners could be held liable under the antitrust laws for a conspiracy in part compelled by a foreign sovereign. We reverse on the first issue, but do not reach the second.

II

We begin by emphasizing what respondents' claim is *not*. Respondents cannot recover antitrust damages based solely on an alleged cartelization of the Japanese market, because American antitrust laws do not regulate the competitive conditions of other nations' economies.[148] Nor can

---

[148]   The Sherman Act does reach conduct outside our borders, but only when the conduct has an effect on American commerce. Continental Ore Co. v. Union Carbide & Carbon Corp., 370 U.S. 690, 704 (1962). The effect on which respondents rely is the artificially depressed level of prices for CEPs in the United States.

Petitioners' alleged cartelization of the Japanese market could not have caused that effect
* * * . * * * On the contrary, were the Japanese market perfectly competitive petitioners would still have to choose whether to sell goods overseas, and would still presumably make that choice

respondents recover damages for any conspiracy by petitioners to charge higher than competitive prices in the American market. Such conduct would indeed violate the Sherman Act, but it could not injure respondents: as petitioners' competitors, respondents stand to gain from any conspiracy to raise the market price in CEPs. Finally, for the same reason, respondents cannot recover for a conspiracy to impose non-price restraints that have the effect of either raising market price or limiting output. Such restrictions, though harmful to competition, actually *benefit* competitors by making supracompetitive pricing more attractive. Thus, neither petitioners' alleged supracompetitive pricing in Japan, nor the five company rule that limited distribution in this country, nor the check prices insofar as they established minimum prices in this country, can by themselves give respondents a cognizable claim against petitioners for antitrust damages. The Court of Appeals therefore erred to the extent that it found evidence of these alleged conspiracies to be "direct evidence" of a conspiracy that injured respondents.

Respondents nevertheless argue that these supposed conspiracies, if not themselves grounds for recovery of antitrust damages, are circumstantial evidence of another conspiracy that *is* cognizable: a conspiracy to monopolize the American market by means of pricing below the market level. The thrust of respondents' argument is that petitioners used their monopoly profits from the Japanese market to fund a concerted campaign to price predatorily and thereby drive respondents and other American manufacturers of CEPs out of business. Once successful, according to respondents, petitioners would cartelize the American CEP market, restricting output and raising prices above the level that fair competition would produce. The resulting monopoly profits, respondents contend, would more than compensate petitioners for the losses they incurred through years of pricing below market level.

The Court of Appeals found that respondents' allegation of a horizontal conspiracy to engage in predatory pricing,[149] if proved,[150] would be a per se

---

based on their profit expectations. For this reason, respondents' theory of recovery depends on proof of the asserted price-cutting conspiracy in this country. [Court's fn. 6]

[149]   Throughout this opinion, we refer to the asserted conspiracy as one to price "predatorily." This term has been used chiefly in cases in which a single firm, having a dominant share of the relevant market, cuts its prices in order to force competitors out of the market, or perhaps to deter potential entrants from coming in. In such cases, "predatory pricing" means pricing below some appropriate measure of cost.

There is a good deal of debate * * * about what "cost" is relevant in such cases. We need not resolve this debate here, because * * * this is a Sherman Act § 1 case. For purposes of this case, it is enough to note that respondents have not suffered an antitrust injury unless petitioners conspired to drive respondents out of the relevant markets by (i) pricing below the level necessary to sell their products, or (ii) pricing below some appropriate measure of cost. * * * [Court's fn. 8]

[150]   We do not consider whether recovery should *ever* be available on a theory such as respondents' when the pricing in question is above some measure of incremental cost. See generally Areeda & Turner, Predatory Pricing and Related Practices Under Section 2 of the Sherman Act, 88 Harvard L. Rev. 697, 709–718 (1975) (discussing cost-based test for use in § 2 cases). As a practical matter, it may be that only direct evidence of below-cost pricing is sufficient

violation of § 1 of the Sherman Act. Petitioners did not appeal from that conclusion. The issue in this case thus becomes whether respondents adduced sufficient evidence in support of their theory to survive summary judgment. We therefore examine the principles that govern the summary judgment determination.

III

To survive petitioners' motion for summary judgment, respondents must establish that there is a genuine issue of material fact as to whether petitioners entered into an illegal conspiracy that caused respondents to suffer a cognizable injury. This showing has two components. First, respondents must show more than a conspiracy in violation of the antitrust laws; they must show an injury to them resulting from the illegal conduct. Respondents charge petitioners with a whole host of conspiracies in restraint of trade. Except for the alleged conspiracy to monopolize the American market through predatory pricing, these alleged conspiracies could not have caused respondents to suffer an "antitrust injury," Brunswick Corp. v. Pueblo Bowl-O-Mat, Inc., because they actually tended to benefit respondents. Therefore, unless, in context, evidence of these "other" conspiracies raises a genuine issue concerning the existence of a predatory pricing conspiracy, that evidence cannot defeat petitioners' summary judgment motion.

Second, the issue of fact must be "genuine." When the moving party has carried its burden under Rule 56(c), its opponent must do more than simply show that there is some metaphysical doubt as to the material facts. In the language of the Rule, the nonmoving party must come forward with "specific facts showing that there is a *genuine issue for trial.*" Where the record taken as a whole could not lead a rational trier of fact to find for the non-moving party, there is no "genuine issue for trial."

It follows from these settled principles that if the factual context renders respondents' claim implausible—if the claim is one that simply makes no economic sense—respondents must come forward with more persuasive evidence to support their claim than would otherwise be necessary. * * *

Respondents correctly note that "[o]n summary judgment the inferences to be drawn from the underlying facts * * * must be viewed in the light most favorable to the party opposing the motion." But antitrust law limits the range of permissible inferences from ambiguous evidence in a § 1 case. Thus, in Monsanto Co. v. Spray-Rite Service Corp., we held that conduct as consistent with permissible competition as with illegal conspiracy does not, standing alone, support an inference of antitrust conspiracy. To survive a motion for summary judgment or for a directed

---

to overcome the strong inference that rational businesses would not enter into conspiracies such as this one. See Part IV–A, infra. [Court's fn. 9]

verdict, a plaintiff seeking damages for a violation of § 1 must present evidence "that tends to exclude the possibility" that the alleged conspirators acted independently. Respondents in this case, in other words, must show that the inference of conspiracy is reasonable in light of the competing inferences of independent action or collusive action that could not have harmed respondents.

Petitioners argue that these principles apply fully to this case. According to petitioners, the alleged conspiracy is one that is economically irrational and practically infeasible. * * * Petitioners argue that, in light of the absence of any apparent motive and the ambiguous nature of the evidence of conspiracy, no trier of fact reasonably could find that the conspiracy with which petitioners are charged actually existed. This argument requires us to consider the nature of the alleged conspiracy and the practical obstacles to its implementation.

IV

A

A predatory pricing conspiracy is by nature speculative. Any agreement to price below the competitive level requires the conspirators to forgo profits that free competition would offer them. The forgone profits may be considered an investment in the future. For the investment to be rational, the conspirators must have a reasonable expectation of recovering, in the form of later monopoly profits, more than the losses suffered. As then-Professor Bork, discussing predatory pricing by a single firm, explained:

> "Any realistic theory of predation recognizes that the predator as well as his victims will incur losses during the fighting, but such a theory supposes it may be a rational calculation for the predator to view the losses as an investment in future monopoly profits (where rivals are to be killed) or in future undisturbed profits (where rivals are to be disciplined). The future flow of profits, appropriately discounted, must then exceed the present size of the losses." R. Bork, The Antitrust Paradox 145 (1978).

See also McGee, Predatory Pricing Revisited, 23 J. Law & Econ. 289, 295–297 (1980). As this explanation shows, the success of such schemes is inherently uncertain: the short-run loss is definite, but the long-run gain depends on successfully neutralizing the competition. Moreover, it is not enough simply to achieve monopoly power, as monopoly pricing may breed quick entry by new competitors eager to share in the excess profits. The success of any predatory scheme depends on maintaining monopoly power for long enough both to recoup the predator's losses and to harvest some additional gain. Absent some assurance that the hoped-for monopoly will materialize, and that it can be sustained for a significant period of time, "[t]he predator must make a substantial investment with no assurance that it will pay off." Easterbrook, Predatory Strategies and Counterstrategies, 48 U.Chicago L.Rev. 263, 268 (1981). For this reason, there is a consensus among commentators that predatory pricing schemes are rarely tried, and even more rarely successful.

These observations apply even to predatory pricing by a single firm seeking monopoly power. In this case, respondents allege that a large number of firms have conspired over a period of many years to charge below-market prices in order to stifle competition. Such a conspiracy is incalculably more difficult to execute than an analogous plan undertaken by a single predator. The conspirators must allocate the losses to be sustained during the conspiracy's operation, and must also allocate any gains to be realized from its success. Precisely because success is speculative and depends on a willingness to endure losses for an indefinite period, each conspirator has a strong incentive to cheat, letting its partners suffer the losses necessary to destroy the competition while sharing in any gains if the conspiracy succeeds. The necessary allocation is therefore difficult to accomplish. Yet if conspirators cheat to any substantial extent, the conspiracy must fail, because its success depends on depressing the market price for *all* buyers of CEPs. If there are too few goods at the artificially low price to satisfy demand, the would-be victims of the conspiracy can continue to sell at the "real" market price, and the conspirators suffer losses to little purpose.

Finally, if predatory pricing conspiracies are generally unlikely to occur, they are especially so where, as here, the prospects of attaining monopoly power seem slight. In order to recoup their losses, petitioners must obtain enough market power to set higher than competitive prices, and then must sustain those prices long enough to earn in excess profits what they earlier gave up in below-cost prices. Two decades after their conspiracy is alleged to have commenced, petitioners appear to be far from achieving this goal: the two largest shares of the retail market in television sets are held by RCA and respondent Zenith, not by any of petitioners. Moreover, those shares, which together approximate 40% of sales, did not decline appreciably during the 1970's. Petitioners' collective share rose rapidly during this period, from one-fifth or less of the relevant markets to close to 50%. Neither the District Court nor the Court of Appeals found, however, that petitioners' share presently allows them to charge monopoly prices; to the contrary, respondents contend that the conspiracy is ongoing—that petitioners are still artificially *depressing* the market price in order to drive Zenith out of the market. The data in the record strongly suggest that that goal is yet far distant.[151]

---

[151] Respondents offer no reason to suppose that entry into the relevant market is especially difficult, yet without barriers to entry it would presumably be impossible to maintain supracompetitive prices for an extended time. * * * [Court's fn. 15]

The alleged conspiracy's failure to achieve its ends in the two decades of its asserted operation is strong evidence that the conspiracy does not in fact exist. Since the losses in such a conspiracy accrue before the gains, they must be "repaid" with interest. And because the alleged losses have accrued over the course of two decades, the conspirators could well require a correspondingly long time to recoup. Maintaining supracompetitive prices in turn depends on the continued cooperation of the conspirators, on the inability of other would-be competitors to enter the market, and (not incidentally) on the conspirators' ability to escape antitrust liability for their *minimum* price-fixing cartel.[152] Each of these factors weighs more heavily as the time needed to recoup losses grows. If the losses have been substantial—as would likely be necessary in order to drive out the competition[153]—petitioners would most likely have to sustain their cartel for years simply to break even.

Nor does the possibility that petitioners have obtained supracompetitive profits in the Japanese market change this calculation. Whether or not petitioners have the *means* to sustain substantial losses in this country over a long period of time, they have no *motive* to sustain such losses absent some strong likelihood that the alleged conspiracy in this country will eventually pay off. The courts below found no evidence of any such success, and—as indicated above—the facts actually are to the contrary: RCA and Zenith, not any of the petitioners, continue to hold the largest share of the American retail market in color television sets. More important, there is nothing to suggest any relationship between petitioners' profits in Japan and the amount petitioners could expect to gain from a conspiracy to monopolize the American market. In the absence of any such evidence, the possible existence of supracompetitive profits in Japan simply cannot overcome the economic obstacles to the ultimate success of this alleged predatory conspiracy.[154]

B

In *Monsanto*, we emphasized that courts should not permit factfinders to infer conspiracies when such inferences are implausible, because the

---

[152] The alleged predatory scheme makes sense only if petitioners can recoup their losses. In light of the large number of firms involved here, petitioners can achieve this only by engaging in some form of price fixing after they have succeeded in driving competitors from the market. Such price fixing would, of course, be an independent violation of § 1 of the Sherman Act. United States v. Socony-Vacuum Oil Co. [Court's fn. 16]

[153] The predators' losses must actually increase as the conspiracy nears its objective: the greater the predators' market share, the more products the predators sell; but since every sale brings with it a loss, an increase in market share also means an increase in predatory losses. [Court's fn. 17]

[154] The same is true of any supposed excess production capacity that petitioners may have possessed. The existence of plant capacity that exceeds domestic demand does tend to establish the ability to sell products abroad. It does not, however, provide a motive for selling at prices lower than necessary to obtain sales; nor does it explain why petitioners would be willing to lose money in the United States market without some reasonable prospect of recouping their investment. [Court's fn. 18]

effect of such practices is often to deter procompetitive conduct. Respondents, petitioners' competitors, seek to hold petitioners liable for damages caused by the alleged conspiracy to cut prices. * * *[155] But cutting prices in order to increase business often is the very essence of competition. Thus, mistaken inferences in cases such as this one are especially costly, because they chill the very conduct the antitrust laws are designed to protect. * * *

In most cases, this concern must be balanced against the desire that illegal conspiracies be identified and punished. That balance is, however, unusually one-sided in cases such as this one. As we earlier explained, predatory pricing schemes require conspirators to suffer losses in order eventually to realize their illegal gains; moreover, the gains depend on a host of uncertainties, making such schemes more likely to fail than to succeed. These economic realities tend to make predatory pricing conspiracies self-deterring: unlike most other conduct that violates the antitrust laws, failed predatory pricing schemes are costly to the conspirators. Finally, unlike predatory pricing by a single firm, *successful* predatory pricing conspiracies involving a large number of firms can be identified and punished once they succeed, since some form of minimum price-fixing agreement would be necessary in order to reap the benefits of predation. Thus, there is little reason to be concerned that by granting summary judgment in cases where the evidence of conspiracy is speculative or ambiguous, courts will encourage such conspiracies.

V

* * * The Court of Appeals erred in two [other] respects: (i) the "direct evidence" on which the court relied had little, if any, relevance to the alleged predatory pricing conspiracy; and (ii) the court failed to consider the absence of a plausible motive to engage in predatory pricing.

The "direct evidence" on which the court relied was evidence of *other* combinations, not of a predatory pricing conspiracy. Evidence that petitioners conspired to raise prices in Japan provides little, if any, support for respondents' claims: a conspiracy to increase profits in one market does not tend to show a conspiracy to sustain losses in another. Evidence that petitioners agreed to fix *minimum* prices (through the check-price agreements) for the American market actually works in petitioners' favor,

---

[155] Respondents also rely on an expert study [The DePodwin Report] suggesting that petitioners have sold their products in the American market at substantial losses. The relevant study is not based on actual cost data; rather, it consists of expert opinion based on a mathematical construction that in turn rests on assumptions about petitioners' costs. The District Court analyzed those assumptions in some detail and found them both implausible and inconsistent with record evidence. Although the Court of Appeals reversed the District Court's finding that the expert report was inadmissible, the court did not disturb the District Court's analysis of the factors that substantially undermine the probative value of that evidence. We find the District Court's analysis persuasive. Accordingly, in our view the expert opinion evidence of below-cost pricing has little probative value in comparison with the economic factors, discussed in Part IV–A, supra, that suggest that such conduct is irrational. [Court's fn. 19]

because it suggests that petitioners were seeking to place a floor under prices rather than to lower them. The same is true of evidence that petitioners agreed to limit the number of distributors of their products in the American market—the so-called five company rule. That practice may have facilitated a horizontal territorial allocation, see United States v. Topco Associates, Inc., but its natural effect would be to raise market prices rather than reduce them. Evidence that tends to support any of these collateral conspiracies thus says little, if anything, about the existence of a conspiracy to charge below-market prices in the American market over a period of two decades.

That being the case, the absence of any plausible motive to engage in the conduct charged is highly relevant to whether a "genuine issue for trial" exists within the meaning of Rule 56(e). Lack of motive bears on the range of permissible conclusions that might be drawn from ambiguous evidence: if petitioners had no rational economic motive to conspire, and if their conduct is consistent with other, equally plausible explanations, the conduct does not give rise to an inference of conspiracy. Here, the conduct in question consists largely of (i) pricing at levels that succeeded in taking business away from respondents, and (ii) arrangements that may have limited petitioners' ability to compete with each other (and thus kept prices from going even lower). This conduct suggests either that petitioners behaved competitively, or that petitioners conspired to *raise* prices. Neither possibility is consistent with an agreement among 21 companies to price below market levels. Moreover, the predatory pricing scheme that this conduct is said to prove is one that makes no practical sense: it calls for petitioners to destroy companies larger and better established than themselves, a goal that remains far distant more than two decades after the conspiracy's birth. Even had they succeeded in obtaining their monopoly, there is nothing in the record to suggest that they could recover the losses they would need to sustain along the way. In sum, in light of the absence of any rational motive to conspire, neither petitioners' pricing practices, nor their conduct in the Japanese market, nor their agreements respecting prices and distribution in the American market, suffice to create a "genuine issue for trial."

* * *

The decision of the Court of Appeals is reversed, and the case is remanded for further proceedings consistent with this opinion.

JUSTICE WHITE, with whom JUSTICE BRENNAN, JUSTICE BLACKMUN, and JUSTICE STEVENS join, dissenting.

It is indeed remarkable that the Court, in the face of the long and careful opinion of the Court of Appeals, reaches the result it does. * * *

The Court's opinion today, far from identifying reversible error, only muddies the waters. In the first place, the Court makes confusing and inconsistent statements about the appropriate standard for granting summary judgment. Second, the Court makes a number of assumptions that invade the factfinder's province. Third, the Court faults the Third Circuit for nonexistent errors and remands the case although it is plain that respondents' evidence raises genuine issues of material fact.

I

The Court's initial discussion of summary judgment standards appears consistent with settled doctrine. * * * But other language in the Court's opinion suggests a departure from traditional summary judgment doctrine. * * * [Its] language suggests that a judge hearing a defendant's motion for summary judgment in an antitrust case should go beyond the traditional summary judgment inquiry and decide for himself whether the weight of the evidence favors the plaintiff. * * *

If the Court intends to give every judge hearing a motion for summary judgment in an antitrust case the job of determining if the evidence makes the inference of conspiracy more probable than not, it is overturning settled law. If the Court does not intend such a pronouncement, it should refrain from using unnecessarily broad and confusing language.

II

In defining what respondents must show in order to recover, the Court makes assumptions that invade the factfinder's province. * * *

The DePodwin Report, on which the Court of Appeals relied along with other material, indicates that respondents were harmed in two ways that are independent of whether petitioners priced their products below "the level necessary to sell their products or * * * some appropriate measure of cost." First, the Report explains that the price-raising scheme in Japan resulted in lower consumption of petitioners' goods in that country and the exporting of more of petitioners' goods to this country than would have occurred had prices in Japan been at the competitive level. Increasing exports to this country resulted in depressed prices here, which harmed respondents. Second, the * * * Report explains that petitioners' restrictions on intragroup competition caused respondents to lose business that they would not have lost had petitioners competed with one another.

The DePodwin Report alone creates a genuine factual issue regarding the harm to respondents caused by Japanese cartelization and by agreements restricting competition among petitioners in this country. No doubt the Court prefers its own economic theorizing to Dr. DePodwin's, but that is not a reason to deny the factfinder an opportunity to consider Dr. DePodwin's views on how petitioners' alleged collusion harmed respondents.

The Court, in discussing the unlikelihood of a predatory conspiracy, also consistently assumes that petitioners valued profit-maximization over growth. In light of the evidence that petitioners sold their goods in this country at substantial losses over a long period of time, * * * I believe that this is an assumption that should be argued to the factfinder, not decided by the Court.

* * *

IV

* * * I would affirm the judgment below and remand this case for trial.

NOTES AND QUESTIONS

1.   This case was decided on summary judgment, but on a very substantial paper record. An important part of this case is what it purports to tell us about summary judgment in antitrust cases.

a.   What issues does the Supreme Court say a court should consider at the summary judgment stage of future cases? Do these issues sound like some of those proposed by then-Professor Easterbrook and the FTC, supra?

b.   Are you comfortable having district judges evaluate the plaintiff's claims in light of economic theory? Is economic theory something that can confidently be applied to written statements and a paper record alone?

c.   Do you agree that allegations as consistent with permissible competition as with illegal conspiracy do not raise contested issues of material fact? Is that point of equipoise obvious in most cases? Isn't the resolution of conflicting inferences just what we ask of juries all the time?

d.   What effects on the handling of antitrust cases can you predict as a result of this decision? Will plaintiffs have to do their homework before drafting the complaint lest they lose a motion to dismiss? Will they have to bring experts into the case early and figure out their economic theory before spending time on general discovery?[156] Aren't those desirable effects to encourage?

e.   Do you suppose judges will be more or less critical of a defendant than juries would be? Is there reason to believe that deciding more cases on summary judgment will work more in favor of defendants than plaintiffs?

2.   The analysis of predatory pricing here is at least equally important. What were these defendants accused of having done?

a.   What allegedly gave the Japanese firms both the means and the incentive to drive the American firms out of business? What was the alleged significance, if any, of barriers to U.S. firms' sales in Japan?

---

[156] See, e.g., Michael I. Speigel & Wayne M. Liao, Avoiding Summary Judgment After *Matsushita* and *Monsanto*, 5 Antitrust 12 (Spring 1991); John T. Soma & Andrew P. McCallin, Summary Judgment and Discovery Strategies in Antitrust and RICO Actions After Matsushita v. Zenith, 36 Antitrust Bull. 325 (1991).

b.   If Japanese firms indeed had more capacity than they needed to serve Japan, were you persuaded that they would look for a new market to enter? Was the U.S. market a logical one to choose? Indeed, did the defendants deny that they had every reason to want to sell in America?

c.   Were you entirely convinced the Japanese did not have a plan or that it was not working? Does the fact that the Japanese had not achieved 100% penetration of the American market mean they could not have done so whenever they wished?

d.   Is an interest in selling in America evidence of an illegal conspiracy? Were you convinced that a conspiracy to sell below cost as alleged here would be both "economically irrational and practically infeasible" and thus something that could not have happened?[157]

e.   Is the important insight of this case that predatory pricing would be irrational unless the defendant had reason to think it could later recoup its losses? Is there only one way to look at recoupment, i.e., must the manufacturer be able to charge higher prices later? Would it be enough to show that the defendants had been able to develop distribution networks for their products that they could now use for more than television sets? Put another way, is a firm's evaluation of whether it can recoup losses from predatory pricing different from any other determination of whether it can earn a return on an initial investment?

3.   Finally, although the Court did not reach the point, if the Japanese government had mandated the defendants' conduct, should that have been an absolute defense? In other words, should there be an international version of Parker v. Brown? Why or why not?[158]

JUDGE EASTERBROOK LOOKS AT A CASE OF EGGS

As the debate raged about *Matsushita*, Judge Frank Easterbrook, in A.A. Poultry Farms, Inc. v. Rose Acre Farms, Inc., 881 F.2d 1396 (7th Cir.1989), suggested a relatively simple way to determine when one should be concerned about alleged predatory conduct and when not.

Rose Acre and its competitors were "vertically integrated egg producers and processors." Eggs have a short shelf life; " 'sell 'em or smell 'em' is the industry motto." Because hens regularly lay eggs in sizes and

---

[157] On the *Matsushita* case itself, see Nickolai G. Levin, The Nomos and Narrative of *Matsushita*, 73 Fordham L. Rev. 1627 (2005). The literature on predatory conduct in general also has continued apace. E.g., Thomas J. Campbell, Predation and Competition in Antitrust: The Case of Nonfungible Goods, 87 Columbia L.Rev. 1625 (1987); Eric Rasmusen & John Shepard Wiley, Jr., Antitrust and Spatial Predation: A Response to Thomas J. Campbell, 89 Columbia L.Rev. 1015 (1989). Cf. John J. Tharp, Raising Rivals' Costs: Of Bottlenecks, Bottled Wine, and Bottled Soda, 84 Northwestern U.L.Rev. 321 (1989).

[158] You will see the Court address the issue later in this chapter in Hartford Fire Insurance Co. v. California, 509 U.S. 764, 113 S.Ct. 2891, 125 L.Ed.2d 612 (1993).

grades different from the producers' current orders, firms usually sell their surplus to producers of cake mix and other dried egg products. Rose Acre, however, sold its surplus at a discount to its regular customers. This proved such a successful way of doing business that one of Rose Acre's competitors "squawked," alleging that Rose Acre had violated the Robinson-Patman Act and engaged in predatory conduct in violation of § 2 of the Sherman Act. The plaintiff's expert testified that Rose Acre's prices had been less than its average total cost, and there was evidence that the president of Rose Acre had told a competitor: "We are going to run you out of the egg business. Your days are numbered." A jury awarded the competitor $9.3 million.

The Court of Appeals reversed. Judge Easterbrook, writing for the court, reasoned:[159]

" * * * A price 'too low' for an inefficient rival may be just right from consumers' perspective, showing only that the defendant's costs of production are lower than those of the plaintiff—for which it should receive a reward in the market rather than a penalty in the courthouse. So the plaintiff's observation that it is losing business to a rival that has slashed prices is consistent with both aggressive competition and predatory pricing. How to tell them apart?

"One way is to find out whether the defendant's prices exceed its costs. If the price exceeds cost, then it reflects beneficial aggressive competition. * * * [But] trying to infer (or refute) predatory conduct from the relation between price and cost is difficult business. Often a price below cost reflects only the sacrifice necessary to establish a presence in a competitive market * * * . Measuring costs creates additional problems. Are advertising and research costs expensed or capitalized? How does one allocate the cost of activities that have joint products? Agencies engaged in ratemaking struggle with these problems for years, even decades, without producing clear answers. If we could measure costs, what would be the right benchmark? Any * * * might be best in a given case, depending on the strategy the aggressor has selected and the length of time it will take to succeed.

"A second approach to separating aggressive competition from predation concentrates on the defendant's intent. * * * [But a] drive to succeed lies at the core of a rivalrous economy. * * * [A] desire to extinguish one's rivals is entirely consistent with, often is the motive behind, competition. * * * If courts use the vigorous, nasty pursuit of sales as evidence of a forbidden 'intent', they run

---

[159] In the interest of compressing Judge Easterbrook's analysis, several sentences and even paragraphs of this opinion have been rearranged by the editor.

the risk of penalizing the motive forces of competition. [Finally, looking for] intent * * * also complicates litigation. Lawyers rummage through business records seeking to discover tidbits that will sound impressive (or aggressive) when read to a jury. Traipsing through the warehouses of business in search of misleading evidence both increases the costs of litigation and reduces the accuracy of decisions.

"The third approach looks at the back end, the 'high price later' part of the predatory sequence. Predatory prices are an investment in a future monopoly, a sacrifice of today's profits for tomorrow's. The investment must be recouped. If a monopoly price later is impossible, then the sequence is unprofitable and we may infer that the low price now is not predatory. More importantly, if there can be no 'later' in which recoupment could occur, then the consumer is an unambiguous beneficiary even if the current price is less than the cost of production. * * * Because unsuccessful predation is unprofitable, it is bootless for the legal system to intervene, see *Matsushita*; self-deterring conduct is not apt to be repeated, and if it is the consumer will receive still another boon. * * * [U]nless recoupment lies in store even the most vicious intent is harmless to the competitive system."

Here, recoupment was impossible, the court concluded. Prices of eggs were falling, yet entry into the industry was constant. The industry was extraordinarily diffuse; Rose Acre, for example, had less than 1% of the market. Entry was cheap; any farmer could raise chickens and sell eggs. There was thus no basis for finding that Rose Acre's conduct had been predatory.

1. Are you convinced? Do you agree that analyzing the possibility of recoupment is significantly easier than measuring the defendant's cost of production and sales? Do you agree that we should be suspicious of a business person who does *not* exhort the sales force to beat the competition to every customer, i.e., to try to get a 100% of the market?

2. Is the court's test consistent with the Supreme Court's in *Matsushita*? Does Judge Easterbrook's analysis help your understanding of the Supreme Court's third major case in this line?

BROOKE GROUP LTD. V. BROWN & WILLIAMSON TOBACCO CORP.

Supreme Court of the United States, 1993
509 U.S. 209, 113 S.Ct. 2578, 125 L.Ed.2d 168

JUSTICE KENNEDY delivered the opinion of the Court.

This case stems from a market struggle that erupted in the domestic cigarette industry in the mid-1980's. Petitioner Brooke Group, Inc., whom we, like the parties to the case, refer to as Liggett because of its former corporate name, charges that to counter its innovative development of generic cigarettes, respondent Brown & Williamson Tobacco Corporation introduced its own line of generic cigarettes in an unlawful effort to stifle price competition in the economy segment of the national cigarette market. Liggett contends that Brown & Williamson cut prices on generic cigarettes below cost and offered discriminatory volume rebates to wholesalers to force Liggett to raise its own generic cigarette prices and introduce oligopoly pricing in the economy segment. We hold that Brown & Williamson is entitled to judgment as a matter of law.

I

In 1980, Liggett pioneered the development of the economy segment of the national cigarette market by introducing a line of "black and white" generic cigarettes. * * * By 1984, when Brown & Williamson entered the generic segment and set in motion the series of events giving rise to this suit, Liggett's black and whites represented 97% of the generic segment, which in turn accounted for a little more than 4% of domestic cigarette sales. Prior to Liggett's introduction of black and whites in 1980, sales of generic cigarettes amounted to less than 1% of the domestic cigarette market.

* * *

The cigarette industry * * * has long been one of America's most profitable, in part because for many years there was no significant price competition among the rival firms. * * * Cf. American Tobacco Co. v. United States.

By 1980, however, broad market trends were working against the industry. Overall demand for cigarettes in the United States was declining, and no immediate prospect of recovery existed. As industry volume shrank, all firms developed substantial excess capacity. * * * Liggett was on the verge of going out of business.

At the urging of a distributor, Liggett took an unusual step to revive its prospects: It developed a line of black and white generic cigarettes. When introduced in 1980, black and whites were offered to consumers at a list price roughly 30% lower than the list price of full-priced, branded cigarettes. * * * Liggett's black and whites were an immediate and considerable success, growing from a fraction of a percent of the market at their introduction to over 4% of the total cigarette market by early 1984.

As the market for Liggett's generic cigarettes expanded, the other cigarette companies found themselves unable to ignore the economy segment. * * * Brown & Williamson was hardest hit, because many of Brown & Williamson's brands were favored by consumers who were sensitive to changes in cigarette prices. Although Brown & Williamson sold only 11.4% of the market's branded cigarettes, 20% of the converts to Liggett's black and whites had switched from a Brown & Williamson brand. * * * In the spring of 1984, [Brown & Williamson] introduced its own black and white cigarette.

* * *

* * * Brown & Williamson not only matched Liggett's prices but beat them. * * *

Liggett responded to Brown & Williamson's introduction of black and whites in two ways. First, Liggett increased its own wholesale rebates. This precipitated a price war at the wholesale level, in which Liggett five times attempted to beat the rebates offered by Brown & Williamson. At the end of each round, Brown & Williamson maintained a real advantage over Liggett's prices. Although it is undisputed that Brown & Williamson's original net price for its black and whites was above its costs, Liggett contends that by the end of the rebate war, Brown & Williamson was selling its black and whites at a loss. * * *

Liggett's second response was to file a lawsuit. * * *

* * * Liggett alleged that Brown & Williamson's volume rebates to wholesalers amounted to price discrimination that had a reasonable possibility of injuring competition, in violation of [the Robinson-Patman Act]. Liggett claimed that Brown & Williamson's discriminatory volume rebates were integral to a scheme of predatory pricing, in which Brown & Williamson reduced its net prices for generic cigarettes below average variable costs. According to Liggett, these below-cost prices were not promotional but were intended to pressure it to raise its list prices on generic cigarettes, so that the percentage price difference between generic and branded cigarettes would narrow. * * * The resulting reduction in the list price gap, it was said, would restrain the growth of the economy segment and preserve Brown & Williamson's supracompetitive profits on its branded cigarettes.

* * *

After a 115-day trial involving almost 3,000 exhibits and over a score of witnesses, the jury * * * awarded Liggett $49.6 million in damages, which the District Court trebled to $148.8 million. After reviewing the record, however, the District Court held that Brown & Williamson was entitled to judgment as a matter of law [based on lack of injury to competition]. * * * [T]he District Court found that no slowing of the growth rate of generics, and thus no injury to competition, was possible unless there had been tacit coordination of prices in the economy segment of the cigarette market by the various manufacturers. The District Court held that a reasonable jury could come to but one conclusion about the existence of such coordination among the firms contending for shares of the economy segment: it did not exist, and Brown & Williamson therefore had no reasonable possibility of limiting the growth of the segment.

The United States Court of Appeals for the Fourth Circuit affirmed. * * * In the Court of Appeals' view, "to rely on the characteristics of an oligopoly to assure recoupment of losses from a predatory pricing scheme after one oligopolist has made a competitive move is * * * economically irrational."

We granted certiorari and now affirm.

II

A

* * *

* * * We last addressed primary line injury over 25 years ago, in Utah Pie Co. v. Continental Baking Co. * * *

Utah Pie * * * has been criticized on the grounds that such low standards of competitive injury are at odds with the antitrust laws' traditional concern for consumer welfare and price competition. We do not regard the Utah Pie case itself as having the full significance attributed to it by its detractors. Utah Pie was an early judicial inquiry in this area and did not purport to set forth explicit, general standards for establishing a violation of the Robinson-Patman Act. As the law has been explored since Utah Pie, it has become evident that primary-line competitive injury under the Robinson-Patman Act is of the same general character as the injury inflicted by predatory pricing schemes actionable under § 2 of the Sherman Act. There are, to be sure, differences between the two statutes. * * * But whatever additional flexibility the Robinson-Patman Act standard may imply, the essence of the claim under either statute is the same: A business rival has priced its products in an unfair manner with an object to eliminate or retard competition and thereby gain and exercise control over prices in the relevant market.

Accordingly, whether the claim alleges predatory pricing under § 2 of the Sherman Act or primary-line price discrimination under the Robinson-Patman Act, two prerequisites to recovery remain the same. First, a plaintiff seeking to establish competitive injury resulting from a rival's low prices must prove that the prices complained of are below an appropriate measure of its rival's costs.[160] Although Cargill [Inc. v. Monfort of Colorado, Inc., 479 U.S. 104, 107 S.Ct. 484, 93 L.Ed.2d 427 (1986)], and *Matsushita* reserved as a formal matter the question " 'whether recovery should ever be available * * * when the pricing in question is above some measure of incremental cost,' " the reasoning in both opinions suggests that only below-cost prices should suffice, and we have rejected elsewhere the notion that above-cost prices that are below general market levels or the costs of a firm's competitors inflict injury to competition cognizable under the antitrust laws. As a general rule, the exclusionary effect of prices above a relevant measure of cost either reflects the lower cost structure of the alleged predator, and so represents competition on the merits, or is beyond the practical ability of a judicial tribunal to control without courting intolerable risks of chilling legitimate price-cutting. * * *

Even in an oligopolistic market, when a firm drops its prices to a competitive level to demonstrate to a maverick the unprofitability of straying from the group, it would be illogical to condemn the price cut: The antitrust laws then would be an obstacle to the chain of events most conducive to a breakdown of oligopoly pricing and the onset of competition. Even if the ultimate effect of the cut is to induce or reestablish supracompetitive pricing, discouraging a price cut and forcing firms to maintain supracompetitive prices, thus depriving consumers of the benefits of lower prices in the interim, does not constitute sound antitrust policy.

The second prerequisite to holding a competitor liable under the antitrust laws for charging low prices is a demonstration that the competitor had a reasonable prospect, or, under § 2 of the Sherman Act, a dangerous probability, of recouping its investment in below-cost prices. See *Matsushita*. * * * Recoupment is the ultimate object of an unlawful predatory pricing scheme; it is the means by which a predator profits from predation. Without it, predatory pricing produces lower aggregate prices in the market, and consumer welfare is enhanced. Although unsuccessful predatory pricing may encourage some inefficient substitution toward the product being sold at less than its cost, unsuccessful predation is in general a boon to consumers.

That below-cost pricing may impose painful losses on its target is of no moment to the antitrust laws if competition is not injured: It is axiomatic that the antitrust laws were passed for "the protection of competition, not competitors." *Brown Shoe.* * * * Even an act of pure malice by one business competitor against another does not, without more, state a claim under the federal antitrust laws; those laws do not create a federal law of unfair competition or "purport to afford remedies for all torts committed by or

---

[160] Because the parties in this case agree that the relevant measure of cost is average variable cost, however, we again decline to resolve the conflict among the lower courts over the appropriate measure of cost. [Court's fn. 1]

against persons engaged in interstate commerce." Hunt v. Crumboch, 325 U.S. 821, 826 (1945).

For recoupment to occur, below-cost pricing must be capable, as a threshold matter, of producing the intended effects on the firm's rivals, whether driving them from the market, or, as was alleged to be the goal here, causing them to raise their prices to supracompetitive levels within a disciplined oligopoly. This requires an understanding of the extent and duration of the alleged predation, the relative financial strength of the predator and its intended victim, and their respective incentives and will. The inquiry is whether, given the aggregate losses caused by the below-cost pricing, the intended target would likely succumb. If circumstances indicate that below-cost pricing could likely produce its intended effect on the target, * * * [t]he plaintiff must demonstrate that there is a likelihood that the predatory scheme alleged would cause a rise in prices above a competitive level that would be sufficient to compensate for the amounts expended on the predation, including the time value of the money invested in it. As we have observed on a prior occasion, "in order to recoup their losses, [predators] must obtain enough market power to set higher than competitive prices, and then must sustain those prices long enough to earn in excess profits what they earlier gave up in below-cost prices." *Matsushita.*

* * *

These prerequisites to recovery are not easy to establish, but they are not artificial obstacles to recovery; rather, they are essential components of real market injury. As we have said in the Sherman Act context, "predatory pricing schemes are rarely tried, and even more rarely successful," *Matsushita*, and the costs of an erroneous finding of liability are high. * * * It would be ironic indeed if the standards for predatory pricing liability were so low that antitrust suits themselves became a tool for keeping prices high.

B

Liggett does not allege that Brown & Williamson sought to drive it from the market but that Brown & Williamson sought to preserve supracompetitive profits on branded cigarettes by pressuring Liggett to raise its generic cigarette prices through a process of tacit collusion with the other cigarette companies. Tacit collusion, sometimes called oligopolistic price coordination or conscious parallelism, describes the process, not in itself unlawful, by which firms in a concentrated market might in effect share monopoly power, setting their prices at a profit-maximizing, supracompetitive level by recognizing their shared economic interests and their interdependence with respect to price and output decisions.

In *Matsushita*, we remarked upon the general implausibility of predatory pricing. *Matsushita* observed that such schemes are even more improbable when they require coordinated action among several firms. * * *

However unlikely predatory pricing by multiple firms may be when they conspire, it is even less likely when, as here, there is no express coordination. Firms that seek to recoup predatory losses through the conscious parallelism of oligopoly must rely on uncertain and ambiguous signals to achieve concerted action. The signals are subject to misinterpretation and are a blunt and imprecise means of ensuring smooth cooperation, especially in the context of changing or unprecedented market circumstances. This anticompetitive minuet is most difficult to compose and to perform, even for a disciplined oligopoly.

* * * In addition to the difficulty of achieving effective tacit coordination and the high likelihood that any attempt to discipline will produce an outbreak of competition, the predator's present losses in a case like this fall on it alone, while the later supracompetitive profits must be shared with every other oligopolist in proportion to its market share, including the intended victim. In this case, for example, Brown & Williamson, with its 11–12% share of the cigarette market, would have had to generate around $9 in supracompetitive profits for each $1 invested in predation; the remaining $8 would belong to its competitors, who had taken no risk.

* * *

To the extent that the Court of Appeals may have held that the interdependent pricing of an oligopoly may never provide a means for achieving recoupment and so may not form the basis of a primary-line injury claim, we disagree. A predatory pricing scheme designed to preserve or create a stable oligopoly, if successful, can injure consumers in the same way, and to the same extent, as one designed to bring about a monopoly. However unlikely that possibility may be as a general matter, when the realities of the market and the record facts indicate that it has occurred and was likely to have succeeded, theory will not stand in the way of liability.

* * * We decline to create a per se rule of nonliability for predatory price discrimination when recoupment is alleged to take place through supracompetitive oligopoly pricing.

III

Although Liggett's theory of liability, as an abstract matter, is within the reach of the statute, we agree with the Court of Appeals and the District Court * * * that the anticompetitive scheme Liggett alleged, when judged against the realities of the market, does not provide an adequate basis for a finding of liability.

* * *

* * * [T]he situation facing the cigarette companies in the 1980's would have made * * * tacit coordination unmanageable. Tacit coordination is facilitated by a stable market environment, fungible products, and a small number of variables upon which the firms seeking to coordinate their pricing may focus. Uncertainty is an oligopoly's greatest enemy. By 1984, however, the cigarette market was in an obvious state of flux. * * *

* * *

* * * [A]lthough some of Brown & Williamson's corporate planning documents speak of a desire to slow the growth of the segment, no objective evidence of its conduct permits a reasonable inference that it had any real prospect of doing so through anticompetitive means. * * * It is undisputed that when Brown & Williamson introduced its generic cigarettes, it offered them to a thousand wholesalers who had never before purchased generic cigarettes. The inevitable effect of this marketing effort was to expand the segment, as the new wholesalers recruited retail outlets to carry generic cigarettes. * * *

* * *

IV

* * * We hold that the evidence cannot support a finding that Brown & Williamson's alleged scheme was likely to result in oligopolistic price coordination and sustained supracompetitive pricing in the generic segment of the national cigarette market. Without this, Brown & Williamson had no reasonable prospect of recouping its predatory losses and could not inflict the injury to competition the antitrust laws prohibit. The judgment of the Court of Appeals is affirmed.

JUSTICE STEVENS, with whom JUSTICE WHITE and JUSTICE BLACKMUN join, dissenting.

* * *

In my opinion the evidence is plainly sufficient to support [the jury's] finding.

* * *

* * * When a predator deliberately engages in below-cost pricing targeted at a particular competitor over a sustained period of time, then price-cutting raises a credible inference that harm to competition is likely to ensue. None of our cases disputes that proposition.

Also as a matter of economics, the Court insists that a predatory pricing program in an oligopoly is unlikely to succeed absent actual conspiracy. Though it has rejected a somewhat stronger version of this proposition as a rule of decision, the Court comes back to the same economic theory, relying on the supposition that an "anticompetitive minuet is most difficult to compose and to perform, even for a disciplined oligopoly." I would suppose, however, that the professional performers who had danced the minuet for 40 to 50 years would be better able to predict whether their favorite partners would follow them in the future than would an outsider, who might not know the difference between Haydn and Mozart. * * *

* * * [T]he jury would surely be entitled to infer that B & W's predatory plan, in which it invested millions of dollars for the purpose of achieving an admittedly anticompetitive result, carried a "reasonable possibility" of injuring competition.

Accordingly, I respectfully dissent.

NOTES AND QUESTIONS

1. Where does the law relating to predatory pricing stand after this decision?

a. Could a plaintiff ever prove a violation of § 2 by showing only that the defendant had sold below some measure of cost for a sustained period of time?

b. Could it ever be enough for the plaintiff to prove that documents in the defendant's files showed it had the intent to drive the plaintiff out of business?

2. Is it now clear that proof the defendant could recoup its losses from below-cost pricing is critical to prevailing in a § 2 predatory pricing case?

a. Must the plaintiff prove the exact amount of the defendant's losses? What measure of cost should the plaintiff use? Can the Court responsibly continue to fail to answer that question?

b. On the other hand, will this decision mean that some *plaintiffs* may now be the ones relying on average variable cost as the appropriate measure of predatory pricing? Put another way, now that they clearly have to prove recoupment, will plaintiffs be looking for the measure of cost that shows the *least* loss by the defendant consistent with predation?

3. Was it clear to you that the plaintiff had not proved the defendant's ability to recover its losses here?

a. Were the Court's observations about the difficulty of disciplined coordination of oligopoly pricing more persuasive than the jury's apparent factual finding to the contrary?

b. Should the plaintiff have to prove that the defendant recovered its losses in generic sales from later profits on *generic* sales? Suppose, instead, that it recovered the losses on increased sales of branded cigarettes, i.e., that its total revenues and profits increased by more than its losses on generics. Indeed, isn't that what the jury apparently found had happened here?[161]

4.   If the court was willing to find that this record justified entering a defense judgment notwithstanding the jury verdict for the plaintiff, was the Court disingenuous in failing to announce a rule of per se legality when a predatory pricing scheme is only alleged to have been "designed to preserve or create a stable oligopoly"?

a.   What interest is the Court serving by *failing* to create such rule? The Court flatly says that, in an oligopolistic market, "even if the ultimate effect of [a price] cut is to induce or reestablish supracompetitive pricing, discouraging [the] price cut * * * [deprives] consumers of lower prices in the interim [and] does not constitute sound antitrust policy." If that is true, why keep business people uncertain about whether engaging in price cutting will involve them in a costly antitrust case?

b.   What different facts should lead a court to conclude that it has before it the "unlikely" case in which "a predatory pricing scheme designed to preserve or create a stable oligopoly * * * can injure consumers in the same way, and to the same extent, as one designed to bring about a monopoly"? Might it be significant that a firm with a large market share was engaging in the below-cost pricing, for example? Why or why not?

A NOTE ON POSSIBLE STANDARDS
FOR EXCLUSIONARY CONDUCT

After the results in these first three cases seemed almost to close the door on monopolization cases under Sherman Act § 2, antitrust scholars and policymakers renewed efforts to develop a test for exclusionary conduct that would be easy to apply, identify economically harmful conduct and avoid punishing or deterring conduct that would benefit consumers. Think about some possible candidates for such a test.[162]

1.   *Intent to Monopolize: The Desire to Grow.* Would you want to punish efforts by an already-large firm to increase its market share?

a.   Remember that Judge Hand came close to prohibiting such conduct in *ALCOA* and it is possible to read *Aspen Skiing* as pointing in that same direction. But would you really want to see a world in which firms did not at least have the ambition to be more and more successful?

---

[161] See, e.g., Jonathan B. Baker, Predatory Pricing After Brooke Group: An Economic Perspective, 62 Antitrust L. J. 585 (1994).

[162] See generally, Aaron S. Edlin, Stopping Above-Cost Predatory Pricing, 111 Yale. L.J. 941 (2002); Einer Elhauge, Defining Better Monopolization Standards, 56 Stanford L. Rev. 253 (2003). Earlier articles include Frank H. Easterbrook, Predatory Strategies and Counterstrategies, 48 U. Chicago L. Rev. 263 (1981); Oliver E. Williamson, Predatory Pricing: A Strategic and Welfare Analysis, 87 Yale L.J. 284 (1977).

b.   Suppose that, if a firm could grow, it could achieve economies of scale and produce higher quality products that it could sell for lower prices. Would you want firms to be concerned that their efforts to become more efficient could be used against them in a § 2 case?[163]

2.   *No Economic Sense.* Might you want to prohibit conduct by a dominant firm that makes no "economic sense" other than as a way to exclude competitors? Is that the test used in *Aspen Skiing*? How would you define "economic sense" in such a case?[164]

a.   Should a plaintiff have to show that a firm has sacrificed short-term profits in the hope of long-term gain once its competitors are eliminated? What kind of proof would make that case?

b.   In *Aspen Skiing*, Ski Co. argued publicly that Highlands had inferior ski lifts and other facilities and that identification with Highlands hurt Ski Co.'s image. If the jury found that to be true, should it be a sufficient defense against liability?

3.   *Raising Rivals' Costs.* Suppose a firm's conduct can be shown to raise the costs faced by its rivals and thus allow the firm to raise its own price above marginal cost.[165]

a.   Suppose the dominant firm in a market controls a bottleneck or "essential facility" that competitors need to lower their own costs. Or suppose the firm induces its suppliers to overcharge or not deal with the firm's rivals.

b.   Is there more reason to be concerned about practices that raise rivals' costs than practices that make competition more difficult in some other way? Is it accurate to say that these practices are necessarily without positive benefit to consumers?

4.   *Excluding an Equally-Efficient Competitor.* Might you adopt a test that does not require proof of intent or actual effects but asks instead whether conduct even theoretically *could* exclude an equally efficient competitor from the market?[166] Would such a test be easy to apply? Might the test at least serve as a screen to get rid of implausible cases if one took

---

[163]   See, e.g., Marina Lao, Aspen Skiing and Trinko" Antitrust Intent and "Sacrifice," 73 Antitrust L.J. 171 (2005).

[164]   See, e.g., A. Douglas Melamed, Exclusive Dealing Agreements and Other Exclusionary Conduct—Are There Unifying Principles?, 73 Antitrust L. J. 375 (2006); Gregory J. Werden, Identifying Exclusionary Conduct Under Section 2: The "No Economic Sense" Test, 73 Antitrust L. J. 413 (2006).

[165]   See, Thomas G. Krattenmaker & Steven C. Salop, Anticompetitive Exclusion: Raising Rivals' Costs to Achieve Power Over Price, 96 Yale L. J. 209 (1986). A similar point had been made earlier in Janusz A. Ordover & Robert D. Willig, An Economic Definition of Predation: Pricing and Product Innovation, 91 Yale L.J. 8 (1981).

[166]   See, e.g., Richard A. Posner, Antitrust Law 194–95 (2d ed. 2001); Thomas A. Lambert, *Weyerhaeuser* and the Search for Antitrust's Holy Grail, Cato Sup. Ct. Rev. 277 (2006–2007).

it for granted that all *less-efficient* competitors *should* be eliminated from the marketplace?

5.   *Balancing Social Gains and Harms.* Might you propose a balancing test analogous to rule of reason analysis under Sherman Act § 1? Might such a test ask whether the defendant's acts impair business opportunities of its rivals that exceed corresponding benefit produced for consumers?[167]

a.   Even if such a test might theoretically produce correct answers, could it do so in the context of real litigation? Would the test provide so little advance guidance to business people that it might deter consumer-friendly competitive behavior?

b.   In the waning days of the Bush Administration, the Justice Department proposed that the law should only punish harm that is "disproportionate" to any consumer benefits achieved. Is that approach preferable to one that seeks to find the balance point between harm and benefit? A majority of FTC Commissioners refused to go along with the Department of Justice position.[168] How would you have reacted to it?

Which of these tests does the Court seem to have been applying in *Aspen Skiing, Matsushita* and *Brooke Group*? Was the analysis the same in all three cases? Might more than one of the tests seem to be consistent with the result reached in the cases?

b.   Cases Reinforcing or Developing the Current Approach

ATTEMPTED MONOPOLIZATION: THE *SPECTRUM SPORTS* CASE

What is the current status of the "attempt to monopolize" offense under Sherman Act § 2? You may remember that Swift & Co. v. United States had held in 1905 that the offense requires *both* acts done with an intent to monopolize *and* "a dangerous probability that it [achievement of a monopoly] will happen."[169]

Should a firm be guilty of an attempt to monopolize because it disables a competitor's vehicles, for example? Suppose it blows up the competitor's

---

167   See, e.g., Jeffrey L. Harrison, An Instrumental Theory of Market Power and Antitrust Policy, 59 S.M.U. L.Rev. 1673 (2006) (market power should be assessed in terms of its use to "make others better off as they improve their own positions"); Steven C. Salop, Exclusionary Conduct, Effect on Consumers, and the Flawed Profit-Sacrifice Standard, 73 Antitrust L. J. 311 (2006) (proposes a "consumer welfare" standard). Cf. Einer Elhauge, Defining Better Monopolization Standards, 56 Stanford L. Rev. 253 (2003) (calling for an "efficiency" standard).

168   See U.S. Department of Justice, Competition and Monopoly: Single-Firm Conduct Under Section 2 of the Sherman Act 45–46 (2008).

169   In an important application of this principle, the Supreme Court held that the fraudulent procurement of a patent may violate Sherman Act § 2 because the patent grants the holder a monopoly. Walker Process Equipment, Inc. v. Food Machinery & Chemical Corp., 382 U.S. 172, 86 S.Ct. 347, 15 L.Ed.2d 247 (1965).

plant? Both would clearly constitute business torts, and probably even state crimes, but should every "bad act" by which one firm tries to injure a competitor constitute a violation of Sherman Act § 2?

The Ninth Circuit seemed to answer that question affirmatively in Lessig v. Tidewater Oil Co., 327 F.2d 459 (9th Cir.1964). Lessig was a Tidewater dealer who had been terminated, allegedly because he refused to buy all his tires, batteries and accessories from Tidewater. In reversing the trial court's failure to submit the § 2 case to the jury, the Court seemed to write the "dangerous probability" requirement out of the test. The Court wrote, "specific intent itself is the only evidence of dangerous probability the statute requires—perhaps on the not unreasonable assumption that the actor is better able than others to judge the practical possibility of achieving his illegal objective."

Other circuits tended not to follow the Ninth, see, e.g., United States v. Empire Gas Corp., 537 F.2d 296 (8th Cir.1976), cert.denied 429 U.S. 1122 (1977), but the Ninth Circuit stuck to its guns lest a "firm that did not control something close to 50 percent of the entire market * * * be free to indulge in any activity, however, unreasonable, predatory, or destructive of competition * * * ." Greyhound Computer Corp. v. IBM Corp., 559 F.2d 488, 504 (9th Cir.1977), cert.denied 434 U.S. 1040 (1978).[170]

Was the Ninth Circuit right to eliminate the "dangerous probability of success" requirement? Did its elimination instead transform a world of state-remediable business torts into federal claims with potential recoveries of treble damages plus attorney's fees?[171]

The Supreme Court took up the question in 1993, shortly before it decided *Brooke Group*. In Spectrum Sports, Inc. v. McQuillan, 506 U.S. 447, 113 S.Ct. 884, 122 L.Ed.2d 247 (1993), the plaintiffs had been granted the right to distribute Sorbothane, a shock-absorbing material used in both athletic shoes and horseshoes, in the Southwest. Later, the defendant decided to establish a single national distributor for Sorbothane's uses in athletic shoes, and it asked the plaintiff to give up those rights. When the plaintiff refused, the defendant took back the rights for equestrian products as well.

The Ninth Circuit upheld a jury's verdict finding the franchise termination violated Sherman Act § 2, but the Supreme Court unanimously reversed. A firm "may not be liable for attempted

---

[170] A Commission appointed by President Carter largely endorsed the Ninth Circuit position: "Conduct that cannot serve any competitive purpose and is inherently destructive of competition in any affected market can be held to violate Section 2 without precise definition of the market affected or extensive consideration of the defendant's market position." Report to the President and the Attorney General of the National Commission for the Review of Antitrust Laws and Procedures 148 (1979).

[171] See, e.g., Daniel J. Gifford, The Role of the Ninth Circuit in the Development of the Law of Attempt to Monopolize, 61 Notre Dame L.Rev. 1021 (1986).

monopolization under § 2 of the Sherman Act absent proof of a dangerous probability that they would monopolize a particular market and specific intent to monopolize."

A court must do more than inquire "whether the defendant has engaged in 'unfair' or 'predatory' tactics. Such conduct may be sufficient to prove the necessary intent to monopolize, which is something more than an intent to compete vigorously, but demonstrating the dangerous probability of monopolization in an attempt case also requires inquiry into the relevant product and geographic market and the defendant's economic power in that market."

Are you surprised by this result? Would you have been surprised by any other?

THE SECTION 2 VERDICT AGAINST MICROSOFT

The first important case of the new century was not resolved by the Supreme Court. It was decided by the Court of Appeals for the District of Columbia Circuit in a case against a company many loved to hate. The case was United States v. Microsoft Corporation, 253 F.3d 34 (D.C. Cir. 2001) (en banc) (per curiam).

Microsoft was accused of monopolizing the "licensing of all Intel-compatible PC operating systems worldwide." Seeing the market in a way that—with the benefit of hindsight—looks naïve, the court found that Apple software was outside the market because it was "less appealing to consumers because it costs considerably more and supports fewer applications." Hand-held devices were similarly found not to represent competition for full-size personal computers.

But the court summarized the case law on monopolization in a way that was convincing and that the Supreme Court has not overturned.

> "First, to be condemned as exclusionary, a monopolist's act must have an 'anticompetitive effect.' That is, it must harm the competitive process and thereby harm consumers. In contrast, harm to one or more competitors will not suffice.

> "Second, the plaintiff, on whom the burden of proof of course rests, must demonstrate that the monopolist's conduct indeed has the requisite anticompetitive effect. In a case brought by a private plaintiff, the plaintiff must show that its injury is 'of the type that the statute was intended to forestall,' Brunswick v. Pueblo Bowl-O-Mat; no less in a case brought by the Government, it must demonstrate that the monopolist's conduct harmed competition, not just a competitor.

good 5 part test for prewriter [handwritten marginal note]

"Third, if a plaintiff successfully establishes a prima facie case under § 2 by demonstrating anticompetitive effect, then the monopolist may proffer a "procompetitive justification" for its conduct. If the monopolist asserts a procompetitive justification—a nonpretextual claim that its conduct is indeed a form of competition on the merits because it involves, for example, greater efficiency or enhanced consumer appeal—then the burden shifts back to the plaintiff to rebut that claim.

"Fourth, if the monopolist's procompetitive justification stands unrebutted, then the plaintiff must demonstrate that the anticompetitive harm of the conduct outweighs the procompetitive benefit. In cases arising under § 1 of the Sherman Act, the courts routinely apply a similar balancing approach under the rubric of the "rule of reason." The source of the rule of reason is Standard Oil Co. v. United States, in which the Supreme Court used that term to describe the proper inquiry under both sections of the Act. * * *

"Finally, in considering whether the monopolist's conduct on balance harms competition and is therefore condemned as exclusionary for purposes of § 2, our focus is upon the effect of that conduct, not upon the intent behind it. Evidence of the intent behind the conduct of a monopolist is relevant only to the extent it helps us understand the likely effect of the monopolist's conduct."

In affirming a finding that Microsoft had violated § 2, the Court of Appeals found that Microsoft required Original Equipment Manufacturers (OEMs) to pre-install Microsoft's Internet Explorer browser and thus made it too expensive for OEMs also to install a competing browser. It found that Microsoft also designed the Windows 98 operating system to make it difficult for OEMs to remove Internet Explorer and create opportunities for a competing browser. Microsoft then entered into exclusive dealing arrangements with Internet Access Providers (IAPs) like AOL that limited IAPs to offering alternative browsers to no more than 15% of their customers. All these practices tended to reduce consumer choice and impair development of competing products. — Shortsighted

Microsoft responded that it wanted to keep developers focused on Internet Explorer and not competing browsers. "That is not an unlawful end," the court said, "but neither is it a procompetitive justification." The court acknowledged that "neither plaintiffs nor the court can confidently reconstruct a [competing] product's hypothetical technological development in a world absent the defendant's exclusionary conduct." But a pattern of systematic exclusionary conduct, not justified by pro-competitive considerations, was enough to affirm a violation of § 2.

NOTES AND QUESTIONS

1. What is it about a computer operating system that makes it so hard to displace the market leader?

    a. The court described the problem as the existence of an "applications barrier to entry" in the market for operating systems. That is, programmers tend to write applications for the leading software program because that will get them the most sales. And because consumers want the applications, the process becomes a vicious circle that tends to exclude new market entrants.

    b. Assuming that story is true and such a barrier exists, it is something for which Microsoft was to blame? Did the conditions the court described mean that someone would tend to monopolize this industry, even if it were not Microsoft?[172]

2. What should Microsoft have been permitted to do when it saw public enthusiasm for the Internet in general and a competing browser in particular?

    a. Should it have been permitted to respond at all? Should a market leader's development of a competing product normally be seen as anticompetitive?

    b. What price should Microsoft have been required to charge for Internet Explorer? What was Microsoft's likely marginal cost of adding it to each new copy of its operating system? The D.C. Circuit refused to say there was any required minimum charge. Do you agree that the court was wise to stay away from prescribing minimum prices?

3. Are you convinced that consumers were directly injured by Microsoft's conduct? How serious was the burden to consumers caused by contractual limitations on OEMs' installation of a competing browser? Should the law see contractual restraints imposed on other firms as necessarily more exclusionary than internal pricing decisions that may cause other firms to leave the market? Why or why not?[173]

Thereafter, in a series of three more decisions, the Supreme Court continued imposing limits on the reach of § 2.

---

[172] See, e.g., Gregory J. Werden, Network Effects and Conditions of Entry: Lessons From the Microsoft Case, 69 Antitrust L. J. 87 (2001).

[173] See, e.g., John E. Lopatka & William H. Page, Who Suffered Antitrust Injury in the Microsoft Case?, 69 George Washington L. Rev. 829 (2001); Alan J. Meese, Monopolization, Exclusion, and the Theory of the Firm, 89 Minnesota L. Rev. 743 (2005). On the consequences of the Microsoft prosecution and the remedies imposed, see David A. Heiner, Microsoft: A Remedial Success?, 78 Antitrust L.J. 229 (2012).

VERIZON COMMUNICATIONS INC. V. LAW OFFICES OF CURTIS V. TRINKO, LLP

Supreme Court of the United States, 2004
540 U.S. 398, 124 S.Ct. 872, 157 L.Ed.2d 823

JUSTICE SCALIA delivered the opinion of the Court.

The Telecommunications Act of 1996 imposes certain duties upon incumbent local telephone companies in order to facilitate market entry by competitors, and establishes a complex regime for monitoring and enforcement. In this case we consider whether a complaint alleging breach of the incumbent's duty under the 1996 Act to share its network with competitors states a claim under § 2 of the Sherman Act.

I

Petitioner Verizon Communications Inc. is the incumbent local exchange carrier (LEC) serving New York State. Before the 1996 Act, Verizon, like other incumbent LECs, enjoyed an exclusive franchise within its local service area. The 1996 Act sought to "uproot" the incumbent LECs' monopoly and to introduce competition in its place. Verizon Communications Inc. v. FCC, 535 U.S. 467, 488, 152 L. Ed. 2d 701, 122 S.Ct. 1646 (2002). Central to the scheme of the Act is the incumbent LEC's obligation under 47 U.S.C. § 251(c) to share its network with competitors, including provision of access to individual elements of the network on an "unbundled" basis. New entrants, so-called competitive LECs, resell these unbundled network elements (UNEs), recombined with each other or with elements belonging to the LECs.

Verizon, like other incumbent LECs, has taken two significant steps within the Act's framework in the direction of increased competition. First, Verizon has signed interconnection agreements with rivals such as AT&T, as it is obliged to do under § 252, detailing the terms on which it will make its network elements available. * * * In 1997, the state regulator, New York's Public Service Commission (PSC), approved Verizon's interconnection agreement with AT&T.

Second, Verizon has taken advantage of the opportunity provided by the 1996 Act for incumbent LECs to enter the long-distance market (from which they had long been excluded). That required Verizon to satisfy, among other things, a 14-item checklist of statutory requirements, which includes compliance with the Act's network-sharing duties. Checklist item two, for example, includes "nondiscriminatory access to network elements in accordance with the requirements" of § 251(c). Whereas the state regulator approves an interconnection agreement, for long-distance approval the incumbent LEC applies to the Federal Communications Commission (FCC). In December 1999, the FCC approved Verizon's § 271 application for New York.

Part of Verizon's UNE obligation under § 251(c)(3) is the provision of access to operations support systems (OSS), a set of systems used by incumbent LECs to provide services to customers and ensure quality. Verizon's interconnection agreement and long-distance authorization each specified the mechanics by which its OSS obligation would be met. As relevant here, a competitive LEC sends orders for service through an electronic interface with Verizon's ordering system, and as Verizon completes certain steps in filling the order, it sends confirmation back through the same interface. Without OSS access a rival cannot fill its customers' orders.

In late 1999, competitive LECs complained to regulators that many orders were going unfilled, in violation of Verizon's obligation to provide access to OSS functions. The PSC and FCC opened parallel investigations, which led to a series of orders by the PSC and a consent decree with the FCC. Under the FCC consent decree, Verizon undertook to make a "voluntary contribution" to the U.S. Treasury in the amount of $3 million; under the PSC orders, Verizon incurred liability to the competitive LECs in the amount of $10 million. * * *

Respondent Law Offices of Curtis V. Trinko, LLP, a New York City law firm, was a local telephone service customer of AT&T. The day after Verizon entered its consent decree with the FCC, respondent filed a complaint in the District Court for the Southern District of New York, on behalf of itself and a class of similarly situated customers. The complaint, as later amended, alleged that Verizon had filled rivals' orders on a discriminatory basis as part of an anticompetitive scheme to discourage customers from becoming or remaining customers of competitive LECs, thus impeding the competitive LECs' ability to enter and compete in the market for local telephone service. According to the complaint, Verizon "has filled orders of [competitive LEC] customers after filling those for its own local phone service, has failed to fill in a timely manner, or not at all, a substantial number of orders for [competitive LEC] customers . . . , and has systematically failed to inform [competitive LECs] of the status of their customers' orders." * * * The complaint sought damages and injunctive relief for violation of § 2 of the Sherman Act, pursuant to the remedy provisions of §§ 4 and 16 of the Clayton Act. The complaint also alleged violations of the 1996 Act, § 202(a) of the Communications Act of 1934, and state law.

The District Court dismissed the complaint in its entirety. * * * The Court of Appeals for the Second Circuit reinstated the * * * antitrust claim. * * *

II

To decide this case, we must first determine what effect (if any) the 1996 Act has upon the application of traditional antitrust principles. The

Act imposes a large number of duties upon incumbent LECs—above and beyond those basic responsibilities it imposes upon all carriers, such as assuring number portability and providing access to rights-of-way. Under the sharing duties of § 251(c), incumbent LECs are required to offer three kinds of access. Already noted, and perhaps most intrusive, is the duty to offer access to UNEs on "just, reasonable, and nondiscriminatory" terms, a phrase that the FCC has interpreted to mean a price reflecting long-run incremental cost. A rival can interconnect its own facilities with those of the incumbent LEC, or it can simply purchase services at wholesale from the incumbent and resell them to consumers. The Act also imposes upon incumbents the duty to allow physical "collocation"—that is, to permit a competitor to locate and install its equipment on the incumbent's premises—which makes feasible interconnection and access to UNEs.

That Congress created these duties, however, does not automatically lead to the conclusion that they can be enforced by means of an antitrust claim. Indeed, a detailed regulatory scheme such as that created by the 1996 Act ordinarily raises the question whether the regulated entities are not shielded from antitrust scrutiny altogether by the doctrine of implied immunity. In some respects the enforcement scheme set up by the 1996 Act is a good candidate for implication of antitrust immunity, to avoid the real possibility of judgments conflicting with the agency's regulatory scheme "that might be voiced by courts exercising jurisdiction under the antitrust laws." United States v. National Ass'n. of Sec. Dealers, Inc., 422 U.S. 694, 45 L. Ed. 2d 486, 95 S.Ct. 2427 (1975).

Congress, however, precluded that interpretation. Section 601(b)(1) of the 1996 Act is an antitrust-specific saving clause providing that "nothing in this Act or the amendments made by this Act shall be construed to modify, impair, or supersede the applicability of any of the antitrust laws." This bars a finding of implied immunity. As the FCC has put the point, the saving clause preserves those "claims that satisfy established antitrust standards."

But just as the 1996 Act preserves claims that satisfy existing antitrust standards, it does not create new claims that go beyond existing antitrust standards; that would be equally inconsistent with the saving clause's mandate that nothing in the Act "modify, impair, or supersede the applicability" of the antitrust laws. We turn, then, to whether the activity of which respondent complains violates preexisting antitrust standards.

III

The complaint alleges that Verizon denied interconnection services to rivals in order to limit entry. If that allegation states an antitrust claim at all, it does so under § 2 of the Sherman Act, which declares that a firm shall not "monopolize" or "attempt to monopolize." It is settled law that this offense requires, in addition to the possession of monopoly power in the relevant market, "the willful acquisition or maintenance of that power as distinguished from growth or development as a consequence of a superior product, business acumen, or historic accident." United States v. Grinnell Corp. The mere possession of monopoly power, and the concomitant charging of monopoly prices, is not only not unlawful; it is an important element of the free-market system. The opportunity to charge monopoly prices—at least for a short period—is what attracts "business acumen" in the first place; it induces risk taking that produces innovation and economic growth. To safeguard the incentive to innovate, the possession of monopoly power will not be found unlawful unless it is accompanied by an element of anticompetitive *conduct.*

Firms may acquire monopoly power by establishing an infrastructure that renders them uniquely suited to serve their customers. Compelling such firms to share the source of their advantage is in some tension with the underlying purpose of antitrust law, since it may lessen the incentive for the monopolist, the rival, or both to invest in those economically beneficial facilities. Enforced sharing also requires antitrust courts to act as central planners, identifying the proper price, quantity, and other terms of dealing—a role for which they are ill-suited. Moreover, compelling negotiation between competitors may facilitate the supreme evil of antitrust: collusion. Thus, as a general matter, the Sherman Act "does not restrict the long recognized right of [a] trader or manufacturer engaged in an entirely private business, freely to exercise his own independent discretion as to parties with whom he will deal." United States v. Colgate & Co.

However, "the high value that we have placed on the right to refuse to deal with other firms does not mean that the right is unqualified." Aspen Skiing Co. v. Aspen Highlands Skiing Corp. Under certain circumstances, a refusal to cooperate with rivals can constitute anticompetitive conduct and violate § 2. We have been very cautious in recognizing such exceptions, because of the uncertain virtue of forced sharing and the difficulty of identifying and remedying anticompetitive conduct by a single firm. The question before us today is whether the allegations of respondent's complaint fit within existing exceptions or provide a basis, under traditional antitrust principles, for recognizing a new one.

The leading case for § 2 liability based on refusal to cooperate with a rival, and the case upon which respondent understandably places greatest reliance, is *Aspen Skiing.* * * *

Aspen Skiing is at or near the outer boundary of § 2 liability. The Court there found significance in the defendant's decision to cease participation in a cooperative venture. The unilateral termination of a voluntary (*and thus presumably profitable*) course of dealing suggested a willingness to forsake short-term profits to achieve an anticompetitive end. Similarly, the defendant's unwillingness to renew the ticket *even if compensated at retail price* revealed a distinctly anticompetitive bent.

The refusal to deal alleged in the present case does not fit within the limited exception recognized in *Aspen Skiing*. The complaint does not allege that Verizon voluntarily engaged in a course of dealing with its rivals, or would ever have done so absent statutory compulsion. Here, therefore, the defendant's prior conduct sheds no light upon the motivation of its refusal to deal—upon whether its regulatory lapses were prompted not by competitive zeal but by anticompetitive malice. The contrast between the cases is heightened by the difference in pricing behavior. In *Aspen Skiing*, the defendant turned down a proposal to sell at its own retail price, suggesting a calculation that its future monopoly retail price would be higher. Verizon's reluctance to interconnect at the cost-based rate of compensation available under § 251(c)(3) tells us nothing about dreams of monopoly.

The specific nature of what the 1996 Act compels makes this case different from *Aspen Skiing* in a more fundamental way. In *Aspen Skiing*, what the defendant refused to provide to its competitor was a product that it already sold at retail—to oversimplify slightly, lift tickets representing a bundle of services to skiers. * * * In the present case, by contrast, the services allegedly withheld are not otherwise marketed or available to the public. The sharing obligation imposed by the 1996 Act created "something brand new"—"the wholesale market for leasing network elements." The unbundled elements offered pursuant to § 251(c)(3) exist only deep within the bowels of Verizon; they are brought out on compulsion of the 1996 Act and offered not to consumers but to rivals, and at considerable expense and effort. New systems must be designed and implemented simply to make that access possible—indeed, it is the failure of one of those systems that prompted the present complaint.[174]

We conclude that Verizon's alleged insufficient assistance in the provision of service to rivals is not a recognized antitrust claim under this Court's existing refusal-to-deal precedents. This conclusion would be unchanged even if we considered to be established law the "essential facilities" doctrine crafted by some lower courts, under which the Court of Appeals concluded respondent's allegations might state a claim. See generally Areeda, Essential Facilities: An Epithet in Need of Limiting Principles, 58 Antitrust L. J. 841 (1989). We have never recognized such a doctrine, and we find no need either to recognize it or to repudiate it here. It suffices for present purposes to note that the indispensable requirement

---

[174] Respondent also relies upon United States v. Terminal R. Ass'n, 224 U.S. 383, 56 L.Ed. 810, 32 S.Ct. 507 (1912), and Associated Press v. United States, 326 U.S. 1, 89 L.Ed. 2013, 65 S.Ct. 1416 (1945). These cases involved *concerted* action, which presents greater anticompetitive concerns and is amenable to a remedy that does not require judicial estimation of free-market forces: simply requiring that the outsider be granted nondiscriminatory admission to the club. [Court's fn. 3]

for invoking the doctrine is the unavailability of access to the "essential facilities"; where access exists, the doctrine serves no purpose. Thus, it is said that "essential facility claims should . . . be denied where a state or federal agency has effective power to compel sharing and to regulate its scope and terms." P. Areeda & H. Hovenkamp, Antitrust Law, p. 150, P773e (2003 Supp.). Respondent believes that the existence of sharing duties under the 1996 Act supports its case. We think the opposite: The 1996 Act's extensive provision for access makes it unnecessary to impose a judicial doctrine of forced access. To the extent respondent's "essential facilities" argument is distinct from its general § 2 argument, we reject it.

IV

Finally, we do not believe that traditional antitrust principles justify adding the present case to the few existing exceptions from the proposition that there is no duty to aid competitors. Antitrust analysis must always be attuned to the particular structure and circumstances of the industry at issue. Part of that attention to economic context is an awareness of the significance of regulation. * * * "Antitrust analysis must sensitively recognize and reflect the distinctive economic and legal setting of the regulated industry to which it applies." Concord v. Boston Edison Co., 915 F.2d 17, 22 (1st Cir. 1990) (Breyer, C. J.).

One factor of particular importance is the existence of a regulatory structure designed to deter and remedy anticompetitive harm. Where such a structure exists, the additional benefit to competition provided by antitrust enforcement will tend to be small, and it will be less plausible that the antitrust laws contemplate such additional scrutiny. Where, by contrast, "there is nothing built into the regulatory scheme which performs the antitrust function," Silver v. New York Stock Exchange, the benefits of antitrust are worth its sometimes considerable disadvantages. Just as regulatory context may in other cases serve as a basis for implied immunity, it may also be a consideration in deciding whether to recognize an expansion of the contours of § 2.

The regulatory framework that exists in this case demonstrates how, in certain circumstances, "regulation significantly diminishes the likelihood of major antitrust harm." Concord v. Boston Edison Co. Consider, for example, the statutory restrictions upon Verizon's entry into the potentially lucrative market for long-distance service. To be allowed to enter the long-distance market in the first place, an incumbent LEC must be on good behavior in its local market. Authorization by the FCC requires state-by-state satisfaction of § 271's competitive checklist, which as we have noted includes the nondiscriminatory provision of access to UNEs. Section 271 applications to provide long-distance service have now been approved for incumbent LECs in 47 States and the District of Columbia.

The FCC's § 271 authorization order for Verizon to provide long-distance service in New York discussed at great length Verizon's commitments to provide access to UNEs, including the provision of OSS. Those commitments are enforceable by the FCC through continuing oversight; a failure to meet an authorization condition can result in an order that the deficiency be corrected, in the imposition of penalties, or in the suspension or revocation of long-distance approval. See 47 U.S.C. § 271(d)(6)(A). Verizon also subjected itself to oversight by the PSC under a so-called "Performance Assurance Plan" (PAP). The PAP, which by its terms became binding upon FCC approval, provides specific financial penalties in the event of Verizon's failure to achieve detailed performance requirements. The FCC described Verizon's having entered into a PAP as a significant factor in its § 271 authorization, because that provided "a strong financial incentive for post-entry compliance with the section 271 checklist," and prevented " 'backsliding.' "

The regulatory response to the OSS failure complained of in respondent's suit provides a vivid example of how the regulatory regime operates. When several competitive LECs complained about deficiencies in Verizon's servicing of orders, the FCC and PSC responded. The FCC soon concluded that Verizon was in breach of its sharing duties under § 251(c), imposed a substantial fine, and set up sophisticated measurements to gauge remediation, with weekly reporting requirements and specific penalties for failure. The PSC found Verizon in violation of the PAP even earlier, and imposed additional financial penalties and measurements with *daily* reporting requirements. In short, the regime was an effective steward of the antitrust function.

Against the slight benefits of antitrust intervention here, we must weigh a realistic assessment of its costs. Under the best of circumstances, applying the requirements of § 2 "can be difficult" because "the means of illicit exclusion, like the means of legitimate competition, are myriad." United States v. Microsoft Corp. (D.C. Cir. 2001) (en banc) (per curiam). Mistaken inferences and the resulting false condemnations "are especially costly, because they chill the very conduct the antitrust laws are designed to protect." Matsushita Elec. Industrial Co. v. Zenith Radio Corp. The cost of false positives counsels against an undue expansion of § 2 liability. One false-positive risk is that an incumbent LEC's failure to provide a service with sufficient alacrity might have nothing to do with exclusion. Allegations of violations of § 251(c)(3) duties are difficult for antitrust courts to evaluate, not only because they are highly technical, but also because they are likely to be extremely numerous, given the incessant, complex, and constantly changing interaction of competitive and incumbent LECs implementing the sharing and interconnection obligations. *Amici* States have filed a brief asserting that competitive LECs are threatened with "death by a thousand cuts,"—identification of which would surely be a daunting task for a generalist antitrust court. Judicial oversight under the Sherman Act would seem destined to distort investment and lead to a new layer of interminable litigation, atop the variety of litigation routes already available to and actively pursued by competitive LECs.

Even if the problem of false positives did not exist, conduct consisting of anticompetitive violations of § 251 may be, as we have concluded with respect to above-cost predatory pricing schemes, "beyond the practical ability of a judicial tribunal to control." Brooke Group Ltd. v. Brown & Williamson Tobacco Corp. Effective remediation of violations of regulatory sharing requirements will ordinarily require continuing supervision of a highly detailed decree. We think that Professor Areeda got it exactly right: "No court should impose a duty to deal that it cannot explain or adequately and reasonably supervise. The problem should be deemed irremediable by antitrust law when compulsory access requires the court to assume the day-to-day controls characteristic of a regulatory agency." Areeda, 58 Antitrust L. J., at 853. In this case, respondent has requested an equitable decree to "preliminarily and permanently enjoin [Verizon] from providing access to the local loop market . . . to [rivals] on terms and conditions that are not as favorable" as those that Verizon enjoys. An antitrust court is unlikely to be an effective day-to-day enforcer of these detailed sharing obligations.

The 1996 Act is in an important respect much more ambitious than the antitrust laws. It attempts *to eliminate the monopolies enjoyed by the inheritors of AT&T's local franchises.*" Verizon Communications Inc. v. FCC (emphasis added). Section 2 of the Sherman Act, by contrast, seeks merely to prevent *unlawful monopolization.* It would be a serious mistake to conflate the two goals. The Sherman Act is indeed the "Magna Carta of free enterprise," United States v. Topco Associates, Inc., but it does not give judges *carte blanche* to insist that a monopolist alter its way of doing business whenever some other approach might yield greater competition. We conclude that respondent's complaint fails to state a claim under the Sherman Act.

Accordingly, the judgment of the Court of Appeals is reversed, and the case is remanded for further proceedings consistent with this opinion.

[The opinion of Justices STEVENS, SOUTER AND THOMAS, concurring in the judgment, but finding that the plaintiff-respondent lacked standing, is omitted.]

NOTES AND QUESTIONS

1.   The first point this case illustrates is that federal regulatory policy often builds upon insights developed in antitrust cases. Were you surprised to

see the telecommunications industry being treated as capable of extensive competition? Indeed, is it an even more competitive industry today?

2. Do you agree that a plaintiff in an antitrust case should not be able to cite violations of regulatory requirements as part of the antitrust claim? Why shouldn't Congress' action in passing the Telecommunication Act be deemed a useful construction of antitrust policy for this industry?

3. Is the Court here limiting the reach of the antitrust law that seemed to have been created in *Aspen Skiing*? Is the limitation useful? Was it long overdue? If you were in Congress, would you try to amend § 2 to restore the significance of *Aspen* and its restriction of single-firm refusals to deal?

4. Has the Court read the "essential facilities" doctrine out of antitrust law? If so, was that a good idea? Has the Court left a vestige of the doctrine for really appropriate cases? What do you understand the Court's current standard to be?

5. Were you surprised that the Court not only did not condemn monopoly power, but explicitly praised it? "[P]ossession of monopoly power and the concomitant charging of monopoly prices, is not only not unlawful," the Court said. "[I]t is an important element of the free market system. The opportunity to charge monopoly prices—at least for a short period—is what attracts business acumen in the first place; it induces risk taking that produces innovation and economic growth." Do you agree that the right to achieve monopoly status is an essential element of creating an incentive to innovate?[175]

Most of the cases we have seen to date have involved sellers with market power. Should the analysis be different if a case involves an alleged power buyer? That is the subject of our next case.

WEYERHAEUSER CO. V. ROSS-SIMMONS HARDWOOD

Supreme Court of the United States, 2007
549 U.S. 312, 127 S.Ct. 1069, 166 L.Ed.2d 911

JUSTICE THOMAS delivered the opinion of the Court.

Respondent Ross-Simmons, a sawmill, sued petitioner Weyerhaeuser, alleging that Weyerhaeuser drove it out of business by bidding up the price of sawlogs to a level that prevented Ross-Simmons from being profitable. A jury returned a verdict in favor of Ross-Simmons on its monopolization claim, and the Ninth Circuit affirmed. We granted certiorari to decide whether the test we applied to claims of predatory pricing in Brooke Group Ltd. v. Brown & Williamson Tobacco Corp. also applies to claims of

---

[175] See, e.g., Spencer Weber Waller, *Microsoft* and *Trinko*: A Tale of Two Courts, 2006 Utah L. Rev. 741 (2006).

predatory bidding. We hold that it does. Accordingly, we vacate the judgment of the Court of Appeals.

I

This antitrust case concerns the acquisition of red alder sawlogs by the mills that process those logs in the Pacific Northwest. These hardwood-lumber mills usually acquire logs in one of three ways. Some logs are purchased on the open bidding market. Some come to the mill through standing short-and long-term agreements with timberland owners. And others are harvested from timberland owned by the sawmills themselves. The allegations relevant to our decision in this case relate to the bidding market.

Ross-Simmons began operating a hardwood-lumber sawmill in Longview, Washington, in 1962. Weyerhaeuser entered the Northwestern hardwood-lumber market in 1980 by acquiring an existing lumber company. Weyerhaeuser gradually increased the scope of its hardwood-lumber operation, and it now owns six hardwood sawmills in the region. By 2001, Weyerhaeuser's mills were acquiring approximately 65 percent of the alder logs available for sale in the region.

From 1990 to 2000, Weyerhaeuser made more than $75 million in capital investments in its hardwood mills in the Pacific Northwest. During this period, production increased at every Northwestern hardwood mill that Weyerhaeuser owned. In addition to increasing production, Weyerhaeuser used "state-of-the-art technology," including sawing equipment, to increase the amount of lumber recovered from every log. By contrast, Ross-Simmons appears to have engaged in little efficiency-enhancing investment.

Logs represent up to 75 percent of a sawmill's total costs. And from 1998 to 2001, the price of alder sawlogs increased while prices for finished hardwood lumber fell. These divergent trends in input and output prices cut into the mills' profit margins, and Ross-Simmons suffered heavy losses during this time. Saddled with several million dollars in debt, Ross-Simmons shut down its mill completely in May 2001.

Ross-Simmons blamed Weyerhaeuser for driving it out of business by bidding up input costs, and it filed an antitrust suit against Weyerhaeuser for monopolization and attempted monopolization under § 2 of the Sherman Act. Ross-Simmons alleged that, among other anticompetitive acts, Weyerhaeuser had used "its dominant position in the alder sawlog market to drive up the prices for alder sawlogs to levels that severely reduced or eliminated the profit margins of Weyerhaeuser's alder sawmill competition." Proceeding in part on this "predatory-bidding" theory, Ross-Simmons argued that Weyerhaeuser had overpaid for alder sawlogs to cause sawlog prices to rise to artificially high levels as part of a plan to drive Ross-Simmons out of business. As proof that this practice had occurred, Ross-Simmons pointed to Weyerhaeuser's large share of the alder purchasing market, rising alder sawlog prices during the alleged predation period, and Weyerhaeuser's declining profits during that same period.

Prior to trial, Weyerhaeuser moved for summary judgment on Ross-Simmons' predatory-bidding theory. The District Court denied the motion. At the close of the 9-day trial, Weyerhaeuser moved for judgment as a matter of law, or alternatively, for a new trial. The motions were based in part on Weyerhaeuser's argument that Ross-Simmons had not satisfied the standard this Court set forth in *Brooke Group*. The District Court denied Weyerhaeuser's motion. The District Court also rejected proposed predatory-bidding jury instructions that incorporated elements of the *Brooke Group* test. Ultimately, the District Court instructed the jury that Ross-Simmons could prove that Weyerhaeuser's bidding practices were anticompetitive acts if the jury concluded that Weyerhaeuser "purchased more logs than it needed, or paid a higher price for logs than necessary, in order to prevent [Ross-Simmons] from obtaining the logs they needed at a fair price." Finding that Ross-Simmons had proved its claim for monopolization, the jury returned a $26 million verdict against Weyerhaeuser. The verdict was trebled to approximately $79 million.

Weyerhaeuser appealed to the Court of Appeals for the Ninth Circuit. There, Weyerhaeuser argued that *Brooke Group's* standard for claims of predatory pricing should also apply to claims of predatory bidding. The Ninth Circuit disagreed and affirmed the verdict against Weyerhaeuser.

The Court of Appeals reasoned that "buy-side predatory bidding" and "sell-side predatory pricing," though similar, are materially different in that predatory bidding does not necessarily benefit consumers or stimulate competition in the way that predatory pricing does. Concluding that "the concerns that led the *Brooke Group* Court to establish a high standard of liability in the predatory-pricing context do not carry over to this predatory bidding context with the same force," the Court of Appeals declined to apply *Brooke Group* to Ross-Simmons' claims of predatory bidding. * * * We granted certiorari to decide whether *Brooke Group* applies to claims of predatory bidding. We hold that it does, and we vacate the Court of Appeals' judgment.

II

In *Brooke Group,* we considered what a plaintiff must show in order to succeed on a claim of predatory pricing under § 2 of the Sherman Act.[176] In a typical predatory-pricing scheme, the predator reduces the sale price of its product (its output) to below cost, hoping to drive competitors out of

---

[176] *Brooke Group* dealt with a claim under the Robinson-Patman Act, but as we observed, "primary-line competitive injury under the Robinson-Patman Act is of the same general character as the injury inflicted by predatory pricing schemes actionable under § 2 of the Sherman Act." Because of this similarity, the standard adopted in *Brooke Group* applies to predatory-pricing claims under § 2 of the Sherman Act. [Court's fn. 1]

business. Then, with competition vanquished, the predator raises output prices to a supracompetitive level. For the scheme to make economic sense, the losses suffered from pricing goods below cost must be recouped (with interest) during the supracompetitive-pricing stage of the scheme. Recognizing this economic reality, we established two prerequisites to recovery on claims of predatory pricing. "First, a plaintiff seeking to establish competitive injury resulting from a rival's low prices must prove that the prices complained of are below an appropriate measure of its rival's costs." Second, a plaintiff must demonstrate that "the competitor had . . . a dangerous probabilit[y] of recouping its investment in below-cost prices."

The first prong of the test-requiring that prices be below cost-is necessary because "[a]s a general rule, the exclusionary effect of prices above a relevant measure of cost either reflects the lower cost structure of the alleged predator, and so represents competition on the merits, or is beyond the practical ability of a judicial tribunal to control." We were particularly wary of allowing recovery for above-cost price cutting because allowing such claims could, perversely, "chil[l] legitimate price cutting," which directly benefits consumers. Thus, we specifically declined to allow plaintiffs to recover for above-cost price cutting, concluding that "discouraging a price cut and . . . depriving consumers of the benefits of lower prices . . . does not constitute sound antitrust policy."

The second prong of the *Brooke Group* test—requiring that there be a dangerous probability of recoupment of losses—is necessary because, without a dangerous probability of recoupment, it is highly unlikely that a firm would engage in predatory pricing. As the Court explained in *Matsushita,* a firm engaged in a predatory-pricing scheme makes an investment-the losses suffered plus the profits that would have been realized absent the scheme-at the initial, below-cost-selling phase. For that investment to be rational, a firm must reasonably expect to recoup in the long run at least its original investment with supracompetitive profits. Without such a reasonable expectation, a rational firm would not willingly suffer definite, short-run losses. Recognizing the centrality of recoupment to a predatory-pricing scheme, we required predatory-pricing plaintiffs to "demonstrate that there is a likelihood that the predatory scheme alleged would cause a rise in prices above a competitive level that would be sufficient to compensate for the amounts expended on the predation, including the time value of the money invested in it."

We described the two parts of the *Brooke Group* test as "essential components of real market injury" that were "not easy to establish." We also reiterated that the costs of erroneous findings of predatory-pricing liability were quite high because " '[t]he mechanism by which a firm engages in predatory pricing-lowering prices-is the same mechanism by which a firm stimulates competition,' " and therefore, mistaken findings of liability would " 'chill the very conduct the antitrust laws are designed to protect.' "

III

Predatory bidding, which Ross-Simmons alleges in this case, involves the exercise of market power on the buy side or input side of a market. In a predatory-bidding scheme, a purchaser of inputs "bids up the market price of a critical input to such high levels that rival buyers cannot survive (or compete as vigorously) and, as a result, the predating buyer acquires (or maintains or increases its) monopsony power." Kirkwood, Buyer Power and Exclusionary Conduct, 72 Antitrust L.J. 625, 652 (2005). Monopsony power is market power on the buy side of the market. As such, a monopsony is to the buy side of the market what a monopoly is to the sell side and is sometimes colloquially called a "buyer's monopoly."

A predatory bidder ultimately aims to exercise the monopsony power gained from bidding up input prices. To that end, once the predatory bidder has caused competing buyers to exit the market for purchasing inputs, it will seek to "restrict its input purchases below the competitive level," thus "reduc[ing] the unit price for the remaining input[s] it purchases." The reduction in input prices will lead to "a significant cost saving that more than offsets the profit[s] that would have been earned on the output." If all goes as planned, the predatory bidder will reap monopsonistic profits that will offset any losses suffered in bidding up input prices. (In this case, the plaintiff was the defendant's competitor in the input-purchasing market. Thus, this case does not present a situation of suppliers suing a monopsonist buyer under § 2 of the Sherman Act, nor does it present a risk of significantly increased concentration in the market in which the monopsonist sells, *i.e.,* the market for finished lumber.)

IV

A

Predatory-pricing and predatory-bidding claims are analytically similar. This similarity results from the close theoretical connection between monopoly and monopsony. The kinship between monopoly and monopsony suggests that similar legal standards should apply to claims of monopolization and to claims of monopsonization.

Tracking the economic similarity between monopoly and monopsony, predatory-pricing plaintiffs and predatory-bidding plaintiffs make strikingly similar allegations. A predatory-pricing plaintiff alleges that a predator cut prices to drive the plaintiff out of business and, thereby, to reap monopoly profits from the output market. In parallel fashion, a predatory-bidding plaintiff alleges that a predator raised prices for a key input to drive the plaintiff out of business and, thereby, to reap monopsony profits in the input market. Both claims involve the deliberate use of unilateral pricing measures for anticompetitive purposes.[177] And both claims logically require firms to incur short-term losses on the chance that they might reap supracompetitive profits in the future.

B

More importantly, predatory bidding mirrors predatory pricing in respects that we deemed significant to our analysis in *Brooke Group*. In *Brooke Group*, we noted that " 'predatory pricing schemes are rarely tried, and even more rarely successful.' " Predatory pricing requires a firm to suffer certain losses in the short term on the chance of reaping supracompetitive profits in the future. A rational business will rarely make this sacrifice. The same reasoning applies to predatory bidding. A predatory-bidding scheme requires a buyer of inputs to suffer losses today on the chance that it will reap supracompetitive profits in the future. For this reason, "[s]uccessful monopsony predation is probably as unlikely as successful monopoly predation." R. Blair & J. Harrison, Monopsony 66 (1993).

And like the predatory conduct alleged in *Brooke Group*, actions taken in a predatory-bidding scheme are often " 'the very essence of competition.' " Just as sellers use output prices to compete for purchasers, buyers use bid prices to compete for scarce inputs. There are myriad legitimate reasons—ranging from benign to affirmatively procompetitive— why a buyer might bid up input prices. A firm might bid up inputs as a result of miscalculation of its input needs or as a response to increased consumer demand for its outputs. A more efficient firm might bid up input prices to acquire more inputs as a part of a procompetitive strategy to gain market share in the output market. A firm that has adopted an input-intensive production process might bid up inputs to acquire the inputs necessary for its process. Or a firm might bid up input prices to acquire excess inputs as a hedge against the risk of future rises in input costs or future input shortages. There is nothing illicit about these bidding decisions. Indeed, this sort of high bidding is essential to competition and innovation on the buy side of the market.

Brooke Group also noted that a failed predatory-pricing scheme may benefit consumers. The potential benefit results from the difficulty an aspiring predator faces in recouping losses suffered from below-cost pricing. Without successful recoupment, "predatory pricing produces lower aggregate prices in the market, and consumer welfare is enhanced." Failed

---

[177] Predatory bidding on inputs is not analytically different from predatory overbuying of inputs. Both practices fall under the rubric of monopsony predation and involve an input purchaser's use of input prices in an attempt to exclude rival input purchasers. The economic effect of the practices is identical: input prices rise. In a predatory-bidding scheme, the purchaser causes prices to rise by offering to pay more for inputs. In a predatory-overbuying scheme, the purchaser causes prices to rise by demanding more of the input. Either way, input prices increase. Our use of the term "predatory bidding" is not meant to suggest that different legal treatment is appropriate for the economically identical practice of "predatory overbuying." [Court's fn. 3]

predatory-bidding schemes can also, but will not necessarily, benefit consumers. In the first stage of a predatory-bidding scheme, the predator's high bidding will likely lead to its acquisition of more inputs. Usually, the acquisition of more inputs leads to the manufacture of more outputs. And increases in output generally result in lower prices to consumers.[178] Thus, a failed predatory-bidding scheme can be a "boon to in the same way that we considered a predatory-pricing scheme to be. See *Brooke Group.*

In addition, predatory bidding presents less of a direct threat of consumer harm than predatory pricing. A predatory-pricing scheme ultimately achieves success by charging higher prices to consumers. By contrast, a predatory-bidding scheme could succeed with little or no effect on consumer prices because a predatory bidder does not necessarily rely on raising prices in the output market to recoup its losses. Even if output prices remain constant, a predatory bidder can use its power as the predominant buyer of inputs to force down input prices and capture monopsony profits.

C

The general theoretical similarities of monopoly and monopsony combined with the theoretical and practical similarities of predatory pricing and predatory bidding convince us that our two-pronged *Brooke Group* test should apply to predatory-bidding claims.

The first prong of *Brooke Group's* test requires little adaptation for the predatory-bidding context. A plaintiff must prove that the alleged predatory bidding led to below-cost pricing of the predator's outputs. That is, the predator's bidding on the buy side must have caused the cost of the relevant output to rise above the revenues generated in the sale of those outputs. As with predatory pricing, the exclusionary effect of higher bidding that does not result in below-cost output pricing "is beyond the practical ability of a judicial tribunal to control without courting intolerable risks of chilling legitimate" procompetitive conduct. Given the multitude of procompetitive ends served by higher bidding for inputs, the risk of chilling procompetitive behavior with too lax a liability standard is as serious here as it was in *Brooke Group.* Consequently, only higher bidding that leads to below-cost pricing in the relevant output market will suffice as a basis for liability for predatory bidding.

A predatory-bidding plaintiff also must prove that the defendant has a dangerous probability of recouping the losses incurred in bidding up input prices through the exercise of monopsony power. Absent proof of likely recoupment, a strategy of predatory bidding makes no economic

---

[178] Consumer benefit does not necessarily result at the first stage because the predator might not use its excess inputs to manufacture additional outputs. It might instead destroy the excess inputs. Also, if the same firms compete in the input and output markets, any increase in outputs by the predator could be offset by decreases in outputs from the predator's struggling competitors. [Court's fn. 5]

sense because it would involve short-term losses with no likelihood of offsetting long-term gains. As with predatory pricing, making a showing on the recoupment prong will require "a close analysis of both the scheme alleged by the plaintiff and the structure and conditions of the relevant market." *Brooke Group.*

Ross-Simmons has conceded that it has not satisfied the *Brooke Group* standard. Therefore, its predatory-bidding theory of liability cannot support the jury's verdict.

NOTES AND QUESTIONS

1. Were you surprised that this opinion was unanimous? Does it tend to confirm that *Brooke Group* stated the proper analysis of predatory pricing cases, no matter the form in which they arise?

2. Was there any merit at all to the Ninth Circuit's argument that a large buyer's efforts to obtain control over supply only raises prices to consumers? Might the conduct be seen as a classic example of raising rivals' costs and thus as a basis for serious antitrust concern?

3. Did the Court convince you that arguably predatory buying might allow a firm to plan its production more efficiently or otherwise produce benefits for consumers? Should a defendant be required to prove that its conduct made good business sense?

4. Should a company like Wal-Mart be seen to violate the antitrust laws when it forces suppliers to offer it lower and lower prices that it can then pass on to the consumer? Does there come a time when pressures to send work abroad, possibly cut corners on safety, and the like, should be seen as relevant in antitrust cases.[179]

5. Is part of the problem in these cases that courts are not good at determining what makes business sense and good social policy? Is the "possible recoupment" standard simply a surrogate for an inquiry that would otherwise need to be much more detailed, expensive and controversial?

———————

What do *Trinko* and *Weyerhaeuser* tell us about whether it is an antitrust violation for a seller to impose unfair terms of dealing on a buyer where the seller has no duty apart from a regulatory statute to deal with the buyer at all?

---

[179] An entire issue of The Antitrust Bulletin is devoted to possible problems arising from the conduct of "power buyers." See 53 Antitrust Bull. 233–474 (2008). Cf., Barry C. Lynn, Breaking the Chain: The Antitrust Case Against Wal-Mart, Harper's, July 2006, p. 29.

PACIFIC BELL v. LINKLINE COMMUNICATIONS

Supreme Court of the United States, 2009
555 U.S. 438, 129 S.Ct. 1109, 172 L.Ed.2d 836

CHIEF JUSTICE ROBERTS delivered the opinion of the Court.

The plaintiffs in this case, respondents here, allege that a competitor subjected them to a price squeeze in violation of § 2 of the Sherman Act. They assert that such a claim can arise when a vertically integrated firm sells inputs at wholesale and also sells finished goods or services at retail. If that firm has power in the wholesale market, it can simultaneously raise the wholesale price of inputs and cut the retail price of the finished good. This will have the effect of "squeezing" the profit margins of any competitors in the retail market. Those firms will have to pay more for the inputs they need; at the same time, they will have to cut their retail prices to match the other firm's prices. The question before us is whether such a price-squeeze claim may be brought under § 2 of the Sherman Act when the defendant is under no antitrust obligation to sell the inputs to the plaintiff in the first place. We hold that no such claim may be brought.

I

This case involves the market for digital subscriber line (DSL) service, which is a method of connecting to the Internet at high speeds over telephone lines. AT&T owns much of the infrastructure and facilities needed to provide DSL service in California. In particular, AT&T controls most of what is known as the "last mile"—the lines that connect homes and businesses to the telephone network. Competing DSL providers must generally obtain access to AT&T's facilities in order to serve their customers.

* * *

The plaintiffs are four independent Internet service providers (ISPs) that compete with AT&T in the retail DSL market. Plaintiffs do not own all the facilities needed to supply their customers with this service. They instead lease DSL transport service from AT&T pursuant to the merger conditions described above. AT&T thus participates in the DSL market at both the wholesale and retail levels; it provides plaintiffs and other independent ISPs with wholesale DSL transport service, and it also sells DSL service directly to consumers at retail.

In July 2003, the plaintiffs brought suit in District Court, alleging that AT&T violated § 2 of the Sherman Act, by monopolizing the DSL market in California. The complaint alleges that AT&T refused to deal with the plaintiffs, denied the plaintiffs access to essential facilities, and engaged in a price squeeze. Specifically, plaintiffs contend that AT&T squeezed their profit margins by setting a high wholesale price for DSL transport and a low retail price for DSL Internet service. * * *

In Verizon Communications Inc. v. Law Offices of Curtis V. Trinko, LLP, we held that a firm with no antitrust duty to deal with its rivals at all is under no obligation to provide those rivals with a sufficient level of service. * * * The District Court held [in this case] that AT&T had no antitrust duty to deal with the plaintiffs, but it denied the motion to dismiss with respect to the price-squeeze claims. The court acknowledged that AT&T's argument "has a certain logic to it," but held that *Trinko* "simply does not involve price-squeeze claims." The District Court also noted that price-squeeze claims have been recognized by several Circuits and "are cognizable under existing antitrust standards."

* * *

On interlocutory appeal, the Court of Appeals for the Ninth Circuit * * * emphasized that "*Trinko* did not involve a price squeezing theory." Because "a price squeeze theory formed part of the fabric of traditional antitrust law prior to *Trinko*," the Court of Appeals concluded that "those claims should remain viable notwithstanding either the telecommunications statutes or *Trinko*." Based on the record before it, the court held that plaintiffs' original complaint stated a potentially valid claim under § 2 of the Sherman Act.

Judge Gould dissented, noting that "the notion of a 'price squeeze' is itself in a squeeze between two recent Supreme Court precedents." A price-squeeze claim involves allegations of both a high wholesale price and a low retail price, so Judge Gould analyzed each component separately. He concluded that "*Trinko* insulates from antitrust review the setting of the upstream price." With respect to the downstream price, he argued that "the retail side of a price squeeze cannot be considered to create an antitrust violation if the retail pricing does not satisfy the requirements of *Brooke Group,* which set unmistakable limits on what can be considered to be predatory within the meaning of the antitrust laws." Judge Gould concluded that the plaintiffs' complaint did not satisfy these requirements because it contained no allegations that the retail price was set below cost and that those losses could later be recouped. * * *

We granted certiorari to resolve a conflict over whether a plaintiff can bring price-squeeze claims under § 2 of the Sherman Act when the defendant has no antitrust duty to deal with the plaintiff. We reverse.

* * *

III

A

* * * Simply possessing monopoly power and charging monopoly prices does not violate § 2; rather, the statute targets "the willful acquisition or maintenance of that power as distinguished from growth or development

as a consequence of a superior product, business acumen, or historic accident." United States v. Grinnell Corp.

As a general rule, businesses are free to choose the parties with whom they will deal, as well as the prices, terms, and conditions of that dealing. But there are rare instances in which a dominant firm may incur antitrust liability for purely unilateral conduct. For example, we have ruled that firms may not charge "predatory" prices—below-cost prices that drive rivals out of the market and allow the monopolist to raise its prices later and recoup its losses. *Brooke Group*. Here, however, the complaint at issue does not contain allegations meeting those requirements.

There are also limited circumstances in which a firm's unilateral refusal to deal with its rivals can give rise to antitrust liability. See Aspen Skiing Co. v. Aspen Highlands Skiing Corp. Here, however, the District Court held that AT&T had no such antitrust duty to deal with its competitors, and this holding was not challenged on appeal.

* * * Plaintiffs' price-squeeze claim * * * requires the defendant to be operating in two markets, a wholesale ("upstream") market and a retail ("downstream") market. A firm with market power in the upstream market can squeeze its downstream competitors by raising the wholesale price of inputs while cutting its own retail prices. This will raise competitors' costs (because they will have to pay more for their inputs) and lower their revenues (because they will have to match the dominant firm's low retail price). Price-squeeze plaintiffs assert that defendants must leave them a "fair" or "adequate" margin between the wholesale price and the retail price. * * *

B

1. A straightforward application of our recent decision in *Trinko* forecloses any challenge to AT&T's *wholesale* prices. In *Trinko*, Verizon was required by statute to lease its network elements to competing firms at wholesale rates. * * *

* * *

In this case, as in *Trinko*, the defendant has no antitrust duty to deal with its rivals at wholesale; any such duty arises only from FCC regulations, not from the Sherman Act. There is no meaningful distinction between the "insufficient assistance" claims we rejected in *Trinko* and the plaintiffs' price-squeeze claims in the instant case. The *Trinko* plaintiffs challenged the quality of Verizon's interconnection service, while this case involves a challenge to AT&T's pricing structure. But for antitrust purposes, there is no reason to distinguish between price and nonprice components of a transaction. * * * The nub of the complaint in both *Trinko* and this case is identical the plaintiffs alleged that the defendants (upstream monopolists) abused their power in the wholesale market to prevent rival firms from competing effectively in the retail market. *Trinko* holds that such claims are not cognizable under the Sherman Act in the absence of an antitrust duty to deal.

The District Court and the Court of Appeals did not regard *Trinko* as controlling because that case did not directly address price-squeeze claims. This is technically true, but the reasoning of *Trinko* applies with equal force to price-squeeze claims. AT&T could have squeezed its competitors' profits just as effectively by providing poor-quality interconnection service to the plaintiffs, as Verizon allegedly did in *Trinko*. * * * If AT&T had simply stopped providing DSL transport service to the plaintiffs, it would not have run afoul of the Sherman Act. Under these circumstances, AT&T was not required to offer this service at the wholesale prices the plaintiffs would have preferred.

2.   The other component of a price-squeeze claim is the assertion that the defendant's *retail* prices are "too low." Here too plaintiffs' claims find no support in our existing antitrust doctrine.

"[C]utting prices in order to increase business often is the very essence of competition." Matsushita Elec. Industrial Co. v. Zenith Radio Corp. In cases seeking to impose antitrust liability for prices that are too low, mistaken inferences are "especially costly, because they chill the very conduct the antitrust laws are designed to protect." To avoid chilling aggressive price competition, we have carefully limited the circumstances under which plaintiffs can state a Sherman Act claim by alleging that prices are too low. Specifically, to prevail on a predatory pricing claim, a plaintiff must demonstrate that: (1) "the prices complained of are below an appropriate measure of its rival's costs"; and (2) there is a "dangerous probability" that the defendant will be able to recoup its investment in below-cost prices. "Low prices benefit consumers regardless of how those prices are set, and so long as they are above predatory levels, they do not threaten competition." Atlantic Richfield Co. v. USA Petroleum Co.

In the complaint at issue in this interlocutory appeal, there is no allegation that AT&T's conduct met either of the *Brooke Group* requirements. Recognizing a price-squeeze claim where the defendant's retail price remains above cost would invite the precise harm we sought to avoid in *Brooke Group*: Firms might raise their retail prices or refrain from aggressive price competition to avoid potential antitrust liability.

3.   Plaintiffs' price-squeeze claim, looking to the relation between retail and wholesale prices, is thus nothing more than an amalgamation of a meritless claim at the retail level and a meritless claim at the wholesale level. If there is no duty to deal at the wholesale level and no predatory

pricing at the retail level, then a firm is certainly not required to price *both* of these services in a manner that preserves its rivals' profit margins.[180]

C

Institutional concerns also counsel against recognition of such claims. We have repeatedly emphasized the importance of clear rules in antitrust law. Courts are ill suited "to act as central planners, identifying the proper price, quantity, and other terms of dealing. *Trinko.* " 'No court should impose a duty to deal that it cannot explain or adequately and reasonably supervise. The problem should be deemed irremedia[ble] by antitrust law when compulsory access requires the court to assume the day-to-day controls characteristic of a regulatory agency.' " Id.; see also Town of Concord v. Boston Edison Co., 915 F.2d 17, 25 (1st Cir. 1990) (Breyer, C.J.) ("[A]ntitrust courts normally avoid direct price administration, relying on rules and remedies . . . that are easier to administer").

* * *

IV

* * *

* * * In this case, plaintiffs have not stated a duty-to-deal claim under *Trinko* and have not stated a predatory pricing claim under *Brooke Group*. They have nonetheless tried to join a wholesale claim that cannot succeed with a retail claim that cannot succeed, and alchemize them into a new form of antitrust liability never before recognized by this Court. We decline the invitation to recognize such claims. Two wrong claims do not make one that is right.

The judgment of the Court of Appeals is reversed, and the case is remanded for further proceedings consistent with this opinion.

JUSTICE BREYER, with whom JUSTICE STEVENS, JUSTICE SOUTER, and JUSTICE GINSBURG join, concurring in the judgment.

I would accept respondents' concession that the Ninth Circuit majority's price squeeze holding is wrong, I would vacate the Circuit's decision, and I would remand the case in order to allow the District Court to determine whether respondents may proceed with their predatory

---

[180] Like the Court of Appeals, *amici* argue that price-squeeze claims have been recognized by Courts of Appeals for many years, beginning with Judge Hand's opinion in United States v. Aluminum Co. of America (*Alcoa*). In that case, the Government alleged that Alcoa was using its monopoly power in the upstream aluminum ingot market to squeeze the profits of downstream aluminum sheet fabricators. The court concluded: "That it was unlawful to set the price of 'sheet' so low and hold the price of ingot so high, seems to us unquestionable, provided, as we have held, that on this record the price of ingot must be regarded as higher than a 'fair price.' " Given developments in economic theory and antitrust jurisprudence since *Alcoa*, we find our recent decisions in *Trinko* and *Brooke Group* more pertinent to the question before us. [Court's fn. 3]

pricing claim as set forth in Judge Gould's dissenting Ninth Circuit opinion.

A price squeeze claim finds its natural home in a Sherman Act § 2 monopolization case where the Government as plaintiff seeks to show that a defendant's monopoly power rests, not upon "skill, foresight and industry," United States v. Aluminum Co. of America, but upon exclusionary conduct, United States v. Grinnell Corp. As this Court pointed out in Verizon Communications Inc. v. Law Offices of Curtis V. Trinko, LLP, the " 'means of illicit exclusion, like the means of legitimate competition, are myriad.' " (quoting United States v. Microsoft Corp. (D.C. Cir. 2001 (en banc) (per curiam)). They may involve a "course of dealing" that, even if profitable, indicates a willingness to forsake short-term profits to achieve an anticompetitive end. Trinko. See, e.g., Aspen Skiing Co. v. Aspen Highlands Skiing Corp. And, as Judge Hand wrote many years ago, a "price squeeze" may fall within that latter category. Alcoa. As a matter of logic, it may be that a particular price squeeze can only be exclusionary if a refusal by the monopolist to sell to the squeezed customer would also be exclusionary. But a court, faced with a price squeeze rather than a refusal to deal, is unlikely to find the latter (hypothetical) question any easier to answer than the former.

NOTES AND QUESTIONS

1.   This case provided the Court with an opportunity to summarize what it thought the state of the law is in monopolization cases under Sherman Act § 2.

a.   Was the case worth the Court's time? Do you agree that Trinko and Brooke Group left no room for a separate price-squeeze claim?

b.   Is part of the difference between the majority and concurring opinions over whether Judge Hand should be slapped down once and for all or whether the legacy of Alcoa should be maintained. On which side of that divide do you come down?

2.   Has the Court left any practices that § 2 would condemn? We turn now to the state of tying and exclusive dealing law, but we will return later to some issues of alleged exclusion as to which the Court has not yet entirely closed the door.

2.   TYING AND EXCLUSIVE DEALING IN THE CURRENT PERIOD

In the last chapter, we looked at vertical arrangements characterized as exclusive dealing (Standard Oil (Calif.)) or tying (International Salt, Northern Pacific, Loews and Fortner). We saw the courts declare tying illegal per se, although we raised doubts about whether the arrangements were in fact always primarily exclusionary practices. Tying doctrine in general, the issue of its per se illegality, and its interrelation with both exclusive dealing and monopolization have assumed increased importance in the post-*GTE Sylvania* period.

a. The Principal Case

JEFFERSON PARISH HOSPITAL DISTRICT NO. 2 v. HYDE
Supreme Court of the United States, 1984
466 U.S. 2, 104 S.Ct. 1551, 80 L.Ed.2d 2

JUSTICE STEVENS delivered the opinion of the Court.

At issue in this case is the validity of an exclusive contract between a hospital and a firm of anesthesiologists. We must decide whether the contract gives rise to a per se violation of § 1 of the Sherman Act because every patient undergoing surgery at the hospital must use the services of one firm of anesthesiologists, and, if not, whether the contract is nevertheless illegal because it unreasonably restrains competition among anesthesiologists.

In July 1977, respondent Edwin G. Hyde, a board-certified anesthesiologist, applied for admission to the medical staff of East Jefferson Hospital. The credentials committee and the medical staff executive committee recommended approval, but the hospital board denied the application because the hospital was a party to a contract providing that all anesthesiological services required by the hospital's patients would be performed by Roux & Associates, a professional medical corporation. Respondent then commenced this action seeking a declaratory judgment that the contract is unlawful and an injunction ordering petitioners to appoint him to the hospital staff. After trial, the District Court denied relief, finding that the anticompetitive consequences of the Roux contract were minimal and outweighed by benefits in the form of improved patient care. The Court of Appeals reversed because it was persuaded that the contract was illegal "per se." We granted certiorari and now reverse.

I

In February 1971, shortly before East Jefferson Hospital opened, it entered into an "Anesthesiology Agreement" with Roux & Associates (Roux), a firm that had recently been organized by Dr. Kermit Roux. The contract provided that any anesthesiologist designated by Roux would be admitted to the hospital's medical staff. The hospital agreed to provide the space, equipment, maintenance, and other supporting services necessary to operate the anesthesiology department. It also agreed to purchase all necessary drugs and other supplies. All nursing personnel required by the anesthesia department were to be supplied by the hospital, but Roux had the right to approve their selection and retention. The hospital agreed to "restrict the use of its anesthesia department to Roux & Associates and

[that] no other persons, parties or entities shall perform such services within the Hospital for the ter[m] of this contract."

* * *

The exclusive contract had an impact on two different segments of the economy: consumers of medical services, and providers of anesthesiological services. Any consumer of medical services who elects to have an operation performed at East Jefferson Hospital may not employ any anesthesiologist not associated with Roux. No anesthesiologists except those employed by Roux may practice at East Jefferson.

There are at least 20 hospitals in the New Orleans metropolitan area and about 70 percent of the patients living in Jefferson Parish go to hospitals other than East Jefferson. Because it regarded the entire New Orleans metropolitan area as the relevant geographic market in which hospitals compete, this evidence convinced the District Court that East Jefferson does not possess any significant "market power"; therefore it concluded that petitioners could not use the Roux contract to anticompetitive ends. The same evidence led the Court of Appeals to draw a different conclusion. Noting that 30 percent of the residents of the parish go to East Jefferson Hospital, and that in fact "patients tend to choose hospitals by location rather than price or quality," the Court of Appeals concluded that the relevant geographic market was the East Bank of Jefferson Parish. The conclusion that East Jefferson Hospital possessed market power in that area was buttressed by the facts that the prevalence of health insurance eliminates a patient's incentive to compare costs, that the patient is not sufficiently informed to compare quality, and that family convenience tends to magnify the importance of location.[181]

The Court of Appeals held that the case involves a "tying arrangement" because the "users of the hospital's operating rooms (the tying product) are also compelled to purchase the hospital's chosen anesthesia service (the tied product)." Having defined the relevant geographic market for the tying product as the East Bank of Jefferson Parish, the court held that the hospital possessed "sufficient market power in the tying market to coerce purchasers of the tied product." Since the purchase of the tied product constituted a "not insubstantial amount of interstate commerce," under the

---

[181] While the Court of Appeals did discuss the impact of the contract upon patients, it did not discuss its impact upon anesthesiologists. The District Court had referred to evidence that in the entire State of Louisiana there are 156 anesthesiologists and 345 hospitals with operating rooms. The record does not tell us how many of the hospitals in the New Orleans metropolitan area have "open" anesthesiology departments and how many have closed departments. Respondent, for example, practices with two other anesthesiologists at a hospital which has an open department; he previously practiced for several years in a different New Orleans hospital and, prior to that, had practiced in Florida. The record does not tell us whether there is a shortage or a surplus of anesthesiologists in any part of the country, or whether they are thriving or starving. [Court's fn. 8]

Court of Appeals' reading of our decision in Northern Pacific R. Co. v. United States, the tying arrangement was therefore illegal "per se."

II

* * * It is far too late in the history of our antitrust jurisprudence to question the proposition that certain tying arrangements pose an unacceptable risk of stifling competition and therefore are unreasonable "per se." The rule was first enunciated in International Salt Co. v. United States and has been endorsed by this Court many times since. The rule also reflects congressional policies underlying the antitrust laws. In enacting § 3 of the Clayton Act, Congress expressed great concern about the anticompetitive character of tying arrangements. While this case does not arise under the Clayton Act, the congressional finding made therein concerning the competitive consequences of tying is illuminating, and must be respected.

It is clear, however, that not every refusal to sell two products separately can be said to restrain competition. If each of the products may be purchased separately in a competitive market, one seller's decision to sell the two in a single package imposes no unreasonable restraint on either market, particularly if competing suppliers are free to sell either the entire package or its several parts. For example, we have written that "if one of a dozen food stores in a community were to refuse to sell flour unless the buyer also took sugar it would hardly tend to restrain competition in sugar if its competitors were ready and able to sell flour by itself." Northern Pacific R. Co. v. United States. Buyers often find package sales attractive; a seller's decision to offer such packages can merely be an attempt to compete effectively—conduct that is entirely consistent with the Sherman Act.

Our cases have concluded that the essential characteristic of an invalid tying arrangement lies in the seller's exploitation of its control over the tying product to force the buyer into the purchase of a tied product that the buyer either did not want at all, or might have preferred to purchase elsewhere on different terms. When such "forcing" is present, competition on the merits in the market for the tied item is restrained and the Sherman Act is violated. * * *

* * *

* * * [T]he law draws a distinction between the exploitation of market power by merely enhancing the price of the tying product, on the one hand, and by attempting to impose restraints on competition in the market for a tied product, on the other. When the seller's power is just used to maximize its return in the tying product market, where presumably its product enjoys some justifiable advantage over its competitors, the competitive ideal of the Sherman Act is not necessarily compromised. But if that power

is used to impair competition on the merits in another market, a potentially inferior product may be insulated from competitive pressures. This impairment could either harm existing competitors or create barriers to entry of new competitors in the market for the tied product, and can increase the social costs of market power by facilitating price discrimination, thereby increasing monopoly profits over what they would be absent the tie. And from the standpoint of the consumer—whose interests the statute was especially intended to serve—the freedom to select the best bargain in the second market is impaired by his need to purchase the tying product, and perhaps by an inability to evaluate the true cost of either product when they are available only as a package. * * *

Per se condemnation—condemnation without inquiry into actual market conditions—is only appropriate if the existence of forcing is probable. Thus, application of the per se rule focuses on the probability of anticompetitive consequences. * * * If only a single purchaser were "forced" with respect to the purchase of a tied item, the resultant impact on competition would not be sufficient to warrant the concern of antitrust law. It is for this reason that we have refused to condemn tying arrangements unless a substantial volume of commerce is foreclosed thereby. Similarly, when a purchaser is "forced" to buy a product he would not have otherwise bought even from another seller in the tied-product market, there can be no adverse impact on competition because no portion of the market which would otherwise have been available to other sellers has been foreclosed.

Once this threshold is surmounted, per se prohibition is appropriate if anticompetitive forcing is likely. For example, if the Government has granted the seller a patent or similar monopoly over a product, it is fair to presume that the inability to buy the product elsewhere gives the seller market power. United States v. Loew's Inc. * * *

The same strict rule is appropriate in other situations in which the existence of market power is probable. When the seller's share of the market is high, or when the seller offers a unique product that competitors are not able to offer, the Court has held that the likelihood that market power exists and is being used to restrain competition in a separate market is sufficient to make per se condemnation appropriate. Thus, in Northern Pacific R. Co. v. United States, we held that the railroad's control over vast tracts of western real estate, although not itself unlawful, gave the railroad a unique kind of bargaining power that enabled it to tie the sales of that land to exclusive, long-term commitments that fenced out competition in the transportation market over a protracted period. When, however, the seller does not have either the degree or the kind of market power that enables him to force customers to purchase a second, unwanted product in order to obtain the tying product, an antitrust violation can be established only by evidence of an unreasonable restraint on competition in the relevant market.

* * * Thus, in this case our analysis of the tying issue must focus on the hospital's sale of services to its patients, rather than its contractual arrangements with the providers of anesthesiological services. In making that analysis, we must consider whether petitioners are selling two separate products that may be tied together, and, if so, whether they have used their market power to force their patients to accept the tying arrangement.

III

The hospital has provided its patients with a package that includes the range of facilities and services required for a variety of surgical operations. At East Jefferson Hospital the package includes the services of the anesthesiologist.[182] Petitioners argue that the package does not involve a tying arrangement at all—that they are merely providing a functionally integrated package of services. * * *

Our cases indicate, however, that the answer to the question whether one or two products are involved turns not on the functional relation between them, but rather on the character of the demand for the two items. * * *

* * * The answer to the question whether petitioners have utilized a tying arrangement must be based on whether there is a possibility that the economic effect of the arrangement is that condemned by the rule against tying—that petitioners have foreclosed competition on the merits in a product market distinct from the market for the tying item. Thus, in this case no tying arrangement can exist unless there is a sufficient demand for the purchase of anesthesiological services separate from hospital services to identify a distinct product market in which it is efficient to offer anesthesiological services separately from hospital services.

Unquestionably, the anesthesiological component of the package offered by the hospital could be provided separately and could be selected either by the individual patient or by one of the patient's doctors if the hospital did not insist on including anesthesiological services in the package it offers to its customers. As a matter of actual practice, anesthesiological services are billed separately from the hospital services petitioners provide. There was ample and uncontroverted testimony that patients or surgeons often request specific anesthesiologists to come to a hospital and provide anesthesia, and that the choice of an individual anesthesiologist separate from the choice of a hospital is particularly frequent in respondent's specialty, obstetric anesthesiology. * * * The

---

[182] It is essential to differentiate between the Roux contract and the legality of the contract between the hospital and its patients. The Roux contract is nothing more than an arrangement whereby Roux supplies all of the hospital's needs for anesthesiological services. That contract raises only an exclusive-dealing question. The issue here is whether the hospital's insistence that its patients purchase anesthesiological services from Roux creates a tying arrangement. [Court's fn. 28]

record amply supports the conclusion that consumers differentiate between anesthesiological services and the other hospital services provided by petitioners.

* * * Nevertheless, the fact that this case involves a required purchase of two services that would otherwise be purchased separately does not make the Roux contract illegal. As noted above, there is nothing inherently anticompetitive about packaged sales. Only if patients are forced to purchase Roux's services as a result of the hospital's market power would the arrangement have anticompetitive consequences. If no forcing is present, patients are free to enter a competing hospital and to use another anesthesiologist instead of Roux.[183] The fact that petitioners' patients are required to purchase two separate items is only the beginning of the appropriate inquiry.[184]

IV

The question remains whether this arrangement involves the use of market power to force patients to buy services they would not otherwise purchase. Respondent's only basis for invoking the per se rule against tying and thereby avoiding analysis of actual market conditions is by relying on the preference of persons residing in Jefferson Parish to go to East Jefferson, the closest hospital. A preference of this kind, however, is not necessarily probative of significant market power.

Seventy percent of the patients residing in Jefferson Parish enter hospitals other than East Jefferson. * * * The fact that a substantial majority of the parish's residents elect not to enter East Jefferson means that the geographic data do not establish the kind of dominant market position that obviates the need for further inquiry into actual competitive conditions. The Court of Appeals acknowledged as much * * * and buttressed its conclusion by relying on "market imperfections" that permit petitioners to charge noncompetitive prices for hospital services: the

---

[183] An examination of the reason or reasons why petitioners denied respondent staff privileges will not provide the answer to the question whether the package of services they offered to their patients is an illegal tying arrangement. As a matter of antitrust law, petitioners may give their anesthesiology business to Roux because he is the best doctor available, because he is willing to work long hours, or because he is the son-in-law of the hospital administrator without violating the per se rule against tying. * * * Thus, we reject the view of the District Court that the legality of an arrangement of this kind turns on whether it was adopted for the purpose of improving patient care. [Court's fn. 41]

[184] Petitioners argue and the District Court found that the exclusive contract had what it characterized as procompetitive justifications in that an exclusive contract ensures 24-hour anesthesiology coverage, enables flexible scheduling, and facilitates work routine, professional standards, and maintenance of equipment. * * * In the past, we have refused to tolerate manifestly anticompetitive conduct simply because the health care industry is involved. Petitioners seek no special solicitude. We have also uniformly rejected similar "goodwill" defenses for tying arrangements, finding that the use of contractual quality specifications are generally sufficient to protect quality without the use of a tying arrangement. Since the District Court made no finding as to why contractual quality specifications would not protect the hospital, there is no basis for departing from our prior cases here. [Court's fn. 42]

prevalence of third-party payment for health care costs reduces price competition, and a lack of adequate information renders consumers unable to evaluate the quality of the medical care provided by competing hospitals. While these factors may generate "market power" in some abstract sense, they do not generate the kind of market power that justifies condemnation of tying.

Tying arrangements need only be condemned if they restrain competition on the merits by forcing purchases that would not otherwise be made. A lack of price or quality competition does not create this type of forcing. If consumers lack price consciousness, that fact will not force them to take an anesthesiologist whose services they do not want—their indifference to price will have no impact on their willingness or ability to go to another hospital where they can utilize the services of the anesthesiologist of their choice. Similarly, if consumers cannot evaluate the quality of anesthesiological services, it follows that they are indifferent between certified anesthesiologists even in the absence of a tying arrangement—such an arrangement cannot be said to have foreclosed a choice that would have otherwise been made "on the merits."

Thus, neither of the "market imperfections" relied upon by the Court of Appeals forces consumers to take anesthesiological services they would not select in the absence of a tie. It is safe to assume that every patient undergoing a surgical operation needs the services of an anesthesiologist; at least this record contains no evidence that the hospital "forced" any such services on unwilling patients. The record therefore does not provide a basis for applying the per se rule against tying to this arrangement.

V

In order to prevail in the absence of per se liability, respondent has the burden of proving that the Roux contract violated the Sherman Act because it unreasonably restrained competition. That burden necessarily involves an inquiry into the actual effect of the exclusive contract on competition among anesthesiologists. * * *

* * * [A]ll that the record establishes is that the choice of anesthesiologists at East Jefferson has been limited to one of the four doctors who are associated with Roux and therefore have staff privileges. Even if Roux did not have an exclusive contract, the range of alternatives open to the patient would be severely limited by the nature of the transaction and the hospital's unquestioned right to exercise some control over the identity and the number of doctors to whom it accords staff privileges. If respondent is admitted to the staff of East Jefferson, the range of choice will be enlarged from four to five doctors, but the most significant restraints on the patient's freedom to select a specific anesthesiologist will nevertheless remain. Without a showing of actual adverse effect on

competition, respondent cannot make out a case under the antitrust laws, and no such showing has been made.

VI

* * * It may well be true that the contract made it necessary for Dr. Hyde and others to practice elsewhere, rather than at East Jefferson. But there has been no showing that the market as a whole has been affected at all by the contract. * * * Accordingly, the judgment of the Court of Appeals is reversed, and the case is remanded to that court for further proceedings consistent with this opinion.

JUSTICE BRENNAN, with whom JUSTICE MARSHALL joins, concurring.

As the opinion for the Court demonstrates, we have long held that tying arrangements are subject to evaluation for per se illegality under § 1 of the Sherman Act. Whatever merit the policy arguments against this longstanding construction of the Act might have, Congress, presumably aware of our decisions, has never changed the rule by amending the Act. In such circumstances, our practice usually has been to stand by a settled statutory interpretation and leave the task of modifying the statute's reach to Congress. I see no reason to depart from that principle in this case and therefore join the opinion and judgment of the Court.

JUSTICE O'CONNOR, with whom THE CHIEF JUSTICE, JUSTICE POWELL, and JUSTICE REHNQUIST join, concurring in the judgment.

* * * I concur in the Court's decision to reverse but write separately to explain why I believe the hospital-Roux contract, whether treated as effecting a tie between services provided to patients, or as an exclusive dealing arrangement between the hospital and certain anesthesiologists, is properly analyzed under the rule of reason.

I

* * *

* * * In deciding whether an economic restraint should be declared illegal per se, "[t]he probability that anticompetitive consequences will result from a practice and the severity of those consequences [is] balanced against its procompetitive consequences. Cases that do not fit the generalization may arise, but a per se rule reflects the judgment that such cases are not sufficiently common or important to justify the time and expense necessary to identify them." Continental T.V., Inc. v. GTE Sylvania Inc. Only when there is very little loss to society from banning a restraint altogether is an inquiry into its costs in the individual case considered to be unnecessary.

Some of our earlier cases did indeed declare that tying arrangements serve "hardly any purpose beyond the suppression of competition." Standard Oil Co. of California v. United States (dictum). However, this declaration was not taken literally even by the cases that purported to rely upon it. In practice, a tie has been illegal only if the seller is shown to have "sufficient economic power with respect to the tying product to appreciably restrain free competition in the market for the tied product * * *." *Northern Pacific R. Co.* * * * The Court has never been willing to say of tying arrangements, as it has of price fixing, division of markets, and other agreements subject to per se analysis, that they are always illegal, without proof of market power or anticompetitive effect.

The "per se" doctrine in tying cases has thus always required an elaborate inquiry into the economic effects of the tying arrangement. As a result, tying doctrine incurs the costs of a rule-of-reason approach without achieving its benefits: the doctrine calls for the extensive and time-consuming economic analysis characteristic of the rule of reason, but then may be interpreted to prohibit arrangements that economic analysis would show to be beneficial. Moreover, the per se label in the tying context has generated more confusion than coherent law because it appears to invite lower courts to omit the analysis of economic circumstances of the tie that has always been a necessary element of tying analysis.

The time has therefore come to abandon the "per se" label and refocus the inquiry on the adverse economic effects, and the potential economic benefits, that the tie may have. The law of tie-ins will thus be brought into accord with the law applicable to all other allegedly anticompetitive economic arrangements, except those few horizontal or quasi-horizontal restraints that can be said to have no economic justification whatsoever.[185] * * *

II

Our prior opinions indicate that the purpose of tying law has been to identify and control those tie-ins that have a demonstrable exclusionary impact in the tied-product market, or that abet the harmful exercise of market power that the seller possesses in the tying product market. Under the rule of reason tying arrangements should be disapproved only in such instances.

Market power in the tying product may be acquired legitimately (e.g., through the grant of a patent) or illegitimately (e.g., as a result of unlawful monopolization). In either event, exploitation of consumers in the market for the tying product is a possibility that exists and that may be regulated under § 2 of the Sherman Act without reference to any tying arrangements

---

[185] Tying law is particularly anomalous in this respect because arrangements largely indistinguishable from tie-ins are generally analyzed under the rule of reason. For example, the "per se" analysis of tie-ins subjects restrictions on a franchisee's freedom to purchase supplies to a more searching scrutiny than restrictions on his freedom to sell his products. Compare, e.g., Siegel v. Chicken Delight, Inc., 448 F.2d 43 (9th Cir.1971), with Continental T.V., Inc. v. GTE Sylvania Inc. And exclusive contracts, that, like tie-ins, require the buyer to purchase a product from one seller, are subject only to the rule of reason. [Concur fn. 2]

that the seller may have developed. The existence of a tied product normally does not increase the profit that the seller with market power can extract from sales of the tying product. A seller with a monopoly on flour, for example, cannot increase the profit it can extract from flour consumers simply by forcing them to buy sugar along with their flour. Counterintuitive though that assertion may seem, it is easily demonstrated and widely accepted.

Tying may be economically harmful primarily in the rare cases where power in the market for the tying product is used to create additional market power in the market for the tied product.[186] The antitrust law is properly concerned with tying when, for example, the flour monopolist threatens to use its market power to acquire additional power in the sugar market, perhaps by driving out competing sellers of sugar, or by making it more difficult for new sellers to enter the sugar market. But such extension of market power is unlikely, or poses no threat of economic harm, unless the two markets in question and the nature of the two products tied satisfy three threshold criteria.

First, the seller must have power in the tying-product market. Absent such power tying cannot conceivably have any adverse impact in the tied-product market, and can be only procompetitive in the tying-product market.[187] If the seller of flour has no market power over flour, it will gain none by insisting that its buyers take some sugar as well.

Second, there must be a substantial threat that the tying seller will acquire market power in the tied-product market. No such threat exists if the tied-product market is occupied by many stable sellers who are not likely to be driven out by the tying, or if entry barriers in the tied-product market are low. * * *

---

[186] Tying might be undesirable in two other instances, but the hospital-Roux arrangement involves neither one.

In a regulated industry a firm with market power may be unable to extract a supercompetitive profit because it lacks control over the prices it charges for regulated products or services. Tying may then be used to extract that profit from sale of the unregulated, tied products or services. See Fortner Enterprises, Inc. v. United States Steel Corp. (White, J., dissenting).

Tying may also help the seller engage in price discrimination by "metering" the buyer's use of the tying product. Cf. International Business Machines Corp. v. United States; International Salt Co. v. United States. Price discrimination may be independently unlawful, see 15 U.S.C. § 13. Price discrimination may, however, decrease rather than increase the economic costs of a seller's market power. See, e.g., R. Bork, The Antitrust Paradox 398 (1978); P. Areeda, Antitrust Analysis 608–610 (3d ed. 1981); O. Williamson, Markets and Hierarchies: Analysis and Antitrust Implications 11–13 (1975). * * * [Concur fn. 4]

[187] A common misconception has been that a patent or copyright, a high market share, or a unique product that competitors are not able to offer suffices to demonstrate market power. While each of these three factors might help to give market power to a seller, it is also possible that a seller in these situations will have no market power: for example, a patent holder has no market power in any relevant sense if there are close substitutes for the patented product. Similarly, a high market share indicates market power only if the market is properly defined to include all reasonable substitutes for the product. See generally Landes & Posner, Market Power in Antitrust Cases, 94 Harv. L. Rev. 937 (1981). * * * [Concur fn. 7]

Third, there must be a coherent economic basis for treating the tying and tied products as distinct. All but the simplest products can be broken down into two or more components that are "tied together" in the final sale. Unless it is to be illegal to sell cars with engines or cameras with lenses, this analysis must be guided by some limiting principle. For products to be treated as distinct, the tied product must, at a minimum, be one that some consumers might wish to purchase separately *without also purchasing the tying product*. When the tied product has no use other than in conjunction with the tying product, a seller of the tying product can acquire no *additional* market power by selling the two products together. * * *

Even when the tied product does have a use separate from the tying product, it makes little sense to label a package as two products without also considering the economic justifications for the sale of the package as a unit. When the economic advantages of joint packaging are substantial the package is not appropriately viewed as two products, and that should be the end of the tying inquiry. * * *

These three conditions—market power in the tying product, a substantial threat of market power in the tied product, and a coherent economic basis for treating the products as distinct—are only threshold requirements. Under the rule of reason a tie-in may prove acceptable even when all three are met. Tie-ins may entail economic benefits as well as economic harms, and if the threshold requirements are met these benefits should enter the rule-of-reason balance.

* * *

III

Application of these criteria to the case at hand is straightforward.

Although the issue is in doubt, we may assume that the hospital does have market power in the provision of hospital services in its area. * * *

* * * [W]e may also assume that there is a substantial threat that East Jefferson will acquire market power over the provision of anesthesiological services in its market. * * *

But the third threshold condition for giving closer scrutiny to a tying arrangement is not satisfied here: there is no sound economic reason for treating surgery and anesthesia as separate services. Patients are interested in purchasing anesthesia only in conjunction with hospital services, so the hospital can acquire no additional market power by selling the two services together. Accordingly, the link between the hospital's services and anesthesia administered by Roux will affect neither the amount of anesthesia provided nor the combined price of anesthesia and surgery for those who choose to become the hospital's patients. In these circumstances, anesthesia and surgical services should probably not be characterized as distinct products for tying purposes.

Even if they are, the tying should not be considered a violation of § 1 of the Sherman Act because tying here cannot increase the seller's already absolute power over the volume of production of the tied product, which is an inevitable consequence of the fact that very few patients will choose to undergo surgery without receiving anesthesia. The hospital-Roux contract therefore has little potential to harm the patients. On the other side of the balance, the District Court found, and the Court of Appeals did not dispute, that the tie-in conferred significant benefits upon the hospital and the patients that it served.

The tie-in improves patient care and permits more efficient hospital operation in a number of ways. From the viewpoint of hospital management, the tie-in ensures 24-hour anesthesiology coverage, aids in standardization of procedures and efficient use of equipment, facilitates flexible scheduling of operations, and permits the hospital more effectively to monitor the quality of anesthesiological services. Further, the tying arrangement is advantageous to patients because, as the District Court found, the closed anesthesiology department places upon the hospital, rather than the individual patient, responsibility to select the physician who is to provide anesthesiological services. The hospital also assumes the responsibility that the anesthesiologist will be available, will be acceptable to the surgeon, and will provide suitable care to the patient. In assuming these responsibilities—responsibilities that a seriously ill patient frequently may be unable to discharge—the hospital provides a valuable service to its patients. And there is no indication that patients were dissatisfied with the quality of anesthesiology that was provided at the hospital or that patients wished to enjoy the services of anesthesiologists other than those that the hospital employed. Given this evidence of the advantages and effectiveness of the closed anesthesiology department, it is not surprising that, as the District Court found, such arrangements are accepted practice in the majority of hospitals of New Orleans and in the health care industry generally. Such an arrangement, which has little anticompetitive effect and achieves substantial benefits in the provision of care to patients, is hardly one that the antitrust law should condemn.[188]
* * *

IV

Whether or not the hospital-Roux contract is characterized as a tie between distinct products, the contract unquestionably does constitute exclusive dealing. Exclusive-dealing arrangements are independently subject to scrutiny under § 1 of the Sherman Act, and are also analyzed under the rule of reason. Tampa Electric Co. v. Nashville Coal Co.

---

[188] The Court of Appeals disregarded the benefits of the tie because it found that there were less restrictive means of achieving them. In the absence of an adequate basis to expect any harm to competition from the tie-in, this objection is simply irrelevant. [Concur fn. 13]

* * *

* * * Exclusive dealing can have adverse economic consequences by allowing one supplier of goods or services unreasonably to deprive other suppliers of a market for their goods, or by allowing one buyer of goods unreasonably to deprive other buyers of a needed source of supply. In determining whether an exclusive-dealing contract is unreasonable, the proper focus is on the structure of the market for the products or services in question—the number of sellers and buyers in the market, the volume of their business, and the ease with which buyers and sellers can redirect their purchases or sales to others. Exclusive dealing is an unreasonable restraint on trade only when a significant fraction of buyers or sellers are frozen out of a market by the exclusive deal. Standard Oil Co. of California v. United States. When the sellers of services are numerous and mobile, and the number of buyers is large, exclusive-dealing arrangements of narrow scope pose no threat of adverse economic consequences. To the contrary, they may be substantially procompetitive by ensuring stable markets and encouraging long-term, mutually advantageous business relationships.

At issue here is an exclusive-dealing arrangement between a firm of four anesthesiologists and one relatively small hospital. There is no suggestion that East Jefferson Hospital is likely to create a "bottleneck" in the availability of anesthesiologists that might deprive other hospitals of access to needed anesthesiological services, or that the Roux associates have unreasonably narrowed the range of choices available to other anesthesiologists in search of a hospital or patients that will buy their services. A firm of four anesthesiologists represents only a very small fraction of the total number of anesthesiologists whose services are available for hire by other hospitals, and East Jefferson is one among numerous hospitals buying such services. Even without engaging in a detailed analysis of the size of the relevant markets we may readily conclude that there is no likelihood that the exclusive-dealing arrangement challenged here will either unreasonably enhance the hospital's market position relative to other hospitals, or unreasonably permit Roux to acquire power relative to other anesthesiologists. Accordingly, this exclusive-dealing arrangement must be sustained under the rule of reason.

* * *

NOTES AND QUESTIONS

1. What was the plaintiff's complaint in this case? Had he been compelled to buy something he did not want? Had any patients been so compelled?

a. Should the plaintiff have been held to have standing? Did he suffer antitrust injury? He did on the exclusive dealing claim, of course, but who does the court say is the "victim" of a tying arrangement?

b. Why had the hospital chosen to do business this way? Was it likely to make additional profits by forcing unwanted anesthesiologists on patients selecting among hospitals at which to have surgery?[189]

2. Do you agree that there were two products here?

a. How did Justice Stevens argue that there were? Is Justice Stevens saying that if 50% of automobile buyers say they want a better radio in their car than manufacturers supply, selling a car with a radio as standard equipment would constitute tying?

b. Would Justice O'Connor agree? Is it helpful to ask whether someone would want to buy the tied product without the tying product? Would someone buy a car radio who did not expect to own a car?

c. Was Justice Stevens too quick to dismiss the "functional relation" test? One might buy a car radio other than at the time of buying a car, for example, but one would not buy anesthesia except at the time of surgery.

d. Should the question be whether the seller could increase its return by selling the "extra" product? Could you sell a car for more if it had a radio? How much more? Could you sell surgery for less if no anesthesia were offered? Put another way, would anyone buy surgery without anesthesia?

3. What does Justice Stevens say is the rule defining when tying is illegal per se?

a. Do you agree that it should only be per se illegal to force people to buy what they do not want? Should the fact that they can buy the tying product from others (without being required to buy the tied product) be decisive? Were you persuaded by the Court's example of only one seller's "tying" flour and sugar? Does it follow that the legality of Ford's requiring the purchase of car radios should depend on whether General Motors also requires it?

b. Should illegal forcing be presumptively present where a legal monopoly such as a patent or copyright is involved? Do you agree with Justice O'Connor that such a presumption is overly broad and not realistic? In their Antitrust Guidelines for the Licensing of Intellectual Property (April 1995), the Justice Department and F.T.C. expressly declared that they "will not presume that a patent, copyright, or trade secret necessarily confers market power upon its owner." Guidelines § 5.3.

c. The Guidelines' position was not self evident. Indeed, the Federal Circuit expressly reiterated that a patent creates a rebuttable presumption of market power in a tying case. Independent Ink, Inc. v. Illinois Tool Works, 396

---

[189] See, e.g., Alan J. Meese, Tying Meets the New Institutional Economics: Farewell to the Chimera of Forcing, 146 U. Pennsylvania L.Rev. 1 (1997).

F.3d 1342 (Fed. Cir. 2005).[190] The Supreme Court very quickly granted certiorari, and its opinion follows our next case.

4. Having prevailed on the application of the per se rule and the presence of two products, why did Dr. Hyde lose?

a. Do you agree that Jefferson Parish Hospital did not have market power? Is a 30% market share trivial? Is market "dominance" now required?

b. Do you agree with Justice O'Connor that the per se rule here has all the costs of the rule of reason and none of the benefits? Does it make sense that when one has created a many-factored rule, all of whose factors must be met to create per se illegality, one might as well go to a rule of reason?

c. Do you agree with the majority that there can never be a pro-competitive or efficiency-producing justification for tying? Might it frequently be efficient to sell a package? Should we tailor the analysis to the facts of each case rather than trying to shoehorn facts into categories?

d. Would you be as willing as Justice O'Connor to look at the benefits to patient care that flow from arrangements such as the one here? Where there are few anticompetitive effects and substantial benefits to patient care flowing from an arrangement, might antitrust law properly see its role as limited? Is that approach inconsistent with *Professional Engineers*?

5. Suppose the hospital did not purport to sell anesthesia services but required that any patient using its operating rooms contract separately with a doctor from Roux. Would that present different issues? Would it matter whether the hospital gained financially through a share of the fee of the provider of anesthesia services? See, e.g., Beard v. Parkview Hospital, 912 F.2d 138 (6th Cir.1990) (no § 1 violation where hospital did not benefit financially from its rule).

6. Did Justice O'Connor correctly analyze the exclusive dealing features of the case? Would you have found the exclusivity of the arrangement with Roux to be justifiable? Cf. United States v. Dentsply International, Inc., 399 F.3d 181 (3d Cir.2005) (dominant manufacturer of false teeth's practice of dropping dealers who also sold competing products was not an exclusive dealing violation but did violate Sherman Act § 2).

b. Cases Reinforcing or Developing the Current Approach

After *Jefferson Parish*, one might reasonably have concluded that tying doctrine would be of decreasing interest to antitrust practitioners. That conclusion would have been a little too hasty.

---

[190] The role of the Federal Circuit in deciding these issues is itself the subject of controversy. It clearly has jurisdiction over all patent issues, but extension of that jurisdiction to decide broad antitrust questions may not necessarily follow. See, e.g., Symposium: The Federal Circuit and Antitrust, 69 Antitrust L.J. 627–849 (2002).

EASTMAN KODAK COMPANY V. IMAGE TECHNICAL SERVICES, INC.

Supreme Court of the United States, 1992
504 U.S. 451, 112 S.Ct. 2072, 119 L.Ed.2d 265

JUSTICE BLACKMUN delivered the opinion of the Court.

This is yet another case that concerns the standard for summary judgment in an antitrust controversy. The principal issue here is whether a defendant's lack of market power in the primary equipment market precludes—as a matter of law—the possibility of market power in derivative aftermarkets.

Petitioner Eastman Kodak Company manufactures and sells photocopiers and micrographic equipment. Kodak also sells service and replacement parts for its equipment. Respondents are 18 independent service organizations (ISOs) that in the early 1980s began servicing Kodak copying and micrographic equipment. Kodak subsequently adopted policies to limit the availability of parts to ISOs and to make it more difficult for ISOs to compete with Kodak in servicing Kodak equipment.

Respondents instituted this action in the United States District Court for the Northern District of California alleging that Kodak's policies were unlawful under both §§ 1 and 2 of the Sherman Act. After truncated discovery, the District Court granted summary judgment for Kodak. The Court of Appeals for the Ninth Circuit reversed. * * * [W]e granted certiorari.

I

A

Because this case comes to us on petitioner Kodak's motion for summary judgment, "the evidence of [respondents] is to be believed, and all justifiable inferences are to be drawn in [their] favor." * * *

Kodak manufactures and sells complex business machines—as relevant here, high-volume photocopier and micrographics equipment. Kodak equipment is unique; micrographic software programs that operate on Kodak machines, for example, are not compatible with competitors' machines. Kodak parts are not compatible with other manufacturers' equipment, and vice versa. Kodak equipment, although expensive when new, has little resale value.

Kodak provides service and parts for its machines to its customers. It produces some of the parts itself; the rest are made to order for Kodak by independent original-equipment manufacturers (OEMs). Kodak does not sell a complete system of original equipment, lifetime service, and lifetime parts for a single price. Instead, Kodak provides service after the initial warranty period either through annual service contracts, which include all necessary parts, or on a per-call basis. It charges, through negotiations and bidding, different prices for equipment, service, and parts for different customers. Kodak provides 80% to 95% of the service for Kodak machines.

Beginning in the early 1980s, ISOs began repairing and servicing Kodak equipment. They also sold parts and reconditioned and sold used Kodak equipment. Their customers were federal, state, and local government agencies, banks, insurance companies, industrial enterprises, and providers of specialized copy and microfilming services. ISOs provide service at a price substantially lower than Kodak does. Some customers found that the ISO service was of higher quality.

Some of the ISOs' customers purchase their own parts and hire ISOs only for service. Others choose ISOs to supply both service and parts. ISOs keep an inventory of parts, purchased from Kodak or other sources, primarily the OEMs.[191]

In 1985 and 1986, Kodak implemented a policy of selling replacement parts for micrographic and copying machines only to buyers of Kodak equipment who use Kodak service or repair their own machines.

As part of the same policy, Kodak sought to limit ISO access to other sources of Kodak parts. Kodak and the OEMs agreed that the OEMs would not sell parts that fit Kodak equipment to anyone other than Kodak. Kodak also pressured Kodak equipment owners and independent parts distributors not to sell Kodak parts to ISOs. In addition, Kodak took steps to restrict the availability of used machines.

Kodak intended, through these policies, to make it more difficult for ISOs to sell service for Kodak machines. It succeeded. ISOs were unable to obtain parts from reliable sources, and many were forced out of business, while others lost substantial revenue. Customers were forced to switch to Kodak service even though they preferred ISO service.

* * *

II

* * *

A

For the respondents to defeat a motion for summary judgment on their claim of a tying arrangement, a reasonable trier of fact must be able to find, first, that service and parts are two distinct products, and, second, that Kodak has tied the sale of the two products.

---

[191] In addition to the OEMs, other sources of Kodak parts include (1) brokers who would buy parts from Kodak, or strip used Kodak equipment to obtain the useful parts and resell them, (2) customers who buy parts from Kodak and make them available to ISOs, and (3) used equipment to be stripped for parts. [Court's fn. 2]

For service and parts to be considered two distinct products, there must be sufficient consumer demand so that it is efficient for a firm to provide service separately from parts. Jefferson Parish Hospital Dist. No. 2 v. Hyde. Evidence in the record indicates that service and parts have been sold separately in the past and still are sold separately to self-service equipment owners. Indeed, the development of the entire high-technology service industry is evidence of the efficiency of a separate market for service.

Kodak insists that because there is no demand for parts separate from service, there cannot be separate markets for service and parts. By that logic, we would be forced to conclude that there can never be separate markets, for example, for cameras and film, computers and software, or automobiles and tires. That is an assumption we are unwilling to make. "We have often found arrangements involving functionally linked products at least one of which is useless without the other to be prohibited tying devices." *Jefferson Parish.*

Kodak's assertion also appears to be incorrect as a factual matter. At least some consumers would purchase service without parts, because some service does not require parts, and some consumers, those who self-service for example, would purchase parts without service. Enough doubt is cast on Kodak's claim of a unified market that it should be resolved by the trier of fact.

* * *

B

Having found sufficient evidence of a tying arrangement, we consider the other necessary feature of an illegal tying arrangement: appreciable economic power in the tying market. Market power is the power "to force a purchaser to do something that he would not do in a competitive market." *Jefferson Parish.* It has been defined as "the ability of a single seller to raise price and restrict output." *Fortner Inc.* The existence of such power ordinarily is inferred from the seller's possession of a predominant share of the market.

1

Respondents contend that Kodak has more than sufficient power in the parts market to force unwanted purchases of the tied market, service. Respondents provide evidence that certain parts are available exclusively through Kodak. Respondents also assert that Kodak has control over the availability of parts it does not manufacture. According to respondents' evidence, Kodak has prohibited independent manufacturers from selling Kodak parts to ISOs, pressured Kodak equipment owners and independent parts distributors to deny ISOs the purchase of Kodak parts, and taken steps to restrict the availability of used machines.

* * * Respondents offer evidence that consumers have switched to Kodak service even though they preferred ISO service, that Kodak service was of higher price and lower quality than the preferred ISO service, and that ISOs were driven out of business by Kodak's policies. Under our prior precedents, this evidence would be sufficient to entitle respondents to a trial on their claim of market power.

2

Kodak counters that even if it concedes monopoly share of the relevant parts market, it cannot actually exercise the necessary market power for a Sherman Act violation. This is so, according to Kodak, because competition exists in the equipment market. Kodak argues that it could not have the ability to raise prices of service and parts above the level that would be charged in a competitive market because any increase in profits from a higher price in the aftermarkets at least would be offset by a corresponding loss in profits from lower equipment sales as consumers began purchasing equipment with more attractive service costs.

Kodak does not present any actual data on the equipment, service, or parts markets. Instead, it urges the adoption of a substantive legal rule that "equipment competition precludes any finding of monopoly power in derivative aftermarkets." * * *

Legal presumptions that rest on formalistic distinctions rather than actual market realities are generally disfavored in antitrust law. This Court has preferred to resolve antitrust claims on a case-by-case basis, focusing on the "particular facts disclosed by the record." * * *

Kodak contends that there is no need to examine the facts when the issue is market power in the aftermarkets. A legal presumption against a finding of market power is warranted in this situation, according to Kodak, because the existence of market power in the service and parts markets absent power in the equipment market "simply makes no economic sense," and the absence of a legal presumption would deter procompetitive behavior. *Matsushita.*

* * *

The Court's requirement in *Matsushita* that the plaintiffs' claims make economic sense did not introduce a special burden on plaintiffs facing summary judgment in antitrust cases. * * * *Matsushita* demands only that the nonmoving party's inferences be reasonable in order to reach the jury, a requirement that was not invented, but merely articulated, in that decision. If the plaintiff's theory is economically senseless, no reasonable jury could find in its favor, and summary judgment should be granted.

Kodak, then, bears a substantial burden in showing that it is entitled to summary judgment. It must show that despite evidence of increased prices and excluded competition, an inference of market power is unreasonable. * * *

The extent to which one market prevents exploitation of another market depends on the extent to which consumers will change their consumption of one product in response to a price change in another, i.e., the "cross-elasticity of demand." Kodak's proposed rule rests on a factual assumption about the cross-elasticity of demand in the equipment and aftermarkets: "If Kodak raised its parts or service prices above competitive levels, potential customers would simply stop buying Kodak equipment. Perhaps Kodak would be able to increase short term profits through such a strategy, but at a devastating cost to its long term interests." Kodak argues that the Court should accept, as a matter of law, this "basic economic reality," that competition in the equipment market necessarily prevents market power in the aftermarkets.[192]

Even if Kodak could not raise the price of service and parts one cent without losing equipment sales, that fact would not disprove market power in the aftermarkets. * * * Kodak's claim that charging more for service and parts would be a "short-run game," is based on the false dichotomy that there are only two prices that can be charged—a competitive price or a ruinous one. But there could easily be a middle, optimum price at which the increased revenues from the higher-priced sales of service and parts would more than compensate for the lower revenues from lost equipment sales. The fact that the equipment market imposes a restraint on prices in the aftermarkets by no means disproves the existence of power in those markets. Thus, contrary to Kodak's assertion, there is no immutable physical law—no "basic economic reality"—insisting that competition in the equipment market cannot coexist with market power in the aftermarkets.

We next consider the more narrowly drawn question: Does Kodak's theory describe actual market behavior so accurately that respondents' assertion of Kodak market power in the aftermarkets, if not impossible, is at least unreasonable? Cf. *Matsushita*.

To review Kodak's theory, it contends that higher service prices will lead to a disastrous drop in equipment sales. Presumably, the theory's corollary is to the effect that low service prices lead to a dramatic increase in equipment sales. According to the theory, one would have expected Kodak to take advantage of lower-priced ISO service as an opportunity to expand equipment sales. Instead, Kodak adopted a restrictive sales policy consciously designed to eliminate the lower-priced ISO service, an act that would be expected to devastate either Kodak's equipment sales or Kodak's

---

[192] It is clearly true, as the United States claims, that Kodak "cannot set service or parts prices without regard to the impact on the market for equipment." The fact that the cross-elasticity of demand is not zero proves nothing; the disputed issue is how much of an impact an increase in parts and service prices has on equipment sales and on Kodak's profits. [Court's fn. 17]

faith in its theory. Yet, according to the record, it has done neither. Service prices have risen for Kodak customers, but there is no evidence or assertion that Kodak equipment sales have dropped.

Kodak and the United States attempt to reconcile Kodak's theory with the contrary actual results by describing a "marketing strategy of spreading over time the total cost to the buyer of Kodak equipment." In other words, Kodak could charge subcompetitive prices for equipment and make up the difference with supracompetitive prices for service, resulting in an overall competitive price. This pricing strategy would provide an explanation for the theory's descriptive failings—if Kodak in fact had adopted it. But Kodak never has asserted that it prices its equipment or parts subcompetitively and recoups its profits through service. Instead, it claims that it prices its equipment comparably to its competitors, and intends that both its equipment sales and service divisions be profitable. Moreover, this hypothetical pricing strategy is inconsistent with Kodak's policy toward its self-service customers. If Kodak were underpricing its equipment, hoping to lock in customers and recover its losses in the service market, it could not afford to sell customers parts without service. In sum, Kodak's theory does not explain the actual market behavior revealed in the record.

Respondents offer a forceful reason why Kodak's theory, although perhaps intuitively appealing, may not accurately explain the behavior of the primary and derivative markets for complex durable goods: the existence of significant information and switching costs. These costs could create a less responsive connection between service and parts prices and equipment sales.

For the service-market price to affect equipment demand, consumers must inform themselves of the total cost of the "package"—equipment, service and parts—at the time of purchase; that is, consumers must engage in accurate lifecycle pricing. Lifecycle pricing of complex, durable equipment is difficult and costly. In order to arrive at an accurate price, a consumer must acquire a substantial amount of raw data and undertake sophisticated analysis. The necessary information would include data on price, quality, and availability of products needed to operate, upgrade, or enhance the initial equipment, as well as service and repair costs, including estimates of breakdown frequency, nature of repairs, price of service and parts, length of "down-time" and losses incurred from down-time.

Much of this information is difficult—some of it impossible—to acquire at the time of purchase. During the life of a product, companies may change the service and parts prices, and develop products with more advanced features, a decreased need for repair, or new warranties. In addition, the information is likely to be customer-specific; lifecycle costs will vary from customer to customer with the type of equipment, degrees of equipment use, and costs of down-time.

Kodak acknowledges the cost of information, but suggests, again without evidentiary support, that customer information needs will be satisfied by competitors in the equipment markets. It is a question of fact, however, whether competitors would provide the necessary information. A competitor in the equipment market may not have reliable information about the lifecycle costs of complex equipment it does not service or the needs of customers it does not serve. Even if competitors had the relevant information, it is not clear that their interests would be advanced by providing such information to consumers.

Moreover, even if consumers were capable of acquiring and processing the complex body of information, they may choose not to do so. Acquiring the information is expensive. If the costs of service are small relative to the equipment price, or if consumers are more concerned about equipment capabilities than service costs, they may not find it cost-efficient to compile the information. Similarly, some consumers, such as the Federal Government, have purchasing systems that make it difficult to consider the complete cost of the "package" at the time of purchase. State and local governments often treat service as an operating expense and equipment as a capital expense, delegating each to a different department. These governmental entities do not lifecycle price, but rather choose the lowest price in each market.

As Kodak notes, there likely will be some large-volume, sophisticated purchasers who will undertake the comparative studies and insist, in return for their patronage, that Kodak charge them competitive lifecycle prices. Kodak contends that these knowledgeable customers will hold down the package price for all other customers. * * * [However,] if a company is able to price-discriminate between sophisticated and unsophisticated consumers, the sophisticated will be unable to prevent the exploitation of the uninformed. * * *

Given the potentially high cost of information and the possibility a seller may be able to price-discriminate between knowledgeable and unsophisticated consumers, it makes little sense to assume, in the absence of any evidentiary support, that equipment-purchasing decisions are based on an accurate assessment of the total cost of equipment, service, and parts over the lifetime of the machine.

* * *

A second factor undermining Kodak's claim that supracompetitive prices in the service market lead to ruinous losses in equipment sales is the cost to current owners of switching to a different product. If the cost of switching is high, consumers who already have purchased the equipment, and are thus "locked-in," will tolerate some level of service-price increases before changing equipment brands. Under this scenario, a seller profitably could maintain supracompetitive prices in the aftermarket if the switching costs were high relative to the increase in service prices, and the number of locked-in customers were high relative to the number of new purchasers.

* * *

Respondents have offered evidence that the heavy initial outlay for Kodak equipment, combined with the required support material that works only with Kodak equipment, makes switching costs very high for existing Kodak customers. And Kodak's own evidence confirms that it varies the package price of equipment/parts/service for different customers. In sum, there is a question of fact whether information costs and switching costs foil the simple assumption that the equipment and service markets act as pure complements to one another.

* * *

We need not decide whether Kodak's behavior has any procompetitive effects and, if so, whether they outweigh the anticompetitive effects. We note only that Kodak's service and parts policy is simply not one that appears always or almost always to enhance competition, and therefore to warrant a legal presumption without any evidence of its actual economic impact. In this case, when we weigh the risk of deterring procompetitive behavior by proceeding to trial against the risk that illegal behavior go unpunished, the balance tips against summary judgment.

* * *

[In Part III of its opinion, omitted here, the Court held that Kodak could also be found to have monopolized sales of the parts for its own machines in violation of Sherman Act § 2, even though it lacked any substantial market share in sales of this kind of machine generally.]

* * *

JUSTICE SCALIA, with whom JUSTICE O'CONNOR and JUSTICE THOMAS join, dissenting.

This is not, as the Court describes it, just "another case that concerns the standard for summary judgment in an antitrust controversy." Rather, the case presents a very narrow—but extremely important—question of substantive antitrust law: Whether, for purposes of applying our per se rule condemning "ties," and for purposes of applying our exacting rules governing the behavior of would-be monopolists, a manufacturer's conceded lack of power in the interbrand market for its equipment is somehow consistent with its possession of "market," or even "monopoly," power in wholly derivative aftermarkets for that equipment. In my view, the Court supplies an erroneous answer to this question, and I dissent.

I

* * *

Despite intense criticism of the tying doctrine in academic circles, the stated rationale for our per se rule has varied little over the years. When the defendant has genuine "market power" in the tying product—the power to raise price by reducing output—the tie potentially enables him to extend that power into a second distinct market, enhancing barriers to entry in each. * * *

Our Section 2 monopolization doctrines are similarly directed to discrete situations in which a defendant's possession of substantial market power, combined with his exclusionary or anticompetitive behavior, threatens to defeat or forestall the corrective forces of competition and thereby sustain or extend the defendant's agglomeration of power. Where a defendant maintains substantial market power, his activities are examined through a special lens: Behavior that might otherwise not be of concern to the antitrust laws—or that might even be viewed as procompetitive—can take on exclusionary connotations when practiced by a monopolist.

The concerns, however, that have led the courts to heightened scrutiny both of the "exclusionary conduct" practiced by a monopolist and of tying arrangements subject to per se prohibition, are completely without force when the participants lack market power. * * * And with respect to tying, we have recognized that bundling arrangements not coerced by the heavy hand of market power can serve the procompetitive functions of facilitating new entry into certain markets, permitting "clandestine price cutting in products which otherwise would have no price competition at all because of fear of retaliation from the few other producers dealing in the market," *Fortner I* (White, J., dissenting), assuring quality control, see, e.g., Standard Oil Co. of Cal. v. United States, and, where "the tied and tying products are functionally related, * * * reducing costs through economies of joint production and distribution." *Fortner I* (White, J., dissenting). "Accordingly, we have [only] condemned tying arrangements [under the per se rule] when the seller has some special ability—usually called market power—to force a purchaser to do something that he would not do in a competitive market." *Jefferson Parish*.

The Court today finds in the typical manufacturer's inherent power over its own brand of equipment—over the sale of distinctive repair parts for that equipment, for example—the sort of "monopoly power" sufficient to bring the sledgehammer of § 2 into play. * * * In my opinion, this makes no economic sense. The holding that market power can be found on the present record causes these venerable rules of selective proscription to extend well beyond the point where the reasoning that supports them leaves off. Moreover, because the sort of power condemned by the Court today is possessed by every manufacturer of durable goods with distinctive parts, the Court's opinion threatens to release a torrent of litigation and a flood of commercial intimidation that will do much more harm than good to enforcement of the antitrust laws and to genuine competition. * * *

II

On appeal in the Ninth Circuit, respondents, having waived their "rule of reason" claim, were limited to arguing that the record, construed in the light most favorable to them, supported application of the per se tying prohibition to Kodak's restrictive parts and service policy. As the Court observes, in order to survive Kodak's motion for summary judgment on this claim, respondents bore the burden of proffering evidence on which a reasonable trier of fact could conclude that Kodak possesses power in the market for the alleged "tying" product.

A

We must assume, for purposes of deciding this case, that petitioner is without market, much less monopoly, power in the interbrand markets for its micrographics and photocopying equipment. * * *

Had Kodak—from the date of its entry into the micrographics and photocopying equipment markets—included a lifetime parts and service warranty with all original equipment, or required consumers to purchase a lifetime parts and service contract with each machine, that bundling of equipment, parts and service would no doubt constitute a tie under the tests enunciated in Jefferson Parish Hospital Dist. No. 2 v. Hyde. Nevertheless, it would be immune from per se scrutiny under the antitrust laws because the tying product would be equipment, a market in which (we assume) Kodak has no power to influence price or quantity. The same result would obtain, I think, had Kodak—from the date of its market entry—consistently pursued an announced policy of limiting parts sales in the manner alleged in this case, so that customers bought with the knowledge that aftermarket support could be obtained only from Kodak. The foreclosure of respondents from the business of servicing Kodak's micrographics and photocopying machines in these illustrations would be undeniably complete—as complete as the foreclosure described in respondents' complaint. Nonetheless, we would inquire no further than to ask whether Kodak's market power in the equipment market effectively forced consumers to purchase Kodak micrographics or photocopying machines subject to the company's restrictive aftermarket practices. If not, that would end the case insofar as the per se rule was concerned. The evils against which the tying prohibition is directed would simply not be presented. * * *

* * * It is quite simply anomalous that a manufacturer functioning in a competitive equipment market should be exempt from the per se rule when it bundles equipment with parts-and-service, but not when it bundles

parts with service. This vast difference in the treatment of what will ordinarily be economically similar phenomena is alone enough to call today's decision into question.

B

In the Court of Appeals, respondents sought to sidestep the impediment posed by interbrand competition to their invocation of the per se tying rule by zeroing in on the parts and service "aftermarkets" for Kodak equipment. By alleging a tie of parts to service, rather than of equipment to parts-and-service, they identified a tying product in which Kodak unquestionably held a near-monopoly share: the parts uniquely associated with Kodak's brand of machines. The Court today holds that such a facial showing of market share in a single-brand aftermarket is sufficient to invoke the per se rule. The existence of even vibrant interbrand competition is no defense.

I find this a curious form of market power on which to premise the application of a per se proscription. * * *[193] Under the Court's analysis, the per se rule may now be applied to single-brand ties effected by the most insignificant players in fully competitive interbrand markets, as long as the arrangement forecloses aftermarket competitors from more than a de minimis amount of business. This seems to me quite wrong. * * * As implemented, the Kodak arrangement challenged in this case may have implicated truth-in-advertising or other consumer protection concerns, but those concerns do not alone suggest an antitrust prohibition.

In the absence of interbrand power, a seller's predominant or monopoly share of its single-brand derivative markets does not connote the power to raise derivative market prices generally by reducing quantity. As Kodak and its principal amicus, the United States, point out, a rational consumer considering the purchase of Kodak equipment will inevitably factor into his purchasing decision the expected cost of aftermarket support. * * * True, there are—as the Court notes—occasional irrational consumers that consider only the hardware cost at the time of purchase (a category that regrettably includes the Federal Government, whose "purchasing system," we are told, assigns foremarket purchases and aftermarket purchases to different entities). But we have never before premised the application of antitrust doctrine on the lowest common denominator of consumer.

---

[193] That there exist innumerable parts and service firms in such industries as the automobile industry does not detract from this point. The question whether power to control an aftermarket exists is quite distinct from the question whether the power has been exercised. Manufacturers in some markets have no doubt determined that exclusionary intrabrand conduct works to their disadvantage at the competitive interbrand level, but this in no way refutes the self-evident reality that control over unique replacement parts for single-branded goods is ordinarily available to such manufacturers for the taking. * * * [Dissent fn. 1]

The Court attempts to counter this theoretical point with theory of its own. It says that there are "information costs"—the costs and inconvenience to the consumer of acquiring and processing life-cycle pricing data for Kodak machines—that "could create a less responsive connection between service and parts prices and equipment sales." But this truism about the functioning of markets for sophisticated equipment cannot create "market power" of concern to the antitrust laws where otherwise there is none. "Information costs," or, more accurately, gaps in the availability and quality of consumer information, pervade real-world markets; and because consumers generally make do with "rough cut" judgments about price in such circumstances, in virtually any market there are zones within which otherwise competitive suppliers may overprice their products without losing appreciable market share. We have never suggested that the principal players in a market with such commonplace informational deficiencies (and, thus, bands of apparent consumer pricing indifference) exercise market power in any sense relevant to the antitrust laws. * * *

* * *

* * * There will be consumers who, because of their capital investment in Kodak equipment, "will tolerate some level of service-price increases before changing equipment brands"; this is necessarily true for "every maker of unique parts for its own product." But this "circumstantial" leverage created by consumer investment regularly crops up in smoothly functioning, even perfectly competitive, markets, and in most—if not all—of its manifestations, it is of no concern to the antitrust laws. The leverage held by the manufacturer of a malfunctioning refrigerator (which is measured by the consumer's reluctance to walk away from his initial investment in that device) is no different in kind or degree from the leverage held by the swimming pool contractor when he discovers a 5-ton boulder in his customer's backyard and demands an additional sum of money to remove it; or the leverage held by an airplane manufacturer over an airline that has "standardized" its fleet around the manufacturer's models; * * * or the leverage held by a mobile home park owner over his tenants, who are unable to transfer their homes to a different park except at great expense. Leverage, in the form of circumstantial power, plays a role in each of these relationships; but in none of them is the leverage attributable to the dominant party's market power in any relevant sense. Though that power can plainly work to the injury of certain consumers, it produces only "a brief perturbation in competitive conditions—not the sort of thing the antitrust laws do or should worry about." Parts & Elec. Motors, Inc. v. Sterling Elec., Inc., 866 F.2d 228, 236 (7th Cir.1988) (Posner, J., dissenting).

* * *

We have never before accepted the thesis the Court today embraces: that a seller's inherent control over the unique parts for its own brand amounts to "market power" of a character sufficient to permit invocation of the per se rule against tying. * * * A tie between two aftermarket derivatives does next to nothing to improve a competitive manufacturer's ability to extract monopoly rents from its consumers.[194]

* * *

* * * In the absence of interbrand power, a manufacturer's bundling of aftermarket products may serve a multitude of legitimate purposes: It may facilitate manufacturer efforts to ensure that the equipment remains operable and thus protect the seller's business reputation; it may create the conditions for implicit consumer financing of the acquisition cost of the tying equipment through supracompetitively-priced aftermarket purchases; and it may, through the resultant manufacturer control of aftermarket activity, "yield valuable information about component or design weaknesses that will materially contribute to product improvement," 3 Areeda & Turner para. 733c, at 258–259. Because the interbrand market will generally punish intrabrand restraints that consumers do not find in their interest, we should not—under the guise of a per se rule—condemn such potentially procompetitive arrangements simply because of the antitrust defendant's inherent power over the unique parts for its own brand.

I would instead evaluate the aftermarket tie alleged in this case under the rule of reason, where the tie's actual anticompetitive effect in the tied product market, together with its potential economic benefits, can be fully captured in the analysis. Disposition of this case does not require such an examination, however, as respondents apparently waived any rule-of-reason claim they may have had in the District Court. I would thus reverse the Ninth Circuit's judgment on the tying claim outright.

* * *

---

[194] The Court insists that the record in this case suggests otherwise, i.e., that a tie between parts and service somehow does enable Kodak to increase overall monopoly profits. * * * [T]he suggestion, apparently, is that such a tie facilitates price discrimination between sophisticated, "high-volume" users of Kodak equipment and their unsophisticated counterparts. The sophisticated users (who, the Court presumes, invariably self-service their equipment) are permitted to buy Kodak parts without also purchasing supracompetitively-priced Kodak service, while the unsophisticated are—through the imposition of the tie—compelled to buy both.

While superficially appealing, at bottom this explanation lacks coherence. Whether they self-service their equipment or not, rational foremarket consumers (those consumers who are not yet "locked in" to Kodak hardware) will be driven to Kodak's competitors if the price of Kodak equipment, together with the expected cost of aftermarket support, exceeds competitive levels. This will be true no matter how Kodak distributes the total system price among equipment, parts, and service. * * * [Dissent fn. 3]

[For the same reasons, the dissenters also rejected the Court's finding that Kodak could be said to have monopolized sales of its own parts in violation of Sherman Act § 2.]

NOTES AND QUESTIONS

1. What was alleged to be the tying product and what was tied in this case? Why wasn't the Kodak equipment the tying product?

a.   Do you agree with Justice Scalia that virtually every manufacturer "monopolizes" or "dominates" the market in some of the specialized parts of its product? Can you think of many products that are built *only* from parts that can be bought off-the-shelf from suppliers other than the manufacturer?[195]

b.   Does this case effectively make it per se illegal for a manufacturer to refuse to sell parts to *all* service providers? What defense for not selling to everyone could Kodak assert after what the Court has said about the defenses it has offered so far? Suppose some of the parts were patented; would that help Kodak's position or hurt it?

c.   Might Kodak say that only "authorized" ISOs may buy the parts, i.e., those with service personnel who had taken a course in maintenance of Kodak equipment? Would that practice be upheld under the Court's per se rule? Would it more likely survive a rule of reason analysis?

2. Was the Court right to reject Kodak's "lifecycle pricing" theory? Do you agree that no one can ever know enough facts to predict lifecycle costs fully? Is that enough to dismiss the theory?

a.   When you buy a car, is the sticker price all that you consider? Might you consult analyses of the car's cost to repair and its likely trade-in value? Even if those estimates are far from perfect, does their availability and relevance tend to lend weight to Kodak's argument here?

b.   Is the Court's point simply that the availability of comparative information in this industry is a matter for Kodak to prove at trial? Do you agree that there is enough doubt about the point that the parties should be remanded to incur the costs involved in now getting ready to try this case?

3. What was Kodak trying to accomplish here? Were its motives procompetitive, as Justice Scalia suggests, or did this case present one of the classic motives for tying?

a.   Were you persuaded by the Court's argument that Kodak should have wanted repairs to be cheap so that it could have charged more for machines? If package A + B = $100, won't I necessarily want you to be able to buy B as cheaply as possible so that $100 less the price of B will give me the maximum possible price for A? If not, why not?

---

[195]   Professor Arthur says that what Kodak had was "nonstructural market power," no greater than that possessed by many firms, and he thus suggests that antitrust challenge to it was inappropriate. See Thomas C. Arthur, The Costly Quest for Perfect Competition: *Kodak* and Nonstructural Market Power, 69 N.Y.U. L. Rev. 1 (1994). Would Justice Scalia agree?

b.　Could this arrangement have been a counting device, i.e., a way to charge higher lifecycle costs to people who used the equipment more? Wouldn't that bring the case squarely under *International Salt* and *International Business Machines*? Be careful! What was alleged to be the tying and what the tied product? Do you see why Justice Scalia was arguing that the Court had talked itself into sustaining the cause of action on a theory expressly eschewed by the plaintiffs?

c.　Is the case less about tying than about the unfairness of changing contract conditions after customers were "locked-in" to a relationship? If that is indeed the basis of the decision, why should the plaintiffs have a claim for antitrust treble damages rather than the actual damages available in a breach of contract action?

4.　Would Justice Brandeis approve of this decision? Is it consistent with his understanding of the rule of reason? Is it a decision that will tend to benefit the kinds of small businesses that were plaintiffs here?

a.　What should have been the significance of the fact that Kodak did not make all of its own replacement parts? Did that tend to show that it had no legitimate interest in controlling their distribution? Should we want antitrust rules to discourage contracting out production in this way?

b.　Could Kodak now decide to price its service at a lower cost than the ISOs and thus make it unprofitable for them to remain in business? Would that violate § 2? What *does* the Court want firms in Kodak's position to do?

5.　What was the significance of this case for the plaintiffs' antitrust bar? Did it seem to breathe life into the seemingly moribund body of private antitrust cases?

a.　If you represented antitrust plaintiffs, what would you conclude from the case about your chances of surviving summary judgment in cases generally? Does the Court here reverse the barrier to survival represented by *Matsushita*?

b.　What would improving the odds of getting to trial do to the settlement value of private cases? Would the costs of discovery alone tend to increase the likely settlement offers from defendants? Would that, in turn, tend to encourage the filing of more cases? Would that improve private enforcement of the antitrust laws or simply encourage strike suits?

6.　Did this case mark the end of the relevance of economic analysis in antitrust cases? Would you have expected to see as much economic debate in these opinions if that were true? Remember that, just a year later in *Brooke Group*, the Court expressly relied on economic theory about predatory pricing to affirm a judgment notwithstanding a jury verdict.

But the Court's attitude toward tying has been evolving, as seen in its consideration of the narrow but important issue of whether a patented product should be conclusively presumed to have market power.

ILLINOIS TOOL WORKS, INC. V. INDEPENDENT INK, INC.

Supreme Court of the United States, 2006
547 U.S. 28, 126 S.Ct. 1281, 164 L.Ed.2d 26

JUSTICE STEVENS delivered the opinion of the Court.

In Jefferson Parish Hospital Dist. No. 2 v. Hyde, we repeated the well-settled proposition that "if the Government has granted the seller a patent or similar monopoly over a product, it is fair to presume that the inability to buy the product elsewhere gives the seller market power." This presumption of market power, applicable in the antitrust context when a seller conditions its sale of a patented product (the "tying" product) on the purchase of a second product (the "tied" product), has its foundation in the judicially created patent misuse doctrine. In 1988, Congress substantially undermined that foundation, amending the Patent Act to eliminate the market power presumption in patent misuse cases. See 35 U.S.C. § 271(d). The question presented to us today is whether the presumption of market power in a patented product should survive as a matter of antitrust law despite its demise in patent law. We conclude that the mere fact that a tying product is patented does not support such a presumption.

I

Petitioners, Trident, Inc., and its parent, Illinois Tool Works Inc., manufacture and market printing systems that include three relevant components: (1) a patented piezoelectric impulse ink jet printhead; (2) a patented ink container, consisting of a bottle and valved cap, which attaches to the printhead; and (3) specially designed, but unpatented, ink. Petitioners sell their systems to original equipment manufacturers (OEMs) who are licensed to incorporate the printheads and containers into printers that are in turn sold to companies for use in printing barcodes on cartons and packaging materials. The OEMs agree that they will purchase their ink exclusively from petitioners, and that neither they nor their customers will refill the patented containers with ink of any kind.

Respondent, Independent Ink, Inc., has developed an ink with the same chemical composition as the ink sold by petitioners. After an infringement action brought by Trident against Independent was dismissed for lack of personal jurisdiction, Independent filed suit against Trident seeking a judgment of noninfringement and invalidity of Trident's patents.[196] In an amended complaint, it alleged that petitioners are

---

[196] Illinois Tool did not acquire Trident until February 19, 1999, approximately six months after this action commenced. [Court's fn. 1]

engaged in illegal tying and monopolization in violation of §§ 1 and 2 of the Sherman Act.

After discovery, the District Court granted petitioners' motion for summary judgment on the Sherman Act claims. It rejected respondent's submission that petitioners "necessarily have market power in the market for the tying product as a matter of law solely by virtue of the patent on their printhead system, thereby rendering [the] tying arrangements *per se* violations of the antitrust laws." Finding that respondent had submitted no affirmative evidence defining the relevant market or establishing petitioners' power within it, the court concluded that respondent could not prevail on either antitrust claim. The parties settled their other claims, and respondent appealed.

After a careful review of the "long history of Supreme Court consideration of the legality of tying arrangements," the Court of Appeals for the Federal Circuit reversed the District Court's decision as to respondent's § 1 claim. * * * We granted certiorari to undertake a fresh examination of the history of both the judicial and legislative appraisals of tying arrangements. Our review is informed by extensive scholarly comment and a change in position by the administrative agencies charged with enforcement of the antitrust laws.

II

American courts first encountered tying arrangements in the course of patent infringement litigation. Such a case came before this Court in Henry v. A. B. Dick Co., 224 U.S. 1 (1912), in which, as in the case we decide today, unpatented ink was the product that was "tied" to the use of a patented product through the use of a licensing agreement. Without commenting on the tying arrangement, the Court held that use of a competitor's ink in violation of a condition of the agreement—that the rotary mimeograph " 'may be used only with the stencil, paper, ink and other supplies made by A. B. Dick Co.' "—constituted infringement of the patent on the machine. Chief Justice White dissented, explaining his disagreement with the Court's approval of a practice that he regarded as an "attempt to increase the scope of the monopoly granted by a patent . . . which tends to increase monopoly and to burden the public in the exercise of their common rights." Two years later, Congress endorsed Chief Justice White's disapproval of tying arrangements, enacting § 3 of the Clayton Act. And in this Court's subsequent cases reviewing the legality of tying arrangements we, too, embraced Chief Justice White's disapproval of those arrangements.

In the years since *A. B. Dick*, four different rules of law have supported challenges to tying arrangements. They have been condemned as improper extensions of the patent monopoly under the patent misuse doctrine, as unfair methods of competition under § 5 of the Federal Trade Commission Act, 15 U.S.C. § 45, as contracts tending to create a monopoly under § 3 of the Clayton Act, 15 U.S.C. § 13a, and as contracts in restraint of trade under § 1 of the Sherman Act.[197] In all of those instances, the justification for the challenge rested on either an assumption or a showing that the defendant's position of power in the market for the tying product was being used to restrain competition in the market for the tied product. As we explained in *Jefferson Parish*, "our cases have concluded that the essential characteristic of an invalid tying arrangement lies in the seller's exploitation of its control over the tying product to force the buyer into the purchase of a tied product that the buyer either did not want at all, or might have preferred to purchase elsewhere on different terms."

* * * Our early opinions consistently assumed that "tying arrangements serve hardly any purpose beyond the suppression of competition." *Standard Oil Co. [California]*. In 1962, in *Loew's*, the Court relied on this assumption despite evidence of significant competition in the market for the tying product. And as recently as 1969, Justice Black, writing for the majority, relied on the assumption as support for the proposition "that, at least when certain prerequisites are met, arrangements of this kind are illegal in and of themselves, and no specific showing of unreasonable competitive effect is required." *Fortner Enterprises, Inc. v. United States Steel Corp.* (1969) *(Fortner I).* * * *

Reflecting a changing view of tying arrangements, four Justices dissented in *Fortner I*, arguing that the challenged "tie"—the extension of a $2 million line of credit on condition that the borrower purchase prefabricated houses from the defendant—might well have served a legitimate purpose. In his opinion, Justice White noted that promotional tie-ins may provide "uniquely advantageous deals" to purchasers. And Justice Fortas concluded that the arrangement was best characterized as "a sale of a single product with the incidental provision of financing."

The dissenters' view that tying arrangements may well be procompetitive ultimately prevailed; indeed, it did so in the very same lawsuit. After the Court remanded the suit in *Fortner I*, a bench trial resulted in judgment for the plaintiff, and the case eventually made its way back to this Court. Upon return, we unanimously held that the plaintiff's failure of proof on the issue of market power was fatal to its case—the plaintiff had proved "nothing more than a willingness to provide cheap financing in order to sell expensive houses." *United States Steel Corp. v. Fortner Enterprises, Inc.* (1977) *(Fortner II).*

---

[197] See, *e.g.*, Jefferson Parish Hospital Dist. No. 2 v. Hyde (Sherman Act); Times-Picayune Publishing Co. v. United States, 345 U.S. 594, 609, 73 S.Ct. 872, 97 L. Ed. 1277 (1953) (Federal Trade Commission Act); International Salt Co. v. United States (Clayton Act and Sherman Act); Morton Salt Co. v. G. S. Suppiger Co., 314 U.S. 488, 494, 62 S.Ct. 402, 86 L. Ed. 363 (1942) (patent misuse); Motion Picture Patents Co. v. Universal Film Mfg. Co., 243 U.S. 502, 516, 37 S.Ct. 416, 61 L. Ed. 871 (1917) (same). [Court's fn. 2]

The assumption that "tying arrangements serve hardly any purpose beyond the suppression of competition," rejected in *Fortner II*, has not been endorsed in any opinion since. Instead, it was again rejected just seven years later in *Jefferson Parish*, where, as in *Fortner II*, we unanimously reversed a Court of Appeals judgment holding that an alleged tying arrangement constituted a *per se* violation of § 1 of the Sherman Act. Like the product at issue in the *Fortner* cases, the tying product in *Jefferson Parish*—hospital services—was unpatented, and our holding again rested on the conclusion that the plaintiff had failed to prove sufficient power in the tying product market to restrain competition in the market for the tied product—services of anesthesiologists.

* * *

Notably, nothing in our opinion suggested a rebuttable presumption of market power applicable to tying arrangements involving a patent on the tying good. Instead, it described the rule that a contract to sell a patented product on condition that the purchaser buy unpatented goods exclusively from the patentee is a *per se* violation of § 1 of the Sherman Act.

Justice O'Connor wrote separately in *Jefferson Parish*, concurring in the judgment on the ground that the case did not involve a true tying arrangement because, in her view, surgical services and anesthesia were not separate products. In her opinion, she questioned not only the propriety of treating any tying arrangement as a *per se* violation of the Sherman Act, but also the validity of the presumption that a patent always gives the patentee significant market power, observing that the presumption was actually a product of our patent misuse cases rather than our antitrust jurisprudence. It is that presumption, a vestige of the Court's historical distrust of tying arrangements, that we address squarely today.

III

Justice O'Connor was, of course, correct in her assertion that the presumption that a patent confers market power arose outside the antitrust context as part of the patent misuse doctrine. * * *

Without any analysis of actual market conditions, these patent misuse decisions assumed that, by tying the purchase of unpatented goods to the sale of the patented good, the patentee was "restraining competition," *Morton Salt*, or "securing a limited monopoly of an unpatented material," *Mercoid* [v. Mid Continent Investment Co., 320 U.S. 661 (1944)]. In other words, these decisions presumed "the requisite economic power" over the tying product such that the patentee could "extend [its] economic control to unpatented products." *Loew's*.

The presumption that a patent confers market power migrated from patent law to antitrust law in International Salt Co. v. United States. In that case, we affirmed a District Court decision holding that leases of patented machines requiring the lessees to use the defendant's unpatented salt products violated § 1 of the Sherman Act and § 3 of the Clayton Act as a matter of law. Although the Court's opinion does not discuss market power or the patent misuse doctrine, it assumes that "the volume of business affected by these contracts cannot be said to be insignificant or insubstantial and the tendency of the arrangement to accomplishment of monopoly seems obvious."

* * *

Our opinion in *International Salt* clearly shows that we accepted the Government's invitation to import the presumption of market power in a patented product into our antitrust jurisprudence. While we cited *Morton Salt* only for the narrower proposition that the defendant's patents did not confer any right to restrain competition in unpatented salt or afford the defendant any immunity from the antitrust laws, given the fact that the defendant was selling its unpatented salt at competitive prices, the rule adopted in *International Salt* necessarily accepted the Government's submission that the earlier patent misuse cases supported the broader proposition "that this type of restraint is unlawful on its face under the Sherman Act."

* * * And in subsequent cases we have repeatedly grounded the presumption of market power over a patented device in *International Salt*.

IV

* * *

Three years before we decided *International Salt*, this Court had expanded the scope of the patent misuse doctrine to include not only supplies or materials used by a patented device, but also tying arrangements involving a combination patent and "unpatented material or [a] device [that] is itself an integral part of the structure embodying the patent." *Mercoid*. In reaching this conclusion, the Court explained that it could see "no difference in principle" between cases involving elements essential to the inventive character of the patent and elements peripheral to it; both, in the Court's view, were attempts to "expand the patent beyond the legitimate scope of its monopoly."

Shortly thereafter, Congress codified the patent laws for the first time. At least partly in response to our *Mercoid* decision, Congress included a provision in its codification that excluded some conduct, such as a tying arrangement involving the sale of a patented product tied to an "essential" or "nonstaple" product that has no use except as part of the patented product or method, from the scope of the patent misuse doctrine. § 271(d) . Thus, at the same time that our antitrust jurisprudence continued to rely on the assumption that "tying arrangements generally serve no legitimate business purpose," *Fortner I*, Congress began chipping away at the assumption in the patent misuse context from whence it came.

It is Congress' most recent narrowing of the patent misuse defense, however, that is directly relevant to this case. Four years after our decision in *Jefferson Parish* repeated the patent-equals-market-power presumption, Congress amended the Patent Code to eliminate that presumption in the patent misuse context, 102 Stat. 4674. The relevant provision reads:

> "(d) No patent owner otherwise entitled to relief for infringement or contributory infringement of a patent shall be denied relief or deemed guilty of misuse or illegal extension of the patent right by reason of his having done one or more of the following: . . . (5) conditioned the license of any rights to the patent or the sale of the patented product on the acquisition of a license to rights in another patent or purchase of a separate product, *unless, in view of the circumstances, the patent owner has market power in the relevant market for the patent or patented product on which the license or sale is conditioned.*" 35 U.S.C. § 271(d)(5) (emphasis added).

The italicized clause makes it clear that Congress did not intend the mere existence of a patent to constitute the requisite "market power." Indeed, fairly read, it provides that without proof that Trident had market power in the relevant market, its conduct at issue in this case was neither "misuse" nor an "illegal extension of the patent right."

While the 1988 amendment does not expressly refer to the antitrust laws, it certainly invites a reappraisal of the *per se* rule announced in *International Salt*. A rule denying a patentee the right to enjoin an infringer is significantly less severe than a rule that makes the conduct at issue a federal crime punishable by up to 10 years in prison. See 15 U.S.C. § 1. It would be absurd to assume that Congress intended to provide that the use of a patent that merited punishment as a felony would not constitute "misuse." Moreover, given the fact that the patent misuse doctrine provided the basis for the market power presumption, it would be anomalous to preserve the presumption in antitrust after Congress has eliminated its foundation.

After considering the congressional judgment reflected in the 1988 amendment, we conclude that tying arrangements involving patented products should be evaluated under the standards applied in cases like *Fortner II* and *Jefferson Parish* rather than under the *per se* rule applied in *Morton Salt* and *Loew's*. While some such arrangements are still unlawful, such as those that are the product of a true monopoly or a marketwide conspiracy, that conclusion must be supported by proof of power in the relevant market rather than by a mere presumption thereof.

V

Rather than arguing that we should retain the rule of *per se* illegality, respondent contends that we should endorse a rebuttable presumption that patentees possess market power when they condition the purchase of the patented product on an agreement to buy unpatented goods exclusively from the patentee. Respondent recognizes that a large number of valid patents have little, if any, commercial significance, but submits that those that are used to impose tying arrangements on unwilling purchasers likely do exert significant market power. Hence, in respondent's view, the presumption would have no impact on patents of only slight value and would be justified, subject to being rebutted by evidence offered by the patentee, in cases in which the patent has sufficient value to enable the patentee to insist on acceptance of the tie.

Respondent also offers a narrower alternative, suggesting that we differentiate between tying arrangements involving the simultaneous purchase of two products that are arguably two components of a single product—such as the provision of surgical services and anesthesiology in the same operation, or the licensing of one copyrighted film on condition that the licensee take a package of several films in the same transaction—and a tying arrangement involving the purchase of unpatented goods over a period of time, a so-called "requirements tie." According to respondent, we should recognize a presumption of market power when faced with the latter type of arrangements because they provide a means for charging large volume purchasers a higher royalty for use of the patent than small purchasers must pay, a form of discrimination that "is strong evidence of market power."

The opinion that imported the "patent equals market power" presumption into our antitrust jurisprudence, however, provides no support for respondent's proposed alternative. In *International Salt*, it was the existence of the patent on the tying product, rather than the use of a requirements tie, that led the Court to presume market power. * * * Moreover, the requirements tie in that case did not involve any price discrimination between large volume and small volume purchasers or evidence of noncompetitive pricing. Instead, the leases at issue provided that if any competitor offered salt, the tied product, at a lower price, "the lessee should be free to buy in the open market, unless appellant would furnish the salt at an equal price."

As we have already noted, the vast majority of academic literature recognizes that a patent does not necessarily confer market power. Similarly, while price discrimination may provide evidence of market power, particularly if buttressed by evidence that the patentee has charged an above-market price for the tied package, it is generally recognized that it also occurs in fully competitive markets. We are not persuaded that the combination of these two factors should give rise to a presumption of market power when neither is sufficient to do so standing alone. Rather, the lesson to be learned from *International Salt* and the academic commentary is the same: Many tying arrangements, even those involving patents and requirements ties, are fully consistent with a free, competitive market. For this reason, we reject both respondent's proposed rebuttable presumption and their narrower alternative.

It is no doubt the virtual consensus among economists that has persuaded the enforcement agencies to reject the position that the Government took when it supported the *per se* rule that the Court adopted in the 1940's. In antitrust guidelines issued jointly by the Department of Justice and the Federal Trade Commission in 1995, the enforcement agencies stated that in the exercise of their prosecutorial discretion they "will not presume that a patent, copyright, or trade secret necessarily confers market power upon its owner." U.S. Dept. of Justice and FTC, Antitrust Guidelines for the Licensing of Intellectual Property § 2.2 (Apr. 6, 1995). While that choice is not binding on the Court, it would be unusual for the Judiciary to replace the normal rule of lenity that is applied in criminal cases with a rule of severity for a special category of antitrust cases.

Congress, the antitrust enforcement agencies, and most economists have all reached the conclusion that a patent does not necessarily confer market power upon the patentee. Today, we reach the same conclusion, and therefore hold that, in all cases involving a tying arrangement, the plaintiff must prove that the defendant has market power in the tying product.

VI

In this case, respondent reasonably relied on our prior opinions in moving for summary judgment without offering evidence defining the relevant market or proving that petitioners possess power within it. When the case returns to the District Court, respondent should therefore be given a fair opportunity to develop and introduce evidence on that issue, as well as any other issues that are relevant to its remaining § 1 claims. Accordingly, the judgment of the Court of Appeals is vacated, and the case is remanded for further proceedings consistent with this opinion.

It is so ordered.

JUSTICE ALITO took no part in the consideration or decision of this case.

NOTES AND QUESTIONS

1.   Do you agree with the result in this case? Even though a patent undeniably creates a monopoly over some product or process, is the fact that patents vary widely as to their commercial worth evidence of the fact that many do not create significant market power?

2.   Is the Court correct that the connection between patents and market power in tying cases was grounded solely in the patent misuse doctrine? Does the fact that tying cases followed patent misuse cases chronologically necessarily demonstrate cause and effect?[198]

3.   Were you surprised to see Justice Stevens writing this majority opinion? Does he seem to implicitly acknowledge that Justice O'Connor's concurring opinion in *Jefferson Parish* has carried the day over his own majority opinion?

Earlier, we saw that the D.C. Circuit found that Microsoft had violated § 2 of the Sherman Act in its marketing of Internet Explorer. The court was at least as creative and assertive in its approach to the current state of tying law.

UNITED STATES v. MICROSOFT CORPORATION

United States Court of Appeals, District of Columbia Circuit, 2001
253 F.3d 34

PER CURIAM:

* * *

IV. Tying

* * * The District Court concluded that Microsoft's contractual and technological bundling of the IE web browser (the "tied" product) with its Windows operating system ("OS") (the "tying" product) resulted in a tying arrangement that was per se unlawful. We hold that the rule of reason, rather than per se analysis, should govern the legality of tying arrangements involving platform software products. * * * While every "business relationship" will in some sense have unique features, some represent entire, novel categories of dealings. As we shall explain, the arrangement before us is an example of the latter, offering the first up-close look at the technological integration of added functionality into software that serves as a platform for third-party applications. There being no close parallel in prior antitrust cases, simplistic application of per se tying rules carries a serious risk of harm. * * * Plaintiffs may on remand pursue their tying claim under the rule of reason.

The facts underlying the tying allegation substantially overlap with those set forth * * * in connection with the § 2 monopoly maintenance claim. The key District Court findings are that (1) Microsoft required licensees of Windows 95 and 98 also to license IE as a bundle at a single

---

[198]   The patent misuse doctrine itself is changing and becoming narrower. See Princo Corp. v. International Trade Comm'n, 616 F.3d 1318 (Fed. Cir. 2010). The Federal Circuit noted that conduct might constitute tying under the antitrust law but not constitute patent misuse.

price; (2) Microsoft refused to allow OEMs to uninstall or remove IE from the Windows desktop; (3) Microsoft designed Windows 98 in a way that withheld from consumers the ability to remove IE by use of the Add/Remove Programs utility; and (4) Microsoft designed Windows 98 to override the user's choice of default web browser in certain circumstances. The court found that these acts constituted a per se tying violation. * * *

There are four elements to a per se tying violation: (1) the tying and tied goods are two separate products; (2) the defendant has market power in the tying product market; (3) the defendant affords consumers no choice but to purchase the tied product from it; and (4) the tying arrangement forecloses a substantial volume of commerce. See Eastman Kodak Co. v. Image Tech. Servs; Jefferson Parish Hosp. Dist. No. 2 v. Hyde.

Microsoft does not dispute that it bound Windows and IE in the four ways the District Court cited. Instead it argues that Windows (the tying good) and IE browsers (the tied good) are not "separate products," and that it did not substantially foreclose competing browsers from the tied product market. * * *

* * *

A.   *Separate-Products Inquiry Under the Per Se Test*

The requirement that a practice involve two separate products before being condemned as an illegal tie started as a purely linguistic requirement: unless products are separate, one cannot be "tied" to the other. Indeed, the nature of the products involved in early tying cases—intuitively distinct items such as a movie projector and a film, led courts either to disregard the separate-products question, or to discuss it only in passing. * * *

The first case to give content to the separate-products test was *Jefferson Parish.* * * *

The *Jefferson Parish* court resolved the matter in two steps. First, it clarified that "the answer to the question whether one or two products are involved" does not turn "on the functional relation between them. . . ." In other words, the mere fact that two items are complements, that "one . . . is useless without the other," does not make them a single "product" for purposes of tying law. Second, reasoning that the "definitional question [whether two distinguishable products are involved] depends on whether the arrangement may have the type of competitive consequences addressed by the rule [against tying]," the Court decreed that "no tying arrangement can exist unless there is a sufficient demand for the purchase of anesthesiological services separate from hospital services to identify a distinct product market in which it is efficient to offer anesthesiological services separately from hospital service."

* * *

To understand the logic behind the Court's consumer demand test, consider first the postulated harms from tying. The core concern is that tying prevents goods from competing directly for consumer choice on their merits * * * . * * *

But not all ties are bad. Bundling obviously saves distribution and consumer transaction costs. This is likely to be true, to take some examples from the computer industry, with the integration of math co-processors and memory into microprocessor chips and the inclusion of spell checkers in word processors. Bundling can also capitalize on certain economies of scope. A possible example is the "shared" library files that perform OS and browser functions with the very same lines of code and thus may save drive space from the clutter of redundant routines and memory when consumers use both the OS and browser simultaneously. Indeed, if there were no efficiencies from a tie (including economizing on consumer transaction costs such as the time and effort involved in choice), we would expect distinct consumer demand for each individual component of every good. In a competitive market with zero transaction costs, the computers on which this opinion was written would only be sold piecemeal—keyboard, monitor, mouse, central processing unit, disk drive, and memory all sold in separate transactions and likely by different manufacturers.

Recognizing the potential benefits from tying, the Court in *Jefferson Parish* forged a separate-products test that, like those of market power and substantial foreclosure, attempts to screen out false positives under per se analysis. The consumer demand test is a rough proxy for whether a tying arrangement may, on balance, be welfare-enhancing, and unsuited to per se condemnation. In the abstract, of course, there is always direct separate demand for products: assuming choice is available at zero cost, consumers will prefer it to no choice. Only when the efficiencies from bundling are dominated by the benefits to choice for enough consumers, however, will we actually observe consumers making independent purchases. * * * On the supply side, firms without market power will bundle two goods only when the cost savings from joint sale outweigh the value consumers place on separate choice. So bundling by all competitive firms implies strong net efficiencies. If a court finds either that there is no noticeable separate demand for the tied product or, there being no convincing direct evidence of separate demand, that the entire "competitive fringe" engages in the same behavior as the defendant, then the tying and tied products should be declared one product and per se liability should be rejected.

* * * [W]e should clarify two things. First, *Jefferson Parish* does not endorse a direct inquiry into the efficiencies of a bundle. Rather, it proposes easy-to-administer proxies for net efficiency. In describing the separate-products test we discuss efficiencies only to explain the rationale behind the consumer demand inquiry. To allow the separate-products test to

become a detailed inquiry into possible welfare consequences would turn a screening test into the very process it is expected to render unnecessary.

Second, the separate-products test is not a one-sided inquiry into the cost savings from a bundle. Although *Jefferson Parish* acknowledged that prior lower court cases looked at cost-savings to decide separate products, the Court conspicuously did not adopt that approach in its disposition of tying arrangement before it. Instead it chose proxies that balance costs savings against reduction in consumer choice.

With this background, we now turn to the separate-products inquiry before us. * * *

Microsoft does not dispute that many consumers demand alternative browsers. But * * * Microsoft contends that no other firm * * * has invested the resources to integrate web browsing as deeply into its OS as Microsoft has. * * * Microsoft contends not only that its integration of IE into Windows is innovative and beneficial but also that it requires non-removal of IE. In our discussion of monopoly maintenance we find that these claims fail the efficiency balancing applicable in that context. But the separate-products analysis is supposed to perform its function as a proxy without embarking on any direct analysis of efficiency. Accordingly, Microsoft's implicit argument—that in this case looking to a competitive fringe is inadequate to evaluate fully its potentially innovative technological integration, that such a comparison is between apples and oranges—poses a legitimate objection to the operation of *Jefferson Parish*'s separate-products test for the per se rule.

In fact there is merit to Microsoft's broader argument that *Jefferson Parish*'s consumer demand test would "chill innovation to the detriment of consumers by preventing firms from integrating into their products new functionality previously provided by stand-alone products—and hence, by definition, subject to separate consumer demand." The per se rule's direct consumer demand and indirect industry custom inquiries are, as a general matter, backward-looking and therefore systematically poor proxies for overall efficiency in the presence of new and innovative integration. * * * Both tests compare incomparables—the defendant's decision to bundle in the presence of integration, on the one hand, and consumer and competitor calculations in its absence, on the other. If integration has efficiency benefits, these may be ignored by the *Jefferson Parish* proxies. Because one cannot be sure beneficial integration will be protected by the other elements of the per se rule, simple application of that rule's separate-products test may make consumers worse off.

* * * [W]e do not find that Microsoft's integration is welfare-enhancing or that it should be absolved of tying liability. Rather, we heed Microsoft's warning that the separate-products element of the per se rule may not give newly integrated products a fair shake.

B. *Per Se Analysis Inappropriate for this Case*

We now address directly the larger question as we see it: whether standard per se analysis should be applied "off the shelf" to evaluate the defendant's tying arrangement, one which involves software that serves as a platform for third-party applications. There is no doubt that "it is far too late in the history of our antitrust jurisprudence to question the proposition that certain tying arrangements pose an unacceptable risk of stifling competition and therefore are unreasonable 'per se.' " *Jefferson Parish.* But there are strong reasons to doubt that the integration of additional software functionality into an OS falls among these arrangements. Applying per se analysis to such an amalgamation creates undue risks of error and of deterring welfare-enhancing innovation.

* * * [T]he sort of tying arrangement attacked here is unlike any the Supreme Court has considered. The early Supreme Court cases on tying dealt with arrangements whereby the sale or lease of a patented product was conditioned on the purchase of certain unpatented products from the patentee. Later Supreme Court tying cases did not involve market power derived from patents, but continued to involve contractual ties.

In none of these cases was the tied good physically and technologically integrated with the tying good. Nor did the defendants ever argue that their tie improved the value of the tying product to users and to makers of complementary goods. In those cases where the defendant claimed that use of the tied good made the tying good more valuable to users, the Court ruled that the same result could be achieved via quality standards for substitutes of the tied good. * * * It is unclear how the benefits from IE APIs could be achieved by quality standards for different browser manufacturers. We do not pass judgment on Microsoft's claims regarding the benefits from integration of its APIs. We merely note that these and other novel, purported efficiencies suggest that judicial "experience" provides little basis for believing that, "because of their pernicious effect on competition and lack of any redeeming virtue," a software firm's decisions to sell multiple functionalities as a package should be "conclusively presumed to be unreasonable and therefore illegal without elaborate inquiry as to the precise harm they have caused or the business excuse for their use."

* * *

While the paucity of cases examining software bundling suggests a high risk that per se analysis may produce inaccurate results, the nature of the platform software market affirmatively suggests that per se rules might stunt valuable innovation. We have in mind two reasons.

First, as we explained in the previous section, the separate products test is a poor proxy for net efficiency from newly integrated products. Under per se analysis the first firm to merge previously distinct functionalities (e.g., the inclusion of starter motors in automobiles) or to eliminate entirely the need for a second function (e.g., the invention of the stain resistant carpet) risks being condemned as having tied two separate products because at the moment of integration there will appear to be a robust "distinct" market for the tied product. Rule of reason analysis, however, affords the first mover an opportunity to demonstrate that an efficiency gain from its "tie" adequately offsets any distortion of consumer choice.

The failure of the separate-products test to screen out certain cases of productive integration is particularly troubling in platform software markets such as that in which the defendant competes. Not only is integration common in such markets, but it is common among firms without market power. * * * Firms without market power have no incentive to package different pieces of software together unless there are efficiency gains from doing so. The ubiquity of bundling in competitive platform software markets should give courts reason to pause before condemning such behavior in less competitive markets.

Second, because of the pervasively innovative character of platform software markets, tying in such markets may produce efficiencies that courts have not previously encountered and thus the Supreme Court had not factored into the per se rule as originally conceived. For example, the bundling of a browser with OSs enables an independent software developer to count on the presence of the browser's APIs, if any, on consumers' machines and thus to omit them from its own package. * * *

* * *

These arguments all point to one conclusion: we cannot comfortably say that bundling in platform software markets has so little "redeeming virtue," and that there would be so "very little loss to society" from its ban, that "an inquiry into its costs in the individual case [can be] considered [ ] unnecessary." * * * [W]e will heed the wisdom that "easy labels do not always supply ready answers," and vacate the District Court's finding of per se tying liability under Sherman Act § 1. We remand the case for evaluation of Microsoft's tying arrangements under the rule of reason. * * *

Our judgment regarding the comparative merits of the per se rule and the rule of reason is confined to the tying arrangement before us, where the tying product is software whose major purpose is to serve as a platform for third-party applications and the tied product is complementary software functionality. While our reasoning may at times appear to have broader force, we do not have the confidence to speak to facts outside the record, which contains scant discussion of software integration generally. * * * Nor should we be interpreted as setting a precedent for switching to the rule of reason every time a court identifies an efficiency justification for a tying arrangement. Our reading of the record suggests merely that integration of new functionality into platform software is a common practice and that wooden application of per se rules in this litigation may cast a cloud over platform innovation in the market for PCs, network computers and information appliances.

NOTES AND QUESTIONS

1.   Did the Court convince you that a rule of reason should be applied to the bundling of software functions in this case? If the rule of reason should apply to these facts, should there be any part of the computer software industry where it is not the governing standard?

2.   The Court eschews a claim that the rule of reason should apply in most tying cases, but does its analysis lead you to that conclusion? If the rule of reason is used to assess many multi-firm cooperation practices, does it make sense to adhere strictly to a per se rule where tying is alleged? The Supreme Court decision in *Illinois Tool Works* came five years after this decision, but does it tend to show that the D.C. Circuit was reading the Court's direction properly?

3.   This case was settled before the District Court had to apply the rule of reason to this tie, but how would you approach determining whether requiring consumers to purchase an internet browser along with their operating system is procompetitive or anticompetitive?

a.   In the plaintiff's case, would a competing browser manufacturer have to prove injury to competition rather than just antitrust injury to the plaintiff? Should a court presume that a tying arrangement imposed by an operating system maker that has market power injures competition? Should the real work under the rule of reason be left to be done by the defendant?

b.   How could Microsoft have presented a convincing defense in this case? Might a court find differences in consumer benefit between including a spell-check program in a word processing program and requiring that an internet browser be purchased along with an operating system? To the contrary, given the way personal computers are used today, might the value of integrating the functionality of browsing into computer operations seem obvious?

4.   Just as Microsoft seemed to be getting these issues behind it in the United States, the European Union imposed a 497 million Euro fine against Microsoft for violating Article 82 (now 102) (abuse of dominant position) of the European Community treaty by bundling its Media Player into Windows. Microsoft v. Commission, Case T–201/04, 2007/C 269/80.

a.   The court found that Microsoft, with over a 90% market share, had a dominant position worldwide in the market for PC operating systems. There is a separate demand for streaming media players, the court found, so they constitute a separate product. Thus, by including Media Player software as part of its Windows package, Microsoft had committed a "tying abuse" that denied consumers the right to buy Windows without Media Player and made it harder for non-Windows media players to enter the marketplace.

b.   Microsoft replied that a media player had become a standard part of computer operating system and had been included by competitors Apple, Sun and Linux in their own operating systems. Microsoft also argued there was no evidence there was any customer demand for an operating system without a media player. It might be true that consumers like to have a media player in their computer, the court responded, but Microsoft customers might prefer a Sun media player, for example. When Microsoft made that possibility more costly by requiring purchase of its media player as well, it committed the tying violation.

c.   Who responded more appropriately to Microsoft's practices—the United States or the European Union? In a highly globalized economy, what are the consequences of largely opposing treatment of the same kind of behavior in two such major markets? Can you think of any good way to handle the conflicting signals sent to firms by these different antitrust regimes?[199]

5.   What effect might these developments in tying law have on the courts' approach to cases we saw in the third period (1940–1974) of antitrust enforcement?

a.   Remember *Loew's*? That was the case that prohibited movie distributors' block-booking, i.e., requiring that television stations buy unpopular films as a condition of getting the ones they wanted.

b.   A similar question arose in Brantley v. NBC Universal, Inc., 675 F.3d 1192 (9th Cir.), cert. denied, 133 S.Ct. 573 (2012). Cable subscribers sued NBC and other distributors of television programming, alleging that they sold packages of channels and did not let subscribers buy only the programs they want. In order to watch the excitement of "Law and Order," for example, a person had to also buy the talking heads of MSNBC. The Ninth Circuit affirmed dismissal of the complaint for failure to state a claim.

"[C]ourts distinguish between tying arrangements in which a company exploits its market power by attempting 'to impose restraints on competition in the market for a tied product' (which may threaten an injury to competition) and arrangements that let a company exploit its market power 'by merely enhancing the price of the tying product' (which does not)," the *Brantley* court said, citing *Jefferson Parish*.

Do you agree that the cases you have read go that far? Do you believe the Ninth Circuit has described what the Supreme Court's approach to tying should be?

---

[199] See, e.g., Daniel F. Spulber, Competition Policy and the Incentive to Innovate: The Dynamic Effects of Microsoft v. Commission, 25 Yale J. Regulation 247 (2008); Nicholas Economides & Ioannis Lianos, The Elusive Antitrust Standard on Bundling in Europe and in the United States in the Aftermath of the Microsoft Cases, 76 Antitrust L.J. 483 (2009).

BROADER ISSUES RAISED BY THE *MICROSOFT* CASE

The Antitrust Division devoted a high proportion of its resources to the *Microsoft* case for nearly a decade. The case raises many questions about antitrust law that are broader than the doctrinal issues the D.C. Circuit addressed. As we discuss in section C1, the government succeeded in its attempt to persuade the court that Microsoft had violated Sherman section 2 by using a wide variety of improper tactics to maintain its monopoly with respect to its operating system. Those tactics included bullying ISPs and hardware makers into using its operating system and even sabotaging the efforts of competitors to develop products that threatened Microsoft's monopoly. DOJ failed, however, in its far more important effort to persuade the court that Microsoft was engaged in unlawful tying of its browser and its operating system. That, in turn, doomed its extremely ambitious attempt to obtain its desired remedy of vertical divestiture and left it with nothing but behavioral remedies that had little effect on Microsoft.

DOJ refused to disclose its desired remedy until after the District Judge issued findings and conclusions that were favorable to DOJ on all issues. At that point, DOJ announced for the first time that it sought the unprecedented remedy of vertical divestiture. Microsoft tendered evidence that purported to demonstrate that vertical divestiture of Microsoft would have a variety of severe adverse effects on the U.S. and global economies. The district judge refused to hear Microsoft's evidence based on a surprising explanation. He said that he seldom learned anything new or important as a result of a hearing. He then ordered vertical divestiture without conducting any hearing.

Shortly after the district judge issued his divestiture order, other bizarre actions he had taken came to public attention. He had met regularly during the trial with a group of reporters. He agreed to give them his impressions of the witnesses and the evidence in return for their agreement not to disclose the meetings to the public. During the meetings, he described Microsoft and its management in extremely derogatory terms.

The D.C. Circuit chastised the district judge for engaging in judicial misconduct and removed him from the case. The court then rejected the proposed remedy of vertical divestiture as based on inadequate legal reasoning, inadequate evidence, and a violation of due process. It remanded the case to another district judge for further action consistent with its opinion upholding the government's monopolization claim, rejecting its illegal tying claim, and rejecting the remedy of vertical divestiture.

On remand DOJ agreed to settle the case by accepting Microsoft's offer to be the subject of a variety of behavioral remedies. Basically, Microsoft agreed to refrain from engaging in the bullying and sabotaging tactics that the circuit court had relied on as the basis for its holding that Microsoft had violated Sherman section 2.

That settlement was not acceptable to ten of the nineteen states that had joined DOJ as co-plaintiffs. They sought and obtained a hearing under the Tunney Act in which they challenged the adequacy of the remedies DOJ had agreed to accept. Those states tried to persuade the district court to reject the settlement and to impose another unprecedented remedy. They sought an order that would require Microsoft to redesign its operating system in a way that would allow anyone to plug in a rival search engine. The new district judge rejected the argument of the ten states.

1.   Was DOJ wise or responsible when it pursued this case aggressively without first identifying the remedy it sought if it won?

a.   One of the reasons DOJ did not disclose the remedy it sought was because it had not yet decided what remedy it wanted. One of the authors participated in a meeting during the trial in which DOJ staff asked several experts to provide their views on a wide range of potential remedies, including vertical divestiture, mandatory product redesign, horizontal divestiture, and mandatory provision of the computer code that is the electronic underpinning of Microsoft's operating systems to all firms that develop software and middleware. The experts identified serious problems with each proposed remedy. Should DOJ or FTC pursue a case without first deciding what it wants to get if it wins?

b.   The disagreement among the states and between DOJ and some of the states in the proceedings on remand suggest the likelihood that many of the states would not have agreed with any remedy DOJ urged before or during the trial. Can you explain why 19 states, including California and Utah, joined the U.S. as plaintiffs, while 31 states, including Washington, chose not to sue Microsoft? What might explain the major differences among the plaintiff-states with respect to the remedies sought by each? Does this case raise doubts about the wisdom of Congress's decision to give states standing to bring antitrust actions on behalf of their citizens?

2.   Is it wise for DOJ to put a high proportion of its scarce resources for a decade into an attempt to persuade a court to take unprecedented actions to address a problem in an extraordinarily dynamic market?

3.   SOME CURRENTLY OPEN ISSUES ON EXCLUSIONARY PRACTICES

As we have seen, the Supreme Court has been relatively hostile to § 2 claims in recent years, and one could reasonably question what life is left in the critique of exclusionary practices. Looking ahead, however, several issues stand out as largely unresolved and of continuing interest.

a.   Bundled Pricing and Loyalty Discounts

A producer of office supplies offers the following deal to its customers: "If you buy more than 80% of your monthly needs for four or more of my products, I will give you a 25% discount on each of them." Is that simply price competition or is it an exclusionary practice?

LePage's, Inc. v. Minnesota Mining and Manufacturing Co., 324 F.3d 141 (3d Cir. 2003) (en banc), cert. denied 124 S.Ct. 2932 (2004), raised that issue. The defendant (3M) makes "Scotch"-brand cellophane tape, and many other office products. Plaintiff LePage's makes a similar cellophane tape sold under various private-labels. Until the early 1990s, 3M had over 90% of the market for cellophane tape, but large retailers like Walmart then increased their receptivity to private-label brands. 3M responded with a "bundled rebate" program that gave lower prices to retailers who bought multiple 3M products. None of the 3M products was sold below an appropriate measure of cost, but 3M's package discounts were said to reduce LePage's sales to firms who bought "Scotch" tape in order to get lower prices on the full line of 3M offerings.

3M said that its conduct could not be "predatory" because none of its sales was below cost, but the Third Circuit disagreed. Sales can be above cost but still exclusionary, the court reasoned. The best analogy might be to tying and exclusive dealing contracts. Such contracts also arguably can show that a "monopolist made a deliberate effort to discourage its customers from doing business with its smaller rival." Entry into the cellophane tape market was hard, the court said; no previous competitor had seriously threatened 3M's sales of Scotch-brand tape. The court found no legitimate business reason for 3M's bundled sales other than to increase its total products sold, and the adverse effects on LePage's were held to be a proper basis for awarding treble damages.

Do you agree with the court's analysis?[200] Even if one says that it is not impossible to find predation in the absence of below-cost pricing, are the risks of Type 1 errors, i.e., punishing and deterring pro-competitive conduct, excessively great if one does not have bright-line rules that create safe harbors for some kinds of behavior?

Bundled pricing was again at issue, this time before the Ninth Circuit, in Cascade Health Solutions v. PeaceHealth, 515 F.3d 883 (9th Cir. 2007). PeaceHealth operated three hospitals, all of which provided primary,

---

[200] See, e.g., Daniel L. Rubinfeld, 3M's Bundled Rebates: An Economic Perspective, 72 U. Chicago L. Rev. 229 (2005); Einer Elhauge, Why Above-Cost Price Cuts to Drive Out Entrants Are Not Predatory—And the Implications for Defining Costs and Market Power, 112 Yale L.J. 681 (2003); Benjamin Klein & John Shepard Wiley, Jr., Competitive Price Discrimination as an Antitrust Justification for Intellectual Property Refusals to Deal, 70 Antitrust L.J. 599 (2003); William J. Baumol & Daniel G. Swanson, The New Economy and Ubiquitous *Competitive* Price Discrimination: Identifying Defensible Criteria of Market Power, 70 Antitrust L.J. 661 (2003); James C. Cooper, Luke Froeb, Daniel P. O'Brien, & Steven Tschantz, Does Price Discrimination Intensify Competition? Implications for Antitrust, 72 Antitrust L.J. 327 (2005).

secondary and tertiary care. McKenzie operated one hospital and offered only primary and secondary care. When the time came to renew its preferred provider agreement with Regence BlueCross-BlueShield, PeaceHealth offered to take an 85% reimbursement rate if it remained the only preferred provider, but demanded a 90% rate if McKenzie were also made a preferred provider of primary and secondary services. Regence declined to add McKenzie (now called Cascade Health Solutions), and Cascade sued PeaceHealth alleging that its arrangement with Regence was an illegal bundled discount, citing *LePage's*.

Was PeaceHealth's discount for being given exclusive rights anticompetitive? Could a bundled discount ever be undesirable in the sense of allowing a less efficient producer to outsell a more efficient one? Yes, the Ninth Circuit said, citing an example from Ortho Diagnostic System, Inc. v. Abbott Labs, Inc., 920 F.Supp. 455 (S.D.N.Y. 1996):

> Assume for the sake of simplicity that the case involved the sale of two hair products, shampoo and conditioner, the latter made only by A and the former by both A and B. Assume as well that both must be used to wash one's hair. Assume further that A's average variable cost for conditioner is $2.50, that its average variable cost for shampoo is $1.50, and that B's average variable cost for shampoo is $1.25. B therefore is the more efficient producer of shampoo. Finally, assume that A prices conditioner and shampoo at $5 and $3, respectively, if bought separately but at $3 and $2.25 if bought as part of a package. Absent the package pricing, A's price for both products is $8. B therefore must price its shampoo at or below $3 in order to compete effectively with A, given that the customer will be paying A $5 for conditioner irrespective of which shampoo supplier it chooses. With the package pricing, the customer can purchase both products from A for $5.25, a price above the sum of A's average variable cost for both products. In order for B to compete, however, it must persuade the customer to buy B's shampoo while purchasing its conditioner from A for $5. In order to do that, B cannot charge more than $0.25 for shampoo, as the customer otherwise will find A's package cheaper than buying conditioner from A and shampoo from B. On these assumptions, A would force B out of the shampoo market, notwithstanding that B is the more efficient producer of shampoo, without pricing either of A's products below average variable cost.

But the question remains whether that means all bundled discounts should be illegal. The Ninth Circuit said no. "Bundled discounts are pervasive," the court began. "Season tickets, fast food value meals, all-in-one home theater systems—all are bundled discounts." Consumers like bundled discounts because they receive more goods for less money. And bundled discounts are not tying arrangements; the customer may purchase less than all of the items if he is willing to pay a higher price for each.

The court rejected a rule saying that a firm would always act legally if it sold the bundle of products for a price that exceeded its total average variable cost of each product. That was true in the above example, the court said, and the consequences of such a rule could be inefficient.

The court also rejected a rule that would prohibit a firm's selling its product for a price that an equally-efficient competitor could not match. That would be a better rule, the court said, but a bundler cannot know the average variable costs of its competitors, so the bundling firm would always be at risk that the price it chose would be illegally low.

Instead, the court adopted a "discount attribution" test under which the defendant must add up the discounts on all the items in its bundle and treat those discounts as if they were all taken on the product in the bundle that the allegedly-excluded competitor-plaintiff was trying to sell. If, after so attributing the discounts, the defendant is selling that part of the bundle for more than its average variable cost to produce that part, the bundling should be found to be legal.[201]

Do you agree? Apply the discount attribution test to the *Ortho* shampoo example quoted above. Producer A gives a bundled discount of $2.75 to customers who buy both its shampoo and conditioner. Treating that discount as if taken on the shampoo alone, A is selling shampoo for $0.25 when its average variable cost to produce shampoo is $1.50 and the discount is not within the safe harbor.

Does that mean the package price should necessarily violate Sherman Act § 2? Suppose that, although seller B in the example could not afford to remain in the market, a significant number of other shampoo producers did remain. Should our focus be on the effects on B or on the competitive realities in the marketplace?

Bundled pricing was back before the Third Circuit in Meritor, LLC v. Eaton Corporation, 696 F.3d 254 (3d Cir. 2012). Eaton had long dominated the market for heavy-duty truck transmissions that are sold to America's four heavy-duty truck manufacturers. Meritor entered the market relatively recently, but its market share in one line had grown to 30%. When demand for heavy-duty trucks declined in 1999–2000, Eaton adopted a pricing policy that gave truck makers rebates if they purchased a high proportion—typically 85% or more—of their transmission needs from

---

[201] This result was advocated in the Report and Recommendations of the federal Antitrust Modernization Commission (2007), and it had been urged in Thomas A. Lambert, Evaluating Bundled Discounts, 89 Minnesota L. Rev. 1688 (2005), and Daniel A. Crane, Mixed Bundling, Profit Sacrifice, and Consumer Welfare, 55 Emory L. J. 423 (2006). See also, Timothy J. Muris & Vernon L. Smith, Antitrust and Bundled Discounts: An Experimental Analysis, 75 Antitrust L. J. 399 (2008) (experimental modeling of bundled discount practices in wide variety of situations finds that very few lead to anticompetitive effects).

Eaton. Each truck maker also had to remove the names of all other transmission suppliers from their data books and "preferentially price" trucks built with Eaton transmissions below the price of trucks built with transmissions from other suppliers. Eaton's prices during this period were always below Meritor's prices, but they were never below Eaton's cost.

Was Eaton's loyalty discount program predatory? Does it look more like the Microsoft requirements that the D.C. Circuit found exclusionary than it looks like traditional predatory pricing? That's how the Third Circuit saw the program. "Although the Supreme Court has created a safe harbor for above-cost discounting, it has not established a *per se* rule of non-liability under the antitrust laws for *all* contractual practices that involve above-cost pricing. * * * "In contrast to the price-cost line of cases, here, Plaintiffs do not allege that price itself functioned as the exclusionary tool." Instead, Eaton's contracts functioned more like exclusive dealing arrangements, the court held, and given the proportion of purchases Eaton required, the court upheld the jury's finding of antitrust liability.

Do you agree with the Third Circuit? How should the courts react to bundled pricing and loyalty discounts? As the Ninth Circuit said, they are all around us. They are not tying arrangements even where the seller's market share is large because the buyer is given alternative—albeit less-attractive—sale and pricing options. Exclusive dealing is often a closer analogy, although few programs require complete exclusivity. But until we have some answers from the Supreme Court, these programs are likely to remain simultaneously attractive and controversial.[202]

b. Unilateral Refusal to Deal: The Case of Intellectual Property

We have known since at least *Colgate* that a unilateral refusal to deal does not violate Sherman Act § 1. Should failure to license intellectual property ever be actionable under Sherman Act § 2? The Court's answer, given even before *Colgate,* was no. Continental Paper Bag Co. v. Eastern Paper Bag Co., 210 U.S. 405, 28 S.Ct. 748, 52 L.Ed. 1122 (1908). Even a patent holder who refuses to use the patent itself, the Court said, may enjoin its use by others.

That result has long been accepted as an inevitable corollary of a patent monopoly,[203] but some firms in recent years have argued that in

---

[202]   See, e.g., Einer Elhauge, Tying, Bundled Discounts, and the Death of the Single Monopoly Profit Theory, 123 Harvard L. Rev. 397 (2009); David S. Evans & A. Jorge Padilla, Designing Antitrust Rules for Assessing Unilateral Practices: A Neo-Chicago Approach, 72 U. Chicago L. Rev. 73 (2005); Andrew I. Gavil, Exclusionary Distribution Strategies by Dominant Firms: Striking a Better Balance, 72 Antitrust L. J. 3 (2004); Thomas A. Lambert, Appropriate Liability Rules for Tying and Bundled Discounting, 72 Ohio State L.J. 909 (2011); Daniel L. Rubinfeld, 3M's Bundled Rebates: An Economic Perspective, 72 U. Chicago L. Rev. 243 (2005).

[203]   See, e.g., Hartford-Empire Co. v. United States, 323 U.S. 386, 65 S.Ct. 373, 89 L.Ed. 322 (1945); United States v. Westinghouse Electric Corp., 648 F.2d 642 (9th Cir. 1981). Indeed, under

today's world, access to patents and other intellectual property can be the difference between a company's life and death. Indeed, they argue, failure to license can inhibit basic research and give existing firms monopolies of fields well beyond an individual patent's scope.[204]

The European Union has long been willing to carve out exceptions to the refusal to deal latitude granted U.S. holders of intellectual property rights. In RTE and ITP v. Commission (Magill), 1995 E.C.R. I–743 (1995), a company wanted to publish a comprehensive weekly guide to television programs. To assemble the guide, the company had to use listings copyrighted by the individual television channels. A national court said the station owners could enforce their rights to their own listings, but the European Court of Justice said that doing so would violate Article 86 [now Article 102] of the European Community treaty. Denial of rights to use intellectual property can "in exceptional circumstances" constitute an abuse of a firm's dominant position, the Court said. In this case, the exceptional circumstances were said to be that product innovation for the benefit of consumers was prevented, there was no legitimate business justification for the denial, and the effect was to exclude competition with the copyright holders' own guides.[205]

What do you think? Have the Europeans taken a better approach to intellectual property rights than the Americans? If the circumstances described in *Magill* are held to be "exceptional," what would be routine? Is the greater protection for intellectual property under U.S. law necessary to ensure a dynamic market for research? Have we assumed the U.S. rule is necessary without adequately considering its effect on efficiency seen more broadly?[206]

---

traditional doctrine, a firm may accumulate patents in a given technology in order to deny others the right to use them. See Automatic Radio Mfg. Co. v. Hazeltine Research, Inc., 339 U.S. 827, 70 S.Ct. 894, 94 L.Ed. 1312 (1950).

[204] Where a firm purchases intellectual property rights from another; such purchases may be analyzed under standards usually applied to mergers. See U.S. Dept. of Justice & Federal Trade Commission, Antitrust Guidelines for the Licensing of Intellectual Property § 5.7 (1995). See generally, Joel M. Cohen & Arthur J. Burke, An Overview of the Antitrust Analysis of Suppression of Technology, 66 Antitrust L.J. 421 (1998); John J. Flynn, Antitrust Policy, Innovation Efficiencies and the Suppression of Technology, 66 Antitrust L.J. 487 (1998).

[205] See, e.g., Maurits Dolmans, Restrictions on Innovation: An EU Antitrust Approach, 66 Antitrust L.J. 455 (1998). On essential facilities doctrine in the European Union generally, see John Temple Lang, Defining Legitimate Competition: Companies' Duties to Supply Competitors and Access to Essential Facilities, 18 Fordham Int'l L.J. 437 (1994).

[206] See generally, Martin J. Adelman, Property Rights Theory and Patent-Antitrust: The Role of Compulsory Licensing, 52 N.Y.U. L.Rev. 977 (1977); Rebecca Eisenberg, Patents and the Progress of Science: Exclusive Rights and Experimental Use, 56 U. Chicago L.Rev. 1017 (1989); John J. Flynn, Antitrust Policy, Innovation Efficiencies, and the Suppression of Technology, 66 Antitrust L.J. 487 (1998); Marina Lao, Unilateral Refusals to Sell or License Intellectual Property and the Antitrust Duty to Deal, 9 Cornell J. Law & Public Policy 193 (1999); Simone Rose, On Purple Pills, Stem Cells, and Other Market Failures: A Case for a Limited Compulsory Licensing Scheme for Patent Property, 48 Howard L.J. 579 (2005). See generally, Federal Trade Commission, To Promote Innovation: The Proper Balance of Competition and Patent Law and Policy (October 2003); Report of the Department of Justice's Task Force on Intellectual Property (October 2004).

In the midst of discussion of these issues, a seemingly minor issue about injunctions arose that may affect the way we think about compulsory licensing of intellectual property.

EBAY, INC. v. MERCEXCHANGE, L.L.C.

Supreme Court of the United States, 2006
547 U.S. 388, 126 S.Ct. 1837, 164 L.Ed.2d 641

JUSTICE THOMAS delivered the opinion of the Court.

Ordinarily, a federal court considering whether to award permanent injunctive relief to a prevailing plaintiff applies the four-factor test historically employed by courts of equity. Petitioners eBay Inc. and Half.com, Inc., argue that this traditional test applies to disputes arising under the Patent Act. We agree and, accordingly, vacate the judgment of the Court of Appeals.

I

Petitioner eBay operates a popular Internet Web site that allows private sellers to list goods they wish to sell, either through an auction or at a fixed price. Petitioner Half.com, now a wholly owned subsidiary of eBay, operates a similar Web site. Respondent MercExchange, L.L.C., holds a number of patents, including a business method patent for an electronic market designed to facilitate the sale of goods between private individuals by establishing a central authority to promote trust among participants. MercExchange sought to license its patent to eBay and Half.com, as it had previously done with other companies, but the parties failed to reach an agreement. MercExchange subsequently filed a patent infringement suit against eBay and Half.com * * * . A jury found that MercExchange's patent was valid, that eBay and Half.com had infringed that patent, and that an award of damages was appropriate.[207]

Following the jury verdict, the District Court denied MercExchange's motion for permanent injunctive relief. The Court of Appeals for the Federal Circuit reversed, applying its "general rule that courts will issue permanent injunctions against patent infringement absent exceptional circumstances." 401 F.3d 1323, 1339 (2005). We granted certiorari to determine the appropriateness of this general rule.

II

According to well-established principles of equity, a plaintiff seeking a permanent injunction must satisfy a four-factor test before a court may grant such relief. A plaintiff must demonstrate: (1) that it has suffered an irreparable injury; (2) that remedies available at law, such as monetary damages, are inadequate to compensate for that injury; (3) that,

---

[207] EBay and Half.com continue to challenge the validity of MercExchange's patent in proceedings pending before the United States Patent and Trademark Office. [Court's fn. 1]

considering the balance of hardships between the plaintiff and defendant, a remedy in equity is warranted; and (4) that the public interest would not be disserved by a permanent injunction. The decision to grant or deny permanent injunctive relief is an act of equitable discretion by the district court, reviewable on appeal for abuse of discretion.

These familiar principles apply with equal force to disputes arising under the Patent Act. As this Court has long recognized, "a major departure from the long tradition of equity practice should not be lightly implied." Nothing in the Patent Act indicates that Congress intended such a departure. To the contrary, the Patent Act expressly provides that injunctions "may" issue "in accordance with the principles of equity." 35 U.S.C. § 283.

To be sure, the Patent Act also declares that "patents shall have the attributes of personal property," § 261, including "the right to exclude others from making, using, offering for sale, or selling the invention," § 154(a)(1). According to the Court of Appeals, this statutory right to exclude alone justifies its general rule in favor of permanent injunctive relief. But the creation of a right is distinct from the provision of remedies for violations of that right. Indeed, the Patent Act itself indicates that patents shall have the attributes of personal property "subject to the provisions of this title," 35 U.S.C. § 261, including, presumably, the provision that injunctive relief "may" issue only "in accordance with the principles of equity," § 283.

This approach is consistent with our treatment of injunctions under the Copyright Act. Like a patent owner, a copyright holder possesses "the right to exclude others from using his property." * * * And as in our decision today, this Court has consistently rejected invitations to replace traditional equitable considerations with a rule that an injunction automatically follows a determination that a copyright has been infringed.

Neither the District Court nor the Court of Appeals below fairly applied these traditional equitable principles in deciding respondent's motion for a permanent injunction. Although the District Court recited the traditional four-factor test, it appeared to adopt certain expansive principles suggesting that injunctive relief could not issue in a broad swath of cases. Most notably, it concluded that a "plaintiff's willingness to license its patents" and "its lack of commercial activity in practicing the patents" would be sufficient to establish that the patent holder would not suffer irreparable harm if an injunction did not issue. But traditional equitable principles do not permit such broad classifications. For example, some patent holders, such as university researchers or self-made inventors, might reasonably prefer to license their patents, rather than undertake efforts to secure the financing necessary to bring their works to market themselves. Such patent holders may be able to satisfy the traditional four-factor test, and we see no basis for categorically denying them the opportunity to do so. * * *

In reversing the District Court, the Court of Appeals departed in the opposite direction from the four-factor test. The court articulated a "general rule," unique to patent disputes, "that a permanent injunction will issue once infringement and validity have been adjudged." The court further indicated that injunctions should be denied only in the "unusual" case, under "exceptional circumstances" and " 'in rare instances . . . to protect the public interest.' " Just as the District Court erred in its categorical denial of injunctive relief, the Court of Appeals erred in its categorical grant of such relief.

Because we conclude that neither court below correctly applied the traditional four-factor framework that governs the award of injunctive relief, we vacate the judgment of the Court of Appeals, so that the District Court may apply that framework in the first instance. * * *

Accordingly, we vacate the judgment of the Court of Appeals, and remand for further proceedings consistent with this opinion.

CHIEF JUSTICE ROBERTS, with whom JUSTICE SCALIA and JUSTICE GINSBURG join, concurring.

I agree with the Court's holding that "the decision whether to grant or deny injunctive relief rests within the equitable discretion of the district courts, and that such discretion must be exercised consistent with traditional principles of equity, in patent disputes no less than in other cases governed by such standards," and I join the opinion of the Court. * * *

From at least the early 19th century, courts have granted injunctive relief upon a finding of infringement in the vast majority of patent cases. This "long tradition of equity practice" is not surprising, given the difficulty of protecting a right to *exclude* through monetary remedies that allow an infringer to *use* an invention against the patentee's wishes—a difficulty that often implicates the first two factors of the traditional four-factor test. This historical practice, as the Court holds, does not *entitle* a patentee to a permanent injunction or justify a *general rule* that such injunctions should issue. The Federal Circuit itself so recognized in Roche Products, Inc. v. Bolar Pharmaceutical Co., 733 F.2d 858 (1984). At the same time, there is a difference between exercising equitable discretion pursuant to the established four-factor test and writing on an entirely clean slate. * * *

JUSTICE KENNEDY, with whom JUSTICE STEVENS, JUSTICE SOUTER, and JUSTICE BREYER join, concurring.

The Court is correct, in my view, to hold that courts should apply the well-established, four-factor test—without resort to categorical rules—in deciding whether to grant injunctive relief in patent cases. The Chief Justice is also correct that history may be instructive in applying this test.

The traditional practice of issuing injunctions against patent infringers, however, does not seem to rest on "the difficulty of protecting a right to *exclude* through monetary remedies that allow an infringer to *use* an invention against the patentee's wishes." Both the terms of the Patent Act and the traditional view of injunctive relief accept that the existence of a right to exclude does not dictate the remedy for a violation of that right. To the extent earlier cases establish a pattern of granting an injunction against patent infringers almost as a matter of course, this pattern simply illustrates the result of the four-factor test in the contexts then prevalent.
* * *

In cases now arising trial courts should bear in mind that in many instances the nature of the patent being enforced and the economic function of the patent holder present considerations quite unlike earlier cases. An industry has developed in which firms use patents not as a basis for producing and selling goods but, instead, primarily for obtaining licensing fees. For these firms, an injunction, and the potentially serious sanctions arising from its violation, can be employed as a bargaining tool to charge exorbitant fees to companies that seek to buy licenses to practice the patent. When the patented invention is but a small component of the product the companies seek to produce and the threat of an injunction is employed simply for undue leverage in negotiations, legal damages may well be sufficient to compensate for the infringement and an injunction may not serve the public interest. In addition injunctive relief may have different consequences for the burgeoning number of patents over business methods, which were not of much economic and legal significance in earlier times. The potential vagueness and suspect validity of some of these patents may affect the calculus under the four-factor test.

The equitable discretion over injunctions, granted by the Patent Act, is well suited to allow courts to adapt to the rapid technological and legal developments in the patent system. For these reasons it should be recognized that district courts must determine whether past practice fits the circumstances of the cases before them. With these observations, I join the opinion of the Court.

NOTES AND QUESTIONS

1.   If patents are presumed valid, when will it ever be appropriate to fail to enforce them with an injunction? If a neighbor regularly came uninvited into your back yard, wouldn't you be entitled to enjoin the trespass? May it be that the Court believes that patents are an unusually uncertain and ill-defined form of property rights? Might possession of what seem to be monopoly rights threaten anti-competitive results?[208]

---

[208]   See, e.g., Christopher R. Leslie, The Anticompetitive Effects of Unenforced Invalid Patents, 91 Minnesota L. Rev. 101 (2006).

2. Should the strength of the underlying patent be relevant to a grant of injunctive relief? How should a district court determine that issue without conducting a full trial? By what standard should a court of appeals review the determination? See, e.g., du Pont v. MacDermid, 2007 WL 2332161 (D.N.J. 2007) (denying injunction because priority of patents uncertain), rev'd 525 F.3d 1353 (Fed.Cir. 2008) (finding that du Pont patent had priority). On remand, the district court again denied injunctive relief, 2008 WL 4952450 (D.N.J. 2008), this time because of a substantial question whether the invention was "obvious" and because of a public interest in "continued competition * * * in the market."

3. The *du Pont* court's reference to the "obviousness" standard refers to the requirement that a patent not be granted to an alleged invention that "would have been obvious at the time the invention was made to a person having ordinary skill in the art to which such subject matter pertains." For many years, the Federal Circuit was thought not to have made that standard a real limitation on the granting of patents, but in KSR International Co. v. Teleflex Inc., 550 U.S. 398, 127 S.Ct. 1727, 167 L.Ed.2d 705 (2007), the Supreme Court restored its significance.

4. Further, one technique patent holders had used to avoid direct challenges to a patent's validity was to license the patent to potential challengers. The rule had been that a licensee could not both use the invention under a license and challenge the validity of the patent, but in Medimmune, Inc. v. Genentech, Inc., 549 U.S. 118, 127 S.Ct. 764, 166 L.Ed.2d 604 (2007), the Court upheld licensee challenges.

c. Patents and Standards Setting

One important kind of multi-firm conduct permitted by antitrust enforcement agencies today is standards setting. The agencies recognize that in rapidly evolving fields, particularly those involving high technology, both development and competition may be stimulated by having industry standards to which all companies can work and that will allow interaction of the many companies' products.

But there is a second important issue involving standards setting. Should an industry participant be permitted to advocate adoption of a standard that would require others in the industry to pay a royalty to use the advocate's patented technology? In Rambus Inc. v. Infineon Technologies AG, 318 F.3d 1081 (Fed. Cir.), cert. denied 540 U.S. 874, 124 S.Ct. 227, 157 L.Ed.2d 135 (2003), Rambus had developed a new form of computer memory that it hoped chip makers would license. An industry group, the JEDEC, tried cooperatively to develop a different technology. Rambus allegedly realized that if the industry standard were written in a particular way, Rambus could amend its pending patent application so as to make the new standard infringe it. That would let Rambus collect a royalty on all chips produced under the standard. Rambus joined the JEDEC and got the standard written to its liking.

Infineon resisted paying royalties to Rambus, alleging that Rambus had committed fraud on the standards setting process by failing to disclose the fact of its patent application and the fact that the standard under consideration would infringe it. A closely-divided panel of the Federal Circuit rejected the fraud claim, finding that Rambus had complied with the JEDEC's own disclosure requirements, but the court affirmed the idea that participants in a standards setting process have some requirement of candor about their self interest.[209]

Rambus continued to pursue firms it thought infringed its patents, however, and for doing so, the Federal Trade Commission charged Rambus with both unfair methods of competition and unfair or deceptive acts or practices in violation of FTC Act § 5. Rambus' failure to tell the standards setting body about its existing patents allowed it either to acquire and exploit its monopoly or to avoid the requirement of "reasonable and non-discriminatory" (RAND) royalties that the standards setting body would have imposed had it known of the patents, the Commission found.

What do you think of this argument? Can the Commission ever really know what standard would have been adopted or conditions imposed if Rambus had disclosed its patents? On the other hand, can the Commission properly argue that one of its functions is to prevent all kinds of underhanded conduct by companies?

The D.C. Circuit rejected the FTC position. Rambus Inc. v. Federal Trade Commission, 522 F.3d 456 (D.C.Cir.2008). Mere possession of a monopoly does not violate the law, the court said. Nor does exploitation of that monopoly, citing *Trinko*. All the law forbids is exclusionary conduct, i.e., willfully acquiring or maintaining monopoly power by means other than a superior product, business acumen or historical accident. The government has the burden of proof of anticompetitive effect, the court said, and "use of deception simply to obtain higher prices normally has no particular tendency to exclude rivals and thus to diminish competition."[210]

---

[209] For an excellent analysis of such issues, see Mark A. Lemley, Intellectual Property Rights and Standards-Setting Organizations, 90 California L. Rev. 1889 (2002); see also, M. Sean Royall, Standard Setting and Exclusionary Conduct: The Role of Antitrust in Policing Unilateral Abuses of Standard Setting Processes, 18 ABA Antitrust 44 (Spr. 2004). In 2005, Rambus and Infineon reached a private settlement whereby Infineon would pay Rambus $47 million in royalties for 2-years' rights to all Rambus patents.

[210] 522 F.3d at 464 (citing NYNEX Corp. v. Discon). Earlier, the Third Circuit came out the other way in Broadcom Corp. v. Qualcomm Inc., 501 F.3d 297 (3rd Cir.2007). For more on antitrust issues in standard setting, see, e.g., Joseph Farrell, John Hayes, Carl Shapiro & Theresa Sullivan, Standard Setting, Patents, and Hold-Up, 74 Antitrust L.J. 603 (2007); Herbert Hovenkamp, Standards Ownership and Competition Policy, 48 Boston Coll. L. Rev. 87 (2007); Justin (Gus) Herwitz, The Value of Patents in Industry Standards: Avoiding License Arbitrage With Voluntary Rules, 36 AIPLA Quarterly J. 1 (2008).

Nevertheless, firms in standards setting organizations have recognized that they all have an interest in not being deceived by someone doing what Rambus did. Many SSOs have established rules that any member with a standard-essential patent (one infringed by conforming to the standard) agrees to license it on a RAND (or FRAND (fair, reasonable and non-discriminatory) basis.

Both the Department of Justice and the FTC have indicated that a company's breach of its F/RAND commitment may violate of Sherman Act § 2. See U.S. Dept. of Justice & Federal Trade Comm'n, Antitrust Enforcement and Intellectual Property Rights: Promoting Innovation and Competition 37–38 (2007), and Federal Trade Comm'n, The Evolving IP Marketplace: Aligning Patent Notice and Remedies with Competition 114 (2011).

And the latitude not to grant an injunction conferred by e-Bay v. MercExchange, supra, has started to take away the principal leverage the patent holder has if it fails to honor its commitment. See, e.g., Apple v. Motorola, 869 F.Supp.2d 901 (N.D.Ill. 2012) (FRAND royalty is the patent holder's complete and only remedy). Agreement on the dollar amount of a proper F/RAND royalty is not always a foregone conclusion, but taking the possibility of an injunction off the table seems likely to remove the incentive to exploit the exclusionary potential of a standard-essential patent.

d. Does FTC Act § 5 Give the Commission Authority to Go Beyond the Other Antitrust Laws in Defining Unfair Methods of Competition?

In general, the Federal Trade Commission applies the antitrust laws just as the Justice Department does. That is why the agencies issue joint Guidelines, for example. But the question remains open whether the FTC could interpret the "unfair methods of competition" language of § 5 to reach conduct not prohibited by the Sherman and Clayton Acts. In FTC v. Sperry & Hutchison Co., 405 U.S. 233, 92 S.Ct. 898, 31 L.Ed.2d 170 (1972), the Supreme Court confirmed that the FTC Act gave the Commission some latitude to do so, but the Commission has rarely used the authority, and it has been largely unsuccessful when it has tried.[211]

The FTC's negotiated settlement in the N-Data case,[212] however, has renewed interest in the possible reach of § 5. N-Data has patents on Fast Ethernet technology used to help local area networks interconnect computers and related devices. Unlike the *Rambus* situation, when the

---

[211] See, e.g., Official Airline Guides, Inc. v. FTC, 630 F.2d 920 (2nd Cir. 1980) (dominant company had achieved position innocently); Russell Stover Candies v. FTC, 718 F.2d 256 (8th Cir. 1983) (refusal to deal if sold below suggested price); E.I. du Pont deNemours & Co. v. FTC, 729 F.2d 128 (2nd Cir. 1984) (parallel pricing without proof of agreement).

[212] In the Matter of Negotiated Data Solutions, LLC, Docket No. D–4234 (Sept. 22, 2008).

Institute of Electrical and Electronics Engineers (IEEE) was establishing the standards companies would use for such networks, N-Data revealed its technology and said that if it were used, it would make non-exclusive licenses available for its use for a one-time royalty of $1000 per user. The N-Data technology was adopted and the company adhered to its promise until 2002 when it notified the IEEE that it would instead seek to increase the royalty to all new and existing users.

N-Data got several users to agree to higher royalties, but by a vote of 3 to 2, the FTC intervened to prohibit what it saw as exploitation of a monopoly position established under false pretenses. The FTC majority cited the Commission's consumer protection standard to say that exploiting licensees who are "locked in" to an adopted standard is an "unfair act or practice." The dissenters argued that it was inappropriate to mix the consumer protection and competition functions of the agency in this way, and that it was inappropriate to turn every misrepresentation or breach of contract into a potential violation of § 5.

Because the case was settled, we cannot know how the courts would have reacted to applying § 5 to the *N-Data* facts. What do you think? Would an expanded § 5 provide a way to apply the antitrust laws more expansively than current law seems to permit? Would the FTC's status as an administrative agency give it an ability to hold hearings on the economic effects of practices that the Justice Department arguably lacks?[213]

D. MERGER REVIEW: ANTITRUST AS AN ADMINISTRATIVE PROCESS

As we saw in Chapter III, in the 1960s, no field of antitrust law was more before the courts than challenges to mergers under Clayton Act § 7. Market definitions were flexibly tailored, relatively low market shares led to presumptive invalidity of many mergers, and a perceived loss of "potential competition" became a basis for challenging yet other combinations. All that changed early in the modern period.

1. TRANSITIONAL DEVELOPMENTS

BRINGING REALISM TO MARKET ANALYSIS— THE *GENERAL DYNAMICS* CASE

The essentially unbroken line of successful government merger challenges in the 1960s and early 70s came to an end with the Supreme

---

[213] In 2013, FTC Commissioners Joshua Wright and Maureen Ohlhausen each proposed an expanded role for § 5, but each would apply a test that focuses on harm to the competitive process and a lack of cognizable efficiencies rather than harm to small business or other "non-economic" factors. See www.ftc.gov/speeches/wright/130619umcpolicystatement.pdf and www.ftc.gov/public-statements/2013/07/section-5-principles-navigation.

Court's decision in United States v. General Dynamics Corp., 415 U.S. 486, 94 S.Ct. 1186, 39 L.Ed.2d 530 (1974). The case challenged Material Service Corporation's acquisition of United Electric Coal Companies. Material Service engaged in deep-mining coal and previously had been acquired by General Dynamics; United Electric mined coal from open-pit and strip-mines.

The Government argued that the acquisition violated Clayton Act § 7 by substantially lessening competition in the production and sale of coal both in the State of Illinois and in the geologically-based Eastern Interior Coal Province Sales Area. The proof likely would have satisfied the Court in the 1960s. Based on recent sales of coal, the degree of concentration in the markets was comparable to that in United States v. Von's Grocery Co., 384 U.S. 270, 86 S.Ct. 1478, 16 L.Ed.2d 555 (1966), where the top four firms in the market had controlled 24.4% of the sales and the top eight 40.9%. The increase in concentration among the top firms was also similar to that found in *Von's*.

The District Court found, however, that in the years after World War II, the coal industry had changed profoundly. Railroads no longer used coal, and environmental concerns had made oil and natural gas highly competitive sources of energy for industrial and residential uses. Coal's share of the energy resources consumed in this country had fallen from 78.4% in 1920 to 21.4% in 1968. Thus, the use of coal as a product market was itself questionable.

Next, to the extent coal was used as an energy source at all, it was used primarily by the electric utility industry. In 1968, utilities bought almost 60% of all the coal consumed in the Nation. Further, in that industry, nearly all coal was sold under long-term requirements contracts that guaranteed to meet coal requirements for a fixed period of time and at agreed prices.

Looking at these facts, the Supreme Court found no meaningful lessening of competition in the market for coal. Writing for the Court, Justice Stewart—formerly the lonely dissenter—reasoned:

> "Evidence of past production does not, as a matter of logic, necessarily give a proper picture of a company's future ability to compete. In most situations, of course, the unstated assumption is that * * * [e]vidence of the amount of annual sales is relevant as a prediction of future competitive strength, since in most markets distribution systems and brand recognition are such significant factors that one may reasonably suppose that a company which has attracted a given number of sales will retain that competitive strength.

> "In the coal market * * * , however, statistical evidence of coal *production* was of considerably less significance. * * * The focus of

competition in a given time frame is not on the disposition of coal already produced but on the procurement of new long-term supply contracts. In this situation, a company's past ability to produce is of limited significance, since it is in a position to offer for sale neither its past production nor the bulk of the coal it is presently capable of producing, which is typically already committed under a long-term supply contract. A more significant indicator of a company's power effectively to compete with other companies lies in the state of a company's uncommitted reserves of recoverable coal. * * *

"The testimony and exhibits in the District Court revealed that United Electric's coal reserve prospects were 'unpromising.' * * * While United ranked fifth among Illinois coal producers in terms of annual production, it was 10th in reserve holdings, and controlled less than 1% of the reserves held by coal producers in Illinois, Indiana, and western Kentucky. * * *

"Viewed in terms of present and future reserve prospects—and thus in terms of probable future ability to compete—rather than in terms of past production, the District Court held that United Electric was a far less significant factor in the coal market than the Government contended or the production statistics seemed to indicate. While the company had been and remained a "highly profitable" and efficient producer of relatively large amounts of coal, its current and future power to compete for subsequent long-term contracts was severely limited by its scarce uncommitted resources. Irrespective of the company's size when viewed as a producer, its weakness as a competitor was properly analyzed by the District Court and fully substantiated that court's conclusion that its acquisition by Material Service would not 'substantially * * * lessen competition * * * .' "

The Court rejected the view that its analysis was a misplaced use of the "failing company" defense. The Court was not assuming United Electric was unprofitable; it was saying that the acquisition would not substantially alter future competition for long-term contracts.

Justices Douglas, Brennan, White and Marshall seemed to see that their days of prevailing in merger cases were coming to an end. In dissent, they gamely asserted that United Electric could have acquired additional reserves and in that way remained a future competitor. But no new strip mining reserves were available, the majority answered, and deep mining would have been a new line of business for United Electric. The merger was held not to violate § 7.

MODERATING THE POTENTIAL COMPETITION
DOCTRINE IN *MARINE BANCORPORATION*

The same year that the Court decided *General Dynamics*, it also decided United States v. Marine Bancorporation, 418 U.S. 602, 94 S.Ct. 2856, 41 L.Ed.2d 978 (1974). National Bank of Commerce (NBC), a large national bank in Seattle (and a subsidiary of Marine Bancorporation), had proposed to acquire Washington Trust Bank (WTB), the state's ninth largest bank, operating exclusively on the other side of the state in Spokane.

Before the merger, the banks were not significant competitors anywhere in the state, but the Government argued that NBC might have entered the Spokane market de novo or by acquiring a smaller bank. Further, the Government argued, the merger removed NBC as a perceived potential entrant; whatever effect on the market that status might have created would also be lost.

The District Court found instead that the merger would substantially *increase* competition in Spokane banking and have no anticompetitive effects. It found "no reasonable probability" that NBC would have entered the Spokane market in the "reasonably foreseeable future," and by a vote of 5–3, the Supreme Court affirmed. Spokane was the relevant geographic market, the Court said, not the state as a whole. Spokane residents do not bank in Seattle any more than the Philadelphia residents in *Philadelphia Bank* would have considered banking in Pittsburgh.

The potential competition doctrine looks to questions of likely entry, Justice Powell wrote for the majority. Further, the potential competition doctrine is not controlling where the market of the acquired firm is not concentrated. As Justice Harlan had suggested in *Procter & Gamble*, if a market is competitive and not oligopolistic, there will be no reason for the firms to change their behavior out of fear of potential entry.

Because banking is heavily regulated, banking markets *are* often concentrated. On the other hand, before applying the doctrine to banking markets, one has to look at the legal limitations on banks' expansion or entry into new areas. Here, state law *forbade* NBC's expansion into Spokane by creating branch banks or without overcoming other substantial regulatory barriers. Merger was the *only* effective way for NBC to enter Spokane.

Similarly, NBC would not have been a *perceived* potential entrant. Bankers in Spokane would certainly have known how hard it would be for NBC to enter other than by a merger of this kind, and thus they would not have changed their own behavior out of concern about such entry.

In dissent, Justices White, Brennan, and Marshall again expressed concern at how merger analysis seemed to be changing. Justice Douglas did not participate in the decision.[214]

THE HART-SCOTT-RODINO ACT AND THE MOVE TO ADMINISTRATIVE RESOLUTION OF MERGERS

At about the same time the Supreme Court was changing its substantive analysis of mergers, Congress made a crucial legislative change in the approach to merger review. The Hart-Scott-Rodino Act of 1976, now § 7A of the Clayton Act, requires that firms give the Justice Department and FTC 30 days advance notice if they plan a merger and certain conditions are met—basically that the transaction involves over $200 million in voting securities and assets of the acquired firm, or involves over $50 million in voting securities and assets and one of the companies has annual sales or total assets of over $100 million while the other's annual sales or total assets exceed $10 million.[215]

At least for big companies, the requirement has transformed merger practice. The only "litigation" over most mergers is at the meetings at which the parties try to satisfy possible agency concerns about the transaction. If clearance is obtained, the merger can proceed with only the risk of private challenge. If the agencies are not satisfied, however, they may ask for more information, seek to enjoin the merger, or both. In some cases, the delay caused by this process can cause transactions to fall through because the parties' sources of financing will not continue to put their funds at risk indefinitely.

When Exxon Corporation announced a plan to acquire Mobil Oil, for example, the Federal Trade Commission opened an investigation. Coordinating its work with that of the European Union and several state attorneys' general, the Commission concluded that the merger would substantially lessen retail competition in the Northeastern states and Mid-Atlantic region, Texas, Arizona and California, as well as other products and services in other regions.[216] Prior to filing a complaint seeking a

---

[214] See also, United States v. Citizens & Southern National Bank, 422 U.S. 86, 95 S.Ct. 2099, 45 L.Ed.2d 41 (1975) (no lessening of competition where bank turned banks in which it had a 5% interest into branches of its main bank).

[215] The triggering amounts are subject to annual adjustment. The statutory provision, 15 U.S.C. § 18a, is contained in the Appendix to these materials. The approval process is described in ABA Section of Antitrust Law, Antitrust Law Developments 370–97 (5th Ed. 2002). The agencies decide which kinds of filings each will ordinarily have the responsibility to review. Annual joint reports to Congress from the Department of Justice and Federal Trade Commission, found at www.ftc.gov/, also provide useful information about the review process in action.

[216] In this case, the European Commission had already approved the merger. For a discussion of the circumstance in which a domestic merger with international effects is first approved by the United States, see Daniel J. Gifford & E. Thomas Sullivan, Can International Antitrust Be Saved

preliminary injunction, however, the Commission and the companies negotiated a plan under which Exxon and Mobil would divest themselves of over 2,400 gas stations in the affected areas, as well as a number of other assets. Under the plan, the firms accepted the Commission's jurisdiction, findings and disposition, and 60 days after publication in the Federal Register, the merger went forward.

When "Baby Bells" Bell Atlantic and NYNEX proposed to merge, the issue was potential competition. They provided local telephone service in different regions, so they argued that theirs was simply a market extension merger that could not substantially limit current competition. The Telecommunications Act of 1996, however, potentially had given local carriers a right to offer long distance service; that service would be offered in a competitive national market. Bell Atlantic had studied entering the NYNEX market with such service, but had not done so. Nor did anyone know how many and which firms would offer long distance service in the future. Indeed, it was not clear whether substantially new technologies might render the question moot. It seems to have been this uncertainty that led ultimately to the merger's final approval. There was simply no basis for showing that the loss of competition between Bell Atlantic and NYNEX long distance services would be significant.[217]

In the Time Warner/Turner merger, the concern was a loss of competition in providing content for cable television. Turner owned CNN and a large movie library; Time Warner owned HBO, Cinemax and Comedy Central; TCI, which already owned 23% of Turner, owned Encore, QVC and The Learning Channel. The proposed merger, opponents feared, could result in the new company's denial of popular programming to competing cable and satellite providers and lead to their monopoly of news and entertainment going into consumers' homes. Creation of the competing Fox News Channel and MSNBC ultimately lowered the intensity of the concerns, so in the end, the FTC approved the merger with limits on the ownership interest TCI could thereafter obtain in the new corporation.[218]

The subject of merger regulation remains controversial, in large part because the wave of mergers in the 1980s and 90s arguably created a new

---

for the Post-Boeing Merger World? A Proposal to Minimize International Conflict and to Rescue Antitrust From Misuse, 45 Antitrust Bulletin 55 (Spring 2000). See also, Douglas H. Ginsburg & Scott H. Angstreich, Multinational Merger Review: Lessons From Our Federalism, 68 Antitrust L.J. 219 (2000).

[217] The case is discussed in Steven R. Brenner, Potential Competition in Local Telephone Service: Bell Atlantic-NYNEX (1997), in John E. Kwoka & Lawrence J. White, eds., The Antitrust Revolution: Economics, Competition and Policy (3d Ed. 1999), p. 116.

[218] See generally, Stanley M. Besen, E. Jane Murdoch, Daniel P. O'Brien, Steven C. Salop & John Woodbury, Vertical and Horizontal Ownership in Cable TV: Time Warner-Turner (1996), in John E. Kwoka & Lawrence J. White, eds., The Antitrust Revolution: Economics, Competition and Policy (3d Ed. 1999), p. 452. For a criticism of the "regulatory" rather than enforcement posture now assumed by the Justice Department and Federal Trade Commission, see Spencer Weber Waller, Prosecution by Regulation: The Changing Nature of Antitrust Enforcement, 77 Oregon L.Rev. 1383 (1998).

tendency toward concentration in the economy. Successive administrations have asserted they would challenge high-risk mergers more aggressively, but evidence of that in practice is not clear.[219]

2. THE HORIZONTAL MERGER GUIDELINES

As they have done in other areas of antitrust interest, the Department of Justice and Federal Trade Commission have issued joint Guidelines to explain how they will exercise their discretion concerning mergers. Merger Guidelines have been around since 1968. The latest Horizontal Merger Guidelines were issued in 2010.[220] The Merger Guidelines are so central to the process of merger review that they are quoted here at length.[221] You should also find them useful as a review of current thinking on a number of more general competition issues covered in this course.

a. The Market Power Issue

The overarching question addressed in the Merger Guidelines is the extent to which a proposed merger will increase the parties' market power. Part 1 of the Guidelines explains:

> "The unifying theme of these Guidelines is that mergers should not be permitted to create, enhance, or entrench market power or to facilitate its exercise. For simplicity of exposition, these Guidelines generally refer to all of these effects as enhancing market power. A merger enhances market power if it is likely to encourage one or more firms to raise price, reduce output, diminish innovation, or otherwise harm customers as a result of diminished competitive constraints or incentives. In evaluating how a merger will likely change a firm's behavior, the

---

[219] Good data is provided in Malcolm B. Coate & Shawn W. Ulrick, Transparency at the Federal Trade Commission: The Horizontal Merger Review Process 1996–2003 (FTC 2005). See also, e.g., Robert B. Bell & John A. Herfort, Justice, FTC Signal Tougher Merger Enforcement Standards, 4 Antitrust 5 (Summer 1990); Arthur Austin, Antitrust Reaction to the Merger Wave: The Revolution vs. the Counterrevolution, 66 N. Carolina L. Rev. 931 (1988). Cf. E. Thomas Sullivan, The Antitrust Division as a Regulatory Agency: An Enforcement Policy in Transition, 64 Washington U.L.Q. 997 (1986).

[220] Corresponding standards of the National Association of [State] Attorneys General may be found on the NAAG web site, www.naag.org.

Guidelines for evaluation of *vertical* mergers were issued by the Justice Department in 1984. The enforcement agencies have shown far less interest in such mergers, and President Clinton's first Antitrust chief, Anne Bingamin, purported to repeal the vertical merger guidelines, but the now-called Non-Horizontal Merger Guidelines may be found at www.usdoj.gov. Calls to renew interest in vertical mergers can be found in Michael H. Riordan & Steven C. Salop, Evaluating Vertical Mergers: A Post-Chicago Approach, 63 Antitrust L.J. 513 (1995); David Reiffen & Michael Vita, Is There New Thinking on Vertical Mergers?, 63 Antitrust L.J. 917 (1995).

[221] But Part 1 of the Merger Guidelines cautions: "These Guidelines should be read with the awareness that merger analysis does not consist of uniform application of a single methodology. Rather, it is a fact-specific process through which the Agencies, guided by their extensive experience, apply a range of analytical tools to the reasonably available and reliable evidence to evaluate competitive concerns in a limited period of time."

Agencies focus primarily on how the merger affects conduct that would be most profitable for the firm.

"A merger can enhance market power simply by eliminating competition between the merging parties. This effect can arise even if the merger causes no changes in the way other firms behave. Adverse competitive effects arising in this manner are referred to as "unilateral effects." A merger also can enhance market power by increasing the risk of coordinated, accommodating, or interdependent behavior among rivals. Adverse competitive effects arising in this manner are referred to as "coordinated effects." In any given case, either or both types of effects may be present, and the distinction between them may be blurred.

" * * * Enhancement of market power by sellers often elevates the prices charged to customers. For simplicity of exposition, these Guidelines generally discuss the analysis in terms of such price effects. * * * "222

b.   Product Market Definition

Part 4 of the Guidelines focus attention on market definition—an issue we have seen in monopolization cases, as well as cases involving multi-firm cooperation. At the outset, however, Part 4 disclaims being a prisoner of market definition analysis.

"The Agencies' analysis need not start with market definition. Some of the analytical tools used by the Agencies to assess competitive effects do not rely on market definition, although evaluation of competitive alternatives available to customers is always necessary at some point in the analysis.

"Evidence of competitive effects can inform market definition, just as market definition can be informative regarding competitive effects. For example, evidence that a reduction in the number of significant rivals offering a group of products causes prices for those products to rise significantly can itself establish that those products form a relevant market. Such evidence also may more directly predict the competitive effects of a merger,

---

222 [Ed. note] Part 3 of the Guidelines says that "When price discrimination is feasible, adverse competitive effects on targeted customers can arise, even if such effects will not arise for other customers. A price increase for targeted customers may be profitable even if a price increase for all customers would not be profitable because too many other customers would substitute away. When discrimination is reasonably likely, the Agencies may evaluate competitive effects separately by type of customer. * * * " Part 3 explains: "For price discrimination to be feasible, two conditions typically must be met: differential pricing and limited arbitrage. First, the suppliers engaging in price discrimination must be able to price differently to targeted customers than to other customers. * * * Second, the targeted customers must not be able to defeat the price increase of concern by arbitrage, e.g., by purchasing indirectly from or through other customers."

reducing the role of inferences from market definition and market shares. * * * "

Part 4 of the Guidelines continues:

"Market definition focuses solely on demand substitution factors, i.e., on customers' ability and willingness to substitute away from one product to another in response to a price increase or a corresponding non-price change such as a reduction in product quality or service. The responsive actions of suppliers are also important in competitive analysis. They are considered in these Guidelines in the sections addressing the identification of market participants, the measurement of market shares, the analysis of competitive effects, and entry.

"Customers often confront a range of possible substitutes for the products of the merging firms. Some substitutes may be closer, and others more distant, either geographically or in terms of product attributes and perceptions. * * * The principles of market definition outlined below seek to make this inevitable simplification as useful and informative as is practically possible. Relevant markets need not have precise metes and bounds."

The Guidelines take up product market definition in Part 4.1.1 by describing the hypothetical monopolist test.

"The Agencies * * * use the hypothetical monopolist test to identify a set of products that are reasonably interchangeable with a product sold by one of the merging firms.

" * * * [T]he test requires that a hypothetical profit-maximizing firm, not subject to price regulation, that was the only present and future seller of those products ("hypothetical monopolist") likely would impose at least a small but significant and non-transitory increase in price ("SSNIP") on at least one product in the market, including at least one product sold by one of the merging firms.[223] For the purpose of analyzing this issue, the terms of sale of products outside the candidate market are held constant. The SSNIP is employed solely as a methodological tool for performing the hypothetical monopolist test; it is not a tolerance level for price increases resulting from a merger.

"Groups of products may satisfy the hypothetical monopolist test without including the full range of substitutes from which customers choose. The hypothetical monopolist test may identify

---

[223] If the pricing incentives of the firms supplying the products in the candidate market differ substantially from those of the hypothetical monopolist, for reasons other than the latter's control over a larger group of substitutes, the Agencies may instead employ the concept of a hypothetical profit-maximizing cartel comprised of the firms (with all their products) that sell the products in the candidate market. * * * [Guidelines fn. 4]

a group of products as a relevant market even if customers would substitute significantly to products outside that group in response to a price increase.

> *"Example 5:* Products A and B are being tested as a candidate market. Each sells for $100, has an incremental cost of $60, and sells 1200 units. For every dollar increase in the price of Product A, for any given price of Product B, Product A loses twenty units of sales to products outside the candidate market and ten units of sales to Product B, and likewise for Product B. Under these conditions, economic analysis shows that a hypothetical profit-maximizing monopolist controlling Products A and B would raise both of their prices by ten percent, to $110. Therefore, Products A and B satisfy the hypothetical monopolist test using a five percent SSNIP, and indeed for any SSNIP size up to ten percent. This is true even though two-thirds of the sales lost by one product when it raises its price are diverted to products outside the relevant market.

* * *

"The hypothetical monopolist test ensures that markets are not defined too narrowly, but it does not lead to a single relevant market. The Agencies may evaluate a merger in any relevant market satisfying the test, guided by the overarching principle that the purpose of defining the market and measuring market shares is to illuminate the evaluation of competitive effects. Because the relative competitive significance of more distant substitutes is apt to be overstated by their share of sales, when the Agencies rely on market shares and concentration, they usually do so in the smallest relevant market satisfying the hypothetical monopolist test."

The Guidelines go on in Part 4.1.2 to discuss benchmark prices and SSNIP size.

"The Agencies apply the SSNIP starting from prices that would likely prevail absent the merger. * * *

"The SSNIP is intended to represent a "small but significant" increase in the prices charged by firms in the candidate market for the value they contribute to the products or services used by customers. This properly directs attention to the effects of price changes commensurate with those that might result from a significant lessening of competition caused by the merger. * * *

"The Agencies most often use a SSNIP of five percent of the price paid by customers for the products or services to which the merging firms contribute value. However, what constitutes a "small but significant" increase in price, commensurate with a significant loss of competition caused by the merger, depends upon the nature of the industry and the merging firms' positions in it, and the Agencies may accordingly use a price increase that is larger or smaller than five percent. * * * "

* * *

c. Critical Loss Analysis

Part 4.1.3 of the Guidelines explores how consumers would likely respond to a price increase and describes the idea of critical loss analysis.

"The hypothetical monopolist's incentive to raise prices depends both on the extent to which customers would likely substitute away from the products in the candidate market in response to such a price increase and on the profit margins earned on those products. The profit margin on incremental units is the difference between price and incremental cost on those units. * * * Incremental cost is measured over the change in output that would be caused by the price increase under consideration.

"In considering customers' likely responses to higher prices, the Agencies take into account any reasonably available and reliable evidence, including, but not limited to:

"how customers have shifted purchases in the past in response to relative changes in price or other terms and conditions;

"information from buyers, including surveys, concerning how they would respond to price changes;

* * *

"objective information about product characteristics and the costs and delays of switching products, especially switching from products in the candidate market to products outside the candidate market;

"the percentage of sales lost by one product in the candidate market, when its price alone rises, that is recaptured by other products in the candidate market, with a higher recapture percentage making a price increase more profitable for the hypothetical monopolist;

* * *

"When the necessary data are available, the Agencies also may consider a 'critical loss analysis' to assess the extent to which it corroborates inferences drawn from the evidence noted above. Critical loss analysis asks whether imposing at least a SSNIP on one or more products in a candidate market would raise or lower the hypothetical monopolist's profits. * * * A price increase raises profits on sales made at the higher price, but this will be offset to the extent customers substitute away from products in the candidate market. Critical loss analysis compares the magnitude of these two offsetting effects resulting from the price increase. The "critical loss" is defined as the number of lost unit sales that would leave profits unchanged. The "predicted loss" is defined as the number of unit sales that the hypothetical monopolist is predicted to lose due to the price increase. The price increase raises the hypothetical monopolist's profits if the predicted loss is less than the critical loss.

"* * * Unless the firms are engaging in coordinated interaction (see Section 7), high pre-merger margins normally indicate that each firm's product individually faces demand that is not highly sensitive to price.[224] Higher pre-merger margins thus indicate a smaller predicted loss as well as a smaller critical loss. The higher the pre-merger margin, the smaller the recapture percentage necessary for the candidate market to satisfy the hypothetical monopolist test.

"Even when the evidence necessary to perform the hypothetical monopolist test quantitatively is not available, the conceptual framework of the test provides a useful methodological tool for gathering and analyzing evidence pertinent to customer substitution and to market definition. The Agencies follow the hypothetical monopolist test to the extent possible given the available evidence, bearing in mind that the ultimate goal of market definition is to help determine whether the merger may substantially lessen competition."[225]

* * *

d. Geographic Market Analysis

Defining the geographic market is described by the Guidelines in Part 4.2.

---

[224] While margins are important for implementing the hypothetical monopolist test, high margins are not in themselves of antitrust concern. [Guidelines fn. 6]

[225] [Ed. note] Part 4.1.4 of the Guidelines says that if "a hypothetical monopolist could profitably target a subset of customers for price increases, the Agencies may identify relevant markets defined around those targeted customers, to whom a hypothetical monopolist would profitably and separately impose at least a SSNIP. Markets to serve targeted customers are also known as price discrimination markets."

"The arena of competition affected by the merger may be geographically bounded if geography limits some customers' willingness or ability to substitute to some products, or some suppliers' willingness or ability to serve some customers. Both supplier and customer locations can affect this. * * *

"The scope of geographic markets often depends on transportation costs. Other factors such as language, regulation, tariff and non-tariff trade barriers, custom and familiarity, reputation, and service availability may impede long-distance or international transactions. The competitive significance of foreign firms may be assessed at various exchange rates, especially if exchange rates have fluctuated in the recent past.

* * *

"The hypothetical monopolist test requires that a hypothetical profit-maximizing firm that was the only present or future producer of the relevant product(s) located in the region would impose at least a SSNIP from at least one location, including at least one location of one of the merging firms. In this exercise the terms of sale for all products produced elsewhere are held constant. A single firm may operate in a number of different geographic markets, even for a single product.

* * *

"When the hypothetical monopolist could discriminate based on customer location, the Agencies may define geographic markets based on the locations of targeted customers. Geographic markets of this type often apply when suppliers deliver their products or services to customers' locations. * * * Some suppliers that sell into the relevant market may be located outside the boundaries of the geographic market.

"The hypothetical monopolist test requires that a hypothetical profit-maximizing firm that was the only present or future seller of the relevant product(s) to customers in the region would impose at least a SSNIP on some customers in that region. A region forms a relevant geographic market if this price increase would not be defeated by substitution away from the relevant product or by arbitrage, e.g., customers in the region travelling outside it to purchase the relevant product. In this exercise, the terms of sale for products sold to all customers outside the region are held constant."

* * *

e.   Market Participants & Concentration

Part 5 of the Guidelines examines market participants (part 5.1), market shares (part 5.2), and market concentration (part 5.3).

"All firms that currently earn revenues in the relevant market are considered market participants. Vertically integrated firms are also included to the extent that their inclusion accurately reflects their competitive significance. Firms not currently earning revenues in the relevant market, but that have committed to entering the market in the near future, are also considered market participants.

"Firms that are not current producers in a relevant market, but that would very likely provide rapid supply responses with direct competitive impact in the event of a SSNIP, without incurring significant sunk costs, are also considered market participants. These firms are termed "rapid entrants." Sunk costs are entry or exit costs that cannot be recovered outside the relevant market. * * *

"Firms that produce the relevant product but do not sell it in the relevant geographic market may be rapid entrants. Other things equal, such firms are most likely to be rapid entrants if they are close to the geographic market.

* * *

"Firms that clearly possess the necessary assets to supply into the relevant market rapidly may also be rapid entrants. In markets for relatively homogeneous goods where a supplier's ability to compete depends predominantly on its costs and its capacity, and not on other factors such as experience or reputation in the relevant market, a supplier with efficient idle capacity, or readily available "swing" capacity currently used in adjacent markets that can easily and profitably be shifted to serve the relevant market, may be a rapid entrant. However, idle capacity may be inefficient, and capacity used in adjacent markets may not be available, so a firm's possession of idle or swing capacity alone does not make that firm a rapid entrant.

* * *

"In most contexts, the Agencies measure each firm's market share based on its actual or projected revenues in the relevant market. Revenues in the relevant market tend to be the best measure of attractiveness to customers, since they reflect the real-world ability of firms to surmount all of the obstacles necessary to offer products on terms and conditions that are attractive to customers. * * *

"In markets for homogeneous products, a firm's competitive significance may derive principally from its ability and incentive to rapidly expand production in the relevant market in response to a price increase or output reduction by others in that market. As a result, a firm's competitive significance may depend upon its level of readily available capacity to serve the relevant market if that capacity is efficient enough to make such expansion profitable. In such markets, capacities or reserves may better reflect the future competitive significance of suppliers than revenues, and the Agencies may calculate market shares using those measures. * * *

* * *

"In analyzing mergers between an incumbent and a recent or potential entrant, to the extent the Agencies use the change in concentration to evaluate competitive effects, they will do so using projected market shares. A merger between an incumbent and a potential entrant can raise significant competitive concerns. The lessening of competition resulting from such a merger is more likely to be substantial, the larger is the market share of the incumbent, the greater is the competitive significance of the potential entrant, and the greater is the competitive threat posed by this potential entrant relative to others.

* * *

"The Agencies may measure market concentration using the number of significant competitors in the market. This measure is most useful when there is a gap in market share between significant competitors and smaller rivals or when it is difficult to measure revenues in the relevant market. The Agencies also may consider the combined market share of the merging firms as an indicator of the extent to which others in the market may not be able readily to replace competition between the merging firms that is lost through the merger.

"The Agencies often calculate the Herfindahl-Hirschman Index ("HHI") of market concentration. The HHI is calculated by summing the squares of the individual firms' market shares,[226]

---

[226] For example, a market consisting of four firms with market shares of thirty percent, thirty percent, twenty percent, and twenty percent has an HHI of 2600 (900 + 900 + 400 + 400) = 2600). The HHI ranges from 10,000 (in the case of a pure monopoly) to a number approaching zero (in the case of an atomistic market). Although it is desirable to include all firms in the calculation, lack of information about firms with small shares is not critical because such firms do not affect the HHI significantly. [Guidelines fn. 9]

and thus gives proportionately greater weight to the larger market shares. When using the HHI, the Agencies consider both the post-merger level of the HHI and the increase in the HHI resulting from the merger. The increase in the HHI is equal to twice the product of the market shares of the merging firms.[227]

"Based on their experience, the Agencies generally classify markets into three types:

"Unconcentrated Markets: HHI below 1500

"Moderately Concentrated Markets: HHI between 1500 and 2500

"Highly Concentrated Markets: HHI above 2500

"The Agencies employ the following general standards for the relevant markets they have defined:

"*Small Change in Concentration*: Mergers involving an increase in the HHI of less than 100 points are unlikely to have adverse competitive effects and ordinarily require no further analysis.

"*Unconcentrated Markets*: Mergers resulting in unconcentrated markets are unlikely to have adverse competitive effects and ordinarily require no further analysis.

"*Moderately Concentrated Markets*: Mergers resulting in moderately concentrated markets that involve an increase in the HHI of more than 100 points potentially raise significant competitive concerns and often warrant scrutiny.

"*Highly Concentrated Markets*: Mergers resulting in highly concentrated markets that involve an increase in the HHI of between 100 points and 200 points potentially raise significant competitive concerns and often warrant scrutiny. Mergers resulting in highly concentrated markets that involve an increase in the HHI of more than 200 points will be presumed to be likely to enhance market power. The presumption may be rebutted by persuasive evidence showing that the merger is unlikely to enhance market power.

"The purpose of these thresholds is not to provide a rigid screen to separate competitively benign mergers from anticompetitive ones, although high levels of concentration do raise concerns. Rather, they provide one way to identify some mergers unlikely to raise competitive concerns and some others

---

[227] For example, the merger of firms with shares of five percent and ten percent of the market would increase the HHI by 100 ($5 \times 10 \times 2 = 100$). [Guidelines fn. 10]

for which it is particularly important to examine whether other competitive factors confirm, reinforce, or counteract the potentially harmful effects of increased concentration. The higher the post-merger HHI and the increase in the HHI, the greater are the Agencies' potential competitive concerns and the greater is the likelihood that the Agencies will request additional information to conduct their analysis."

f. Unilateral Effects

After determining market definition and market shares, the question becomes what negative effects a merger might produce. Part 6 of the Guidelines examines "unilateral effects."

"The elimination of competition between two firms that results from their merger may alone constitute a substantial lessening of competition. Such unilateral effects are most apparent in a merger to monopoly in a relevant market, but are by no means limited to that case. * * *

* * *

"A merger may result in different unilateral effects along different dimensions of competition. For example, a merger may increase prices in the short term but not raise longer-term concerns about innovation, either because rivals will provide sufficient innovation competition or because the merger will generate cognizable research and development efficiencies. * * *

* * *

"A merger between firms selling differentiated products may diminish competition by enabling the merged firm to profit by unilaterally raising the price of one or both products above the pre-merger level. Some of the sales lost due to the price rise will merely be diverted to the product of the merger partner and, depending on relative margins, capturing such sales loss through merger may make the price increase profitable even though it would not have been profitable prior to the merger.

"The extent of direct competition between the products sold by the merging parties is central to the evaluation of unilateral price effects. Unilateral price effects are greater, the more the buyers of products sold by one merging firm consider products sold by the other merging firm to be their next choice. * * * The types of evidence relied on often overlap substantially with the types of evidence of customer substitution relevant to the hypothetical monopolist test. * * *

* * *

"In some cases, the Agencies may seek to quantify the extent of direct competition between a product sold by one merging firm and a second product sold by the other merging firm by estimating the diversion ratio from the first product to the second product. The diversion ratio is the fraction of unit sales lost by the first product due to an increase in its price that would be diverted to the second product. Diversion ratios between products sold by one merging firm and products sold by the other merging firm can be very informative for assessing unilateral price effects, with higher diversion ratios indicating a greater likelihood of such effects. * * *

" * * * Diagnosing unilateral price effects based on the value of diverted sales need not rely on market definition or the calculation of market shares and concentration. The Agencies rely much more on the value of diverted sales than on the level of the HHI for diagnosing unilateral price effects in markets with differentiated products. If the value of diverted sales is proportionately small, significant unilateral price effects are unlikely.[228]

"Where sufficient data are available, the Agencies may construct economic models designed to quantify the unilateral price effects resulting from the merger. These models often include independent price responses by non-merging firms. They also can incorporate merger-specific efficiencies. These merger simulation methods need not rely on market definition. The Agencies do not treat merger simulation evidence as conclusive in itself, and they place more weight on whether their merger simulations consistently predict substantial price increases than on the precise prediction of any single simulation.

* * *

"In markets involving relatively undifferentiated products, the Agencies may evaluate whether the merged firm will find it profitable unilaterally to suppress output and elevate the market price. A firm may leave capacity idle, refrain from building or obtaining capacity that would have been obtained absent the merger, or eliminate pre-existing production capabilities. A firm may also divert the use of capacity away from one relevant market and into another so as to raise the price in the former market. The

---

[228] For this purpose, the value of diverted sales is measured in proportion to the lost revenues attributable to the reduction in unit sales resulting from the price increase. Those lost revenues equal the reduction in the number of units sold of that product multiplied by that product's price. [Guidelines fn. 11]

competitive analyses of these alternative modes of output suppression may differ.

"A unilateral output suppression strategy is more likely to be profitable when (1) the merged firm's market share is relatively high; (2) the share of the merged firm's output already committed for sale at prices unaffected by the output suppression is relatively low; (3) the margin on the suppressed output is relatively low; (4) the supply responses of rivals are relatively small; and (5) the market elasticity of demand is relatively low.

* * *

"In some cases, a merger between a firm with a substantial share of the sales in the market and a firm with significant excess capacity to serve that market can make an output suppression strategy profitable. This can occur even if the firm with the excess capacity has a relatively small share of sales, if that firm's ability to expand, and thus keep price from rising, has been making an output suppression strategy unprofitable for the firm with the larger market share.

" * * * The Agencies may consider whether a merger is likely to diminish innovation competition by encouraging the merged firm to curtail its innovative efforts below the level that would prevail in the absence of the merger. That curtailment of innovation could take the form of reduced incentive to continue with an existing product-development effort or reduced incentive to initiate development of new products.

* * *

If the merged firm would withdraw a product that a significant number of customers strongly prefer to those products that would remain available, this can constitute a harm to customers over and above any effects on the price or quality of any given product. * * * "

* * *

g.   Coordination Effects

Part 7 of the Guidelines, in turn, considers a merger's "coordination effects."

"A merger may diminish competition by enabling or encouraging post-merger coordinated interaction among firms in the relevant market that harms customers. Coordinated interaction involves conduct by multiple firms that is profitable for each of them only as a result of the accommodating reactions of the others. These reactions can blunt a firm's incentive to offer customers better deals by undercutting the extent to which such a move would win business away from rivals. They also can enhance a firm's incentive to raise prices, by assuaging the fear that such a move would lose customers to rivals.

"Coordinated interaction includes a range of conduct. Coordinated interaction can involve the explicit negotiation of a common understanding of how firms will compete or refrain from competing. Such conduct typically would itself violate the antitrust laws. Coordinated interaction also can involve a similar common understanding that is not explicitly negotiated but would be enforced by the detection and punishment of deviations that would undermine the coordinated interaction. Coordinated interaction alternatively can involve parallel accommodating conduct not pursuant to a prior understanding. Parallel accommodating conduct includes situations in which each rival's response to competitive moves made by others is individually rational, and not motivated by retaliation or deterrence nor intended to sustain an agreed-upon market outcome, but nevertheless emboldens price increases and weakens competitive incentives to reduce prices or offer customers better terms. Coordinated interaction includes conduct not otherwise condemned by the antitrust laws.

"The ability of rival firms to engage in coordinated conduct depends on the strength and predictability of rivals' responses to a price change or other competitive initiative. Under some circumstances, a merger can result in market concentration sufficient to strengthen such responses or enable multiple firms in the market to predict them more confidently, thereby affecting the competitive incentives of multiple firms in the market, not just the merged firm.

* * *

"Pursuant to the Clayton Act's incipiency standard, the Agencies may challenge mergers that in their judgment pose a real danger of harm through coordinated effects, even without specific evidence showing precisely how the coordination likely would take place. The Agencies are likely to challenge a merger if the following three conditions are all met: (1) the merger would significantly increase concentration and lead to a moderately or highly concentrated market; (2) that market shows signs of vulnerability to coordinated conduct; and (3) the Agencies have a credible basis on which to conclude that the merger may enhance that vulnerability. An acquisition eliminating a maverick firm in a market vulnerable to coordinated conduct is likely to cause adverse coordinated effects.

"The Agencies presume that market conditions are conducive to coordinated interaction if firms representing a substantial share in the relevant market appear to have previously engaged in express collusion affecting the relevant market, unless competitive conditions in the market have since changed significantly. * * *

"A market typically is more vulnerable to coordinated conduct if each competitively important firm's significant competitive initiatives can be promptly and confidently observed by that firm's rivals. This is more likely to be the case if the terms offered to customers are relatively transparent. * * * Regular monitoring by suppliers of one another's prices or customers can indicate that the terms offered to customers are relatively transparent.

"A market typically is more vulnerable to coordinated conduct if a firm's prospective competitive reward from attracting customers away from its rivals will be significantly diminished by likely responses of those rivals. This is more likely to be the case, the stronger and faster are the responses the firm anticipates from its rivals. The firm is more likely to anticipate strong responses if there are few significant competitors, if products in the relevant market are relatively homogeneous, if customers find it relatively easy to switch between suppliers, or if suppliers use meeting-competition clauses.

* * *

"A market is more apt to be vulnerable to coordinated conduct if the firm initiating a price increase will lose relatively few customers after rivals respond to the increase. Similarly, a market is more apt to be vulnerable to coordinated conduct if a firm that first offers a lower price or improved product to customers will retain relatively few customers thus attracted away from its rivals after those rivals respond.

" * * * Coordination generally is more profitable, the lower is the market elasticity of demand."

* * *

h. Power Buyers

Part 8 of the Guidelines takes up the role of powerful buyers in controlling any anti-competitive effect of a merger.

"The Agencies consider the possibility that powerful buyers may constrain the ability of the merging parties to raise prices. This can occur, for example, if powerful buyers have the ability and incentive to vertically integrate upstream or sponsor entry, or if the conduct or presence of large buyers undermines coordinated effects. However, the Agencies do not presume that the presence of powerful buyers alone forestalls adverse competitive effects flowing from the merger. Even buyers that can negotiate favorable terms may be harmed by an increase in market power. * * * Normally, a merger that eliminates a supplier whose presence contributed significantly to a buyer's negotiating leverage will harm that buyer."

* * *

i.   New Entry

The Guidelines take up the effect of new entry in Part 9.

" * * * The prospect of entry into the relevant market will alleviate concerns about adverse competitive effects only if such entry will deter or counteract any competitive effects of concern so the merger will not substantially harm customers.

* * *

"The Agencies examine the timeliness, likelihood, and sufficiency of the entry efforts an entrant might practically employ. An entry effort is defined by the actions the firm must undertake to produce and sell in the market. * * * Recent examples of entry, whether successful or unsuccessful, generally provide the starting point for identifying the elements of practical entry efforts. They also can be informative regarding the scale necessary for an entrant to be successful, the presence or absence of entry barriers, the factors that influence the timing of entry, the costs and risk associated with entry, and the sales opportunities realistically available to entrants.

"If the assets necessary for an effective and profitable entry effort are widely available, the Agencies will not necessarily attempt to identify which firms might enter. * * * Firms operating in adjacent or complementary markets, or large customers themselves, may be best placed to enter. However, the Agencies will not presume that a powerful firm in an adjacent market or a large customer will enter the relevant market unless there is reliable evidence supporting that conclusion.

* * *

"In order to deter the competitive effects of concern, entry must be rapid enough to make unprofitable overall the actions causing those effects and thus leading to entry, even though those actions would be profitable until entry takes effect.

* * *

"Even where timely and likely, entry may not be sufficient to deter or counteract the competitive effects of concern. For example, in a differentiated product industry, entry may be insufficient because the products offered by entrants are not close enough substitutes to the products offered by the merged firm to render a price increase by the merged firm unprofitable. Entry may also be insufficient due to constraints that limit entrants' competitive effectiveness, such as limitations on the capabilities of the firms best placed to enter or reputational barriers to rapid expansion by new entrants. Entry by a single firm that will replicate at least the scale and strength of one of the merging firms is sufficient. Entry by one or more firms operating at a smaller scale may be sufficient if such firms are not at a significant competitive disadvantage."

j. Efficiencies

Part 10 of the Guidelines takes up the question of efficiencies.

"The Agencies credit only those efficiencies likely to be accomplished with the proposed merger and unlikely to be accomplished in the absence of either the proposed merger or another means having comparable anticompetitive effects. These are termed merger-specific efficiencies.[229] Only alternatives that are practical in the business situation faced by the merging firms are considered in making this determination. The Agencies do not insist upon a less restrictive alternative that is merely theoretical.

"Efficiencies are difficult to verify and quantify, in part because much of the information relating to efficiencies is uniquely in the possession of the merging firms. * * * Therefore, it is incumbent upon the merging firms to substantiate efficiency claims so that the Agencies can verify by reasonable means the likelihood and magnitude of each asserted efficiency, how and when each would be achieved (and any costs of doing so), how each would enhance the merged firm's ability and incentive to compete, and why each would be merger-specific.

---

[229] The Agencies will not deem efficiencies to be merger-specific if they could be attained by practical alternatives that mitigate competitive concerns, such as divestiture or licensing. * * * [Guidelines fn. 13]

* * *

"Cognizable efficiencies are merger-specific efficiencies that have been verified and do not arise from anticompetitive reductions in output or service. Cognizable efficiencies are assessed net of costs produced by the merger or incurred in achieving those efficiencies.

"The Agencies will not challenge a merger if cognizable efficiencies are of a character and magnitude such that the merger is not likely to be anticompetitive in any relevant market.[230] To make the requisite determination, the Agencies consider whether cognizable efficiencies likely would be sufficient to reverse the merger's potential to harm customers in the relevant market, e.g., by preventing price increases in that market.[231] In conducting this analysis, the Agencies will not simply compare the magnitude of the cognizable efficiencies with the magnitude of the likely harm to competition absent the efficiencies. The greater the potential adverse competitive effect of a merger, the greater must be the cognizable efficiencies, and the more they must be passed through to customers, for the Agencies to conclude that the merger will not have an anticompetitive effect in the relevant market. When the potential adverse competitive effect of a merger is likely to be particularly substantial, extraordinarily great cognizable efficiencies would be necessary to prevent the merger from being anticompetitive. In adhering to this approach, the Agencies are mindful that the antitrust laws give competition, not internal operational efficiency, primacy in protecting customers.

"In the Agencies' experience, efficiencies are most likely to make a difference in merger analysis when the likely adverse competitive effects, absent the efficiencies, are not great. Efficiencies almost never justify a merger to monopoly or near-monopoly. * * *

"The Agencies have found that certain types of efficiencies are more likely to be cognizable and substantial than others. For example, efficiencies resulting from shifting production among

---

[230] The Agencies normally assess competition in each relevant market affected by a merger independently and normally will challenge the merger if it is likely to be anticompetitive in any relevant market. In some cases, however, the Agencies in their prosecutorial discretion will consider efficiencies not strictly in the relevant market, but so inextricably linked with it that a partial divestiture or other remedy could not feasibly eliminate the anticompetitive effect in the relevant market without sacrificing the efficiencies in the other market(s). * * * [Guidelines fn. 14]

[231] The Agencies normally give the most weight to the results of this analysis over the short term. * * * Delayed benefits from efficiencies * * * will be given less weight because they are less proximate and more difficult to predict. Efficiencies relating to costs that are fixed in the short term are unlikely to benefit customers in the short term, but can benefit customers in the longer run, e.g., if they make new product introduction less expensive. [Guidelines fn. 15]

facilities formerly owned separately, which enable the merging firms to reduce the incremental cost of production, are more likely to be susceptible to verification and are less likely to result from anticompetitive reductions in output. Other efficiencies, such as those relating to research and development, are potentially substantial but are generally less susceptible to verification and may be the result of anticompetitive output reductions. Yet others, such as those relating to procurement, management, or capital cost, are less likely to be merger-specific or substantial, or may not be cognizable for other reasons.

"When evaluating the effects of a merger on innovation, the Agencies consider the ability of the merged firm to conduct research or development more effectively. Such efficiencies may spur innovation but not affect short-term pricing. The Agencies also consider the ability of the merged firm to appropriate a greater fraction of the benefits resulting from its innovations. Licensing and intellectual property conditions may be important to this enquiry, as they affect the ability of a firm to appropriate the benefits of its innovation. * * * "

k. Failing Firms

Part 11 of the Guidelines articulates today's failing firm doctrine.

" * * *[A] merger is not likely to enhance market power if imminent failure, as defined below, of one of the merging firms would cause the assets of that firm to exit the relevant market. This is an extreme instance of the more general circumstance in which the competitive significance of one of the merging firms is declining: the projected market share and significance of the exiting firm is zero. If the relevant assets would otherwise exit the market, customers are not worse off after the merger than they would have been had the merger been enjoined.

"The Agencies do not normally credit claims that the assets of the failing firm would exit the relevant market unless all of the following circumstances are met: (1) the allegedly failing firm would be unable to meet its financial obligations in the near future; (2) it would not be able to reorganize successfully under Chapter 11 of the Bankruptcy Act; and (3) it has made unsuccessful good-faith efforts to elicit reasonable alternative offers that would keep its tangible and intangible assets in the relevant market and pose a less severe danger to competition than does the proposed merger.[232]

"Similarly, a merger is unlikely to cause competitive harm if the risks to competition arise from the acquisition of a failing division. The Agencies do not normally credit claims that the assets of a division would exit the relevant market in the near future unless both of the following conditions are met: (1) applying cost allocation rules that reflect true economic costs, the division has a persistently negative cash flow on an operating basis, and such negative cash flow is not economically justified for the firm by benefits such as added sales in complementary markets or enhanced customer goodwill; and (2) the owner of the failing division has made unsuccessful good-faith efforts to elicit reasonable alternative offers that would keep its tangible and intangible assets in the relevant market and pose a less severe danger to competition than does the proposed acquisition."

l. Partial Integration

Part 12 of the Guidelines makes clear that mergers of competing buyers will be analyzed by the same basic standards that apply to a merger of sellers, while Part 13 confirms that the Guidelines apply to partial acquisitions as well as complete integration of two firms.

" * * * While the Agencies will consider any way in which a partial acquisition may affect competition, they generally focus on three principal effects.

"First, a partial acquisition can lessen competition by giving the acquiring firm the ability to influence the competitive conduct of the target firm. A voting interest in the target firm or specific governance rights, such as the right to appoint members to the board of directors, can permit such influence. * * *

"Second, * * * acquiring a minority position in a rival might significantly blunt the incentive of the acquiring firm to compete aggressively because it shares in the losses thereby inflicted on that rival. This reduction in the incentive of the acquiring firm to compete arises even if cannot influence the conduct of the target firm. * * *

"Third, a partial acquisition can lessen competition by giving the acquiring firm access to non-public, competitively sensitive information from the target firm. Even absent any ability to influence the conduct of the target firm, access to competitively

---

[232] Any offer to purchase the assets of the failing firm for a price above the liquidation value of those assets will be regarded as a reasonable alternative offer. Liquidation value is the highest value the assets could command for use outside the relevant market. [Guidelines fn. 16]

sensitive information can lead to adverse unilateral or coordinated effects. * * * "

"Partial acquisitions, like mergers, vary greatly in their potential for anticompetitive effects. Accordingly, the specific facts of each case must be examined to assess the likelihood of harm to competition. While partial acquisitions usually do not enable many of the types of efficiencies associated with mergers, the Agencies consider whether a partial acquisition is likely to create cognizable efficiencies."

NOTES AND QUESTIONS

1.   There is a tendency for our eyes to glaze over when we read a document as densely written as the Merger Guidelines. Do you see, however, that the Merger Guidelines present a careful approach to questions we have been discussing since literally the first days of this course?

a.   Should the Merger Guidelines be seen as authoritative? Should the courts' understanding of antitrust principles be influenced by the Guidelines?

b.   Should private plaintiffs be permitted to assert a more aggressive reading of Clayton Act § 7?

c.   Should the Justice Department and FTC be permitted to change their mind on particular provisions without issuing amendments to the Guidelines? The agencies elaborated on the 1992 Guidelines and provided a number of examples in Commentary on the Horizontal Merger Guidelines (2006), http://www.usdoj.gov/atr/public/guidelines/215247.htm.

2.   The first challenge in any merger case is to define both a product and a geographic market. Animating the Merger Guidelines' approach to those questions is the sense that the relevant market is the smallest in which a sole seller could make a "small but significant and nontransitory increase in price," assuming prices of all other products are held constant.

a.   As the Guidelines say, that standard has been understood to mean that a sole seller could raise price at least 5% and sustain the increase for at least a year. What do you think of that definition? Is its terminology more confusing than helpful?

b.   As a practical matter, how would you go about proving that character of pricing a product when in fact there have historically been multiple firms, not a "sole seller," in the field? Is the standard any more than a theoretical exercise requiring the expertise of dueling economists?[233]

c.   Even given the practical limitations of the standard, can you come up with one that would be preferable?

---

[233] See, e.g., Gregory J. Werden, The 1982 Merger Guidelines and the Ascent of the Hypothetical Monopolist Paradigm, 71 Antitrust L. J. 253 (2003).

3.   An important concept in the 2010 Merger Guidelines § 5.3 is the Herfindahl-Hirschman Index, or HHI. As you saw in the text of the Merger Guidelines, one calculates an HHI by *squaring* the market shares of each of the firms in the industry and adding the results together. For example:

a.   Imagine 10 firms, each with 10% of the industry. 10% squared is 100 for each firm's part of the HHI; adding 100 ten times, one gets a 1000 HHI for the industry.

b.   Imagine instead that there are 10 firms whose market shares are 25%+20%+15%+15%+10%+5%+4%+3%+2%+1%. Squaring each market share and adding the results together, one gets 625+400+225+225+100+25+16+9+4+ 1, or an industry HHI of 1630.

c.   Why does it matter whether we use the HHI or the former 4-firm or 8-firm market share totals? You can see some differences using the numbers in the above examples, but one should be cautious about assuming that this new measure of concentration is dramatically better than the old ones.[234] The principal improvement is that the relative size of *each* firm is measured, not just an arbitrary number of firms, and that one thus gets the equivalent of a 2-firm, 3-firm, etc., calculation all rolled into one number.

4.   The Merger Guidelines offer specific standards for merger review using the HHI numbers. An industry will be defined as not concentrated, concentrated, or in-between. It is possible to calculate whether, at least on the basis of their HHI, some of the mergers we have seen before would be challenged under the Merger Guidelines.

a.   In *Brown Shoe*, we know that the top 4 firms produced 23% and that Brown was #4 with 4%. Assume the first three had 8%, 6% & 5% respectively. We then know that the next 20 firms had a total of 11% of the market. Herfindahls below 1% are not worth computing so we can discount everyone else. Thus, this market would be 64 + 36 + 25 + 16 + (say) 50 total for everyone else. That's a pre-merger HHI less than 200. Post merger would be little different and there would have been no government intervention.

b.   In *Philadelphia Bank*, taking assets as the measure of size, the largest bank had 23% of the market, the 2d had 20%, the 3d had 16%, the 4th & 5th about 10% each, the 6th & 7th about 5% each, and the rest were below 1% each. Thus, this pre-merger HHI would be 529 + 400 + 256 + 100 + 100 + 25 + 25 = 1435. The post-merger HHI would be 529 + 1296 + 250 = 2075. Looking at Standard 3.11(c), we see that Philadelphia would have been defined as a moderately concentrated market with a 640 jump in HHI, and the merger "potentially" would raise competitive concerns. But unlike the actual case, the

---

[234] The Index was suggested in the mid-1940s but largely lay dormant until George Stigler and Richard Posner started to use it to help them analyze whether markets were sufficiently concentrated to worry about oligopoly pricing. Use of the Index, as well as its origins and competitors, is discussed in Stephen Calkins, The New Merger Guidelines and the Herfindahl-Hirschman Index, 71 California L.Rev. 402 (1983). See also, John E. Kwoka, Jr., The Herfindahl Index in Theory and Practice, 30 Antitrust Bull. 915 (1985).

defendants might not have had to sustain the burden of justifying the merger.[235]

5.   Why is it necessary to examine the competitive effect of a merger after one knows the HHI numbers? If concentration is no longer the presumptive measure of competitive effect, what tests have replaced it?

6.   Why is ease of entry a separate criterion for evaluating a merger? Is it helpful to distinguish it from the market-defining question of whether a hypothetical monopolist would be able to sustain a 5% price increase for a year?[236]

7.   Expansion of the recognition of merger efficiencies was a principal effect of the 1997 amendments to the 1992 Merger Guidelines. Do you agree that acknowledging the importance of efficiencies was a positive step? Do antitrust enforcers typically have enough data to effectively balance anticompetitive effects of a merger against the increased efficiencies it might generate?[237]

3.   A SERIES OF REPRESENTATIVE CASES

As we have seen, antitrust challenges can come from four directions— the Justice Department, the Federal Trade Commission, private parties, and state Attorneys General. As suggested earlier, however, the Hart-Scott-Rodino negotiated review process reduces the likelihood that a merger will actually become the subject of contested litigation. Further, when one does, it often will not go beyond a District Court. The cases in this section illustrate, however, the bases on which courts exercise review when a merger challenge comes before them.[238]

---

[235] On expanding the relevant issues considered during merger review, see Richard J. Gilbert & Steven C. Sunshine, Incorporating Dynamic Efficiency Concerns in Merger Analysis: The Use of Innovation Markets, 63 Antitrust L.J. 569 (1995).

[236] See, e.g., Jonathan B. Baker, Responding to Developments in Economics and the Courts: Entry in the Merger Guidelines, 71 Antitrust L. J. 189 (2003).

[237] See, e.g., William J. Kolasky & Andrew R. Dick, The Merger Guidelines and the Integration of Efficiencies into Antitrust Review of Horizontal Mergers, 71 Antitrust L. J. 207 (2003).

[238] In a series of studies over several years, Congressional pressure and public notoriety of particular cases have proved to be more reliable predictors of public enforcement activity than the Merger Guidelines or other economically significant indicia of when the public would be served by a challenge. See, e.g., Malcolm B. Coate, Richard S. Higgins & Fred S. McChesney, Bureaucracy and Politics in FTC Merger Challenges, 33 J.Law & Econ. 463 (1990). But see, Malcolm B. Coate & Shawn W. Ulrick, Transparency at the Federal Trade Commission: The Horizontal Merger Review Process 1996–2003 (FTC 2005). The work builds on William F. Long, Richard Schramm & Robert Tollison, The Economic Determinants of Antitrust Activity, 16 J.Law & Econ. 351 (1973); John J. Siegfried, The Determinants of Antitrust Activity, 17 J.Law & Econ. 559 (1975). See also, Roger L. Faith, Donald R. Leavens & Robert D. Tollison, Antitrust Pork Barrel, 25(2) J.Law & Econ. 329 (1982); Jonathan Rose, State Antitrust Enforcement, Mergers & Politics, 41 Wayne L. Rev. 71 (1994). Cf. Howard P. Marvel, Jeffrey M. Netter & Anthony M. Robinson, Price Fixing and Civil Damages: An Economic Analysis, 40 Stanford L.Rev. 561 (1988) (enforcers tend to bring easy cases rather than cases against cartels that threaten to produce more significant economic harm).

a. Private Party Standing to Challenge a Merger—The *Cargill* Case

While public review of mergers presents the most common hurdle most firms face, there remains the possibility that a competitor, customer, or other private party might seek to block the acquisition. The ground rules for such challenges were analyzed by the Supreme Court in Cargill, Inc. v. Monfort of Colorado, Inc., 479 U.S. 104, 107 S.Ct. 484, 93 L.Ed.2d 427 (1986).

Clayton Act § 16 gives federal courts jurisdiction to hear private suits seeking injunctive relief. We have seen that the Court has required that, to bring a suit for damages under Clayton Act § 4, a plaintiff must show it has suffered "antitrust injury, [i.e.,] * * * injury of the type the antitrust laws were intended to prevent * * *." Brunswick v. Pueblo Bowl-O-Mat. The first question for the Court in *Cargill* was thus whether, in a case under § 16, plaintiff Monfort must also show antitrust injury. The Court said yes. "Sections 4 and 16 are * * * best understood as providing complementary remedies for a single set of injuries," the Court concluded, and thus the jurisdictional requirements are the same.

The industry in *Cargill* was beef-packing, i.e., the slaughter of beef and the "fabrication" of steaks and ground beef products. The injury alleged by Monfort was that the merged firm, Cargill, would be so financially strong that it could bid up the price of cattle and cut the price of packaged beef. The resulting cost-price squeeze, although always profitable for Cargill, would severely cut into Monfort's profits and thus allegedly be a form of predatory pricing.

In an opinion by Justice Brennan, the Court rejected Monfort's claim.

" * * * *Brunswick* holds that the antitrust laws do not require the courts to protect small businesses from the loss of profits due to continued competition, but only against the loss of profits from practices forbidden by the antitrust laws. The kind of competition that Monfort alleges here, competition for increased market share, is not activity forbidden by the antitrust laws. It is simply, as petitioners claim, vigorous competition. To hold that the antitrust laws protect competitors from the loss of profits due to such price competition would, in effect, render illegal any decision by a firm to cut prices in order to increase market share. The antitrust laws require no such perverse result * * * ."

In dissent, Justices Stevens and White would have limited *Brunswick* to suits for damages.

" * * * [G]iven the statutory purposes to protect small businesses and to stem the rising tide of concentration in particular markets, a competitor trying to stay in business in a changing market must have standing to ask a court to set aside a merger that has changed the character of the market in an illegal way. Certainly the businesses—small or large—that must face competition in a market altered by an illegal merger are directly affected by that transaction. Their inability to prove exactly how or why they may be harmed does not place them outside the circle of interested parties whom the statute was enacted to protect."

As the dissenters foresaw, the practical effect of *Cargill* has tended toward limiting decisions about enforcement of Clayton Act § 7 to public officials. Insofar as those officials have chosen to limit vigorous enforcement of § 7, in turn, there has been little independent review of those decisions. Are you concerned about that development? Suppose the Court had come out the other way. What would be the possibilities for corporate blackmail if competitors or even customers of the merger partners could file suit to put a combination on indefinite hold?[239]

b. The Challenge of Market Analysis: The Staples-Office Depot Merger

During the 1990s, the formerly staid world of retail office supply sales was transformed by "superstores" in the same way Walmart transformed the retail sale of almost everything else. In 1997, the Federal Trade Commission considered the merger of Staples and Office Depot, the two largest superstore retailers of office products. District Judge Thomas F. Hogan, granted the Commission's request for a preliminary injunction to stop the merger pending completion of its administrative review. Federal Trade Commission v. Staples, Inc. & Office Depot, Inc., 970 F.Supp. 1066 (D.D.C. 1997). The court explained:

> "Defendants are both corporations which sell office products—including office supplies, business machines, computers and furniture—through retail stores, commonly described as office supply superstores, as well as through direct mail delivery and contract stationer operations. Staples is the second largest office superstore chain in the United States with approximately 550 retail stores located in 28 states and the District of Columbia, primarily in the Northeast and California. In 1996 Staples' revenues from those stores were approximately $4 billion through all operations. Office Depot, the largest office superstore chain, operates over 500 retail office supply superstores that are located in 38 states and the District of Columbia, primarily in the South and Midwest. Office Depot's

---

[239] See, e.g., Jonathan L. Diesenhaus, Competitor Standing to Challenge a Merger of Rivals: The Applicability of Strategic Behavior Analysis, 75 California L.Rev. 2057 (1987). The right of a private party to sue to set aside a completed merger was later confirmed in California v. American Stores Co., 495 U.S. 271, 110 S.Ct. 1853, 109 L.Ed.2d 240 (1990).

1996 sales were approximately $6.1 billion. OfficeMax. Inc., is the only other office supply superstore firm in the United States."

Everyone agreed that the appropriate geographic markets were 42 large metropolitan areas. The parties differed mightily, however, about what product market was appropriate. Staples and Office Depot sold only 5.5% of all office products in North America, for example, but the court accepted that "the appropriate relevant product market definition in this case is, as the Commission has argued, the sale of consumable office supplies through office supply superstores." The Court reasoned that

"Whether there are other products available to consumers which are similar in character or use to the products in question may be termed 'functional interchangeability.' This case, of course, is an example of perfect 'functional interchangeability.' The consumable office products at issue here are identical whether they are sold by Staples or Office Depot or another seller of office supplies. A legal pad sold by Staples or Office Depot is 'functionally interchangeable' with a legal pad sold by Wal-Mart. * * * No one disputes the functional interchangeability of consumable office supplies. However, as the government has argued, functional interchangeability should not end the Court's analysis."

The Commission argued and the court accepted

"that a slight but significant increase in Staples-Office Depot's prices will not cause a considerable number of Staples-Office Depot's customers to purchase consumable office supplies from other non-superstore alternatives such as Wal-Mart, Best Buy, Quill, or Viking. On the other hand, the Commission has argued that an increase in price by Staples would result in consumers turning to another office superstore, especially Office Depot, if the consumers had that option. * * *

* * *

"The Court acknowledges that there is, in fact, a broad market encompassing the sale of consumable office supplies by all sellers of such supplies, and that those sellers must, at some level, compete with one another. However, the mere fact that a firm may be termed a competitor in the overall marketplace does not necessarily require that it be included in the relevant product market for antitrust purposes. The Supreme Court has recognized that within a broad market, 'well-defined submarkets may exist which, in themselves, constitute product markets for antitrust purposes.' Brown Shoe Co. v. United States. * * * There is a possibility, therefore, that the sale of consumable office supplies by office superstores may qualify as a submarket within a larger market of retailers of office supplies in general.

"The Court in *Brown Shoe* provided a series of factors or 'practical indicia' for determining whether a submarket exists including 'industry or public recognition of the submarket as a separate economic entity, the product's peculiar characteristics and uses, unique production facilities, distinct customers, distinct prices, sensitivity to price changes, and specialized vendors.' * * *

"The Commission discussed several of the *Brown Shoe* 'practical indicia' in its case, such as industry recognition, and the special characteristics of superstores which make them different from other sellers of office supplies, including distinct formats, customers, and prices. Primarily, however, the FTC focused on what it termed the 'pricing evidence,' which the Court finds corresponds with *Brown Shoe*'s 'sensitivity to price changes' factor. First, the FTC presented evidence comparing Staples' prices in geographic markets where Staples is the only office superstore, to markets where Staples competes with Office Deport or OfficeMax, or both. Based on the FTC's calculations, in markets where Staples faces no office superstore competition at all, something which was termed a one firm market during the hearing, prices are 13% higher than in three firm markets where it competes with both Office Depot and OfficeMax. * * * The FTC presented similar evidence based on Office Depot's prices of a sample of 500 items * * * . Similarly, the evidence showed that Office Depot's prices are significantly higher, well over 5% higher, in Depot-only markets than they are in three firm markets.

* * *

"This evidence all suggests that office superstore prices are affected primarily by other office superstores and not by non-superstore competitors such as mass merchandisers like Wal-Mart, Kmart, or Target, wholesale clubs such as BJ's, Sam's, and Price Costco, computer or electronic stores such as Computer City and Best Buy, independent retail office supply stores, mail orders firms like Quill and Viking, and contract stationers. Though the FTC did not present the Court with evidence regarding the precise amount of non-superstore competition in each of Staples' and Office Depot's one, two, and three firm markets, it is clear to the Court that these competitors, albeit in different combinations and concentrations, are present in every one of these markets. * * * [O]n average, Staples' prices were higher where there was a Staples and a Wal-Mart but no other superstore than where there was a Staples, a Wal-Mart, and another superstore.

* * *

The Court has observed that office supply superstores look far different from other sellers of office supplies. Office supply superstores are high volume, discount office supply chain stores averaging in excess of 20,000 square feet, with over 11,000 of those square feet devoted to traditional office supplies, and carrying over 5,000 SKUs [Stock Keeping Units] of consumable office supplies in addition to computers, office furniture, and other non-consumables. In contrast, stores such as Kmart devote approximately 210 square feet to the sale of approximately 250 SKUs of consumable office supplies. Kinko's devotes approximately 50 square feet to the sale of 150 SKUs. Target sells only 400 SKUs. Both Sam's Club and Computer City each sell approximately 200 SKUs. Even if these SKU totals are low estimates as the defendants have argued, there is still a huge difference between the superstores and the rest of the office supply sellers.

* * *

* * * Based on the Court's observations, the Court finds that the unique combination of size, selection, depth and breadth of inventory offered by the superstores distinguishes them from other retailers. * * * No one entering a Wal-Mart would mistake it for an office superstore. No one entering Staples or Office Depot would mistakenly think he or she was in Best Buy or CompUSA. You certainly know an office superstore when you see one.

Another of the "practical indicia" for determining the presence of a submarket suggested by Brown Shoe is "industry or public recognition of the submarket as a separate economic entity." The Commission offered abundant evidence on this factor from Staples' and Office Depot's documents which shows that both Staples and Office Depot focus primarily on competition from other superstores. * * * Staples uses the phrase "office superstore industry" in strategic planning documents. Staples' 1996 Strategy Update refers to the "Big Three" and "improved relative competitive position" since 1993 and states that Staples is "increasingly recognized as [the] industry leader." A document analyzing a possible acquisition of OfficeMax referenced the "benefits from pricing in [newly] noncompetitive markets," and also the fact that there was "a potential margin lift overall as the industry moves to 2 players."

* * *

* * * [A]llowing the defendants to merge would eliminate significant future competition. Absent the merger, the firms are likely, and in fact have planned, to enter more of each other's markets, leading to a deconcentration of the market and, therefore, increased competition between the superstores.

In addition, direct evidence shows that by eliminating Staples' most significant, and in many markets only, rival, this merger would allow Staples to increase prices or otherwise maintain prices at an anti-competitive level.[240] The merger would eliminate significant head-to-head competition between the two lowest cost and lowest priced firms in the superstore market. Thus, the merger would result in the elimination of a particularly aggressive competitor in a highly concentrated market, a factor which is certainly an important consideration when analyzing possible anti-competitive effects. It is based on all of this evidence as well that the Court finds that the Commission has shown a likelihood of success on the merits and a "reasonable probability" that the proposed transaction will have an anti-competitive effect.

By showing that the proposed transaction between Staples and Office Depot will lead to undue concentration in the market for consumable office supplies sold by office superstores in the geographic markets agreed upon by the parties, the Commission establishes a presumption that the transaction will substantially lessen competition. See United States v. Philadelphia Nat'l Bank. Once such a presumption has been established, the burden of producing evidence to rebut the presumption shifts to the defendants. To meet this burden, the defendants must show that the market-share statistics give an inaccurate prediction of the proposed acquisition's probable effect on competition. * * *

The court concluded that, given the market definition thus used, the defendants' had not overcome the presumption. Judge Hogan recognized the irony and implications of his decision, but concluded that he had no choice but to enjoin the merger.

---

[240] There has been tremendous argument regarding whether the FTC actually contends that prices will go up after the merger. The Court understands that that is not precisely the Commission's contention. Rather, the Commission argues that the merger will have an anti-competitive effect such that the combined firm's prices will be higher after the merger than they would be absent the merger. This does not necessarily mean that prices would rise from the levels they are now. Instead, according to the Commission, prices would simply not decrease as much as they would have on their own absent the merger. It is only in this sense that the Commission has contended that prices would go up—prices would go up compared to where they would have been absent the merger. It is only in this sense that consumers would be faced with "higher" prices. Therefore, when the Court discusses "raising" prices it is also with respect to raising prices with respect to where prices would have been absent the merger, not actually an increase from present price levels. [Court's fn. 14]

"In light of the undeniable benefits that Staples and Office Depot have brought to consumers, it is with regret that the Court reaches the decision that it must in this case. This decision will most likely kill the merger. The Court feels, to some extent, that the defendants are being punished for their own successes and for the benefits that they have brought to consumers. In effect, they have been hoisted with their own petards. See William Shakespeare, Hamlet act 3, sc. 4. In addition, the Court is concerned with the broader ramifications of this case. The superstore or 'category killer' like office supply superstores are a fairly recent phenomenon and certainly not restricted to office supplies. There are a host of superstores or 'category killers' in the United States today, covering such areas as pet supplies, home and garden products, bed, bath, and kitchen products, toys, music, books, and electronics. Indeed, such 'category killer' stores may be the way of retailing for the future. It remains to be seen if this case is sui generis or is the beginning of a new wave of FTC activism. For these reasons, the Court must emphasize that the ruling in this case is based strictly on the facts of this particular case, and should not be construed as this Court's recognition of general superstore relevant product markets."[241]

NOTES AND QUESTIONS

1.   Were you persuaded that the court had no choice in this case? Was its conclusion as to the product market inevitable?

2.   What is the product market the court identified? Should we define products in terms of the companies from which they are sold? Does even the court concede that a ream of copy paper is the same whether it comes from Staples or comes from "Family Co."? Might one say that while the paper itself is the same wherever bought, the true "product" being sold is the manner and efficiency of distribution?

3.   Did the court's use of the Merger Guidelines help dictate the result in this case? Did the *Guidelines* method of market definition sharpen the court's analysis? Was this a case where the 5%-price-increase-for-one-year standard might have led the court astray?

4.   Might the court have approached the case differently, conceding that the market is larger than "superstores" but saying that there would be unilateral effects of this merger, i.e., that Staples' customers considered Office Depot their second choice, and vice versa? Why should it matter which analysis the court uses in a case like this?

---

[241]   [Ed. note] After losing this case in the District Court, Staples and Office Depot announced they were dropping plans for the merger. See Barrons, July 7, 1997, at p. 46. In 2013, Office Depot and OfficeMax merged with little or no government opposition.

5.   Look again at the court's conclusion. Is the court right to be troubled that the firms' very efficiency and creativity condemns their merger? Has the court committed a Type 1 error here? Has it let concerns about allocative efficiency trump issues of productive and dynamic efficiency? What might the result in this case do to the incentives for others to take similar risks and initiative?

6.   In 2013, two of the superstores, Office Depot and Officemax, proposed to merge. FTC decided not to attempt to block the merger. Can you explain that FTC decision with reference to changes in the functioning of retail markets between 1997 and 2013?

c.   Special Problems of Hospital Mergers

In recent years, many merger cases have involved hospitals. That is in part because of the many significant hospital acquisitions by HMOs and other large medical care organizations. In part, it may be because in many hospital mergers at least one of the partners is in financial trouble and dropping the merger plans without a fight is an unattractive option.

A recurring question in such cases is again market definition. The product market is usually fairly straightforward, typically being defined as "acute care" health facilities. The increase in outpatient treatment and the growth of centers that specialize in outpatient surgical care makes the product market less than precise, but "if you need a kidney transplant, or a mastectomy, or if you have a stroke or a heart attack or a gunshot wound, you will go (or be taken) to an acute care hospital for inpatient treatment."[242] The fact that hospitals face competition for treatment of less serious conditions does not affect their ability to raise prices on services as to which they have no substitutes.

But most cases turn on defining the geographic market. People will travel around the country or around the world for truly life-saving care, but most would prefer to go to a hospital near their home, where their own doctor practices and their family can come to visit. How big that service area is becomes the issue in dispute.

Some courts have relied upon the so-called Elzinga-Hogarty test for market definition.[243] Using zip code data, the test asks where patients reside who account for 75–90% of admissions to an area's hospitals. It then tries to confirm that finding by asking what proportion of persons from within that area go to local hospitals.[244]

---

[242]   United States v. Rockford Memorial Corporation, 898 F.2d 1278, 1284 (7th Cir. 1990).

[243]   The sources of these tests are Kenneth G. Elzinga & Thomas F. Hogarty, The Problem of Geographic Market Deliniation in Antimerger Suits, 18 Antitrust Bull. 45 (1973), and Kenneth G. Elzinga & Thomas F. Hogarty, The Problem of Geographic Market Deliniation Revisited: The Case of Coal, 23 Antitrust Bull. 1 (1978).

[244]   For cases using this test, see Federal Trade Commission v. Freeman Hospital, 69 F.3d 260 (8th Cir. 1995); United States v. Rockford Hospital Corp., 717 F.Supp. 1251 (N.D.Ill. 1989), aff'd

Now, because of the importance of the health care industry and the costs inherent in the uncertainty of litigation, the enforcement agencies have announced an "antitrust safety zone" within any relevant market. For example, the Justice Department and Federal Trade Commission have said that they will not challenge any merger between two general acute care hospitals where, over the most recent 3 years, one of the hospitals has both an average of fewer than 100 licensed beds and an average daily inpatient census of less than 40 patients. See U.S. Department of Justice & Federal Trade Commission, Statements of Antitrust Enforcement Policy in Health Care 5 (1996).

After losing seven hospital merger cases in a row, FTC stopped challenging proposed hospital mergers until it completed a study of the effects of the mergers it had unsuccessfully opposed. That study found that hospital prices in the markets in which those mergers took place had increased by 20 to 44%. FTC then returned to its practice of challenging the proposed hospital mergers that would create highly concentrated markets. Armed with the results of its study, it fared much better in court, as the following opinion illustrates.

FEDERAL TRADE COMMISSION v. PENN STATE HERSHEY MEDICAL CENTER

United States Court of Appeals, Third Circuit, 2016
838 F.3d 327

Before: FISHER, GREENAWAY, JR., and KRAUSE, CIRCUIT JUDGES.

OPINION OF THE COURT

FISHER, CIRCUIT JUDGE.

At issue in this case is the proposed merger of the two largest hospitals in the Harrisburg, Pennsylvania area: Penn State Hershey Medical Center and PinnacleHealth System. The Federal Trade Commission ("FTC") opposes their merger and filed an administrative complaint alleging that it violates Section 7 of the Clayton Act because it is likely to substantially lessen competition. In order to maintain the status quo and prevent the parties from merging before the administrative adjudication could occur, the FTC, joined by the Commonwealth of Pennsylvania, filed suit in the Middle District of Pennsylvania under Section 13(b) of the Federal Trade Commission Act ("FTC Act") and Section 16 of the Clayton Act, which authorize the FTC and the Commonwealth, respectively, to seek a preliminary injunction pending the outcome of the FTC's adjudication on the merits. The District Court denied the FTC and the Commonwealth's

---

898 F.2d 1278 (7th Cir. 1990); State of California v. Sutter Health System, 84 F.Supp.2d 1057 (N.D.Cal. 2000). See also, H.E. Frech III, James Langenfeld & R. Forrest McCluer, Elzinga-Hogarty Tests and Alternative Approaches for Market Share Calculations in Hospital Markets, 71 Antitrust L. J. 921 (2004).

motion for a preliminary injunction, holding that they did not properly define the relevant geographic market—a necessary prerequisite to determining whether a proposed combination is sufficiently likely to be anticompetitive as to warrant injunctive relief. For the reasons that follow, we will reverse.

I. Background

A. Factual Background

Penn State Hershey Medical Center ("Hershey") is a leading academic medical center and the primary teaching hospital of the Penn State College of Medicine. It is located in Hershey, and it offers 551 beds and employs more than 800 physicians, many of whom are highly specialized. Hershey offers all levels of care, but it specializes in more complex, specialized services that are unavailable at most other hospitals. Because of its advanced services, Hershey draws patients from a broad area both inside and outside Dauphin County.

PinnacleHealth System ("Pinnacle") is a health system with three hospital campuses—two located in Harrisburg in Dauphin County, and the third located in Mechanicsburg in Cumberland County. It focuses on cost-effective primary and secondary services and offers only a limited range of more complex services. It employs fewer than 300 physicians and provides 646 beds.

In June 2014, Hershey and Pinnacle (collectively, the "Hospitals") signed a letter of intent for the proposed merger. Their respective boards subsequently approved the merger in March 2015. The following month, the Hospitals notified the FTC of their proposed merger."

B. Procedural History

After receiving notification of the proposed merger, the FTC began investigating the combination. Following the investigation, on December 7, 2015, the FTC filed an administrative complaint alleging that the merger violates Section 7 of the Clayton Act. On December 9, 2015, the FTC and the Commonwealth of Pennsylvania (collectively, the "Government") filed suit in the Middle District of Pennsylvania. Invoking Section 13(b) of the FTC Act, and Section 16 of the Clayton Act, the Government sought a preliminary injunction pending resolution of the FTC's administrative adjudication. In its complaint, the Government alleged that the Hospitals' merger would substantially lessen competition in the market for general acute care services sold to commercial insurers in the Harrisburg, Pennsylvania market. According to the Government, the combined Hospitals would control 76% of the market in Harrisburg.

The District Court conducted expedited discovery and held five days of evidentiary hearings. During the hearings, the District Court heard testimony from sixteen witnesses and admitted thousands of pages of exhibits into evidence.

Following the hearings, the District Court denied the Government's request for a preliminary injunction on the basis that the Government had failed to meet its burden to properly define the relevant geographic market. Without a properly defined relevant geographic market, the District Court held there was no way to determine whether the proposed merger was likely to be anticompetitive. Thus, the Government could not show a likelihood of success on the merits, and its failure to properly define the relevant geographic market was fatal to its motion. The Government timely appealed.

IV. Analysis

The Government alleges that the proposed merger of Hershey and Pinnacle violates Section 7 of the Clayton Act. In order to prevent the parties from merging until the FTC can conduct an administrative adjudication on the merits to determine whether the merger violates Section 7, the Government seeks a preliminary injunction under Section 13(b) of the FTC Act.

Section 13(b) of the FTC Act empowers the FTC to file suit in the federal district courts and seek a preliminary injunction to prevent a merger pending a FTC administrative adjudication "[w]henever the Commission has reason to believe that a corporation is violating, or is about to violate, Section 7 of the Clayton Act."

A district court may issue a preliminary injunction "[u]pon a proper showing that, weighing the equities and considering the Commission's likelihood of ultimate success, such action would be in the public interest." The public interest standard is not the same as the traditional equity standard for injunctive relief. Under Section 13(b), we first consider the FTC's likelihood of success on the merits and then weigh the equities to determine whether a preliminary injunction would be in the public interest.

A. Likelihood of Success on the Merits

We first consider the FTC's likelihood of success on the merits. In its administrative adjudication, the FTC must show that the proposed merger violates Section 7 of the Clayton Act. Section 7 bars mergers whose effect "may be substantially to lessen competition, or to tend to create a monopoly." "Congress used the words '*may be* substantially to lessen competition' . . . to indicate that its concern was with probabilities, not certainties," rendering Section 7's definition of antitrust liability "relatively expansive." At this stage, "[t]he FTC is not required to *establish* that the proposed merger would in fact violate section 7 of the Clayton Act."

Accordingly, "[a] certainty, even a high probability, need not be shown," and any "doubts are to be resolved against the transaction."

We assess Section 7 claims under a burden-shifting framework. First, the Government must establish a prima facie case that the merger is anticompetitive. If the Government establishes a prima facie case, the burden then shifts to the Hospitals to rebut it. If the Hospitals successfully rebut the Government's prima facie case, "the burden of production shifts back to the Government and merges with the ultimate burden of persuasion, which is incumbent on the Government at all times."

To establish a prima facie case, the Government must (1) propose the proper relevant market and (2) show that the effect of the merger in that market is likely to be anticompetitive.

1. Relevant Market

"Determination of the relevant product and geographic markets is 'a necessary predicate' to deciding whether a merger contravenes the Clayton Act." "Without a well-defined relevant market," an examination of the merger's competitive effects would be "without context or meaning." The relevant market is defined in terms of two components: the product market and the geographic market.

a. Relevant Product Market

There is no dispute as to the relevant product market. The District Court found, and the parties stipulated, that the relevant product market is general acute care ("GAC") services sold to commercial payors. GAC services comprise a number of "medical and surgical services that require an overnight hospital stay." Though the parties agree as to the relevant product market, the Hospitals strongly dispute the relevant geographic market put forth by the Government.

b. Relevant Geographic Market

The relevant geographic market "is that area in which a potential buyer may rationally look for the goods or services he seeks." Determined within the specific context of each case, a market's geographic scope must "correspond to the commercial realities of the industry" being considered and "be economically significant." The plaintiff (here, the Government) bears the burden of establishing the relevant geographic market.

A common method employed by courts and the FTC to determine the relevant geographic market is the hypothetical monopolist test. Under the *Horizontal Merger Guidelines* issued by the U.S. Department of Justice's Antitrust Division and the FTC, if a hypothetical monopolist could impose a small but significant non-transitory increase in price ("SSNIP") in the proposed market, the market is properly defined. If, however, consumers would respond to a SSNIP by purchasing the product from outside the proposed market, thereby making the SSNIP unprofitable, the proposed market definition is too narrow. Important for our purposes, both the Government and the Hospitals agree that this test should govern the instant appeal.

The Government argues, as it did before the District Court, that the relevant geographic market is the "Harrisburg area." More specifically, the four counties encompassing and immediately surrounding Harrisburg, Pennsylvania: Dauphin, Cumberland, Lebanon, and Perry counties.

The District Court rejected the Government's proposed geographic market. It first observed that 43.5% of Hershey's patients—11,260 people— travel to Hershey from outside the four-county area, which "strongly indicate [d] that the FTC had created a geographic market that [was] too narrow because it does not appropriately account for where the Hospitals, particularly Hershey, draw their business." Second, it held that the nineteen hospitals within a sixty-five-minute drive of Harrisburg "would readily offer consumers an alternative" to accepting a SSNIP. Finally, the District Court found it "extremely compelling" that the Hospitals had entered into private agreements with the two largest insurers in Central Pennsylvania, ensuring that post-merger rates would not increase for five years with one insurer and ten years with the other. Refusing to "blind [itself] to this reality," the District Court declined to "prevent [the] merger based on a prediction of what might happen to negotiating position and rates in 5 years." The failure to propose the proper relevant geographic market was fatal to the Government's motion, and the District Court denied the preliminary injunction request.

We conclude that the District Court erred in both its formulation and its application of the proper legal test. Although the District Court correctly identified the hypothetical monopolist test, its decision reflects neither the proper formulation nor the correct application of that test. We find three errors in the District Court's analysis. First, by relying almost exclusively on the number of patients that enter the proposed market, the District Court's analysis more closely aligns with a discredited economic theory, not the hypothetical monopolist test. Second, the District Court focused on the likely response of patients to a price increase, completely neglecting any mention of the likely response of insurers. Third, the District Court grounded its reasoning, in part, on the private agreements between the Hospitals and two insurers, even though these types of private contracts are not relevant to the hypothetical monopolist test.

i.   Formulation of the Legal Test

According to the District Court, to determine the geographic market, a court must apply a two-part test. First, it must determine "the market area in which the seller operates, its trade area." Second, it "must then determine whether a plaintiff has alleged a geographic market in which only a small percentage of purchasers have alternative suppliers to whom they could practically turn in the event that a defendant supplier's anticompetitive actions result in a price increase." Under the District Court's inquiry, the "end goal" of the relevant geographic market analysis is "to delineate a geographic area where, in the medical setting, few patients leave . . . and few patients enter."

The district court's formulation of the relevant geographic market test is inconsistent with the hypothetical monopolist test. Rather, it is one-half of a different test utilized in non-healthcare markets to define the relevant geographic market: the Elzinga-Hogarty test. The Elzinga-Hogarty test consists of two separate measurements: first, the number of customers who come from outside the proposed market to purchase goods and services from inside of it, and, second, the number of customers who reside inside the market but leave that market to purchase goods and services.

The Elzinga-Hogarty test was once the preferred method to analyze the relevant geographic market and was employed by many courts. But subsequent empirical research demonstrated that utilizing patient flow data to determine the relevant geographic market resulted in overbroad markets with respect to hospitals. Professor Elzinga himself testified before the FTC that this method "was not an appropriate method to define geographic markets in the hospital sector."

As the *amici curiae* Economics Professors have persuasively demonstrated, patient flow data—such as the 43.5% number emphasized by the District Court—is particularly unhelpful in hospital merger cases because of two problems: the "silent majority fallacy" and the "payor problem." "The silent majority fallacy is the false assumption that patients who travel to a distant hospital to obtain care significantly constrain the prices that the closer hospital charges to patients who will not travel to other hospitals." The constraining effect is non-existent because patient decisions are based mostly on non-price factors, such as location or quality of services. This fallacy is particularly salient here, where the District Court relied almost exclusively on the fact that Hershey attracts many patients from outside of the Harrisburg area. In deciding that patients who travel to Hershey would turn to other hospitals outside of Harrisburg if the merger gave rise to higher prices, the District Court did not consider that Hershey is a leading academic medical center that provides highly complex medical services. We are skeptical that patients who travel to Hershey for these complex services would turn to other hospitals in the area.

ii. Likely Response of Payors

The next problem with utilizing patient flow data—the payor problem—underscores the second error committed by the District Court. By utilizing patient flow data as its primary evidence that the relevant market was too narrow, the District Court failed to properly account for the likely response of insurers in the face of a SSNIP. In fact, it completely neglected any mention of the insurers in the healthcare market. This incorrect focus reflects a misunderstanding of the "commercial realities" of the healthcare market.

As the FTC and several courts have recognized, the healthcare market is represented by a two-stage model of competition. In the first stage, hospitals compete to be included in an insurance plan's hospital network. In the second stage, hospitals compete to attract individual members of an insurer's plan. Patients are largely insensitive to healthcare prices because they utilize insurance, which covers the majority of their healthcare costs. Because of this, our analysis must focus, at least in part, on the payors who will feel the impact of any price increase.

The Hospitals argue that there is no fundamental difference between analyzing the likely response of consumers through the patient or the payor perspective. We disagree. Patients are relevant to the analysis, especially to the extent that their behavior affects the relative bargaining positions of insurers and hospitals as they negotiate rates. But patients, in large part, do not feel the impact of price increases. Insurers do. And they are the ones who negotiate directly with the hospitals to determine both reimbursement rates and the hospitals that will be included in their networks.

Imagine that a hospital raised the cost of a procedure from $1,000 to $2,000. The patient who utilizes health insurance will still have the same out-of-pocket costs before and after the price increase. It is the insurer who will bear the immediate impact of that price increase. Not until the insurer passes that cost on to the patient in the form of higher premiums will the patient feel the impact of that price increase. And even then, the cost will be spread among many insured patients; it will not be felt solely by the patient who receives the higher-priced procedure. This is the commercial reality of the healthcare market as it exists today.

Thus, consistent with the mandate to determine the relevant geographic market taking into account the commercial realities of the specific industry involved, when we apply the hypothetical monopolist test, we must also do so through the lens of the insurers: if enough insurers, in the face of a small but significant non-transitory price increase, would avoid the price increase by looking to hospitals outside the proposed geographic market, then the market is too narrow. It was error for the District Court to completely disregard the role that insurers play in the healthcare market.

iii.   Private Pricing Agreements

Finally, the District Court erred in resting part of its analysis of the relevant geographic market on the private agreements between the Hospitals and the payors. The District Court found it "extremely compelling" that the Hospitals had already entered into contractual agreements with two of Central Pennsylvania's largest payors to maintain the existing rate structure for five years with Payor A and ten years with Payor B. Because of the agreements, the District Court believed that the FTC was "asking the Court [to] prevent this merger based on a prediction of what might happen to negotiating position and rates in 5 years." It declined to make such a prediction "[i]n the rapidly-changing arena of healthcare and health insurance."

This reasoning is flawed. We have previously cautioned that, in determining the relevant product market, private contracts are not to be considered. This same reasoning applies to the relevant geographic market. In determining the relevant market, we "look[ ] not to the contractual restraints assumed by a particular plaintiff," but instead, we answer whether a *hypothetical* monopolist could profitably impose a SSNIP.

For this reason, private contracts between merging parties and their customers have no place in the relevant geographic market analysis. The hypothetical monopolist test is exactly what its name suggests: hypothetical. This is for good reason. If we considered the agreements, then our inquiry would be simple: the Hospitals would not be able to profitably impose a SSNIP because the agreements forbid them from doing so. Determination of the relevant geographic market is a task for the courts, not for the merging entities. Although the District Court declined to predict what might happen to negotiating position and rates, making predictions about parties' and consumers' behavior is exactly what we are asked to do.

Moreover, if we allowed such private contracts to impact our analysis, any merging entity could enter into similar agreements—that may or may not be enforceable—to impermissibly broaden the scope of the relevant geographic market. This would enable antitrust defendants to escape effective enforcement of the antitrust laws.

These errors together render the District Court's analysis economically unsound and not reflective of the commercial reality of the healthcare market. In recent years, economists have concluded that the use of patient flow data does not accurately portray the relevant geographic market in the hospital merger context. Instead, economists have proposed, and the FTC has implemented, the hypothetical monopolist test. The realities of the healthcare market—in which payors negotiate prices for GAC services and will therefore feel the impact of any price increase— dictate that we consider the payors in our analysis. The District Court did not properly formulate the hypothetical monopolist test, nor did it properly apply that test. Because our antitrust analysis must be consistent with the evolution of economic understanding, and must be tied to the commercial realities of the specific industry at issue, we hold that the District Court committed legal error in failing to properly formulate and apply the hypothetical monopolist test.

We therefore conclude that, after determining the Government's likelihood of success and weighing the equities, a preliminary injunction would be in the public interest. Accordingly, we will reverse the District Court's denial of the Government's motion for a preliminary injunction. We will also remand the case and direct the District Court to preliminarily enjoin the proposed merger between Hershey and Pinnacle pending the outcome of the FTC's administrative adjudication.

NOTES AND QUESTIONS

1.   Unfortunately, by the time FTC regained its footing and began to succeed in hospital merger cases, 80% of the markets for many types of hospital care had become highly concentrated. FTC can do nothing effective about that problem because it is extremely difficult to unwind a merger.

2.   Note that this case and all of the other modern merger cases we have excerpted ended at the preliminary injunction stage. Merger agreements are too time-sensitive to survive the lengthy process of adjudicating the merits of a proposed merger.

3.   Note that the standard FTC must meet to obtain a preliminary injunction is much easier to meet than the standard the government must meet to obtain a preliminary injunction in any other context. The relative ease with which the FTC can enjoin a proposed merger combines with two other characteristics of the legal regime applicable to mergers that are within FTC's areas of responsibility to create a controversial situation. FTC usually assigns the task of adjudicating the merits of a merger dispute to one of its Administrative Law Judges, rather than asking a federal court to adjudicate the dispute, as DOJ must do. Moreover, the process of FTC adjudication of the merits of a merger dispute is so long that the parties know it can never be completed before the time-sensitive merger agreement expires. As a result, the parties to the proposed merger give up their efforts to merge if they lose at the preliminary injunction stage. Does this combination of characteristics seem fair to firms that propose to merge?

d.   An Industry Goes from Three Firms to Two

There is no serious question that the likelihood of antitrust challenge increases the closer a merger is to monopoly, i.e., reducing an industry from two firms to one. A merger from three firms to two is probably next worst, although in all cases, the concrete facts make a difference.

Federal Trade Commission v. H.J. Heinz Co., 246 F.3d 708 (D.C. Cir. 2001), involved the baby food industry. Gerber was the industry leader with a 65% market share, while Heinz was second with 17.4% and Beech-Nut third with 15.4%. Most grocery stores sold Gerber and one other brand, i.e., either Heinz or Beech-Nut but not both.

When Heinz and Beech-Nut proposed to merge, the FTC sought an injunction, alleging the merger would reduce the industry from three firms to two. In response, the companies said that consumers would hardly notice the difference. They have two choices today at any grocery store and they would have two choices in the future. Further, by keeping the best of both Heinz and Beech-Nut, the new company could be an even stronger competitor for Gerber and possibly bring even lower prices to consumers.

The District Court sided with the companies, but the D.C. Circuit reversed. The post-merger HHI would be almost 5300 with an increase of over 500. And while the retail consumer might not see a loss of competition, grocery stores would lose the benefit of competition between Heinz and Beech-Nut for the second spot on store shelves. The need to develop a consumer's trust over a long term makes baby food a hard market to enter, and the court thought the alleged efficiency gains might be gained without merger.

"The creation of a durable duopoly affords both the opportunity and incentive for both firms to coordinate to increase prices," the court said. "Tacit coordination is feared by antitrust policy even more than express collusion, for tacit coordination, even when observed, cannot easily be controlled directly by the antitrust laws. It is a central object of merger policy to obstruct the creation or reinforcement by merger of such oligopolistic market structures in which tacit coordination can occur."

Finally, the court said that its holding was narrow. "We do not decide whether the FTC will ultimately prove its case or whether the defendants' claimed efficiencies will carry the day. * * * Our task is [only] to review the district court's order to determine whether * * * preliminary injunctive relief would be in the public interest."

Do you agree that the court was not affecting the viability of the merger? Suppose you knew that it might take the FTC six to nine months to issue a decision on the merits of the case?

e.   Tough District Court Review but D.C. Circuit Gives the FTC New Life

FEDERAL TRADE COMMISSION V. WHOLE FOODS MARKET, INC.

United States Court of Appeals, District of Columbia Circuit, 2008
548 F.3d 1028

Before: TATEL, BROWN and KAVANAUGH, CIRCUIT JUDGES.

BROWN, CIRCUIT JUDGE:

The FTC sought a preliminary injunction, under 15 U.S.C. § 53(b), to block the merger of Whole Foods and Wild Oats. It appeals the district court's denial of the injunction. I conclude the district court should be reversed, though I do so reluctantly, admiring the thoughtful opinion the district court produced under trying circumstances in which the defendants were rushing to a financing deadline and the FTC presented, at best, poorly explained evidence. Nevertheless, the district court committed legal error in assuming market definition must depend on marginal consumers; consequently, it underestimated the FTC's likelihood of success on the merits.

I

Whole Foods Market, Inc. ("Whole Foods") and Wild Oats Markets, Inc. ("Wild Oats") operate 194 and 110 grocery stores, respectively, primarily in the United States. In February 2007, they announced that Whole Foods would acquire Wild Oats in a transaction closing before August 31, 2007. They notified the FTC, as the Hart-Scott-Rodino Act required for the $565 million merger, and the FTC investigated the merger through a series of hearings and document requests. On June 6, 2007, the FTC sought a temporary restraining order and preliminary injunction to block the merger temporarily while the FTC conducted an administrative proceeding to decide whether to block it permanently under § 7 of the Clayton Act. The parties conducted expedited discovery, and the district court held a hearing on July 31 and August 1, 2007.

The FTC contended Whole Foods and Wild Oats are the two largest operators of what it called premium, natural, and organic supermarkets ("PNOS"). Such stores "focus on high-quality perishables, specialty and natural organic produce, prepared foods, meat, fish[,] and bakery goods; generally have high levels of customer services; generally target affluent and well educated customers [and] . . . are mission driven with an emphasis on social and environmental responsibility." FTC v. Whole Foods Market, Inc., 502 F.Supp.2d 1, 28 (D.D.C.2007). In eighteen cities, asserted the FTC, the merger would create monopolies because Whole Foods and Wild Oats are the only PNOS. To support this claim, the FTC relied on emails Whole Foods's CEO John Mackey sent to other Whole Foods executives and directors, suggesting the purpose of the merger was to eliminate a competitor. In addition the FTC produced pseudonymous blog postings in which Mr. Mackey touted Whole Foods and denigrated other supermarkets as unable to compete. The FTC's expert economist, Dr. Kevin Murphy, analyzed sales data from the companies to show how entry by various supermarkets into a local market affected sales at a Whole Foods or Wild Oats store.

* * * [D]eposition testimony from other supermarkets indicated they regarded Whole Foods and Wild Oats as critical competition. Internal documents from the two defendants reflected their extensive monitoring of other supermarkets' prices as well as each other's.

The district court concluded that PNOS was not a distinct market and that Whole Foods and Wild Oats compete within the broader market of grocery stores and supermarkets. Believing such a basic failure doomed any chance of the FTC's success, the court denied the preliminary injunction without considering the balance of the equities.

On August 17, the FTC filed an emergency motion for an injunction pending appeal, which this court denied on August 23. Freed to proceed, Whole Foods and Wild Oats consummated their merger on August 28. The dissent argues that a reversal today contradicts this earlier decision, but our standard of review then was very different, requiring the FTC to show "such a substantial indication of probable success" that there would be "justification for the court's intrusion into the ordinary processes of . . . judicial review." It is hardly remarkable that the FTC could fail to meet such a stringent standard and yet persuasively show the district court erred in applying the much less demanding § 53(b) preliminary injunction standard.

II

At the threshold, Whole Foods questions our jurisdiction to hear this appeal. The merger is a *fait accompli,* and Whole Foods has already closed some Wild Oats stores and sold others. In addition, Whole Foods has sold two complete lines of stores, Sun Harvest and Harvey's, as well as some unspecified distribution facilities. Therefore, argues Whole Foods, the transaction is irreversible and the FTC's request for an injunction blocking it is moot.

Only in a rare case would we agree a transaction is truly irreversible, for the courts are "clothed with large discretion" to create remedies "effective to redress [antitrust] violations and to restore competition." Indeed, "divestiture is a common form of relief" from unlawful mergers. * * * Even remedies which "entail harsh consequences" would be appropriate to ameliorate the harm to competition from an antitrust violation. United States v. E.I. du Pont de Nemours & Co.

Of course, neither court nor agency has found Whole Foods's acquisition of Wild Oats to be unlawful. Therefore, the FTC may not yet claim the right to have any remedy necessary to undo the effects of the merger, as it could after such a determination. But the whole point of a preliminary injunction is to avoid the need for intrusive relief later, since even with the considerable flexibility of equitable relief, the difficulty of "unscrambl[ing] merged assets" often precludes "an effective order of divestiture." * * * At a minimum, the courts retain the power to preserve the *status quo nunc,* for example by means of a hold separate order, and perhaps also to restore the *status quo ante.*

Thus, the courts have the power to grant relief on the FTC's complaint, despite the merger's having taken place, and this case is therefore not moot. * * *

III

* * *

In deciding the FTC's request for a preliminary injunction blocking a merger under § 53(b), a district court must balance the likelihood of the FTC's success against the equities, under a sliding scale. The equities will often weigh in favor of the FTC, since the public interest in effective enforcement of the antitrust laws was Congress's specific public equity consideration in enacting the provision. Therefore, the FTC will usually be able to obtain a preliminary injunction blocking a merger by rais[ing] questions going to the merits so serious, substantial, difficult[,] and doubtful as to make them fair ground for thorough investigation. By meeting this standard, the FTC creates a presumption in favor of preliminary injunctive relief; but the merging parties may rebut that presumption, requiring the FTC to demonstrate a greater likelihood of success, by showing equities weighing in favor of the merger. * * *

* * *

The district court did not apply the sliding scale, instead declining to consider the equities. To be consistent with the § 53(b) standard, this decision must have rested on a conviction the FTC entirely failed to show a likelihood of success. Indeed, the court concluded the relevant product market in this case is not premium natural and organic supermarkets . . . as argued by the FTC but . . . at least all supermarkets. It also observed that several supermarkets "have already repositioned themselves to compete vigorously with Whole Foods and Wild Oats for the consumers' premium natural and organic food business." Thus, considering the defendants' evidence as well as the FTC's, as it was obligated to do, the court was in no doubt that this merger would not substantially lessen competition, because it found the evidence proved Whole Foods and Wild Oats compete among supermarkets generally. If, and only if, the district court's certainty was justified, it was appropriate for the court not to balance the likelihood of the FTC's success against the equities.

IV

However, the court's conclusion was in error. The FTC contends the district court abused its discretion in two ways: first, by treating market definition as a threshold issue; and second, by ignoring the FTC's main evidence. We conclude the district court acted reasonably in focusing on the market definition, but it analyzed the product market incorrectly.

A

First, the FTC complains the district court improperly focused on whether Whole Foods and Wild Oats operate within a PNOS market. However, this was not an abuse of discretion given that the district court was simply following the FTC's outline of the case.

Inexplicably, the FTC now asserts a market definition is not necessary in a § 7 case, in contravention of the statute itself, see 15 U.S.C. § 18 (barring an acquisition "where in any line of commerce . . . the effect of such acquisition may be substantially to lessen competition") * * * .

That is not to say market definition will always be crucial to the FTC's likelihood of success on the merits. Nor does the FTC necessarily need to settle on a market definition at this preliminary stage. * * * For example, the FTC may have alternate theories of the merger's anticompetitive harm, depending on inconsistent market definitions. While on the merits, the FTC would have to proceed with only one of those theories, at this preliminary phase it just has to raise substantial doubts about a transaction. One may have such doubts without knowing exactly what arguments will eventually prevail. Therefore, a district court's assessment of the FTC's chances will not depend, in every case, on a threshold matter of market definition.

In this case, however, the FTC itself made market definition key. It claimed [t]he operation of premium natural and organic supermarkets is a distinct line of commerce within the meaning of Section 7, and its theory of anticompetitive effect was that the merger would substantially increase concentration in the operation of [PNOS]. * * *

B

Thus, the FTC assumed the burden of raising some question of whether PNOS is a well-defined market. As the FTC presented its case, success turned on whether there exist core customers, committed to PNOS, for whom one should consider PNOS a relevant market. The district court assumed "the 'marginal' consumer, not the so-called 'core' or 'committed' consumer, must be the focus of any antitrust analysis." To the contrary, core consumers can, in appropriate circumstances, be worthy of antitrust protection. See Horizontal Merger Guidelines § 1.12 (explaining the possibility of price discrimination for targeted buyers). The district court's error of law led it to ignore FTC evidence that strongly suggested Whole Foods and Wild Oats compete for core consumers within a PNOS market, even if they also compete on individual products for marginal consumers in the broader market.

* * *

Experts for the two sides disagreed about how to do the SSNIP of the proposed PNOS market. Dr. Scheffman [for the defense] used a method called critical loss analysis, in which he predicted the loss that would result when marginal customers shifted purchases to conventional supermarkets in response to a SSNIP. He concluded a hypothetical monopolist could not profit from a SSNIP, so that conventional supermarkets must be within the same market as PNOS. In contrast, Dr. Murphy [for the FTC] disapproved of critical loss analysis generally, preferring a method called critical diversion that asked how many customers would be diverted to Whole Foods and how many to conventional supermarkets if a nearby Wild Oats closed. Whole Foods's internal planning documents indicated at least a majority of these customers would switch to Whole Foods, thus making the closure profitable for a hypothetical PNOS monopolist. One crucial difference between these approaches was that Dr. Scheffman's analysis depended only on the *marginal* loss of sales, while Dr. Murphy's used the *average* loss of customers. Dr. Murphy explained that focusing on the average behavior of customers was appropriate because a core of committed customers would continue to shop at PNOS stores despite a SSNIP.

In appropriate circumstances, core customers can be a proper subject of antitrust concern. In particular, when one or a few firms differentiate themselves by offering a particular package of goods or services, it is quite possible for there to be a central group of customers for whom only [that package] will do. What motivates antitrust concern for such customers is the possibility that fringe competition for individual products within a package may not protect customers who need the whole package from market power exercised by a sole supplier of the package.

Such customers may be captive to the sole supplier, which can then, by means of price discrimination, extract monopoly profits from them while competing for the business of marginal customers. Not that prices that segregate core from marginal consumers are in themselves anticompetitive; such pricing simply indicates the existence of a submarket of core customers, operating in parallel with the broader market but featuring a different demand curve. Sometimes, for some customers a package provides "access to certain products or services that would otherwise be unavailable to them." Because the core customers require the whole package, they respond differently to price increases from marginal customers who may obtain portions of the package elsewhere. Of course, core customers may constitute a submarket even without such an extreme difference in demand elasticity. After all, market definition focuses on what products are *reasonably* substitutable; what is reasonable must ultimately be determined by "settled consumer preference." United States v. Philadelphia Nat'l Bank.

In short, a core group of particularly dedicated, distinct customers, paying distinct prices, may constitute a recognizable submarket, *Brown Shoe*, whether they are dedicated because they need a complete cluster of products, *Phila. Nat'l Bank,* because their particular circumstances dictate that a product is the only realistic choice, or because they find a particular product uniquely attractive, [*NCAA*]. * * *

The FTC's evidence delineated a PNOS submarket catering to a core group of customers who have decided that natural and organic is important, lifestyle of health and ecological sustainability is important. It was undisputed that Whole Foods and Wild Oats provide higher levels of customer service than conventional supermarkets, a "unique environment," and a particular focus on the "core values" these customers espoused. The FTC connected these intangible properties with concrete aspects of the PNOS model, such as a much larger selection of natural and organic products.

Further, the FTC documented exactly the kind of price discrimination that enables a firm to profit from core customers for whom it is the sole supplier. Dr. Murphy compared the margins of Whole Foods stores in cities where they competed with Wild Oats. He found the presence of a Wild Oats depressed Whole Foods's margins significantly. Notably, while there was no effect on Whole Foods's margins in the product category of "groceries," where Whole Foods and Wild Oats compete on the margins with conventional supermarkets, the effect on margins for perishables was substantial. Confirming this price discrimination, Whole Foods's documents indicated that when it price-checked conventional supermarkets, the focus was overwhelmingly on "dry grocery," rather than on the perishables that were 70% of Whole Foods's business. Thus, in the high-quality perishables on which both Whole Foods and Wild Oats made most of their money, they competed directly with each other, and they competed with supermarkets only on the dry grocery items that were the fringes of their business.

Additionally, the FTC provided direct evidence that PNOS competition had a greater effect than conventional supermarkets on PNOS prices. Dr. Murphy showed the opening of a new Whole Foods in the vicinity of a Wild Oats caused Wild Oats's prices to drop, while entry by non-PNOS stores had no such effect. * * *

Finally, evidence of consumer behavior supported the conclusion that PNOS serve a core consumer base. Whole Foods's internal projections, based on market experience, suggested that if a Wild Oats near a Whole Foods were to close, the majority (in some cases nearly all) of its customers would switch to the Whole Foods rather than to conventional supermarkets. Since Whole Foods's prices for perishables are higher than those of conventional supermarkets, such customers must not find shopping at the latter interchangeable with PNOS shopping. They are the core customers. Moreover, market research, including Dr. Scheffman's own studies, indicated 68% of Whole Foods customers are core customers who share the Whole Foods "core values."

Against this conclusion the defendants posed evidence that customers cross-shop between PNOS and other stores and that Whole Foods and Wild Oats check the prices of conventional supermarkets. But the fact that PNOS and ordinary supermarkets are direct competitors in some submarkets . . . is not the end of the inquiry. Of course customers cross-shop; PNOS carry comprehensive inventories. The fact that a customer might buy a stick of gum at a supermarket or at a convenience store does not mean there is no definable groceries market. Here, cross-shopping is entirely consistent with the existence of a core group of PNOS customers. Indeed, Dr. Murphy explained that Whole Foods competes actively with conventional supermarkets for dry groceries sales, even though it ignores their prices for high-quality perishables.

* * *

In sum, the district court believed the antitrust laws are addressed only to marginal consumers. This was an error of law, because in some situations core consumers, demanding exclusively a particular product or package of products, distinguish a submarket. The FTC described the core PNOS customers, explained how PNOS cater to these customers, and showed these customers provided the bulk of PNOS's business. The FTC put forward economic evidence—which the district court ignored—showing directly how PNOS discriminate on price between their core and marginal customers, thus treating the former as a distinct market. Therefore, we cannot agree with the district court that the FTC would never be able to prove a PNOS submarket. We do not say the FTC has in fact proved such a market, which is not necessary at this point. To obtain a preliminary injunction under § 53(b), the FTC need only show a likelihood of success sufficient, using the sliding scale, to balance any equities that might weigh against the injunction.

V

It remains to address the equities, which the district court did not reach, and see whether for some reason there is a balance against the FTC that would require a greater likelihood of success. * * * Although the equities in a § 53(b) preliminary injunction proceeding will usually favor the FTC, the district court must independently exercise its discretion considering the circumstances of this case, including the fact that the merger has taken place. We remind the district court that a risk that the transaction will not occur at all, by itself, is a private consideration that cannot alone defeat the preliminary injunction.

* * * For the reasons stated above, we reverse the district court's conclusion that the FTC showed no likelihood of success in an eventual § 7 case, and we remand for proceedings consistent with this opinion.

TATEL, CIRCUIT JUDGE, concurring in the judgment.

* * * I believe the district court overlooked or mistakenly rejected evidence supporting the FTC's view that Whole Foods and Wild Oats occupy a separate market of premium natural and organic supermarkets.

I

* * * Congress used the words *may be* substantially to lessen competition, to indicate that its concern was with probabilities, not certainties. Brown Shoe Co. v. United States.

When the FTC believes an acquisition violates section 7 and that enjoining the acquisition pending an investigation would be in the interest of the public, section 13(b) of the Federal Trade Commission Act authorizes the Commission to ask a federal district court to block the acquisition. Because Congress concluded that the FTC—an expert agency acting on the public's behalf—should be able to obtain injunctive relief more readily than private parties, it incorporat[ed] a unique public interest standard in 15 U.S.C. § 53(b), rather than the more stringent, traditional equity standard for injunctive relief. * * *

* * *

II

In this case the district court concluded that the FTC had failed to raise the serious, substantial questions necessary to show a likelihood of success on the merits. FTC v. Whole Foods Market, Inc., 502 F.Supp.2d 1, 49 (D.D.C.2007). Following the FTC's lead, the court focused on defining the product market in which Whole Foods and Wild Oats operate, saying:

> [I]f the relevant product market is, as the FTC alleges, a product market of premium natural and organic supermarkets . . . , there can be little doubt that the acquisition of the second largest firm in the market by the largest firm in the market will tend to harm competition in that market. If, on the other hand, the defendants are merely differentiated firms operating within the larger relevant product market of supermarkets, the proposed merger will not tend to harm competition.

* * * And after reviewing the evidence, the district court concluded that [t]here is no substantial likelihood that the FTC can prove its asserted product market and thus no likelihood that it can prove that the proposed merger may substantially lessen competition or tend to create a monopoly.

I agree with the district court that this case hinges—almost entirely—on the proper definition of the relevant product market, for if a separate natural and organic market exists, there can be little doubt that the acquisition of the second largest firm in the market by the largest firm in the market will tend to harm competition in that market. But I respectfully part ways with the district court when it comes to assessing the FTC's evidence in support of its contention that Whole Foods and Wild Oats occupy a distinct market. * * * In this case the FTC presented a great deal of credible evidence—either unmentioned or rejected by the district court—suggesting that Whole Foods and Wild Oats are not reasonabl[y] interchangeab[le] with conventional supermarkets and do not compete directly with them.

To begin with, the FTC's expert prepared a study showing that when a Whole Foods opened near an existing Wild Oats, it reduced sales at the Wild Oats store dramatically. By contrast, when a conventional supermarket opened near a Wild Oats store, Wild Oats's sales were virtually unaffected. This strongly suggests that although Wild Oats customers consider Whole Foods an adequate substitute, they do not feel the same way about conventional supermarkets. * * *

The FTC also highlighted Whole Foods's own study—called "Project Goldmine"—showing what Wild Oats customers would likely do after the proposed merger in cities where Whole Foods planned to close Wild Oats stores. According to the study, the average Whole Foods store would capture most of the revenue from the closed Wild Oats store, even though virtually every city contained multiple conventional retailers closer to the shuttered Wild Oats store. This high diversion ratio further suggests that many consumers consider conventional supermarkets inadequate substitutes for Wild Oats and Whole Foods. * * *

Several industry studies predating the merger also suggest that Whole Foods and Wild Oats never truly competed with conventional supermarkets. For example, a study * * * concludes that "[w]hile th[e] same consumer shops" at both "mainstream grocers such as Safeway" and "large-format natural foods store[s] such as Wild Oats or Whole Foods Market," they tend to shop at each for different things (e.g., Wild Oats for fresh and specialty items, Safeway for canned and packaged goods). In addition, Wild Oats's former CEO, Perry Odak, explained in a deposition why conventional stores have difficulty competing with Whole Foods and Wild Oats: if conventional stores offer a lot of organic products, they don't sell enough to their existing customer base, leaving the stores with spoiled products and reduced profits. But if conventional stores offer only a narrow range of organic products, customers with a high demand for organic items refuse to shop there. Thus, "the conventionals have a very difficult time getting into this business." The district court mentioned none of this.

In addition to all this direct evidence that Whole Foods and Wild Oats occupy a separate market from conventional supermarkets, the FTC presented an enormous amount of evidence of industry or public recognition of the natural and organic market as a separate economic entity—one of the practical indicia the Supreme Court has said can be used to determine the boundaries of a distinct market. *Brown Shoe.* For example, dozens of record studies about the grocery store industry—including many prepared for Whole Foods or Wild Oats—distinguish between traditional or conventional grocery stores on the one hand and natural food or organic stores on the other. Moreover, record evidence indicates that the Whole Foods and Wild Oats CEOs both believed that their companies occupied a market separate from the conventional grocery store industry. In an email to his company's board, Whole Foods CEO John Mackey explained that "[Wild Oats] is the only existing company that has the brand and number of stores to be a meaningful springboard for another player to get into this space. Eliminating them means eliminating this threat forever, or almost forever." Echoing this point, former Wild Oats CEO Perry Odak said that "there's really only two players of any substance in the organic and all natural [market], and that's Whole Foods and Wild Oats. . . . [T]here's really nobody else in that particular space." * * * As Judge Bork explained, this evidence of "industry or public recognition of the submarket as a separate economic unit matters because we assume that economic actors usually have accurate perceptions of economic realities." Rothery Storage & Van Co. v. Atlas Van Lines, Inc.

* * *

Insisting that all this evidence of a separate market is irrelevant, Whole Foods and the dissent argue that the FTC's case must fail because the record contains no evidence that Whole Foods or Wild Oats charged higher prices in cities where the other was absent—i.e., where one had a local monopoly on the asserted natural and organic market—than they did in cities where the other was present. This argument is both legally and factually incorrect.

As a legal matter, although evidence that a company charges more when other companies in the alleged market are absent certainly indicates that the companies operate in a distinct market, see, e.g., *Staples,* that is not the *only* way to prove a separate market. Indeed, *Brown Shoe* lists distinct prices as only one of a non-exhaustive list of seven practical indicia that may be examined to determine whether a separate market exists. Furthermore, even if the FTC could *prove* a section 7 violation only by showing evidence of higher prices in areas where a company had a local monopoly in an alleged market, the FTC need not *prove* a section 7 violation to obtain a preliminary injunction; rather, it need only raise "serious, substantial" questions as to the merger's legality. Thus, the dissent misses the mark when it cites the FTC's Horizontal Merger Guidelines to assert that the Commission may obtain a preliminary injunction only by "mak[ing] a sufficient showing that the merged company could . . . profitably impose a significant nontransitory increase in price" of 5% or more. Such evidence in a case like this, which turns entirely on market definition, would be enough *to prove* a section 7 violation in the FTC's administrative proceeding. Yet our precedent clearly holds that to obtain a preliminary injunction, "[t]he FTC is not required to *establish* that the proposed merger would in fact violate section 7 of the Clayton Act." * * *

In any event, the FTC did present evidence indicating that Whole Foods and Wild Oats charged more when they were the only natural and organic supermarket present. The FTC's expert looked at prices Whole Foods charged in several of its North Carolina stores before and after entry of a regional natural food chain called Earth Fare. Before any Earth Fare stores opened, Whole Foods charged essentially the same prices at its five North Carolina stores, but when an Earth Fare opened near the Whole Foods in Chapel Hill, that store's prices dropped 5% below those at the other North Carolina Whole Foods. * * * In addition to this quantitative evidence, the FTC pointed to Whole Foods CEO John Mackey's statement explaining to the company's board why the merger made sense: By buying [Wild Oats] we will . . . avoid nasty price wars in [several cities where both companies have stores].

* * *

The district court * * * emphasized that when a new Whole Foods store opens, it takes business from conventional grocery stores, and even when an existing Wild Oats is nearby, most of the new Whole Foods store's revenue comes from customers who previously shopped at conventional stores. According to the district court, this led "to the inevitable conclusion that Whole Foods' and Wild Oats' main competitors are other supermarkets, not just each other." As the FTC points out, however, "an innovative [product] can create a new product market for antitrust purposes" by "satisfy[ing] a previously-unsatisfied consumer demand." To use the Commission's example, when the automobile was first invented, competing auto manufacturers obviously took customers primarily from companies selling horses and buggies, not from other auto manufacturers, but that hardly shows that cars and horse-drawn carriages should be treated as the same product market. That Whole Foods and Wild Oats have attracted many customers away from conventional grocery stores by offering extensive selections of natural and organic products thus tells us nothing about whether Whole Foods and Wild Oats should be treated as operating in the same market as conventional grocery stores. Indeed, courts have often found that sufficiently innovative retailers can constitute a distinct product market even when they take customers from existing retailers.

* * *

III

* * *

Given the novel and significant task the district court faces on remand, I think it important to emphasize the principles that should guide its weighing of the equities. To begin with, as this court has held, "a likelihood of success finding weighs heavily in favor of a preliminary injunction blocking the acquisition, creat[ing] a presumption in favor of preliminary injunctive relief." * * *

* * * [I]f Whole Foods can show no public equities in favor of allowing the merger to proceed immediately—such as increased employment or reduced prices—the district court should go no further, for "[w]hen the Commission demonstrates a likelihood of ultimate success, a countershowing of private equities alone [does] not suffice to justify denial of a preliminary injunction barring the merger." But if Whole Foods can show some public equity favoring the merger, then the court should also consider private equities on Whole Foods's side of the ledger, such as whether it would allow an otherwise failing firm to survive. That said, "[w]hile it is proper to consider private equities in deciding whether to enjoin a particular transaction, we must afford such concerns little weight, lest we undermine section 13(b)'s purpose of protecting the public-at-large, rather than the individual private competitors." Moreover, "[w]e do not rank as a private equity meriting weight a mere expectation of private gain from a transaction the FTC has shown is likely to violate the antitrust laws." In other words, even if allowing the merger to proceed would increase Whole Foods's profits, that is irrelevant to the private equities under section 13(b).

KAVANAUGH, CIRCUIT JUDGE, dissenting:

* * *

A year ago, after a lengthy evidentiary hearing and in an exhaustive and careful opinion, the District Court found that the record evidence overwhelmingly supports the following conclusions: Whole Foods competes against all supermarkets and not just so-called organic stores; the relevant market for evaluating this merger for antitrust purposes is all supermarkets; and the merger of Whole Foods and Wild Oats would not substantially lessen competition in a market that includes all supermarkets. The court therefore denied the FTC's motion for a preliminary injunction.

And more than a year ago, a three-judge panel of this Court unanimously denied the FTC's request for an injunction pending appeal, thereby allowing the Whole Foods-Wild Oats deal to close. Since then, the merged entity has shut down, sold, or converted numerous Wild Oats stores and otherwise effectuated the merger through many changes in supplier contracts, leases, distribution, and the like.

The court's splintered decision in this case seeks to unring the bell. In my judgment, this Court got it right a year ago in refusing to enjoin the merger, and there is no basis for a changed result now. Both a year ago and now, the same central question has been before the Court in determining whether to approve an injunction: whether the FTC demonstrated the necessary likelihood of success on its § 7 case. A year ago, the Court said no. Now, the Court says yes. The now-merged entity and the markets no doubt will be confused by this apparent judicial about-face.

* * *

I

* * *

B

Consistent with the statute, the Executive Branch's Merger Guidelines, and Judge Hogan's convincing opinion in *Staples,* the District Court here carefully analyzed the economics of supermarkets, including so-called organic supermarkets. The court considered whether Whole Foods charged higher prices in areas without Wild Oats than in areas with Wild Oats. After an evidentiary hearing and based on a painstaking review of the evidence in the record, the court concluded that Whole Foods prices are essentially the same at all of its stores in a region, regardless of whether there is a Wild Oats store nearby. That factual conclusion was supported by substantial evidence offered by Dr. Scheffman, Whole Foods's expert, and by the lack of any credible evidence to the contrary.

* * *

Moreover, the record evidence in this case does not show that Whole Foods changed its prices in any significant way in response to exit from an area by Wild Oats. In the four cases where Wild Oats exited and a Whole Foods store remained, there is no evidence in the record that Whole Foods then raised prices. Nor was there any evidence of price increases after Whole Foods took over two Wild Oats stores.

* * *

The record * * * demonstrates that conventional supermarkets and so-called organic supermarkets are aggressively competing to attract customers from one another. After reviewing a wide variety of industry information and trade journals, Dr. Scheffman concluded that "[o]ther supermarkets are competing vigorously for the purchases made by shoppers at [Whole Foods] and [Wild Oats]." Whole Foods recognizes the fact that it has to appeal to a significantly broader group of consumers than organic and natural focused consumers. The record shows that Whole Foods has made progress: Most products that Whole Foods sells are not organic. Conversely, conventional supermarkets have shifted towards emphasizing fresh, natural and organic products. * * *

So the dividing line between "organic" and conventional supermarkets has been blurred. As the District Court aptly put it, the "train has already left the station." The convergence undermines the threshold premise of the FTC's case. This is an industry in transition, and Whole Foods has pioneered a product differentiation that in turn has caused other supermarket chains to update their offerings. These are not separate product markets; this is a market where all supermarkets including so-called organic supermarkets are clawing tooth and nail to differentiate themselves, beat the competition, and make money.

* * *

II

In an attempt to save its merger case despite its inability to meet the test reflected in the Merger Guidelines and applied in *Staples,* the FTC cites marginally relevant evidence and advances seriously flawed arguments.

First, the FTC says that so-called organic supermarkets like Whole Foods and Wild Oats constitute their own product market because they are characterized by factors that differentiate them from conventional supermarkets. Those factors include intangible qualities such as customer service and tangible factors such as a focus on perishables.

This argument reflects the key error that permeates the FTC's flawed approach to this case. Those factors demonstrate only product differentiation, and product differentiation does not mean different product markets. * * * As the District Court noted, supermarkets including so-called organic supermarkets differentiate themselves by emphasizing specific benefits or characteristics to attract customers to their stores. They may differentiate themselves along dimensions such as low price, ethnic appeal, prepared foods, health and nutrition, variety within a product category, customer service, or perishables such as meats or produce.

The key to distinguishing product differentiation from separate product markets lies in price information. * * * To distinguish differentiation from separate product markets, courts thus must ask whether one seller could maximize profit by charging more than the competitive price without losing too much patronage to other sellers. Here, in other words, could so-called organic supermarkets maximize profit by charging more than a competitive price without losing too much patronage to conventional supermarkets? Based on the evidence regarding Whole

Foods's pricing practices, the District Court correctly found that the answer to that question is no. So-called organic supermarkets are engaged in product differentiation; they do not constitute a product market separate from all supermarkets.

Second, the FTC points to internal Whole Foods studies and other evidence showing that if a Wild Oats near a Whole Foods were to close, most of the Wild Oats customers would shift to Whole Foods. But that says nothing about whether Whole Foods could impose a five percent or more price increase and still retain those customers (and its other customers), which is the relevant antitrust question. In other words, the fact that many Wild Oats customers would shift to Whole Foods does not mean that those customers would stay with Whole Foods, as opposed to shifting to conventional supermarkets, if Whole Foods significantly raised its prices. And even if one could infer that all of those former Wild Oats customers would so prefer Whole Foods that they would shop there even in the face of significant price increases, that would not show whether Whole Foods could raise prices without driving out a sufficient number of *other* customers as to make the price increases unprofitable. In sum, this argument is a diversion from the economic analysis that must be conducted in antitrust cases like this. The District Court properly found that the expert evidence in the record leads to the conclusion that Whole Foods could not profitably impose such a significant price increase.

Third, the FTC points to comments by Whole Foods CEO John Mackey as evidence that Whole Foods perceived Wild Oats to be a unique competitor. Even if Mackey's comments were directed only to Wild Oats, that would not be evidence that Whole Foods and Wild Oats are in their own product market separate from all other supermarkets. It just as readily suggests that Whole Foods and Wild Oats are two supermarkets that have similarly *differentiated* themselves from the rest of the market, such that Mackey would be especially pleased to see that competitor vanish. Beating the competition from similarly differentiated competitors in a product market is ordinarily an entirely permissible competitive goal. Saying as much, as Mackey did here, does not mean that the similarly differentiated competitor is the *only* relevant competition in the marketplace. Moreover, Mackey nowhere says that the merger would allow Whole Foods to significantly raise prices, which of course is the issue here. In any event, intent is not an element of a § 7 claim, and a CEO's bravado with regard to one rival cannot alter the laws of economics: Mere boasts cannot vanquish real-world competition—here, from Safeway, Albertson's, and the like. As Judge Easterbrook has explained, "Firms need not like their competitors; they need not cheer them on to success; a desire to extinguish one's rivals is entirely consistent with, often is the motive behind, competition." A.A. Poultry Farms, Inc. v. Rose Acre Farms, Inc. And [i]f courts use the vigorous, nasty pursuit of sales as evidence of a forbidden intent, they run the risk of penalizing the motive forces of competition. * * *

* * *

The bottom line is that, as the District Court found, there is no evidence in the record suggesting that Whole Foods priced differently based on the presence or absence of a Wild Oats store in the area. That is a conspicuous—and all but dispositive—omission in Dr. Murphy's analysis and in the FTC's case.

* * *

III

A

* * *

* * * [T]he court's decision resuscitates the loose antitrust standards of Brown Shoe Co. v. United States, the 1960s relic. * * *

As demonstrated in this court's most recent merger case, the practical indicia test of Brown Shoe no longer guides courts' merger analysis because it does not sufficiently account for the basic economic principles that, according to the Supreme Court, must be considered under modern antitrust doctrine. See FTC v. H.J. Heinz Co. * * *

The court's revival of the loose *Brown Shoe* standard threatens to * * * upend modern merger practice.

* * *

B

In reaching her conclusion, Judge Brown also relies on a distinction between marginal consumers and core consumers. But the FTC never once referred to, much less relied on, the distinction * * * .

In any event, I respectfully disagree with Judge Brown's emphasis on core customers. For a business to exert market power as a result of a merger, it must be able to increase prices (usually by five percent or more) while retaining enough customers to make that price increase profitable. If too many "marginal" customers are turned off by a price hike, then the hike will be unprofitable even if a large group of die-hard "core" customers remain active clients. Therefore, a focus on core customers alone cannot resolve a merger case. * * * [V]irtually *every* merger involves some core customers who would stick with the company regardless of a significant price increase. So under this "core customer" approach, many heretofore permissible mergers presumably could be blocked as anticompetitive. That cannot be the law, and it is not the law.

* * *

IV

In the end, the FTC's case is weak and seems a relic of a bygone era when antitrust law was divorced from basic economic principles. The record does not show that Whole Foods priced differently based on the presence or absence of Wild Oats in the same area. The reason for that and the conclusion that follows from that are the same: Whole Foods competes in an extraordinarily competitive market that includes all supermarkets, not just so-called organic supermarkets. The merged entity thus could not exercise market power such that it could profitably impose a significant and nontransitory price increase. Therefore, there is no sound legal basis to block this merger.

* * *

I respectfully dissent.

NOTES AND QUESTIONS

1.   Do you agree with Judge Brown's focus on the difference between "core" and "marginal" customers? Why did she believe the lower court's focus on the latter was not consistent with Section 7?

a.   A marginal customer is one who will only buy if a seller lowers its price a little more and is thus among the customers who theoretically drive prices to a competitive level. Did Judge Tatel's failure to follow Judge Brown's lead and Judge Kavanaugh's outright rejection of her position persuade you that the effect of the merger on marginal customers should be the real measure of whether the merger caused a substantial lessening of competition?

b.   A core customer, on the other hand, is thoroughly committed to the seller and will continue to buy even as prices rise. Do you agree with Judge Brown that protecting consumers who are locked into a particular seller by such strong feelings should be an important element of antitrust policy?

2.   Were you surprised by the deference Judge's Tatel and Brown were willing to show the FTC?

a.   Do you agree with Judge Kavanaugh that the DOJ and FTC are both "executive branch agencies" and should be given no implicit presumption that their request for injunctive relief is justified?

b.   Is the fact that a merger has been singled out for challenge from among the many HSR notifications filed itself a basis for giving weight to the government's position? In 2007, for example, the enforcement agencies received 2,201 Hart-Scott-Rodino filings. They issued a "second request" (for additional data) in only 63 of those, about 3% of the total. And the agencies took only 7 cases to federal district court. Might the fine screen through which cases must pass make courts less quick to second-guess the agencies' request for an injunction?

c.   On the other hand, is it fair to say that a preliminary injunction simply requires that the proposed merger be delayed? Might enjoining a merger mean as a practical matter that the merger will fall through no matter how the case might properly be resolved?

3.   Do you agree with Judges Brown and Tatel that "premium natural and organic supermarkets (PNOS)" constitute a separate market for antitrust purposes? Is Judge Kavanaugh right that the designation simply represents predictable product differentiation within a larger market for groceries? Does the distinction between core and marginal consumers suggest that no single market definition makes sense for all customers?

4.   To what extent did the *Whole Foods* case likely turn on CEO Mackey's emails that the merger would eliminate competition?

a.   Should such statements by executives be taken virtually as confessions of wrongdoing? Might they instead be seen as puffing by an executive trying to impress associates with the wisdom of the merger?

b.   How have the courts in exclusion cases treated executive statements about the intent to drive a competitor out of business? Should the statements be given any more weight in merger cases?

f.   The Justice Department Makes a Taxing Decision

UNITED STATES V. H & R BLOCK, INC.

United States District Court for the District of Columbia, 2011
833 F.Supp.2d 36

MEMORANDUM OPINION

BERYL A. HOWELL, DISTRICT JUDGE.

* * *

[A]pproximately 140 million Americans filed tax returns with the IRS in 2010. Broadly speaking, there are three methods for preparing a tax return. The pen and paper or manual method includes preparation by hand and with free, electronically fillable forms available on the IRS website. A second method, known as assisted preparation, involves hiring a tax professional—typically either a certified public accountant (CPA) or a specialist at a retail tax store. HRB operates the largest retail tax store chain in the United States. The companies Jackson Hewitt and Liberty Tax Service also operate well-known retail tax stores. Finally, many taxpayers now prepare their returns using digital do-it-yourself tax preparation products (DDIY), such as the popular software product TurboTax. DDIY preparation is becoming increasingly popular and an estimated 35 to 40 million taxpayers used DDIY in 2010.

The three most popular DDIY providers are HRB, TaxACT, and Intuit, the maker of TurboTax. According to IRS data, these three firms accounted for approximately 90 percent of the DDIY-prepared federal returns filed in tax season 2010. The next largest firm is TaxHawk, also known as FreeTaxUSA, with 3.2 percent market share, followed by TaxSlayer, with 2.7 percent. The remainder of the market is divided among numerous smaller firms. Intuit accounted for 62.2 percent of DDIY returns, HRB for 15.6 percent, and TaxACT for 12.8 percent. DDIY products are offered to consumers through three channels: (1) online through an internet browser; (2) personal computer software downloaded from a website; and (3) personal computer software installed from a disk, which is either sent directly to the consumer or purchased by the consumer from a third-party retailer. In industry parlance, DDIY products provided through an internet browser are called online products, while software applications downloaded onto the user's computer via the web or installed from a disk are referred to as software products.

The proposed acquisition challenged in this case would combine HRB and TaxACT, the second and third most popular providers of DDIY products, respectively. According to the government, this combination would result in an effective duopoly between HRB and Intuit in the DDIY market, in which the next nearest competitor will have an approximately 3 percent market share, and most other competitors will have less than a 1 percent share. The government also alleges that unilateral anticompetitive effects would result from the elimination of head-to-head competition between the merging parties.

Thus, the DOJ alleges that because the proposed acquisition would reduce competition in the DDIY industry by eliminating head-to-head competition between the merging parties and by making anticompetitive coordination between the two major remaining market participants substantially more likely, the proposed acquisition violates Section 7 of the Clayton Act. Accordingly, the government seeks a permanent injunction blocking HRB from acquiring TaxACT.

* * *

TaxACT was founded in 1998 by Lance Dunn and three others, with Mr. Dunn serving as president. Before founding TaxACT, Mr. Dunn and the other co-founders of the company had worked at Parsons Technology, a software company that had created a DDIY tax preparation product called Personal Tax Edge. In 1994, Intuit acquired Parsons Technology and continued to operate Personal Tax Edge as a separate product for approximately two years before merging it into its TurboTax product line. Mr. Dunn testified that the business objective of founding TaxACT was to make money selling value tax software which . . . was a category that did not exist at that time because Intuit's acquisition of Parsons Technology had eliminated Personal Tax Edge, which had previously occupied a value tax software niche. Thus, TaxACT recreated the category or "niche" that the Personal Tax Edge product line filled when it existed.

Over the years, TaxACT has emphasized high-quality free product offerings as part of its business strategy. TaxACT initially offered a DDIY tax preparation product that made it free to prepare and print a federal tax return, but TaxACT charged a fee for electronic filing ("e-filing") or preparation of a state tax return. Thus, from the beginning, TaxACT's business strategy relied on promoting free or freemium products, in which a basic part of the service is offered for free and add-ons and extra features are sold for a price. * * *

* * *

In October 2010, the HRB Board of Directors approved a plan for HRB to acquire TaxACT. * * * HRB's stated post-merger plan is to maintain both the HRB and TaxACT brands with the HRB-brand focusing on higher priced-products and the TaxACT brand focusing on the lower-priced products. HRB plans ultimately to rely on TaxACT's current technological platform and intends to give Mr. Dunn responsibility for running the combined firm's entire DDIY business operation from Cedar Rapids, Iowa.

* * *

II. STANDARD OF REVIEW

* * *

* * * [T]he decision in United States v. Baker Hughes Inc., 908 F.2d 981 (D.C. Cir. 1990), sets forth the analytical approach for establishing a Section 7 violation.[245] To establish [a] * * * presumption [that a merger will substantially limit competition], the government must "show that the merger would produce 'a firm controlling an undue percentage share of the relevant market, and [would] result in a significant increase in the concentration of firms in that market.'" Once the government has established this presumption, the burden shifts to the defendants to rebut the presumption by "show[ing] that the market-share statistics give an inaccurate account of the merger's probable effects on competition in the relevant market." If the defendant successfully rebuts the presumption [of illegality], the burden of producing additional evidence of anticompetitive effect shifts to the government, and merges with the ultimate burden of persuasion, which remains with the government at all times. Ultimately,

---

[245] In their closing argument, the defendants chided the government for citing Clayton Act Section 7 cases brought by the Federal Trade Commission for the relevant standard to apply in this case rather than citing to *Baker Hughes*, a case brought by the DOJ. Since this Circuit's FTC precedents themselves rely heavily on the analytical approach set forth in *Baker Hughes*, the defendants' distinction on this point is ultimately of little import. While a lesser showing is required to obtain preliminary relief in an FTC preliminary injunction case, as opposed to a full merits trial like this case, the Court must apply the *Baker Hughes* analytical framework in either type of Section 7 case.

"[t]he Supreme Court has adopted a totality-of-the-circumstances approach to the statute, weighing a variety of factors to determine the effects of particular transactions on competition." *Baker Hughes.*

III. DISCUSSION

A. The Relevant Product Market

* * *

The government argues that the relevant market in this case consists of all DDIY products, but does not include assisted tax preparation or pen-and-paper. Under this view of the market, the acquisition in this case would result in a DDIY market that is dominated by two large players—H & R Block and Intuit—that together control approximately 90 percent of the market share, with the remaining 10 percent of the market divided amongst a plethora of smaller companies. In contrast, the defendants argue for a broader market that includes all tax preparation methods (all methods), comprised of DDIY, assisted, and pen-and-paper. Under this view of the market, the market concentration effects of this acquisition would be much smaller and would not lead to a situation in which two firms control 90 percent of the market. This broader view of the market rests primarily on the premise that providers of all methods of tax preparation compete with each other for the patronage of the same pool of customers U.S. taxpayers. After carefully considering the evidence and arguments presented by all parties, the Court has concluded that the relevant market in this case is, as the DOJ contends, the market for digital do-it-yourself tax preparation products.

* * *

An analytical method often used by courts to define a relevant market is to ask hypothetically whether it would be profitable to have a monopoly over a given set of substitutable products. If so, those products may constitute a relevant market. This approach—sometimes called the hypothetical monopolist test—is endorsed by the Horizontal Merger Guidelines issued by the DOJ and [FTC]. * * *

Thus, the question here is whether it would be hypothetically useful to have a monopoly over all DDIY tax preparation products because the monopolist could then profitably raise prices for those products by five percent or more; or whether, to the contrary, there would be no reason to monopolize all DDIY tax preparation products because substitution and price competition with other methods of tax preparation would restrain any potential DDIY monopolist from profitably raising prices. In other words, would enough DDIY users switch to the assisted or pen-and-paper methods of tax preparation in response to a five-to-ten percent increase in DDIY prices to make such a price increase unprofitable?

* * *

1. The Defendants' Documents Show That DDIY Is the Relevant Product Market

When determining the relevant product market, courts often pay close attention to the defendants' ordinary course of business documents. The government argues that the defendants' ordinary course of business documents in this case conclusively demonstrate that competition with other [DDIY] firms drive Defendants' pricing decisions, quality improvements, and corporate strategy for their own DDIY products thus supporting the government's view of the relevant market. * * *

Internal TaxACT documents establish that TaxACT has viewed DDIY offerings by HRB and TurboTax as its primary competitors, that it has tracked their marketing, product offerings, and pricing, and that it has determined its own pricing and business strategy in relation to those companies' DDIY products. Confidential memoranda prepared by TaxACT's investment bankers for potential private equity buyers of TaxACT identify HRB and TurboTax as TaxACT's primary competitors in a DDIY market. These documents also recognize that TaxACT's strategy for competing with Intuit and HRB is to offer a lower price for what it deems a superior product.

While, as defendants point out, parts of these TaxACT documents also discuss the broader tax preparation industry, these documents make clear that TaxACT's own view and that conveyed by its investment bankers to potential buyers is that the company primarily competes in a DDIY market against Intuit and HRB and that it develops its pricing and business strategy with that market and those competitors in mind. These documents are strong evidence that DDIY is the relevant product market. *See Whole Foods* (Tatel, J.) ([E]vidence of industry or public recognition of the submarket as a separate economic unit matters because we assume that economic actors usually have accurate perceptions of economic realities).

* * *

2. The Relevant Product Market Does Not Include Assisted Tax Preparation or Manual Preparation

It is beyond debate and conceded by the plaintiff that all methods of tax preparation are, to some degree, in competition. All tax preparation methods provide taxpayers with a means to perform the task of completing a tax return, but each method is starkly different. Thus, while providers of all tax preparation methods may compete at some level, this does not necessarily require that [they] be included in the relevant product market for antitrust purposes. *Staples.* DDIY tax preparation products differ from manual tax preparation and assisted tax preparation products in a number of meaningful ways. As compared to manual and assisted methods, DDIY products involve different technology, price, convenience level, time investment, mental effort and type of interaction by the consumer. Taken together, these different attributes make the consumer experience of using DDIY products quite distinct from other methods of tax preparation. *See Whole Foods* (Brown, J.) (noting that a product's peculiar characteristics and uses and distinct prices may distinguish a relevant market). The question for this court is whether DDIY and other methods of tax preparation are reasonably interchangeable so that it would not be profitable to have a monopoly over only DDIY products.

a.   Assisted Tax Preparation Is Not in the Relevant Product Market

* * * [T]he defendants' main argument for inclusion of assisted tax preparation in the relevant market is that DDIY and assisted companies compete for customers. As evidence for this point, the defendants emphasize that Intuit's marketing efforts have targeted HRB's assisted customers. While the evidence does show that companies in the DDIY and assisted markets all generally compete with each other for the same overall pool of potential customers—U.S. taxpayers—that fact does not necessarily mean that DDIY and assisted must be viewed as part of the same relevant product market. DDIY provides customers with tax preparation services through an entirely different method, technology, and user experience than assisted preparation. As Judge Tatel explained in *Whole Foods:*

> [W]hen the automobile was first invented, competing auto manufacturers obviously took customers primarily from companies selling horses and buggies, not from other auto manufacturers, but that hardly shows that cars and horse-drawn carriages should be treated as the same product market. * * *

The key question for the Court is whether DDIY and assisted products are sufficiently close substitutes to constrain any anticompetitive DDIY pricing after the proposed merger. Evidence of the absence of close price competition between DDIY and assisted products makes clear that the answer to that question is no and that DDIY is the relevant product market here. Significantly, despite some DDIY efforts to capture tax store customers, none of the major DDIY competitors sets their prices based on consideration of assisted prices. Indeed, there are quite significant price disparities between the average prices of DDIY and assisted products. The average price of TurboTax, the most popular DDIY brand is approximately $55. The average price of HRB's DDIY products is approximately $25. Overall, the DDIY industry average price is $44.13. In contrast, the typical price of an assisted tax return is significantly higher, in the range of $150–200. A 10 percent or even 20 percent price increase in the average price of DDIY would only move the average price up to $48.54 or $52.96, respectively—still substantially below the average price of assisted tax products. The overall lack of evidence of price competition between DDIY and assisted products supports the conclusion that DDIY is a separate relevant product market for evaluating this transaction, despite the fact that DDIY and assisted firms target their marketing efforts at the same pool of customers.

* * *

b.   Manual Tax Preparation Is Not in the Relevant Product Market

The defendants also argue that manual tax preparation, or pen-and-paper, should be included in the relevant product market. At the outset, the Court notes that pen-and-paper is not a product at all; it is the task of filling out a tax return by oneself without any interactive assistance. Even so, the defendants argue pen-and-paper should be included in the relevant product market because it acts as a significant competitive constraint on DDIY. * * *

The Court finds that pen-and-paper is not part of the relevant market because it does not believe a sufficient number of consumers would switch to pen-and-paper in response to a small, but significant increase in DDIY prices. The possibility of preparing one's own tax return necessarily constrains the prices of other methods of preparation at some level. For example, if the price of DDIY and assisted products were raised to $1 million per tax return, surely all but the most well-heeled taxpayers would switch to pen-and-paper. Yet, at the more practical price increase levels that trigger antitrust concern—the typical five to ten percent price increase of the SSNIP test—pen-and-paper preparation is unlikely to provide a meaningful restraint for DDIY products, which currently sell for an average price of $44.13.

The government well illustrated the overly broad nature of defendants' proposed relevant market by posing to the defendants' expert the hypothetical question of whether sitting at home and drinking chicken soup [would be] part of the market for [manufactured] cold remedies? The defendants' expert responded that the real question is if the price of cold medicines went up sufficiently, would people turn to chicken soup? As an initial matter, in contrast to the defendants' expert, the Court doubts that it would ever be legally appropriate to define a relevant product market that included manufactured cold remedies and ordinary chicken soup. This conclusion flows from the deep functional differences between those products. Setting that issue aside, however, a price has increased sufficiently to trigger antitrust concern at the level of a five to ten percent small, but significant non-transitory increase in price. Just as chicken soup is unlikely to constrain the price of manufactured cold remedies sufficiently, the Court concludes that a SSNIP in DDIY would not be constrained by people turning to pen-and-paper. First, the share of returns prepared via pen-and-paper has dwindled over the past decade, as the

DDIY market has grown. Second, while pen-and-paper filers have been a net source of new customers for DDIY companies, * * * executives have testified that they do not believe their DDIY products compete closely with pen-and-paper methods. Third, courts in antitrust cases frequently exclude similar self-supply substitutes from relevant product markets. See, e.g., FTC v. H.J. Heinz Co. (noting that homemade baby food and breast milk should not be included in the jarred baby food market even though substitution was possible because the Supreme Court's interchangeability test refers to *products*).

* * *

While some diversion from DDIY to manual filing may occur in response to a SSNIP, the Court finds that it would likely be limited and marginal. The functional experience of using a DDIY product is meaningfully different from the self-service task of filling out tax forms independently. Manual completion of a tax return requires different tools, effort, resources, and time investment by a consumer than use of either DDIY or assisted methods. * * *

* * * Indeed, the pen-and-paper method, in which the consumer essentially relies on his or her own labor to prepare a tax return, is perhaps most analogous to walking as opposed to purchasing a ride on any means of transportation. In sum, filling out a tax return manually is not reasonably interchangeable with DDIY products that effectively fill out the tax return with data input provided by the consumer.

* * *

3. The Economic Expert Testimony Tends to Confirm That DDIY Is the Relevant Product Market

* * *

The Court finds that the analysis performed by the plaintiff's expert tends to confirm that DDIY is a relevant product market, although the available data in this case limited the predictive power of the plaintiff's expert's economic models. * * *

a. Plaintiff's Expert Dr. Warren-Boulton

* * *

The plaintiff's expert, Dr. Warren-Boulton, * * * began his analysis by postulating that DDIY was the relevant product market and then he used two principal analytical tests to confirm the validity of that assumption. * * *

* * *

i.   Critical Loss Analysis

The first economic test Dr. Warren-Boulton performed is known as a critical loss analysis. This test attempts to calculate the largest amount of sales that a monopolist can lose before a price increase becomes unprofitable. Dr. Warren Boulton calculated that for a 10 percent price increase in DDIY, the price increase would be profitable if the resulting lost sales did not surpass 16.7 percent.[246]

Dr. Warren-Boulton then sought to compare this critical loss threshold with aggregate diversion ratios. The aggregate diversion ratio for any given product represents the proportion of lost sales that are recaptured by all other firms in the proposed market as the result of a price increase. Since these lost sales are recaptured within the proposed market, they are not lost to the hypothetical monopolist. According to Dr. Warren-Boulton, economists have shown that if the aggregate diversion ratio to products inside the proposed relevant market exceeds the critical loss threshold, then the critical loss analysis indicates that a SSNIP at that level would be profitable for a hypothetical monopolist.

Because no diversion data is available, Dr. Warren-Boulton relied instead on IRS switching data to estimate aggregate diversion ratios. These data show that of the taxpayers who left HRB's DDIY products between tax year 2007 and 2008, 57 percent went to other DDIY providers. Of those who left TaxACT, 53 percent stayed in DDIY, and for TurboTax, 39 percent stayed in DDIY. Since these numbers are all well above the 16.7 percent critical loss threshold, Dr. Warren-Boulton concluded a 10 percent SSNIP in the DDIY market would be profitable for a hypothetical monopolist.

In cross-examining Dr. Warren-Boulton, the defendants suggested that the critical loss test is meaningless because it would seem to validate numerous different candidate markets consisting of various assortments of tax preparation businesses. For example, the defendants demonstrated that the test could also validate a market consisting of just HRB and Intuit or a market consisting of just TaxACT and Intuit. Dr. Warren-Boulton noted in his testimony, however, that such markets are smaller, irrelevant markets for evaluating the proposed transaction between HRB and TaxACT. The fact that critical loss analysis would validate other groupings of businesses does not undermine Dr. Warren-Boulton's reliance on it to validate DDIY as the relevant market in this case. * * * Nonetheless, the Court appreciates the defendants' point that the critical loss test alone cannot answer the relevant market inquiry. While some inappropriate

---

[246] The formula for critical loss is $L = X/(X + M)$, where L is the critical loss, X is the percentage price increase, and M is the hypothetical monopolist's gross margin. Assuming a 50 percent margin, which Dr. Warren-Boulton claims is a conservative estimate for firms in the DDIY market, then the critical loss for a 10 percent SSNIP is 16.7 percent. 16.7 percent is the result of applying 10 percent and 50 percent in the formula $X/(X+M)$: $.167 = .1/(.1+.5)$. [Court's fn. 17]

proposed relevant markets would be ruled out by the critical loss test, the fact that the test could still confirm multiple relevant markets means that the Court must rely on additional evidence in reaching the single, appropriate market definition.

ii. Merger Simulation

In addition to the critical loss analysis, Dr. Warren-Boulton also performed an economic simulation of a merger among the HRB, TaxACT, and Intuit. This simulation, known as a Bertrand model, predicted that a monopolist of the DDIY products of these three companies would find it profit-maximizing to raise TaxACT's price by 83 percent, HRB's price by 37 percent and TurboTax's price by 11 percent absent efficiencies. Dr. Warren-Boulton concluded that this simulation also confirms that DDIY is the relevant product market.

* * *

B. Likely Effect on Competition

1. The Plaintiff's Prima Facie Case

Having defined the relevant market as DDIY tax preparation products, the Court must next consider the likely effects of the proposed acquisition on competition within that market. * * *

Market concentration, or the lack thereof, is often measured by the Herfindahl-Hirschmann Index (HHI). * * * Sufficiently large HHI figures establish the government's prima facie case that a merger is anticompetitive. * * *

* * *

The proposed acquisition in this case would give the combined firm a 28.4 percent market share and will increase the HHI by approximately 400, resulting in a post-acquisition HHI of 4,691. These HHI levels are high enough to create a presumption of anticompetitive effects. *See, e.g., Heinz* (three-firm to two-firm merger that would have increased HHI by 510 points from 4,775 created presumption of anticompetitive effects by a wide margin). Accordingly, the government has established a prima facie case of anticompetitive effects.

Upon the showing of a *prima facie* case, the burden shifts to defendants to show that traditional economic theories of the competitive effects of market concentration are not an accurate indicator of the merger's probable effect on competition in these markets or that the procompetitive effects of the merger are likely to outweigh any potential anticompetitive effects. * * * Even in cases where the government has made a strong prima facie showing:

[i]mposing a heavy burden of production on a defendant would be particularly anomalous where, as here, it is easy to establish a prima facie case. The government, after all, can carry its initial burden of production simply by presenting market concentration statistics. To allow the government virtually to rest its case at that point, leaving the defendant to prove the core of the dispute, would grossly inflate the role of statistics in actions brought under section 7. The Herfindahl-Hirschman Index cannot guarantee litigation victories. *Baker-Hughes.*

* * * With these observations in mind, the Court will evaluate the parties' evidence and arguments about the likely effect of the transaction on competition in the DDIY market.

2. Defendants' Rebuttal Arguments

a. Barriers to Entry

Defendants argue that the likelihood of expansion by existing DDIY companies besides Intuit, HRB, and TaxACT will offset any potential anticompetitive effects from the merger. Courts have held that likely entry or expansion by other competitors can counteract anticompetitive effects that would otherwise be expected. According to the Merger Guidelines, entry or expansion must be timely, likely, and sufficient in its magnitude, character, and scope to deter or counteract the competitive effects of concern. Merger Guidelines § 9. In this case, the parties essentially agree that the proper focus of this inquiry is on the likelihood of expansion by existing competitors rather than new entry into the market. * * *

In describing the competitive landscape, the defendants note there are eighteen companies offering various DDIY products * * * . Most of these companies are very small-time operators. The defendants acknowledge this fact, but nevertheless contend that the companies TaxSlayer and TaxHawk are the two largest and most poised to replicate the scale and strength of TaxACT. * * *

TaxHawk runs five different websites, including FreeTaxUSA.com, that all market the same underlying DDIY product. TaxHawk was founded in 2001, three years after TaxACT, although it has a significantly smaller market share of 3.2 percent. TaxHawk's vice-president and co-founder, Mr. Dane Kimber, testified that the company has the technical infrastructure to grow by five to seven times the number of customers in any given year. * * * Despite having been in business for a decade, its products are functionally more limited than those of Intuit, HRB, and TaxACT in various ways. Although TaxHawk services the forms that cover most taxpayers, its program does not service all federal forms, it excludes two states' forms in their entirety, and it does not service city income tax forms for major cities that have income taxes—notably, New York City. In fact, Mr. Kimber testified that the company would likely need another decade before its DDIY products could fully support all the tax forms. The reason is that TaxHawk is what Mr. Kimber "like[s] to call . . . a 'lifestyle' company. We like the lifestyle we have as owners. We want our employees to have a life, if you will. I do feel we have the expertise to [expand functionality] more rapidly, but we choose not to." * * *

TaxHawk's relaxed attitude toward its business stands in stark contrast to the entrepreneurial verve that was apparent throughout the testimony of Mr. Dunn and that has been rewarded by the impressive growth of TaxACT over the years. * * * While TaxHawk's decision to prioritize a relaxed lifestyle over robust competition and innovation is certainly a valid one, expansion from TaxHawk that would allow it to compete on the same playing field as the merged company appears unlikely.

After TaxHawk, TaxSlayer is the next largest DDIY competitor, with a 2.7 percent market share. * * * TaxSlayer is part of the same corporate family as Rhodes Murphy, a tax firm that provides assisted tax preparation through sixteen retail offices in the Augusta, Georgia area. The company is a family business * * * . TaxSlayer's marketing strategy relies heavily on sponsorship of sporting events, including the Gator Bowl and NASCAR. * * * Despite this [high] level of marketing spending, TaxSlayer's DDIY market share has not changed substantially since 2006, despite steady growth in TaxSlayer's revenue and number of units sold. Rather, TaxSlayer's growth in unit sales and revenue has come from maintaining the same slice of an expanding pie the growing DDIY market.

TaxSlayer's stable market share despite its significant marketing expenditure as a proportion of revenue points to what the government considers the key barrier to entry in this market—the importance of reputation and brand in driving consumer behavior in purchasing DDIY products. Simply put, tax returns are highly personal documents that carry significant financial and legal consequences for consumers. Consumers, therefore, must trust and have confidence in their tax service provider. * * *

Building a reputation that a significant number of consumers will trust requires time and money. * * * In the DDIY industry, the Big Three incumbent players spend millions on marketing and advertising each year to build and maintain their brands, dwarfing the combined spending of the smaller companies. For example, in tax year 2009, Intuit, HRB, and TaxACT collectively spent approximately [over $100 million] on marketing and advertising. By contrast, TaxSlayer and TaxHawk spent a significantly smaller amount.

* * *

Upon consideration of all of the evidence relating to barriers to entry or expansion, the Court cannot find that expansion is likely to avert anticompetitive effects from the transaction. * * *

b.   Coordinated Effects

Merger law rests upon the theory that, where rivals are few, firms will be able to coordinate their behavior, either by overt collusion or implicit understanding in order to restrict output and achieve profits above competitive levels. The government argues that the elimination of TaxACT, one of the Big 3 Digital DIY firms will facilitate tacit coordination between Intuit and HRB. Whether a merger will make coordinated interaction more likely depends on whether market conditions, on the whole, are conducive to reaching terms of coordination and detecting and punishing deviations from those terms. Since the government has established its prima facie case, the burden is on the defendants to produce evidence of structural market barriers to collusion specific to this industry that would defeat the ordinary presumption of collusion that attaches to a merger in a highly concentrated market. *See Heinz.*

The defendants argue the primary reason that coordinated effects will be unlikely is that Intuit will have no incentive to compete any less vigorously post-merger. The defendants assert that the competition between Intuit and HRB's retail stores would be fundamentally nullified if Intuit decided to reduce the competitiveness of TurboTax. Further, defendants contend that Intuit has no incentive to reduce the competitiveness of its free product because it views its free product as a critical driver of new customers. Therefore, the defendants conclude that if HRB does not compete as aggressively as possible with its post-merger products, it will lose customers to Intuit.

The most compelling evidence the defendants marshal in support of these arguments consists of documents and testimony indicating that Intuit engaged in a series of war games designed to anticipate and defuse new competitive threats that might emerge from HRB post-merger. The documents and testimony do indicate that Intuit and HRB will continue to compete for taxpayers' patronage after the merger—indeed, in the DDIY market, they would be the only major competitors. This conclusion, however, is not necessarily inconsistent with some coordination. As the Merger Guidelines explain, coordinated interaction involves a range of conduct, including unspoken understandings about *how* firms will compete or refrain from competing.

In this case, the government contends that coordination would likely take the form of mutual recognition that neither firm has an interest in an overall race to free in which high-quality tax preparation software is provided for free or very low prices. Indeed, the government points to an outline created as part of the Intuit war games regarding post-merger competition with HRB that also indicates an Intuit employee's perception that part of HRB's post-merger strategy would be to not escalate free war: Make free the starting point not the end point for customers. Since, as defendants point out, DDIY companies have found free offers to be a useful marketing tool, it is unlikely that free offers would be eliminated. Rather, the government argues, it is more likely that HRB and Intuit may find it in their mutual interest to reduce the quality of their free offerings . . . offer a lower quality free product and maintain higher prices for paid products. . . .

* * *

The defendants also argue that coordinated effects are unlikely because the DDIY market consists of differentiated products and has low price transparency. To the contrary, the record clearly demonstrates that the players in the DDIY industry are well aware of the prices and features offered by competitors. Since DDIY products are marketed to a large swath of the American population and available via the Internet, DDIY firms can easily monitor their competitors' offerings and pricing. The fact that competitors may offer various discounts and coupons to some customers via email hardly renders industry pricing not transparent, as defendants submit. Moreover, while collusion may, in some instances, be more likely in markets for homogenous products than differentiated products, product differentiation in this market would not necessarily make collusion more difficult.

* * *

Finally, the Court notes that the "merger would result in the elimination of a particularly aggressive competitor in a highly concentrated market, a factor which is certainly an important consideration when analyzing possible anti-competitive effects." *Staples.* The evidence presented at the hearing from all parties demonstrated TaxACT's impressive history of innovation and competition in the DDIY market. Mr. Dunn's trial testimony revealed him to be a dedicated and talented entrepreneur and businessman, with deep knowledge and passion for providing high-quality, low-cost tax solutions. * * *

The government presses the argument that TaxACT's role as an aggressive competitor is particularly important by urging this Court to find that TaxACT is a maverick. In the context of antitrust law, a maverick has been defined as a particularly aggressive competitor that plays a disruptive role in the market to the benefit of customers. Merger Guidelines § 2.1.5. * * *

* * *

The government has not set out a clear standard, based on functional or economic considerations, to distinguish a maverick from any other aggressive competitor. At times, the government has emphasized TaxACT's low pricing as evidence of its maverick status, while, at other times, the government seems to suggest that almost any competitive activity on TaxACT's part is a disruptive indicator of a maverick. * * *

What the Court finds particularly germane for the maverick or particularly aggressive competitor analysis in this case is this question: Does TaxACT consistently play a role within the competitive structure of this market that constrains prices? * * * Not only did TaxACT buck prevailing pricing norms by introducing the free-for-all offer, which others later matched, it has remained the only competitor with significant market share to embrace a business strategy that relies primarily on offering high-quality, full-featured products for free with associated products at low prices.

* * *

c.   Unilateral Effects

* * *

vi. Merger Simulation Shows Likely Unilateral Price Increase

The government's expert economist, Dr. Warren-Boulton, did a merger simulation analysis that suggests a unilateral price increase is likely. * * *

Unless there are significant efficiencies from the merger that are passed on to consumers, this simulation predicts a unilateral price increase. Assuming diversion ratios according to market share, the model predicts TaxACT's price will increase by 12.2 percent and HRB's price by 2.5 percent. Assuming diversion ratios based on the IRS switching data as discussed above, the model predicts TaxACT's price will increase by 10.5 percent and HRB's price by 2.2 percent.

* * *

d.   Post Merger Efficiencies

One of the key benefits of a merger to the economy is its potential to generate efficiencies. As the Merger Guidelines recognize, merger-generated efficiencies can enhance the merged firm's ability and incentive to compete, which may result in lower prices, improved quality, enhanced service, or new products. Merger Guidelines § 10. Courts have recognized that a showing of sufficient efficiencies may rebut the government's showing of likely anticompetitive effects. High market concentration levels require proof of extraordinary efficiencies, however * * * .

* * *

Dr. Mark E. Zmijewski, an expert witness for the government, analyzed the defendants' alleged efficiencies and concluded that—with the exception of one efficiency related to eliminating third-party contracts—

the proposed efficiencies identified by the defendants are either not merger-specific or not verifiable.

The Court agrees with Dr. Zmijewski that the defendants have not demonstrated that their claimed efficiencies are merger-specific. * * * The reasons HRB claims it has higher costs than TaxACT include (1) that TaxACT has lower labor costs in Cedar Rapids than HRB has in Kansas City and (2) that TaxACT is simply more cost conscious. Plainly, then, HRB could therefore achieve at least some of the cost savings on its own by relocating and taking a more cost conscious attitude toward them. Likewise, the efficiencies related to bringing HRB's outsourced functions in-house are unlikely to be wholly merger-specific.

* * *

Even if the efficiencies were entirely merger-specific, many of them are also not independently verifiable. As Dr. Zmijewski explained, for the various efficiencies that involve the activities now performed by HRB or its vendors that are proposed to be transferred to TaxACT, TaxACT's predicted cost figures for taking over these activities were not based on an analysis of facts that could be verified by a third party. Instead, TaxACT based its cost estimates on management judgments. By comparison, HRB's estimated costs for the relevant activities were rooted in accounting and planning documents prepared in the ordinary course of business.

* * * While reliance on the estimation and judgment of experienced executives about costs may be perfectly sensible as a business matter, the lack of a verifiable method of factual analysis resulting in the cost estimates renders them not cognizable by the Court. If this were not so, then the efficiencies defense might well swallow the whole of Section 7 of the Clayton Act because management would be able to present large efficiencies based on its own judgment and the Court would be hard pressed to find otherwise. * * *

* * *

IV. CONCLUSION

The Court concludes that the proposed merger between HRB and TaxACT violates Section 7 of the Clayton Act because it is reasonably likely to cause anticompetitive effects. The law of this Circuit supports this conclusion. In *Heinz,* the Court of Appeals reversed a district court's denial of a preliminary injunction against a merger involving the second-and third-largest jarred baby food companies. After noting the high barriers to entry and high HHI figures that characterized the market, the D.C. Circuit observed that [a]s far as we can determine, no court has ever approved a merger to duopoly under similar circumstances. The situation in this case is similar. The government established a prima facie case indicating that anticompetitive effects are likely to result from the merger. The defendants have not made a showing of evidence that rebuts the presumption of anticompetitive effects by demonstrating that the government's market share statistics give an inaccurate account of the merger's probable effects on competition in the relevant market. To the contrary, the totality of the evidence confirms that anticompetitive effects are a likely result of the merger, which would give H & R Block and Intuit control over 90 percent of the market for digital do-it-yourself tax preparation products.

Accordingly, the Court will enjoin H & R Block's proposed acquisition of TaxACT. * * *

NOTES AND QUESTIONS

1. Do you agree with the court that digital do-it-yourself software is the relevant market in this case?

a. Would you have reached that result instinctively, just based on the common sense idea that people who use software today probably wouldn't be comfortable doing their taxes with paper and pencil? Would it follow that people whose tax situation is complex enough to require preparation by an accountant are not going to buy TurboTax no matter how high or low its price gets?

b. Did the hypothetical monopolist test give you more confidence in the conclusion? Was its invocation more than a framework within which the court in fact looked at a variety of factors such as internal documents of the defendant that didn't talk about hypothetical monopoly at all?

c. Was the government's use of critical loss analysis convincing? How about its use of aggregate diversion ratios? Did Dr. Warren-Boulton's data suggesting the profitability of large price increases persuade you that the market definition was correct? Should the defendants' showing that the numbers led to a wide variety of market definitions have been given greater weight by the court?

2. Given the market definition the court accepted, was it any surprise that the government could make a prima facie case the merger was illegal?

a. Was the dramatic increase in the HHI a foregone conclusion? Would the court have been wise to ask for more and to rely more on the fact that "the Herfindahl Hirschman Index cannot guarantee litigation victories"?

b. What additional evidence did the court have before it? Were Dr. Warren-Boulton merger simulation numbers convincing? How did Dr. Warren-Boulton come up with his numbers?

c. Were you persuaded that new entry in this industry was unlikely? Why should the possibility of expansion by existing firms be the controlling issue? Should the personalities of current owners of existing firms in an industry end the analysis?

d.   Is marketing computer software an inherently high-cost activity? Indeed, is the world full of companies who sell software? If a private equity firm bought one of the sleepy "lifestyle" companies and marketed its software vigorously, might the barriers to entry seem to melt away? What should a court do when such a result is possible but no candidate for entry has yet appeared?

3.   Were the defenses offered for this merger inherently unconvincing?

a.   Should it be important that Intuit had "war gamed" how it would respond competitively to the merger? Are such planning documents inherently less reliable than reports of past competitive conduct? Do such plans inherently fail to capture what might happen as competitors see the benefits of greater cooperation?

b.   Were the defendants' efficiency arguments more convincing? Was the court too quick to say that HRB could simply move its operations to Cedar Rapids and get the same efficiencies?

4.   Would the court have reached the same result if this merger had reduced the relevant market—as the court defined it—from five firms to four, or four firms to three, instead of three firms to two? Put another way, even though the government won this case, does the challenging road it traveled to get the victory suggest why so many mergers are approved by the agencies without challenge, and why their challenges to mergers often fail?

5.   The airline industry has seen several mergers in recent years—Delta-Northwest and United-Continental—being the largest.

a.   In 2013, the Justice Department sued to challenge the merger of American Airlines and U.S. Airways. Opposition to the challenge was based on two ideas. First, agencies that did not challenge the earlier mergers should not be able to now "change the rules." Second, if Southwest Airlines and Jet Blue are included in the market, this merger would only reduce the number of major U.S. airlines from six to five. Ultimately, the government retreated and the merger was approved with only minor conditions.

b.   Have we reached a point in merger enforcement where industries can become highly concentrated before hoped-for benefits of merger regulation can in fact be achieved?[247]

E. THE INTERPLAY BETWEEN REGULATION AND THE ANTITRUST LAWS

We first saw the interplay of regulation and the antitrust laws at the outset of this course. Queen Elizabeth's grant of the playing card monopoly was in effect a government attempt to structure a small industry. The *Trans-Missouri* case, in turn, discussed the tension between Congress'

---

[247] See generally, James A Keyte, United States v. H & R Block: The DOJ Invokes Brown Shoe to Shed the Oracle Albatross, 26 Antitrust L.J. 32 (Spring 2012); John E. Kwoka, Jr., Does Merger Control Work?: A Retrospective on U.S. Enforcement Actions and Merger Outcomes, 78 Antitrust L.J. 619 (2013).

desire to have railroads regulated by the Interstate Commerce Commission as to some matters but by the antitrust laws as to others.

1. FEDERAL REGULATION

When the conflict is between antitrust law and direct federal regulation, its resolution is often largely a matter of statutory interpretation, i.e., discerning the overall regulatory plan. In United States v. American Telephone & Telegraph Co., 461 F.Supp. 1314 (D.D.C. 1978), Judge Harold Greene concluded that, as a practical matter, the Federal Communications Commission was in no position to regulate the conduct with which AT&T was charged. Thus, the antitrust case was allowed to continue and was settled in 1982 by the consent decree breaking up AT&T, discussed earlier in this chapter.[248]

Issues also arise because "deregulation" often does not describe an absence of regulation. Instead, we increasingly find industries in which some practices remain required by direct regulation while others are now governed by antitrust standards.[249] The challenge for the courts is deciding which of these often inconsistent approaches to regulation apply. See, e.g., Town of Norwood v. New England Power Company, 202 F.3d 408 (1st Cir. 2000) (effect of partial rate approval on allegation of attempt to monopolize by price squeeze).[250]

CREDIT SUISSE SECURITIES (USA) L.L.C. v. BILLING

Supreme Court of the United States, 2007
551 U.S. 264, 127 S.Ct. 2383, 168 L.Ed.2d 145

JUSTICE BREYER delivered the opinion of the Court.

A group of buyers of newly issued securities have filed an antitrust lawsuit against underwriting firms that market and distribute those

---

[248] Additional cases involving the interplay of federal regulation and the antitrust laws include National Broiler Marketing Ass'n v. United States, 436 U.S. 816, 98 S.Ct. 2122, 56 L.Ed.2d 728 (1978) (defining who qualifies as a chicken farmer); National Gerimedical Hospital & Gerontology Center v. Blue Cross, 452 U.S. 378, 101 S.Ct. 2415, 69 L.Ed.2d 89 (1981) (deciding which activities of Blue Cross can be defined as part of the implementation of plans of a health system agency). See also, Jung v. Ass'n of American Medical Colleges, 339 F.Supp.2d 26 (D.D.C. 2004) (upholds specially-passed law, 15 U.S.C. § 37b (2004), exempting physician residency matching program from antitrust charges).

[249] See generally, Jeffrey L. Harrison, Thomas D. Morgan & Paul R. Verkuil, Regulation and Deregulation: Cases and Materials (2nd ed. 2004).

[250] See also, Bristol-Myers Squibb v. IVAX Corp., 77 F.Supp.2d 606 (D.N.J. 2000) (allegation that commercial interest of the National Cancer Institute in one producer's anti-cancer drug led to improper approval of the drug to detriment of competitor); PGMedia, Inc. v. Network Solutions, Inc., 51 F.Supp.2d 389 (S.D.N.Y. 1999) (licensee of National Science Foundation held immune from liability for monopolizing issuance of internet domain names).

Yet another set of problems arise when companies use laws intended for one purpose in a way that is anticompetitive. See, e.g., Cheminor Drugs, Ltd. v. Ethyl Corporation, 168 F.3d 119 (3d Cir. 1999) (alleged filing of antidumping cases to exclude cheaper generic drugs); Richard J. Pierce, Antidumping Law as a Means of Facilitating Cartelization, 67 Antitrust L.J. 725 (2000).

issues. The buyers claim that the underwriters unlawfully agreed with one another that they would not sell shares of a popular new issue to a buyer unless that buyer committed (1) to buy additional shares of that security later at escalating prices (a practice called "laddering"), (2) to pay unusually high commissions on subsequent security purchases from the underwriters, or (3) to purchase from the underwriters other less desirable securities (a practice called "tying"). The question before us is whether there is a " 'plain repugnancy' " between these antitrust claims and the federal securities law. We conclude that there is. Consequently we must interpret the securities laws as implicitly precluding the application of the antitrust laws to the conduct alleged in this case.

I

A

The underwriting practices at issue take place during the course of an initial public offering (IPO) of shares in a company. An IPO presents an opportunity to raise capital for a new enterprise by selling shares to the investing public. A group of underwriters will typically form a syndicate to help market the shares. The syndicate will investigate and estimate likely market demand for the shares at various prices. It will then recommend to the firm a price and the number of shares it believes the firm should offer. Ultimately, the syndicate will promise to buy from the firm all the newly issued shares on a specified date at a fixed, agreed-upon price, which price the syndicate will then charge investors when it resells the shares. When the syndicate buys the shares from the issuing firm, however, the firm gives the syndicate a price discount, which amounts to the syndicate's commission.

At the heart of the syndicate's IPO marketing activity lie its efforts to determine suitable initial share prices and quantities. At first, the syndicate makes a preliminary estimate that it submits in a registration statement to the Securities and Exchange Commission (SEC). It then conducts a "road show" during which syndicate underwriters and representatives of the offering firm meet potential investors and engage in a process that the industry calls "book building." During this time, the underwriters and firm representatives present information to investors about the company and the stock. And they attempt to gauge the strength of the investors' interest in purchasing the stock. For this purpose, underwriters might well ask the investors how their interest would vary depending upon price and the number of shares that are offered. They will learn, among other things, which investors might buy shares, in what quantities, at what prices, and for how long each is likely to hold purchased shares before selling them to others.

On the basis of this kind of information, the members of the underwriting syndicate work out final arrangements with the issuing firm, fixing the price per share and specifying the number of shares for which the underwriters will be jointly responsible. As we have said, after buying the shares at a discounted price, the syndicate resells the shares to investors at the fixed price, in effect earning its commission in the process.

B

In January 2002, respondents, a group of 60 investors, filed two antitrust class-action lawsuits against the petitioners, 10 leading investment banks. They sought relief under § 1 of the Sherman Act; § 2(c) of the * * * Robinson-Patman Act; and state antitrust laws. The investors stated that between March 1997 and December 2000 the banks had acted as underwriters, forming syndicates that helped execute the IPOs of several hundred technology-related companies. Respondents' antitrust complaints allege that the underwriters "abused the . . . practice of combining into underwriting syndicates" by agreeing among themselves to impose harmful conditions upon potential investors—conditions that the investors apparently were willing to accept in order to obtain an allocation of new shares that were in high demand.

These conditions, according to respondents, consist of a requirement that the investors pay "additional anticompetitive charges" over and above the agreed-upon IPO share price plus underwriting commission. In particular, these additional charges took the form of (1) investor promises "to place bids . . . in the aftermarket at prices above the IPO price" (i.e., "laddering" agreements); (2) investor "commitments to purchase other, less attractive securities" (i.e., "tying" arrangements); and (3) investor payment of "non-competitively determined" (i.e., excessive) "commissions," including the "purchas[e] of an issuer's shares in follow-up or 'secondary' public offerings (for which the underwriters would earn underwriting discounts)." The complaint added that the underwriters' agreement to engage in some or all of these practices artificially inflated the share prices of the securities in question.

The underwriters moved to dismiss the investors' complaints on the ground that federal securities law impliedly precludes application of antitrust laws to the conduct in question. * * * The District Court agreed with petitioners and dismissed the complaints against them. The Court of Appeals for the Second Circuit reversed, however, and reinstated the complaints. We granted the underwriters' petition for certiorari. And we now reverse the Court of Appeals.

II

A

Sometimes regulatory statutes explicitly state whether they preclude application of the antitrust laws. * * * Where regulatory statutes are silent in respect to antitrust, however, courts must determine whether, and in what respects, they implicitly preclude application of the antitrust laws. Those determinations may vary from statute to statute, depending upon the relation between the antitrust laws and the regulatory program set forth in the particular statute, and the relation of the specific conduct at issue to both sets of laws.

Three decisions from this Court specifically address the relation of securities law to antitrust law. In Silver [v. New York Stock Exchange (1963),] the Court considered a dealer's claim that, by expelling him from the New York Stock Exchange, the Exchange had violated the antitrust prohibition against group "boycott[s]." The Court wrote that, where possible, courts should "reconcil[e] the operation of both [*i.e.,* antitrust and securities] statutory schemes rather than holding one completely ousted." It also set forth a standard, namely that "[r]epeal of the antitrust laws is to be regarded as implied only if necessary to make the Securities Exchange Act work, and even then only to the minimum extent necessary." And it held that the securities law did *not* preclude application of the antitrust laws to the claimed boycott *insofar as the Exchange denied the expelled dealer a right to fair procedures.* (emphasis added).

In reaching this conclusion, the Court noted that the SEC lacked jurisdiction under the securities law "to review particular instances of enforcement of exchange rules"; that "nothing [was] built into the regulatory scheme which performs the antitrust function of insuring" that rules that injure competition are nonetheless "justified as furthering" legitimate regulatory "ends"; that the expulsion "would clearly" violate "the Sherman Act unless justified by reference to the purposes of the Securities Exchange Act"; and that it could find *no such justifying purpose* where the Exchange took "anticompetitive collective action . . . *without according fair procedures.*" (emphasis added).

In Gordon [v. New York Stock Exchange (1975),] the Court considered an antitrust complaint that essentially alleged "price fixing" among stockbrokers. It charged that members of the New York Stock Exchange had agreed to fix their commissions on sales under $500,000. And it sought damages and an injunction forbidding future agreements. The lawsuit was filed at a time when regulatory attitudes toward fixed stockbroker commissions were changing. The fixed commissions challenged in the complaint were applied during a period when the SEC approved of the practice of fixing broker-commission rates. But Congress and the SEC had both subsequently disapproved for the future the fixing of some of those rates.

In deciding whether antitrust liability could lie, the Court repeated *Silver's* general standard in somewhat different terms: It said that an "implied repeal" of the antitrust laws would be found only "where there is a 'plain repugnancy between the antitrust and regulatory provisions.'" It then held that the securities laws impliedly precluded application of the antitrust laws in the case at hand. The Court rested this conclusion on three sets of considerations. For one thing, the securities law "gave the SEC direct regulatory power over exchange rules and practices with respect to the fixing of reasonable rates of commission." For another, the SEC had "taken an active role in review of proposed rate changes during the last 15 years," and had engaged in "continuing activity" in respect to the regulation of commission rates. Finally, without antitrust immunity, "the exchanges and their members" would be subject to "conflicting standards."

* * *

In [U.S. v.] NASD [(1975)], the Court considered a Department of Justice antitrust complaint claiming that mutual fund companies had agreed with securities broker-dealers (1) to fix "resale" prices, *i.e.,* the prices at which a broker-dealer would sell a mutual fund's shares to an investor or buy mutual fund shares from a fund investor (who wished to redeem the shares); (2) to fix other terms of sale including those related to when, how, to whom, and from whom the broker-dealers might sell and buy mutual fund shares; and (3) to forbid broker-dealers from freely selling to, and buying shares from, one another.

The Court again found "clear repugnancy," and it held that the securities law, by implication, precluded all parts of the antitrust claim. * * *

* * *

As an initial matter these cases make clear that JUSTICE THOMAS is wrong to regard §§ 77p(a) and 78bb(a) as saving clauses so broad as to preserve all antitrust actions. The United States advanced the same argument in *Gordon.* Although one party has made the argument in this Court, it was not presented in the courts below. And we shall not reexamine it.

This Court's prior decisions also make clear that, when a court decides whether securities law precludes antitrust law, it is deciding whether, given context and likely consequences, there is a "clear repugnancy" between the securities law and the antitrust complaint—or as we shall subsequently describe the matter, whether the two are "clearly incompatible." Moreover, *Gordon* and *NASD,* in finding sufficient incompatibility to warrant an implication of preclusion, have treated the following factors as critical: (1) the existence of regulatory authority under the securities law to supervise the activities in question; (2) evidence that the responsible regulatory entities exercise that authority; and (3) a resulting risk that the securities and antitrust laws, if both applicable, would produce conflicting guidance, requirements, duties, privileges, or standards of conduct. We also note (4) that in *Gordon* and *NASD* the possible conflict affected practices that lie squarely within an area of financial market activity that the securities law seeks to regulate.

B

These principles, applied to the complaints before us, considerably narrow our legal task. For the parties cannot reasonably dispute the existence here of several of the conditions that this Court previously regarded as crucial to finding that the securities law impliedly precludes the application of the antitrust laws.

First, the activities in question here—the underwriters' efforts jointly to promote and to sell newly issued securities—is central to the proper functioning of well-regulated capital markets. The IPO process supports new firms that seek to raise capital; it helps to spread ownership of those firms broadly among investors; it directs capital flows in ways that better correspond to the public's demand for goods and services. Moreover, financial experts, including the securities regulators, consider the general kind of joint underwriting activity at issue in this case, including road shows and book-building efforts essential to the successful marketing of an IPO. Thus, the antitrust complaints before us concern practices that lie at the very heart of the securities marketing enterprise.

Second, the law grants the SEC authority to supervise all of the activities here in question. Indeed, the SEC possesses considerable power to forbid, permit, encourage, discourage, tolerate, limit, and otherwise regulate virtually every aspect of the practices in which underwriters engage. * * * Private individuals who suffer harm as a result of a violation of pertinent statutes and regulations may also recover damages.

Third, the SEC has continuously exercised its legal authority to regulate conduct of the general kind now at issue. It has defined in detail, for example, what underwriters may and may not do and say during their road shows. It has brought actions against underwriters who have violated these SEC regulations. And private litigants, too, have brought securities actions complaining of conduct virtually identical to the conduct at issue here; and they have obtained damages.

The preceding considerations show that the first condition (legal regulatory authority), the second condition (exercise of that authority), and the fourth condition (heartland securities activity) that were present in *Gordon* and *NASD* are satisfied in this case as well. Unlike *Silver,* there is here no question of the existence of appropriate regulatory authority, nor is there doubt as to whether the regulators have exercised that authority. Rather, the question before us concerns the third condition: Is there a conflict that rises to the level of incompatibility? Is an antitrust suit such as this likely to prove practically incompatible with the SEC's administration of the Nation's securities laws?

III

A

Given the SEC's comprehensive authority to regulate IPO underwriting syndicates, its active and ongoing exercise of that authority, and the undisputed need for joint IPO underwriter activity, we do not read the complaints as attacking the bare existence of IPO underwriting syndicates or any of the joint activity that the SEC considers a necessary component of IPO-related syndicate activity. Nor do we understand the complaints as questioning underwriter agreements to fix the levels of their commissions, whether or not the resulting price is "excessive."

We nonetheless can read the complaints as attacking the *manner* in which the underwriters jointly seek to collect "excessive" commissions. The complaints attack underwriter efforts to collect commissions through certain practices (*i.e.,* laddering, tying, collecting excessive commissions in the form of later sales of the issued shares), which according to respondents the SEC itself has already disapproved and, in all likelihood, will not approve in the foreseeable future. In respect to this set of claims, they contend that there is no possible "conflict" since both securities law and antitrust law aim to prohibit the same undesirable activity. Without a conflict, they add, there is no "repugnance" or "incompatibility," and this Court may not imply that securities law precludes an antitrust suit.

B

We accept the premises of respondents' argument—that the SEC has full regulatory authority over these practices, that it has actively exercised that authority, but that the SEC has *disapproved* (and, for argument's sake, we assume that it will continue to disapprove) the conduct that the antitrust complaints attack. Nonetheless, we cannot accept respondents' conclusion. Rather, several considerations taken together lead us to find that, even on these prorespondent assumptions, securities law and antitrust law are clearly incompatible.

First, to permit antitrust actions such as the present one *still* threatens serious securities-related harm. For one thing, an unusually serious legal line-drawing problem remains unabated. In the present context only a fine, complex, detailed line separates activity that the SEC permits or encourages (for which respondents must concede antitrust immunity) from activity that the SEC must (and inevitably will) forbid (and which, on respondents' theory, should be open to antitrust attack).

For example, in respect to "laddering" the SEC forbids an underwriter to "solicit customers prior to the completion of the distribution regarding whether and at what price and in what quantity they intend to place immediate aftermarket orders for IPO stock." But at the same time the SEC permits, indeed encourages, underwriters (as part of the "book building" process) to "inquir[e] as to a customer's desired future position in the longer term (for example, three to six months), and the price or prices at which the customer might accumulate that position without reference to immediate aftermarket activity."

It will often be difficult for someone who is not familiar with accepted syndicate practices to determine with confidence whether an underwriter has insisted that an investor buy more shares in the immediate aftermarket (forbidden), or has simply allocated more shares to an investor willing to purchase additional shares of that issue in the long run (permitted). And who but a securities expert could say whether the present SEC rules set forth a virtually permanent line, unlikely to change in ways that would permit the sorts of "laddering-like" conduct that it now seems to forbid?

Similarly, in respect to "tying" and other efforts to obtain an increased commission from future sales, the SEC has sought to prohibit an underwriter "from demanding . . . an offer from their customers of any payment or other consideration [such as the purchase of a different security] in addition to the security's stated consideration." But the SEC would permit a firm to "allocat[e] IPO shares to a customer because the customer has separately retained the firm for other services, when the customer has not paid excessive compensation in relation to those services." The National Association of Securities Dealers (NASD), over which the SEC exercises supervisory authority, has also proposed a rule that would prohibit a member underwriter from "offering or threatening to withhold" IPO shares "as consideration or inducement for the receipt of compensation that is excessive in relation to the services provided." The NASD would allow, however, a customer legitimately to compete for IPO shares by increasing the level and quantity of compensation it pays to the underwriter.

Under these standards, to distinguish what is forbidden from what is allowed requires an understanding of just when, in relation to services provided, a commission is "excessive," indeed, so "excessive" that it will remain *permanently* forbidden, see *Gordon*. And who but the SEC itself could do so with confidence?

For another thing, evidence tending to show unlawful antitrust activity and evidence tending to show lawful securities marketing activity may overlap, or prove identical. Consider, for instance, a conversation between an underwriter and an investor about how long an investor intends to hold the new shares (and at what price), say a conversation that elicits comments concerning both the investor's short and longer term plans. That exchange might, as a plaintiff sees it, provide evidence of an underwriter's insistence upon "laddering" or, as a defendant sees it, provide evidence of a lawful effort to allocate shares to those who will hold them for a longer time.

Similarly, the same somewhat ambiguous conversation might help to establish an effort to collect an unlawfully high commission through atypically high commissions on later sales or through the sales of less popular stocks. Or it might prove only that the underwriter allocates more popular shares to investors who will help stabilize the aftermarket share price.

Further, antitrust plaintiffs may bring lawsuits throughout the Nation in dozens of different courts with different nonexpert judges and different nonexpert juries. In light of the nuanced nature of the evidentiary evaluations necessary to separate the permissible from the impermissible, it will prove difficult for those many different courts to reach consistent results. And, given the fact-related nature of many such evaluations, it will also prove difficult to assure that the different courts evaluate similar fact patterns consistently. The result is an unusually high risk that different courts will evaluate similar factual circumstances differently.

Now consider these factors together—the fine securities-related lines separating the permissible from the impermissible; the need for securities-related expertise (particularly to determine whether an SEC rule is likely permanent); the overlapping evidence from which reasonable but contradictory inferences may be drawn; and the risk of inconsistent court results. Together these factors mean there is no practical way to confine antitrust suits so that they challenge only activity of the kind the investors seek to target, activity that is presently unlawful and will likely remain unlawful under the securities law. Rather, these factors suggest that antitrust courts are likely to make unusually serious mistakes in this respect. And the threat of antitrust mistakes, *i.e.,* results that stray outside the narrow bounds that plaintiffs seek to set, means that underwriters must act in ways that will avoid not simply conduct that the securities law forbids (and will likely continue to forbid), but also a wide range of joint conduct that the securities law permits or encourages (but which they fear could lead to an antitrust lawsuit and the risk of treble damages). And therein lies the problem.

This kind of problem exists to some degree in respect to other antitrust lawsuits. But here the factors we have mentioned make mistakes unusually likely (a matter relevant to Congress' determination of which institution should regulate a particular set of market activities). And the role that joint conduct plays in respect to the marketing of IPOs, along with the important role IPOs themselves play in relation to the effective functioning of capital markets, means that the securities-related costs of mistakes is unusually high. It is no wonder, then, that the SEC told the District Court (consistent with what the Government tells us here) that a "failure to hold that the alleged conduct was immunized would threaten to disrupt the full range of the Commission's ability to exercise its regulatory authority," adding that it would have a "chilling effect" on "lawful joint activities . . . of tremendous importance to the economy of the country."

We believe it fair to conclude that, where conduct at the core of the marketing of new securities is at issue; where securities regulators proceed with great care to distinguish the encouraged and permissible from the forbidden; where the threat of antitrust lawsuits, through error and disincentive, could seriously alter underwriter conduct in undesirable ways, to allow an antitrust lawsuit would threaten serious harm to the efficient functioning of the securities markets.

Second, any enforcement-related need for an antitrust lawsuit is unusually small. For one thing, the SEC actively enforces the rules and regulations that forbid the conduct in question. For another, as we have said, investors harmed by underwriters' unlawful practices may bring lawsuits and obtain damages under the securities law. Finally, the SEC is itself required to take account of competitive considerations when it creates securities-related policy and embodies it in rules and regulations. And that fact makes it somewhat less necessary to rely upon antitrust actions to address anticompetitive behavior.

We also note that Congress, in an effort to weed out unmeritorious securities lawsuits, has recently tightened the procedural requirements that plaintiffs must satisfy when they file those suits. To permit an antitrust lawsuit risks circumventing these requirements by permitting plaintiffs to dress what is essentially a securities complaint in antitrust clothing. See generally Private Securities Litigation Reform Act of 1995; Securities Litigation Uniform Standards Act of 1998.

In sum, an antitrust action in this context is accompanied by a substantial risk of injury to the securities markets and by a diminished need for antitrust enforcement to address anticompetitive conduct. Together these considerations indicate a serious conflict between, on the one hand, application of the antitrust laws and, on the other, proper enforcement of the securities law.

* * *

The upshot is that all four elements present in *Gordon* are present here: (1) an area of conduct squarely within the heartland of securities regulations; (2) clear and adequate SEC authority to regulate; (3) active and ongoing agency regulation; and (4) a serious conflict between the antitrust and regulatory regimes. We therefore conclude that the securities laws are "clearly incompatible" with the application of the antitrust laws in this context.

The Second Circuit's contrary judgment is *reversed*.

JUSTICE KENNEDY took no part in the consideration or decision of this case.

JUSTICE STEVENS, concurring in the judgment.

When investment bankers cooperate in underwriting an initial public offering (IPO), they increase the amount of capital available to firms producing goods and services and make additional securities available for purchase. By agglomerating networks of investors and spreading the risk of overvaluation, syndicates make positive contributions to the economy that could not be achieved through independent action. In my view, agreements among underwriters on how best to market IPOs, including agreements on price and other terms of sale to initial investors, should be treated as procompetitive joint ventures for purposes of antitrust analysis. In all but the rarest of cases, they cannot be conspiracies in restraint of trade within the meaning of § 1 of the Sherman Act.

After the initial purchase, the prices of newly issued stocks or bonds are determined by competition among the vast multitude of other securities traded in a free market. To suggest that an underwriting syndicate can restrain trade in that market by manipulating the terms of IPOs is frivolous. It is possible of course that the practices described in the complaints in these two cases may have enabled the underwriters to divert some of the benefits of the offerings from the issuers to themselves, thus breaching the agents' fiduciary obligations to their principals. But if such an injury did occur, it is not an "antitrust injury" giving rise to a damages claim by investors.

* * *

The defendants moved to dismiss for failure to state a claim on the ground, among others, that the plaintiffs' claims challenge "the ordinary activities of participants in underwriting syndicates, which are recognized to be completely lawful and pro-competitive." I agree and would hold, as we did in Parker v. Brown (1943), that the defendants' alleged conduct does not violate the antitrust laws, rather than holding that Congress has implicitly granted them immunity from those laws. Surely I would not suggest, as the Court did in *Twombly*, and as it does again today, that either the burdens of antitrust litigation or the risk "that antitrust courts are likely to make unusually serious mistakes," should play any role in the analysis of the question of law presented in a case such as this.

Accordingly, I concur in the Court's judgment but not in its opinion.

JUSTICE THOMAS, dissenting.

The Court believes it must decide whether the securities laws implicitly preclude application of the antitrust laws because the securities statutes "are silent in respect to antitrust." I disagree with that basic premise. The securities statutes are not silent. Both the Securities Act and the Securities Exchange Act contain broad saving clauses that preserve rights and remedies existing outside of the securities laws.

Section 16 of the Securities Act of 1933 states that "the rights and remedies provided by this subchapter shall be in addition to any and all other rights and remedies that may exist in law or in equity." In parallel fashion, § 28 of the Securities Exchange Act of 1934 states that "the rights and remedies provided by this chapter shall be in addition to any and all other rights and remedies that may exist at law or in equity." * * *

The Sherman Act was enacted in 1890. Accordingly, rights and remedies under the federal antitrust laws certainly would have been thought of as "rights and remedies" that existed "at law or in equity" by the Congresses that enacted that Securities Act and the Securities Exchange Act in the early 1930's. Therefore, both statutes explicitly save the very remedies the Court holds to be impliedly precluded. There is no convincing argument for why these saving provisions should not resolve this case in respondents' favor.

The Court's opinion overlooks the saving clauses seemingly because they do not "explicitly state whether they preclude application of the antitrust laws." As the Court observes, some statutes contain saving clauses specific to antitrust. But the mere existence of targeted saving clauses does not demonstrate—or even suggest—that antitrust remedies are not included within the "any and all" other remedies to which the securities saving clauses refer. * * *

Petitioners also argue that the saving clauses should not apply because the clauses did not play a role in the Court's prior securities-antitrust pre-emption cases. Be that as it may, none of the opinions in *Silver, Gordon,* or *NASD*—majority or dissent—offered any analysis of the saving clauses. Omitted reasoning has little claim to precedential value. * * *

* * *

* * * Accordingly, we do not need to reconcile any conflict between the securities laws and the antitrust laws. I respectfully dissent.

NOTES AND QUESTIONS

1.   Do you agree with Justice Stevens that syndication by multiple underwriters is so valuable to the securities marketplace that jointly imposing conditions of the kind seen here is not an antitrust violation at all? Should syndicates be required to register as joint ventures in order to receive that characterization of their activities?

2.   Should the SEC's failure to prohibit the conditions imposed by the underwriters in this case constitute an affirmation of their legality? Is there probably lots of illegal conduct that is simply not noticed by administrative

agencies? If there were no way for private parties to bring such conduct to the SEC's attention, should the Court have reached a different result in this case?

3. Do you agree that, as the Court held in *Trinko*, violation of an administrative standard—even one that is pro-competitive—should not have an antitrust remedy? Is Justice Stevens correct that *Trinko*'s concern about inconsistent results and uninformed courts should be quietly buried?

4. Justice Thomas focuses on the savings clause in the Securities Exchange Act of 1934 to say there is no conflict between antitrust law and securities law here. Do you agree? Are savings clauses necessarily a complete answer to the question of how two laws relate? Do you agree with Justice Thomas' implicit view that antitrust enforcement here would not disrupt the Commission's work?

2. STATE REGULATION

AN INTRODUCTORY NOTE

Do you remember the Supreme Court's 1943 decision in Parker v. Brown? It came not long after *Socony-Vacuum*. During the Depression, California regulations had tried to restrict the marketing of "excess" raisins. The antitrust laws were designed to deal with private actions by private firms, the Court held, not the actions of sovereign states. Furthermore, it would be unfair to sanction a firm under federal law for complying with a requirement of state law.

Basically, except for United States v. South-Eastern Underwriters, 322 U.S. 533 (1944), and Schwegmann Bros. v. Calvert Distillers Corp., 341 U.S. 384, 71 S.Ct. 745, 95 L.Ed. 1035 (1951), both of which read *Parker* very narrowly, little more was said about this issue for over twenty years. The exceptions, of course, were the *Noerr*, *Pennington* and *California Motor Transport* cases, which decided that seeking anticompetitive regulation did not constitute an antitrust violation.[251]

Then, in 1975, the Supreme Court decided Goldfarb v. Virginia State Bar, which we read at the outset of this Chapter. The State Bar had been granted authority to issue ethics opinions by the state Supreme Court, and had promulgated a minimum fee schedule, but the Court itself did not approve or issue the schedule. Thus, the Court found that the fee schedule was not a regulation protected against antitrust liability by *Parker*. "It is not enough that * * * anticompetitive conduct is 'prompted' by state action," the Court wrote, "rather, anticompetitive activities must be *compelled* by direction of the State acting as a sovereign." 421 U.S. at 791, 95 S.Ct. at 2015 (1975) (emphasis added).

---

[251] The cases are discussed in a note following Parker v. Brown in Chapter III, supra. On the current interpretation of the *Noerr-Pennington* doctrine, see Professional Real Estate Investors, Inc. v. Columbia Pictures Industries, Inc., infra.

Since *Goldfarb*, defining circumstances under which the dictates of state regulation may be cited as a defense to an antitrust violation has occupied as much Supreme Court time as any other single aspect of antitrust doctrine.

In Cantor v. Detroit Edison Co., 428 U.S. 579, 96 S.Ct. 3110, 49 L.Ed.2d 1141 (1976), for example, Detroit Edison gave light bulbs away free to its electric service customers pursuant to a tariff approved by the Michigan Public Service Commission. Plaintiff, the owner of a store that wanted to sell light bulbs, accused the defendant of thus monopolizing the market for light bulbs and tying bulbs to electric service. The District Court dismissed the complaint based on *Parker* and *Goldfarb*.

The Supreme Court reversed. This regulation had been sought by Detroit Edison, Justice Stevens wrote for the Court, i.e., it had filed the challenged tariff for Commission approval as it had all its other tariffs relating to rates and terms of service. State regulation may not exempt action from the federal antitrust laws unless the anticompetitive conduct is "necessary in order to make the regulatory act work" and then only to "the minimum extent necessary." This, the Court said, would make the state regulation rule consistent with *Philadelphia Bank*, Silver v. New York Stock Exchange, and other cases involving the conflict between *federal* regulation and antitrust policy. Justices Stewart, Powell and Rehnquist dissented, urging that a clear line render lawful any firm's compliance with state regulatory law. That, they said, was required by Parker v. Brown itself, and to keep this line of cases consistent with *Noerr* and other cases permitting lobbying.

Bates v. State Bar of Arizona, 433 U.S. 350, 97 S.Ct. 2691, 53 L.Ed.2d 810 (1977), was the next case in the series. If the name sounds familiar, it may be because it is the case that will allow you to advertise your professional services. Absent state authority, the rules prohibiting such lawyer advertising were presumed to be restraints of trade in violation of § 1, but the Supreme Court unanimously held that the prohibitions did not violate the Sherman Act. *Cantor* had involved a suit against a private party, the Court said; here the defendant was an agent of the Arizona Supreme Court. Further, in *Cantor*, there was no reason for the state to want to regulate light bulbs; here, regulation of lawyer advertising was part of protecting the public. Finally, while the bar did seek these rules, the regulatory authority had thought about them and actually applied them in discipline cases. Thus, although the restrictions were held to be unconstitutional regulations of commercial speech, they did not violate the antitrust laws.[252]

---

[252] Later decisions finding regulation of the legal profession by state supreme courts acting through administrative agencies to be immune from Sherman Act liability include Hoover v. Ronwin, 466 U.S. 558, 104 S.Ct. 1989, 80 L.Ed.2d 590 (1984) (suit against bar examiners for limiting entry into profession), and Lawline v. American Bar Ass'n, 956 F.2d 1378 (7th Cir.1992)

California Retail Liquor Dealers Assn. v. Midcal Aluminum, Inc., 445 U.S. 97, 100 S.Ct. 937, 63 L.Ed.2d 233 (1980), involved a challenge to California's program under which each wine producer or wholesaler was required to file a price schedule with the state and require that its retailers adhere to it. Midcal had allegedly sold 27 cases of wine for less than the posted price. Citing *Schwegmann*, the Court held that the California program clearly violated the Sherman Act. However, citing *Parker* for the proposition that the Sherman Act had "no purpose to nullify state powers", the Court went on to detail the circumstances required for antitrust immunity.

> "First, the challenged restraint must be 'one clearly articulated and affirmatively expressed as state policy'; second, the policy must be 'actively supervised' by the State itself."

The Court found that the California program did not involve the requisite active state supervision.[253]

But even these cases were really only the beginning of what has been a continuing series of efforts by the Supreme Court to find an accommodation between state regulation and federal antitrust policy.

SOUTHERN MOTOR CARRIERS RATE CONFERENCE v. UNITED STATES

Supreme Court of the United States, 1985
471 U.S. 48, 105 S.Ct. 1721, 85 L.Ed.2d 36

JUSTICE POWELL delivered the opinion of the Court.

Southern Motor Carriers Rate Conference, Inc. (SMCRC) and North Carolina Motor Carriers Association, Inc. (NCMCA), petitioners, are "rate bureaus" composed of motor common carriers operating in four Southeastern States. The rate bureaus, on behalf of their members, submit joint rate proposals to the Public Service Commissions in each State for approval or rejection. This collective rate-making is authorized, but not compelled, by the States in which the rate bureaus operate. The United

---

(challenge to disciplinary rules limiting non-lawyers from practicing law). Cf. Earles v. State Board of Certified Public Accountants, 139 F.3d 1033 (5th Cir. 1998) (immunity found).

Because each state must decide whether to require that its bar applicants have attended an accredited law school, a challenge to the accreditation process was rejected in Massachusetts School of Law at Andover, Inc. v. American Bar Association, 107 F.3d 1026 (3rd Cir. 1997). However, a separate action brought by the Department of Justice resulted in a consent decree that now governs the process. United States v. American Bar Association, 934 F.Supp. 435 (D.D.C. 1996). Cf. George B. Shepard, Cartels and Controls in Legal Training, 45 Antitrust Bulletin 436 (2000) (arguing law school accreditation is not necessarily in the public interest).

[253] As an earlier case finding adequate state involvement, the Court cited New Motor Vehicle Bd. of California v. Orrin W. Fox Co., 439 U.S. 96, 99 S.Ct. 403, 58 L.Ed.2d 361 (1978), where the State guaranteed a hearing to any automobile dealer who protested the establishment or relocation of a competing dealership. However, see 324 Liquor Corp. v. Duffy, 479 U.S. 335, 107 S.Ct. 720, 93 L.Ed.2d 667 (1987) (N.Y. program requiring liquor retailers to charge at least 112% of wholesaler's posted bottle price not actively supervised by state).

States, contending that collective rate-making violates the federal antitrust laws, filed this action to enjoin the rate bureaus' alleged anticompetitive practices. We here consider whether the petitioners' collective rate-making activities, though not compelled by the States, are entitled to Sherman Act immunity under the "state action" doctrine of Parker v. Brown.

I

A

In North Carolina, Georgia, Mississippi, and Tennessee, Public Service Commissions set motor common carriers' rates for the intrastate transportation of general commodities.[254] Common carriers are required to submit proposed rates to the relevant Commission for approval. A proposed rate becomes effective if the state agency takes no action within a specified period of time. If a hearing is scheduled, however, a rate will become effective only after affirmative agency approval. The State Public Service Commissions thus have and exercise ultimate authority and control over all intrastate rates.

In all four States, common carriers are allowed to agree on rate proposals prior to their joint submission to the regulatory agency. By reducing the number of proposals, collective rate-making permits the agency to consider more carefully each submission. In fact, some public service commissions have stated that without collective rate-making they would be unable to function effectively as rate-setting bodies.[255] Nevertheless, collective rate-making is not compelled by any of the States; every common carrier remains free to submit individual rate proposals to the Public Service Commissions.

As indicated above, SMCRC and NCMCA are private associations composed of motor common carriers operating in North Carolina, Georgia, Mississippi, and Tennessee. Both organizations have committees that consider possible rate changes. If a rate committee concludes that an intrastate rate should be changed, a collective proposal for the changed rate is submitted to the State Public Service Commission. Members of the Bureau, however, are not bound by the joint proposal. Any disapproving member may submit an independent rate proposal to the state regulatory commission.

---

[254] The Interstate Commerce Commission has the power to fix common carriers' rates for the interstate transportation of general commodities. The Interstate Commerce Act, however, expressly reserves to the States the regulation of common carriers' intrastate rates, even if these rates affect interstate commerce. 49 U.S.C. § 10521(b). [Court's fn. 1]

[255] Moreover, the uniformity in prices that collective rate-making tends to produce is considered desirable by the legislature of at least one State [North Carolina] and the Public Service Commission of another [Mississippi]. [Court's fn. 5]

B

On November 17, 1976, the United States instituted this action against SMCRC and NCMCA in the United States District Court for the Northern District of Georgia. The United States charged that the two rate bureaus had violated § 1 of the Sherman Act by conspiring with their members to fix rates for the intrastate transportation of general commodities. The rate bureaus responded that their conduct was exempt from the federal antitrust laws by virtue of the state action doctrine. See Parker v. Brown.[256] They further asserted that their collective rate-making activities did not violate the Sherman Act because the rates ultimately were determined by the appropriate state agencies. The District Court found the rate bureaus' arguments meritless, and entered a summary judgment in favor of the Government. The defendants were enjoined from engaging in collective rate-making activities with their members.

The Court of Appeals for the Fifth Circuit, sitting en banc, affirmed the judgment of the District Court. * * *

* * *

We granted certiorari to decide whether petitioners' collective rate-making activities, though not compelled by the States in which they operate, are entitled to *Parker* immunity.

II

In Parker v. Brown, this Court held that the Sherman Act was not intended to prohibit States from imposing restraints on competition. There, a raisin producer filed an action against the California director of agriculture to enjoin the enforcement of the State's Agricultural Prorate Act. * * * The Court recognized that the State's program was anticompetitive, and it assumed that Congress, "in the exercise of its commerce power, [could] prohibit a state from maintaining [such] a stabilization program * * * ." Nevertheless, the Court refused to find in the Sherman Act "an unexpressed purpose to nullify a state's control over its officers and agents * * * ."

Although *Parker* involved an action against a state official, the Court's reasoning extends to suits against private parties. The *Parker* decision was premised on the assumption that Congress, in enacting the Sherman Act, did not intend to compromise the States' ability to regulate their domestic commerce. If *Parker* immunity were limited to the actions of public officials, this assumed congressional purpose would be frustrated, for a State would be unable to implement programs that restrain competition among private parties. A plaintiff could frustrate any such program merely

---

[256] The defendants also contended that their collective rate-making activities were protected by the *Noerr-Pennington* doctrine. Both the District Court and the Court of Appeals rejected this defense, and we do not address it. [Court's fn. 11]

by filing suit against the regulated private parties, rather than the state officials who implement the plan. We decline to reduce Parker's holding to a formalism that would stand for little more than the proposition that Porter Brown sued the wrong parties. Cantor v. Detroit Edison Co. (Stewart, J., dissenting).

The circumstances in which *Parker* immunity is available to private parties, and to state agencies or officials regulating the conduct of private parties, are defined most specifically by our decision in California Retail Liquor Dealers Assn. v. Midcal Aluminum, Inc. In *Midcal*, we affirmed a state-court injunction prohibiting officials from enforcing a statute requiring wine producers to establish resale price schedules. We set forth a two-pronged test for determining whether state regulation of private parties is shielded from the federal antitrust laws. First, the challenged restraint must be "one clearly articulated and affirmatively expressed as state policy." Second, the State must supervise actively any private anticompetitive conduct. This supervision requirement prevents the state from frustrating the national policy in favor of competition by casting a "gauzy cloak of state involvement" over what is essentially private anticompetitive conduct.[257]

III

The *Midcal* test does not expressly provide that the actions of a private party must be compelled by a State in order to be protected from the federal antitrust laws. The Court of Appeals, however, held that compulsion is a threshold requirement to a finding of *Parker* immunity. * * *

A

The Court of Appeals held that *Midcal*, that involved a suit against a state agency, is inapplicable where a private party is the named defendant. *Midcal*, however, should not be given such a narrow reading. In that case we were concerned, as we are here, with state regulation restraining competition among private parties. Therefore, the two-pronged test set forth in *Midcal* should be used to determine whether the private rate bureaus' collective rate-making activities are protected from the federal antitrust laws. The success of an antitrust action should depend upon the

---

[257] The dissent argues that a state regulatory program is entitled to *Parker* immunity only if an antitrust exemption is "necessary to make the * * * [program] work * * * ." (quoting Cantor v. Detroit Edison Co.) This argument overlooks the fact that, with the exception of a questionable dictum in *Cantor*, the dissent's proposed test has been used only in deciding whether Congress intended to immunize a federal regulatory program from the Sherman Act's proscriptions. See, e.g., Silver v. New York Stock Exchange. In this context, if the federal courts wrongly conclude that an antitrust exemption is "unnecessary," Congress can correct the error. As the dissent recognizes, however, the Supremacy Clause would prevent state legislatures taking similar remedial action. Moreover, the proposed test would prompt the "kind of interference with state sovereignty * * * that * * * *Parker* was intended to prevent." Therefore, we hold that state action immunity is not dependent on a finding that an exemption from the federal antitrust laws is "necessary." [Court's fn. 21]

nature of the activity challenged, rather than on the identity of the defendant.

B

The Court of Appeals held that even if *Midcal* were applicable here, the rate bureaus would not be immune from federal antitrust liability. * * * In the four States in which petitioners operate, all common carriers are free to submit proposals individually. The court therefore reasoned that the States' policies are neutral with respect to collective ratemaking, and that these policies will not be frustrated if the federal antitrust laws are construed to require individual submissions.

In reaching its conclusion, the Court of Appeals assumed that if anticompetitive activity is not compelled, the State can have no interest in whether private parties engage in that conduct. This type of analysis ignores the manner in which the States in this case clearly have intended their permissive policies to work. Most common carriers probably will engage in collective rate-making, as that will allow them to share the cost of preparing rate proposals. If the joint rates are viewed as too high, however, carriers individually may submit lower proposed rates to the commission in order to obtain a larger share of the market. Thus, through the self-interested actions of private common carriers, the States may achieve the desired balance between the efficiency of collective rate-making and the competition fostered by individual submissions. Construing the Sherman Act to prohibit collective rate proposals eliminates the free choice necessary to ensure that these policies function in the manner intended by the States. The federal antitrust laws do not forbid the States to adopt policies that permit, but do not compel, anticompetitive conduct by regulated private parties. As long as the State clearly articulates its intent to adopt a permissive policy, the first prong of the *Midcal* test is satisfied.[258]

C

In Goldfarb v. Virginia State Bar, this Court said that "[t]he threshold inquiry in determining if an anticompetitive activity is state action of the type the Sherman Act was not meant to proscribe is whether the activity is required by the State acting as sovereign." * * * *Goldfarb*, however, is not properly read as making compulsion a sine qua non to state action immunity. * * *

Although *Goldfarb* did employ language of compulsion, it is beyond dispute that the Court would have reached the same result had it applied the two-pronged test later set forth in *Midcal*. * * * Virginia "as sovereign" did not have a "clearly articulated policy" designed to displace price

---

[258] Under the Interstate Commerce Act, motor common carriers are permitted, but not compelled, to engage in collective interstate rate-making. It is clear, therefore, that Congress has recognized the advantages of a permissive policy. We think it unlikely that Congress intended to prevent the States from adopting virtually identical policies at the intrastate level. [Court's fn. 22]

competition among lawyers. In fact, the Supreme Court of Virginia had explicitly directed lawyers not "to be controlled" by minimum fee schedules. Although we recognize that the language in *Goldfarb* is not without ambiguity, we do not read that opinion as making compulsion a prerequisite to a finding of state action immunity.

D

The *Parker* doctrine represents an attempt to resolve conflicts that may arise between principles of federalism and the goal of the antitrust laws, unfettered competition in the marketplace. A compulsion requirement is inconsistent with both values. It reduces the range of regulatory alternatives available to the State. At the same time, insofar as it encourages States to require, rather than merely permit, anticompetitive conduct, a compulsion requirement may result in *greater* restraints on trade. We do not believe that Congress intended to resolve conflicts between two competing interests by impairing both more than necessary.

* * * Our holding today does not suggest, however, that compulsion is irrelevant. To the contrary, compulsion often is the best evidence that the State has a clearly articulated and affirmatively expressed policy to displace competition. Nevertheless, when other evidence conclusively shows that a State intends to adopt a permissive policy, the absence of compulsion should not prove fatal to a claim of *Parker* immunity.

IV

A

Our holding that there is no inflexible "compulsion requirement" does not suggest necessarily that petitioners' collective ratemaking activities are shielded from the federal antitrust laws. A private party may claim state action immunity only if both prongs of the *Midcal* test are satisfied. Here the Court of Appeals found, and the Government concedes, that the State Public Service Commissions actively supervise the collective ratemaking activities of the rate bureaus. Therefore, the only issue left to resolve is whether the petitioners' challenged conduct was taken pursuant to a clearly articulated state policy.

The Public Service Commissions in North Carolina, Georgia, Mississippi, and Tennessee permit collective ratemaking. Acting alone, however, these agencies could not immunize private anticompetitive conduct. * * * *Parker* immunity is available only when the challenged activity is undertaken pursuant to a clearly articulated policy of the State itself, such as a policy approved by a state legislature or a State Supreme Court.

In this case, therefore, the petitioners are entitled to *Parker* immunity only if collective ratemaking is clearly sanctioned by the legislatures of the four States in which the rate bureaus operate. North Carolina, Georgia, and Tennessee have statutes that explicitly permit collective ratemaking by common carriers. The rate bureaus' challenged actions, at least in these States, are taken pursuant to an express and clearly articulated state policy. Mississippi's legislature, however, has not specifically addressed collective ratemaking. We therefore must consider whether, in the absence of a statute expressly permitting the challenged conduct, the first prong of the *Midcal* test can be satisfied.

B

The Mississippi Motor Carrier Regulatory Law of 1938 gives the State Public Service Commission authority to regulate common carriers. The statute provides that the commission is to prescribe "just and reasonable" rates for the intrastate transportation of general commodities. The legislature thus made clear its intent that intrastate rates would be determined by a regulatory agency, rather than by the market. The details of the inherently anticompetitive rate-setting process, however, are left to the agency's discretion. The state commission has exercised its discretion by actively encouraging collective ratemaking among common carriers. We do not believe that the actions petitioners took pursuant to this regulatory program should be deprived of *Parker* immunity.

A private party acting pursuant to a anticompetitive regulatory program need not "point to a specific, detailed legislative authorization" for its challenged conduct. As long as the State as sovereign clearly intends to displace competition in a particular field with a regulatory structure, the first prong of the *Midcal* test is satisfied. * * *

If more detail than a clear intent to displace competition were required of the legislature, States would find it difficult to implement through regulatory agencies their anticompetitive policies. Agencies are created because they are able to deal with problems unforeseeable to, or outside the competence of, the legislature. Requiring express authorization for every action that an agency might find necessary to effectuate state policy would diminish, if not destroy, its usefulness. Therefore, we hold that if the State's intent to establish an anticompetitive regulatory program is clear, as it is in Mississippi, the State's failure to describe the implementation of its policy in detail will not subject the program to the restraints of the federal antitrust laws.

* * *

V

We conclude that the petitioners' collective rate-making activities, although not compelled by the States, are immune from antitrust liability under the doctrine of Parker v. Brown. Accordingly, the judgment of the Court of Appeals is reversed.

JUSTICE STEVENS, with whom JUSTICE WHITE joins, dissenting.

* * *

I

* * * [A]greements and combinations tampering with competitive price structures are unlawful. State legislatures, whose powers are limited by the Supremacy Clause, may not expressly modify the obligations of any person under this federal law. Only Congress, expressly or by implication, may authorize price fixing, and has done so in particular industries or compelling circumstances. Implied antitrust immunities, however, are disfavored, and any exemptions from the antitrust laws are to be strictly construed. * * *

Applying these principles, this Court has consistently embraced the view that "[r]egulated industries are not per se exempt from the Sherman Act." Georgia v. Pennsylvania R. Co., 324 U.S. 439, 456 (1945). For many years prior to the enactment of the Sherman Act, state agencies regulated the business of insurance, but we rejected the view that these programs of public scrutiny supported "our reading into the Act an exemption" allowing insurance businesses to fix premium rates and agents' commissions. United States v. South-Eastern Underwriters Assn., 322 U.S. 533, 559 (1944). * * * Thereafter, in the McCarran-Ferguson Act of 1945, Congress decided, as a matter of policy, that the Sherman Act's prohibition of price fixing "shall [only] be applicable to the business of insurance to the extent that such business is not regulated by State Law." 15 U.S.C. § 1012(b).

Consistent with its treatment of the insurance business in *South-Eastern Underwriters*, this Court has repeatedly held that collusive price fixing by railroads is unlawful even though the end result is a reasonable charge approved by a public rate commission. Georgia v. Pennsylvania R. Corp.; United States v. Trans-Missouri Freight Assn. In the *Pennsylvania Railroad* case, the Court explained why this is so:

> "* * * [T]he Interstate Commerce Act does not provide remedies for the correction of all the abuses of rate-making which might constitute violations of the anti-trust laws. Thus a 'zone of reasonableness exists between maxima and minima within which a carrier is ordinarily free to adjust its charges for itself.' Within that zone the Commission lacks power to grant relief even though the rates are raised to the maxima by a conspiracy among carriers who employ unlawful tactics. * * * Damage must be presumed to flow from a conspiracy to manipulate rates within that zone."

Collusive price fixing by regulated carriers causes upward pressure on rates within the zone of reasonableness, and such combinations and conspiracies are generally actionable under the Sherman Act on the theory of the *Pennsylvania Railroad* case.

* * *

The defendants have stipulated that their price fixing arrangements are identical to those followed by the Carrier Rate Committees in the *Pennsylvania Railroad* case which were declared unlawful under the Sherman Act. They also acknowledge that neither the Reed-Bulwinkle Act, nor any other federal statute expressly exempts their price fixing from the antitrust laws. Nevertheless, they contend that Congress would not have intended to prohibit collective rate-making by intrastate motor carriers when it is permitted, but not required, by state law.

II

The basis for the defendant's claim of implied immunity from the antitrust laws is the state-action doctrine of Parker v. Brown. This Court, however, has repeatedly recognized that private entities may not claim the state-action immunity unless their unlawful conduct is compelled by the State.

* * *

The Court's unanimous decision in California Retail Liquor Dealers Assn. v. Midcal Aluminum, Inc. signaled no departure from settled principals in this area. In discussing the principles of law applicable to state-action immunity, the Court quoted extensively from the language in *Parker* and *Goldfarb* that recognized the compulsion requirement. * * *

III

* * *

The Court's reliance today on vague "principles of federalism" obscures our traditional disfavor for implied exemptions to the Sherman Act. We have only authorized exemptions from the Sherman Act for businesses regulated by federal law when "that exemption was necessary in order to make the regulatory Act work 'and even then only to the minimum extent necessary.'" No lesser showing of repugnancy should be sufficient to justify an implied exemption based on a state regulatory program.

Any other view separates the state-action exemption from the reason for its existence. The program involved in the *Parker* case was designed to enhance the market price of raisins by regulating both output and price. In other words, the state policy was one that replaced price competition with economic regulation. Price support programs like the one involved in *Parker* can not possibly succeed if every individual producer is free to participate or not participate in the program at his option. In *Parker*, the challenged price fixing was the heart of California's support program for agriculture; without immunity from the Sherman Act, the State would have had to abandon the project.

* * * When, as here, state regulatory policies are permissive rather than mandatory, there is no necessary conflict between the antitrust laws and the regulatory systems; the regulated entity may comply with the edicts of each sovereign. Indeed, it is almost meaningless to contemplate a "regulatory" policy that gives every regulated entity carte blanche to excuse itself from the consequences of the regulation. Even a policy against speeding could not be enforced if every motorist could drive as fast as he chose. When a State declares that a regulated entity need not follow a regulatory procedure, it as much as admits that this element is inconsequential to the ultimate success of the regulatory program.

* * *

The Court embraces the defendants' specious argument that "insofar as it encourages States to require, rather than merely permit, anticompetitive conduct, a compulsion requirement may result in greater restraints on trade." * * * This argument is seriously flawed.

On a practical level, the Court's argument assumes that a decision for the Government today would cause the States to rush into enactment legislation compelling price fixing in the motor carrier industry. Moreover, the Court's argument assumes that a Congress that only recently has acted to increase competition in the interstate motor carrier field would remain silent in the face of anticompetitive legislation at the intrastate level. These assumptions are wholly speculative.

On a more theoretical level, the Court ignores the anticompetitive effect of the collective ratemaking practices challenged in this litigation. * * * The increased rates for transportation caused by this behavior are especially grave in a basic industry, like transportation, where the ripple effects of the increased rates are magnified as raw materials, semifinished and finished goods are transported at various stages of production and distribution.

Active supervision of the rate bureau process—like that provided in the Motor Carrier Act of 1980—might minimize the anticompetitive effects of collective ratemaking. To the extent that the state regulatory commissions are structured like the ICC in the *Pennsylvania Railroad* case, however, they only have the power to reject the rates proposed by the carriers if those rates fall outside the "zone of reasonableness." Unless the commissions "actively supervise" the price-fixing process itself, they cannot eliminate the upward pressure on rates caused by collusive rate-making. Unfortunately, the nature of the "active supervision" of those carriers who take part in collective rate-making is not fully disclosed by the record.

IV

Whether it is wise or unwise policy for the Federal Government to seek to enforce the Sherman Act in this case is not a question that this Court is authorized to consider. The District Court and the Court of Appeals correctly applied established precedent in holding that the Government is entitled to an injunction against the defendant's price fixing. Such price fixing is unlawful unless it is expressly authorized by statute, or required by a State's regulatory program. Today the Court authorizes collective rate-making by intrastate motor carriers even though the State has only permitted it in a program regulating the reasonableness of prices in the industry. Immunity of this type was rejected by the Court in the *South-Eastern Underwriters* and *Pennsylvania Railroad* cases, but today, under the shroud of the state-action doctrine, it is resurrected.

Accordingly, I respectfully dissent.

NOTES AND QUESTIONS

1. Does all this sound familiar? We read this case near the end of the course because it should remind you that the western railroads made a similar argument almost a century earlier in *Trans-Missouri*. How did the argument fare there? How did it fare in Georgia v. Pennsylvania Railroad, the case that sought to accommodate *federal* regulation and the antitrust laws? Why should it fare better here?

2. Is motor carrier price setting something that inherently requires collective action?

a. Are you convinced by the dissenters that even if the rates later have to be approved by the state, this collective process will have an upward effect on rates? If you are not convinced, why do you suppose the truck lines were engaged in this activity?

b. Are trucks "natural monopolies," as railroads have been thought to be? Do truck lines have high fixed costs relative to their variable costs? Do they need the same protection against "cut-throat competition" that the railroads have asserted and about which we earlier expressed some sympathy?

c. Are truck lines, in fact, quintessential low overhead, flexible operations that do *not* need collective ratemaking except for their understandable self-interest in pricing in the manner of a cartel?

3. Had a substantial shift in the Court's approach in fact occurred during the decade between *Goldfarb* and *Southern Motor Carriers*?[259]

a. What had happened to the idea that private action must be compelled by the state in order not to be conspiratorial and thus violate the Sherman Act?

b. What had happened to the concern about whether the state had expressly authorized a regulatory initiative?

---

[259] Whatever shift had occurred was not the result of a change in court membership. The only new Supreme Court justice between 1975 and 1985 was Justice O'Connor who replaced Justice Stewart in 1982.

c.   What had happened to the *Midcal* requirement that the states "actively supervise" the regulatory process?

d.   Whatever happened to the concern in The Case of Monopolies that sovereigns would be tempted to grant monopoly privileges to their friends? Is there reason to have a corresponding concern about state officials today?[260]

4.   Can you see good reasons why the Court has abandoned some of its prior positions?

a.   Does the approach taken here make the tests any easier to apply? After this case, for example, do you know how *little* state review would qualify as "active" supervision?

b.   Are the new standards any more principled? Do they give any greater weight to principles of federalism? Do they reflect greater appreciation for the fact that not all parties in the political process may believe competition is the highest value? See, e.g., Massachusetts Food Ass'n v. Massachusetts Alcoholic Beverages Control Commission, 197 F.3d 560 (1st Cir. 1999), cert.denied 529 U.S. 1105 (2000) (making such arguments in upholding anticompetitive liquor control legislation).

THE PROBLEM OF ACTIVE SUPERVISION— *PATRICK v. BURGET* AND *TICOR TITLE*

As suggested by Justice Stevens' dissent in *Southern Motor Carriers*, a compromise short of required compulsion by the state would be to put greater emphasis on the "active supervision" element of the *Midcal* test.

Patrick v. Burget, 486 U.S. 94, 108 S.Ct. 1658, 100 L.Ed.2d 83 (1988), adopted this approach. Hospitals around the country are under a statutory obligation to establish peer-review procedures to assure the competence of doctors practicing there. State Health Departments are required to assure such procedures are in place, but in most states they do no more. In *Patrick*,

---

[260] There is a large body of economic theory that analyzes the incentives of legislators, executive branch officials, judges, and the persons who try to influence them. Most often, it goes by the name of "public choice" theory. Among the classics of this literature are James M. Buchanan & Gordon Tullock, The Calculus of Consent (1962); Mancur Olson, The Logic of Collective Action (1965); George J. Stigler, The Theory of Economic Regulation, 2 Bell J.Econ. & Mgmt. Sci. 3 (1971); Sam Peltzman, Toward a More General Theory of Regulation, 19 J.Law & Econ. 211 (1976); Gary S. Becker, A Theory of Competition Among Pressure Groups for Political Influence, 98 Q.J. Econ. 371 (1983).

The law reviews have seen an active debate on whether this theory suggests limits on how far the Sherman Act should yield to state regulation. E.g., Frank H. Easterbrook, Antitrust and the Economics of Federalism, 26 J. Law & Econ. 23 (1983); John S. Wiley, Jr., A Capture Theory of Antitrust Federalism, 99 Harvard L.Rev. 713 (1986); Merrick B. Garland, Antitrust and State Action: Economic Efficiency and the Political Process, 96 Yale L.J. 486 (1987); William H. Page, Interest Groups, Antitrust, and State Regulation: Parker v. Brown in the Economic Theory of Legislation, 1987 Duke L.J. 618; Matthew L. Spitzer, Antitrust Federalism and Rational Choice Political Economy: A Critique of Capture Theory, 61 S.California L.Rev. 1293 (1988); Einer Richard Elhauge, The Scope of Antitrust Process, 104 Harvard L.Rev. 668 (1991).

a doctor had been denied hospital privileges after an incident in which the doctor had allegedly left a patient unattended. The doctor alleged the real reason was because he had refused to join the medical clinic to which a majority of the hospital's doctors belonged. He filed suit under Sherman Act §§ 1 & 2, alleging the action was taken to protect the Board members' competitive position rather than to improve patient care. A jury agreed and a unanimous Supreme Court approved the result. Hospital peer-review is mandated, the Court said, but it is not actively supervised by independent state officials. Even state courts review only procedural issues; they do not assess underlying medical judgments. The regulatory system thus has no protection against anticompetitive action such as that alleged.

What do you think of this result? The next time you are in the hospital, would you be pleased to know that it had been deterred from reviewing the quality of care provided by the doctors who treat you? Congress was so concerned about the implications of this decision that it purported to insulate medical peer-review activities from antitrust liability in the Health Care Quality Improvement Act of 1986, 42 U.S.C. § 11101. The Act creates immunity from liability if peer-review action was taken "in the reasonable belief that [it] was in the furtherance of quality health care." Would that standard necessarily have defeated Dr. Patrick's claim?

"Active state supervision" of the regulatory process was again addressed in Federal Trade Commission v. Ticor Title Insurance Company, 504 U.S. 621, 112 S.Ct. 2169, 119 L.Ed.2d 410 (1992). Title insurers had agreed upon common charges for a title search and examination. The charges for the title search and the examination were billed separately and both were conceded to be within the regulatory jurisdiction of the state agencies involved. The problem was that all four states used a "negative option" system of review. That is, companies filed their rates and they went into effect unless the state objected within specified periods.

Writing for the Court, Justice Kennedy asserted:

"Our decisions make clear that the purpose of the active supervision inquiry is not to determine whether the State has met some normative standard, such as efficiency, in its regulatory practices. Its purpose is to determine whether the State has exercised sufficient independent judgment and control so that the details of the rates or prices have been established as a product of deliberate state intervention, not simply by agreement among private parties. Much as in causation inquiries, the analysis asks whether the State has played a substantial role in determining the specifics of the economic policy. The question is not how well state regulation works but whether the anticompetitive scheme is the State's own."

Applying this standard, the Court concluded that in two of the states there was insufficient review to constitute active state supervision. The Court of Appeals was asked to apply the newly-articulated standard to the systems in the other two states.[261]

Justice Scalia concurred, asserting himself both "skeptical" about the Parker v. Brown rule itself and troubled that under the Court's approach, "conspirators" can find out only after the fact whether their conduct was protected by sufficiently active supervision. However, he believed the Court's result was about the best that could be expected given the current state of the law.

Chief Justice Rehnquist, joined by Justices O'Connor and Thomas, dissented, asserting that the Court's test departed from that applied in both *Midcal* and Patrick v. Burget. The dissenters feared that the new test would undercut states' flexibility in choosing ways to regulate conduct clearly within their jurisdiction and would leave firms uncertain about when state officials' review of their conduct had been sufficient that obeying the regulation would not lead to Sherman Act liability.[262]

3. MUNICIPAL REGULATION

We now know that regulation by state government can create important protection against federal antitrust liability. Should the same be true of municipal regulation? Should a city or one of its agencies ever be found guilty of an antitrust violation?

In City of Lafayette v. Louisiana Power & Light Co., 435 U.S. 389, 98 S.Ct. 1123, 55 L.Ed.2d 364 (1978), a municipal electric company was alleged to have engaged in sham litigation against a private utility and to have required purchasers of city water service to also buy city power. The city responded that it was not a "person" that could violate the Sherman Act. The Court, however, disagreed. Exceptions to the antitrust laws are to be narrowly construed, the Court asserted. A city can be an antitrust plaintiff, so it can also be a defendant. Justice Brennan wrote for a plurality of the Court:

> "Cities are not themselves sovereign; they do not receive all the federal deference of the States that create them. * * * In light of the serious economic dislocation which could result if cities were free to place their own parochial interests above the Nation's economic goals reflected in the antitrust laws, we are especially

---

[261] On remand, the Third Circuit found that Arizona and Connecticut inadequately supervised their regulation to receive state action protection as well. Ticor Title Insurance Co. v. Federal Trade Commission, 998 F.2d 1129 (3d Cir.1993). Cf. Brown v. Ticor Title Insurance Co., 982 F.2d 386 (9th Cir.1992) (private action by Arizona and Wisconsin consumers).

[262] A good review of legal and policy issues raised by the state action exception is provided in Federal Trade Commission, Report of the State Action Task Force (Sept. 2003).

unwilling to presume that Congress intended to exclude anticompetitive municipal action from their reach.

* * *

" * * * We therefore conclude that the *Parker* doctrine exempts only anticompetitive conduct engaged in as an act of government by the State as sovereign, or, by its subdivisions, pursuant to state policy to displace competition with regulation or monopoly public service."

Justices Stewart, White, Blackmun, and Rehnquist dissented. They saw no principled basis to distinguish states from their constituent units. They did not believe that the 1890 Congress would have thought municipalities represented the evils against which the antitrust laws were directed, and they feared what treble damage sanctions could do to municipal treasuries. Chief Justice Burger broke the tie, saying he would apply antitrust standards only to a city's "business activity." He believed this power company clearly was such a business.

Community Communications Co. v. City of Boulder, 455 U.S. 40, 102 S.Ct. 835, 70 L.Ed.2d 810 (1982), raised similar issues in the context of a "home rule" city, i.e., one that had "the full right of self-government" with the power to adopt ordinances that superceded even state law. Boulder had awarded the plaintiff a cable television franchise to serve a small area of the city. As technology improved, the firm wanted to serve more citizens with a wider range of services. A competing company also proposed service, however, and the city adopted an ordinance prohibiting the plaintiff's expansion until the city could explore letting more cable companies provide service. Plaintiff's response was to charge the city with a violation of § 1. The city's response was to cite *Parker*.

The Supreme Court, again in an opinion by Justice Brennan, held that home rule status did not meet the *City of Lafayette* requirement of specific state authorization of the anticompetitive activity. Thus the *Parker* defense was unavailable. Justice Stevens, concurring, noted that this was not the same as saying that opening up the cable television market to competition was substantively a violation of the Sherman Act.

Justices Rehnquist and O'Connor and Chief Justice Burger dissented, arguing that the real analysis should be whether the Sherman Act *preempts* particular state or local law, not whether a city or state may "exempt" persons from complying with the federal statute. The effect of this decision, they said, would be to force cities to defend countless cases brought by citizens unhappy with local ordinances. Would *Professional Engineers* mean that local law could only be defended on the ground it was "procompetitive," they asked, rather than on the ground it served some other public interest?[263]

Town of Hallie v. City of Eau Claire, 471 U.S. 34, 105 S.Ct. 1713, 85 L.Ed.2d 24 (1985), decided the same day as *Southern Motor Carriers*, involved a battle between municipalities. The City of Eau Claire had a sewage treatment system; neighboring towns did not. Eau Claire said the towns could use its sewage treatment facility only if they also let Eau Claire pick up their garbage. The nearby towns said this was both an attempt to monopolize and a tying arrangement.

In a unanimous opinion written by Justice Powell, the Court found Eau Claire entitled to *Parker* protection. The state of Wisconsin had granted its cities authority to refuse to collect garbage in unincorporated areas, the Court said, and thus had thought about the anticompetitive consequences that might have. Further, none of the cases involving cities had required that the state compel local activity, as opposed to permit it. Finally, the Court may "presume" a municipality acts in the public interest. Thus, while there is a requirement of active state supervision of regulation of *private* parties, there is no similar requirement that the state actively supervise a municipality's regulatory program.

Fisher v. City of Berkeley, 475 U.S. 260, 106 S.Ct. 1045, 89 L.Ed.2d 206 (1986), involved a rent-control ordinance enacted by ballot initiative. Local landlords asserted that an ordinance which limited competitive setting of rent levels necessarily violated §§ 1 and 2 of the Sherman Act. Citing preemption analysis used in Rice v. Norman Williams Co., 458 U.S. 654, 102 S.Ct. 3294, 73 L.Ed.2d 1042 (1982), the Court said that this kind of regulation was "unilaterally" imposed by the city and not a conspiracy among the residents themselves, or the residents and the city. Unless the city becomes a "participant in a private agreement or combination," there could be no agreement and no violation of § 1.

Justice Powell, concurring, would have upheld the plan as state-authorized; Justice Brennan argued that the Court was departing from the more desirable limits on *Parker* established in *City of Lafayette* and *City of Boulder*.[264]

That, then, was the state of the law when the Court considered our next case.

---

[263] In response to this concern, Congress adopted the Local Government Antitrust Act of 1984, 98 Stat. 2750, 15 U.S.C. §§ 34–36, to limit the liability of municipalities.

[264] Among the articles critically analyzing these cases are John E. Lopatka, State Action and Municipal Antitrust Immunity: An Economic Approach, 53 Fordham L. Rev. 23 (1984); Daniel J. Gifford, The Antitrust State-Action Doctrine After Fisher v. Berkeley, 39 Vanderbilt L.Rev. 1257 (1986); John F. Hart, "Sovereign" State Policy and State Action Antitrust Immunity, 56 Fordham L.Rev. 535 (1988).

CITY OF COLUMBIA V. OMNI OUTDOOR ADVERTISING, INC.

Supreme Court of the United States, 1991
499 U.S. 365, 111 S.Ct. 1344, 113 L.Ed.2d 382

JUSTICE SCALIA delivered the opinion of the Court.

This case requires us to clarify the application of the Sherman Act to municipal governments and to the citizens who seek action from them.

I

Petitioner Columbia Outdoor Advertising, Inc. (COA), a South Carolina corporation, entered the billboard business in the city of Columbia, South Carolina (also a petitioner here), in the 1940's. By 1981 it controlled more than 95% of what has been conceded to be the relevant market. COA was a local business owned by a family with deep roots in the community, and enjoyed close relations with the city's political leaders. The mayor and other members of the city council were personal friends of COA's majority owner, and the company and its officers occasionally contributed funds and free billboard space to their campaigns. According to respondent, these beneficences were part of a "longstanding" "secret anticompetitive agreement" whereby "the City and COA would each use their [sic] respective power and resources to protect * * * COA's monopoly position," in return for which "City Council members received advantages made possible by COA's monopoly."

In 1981, respondent Omni Outdoor Advertising, Inc., a Georgia corporation, began erecting billboards in and around the city. COA responded to this competition in several ways. First, it redoubled its own billboard construction efforts and modernized its existing stock. Second—according to Omni—it took a number of anticompetitive private actions, such as offering artificially low rates, spreading untrue and malicious rumors about Omni, and attempting to induce Omni's customers to break their contracts. Finally (and this is what gives rise to the issue we address today), COA executives met with city officials to seek the enactment of zoning ordinances that would restrict billboard construction. COA was not alone in urging this course; a number of citizens concerned about the city's recent explosion of billboards advocated restrictions, including writers of articles and editorials in local newspapers.

In the spring of 1982, the city council passed an ordinance requiring the council's approval for every billboard constructed in downtown Columbia. * * * A state court invalidated this ordinance on the ground that its conferral of unconstrained discretion upon the city council violated both the South Carolina and Federal Constitutions. The city then requested the State's regional planning authority to conduct a comprehensive analysis of the local billboard situation as a basis for developing a final, constitutionally valid, ordinance. In September 1982, after a series of public hearings and numerous meetings involving city officials, Omni, and

COA (in all of which, according to Omni, positions contrary to COA's were not genuinely considered), the city council passed a new ordinance restricting the size, location, and spacing of billboards. These restrictions, particularly those on spacing, obviously benefited COA, which already had its billboards in place; they severely hindered Omni's ability to compete.

In November 1982, Omni filed suit against COA and the city in Federal District Court, charging that they had violated §§ 1 and 2 of the Sherman Act, as well as South Carolina's Unfair Trade Practices Act. Omni contended, in particular, that the city's billboard ordinances were the result of an anticompetitive conspiracy between city officials and COA that stripped both parties of any immunity they might otherwise enjoy from the federal antitrust laws. In January 1986, after more than two weeks of trial, a jury returned general verdicts against the city and COA on both the federal and state claims. It awarded damages, before trebling, of $600,000 on the § 1 Sherman Act claim, and $400,000 on the § 2 claim. The jury also answered two special interrogatories, finding specifically that the city and COA had conspired both to restrain trade and to monopolize the market. Petitioners moved for judgment notwithstanding the verdict, contending among other things that their activities were outside the scope of the federal antitrust laws. In November 1988, the District Court granted the motion.

A divided panel of the United States Court of Appeals for the Fourth Circuit reversed * * * and reinstated the jury verdict on all counts. We granted certiorari.

II

In the landmark case of Parker v. Brown, we rejected the contention that a program restricting the marketing of privately produced raisins, adopted pursuant to California's Agricultural Prorate Act, violated the Sherman Act. Relying on principles of federalism and state sovereignty, we held that the Sherman Act did not apply to anticompetitive restraints imposed by the States "as an act of government."

Since *Parker* emphasized the role of sovereign States in a federal system, it was initially unclear whether the governmental actions of political subdivisions enjoyed similar protection. In recent years, we have held that *Parker* immunity does not apply directly to local governments, see Hallie v. Eau Claire; Community Communications Co. v. Boulder; Lafayette v. Louisiana Power & Light Co. We have recognized, however, that a municipality's restriction of competition may sometimes be an authorized implementation of state policy, and have accorded *Parker* immunity where that is the case.

The South Carolina statutes under which the city acted in the present case authorize municipalities to regulate the use of land and the construction of buildings and other structures within their boundaries. It is undisputed that, as a matter of state law, these statutes authorize the city to regulate the size, location, and spacing of billboards. It could be argued, however, that a municipality acts beyond its delegated authority, for *Parker* purposes, whenever the nature of its regulation is substantively or even procedurally defective. On such an analysis it could be contended, for example, that the city's regulation in the present case was not "authorized" by S.C. Code § 5–23–10 (1976), if it was not, as that statute requires, adopted "for the purpose of promoting health, safety, morals or the general welfare of the community." * * * [S]uch an expansive interpretation of the *Parker*-defense authorization requirement would have unacceptable consequences.

* * * We * * * believe that in order to prevent *Parker* from undermining the very interests of federalism it is designed to protect, it is necessary to adopt a concept of authority broader than what is applied to determine the legality of the municipality's action under state law. * * * It suffices for the present to conclude that here no more is needed to establish, for *Parker* purposes, the city's authority to regulate than its unquestioned zoning power over the size, location, and spacing of billboards.

Besides authority to regulate, however, the *Parker* defense also requires authority to suppress competition—more specifically, "clear articulation of a state policy to authorize anticompetitive conduct" by the municipality in connection with its regulation. *Hallie.* We have rejected the contention that this requirement can be met only if the delegating statute explicitly permits the displacement of competition. It is enough, we have held, if suppression of competition is the "foreseeable result" of what the statute authorizes. That condition is amply met here. The very purpose of zoning regulation is to displace unfettered business freedom in a manner that regularly has the effect of preventing normal acts of competition, particularly on the part of new entrants. A municipal ordinance restricting the size, location, and spacing of billboards (surely a common form of zoning) necessarily protects existing billboards against some competition from newcomers.

The Court of Appeals was therefore correct in its conclusion that the city's restriction of billboard construction was prima facie entitled to *Parker* immunity. The Court of Appeals upheld the jury verdict, however, by invoking a "conspiracy" exception to *Parker* that has been recognized by several Courts of Appeals. That exception is thought to be supported by * * * statements in *Parker* * * * . *Parker* does not apply, according to the Fourth Circuit, "where politicians or political entities are involved as conspirators" with private actors in the restraint of trade.

There is no such conspiracy exception. The rationale of *Parker* was that, in light of our national commitment to federalism, the general language of the Sherman Act should not be interpreted to prohibit anticompetitive actions by the States in their governmental capacities as sovereign regulators. * * * [T]his immunity does not necessarily obtain where the State acts not in a regulatory capacity but as a commercial participant in a given market. * * * [But *Parker*] should not be read to suggest the general proposition that even governmental regulatory action may be deemed private—and therefore subject to antitrust liability—when it is taken pursuant to a conspiracy with private parties. The impracticality of such a principle is evident if, for purposes of the exception, "conspiracy" means nothing more than an agreement to impose the regulation in question. Since it is both inevitable and desirable that public officials often agree to do what one or another group of private citizens urges upon them, such an exception would virtually swallow up the *Parker* rule: All anticompetitive regulation would be vulnerable to a "conspiracy" charge.[265]

Omni suggests, however, that "conspiracy" might be limited to instances of governmental "corruption," defined variously as "abandonment of public responsibilities to private interests," "corrupt or bad faith decisions," and "selfish or corrupt motives." Ultimately, Omni asks us not to define "corruption" at all, but simply to leave that task to the jury: "at bottom, however, it was within the jury's province to determine what constituted corruption of the governmental process in their community." Omni's amicus eschews this emphasis on "corruption," instead urging us to define the conspiracy exception as encompassing any governmental act "not in the public interest."

A conspiracy exception narrowed along such vague lines is similarly impractical. Few governmental actions are immune from the charge that they are "not in the public interest" or in some sense "corrupt." The California marketing scheme at issue in *Parker* itself, for example, can readily be viewed as the result of a "conspiracy" to put the "private" interest of the State's raisin growers above the "public" interest of the State's consumers. The fact is that virtually all regulation benefits some segments of the society and harms others; and that it is not universally considered contrary to the public good if the net economic loss to the losers exceeds the net economic gain to the winners. *Parker* was not written in ignorance of

---

265 The dissent is confident that a jury composed of citizens of the vicinage will be able to tell the difference between "independent municipal action and action taken for the sole purpose of carrying out an anticompetitive agreement for the private party." No doubt. But those are merely the polar extremes, which like the geographic poles will rarely be seen by jurors of the vicinage. Ordinarily the allegation will merely be (and the dissent says this is enough) that the municipal action was not prompted "exclusively by a concern for the general public interest." Thus, the real question is whether a jury can tell the difference—whether Solomon can tell the difference— between municipal-action-not-entirely-independent-because-based-partly-on-agreement-with-private-parties that is lawful and municipal-action-not-entirely-independent-because-based-partly-on-agreement-with-private-parties that is unlawful. The dissent does not tell us how to put this question coherently, much less how to answer it intelligently. "Independent municipal action" is un-objectionable, "action taken for the sole purpose of carrying out an anticompetitive agreement for the private party" is un-lawful, and everything else (that is, the known world between the two poles) is unaddressed. * * * [Court's fn. 5]

the reality that determination of "the public interest" in the manifold areas of government regulation entails not merely economic and mathematical analysis but value judgment, and it was not meant to shift that judgment from elected officials to judges and juries. If the city of Columbia's decision to regulate what one local newspaper called "billboard jungles," is made subject to ex post facto judicial assessment of "the public interest," with personal liability of city officials a possible consequence, we will have gone far to "compromise the States' ability to regulate their domestic commerce," Southern Motor Carriers Rate Conference, Inc. v. United States. The situation would not be better, but arguably even worse, if the courts were to apply a subjective test: not whether the action was in the public interest, but whether the officials involved thought it to be so. This would require the sort of deconstruction of the governmental process and probing of the official "intent" that we have consistently sought to avoid. * * *

The foregoing approach to establishing a "conspiracy" exception at least seeks (however impractically) to draw the line of impermissible action in a manner relevant to the purposes of the Sherman Act and of *Parker*: prohibiting the restriction of competition for private gain but permitting the restriction of competition in the public interest. Another approach is possible, which has the virtue of practicality but the vice of being unrelated to those purposes. That is the approach which would consider *Parker* inapplicable only if, in connection with the governmental action in question, bribery or some other violation of state or federal law has been established. Such unlawful activity has no necessary relationship to whether the governmental action is in the public interest. A mayor is guilty of accepting a bribe even if he would and should have taken, in the public interest, the same action for which the bribe was paid. * * * When, moreover, the regulatory body is not a single individual but a state legislature or city council, there is even less reason to believe that violation of the law (by bribing a minority of the decisionmakers) establishes that the regulation has no valid public purpose. To use unlawful political influence as the test of legality of state regulation undoubtedly vindicates (in a rather blunt way) principles of good government. But the statute we are construing is not directed to that end.

III

While *Parker* recognized the States' freedom to engage in anticompetitive regulation, it did not purport to immunize from antitrust liability the private parties who urge them to engage in anticompetitive regulation. However, it is obviously peculiar in a democracy, and perhaps in derogation of the constitutional right "to petition the Government for a redress of grievances," to establish a category of lawful state action that citizens are not permitted to urge. Thus, beginning with Eastern Railroad Presidents Conference v. Noerr Motor Freight, Inc., we have developed a corollary to *Parker*: the federal antitrust laws also do not regulate the conduct of private individuals in seeking anticompetitive action from the government. This doctrine, like *Parker*, rests ultimately upon a recognition that the antitrust laws, "tailored as they are for the business world, are not at all appropriate for application in the political arena." That a private party's political motives are selfish is irrelevant: "*Noerr* shields from the Sherman Act a concerted effort to influence public officials regardless of intent or purpose." United Mine Workers of America v. Pennington.

Noerr recognized, however, what has come to be known as the "sham" exception to its rule. * * * The Court of Appeals concluded that the jury in this case could have found that COA's activities on behalf of the restrictive billboard ordinances fell within this exception. In our view that was error.

The "sham" exception to *Noerr* encompasses situations in which persons use the governmental process—as opposed to the outcome of that process—as an anticompetitive weapon. A classic example is the filing of frivolous objections to the license application of a competitor, with no expectation of achieving denial of the license but simply in order to impose expense and delay. See California Motor Transport Co. v. Trucking Unlimited. A "sham" situation involves a defendant whose activities are "not genuinely aimed at procuring favorable government action" at all, Allied Tube & Conduit Corp. v. Indian Head, Inc., not one "who 'genuinely seeks to achieve his governmental result, but does so through improper means.'"

* * *

Omni urges that if, as we have concluded, the "sham" exception is inapplicable, we should use this case to recognize another exception to Noerr immunity—a "conspiracy" exception, which would apply when government officials conspire with a private party to employ government action as a means of stifling competition. We have left open the possibility of such an exception, see, e.g., *Allied Tube*. * * *

Giving full consideration to this matter for the first time, we conclude that a "conspiracy" exception to *Noerr* must be rejected. We need not describe our reasons at length, since they are largely the same as those set forth in Part II above for rejecting a "conspiracy" exception to *Parker*. As we have described, *Parker* and *Noerr* are complementary expressions of the principle that the antitrust laws regulate business, not politics; the former decision protects the States' acts of governing, and the latter the citizens' participation in government. Insofar as the identification of an immunity-destroying "conspiracy" is concerned, *Parker* and *Noerr* generally present two faces of the same coin. The *Noerr*-invalidating conspiracy alleged here is just the *Parker*-invalidating conspiracy viewed from the standpoint of the private-sector participants rather than the governmental participants. The same factors which, as we have described above, make it impracticable or beyond the purpose of the antitrust laws to identify and invalidate lawmaking that has been infected by selfishly motivated agreement with private interests likewise make it impracticable or beyond that scope to identify and invalidate lobbying that has produced selfishly motivated agreement with public officials. * * * And if the invalidating "conspiracy" is limited to one that involves some element of unlawfulness (beyond mere anticompetitive motivation), the invalidation would have nothing to do with the policies of the antitrust laws. In *Noerr* itself, where the private party "deliberately deceived the public and public officials" in its successful lobbying campaign, we said that "deception, reprehensible as it is, can be of no consequence so far as the Sherman Act is concerned."

IV

* * *

* * * The judgment of the Court of Appeals is reversed, and the case is remanded for further proceedings consistent with this opinion.

JUSTICE STEVENS, with whom JUSTICE WHITE and JUSTICE MARSHALL join, dissenting.

* * * [T]he Court today [decides] * * * that agreements between municipalities, or their officials, and private parties to use the zoning power to confer exclusive privileges in a particular line of commerce are beyond the reach of § 1. History, tradition, and the facts of this case all demonstrate that the Court's attempt to create a "better" and less inclusive Sherman Act is ill advised.

I

As a preface to a consideration of the "state action" and so-called "*Noerr-Pennington*" exemptions to the Sherman Act, it is appropriate to remind the Court that one of the classic common-law examples of a prohibited contract in restraint of trade involved an agreement between a public official and a private party. The public official—the Queen of England—had granted one of her subjects a monopoly in the making, importation, and sale of playing cards in order to generate revenues for the crown. A competitor challenged the grant in The Case of Monopolies and prevailed. * * *

In the case before us today, respondent alleges that the city of Columbia, South Carolina, has entered into a comparable agreement to give respondent a monopoly in the sale of billboard advertising. After a three-week trial, a jury composed of citizens of the vicinage found that, despite the city fathers' denials, there was indeed such an agreement, presumably motivated in part by past favors in the form of political advertising, in part by friendship, and in part by the expectation of a beneficial future relationship—and in any case, not exclusively by a concern for the general public interest. Today the Court acknowledges the anticompetitive consequences of this and similar agreements but decides that they should be exempted from the coverage of the Sherman Act because it fears that enunciating a rule that allows the motivations of public officials to be probed may mean that innocent municipal officials may be harassed with baseless charges. The holding evidences an unfortunate lack of confidence in our judicial system and will foster the evils the Sherman Act was designed to eradicate.

II

There is a distinction between economic regulation, on the one hand, and regulation designed to protect the public health, safety, and environment. In antitrust parlance a "regulated industry" is one in which decisions about prices and output are made not by individual firms, but rather by a public body or a collective process subject to governmental approval. * * *

The antitrust laws reflect a basic national policy favoring free markets over regulated markets. In essence, the Sherman Act prohibits private unsupervised regulation of the prices and output of goods in the marketplace. That prohibition is inapplicable to specific industries which Congress has exempted from the antitrust laws and subjected to regulatory supervision over price and output decisions. Moreover, the so-called "state action" exemption from the Sherman Act reflects the Court's understanding that Congress did not intend the statute to preempt a State's economic regulation of commerce within its own borders.

* * *

Underlying the Court's recognition of this state action exemption has been respect for the fundamental principle of federalism. As we stated in *Parker*, "In a dual system of government in which, under the Constitution, the states are sovereign, save only as Congress may constitutionally subtract from their authority, an unexpressed purpose to nullify a state's control over its officers and agents is not lightly to be attributed to Congress."

However, this Court recognized long ago that the deference due States within our federal system does not extend fully to conduct undertaken by municipalities. * * *

Unlike States, municipalities do not constitute bedrocks within our system of federalism. And also unlike States, municipalities are more apt to promote their narrow parochial interests "without regard to extraterritorial impact and regional efficiency." Lafayette v. Louisiana Power & Light Co., 435 U.S. 389 (1978); see also The Federalist No. 10 (J. Madison) (describing the greater tendency of smaller societies to promote oppressive and narrow interests above the common good). * * *

* * *

III

Today the Court adopts a significant enlargement of the state action exemption. The South Carolina statutes that confer zoning authority on municipalities in the State do not articulate any state policy to displace competition with economic regulation in any line of commerce or in any specific industry. * * * Like Colorado's grant of "home rule" powers to the city of Boulder, they are simply neutral on the question whether the municipality should displace competition with economic regulation in any industry. There is not even an arguable basis for concluding that the State authorized the city of Columbia to enter into exclusive agreements with any person, or to use the zoning power to protect favored citizens from competition. * * *

In this case, the jury found that the city's ordinance—ostensibly one promoting health, safety, and welfare—was in fact enacted pursuant to an agreement between city officials and a private party to restrict competition. In my opinion such a finding necessarily leads to the conclusion that the city's ordinance was fundamentally a form of economic regulation of the billboard market rather than a general welfare regulation having incidental anticompetitive effects. Because I believe our cases have wisely held that the decision to embark upon economic regulation is a nondelegable one that must expressly be made by the State in the context of a specific industry in order to qualify for state action immunity, I would hold that the city of Columbia's economic regulation of the billboard market pursuant to a general state grant of zoning power is not exempt from antitrust scrutiny.

* * *

The difficulty of proving whether an agreement motivated a course of conduct should not in itself intimidate this Court into exempting those illegal agreements that are proven by convincing evidence. Rather, the Court should, if it must, attempt to deal with these problems of proof as it has in the past—through heightened evidentiary standards rather than through judicial expansion of exemptions from the Sherman Act. See, e.g., Matsushita Electric Industrial Co. v. Zenith Radio Corp.

* * * Unlike the previous limitations this Court has imposed on Congress' sweeping mandate in § 1, which found support in our common-law traditions or our system of federalism, the Court's wholesale exemption of municipal action from antitrust scrutiny amounts to little more than a bold and disturbing act of judicial legislation which dramatically curtails the statutory prohibition against "every" contract in restraint of trade.

* * *

I respectfully dissent.

NOTES AND QUESTIONS

1.   Are you persuaded that the Court should have closed the door apparently left open in *Fisher* for suits alleging a conspiracy between a city and its favored corporate citizens?

a.   Are dissenting Justices Stevens, Brennan and Marshall correct to remind us that monopolies granted by the state have been subject to antitrust challenge at least since The Case of Monopolies with which we began this course? Is such an appeal to English history relevant to the problems of federalism today?

b.   Was the plaintiff's story implausible here? Does one have to be a cynic to believe that a city council might try to protect a South Carolina business against a sophisticated operation from Atlanta?

c.   What would be the likely effect of the city council's action on the price of advertising in Columbia? Is this, then, the sort of conduct the antitrust laws were designed to prevent?

2.   Were you convinced by the Court's conclusion that the state grant of authority to enact a zoning ordinance constituted a grant of authority to limit billboard competition?

a.   Is the controlling test whether it was inevitable that any exercise of zoning authority would affect competition in some way?

b.   Is it whether the state might reasonably foresee that its grant of authority could be used to limit competition? See Surgical Care Center of Hammond v. Hospital Service District No. 1 of Tangipahoa Parish, 171 F.3d 231 (5th Cir.) (en banc), cert.denied 528 U.S. 964 (1999) (grant of authority to form medical facility joint ventures did not authorize hospital district's limiting plaintiff's right to offer outpatient surgical care services).

3.   Is the real problem here that it is too easy to allege a conspiracy and thus to get a case to the jury?

a.   How do you think juries would tend to react to stories of conspiracies by municipal officials? Would cynicism about government decision makers tend to lead to finding conspiracy behind a great many decisions? Would jurors' liability as taxpayers for paying at least part of some antitrust judgments tend to overcome such a tendency?[266]

b.   Is this a problem of federalism? Is the majority right that decisions of state officials should not be reviewable in the federal courts? Do we adhere to that principle in many other areas of the law?

c.   Is this a case where doctrinal consistency is less important than reducing the burden on cities of what could become very expensive blackmail-

---

[266] On remand, the Court of Appeals did not send the case back for a new trial. It found that Omni had relied so heavily on the conspiracy theory rejected by the Supreme Court that there was no cause of action left pleaded against Columbia Outdoor Advertising, the private defendant. Omni Outdoor Advertising v. Columbia Outdoor Advertising, 974 F.2d 502 (4th Cir.1992).

by-litigation? Such a concern lay behind adoption of the Local Government Antitrust Act of 1984, 15 U.S.C.A. §§ 34–36 (eliminates damage liability of governmental bodies and their officials).

But concern remained that the state action immunity and its extension to local entities might be going too far. See if you think the Court's most recent decision may have narrowed the scope of the doctrine.

FEDERAL TRADE COMMISSION V. PHOEBE PUTNEY HEALTH SYSTEM

Supreme Court of the United States, 2013
568 U.S. 216, 133 S.Ct. 1003, 185 L.Ed.2d 43

JUSTICE SOTOMAYOR delivered the opinion of the Court.

Under this Court's state-action immunity doctrine, when a local governmental entity acts pursuant to a clearly articulated and affirmatively expressed state policy to displace competition, it is exempt from scrutiny under the federal antitrust laws. * * * Because Georgia's grant of general corporate powers to hospital authorities does not include permission to use those powers anticompetitively, we hold that the clear-articulation test is not satisfied and state-action immunity does not apply.

I

A

In 1941, the State of Georgia amended its Constitution to allow political subdivisions to provide health care services. The State concurrently enacted the Hospital Authorities Law (Law), "to provide a mechanism for the operation and maintenance of needed health care facilities in the several counties and municipalities of th[e] state." * * * As amended, the Law authorizes each county and municipality, and certain combinations of counties or municipalities, to create "a public body corporate and politic" called a "hospital authority." Hospital authorities are governed by 5- to 9-member boards that are appointed by the governing body of the county or municipality in their area of operation.

Under the Law, a hospital authority "exercise[s] public and essential governmental functions" and is delegated "all the powers necessary or convenient to carry out and effectuate" the Law's purposes. Giving more content to that general delegation, the Law enumerates 27 powers conferred upon hospital authorities, including the power "[t]o acquire by purchase, lease, or otherwise and to operate projects," which are defined to include hospitals and other public health facilities; "[t]o construct, reconstruct, improve, alter, and repair projects;" "[t]o lease . . . for operation by others any project" provided certain conditions are satisfied; and "[t]o establish rates and charges for the services and use of the facilities of the authority." Hospital authorities may not operate or construct any project for profit, and accordingly they must set rates so as only to cover operating expenses and create reasonable reserves.

B

In the same year that the Law was adopted, the city of Albany and Dougherty County established the Hospital Authority of Albany-Dougherty County (Authority) and the Authority promptly acquired Phoebe Putney Memorial Hospital (Memorial), which has been in operation in Albany since 1911. In 1990, the Authority restructured its operations by forming two private nonprofit corporations to manage Memorial: Phoebe Putney Health System, Inc. (PPHS), and its subsidiary, Phoebe Putney Memorial Hospital, Inc. (PPMH). * * * Consistent with [the Law], PPMH is subject to lease conditions that require provision of care to the indigent sick and limit its rate of return.

Memorial is one of two hospitals in Dougherty County. The second, Palmyra Medical Center (Palmyra), was established in Albany in 1971 and is located just two miles from Memorial. At the time suit was brought in this case, Palmyra was operated by a national for-profit hospital network, HCA, Inc. (HCA). Together, Memorial and Palmyra account for 86 percent of the market for acute-care hospital services provided to commercial health care plans and their customers in the six counties surrounding Albany. Memorial accounts for 75 percent of that market on its own.

In 2010, PPHS began discussions with HCA about acquiring Palmyra. * * * The Authority unanimously approved the transaction.

The Federal Trade Commission (FTC) shortly thereafter issued an administrative complaint alleging that the proposed * * * transaction would create a virtual monopoly and would substantially reduce competition in the market for acute-care hospital services, in violation of § 5 of the Federal Trade Commission Act, and § 7 of the Clayton Act. The FTC, along with the State of Georgia, subsequently filed suit * * * seeking to enjoin the transaction pending administrative proceedings.

The United States District Court for the Middle District of Georgia denied the request for a preliminary injunction and granted respondents' motion to dismiss. The District Court held that respondents are immune from antitrust liability under the state-action doctrine.

The United States Court of Appeals for the Eleventh Circuit affirmed. As an initial matter, the court "agree[d] with the [FTC] that, on the facts alleged, the joint operation of Memorial and Palmyra would substantially lessen competition or tend to create, if not create, a monopoly." But the * * * Court of Appeals explained that as a local governmental entity, the Authority was entitled to state-action immunity if the challenged anticompetitive conduct was a " 'foreseeable result' " of Georgia's legislation. According to the court, anticompetitive conduct is foreseeable if it could have been " 'reasonably anticipated' " by the state legislature; it is not necessary, the court reasoned, for an anticompetitive effect to "be 'one that ordinarily occurs, routinely occurs, or is inherently likely to occur as a result of the empowering legislation.' " Applying that standard, the Court of Appeals concluded that the Law contemplated the anticompetitive conduct challenged by the FTC. The court noted the "impressive breadth" of the powers given to hospital authorities, which include traditional powers of private corporations and a few additional capabilities, such as the power to exercise eminent domain. More specifically, the court reasoned that the Georgia Legislature must have anticipated that the grant of power to hospital authorities to acquire and lease projects would produce anticompetitive effects because "[f]oreseeably, acquisitions could consolidate ownership of competing hospitals, eliminating competition between them."

* * *

We granted certiorari on two questions: whether the Georgia Legislature, through the powers it vested in hospital authorities, clearly articulated and affirmatively expressed a state policy to displace competition in the market for hospital services; and if so, whether state-action immunity is nonetheless inapplicable as a result of the Authority's minimal participation in negotiating the terms of the sale of Palmyra and the Authority's limited supervision of the two hospitals' operations. Concluding that the answer to the first question is "no," we reverse without reaching the second question.

II

In Parker v. Brown, this Court held that because "nothing in the language of the Sherman Act or in its history" suggested that Congress intended to restrict the sovereign capacity of the States to regulate their economies, the Act should not be read to bar States from imposing market restraints "as an act of government." Following *Parker*, we have held that under certain circumstances, immunity from the federal antitrust laws may extend to non-state actors carrying out the State's regulatory program.

But given the fundamental national values of free enterprise and economic competition that are embodied in the federal antitrust laws, "state-action immunity is disfavored, much as are repeals by implication." FTC v. Ticor Title Ins. Co. Consistent with this preference, we recognize state-action immunity only when it is clear that the challenged anticompetitive conduct is undertaken pursuant to a regulatory scheme that "is the State's own." * * *

This case involves allegedly anticompetitive conduct undertaken by a substate governmental entity. Because municipalities and other political subdivisions are not themselves sovereign, state-action immunity under *Parker* does not apply to them directly. See Columbia v. Omni Outdoor Advertising, Inc.; Lafayette v. Louisiana Power & Light Co. At the same time, however, substate governmental entities do receive immunity from antitrust scrutiny when they act "pursuant to state policy to displace competition with regulation or monopoly public service." This rule "preserves to the States their freedom . . . to use their municipalities to administer state regulatory policies free of the inhibitions of the federal antitrust laws without at the same time permitting purely parochial interests to disrupt the Nation's free-market goals."

As with private parties, immunity will only attach to the activities of local governmental entities if they are undertaken pursuant to a "clearly articulated and affirmatively expressed" state policy to displace competition. But unlike private parties, such entities are not subject to the "active state supervision requirement" because they have less of an incentive to pursue their own self-interest under the guise of implementing state policies.

"[T]o pass the 'clear articulation' test," a state legislature need not "expressly state in a statute or its legislative history that the legislature intends for the delegated action to have anticompetitive effects." Rather, we explained in Hallie [v. Eau Claire] that state-action immunity applies if the anticompetitive effect was the "foreseeable result" of what the State authorized. We applied that principle in *Omni*, where we concluded that the clear-articulation test was satisfied because the suppression of competition in the billboard market was the foreseeable result of a state statute authorizing municipalities to adopt zoning ordinances regulating the construction of buildings and other structures.

III

A

Applying the clear-articulation test to the Law before us, we conclude that respondents' claim for state-action immunity fails because there is no evidence the State affirmatively contemplated that hospital authorities would displace competition by consolidating hospital ownership. The acquisition and leasing powers exercised by the Authority in the challenged transaction, which were the principal powers relied upon by the Court of Appeals in finding state-action immunity, mirror general powers routinely conferred by state law upon private corporations. Other powers possessed by hospital authorities that the Court of Appeals characterized as having "impressive breadth," also fit this pattern, including the ability to make and execute contracts, to set rates for services, to sue and be sued, to borrow money, and the residual authority to exercise any or all powers possessed by private corporations.

Our case law makes clear that state-law authority to act is insufficient to establish state-action immunity; the substate governmental entity must also show that it has been delegated authority to act or regulate anticompetitively. In [Community Communications Co. v. City of] Boulder, we held that Colorado's Home Rule Amendment allowing municipalities to govern local affairs did not satisfy the clear-articulation test. There was no doubt in that case that the city had authority as a matter of state law to pass an ordinance imposing a moratorium on a cable provider's expansion of service. But we rejected the proposition that "the general grant of power to enact ordinances necessarily implies state authorization to enact specific anticompetitive ordinances" because such an approach "would wholly eviscerate the concepts of 'clear articulation and affirmative expression' that our precedents require." We explained that when a State's position "is one of mere neutrality respecting the municipal actions challenged as anticompetitive," the State cannot be said to have " 'contemplated' " those anticompetitive actions.

The principle articulated in *Boulder* controls this case. Grants of general corporate power that allow substate governmental entities to participate in a competitive marketplace should be, can be, and typically are used in ways that raise no federal antitrust concerns. As a result, a State that has delegated such general powers "can hardly be said to have 'contemplated' " that they will be used anti-competitively. * * * Thus, while the Law does allow the Authority to acquire hospitals, it does not clearly articulate and affirmatively express a state policy empowering the Authority to make acquisitions of existing hospitals that will substantially lessen competition.

B

* * *

In *Hallie*, we recognized that it would "embod[y] an unrealistic view of how legislatures work and of how statutes are written" to require state legislatures to explicitly authorize specific anticompetitive effects before state-action immunity could apply. "No legislature," we explained, "can be expected to catalog all of the anticipated effects" of a statute delegating authority to a substate governmental entity. Instead, we have approached the clear-articulation inquiry more practically, but without diluting the ultimate requirement that the State must have affirmatively contemplated the displacement of competition such that the challenged anti-competitive effects can be attributed to the "state itself." *Parker*. Thus, we have concluded that a state policy to displace federal antitrust law was sufficiently expressed where the displacement of competition was the inherent, logical, or ordinary result of the exercise of authority delegated by the state legislature. In that scenario, the State must have foreseen and implicitly endorsed the anticompetitive effects as consistent with its policy goals.

For example, in *Hallie*, Wisconsin statutory law regulating the municipal provision of sewage services expressly permitted cities to limit their service to surrounding unincorporated areas. While unincorporated towns alleged that the city's exercise of that power constituted an unlawful tying arrangement, an unlawful refusal to deal, and an abuse of monopoly power, we had no trouble concluding that these alleged anticompetitive effects were affirmatively contemplated by the State because it was "clear" that they "logically would result" from the grant of authority. As described by the Wisconsin Supreme Court, the state legislature " 'viewed annexation by the city of a surrounding unincorporated area as a reasonable quid pro quo that a city could require before extending sewer services to the area.' " Without immunity, federal antitrust law could have undermined that arrangement and taken completely off the table the policy option that the State clearly intended for cities to have.

Similarly, in *Omni*, where the respondents alleged that the city had used its zoning power to protect an incumbent billboard provider against competition, we found that the clear-articulation test was easily satisfied even though the state statutes delegating zoning authority to the city did not explicitly permit the suppression of competition. * * *

By contrast, "simple permission to play in a market" does not "foreseeably entail permission to roughhouse in that market unlawfully." Kay Elec. Cooperative v. Newkirk, 647 F.3d 1039, 1043 (10th Cir. 2011). When a State grants some entity general power to act, whether it is a private corporation or a public entity like the Authority, it does so against the backdrop of federal antitrust law. See *Ticor Title*. Of course, both private parties and local governmental entities conceivably may transgress antitrust requirements by exercising their general powers in anticompetitive ways. But a reasonable legislature's ability to anticipate that (potentially undesirable) possibility falls well short of clearly articulating an affirmative state policy to displace competition with a regulatory alternative.

Believing that this case falls within the scope of the foreseeability standard applied in *Hallie* and *Omni*, the Court of Appeals stated that "[i]t defies imagination to suppose the [state] legislature could have believed that every geographic market in Georgia was so replete with hospitals that authorizing acquisitions by the authorities could have no serious anticompetitive consequences." Respondents echo this argument, noting that each of Georgia's 159 counties covers a small geographical area and that most of them are sparsely populated, with nearly three-quarters having fewer than 50,000 residents as of the 2010 Census.

Even accepting, arguendo, the premise that facts about a market could make the anticompetitive use of general corporate powers "foreseeable," we reject the Court of Appeals' and respondents' conclusion because only a relatively small subset of the conduct permitted as a matter of state law * * * has the potential to negatively affect competition. Contrary to the Court of Appeals' and respondents' characterization, [the Law] is not principally concerned with hospital authorities' ability to acquire multiple hospitals and consolidate their operations. [It] allows authorities to acquire "projects," which includes not only "hospitals," but also "health care facilities, dormitories, office buildings, clinics, housing accommodations, nursing homes, rehabilitation centers, extended care facilities, and other public health facilities." Narrowing our focus to the market for hospital services, the power to acquire hospitals still does not ordinarily produce anticompetitive effects. [The Law] was, after all, the source of power for newly formed hospital authorities to acquire a hospital in the first instance—a transaction that was unlikely to raise any antitrust concerns even in small markets because the transfer of ownership from private to public hands does not increase market concentration. * * * While subsequent acquisitions by authorities have the potential to reduce competition, they will raise federal antitrust concerns only in markets that are large enough to support more than one hospital but sufficiently small that the merger of competitors would lead to a significant increase in market concentration. This is too slender a reed to support the Court of Appeals' and respondents' inference.

IV

A

Taking a somewhat different approach than the Court of Appeals, respondents * * * argue that in view of hospital authorities' statutory objective, their specific attributes, and the regulatory context in which they operate, it was foreseeable that authorities facing capacity constraints would decide they could best serve their communities' needs by acquiring an existing local hospital rather than incur the additional expense and regulatory burden of expanding a facility or constructing a new one.

In support of this argument, respondents observe that hospital authorities are simultaneously empowered to act in ways private entities cannot while also being subject to significant regulatory constraints. * * * [H]ospital authorities are managed by a publicly accountable board, they must operate on a nonprofit basis, and they may only lease a project for others to operate after determining that doing so will promote the community's public health needs and that the lessee will not receive more than a reasonable rate of return on its investment. Moreover, hospital authorities operate within a broader regulatory context in which Georgia requires any party seeking to establish or significantly expand certain medical facilities, including hospitals, to obtain a certificate of need from state regulators.

We have no doubt that Georgia's hospital authorities differ materially from private corporations that offer hospital services. But nothing in the Law or any other provision of Georgia law clearly articulates a state policy to allow authorities to exercise their general corporate powers, including their acquisition power, without regard to negative effects on competition. The state legislature's objective of improving access to affordable health care does not logically suggest that the State intended that hospital authorities pursue that end through mergers that create monopolies. Nor do the restrictions imposed on hospital authorities, including the requirement that they operate on a nonprofit basis, reveal such a policy. * * * The legislature may have viewed profit generation as incompatible with its goal of providing care for the indigent sick. In addition, the legislature may have believed that some hospital authorities would operate in markets with characteristics of natural monopolies in which case the legislature could not rely on competition to control prices.

We recognize that Georgia, particularly through its certificate of need requirement, does limit competition in the market for hospital services in some respects. But regulation of an industry, and even the authorization of discrete forms of anticompetitive conduct pursuant to a regulatory structure, does not establish that the State has affirmatively contemplated other forms of anticompetitive conduct that are only tangentially related. Thus, in Goldfarb v. Virginia State Bar, we rejected a state-action defense to price-fixing claims where a state bar adopted a compulsory minimum fee schedule. Although the State heavily regulated the practice of law, we found no evidence that it had adopted a policy to displace price competition among lawyers. * * *

In this case, the fact that Georgia imposes limits on entry into the market for medical services, which apply to both hospital authorities and private corporations, does not clearly articulate a policy favoring the consolidation of existing hospitals that are engaged in active competition. * * *

B

Finally, respondents contend that to the extent there is any doubt about whether the clear-articulation test is satisfied in this context, federal courts should err on the side of recognizing immunity to avoid improper interference with state policy choices. But we do not find the Law ambiguous on the question whether it clearly articulates a policy authorizing anticompetitive acquisitions; it does not.

More fundamentally, respondents' suggestion is inconsistent with the principle that "state-action immunity is disfavored." *Ticor Title. Parker* and its progeny are premised on an understanding that respect for the States' coordinate role in government counsels against reading the federal antitrust laws to restrict the States' sovereign capacity to regulate their economies and provide services to their citizens. But federalism and state sovereignty are poorly served by a rule of construction that would allow "essential national policies" embodied in the antitrust laws to be displaced by state delegations of authority "intended to achieve more limited ends." As an amici brief filed by 20 States in support of the FTC contends, loose application of the clear-articulation test would attach significant unintended consequences to States' frequent delegations of corporate authority to local bodies, effectively requiring States to disclaim any intent to displace competition to avoid inadvertently authorizing anticompetitive conduct. We decline to set such a trap for unwary state legislatures.

* * *

* * * The judgment of the Court of Appeals is reversed, and the case is remanded for further proceedings consistent with this opinion.

NOTES AND QUESTIONS

1. Are you convinced that the Georgia Legislature did not intend to give the hospital authorities an ability to manage costs by merging small hospitals into more efficient ones?

a. Is the problem that the statute did not affirmatively articulate that intention? Did the earlier cases establish a requirement that the intent to authorize anti-competitive conduct be explicit?

b. Were hospital mergers a "foreseeable result" of creating the hospital authorities? Did the Court of Appeals reasonably read *Omni* as applying that test to the relationship between zoning authority and passing an ordinance limiting the number of billboards?

2. What might lead the Court to give a narrow reading to a hospital authority's power to act anticompetitively?

a. Is health care a field where competition is of particular concern these days? Remember the issues raised by creation of Accountable Care Organizations under the Affordable Care Act.

b. In fields where public agencies and private companies operate side-by-side, might there be concern that public agencies not be able to benefit their private competitors? In this case, for example, for-profit HCA would be able to avoid future competition with Phoebe Putney if the otherwise-illegal merger had been given state action immunity.

3. Whatever the value of *Phoebe Putney* as precedent on state action standards, it had little practical effect on hospital care in Georgia.

a. After the Supreme Court decision, the FTC acknowledged that Georgia's Certificate-of-Need law deems the Albany area "over-bedded," so the merger cannot be unwound.

b.   Phoebe Putney and the Authority have agreed simply not to oppose any other hospital's application to open in the area and to give the FTC prior notice of any transactions they plan, including any transactions with physician practice groups.

WHAT IS "SHAM" LITIGATION?: AN UPDATE ON *NOERR-PENNINGTON*

Omni seems to acknowledge that lobbying for protective state legislation is an entrenched part of our governmental system. So is litigation to confirm and assert one's legal rights. In 1993, the Supreme Court had to decide when such efforts went beyond the protection of the *Noerr-Pennington* doctrine.

Professional Real Estate Investors v. Columbia Pictures Industries, 508 U.S. 49, 113 S.Ct. 1920, 123 L.Ed.2d 611 (1993), was brought by an operator of resort hotels that wanted to rent videodisks to its guests to be played in their rooms. Columbia was not only one of the world's largest producers of motion pictures; it also operated the "Spectradyne" system of pay-per-view movies for hotel rooms. Columbia sued PRE, saying that its disk rental program violated Columbia's copyright on its films; PRE countered that Columbia's lawsuit was an effort to monopolize the industry.

PRE's claims were rejected by the lower courts, relying on *Noerr*. The Supreme Court affirmed. "Whether applying *Noerr* as an antitrust doctrine or invoking it in other contexts," Justice Thomas wrote for the Court, "we have repeatedly reaffirmed that evidence of anticompetitive intent or purpose alone cannot transform otherwise legitimate activity into a sham. * * * In Columbia v. Omni Outdoor Advertising, Inc., we similarly held that challenges to allegedly sham petitioning activity must be resolved according to objective criteria."

Litigation will not be a sham under *Noerr* unless two conditions are met:

> " * * * First, the lawsuit must be objectively baseless in the sense that no reasonable litigant could realistically expect success on the merits. If an objective litigant could conclude that the suit is reasonably calculated to elicit a favorable outcome, the suit is immunized under *Noerr*, and an antitrust claim premised on the sham exception must fail.[267] Only if challenged litigation is

---

[267] A winning lawsuit is by definition a reasonable effort at petitioning for redress and therefore not a sham. On the other hand, when the antitrust defendant has lost the underlying litigation, a court must "resist the understandable temptation to engage in post hoc reasoning by concluding" that an ultimately unsuccessful "action must have been unreasonable or without foundation." Christiansburg Garment Co. v. EEOC, 434 U.S. 412 (1978). The court must remember

objectively meritless may a court examine the litigant's subjective motivation. * * * [Second,] the court should focus on whether the baseless lawsuit conceals "an attempt to interfere *directly* with the business relationships of a competitor," *Noerr* (emphasis added), through the "use [of] the governmental *process*—as opposed to the *outcome* of that process—as an anticompetitive weapon," *Omni* (emphasis in original).

"This two-tiered process requires the plaintiff to disprove the challenged lawsuit's legal viability before the court will entertain evidence of the suit's economic viability. Of course, even a plaintiff who defeats the defendant's claim to *Noerr* immunity by demonstrating both the objective and the subjective components of a sham must still prove a substantive antitrust violation."

Justices Souter, Stevens and O'Connor concurred but considered the Court's rhetoric too sweeping and absolute. The latter two cited Judge Posner's distinction between a suit brought to obtain damages and one brought to burden a competitor.

"Many claims not wholly groundless would never be sued on for their own sake; the stakes, discounted by the probability of winning, would be too low to repay the investment in litigation," Judge Posner had written. He posited a monopolist who "brought a tort action against its single, tiny competitor; the action had a colorable basis in law; but in fact the monopolist would never have brought the suit * * * except that it wanted to use pretrial discovery to discover its competitor's trade secrets; or hoped that the competitor would be required to make public disclosure of its potential liability in the suit and that this disclosure would increase the interest rate that the competitor had to pay for bank financing; or just wanted to impose heavy legal costs on the competitor in the hope of deterring entry by other firms." Grip-Pak, Inc. v. Illinois Tool Works, Inc., 694 F.2d 466 (1982).

What do you think? Should the case described by Judge Posner be deemed a "mere sham" and thus constitute proof of an attempt to monopolize? Was the Court correct in deciding that it never should raise antitrust concerns?

Does the rationale of *Professional Real Estate Investors* also apply where the defendant is accused of making misrepresentations to an administrative agency? Over a vigorous dissent, Armstrong Surgical Center, Inc. v. Armstrong County Memorial Hospital, 185 F.3d 154 (3d Cir.

---

that "even when the law or the facts appear questionable or unfavorable at the outset, a party may have an entirely reasonable ground for bringing suit." [Court's fn. 5]

1999), cert.denied 530 U.S. 1261 (2000), relying heavily on *Omni Outdoor Advertising*, said that it does.[268]

THE FTC'S ATTEMPT TO REIN IN THE TREND TOWARD STATE SPONSORED CARTELS

In recent years, states have increased dramatically the number of occupations that must be licensed and regulated by a state agency, and state professional licensing agencies have become aggressive in their efforts to protect their members from competition. FTC has responded to this growth in state-sponsored cartels by challenging many of the actions taken by state licensing authorities that FTC considers to be blatantly anticompetitive. The following opinion is FTC's greatest success so far in this effort.

NORTH CAROLINA STATE BOARD OF DENTAL EXAMINERS, PETITIONER v. FEDERAL TRADE COMMISSION

Supreme Court of the United States, 2015
___ U.S. ___, 135 S.Ct. 1101, 191 L.Ed.2d 35

KENNEDY, J., delivered the opinion of the Court, in which ROBERTS, C.J., and GINSBURG, BREYER, SOTOMAYOR, and KAGAN, JJ., joined. ALITO, J., filed a dissenting opinion, in which SCALIA and THOMAS, JJ., joined.

JUSTICE KENNEDY delivered the opinion of the Court.

This case arises from an antitrust challenge to the actions of a state regulatory board. A majority of the board's members are engaged in the active practice of the profession it regulates. The question is whether the board's actions are protected from Sherman Act regulation under the doctrine of state-action antitrust immunity, as defined and applied in this Court's decisions beginning with *Parker v. Brown.*

I

A

In its Dental Practice Act (Act), North Carolina has declared the practice of dentistry to be a matter of public concern requiring regulation. Under the Act, the North Carolina State Board of Dental Examiners (Board) is "the agency of the State for the regulation of the practice of dentistry."

---

[268] This and related issues are discussed in C. Douglas Floyd, Antitrust Liability for the Anticompetitive Effects of Governmental Action Induced by Fraud, 69 Antitrust L. J. 403 (2001). See also, Marina Lao, Reforming the *Noerr-Pennington* Antitrust Immunity Doctrine, 55 Rutgers L. Rev. 965 (2003).

The Board's principal duty is to create, administer, and enforce a licensing system for dentists. To perform that function it has broad authority over licensees. The Board's authority with respect to unlicensed persons, however, is more restricted: like "any resident citizen," the Board may file suit to "perpetually enjoin any person from . . . unlawfully practicing dentistry."

The Act provides that six of the Board's eight members must be licensed dentists engaged in the active practice of dentistry. They are elected by other licensed dentists in North Carolina, who cast their ballots in elections conducted by the Board. The seventh member must be a licensed and practicing dental hygienist, and he or she is elected by other licensed hygienists. The final member is referred to by the Act as a "consumer" and is appointed by the Governor. All members serve 3-year terms, and no person may serve more than two consecutive terms. The Act does not create any mechanism for the removal of an elected member of the Board by a public official.

The Board may promulgate rules and regulations governing the practice of dentistry within the State, provided those mandates are not inconsistent with the Act and are approved by the North Carolina Rules Review Commission, whose members are appointed by the state legislature.

B

In the 1990's, dentists in North Carolina started whitening teeth. Many of those who did so, including 8 of the Board's 10 members during the period at issue in this case, earned substantial fees for that service. By 2003, nondentists arrived on the scene. They charged lower prices for their services than the dentists did. Dentists soon began to complain to the Board about their new competitors. Few complaints warned of possible harm to consumers. Most expressed a principal concern with the low prices charged by nondentists.

Responding to these filings, the Board opened an investigation into nondentist teeth whitening. A dentist member was placed in charge of the inquiry. Neither the Board's hygienist member nor its consumer member participated in this undertaking. The Board's chief operations officer remarked that the Board was "going forth to do battle" with nondentists. The Board's concern did not result in a formal rule or regulation reviewable by the independent Rules Review Commission, even though the Act does not, by its terms, specify that teeth whitening is "the practice of dentistry."

Starting in 2006, the Board issued at least 47 cease-and-desist letters on its official letterhead to nondentist teeth whitening service providers and product manufacturers. Many of those letters directed the recipient to cease "all activity constituting the practice of dentistry"; warned that the unlicensed practice of dentistry is a crime; and strongly implied (or expressly stated) that teeth whitening constitutes "the practice of dentistry." In early 2007, the Board persuaded the North Carolina Board of Cosmetic Art Examiners to warn cosmetologists against providing teeth whitening services. Later that year, the Board sent letters to mall operators, stating that kiosk teeth whiteners were violating the Dental Practice Act and advising that the malls consider expelling violators from their premises.

These actions had the intended result. Nondentists ceased offering teeth whitening services in North Carolina.

C

In 2010, the Federal Trade Commission (FTC) filed an administrative complaint charging the Board with violating § 5 of the Federal Trade Commission Act. The FTC alleged that the Board's concerted action to exclude nondentists from the market for teeth whitening services in North Carolina constituted an anticompetitive and unfair method of competition. The Board moved to dismiss, alleging state-action immunity. An Administrative Law Judge (ALJ) denied the motion. On appeal, the FTC sustained the ALJ's ruling. It reasoned that, even assuming the Board had acted pursuant to a clearly articulated state policy to displace competition, the Board is a "public/private hybrid" that must be actively supervised by the State to claim immunity. The FTC further concluded the Board could not make that showing.

Following other proceedings not relevant here, the ALJ conducted a hearing on the merits and determined the Board had unreasonably restrained trade in violation of antitrust law. On appeal, the FTC again sustained the ALJ. The FTC rejected the Board's public safety justification, noting, *inter alia,* "a wealth of evidence . . . suggesting that non-dentist provided teeth whitening is a safe cosmetic procedure."

The FTC ordered the Board to stop sending the cease-and-desist letters or other communications that stated nondentists may not offer teeth whitening services and products. It further ordered the Board to issue notices to all earlier recipients of the Board's cease-and-desist orders advising them of the Board's proper sphere of authority and saying, among other options, that the notice recipients had a right to seek declaratory rulings in state court.

On petition for review, the Court of Appeals for the Fourth Circuit affirmed the FTC in all respects. This Court granted certiorari.

II

Federal antitrust law is a central safeguard for the Nation's free market structures. In this regard it is "as important to the preservation of economic freedom and our free-enterprise system as the Bill of Rights is to the protection of our fundamental personal freedoms." The antitrust laws declare a considered and decisive prohibition by the Federal Government of cartels, price fixing, and other combinations or practices that undermine the free market.

The Sherman Act serves to promote robust competition, which in turn empowers the States and provides their citizens with opportunities to pursue their own and the public's welfare. The States, however, when acting in their respective realm, need not adhere in all contexts to a model of unfettered competition. While "the States regulate their economies in many ways not inconsistent with the antitrust laws,", in some spheres they impose restrictions on occupations, confer exclusive or shared rights to dominate a market, or otherwise limit competition to achieve public objectives. If every duly enacted state law or policy were required to conform to the mandates of the Sherman Act, thus promoting competition at the expense of other values a State may deem fundamental, federal antitrust law would impose an impermissible burden on the States' power to regulate.

For these reasons, the Court in *Parker v. Brown* interpreted the antitrust laws to confer immunity on anticompetitive conduct by the States when acting in their sovereign capacity. That ruling recognized Congress' purpose to respect the federal balance and to "embody in the Sherman Act the federalism principle that the States possess a significant measure of sovereignty under our Constitution." Since 1943, the Court has reaffirmed the importance of *Parker* 's central holding.

III

In this case the Board argues its members were invested by North Carolina with the power of the State and that, as a result, the Board's actions are cloaked with *Parker* immunity. This argument fails, however. A nonsovereign actor controlled by active market participants—such as the Board—enjoys *Parker* immunity only if it satisfies two requirements: "first that 'the challenged restraint . . . be one clearly articulated and affirmatively expressed as state policy,' and second that 'the policy . . . be actively supervised by the State.' " The parties have assumed that the clear articulation requirement is satisfied, and we do the same. While North Carolina prohibits the unauthorized practice of dentistry, however, its Act is silent on whether that broad prohibition covers teeth whitening. Here, the Board did not receive active supervision by the State when it interpreted the Act as addressing teeth whitening and when it enforced that policy by issuing cease-and-desist letters to nondentist teeth whiteners.

A

Although state-action immunity exists to avoid conflicts between state sovereignty and the Nation's commitment to a policy of robust competition, *Parker* immunity is not unbounded. "[G]iven the fundamental national values of free enterprise and economic competition that are embodied in the federal antitrust laws, 'state action immunity is disfavored, much as are repeals by implication.' "

An entity may not invoke *Parker* immunity unless the actions in question are an exercise of the State's sovereign power. State legislation and "decision[s] of a state supreme court, acting legislatively rather than judicially," will satisfy this standard, and "*ipso facto* are exempt from the operation of the antitrust laws" because they are an undoubted exercise of state sovereign authority.

But while the Sherman Act confers immunity on the States' own anticompetitive policies out of respect for federalism, it does not always confer immunity where, as here, a State delegates control over a market to a non-sovereign actor. For purposes of *Parker,* a nonsovereign actor is one whose conduct does not automatically qualify as that of the sovereign State itself. State agencies are not simply by their governmental character sovereign actors for purposes of state-action immunity. Immunity for state agencies, therefore, requires more than a mere facade of state involvement, for it is necessary in light of *Parker* 's rationale to ensure the States accept political accountability for anticompetitive conduct they permit and control.

Limits on state-action immunity are most essential when the State seeks to delegate its regulatory power to active market participants, for established ethical standards may blend with private anticompetitive motives in a way difficult even for market participants to discern. Dual allegiances are not always apparent to an actor. In consequence, active market participants cannot be allowed to regulate their own markets free from antitrust accountability. "The national policy in favor of competition cannot be thwarted by casting [a] gauzy cloak of state involvement over what is essentially a private price-fixing arrangement". Indeed, prohibitions against anticompetitive self-regulation by active market participants are an axiom of federal antitrust policy. So it follows that, under *Parker* and the Supremacy Clause, the States' greater power to attain an end does not include the lesser power to negate the congressional judgment embodied in the Sherman Act through unsupervised delegations to active market participants.

Parker immunity requires that the anticompetitive conduct of nonsovereign actors, especially those authorized by the State to regulate their own profession, result from procedures that suffice to make it the State's own. The question is not whether the challenged conduct is efficient, well-functioning, or wise. Rather, it is "whether anticompetitive conduct engaged in by [nonsovereign actors] should be deemed state action and thus shielded from the antitrust laws."

To answer this question, the Court applies the two-part test set forth in, a case arising from California's delegation of price-fixing authority to wine merchants. Under *Midcal,* "[a] state law or regulatory scheme cannot be the basis for antitrust immunity unless, first, the State has articulated a clear policy to allow the anticompetitive conduct, and second, the State provides active supervision of [the] anticompetitive conduct."

Midcal's clear articulation requirement is satisfied "where the displacement of competition [is] the inherent, logical, or ordinary result of the exercise of authority delegated by the state legislature. In that scenario, the State must have foreseen and implicitly endorsed the anticompetitive effects as consistent with its policy goals." The active supervision requirement demands, *inter alia,* "that state officials have and exercise power to review particular anticompetitive acts of private parties and disapprove those that fail to accord with state policy."

The two requirements set forth in *Midcal* provide a proper analytical framework to resolve the ultimate question whether an anticompetitive policy is indeed the policy of a State. The first requirement—clear articulation—rarely will achieve that goal by itself, for a policy may satisfy this test yet still be defined at so high a level of generality as to leave open critical questions about how and to what extent the market should be regulated. Entities purporting to act under state authority might diverge from the State's considered definition of the public good. The resulting asymmetry between a state policy and its implementation can invite private self-dealing. The second *Midcal* requirement—active supervision—seeks to avoid this harm by requiring the State to review and approve interstitial policies made by the entity claiming immunity.

Midcal's supervision rule "stems from the recognition that '[w]here a private party is engaging in anticompetitive activity, there is a real danger that he is acting to further his own interests, rather than the governmental interests of the State.'" Concern about the private incentives of active market participants animates *Midcal's* supervision mandate, which demands "realistic assurance that a private party's anticompetitive conduct promotes state policy, rather than merely the party's individual interests."

B

In determining whether anticompetitive policies and conduct are indeed the action of a State in its sovereign capacity, there are instances in which an actor can be excused from *Midcal's* active supervision requirement. In *Hallie v. Eau Claire,* the Court held municipalities are subject exclusively to *Midcal's* "'clear articulation'" requirement. That rule, the Court observed, is consistent with the objective of ensuring that the policy at issue be one enacted by the State itself. *Hallie* explained that "[w]here the actor is a municipality, there is little or no danger that it is involved in a private price-fixing arrangement. The only real danger is that it will seek to further purely parochial public interests at the expense of more overriding state goals." *Hallie* further observed that municipalities are electorally accountable and lack the kind of private incentives characteristic of active participants in the market. Critically, the municipality in *Hallie* exercised a wide range of governmental powers across different economic spheres, substantially reducing the risk that it would pursue private interests while regulating any single field. That *Hallie* excused municipalities from *Midcal*'s supervision rule for these reasons all but confirms the rule's applicability to actors controlled by active market participants, who ordinarily have none of the features justifying the narrow exception *Hallie* identified.

Following *Goldfarb, Midcal,* and *Hallie,* which clarified the conditions under which *Parker* immunity attaches to the conduct of a nonsovereign actor, the Court in *Columbia v. Omni Outdoor Advertising, Inc.* addressed whether an otherwise immune entity could lose immunity for conspiring with private parties. In *Omni,* an aspiring billboard merchant argued that the city of Columbia, South Carolina, had violated the Sherman Act—and forfeited its *Parker* immunity—by anticompetitively conspiring with an established local company in passing an ordinance restricting new billboard construction. The Court disagreed, holding there is no "conspiracy exception" to *Parker.*

Omni, like the cases before it, recognized the importance of drawing a line "relevant to the purposes of the Sherman Act and of *Parker*: prohibiting the restriction of competition for private gain but permitting the restriction of competition in the public interest." In the context of a municipal actor which, as in *Hallie,* exercised substantial governmental powers, *Omni* rejected a conspiracy exception for "corruption" as vague and unworkable, since "virtually all regulation benefits some segments of the society and harms others" and may in that sense be seen as " 'corrupt.' " *Omni* also rejected subjective tests for corruption that would force a "deconstruction of the governmental process and probing of the official 'intent' that we have consistently sought to avoid." Thus, whereas the cases preceding it addressed the preconditions of *Parker* immunity and engaged in an objective, *ex ante* inquiry into nonsovereign actors' structure and incentives, *Omni* made clear that recipients of immunity will not lose it on the basis of ad hoc and *ex post* questioning of their motives for making particular decisions.

Omni's holding makes it all the more necessary to ensure the conditions for granting immunity are met in the first place. The Court's two state-action immunity cases decided after *Omni* reinforce this point. In *Ticor* the Court affirmed that *Midcal*'s limits on delegation must ensure that "[a]ctual state involvement, not deference to private price-fixing arrangements under the general auspices of state law, is the precondition for immunity from federal law." And in *Phoebe Putney* the Court observed that *Midcal's* active supervision requirement, in particular, is an essential condition of state-action immunity when a nonsovereign actor has "an incentive to pursue [its] own self-interest under the guise of implementing state policies." The lesson is clear: *Midcal's* active supervision test is an essential prerequisite of *Parker* immunity for any nonsovereign entity—public or private—controlled by active market participants.

C

The Board argues entities designated by the States as agencies are exempt from *Midcal's* second requirement. That premise, however, cannot be reconciled with the Court's repeated conclusion that the need for supervision turns not on the formal designation given by States to regulators but on the risk that active market participants will pursue private interests in restraining trade.

State agencies controlled by active market participants, who possess singularly strong private interests, pose the very risk of self-dealing *Midcal's* supervision requirement was created to address. This conclusion does not question the good faith of state officers but rather is an assessment of the structural risk of market participants' confusing their own interests with the State's policy goals.

The Court applied this reasoning to a state agency in *Goldfarb*. There the Court denied immunity to a state agency (the Virginia State Bar) controlled by market participants (lawyers) because the agency had "joined in what is essentially a private anticompetitive activity" for "the benefit of its members." This emphasis on the Bar's private interests explains why *Goldfarb*, though it predates *Midcal*, considered the lack of supervision by the Virginia Supreme Court to be a principal reason for denying immunity.

While *Hallie* stated "it is likely that active state supervision would also not be required" for agencies, the entity there, as was later the case in *Omni*, was an electorally accountable municipality with general regulatory powers and no private price-fixing agenda. In that and other respects the municipality was more like prototypical state agencies, not specialized boards dominated by active market participants. In important regards, agencies controlled by market participants are more similar to private trade associations vested by States with regulatory authority than to the agencies *Hallie* considered. And as the Court observed three years after *Hallie*, "[t]here is no doubt that the members of such associations often have economic incentives to restrain competition and that the product standards set by such associations have a serious potential for anticompetitive harm." For that reason, those associations must satisfy *Midcal*'s active supervision standard.

The similarities between agencies controlled by active market participants and private trade associations are not eliminated simply because the former are given a formal designation by the State, vested with a measure of government power, and required to follow some procedural rules. *Parker* immunity does not derive from nomenclature alone. When a State empowers a group of active market participants to decide who can participate in its market, and on what terms, the need for supervision is manifest. The Court holds today that a state board on which a controlling number of decisionmakers are active market participants in the occupation the board regulates must satisfy *Midcal*'s active supervision requirement in order to invoke state-action antitrust immunity.

D

The State argues that allowing this FTC order to stand will discourage dedicated citizens from serving on state agencies that regulate their own occupation. If this were so—and, for reasons to be noted, it need not be so—there would be some cause for concern. The States have a sovereign interest in structuring their governments, and may conclude there are substantial benefits to staffing their agencies with experts in complex and technical subjects. There is, moreover, a long tradition of citizens esteemed by their professional colleagues devoting time, energy, and talent to enhancing the dignity of their calling.

Adherence to the idea that those who pursue a calling must embrace ethical standards that derive from a duty separate from the dictates of the State reaches back at least to the Hippocratic Oath. In the United States, there is a strong tradition of professional self-regulation, particularly with respect to the development of ethical rules. Dentists are no exception. The American Dental Association, for example, in an exercise of "the privilege and obligation of self-government," has "call[ed] upon dentists to follow high ethical standards," including "honesty, compassion, kindness, integrity, fairness and charity." State laws and institutions are sustained by this tradition when they draw upon the expertise and commitment of professionals.

Today's holding is not inconsistent with that idea. The Board argues, however, that the potential for money damages will discourage members of regulated occupations from participating in state government. But this case, which does not present a claim for money damages, does not offer occasion to address the question whether agency officials, including board members, may, under some circumstances, enjoy immunity from damages liability. And, of course, the States may provide for the defense and indemnification of agency members in the event of litigation.

States, furthermore, can ensure *Parker* immunity is available to agencies by adopting clear policies to displace competition; and, if agencies controlled by active market participants interpret or enforce those policies, the States may provide active supervision. Precedent confirms this principle. The Court has rejected the argument that it would be unwise to apply the antitrust laws to professional regulation absent compliance with the prerequisites for invoking *Parker* immunity ... The reasoning of *Patrick v. Burget* applies to this case with full force, particularly in light of the risks licensing boards dominated by market participants may pose to the free market. The Board does not contend in this Court that its anticompetitive conduct was actively supervised by the State or that it should receive *Parker* immunity on that basis.

By statute, North Carolina delegates control over the practice of dentistry to the Board. The Act, however, says nothing about teeth whitening, a practice that did not exist when it was passed. After receiving complaints from other dentists about the nondentists' cheaper services, the Board's dentist members—some of whom offered whitening services— acted to expel the dentists' competitors from the market. In so doing the Board relied upon cease-and-desist letters threatening criminal liability, rather than any of the powers at its disposal that would invoke oversight by a politically accountable official. With no active supervision by the State, North Carolina officials may well have been unaware that the Board had decided teeth whitening constitutes "the practice of dentistry" and sought to prohibit those who competed against dentists from participating in the teeth whitening market. Whether or not the Board exceeded its powers under North Carolina law, there is no evidence here of any decision by the State to initiate or concur with the Board's actions against the nondentists.

IV

The Board does not claim that the State exercised active, or indeed any, supervision over its conduct regarding nondentist teeth whiteners; and, as a result, no specific supervisory systems can be reviewed here. It suffices to note that the inquiry regarding active supervision is flexible and context-dependent. Active supervision need not entail day-to-day involvement in an agency's operations or micromanagement of its every decision. Rather, the question is whether the State's review mechanisms provide "realistic assurance" that a nonsovereign actor's anticompetitive conduct "promotes state policy, rather than merely the party's individual interests."

The Court has identified only a few constant requirements of active supervision: The supervisor must review the substance of the anticompetitive decision, not merely the procedures followed to produce it, the supervisor must have the power to veto or modify particular decisions to ensure they accord with state policy, and the "mere potential for state supervision is not an adequate substitute for a decision by the State," Further, the state supervisor may not itself be an active market participant. In general, however, the adequacy of supervision otherwise will depend on all the circumstances of a case.

* * *

The Sherman Act protects competition while also respecting federalism. It does not authorize the States to abandon markets to the unsupervised control of active market participants, whether trade associations or hybrid agencies. If a State wants to rely on active market participants as regulators, it must provide active supervision if state-action immunity under *Parker* is to be invoked.

The judgment of the Court of Appeals for the Fourth Circuit is affirmed.

It is so ordered.

JUSTICE ALITO, with whom JUSTICE SCALIA and JUSTICE THOMAS join, dissenting.

The Court's decision in this case is based on a serious misunderstanding of the doctrine of state-action antitrust immunity that this Court recognized more than 60 years ago in *Parker v. Brown.* In *Parker,* the Court held that the Sherman Act does not prevent the States from continuing their age-old practice of enacting measures, such as licensing requirements, that are designed to protect the public health and welfare. It is precisely this type of state regulation—North Carolina's laws governing the practice of dentistry, which are administered by the North Carolina Board of Dental Examiners.

Today, however, the Court takes the unprecedented step of holding that *Parker* does not apply to the North Carolina Board because the Board is not structured in a way that merits a good-government seal of approval; that is, it is made up of practicing dentists who have a financial incentive to use the licensing laws to further the financial interests of the State's dentists. There is nothing new about the structure of the North Carolina Board. When the States first created medical and dental boards, well before the Sherman Act was enacted, they began to staff them in this way. Nor is there anything new about the suspicion that the North Carolina Board—in attempting to prevent persons other than dentists from performing teeth-whitening procedures—was serving the interests of dentists and not the public. Professional and occupational licensing requirements have often been used in such a way. But that is not what *Parker* immunity is about. Indeed, the very state program involved in that case was unquestionably designed to benefit the regulated entities, California raisin growers.

The question before us is not whether such programs serve the public interest. The question, instead, is whether this case is controlled by *Parker,* and the answer to that question is clear. Under *Parker,* the Sherman Act and the Federal Trade Commission Act do not apply to state agencies; the North Carolina Board of Dental Examiners is a state agency; and that is the end of the matter. By straying from this simple path, the Court has not only distorted *Parker*; it has headed into a morass. Determining whether a state agency is structured in a way that militates against regulatory capture is no easy task, and there is reason to fear that today's decision will spawn confusion. The Court has veered off course, and therefore I cannot go along.

I

In order to understand the nature of *Parker* state-action immunity, it is helpful to recall the constitutional landscape in 1890 when the Sherman Act was enacted. At that time, this Court and Congress had an understanding of the scope of federal and state power that is very different from our understanding today. The States were understood to possess the exclusive authority to regulate "their purely internal affairs." In exercising their police power in this area, the States had long enacted measures, such as price controls and licensing requirements, that had the effect of restraining trade.

The Sherman Act was enacted pursuant to Congress' power to regulate interstate commerce, and in passing the Act, Congress wanted to exercise that power "to the utmost extent." But in 1890, the understanding of the commerce power was far more limited than it is today. As a result, the Act did not pose a threat to traditional state regulatory activity.

By 1943, when *Parker* was decided, however, the situation had changed dramatically. This Court had held that the commerce power permitted Congress to regulate even local activity if it "exerts a substantial economic effect on interstate commerce." This meant that Congress could regulate many of the matters that had once been thought to fall exclusively within the jurisdiction of the States. The new interpretation of the commerce power brought about an expansion of the reach of the Sherman Act. And the expanded reach of the Sherman Act raised an important question. The Sherman Act does not expressly exempt States from its scope. Does that mean that the Act applies to the States and that it potentially outlaws many traditional state regulatory measures? The Court confronted that question in *Parker*.

In *Parker,* a raisin producer challenged the California Agricultural Prorate Act, an agricultural price support program. The California Act authorized the creation of an Agricultural Prorate Advisory Commission to establish marketing plans for certain agricultural commodities within the State. Raisins were among the regulated commodities, and so the Commission established a marketing program that governed many aspects of raisin sales, including the quality and quantity of raisins sold, the timing of sales, and the price at which raisins were sold. The *Parker* Court assumed that this program would have violated "the Sherman Act if it were organized and made effective solely by virtue of a contract, combination or conspiracy of private persons," and the Court also assumed that Congress could have prohibited a State from creating a program like California's if it had chosen to do so. Nevertheless, the Court concluded that the California program did not violate the Sherman Act because the Act did not circumscribe state regulatory power.

The Court's holding in *Parker* was not based on either the language of the Sherman Act or anything in the legislative history affirmatively showing that the Act was not meant to apply to the States. Instead, the Court reasoned that "[i]n a dual system of government in which, under the Constitution, the states are sovereign, save only as Congress may constitutionally subtract from their authority, an unexpressed purpose to nullify a state's control over its officers and agents is not lightly to be attributed to Congress." For the Congress that enacted the Sherman Act in 1890, it would have been a truly radical and almost certainly futile step to attempt to prevent the States from exercising their traditional regulatory authority, and the *Parker* Court refused to assume that the Act was meant to have such an effect.

When the basis for the *Parker* state-action doctrine is understood, the Court's error in this case is plain. In 1890, the regulation of the practice of medicine and dentistry was regarded as falling squarely within the States' sovereign police power. By that time, many States had established medical and dental boards, often staffed by doctors or dentists, and had given those boards the authority to confer and revoke licenses. This was quintessential police power legislation, and although state laws were often challenged during that era under the doctrine of substantive due process, the licensing of medical professionals easily survived such assaults. . . . Thus, the North Carolina statutes establishing and specifying the powers of the State Board of Dental Examiners represent precisely the kind of state regulation that the *Parker* exemption was meant to immunize.

II

As noted above, the only question in this case is whether the North Carolina Board of Dental Examiners is really a state agency, and the answer to that question is clearly yes.

. . . North Carolina's Board of Dental Examiners is unmistakably a state agency created by the state legislature to serve a prescribed regulatory purpose and to do so using the State's power in cooperation with other arms of state government.

The Board is not a private or "nonsovereign" entity that the State of North Carolina has attempted to immunize from federal antitrust scrutiny. . . . North Carolina did not authorize a private entity to enter into an anticompetitive arrangement; rather, North Carolina *created a state agency* and gave that agency the power to regulate a particular subject affecting public health and safety.

Nothing in *Parker* supports the type of inquiry that the Court now prescribes. The Court crafts a test under which state agencies that are "controlled by active market participants" must demonstrate active state supervision in order to be immune from federal antitrust law. The Court thus treats these state agencies like private entities. But in *Parker,* the Court did not examine the structure of the California program to determine if it had been captured by private interests. If the Court had done so, the case would certainly have come out differently, because California conditioned its regulatory measures on the participation and approval of market actors in the relevant industry.

Establishing a prorate marketing plan under California's law first required the petition of at least 10 producers of the particular commodity. If the Commission then agreed that a marketing plan was warranted, the Commission would "select a program committee *from among nominees chosen by the qualified producers.*" That committee would then formulate the proration marketing program, which the Commission could modify or approve. But even after Commission approval, the program became law (and then, automatically) only if it gained the approval of 65 percent of the relevant producers, representing at least 51 percent of the acreage of the regulated crop. This scheme gave decisive power to market participants. But despite these aspects of the California program, *Parker* held that California was acting as a "sovereign" when it "adopt[ed] and enforc[ed] the prorate program." This reasoning is irreconcilable with the Court's today.

III

The Court goes astray because it forgets the origin of the *Parker* doctrine and is misdirected by subsequent cases that extended that doctrine (in certain circumstances) to private entities.

This case [involves the action of a state agency] . . . , and therefore *Midcal* is inapposite. The North Carolina Board is not a private trade association. It is a state agency, created and empowered by the State to regulate an industry affecting public health. It would not exist if the State had not created it. And for purposes of *Parker,* its membership is irrelevant; what matters is that it is part of the government of the sovereign State of North Carolina.

* * *

The Court's analysis seems to be predicated on an assessment of the varying degrees to which a municipality and a state agency like the North Carolina Board are likely to be captured by private interests. But until today, *Parker* immunity was never conditioned on the proper use of state regulatory authority.

IV

Not only is the Court's decision inconsistent with the underlying theory of *Parker*; it will create practical problems and is likely to have far-reaching effects on the States' regulation of professions. As previously noted, state medical and dental boards have been staffed by practitioners since they were first created, and there are obvious advantages to this approach. It is reasonable for States to decide that the individuals best able to regulate technical professions are practitioners with expertise in those very professions. Staffing the State Board of Dental Examiners with certified public accountants would certainly lessen the risk of actions that place the well-being of dentists over those of the public, but this would also compromise the State's interest in sensibly regulating a technical profession in which lay people have little expertise.

As a result of today's decision, States may find it necessary to change the composition of medical, dental, and other boards, but it is not clear what sort of changes are needed to satisfy the test that the Court now adopts. The Court faults the structure of the North Carolina Board because "active market participants" constitute "a controlling number of [the] decisionmakers," but this test raises many questions.

NOTES AND QUESTIONS

1.   The majority gives states two ways of continuing to regulate occupations. They can change the composition of the licensing boards so that they are no longer "controlled" by practitioners of the occupation or they can subject them to "active supervision" by other state officials who have no conflict of interest. Identify the advantages and disadvantages of each approach. Which do you prefer?

2.   Are the dissenting Justices right when they argue that the California Raisin Board at issue in *Parker* could not survive the majority's test?

3.   Until this case was decided, most people believed that the state action doctrine was created by the Court and could be changed or eliminated by the Court. The dissenting Justices argue that the doctrine is required by the Constitution. What would be the results if a majority of Justices adopt the reasoning of the dissenting Justices.

4.   THE STATE OF THE INTERSTATE COMMERCE REQUIREMENT

Summit Health, Ltd. v. Pinhas, 500 U.S. 322, 111 S.Ct. 1842, 114 L.Ed.2d 366 (1991), involved another doctor who had lost his hospital privileges, this time an ophthalmologist who refused to use a second doctor in the operating room during eye surgery. He said he believed the practice unnecessarily padded patients' bills and was required as a way to keep less skilled doctors employed. The hospital defended in part by saying that termination of a single California doctor by a single California hospital for conduct that occurred only in California had insufficient effect on interstate commerce to create Sherman Act jurisdiction.

A majority of the Court disagreed with the hospital, citing McLain v. Real Estate Bd. of New Orleans, Inc., 444 U.S. 232, 100 S.Ct. 502, 62 L.Ed.2d 441 (1980). As a "matter of practical economics," the activities of a hospital in purchasing medicine and supplies and accepting reimbursement from out-of-state insurance companies establish "the necessary interstate nexus." Further, even if termination of a single doctor might not have measurable interstate effects, that could not defeat jurisdiction any more than it had when a single merchant had been the victim of a boycott in *Klor's*. "The competitive significance of respondent's exclusion from the market must be measured," the Court said, quoting *McLain*, "not just by a particularized evaluation of his own practice, but rather, by a general evaluation of the impact of the restraint on other participants and potential participants in the market from which he has been excluded."

The surprise was not the majority opinion but the fact that four justices—Justices Scalia, O'Connor, Kennedy and Souter—dissented. The issue, Justice Scalia wrote, is not whether Congress could reach this conduct, but whether the Sherman Act does so. The Act prohibits only conduct "in restraint of trade or commerce among the several States." This, the dissenters said, "commands a judicial inquiry into the nature and potential effect of each particular restraint." The boycott in *Klor's* had prevented shipments of appliances across state lines. In this case, even if the hospital had hired someone to kill Dr. Pinhas—i.e., exclude him from the market forever—the dissenters said, "it would be absurd to think" that the economic effects would be felt outside California. Do you agree?

F. APPLYING ANTITRUST LAW TO CONDUCT THAT CROSSES NATIONAL BORDERS

1. U.S. JURISDICTION OVER ACTS IN FOREIGN COMMERCE

The days in which *American Banana*, discussed in Chapter I, limited the reach of the antitrust laws are long over. Since at least Judge Hand's opinion in the *Alcoa* case in 1945, it has been enough for antitrust jurisdiction that conduct outside U.S. borders be "shown actually to have some effects" on U.S. exports or imports.

Thus, it should not be surprising that price fixing by a cartel of non-U.S. vitamin producers that affected sales in the United States was charged as a violation of Sherman Act § 1. In 1999, the Justice Department obtained guilty pleas from some of the world's largest vitamin producers for that conduct. The large Swiss pharmaceutical firm, F. Hoffman-LaRoche, Ltd., paid a fine of $500 million and one its executives served a 4-month prison term. The German producer, BASF Aktiengesellschaft, paid a fine of $225 million. Japanese producer, Takeda Chemical Industries, Ltd., paid $72 million. Large private class action civil cases followed the criminal convictions.[269]

Similar civil and criminal prosecutions of foreign producers in U.S. courts have followed for cartels ranging from citric acid to copper to fine arts. The jurisdictional standard now used in the Foreign Trade Antitrust Improvements Act of 1982, 15 U.S.C. § 6a, is that the conduct have "a direct, substantial, and reasonably foreseeable effect" on U.S. domestic commerce, imports or exports.

Two key questions have arisen in recent years about the reach of U.S. law. The first returns us to an issue we had put off earlier. How does the Sherman Act apply to concerted action that is permitted or mandated, not by a U.S. state, but by another national sovereign? Our next case gave what is still the most authoritative current answer.

HARTFORD FIRE INSURANCE CO. v. CALIFORNIA

Supreme Court of the United States, 1993
509 U.S. 764, 113 S.Ct. 2891, 125 L.Ed.2d 612

JUSTICE SOUTER * * * delivered the opinion of the Court * * * .

* * * These consolidated cases present questions about the application of [the Sherman] Act to the insurance industry, both here and abroad. The plaintiffs (respondents here) allege that both domestic and foreign defendants (petitioners here) violated the Sherman Act by engaging in various conspiracies to affect the American insurance market. * * * We hold that * * * the principle of international comity does not preclude District Court jurisdiction over the foreign conduct alleged.

I

The two petitions before us stem from consolidated litigation comprising the complaints of 19 States and many private plaintiffs alleging that the defendants, members of the insurance industry, conspired in violation of § 1 of the Sherman Act to restrict the terms of coverage of commercial general liability (CGL) insurance available in the United States. Because the cases come to us on motions to dismiss, we take the allegations of the complaints as true.

---

[269] See, e.g., Harry First, The Vitamins Case: Cartel Prosecutions and the Coming of International Competition Law, 68 Antitrust L. J. 711 (2001). See also, Margaret Levenstein & Valerie Y. Suslow, Contemporary International Cartels and Developing Countries: Economic Effects and Implications for Competition Policy, 71 Antitrust L.J. 801 (2004).

A

According to the complaints, the object of the conspiracies was to force certain primary insurers (insurers who sell insurance directly to consumers) to change the terms of their standard CGL insurance policies to conform with the policies the defendant insurers wanted to sell. The defendants wanted four changes.

First, CGL insurance has traditionally been sold in the United States on an "occurrence" basis, through a policy obligating the insurer "to pay or defend claims, whenever made, resulting from an * * * [event] that occurred during the * * * period the policy was in effect." In place of this traditional "occurrence" trigger of coverage, the defendants wanted a "claims-made" trigger, obligating the insurer to pay or defend only those claims made during the policy period. Such a policy has the distinct advantage for the insurer that when the policy period ends without a claim having been made, the insurer can be certain that the policy will not expose it to any further liability. Second, the defendants wanted the "claims-made" policy to have a "retroactive date" provision, which would further restrict coverage to claims based on incidents that occurred after a certain date. Such a provision eliminates the risk that an insurer, by issuing a claims-made policy, would assume liability arising from incidents that occurred before the policy's effective date, but remained undiscovered or caused no immediate harm. Third, CGL insurance has traditionally covered "sudden and accidental" pollution; the defendants wanted to eliminate that coverage. Finally, CGL insurance has traditionally provided that the insurer would bear the legal costs of defending covered claims against the insured without regard to the policy's stated limits of coverage; the defendants wanted legal defense costs to be counted against the stated limits (providing a "legal defense cost cap").

To understand how the defendants are alleged to have pressured the targeted primary insurers to make these changes, one must be aware of two important features of the insurance industry. First, most primary insurers rely on certain outside support services for the type of insurance coverage they wish to sell. Defendant Insurance Services Office, Inc. (ISO), an association of approximately 1,400 domestic property and casualty insurers (including the primary insurer defendants * * *), is the almost exclusive source of support services in this country for CGL insurance. ISO develops standard policy forms and files or lodges them with each State's insurance regulators; most CGL insurance written in the United States is written on these forms. All of the "traditional" features of CGL insurance relevant to this case were embodied in the ISO standard CGL insurance form that had been in use since 1973 * * * . For each of its standard policy forms, ISO also supplies actuarial and rating information * * * . Most ISO members cannot afford to continue to use a form if ISO withdraws these support services.

Second, primary insurers themselves usually purchase insurance to cover a portion of the risk they assume from the consumer. This so-called "reinsurance" may serve at least two purposes, protecting the primary insurer from catastrophic loss, and allowing the primary insurer to sell more insurance than its own financial capacity might otherwise permit. Thus, "the availability of reinsurance affects the ability and willingness of primary insurers to provide insurance to their customers." * * * Many of the defendants here are reinsurers or * * * play some other specialized role in the reinsurance business * * * .

B

The prehistory of events claimed to give rise to liability starts in 1977, when ISO began the process of revising its 1973 CGL form. For the first time, it proposed two CGL forms (1984 ISO CGL forms), one the traditional "occurrence" type, the other "with a new 'claims-made' trigger." The "claims-made" form did not have a retroactive date provision, however, and both 1984 forms covered " 'sudden and accidental' pollution" damage and provided for unlimited coverage of legal defense costs by the insurer. Within the ISO, defendant Hartford Fire Insurance Company objected to the proposed 1984 forms * * * . Defendant Allstate Insurance Company also [desired] * * * a retroactive date provision on the "claims-made" form. Majorities in the relevant ISO committees, however, supported the proposed 1984 CGL forms and rejected the changes proposed by Hartford and Allstate. In December 1983, the ISO Board of Directors approved the proposed 1984 forms, and ISO filed or lodged the forms with state regulators in March 1984.

Dissatisfied with this state of affairs, the defendants began to take other steps to force a change in the terms of coverage of CGL insurance generally available, steps that, the plaintiffs allege, implemented a series of conspiracies in violation of § 1 of the Sherman Act. * * *

* * * [The complaints charge that in] March 1984, primary insurer Hartford persuaded General Reinsurance Corporation (General Re), the largest American reinsurer, to take steps either to procure desired changes in the ISO CGL forms, or "failing that, [to] 'derail' the entire ISO CGL forms program." General Re took up the matter with its trade association, RAA, which created a special committee that met and agreed to "boycott" the 1984 ISO CGL forms unless a retroactive-date provision was added to the claims-made form, and a pollution exclusion and defense cost cap were added to both forms. RAA then sent a letter to ISO "announcing that its members would not provide reinsurance for coverages written on the 1984 CGL forms," and Hartford and General Re enlisted a domestic reinsurance broker to give a speech to the ISO Board of Directors, in which he stated that no reinsurers would "break ranks" to reinsure the 1984 ISO CGL forms.

The four primary insurer defendants (Hartford, Aetna, CIGNA, and Allstate) also encouraged key actors in the London reinsurance market, an important provider of reinsurance for North American risks, to withhold reinsurance for coverages written on the 1984 ISO CGL forms. As a consequence, many London-based underwriters, syndicates, brokers, and reinsurance companies informed ISO of their intention to withhold reinsurance on the 1984 forms, and at least some of them told ISO that they would withhold reinsurance until ISO incorporated all four desired changes into the ISO CGL forms.

For the first time ever, ISO invited representatives of the domestic and foreign reinsurance markets to speak at an ISO Executive Committee meeting. At that meeting, the reinsurers "presented their agreed upon positions that there would be changes in the CGL forms or no reinsurance." The ISO Executive Committee then voted to include a retroactive-date provision in the claims-made form, and to exclude all pollution coverage from both new forms. (But it neither eliminated the occurrence form, nor added a legal defense cost cap.) The 1984 ISO CGL forms were then withdrawn from the marketplace, and replaced with forms (1986 ISO CGL forms) containing the new provisions. After ISO got regulatory approval of the 1986 forms in most States where approval was needed, it eliminated its support services for the 1973 CGL form, thus rendering it impossible for most ISO members to continue to use the form.

The [complaints also] * * * charge a conspiracy among a group of London reinsurers and brokers to coerce primary insurers in the United States to offer CGL coverage only on a claims-made basis. The reinsurers collectively refused to write new reinsurance contracts for, or to renew long-standing contracts with, "primary * * * insurers unless they were prepared to switch from the occurrence to the claims-made form;" they also amended their reinsurance contracts to cover only claims made before a " 'sunset date,' " thus eliminating reinsurance for claims made on occurrence policies after that date.

[Further, the complaints] charge another conspiracy among a somewhat different group of London reinsurers to withhold reinsurance for pollution coverage. * * * In accordance with this agreement, the parties have in fact excluded pollution liability coverage from CGL reinsurance contracts since at least late 1985.

* * *

C

Nineteen States and a number of private plaintiffs filed 36 complaints against the insurers involved in this course of events, charging that the conspiracies described above violated § 1 of the Sherman Act. [T]he defendants moved to dismiss for failure to state a cause of action * * * . The

District Court granted the motions to dismiss. It * * * dismissed the three claims that named only certain London-based defendants, invoking international comity * * * .

The Court of Appeals reversed. * * * [A]s to the three claims brought solely against foreign defendants, the court * * * concluded that the principle of international comity was no bar to exercising Sherman Act jurisdiction.

We granted certiorari * * * to address * * * the application of the Sherman Act to the foreign conduct at issue. * * *

* * *270

III

Finally, we take up the question * * * whether certain claims against the London reinsurers should have been dismissed as improper applications of the Sherman Act to foreign conduct. * * *

At the outset, we note that the District Court undoubtedly had jurisdiction of these Sherman Act claims, as the London reinsurers apparently concede. * * * Although the proposition was perhaps not always free from doubt, see American Banana Co. v. United Fruit Co., it is well established by now that the Sherman Act applies to foreign conduct that was meant to produce and did in fact produce some substantial effect in the United States. See Matsushita Elec. Industrial Co. v. Zenith Radio Corp.[271] Such is the conduct alleged here: that the London reinsurers engaged in unlawful conspiracies to affect the market for insurance in the United States and that their conduct in fact produced substantial effect.

According to the London reinsurers, the District Court should have declined to exercise such jurisdiction under the principle of international comity. The Court of Appeals agreed * * * . This availed the London reinsurers nothing, however. To be sure, the Court of Appeals believed that "application of [American] antitrust laws to the London reinsurance market 'would lead to significant conflict with English law and policy,'" and that "such a conflict, unless outweighed by other factors, would by itself be reason to decline exercise of jurisdiction." But other factors, in the court's view, including the London reinsurers' express purpose to affect United States commerce and the substantial nature of the effect produced, outweighed the supposed conflict and required the exercise of jurisdiction in this case.

---

[270] [Ed. note] In Part II of the opinion, not included here, all members of the Court agreed that there were sufficient allegations of "boycott" that the McCarran-Ferguson Act did not grant antitrust immunity, although they differed about what conduct the term "boycott" includes.

[271] Justice Scalia believes that what is at issue in this case is prescriptive, as opposed to subject-matter, jurisdiction. The parties do not question prescriptive jurisdiction, however, and for good reason: it is well established that Congress has exercised such jurisdiction under the Sherman Act. [Court's fn. 22]

When it enacted the Foreign Trade Antitrust Improvements Act of 1982 (FTAIA), Congress expressed no view on the question whether a court with Sherman Act jurisdiction should ever decline to exercise such jurisdiction on grounds of international comity. We need not decide that question here, however, for even assuming that in a proper case a court may decline to exercise Sherman Act jurisdiction over foreign conduct * * *, international comity would not counsel against exercising jurisdiction in the circumstances alleged here.

The only substantial question in this case is whether "there is in fact a true conflict between domestic and foreign law." The London reinsurers contend that applying the Act to their conduct would conflict significantly with British law, and the British Government, appearing before us as amicus curiae, concurs. They assert that Parliament has established a comprehensive regulatory regime over the London reinsurance market and that the conduct alleged here was perfectly consistent with British law and policy. But this is not to state a conflict. "The fact that conduct is lawful in the state in which it took place will not, of itself, bar application of the United States antitrust laws," even where the foreign state has a strong policy to permit or encourage such conduct. Restatement (Third) Foreign Relations Law § 415, Comment j. No conflict exists, for these purposes, "where a person subject to regulation by two states can comply with the laws of both." Restatement (Third) Foreign Relations Law § 403, Comment e. Since the London reinsurers do not argue that British law requires them to act in some fashion prohibited by the law of the United States, or claim that their compliance with the laws of both countries is otherwise impossible, we see no conflict with British law. We have no need in this case to address other considerations that might inform a decision to refrain from the exercise of jurisdiction on grounds of international comity.

IV

The judgment of the Court of Appeals is affirmed in part and reversed in part, and the case is remanded for further proceedings consistent with this opinion.

JUSTICE SCALIA delivered [the opinion of the Court in Part I of this opinion (omitted here) and] * * * a dissenting opinion * * * [in] Part II, in which JUSTICE O'CONNOR, JUSTICE KENNEDY, and JUSTICE THOMAS have joined.

* * *

II

The petitioners [who are] * * * British corporations and other British subjects argue that certain of the claims against them constitute an inappropriate extraterritorial application of the Sherman Act. It is important to distinguish two distinct questions raised by this petition:

whether the District Court had jurisdiction, and whether the Sherman Act reaches the extraterritorial conduct alleged here. On the first question, I believe that the District Court had subject-matter jurisdiction over the Sherman Act claims against all the defendants (personal jurisdiction is not contested). The respondents asserted nonfrivolous claims under the Sherman Act, and 28 U.S.C. § 1331 vests district courts with subject-matter jurisdiction over cases "arising under" federal statutes. * * * [T]hat is sufficient to establish the District Court's jurisdiction over these claims. * * *

The second question—the extraterritorial reach of the Sherman Act—has nothing to do with the jurisdiction of the courts. It is a question of substantive law turning on whether, in enacting the Sherman Act, Congress asserted regulatory power over the challenged conduct. If a plaintiff fails to prevail on this issue, the court does not dismiss the claim for want of subject-matter jurisdiction—want of power to adjudicate; rather, it decides the claim, ruling on the merits that the plaintiff has failed to state a cause of action under the relevant statute.

There is, however, a type of "jurisdiction" relevant to determining the extraterritorial reach of a statute; it is known as "legislative jurisdiction," Restatement (First) Conflict of Laws § 60 (1934), or "jurisdiction to prescribe," 1 Restatement (Third) of Foreign Relations Law of the United States 235 (1987). This refers to "the authority of a state to make its law applicable to persons or activities," and is quite a separate matter from "jurisdiction to adjudicate." There is no doubt, of course, that Congress possesses legislative jurisdiction over the acts alleged in this complaint: Congress has broad power under Article I, § 8, cl. 3 "to regulate Commerce with foreign Nations," and this Court has repeatedly upheld its power to make laws applicable to persons or activities beyond our territorial boundaries where United States interests are affected. But the question in this case is whether, and to what extent, Congress has exercised that undoubted legislative jurisdiction in enacting the Sherman Act.

Two canons of statutory construction are relevant in this inquiry. The first is the "long-standing principle of American law 'that legislation of Congress, unless a contrary intent appears, is meant to apply only within the territorial jurisdiction of the United States.' " *Aramco.* [EEOC v. Arabian American Oil Co., 499 U.S. 244 (1991).] Applying that canon in *Aramco*, we held that the version of Title VII of the Civil Rights Act of 1964 then in force did not extend outside the territory of the United States even though the statute contained broad provisions extending its prohibitions to, for example, " 'any activity, business, or industry in commerce.' " We held such "boilerplate language" to be an insufficient indication to override the presumption against extraterritoriality. The Sherman Act contains similar "boilerplate language," and if the question were not governed by precedent, it would be worth considering whether that presumption controls the outcome here. We have, however, found the presumption to be overcome with respect to our antitrust laws; it is now well established that the Sherman Act applies extraterritorially. See Matsushita Elec. Industrial Co. v. Zenith Radio Corp.

But if the presumption against extraterritoriality has been overcome or is otherwise inapplicable, a second canon of statutory construction becomes relevant: "An act of congress ought never to be construed to violate the law of nations if any other possible construction remains." Murray v. The Charming Betsy, 2 Cranch 64, 118 (1804) (Marshall, C.J.). This canon is "wholly independent" of the presumption against extraterritoriality. It is relevant to determining the substantive reach of a statute because "the law of nations," or customary international law, includes limitations on a nation's exercise of its jurisdiction to prescribe. Though it clearly has constitutional authority to do so, Congress is generally presumed not to have exceeded those customary international-law limits on jurisdiction to prescribe.

Consistent with that presumption, this and other courts have frequently recognized that, even where the presumption against extraterritoriality does not apply, statutes should not be interpreted to regulate foreign persons or conduct if that regulation would conflict with principles of international law. * * *

* * *

* * * More specifically, the principle was expressed in United States v. Aluminum Co. of America * * * . In his opinion for the court, Judge Learned Hand cautioned "we are not to read general words, such as those in [the Sherman] Act, without regard to the limitations customarily observed by nations upon the exercise of their powers; limitations which generally correspond to those fixed by the 'Conflict of Laws.'"

More recent lower court precedent has also tempered the extraterritorial application of the Sherman Act with considerations of "international comity." See Timberlane Lumber Co. v. Bank of America, N.T. & S.A., 549 F.2d 597 (9th Cir.1976). The "comity" they refer to is not the comity of courts, whereby judges decline to exercise jurisdiction over matters more appropriately adjudged elsewhere, but rather what might be termed "prescriptive comity": the respect sovereign nations afford each other by limiting the reach of their laws. * * *[272]

---

[272] Some antitrust courts, including the Court of Appeals in the present case, have mistaken the comity at issue for the "comity of courts," which has led them to characterize the question presented as one of "abstention," that is, whether they should "exercise or decline jurisdiction." * * * [T]hat seems to be the error the Court has fallen into today. Because courts are generally reluctant to refuse the exercise of conferred jurisdiction, confusion on this seemingly theoretical point can have the very practical consequence of greatly expanding the extraterritorial reach of the Sherman Act. [Dissent fn. 9]

* * *

Under the Restatement [(Third) of Foreign Relations Law], a nation having some "basis" for jurisdiction to prescribe law should nonetheless refrain from exercising that jurisdiction "with respect to a person or activity having connections with another state when the exercise of such jurisdiction is unreasonable." Restatement (Third) § 403(1). The "reasonableness" inquiry turns on a number of factors including, but not limited to: "the extent to which the activity takes place within the territory [of the regulating state]," § 403(2)(a); "the connections, such as nationality, residence, or economic activity, between the regulating state and the person principally responsible for the activity to be regulated," § 403(2)(b) ; "the character of the activity to be regulated, the importance of regulation to the regulating state, the extent to which other states regulate such activities, and the degree to which the desirability of such regulation is generally accepted," § 403(2)(c); "the extent to which another state may have an interest in regulating the activity," § 403(2)(g); and "the likelihood of conflict with regulation by another state," § 403(2)(h). Rarely would these factors point more clearly against application of United States law. The activity relevant to the counts at issue here took place primarily in the United Kingdom, and the defendants in these counts are British corporations and British subjects having their principal place of business or residence outside the United States. Great Britain has established a comprehensive regulatory scheme governing the London reinsurance markets, and clearly has a heavy "interest in regulating the activity." Finally, § 2(b) of the McCarran-Ferguson Act allows state regulatory statutes to override the Sherman Act in the insurance field, subject only to the narrow "boycott" exception set forth in § 3(b)—suggesting that "the importance of regulation to the [United States]," is slight. Considering these factors, I think it unimaginable that an assertion of legislative jurisdiction by the United States would be considered reasonable, and therefore it is inappropriate to assume, in the absence of statutory indication to the contrary, that Congress has made such an assertion.

It is evident from what I have said that the Court's comity analysis, which proceeds as though the issue is whether the courts should "decline to exercise * * * jurisdiction," rather than whether the Sherman Act covers this conduct, is simply misdirected. * * * [The Court] concludes that no "true conflict" counseling nonapplication of United States law (or rather, as it thinks, United States judicial jurisdiction) exists unless compliance with United States law would constitute a violation of another country's law. That breathtakingly broad proposition, which contradicts the many cases discussed earlier, will bring the Sherman Act and other laws into sharp and unnecessary conflict with the legitimate interests of other countries—particularly our closest trading partners.

* * *

Literally the only support that the Court adduces for its position is § 403 of the Restatement (Third) of Foreign Relations Law—or more precisely Comment e * * * . The Court has completely misinterpreted this provision. Subsection (3) of § 403 (requiring one State to defer to another in the limited circumstances just described) comes into play only after subsection (1) of § 403 has been complied with—i.e., after it has been determined that the exercise of jurisdiction by both of the two states is not "unreasonable." That prior question is answered by applying the factors (inter alia) set forth in subsection (2) of § 403, that is, precisely the factors that I have discussed in text and that the Court rejects.

I would reverse the judgment of the Court of Appeals on this issue, and remand to the District Court with instructions to dismiss for failure to state a claim on the three counts at issue * * * .

NOTES AND QUESTIONS

1.   Were you convinced by the Court that jurisdiction over the London reinsurers was clear? Should it be enough to ask whether the antitrust laws will require the foreign firms to violate their own law?

a.   Put the matter in a domestic setting. When we ask whether state regulation creates an antitrust immunity under Parker v. Brown, do we ask only whether compliance with the Sherman Act would require violation of the state law? Think of *Southern Motor Carriers*; were the trucking firms *required* to act through the rate bureau?

b.   Why have the cases accommodating state and federal regulation developed in this way? Is it because of Constitutional requirements or an express exception written into the antitrust laws? Is it because the courts have been trying to accommodate parallel and often-inconsistent systems of regulation? Does the variety of regulatory systems around the world present a similar set of issues?

c.   Do you agree with Justice Scalia that each case should require a balancing of the factors set forth in the Restatement (Third) of Foreign Relations Law? Might that give too little guidance to business persons? Is he right that as we enter the global economy, the majority's analysis is too simplistic and likely to put the courts in the position of offending foreign governments?[273]

2.   A number of cases decided since *Hartford Fire Insurance* have continued its expansive view of U.S. jurisdiction.

a.   United States v. Nippon Paper Industries Co., 109 F.3d 1 (1st Cir. 1997), cert. denied 522 U.S. 1044 (1998), was a United States criminal prosecution of a Japanese company for allegedly conspiring to fix the price of thermal fax paper throughout North America. The District Court said that a

---

[273] For a highly critical assessment of *Hartford*, for example, see Eleanor M. Fox, National Law, Global Markets, and *Hartford*: Eyes Wide Shut, 68 Antitrust L.J. 73 (2000).

Sherman Act criminal prosecution could not be based on wholly extraterritorial conduct. A civil suit could be based on such conduct, the Court of Appeals wrote, and the same words of the Sherman Act impose criminal liability as well. The conduct was illegal in both Japan and the United States, so the indictment was reinstated.

b.   Caribbean Broadcasting System, Ltd. v. Cable & Wireless PLC, 148 F.3d 1080 (D.C. Cir. 1998), was a suit brought in a U.S. court by one Caribbean company against another alleging monopolization of English language radio broadcasting in the Eastern Caribbean. The District Court dismissed the complaint, finding no effect on U.S. commerce. Puerto Rico and the U.S. Virgin Islands are in the Eastern Caribbean, the Court of Appeals answered, and reinstated the cause of action.

c.   Filetech S.A. v. France Telecom S.A., 157 F.3d 922 (2d Cir. 1998), was brought by a French seller of marketing lists against the operator of the French telephone system alleging monopolization of the U.S. market for French marketing lists. The defendant denied doing any substantial marketing list business in the United States, but the Court of Appeals concludes that substantiality is a matter for proof in further proceedings in the District Court.

THE ENFORCEMENT GUIDELINES FOR
INTERNATIONAL OPERATIONS (1995)

In the years since *Hartford Fire Insurance*, the United States has taken seriously its authority to enforce violations of U.S. antitrust policy that take place outside our borders, both by entering into bilateral enforcement agreements with other nations and the European Union, and by domestic enforcement of U.S. law against foreign firms.[274] In 1995, the Justice Department and Federal Trade Commission issued yet another set of enforcement Guidelines, this time to explain how they would deal with the sensitive issues arising in the increasingly international marketplace.

The International Guidelines begin (Part 2) with an extended discussion of the many statutes dealing with trade issues that have antitrust implications. The discussion includes many bilateral and multilateral enforcement agreements that competition authorities have entered into in recent years, as now authorized by the International Antitrust Enforcement Assistance Act of 1994.

---

[274] See, e.g., Joseph P. Griffin, Extraterritoriality in U.S. and E.U. Antitrust Enforcement, 67 Antitrust L.J. 159 (1999); Spencer Weber Waller, The Internationalization of Antitrust Enforcement, 77 B.Y.U. L.Rev. 343 (1997); Robert D. Shank, The Justice Department's Recent Antitrust Enforcement Policy: Toward a "Positive Comity" Solution to International Competition Problems?, 29 Vanderbilt J. Transnational L. 155 (1996).

The *Guidelines* (Part 3) rely on "direct, substantial and reasonably foreseeable effects" of conduct as the test for jurisdiction, citing both *Hartford Fire Insurance* and the Foreign Trade Improvements Act of 1982.

A cartel of foreign producers who make substantial sales in the United States thus could violate the Sherman Act, for example (Part 3.11).[275] An agreement by foreign companies not to deal with an American firm who wants to export to a foreign market could also be prosecuted by the United States (Part 3.122). Even a merger of foreign firms could be attacked under Clayton Act § 7 if the firms account for a substantial percentage of U.S. sales of a product (Part 3.14).[276]

In terms of comity, the *Guidelines* (Part 3.2) stake out the full authority granted by *Hartford* to pursue any conduct not compelled by foreign law. However, the agencies say they will exercise their discretion to consider other foreign policy issues such as whether a foreign nation will prosecute the activity itself and whether a prosecution would injure relations between the United States and a foreign government.

The effect of foreign government involvement in prohibited conduct is broken down into four issues discussed in Part 3.3 of the *Guidelines*. These are foreign sovereign immunity, foreign sovereign compulsion, the act of state doctrine, and the application of *Noerr-Pennington* to lobbying of foreign governments. On the last of these, the *Guidelines* say that a genuine effort to obtain or influence the action of governments abroad will be protected to the same extent as a similar effort would be in the United States.

2. REMEDIES FOR FOREIGN CITIZENS IN U.S. COURTS

The second major question that has arisen is to what extent U.S. courts should be open to non-U.S. litigants seeking damages for conduct that occurred outside the United States. The substantive setting is the vitamin cartel litigation discussed earlier. In many areas of domestic law, of course, "forum shopping" is decried in theory but widely practiced. Our next case examined forum shopping in an international antitrust setting.

---

[275] Issues of subjecting the firms to personal jurisdiction are addressed in the Guidelines, Part 4.

[276] Application of the Hart-Scott-Rodino Act's notice requirements to foreign mergers is addressed in Part 4.22 of the Guidelines.

F. HOFFMANN-LA ROCHE LTD. v. EMPAGRAN S. A.

Supreme Court of the United States, 2004
542 U.S. 155, 124 S.Ct. 2359, 159 L.Ed.2d 226

JUSTICE BREYER delivered the opinion of the Court.

The Foreign Trade Antitrust Improvements Act of 1982 (FTAIA) excludes from the Sherman Act's reach much anticompetitive conduct that causes only foreign injury. It does so by setting forth a general rule stating that the Sherman Act "shall not apply to conduct involving trade or commerce . . . with foreign nations." 15 U.S.C. § 6a. It then creates exceptions to the general rule, applicable where (roughly speaking) that conduct significantly harms imports, domestic commerce, or American exporters.

* * *

* * * [T]his case involves vitamin sellers around the world that agreed to fix prices, leading to higher vitamin prices in the United States and independently leading to higher vitamin prices in other countries such as Ecuador. We conclude that, in this scenario, a purchaser in the United States could bring a Sherman Act claim under the FTAIA based on domestic injury, but a purchaser in Ecuador could not bring a Sherman Act claim based on foreign harm.

I

The plaintiffs in this case originally filed a class-action suit on behalf of foreign and domestic purchasers of vitamins under, *inter alia*, § 1 of the Sherman Act, and §§ 4 and 16 of the Clayton Act. Their complaint alleged that petitioners, foreign and domestic vitamin manufacturers and distributors, had engaged in a price-fixing conspiracy, raising the price of vitamin products to customers in the United States and to customers in foreign countries.

As relevant here, petitioners moved to dismiss the suit as to the *foreign* purchasers (the respondents here), five foreign vitamin distributors located in Ukraine, Australia, Ecuador, and Panama, each of which bought vitamins from petitioners for delivery outside the United States. Respondents have never asserted that they purchased any vitamins in the United States or in transactions in United States commerce, and the question presented assumes that the relevant "transactions occurr[ed] entirely outside U. S. commerce." The District Court dismissed their claims. * * *

A divided panel of the Court of Appeals [for the D.C. Circuit] reversed. The panel concluded that the FTAIA's general exclusionary rule applied to the case, but that its domestic-injury exception also applied. It basically read the plaintiffs' complaint to allege that the vitamin manufacturers' price-fixing conspiracy (1) had "a direct, substantial, and reasonably foreseeable effect" on ordinary domestic trade or commerce, *i.e.*, the conspiracy brought about higher domestic vitamin prices, and (2) "such effect" gave "rise to a [Sherman Act] claim," *i.e.*, an injured *domestic* customer could have brought a Sherman Act suit. Those allegations, the court held, are sufficient to meet the exception's requirements.

The court assumed that the foreign effect, *i.e.*, higher prices in Ukraine, Panama, Australia, and Ecuador, was independent of the domestic effect, *i.e.*, higher domestic prices. But it concluded that, in light of the FTAIA's text, legislative history, and the policy goal of deterring harmful price-fixing activity, this lack of connection does not matter. * * *

We granted certiorari to resolve a split among the Courts of Appeals about the exception's application.

II

The FTAIA seeks to make clear to American exporters (and to firms doing business abroad) that the Sherman Act does not prevent them from entering into business arrangements (say, joint-selling arrangements), however anticompetitive, as long as those arrangements adversely affect only foreign markets. * * *

The FTAIA says:

> "Sections 1 to 7 of this title [the Sherman Act] shall not apply to conduct involving trade or commerce (other than import trade or import commerce) with foreign nations unless—
>
>> "(1) such conduct has a direct, substantial, and reasonably foreseeable effect—
>>
>>> "(A) on trade or commerce which is not trade or commerce with foreign nations [*i.e.*, domestic trade or commerce], or on import trade or import commerce with foreign nations; or
>>>
>>> "(B) on export trade or export commerce with foreign nations, of a person engaged in such trade or commerce in the United States [*i.e.*, on an American export competitor]; and
>>
>> (2) such effect gives rise to a claim under the provisions of sections 1 to 7 of this title, other than this section.
>
> "If sections 1 to 7 of this title apply to such conduct only because of the operation of paragraph (1)(B), then sections 1 to 7 of this title shall apply to such conduct only for injury to export business in the United States." 15 U.S.C. § 6a.

This technical language initially lays down a general rule placing *all* (non-import) activity involving foreign commerce outside the Sherman

Act's reach. It then brings such conduct back within the Sherman Act's reach *provided that* the conduct *both* (1) sufficiently affects American commerce, *i.e.*, it has a "direct, substantial, and reasonably foreseeable effect" on American domestic, import, or (certain) export commerce, *and* (2) has an effect of a kind that antitrust law considers harmful, *i.e.*, the "effect" must "giv[e] rise to a [Sherman Act] claim."

We ask here how this language applies to price-fixing activity that is in significant part foreign, that has the requisite domestic effect, and that also has independent foreign effects giving rise to the plaintiff's claim.

III

Respondents make a threshold argument. They say that the transactions here at issue fall outside the FTAIA because the FTAIA's general exclusionary rule applies only to conduct involving exports. * * *

The difficulty with respondents' argument is that the FTAIA originated in a bill that initially referred only to "export trade or export commerce." But the House Judiciary Committee subsequently changed that language to "trade or commerce (other than import trade or import commerce)." And it did so deliberately to include commerce that did not involve American exports but which was wholly foreign.

* * *

For those who find legislative history useful, the House Report's account should end the matter. Others, by considering carefully the amendment itself and the lack of any other plausible purpose, may reach the same conclusion, namely that the FTAIA's general rule applies where the anticompetitive conduct at issue is foreign.

IV

We turn now to the basic question presented, that of the exception's application. Because the underlying antitrust action is complex, potentially raising questions not directly at issue here, we reemphasize that we base our decision upon the following: The price-fixing conduct significantly and adversely affects both customers outside the United States and customers within the United States, but the adverse foreign effect is independent of any adverse domestic effect. In these circumstances, we find that the FTAIA exception does not apply (and thus the Sherman Act does not apply) for two main reasons.

First, this Court ordinarily construes ambiguous statutes to avoid unreasonable interference with the sovereign authority of other nations. This rule of construction reflects principles of customary international law—law that (we must assume) Congress ordinarily seeks to follow. See Restatement (Third) of Foreign Relations Law of the United States §§ 403(1), 403(2) (1986) (hereinafter Restatement) (limiting the unreasonable exercise of prescriptive jurisdiction with respect to a person or activity having connections with another State); Murray v. Schooner Charming Betsy, 6 U.S. 64, 2 Cranch 64, 2 L. Ed. 208 (1804); Hartford Fire Insurance Co. v. California (1993) (Scalia, J., dissenting) (identifying rule of construction as derived from the principle of "prescriptive comity").

This rule of statutory construction cautions courts to assume that legislators take account of the legitimate sovereign interests of other nations when they write American laws. It thereby helps the potentially conflicting laws of different nations work together in harmony—a harmony particularly needed in today's highly interdependent commercial world.

No one denies that America's antitrust laws, when applied to foreign conduct, can interfere with a foreign nation's ability independently to regulate its own commercial affairs. But our courts have long held that application of our antitrust laws to foreign anticompetitive conduct is nonetheless reasonable, and hence consistent with principles of prescriptive comity, insofar as they reflect a legislative effort to redress *domestic* antitrust injury that foreign anticompetitive conduct has caused. See United States v. Aluminum Co. of America.

But why is it reasonable to apply those laws to foreign conduct *insofar as that conduct causes independent foreign harm and that foreign harm alone gives rise to the plaintiff's claim?* Like the former case, application of those laws creates a serious risk of interference with a foreign nation's ability independently to regulate its own commercial affairs. But, unlike the former case, the justification for that interference seems insubstantial. * * * Why should American law supplant, for example, Canada's or Great Britain's or Japan's own determination about how best to protect Canadian or British or Japanese customers from anticompetitive conduct engaged in significant part by Canadian or British or Japanese or other foreign companies?

We recognize that principles of comity provide Congress greater leeway when it seeks to control through legislation the actions of *American* companies, see Restatement § 402; and some of the anticompetitive price-fixing conduct alleged here took place in *America*. But the higher foreign prices of which the foreign plaintiffs here complain are not the consequence of any domestic anticompetitive conduct *that Congress sought to forbid*, for Congress did not seek to forbid any such conduct insofar as it is here relevant, *i.e.*, insofar as it is intertwined with foreign conduct that causes independent foreign harm. Rather Congress sought to *release* domestic (and foreign) anticompetitive conduct from Sherman Act constraints when that conduct causes foreign harm. Congress, of course, did make an exception where that conduct also causes domestic harm. But any independent domestic harm the foreign conduct causes here has, by definition, little or nothing to do with the matter.

We thus repeat the basic question: Why is it reasonable to apply this law to conduct that is significantly foreign *insofar as that conduct causes independent foreign harm and that foreign harm alone gives rise to the plaintiff's claim?* We can find no good answer to the question.

The Areeda and Hovenkamp treatise notes that under the Court of Appeals' interpretation of the statute

> "a Malaysian customer could . . . maintain an action under United States law in a United States court against its own Malaysian supplier, another cartel member, simply by noting that unnamed third parties injured [in the United States] by the American [cartel member's] conduct would also have a cause of action. Effectively, the United States courts would provide worldwide subject matter jurisdiction to any foreign suitor wishing to sue its own local supplier, but unhappy with its own sovereign's provisions for private antitrust enforcement, provided that a different plaintiff had a cause of action against a different firm for injuries that were within U. S. [other-than-import] commerce. It does not seem excessively rigid to infer that Congress would not have intended that result." P. Areeda & H. Hovenkamp, Antitrust Law P 273, pp. 51–52 (Supp. 2003).

We agree with the comment. We can find no convincing justification for the extension of the Sherman Act's scope that it describes.

Respondents reply that many nations have adopted antitrust laws similar to our own, to the point where the practical likelihood of interference with the relevant interests of other nations is minimal. Leaving price fixing to the side, however, this Court has found to the contrary. See, *e.g., Hartford Fire* (noting that the alleged conduct in the London reinsurance market, while illegal under United States antitrust laws, was assumed to be perfectly consistent with British law and policy).

Regardless, even where nations agree about primary conduct, say price fixing, they disagree dramatically about appropriate remedies. The application, for example, of American private treble-damages remedies to anticompetitive conduct taking place abroad has generated considerable controversy. And several foreign nations have filed briefs here arguing that to apply our remedies would unjustifiably permit their citizens to bypass their own less generous remedial schemes, thereby upsetting a balance of competing considerations that their own domestic antitrust laws embody.
* * *

These briefs add that a decision permitting independently injured foreign plaintiffs to pursue private treble-damages remedies would undermine foreign nations' own antitrust enforcement policies by diminishing foreign firms' incentive to cooperate with antitrust authorities in return for prosecutorial amnesty.

Respondents alternatively argue that comity does not demand an interpretation of the FTAIA that would exclude independent foreign injury cases *across the board*. Rather, courts can take (and sometimes have taken) account of comity considerations case by case, abstaining where comity considerations so dictate.

In our view, however, this approach is too complex to prove workable. The Sherman Act covers many different kinds of anticompetitive agreements. Courts would have to examine how foreign law, compared with American law, treats not only price fixing but also, say, information-sharing agreements, patent-licensing price conditions, territorial product resale limitations, and various forms of joint venture, in respect to both primary conduct and remedy. The legally and economically technical nature of that enterprise means lengthier proceedings, appeals, and more proceedings—to the point where procedural costs and delays could themselves threaten interference with a foreign nation's ability to maintain the integrity of its own antitrust enforcement system. Even in this relatively simple price-fixing case, for example, competing briefs tell us (1) that potential treble-damage liability would help enforce widespread anti-price-fixing norms (through added deterrence) and (2) the opposite, namely that such liability would hinder antitrust enforcement (by reducing incentives to enter amnesty programs). How could a court seriously interested in resolving so empirical a matter—a matter potentially related to impact on foreign interests—do so simply and expeditiously?

We conclude that principles of prescriptive comity counsel against the Court of Appeals' interpretation of the FTAIA. Where foreign anticompetitive conduct plays a significant role and where foreign injury is independent of domestic effects, Congress might have hoped that America's antitrust laws, so fundamental a component of our own economic system, would commend themselves to other nations as well. But, if America's antitrust policies could not win their own way in the international marketplace for such ideas, Congress, we must assume, would not have tried to impose them, in an act of legal imperialism, through legislative fiat.

Second, the FTAIA's language and history suggest that Congress designed the FTAIA to clarify, perhaps to limit, but not *to expand* in any significant way, the Sherman Act's scope as applied to foreign commerce. And we have found no significant indication that at the time Congress wrote this statute courts would have thought the Sherman Act applicable in these circumstances.

The Solicitor General and petitioners tell us that they have found no case in which any court applied the Sherman Act to redress foreign injury in such circumstances. And respondents themselves apparently conceded as much * * * before the District Court below.

* * *

The upshot is that no pre-1982 case provides significant authority for application of the Sherman Act in the circumstances we here assume. Indeed, a leading contemporaneous lower court case contains language suggesting the contrary. See Timberlane Lumber Co. v. Bank of America, 549 F.2d 597, 613 (9th Cir. 1976) (insisting that the foreign conduct's domestic effect be "sufficiently large to present a cognizable injury *to the plaintiffs*" (emphasis added)).

Taken together, these two sets of considerations, the one derived from comity and the other reflecting history, convince us that Congress would not have intended the FTAIA's exception to bring independently caused foreign injury within the Sherman Act's reach.

V

Respondents point to several considerations that point the other way. For one thing, * * * [h]ow can the Sherman Act both *apply to the conduct* when one person sues but *not apply to the same conduct* when another person sues? * * *

* * *

* * * Linguistically speaking, a statute can apply and not apply to the same conduct, depending upon other circumstances; and those other circumstances may include the nature of the lawsuit (or of the related underlying harm). It also makes linguistic sense to read the words "a claim" as if they refer to the "plaintiff's claim" or "the claim at issue."

At most, respondents' linguistic arguments might show that respondents' reading is the more natural reading of the statutory language. But those arguments do not show that we *must* accept that reading. And that is the critical point. The considerations previously mentioned—those of comity and history—make clear that the respondents' reading is not consistent with the FTAIA's basic intent. If the statute's language reasonably permits an interpretation consistent with that intent, we should adopt it. And, for the reasons stated, we believe that the statute's language permits the reading that we give it.

* * *

For these reasons, the judgment of the Court of Appeals is vacated, and the case is remanded for further proceedings consistent with this opinion.

JUSTICE O'CONNOR took no part in the consideration or decision of the case.

JUSTICE SCALIA, with whom JUSTICE THOMAS joins, concurring in the judgment.

I concur in the judgment of the Court because the language of the statute is readily susceptible of the interpretation the Court provides and because only that interpretation is consistent with the principle that statutes should be read in accord with the customary deference to the application of foreign countries' laws within their own territories.

NOTES AND QUESTIONS

1. Did the conduct of the defendants have effects in the United States? Could the defendants have been sued for the same conduct by U.S. citizens? Then why should the defendants not have been subject to suit by these plaintiffs?

2. Was the conduct of which the defendants were accused illegal in the countries in which the plaintiffs were resident? Were remedies available to the plaintiffs in those countries? If so, why should resources of the U.S. courts be expended to give a forum to these plaintiffs?

3. The Court of Appeals had relied heavily on an argument that to achieve optimal deterrence of the price fixing, *all* of its consequences had to be redressed in U.S. courts. Put another way, if defendants could make monopoly profits on world-wide sales but pay treble damages only on their U.S. sales, they would do more price fixing than if the damages were assessed on their entire profits. What do you think of that argument? Did the Supreme Court adequately answer that concern?

4. Think back to *Hartford Fire Insurance*. Do you think the policy underlying the antitrust laws in the plaintiffs' home countries would be seriously infringed if this suit were permitted to go forward?

a. Should briefs filed by European countries expressing concern about such conflicts compel the Court to reach the result it did? In deferring to the positions taken in those briefs, has the Court ceded jurisdiction over U.S. law to foreign nations?

b. Does it seem that the Court has in effect concluded that Justice Scalia's dissent in *Hartford Fire Insurance* was right?[277]

---

[277] Support for such an argument is found in Herbert Hovenkamp, Antitrust as Extraterritorial Regulatory Policy, 48 Antitrust Bulletin 629 (2003). On remand, the D.C. Circuit held that a plaintiff may only recover for foreign loss that was proximately caused by the U.S. domestic effects of the defendants' conduct; but-for causation is not enough. Empagran S.A. v. F. Hoffmann-LaRoche Ltd., 417 F.3d 1267 (D.C. Cir. 2005). The same standard was adopted by the Ninth Circuit in In re Dynamic Random Access Memory (DRAM), 546 F.3d 981 (9th Cir. 2008).

3. THE CHALLENGE OF ANTITRUST POLICY DIVERGENCE

This course has been primarily about American antitrust law. But commerce is not limited by national borders, and Americans no longer monopolize development of antitrust policy. Over 100 nations all over the world now have competition laws—indeed, creating new competition laws became something of a cottage industry even for countries that did not yet have developed competitive economies[278]—and the content and enforcement of those laws continues to evolve.

a. The European Union

The European Union[279] provides the most developed counterpart to the U.S. antitrust laws. Its three important provisions address the same issues that we have seen in this course.[280] Article 101 is the counterpart to Sherman Act § 1. It attacks agreements that we would call price fixing, output limitation, market division, discriminatory dealing, and tying arrangements, but it also provides for categorical exemptions of certain kinds of transactions thought to be more beneficial than harmful. Exemptions include certain vertical arrangements,[281] some agreements to specialize in particular work, as well as some research and development agreements.

Article 102 is the EU counterpart to Sherman Act § 2, but its prohibition of "abuse of a dominant position" has been seen to encompass considerably more than practices reached by § 2 as interpreted by the U.S. courts in the current period. The term "abuse of a dominant position" can reach "unfair prices," for example, and can prohibit failing to license patent rights to other producers.[282]

Finally, the Merger Regulations are the European version of Clayton Act § 7. The regulations condemn any "concentration," i.e., a merger or purchase of stock or assets, that creates or strengthens a dominant position and "significantly impedes" competition. Planned concentrations with

---

[278] See, e.g., William E. Kovacic, Getting Started: Creating New Competition Policy Institutions in Transition Economies, 23 Brooklyn J. Inter. Law 403 (1997); Manisha M. Sheth, Formulating Antitrust Policy in Emerging Economies, 86 Georgetown L.J. 451 (1997).

[279] The European Commission is technically the part of the European Union with responsibility for antitrust enforcement. Thus, some references in this section will be to the EC while others will be to the more comprehensive EU.

[280] EU competition law will be well worth your further study. Available materials include George A. Bermann, Roger J. Goebel, William J. Davey & Eleanor M. Fox, Cases and Materials on European Union Law (3rd ed. 2010).

[281] See generally, Vincent Verouden, Vertical Agreements and Article 81(1) EC: The Evolving Role of Economic Analysis, 71 Antitrust L. J. 525 (2003).

[282] See, e.g., Brian A. Facey & Dany H. Assaf, Monopolization and Abuse of Dominance in Canada, the United States, and the European Union: A Survey, 70 Antitrust L. J. 513 (2002).

turnover in excess of particular figures must be reported to competition authorities in advance, similar to practice in the United States.[283]

The proposed merger of General Electric and Honeywell, however, illustrates how similar processes can lead to different results. Both General Electric and Honeywell make a wide array of products, but their only serious overlap is in aircraft engines and related items. The U.S. Justice Department approved the merger on condition that Honeywell sell its helicopter-engine unit, thus preserving a competitor for General Electric in that line of business.

European regulators, however, blocked the merger, causing the firms to abandon their plans. While the U.S. had seen the increased diversity and competitive strength of the combined firms as a plus, Europe had seen it as a threat. As we have seen, creation or strengthening of a "dominant position" is the key concept under European law, and EC Competition Commissioner Mario Monti concluded that the merger would excessively strengthen the new firm's position in markets for a number of aircraft items such as jet engines and electronic guidance systems.[284]

The merger had been opposed by a number of the possible new firm's competitors. As we have seen, U.S. regulators often view such opposition as a positive sign that the new firm will be more efficient. Europeans, however, tended to see it more as a sign of increased dominance if the merger were consummated.

b.   U.S. Assistance to Foreign Antitrust Proceedings

One question that inevitably arises in a world of parallel but different antitrust regimes is whether courts in one country may be employed in support of cases in another. Government enforcement agencies often share information through a series of bilateral agreements,[285] but civil cases are different.

Intel Corp. v. Advanced Micro Devices, Inc., 542 U.S. 241, 124 S.Ct. 2466, 159 L.Ed.2d 355 (2004), involved a private grievance that had been filed by AMD before the EU Directorate-General for Competition (DG). After the DG declined to seek documents that Intel had produced in a case

---

[283] The European Union program is found in Council Regulation (EC) No. 139/2004, published at OJ [Official Journal] L 24, 29.1.2004. See, e.g., Daniel J. Gifford & Robert T. Kudrle, Rhetoric and Reality in the Merger Standards of the United States, Canada, and the European Union, 72 Antitrust L. J. 423 (2005).

[284] E.g., Monti Tries to Limit GE Fallout After Veto, Financial Times, July 4, 2001, p. 1. Pincar Karacan, Differences in Merger Analysis Between the United States and the European Union, Highlighted in the Context of the Boeing/McDonnell Douglas and GE/Honeywell Mergers, 17 Transnational Lawyer 209 (2004); Donna E. Patterson & Carl Shapiro, Transatlantic Divergence in *GE/Honeywell*: Causes and Lessons, 16 Antitrust 18 (Fall 2001). See also, Robert J. Reynolds & Janusz A. Ordover, Archimedean Leveraging and the GE/Honeywell Transaction, 70 Antitrust L. J. 171 (2002).

[285] See, e.g., OJ 1995 L95/47 (information sharing agreement between United States and Commission of the European Communities).

filed in Alabama, AMD sought an order from a federal court in California (Intel's home district) directing Intel to produce the documents for transmittal to the DG.

28 U.S.C. § 1782(a) provides that a federal court "may order" a person "found" in the district to produce documents "for use in a proceeding in a foreign or international tribunal * * * upon the application of any interested person." The California Federal District Court concluded that the statute did not support issuing the requested order, but the Supreme Court disagreed. In an opinion by Justice Ginsburg, the Court held 7–1 that under § 1782(a), the federal court's help was available even though the DG had begun no proceeding and, at least as yet, AMR had no standing as a litigant in any foreign court. Further, the Court held, the statute did not require that a foreign state have any stake in the proceeding before the federal court could act.

Complainants before the European Commission have a significant role, the Court said. They may later go to court themselves if the Directorate General dismisses the complaint. That clearly makes a complainant in the position of AMD an "interested person" within the meaning of the statute. The fact that the DG does not seem to want the documents does not mean that AMD may not seek to require their production.

Justice Breyer dissented, saying that discovery is expensive and that U.S. courts should not extend rights to it any farther than necessary. In this case, the DG does not consider itself a "tribunal" and thus the express language of 28 U.S.C. § 1782(a) has not been satisfied. Further, no discovery should be available under § 1782(a) where, as here, it would not be available to AMR in the foreign jurisdiction or in an American court (because AMR had not yet filed a civil complaint). Might Justice Breyer justifiably wonder why the Court that shared his deferential views in *Empagran*, decided in the same Term, seemed to depart so far from them here?

c. The Chinese Anti-Monopoly Law

Antitrust laws are not new to Asia. Japan and Korea have long had antitrust regimes, and India, Indonesia, Singapore and Taiwan now have laws in place that multinational companies must acknowledge when doing business in these economically-dynamic parts of the world.

But the most-awaited and potentially-significant antitrust development in Asia was promulgation of the new Chinese anti-monopoly law in August 2007. Integration of such a law into what was once a planned economy and still is a communist political system is largely unprecedented, and how the law will work and be enforced are matters of great interest and some apprehension.

Article 1 of the new law describes its purposes as "[1] preventing and prohibiting monopolistic conduct, [2] protecting fair market competition, [3] promoting efficiency of economic operation, [4] safeguarding the interests of consumers and the public interests, and [5] promoting the healthy development of the socialist market economy."[286] It does not take much imagination to see that those purposes do not all point the same way in most cases, so the Anti-Monopoly Law Enforcement Authority, appointed by the State Council, is likely to have substantial discretion.

Article 2 extends the reach of the law to conduct anywhere in the world "that has eliminative or restrictive effects on competition in the domestic market" of China. The Chinese law has four broad prohibitions, each considered in a separate chapter of the law and each subject to expansion by the Authority.

First, the law prohibits "monopoly agreements," defined as including price fixing, limiting output, allocating markets, resale price maintenance, agreements restricting technological development, and group boycotts.

Second, the law prohibits "abuse of dominant market position," defined as selling at "unfair high prices" or buying at "unfair low prices," below cost sales, unilateral refusal to deal, tying arrangements, exclusive dealing and price discrimination. Intellectual property rights are preserved, but "abuse" of the rights is prohibited, thus preserving a substantial area for further interpretation.

Third, the law regulates mergers or other "concentration of undertakings." A review process is established that is much like Hart-Scott-Rodino review for entities with combined global annual revenue over about $1.5 billion if at least two of the firms have sales in China greater than about $60 million each. The Authority is permitted to condition its approval of a concentration or merger.

Fourth, the new law expressly prohibits administrative agencies and other state organizations from preventing the free flow of goods throughout China.

Substantial fines, potential civil liability, and loss of the right to do business are among remedies specified in the new law. Given China's place in the world economy, it seems likely that multinational companies will have to factor Chinese anti-monopoly law into their plans just as they now focus attention on U.S. and European Union antitrust regulation.

---

[286] For more about the Chinese law, see Adrian Emch & David Stallibrass, eds., China's Anti-Monopoly Law: The First Five Years (2013); Symposium: The Anti-Monopoly Law of the People's Republic of China, 75 Antitrust L. J. 67–265 (2008).

d. Attempts to Achieve Policy Convergence

Differences among antitrust regimes are probably inevitable. Countries vary in the size of their economies; they also vary in their history of centralized economies and fear of multinational corporations. But the effort to identify at least common antitrust norms continues.[287] Two examples are the Global Administrative Law (GAL) Competition Project and the International Competition Network (ICN).[288]

As its name suggests, the GAL concentrates on process norms for antitrust enforcement, including timeliness, expertise, transparency and accountability.[289] The ICN, in turn, is a decentralized collection of agencies from more than 100 countries that meets largely by email, conference calls and working groups. By design, it is not dominated by a single nation or point of view. It began by identifying areas of widespread agreement such as anti-cartel enforcement, but it has moved on to tougher issues such as unilateral conduct and its work is widely watched.[290]

There is little sign of a world-wide antitrust policy in our future, but efforts at policy coordination and moves toward convergence are likely to remain important.[291] In that effort, U.S. approaches to antitrust policy likely will not always prevail.

G. THE FORESEEABLE FUTURE OF ANTITRUST LAW

Federal antitrust law in the United States is over 125 years old. It has been a fascinating thirteen decades, a period in which American and world industry has been transformed several times and a period in which economic understanding has become increasingly sophisticated.

Will the United States and other nations continue to rely on competition to answer key questions of what products to produce and what prices to charge? Have the growth of network industries, international conglomerates, and the speed of technological change made antitrust law obsolete or more important than ever? Will antitrust concepts that evolved

---

[287] For an excellent introduction to the issues of antitrust diversity and convergence, see Eleanor Fox & Michael Trebilcock, eds., The Design of Competition Law Institutions (2013).

[288] Others in the convergence dialogue include the Organization for Economic Cooperation and Development (OECD) Competition Law and Policy Committee and the United Nations Conference on Trade and Development (UNCTAD).

[289] Professor William Kovacic has been among the most engaged analysts of institutional design. See, e.g., William E. Kovacic, Rating the Competition Agencies: What Constitutes Good Performance?, 16 George Mason L. Rev. 903 (2009).

[290] See, e.g., Ian G. John & Joshua B. Gray, The International Competition Network: A Decennial Retrospective, 26 Antitrust 54 (Spring 2012); Larry Fullerton & Megan Alvarez, Convergence in International Merger Control, 26 Antitrust 20 (Spring 2012).

[291] See, e.g., Diane P. Wood, Antitrust at the Global Level, 72 U. Chicago L. Rev. 309 (2005).

in the 20th Century survive in their present form for even another decade, much less another 100 years? The truth is, of course, that we cannot know.

The fourth period of our antitrust history has represented an almost inevitable response to the rigidity of broad per se rules. Current judges did not invent reliance on economic orthodoxy; they simply changed some of the doctrines of the faith. But now the fourth period itself has lasted over thirty years, and one might argue that the time has come for yet another turn in antitrust analysis.[292]

Is the direction of antitrust law about to change significantly? Obviously, anything could happen. It does seem likely that more mergers may be challenged than in recent years,[293] but radical change in the direction of antitrust law seems unlikely.

The same basic questions will face future administrations that faced President Harrison when the Sherman Act was adopted:

How can the antitrust laws contribute to the kinds of economic efficiency that we identified at the outset of these materials—the productive and dynamic efficiency of individual firms, and allocative efficiency within the economy as a whole?

How can antitrust help reduce economic concentration and increase business fairness?

How can the laws frame issues so that judges and juries can render decisions within a reasonable time and without incurring litigation costs that tend to make all sides losers?[294]

Courts have handled those questions less than perfectly in the period since the mid-1970s, but they tend to have done much better than during the previous thirty-five years. With continued effort at identifying relevant indicia of economic harm or lack of it, antitrust decisions may get better still.

---

[292] Many such calls came in essays written at the time of the Sherman Act's centennial in 1990. See, e.g., Robert Pitofsky, The Renaissance of Antitrust, 45 A.B.C.N.Y. Record 851 (1990); Rudolph Peritz, A Counter-History of Antitrust Law, 1990 Duke L.J. 263; Richard S. Markovits, The American Antitrust Laws on the Centennial of the Sherman Act: A Critique of the Statutes Themselves, Their Interpretation, and Their Operationalization, 38 Buffalo L. Rev. 673 (1990); David W. Barnes, Revolutionary Antitrust: Efficiency, Ideology, and Democracy, 58 U. Cincinnati L. Rev. 59 (1989). The fact that it is almost impossible to observe any impact of these articles may suggest that the current approach to antitrust law has staying power.

[293] For background on this development, compare Jonathan B. Baker & Carl Shapiro, Detecting and Reversing the Decline in Horizontal Merger Enforcement, 22 Antitrust 29 (Summer 2008), with Timothy J. Muris, Facts Trump Politics: The Complexities of Comparing Merger Enforcement Over Time and Between Agencies, 22 Antitrust 37 (Summer 2008).

[294] See generally, William E. Kovacic, The Modern Evolution of U.S. Competition Policy Enforcement Norms, 71 Antitrust L. J. 377 (2003).

A NOTE ON THE ANTITRUST MODERNIZATION COMMISSION

The Antitrust Modernization Commission was created by Congress to conduct a comprehensive, bipartisan review of the antitrust laws with an eye to needed amendments. After holding extensive hearings, its report, issued in 2007, concludes that the substantive antitrust laws are "sound." While the Commission made 80 recommendations, antitrust practitioners keep their eyes on 10 of its most important.

1. The Antitrust Division should continue to focus its criminal enforcement efforts on "naked" price fixing, bid rigging, and market or customer allocation agreements that inevitably harm consumers.

2. Federal and state enforcement agencies should coordinate their efforts to avoid subjecting companies to multiple and possibly inconsistent requirements.

3. There should be joint and several liability in civil cases with multiple defendants, and non-settling defendants should have their liability reduced by the amount of prior settlements or the share of liability of settling defendants, whichever is greater.

4. Congress should repeal the Robinson-Patman Act in its entirety.

5. The Antitrust Division and the FTC should develop a new merger clearance agreement. At the moment, there is often infighting over which agency will consider a given merger. Areas of responsibility should be clear, and focus on the merits of the merger should begin promptly.

6. If the FTC challenges a merger in court, it should seek a permanent injunction and should not later itself conduct an administrative hearing. The standard for judicial evaluation of a merger should be the same whether the case is brought by the Justice Department or the FTC.

7. Statutory antitrust immunities should be disfavored and regulatory statutes should clearly state whether and to what extent they are intended to displace the antitrust laws.

8. Congress should overrule both *Hanover Shoe* and *Illinois Brick* concerning suits by direct and indirect purchasers. Cases for all purchasers should be consolidated and total damages should not exceed three times the damages suffered by direct purchasers. Proceeds recovered should then be fairly divided among the direct and indirect purchasers.

9. The agencies should work with their counterparts in other countries to establish comity principles and minimize duplicative or inconsistent international antitrust enforcement.

10. The Patent and Trademark Office should be staffed to approve only "quality" patents and to do so within a reasonable time.

Do many of these recommendations raise familiar issues? Does the relative modesty of the proposals suggest that there is substantial bipartisan support for the general outlines of the current antitrust laws and their enforcement?

Some other open issues can also be identified as ones with which you will be struggling in at least the early years of your practice. Some will affect only domestic markets, but increasingly the issues will involve the place of antitrust in regulating firms that face global competition.[295]

First, what should be the role of competition in the transformation of our health care system? Has the relatively recent role of antitrust law in stimulating competition improved medical care? Has it lowered health care costs? Have very large insurance companies, health maintenance organizations, and hospital networks actually decreased competition in that industry? Should health care receive a statutory antitrust exemption and rely on direct regulation to keep costs down and the quality of patient service high? Might other service providers seek similar antitrust exemptions for themselves?

Second, what is the appropriate balance between protection of intellectual property and the role of competition? Should patent holders be required to exploit inventions or to license them to those who will? Should patent rights continue to include the right to prevent others from doing research into improvements on existing patents? Should territorial limitations on patent licenses include the right to prevent sale of a patented item in countries other than the one in which the item is made?[296]

Third, should states enforce their own resale price maintenance laws and should Congress reverse *Leegin* to make resale price maintenance again illegal? Given the secure presence of discount merchandising in the American economy, if a manufacturer wants to resist the trend and impose price or distribution restraints, will the broad availability of market

---

[295] Ultimately, the future of antitrust may come down to our assessment of its effect on American productivity. Professors Jorde and Teece, for example, have concluded that the conceded public benefit from antitrust enforcement could still be a net loss for society if that enforcement were to suppress the innovation that would stimulate 1% more economic growth in the country each year. Thomas M. Jorde & David J. Teece, eds., Antitrust, Innovation and Competitiveness (1992). See also, Janusz A. Ordover & Robert D. Willig, Antitrust for High-Technology Industries: Assessing Research Joint Ventures and Mergers, 28 J.Law & Econ. 311 (1985); Ward Bowman, The Incentive to Invent in Competitive as Contrasted to Monopolistic Industries, 20 J.Law & Econ. 227 (1977).

[296] See, e.g., Robert Pitofsky, Challenges of the New Economy: Issues at the Intersection of Antitrust and Intellectual Property, 68 Antitrust L. J. 913 (2001); Richard A. Posner, Antitrust in the New Economy, 68 Antitrust L. J. 925 (2001); E. Thomas Sullivan, The Confluence of Antitrust and Intellectual Property at the New Century, 1 Minnesota Intell.Prop.Rev. 1 (2000).

alternatives protect the public? Can you think of any conditions under which they might not?[297]

Fourth, what should the effect of globalization of many markets be on competition policy?[298] Will antitrust law and related concepts be used to open markets to American firms? Might antitrust laws instead be used as weapons in a new round of trade protectionism? Does *Hartford* portend the use of U.S. antitrust law to attack the activities of foreign firms acting abroad?[299] Might we use provisions such as Section 337 of the Tariff Act of 1930,[300] or Section 301 of the Trade Act of 1974,[301] increasingly to challenge "dumping" and other "unfair" trade by foreign firms?

Fifth, do enforcement authorities and judges have the capacity to respond as quickly to economic problems as the market does? If not, might courts make problems worse by ordering responses to last year's, not next year's, issues?

Almost a quarter-century ago, Professor Michael Porter of the Harvard Business School called our attention to what is at stake. Firms tend to become strong world competitors, he said, by first effectively competing at home.

> "Few roles of government are more important to the upgrading of an economy than ensuring vigorous domestic rivalry. * * * Maintaining vigorous domestic competition * * * [ensures] that a nation's firms gain advantages from * * * demanding buyers * * * instead of harvesting market positions, seeking

---

[297] See, e.g., Joel M. Mitnick, John J. Lavelle, William V. Reiss & Owen H. Smith, On Life Support from *Leegin*aire's Disease: Can the States Resuscitate *Dr. Miles*, 22 Antitrust 63 (Summer 2008). Vertical restraints generally remain of interest to academics, e.g., Andy C. M. Chen & Keith Hylton, Procompetitive Theories of Vertical Control, 50 Hastings L.J. 573 (1999); Mark A. Glick & Duncan Cameron, When Do Proprietary Aftermarkets Benefit Consumers, 67 Antitrust L.J. 357 (1999); Warren S. Grimes, Brand Marketing, Intrabrand Competition, and the Multibrand Retailer: The Antitrust Law of Vertical Restraints, 64 Antitrust L.J. 83 (1995); Michael H. Riordan & Steven C. Salop, Evaluating Vertical Mergers: A Post-Chicago Approach, 63 Antitrust L.J. 513 (1995).

[298] Both the Justice Department and the FTC have been studying such issues. See, e.g., Antitrust Division, U.S. Department of Justice, International Competition Policy Advisory Committee to the Attorney General and Assistant Attorney General for Antitrust: Final Report (2000); Richard J. Pierce, Antidumping Law as a Means of Facilitating Cartelization, 67 Antitrust L.J. 725 (2000); Mark A.A. Warner, International Competition Policy After ICPAC: Where Next?, 14 Antitrust 46 (Summer 2000).

[299] See, e.g., "Possible Violations of U.S. Antitrust Laws by Foreign Corporations", Hearings before the Subcommittee on Economic and Commercial Law, Committee on the Judiciary, U.S. House of Representatives, 101 Cong., 1st Sess., May 3, 1990. There is no consensus on the wisdom of applying U.S. law to extraterritorial economic activity. See, e.g., Pamela B. Gann, ed., Symposium: Extraterritoriality of Economic Legislation, 50 Law & Contemp.Probs. 1 (1987); Eleanor M. Fox, Extraterritoriality, Antitrust, and the New Restatement: Is "Reasonableness" the Answer?, 19 N.Y.U.J.Inter.L. & Politics 565 (1987); Donald I. Baker, The Proper Role for Antitrust in a Not-Yet-Global Economy, 9 Cardozo L.Rev. 1135 (1988).

[300] 19 U.S.C. § 1337.

[301] 19 U.S.C. § 2411.

government assistance, or outsourcing high-productivity manufacturing abroad.

* * *

"* * * [C]reating a dominant domestic competitor rarely results in international competitive advantage. Firms that do not have to compete at home rarely succeed abroad. Economies of scale are best gained through selling globally, not through dominating the home market.

* * *

"* * * Company behavior that leads to innovation and productivity growth, such as aggressive capital investment and new product introduction, should not be deterred even if rivals lose market share as a result.

"* * * American antitrust laws toward trade associations have been especially counterproductive * * * . With nothing else to do, too many associations spend all their energy on lobbying."[302]

What do you think? What should be the shape of antitrust in the future? If preservation of domestic competition is indeed critical to the international success of American firms, it just may be that the most important years for antitrust law and competition policy are those that are yet to come.

A NASCENT COUNTER-REVOLUTION?

In July 2017, the Democratic Party issued a document titled, "A Better Deal," in which it outlined its goals for the nation. In a section titled "Cracking Down on Corporate Monopolies," it proposed dramatic revisions to antitrust law:

"A Better Deal on competition means that we will revisit our antitrust laws to ensure that the economic freedom of all Americans—consumers, workers, and small businesses—come before big corporations that are getting even bigger.

Specifically, the Better Deal plan will:

Prevent big mergers that would harm consumers, workers, and competition.

---

[302] Michael E. Porter, The Competitive Advantage of Nations 662–64 (1990). The Porter analysis is developed and applied to antitrust principles in Charles D. Weller, Harmonizing Antitrust Worldwide by Evolving to Michael Porter's Dynamic Productivity Growth Analysis, 46 Antitrust Bulletin 879 (2001).

Require regulators to review mergers after completion to ensure they continue to promote competition.

Create a 21st century "Trust Buster" to stop abusive corporate conduct and the exploitation of market power where it already exists.

New standards to limit large mergers that unfairly consolidate corporate power: Currently, it is too easy for companies to unfairly harm competition by merging, squeezing competitors, workers, customers, and suppliers. Today, antitrust regulators and other federal oversight authorities can only consider the narrow interests of a merger on prices and output, and have the burden of proving that consolidation would be anticompetitive.

We propose establishing new merger standards that require a broader, longer term view and strong presumptions that market concentration can result in anticompetitive conduct. These standards will prevent mergers that unfairly increase prices but also those that unfairly reduce competition—they will ensure that regulators carefully scrutinize whether mergers reduce wages, cut jobs, lower product quality, limit access to services, stifle innovation, or hinder the ability of small businesses and entrepreneurs to compete. In an increasingly data-driven society, merger standards must explicitly consider the ways in which control of consumer data can be used to stifle competition or jeopardize consumer privacy."

One possible avenue for change is suggested by a book written by a well-regarded economist and published by MIT Press in 2015, John Kwoka, *Mergers, Merger Control, and Remedies in the United States: A Retrospective Analysis.* Kwoka studied the results of the forty largest recent mergers that antitrust authorities permitted. He found that in three quarters of those cases, price increased significantly after the merger. In some cases, the price increases were 10 to 20 per cent. Kwoka's work suggests that the methods of predicting the effects of mergers on prices that we have been using are faulty. If Kwoka is right, the logical solution to the problem would seem to be to adopt improved methods of predicting the effects of mergers on prices.

The "Better Deal" urged by the Democratic Party would go far beyond Kwoka's proposed solution, however. The Better Deal urges changes to antitrust law that would add the goals of protecting workers, protecting suppliers, protecting privacy and protecting competitors to the goal of protecting consumers. Do you believe that antitrust law can simultaneously further the goal of maximizing consumer welfare and the goals of protecting workers, protecting suppliers, protecting privacy and protecting small businesses? If so, how would you go about designing such a legal regime?

A student Note in the January 2017 issue of Yale Law Journal argues in support of one possible method of implementing the changes urged in the Better Deal. In *Amazon's Antitrust Paradox*, Lina Khan argues that "the current framework in antitrust—specifically its pegging competition to 'consumer welfare,' defined as short term price effects—is unequipped to capture the architecture of market power in the modern economy.... Specifically, current doctrine underappreciates the risk of predatory pricing and how integration across distinct business lines may prove anticompetitive."

Khan recognizes that the entry of Amazon into many product markets has dramatically reduced the price of those products, but she argues that Amazon is doing far more harm than good if we consider all of the effects of its behavior on society. She refers to the persuasive evidence that the antitrust statutes were enacted to address perceived political problems caused by concentration of power in large corporations as well as economic problems caused by the trend toward creation of large corporations. She urges adoption of a new legal regime that would address both the economic problems and the political problems that are potentially caused by the growth of big businesses, particualrly in platform markets.

Khan illustrates her points by referring to the effects that the Amazon Kindle has had on the book market. It has reduced the price of books significantly but it has also inflicted harm on competitors, authors and publishers. She argues that the Amazon Kindle has harmed society by reducing the quality and variety of books that are published.

The legal regime Khan urges would reflect her view that predatory pricing and vertical integration are both common practices and socially unacceptable practices. She would implement a merger law regime that would have the effect of barring mergers that would create a firm that would be able to misuse its power by engaging in predatory pricing and/or leveraging a position of dominance in one market into a position of dominance in another market. She would supplement that merger regime with a system of pervasive price regulation modeled after public utility law or common carrier law applicable to any firm that is in a position to engage in predatory pricing or monopoly leveraging.

Do you think it is possible to design and implement a legal regime based on Khan's argument? If so, how would you go about that task? What would expect to be the results of the adoption of such a legal regime? Would we be better off without Amazon, Google, Facebook, and Microsoft? We would be better off if each of those firms was regulated as a public utility?

INDEX

References are to Pages